FREQUENTLY USED SYMBOLS AND ABBREVIATIONS (CONTINUED)

LBO	Leverage Buyout
m	Number of times per year interest is compounded
M	Bond's Par
M_e	Market Val
M_w	Market Val
MACRS	Modified A
MNC	Multination
MPR	Market Pric
MRP	Materials R
n	• Number o
	• Number o
	• Years to M
N	• Number o by Giving
	• Number o Share of S
	• Number o Obtainabl
N_d	Net Proceed
N_n	Net Proceed Stock
N_p	Net Proceed Stock
NE	Number of Number of
NPV	Net Present
O	• Order Cos
	• Total Num Outstandi
OC	Operating C
P	Price (value)
P_0	Value of Co
PAC	Preauthorize
$PBDT_t$	Profits Befo
PD	Preferred St
P/E	Price/Earnings Ratio
PMT	Amount of Payment
Pr	Probability
PV	Present Value
PVA_n	Present Value of an n-Year Annuity

$PVIF_{k,n}$	Present Value Interest Factor for a Single Amount Discounted at k Percent for n Periods
$PVIFA_{k,n}$	Present Value Interest Factor for an Annuity annually at k

YTM	Yield to Maturity
α_t	Certainty Equivalent Factor in Year t
σ	Standard Deviation
σ^2	Variance
Σ	Summation Sign

PRINCIPLES OF

MANAGERIAL
FINANCE

ADDISON-WESLEY

An Imprint of Addison Wesley Longman, Inc.

Reading, Massachusetts • Menlo Park, California • New York • Harlow, England
Don Mills, Ontario • Sydney • Mexico City • Madrid • Amsterdam

Lawrence J. Gitman

San Diego State University

PRINCIPLES OF

MANAGERIAL FINANCE

Ninth Edition

Executive Editor: Denise Clinton
Sponsoring Editor: Julie Lindstrom
Deveopment Editor: Ann Torbert
Managing Editor: Jim Rigney
Production Supervisor: Nancy Fenton
Marketing Manager: Amy Cronin
Supplements Editor: Deb Kiernan
Associate Media Producer: Jennifer Pelland
Editorial Assistant: Greta Brogna
Project Coordination, Text Design, Art Studio,
    and Electronic Page Makeup: Thompson Steele, Inc.
Design Manager: Regina Hagen
Cover Designer: Leslie Haimes
Cover Photograph: Image ©1999 PhotoDisc Inc.
Manufacturing Coordinator: Tim McDonald
Printer and Binder: RR Donnelley & Sons Company
Cover Printer: The Lehigh Press

For permission to use copyrighted material, grateful acknowledgment is made to the copyright holders on pp. S-1– S-2 , which are hereby made part of this copyright page.

Library of Congress Cataloging-in-Publication Data
Gitman, Lawrence J.
    Principles of managerial finance / Lawrence J. Gitman.—9th ed.
      p. cm.
    Includes bibliographical references and index.
    ISBN 0-321-04308-1 (alk. paper)
    1. Corporations—Finance. 2. Business enterprises—Finance.
  I. Title.
  HG4011.G5 2000   99-25883
  658.15-dc21   CIP

ISBN 0-321-04308-1

12345678910—DOW—0302010099

*Dedicated to the memory
of my mother, Dr. Edith Gitman,
who instilled in me the importance
of education and hard work*

Brief Contents

Detailed Contents

CHAPTER 2

Institutions, Securities, Markets, and Rates 30

Financial Fabric

Part 2   *Important Financial Concepts*   175

CHAPTER 5

Time Value of Money   176

Money Time

Part 3   *Long-Term Investment Decisions   331*

CHAPTER 8

Capital Budgeting and Cash Flow Principles 332

Such Stuff as Dreams Are Made of

Part 4   *Long-Term Financial Decisions*   447

Part 5 *Short-Term Financial Decisions* 577

CHAPTER 14

*Financial
Planning
578*

*"If Only I'd
Known . . ."*

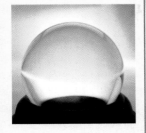

CHAPTER 17

*Accounts
Receivable
and Inventory*
698

*"The Check's in
the Mail"*

Part 6   *Special Topics in Managerial Finance*   *739*

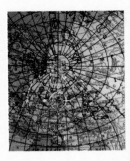

Appendixes

List of Companies

Page numbers in italics indicate figures; page numbers followed by n indicate notes; page numbers followed by t indicate tables.

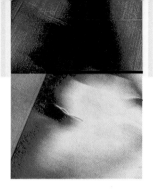

To the Instructor

This textbook, *Principles of Managerial Finance,* has consistently met the needs of the introductory finance course at the undergraduate level over the course of eight editions. In 24 years, over half a million students have used the book. As the needs of instructors and students in the introductory course have changed in that time, so too has the book. I believe that this new, ninth edition will continue to satisfy the needs of both instructors and students for a textbook that is firmly grounded in the theory and practice of finance and at the same time is user-friendly.

The ninth edition continues to satisfy market needs—and more. Incorporating a proven learning system, which integrates pedagogy and color with concepts and practical applications, this edition equips instructors to concentrate on the concepts, techniques, and practices that are needed to make keen financial decisions in an increasingly competitive business environment. The strong pedagogy and generous use of examples also make the text an easily accessible resource for long-distance learning and self-study programs. The book has also been exceptionally well received in the core M.B.A. course and in management development and executive training programs. From classroom to boardroom, the ninth edition of *Principles of Managerial Finance* can help users get to where they want to be.

Distinguishing Features of the Ninth Edition

Numerous features distinguish the ninth edition of *Principles of Managerial Finance* from its many excellent competitors. Among them are the book's flexible organization, proven teaching/learning system, strong ties to practice, and important content improvements.

Flexible Organization

The text's organization conceptually links the firm's actions and its value as determined in the securities markets. Each major decision area is presented in terms of both risk and return factors and their potential impact on the owners' wealth, as reflected by share value.

In organizing each chapter, I have adhered to a managerial decision-making perspective. That is, I have described a concept such as present value or operating leverage and have also related it to the financial manager's overall goal of wealth maximization. Once a particular concept has been developed, its application is illustrated by an example. The student is not left with just an abstract definition or discussion, but truly senses the related decision-making considerations and consequences.

The ninth edition of *Principles of Managerial Finance* contains 20 chapters, in six parts. We've eliminated one part by integrating some of the descriptive material on corporate securities into Chapter 2, attaching the chapter on dividend policy to the part on long-term financial decisions, and moving the chapter on hybrid and derivative securities into the final part that deals with special topics in managerial finance. In addition, we've expanded the coverage of capital budgeting in the ninth edition to three chapters. For an overview of the book's part and chapter organization, see the Brief Contents listing on page vii. Although the text is sequential, instructors can assign almost any chapter as a self-contained unit. This flexibility enables instructors to customize the text to various teaching strategies and course lengths.

Proven Teaching/Learning System

Feedback from users has praised the effectiveness of the book's teaching/learning system, which has been one of its hallmarks for a couple of editions. This system has been retained and polished in the ninth edition. The system is driven by a set of carefully developed learning goals that help guide and organize student reading and study. In addition, numerous other features facilitate teaching and reinforce student learning to promote achievement of the learning goals. Each of the system's key elements is described in what follows.

Learning Goals   The *PMF* Teaching/Learning System is anchored in a set of six proven *Learning Goals* (LGs) per chapter. Marked by a special icon, shown here in the margin, the learning goals are listed at the start of each chapter, tied to first-level headings, reviewed point by point at the chapter's end, and noted in assignment material and supplements such as the *Test Bank* and *Study Guide*. These goals focus student attention on what material he or she needs to learn, where it can be found in the chapter, and whether it has been mastered by the end of the chapter. In addition, instructors can easily build lectures and assignments around the LGs.

***PMF* Toolbox**   A key visual aid in the *PMF* Teaching/Learning System is the *PMF Toolbox,* a cluster of icons at the beginning of every major chapter section. Inside the Toolbox, students will find learning tools and resources that are available to them as they attempt to master each learning goal. These tools and resources consist of learning goals, software tutorials, problem-solving disk routines, and spreadsheet templates, where these apply to the topic at hand. An example of the Toolbox appears in Chapter 5 ("Time Value of Money"), on page 197, next to the heading "Present Value of a Single Amount."

***PMF* Example Method**   The *PMF Example Method* is an important component of the *PMF* Teaching/Learning System because it infuses practical demonstrations into the learning process. Seeing a financial concept or technique applied in a realistic example provides students with immediate reinforcement that helps cement their understanding of that concept or technique. Where applicable, the solution of each example shows the use of time lines, tables, and financial calculators. Calculator keystrokes of inputs, functions, and outputs are highlighted in discussions and examples of time value techniques in Chapter 5 and in the application of those techniques in subsequent chapters. Appendix A and the laminated table card included in all new books contain financial tables and note the basic calculator keystrokes for the most popular financial calculators.

Key Equations   Key equations are printed in blue throughout the text to help students identify the most important mathematical relationships. The variables used in these equations are for convenience printed on the front endpapers of the book.

Marginal Glossary   Throughout the text, key terms and their definitions appear in the text margin when they are first introduced. In addition, these terms are **boldfaced** in the index for easy access to the glossary entry.

Marginal Hints   Marginal *Hints,* new in this edition, add useful pieces of information to enrich the text discussion and help student learning.

International Coverage   Discussions of international dimensions of chapter topics are integrated throughout the book. For example, Chapter 6 discusses the risks and returns associated with international diversification. Similarly, Chapter 10 addresses the international aspects of capital budgeting and long-term investments. In each chapter in which international coverage is included, the international material is integrated into chapter learning goals and the end-of-chapter summary and problem material.

Review Questions   *Review Questions* appear at the end of each section of the chapter (positioned before the next first-level heading) and are marked with a special design element. As students progress through the chapter, they can test their understanding of each key concept, technique, and practice before moving on to the next section.

Summary   End-of-chapter summaries are keyed to the learning goals, which are restated for reinforcement at the beginning of each *Summary* paragraph. The learning-goal-driven summary facilitates the student's review of the key material that was presented to support mastery of the given goal.

Self-Test Problems   At the end of most chapters, one or more *Self-Test Problems* are included. Each problem is keyed to the appropriate learning goal and the *PMF* disk icons from the Toolbox. Appendix B contains all worked-out solutions to Self-Test Problems in one location, marked with an easy-to-spot green stripe on the edge of the page. These demonstration problems with solutions help to strengthen students' understanding of the topics and the techniques presented.

Chapter Problems   A comprehensive set of *Problems,* containing more than one problem for each concept or technique, provides students with multiple self-testing opportunities and gives professors a wide choice of assignable material. The ninth edition offers more problems than ever before—with the addition of 80 interesting new problems. A short descriptor at the beginning of every problem identifies the concept or technique that the problem has been designed to test. In addition, new in this edition, the problems are graded by difficulty level—warm-up, intermediate, and challenge—to indicate the amount of work that should be involved in solving each problem. Some of the end-of-chapter problems are captioned "integrative" because they tie together related topics. All problems are keyed to the learning goals and the *PMF* disk using icons from the Toolbox. Guideline answers to selected end-of-chapter problems appear in Appendix C.

Chapter Cases   Chapter *Cases* enable students to apply what they've learned in the chapter to realistic situations. For example, at the end of Chapter 7 ("Bond and Stock Valuation"), students are asked to assess the impact of a proposed risky investment on a firm's bond and stock values. These end-of-chapter cases help strengthen practical understanding of financial tools and techniques without the added expense of a separate casebook.

Web Exercises   New in the ninth edition, a *Web Exercise* at the end of each chapter links the chapter topic to a related site on the Internet and asks students to use information located there to answer various questions. These exercises will capture student interest in using the Internet while educating them about finance-related sites.

End-of-Part Cases   At the end of each of the book's six parts is an integrative case that challenges students to use what they've learned in the several chapters in the part in a realistic business context. At the end of Part 1, for example, students can apply a variety of concepts from Chapters 1 through 4 to assess and make recommendations with regard to the financial strategy of a software company.

Contemporary Design   A vibrant, contemporary design, with pedagogical use of colors in most charts and graphs, draws reader attention to features of the learning system. Bars of data are highlighted with color in tables and then graphed in the same color so that visual learners can immediately see relationships among data. Additionally, new attention-getting photographs and related short vignettes at the beginning of each chapter connect to key points in the chapter.

Strong Ties to Practice

A variety of features are used in the ninth edition to anchor student understanding in the operational aspects of topics presented. Many textual discussions present practical insights and applications of concepts and techniques. In addition, a number of special features are used both to assure realism and to stimulate student interest.

Cross-Disciplinary Focus   We have kept the idea from the eighth edition of an element that helps students understand the importance of the chapter material to other major business disciplines. In the ninth edition, *Career Keys* are placed in the margins to indicate the benefit or interactions that those in other disciplines would have with the topic covered at that point in the text. This feature allows students who are not finance majors to see how various finance topics relate to their chosen business major. In addition, this element gives students a better appreciation for the numerous cross-disciplinary interactions that routinely occur in business.

In Practice   Each chapter contains two *In Practice* boxes, which offer insight into important topics in finance through experiences of individuals and of real companies, both large and small. *Small Business* In Practice boxes are light blue. For example, an In Practice box in Chapter 7 discusses how to apply valuation techniques to value a small business. Similarly, to help students appreciate the pervasive nature of finance, there are light green *Personal Finance* In Practice boxes that apply to the financial decisions of individuals. One in the time value of money chapter (Chapter 5), for example, discusses 15-year mortgages; another in Chapter 18 discusses car leasing. Specific topics and companies covered in these In Practice boxes are listed in the next section. All of the In Practice boxes provide students with a solid grounding in the practice of finance in the real world.

Important Content Improvements

The publication of each new edition of a textbook offers the opportunity to update material in terms of important current and emerging issues, instruments, and techniques affecting the practice of financial management. Consistent exposure to current practical applications throughout the text enables students to walk away from the book and onto the job well-prepared with forward-looking, practical insight, rather than merely a conceptual grasp of the finance function. Each new edition also offers the opportunity to fine-tune material based on the considered comments of the book's users and potential users.

Because users and potential users often like to know where new material appears, here are the significant changes made in the ninth edition:

Chapter 1, which provides a newly streamlined overview of managerial finance, now includes

- a brief presentation of limited liability organizations other than corporations
- revised discussion of the relationship among profits, cash flows, and stock price
- the agency issue covered in a major section on its own
- revised discussion of incentive and performance plans (in the compensation discussion)
- an In Practice box on what it takes to be a CFO (highlights Allstate Insurance Co.)
- an In Practice box on social responsibility (Levi Strauss)

Chapter 2 has been retitled "Institutions, Securities, Markets, and Rates." The discussion of business taxation has been moved from this chapter into Chapter 3. In its place have been added sections on the basic corporate securities—bonds and stocks—and the difference between debt and equity capital. This new organization will give students a better understanding of these important securities from early in the course. In addition, the chapter now features

- streamlined coverage of investment banking
- an In Practice box on investment banking (using the example of Multicom Publishing Co.)
- an In Practice box on the inverted yield curve in 1998

Chapter 3 now covers financial statements, taxes, depreciation, and cash flow. Taxes were moved from Chapter 3 in order to bring them closer to the related discussions of depreciation and cash flow. Chapter 3 now contains

- an updated Intel letter to stockholders
- a new explanation of double taxation
- an In Practice box on how accounting methods affect a firm's reported profit performance (Microsoft)
- a personal finance In Practice box on tax planning principles

Chapter 4's coverage of financial statement analysis has been streamlined by the elimination of the fixed asset turnover and debt-equity ratios. Other changes include

- Table 4.1 now focuses primarily on ratios covered in the chapter
- an In Practice box on cash flow–based ratios (EBITDA and free cash flow)
- an In Practice box on the continuing popularity of the DuPont system (Caterpillar Inc. and Nucor)

Chapter 5 on time value of money has

- a revised discussion of nominal annual rate and effective annual rate (EAR)
- streamlined presentation of calculator-use examples
- simplified headings to improve understanding of chapter structure
- an In Practice box on new uses of time value of money techniques to value customers and brands
- a personal finance In Practice box on 15-year mortgages

Chapter 6 on risk and return now contains

- an In Practice box on reducing risk through diversification (GE Capital)
- an In Practice box on value-at-risk (VAR) techniques

Chapter 7 on bond and stock valuation now includes

- a definition of interest-rate risk in the section on changing required returns
- an In Practice box on how to value a small business
- an In Practice box on valuing zero-coupon bonds

Chapter 8 on capital budgeting and cash flow principles has

- a new figure that illustrates the relevant cash flows for replacement decisions
- an improved format for tables that show how to determine initial investment and the terminal cash flow
- an In Practice box on the need to evaluate investment in information technology (Boston Market, Pink Jeep Tours)
- an In Practice box on capital spending (Coors Brewing)

Chapter 9 on capital budgeting techniques in this edition has been revised to cover only the specific techniques. The coverage of capital budgeting risk and refinements has been moved to a new Chapter 10. Chapter 9 also includes

- a revised format that sets off the capital budgeting decision criteria more clearly
- a new example that demonstrates the failure of payback period to take fully into account the time value of money
- an In Practice box on creating value with EVA

New *Chapter 10* on risk and refinements in capital budgeting covers the behavioral approaches for dealing with risk, risk-adjustment techniques (CEs and RADRs), comparison of unequal-lived projects, and capital rationing. Coverage of these topics in a separate chapter helps to solidify student learning by presenting this important material in smaller chunks. The chapter also contains

- an In Practice box on payoffs of capital investment (Loanshop.com)
- an In Practice box on capital rationing (US West)

Chapter 11 on the cost of capital leads off a three-chapter part on "Long-Term Financial Decisions." Now included in this part is Chapter 13 on dividend policy. Changes in Chapter 11 are

- a clearer explanation of the cost of retained earnings
- a new discussion of the reasons for underpricing new common stock issues
- an In Practice box on how a CFO reduced outstanding debt and raised new financing (Continental Airlines)
- an In Practice box on international hurdle rates (General Motors)

Chapter 12 on leverage and capital structure now includes

- a new, clearer illustration showing capital costs and the optimal capital structure
- an In Practice box comparing leverage measures of same-industry companies (Barnes & Noble and Borders)
- an In Practice box on improving the capital structure of an overleveraged company (USG Corporation)

Chapter 13 now focuses exclusively on dividend policy. Other changes include

- an In Practice box on whether dividends matter to stockholders (Comcast)
- a personal finance In Practice box on investors' reactions to stock splits

Chapter 14 on financial planning is the first of four chapters on short-term financial decisions. These chapters now precede the discussion of hybrid and derivative securities (now Chapter 18) in order to cover fundamental material prior to more specialized topics. Chapter 14 changes include

- the example of cash flow within the month has been moved to the book's homepage
- an In Practice box on the importance of relevant and useful planning procedures (Nationwide Financial Services)
- a small-business In Practice box on the importance of timely management reports for financial planning in small businesses

Chapter 15 on working capital and short-term financing now includes the following changes:

- coverage has been streamlined to focus on core concepts and eliminate unnecessary technical details and demonstrations
- an In Practice box discussing working capital benchmarks (USX-US Steel, Nucor)
- a small-business In Practice box on the difficulties small businesses have in getting bank loans

Chapter 16 on cash and marketable securities has been changed as follows:

- coverage of check clearing time has been shortened
- the section on the Baumol model has been tightened
- an In Practice box examines changes made to improve one company's cash conversion cycle cash management (Dell Computer)
- a personal finance In Practice box discusses online banking

Chapter 17 on accounts receivable and inventory now includes

- a personal finance In Practice box on managing personal credit
- a small-business In Practice box on the importance of credit and collections policies in small firms

Chapter 18 on hybrid and derivative securities introduces the final part of the book, which deals with special topics in managerial finance. This chapter (which was Chapter 14 in the eighth edition) provides an overview of hybrids and derivatives and discusses leasing, convertible securities, stock purchase warrants, and options. Changes include

- tighter coverage of leasing
- advantages of leasing are presented in order of significance
- updated coverage of reporting of contingent securities, consistent with new FASB financial reporting standards—now includes basic EPS and diluted EPS
- a personal finance In Practice box on car leasing
- an In Practice box on convertible bonds (Amazon.com)

Chapter 19 on mergers, LBOs, divestitures, and business failure has been updated to reflect recent high-profile mergers. Other changes include

- the example of priority claims has been moved to homepage
- an In Practice box on mergers of small businesses (PhotoDisc)
- an In Practice box on bankruptcy and reorganization (J. Peterman Co.)

Chapter 20 on international managerial finance has been revised by the following changes:

- new material on emerging trading blocs—NAFTA, the European Union, and Mercosur
- updated coverage of monetary union and the Euro
- the discussion of GATT now considers China's current status
- a revised presentation of foreign exchange relationships
- updated information on foreign direct investment
- expanded discussion of using options to hedge exchange rate risk
- an In Practice box on investing in the Russian stock market
- an In Practice box on the merger that produced the world's largest wireless phone company (Vodafone Group)

In addition, references throughout the book point students to the textbook's *Homepage* where they can find additional examples, further discussion of topics, or more technical detail.

Supplements to the *PMF* Teaching/Learning System

The *PMF* Teaching/Learning System includes a variety of useful supplements for teachers and for students.

Teaching Tools for Instructors

The key teaching tools available to instructors are the *Instructor's Manual,* testing materials, and *PowerPoint Lecture Presentations.*

Instructor's Manual   *Compiled by Dev Prasad,* Texas A&M University–Corpus Christi. This comprehensive resource pulls together the teaching tools so that instructors can use the textbook easily and effectively in the classroom. Each chapter provides an overview of key topics and detailed answers and solutions to all Review Questions, end-of-chapter problems, and chapter cases. At the end of the manual are practice quizzes and solutions.

Testing Material   *Created by Hadi Salavitabar, SUNY–New Paltz.* Thoroughly revised to accommodate changes in the text, the Test Bank contains 2,500 questions made up of a mix of true/false, multiple choice, and essay questions. For quick test selection and construction, each chapter features a handy chart for identifying type of question, skill tested by learning goal, and level of difficulty. Because the Test Bank is available in both printed and electronic formats—word processing files and Windows or Macintosh *TestGen EQ* files—instructors should contact their Addison Wesley Longman sales representative to determine which format best meets their testing needs.

Instructors can download the *TestGen EQ* version of the Test Bank into *QuizMaster,* an online testing program for Windows and Macintosh that enables users to conduct timed or untimed exams at computer workstations. After completing tests, students can see their scores and view or print a diagnostic report of those topics or objectives requiring more attention. When installed on a local-area network, *QuizMaster* allows instructors to save the scores on disk, print study diagnoses, and monitor progress of students individually or by class section and by all sections of the course.

PowerPoint Lecture Presentation   *Created by Daniel Borgia, Florida Gulf Coast University.* Available for Windows or Macintosh on the Instructor's Resource CD-ROM, this presentation combines lecture notes with art from the textbook. The lecture presentations for each chapter can be viewed electronically in the classroom or can be printed as black-and-white transparency masters.

Instructor's Resource CD-ROM   Electronic files of the *Instructor's Manual,* Test Bank, and PowerPoint Lecture Presentation are available on one convenient CD-ROM, compatible with both Windows and Macintosh computers. The electronic versions allow instructors to customize the support materials to their individual classroom needs.

Learning Tools for Students

Beyond the book itself, students have access to several resources for success in this course: the *PMF* CD-ROM, *Study Guide,* and the *Principles of Managerial Finance: Ninth Edition Web Site.*

PMF CD-ROM Software   Packaged with new copies of the text at no additional cost, the *PMF* CD-ROM Software, created by KMT Software, contains three state-of-the-art software tools: the *PMF Tutor,* the *PMF Problem-Solver,* and the *PMF Excel Spreadsheet Templates.* Documentation and practical advice for using the *PMF* CD-ROM appears in Appendix D of the textbook.

PMF Tutor   The *PMF Tutor* extends self-testing opportunities beyond those of the printed page. The Tutor helps students to identify and solve various types of managerial finance problems. Part of the *PMF* Toolbox, the Tutor icon flags all the Tutor applications in the text. Through user-friendly menus, students can access over 55 different problem types, constructed by random-number generation for an inexhaustible supply of problems with little chance of repetition. Routines include financial ratios, time value of money, valuation, capital budgeting, and cost of capital.

PMF Problem-Solver   The *PMF Problem-Solver* contains seven short menu-driven programs to accelerate learning by providing an efficient away to perform financial computations. The Problem-Solver icon points out all the related applications throughout the text of this popular provision of the *PMF* Toolbox. Referenced to specific text pages for quick review of techniques, the routines include financial ratios, time value of money, bond and stock valuation, capital budgeting techniques, cost of capital, and cash budgets.

PMF Excel Spreadsheet Templates   The *PMF Excel Spreadsheet Templates* provide users with preprogrammed spreadsheet templates for inputting data and solving problems using perhaps the most popular and widely accepted practical software application. The template files correspond to selected end-of-chapter problems. The Excel Spreadsheet Template icon appears in the *PMF* Toolbox to note related applications throughout the text.

Study Guide   *Prepared by Stanley G. Eakins of East Carolina University.* The *Study Guide* is an integral component of the *PMF* Learning System. It offers many tools for studying finance. Each chapter contains the following features: chapter summary enumerated by learning goals; topical chapter outline, also broken down by learning goals for quick review; sample problem solutions; study tips; a full sample exam with the answers at the end of the chapter; and thumbnail printouts of the PowerPoint Lecture Presentations to facilitate classroom note taking.

Principles of Managerial Finance: Ninth Edition Web Site   The Web site to accompany this textbook, located at **http://www.awlonline/gitman,** contains valuable links, self-assessment quizzes, threaded discussion boards, and much more. The site will be updated on a regular basis, so check frequently for new features.

To My Colleagues, Friends, and Family

No textbook can consistently meet market needs without continual feedback from colleagues, students, practitioners, and members of the publishing team. Once again, I invite colleagues to relate their classroom experiences using this book and its package to me at San Diego State University, or in care of the Acquisitions Editor in Finance, Addison Wesley Longman, One Jacob Way, Reading, Massachusetts 01867-3999. Your constructive criticism will help me to continue to improve the textbook and its Teaching/Learning System still further.

Addison Wesley Longman and former publisher HarperCollins sought the advice of a great many excellent reviewers, all of whom strongly influenced various aspects of this book. My special thanks go to the following individuals who analyzed the manuscript in previous editions:

Saul W. Adelman

Lee E. Davis

M. Fall Ainina

Richard F. DeMong

Gary A. Anderson

Peter A. DeVito

Ronald F. Anderson

James P. D'Mello

Gene L. Andrusco

R. Gordon Dippel

Antonio Apap

Thomas W. Donohue

David A. Arbeit

Vincent R. Driscoll

Allen Arkins

Betty A. Driver

Saul H. Auslander

Lorna Dotts

Peter W. Bacon

David R. Durst

Richard E. Ball

Dwayne O. Eberhardt

Alexander Barges

Ronald L. Ehresman

Charles Barngrover

Ted Ellis

Michael Becker

F. Barney English

Scott Besley

Greg Filbeck

Douglas S. Bible

Ross A. Flaherty

Charles W. Blackwell

Rich Fortin

Russell L. Block

Timothy J. Gallagher

Calvin M. Boardman

George W. Gallinger

Paul Bolster

Gerald D. Gay

Robert J. Bondi

R. H. Gilmer

Jeffrey A. Born

Anthony J. Giovino

Jerry D. Boswell

Philip W. Glasgo

Denis O. Boudreaux

Jeffrey W. Glazer

Kenneth J. Boudreaux

Joel Gold

Wayne Boyet

Ron B. Goldfarb

Ron Braswell

Dennis W. Goodwin

Christopher Brown

David A. Gordon

William Brunsen

J. Charles Granicz

Samuel B. Bulmash

C. Ramon Griffin

Francis E. Canda

Reynolds Griffith

Omer Carey

Melvin W. Harju

Patrick A. Casabona

Phil Harrington

Robert Chatfield

George F. Harris

K. C. Chen

George T. Harris

Roger G. Clarke

John D. Harris

Terrence M. Clauretie

R. Stevenson Hawkey

Mark Cockalingam

Roger G. Hehman

Thomas Cook

Harvey Heinowitz

Maurice P. Corrigan

Glenn Henderson

Mike Cudd

Russell H. Hereth

Donnie L. Daniel

Kathleen T. Hevert

Prabir Datta

J. Lawrence Hexter

Joel J. Dauten

Douglas A. Hibbert

Roger P. Hill
Linda C. Hittle
James Hoban
Hugh A. Hobson
Keith Howe
Kenneth M. Huggins
Jerry G. Hunt
Mahmood Islam
James F. Jackson
Stanley Jacobs
Dale W. Janowsky
Jeannette R. Jesinger
Nalina Jeypalan
Timothy E. Johnson
Roger Juchau
Ashok K. Kapoor
Daniel J. Kaufman, Jr.
Joseph K. Kiely
Terrance E. Kingston
Thomas M. Krueger
Lawrence Kryzanowski
Harry R. Kuniansky
Richard E. La Near
William R. Lane
James Larsen
B. E. Lee
Scott Lee
Michael A. Lenarcic
A. Joseph Lerro
Thomas J. Liesz
Timothy Hoyt McCaughey
Christopher K. Ma
James C. Ma
Dilip B. Madan
Judy Maese
Brian Maris
Daniel S. Marrone
William H. Marsh
John F. Marshall
Linda J. Martin
Stanley A. Martin
Charles E. Maxwell
Jay Meiselman
Vincent A. Mercurio
Joseph Messina
Gene P. Morris
Edward A. Moses
Tarun K. Mukherjee
William T. Murphy

Randy Myers
Donald A. Nast
G. Newbould
Gary Noreiko
Dennis T. Officer
Kathleen J. Oldfather
Kathleen F. Oppenheimer
Richard M. Osborne
Jerome S. Osteryoung
Prasad Padmanabhan
Roger R. Palmer
Don B. Panton
John Park
Ronda S. Paul
Bruce C. Payne
Gerald W. Perritt
Gladys E. Perry
Stanley Piascik
D. Anthony Plath
Jerry B. Poe
Gerald A. Pogue
Ronald S. Pretekin
Fran Quinn
Walter J. Reinhart
Jack H. Reubens
William B. Riley, Jr.
Ron Rizzuto
Murray Sabrin
Kanwal S. Sachedeva
R. Daniel Sadlier
Hadi Salavitibar
Gary Sanger
William L. Sartoris
Carl J. Schwendiman
Carl Schweser
Jim Scott
John W. Settle
Richard A. Shick
A. M. Sibley
Surendra S. Singhvi
Stacy Sirmans
Barry D. Smith
Gerald Smolen
Ira Smolowitz
Jean Snavely
Joseph V. Stanford
John A. Stocker
Lester B. Strickler
Elizabeth Strock

Philip R. Swensen
John C. Talbott
Gary Tallman
Harry Tamule
Rolf K. Tedefalk
Richard Teweles
Kenneth J. Thygerson
Robert D. Tollen
Emery A. Trahan
Pieter A. Vandenberg
Nikhil P. Varaiya
Oscar Varela
Kenneth J. Venuto
James A. Verbrugge
Ronald P. Volpe
John M. Wachowicz, Jr.
William H. Weber III
Herbert Weinraub
Jonathan B. Welch
Grant J. Wells
Larry R. White
Peter Wichert
C. Don Wiggins
Howard A. Williams
Richard E. Williams
Glenn A. Wilt, Jr.
Bernard J. Winger
Tony R. Wingler
I. R. Woods
John C. Woods
Robert J. Wright
Richard H. Yanow
Seung J. Yoon
Charles W. Young
Philip J. Young
Joe W. Zeman
J. Kenton Zumwalt
John T. Zietlow
Tom Zwirlein

The following individuals provided extremely useful commentary on the eighth edition and its package:

The following individuals provided extremely useful comments on the ninth edition and its supplements package:

Lewell F. Gunter, *University of Georgia*
Mary L. Piotrowski, *Northern Arizona University*
Rick LeCompte, *Wichita State University*
Gayle A. Russell, *Eastern Connecticut State University*
John B. Mitchell, *Central Michigan University*
Patricia A. Ryan, *Drake University*
Lance Nail, *University of Alabama–Birmingham*
Richard W. Taylor, *Arkansas State University*
Prasad Padmanabahn, *San Diego State University*
Emery A. Trahan, *Northeastern University*

My special thanks goes to all members of my book team whose vision, creativity, and ongoing support helped me to engineer all elements of the Teaching/Learning System: to Marlene Bellamy of Writeline Associates for preparing the In Practice boxes; to Bernard W. Weinrich of St. Louis Community College, Forest Park Campus, for preparing the marginal annotations and the Web exercises; to Mary L. Piotrowski of Northern Arizona University for writing new end-of-chapter problems; to Dev Prasad of Texas A&M University–Corpus Christi for updating the *Instructor's Manual;* to Stanley G. Eakins of East Carolina University for revising and updating the *Study Guide;* to Hadi Salavitabar of the State University of New York at New Paltz for cultivating the now huge database of test items; to Daniel Borgia of Florida Gulf Coast University for preparing the *PowerPoint Lecture Presentation;* to Bill Megginson of the University of Oklahoma for revising the final chapter on international managerial finance, which was originally prepared by Mehdi Salehizadeh of San Diego State University; and to KMT Software for developing the *PMF CD-ROM software.*

I'm pleased by and proud of all their efforts, and I'm confident that those who use the book—both instructors and students—will appreciate everything they've done to add new features of interest and to ensure accuracy, consistency, and accessibility throughout the package.

A standing ovation and hearty round of applause also go to the publishing team assembled by Addison Wesley—including Greta Brogna, Amy Cronin, Nancy Fenton, Deb Kiernan, Julie Lindstrom, Jennifer Pelland, and others who worked on the book—for the inspiration and the perspiration that define teamwork. Elinor Stapleton and all the people at Thompson Steele Production Services deserve an equally resounding ovation. Applause is also due Ann Torbert, whose development skills, creativity, expertise, and hard work have contributed to the book's standard of excellence. Also, special thanks to the formidable Addison Wesley sales force in finance, whose ongoing efforts keep the business fun!

Finally, and most important, many thanks to my wife, Robin, and to our children, Zachary and Jessica, for patiently providing support, understanding, and good humor throughout the revision process. To them, I will be forever grateful.

—*Lawrence J. Gitman*

To the Student

Because you have a good many options for getting your assigned reading materials, I appreciate your choosing this textbook as the best means for learning. You shouldn't be disappointed. To meet your increasingly diverse needs and time constraints, my product team and I have put together in this textbook an effective learning system. It integrates a variety of learning tools with the concepts, techniques, and practical applications you'll need to learn about managerial finance. We have carefully listened to the compliments and complaints of professors and of students who have used earlier editions of this textbook in their coursework, and we have worked hard to present the most important concepts and practices of managerial finance in a clear and interesting way.

Each chapter begins with a photo and short paragraph that introduce a key idea of the chapter. These brief introductions won't take long to read, but they will give you a useful preview of the chapter topic. Also at the beginning of the chapter, you will find a list of six *Learning Goals*. Marked by a special icon, shown here in the margin, the Learning Goals are tied to first-level headings in the chapter and are reviewed point by point in the end-of-chapter summary. These goals will help you focus attention on what material you need to learn, where you can find it in the chapter, and whether you've mastered it by the end of the chapter.

Other features are included to support your learning experience. At the end of each major text section are *Review Questions*. Although it may be tempting to

Lawrence J. Gitman

rush past these questions, try to resist doing so. Pausing briefly to test your understanding of the key concepts, techniques, and practices in the section you've just read will help you cement your understanding of that material.

Other features in the body of each chapter are intended to motivate your study. In Practice boxes offer practical insights into the topic at hand through real company experiences. Some provide applications of the chapter material to typical personal financial situations, and others relate specifically to small businesses. Both these types of special applications are marked by headings. *Career Keys*, set in the margins, help you understand the importance of the material being covered to business majors other than finance. After all, managerial finance is an essential component not just in the business curriculum or in professional training programs, but in your daily job activities, *regardless of your major*. Other marginal items are *Hints* and *Key Terms*. Hints are just what their name implies—ideas and comments that help clarify important concepts. Key Terms and their definitions also appear in the margin when they are first introduced. These terms are the basic vocabulary of finance; you should be sure you know the

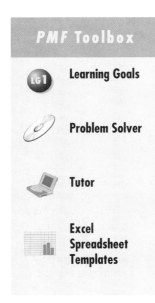

PMF Toolbox

Learning Goals

Problem Solver

Tutor

Excel Spreadsheet Templates

key terms in any section of the text covered in your coursework. In addition, these terms are **boldfaced** in the index for easy access to the glossary entry.

At the beginning of each major chapter section, you'll find a cluster of icons, which we call the *PMF* Toolbox. These icons represent learning tools and resources—learning goals, software tutorials, problem-solving disk routines, and spreadsheet templates—that are available to you in conjunction with the text section. We've already discussed the Learning Goals and how they work. The other items are described in what follows:

PMF CD-ROM Software Packaged with new copies of the text at no additional cost, your disk contains three useful tools: the *PMF Tutor*, the *PMF Problem-Solver*, and the *PMF Excel Spreadsheet Templates*. Documentation and practical advice for using the *PMF* CD-ROM appears at the end of the textbook in Appendix D.

The *PMF Tutor* extends self-testing opportunities beyond those on the printed page. The Tutor helps you identify and solve various types of managerial finance problems. Part of the *PMF* Toolbox, the Tutor icon flags all Tutor applications in the text. Through user-friendly menus, you can access over 55 different problem types, constructed by random-number generation for an inexhaustible supply of problems with little chance of repetition.

The *PMF Problem-Solver* contains seven short menu-driven programs to accelerate learning by providing an efficient way to perform financial computations. The Problem-Solver icon points out all related applications throughout the text of this popular provision of the *PMF* Toolbox. Once you have learned the concept needed to solve a particular problem, you can use the Problem-Solver to do the mathematical computations using the input data you supply.

The *PMF Excel Spreadsheet Templates* provide users with preprogrammed spreadsheet templates for inputting data and solving problems using perhaps the most popular and widely accepted practical software application. The template files correspond to selected end-of-chapter problems, and the template file names follow the chapter number and the problem number.

Study Guide (**ISBN** 0-321-05066-5) *Created by Stanley G. Eakins of East Carolina University.* The *Study Guide to accompany Principles of Managerial Finance,* ninth edition, is an integral component of the *PMF* Learning System. It offers many good tools for studying finance. Each chapter includes the following features: chapter summary enumerated by learning goals; topical chapter outline, also broken down by learning goals for quick review; sample problem solutions and a full sample exam with the answers at the end of the chapter; and thumbnail printouts of the PowerPoint Lecture Presentations to facilitate classroom note taking.

Given today's rapidly changing technology, who knows what might be available next semester? If you'd prefer electronic versions of texts—on disk or CD-ROM or any other platform—please let my publisher know by writing to the attention of the Acquisitions Editor in Finance, Addison Wesley Longman, One Jacob Way, Reading, Massachusetts 01867-3999. We are striving daily to keep apace of your needs and interests, and are interested in your ideas for improving the teaching and learning of finance. We wish you all the best in both your academic and professional careers.

PRINCIPLES OF

MANAGERIAL
FINANCE

PART

1

Introduction to Managerial Finance

Overview of Managerial Finance

LEARNING GOALS

LG1 Define *finance* and describe its major areas—financial services and managerial finance—and the career opportunities within them.

LG2 Review the basic forms of business organization and their respective strengths and weaknesses.

LG3 Describe the managerial finance function and differentiate managerial finance from the closely related disciplines of economics and accounting.

LG4 Identify the key activities of the financial manager within the firm.

LG5 Explain why wealth maximization, rather than profit maximization, is the firm's goal and how economic value added (EVA), a focus on stakeholders, and ethical behavior relate to its achievement.

LG6 Discuss the agency issue as it relates to owner wealth maximization.

LG1

1.1 Finance as an Area of Study

The field of finance is broad and dynamic. It directly affects the lives of every person and every organization. There are many areas for study, and a large number of career opportunities are available in the field of finance.

What Is Finance?

finance
The art and science of managing money.

Finance can be defined as the art and science of managing money. Virtually all individuals and organizations earn or raise money and spend or invest money. Finance is concerned with the process, institutions, markets, and instruments

The Balance of Power

MOST BUSINESSES ARE STRUCTURED like pyramids—with power to set policies concentrated at the top and spreading toward the bottom where day-to-day operations are carried out. However, the ultimate authority over all management of the organization resides in the owners of a corporation—its stockholders. The goal of the business organization, and the goal of its financial managers, is to achieve the objectives of the firm's owners. This chapter will explain corporate organization and the managerial finance function within the organization. It also will explore the key goal of the firm's owners—to maximize shareholder wealth—and the role of the financial manager in meeting that goal.

involved in the transfer of money among and between individuals, businesses, and governments. An understanding of finance will benefit most adults by allowing them to make better personal financial decisions. Those who work in financial jobs will benefit from an understanding of finance by being able to interface effectively with the firm's financial personnel, processes, and procedures.

Major Areas and Opportunities in Finance

The major areas of finance can be summarized by reviewing the career opportunities in finance. These opportunities can, for convenience, be divided into two broad parts: financial services and managerial finance.

Financial Services

financial services
The part of finance concerned with design and delivery of advice and financial products to individuals, business, and government.

Financial services is the area of finance concerned with the design and delivery of advice and financial products to individuals, business, and government. It involves a variety of interesting career opportunities within the areas of banking and related institutions, personal financial planning, investments, real estate, and insurance. Career opportunities available in each of these areas are described briefly at this textbook's homepage at **www.awlonline.com/gitman.**

Managerial Finance

managerial finance
Concerns the duties of the financial manager in the business firm.

financial manager
Actively manages the financial affairs of any type of business, whether financial or nonfinancial, private or public, large or small, profit-seeking or not-for-profit.

Managerial finance is concerned with the duties of the financial manager in the business firm. **Financial managers** actively manage the financial affairs of many types of business—financial and nonfinancial, private and public, large and small, profit-seeking and not-for-profit. They perform such varied financial tasks as planning, extending credit to customers, evaluating proposed large expenditures, and raising money to fund the firm's operations. In recent years, the changing economic and regulatory environments have increased the importance and complexity of the financial manager's duties. As a result, many top executives in industry and government have come from the finance area.

Another important recent trend has been the globalization of business activity. U.S. corporations have dramatically increased their sales, purchases, investments, and fund raising in other countries, and foreign corporations have likewise increased these activities in the United States. These changes have created a need for financial managers who can help a firm to manage cash flows in different currencies and protect against the risks that naturally arise from international transactions. Although this need makes the managerial finance function more complex, it can also lead to a more rewarding and fulfilling career.

The Study of Managerial Finance

An understanding of the theories, concepts, techniques, and practices presented throughout this text will fully acquaint you with the financial manager's activities and decisions. Because most business decisions are measured in financial terms, the financial manager plays a key role in the operation of the firm. People in all areas of responsibility—accounting, information systems, management, marketing, operations, and so forth—need a basic understanding of the managerial finance function.

All managers in the firm, regardless of their job descriptions, work with financial personnel to justify manpower requirements, negotiate operating budgets, deal with financial performance appraisals, and sell proposals based at least in part on their financial merits. Clearly, those managers who understand the financial decision-making process will be better able to address financial concerns and will therefore more often get the resources they need to accomplish their own goals. Throughout the text, "career keys" are positioned in the text margin. These are brief discussions (preceded by the icon   ) that highlight the relationship between the topic being discussed and one or more nonfinancial area of business responsibility. These marginal notes should help you understand some of the many interactions between managerial finance and other business careers.

TABLE 1.1	**Career Opportunities in Managerial Finance**
Position	Description
Financial analyst	Primarily responsible for preparing and analyzing the firm's financial plans and budgets. Other duties include financial forecasting, performing financial ratio analysis, and working closely with accounting.
Capital budgeting analyst/manager	Responsible for the evaluation and recommendation of proposed asset investments. May be involved in the financial aspects of implementation of approved investments.
Project finance manager	In large firms, arranges financing for approved asset investments. Coordinates consultants, investment bankers, and legal counsel.
Cash manager	Responsible for maintaining and controlling the firm's daily cash balances. Frequently manages the firm's cash collection, short-term investment, transfer, and disbursement activities and coordinates short-term borrowing and banking relationships.
Credit analyst/manager	Administers the firm's credit policy by analyzing or managing the evaluation of credit applications, extending credit, and monitoring and collecting accounts receivable.
Pension fund manager	In large companies, responsible for coordinating the assets and liabilities of the employees' pension fund. Either performs investment management activities or hires and oversees the performance of these activities by a third party.

As you study this text, you will learn about the career opportunities in managerial finance. These are briefly described in Table 1.1. Although this text focuses on profit-seeking firms, the principles presented here are equally applicable to public and nonprofit organizations. The decision-making principles developed in this text can also be applied to personal financial decisions. I hope that this first exposure to the exciting field of finance will provide the foundation and initiative for further study and possibly even a future career.

? Review Questions

1–1   What is *finance?* Explain how this field affects the lives of everyone and every organization.

1–2   What is the *financial services* area of finance?

1–3   Describe the field of *managerial finance.* Why is the study of managerial finance important regardless of the specific area of responsibility one has within the business firm?

1.2 Basic Forms of Business Organization

The three basic legal forms of business organization are the *sole proprietorship,* the *partnership,* and the *corporation.* In addition, other specialized forms of business organization exist. The sole proprietorship is the most common form of organization. However, the corporation is by far the dominant form with respect to receipts and net profits. Corporations are given primary emphasis in this textbook.

Sole Proprietorships

sole proprietorship
A business owned by one person and operated for his or her own profit.

unlimited liability
The condition of a sole proprietorship (or general partnership) allowing the owner's total wealth to be taken to satisfy creditors.

A **sole proprietorship** is a business owned by one person who operates it for his or her own profit. About 75 percent of all business firms are sole proprietorships. The typical sole proprietorship is a small business, such as a bike shop, personal trainer, or plumber. Typically, the proprietor, along with a few employees, operates the proprietorship. He or she normally raises capital from personal resources or by borrowing and is responsible for all business decisions. The sole proprietor has **unlimited liability;** his or her total wealth, not merely the amount originally invested, can be taken to satisfy creditors. The majority of sole proprietorships are found in the wholesale, retail, service, and construction industries. The key strengths and weaknesses of sole proprietorships are summarized in Table 1.2.

TABLE 1.2	**Strengths and Weaknesses of the Basic Legal Forms of Business Organization**		
		Legal form	
	Sole proprietorship	Partnership	Corporation
Strengths	Owner receives all profits (as well as losses)	Can raise more funds than sole proprietorships	Owners have *limited liability,* which guarantees that they cannot lose more than they invested
	Low organizational costs	Borrowing power enhanced by more owners	Can achieve large size due to sale of stock
	Income included and taxed on proprietor's personal tax return	More available brain power and managerial skill	Ownership (stock) is readily transferable
	Independence	Income included and taxed on partner's tax return	Long life of firm
	Secrecy		Can hire professional managers
	Ease of dissolution		Has better access to financing
			Receives certain tax advantages
Weaknesses	Owner has *unlimited liability*— total wealth can be taken to satisfy debts	Owners have *unlimited liability* and may have to cover debts of other partners	Taxes generally higher, because corporate income is taxed and dividends paid to owners are also taxed
	Limited fund-raising power tends to inhibit growth	Partnership is dissolved when a partner dies	More expensive to organize than other business forms
	Proprietor must be jack-of-all-trades	Difficult to liquidate or transfer partnership	Subject to greater government regulation
	Difficult to give employees long-run career opportunities		Lacks secrecy, because stockholders must receive financial reports
	Lacks continuity when proprietor dies		

Partnerships

partnership
A business owned by two or more people and operated for profit.

A **partnership** consists of two or more owners doing business together for profit. Partnerships, which account for about 10 percent of all businesses, are typically larger than sole proprietorships. Finance, insurance, and real estate firms are the most common types of partnership. Public accounting and stock brokerage partnerships often have large numbers of partners.

articles of partnership
The written contract used to formally establish a business partnership.

Most partnerships are established by a written contract known as **articles of partnership.** In a *general* (or *regular*) *partnership*, all partners have unlimited liability, and each partner is legally liable for all of the debts of the partnership. Strengths and weaknesses of partnerships are summarized in Table 1.2.

Corporations

corporation
An intangible business entity created by law (often called a "legal entity").

A **corporation** is an artificial being created by law. Often called a "legal entity," a corporation has the powers of an individual in that it can sue and be sued, make and be party to contracts, and acquire property in its own name. Although only about 15 percent of all businesses are incorporated, the corporation is the dominant form of business organization. It accounts for nearly 90 percent of business receipts and 80 percent of net profits. Although corporations are involved in all types of business, manufacturing corporations account for the largest portion of corporate business receipts and net profits. The key strengths and weaknesses of large corporations are summarized in Table 1.2.

Hint   For many small corporations, as well as small proprietorships and partnerships, there is no access to financial markets. In addition, whenever the owners make a loan, they usually must personally cosign the loan.

The owners of a corporation are its **stockholders,** whose ownership or "equity" is evidenced by either *common stock* or *preferred stock.*[1] These forms of ownership are defined and discussed in Chapter 2; at this point suffice it to say that **common stock** is the purest and most basic form of corporate ownership. Stockholders expect to earn a return by receiving **dividends**—periodic distributions of earnings—or by realizing gains through increases in share price. As noted in the upper portion of Figure 1.1, the stockholders vote periodically to elect the members of the board of directors and to amend the firm's corporate charter.

stockholders
The owners of a corporation, whose ownership or "equity" is evidenced by either *common stock* or *preferred stock.*

common stock
The purest and most basic form of corporate ownership.

dividends
Periodic distributions of earnings to the stockholders of a firm.

The **board of directors** has the ultimate authority in guiding corporate affairs and in making general policy. The directors include key corporate personnel as well as outside individuals who typically are successful businesspeople and executives of other major organizations. Outside directors for major corporations are typically paid an annual fee of $10,000 to $20,000 or more and are frequently granted options to buy a specified number of shares of the firm's stock at a stated—and often attractive—price.

board of directors
Group elected by the firm's stockholders and having ultimate authority to guide corporate affairs and make general policy.

president or chief executive officer (CEO)
Corporate official responsible for managing the firm's day-to-day operations and carrying out the policies established by the board of directors.

The **president or chief executive officer (CEO)** is responsible for managing day-to-day operations and carrying out the policies established by the board. The CEO is required to report periodically to the firm's directors. It is important to note the division between owners and managers in a large corporation, as shown by the dashed horizontal line in Figure 1.1. This separation and some of the

---

1. Some corporations do not have stockholders but rather have "members" who often have rights similar to those of stockholders—they are entitled to vote and receive dividends. Examples include mutual savings banks, credit unions, mutual insurance companies, and a whole host of charitable organizations.

FIGURE 1.1   **Corporate Organization**

The general organization of a corporation and the finance function (which is shown in yellow).

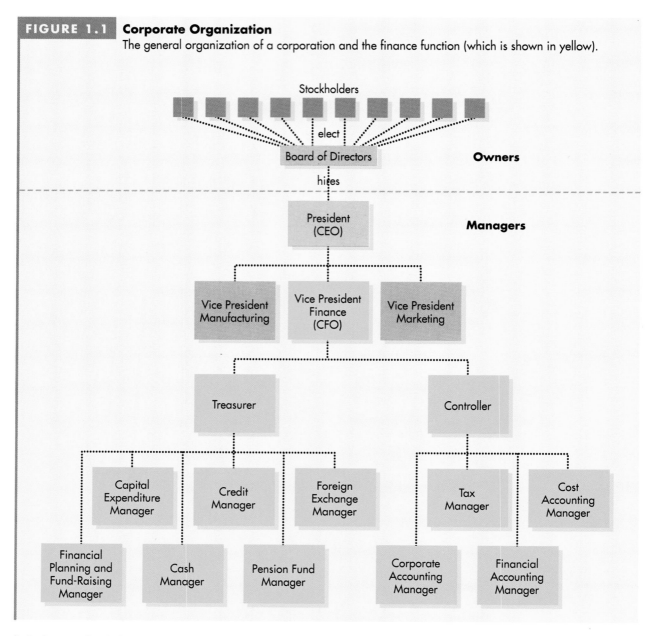

limited partnership (LP)
See Table 1.3.

S corporation (S corp)
See Table 1.3.

limited liability corporation (LLC)
See Table 1.3.

limited liability partnership
(LLP)
See Table 1.3.

issues surrounding it will be addressed in the discussion of *the agency issue* later in this chapter.

Other Limited Liability Organizations

A number of other organizational forms provide owners with limited liability. The most popular include **limited partnerships (LPs)**, **S corporations (S corps)**, **limited liability corporations (LLCs)**, and **limited liability partnerships (LLPs)**.

TABLE 1.3   Other Limited Liability Organizations

Organization	Description
Limited partnership (LP)	A partnership in which one or more partners can be designated as having limited liability as long as at least *one* partner (the general partner) has unlimited liability. The *limited partners* are prohibited from being active in the firm's management; they are passive investors.
S corporation (S corp)	A tax-reporting entity that (under Subchapter S of the Internal Revenue Code) allows corporations that meet specified requirements and have 75 or fewer stockholders to elect to be taxed as partnerships. Its stockholders receive all of the organizational benefits of a corporation and the tax advantages of a partnership. But S corps lose certain tax advantages related to pension plans that are available to the traditional corporation.
Limited liability corporation (LLC)	Permitted in most states, the LLC's owners, like those of S corps, have limited liability and are taxed as a partnership. But unlike an S corp, the LLC can own more than 80 percent of another corporation, and corporations, partnerships, or non-U.S. residents can own LLC shares. LLCs work well for corporate joint ventures or projects developed through a subsidiary, by allowing the venture's risk to be isolated while getting favorable tax treatment.
Limited liability partnership (LLP)[a]	A partnership registered with the state, which has governing statutes that specify the types of business entities that qualify. It is permitted in many states, but the governing statutes vary. All LLP partners have limited liability with regard to the business—they are not personally liable for other partners' malpractice—and the LLP is taxed as a partnership. The liability protection does not protect partners from their individual acts of malpractice. LLPs are frequently used by legal and accounting professionals.

[a]During the past few years this organizational form has begun to replace *professional corporations* or *associations*—corporations formed by groups of professionals such as attorneys and accountants that provide limited liability except for that related to malpractice—because of their tax advantages.

Each represents a specialized form or blending of the characteristics of the organizational forms described before. What they have in common is that their owners receive limited liability and they typically have fewer than 100 owners. Each of these limited liability organizations is briefly described in Table 1.3.

? Review Questions

1–4 What are the three basic forms of business organization? Which form is most common? Which form is dominant in terms of business receipts and net profits? Why?

1–5 Describe the role and basic relationship among the major parties in a corporation—stockholders, board of directors, and president. How are corporate owners compensated?

1–6 Briefly name and describe some organizational forms other than corporations that provide owners with limited liability. Do these organizations typically have a large number of owners?

1.3 The Managerial Finance Function

As noted earlier, people in all areas of responsibility within the firm will interact with finance personnel, processes, and procedures to get their jobs done. For financial personnel to make useful forecasts and decisions, they must talk to individuals in other areas of the firm. The managerial finance function can be broadly described by considering its role within the organization, its relationship to economics and accounting, and the key activities of the financial manager.

Organization of the Finance Function

Career Key

Management will define the tasks that will be performed by the finance department. It will also choose how the finance function fits within the total structure of the firm.

The size and importance of the managerial finance function depend on the size of the firm. In small firms, the finance function is generally performed by the accounting department. As a firm grows, the finance function typically evolves into a separate department linked directly to the company president or chief executive officer (CEO) through a vice president of finance, commonly called the chief financial officer (CFO). The lower portion of the organizational chart in Figure 1.1 showed the structure of the finance function in a typical medium-to-large-size firm. Reporting to the vice president of finance are the treasurer and the controller. The **treasurer** is commonly responsible for handling financial activities, such as financial planning and fund raising, making capital expenditure decisions, managing cash, managing credit activities, managing the pension fund, and managing foreign exchange. The **controller** typically handles the accounting activities, such as corporate accounting, tax management, financial accounting, and cost accounting. The treasurer's focus tends to be more external, whereas the controller's focus is more internal. *The activities of the treasurer, or financial manager, are the primary concern of this text.*

treasurer
The officer responsible for the firm's financial activities such as financial planning and fund raising, making capital expenditure decisions, and managing cash, credit, the pension fund, and foreign exchange.

controller
The officer responsible for the firm's accounting activities, such as corporate accounting, tax management, financial accounting, and cost accounting.

Hint A *controller* is sometimes referred to as a *comptroller*. Nonprofit and governmental organizations frequently use the title of comptroller.

If international sales or purchases are important to a firm, it may well employ one or more finance professionals whose job is to monitor and manage the firm's exposure to loss from currency fluctuations. A trained financial manager can "hedge," or protect against, this and similar risks, at reasonable cost, using a variety of financial instruments. These **foreign exchange managers** (or traders) typically report to the firm's treasurer.

foreign exchange manager
The manager responsible for monitoring and managing the firm's exposure to loss from currency fluctuations.

Relationship to Economics

The field of finance is closely related to economics. Financial managers must understand the economic framework and be alert to the consequences of varying levels of economic activity and changes in economic policy. They must also be able to use economic theories as guidelines for efficient business operation. Examples include supply-and-demand analysis, profit-maximizing strategies, and price theory. The primary economic principle used in managerial finance is **marginal analysis,** the principle that financial decisions should be made and actions taken only when the added benefits exceed the added costs. Nearly all financial decisions ultimately come down to an assessment of their marginal benefits and marginal costs. A basic knowledge of economics is therefore necessary to understand both the environment and the decision techniques of managerial finance.

marginal analysis
Economic principle that states that financial decisions should be made and actions taken only when the added benefits exceed the added costs.

Example ▼ Jamie Teng is a financial manager for Nord Department Stores—a large chain of upscale department stores operating primarily in the western United States. She is currently trying to decide whether to replace one of the firm's on-line computers with a new, more sophisticated one that would both speed processing time and handle a larger volume of transactions. The new computer would require a cash outlay of $80,000, and the old computer could be sold to net $28,000. The total benefits from the new computer (measured in today's dollars) would be $100,000, and the benefits over a similar time period from the old computer (measured in today's dollars) would be $35,000. Applying marginal analysis to this data, we get

Benefits with new computer	$100,000	
Less: Benefits with old computer	35,000	
(1) Marginal (added) benefits		$65,000
Cost of new computer	$ 80,000	
Less: Proceeds from sale of old computer	28,000	
(2) Marginal (added) costs		52,000
Net benefit [(1) − (2)]		$13,000

Because the marginal (added) benefits of $65,000 exceed the marginal (added) costs of $52,000, the purchase of the new computer to replace the old one is recommended. The firm will experience a net benefit of $13,000 as a result of this ▲ action.

Relationship to Accounting

The firm's finance (treasurer) and accounting (controller) activities, shown in the lower portion of Figure 1.1, are closely related and generally overlap. Indeed, managerial finance and accounting are not often easily distinguishable. In small firms the controller often carries out the finance function, and in large firms many accountants are closely involved in various finance activities. However, there are two basic differences between finance and accounting; one relates to the emphasis on cash flows and the other to decision making.

Emphasis on Cash Flows

The accountant's primary function is to develop and provide data for measuring the performance of the firm, assessing its financial position, and paying taxes. Using certain standardized and generally accepted principles, the accountant prepares financial statements that recognize revenue at the point of sale and expenses when incurred. This approach is referred to as the **accrual basis.**

The financial manager, on the other hand, places primary emphasis on *cash flows*, the intake and outgo of cash. He or she maintains the firm's solvency by planning the cash flows necessary to satisfy its obligations and to acquire assets needed to achieve the firm's goals. The financial manager uses this **cash basis** to recognize the revenues and expenses only with respect to actual inflows and outflows

accrual basis
Recognizes revenue at the point of sale and recognizes expenses when incurred.

cash basis
Recognizes revenues and expenses only with respect to actual inflows and outflows of cash.

of cash. Regardless of its profit or loss, a firm must have a sufficient flow of cash to meet its obligations as they come due.

E x a m p l e ▼ Nassau Corporation, a small yacht dealer, in the calendar year just ended sold one yacht for $100,000; the yacht was purchased during the year at a total cost of $80,000. Although the firm paid in full for the yacht during the year, at year end it has yet to collect the $100,000 from the customer. The accounting view and the financial view of the firm's performance during the year are given by the following income and cash flow statements, respectively.

Accounting (accrual basis) view		Financial (cash basis) view	
Income Statement Nassau Corporation for the year ended 12/31		**Cash Flow Statement Nassau Corporation for the year ended 12/31**	
Sales revenue	$100,000	Cash inflow	$ 0
Less: Costs	80,000	Less: Cash outflow	80,000
Net profit	$ 20,000	Net cash flow	($80,000)

In an accounting sense Nassau Corporation is profitable, but it is a financial failure in terms of actual cash flow. Its lack of cash flow resulted from the uncollected account receivable of $100,000. Without adequate cash inflows to meet its obligations the firm will not survive, regardless of its level of profits. ▲

Hint The primary emphasis of accounting is on accrual methods; the primary emphasis of financial management is on cash flow methods.

The preceding example shows that accrual accounting data do not fully describe the circumstances of a firm. Thus, the financial manager must look beyond financial statements to obtain insight into developing or existing problems. The financial manager, by concentrating on cash flows, should be able to avoid insolvency and achieve the firm's financial goals.

Decision Making

We come now to the second major difference between finance and accounting: decision making. Whereas accountants devote most of their attention to the collection and presentation of financial data, financial managers evaluate the accounting statements, develop additional data, and make decisions based on their assessment of the associated returns and risks. Accountants provide consistently developed and easily interpreted data about the firm's past, present, and future operations. Financial managers use these data, either in raw form or after adjustments and analyses, as inputs to the decision-making process.

Key Activities of the Financial Manager

The financial manager's primary activities are (1) performing financial analysis and planning, (2) making investment decisions, and (3) making financing decisions. Figure 1.2 relates each of these financial activities to the firm's balance

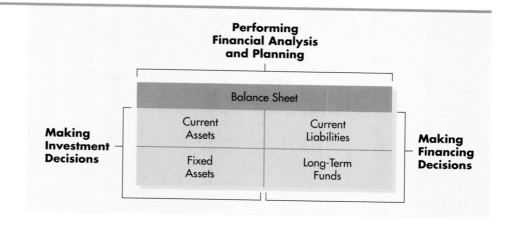

FIGURE 1.2

Financial Activities
Key activities of the
financial manager

sheet. Although investment and financing decisions can be conveniently viewed in
terms of the balance sheet, these decisions are made on the basis of their cash flow
effects. This focus on cash flow will become clearer in later chapters.

Performing Financial Analysis and Planning

Financial analysis and planning is concerned with (1) monitoring the firm's
financial condition, (2) evaluating the need for increased (or reduced) productive
capacity, and (3) determining what financing is required. These functions encom-
pass the entire balance sheet as well as the firm's income statement and other
financial statements. Although this activity relies heavily on accrual-based financial statements, its underlying objective is to assess the firm's cash flows and
develop plans that ensure adequate cash flow to support goal achievement.

Making Investment Decisions

Investment decisions determine both the mix and the type of assets found on the
left-hand side of the firm's balance sheet. *Mix* refers to the number of dollars of
current and fixed assets. Once the mix is established, the financial manager
attempts to maintain optimal levels of each type of current asset. The financial
manager also decides which fixed assets to acquire and when existing fixed assets
need to be modified, replaced, or liquidated. These decisions are important
because they affect the firm's success in achieving its goals.

Making Financing Decisions

Financing decisions deal with the right-hand side of the firm's balance sheet and
involve two major areas. First, the most appropriate mix of short-term and long-
term financing must be established. A second and equally important concern is
which individual short-term or long-term sources of financing are best at a given
point in time. Many of these decisions are dictated by necessity, but some require
in-depth analysis of the financing alternatives, their costs, and their long-run

In Practice

All in a Day's Work

What does it take to be a successful chief financial officer (CFO)? Today's CFOs are key members of the executive team, setting the firm's overall financial strategy and participating in managerial activities of all sorts. Based on a recent survey of Fortune 1000 companies, the three most important qualities, wanted by more than half of the CEOs surveyed, are analytical thinking, strategic planning, and leadership. More than half of the CEOs cited general management as the most important area in which CFOs should have experience.

Thomas J. Wilson, CFO of Allstate Insurance Co., exemplifies the new financial leader. Joining Allstate in 1995, when it became independent from Sears, Roebuck and Co., he inherited a finance organization that looked to Sears' corporate finance department to raise external funding, acquire other companies, and manage cash. "I had some great people, but they didn't know much about the public market or external reporting," Wilson says. Building a new finance team was his first priority, and broad coverage of all financial areas was the goal. First, he promoted to treasurer a manager with 20 years' experience in Allstate's finance and marketing departments. Next, he hired two assistant treasurers with expertise in cash management, capital markets, and acquisitions to fill in the knowledge gaps.

A newcomer to the insurance industry, Wilson learned about Allstate's operations by asking difficult questions of colleagues in all areas of the company. "Tom is someone who doesn't necessarily accept the way things have been done previously, even though things may be looking okay," says Allstate chairman and CEO Jerry Choate. For example, Wilson recommended that Allstate concentrate on its core businesses—auto, homeowners, and life insurance, and selected personal savings products—to strengthen the Allstate brand. He sold all other business units and acquired several new companies to expand Allstate's market presence and product lines.

Team building, strategic and operational planning, raising and allocating capital to achieve corporate goals, managing risks, selling and acquiring companies—it's all in a day's work for CFOs like Tom Wilson.

implications. Again, it is the effect of these decisions on the firm's goal achievement that is most important.

? Review Questions

1–7 What financial activities does the treasurer, or financial manager, perform in the mature firm?

1–8 Explain why the financial manager should possess a basic knowledge of economics. What is the primary economic principle used in managerial finance?

fidelity bond
A contract under which a bonding company agrees to reimburse a firm for up to a stated amount if a bonded manager's dishonest act results in a financial loss to the firm.

2. *Bonding expenditures* protect against the potential consequences of dishonest acts by managers. Typically, the owners pay a third-party bonding company to obtain a **fidelity bond.** This bond is a contract under which the bonding company agrees to reimburse the firm for up to a stated amount if a bonded manager's dishonest act results in financial loss to the firm.
3. *Opportunity costs* result from the difficulties that large organizations typically have in responding to new opportunities. The firm's necessary organizational structure, decision hierarchy, and control mechanisms may cause profitable opportunities to be forgone because of management's inability to seize upon them quickly.
4. *Structuring expenditures* are the most popular, powerful, and expensive agency costs incurred by firms. They result from structuring managerial compensation to correspond with share price maximization. The objective is to give managers incentives to act in the best interests of the owners and to compensate them for such actions. In addition, the resulting compensation packages allow firms to compete for and hire the best managers available. Compensation plans can be divided into two groups—incentive plans and performance plans.

incentive plans
Management compensation plans that tend to tie management compensation to share price; most popular incentive plan involves the grant of *stock options.*

stock options
An incentive allowing managers to purchase stock at the market price set at the time of the grant.

Incentive plans tend to tie management compensation to share price. The most popular incentive plan is the granting of **stock options** to management. These options allow managers to purchase stock at the market price set at the time of the grant. If the market price rises, they will be rewarded by being able to resell the shares subsequently at the higher market price. Although in theory these options should motivate, they are sometimes criticized because positive management performance can be masked in a poor stock market in which share prices in general have declined due to economic and behavioral "market forces" outside of management's control.

performance plans
Plans that compensate managers on the basis of proven performance measured by EPS, growth in EPS, and other ratios of return. *Performance shares and/or cash bonuses* are used as compensation under these plans.

performance shares
Shares of stock given to management for meeting stated performance goals.

cash bonuses
Cash paid to management for achieving certain performance goals.

The use of **performance plans** has grown in popularity in recent years due to their relative independence from market forces. These plans compensate managers on the basis of their proven performance measured by earnings per share (EPS), growth in EPS, and other ratios of return. **Performance shares,** shares of stock given to management as a result of meeting the stated performance goals, are often used in these plans. Another form of performance-based compensation is **cash bonuses,** cash payments tied to the achievement of certain performance goals. Under performance plans, management understands in advance the formula used to determine the amount of performance shares or cash bonus it can earn during the period. In addition, the minimum benefit (typically, $0) and maximum benefit available under the plan are specified.

The Current View

Although experts agree that an effective way to motivate management is to tie compensation to performance, the execution of many compensation plans has been closely scrutinized in recent years. Stockholders—both individuals and institutions—as well as the Securities and Exchange Commission (SEC) have publicly questioned the appropriateness of the multimillion-dollar compensation packages (including salary, bonus, and long-term compensation) that many corporate executives receive. For example, the three highest-paid CEOs in 1998 were (1) Michael Eisner, of Walt Disney, who earned $575.6 million; (2) Mel Karmazin, of CBS, who earned $201.9 million; and (3) Sanford Weill, of Citigroup, who earned $167.1 million. Tenth on the same list was M. Douglas Ivester of Coca-Cola, who earned $57.3 million. During 1998, the compensation of the average CEO of a major U.S. corporation rose by about 36 percent over 1997. CEOs of 365 of the largest U.S. companies surveyed by *Business Week,* using data from Standard & Poor's Compusat, earned an average of $10.6 million in total compensation; the average for the 20 highest paid CEOs was $101.2 million.

Although these sizable compensation packages may be justified by significant increases in shareholder wealth, recent studies have failed to find a strong relationship between CEO compensation and share price. The publicity surrounding these large compensation packages (without corresponding share price performance) is expected to drive down executive compensation in the future. Contributing to this publicity is the relatively recent SEC requirement that publicly traded companies disclose to shareholders and others both the amount of and method used to determine compensation to their highest paid executives. At the same time, new compensation plans that better link management performance with regard to shareholder wealth to its compensation are expected to be developed and implemented.

Of course, in addition to incurring structuring costs to link management compensation to performance, many firms incur additional agency costs for monitoring, bonding, and streamlining organizational decision making to further ensure congruence of management and owner objectives. Unconstrained, managers may have other goals in addition to share price maximization, but much of the evidence suggests that share price maximization—the focus of this book—is the primary goal of most firms.

? Review Questions

1–16 What is the *agency problem?* How do market forces, both shareholder activism and the threat of hostile takeover, act to prevent or minimize this problem?

1–17 Define *agency costs,* and explain why firms incur them. What are *structuring expenditures,* and how are they used? Describe and differentiate between *incentive* and *performance* compensation plans. What is the current view with regard to the execution of many compensation plans?

1.6 Using This Text

The text's organization links the firm's activities to its value, as determined in the securities markets. The activities of the financial manager are described in six parts:

Part 1: Introduction to Managerial Finance
Part 2: Important Financial Concepts
Part 3: Long-Term Investment Decisions
Part 4: Long-Term Financing Decisions
Part 5: Short-Term Financial Decisions
Part 6: Special Topics in Managerial Finance

Each major decision area is presented in terms of both return and risk factors and their potential impact on the owners' wealth. Coverage of international events and topics is integrated into the chapter discussions. A separate international managerial finance chapter is also included.

The text has been developed around a group of about 120 learning goals—6 per chapter. Mastery of these goals results in a broad understanding of the theories, concepts, techniques, and practices of managerial finance. These goals have been carefully integrated into a learning system. Each chapter begins with a numbered list of learning goals. Next to each major text heading is a *toolbox,* which notes by number the specific learning goal(s) addressed in that section. At the end of each section of the chapter (positioned before the next major heading) are review questions that test your understanding of key theories, concepts, techniques, and practices in that section. At the end of each chapter, the chapter summaries, self-test problems, and problems are also keyed by number to each chapter's learning goals. By linking all elements to the learning goals, the integrated learning system facilitates the mastery of those goals.

Also keyed to various parts of the text is the *PMF CD-ROM Software,* a disk for use with IBM PCs and compatible microcomputers. The disk contains three different sets of routines:

1. The *PMF Tutor* is a user-friendly program that extends self-testing opportunities in the more quantitative chapters beyond those included in the end-of-chapter materials. It gives immediate feedback with detailed solutions and provides tutorial assistance (including text page references). Text discussions and end-of-chapter problems with which the *PMF Tutor* can be used are marked with a ✒.
2. The *PMF Problem-Solver* can be used as an aid in performing many of the routine financial calculations presented in the book. A disk symbol, ✐, identifies those text discussions and end-of-chapter problems that can be solved with the *PMF Problem-Solver.*
3. The *PMF Excel Spreadsheet Templates* can be used with Microsoft Excel to input data and carry out "what-if" types of analyses in selected chapters. These problems are marked by the symbol ▦.

A detailed discussion of how to use the *PMF CD-ROM Software*—the *Tutor,* the *Problem-Solver,* and the *Excel Spreadsheet Templates*—is included in Appendix D at the back of this book.

Each chapter ends with a case that integrates the chapter materials, and each part ends with an integrative case that ties together the key topical material covered in the chapters within that part. Where applicable, the symbols for the *PMF*

Problem-Solver and/or the *PMF Tutor* identify case questions that can be solved with the aid of these programs. Both the chapter-end and part-end cases can be used to synthesize and apply related concepts and techniques.

SUMMARY

 Define *finance* and describe its major areas—financial services and managerial finance—and the career opportunities within them. Finance, the art and science of managing money, affects the lives of every person and every organization. Major opportunities in financial services exist within banking and related institutions, personal financial planning, investments, real estate, and insurance. Managerial finance, concerned with the duties of the financial manager in the business firm, offers numerous career opportunities such as financial analyst, capital budgeting analyst/manager, project finance manager, cash manager, credit analyst/manager, and pension fund manager. The recent trend toward globalization of business activity has created new demands and opportunities in managerial finance.

 Review the basic forms of business organization and their respective strengths and weaknesses. The basic forms of business organization are the sole proprietorship, the partnership, and the corporation. Although there are more sole proprietorships than any other form of business organization, the corporation is dominant in terms of business receipts and profits. The owners of a corporation are its stockholders, evidenced by either common stock or preferred stock. Stockholders expect to earn a return by receiving dividends or by realizing gains through increases in share price. The key strengths and weaknesses of each form of business organization are summarized in Table 1.2. Other popular limited liability organizations are listed and described in Table 1.3.

 Describe the managerial finance function and differentiate managerial finance from the closely related disciplines of economics and accounting. All areas of responsibility within a firm interact with finance personnel, processes, and procedures. In large firms, the managerial finance function might be handled by a separate department headed by the vice president of finance (CFO), to whom the treasurer and controller report; in small firms, the finance function is generally performed by the accounting department. The financial manager must understand the economic environment and relies heavily on the economic principle of marginal analysis when making decisions. Financial managers use accounting data but differ from accountants, who devote primary attention to accrual methods and to gathering and presenting data, by concentrating on cash flows and decision making.

 Identify the key activities of the financial manager within the firm. The three key activities of the financial manager are (1) performing financial analysis and planning, (2) making investment decisions, and (3) making financing decisions.

 Explain why wealth maximization, rather than profit maximization, is the firm's goal and how economic value added (EVA), a focus on stakeholders, and ethical behavior relate to its achievement. The goal of the financial manager is to maximize the owners' wealth (dependent on stock price) rather than profits, because profit maximization ignores the timing of returns, does not directly consider cash flows, and ignores risk. Because return and risk are the key determinants of share price, both must be assessed by the financial manager when evaluating decision alternatives or actions. EVA is a popular measure used by many firms to determine whether an investment positively contributes to the owners' wealth. The wealth maximizing actions of financial managers should be consistent with the preservation of the wealth of *stakeholders,* groups such as employees, customers, suppliers, creditors, owners, and others who have a direct economic link to the firm. Positive ethical practices by the firm and its managers are believed

Financial Fabric

The financial environment is like a fabric woven from many different threads—savers (suppliers) and investors (demanders) of funds, financial institutions (like banks), financial markets such as stock exchanges, and the federal government and its regulatory agencies. The common thread running through the entire fabric is money. Those who have excess money are willing to put it to use in ways that make it possible for those who need money to obtain it, for a cost. This chapter will describe the prominent threads in the fabric of the financial environment—the institutions and markets that channel money into loans and investments, the common debt and equity securities issued by businesses to raise money, and the interest rates that regulate the flow of money between suppliers and demanders of funds.

Financial Institutions

financial institution
An intermediary that channels the savings of individuals, businesses, and governments into loans or investments.

Hint Think about how inefficient it would be if each individual saver had to negotiate with each potential user of savings. Institutions make the process very efficient by becoming intermediaries between savers and users.

Financial institutions are intermediaries that channel the savings of individuals, businesses, and governments into loans or investments. Many financial institutions directly or indirectly pay savers interest on deposited funds; others provide services for a fee (for example, checking accounts for which customers pay service charges). Some financial institutions accept customers' savings deposits and lend this money to other customers; others invest customers' savings in earning assets such as real estate or stocks and bonds; and some do both. Financial institutions are required by the government to operate within established regulatory guidelines.

Key Participants in Financial Institution Transactions

The key suppliers and demanders of funds are individuals, businesses, and governments. The savings of individual consumers provide financial institutions with a large portion of their funds. Individuals not only supply funds to financial institutions but also demand funds from them in the form of loans. However, individuals as a group are the *net suppliers* for financial institutions: They save more money than they borrow.

Business firms also deposit some of their funds in financial institutions, primarily in checking accounts with various commercial banks. Firms, like individuals, also borrow funds from these institutions. As a group, business firms are *net demanders* of funds: They borrow more money than they save.

Governments maintain deposits of temporarily idle funds, certain tax payments, and Social Security payments in commercial banks. They do not borrow funds *directly* from financial institutions, but by selling their securities to various institutions, governments indirectly borrow from them. The government also is typically a *net demander* of funds: It borrows more than it saves. We've all heard about the federal budget deficit.

Major Financial Institutions

The major financial institutions in the U.S. economy are commercial banks, savings and loans, credit unions, savings banks, life insurance companies, pension funds, and mutual funds. These institutions attract funds from individuals, businesses, and governments, combine them, and make loans available to individuals and businesses. A brief description of the major financial institutions is found in Table 2.1.

The Changing Role of Financial Institutions

Depository Institutions Deregulation and Monetary Control Act of 1980 (DIDMCA) Signaled the beginning of the "financial services revolution" by eliminating interest-rate ceilings on all accounts and permitting certain institutions to offer new types of accounts and services.

A revolution in the delivery of financial services began with passage of the **Depository Institutions Deregulation and Monetary Control Act of 1980 (DIDMCA).** Nearly two decades later, financial institutions are today still reacting to this law. By eliminating interest-rate ceilings on all accounts and permitting certain institutions to offer new types of services, DIDMCA intensified competition and blurred traditional distinctions among financial institutions.

The trend today is toward the elimination of smaller financial institutions through acquisition or merger. In addition, mergers of large financial institutions, such as BankAmerica and NationsBank Corp. (now called BankAmerica); Bank One and First Chicago NBD (now called Bank One); Wells Fargo and Norwest Bank (now called Wells Fargo); and Washington Mutual, American Savings, and Ahmanson Corp. (now called Washington Mutual), are creating large national institutions that are rapidly displacing regional and local financial institutions. Contributing to this growth is new technology, particularly services such as ATMs, debit cards, checkless electronic banking, and Internet access. Large institutions that can afford to build and support the necessary technological infrastructure will be able to perpetuate their growth.

TABLE 2.1	Major Financial Institutions

Institution	Description
Commercial bank	Accepts both demand (checking) and time (savings) deposits. Also offers negotiable order of withdrawal (NOW) accounts, which are interest-earning savings accounts against which checks can be written, and money market deposit accounts. Makes loans directly to borrowers or through the financial markets.
Savings and loan	Similar to a commercial bank except that it may not hold demand (checking) deposits. Obtains funds from savings, NOW, and money market deposit accounts. Lends funds primarily to individuals and businesses for real estate mortgage loans.
Credit union	Deals primarily in transfer of funds between consumers. Membership is generally based on some common bond, such as working for a given employer. Accepts members' savings deposits, NOW account deposits, and money market deposit accounts. Lends funds to other members, typically to finance automobile or appliance purchases or home improvements.
Savings bank	Similar to a savings and loan in that it holds savings, NOW, and money market deposit accounts. Generally lends or invests funds through financial markets, although some mortgage loans are made to individuals. Located primarily in the Northeast.
Life insurance company	The largest type of financial intermediary handling individual savings. Receives premium payments and invests them to accumulate funds to cover future benefit payments. Lends funds to individuals, businesses, and governments, typically through the financial markets.
Pension fund	Set up so that employees can receive income after retirement. Often employers match the contributions of their employees. The majority of funds is lent or invested via the financial markets.
Mutual fund	Pools funds from the sale of shares and uses them to acquire bonds and stocks of business and governmental units. Creates a professionally managed portfolio of securities to achieve a specified investment objective, such as liquidity with a high return. Hundreds of funds, with a variety of investment objectives, exist. Money market mutual funds provide competitive returns with very high liquidity.

Financial Markets

financial markets
Provide a forum in which suppliers of funds and demanders of funds can transact business directly.

Financial markets provide a forum in which suppliers of funds and demanders of funds can transact business directly. Whereas the loans and investments of institutions are made without the direct knowledge of the suppliers of funds (savers), suppliers in the financial markets know where their funds are being lent or invested. The two key financial markets are the *money market* and the *capital market*. Transactions in short-term debt instruments, or marketable securities, take place in the money market. Long-term securities—bonds and stocks—are traded in the capital market.

private placement
The sale of a new security issue, typically bonds or preferred stock, directly to an investor or group of investors.

public offering
The nonexclusive sale of either bonds or stocks to the general public.

To raise money, firms can use either private placements or public offerings. **Private placement** involves the sale of a new security issue, typically bonds or preferred stock, directly to an investor or group of investors, such as an insurance company or pension fund. However, most firms raise money through a **public offering** of securities, which is the nonexclusive sale of either bonds or stocks to the general public.

primary market
Financial market in which securities are initially issued; the only market in which the issuer is directly involved in the transaction.

All securities, whether in the money or capital market, are initially issued in the **primary market.** This is the only market in which the corporate or government issuer is directly involved in the transaction and receives direct benefit from the issue. That is, the company actually receives the proceeds from the sale of

FIGURE 2.1

FIGURE 2.1

Flow of Funds

Flow of funds for financial institutions and markets

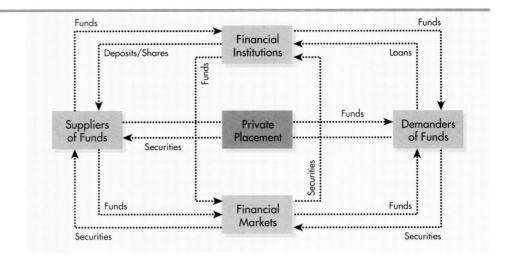

securities. Once the securities begin to trade between savers and investors, they become part of the **secondary market.** The primary market is the one in which "new" securities are sold; the secondary market can be viewed as a "used," or "preowned," securities market.

secondary market
Financial market in which preowned securities (those that are not new issues) are traded.

The Relationship Between Institutions and Markets

Financial institutions actively participate in the money market and the capital market as both suppliers and demanders of funds. Figure 2.1 depicts the general flow of funds through and between financial institutions and financial markets; private placement transactions are also shown. The individuals, businesses, and governments that supply and demand funds may be domestic or foreign. We end this section with a brief description of the money market, including its international equivalent—the *Eurocurrency market*. A later section of the chapter is devoted to discussion of the capital market because of its key importance to the firm.

The Money Market

money market
A financial relationship created between suppliers and demanders of *short-term funds.*

The **money market** is created by a financial relationship between suppliers and demanders of *short-term funds,* which have maturities of one year or less. The money market exists because certain individuals, businesses, governments, and financial institutions have temporarily idle funds that they wish to place in some type of short-term, interest-earning instrument. At the same time, other individuals, businesses, governments, and financial institutions find themselves in need of seasonal or temporary financing. The money market thus brings together these suppliers and demanders of short-term liquid funds.

marketable securities
Short-term debt instruments, such as U.S. Treasury bills, commercial paper, and negotiable certificates of deposit issued by government, business, and financial institutions, respectively.

Most money market transactions are made in **marketable securities**—short-term debt instruments, such as U.S. Treasury bills, commercial paper, and negotiable certificates of deposit issued by government, business, and financial institutions, respectively. (Marketable securities are described in Chapter 16.)

The Operation of the Money Market

The money market is not an actual organization housed in some central location. How, then, are suppliers and demanders of short-term funds brought together? Typically, they are matched through the facilities of large New York banks and through government securities dealers. A number of stock brokerage firms purchase various money market instruments for resale to customers. In addition, financial institutions such as banks and mutual funds purchase money market instruments for their portfolios to provide attractive returns on their customers' deposits and share purchases. Additionally, the Federal Reserve banks become involved in the money market but only in loans from one commercial bank to another; these loans are referred to as transactions in **federal funds.**

Regardless of whether a business or government is *issuing* a money market instrument (demanding short-term funds) or *purchasing* a money market instrument (supplying short-term funds), one party must go directly to another party or use an intermediary, such as banks or brokerage firms, to make a transaction. The secondary (or resale) market for marketable securities is no different from the primary (or initial issue) market with respect to the basic transactions that are made.

Individuals participate in the money market as purchasers and as sellers of money market instruments. Because the instruments are typically traded in denominations of $100,000 or more, banks and stock brokerage firms will "break down" marketable securities to make them available in smaller denominations. Individuals sell marketable securities in the money market to liquidate the securities before maturity. Individuals do not issue marketable securities.

Business firms, governments, and financial institutions both buy and sell marketable securities. They may be the primary issuers, or they may sell securities that they have purchased from others. Of course, each of these parties can issue only certain money market instruments; a business firm, for example, cannot issue a U.S. Treasury bill. Some financial institutions purchase marketable securities specifically for resale, whereas others purchase them as short-term investments. Businesses and governments purchase marketable securities to earn a return on temporarily idle funds.

The Eurocurrency Market

The international equivalent of the domestic money market is called the **Eurocurrency market.** This is a market for short-term bank deposits denominated in U.S. dollars or other easily convertible currencies. Historically, the Eurocurrency market has been centered in London, but it has evolved into a large, truly global market.

Eurocurrency deposits arise when a corporation or individual makes a bank deposit in a currency other than the local currency of the country where the bank is located. If, for example, a multinational corporation were to deposit U.S. dollars in a London bank, this would create a Eurodollar deposit (a dollar deposit at a bank in Europe). Almost all Eurodollar deposits are *time deposits*, meaning that the bank would promise to repay the deposit, with interest, at a fixed date in the future—say, 6 months. During the interim, the bank is free to lend this dollar deposit to creditworthy corporate or government borrowers. If the bank cannot

federal funds
Loan transactions between commercial banks in which the Federal Reserve banks become involved.

Hint   Remember that the *money market* is for short-term fund-raising and is represented by current liabilities on the balance sheet. The *capital market* is for long-term fund-raising and is reflected by long-term debt and equity on the balance sheet.

Eurocurrency market
International equivalent of the domestic money market.

London Interbank Offered Rate (LIBOR)
The base rate that is used to price all Eurocurrency loans.

find a borrower on its own, it may loan the deposit to another international bank. The rate charged on these "interbank loans" is called the **London Interbank Offered Rate (LIBOR),** and this is the base rate that is used to price all Eurocurrency loans.

The Eurocurrency market has grown rapidly, primarily because it is an unregulated, wholesale, and global market that fills the needs of both borrowers and lenders. Investors with excess cash to lend are able to make large, short-term, and safe deposits at attractive interest rates, and borrowers are able to arrange large loans, quickly and confidentially, also at attractive interest rates.

? Review Questions

2–1   Who are the key participants in the transactions of financial institutions? Indicate who are net suppliers and who are net demanders.

2–2   What did the *Depository Institutions Deregulation and Monetary Control Act of 1980 (DIDMCA)* do to begin the "financial services revolution"? What appears to be the trend in terms of the size of financial institutions and the services they provide?

2–3   What role do *financial markets* play in our economy? What are *primary* and *secondary* markets? What relationship exists between financial institutions and financial markets?

2–4   What is the *money market?* How does it differ from the capital market?

2–5   What is the *Eurocurrency market?* What is the *London Interbank Offered Rate (LIBOR)* and how is it used in this market?

2.2 Corporate Bonds

corporate bond
A debt instrument indicating that a corporation has borrowed a certain amount of money and promises to repay it in the future under clearly defined terms.

A **corporate bond** is a debt instrument indicating that a corporation has borrowed a certain amount of money and promises to repay it in the future under clearly defined terms. Most bonds are issued with maturities of 10 to 30 years and with a par, or face, value of $1,000. The *coupon interest rate* on a bond represents the percentage of the bond's par value that will be paid annually, typically in two equal semiannual payments. The bondholders, who are the lenders, are promised the semiannual interest payments and, at maturity, repayment of the principal amount (par value).

Legal Aspects of Corporate Bonds

Certain legal arrangements are required to protect purchasers of bonds. Bondholders are protected legally primarily through the indenture and the trustee.

Bond Indenture

bond indenture
A complex legal document stating the conditions under which a bond has been issued.

A **bond indenture** is a complex legal document stating the conditions under which a bond has been issued. It specifies both the rights of the bondholders and the duties of the issuing corporation. Included in the indenture are the interest and principal payments, various standard and restrictive provisions, and, frequently, sinking-fund requirements and security interest provisions.

standard debt provisions
Provisions in a bond indenture specifying certain criteria of satisfactory record keeping and general business maintenance on the part of the borrower (issuer); normally, they do not place a burden on the financially sound business.

Standard Provisions   The **standard debt provisions** included in the bond indenture specify certain criteria of satisfactory record keeping and general business maintenance on the part of the borrower (the issuer). Standard debt provisions do not normally place a burden on a financially sound business.

The borrower commonly must (1) *maintain satisfactory accounting records* in accordance with generally accepted accounting principles (GAAP); (2) periodically *supply audited financial statements*; (3) *pay taxes and other liabilities when due*; and (4) *maintain all facilities in good working order*.

restrictive covenants
Contractual clauses in a *bond indenture* that place operating and financial constraints on the borrower.

Restrictive Provisions   Bond indentures normally include certain **restrictive covenants**—contractual clauses that place operating and financial constraints on the borrower. Restrictive covenants, coupled with standard debt provisions, help protect the bondholder against increases in borrower risk. Without these provisions, the borrower could increase the firm's risk but not have to pay an increased return (interest).

The most common restrictive covenants:

1. Require the borrower to *maintain a minimum level of liquidity*, to ensure against loan default and ultimate failure.
2. *Prohibit borrowers from selling accounts receivable* to generate cash. Doing so could cause a long-run cash shortage if proceeds are used to meet current obligations.
3. Impose *fixed asset restrictions* on the borrower. The liquidation or encumbrance of fixed assets could damage the firm's ability to repay the bonds.
4. *Constrain subsequent borrowing*. Additional long-term debt may be prohibited, or additional borrowing may be *subordinated* to the original loan. **Subordination** means that subsequent creditors agree to wait until all claims of the *senior debt* are satisfied.
5. *Limit the firm's annual cash dividend payments* to a specified percentage or amount.

subordination
In a bond indenture, the stipulation that subsequent creditors agree to wait until all claims of the *senior debt* are satisfied.

Other restrictive covenants may sometimes be included in bond indentures. All restrictive covenants are intended to protect bondholders' funds against increased risk.

The violation of any standard or restrictive provision by the borrower gives the bondholders the right to demand immediate repayment of the debt. Generally, the bondholders' representative will evaluate any violation to determine whether it is serious enough to jeopardize the loan. The bondholders may then decide to demand immediate repayment, continue the loan, or alter the terms of the bond indenture.

sinking-fund requirement
A restrictive provision that is often included in a bond indenture providing for the systematic retirement of bonds prior to their maturity.

Sinking-Fund Requirements   An additional restrictive provision often included in a bond indenture is a **sinking-fund requirement**. Its objective is to provide for the systematic retirement of bonds prior to their maturity. To carry out this requirement, the corporation makes semiannual or annual payments to a *trustee*, who uses these funds to retire bonds by purchasing them in the marketplace.

Security Interest   The bond indenture identifies any collateral pledged against the bond. Usually, the disposition of the collateral in various circumstances is specified. The protection of bond collateral is crucial to increase the safety of a bond issue.

Trustee

trustee
A paid individual, corporation, or commercial bank trust department that acts as the third party to a bond indenture to ensure that the issuer does not default on its contractual responsibilities to the bondholders.

A **trustee** is a third party to a bond indenture. The trustee can be an individual, a corporation, or, most often, a commercial bank trust department. The trustee is paid to act as a "watchdog" on behalf of the bondholders and is empowered to take specified actions on behalf of the bondholders if the terms of the indenture are violated.

Cost of Bonds

The cost of bond financing is generally greater than that of short-term borrowing. The bond indenture specifies the interest rate, the timing of payments, and the dollar amount of payments. The major factors affecting the cost, or interest rate, on a bond are its maturity, size of the offering, and, more important, issuer risk and the basic cost of money.

Generally, *long-term debt has higher interest rates than short-term debt*. In a practical sense, the longer the maturity of a bond, the less accuracy there is in predicting future interest rates, and therefore the greater the bondholders' risk of giving up an opportunity to loan money at a higher rate. In addition, the longer the term, the greater the default risk associated with the bond. The *size of the bond offering* also affects the interest cost of borrowing, but in an inverse manner: Bond flotation and administration costs per dollar borrowed are likely to decrease with increasing offering size. On the other hand, the risk of the bondholders may increase, because larger offerings result in greater risk of default. The greater the *issuer's default risk,* the higher the interest rate. Clearly, bondholders must be compensated for taking this risk.

The *cost of money in the capital market* is the basis for determining the coupon interest rate. Generally, the rate on U.S. Treasury securities with *equivalent maturities* is used as the basic (lowest-risk) cost of money. To determine the coupon interest rate, a *risk premium* reflective of the maturity, offering size, and, most important, the issuer's default risk is added to the basic cost of money. Frequently, bond buyers rely on *bond ratings* (discussed later) to determine the issuer's overall risk and the required return. Instead of having to determine a risk premium, the bond buyer relies on the risk premium prevailing in the marketplace for similar-risk bonds.

General Features of a Bond Issue

Three common features of a bond issue are a conversion feature, a call feature, and stock purchase warrants. These features provide both the issuer and the purchaser with certain opportunities for replacing, retiring, and (or) supplementing the bond with some type of equity issue.

conversion feature
A feature of *convertible bonds* that allows bondholders to change each bond into a stated number of shares of common stock.

call feature
A feature that is included in almost all corporate bond issues that gives the issuer the opportunity to repurchase bonds at a stated *call price* prior to maturity.

call price
The stated price at which a bond may be repurchased, by use of a *call feature*, prior to maturity.

call premium
The amount by which a bond's call price exceeds its par value.

The **conversion feature** of *convertible bonds* allows bondholders to change each bond into a stated number of shares of common stock. Bondholders will convert their bonds only when the market price of the stock is greater than the conversion price, thus providing a profit.

The **call feature** is included in almost all corporate bond issues. It gives the issuer the opportunity to repurchase bonds prior to maturity. The **call price** is the stated price at which bonds may be repurchased prior to maturity. Sometimes the call feature can be exercised only during a certain period. As a rule, the call price exceeds the par value of a bond by an amount equal to 1 year's interest. For example, a $1,000 bond with a 10 percent coupon interest rate would be callable for around $1,100 [$1,000 + (10% × $1,000)]. The amount by which the call price exceeds the bond's par value is commonly referred to as the **call premium.** This premium compensates bondholders for having the bond called away from them, and it is the cost to the issuer of calling the bonds.

The call feature enables the issuer to retire outstanding debt prior to maturity. Thus, when interest rates fall, an issuer can call an outstanding bond and re-issue a new bond at a lower interest rate. When interest rates rise, the call privilege will not be exercised, except possibly to meet sinking-fund requirements. Of course, to sell a callable bond, the issuer must pay a higher interest rate than on noncallable bonds of equal risk, to compensate bondholders for the risk of having the bonds called away from them.

stock purchase warrants
Instruments that give their holders the right to purchase a certain number of shares of the firm's common stock at a specified price over a certain period of time.

Bonds occasionally have stock purchase warrants attached as "sweeteners" to make them more attractive to prospective buyers. **Stock purchase warrants** are instruments that give their holders the right to purchase a certain number of shares of the firm's common stock at a specified price over a certain period of time. Their inclusion typically allows the firm to raise needed funds at a slightly lower coupon interest rate than would otherwise be required.

Bond Ratings

Independent agencies such as Moody's and Standard & Poor's assess the riskiness of publicly traded bond issues. These agencies derive the ratings by using financial ratio and cash flow analyses to assess the likely payment of bond interest and principal. Table 2.2 summarizes these ratings. Normally an inverse relationship exists between the quality of a bond and the rate of return that it must provide bondholders: High-quality (high-rated) bonds provide lower returns than lower-quality (low-rated) bonds. This reflects the lender's risk-return trade-off. When considering bond financing, the financial manager must be concerned with the expected ratings of the bond issue, because these ratings affect salability and cost.

Popular Types of Bonds

debentures
See Table 2.3.

subordinated debentures
See Table 2.3.

Bonds can be classified in a variety of ways. Here we break them into traditional bonds—the basic types that have been around for years—and contemporary bonds—newer, more innovative types. The traditional types of bonds are summarized in terms of their key characteristics and priority of lender's claim in Table 2.3. Note that the first three types—**debentures, subordinated debentures,**

TABLE 2.2	Moody's and Standard & Poor's Bond Ratings[a]		
Moody's	Interpretation	Standard & Poor's	Interpretation
Aaa	Prime quality	AAA	Bank investment quality
Aa	High grade	AA	
A	Upper medium grade	A	
Baa	Medium grade	BBB	
Ba	Lower medium grade or speculative	BB	Speculative
		B	
B	Speculative		
Caa	From very speculative	CCC	
Ca	to near or in default	CC	
C	Lowest grade	C	Income bond
		D	In default

[a]Some ratings may be modified to show relative standing within a major rating category; for example, Moody's uses numerical modifiers (1, 2, 3), whereas Standard & Poor's uses plus (+) and minus (−) signs.

Sources: Moody's Investors Services, Inc. and Standard & Poor's Corporation.

Hint   Note that Moody's has 9 major ratings; Standard & Poor's has 10.

income bonds
See Table 2.3.

mortgage bonds
See Table 2.3.

collateral trust bonds
See Table 2.3.

equipment trust certificates
See Table 2.3.

zero (or low) coupon bonds
See Table 2.4.

junk bonds
See Table 2.4.

floating-rate bonds
See Table 2.4.

extendible notes
See Table 2.4.

putable bonds
See Table 2.4.

Eurobond
A bond issued by an international borrower and sold to investors in countries with currencies other than the currency in which the bond is denominated.

and **income bonds**—are unsecured, whereas the last three—**mortgage bonds, collateral trust bonds,** and **equipment trust certificates**—are secured.

Table 2.4 describes the key characteristics of five contemporary types of bonds—**zero (or low) coupon bonds, junk bonds, floating-rate bonds, extendible notes,** and **putable bonds.** These bonds can be either unsecured or secured. In recent years, changing capital market conditions and investor preferences, along with corporate financing needs, have spurred development of innovations in bond financing and will likely continue to do so.

International Bond Issues

Companies and governments borrow internationally by issuing bonds in two principal financial markets: the Eurobond and the foreign bond. Both of these provide creditworthy borrowers the opportunity to obtain large amounts of long-term debt financing quickly, in their choice of currency and with flexible repayment terms.

A **Eurobond** is issued by an international borrower and sold to investors in countries with currencies other than the currency in which the bond is denominated. An example would be a dollar-denominated bond issued by a U.S. corporation and sold to Belgian investors. From the founding of the Eurobond market in the 1960s until the mid-1980s, "blue chip" U.S. corporations were the largest single class of Eurobond issuers. Many of these companies were able to borrow in this market at interest rates below those the U.S. government paid on Treasury bonds it issued. As the market matured, issuers became able to choose the cur-

TABLE 2.3	Characteristics and Priority of Lender's Claim of Traditional Types of Bonds		
Bond type	**Characteristics**	**Priority of lender's claim**
Unsecured Bonds		
Debentures	Unsecured bonds that only creditworthy firms can issue. Convertible bonds are normally debentures.	Claims are the same as those of any general creditor. May have other unsecured bonds subordinated to them.
Subordinated debentures	Claims are not satisfied until those of the creditors holding certain (senior) debts have been fully satisfied.	Claim is that of a general creditor but not as good as a senior debt claim.
Income bonds	Payment of interest is required only when earnings are available. Commonly issued in reorganization of a failing firm.	Claim is that of a general creditor. Are not in default when interest payments are missed, because they are contingent only on earnings being available.
Secured Bonds		
Mortgage bonds	Secured by real estate or buildings.	Claim is on proceeds from sale of mortgaged assets; if not fully satisfied, the lender becomes a general creditor. The *first-mortgage* claim must be fully satisfied before distribution of proceeds to *second-mortgage* holders, and so on. A number of mortgages can be issued against the same collateral.
Collateral trust bonds	Secured by stock and (or) bonds that are owned by the issuer. Collateral value is generally 25 to 35% greater than bond value.	Claim is on proceeds from stock and (or) bond collateral; if not fully satisfied, the lender becomes a general creditor.
Equipment trust certificates	Used to finance "rolling stock"—airplanes, trucks, boats, railroad cars. A trustee buys such an asset with funds raised through the sale of trust certificates and then leases it to the firm, which, after making the final scheduled lease payment, receives title to the asset. A type of leasing.	Claim is on proceeds from the sale of the asset; if proceeds do not satisfy outstanding debt, trust certificate lenders become general creditors.

rency in which they borrowed, and European and Japanese borrowers rose to prominence. In more recent years, the Eurobond market has become much more balanced in terms of the mix of borrowers, total issue volume, and currency of denomination.

foreign bond
A bond issued in a host country's financial market, in the host country's currency, by a foreign borrower.

Unlike a Eurobond, a **foreign bond** is issued in a host country's financial market, in the host country's currency, by a foreign borrower. A Deutschemark–denominated bond issued in Germany by a U.S. company is an example of a foreign bond. The three largest foreign bond markets are Japan, Switzerland, and the United States.

? Review Questions

2–6 What are typical maturities, denominations, and interest payments associated with a corporate bond? Describe the role of the *bond indenture* and the *trustee*.

TABLE 2.4	Characteristics of Contemporary Types of Bonds
Bond type	**Characteristics**[a]
Zero (or low) coupon bonds	Issued with no (zero) or a very low coupon (stated interest) rate and sold at a large discount from par. A significant portion (or all) of the investor's return comes from gain in value (i.e., par value minus purchase price). Generally callable at par value. Because the issuer can annually deduct the current year's interest accrual without having to pay the interest until the bond matures (or is called), its cash flow each year is increased by the amount of the tax shield provided by the interest deduction.
Junk bonds	Debt rated Ba or lower by Moody's or BB or lower by Standard & Poor's. Commonly used during the 1980s by rapidly growing firms to obtain growth capital, most often as a way to finance mergers and takeovers. High-risk bonds with high yields—typically yielding 3% more than the best-quality corporate debt.
Floating-rate bonds	Stated interest rate is adjusted periodically within stated limits in response to changes in specified money or capital market rates. Popular when future inflation and interest rates are uncertain. Tend to sell at close to par due to the automatic adjustment to changing market conditions. Some issues provide for annual redemption at par at the option of the bondholder.
Extendible notes	Short maturities, typically 1 to 5 years, that can be renewed for a similar period at the option of holders. Similar to a floating-rate bond. An issue might be a series of 3-year renewable notes over a period of 15 years; every 3 years, the notes could be extended for another 3 years, at a new rate competitive with market interest rates at the time of renewal.
Putable bonds	Bonds that can be redeemed at par (typically, $1,000) at the option of their holder either at specific dates after the date of issue and every 1 to 5 years thereafter or when and if the firm takes specified actions such as being acquired, acquiring another company, or issuing a large amount of additional debt. In return for the right to "put the bond" at specified times or actions by the firm, the bond's yield is lower than that of a nonputable bond.

[a]The claims of lenders (i.e., bondholders) against issuers of each of these types of bonds vary, depending on their other features. Each of these bonds can be unsecured or secured.

2–7 Differentiate between *standard debt provisions* and *restrictive covenants* included in a bond indenture. What are the consequences of violation of them by the bond issuer?

2–8 What is a *conversion feature?* A *call feature? Stock purchase warrants?* How are bonds rated, and why?

2–9 How does the cost of bond financing typically relate to the cost of short-term borrowing? In addition to a bond's maturity, what other major factors affect its coupon interest rate?

2–10 Describe and compare the basic characteristics of *Eurobonds* and *foreign bonds.*

2.3 Differences Between Debt and Equity Capital

capital
The long-term funds of a firm; all items on the right-hand side of the balance sheet, *excluding current liabilities.*

debt capital
All long-term borrowing incurred by the firm, including bonds.

The term **capital** denotes the long-term funds of the firm. All items on the right-hand side of the firm's balance sheet, *excluding current liabilities,* are sources of capital. **Debt capital** includes all long-term borrowing incurred by the firm,

TABLE 2.5	Key Differences Between Debt and Equity Capital	

	Type of capital	
Characteristic	**Debt**	**Equity**
Voice in management[a]	No	Yes
Claims on income and assets	Senior to equity	Subordinate to debt
Maturity	Stated	None
Tax treatment	Interest deduction	No deduction

[a]In the event the issuer violates its stated contractual obligations to them, debtholders and preferred stock-holders *may* receive a voice in management; otherwise, only common stockholders have voting rights.

equity capital
The long-term funds provided by the firm's owners, the stockholders.

including bonds. **Equity capital** consists of long-term funds provided by the firm's owners, the stockholders. Equity capital can be raised *internally* through retained earnings, or *externally* by selling common or preferred stock. The key differences between debt and equity capital are summarized in Table 2.5. These differences relate to voice in management, claims on the firm's income and assets, maturity, and tax treatment.

Voice in Management

Unlike creditors (lenders), holders of equity capital (common and preferred stockholders) are owners of the firm. Holders of common stock have voting rights that permit them to select the firm's directors and to vote on special issues. In contrast, debtholders and preferred stockholders may receive voting privileges only when the firm has violated its stated contractual obligations to them.

Claims on Income and Assets

Holders of equity have claims on both income and assets that are secondary to the claims of creditors. Their *claims on income* cannot be paid until the claims of all creditors, including both interest and scheduled principal payments, have been satisfied. Once these claims have been satisfied, the firm's board of directors decides whether to distribute dividends to the owners.

The equity holders' *claims on assets* of the firm also are secondary to the claims of creditors. If the firm fails, assets are sold, and the proceeds are distributed in this order: employees and customers, the government, creditors, and finally equity holders. Because equity holders are the last to receive any distribution of assets during bankruptcy proceedings, they expect greater returns from dividends and/or increases in stock price.

As will be explained in Chapter 12, the costs of the various forms of equity financing are generally higher than debt costs. One reason is that the suppliers of equity capital take more risk because of their subordinate claims on income and assets. Despite being more costly, equity capital is necessary for the firm to grow. All firms must initially be financed with some common stock equity.

Maturity

Unlike debt, equity capital is a *permanent form* of financing. It does not "mature," and therefore repayment is not required. Because equity does not mature and will be liquidated only during bankruptcy proceedings, the owners must recognize that although a ready market may exist for the firm's shares, the price that can be realized may fluctuate. This potential fluctuation of the market price of equity makes the overall returns to a firm's owners even more risky.

Tax Treatment

Interest payments to debtholders are treated as tax-deductible expenses on the firm's income statement, whereas dividend payments to common and preferred stockholders are not tax-deductible. The tax deductibility of interest lowers the cost of debt financing, thereby further causing the cost of debt financing to be lower than the cost of equity financing.

? Review Question

2–11   What are *debt capital* and *equity capital?* What are the key differences between them with respect to voice in management, claims on income and assets, maturity, and tax treatment?

2.4 Common and Preferred Stock

The equity, or ownership, capital of the firm can be raised through the sale of common and preferred stock. All corporations initially issue common stock to raise equity capital. Some of these firms later issue preferred stock to raise additional equity capital. Although both common and preferred stock are forms of equity capital, preferred stock has some similarities to debt capital that significantly differentiate it from common stock. Here we consider the key features and behaviors of both common and preferred stock.

Common Stock

The true owners of business firms are the common stockholders. Common stockholders are sometimes referred to as *residual owners:* In essence they have no guarantee of receiving any cash inflows, but receive what is left—the residual—after all other claims on the firm's income and assets have been satisfied. They are assured of only one thing: that they cannot lose any more than they have invested in the firm. As a result of this generally uncertain position, common stockholders expect to be compensated with adequate dividends and, ultimately, capital gains. Here we discuss the fundamental aspects of common stock.

Ownership

privately owned (stock)
All common stock of a firm owned by a single individual.

The common stock of a firm can be **privately owned** by a single individual, **closely owned** by a small group of investors (such as a family), or **publicly owned** by a broad group of unrelated individual or institutional investors. Typically, small corporations are privately or closely owned, and if their shares are traded, this occurs infrequently and in small amounts. Large corporations, which are emphasized in the following discussions, are publicly owned, and their shares are generally actively traded on major securities exchanges (discussed later).

closely owned (stock)
All common stock of a firm owned by a small group of investors (such as a family).

publicly owned (stock)
Common stock of a firm owned by a broad group of unrelated individual or institutional investors.

Par Value

par value
A relatively useless value established in the firm's corporate charter.

Unlike bonds, which always have a par value, common stock may be sold with or without a par value. The **par value** of a common stock is a relatively useless value established in the firm's corporate charter. It is generally quite low, about $1.

Firms often issue stock with no par value, in which case they may assign it a value or record it on the books at the price at which it is sold. A low par value may be advantageous in states where certain corporate taxes are based on the par value of stock; if a stock has no par value, the tax may be based on an arbitrarily determined per-share figure.

Preemptive Rights

preemptive right
Allows common stockholders to maintain their *proportionate* ownership in the corporation when new shares are issued.

The **preemptive right** allows common stockholders to maintain their *proportionate* ownership in the corporation when new shares are issued. The preemptive right allows existing shareholders to maintain voting control and protect against the dilution of their ownership. **Dilution of ownership** usually results in the dilution of earnings, because each present shareholder has a claim on a *smaller* part of the firm's earnings than previously.

dilution of ownership
Occurs when a new stock issue results in each present shareholder having a claim on a *smaller* part of the firm's earnings than previously.

In a *rights offering*, the firm grants **rights** to its shareholders. These financial instruments permit stockholders to purchase additional shares at a price below the market price, in direct proportion to their number of owned shares. Rights are primarily used by smaller corporations whose shares are either *closely owned* or *publicly owned* and not actively traded. In these situations, rights are an important financing tool without which shareholders would run the risk of losing their proportionate control of the corporation. From the firm's viewpoint, the use of rights offerings to raise new equity capital may be less costly and generate more interest than a public offering of stock.

rights
Financial instruments that permit stockholders to purchase additional shares at a price below the market price, in direct proportion to their number of owned shares.

Authorized, Outstanding, and Issued Shares

authorized shares
The number of shares of common stock that a firm's corporate charter allows without further shareholder approval.

A firm's corporate charter defines the number of **authorized shares** that it can issue. The firm cannot sell more shares than the charter authorizes without obtaining approval through a shareholder vote. To avoid later having to amend the charter, firms generally attempt to authorize more shares than they initially plan to issue. Authorized shares become **outstanding shares** when they are held by the public. If the *firm* repurchases any of its outstanding shares, these shares are recorded as **treasury stock** (and shown as a deduction from stockholders' equity on the firm's balance sheet). **Issued shares** are the shares of common stock

outstanding shares
The number of shares of common stock held by the public.

treasury stock
The number of shares of outstanding stock that have been repurchased by the firm (shown as a deduction from stockholders' equity on the firm's balance sheet).

issued shares
The number of shares of common stock that have been put into circulation; they represent the sum of outstanding shares and treasury stock.

that have been put into circulation; they represent the sum of outstanding shares and treasury stock.

Example ▼   Golden Enterprises, a producer of medical pumps, has the following stockholders' equity account on December 31:

Stockholders' equity	
Common stock—$.80 par value:	
Authorized 35,000,000 shares; issued 15,000,000 shares	$ 12,000,000
Paid-in capital in excess of par	63,000,000
Retained earnings	31,000,000
	$106,000,000
Less: Cost of treasury stock (1,000,000 shares)	4,000,000
Total stockholders' equity	$102,000,000

How many shares of additional common stock can Golden sell without gaining approval from its shareholders? The firm has 35 million authorized shares, 15 million issued shares, and 1 million shares of treasury stock. Thus, 14 million shares are outstanding (15 million issued shares − 1 million shares of treasury stock), and Golden can issue 21 million additional shares (35 million authorized shares − 14 million outstanding shares) without seeking shareholder approval. This total includes the treasury shares currently held, which the firm can reissue
▲   to the public without obtaining shareholder approval.

Voting Rights

Generally, each share of common stock entitles the holder to one vote in the election of directors and on special issues. Votes are generally assignable and must be cast at the annual stockholders' meeting.

In recent years, many firms have issued two or more classes of common stock, unequal voting rights being their key difference. The issuance of different classes of stock has been frequently used as a defense against a *hostile takeover* in which an outside group, without management support, tries to gain voting control of the firm by buying its shares in the marketplace. At other times, a class of **nonvoting common stock** is issued when the firm wishes to raise capital through the sale of common stock but does not want to give up its voting control. Issuing classes of stock with unequal voting rights results in some **supervoting shares,** which give their holders more votes per share than a regular share of common stock and allow them to better control the firm's future.

When different classes of common stock are issued on the basis of unequal voting rights, class A common is typically—but not universally—designated as nonvoting, and class B common would have voting rights. Generally, higher classes of shares are given preference in the distribution of earnings (dividends) and assets (in liquidation); lower-class shares, in exchange, receive voting rights. Treasury stock, which is held within the corporation, generally *does not* have voting rights, *does not* earn dividends, and *does not* have a claim on assets in liquidation.

Because most small stockholders do not attend the annual meeting to vote, they may sign a **proxy statement** giving their votes to another party. The solicita-

nonvoting common stock
Common stock that carries no voting rights; issued when the firm wishes to raise capital through the sale of common stock but does not want to give up its voting control.

supervoting shares
Stock that carries with it more votes per share than a regular share of common stock.

proxy statement
A statement giving the votes of a stockholder to another party.

tion of proxies from shareholders is closely controlled by the Securities and Exchange Commission, to protect against proxies being solicited on the basis of misleading information. Existing management generally receives the stockholders' proxies, because it is able to solicit them at company expense.

proxy battle
The attempt by a nonmanagement group to gain control of the management of a firm by soliciting a sufficient number of proxy votes.

Occasionally, when the firm is widely owned, outsiders may wage a **proxy battle** to unseat the existing management and gain control. To win a corporate election, votes from a majority of the shares voted are required. However, the odds of a nonmanagement group winning a proxy battle are generally slim.

Dividends

The payment of corporate dividends is at the discretion of the board of directors. Most corporations pay dividends quarterly. Dividends may be paid in cash, stock, or merchandise. Cash dividends are the most common; merchandise dividends are the least common. Common stockholders are not promised a dividend, but they come to expect certain payments based on the historical dividend pattern of the firm. Before dividends are paid to common stockholders, the claims of the government, all creditors, and preferred stockholders must be satisfied. Because of the importance of the dividend decision to the growth and valuation of the firm, detailed discussion of dividends is included in Chapter 13.

International Stock Issues

Although the international market for common stock is not as large as the international market for debt securities, cross-border trading and issuance of common stock have increased dramatically in the past 20 years. Much of this increase is due to a growing desire on the part of securities investors to diversify their investment portfolios internationally.

Today, some corporations *issue stock in foreign markets.* For example, several top U.S. multinational companies have listed their stock in half a dozen or more stock markets. The London, Frankfurt, and Tokyo markets are the most popular. Issuing stock internationally both broadens the ownership base and helps a company to integrate itself into the local business scene. A listing on a foreign stock exchange both increases local business press coverage and serves as effective corporate advertising. Having locally traded stock can also facilitate corporate acquisitions because shares can be used as an acceptable method of payment.

Foreign corporations have also discovered the benefits of trading their stock in the United States. The disclosure and reporting requirements mandated by the U.S. Securities and Exchange Commission have historically discouraged all but the largest foreign firms from directly listing their shares on the New York or American Stock Exchanges. For example, in 1993, Daimler-Benz became the first large German company to be listed on the NYSE.

American Depositary Receipts (ADRs)
Claims issued by U.S. banks representing ownership of shares of a foreign company's stock held on deposit by the U.S. bank in the foreign market and issued in dollars to U.S. investors.

Alternatively, most foreign companies tap the U.S. market through **American Depositary Receipts (ADRs).** These are claims issued by U.S. banks representing ownership of shares of a foreign company's stock held on deposit by the U.S. bank in the foreign market. Because ADRs are issued, in dollars, by a U.S. bank to U.S. investors, they are subject to U.S. securities laws yet still give investors the opportunity to diversify their portfolios internationally.

Preferred Stock

Preferred stock gives its holders certain privileges that make them senior to common stockholders. Preferred stockholders are promised a fixed periodic return, which is stated either as a percentage or as a dollar amount. The way the dividend is specified depends on whether the preferred stock has a par value. **Par-value preferred stock** has a stated face value, and its annual dividend is specified as a percentage. **No-par preferred stock** has no stated face value, but its annual dividend is stated in dollars. Preferred stock is most often issued by public utilities, by acquiring firms in merger transactions, or by firms that are experiencing losses and need additional financing.

par-value preferred stock
Preferred stock with a stated face value that is used with the specified dividend percentage to determine the annual dollar dividend.

no-par preferred stock
Preferred stock with no stated face value but with a stated annual dollar dividend.

Basic Rights of Preferred Stockholders

The basic rights of preferred stockholders are somewhat more favorable than the rights of common stockholders. Preferred stock is often considered *quasi-debt* because, much like interest on debt, it specifies a fixed periodic (dividend) payment. Of course, as ownership, preferred stock is unlike debt in that it has no maturity date. Because their claim on the firm's income is fixed and takes precedence over the claim of common stockholders, preferred stockholders are not exposed to the same degree of risk as common stockholders. They are consequently *not normally given a voting right*.

Preferred stockholders have *preference over common stockholders with respect to the distribution of earnings*. If the stated preferred stock dividend is passed (not paid) by the board of directors, the payment of dividends to common stockholders is prohibited. It is this preference in dividend distribution that makes common stockholders the true risk takers with respect to receipt of periodic returns. Preferred stockholders are also usually given *preference over common stockholders in the liquidation of assets* as a result of a firm's bankruptcy, although they must "stand in line" behind creditors. The amount of the claim of preferred stockholders in liquidation is normally equal to the par value of the preferred stock.

Features of Preferred Stock

A number of features are generally included as part of a preferred stock issue. These features, along with a statement of the stock's par value, the amount of dividend payments, the dividend payment dates, and any restrictive covenants, are specified in an agreement similar to a *bond indenture*.

Restrictive Covenants   The restrictive covenants commonly found in a preferred stock issue are aimed at ensuring the continued existence of the firm and regular payment of the stated dividend. These covenants include provisions related to passing dividends, the sale of senior securities, mergers, sales of assets, minimum liquidity requirements, and the payment of common stock dividends or common stock repurchases. The violation of preferred stock covenants usually permits preferred stockholders either to obtain representation on the firm's board of directors or to force the retirement of their stock at or above its par value.

In Practice

To Market, To Market

When making a securities offering, whether private or public, most firms hire an investment banker. The term is somewhat misleading because an investment banker neither makes long-term investments nor guards the savings of others. Instead, acting as an intermediary, the investment banker purchases securities from corporate and government issuers and resells them to the general public in the primary market—thus bearing the risk of selling a security issue. The investment banker is compensated by purchasing the security issue at a discount from the proposed sale price. The difference between the price the investment banker pays for a security and the sale price in the market is referred to as the spread. *The overall cost for common stock is the highest, followed by preferred stock and bonds in that order. The cost ranges from about 1.6 percent of the total proceeds on a large bond issue ($500 billion or more) to as much as 17 percent on a small common stock issue.*

For many small companies, selling stock to the public is a dream come true that enables the founders and other early investors to recoup some of their investment. However, the final tally of an initial public offering can be surprising. For example, Multicom Publishing Co., a Seattle-based developer of interactive CD-ROM software, went public in June 1996. The company netted about $5.9 million, or 82 percent, of the $7.2 million raised. Where did the rest go? The biggest chunk—about 10 percent—went to Multicom's investment banker, who purchased shares at $5.98 a share to resell at the $6.50 offering price. Legal and accounting costs ate up another 5 percent. Costs for liability insurance, printing and investor presentations, and registration and application fees consumed another 3 percent.

Going public is not a sure thing by any means. During periods of stock market volatility, many companies cancel or postpone potential public offerings when the market heads south. "Only the best need apply," comments Dick Smith, head of equity syndications for NationsBanc Montgomery Securities.

---

cumulative preferred stock
Preferred stock for which all passed (unpaid) dividends in arrears must be paid along with the current dividend prior to the payment of dividends to common stockholders.

noncumulative preferred stock
Preferred stock for which passed (unpaid) dividends do not accumulate.

Cumulation   Most preferred stock is **cumulative** with respect to any dividends passed. That is, all dividends in arrears must be paid along with the current dividend prior to the payment of dividends to common stockholders. If preferred stock is **noncumulative,** passed (unpaid) dividends do not accumulate. In this case, only the current dividend must be paid prior to paying dividends to common stockholders. Because the common stockholders can receive dividends only after the dividend claims of preferred stockholders have been satisfied, it is in the firm's best interest to pay preferred dividends when they are due.[1]

---

1. Most preferred stock is cumulative, because it is difficult to sell noncumulative stock. Common stockholders obviously prefer issuance of noncumulative preferred stock, because it does not place them in quite as risky a position. But it is often in the best interest of the firm to sell cumulative preferred stock due to its lower cost.

Most preferred stock has a fixed dividend, but some firms issue adjustable-rate (floating-rate) preferred stock whose dividend rate is tied to interest rates on specific government securities. Rate adjustments are commonly made quarterly. ARPS offers investors protection against sharp rises in interest rates, which means the issue can be sold at an initially lower dividend rate.

Other Features   Preferred stock is generally *callable*—the issuer can retire outstanding stock within a certain period of time at a specified price. The call option generally cannot be exercised until a specified date. The call price is normally set above the initial issuance price but may decrease as time passes. Making preferred stock callable provides the issuer with a method of bringing the fixed-payment commitment of the preferred issue to an end.

Preferred stock quite often contains a **conversion feature** that allows *holders of convertible preferred stock* to change each share into a stated number of shares of common stock. Sometimes the number of shares of common stock that the preferred stock can be exchanged for changes according to a prespecified formula.

conversion feature
A feature of *convertible preferred stock* that allows its holders to change each share into a stated number of shares of common stock.

❓ Review Questions

2–12 Why is the common stockholder considered the true owner of a firm? What risks do common stockholders take that other suppliers of long-term capital do not?

2–13 What is *the preemptive right?* How does it protect against *dilution of ownership?* What are *rights?*

2–14 Explain the relationships among the following: (**a**) authorized shares; (**b**) outstanding shares; (**c**) treasury stock; and (**d**) issued shares.

2–15 What are the advantages, to both U.S.-based and foreign corporations, of issuing stock outside of their home markets? What are *American Depositary Receipts (ADRs)?*

2–16 What is *preferred stock?* What claims do preferred stockholders have with respect to the distribution of earnings (dividends) and assets?

2–17 What are *cumulative* and *noncumulative* preferred stock? What is a *call feature* in a preferred stock issue?

2.5 The Capital Market

capital market
A financial relationship created by institutions and arrangements that allows suppliers and demanders of *long-term funds* to make transactions.

The **capital market** is a financial relationship created by a number of institutions and arrangements that allows suppliers and demanders of *long-term funds* to make transactions. Included are securities issues of business and government. The backbone of the capital market is formed by the various *securities exchanges* that provide a forum for bond and stock transactions.

Major Securities Exchanges

securities exchanges
Organizations that provide the marketplace in which firms can raise funds through the sale of new securities and purchasers can resell securities.

Securities exchanges provide the marketplace in which firms can raise funds through the sale of new securities and purchasers of securities can maintain liquidity by being able to easily resell them when necessary. Many people call securities exchanges "stock markets," but this label is somewhat misleading: bonds, common stock, preferred stock, and a variety of other investment vehicles are all traded on these exchanges. The two key types of securities exchange are the organized exchange and the over-the-counter exchange. In addition, important markets exist outside the United States.

Organized Securities Exchanges

organized securities exchanges
Tangible organizations that act as *secondary markets* where outstanding securities are resold.

Organized securities exchanges are tangible organizations that act as *secondary markets* where outstanding securities are resold. Organized exchanges account for about 59 percent of the *total dollar volume* of domestic shares traded. The best-known organized exchanges are the New York Stock Exchange (NYSE) and the American Stock Exchange (AMEX), both headquartered in New York City. There are also regional exchanges, such as the Chicago Stock Exchange and the Pacific Stock Exchange (co-located in Los Angeles and San Francisco).

Most exchanges are modeled after the New York Stock Exchange, which accounts for about 90 percent of the total annual dollar volume of shares traded on organized exchanges. In order for a firm's securities to be listed for trading on an organized exchange, a firm must file an application for listing and meet a number of requirements. For example, to be eligible for listing on the NYSE, a firm must have at least 2,000 stockholders owning 100 or more shares, a minimum of 1.1 million shares of publicly held stock, earnings of at least $15 million over the previous 3 years, with no loss in the previous 2 years; and a minimum of $100 million in stockholders' equity. Clearly, only large, widely held firms are candidates for listing on the NYSE.

To make transactions on the "floor" of the New York Stock Exchange, an individual or firm must own a "seat" on the exchange. There are a total of 1,366 seats on the NYSE, most of which are owned by brokerage firms. Trading is carried out on the floor of the exchange through an *auction process.* The goal of trading is to fill *buy orders* (orders to purchase securities) at the lowest price and to fill *sell orders* (orders to sell securities) at the highest price, thereby giving both purchasers and sellers the best possible deal. Once placed, an order to buy or sell can be executed in minutes, thanks to sophisticated telecommunication devices. New Internet-based brokerage systems enable investors to electronically place their buy and sell orders. Information on the daily trading of securities is reported in various media, including financial publications such as the *Wall Street Journal.*

The Over-the-Counter Exchange

over-the-counter (OTC) exchange
An intangible market for the purchase and sale of securities not listed by the organized exchanges.

The **over-the-counter (OTC) exchange** is an intangible market for the purchase and sale of securities not listed by the organized exchanges. OTC traders, known as *dealers,* are linked with the purchasers and sellers of securities through the *National Association of Securities Dealers Automated Quotation (Nasdaq) System.* This sophisticated telecommunications network provides current bid and ask prices on thousands of actively traded OTC securities. The *bid price* is the highest price offered by a dealer to purchase a given security, and the *ask price* is the lowest price at which the dealer is willing to sell the security. The dealer in effect adds securities to his or her inventory by purchasing them at the bid price and sells securities from the inventory at the ask price, hoping to profit from the *spread* between the bid and ask price. Unlike the auction process on the organized securities exchanges, the prices at which securities are traded in the OTC market result from both competitive bids and negotiation.

Unlike the organized exchanges, the OTC handles *both* outstanding securities and new public issues, making it both a *secondary* and a *primary market.* The OTC accounts for about 41 percent of the *total dollar volume* of domestic shares traded.

International Capital Markets

Eurobond market
The oldest and largest international bond market, in which bonds, typically denominated in dollars, are issued and sold to investors outside the United States.

Although U.S. capital markets are by far the world's largest, there are important debt and equity markets outside the United States. In the **Eurobond market,** the oldest and largest international bond market, corporations and governments typically issue bonds denominated in dollars and sell them to investors located outside the United States. A U.S. corporation might, for example, issue dollar-denominated bonds that would be purchased by investors in Belgium, Germany, or Switzerland. Through the Eurobond market, issuing firms and governments can tap a much larger pool of investors than would be generally available in the local market.

The foreign bond market is another international market for long-term debt securities. As indicated earlier, a *foreign bond* is a bond issued by a foreign corporation or government that is denominated in the investor's home currency and sold in the investor's home market. A bond issued by a U.S. company that is denominated in Swiss francs and sold in Switzerland is an example of a foreign bond. Although the foreign bond market is much smaller than the Eurobond market, many issuers have found this to be an attractive way of tapping debt markets in Germany, Japan, Switzerland, and the United States.

international equity market
A vibrant equity market that emerged during the past decade to allow corporations to sell blocks of shares in several different countries simultaneously.

Finally, a vibrant **international equity market** has emerged in the past decade. Many corporations have discovered that they can sell blocks of shares to investors in a number of different countries simultaneously. This market has enabled corporations to raise far larger amounts of capital than they could have raised in any single national market. International equity sales have also proven to be indispensable to governments that have sold state-owned companies to private investors in recent years.

The Role of Securities Exchanges

efficient market
A market that allocates funds to their most productive uses as a result of competition among wealth-maximizing investors that determines and publicizes prices that are believed to be close to their true value.

Securities exchanges create continuous liquid markets in which firms can obtain needed financing. They also create **efficient markets** that allocate funds to their most productive uses. This is especially true for securities that are actively traded on major exchanges, where the competition among wealth-maximizing investors determines and publicizes prices that are believed to be close to their true value. The price of an individual security is determined by the demand for and supply of the security. Figure 2.2 depicts the interaction of the forces of demand (represented by line D_0) and supply (represented by line S) for a given security currently selling at an equilibrium price P_0. At that price, Q_0 shares of the stock are traded.

Changing evaluations of a firm cause changes in the demand for and supply of its securities and ultimately result in a new price for the securities. Suppose, for example, that a favorable discovery by the firm shown in Figure 2.2 is

FIGURE 2.2

Supply and Demand
Supply and demand for a
security

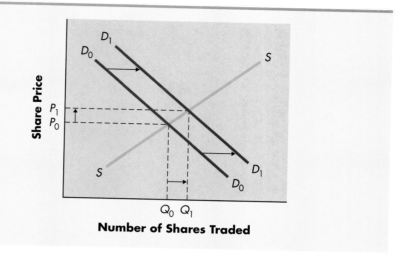

announced and investors in the marketplace increase their valuations of the firm's shares. The changing evaluation results in a shift in demand from D_0 to D_1; Q_1 shares will be traded; and a new, higher equilibrium price of P_1 will result. The competitive market created by the major securities exchanges provides a forum in which share price is continuously adjusted to changing demand and supply.

Interpreting Bond and Stock Price Quotations

The financial manager needs to stay abreast of the market values of the firm's outstanding bonds and stocks, whether they are traded on an organized exchange, over the counter, or in international markets. Similarly, existing and prospective bondholders and stockholders need to monitor the prices of the securities they own because these prices represent the current value of their investment. Information on bonds, stocks, and other securities is contained in **quotations,** which include current price data along with statistics on recent price behavior. Security price quotations are readily available for actively traded bonds and stocks. The most up-to-date "quotes" can be obtained electronically, via a personal computer. Price information is available from stockbrokers and is widely published in news media. Popular sources of daily security price quotations are financial newspapers, such as the *Wall Street Journal* and *Investor's Business Daily*, or the business sections of daily general newspapers.

quotations
Information on bonds, stocks, and other securities, including current price data and statistics on recent price behavior.

Bond Quotations

Part A of Figure 2.3 includes an excerpt from the New York Stock Exchange (NYSE) bond quotations reported in the April 2, 1999, *Wall Street Journal* for transactions through the close of trading on Thursday, April 1, 1999. We'll look at the corporate bond quotation for IBM, which is highlighted in Figure 2.3. The numbers following the company name—IBM—represent the bond's coupon

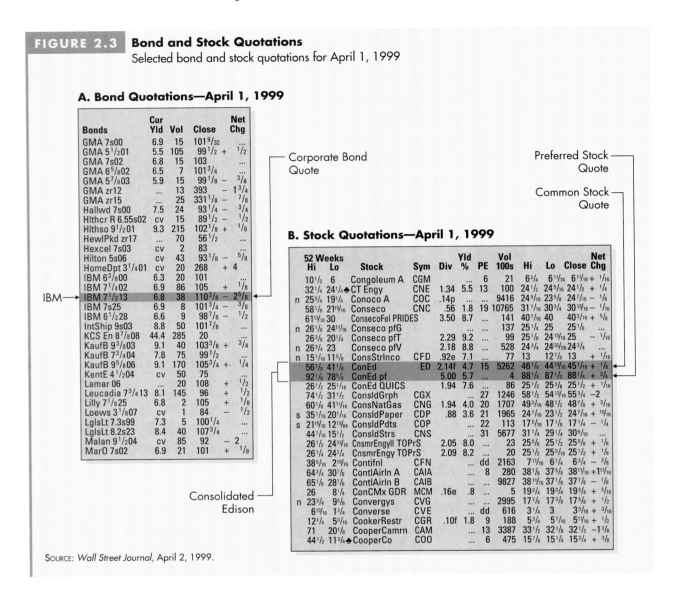

FIGURE 2.3   **Bond and Stock Quotations**
Selected bond and stock quotations for April 1, 1999

A. Bond Quotations—April 1, 1999

Bonds	Cur Yld	Vol	Close	Net Chg
GMA 7s00	6.9	15	$101^9/_{32}$	...
GMA $5^1/_2$01	5.5	105	$99^1/_2$ +	$^1/_2$
GMA 7s02	6.8	15	103	...
GMA $6^5/_8$02	6.5	7	$101^3/_4$	...
GMA $5^7/_8$03	5.9	15	$99^1/_8$ −	$^3/_8$
GMA zr12	...	13	393	− $1^3/_4$
GMA zr15	...	25	$331^1/_8$ −	$^7/_8$
Hallwd 7s00	7.5	24	$93^1/_4$ −	$^3/_4$
Hlthcr R 6.55s02	cv	15	$89^1/_2$ −	$^1/_2$
Hlthso $9^1/_2$01	9.3	215	$102^1/_8$ +	$^1/_8$
HewlPkd zr17	...	70	$56^1/_2$	...
Hexcel 7s03	cv	2	83	...
Hilton 5s06	cv	43	$93^1/_8$ −	$^5/_8$
HomeDpt $3^1/_4$01	cv	20	268	+ 4
IBM $6^3/_8$00	6.3	20	101	...
IBM $7^1/_4$02	6.9	86	105	+ $^1/_8$
IBM $7^1/_2$13	6.8	38	$110^3/_8$ −	$2^5/_8$
IBM 7s25	6.9	8	$101^3/_4$ −	$^3/_8$
IBM $6^1/_2$28	6.6	9	$98^7/_8$ −	$^1/_2$
IntShip 9s03	8.8	50	$101^7/_8$	...
KCS En $8^7/_8$08	44.4	285	20	...
KaufB $9^3/_8$03	9.1	40	$103^3/_8$ +	$^3/_4$
KaufB $7^3/_4$04	7.8	75	$99^1/_2$	...
KaufB $9^5/_8$06	9.1	170	$105^3/_4$ +.	$^1/_4$
KentE $4^1/_2$04	cv	50	75	...
Lamar 06	...	20	108	+ $^1/_2$
Leucadia $7^3/_4$13	8.1	145	96	+ $^1/_2$
Lilly $7^1/_8$25	6.8	2	105	+ $^1/_8$
Loews $3^1/_8$07	cv	1	84	− $^1/_2$
LglsLt 7.3s99	7.3	5	$100^1/_4$	...
LglsLt 8.2s23	8.4	40	$107^3/_4$	...
Malan $9^1/_2$04	cv	85	92	− 2
MarO 7s02	6.9	21	101	+ $^1/_8$

IBM →

Corporate Bond Quote

Consolidated Edison

B. Stock Quotations—April 1, 1999

52 Weeks Hi	52 Weeks Lo	Stock	Sym	Div	Yld %	PE	Vol 100s	Hi	Lo	Close	Net Chg
$10^1/_2$	6	Congoleum A	CGM	...	...	6	21	$6^3/_4$	$6^{11}/_{16}$	$6^{11}/_{16}$ +	$^1/_{16}$
$32^1/_2$	$24^1/_4$ ♣ CT Engy	CNE		1.34	5.5	13	100	$24^1/_2$	$24^5/_{16}$	$24^1/_2$ +	$^1/_4$
n $25^3/_4$	$19^1/_4$	Conoco A	COC	.14p	...	...	9416	$24^9/_{16}$	$23^5/_8$	$24^7/_{16}$ −	$^1/_8$
$58^1/_8$	$21^{15}/_{16}$	Conseco	CNC	.56	1.8	19	10765	$31^7/_{16}$	$30^3/_4$	$30^{13}/_{16}$ −	$^1/_{16}$
$61^{13}/_{16}$	30	ConsecoFel PRIDES		3.50	8.7	...	141	$40^7/_{16}$	40	$40^3/_{16}$ +	$^5/_8$
n $26^1/_8$	$24^{11}/_{16}$	Conseco pfG		...	...	...	137	$25^1/_4$	25	$25^1/_8$	...
$26^3/_8$	$20^1/_4$	Conseco pfT		2.29	9.2	...	99	$25^1/_8$	$24^{15}/_{16}$ 25	−	$^1/_{16}$
n $26^3/_4$	23	Conseco pfV		2.18	8.8	...	528	$24^3/_4$	$24^{133}/_{256}$ $24^3/_4$	...
n $15^1/_8$	$11^5/_8$	ConsStrInco	CFD	.92e	7.1	...	77	13	$12^7/_8$	13 +	$^1/_{16}$
$56^1/_8$	$41^1/_8$	ConEd	ED	2.14f	4.7	15	5262	$46^1/_8$	$44^{13}/_{16}$ $45^7/_{16}$ +	$^1/_8$
$92^1/_8$	$78^5/_8$	ConEd pf		5.00	5.7	...	4	$88^1/_4$	$87^1/_2$	$88^1/_8$ +	$^3/_4$
$26^1/_2$	$25^1/_{16}$	ConEd QUICS		1.94	7.6	...	86	$25^1/_2$	$25^3/_8$	$25^1/_2$ +	$^1/_{16}$
$74^1/_2$	$31^1/_2$	ConsldGrph	CGX	...	...	27	1246	$58^1/_2$	$54^{13}/_{16}$ $55^3/_4$	−2	
$60^1/_8$	$41^{11}/_{16}$	ConsNatGas	CNG	1.94	4.0	20	1707	$49^3/_{16}$	$48^1/_2$	$48^7/_8$ +	$^3/_{16}$
s $35^1/_{16}$	$20^1/_{16}$	ConsldPaper	CDP	.88	3.6	21	1965	$24^7/_{16}$	$23^1/_2$	$24^7/_{16}$ +	$^{15}/_{16}$
s $21^{15}/_{16}$	$12^{19}/_{64}$	ConsldPdts	COP	...	...	22	113	$17^5/_{16}$	$17^1/_8$	$17^1/_4$ −	$^1/_4$
$44^7/_{16}$	$15^1/_2$	ConsldStrs	CNS	...	...	31	5677	$31^1/_4$	$29^1/_4$	$30^5/_{16}$	...
$26^1/_2$	$24^{13}/_{16}$	CnsmrEngyll TOPrS		2.05	8.0	...	23	$25^5/_8$	$25^1/_2$	$25^5/_8$ +	$^1/_8$
$26^1/_4$	$24^3/_4$	CnsmrEngy TOPrS		2.09	8.2	...	20	$25^1/_2$	$25^5/_{16}$ $25^1/_2$ +	$^1/_8$
$38^9/_{16}$	$2^{15}/_{16}$	Contifnl	CFN	...	...	dd	2163	$7^{11}/_{16}$	$6^1/_4$	$6^3/_4$ −	$^3/_8$
$64^3/_4$	$30^7/_8$	ContlAirln A	CAIA	...	...	8	280	$38^7/_8$	$37^5/_8$	$38^{11}/_{16}$ +$1^{11}/_{16}$
$65^1/_8$	$28^7/_8$	ContlAirln B	CAIB	...	...	...	9827	$38^{11}/_{16}$ $37^1/_8$	$37^7/_8$ −	$^1/_8$
26	$8^1/_4$	ConCMx GDR	MCM	.16e	.8	...	5	$19^3/_4$	$19^3/_4$	$19^3/_4$ +	$^3/_{16}$
n $23^3/_4$	$9^5/_8$	Convergys	CVG	...	...	...	2995	$17^7/_8$	$17^3/_8$	$17^5/_8$ +	$^1/_2$
$6^{13}/_{16}$	$1^3/_4$	Converse	CVE	...	...	dd	616	$3^1/_4$	3	$3^3/_{16}$ +	$^3/_{16}$
$12^1/_4$	$5^3/_{16}$	CookerRestr	CGR	.10f	1.8	9	188	$5^3/_4$	$5^7/_{16}$	$5^{11}/_{16}$ +	$^1/_2$
71	$20^1/_8$	CooperCamrn	CAM	...	...	13	3387	$33^1/_2$	$32^1/_8$	$32^1/_2$ − $1^3/_8$
$44^1/_2$	$11^3/_4$ ♣ CooperCo	COO	...	...	6	475	$15^7/_8$	$15^1/_4$	$15^3/_4$ +	$^3/_8$

Preferred Stock Quote

Common Stock Quote

Source: *Wall Street Journal*, April 2, 1999.

interest rate and the year it matures: "$7^1/_2$ 13" means that the bond has a stated coupon interest rate of $7^1/_2$ percent and matures sometime in the year 2013. This information allows investors to differentiate between the various bonds issued by the corporation. Note that on the day of this quote IBM had five bonds listed. The next column, labeled "Cur Yld," gives the bond's *current yield*, which is found by dividing its annual coupon ($7^1/_2$%, or 7.500%) by its closing price ($110^3/_8$), which in this case turns out to be 6.8 percent ($7.500 \div 110.375 = .0680 = 6.8\%$).

The "Vol" column indicates the actual number of bonds that traded on the given day; 38 IBM bonds traded on Thursday, April 1, 1999. The final two columns include price information—the closing price and the net change in closing price from the prior trading day. Although most corporate bonds are issued with a *par*, or *face, value* of $1,000, *all bonds are quoted as a percentage of par.* A $1,000-par-value bond quoted at 92⅝ is priced at $926.25 (92.625% × $1,000). Corporate bonds trade in fractions of ⅛, which for $1,000-par-value bonds represents 1.25 *dollars*. Note that fractions are reduced to their lowest common denominator—²⁄₈, ⁴⁄₈, and ⁶⁄₈ are expressed as ¼, ½, and ¾, respectively. Thus, IBM's closing price of 110⅜ for the day was $1,1103.75, that is, 110.375% × $1,000. Because a "Net Chg." of −2⅝ is given in the final column, the bond must have closed at 113 or $1,130.00 (113.000% × $1,000) on the prior day. Its price decreased by 2⅝, or $26.25 (2.625% × $1,000), on Thursday, April 1, 1999. Additional information may be included in a bond quotation but we have looked at the basic elements.

Stock Quotations

Part B of Figure 2.3 includes an excerpt from the NYSE stock quotations, also reported in the April 2, 1999, *Wall Street Journal* for transactions through the close of trading on Thursday, April 1, 1999. We'll look at both the common stock and preferred stock quotations for Consolidated Edison, highlighted in Figure 2.3. The quotations show that most stock prices are quoted in sixteenths of a dollar, with the fractions reduced to their lowest common denominator. The first two columns, labeled "Hi" and "Lo," contain the highest and lowest price at which the stock sold during the preceding 52 weeks. Consolidated Edison (abbreviated "ConEd") common stock, for example, traded between 41⅛ and 56⅛ during the 52-week period ending April 1, 1999. Listed to the right of the company's abbreviated name is its *stock symbol*—Consolidated Edison goes by "ED." The figure listed right after the stock symbol under "Div" is the annual cash dividend paid on each share of stock. The dividend for Consolidated Edison was $2.14 per share. The next item, labeled "Yld%," is the *dividend yield*, which is found by dividing the stated dividend by the closing share price. The dividend yield for Consolidated Edison is 4.7 percent (2.14 ÷ 45⁷⁄₁₆ = 2.14 ÷ 45.4375 = .0471 ≈ 4.7%).

The **price/earnings (P/E) ratio**, labeled "PE," is next. It is calculated by dividing the closing market price by the firm's most recent annual earnings per share (EPS). The price/earnings (P/E) ratio measures the amount investors are willing to pay for each dollar of the firm's earnings. Consolidated Edison's P/E ratio was 15—the stock was trading at 15 times its earnings. The P/E ratio is believed to reflect investor expectations concerning the firm's future prospects: Higher P/E ratios reflect investor optimism and confidence; lower P/E ratios reflect investor pessimism and concern.

The daily volume, labeled "Vol 100s," follows the P/E ratio. Here the day's sales are quoted in lots of 100 shares. The value 5262 for Consolidated Edison indicates that 526,200 shares of its common stock were traded on April 1, 1999. The "Hi," "Lo," and "Close" columns contain the highest, lowest, and closing (last) price, respectively, at which the stock sold on the given day. These values for Consolidated Edison were a high of $46.125, a low of $44.8125, and a closing price of $45.4375. The final column, "Net Chg," indicates the change in the

Hint Occasionally shares of stock will be quoted in thirty-seconds or sixty-fourths.

price/earnings (P/E) ratio Measures the amount common stock investors are willing to pay for each dollar of the firm's earnings.

closing price from that on the prior trading day. Consolidated Edison closed up
⅛ ($.125) from March 31, 1999, which means the closing price on that day was
$45.3125 (45⁵⁄₁₆).

Note that preferred stocks are listed with common stocks. For example, following Consolidated Edison's common stock in the quotes in part B of Figure 2.3 is its preferred stock, which is identified by the letters "pf." The quotation for preferred stock is nearly identical to that of common stock except that the value for the P/E ratio is left blank because it is irrelevant in the case of preferred stock.

Similar quotation systems are used for stocks that trade on other exchanges such as the American Stock Exchange (AMEX) and for the over-the-counter (OTC) exchange's Nasdaq national market issues. Also note that when a bond or stock issue is not traded on a given day it generally is not quoted in the financial and business press.

? Review Questions

2–16   What is the *capital market?* What role do securities exchanges play in the capital market?

2–17   How does the over-the-counter exchange operate? How does it differ from the organized securities exchanges?

2–18   Briefly describe the international capital markets, particularly the *Eurobond market* and the *international equity market.*

2–19   What information is found in a bond quotation? What unit of measurement is used to quote bond price data?

2–20   Describe the key items of information included in a stock quotation. What information does the stock's price/earnings (P/E) ratio provide? How are preferred stock quotations differentiated from those of common stock?

2.6 Interest Rates and Required Returns

Financial institutions and markets create the mechanism through which funds flow between savers (funds suppliers) and investors (funds demanders). The level of funds flow between suppliers and demanders can significantly affect economic growth. Growth results from the interaction of a variety of economic factors (such as the money supply, trade balances, and economic policies) that affect the cost of money—the interest rate or required return. The interest rate level acts as a regulating device that controls the flow of funds between suppliers and demanders. The *Board of Governors of the Federal Reserve System* regularly assesses economic conditions and, when necessary, initiates actions to raise or lower interest rates to control inflation and economic growth. Generally, the lower the interest rate, the greater the funds flow and therefore the greater the economic growth; the higher the interest rate, the lower the funds flow and economic growth.

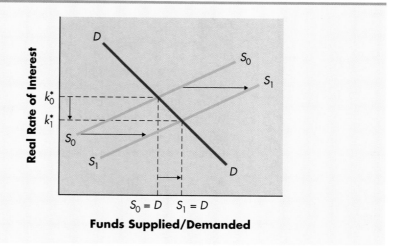

FIGURE 2.4

Supply–Demand Relationship
Supply of savings and demand for investment funds

Interest Rate Fundamentals

The interest rate or required return represents the cost of money. It is the compensation that a demander of funds must pay a supplier. When funds are lent, the cost of borrowing the funds is the **interest rate.** When funds are obtained by selling an ownership interest—as in the sale of stock—the cost to the issuer (demander) is commonly called the **required return,** which reflects the funds supplier's level of expected return. In both cases the supplier is compensated for providing funds. Ignoring risk factors, the cost of funds results from the *real rate of interest* adjusted for inflationary expectations and **liquidity preferences**—general preferences of investors for shorter-term securities.

interest rate
The compensation paid by the borrower of funds to the lender; from the borrower's point of view, the cost of borrowing funds.

required return
The cost of funds obtained by selling an ownership interest; it reflects the funds supplier's level of expected return.

liquidity preferences
General preferences of investors for shorter-term securities.

real rate of interest
The rate that creates an equilibrium between the supply of savings and the demand for investment funds in a perfect world, without inflation, where funds suppliers and demanders have no liquidity preference and all outcomes are certain.

The Real Rate of Interest

Assume a *perfect world* in which there is no inflation and in which funds suppliers and demanders are indifferent to the term of loans or investments because they have no liquidity preference and all outcomes are certain.[2] At any given point in time in that perfect world, there would be one cost of money—the **real rate of interest.** The real rate of interest creates an equilibrium between the supply of savings and the demand for investment funds. It represents the most basic cost of money. The real rate of interest in the United States is assumed to be stable and equal to around 2 percent.[3] This supply–demand relationship is shown in Figure 2.4 by the supply function (labeled S_0) and the demand function (labeled D). An

2. These assumptions are made to describe the most basic interest rate, the *real rate of interest.* Subsequent discussions relax these assumptions to develop the broader concept of the interest rate and required return.

3. Data in Roger G. Ibbotson and Rex A. Sinquefield, *Stocks, Bonds, Bills and Inflation: Historical Returns* (Chicago: Dow-Jones Irwin, 1989), updated in *SBBI 1998 Yearbook* (Chicago: Ibbotson Associates, 1999), show that over the period 1926–1997, U.S. Treasury bills provided an average annual real rate of return of about .6 percent. Because of certain major economic events that occurred during the 1926–1997 period, many economists believe that the real rate of interest during recent years has been about 2 percent.

equilibrium between the supply of funds and the demand for funds ($S_0 = D$) occurs at a rate of interest k_0^*, the real rate of interest.

Clearly, the real rate of interest changes with changing economic conditions, tastes, and preferences. A trade surplus could result in an increased supply of funds, causing the supply function in Figure 2.4 to shift to, say, S_1. This could result in a lower real rate of interest, k_1^*, at equilibrium ($S_1 = D$). Likewise, a change in tax laws or other factors could affect the demand for funds, causing the real rate of interest to rise or fall to a new equilibrium level.

Nominal or Actual Rate of Interest (Return)

nominal rate of interest
The actual rate of interest charged by the supplier of funds and paid by the demander.

The **nominal rate of interest** is the actual rate of interest charged by the supplier of funds and paid by the demander. *Throughout this book, interest rates and required rates of return are nominal rates unless otherwise noted.* The nominal rate of interest differs from the real rate of interest, k^*, as a result of two factors: (1) inflationary expectations reflected in an inflation premium (IP), and (2) issuer and issue characteristics, such as default risk and contractual provisions, reflected in a risk premium (RP). By using this notation, the nominal rate of interest for security 1, k_1, is given in Equation 2.1:

$$k_1 = \underbrace{k^* + IP}_{\substack{\text{risk-free} \\ \text{rate, } R_F}} + \underbrace{RP_1}_{\substack{\text{risk} \\ \text{premium}}} \qquad (2.1)$$

As the horizontal braces below the equation indicate, the nominal rate, k_1, can be viewed as having two basic components: a risk-free rate of interest, R_F, and a risk premium, RP_1:

$$k_1 = R_F + RP_1 \qquad (2.2)$$

To simplify the discussion, we will assume that the risk premium, RP_1, is equal to zero. By drawing from Equation 2.1,[4] the risk-free rate can be represented as:

$$R_F = k^* + IP \qquad (2.3)$$

risk-free rate of interest, R_F
The required return on a risk-free asset, typically a 3-month *U.S. Treasury bill.*

U.S. Treasury bills (T-bills)
Short-term IOUs issued by the U.S. Treasury; considered the risk-free asset.

Thus, we concern ourselves only with the **risk-free rate of interest, R_F,** which is defined as the required return on a risk-free asset.[5] The risk-free rate (as shown in Equation 2.3) embodies the real rate of interest plus the inflationary expectation. Three-month **U.S. Treasury bills (T-bills),** which are short-term IOUs issued by

---

4. This equation is commonly called the *Fisher equation*, named for the renowned economist Irving Fisher, who first presented this approximate relationship between nominal interest and the rate of inflation. See Irving Fisher, *The Theory of Interest* (New York: Macmillan, 1930).

5. In a later part of this discussion the risk premium and its effect on the nominal rate of interest are discussed and illustrated.

the U.S. Treasury, are commonly considered the risk-free asset. *The real rate of interest can be estimated by subtracting the inflation premium from the nominal rate of interest.* For the risk-free asset in Equation 2.3, the real rate of interest, k^*, would equal $R_F - IP$. A simple example can demonstrate the practical distinction between nominal and real rates of interest.

E x a m p l e ▼ Marilyn Carbo has $10 that she can spend on candy costing $.25 per piece. She could therefore buy 40 pieces of candy ($10.00/$.25) today. The nominal rate of interest on a 1-year deposit is currently 7% and the expected rate of inflation over the coming year is 4%. Instead of buying the 40 pieces of candy today, Marilyn can invest the $10 in a 1-year deposit account now. At the end of 1 year she would have $10.70 because she would have earned 7% interest—an additional $.70 (.07 × $10.00)—on her $10 deposit. The 4% inflation rate would over the 1-year period increase the cost of the candy by 4%—an additional $.01 (.04 × $.25)—to $.26 per piece. As a result, at the end of the 1-year period Marilyn would be able to buy about 41.2 pieces of candy ($10.70/$.26), or roughly 3% more (41.2/40.0 = 1.03). The increase in the amount of money available to Marilyn at the end of 1 year is merely her nominal rate of return (7%), which must be reduced by the rate of inflation (4%) during the period to determine her real rate of return of 3%. Marilyn's increased buying power therefore
▲ equals her 3% real rate of return.

The premium for *inflationary expectations* in Equation 2.3 represents the average rate of *inflation* expected over the life of a loan or investment. It is *not* the rate of inflation experienced over the immediate past; rather, it reflects the forecasted rate. Take, for example, the risk-free asset. During the week ended July 31, 1998, 3-month T-bills earned a 4.95 percent rate of return. Assuming an approximate 2 percent real rate of interest, funds suppliers were forecasting a 2.95 percent (annual) rate of inflation (4.95% − 2.00%) over the next 3 months. This expectation was in striking contrast to the expected rate of inflation 17 years earlier in the week ending May 22, 1981. At that time the 3-month T-bill rate was 16.60 percent, which meant an expected (annual) inflation rate of 14.60 percent (16.60% − 2.00%). The inflationary expectation premium changes over time in response to many factors, including recent rates, government policies, and international events.

Figure 2.5 illustrates the movement of the rate of inflation and the risk-free rate of interest during the 20-year period 1978–1998. During this period the two rates tended to move in a similar fashion. Between 1978 and the early 1980s, inflation and interest rates were quite high, peaking at over 13 percent in 1980–1981. Since 1981 these rates have declined to levels generally below those in 1978. The data clearly illustrate the significant impact of inflation on the nominal rate of interest for the risk-free asset.

Term Structure of Interest Rates

term structure of interest rates
The relationship between the interest rate or rate of return and the time to maturity.

For any class of similar-risk securities, the **term structure of interest rates** relates the interest rate or rate of return to the time to maturity. For convenience we will use Treasury securities as a class, but other classes could include securities that

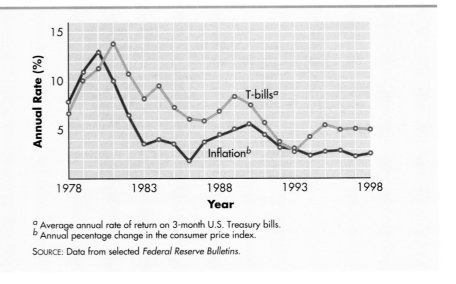

FIGURE 2.5

Impact of Inflation
Relationship between annual rate of inflation and 3-month U.S. Treasury bill average annual returns, 1978–1998

[a] Average annual rate of return on 3-month U.S. Treasury bills.
[b] Annual pecentage change in the consumer price index.
SOURCE: Data from selected *Federal Reserve Bulletins*.

have similar overall quality or risk ratings, as determined by independent agencies like Moody's and Standard & Poor's. The riskless nature of Treasury securities also provides a laboratory in which to develop the term structure.

Yield Curves

yield to maturity
Annual rate of interest earned on a security purchased on a given day and held to maturity.

yield curve
A graph of the *term structure of interest rates* that depicts the relationship between the *yield to maturity* of a security (*y* axis) and the time to maturity (*x* axis); it shows the pattern of interest rates on securities of equal quality and different maturity.

inverted yield curve
A downward-sloping yield curve that indicates generally cheaper long-term borrowing costs than short-term borrowing costs.

normal yield curve
An upward-sloping yield curve that indicates generally cheaper short-term borrowing costs than long-term borrowing costs.

flat yield curve
A yield curve that reflects relatively similar borrowing costs for both short- and longer-term loans.

The annual rate of interest earned on a security purchased on a given day and held to maturity is its **yield to maturity.** At any point in time, the relationship between yield to maturity and the remaining time to maturity can be represented by a graph called the **yield curve.** The yield curve shows the pattern of interest rates on securities of equal quality and different maturity; it is a graphic depiction of the *term structure of interest rates*. Figure 2.6 shows three yield curves for all U.S. Treasury securities—one at May 22, 1981, a second one at September 29, 1989, and a third one at July 31, 1998. Note that both the position and the shape of the yield curves change over time. The May 22, 1981, curve indicates high short-term interest rates and lower longer-term rates. This curve is described as *downward-sloping,* reflecting generally cheaper long-term borrowing costs than short-term borrowing costs. Historically, the downward-sloping yield curve, which is often called an **inverted yield curve,** has been the exception. More frequently, yield curves similar to (but steeper than) that of July 31, 1998, have existed. These *upward-sloping* or **normal yield curves** indicate that short-term borrowing costs are below long-term borrowing costs. Sometimes, a **flat yield curve,** similar to that of September 29, 1989, exists. It reflects relatively similar borrowing costs for both short- and longer-term loans.

The shape of the yield curve affects the firm's financing decisions. A financial manager who faces a downward-sloping yield curve is likely to rely more heavily on cheaper, long-term financing; when the yield curve is upward-sloping, the manager is more likely to use cheaper, short-term financing. Although a variety of other factors also influence the choice of loan maturity, the shape of the yield curve provides useful insights into future interest-rate expectations.

FIGURE 2.6

Treasury Yield Curves
Yield curves for U.S.
Treasury securities: May 22,
1981; September 29, 1989;
and July 31, 1998

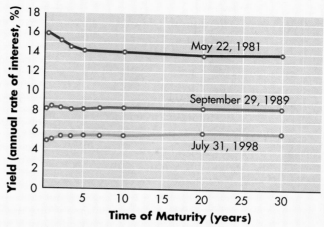

SOURCE: Data from *Federal Reserve Bulletin* (June 1981), p. A25;
(December 1989), p. A24; and (October 1998), p. A23.

In Practice

Watch Those Curves!

In fall 1998, warning bells went off amongst economy watchers. The yield curve—a chart of the gap between short- and long-term interest rates—changed from the typical upward-sloping curve to an inverted curve, as short-term interest rates rose above long-term rates. In early September 1998, the difference between 3-month T-bills and 10-year Treasury notes was almost nonexistent. Yields of government securities at all maturities fell below the federal funds rate, another key short-term interest rate, for the first time since 1991.

Why was the inverted yield curve alarming? The shape of the yield curve has been an excellent predictor of future economic growth. In general, sharp upward-sloping curves signal a substantial rise in economic activity within a year, whereas inverted yield curves preceded every recession since 1955. Most periods of flat or inverted yield curves occur when the Federal Reserve increases short-term rates, tightening monetary policy to control inflation. These higher rates curtail business growth.

However, 1998's inverted yield curve resulted not from increases in short-term rates to control inflation, but from falling long-term rates in the global economy. Financial turmoil in Asia, Latin America, and Russia pushed investors toward higher-quality, lower-risk securities, reducing the demand for long-term bonds both in the United States and abroad. As global problems began affecting the United States, economists and central bank officials around the world urged the Federal Reserve to cut U.S. interest rates. Despite the risk that lower rates could once again heat up the U.S. economy and increase inflation, the continuing worldwide economic chaos led the Fed to cut the federal funds rate from 5.50 to 5.25 percent at the end of September. Two weeks later, the Fed cut the rate to 5.0 percent, to ward off further weakening of the U.S. economy and avoid recession.

Theories of Term Structure

The dominance of the upward-sloping yield curve can be simply explained: Short-term securities are less risky than long-term securities because near-term events are more certain than future events, and therefore they have lower returns. However, this explanation fails to explain why yield curves often take on different shapes, such as those shown in Figure 2.6. Three theories are frequently cited to better explain the general shape of the yield curve: the expectations hypothesis, liquidity preference theory, and market segmentation theory.

expectations hypothesis
Theory suggesting that the yield curve reflects investor expectations about future interest rates; an increasing inflation expectation results in an upward-sloping yield curve and a decreasing inflation expectation results in a downward-sloping yield curve.

Expectations Hypothesis   The **expectations hypothesis** suggests that the yield curve reflects investor expectations about future interest rates and inflation. Higher future rates of expected inflation will result in higher, long-term interest rates; the opposite occurs with lower future rates. This widely accepted explanation of the term structure can be applied to the securities of any issuer. For example, take the case of U.S. Treasury securities. Thus far, we have concerned ourselves solely with the 3-month Treasury bill. In fact, all Treasury securities are *riskless* in terms of (1) the chance that the Treasury will default on the issue and (2) the ease with which they can be liquidated for cash without losing value. Because it is believed to be easier to forecast inflation over shorter periods of time, the shorter-term 3-month U.S. Treasury bill is considered the risk-free asset. Of course, differing inflation expectations associated with different maturities will cause nominal interest rates to vary. With the addition of a maturity subscript, *t*, Equation 2.3 can be rewritten as:

$$R_{F_t} = k^* + IP_t \qquad (2.4)$$

In other words, for U.S. Treasury securities the nominal, or risk-free, rate for a given maturity varies with the inflation expectation over the term of the security.[6]

E x a m p l e ▼ The nominal interest rate, R_F, for four maturities of U.S. Treasury securities on July 31, 1998, is given in column 1 of the following table. Assuming that the real rate of interest is 2%, as noted in column 2, the inflation expectation for each maturity in column 3 is found by solving Equation 2.4 for IP_t. Although a 2.95% rate of inflation was expected over the 3-month period, beginning July 31, 1998, a 3.09% average rate of inflation was expected over the 1-year period, and so on. An analysis of the inflation expectations in column 3 for July 31, 1998, suggests that at that time a general expectation of slightly increasing inflation existed. Simply stated, the July 31, 1998, yield curve for U.S. Treasury securities shown in Figure 2.6 was upward-sloping as a result of the expectation that the rate of inflation would increase slightly in the future.[7]

---

6. Although U.S. Treasury securities have no risk of default or illiquidity, they do suffer from "maturity, or interest rate, risk"—the risk that interest rates will change in the future and thereby affect longer maturities more than shorter maturities. Therefore the longer the maturity of a Treasury (or any other) security, the greater its interest rate risk. The impact of interest-rate changes on bond values is discussed in Chapter 7; here we ignore this effect.

7. It is interesting to note (in Figure 2.6) that the expectations reflected by the September 29, 1989, yield curve were not fully borne out by actual events. By July 1998, interest rates had fallen for all maturities, and the yield curve at that time had shifted downward and become somewhat upward-sloping, reflecting an expectation of slightly increasing future interest rates and inflation rates.

Maturity, t	Nominal interest rate, R_{F_t} (1)	Real interest rate, k^* (2)	Inflation expectation, IP_t [(1) − (2)] (3)
3 months	4.95%	2.00%	2.95%
1 year	5.09	2.00	3.09
5 years	5.51	2.00	3.51
30 years	5.73	2.00	3.73

Generally, under the expectations hypothesis, an increasing inflation expectation results in an upward-sloping yield curve; a decreasing inflation expectation results in a downward-sloping yield curve; and a stable inflation expectation results in a flat yield curve. Although, as we'll see, other theories exist, the observed strong relationship between inflation and interest rates (see Figure 2.5) supports this widely accepted theory.

Liquidity Preference Theory The tendency for yield curves to be upward-sloping can be further explained by **liquidity preference theory**. This theory indicates that for a given issuer, such as the U.S. Treasury, long-term rates tend to be higher than short-term rates. This belief is based on two behavioral facts:

liquidity preference theory
Theory suggesting that for any given issuer, long-term interest rates tend to be higher than short-term rates due to the lower liquidity and higher responsiveness to general interest rate movements of longer-term securities; causes the yield curve to be upward-sloping.

1. Investors perceive less risk in short-term securities than in longer-term securities and are therefore willing to accept lower yields on them. The reason is that shorter-term securities are more liquid and less responsive to general interest rate movements.[8]
2. Borrowers are generally willing to pay a higher rate for long-term than for short-term financing. By locking in funds for a longer period of time, they can eliminate the potential adverse consequences of having to roll over short-term debt at unknown costs to obtain long-term financing.

Investors (lenders) tend to require a premium for tying up funds for longer periods, whereas borrowers are generally willing to pay a premium to obtain longer-term financing. These preferences of lenders and borrowers cause the yield curve to tend to be upward-sloping. Simply stated, longer maturities tend to have higher interest rates than shorter maturities.

market segmentation theory
Theory suggesting that the market for loans is segmented on the basis of maturity and that the supply of and demand for loans within each segment determine its prevailing interest rate; the slope of the yield curve is determined by the general relationship between the prevailing rates in each segment.

Market Segmentation Theory The **market segmentation theory** suggests that the market for loans is segmented on the basis of maturity and that the supply of and demand for loans within each segment determine its prevailing interest rate. In other words, the equilibrium between suppliers and demanders of short-term funds, such as seasonal business loans, would determine prevailing short-term interest rates, and the equilibrium between suppliers and demanders

8. Chapter 7 demonstrates that debt instruments with longer maturities are more sensitive to changing market interest rates. For a given change in market rates, the price or value of longer-term debts will be more significantly changed (up or down) than those with shorter maturities.

of long-term funds, such as real estate loans, would determine prevailing long-term interest rates. The slope of the yield curve would be determined by the general relationship between the prevailing rates in each market segment. Simply stated, low rates in the short-term segment and high rates in the long-term segment cause the yield curve to be upward-sloping. The opposite occurs for high short-term rates and low long-term rates.

All three theories of term structure have merit. From them we can conclude that at any time the slope of the yield curve is affected by (1) inflationary expectations, (2) liquidity preferences, and (3) the comparative equilibrium of supply and demand in the short- and long-term market segments. Upward-sloping yield curves result from higher future inflation expectations, lender preferences for shorter-maturity loans, and greater supply of short-term loans than of long-term loans relative to demand. The opposite behaviors would result in a downward-sloping yield curve. At any point in time, the interaction of these three forces will determine the prevailing slope of the yield curve.

Risk Premiums: Issuer and Issue Characteristics

So far we have considered only risk-free U.S. Treasury securities. We now re-introduce the risk premium and assess it in view of risky non-Treasury issues. Recall Equation 2.1, restated here:

$$k_1 = \underbrace{k^* + IP}_{\substack{\text{risk-free} \\ \text{rate, } R_F}} + \underbrace{RP_1}_{\substack{\text{risk} \\ \text{premium}}}$$

In words, the nominal rate of interest for security 1 (k_1) is equal to the risk-free rate, consisting of the real rate of interest (k^*) plus the inflation expectation premium (IP), plus the risk premium (RP_1). The *risk premium* varies with specific issuer and issue characteristics; it causes similar-maturity securities[9] to have differing nominal rates of interest.

E x a m p l e ▼ The nominal interest rates on a number of classes of long-term securities on July 31, 1998, were as follows:[10]

Security	Nominal interest
U.S. Treasury bonds (average)	5.81%
Corporate bonds (by rating):	
Aaa	6.60
Aa	6.82
A	6.93
Baa	7.20
Utility bonds (A-rated)	7.04

---

9. To provide for the same risk-free rate of interest, $k^* + IP$, it is necessary to assume equal maturities. By doing this the inflationary expectations premium, IP, and therefore R_F, will be held constant, and the issuer and issue characteristics premium, RP, becomes the key factor differentiating the nominal rates of interest on various securities.

10. These yields were obtained from the *Federal Reserve Bulletin* (October 1998), p. A23.

Because the U.S. Treasury bond would represent the risk-free, long-term security, we can calculate the risk premium of the other securities by subtracting the risk-free rate, 5.81%, from each nominal rate (yield):

Security	Risk premium
Corporate bonds (by rating):	
Aaa	6.60 − 5.81 = 0.79%
Aa	6.82 − 5.81 = 1.01
A	6.93 − 5.81 = 1.12
Baa	7.20 − 5.81 = 1.39
Utility bonds (A-rated)	7.04 − 5.81 = 1.23

These risk premiums reflect differing issuer and issue risks. The lower-rated corporate issues (A and Baa) have higher risk premiums than those of the higher-rated corporates (Aaa and Aa), and the utility issue has a risk premium near that of the A corporates.

The risk premium consists of a number of issuer- and issue-related components including default risk, maturity risk, liquidity risk, contractual provisions, and tax risk. Each of these components is briefly defined in Table 2.6. In general,

TABLE 2.6   Issuer- and Issue-Related Risk Components

Component	Description
Default risk	The possibility that the issuer of debt will not pay the contractual interest or principal as scheduled. The greater the uncertainty as to the borrower's ability to meet these payments, the greater the risk premium. High bond ratings reflect low default risk, and low bond ratings reflect high default risk.
Maturity risk (also called *interest-rate risk*)	The fact that the longer the maturity, the more the value of a security will change in response to a given change in interest rates. If interest rates on otherwise similar-risk securities suddenly rise due to a change in the money supply, the prices of long-term bonds will decline by more than the prices of short-term bonds, and vice versa.[a]
Liquidity risk	The ease with which securities can be converted into cash without experiencing a loss in value. Generally, securities actively traded on major exchanges and over-the-counter have low liquidity risk, and less actively traded securities in a "thin market" have high liquidity risk.
Contractual provisions	Conditions that are often included in a debt agreement or a stock issue. Some of these reduce risk, whereas others may increase risk. For example, a provision allowing a bond issuer to retire its bonds prior to their maturity under favorable terms would increase the bond's risk.
Tax risk	The chance that Congress will make unfavorable changes in tax laws. The greater the potential impact of a tax law change on the return of a given security, the greater its tax risk. Generally, long-term securities are subject to greater tax risk than are those that are closer to their maturity dates.

[a]A detailed discussion of the effects of interest rates on the price or value of bonds and other fixed-income securities is presented in Chapter 7.

FIGURE 2.7

Risk-Return Trade-off
Risk-return profile for popular securities

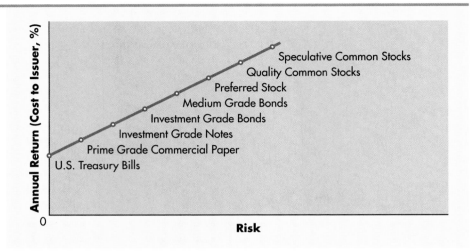

the highest risk premiums and therefore the highest returns are to be found in securities issued by firms with a high risk of default and in long-term maturities that are not actively traded, have unfavorable contractual provisions, and are not tax-exempt.

Risk and Return

The fact that a positive relationship exists between risk and the nominal or expected return should be evident. Investors tend to purchase those securities that are expected to provide a return commensurate with the perceived risk. The actual return earned on the security will affect whether investors sell, hold, or buy additional securities. In addition, most investors look to certain types of securities to provide a given range of risk-return behaviors.

risk-return trade-off
The expectation that for accepting greater risk, investors must be compensated with greater returns.

Career Key
The *marketing* department is particularly concerned about the risk-return relationship because it might be used by top management to reject new product proposals. Management might feel that if it accepted these proposals, the firm's risk would be too high.

A **risk-return trade-off** exists: Investors must be compensated for accepting greater risk with the expectation of greater returns.[11] Figure 2.7 illustrates the typical relationship between risk and return for several popular securities. Clearly, higher returns are expected with greater risk. Financial managers must attempt to keep revenues up and costs down, but they must also consider the risks associated with each investment and financing alternative. Decisions will ultimately rest on an analysis of the impact of risk and return on share price.

❓ Review Questions

2–22 What is the *real rate of interest?* Differentiate it from the *nominal rate of interest* for the risk-free asset, a 3-month U.S. Treasury bill. How can the real rate of interest be estimated?

11. The risk-return tradeoff is discussed in detail in Chapter 6, where certain refinements are introduced to explain why investors are actually rewarded with higher returns for taking only certain types of "nondiversifiable" or inescapable risks.

Amount of funds supplied/demanded ($ billion)	Currently		With passage of tax legislation
	Interest rate required by funds suppliers	Interest rate required by funds demanders	Interest rate required by funds demanders
$ 1	2%	7%	9%
5	3	6	8
10	4	4	7
20	6	3	6
50	7	2	4
100	9	1	3

b. Using your graph, label and note the real rate of interest using current data.

c. Add to the graph drawn in **a** the new demand curve expected in the event the proposed tax legislation becomes effective.

d. What is the new real rate of interest? Compare and analyze this finding in light of your analysis in **b**.

  2–9   **Real and nominal rates interest**   Zane Perelli currently has $100 that he can spend today on polo shirts costing $25 each. Instead he could invest the $100 in a risk-free U.S. Treasury security that is expected to earn a 9% nominal rate of interest. The consensus forecast of leading economists is a 5% rate of inflation over the coming year.

a. How many polo shirts can Zane purchase today?

b. How much money would Zane have at the end of 1 year if he forgoes purchasing the polo shirts today?

c. How much would you expect the polo shirts to cost at the end of 1 year in light of the expected inflation?

d. Use your findings in **b** and **c** to determine how many polo shirts (fractions are OK) Zane could purchase at the end of 1 year? In percentage terms, how many more or fewer polo shirts can Zane buy at the end of 1 year?

e. What is Zane's real rate of return over the year? How does it relate to the percentage change in Zane's buying power found in **d**? Explain.

  2–10   **Yield curve**   A firm wishing to evaluate interest rate behavior has gathered yield data on five U.S. Treasury securities, each having a different maturity and all measured at the same point in time. The summarized data follows:

U.S. Treasury security	Time to maturity	Yield
A	1 year	12.6%
B	10 years	11.2
C	6 months	13.0
D	20 years	11.0
E	5 years	11.4

a. Draw the yield curve associated with the data given.

b. Describe the resulting yield curve in **a**, and explain the general expectations embodied in it.

  2–11 **Nominal interest rates and yield curves** A recent study of inflationary expectations has disclosed that the consensus among economic forecasters yields the following average annual rates of inflation expected over the periods noted. (*Note:* Assume that the risk that future interest rate movements will affect longer maturities more than shorter maturities is zero; that is, there is no *maturity risk*.)

Period	Average annual rate of inflation
3 months	5%
1 year	6
5 years	8
10 years	8.5
20 years	9

a. If the real rate of interest is currently 2.5%, find the nominal interest rate on each of the following U.S. Treasury issues: 20-year bond, 3-month bill, 1-year note, and 5-year bond.

b. If the real rate of interest suddenly drops to 2% without any change in inflationary expectations, what effect, if any, would this have on your answers in **a?** Explain.

c. Using your findings in **a**, draw a yield curve for U.S. Treasury securities. Describe the general shape and expectations reflected by the curve.

d. What would a follower of the *liquidity preference theory* say about how the preferences of lenders and borrowers tend to affect the shape of the yield curve drawn in item **c?** Illustrate that effect by placing a dotted line on your graph that approximates the yield curve without the effect of liquidity preference.

e. What would a follower of the *market segmentation theory* say about the supply and demand for long-term loans versus the supply and demand for short-term loans given the yield curve constructed for part **c** of this problem?

  2–12 **Nominal and real rates and yield curves** A firm wishing to evaluate interest rate behavior has gathered nominal rate of interest and inflationary expectation data on five U.S. Treasury securities, each having a different maturity and each measured at a different point in time during the year just ended. (*Note:* Assume that the risk that future interest rate movements will affect longer maturities more than shorter maturities is zero; that is, there is no *maturity risk*.) These data are summarized in the following table.

U.S. Treasury security	Point in time	Maturity	Nominal rate of interest	Inflationary expectation
A	Jan. 7	1 year	12.6%	9.5%
B	Mar. 12	10 years	11.2	8.2
C	May 30	6 months	13.0	10.0
D	Aug. 15	20 years	11.0	8.1
E	Dec. 30	5 years	11.4	8.3

a. Using the preceding data, find the real rate of interest at each point in time.
b. Describe the behavior of the real rate of interest over the year. What forces might be responsible for such behavior?
c. Draw the yield curve associated with these data, assuming that the nominal rates were measured at the same point in time.
d. Describe the resulting yield curve in c, and explain the general expectations embodied in it.

INTERMEDIATE   **2–13   Term structure of interest rates**   The following yield data for a number of highest quality corporate bonds existed at each of the three points in time noted.

Time to maturity (years)	Yield		
	5 years ago	2 years ago	Today
1	9.1%	14.6%	9.3%
3	9.2	12.8	9.8
5	9.3	12.2	10.9
10	9.5	10.9	12.6
15	9.4	10.7	12.7
20	9.3	10.5	12.9
30	9.4	10.5	13.5

a. On the same set of axes, draw the yield curve at each of the three given times.
b. Label each curve in **a** as to its general shape (downward-sloping, upward-sloping, flat).
c. Describe the general inflationary and interest rate expectation existing at each of the three times.

WARM-UP   **2–14   Risk-free rate and risk premiums**   The real rate of interest is currently 3%; the inflation expectation and risk premiums for a number of securities follow:

Security	Inflation expectation premium	Risk premium
A	6%	3%
B	9	2
C	8	2
D	5	4
E	11	1

a. Find the risk-free rate of interest, R_F, that is applicable to each security.
b. Although not noted, what factor must be the cause of the differing risk-free rates found in **a**?
c. Find the nominal rate of interest for each security.

INTERMEDIATE 2–15　**Risk premiums**　Eleanor Burns is attempting to find the nominal rate of interest for each of two securities—A and B—issued by different firms at the same point in time. She has gathered the following data:

Characteristic	Security A	Security B
Time to maturity	3 years	15 years
Inflation expectation premium	9.0%	7.0%
Risk premium for:		
Default risk	1.0%	2.0%
Maturity risk	.5%	1.5%
Liquidity risk	1.0%	1.0%
Other risk	.5%	1.5%

a. If the real rate of interest is currently 2%, find the risk-free rate of interest applicable to each security.

b. Find the total risk premium attributable to each security's issuer and issue characteristics.

c. Calculate the nominal rate of interest for each security. Compare and discuss your findings.

CASE　CHAPTER 2　　　　Financing Lobo Enterprises' Expansion Program

Lobo Enterprises, based in Dallas, began as a small radio station. In 1985, it used a sizable loan to purchase a much larger company involved in the exterminating business and has acquired other businesses since then. Net earnings have risen continuously through 2000, 12 years since Lobo Enterprises first went public. Currently, the firm's equity base is quite small in comparison to the amount of debt financing on its books. The company is also doing well in its media, wallcovering, and burglary and fire protection systems businesses. Most important, the exterminating business—benefiting from wider markets, new customers, and higher fees—is performing magnificently. In the fiscal year ended June 30, 2000, gross income at Lobo Enterprises rose 17 percent; profits were held down somewhat by startup costs in several new businesses. Lobo's capital outlays have approximated $11 million in each of the past two fiscal years, but higher expansion levels are likely in the near future and are expected to require an additional $23 million of financing.

A few years ago, Lobo's long-term debt equaled 85 percent of total capital, but debt has since been reduced to 70 percent of total capital. The debt carries an average interest rate of 11.7 percent before taxes. The debt reduction was partially financed through issuance of $7.7 million of 10 percent (annual dividend) preferred stock.

Currently, the directors must decide on a method of financing the $23 million expansion. They are primarily interested in an equity financing plan, because funds could be obtained without incurring added mandatory interest payments that would result in greater risk. Additional equity would allow Lobo Enterprises to avoid restrictive covenants that are often tied to bond financing and would provide a more flexible foundation from which bonds could be issued when interest rates fall. The decision, however, could result in lowering earnings per share (EPS) as well as diluting the current stockholders' control of the company. Rebecca Marks, the chief financial officer, has been charged with advising Lobo's board with regard to common and preferred stock financing alternatives.

Required

a. Discuss the overall advantages of equity financing for Lobo Enterprises at this time.
b. Discuss the advantages and disadvantages of selling common stock. Compare and contrast its use to the use of bond financing.
c. Discuss the advantages and disadvantages of selling preferred stock. Compare and contrast its use to the use of common stock financing.
d. In the event Lobo Enterprises decides to use common stock financing, discuss the advantages and disadvantages of using a rights offering rather than the public sale of new common stock.
e. Based solely on the nonquantitative factors discussed in **a** through **d,** what recommendation should Rebecca Marks make to Lobo's board about how to finance the firm's $23 million need? Justify your recommendation in light of the alternatives.

WEB EXERCISE

GOTO web site www.corpfinet.com and click on Companies.

1. What are the headings in the left column under the title, Companies?

Now, click on Banks and then click on Top 25.

2. What are the five largest U.S. commercial banks, and what are their asset sizes?
3. Out of the list of top 25 banks, which bank is located geographically closest to you?
4. Prepare a bar graph that indicates how many of these 25 banks' principal offices are located in each state. Do not include in your graph states that have zero or one bank.
5. Which of these banks offer services to small businesses?
6. Name the banks that would help a business that has major international operations.

Under World Listings in the left column, click on Top 10.

7. How large are these banks compared to the banks in the U.S. top 25? *Hint*: Compare asset sizes.
8. How many of these banks have their principal offices in Japan? In the United States?

Financial Statements, Taxes, Depreciation, and Cash Flow

3

LEARNING GOALS

LG1 Describe the purpose and basic components of the stockholders' report.

LG2 Review the format and key components of the income statement, the balance sheet, the statement of retained earnings, the statement of cash flows, and the procedures for consolidating international financial statements.

LG3 Discuss the fundamentals of business taxation of ordinary income and capital gains, and the treatment of tax losses.

LG4 Understand the effect of depreciation and other noncash charges on the firm's cash flows.

LG5 Determine the depreciable value of an asset, its depreciable life, and the amount of depreciation allowed each year for tax purposes using the modified accelerated cost recovery system (MACRS).

LG6 Analyze the firm's cash flows, and develop and interpret the statement of cash flows.

LG1

3.1 The Stockholders' Report

Every corporation has many and varied uses for the standardized records and reports of its financial activities. Periodically, reports must be prepared for regulators, creditors (lenders), owners, and management. Regulators, such as federal and state securities commissions, enforce the accurate disclosure of corporate financial data. Creditors use financial data to evaluate the firm's ability to meet scheduled debt payments. Owners use financial data to decide whether to buy, sell, or hold its stock. Management is concerned with regulatory compliance, satisfying creditors and owners, and monitoring the firm's performance.

What's It Worth?

As a stockholder of a corporation, would you be interested in the value of the firm's aging trucks, computers, or other equipment? If you are finance-savvy, you would, and you would look to the firm's financial statements for the information. On the balance sheet, you would find the original cost and the current value of these assets. On the income statement, you would find an entry for depreciation expense—a portion of the assets' original cost charged against this period's revenues. Depreciation on those old trucks matters because it lowers taxable income, shields the firm from taxes, and thereby improves cash flow. The purpose of this chapter is to review the content of the basic financial statements and to describe the impact of business taxation and depreciation on the firm's cash flows.

The guidelines used to prepare and maintain financial records and reports are known as **generally accepted accounting principles (GAAP)**. These accounting practices and procedures are authorized by the accounting profession's rule-setting body, the **Financial Accounting Standards Board (FASB)**. *Publicly owned corporations* with more than $5 million in assets and 500 or more stockholders[1] are required by the **Securities and Exchange Commission (SEC)**—the

1. Although the Securities and Exchange Commission (SEC) does not have an official definition of "publicly owned," these financial measures mark the cutoff point it uses to require informational reporting, regardless of whether the firm publicly sells its securities. Firms that do not meet these requirements are commonly called "closely owned" firms.

Securities and Exchange Commission (SEC)
The federal regulatory body that governs the sale and listing of securities.

stockholders' report
Annual report required of publicly owned corporations that summarizes and documents for stockholders the firm's financial activities during the past year.

letter to stockholders
Typically, the first element of the annual stockholders' report and the primary communication from management to the firm's owners.

federal regulatory body that governs the sale and listing of securities—to provide their stockholders with an annual **stockholders' report.** The annual report summarizes and documents the firm's financial activities during the past year. It begins with a letter to the stockholders from the firm's president and/or chairman of the board.

The Letter to Stockholders

The **letter to stockholders** is the primary communication from management to the firm's owners. It describes the events that are considered to have had the greatest impact on the firm during the year. In addition, the letter generally discusses management philosophy, strategies, and actions as well as plans for the coming year and their anticipated effects on the firm's financial condition. Figure 3.1 shows the letter to the stockholders of Intel Corporation, a major supplier (1998 sales of about $26.3 billion) to the personal computing industry of chips, boards, systems, and software that are the "ingredients" of the most popular computing architecture. The letter appears in Intel's 1998 annual stockholders' report. It discusses Intel's 1998 results, basic strategies, business focus, competitive position, and challenges.

Financial Statements

Career Key

Accounting personnel have the major responsibility in knowing and setting up systems so that the financial records and reports conform to the generally accepted accounting principles (GAAP).

Following the letter to stockholders will be, at minimum, the four key financial statements required by the SEC: (1) the income statement, (2) the balance sheet, (3) the statement of retained earnings, and (4) the statement of cash flows.[2] The annual corporate report must contain these statements for at least the 3 most recent years of operation (2 years for balance sheets). Following the financial statements are *Notes to Financial Statements*—an important source of information on the accounting policies, procedures, calculations, and transactions underlying entries in the financial statements. Historical summaries of key operating statistics and financial ratios (discussed in Chapter 4) for the past 5 to 10 years are also commonly included with the financial statements.

Other Features

The stockholders' reports of most widely held corporations also include discussions of the firm's activities, new products, research and development, and the like. Most companies view the annual report not only as a requirement, but also as an important vehicle for influencing owners' perceptions of the company.

---

2. Whereas these statement titles are consistently used throughout this text, it is important to recognize that in practice, companies frequently use different statement titles. For example, General Electric uses "Statement of Earnings" rather than "Income Statement" and "Statement of Financial Position" rather than "Balance Sheet"; Bristol Myers Squibb uses "Statement of Earnings and Retained Earnings" rather than "Income Statement"; and Pfizer uses "Statement of Shareholders' Equity" rather than "Statement of Retained Earnings."

FIGURE 3.1   Letter to Stockholders

Intel Corporation's 1995 letter to stockholders

To our stockholders,

We faced extraordinary conditions in 1998. Competition in the value PC market segment, inventory corrections among some of our large customers in the first half of the year and an economic slowdown in some parts of the world all took their toll. As a consequence, our financial results in the first half of the year were not as strong as we would have liked. Revenues for the year were up 5%, with net income down 13% to $6.1 billion. At the same time, beneath these choppy waters, we were undergoing a fundamental sea change in how we see our business. The Internet is transforming the nature of the computing industry. As a leading provider of key computing and communications building blocks, we play a central role in this revolution. We are confident that our actions have helped us ride out the turbulence of 1998, and we are excited about our strategic plans to help drive the development of an increasingly connected computing world.

New products for all levels. With hindsight, it's clear that we were caught off guard by the increase in demand for low-cost PCs. We were late in recognizing the emergence of this value PC market segment—and the competition took advantage of our delay. While our global position remains strong, we lost market share in the U.S. retail segment of the market (which is about 10% of the worldwide PC market). We have redoubled our efforts to regain that share, with focused product development.

In response to the evolving computing marketplace, it was clear that we had to drive our business in a new way. We developed a broad game plan that would enable us to participate in every level of the newly segmented computing market. We revamped our microprocessor lineup with new products created specifically for each computing segment:

• Our Intel® Celeron™ microprocessor, introduced in April and followed in August by an enhanced version, offers entry-level PC buyers good value and reliable Intel technology. By the end of 1998, it was the second-highest volume PC microprocessor in the world, second only to the Pentium® II microprocessor.

• Our Pentium II microprocessor remains the heart of our business. Ideal for the performance desktop and entry-level servers and workstations, this powerful processor makes up the majority of units we sold worldwide in 1998.

• The powerhouse Pentium® II Xeon™ microprocessor, introduced in August, is specifically designed for mid- and high-range servers and workstations. Manufacturers can benefit by designing systems to harness the power of multiple high-performance processors. Demand for servers and workstations is increasing, and within both of these segments, sales of systems based on Intel architecture are growing much faster than the overall segment.

Our segmentation strategy is designed to allow us to participate profitably in various segments of the computing market and to pursue new growth opportunities in the high-end server and workstation market segments. Supported by our strong branding program, which conveys the benefits of Intel technology and the attributes of the products at each level, our segmentation strategy is working as intended.

1998 Geographic breakdown of revenues

Adjusting to a cost-competitive environment. 1998 found us operating in a more cost-competitive marketplace. We responded by setting aggressive new targets in cost management and manufacturing efficiency. With belt tightening in discretionary spending and some headcount reductions, we adjusted to an environment that demands leaner operations. We ended the year with headcount down 2% (excluding acquisitions) and our human resources employed in the areas of maximum return.

We also made great strides in manufacturing efficiency through a successful and rapid ramp to our new 0.25-micron process technology. With each new generation of our manufacturing process, the dimensions shrink on the finished chip, giving higher product yields as well as more powerful products.

In 1998, we also developed an innovative new packaging technology for our microprocessors, the Organic LAN Grid Array, that provides higher performance and versatility at lower cost for the final product. We are the only major chip maker using this packaging. We continue to invest in the state-of-the-art manufacturing facilities and R&D programs that make such innovations possible, spending $4 billion for capital additions and $2.7 billion for R&D in 1998.

The Internet drives an industry shift. Throughout the turbulence of the first half of the year, we were also adapting to a more fundamental shift in our business. Ten years ago, people bought PCs for personal productivity needs—spreadsheets, word processing and the like. Today, the number one reason people buy PCs is to get on the Internet. As the computing universe becomes connected, the demands on PCs and the entire computing infrastructure are expanding.

On a networked PC, every click of the mouse sets in motion a series of invisible and demanding tasks: compression and decompression of bulky downloads, encryption, virus scans and security checks, among others. These tasks have to be executed quickly and accurately behind the scenes, and they require powerful PCs. At the same time, behind the connected PCs is a large number of powerful servers, delivering data to the desktop and performing some of those compute-intensive functions. The number of servers is increasing as the Internet expands, providing a growing market segment for our products. We consider this opportunity so significant that more than half of Intel's microprocessor R&D investment is now committed to workstations and servers.

We also have a rapidly growing network products business, with software and hardware products designed to make it easier to connect and manage networked PCs for small businesses, large enterprises and home users. As part of our commitment to networking, we acquired Case Technology and Dayna Communications Inc. in 1997, and have entered into an agreement to acquire Shiva Corporation. These companies provide key technologies for improving Internet performance.

In addition to providing the powerful processors that are the key building blocks of the Internet and network products, we are engaging with other industry leaders in initiatives to expand Internet capabilities and product offerings. In 1998, our Corporate Business Development group made more than 100 new equity investments to help spur development of computer and Internet capabilities.

The Internet has stimulated the most intensely competitive cycle and development boom in the history of the computing industry. Being connected is now at the center of people's computing experience. The resulting opportunities have made our direction clear: to help drive the growth of the connected world. In 1999 and beyond, we will pursue our strategic intent to be a major force behind the Internet revolution.

Gordon E. Moore
Gordon E. Moore
Chairman Emeritus

A. S. Grove
Andrew S. Grove
Chairman

Craig R. Barrett
Craig R. Barrett
President and CEO

Source: Intel Corporation, *1998 Annual Report*, pp. 1–2. Reprinted by permission of Intel Corporation. © Intel Corporation 1999.

? Review Questions

3–1   What are *generally accepted accounting principles (GAAP)* and who authorizes them? What role does the *Securities and Exchange Commission (SEC)* play in the financial reporting activities of U.S. corporations?

3–2   Describe the basic contents, including the key financial statements, of the stockholders' reports of publicly owned corporations.

3.2 Basic Financial Statements

Our chief concern in this section is to understand the factual information presented in the four required corporate financial statements. We use the financial statements from the 2000 stockholders' report of a hypothetical firm, Baker Corporation. The procedures for consolidating international financial statements are also briefly described.

Income Statement

income statement
Provides a financial summary of the firm's operating results during a specified period.

Hint Some firms, such as retailers and agricultural firms, end their fiscal year at the end of their operating cycle rather than at the end of the calendar year—for example, retailers at the end of January and agricultural firms at the end of September.

The **income statement** provides a financial summary of the firm's operating results during a specified period. Most common are income statements covering a 1-year period ending at a specified date, ordinarily December 31 of the calendar year. Many large firms, however, operate on a 12-month financial cycle, or *fiscal year,* that ends at a time other than December 31. Monthly income statements are typically prepared for use by management, and quarterly statements must be made available to the stockholders of publicly owned corporations.

Table 3.1 presents Baker Corporation's income statement for the year ended December 31, 2000. The statement begins with *sales revenue*—the total dollar amount of sales during the period—from which the *cost of goods sold* is deducted. The resulting *gross profits* of $700,000 represent the amount remaining to satisfy operating, financial, and tax costs after meeting the costs of producing or purchasing the products sold. Next, *operating expenses,* which include selling expense, general and administrative expense, and depreciation expense, are deducted from gross profits.[3] The resulting *operating profits* of $370,000 represent the profits earned from producing and selling products; this amount does not consider financial and tax costs. (Operating profit is often called *earnings before interest and taxes,* or *EBIT.*) Next, the financial cost—*interest expense*—is subtracted from operating profits to find *net profits* (or *earnings*) *before taxes.* After subtracting $70,000 in 2000 interest, Baker Corporation had $300,000 of net profits before taxes.

After the appropriate tax rates have been applied to before-tax profits, taxes are calculated and deducted to determine *net profits* (or *earnings*) *after taxes.*

---

3. Depreciation expense can be, and frequently is, included in manufacturing costs—cost of goods sold—to calculate gross profits. Depreciation is shown as an expense in this text to isolate its impact on cash flows.

TABLE 3.1	Baker Corporation Income Statement ($000) for the Year Ended December 31, 2000

Sales revenue		$1,700
Less: Cost of goods sold		1,000
Gross profits		$ 700
Less: Operating expenses		
Selling expense	$ 80	
General and administrative expense	150	
Depreciation expense	100	
Total operating expense		330
Operating profits		$ 370
Less: Interest expense[a]		70
Net profits before taxes		$ 300
Less: Taxes (rate = 40%)		120
Net profits after taxes		$ 180
Less: Preferred stock dividends		10
Earnings available for common stockholders		$ 170
Earnings per share (EPS)[b]		$ 1.70

[a]Interest expense includes the interest component of the annual financial lease payment as specified by the Financial Accounting Standards Board (FASB).

[b]Calculated by dividing the earnings available for common stockholders by the number of shares of common stock outstanding ($170,000 ÷ 100,000 shares = $1.70 per share).

Baker Corporation's net profits after taxes for 2000 were $180,000. Next, any preferred stock dividends must be subtracted from net profits after taxes to arrive at *earnings available for common stockholders*. This is the amount earned by the firm on behalf of the common stockholders during the period. Dividing earnings available for common stockholders by the number of shares of common stock outstanding results in *earnings per share (EPS)*. EPS represents the amount earned during the accounting period on each outstanding share of common stock. In 2000, Baker Corporation earned $170,000 for its common stockholders, which represents $1.70 for each outstanding share.

Balance Sheet

balance sheet
Summary statement of the firm's financial position at a given point in time.

The **balance sheet** presents a summary statement of the firm's financial position at a given point in time. The statement balances the firm's *assets* (what it owns) against its financing, which can be either *debt* (what it owes) or *equity* (what was provided by owners). Baker Corporation's balance sheets on December 31 of 2000 and 1999 are presented in Table 3.2. They show a variety of asset, liability (debt), and equity accounts. An important distinction is made between short-term and long-term assets and liabilities. The **current assets** and **current liabilities**

In Practice

Too Much Profit?

For the first quarter of fiscal year 1999, ending September 30, 1998, Microsoft Corp. reported record results: revenues of $3.95 billion and net income from continuing operations of $1.52 billion. This represents an unusually high net profit margin (net income after taxes divided by sales) of 38.5 percent—many times higher than other software companies' ratios.

Microsoft's accounting methods are one reason for its outstanding profit performance. The software giant excludes from quarterly income statements gross revenues and expenses for units that operate at a loss or just break even. Only the net results show up as operating expenses. This practice boosts profit margins by eliminating from the consolidated income statement the low revenues and high expenses of some of Microsoft's noncore businesses, such as Microsoft Network, its online service, and its small professional consulting business.

According to a Microsoft spokesperson, these accounting methods are "designed to present results fairly to shareholders and as required by generally accepted accounting practices." However, in the face of the government's antitrust trial against the company, charging that Microsoft is a monopoly, some securities analysts expect Microsoft to eventually change to the more commonly used method that shows revenue and expense from all operating units, not just the profitable ones.

current assets
Short-term assets, expected to be converted into cash within 1 year or less.

current liabilities
Short-term liabilities, expected to be paid within 1 year or less.

are *short-term* assets and liabilities. This means that they are expected to be converted into cash (current assets) or paid (current liabilities) within 1 year or less. All other assets and liabilities, along with stockholders' equity, which is assumed to have an infinite life, are considered *long-term*, or *fixed*, because they are expected to remain on the firm's books for 1 year or more.

As is customary, the assets are listed beginning with the most liquid down to the least liquid. Current assets therefore precede fixed assets. *Marketable securities* represent very liquid short-term investments, such as U.S. Treasury bills or certificates of deposit, held by the firm. Because of their highly liquid nature, marketable securities are frequently viewed as a form of cash. *Accounts receivable* represent the total monies owed the firm by its customers on credit sales made to them. *Inventories* include raw materials, work in process (partially finished goods), and finished goods held by the firm. The entry for *gross fixed assets* is the original cost of all fixed (long-term) assets owned by the firm.[4] *Net fixed*

---

[4]For convenience the term *fixed assets* is used throughout this text to refer to what, in a strict accounting sense, is captioned "property, plant, and equipment." This simplification of terminology permits certain financial concepts to be more easily developed.

TABLE 3.4   Corporate Tax Rate Schedule

Range of taxable income		Tax calculation		
		Base tax	+	(Rate × amount over base bracket)
$ 0 to $ 50,000		$ 0	+	(15% × amount over $ 0)
50,000 to 75,000		7,500	+	(25 × amount over 50,000)
75,000 to 100,000		13,750	+	(34 × amount over 75,000)
100,000 to 335,000 [a]		22,250	+	(39 × amount over 100,000)
335,000 to 10,000,000		113,900	+	(34 × amount over 335,000)
Over $10,000,000 [b]		3,400,000	+	(35 × amount over 10,000,000)

[a]Because corporations with taxable income in excess of $100,000 must increase their tax by the lesser of $11,750 or 5% of the taxable income in excess of $100,000, they will end up paying a 39% tax on taxable income between $100,000 and $335,000. The 5% surtax that raises the tax rate from 34% to 39% causes all corporations with taxable income between $335,000 and $10,000,000 to have an *average tax rate* of 34%, as can be seen in Table 3.5.

[b]This bracket and its associated 35% tax rate was created with passage of the *Omnibus Budget Reconciliation Act of 1993*, which was signed into law by President Clinton on August 10, 1993, and was retroactive to its effective date of January 1, 1993.

this text is published. Because the corporation is financially dominant in our economy, *emphasis here is given to corporate taxation.*

Ordinary Income

ordinary income
Income earned through the sale of a firm's goods or services.

The **ordinary income** of a corporation is income earned through the sale of a firm's goods or services. Ordinary income is currently taxed subject to the rates depicted in the corporate tax rate schedule given in Table 3.4.

Example ▼ Webster Manufacturing, Inc., a small manufacturer of kitchen knives, has before-tax earnings of $250,000. The tax on these earnings can be found by using the tax rate schedule given in Table 3.4:

$$\text{Total taxes due} = \$22,250 + [.39 \times (\$250,000 - \$100,000)]$$
$$= \$22,250 + (.39 \times \$150,000)$$
$$= \$22,250 + \$58,500 = \underline{\$80,750}$$

▲

From a financial point of view it is important to understand the difference between average and marginal tax rates, the treatment of interest and dividend income, and the effect of tax deductibility on the after-tax cost of expenses.

Average Versus Marginal Tax Rates

average tax rate
A firm's taxes divided by its taxable income.

The **average tax rate** paid on the firm's ordinary income can be calculated by dividing its taxes by its taxable income. For firms with taxable income of $10,000,000 or less, the average tax rate ranges from 15 to 34 percent, reaching 34 percent when taxable income equals or exceeds $335,000. For firms with

TABLE 3.5   Pretax Income, Tax Liabilities, and Average Tax Rates

Pretax income (1)	Tax liability (2)	Average tax rate [(2) ÷ (1)] (3)
$ 50,000	$ 7,500	15.00%
75,000	13,750	18.33
100,000	22,250	22.25
200,000	61,250	30.63
335,000	113,900	34.00
500,000	170,000	34.00
1,000,000	340,000	34.00
2,500,000	850,000	34.00
10,000,000	3,400,000	34.00
12,000,000	4,100,000	34.17
25,000,000	8,650,000	34.60

taxable income in excess of $10,000,000, the average tax rate ranges between 34 and 35 percent. The average tax rate paid by Webster Manufacturing, Inc., in our preceding example was 32.3 percent ($80,750 ÷ $250,000). Table 3.5 presents the firm's tax liability and average tax rate for various levels of pretax income; as income increases, the rate approaches and finally reaches 34 percent. It remains at that level up to $10,000,000 of taxable income, beyond which it rises toward but never reaches an average tax rate of 35 percent.

marginal tax rate
The rate at which additional income is taxed.

The **marginal tax rate** represents the rate at which additional income is taxed. In the current corporate tax structure, the marginal tax rate on income up to $50,000 is 15 percent; from $50,000 to $75,000 it is 25 percent; and so on, as shown in Table 3.4. To simplify calculations in the text, *a fixed 40 percent tax rate is assumed to be applicable to ordinary corporate income.*

Example ▼ If Webster Manufacturing's earnings go up to $300,000, the marginal tax rate on the additional $50,000 of income will be 39 percent. The company will therefore have to pay additional taxes of $19,500 (.39 × $50,000). Total taxes on the $300,000, then, will be $100,250 ($80,750 + $19,500). To check this figure using the tax rate schedule in Table 3.4, we would get a total tax liability of $22,250 + [.39 × ($300,000 − $100,000)] = $22,250 + $78,000 = $100,250—the same value obtained by applying the marginal tax rate to the added income
▲ and adjusting the known tax liability.

The *average tax rate* tends to be most useful in evaluating taxes historically, and the *marginal tax rate* is more frequently used in financial decision making. For example, it is often helpful to know the average tax rate at which taxes were paid over a given period. But in making decisions the important concern is the rate at which the earnings from alternative proposals will *actually* be taxed, that is, the marginal tax rate. With *progressive tax rates*—higher rates for higher levels of taxable income—the average tax rate is always less than or equal to the marginal tax rate. Given our focus on financial decision making, *the tax rates used throughout this text are assumed to represent marginal tax rates.*

Interest and Dividend Income

In the process of determining taxable income, any *interest received* by the corporation is included as ordinary income and is therefore taxed at the firm's applicable tax rates. Dividends, on the other hand, are treated differently due to **double taxation,** which occurs when the already once-taxed earnings of a corporation are distributed as cash dividends to stockholders, who must pay taxes on them. Therefore, dividends received on common and preferred stock held in other corporations, and representing less than 20 percent ownership in them, are subject to a 70 percent exclusion for tax purposes.[5] Because of the dividend exclusion, only 30 percent of these **intercorporate dividends** are included as ordinary income. The tax law provides this exclusion to avoid *triple taxation*—the first and second corporations are taxed on income before paying the dividend, and the dividend recipient must include the dividend in his or her taxable income. This feature in effect eliminates most of the potential tax liability from the dividend received by the second and any subsequent corporations.

double taxation
Occurs when the already once-taxed earnings of a corporation are distributed as cash dividends to stockholders, who must pay taxes on them.

intercorporate dividends
Dividends received by one corporation on common and preferred stock held in other corporations.

E x a m p l e ▼ Charnes Industries, a large foundry that makes custom castings for the automobile industry, during the year just ended received $100,000 in interest on bonds it held and $100,000 in dividends on common stock it owned in other corporations. The firm is subject to a 40% marginal tax rate and is eligible for a 70% exclusion on its intercorporate dividend receipts. The after-tax income realized by Charnes from each of these sources of investment income is found as follows:

	Interest income		Dividend income
(1) Before-tax amount	$100,000		$100,000
Less: Applicable exclusion	0	(.70 × $100,000) =	70,000
Taxable amount	$100,000		$ 30,000
(2) Tax (40%)	40,000		12,000
After-tax amount [(1) − (2)]	$ 60,000		$ 88,000

As a result of the 70% dividend exclusion, the after-tax amount is greater for the dividend income than for the interest income. Clearly, the dividend exclusion enhances the attractiveness of stock investments relative to bond investments ▲ made by one corporation in another corporation.

Tax-Deductible Expenses

In calculating their taxes, corporations are allowed to deduct operating expenses, as well as interest expense. The tax deductibility of these expenses reduces their after-tax cost. The following example illustrates the benefit of tax deductibility.

---

5. The exclusion is 80% if the corporation owns between 20 and 80% of the stock in the corporation paying it dividends; 100% of the dividends received are excluded if it owns more than 80% of the corporation paying it dividends. For convenience, we are assuming here that the ownership interest in the dividend-paying corporation is less than 20%.

Example ▼ Companies X and Y each expect in the coming year to have earnings before interest and taxes of $200,000. Company X during the year will have to pay $30,000 in interest; Company Y has no debt and therefore will have no interest expense. Calculations of the earnings after taxes for these two firms are as follows:

	Company X	Company Y
Earnings before interest and taxes	$200,000	$200,000
Less: Interest expense	30,000	0
Earnings before taxes	$170,000	$200,000
Less: Taxes (40%)	68,000	80,000
Earnings after taxes	$102,000	$120,000
Difference in earnings after taxes	$18,000	

The data demonstrate that whereas Company X had $30,000 more interest expense than Company Y, Company X's earnings after taxes are only $18,000 less than those of Company Y ($102,000 for Company X versus $120,000 for Company Y). This difference is attributable to the fact that Company X's $30,000 interest expense deduction provided a tax savings of $12,000 ($68,000 for Company X versus $80,000 for Company Y). This amount can be calculated directly by multiplying the tax rate by the amount of interest expense (.40 × $30,000 = $12,000). Similarly, the $18,000 *after-tax cost* of the interest expense can be calculated directly by multiplying one minus the tax rate by the amount of

▲ interest expense [(1 − .40) × $30,000 = $18,000].

The tax deductibility of certain expenses reduces their actual (after-tax) cost to the profitable firm. Note that both for accounting and tax purposes *interest is a tax-deductible expense, whereas dividends are not.* Because dividends are not tax deductible, their after-tax cost is equal to the amount of the dividend. Thus, a $30,000 cash dividend would have an after-tax cost of $30,000.

Capital Gains

capital gain
The amount by which the sale price of an asset exceeds the asset's initial purchase price.

If a firm sells a capital asset[6] such as stock held as an investment for more than its initial purchase price, the difference between the sale price and the purchase price is called a **capital gain.** For corporations, capital gains are added to ordinary corporate income and taxed at the regular corporate rates, with a maximum marginal tax rate of 39 percent.[7] To simplify the computations presented in later chapters of the text, as for ordinary income, *a fixed 40 percent tax rate is assumed to be applicable to corporate capital gains.*

---

6. To simplify the discussion, only capital assets are considered here. The full tax treatment of gains and losses on depreciable assets is presented as part of the discussion of capital budgeting cash flows in Chapter 8.

7. The *Omnibus Budget Reconciliation Act of 1993* included a provision that allows the capital gains tax to be halved on gains resulting from investments made after January 1, 1993, in startup firms with a value of less than $50 million that have been held for at least 5 years. This special provision, which is intended to help startup firms, is ignored throughout this text.

TABLE 3.6	Baker Corporation Income Statement Calculated on a Cash Basis ($000) for the Year Ended December 31, 2000

Sales revenue		$1,700
Less: Cost of goods sold		1,000
Gross profits		$ 700
Less: Operating expenses		
Selling expense	$ 80	
General and administrative expense	150	
Depreciation expense (noncash charge)	0	
Total operating expense		230
Operating profits		$ 470
Less: Interest expense		70
Net profits before taxes		$ 400
Less: Taxes (from Table 3.1)		120
Cash flow from operations		$ 280

Example ▼
▲
Baker Corporation acquired a new machine at a cost of $38,000, with installation costs of $2,000. Regardless of its expected salvage value, the depreciable value of the machine is $40,000: $38,000 cost + $2,000 installation cost.

Depreciable Life of an Asset

depreciable life
Time period over which an asset is depreciated.

The time period over which an asset is depreciated—its **depreciable life**—can significantly affect the pattern of cash flows. The shorter the depreciable life, the more quickly the cash flow created by the depreciation write-off will be received. Given the financial manager's preference for faster receipt of cash flows, a shorter depreciable life is preferred to a longer one. However, the firm must abide by certain Internal Revenue Service (IRS) requirements for determining depreciable life. These MACRS standards, which apply to both new and used assets, require the taxpayer to use as an asset's depreciable life the appropriate MACRS **recovery period**.[10] There are six MACRS recovery periods—3, 5, 7, 10, 15, and 20 years—excluding real estate. It is customary to refer to the property classes (excluding real estate), in accordance with their recovery periods, as 3-, 5-, 7-, 10-, 15-, and 20-year property. The first four property classes—those routinely used by business—are defined in Table 3.7.

recovery period
The appropriate depreciable life of a particular asset as determined by MACRS.

Depreciation Methods

For *financial reporting purposes*, a variety of depreciation methods—straight-line, double-declining balance, and sum-of-the-years'-digits[11]—can be used. For *tax purposes*, using MACRS recovery periods, assets in the first four property

---

10. An exception occurs in the case of assets depreciated under the *alternative depreciation system*. For convenience, we ignore the depreciation of assets under this system in this text.

11. For a review of these depreciation methods as well as other aspects of financial reporting, see any recently published financial accounting text.

| TABLE 3.7 | First Four Property Classes Under MACRS |

Property class (recovery period)	Definition
3 years	Research equipment and certain special tools.
5 years	Computers, typewriters, copiers, duplicating equipment, cars, light-duty trucks, qualified technological equipment, and similar assets.
7 years	Office furniture, fixtures, most manufacturing equipment, railroad track, and single-purpose agricultural and horticultural structures.
10 years	Equipment used in petroleum refining or in the manufacture of tobacco products and certain food products.

classes are depreciated by the double-declining balance (200 percent) method using the half-year convention and switching to straight-line when advantageous. Although tables of depreciation percentages are not provided by law, the *approximate percentages* (i.e., rounded to nearest whole percent) written off each year for the first four property classes are given in Table 3.8. Rather than

| TABLE 3.8 | Rounded Depreciation Percentages by Recovery Year Using MACRS for First Four Property Classes |

| | Percentage by recovery year[a] | | | |
Recovery year	3 years	5 years	7 years	10 years
1	33%	20%	14%	10%
2	45	32	25	18
3	15	19	18	14
4	7	12	12	12
5		12	9	9
6		5	9	8
7			9	7
8			4	6
9				6
10				6
11				4
Totals	100%	100%	100%	100%

[a]These percentages have been rounded to the nearest whole percent to simplify calculations while retaining realism. To calculate the *actual* depreciation for tax purposes, be sure to apply the actual unrounded percentages or directly apply double-declining balance (200%) depreciation using the half-year convention.

using the percentages in the table, the firm can either use straight-line deprecia-tion over the asset's recovery period with the half-year convention or use the alternative depreciation system. For purposes of this text we will use the MACRS depreciation percentages because they generally provide for the fastest write-off and therefore the best cash flow effects for the profitable firm.

Because MACRS requires use of the half-year convention, assets are assumed to be acquired in the middle of the year, and therefore only one-half of the first year's depreciation is recovered in the first year. As a result, the final half-year of depreciation is recovered in the year immediately following the asset's stated recovery period. In Table 3.8, the depreciation percentages for an *n*-year class asset are given for *n* + 1 years. For example, a 5-year asset is depreciated over 6 recovery years. (*Note:* The percentages in Table 3.8 have been rounded to the nearest whole percentage to simplify calculations while retaining realism.)

Because primary concern in managerial finance centers on cash flows, *only tax depreciation methods will be utilized throughout this textbook*. The applica-tion of the tax depreciation percentages given in Table 3.8 can be demonstrated by a simple example.

Example ▼ Baker Corporation acquired, for an installed cost of $40,000, a machine having a recovery period of 5 years. By using the applicable percentages from Table 3.8, the depreciation in each year is calculated as follows:

Year	Cost (1)	Percentages (from Table 3.8) (2)	Depreciation [(1) × (2)] (3)
1	$40,000	20%	$ 8,000
2	40,000	32	12,800
3	40,000	19	7,600
4	40,000	12	4,800
5	40,000	12	4,800
6	40,000	5	2,000
Totals		100%	$40,000

Column 3 shows that the full cost of the asset is written off over 6 recovery ▲ years.

? Review Questions

3–9   In what sense does depreciation act as cash inflow? How can a firm's after-tax profits be adjusted to determine *cash flow from operations?*

3–10   Briefly describe the first four modified accelerated cost recovery system (MACRS) property classes and recovery periods. Explain how the depre-ciation percentages are determined by using the MACRS recovery periods.

3.5 Analyzing the Firm's Cash Flow

The *statement of cash flows,* briefly described earlier, summarizes the firm's cash flow over a given period of time. Because it can be used to capture historic cash flow, the statement is developed in this section. First, however, we need to discuss cash flow through the firm and the classification of sources and uses of cash.

The Firm's Cash Flows

Hint   Remember that, in finance, cash is king. Income statement profits are good, but they do not pay the bills nor do asset owners accept them in place of cash.

operating flows
Cash flows directly related to production and sale of the firm's products and services.

investment flows
Cash flows associated with purchase and sale of both fixed assets and business interests.

financing flows
Cash flows that result from debt and equity financing transactions; includes incurrence and repayment of debt, cash inflow from the sale of stock, and cash outflows to pay cash dividends or repurchase stock.

Figure 3.2 illustrates the firm's cash flows. Note that marketable securities, because of their highly liquid nature, are considered the same as cash. Both cash and marketable securities represent a reservoir of liquidity that is *increased by cash inflows* and *decreased by cash outflows.* Also note that the firm's cash flows have been divided into (1) operating flows, (2) investment flows, and (3) financing flows. The **operating flows** are cash inflows and outflows directly related to production and sale of the firm's products and services. These flows capture the income statement and current account transactions (excluding notes payable) occurring during the period. **Investment flows** are cash flows associated with purchase and sale of both fixed assets and business interests. Clearly, purchase transactions would result in cash outflows, whereas sales transactions would generate cash inflows. The **financing flows** result from debt and equity financing transactions. Incurring and repaying either short-term debt (notes payable) or long-term debt would result in a corresponding cash inflow or outflow. Similarly, the sale of stock would result in a cash inflow; the payment of cash dividends or repurchase of stock would result in a financing outflow. In combination, the firm's operating, investment, and financing cash flows during a given period will affect the firm's cash and marketable securities balances.

Classifying Sources and Uses of Cash

The statement of cash flows in effect summarizes the sources and uses of cash during a given period. (Table 3.9 on page 100 classifies the basic sources and uses of cash.) For example, if a firm's accounts payable increased by $1,000 during the year, this change would be a *source of cash.* If the firm's inventory increased by $2,500, the change would be a *use of cash.*

A few additional points can be made with respect to the classification scheme in Table 3.9:

1. A *decrease* in an asset, such as the firm's cash balance, is a *source of cash flow* because cash that has been tied up in the asset is released and can be used for some other purpose, such as repaying a loan. On the other hand, an *increase* in the firm's cash balance is a *use of cash flow,* because additional cash is being tied up in the firm's cash balance.
2. Earlier, Equation 3.1 and the related discussion explained why depreciation and other noncash charges are considered cash inflows, or sources of cash. Adding noncash charges back to the firm's net profits after taxes gives cash flow from operations:

Cash flow from operations = net profits after taxes + noncash charges

FIGURE 3.2   Cash Flows
The firm's cash flows

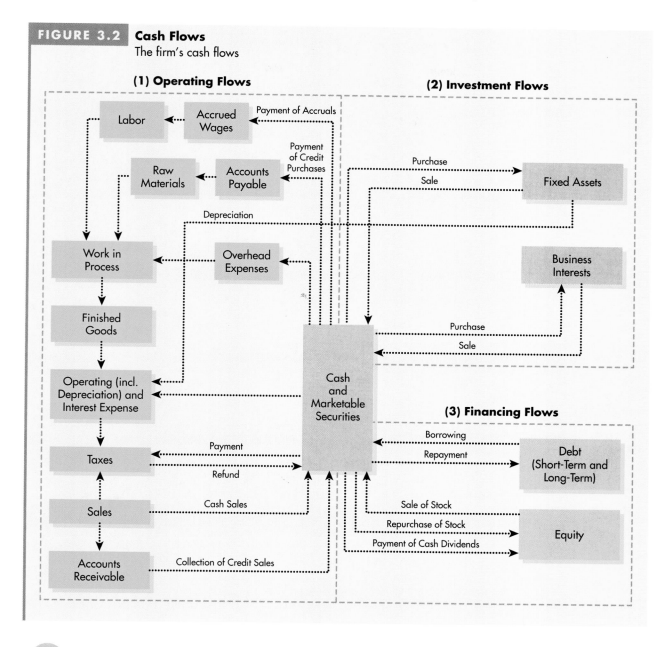

Note that a firm can have a *net loss* (negative net profits after taxes) and still have positive cash flow from operations when noncash charges (typically depreciation) during the period are greater than the net loss. In the statement of cash flows, net profits after taxes (or net losses) and noncash charges are therefore treated as separate entries.

3. Because depreciation is treated as a separate source of cash, only *gross* rather than *net* changes in fixed assets appear on the statement of cash flows. This treatment avoids the potential double counting of depreciation.

TABLE 3.9   The Sources and Uses of Cash

Sources	Uses
Decrease in any asset	Increase in any asset
Increase in any liability	Decrease in any liability
Net profits after taxes	Net loss
Depreciation and other noncash charges	Dividends paid
Sale of stock	Repurchase or retirement of stock

4. Direct entries of changes in retained earnings are not included on the statement of cash flows. Instead, entries for items that affect retained earnings appear as net profits or losses after taxes and dividends paid.

Developing the Statement of Cash Flows

The statement of cash flows can be developed in five steps: (1, 2, and 3) prepare a statement of sources and uses of cash, (4) obtain needed income statement data, and (5) properly classify and present relevant data from Steps 1 through 4. With this five-step procedure we can use the financial statements for Baker Corporation presented in Tables 3.1 and 3.2 to demonstrate the preparation of its December 31, 2000, statement of cash flows.

Preparing the Statement of Sources and Uses of Cash (Steps 1, 2, and 3)

The first three steps in the statement of cash flow preparation process guide the preparation of the statement of sources and uses of cash.

Step 1   Calculate the balance sheet changes in assets, liabilities, and stockholders' equity over the period of concern. (*Note:* Calculate the *gross* fixed asset change for the fixed asset account along with any change in accumulated depreciation.)

Step 2   Using the classification scheme in Table 3.9, classify each change calculated in Step 1 as either a source (S) or a use (U). (*Note:* An increase in accumulated depreciation would be classified as a source, whereas a decrease in accumulated depreciation would be a use. Changes in stockholders' equity accounts are classified in the same way as changes in liabilities—increases are sources and decreases are uses.)

Step 3   Separately sum all sources and all uses found in Steps 1 and 2. If this statement is prepared correctly, *total sources should equal total uses.*

E x a m p l e ▼ Baker Corporation's balance sheets in Table 3.2 can be used to develop its statement of sources and uses of cash for the year ended December 31, 2000.

TABLE 3.10   Baker Corporation Statement of Sources and Uses of Cash ($000) for the Year Ended December 31, 2000

Account (1)	Account balance December 31 (from Table 3.2) 2000 (2)	1999 (3)	Change [(2) − (3)] (4)	Classification Source (5)	Use (6)
Assets					
Cash	$ 400	$ 300	+$100		$ 100
Marketable securities	600	200	+ 400		400
Accounts receivable	400	500	− 100	$ 100	
Inventories	600	900	− 300	300	
Gross fixed assets	2,500	2,200	+ 300		300
Accumulated depreciation[a]	1,300	1,200	+ 100	100	
Liabilities					
Accounts payable	700	500	+ 200	200	
Notes payable	600	700	− 100		100
Accruals	100	200	− 100		100
Long-term debt	600	400	+ 200	200	
Stockholders' equity					
Preferred stock	100	100	0		
Common stock at par	120	120	0		
Paid-in capital in excess of par	380	380	0		
Retained earnings	600	500	+ 100	100	
			Totals	$1,000	$1,000

[a]Because accumulated depreciation is treated as a deduction from gross fixed assets, an increase in it is classified as a source; any decrease would be classified as a use.

Step 1   The key entries from Baker Corporation's balance sheets in Table 3.2 are listed in a stacked format in Table 3.10. Column 1 lists the account name, and columns 2 and 3 give the December 31, 2000 and 1999 values, respectively, for each account. In column 4, the change in the balance sheet account between December 31, 1999, and December 31, 2000, is calculated. Note that for fixed assets, both the gross fixed asset change of +$300,000 and the accumulated depreciation change of +$100,000 are calculated.

Step 2   Based on the classification scheme from Table 3.9 and recognizing that changes in stockholders' equity are classified in the same way as changes in liabilities, each change in column 4 of Table 3.10 is classified as either a source in column 5 or a use in column 6.

Step 3   The sources and uses in columns 5 and 6, respectively, of Table 3.10 are totaled at the bottom. Because total sources of $1,000,000 equal total uses of $1,000,000, it appears that the statement has been correctly prepared.

Obtaining Income Statement Data (Step 4)

Step 4 involves obtaining three important inputs to the statement of cash flows from an income statement for the period of concern. These inputs are (1) net profits after taxes, (2) depreciation and any other noncash charges, and (3) cash dividends paid on both preferred and common stock.

Step 4   Net profits after taxes and depreciation typically can be taken directly from the income statement. Dividends may have to be calculated by using the following equation:

$$\text{Dividends = net profits after taxes − change in retained earnings} \qquad (3.2)$$

The value of net profits after taxes can be obtained from the income statement, and the change in retained earnings can be found in the statement of sources and uses of cash or can be calculated by using the beginning- and end-of-period balance sheets. The dividend value could be obtained directly from the statement of retained earnings, if available.

Example ▼   Baker Corporation's net profits after taxes, depreciation, and dividends can be found in its financial statements.

Step 4   Baker Corporation's net profits after taxes and depreciation for 2000 can be found on its income statement presented in Table 3.1:

Net profits after taxes ($000)	$180
Depreciation ($000)	$100

Substituting the net profits after taxes value of $180,000 and the increase in retained earnings of $100,000 from Baker Corporation's statement of sources and uses of cash for the year ended December 31, 2000, given in Table 3.10, into Equation 3.2, we find the 2000 cash dividends to be

$$\text{Dividends ($000) = $180 − $100 = $80}$$

Note that the $80,000 of dividends just calculated could have been drawn directly from Baker's statement of retained earnings, given in Table 3.3. ▲

Classifying and Presenting Relevant Data (Step 5)

The relevant data from the statement of sources and uses of cash (prepared in Steps 1, 2, and 3) along with the net profit, depreciation, and dividend data from the income statement (obtained in Step 4) can be used to prepare the statement of cash flows.

TABLE 3.11	Categories and Sources of Data Included in the Statement of Cash Flows

Categories and data items	Data source S/U = Statement of sources and uses of cash I/S = Income statement
Cash Flow from Operating Activities	
Net profits (losses) after taxes	I/S
Depreciation and other noncash charges	I/S
Changes in all current assets other than cash and marketable securities	S/U
Changes in all current liabilities other than notes payable	S/U
Cash Flow from Investment Activities	
Changes in gross fixed assets	S/U
Changes in business interests	S/U
Cash Flow from Financing Activities	
Changes in notes payable	S/U
Changes in long-term debt	S/U
Changes in stockholders' equity other than retained earnings	S/U
Dividends paid	I/S

Step 5   Classify relevant data into one of three categories:

1. Cash flow from operating activities
2. Cash flow from investment activities
3. Cash flow from financing activities

These three categories are consistent with the operating, investment, and financing cash flows depicted in Figure 3.2. Table 3.11 lists the items that would be included in each category on the statement of cash flows. In addition the source of each data item is noted. By reviewing Table 3.11, it can be seen that all current asset changes other than cash and marketable securities and all current liability changes other than accounts payable are included under "Cash Flow from Operating Activities." The cash and marketable securities changes are excluded because they represent the period's net cash flow to which the statement is reconciled. Notes payable are included in "Cash Flow from Financing Activities" because they reflect deliberate financing actions rather than the spontaneous financing that results from other current liabilities such as accounts payable and accruals.

Relevant data should be listed in a fashion consistent with the order of the categories and data items given in Table 3.11. All sources as well as net profits after taxes and depreciation would be treated as positive values—cash inflows—whereas all uses, any losses, and dividends paid would be treated as negative values—cash outflows. The items in each category—operating, investment, and financing—should be totaled, and these three totals should be added to get the "net increase (decrease) in cash and marketable securities" for the period. As a check, this value should reconcile with the actual change in cash and marketable securities for the year, which can be obtained from either the beginning- and end-of-period balance sheets or the statement of sources and uses of cash for the period.

Example ▼ The relevant data developed for Baker Corporation for 2000 can be combined by using the procedure described before to create its statement of cash flows.

Step 5 Classifying and listing the relevant data from earlier steps in a fashion consistent with Table 3.11 result in Baker Corporation's Statement of Cash Flows, presented in Table 3.12. This statement shows that the firm experienced a $500,000 increase in cash and marketable securities during 2000. Looking at Baker Corporation's 1999 and 2000 balance sheets in Table 3.2 or its statement of sources and uses of cash in Table 3.10, we can see that the firm's cash increased by $100,000 and its marketable securities increased by $400,000 between December 31, 1999, and December 31, 2000. The $500,000 net increase in cash and marketable securities from the statement of cash flows therefore reconciles with the total change of $500,000 in these accounts during 2000. The statement of cash flows therefore reconciles with the actual balance

▲   sheet changes.

Interpreting the Statement

The statement of cash flows allows the financial manager and other interested parties to analyze the firm's cash flow. The manager should pay special attention to both the major categories of cash flow and the individual items of cash inflow and outflow, to assess whether any developments have occurred that are contrary to the company's financial policies. In addition, the statement can be used to evaluate progress toward projected goals. This statement does not match specific cash inflows with specific cash outflows, but it can be used to isolate inefficiencies. For example, increases in accounts receivable and inventories resulting in major cash outflows may signal credit or inventory problems, respectively.

In addition, the financial manager can prepare a statement of cash flows developed from projected, or pro forma, financial statements. This approach can

Balance Sheets
Technica, Inc.

	December 31	
Assets	**2000**	**1999**
Cash	$ 15,000	$ 16,000
Marketable securities	7,200	8,000
Accounts receivable	34,100	42,200
Inventories	82,000	50,000
Total current assets	$138,300	$116,200
Land and buildings	$150,000	$150,000
Machinery and equipment	200,000	190,000
Furniture and fixtures	54,000	50,000
Other	11,000	10,000
Total gross fixed assets	$415,000	$400,000
Less: Accumulated depreciation	145,000	115,000
Net fixed assets	$270,000	$285,000
Total assets	$408,300	$401,200
Liabilities and stockholders' equity		
Accounts payable	$ 57,000	$ 49,000
Notes payable	13,000	16,000
Accruals	5,000	6,000
Total current liabilities	$ 75,000	$ 71,000
Long-term debt	$150,000	$160,000
Stockholders' equity		
Common stock equity (shares outstanding: 19,500 in 2000 and 20,000 in 1999)	$110,200	$120,000
Retained earnings	73,100	50,200
Total stockholders' equity	$183,300	$170,200
Total liabilities and stockholders' equity	$408,300	$401,200

Statement of Retained Earnings
Technica, Inc.
for the year ended December 31, 2000

Retained earnings balance (January 1, 2000)	$50,200
Plus: Net profits after taxes (for 2000)	42,900
Less: Cash dividends (paid during 2000)	(20,000)
Retained earnings balance (December 31, 2000)	$73,100

3–2   **Financial statement account identification**   Mark each of the accounts listed in the following table as follows:

a. In column (1), indicate in which statement—income statement (IS) or balance sheet (BS)—the account belongs.

b. In column (2), indicate whether the account is a current asset (CA), current liability (CL), expense (E), fixed asset (FA), long-term debt (LTD), revenue (R), or stockholders' equity (SE).

Account name	(1) Statement	(2) Type of account
Accounts payable	_____	_____
Accounts receivable	_____	_____
Accruals	_____	_____
Accumulated depreciation	_____	_____
Administrative expense	_____	_____
Buildings	_____	_____
Cash	_____	_____
Common stock (at par)	_____	_____
Cost of goods sold	_____	_____
Depreciation	_____	_____
Equipment	_____	_____
General expense	_____	_____
Interest expense	_____	_____
Inventories	_____	_____
Land	_____	_____
Long-term debts	_____	_____
Machinery	_____	_____
Marketable securities	_____	_____
Notes payable	_____	_____
Operating expense	_____	_____
Paid-in capital in excess of par	_____	_____
Preferred stock	_____	_____
Preferred stock dividends	_____	_____
Retained earnings	_____	_____
Sales revenue	_____	_____
Selling expense	_____	_____
Taxes	_____	_____
Vehicles	_____	_____

   3–3   **Income statement preparation**   Use the *appropriate items* from the following list to prepare in good form Perry Corporation's income statement for the year ended December 31, 2000.

a. Prepare a statement of retained earnings for the year ended December 31, 2000, for Hayes Enterprises. (*Note:* Be sure to calculate and include the amount of cash dividends paid in 2000.)

b. Calculate the firm's 2000 earnings per share (EPS).

c. How large a per-share cash dividend did the firm pay on common stock during 2000?

INTERMEDIATE **3–11** **Translation of foreign subsidiary's balance sheet** Cummings Products, a multi-national producer of men's clothing, has a major manufacturing subsidiary operating in Switzerland. (The Swiss currency is francs, noted Sf.) The subsidiary has total assets worth Sf 9,000,000, total liabilities of Sf 6,000,000, and Sf 3,000,000 in equity. The exchange rate at the *beginning* of 2000 was Sf 1.50/US$, or alternatively, US$.67/Sf. At the *end* of 2000, the Swiss franc had appreciated to a value of Sf 1.40/US$, or US$.77/Sf.

a. Find the value in US$ of the Swiss subsidiary's assets, liabilities, and equity at the *beginning* of 2000.

b. Find the value in US$ of the Swiss subsidiary's assets and liabilities at the *end* of 2000.

c. Compare your findings in **a** and **b,** and determine the amount, if any, of translation gain or loss experienced by Cummings Products on its Swiss subsidiary during 2000.

d. How should any translation gain or loss found in **c** be treated by Cummings Products?

CHALLENGE **3–12** **Translation of foreign subsidiary statements** Layton Pharmaceuticals, Inc., is a multinational maker of prescription medicines. In 1999, the firm acquired a British subsidiary with assets totaling £25,000,000, liabilities of £12,000,000, and equity of £12,000,000. These values are reflected on Layton's 1999 balance sheet at the then current exchange rate of US$1.60/£. The exchange rate at the end of fiscal 2000 was US$1.70/£. Layton's British subsidiary reported net income of £5,800,000 for fiscal year 2000.

Balance Sheet US$ values for fiscal 1999	
British assets	$40,000,000
British liabilities	19,200,000
British equity	20,800,000

a. Apply FASB 52 to correctly report the British subsidiary's US$ balance sheet values for fiscal year 2000.

b. Calculate the gain (loss) for the year that is to be carried over to the cumulative translation adjustment account.

c. Translate the British subsidiary's income to US$ using the year-end exchange rate.

d. Translate the British subsidiary's income to US$ using the average exchange rate during the fiscal year.
e. Which of the two income figures do you think it is more likely that Layton will report? Why would Layton choose to report the higher or the lower amount?

 3–13 **Changes in stockholders' equity**   Listed are the equity sections of balance sheets for years 1999 and 2000 as reported by Mountain Air Ski Resorts, Inc. The overall value of stockholders' equity has risen from $2,000,000 to $7,500,000. Use the statements to discover how and why this happened.

	Mountain Air Ski Resorts, Inc.	
	1999	2000
Stockholders' equity		
Common stock ($1.00 par)		
Authorized—5,000,000 shares		
Outstanding—1,500,000 shares 2000		
— 500,000 shares 1999	$ 500,000	$1,500,000
Paid-in capital in excess of par	500,000	4,500,000
Retained earnings	1,000,000	1,500,000
Total stockholders' equity	$2,000,000	$7,500,000

The company paid total dividends of $200,000 during fiscal 2000.
a. What was Mountain Air's net income for fiscal 2000?
b. How many new shares did the corporation issue and sell during the year?
c. At what average price per share did the new stock sold during 2000 sell?
d. At what price per share did Mountain Air's original 500,000 shares sell?

 3–14 **Corporate taxes**   Tantor Supply, Inc., is a small corporation acting as the exclusive distributor of a major line of sporting goods. During 2000 the firm earned $92,500 before taxes.
a. Calculate the firm's tax liability using the corporate tax rate schedule given in Table 3.4.
b. How much is Tantor Supply's 2000 after-tax earnings?
c. What was the firm's *average tax rate*, based on your findings in **a**?
d. What is the firm's *marginal tax rate*, based on your findings in **a**?

 3–15 **Average corporate tax rates**   Using the corporate tax rate schedule given in Table 3.4, perform the following:
a. Calculate the tax liability, after-tax earnings, and average tax rates for the following levels of corporate earnings before taxes: $10,000; $80,000; $300,000; $500,000; $1.5 million; $10 million; and $15 million.
b. Plot the average tax rates (measured on the *y* axis) against the pretax income levels (measured on the *x* axis). What generalization can be made concerning the relationship between these variables?

3–16 **Marginal corporate tax rates** Using the corporate tax rate schedule given in Table 3.4, perform the following:

a. Find the marginal tax rate for the following levels of corporate earnings before taxes: $15,000; $60,000; $90,000; $200,000; $400,000; $1 million; and $20 million.

b. Plot the marginal tax rates (measured on the y axis) against the pretax income levels (measured on the x axis). Explain the relationship between these variables.

3–17 **Interest versus dividend income** During the year just ended, Shering Distributors, Inc., had pretax earnings from operations of $490,000. In addition, during the year it received $20,000 in income from interest on bonds it held in Zig Manufacturing and received $20,000 in income from dividends on its 5% common stock holding in Tank Industries, Inc. Shering is in the 40% tax bracket and is eligible for a 70% dividend exclusion on its Tank Industries stock.

a. Calculate the firm's tax on its operating earnings only.

b. Find the tax and after-tax amount attributable to the interest income from Zig Manufacturing bonds.

c. Find the tax and after-tax amount attributable to the dividend income from the Tank Industries, Inc., common stock.

d. Compare, contrast, and discuss the after-tax amounts resulting from the interest income and dividend income calculated in b and c.

e. What is the firm's total tax liability for the year?

3–18 **Interest versus dividend expense** Michaels Corporation expects earnings before interest and taxes to be $40,000 for this period. Assuming an ordinary tax rate of 40 percent, compute the firm's earnings after taxes and earnings available for common stockholders (earnings after taxes and preferred stock dividends, if any) under the following conditions:

a. The firm pays $10,000 in interest.

b. The firm pays $10,000 in preferred stock dividends.

  3–19 **Capital gains taxes** Perkins Manufacturing is considering the sale of two non-depreciable assets, X and Y. Asset X was purchased for $2,000 and will be sold today for $2,250. Asset Y was purchased for $30,000 and will be sold today for $35,000. The firm is subject to a 40% tax rate on capital gains.

a. Calculate the amount of capital gain, if any, realized on each of the assets.

b. Calculate the tax on the sale of each asset.

  3–20 **Capital gains taxes** The following table contains purchase and sale prices for the nondepreciable capital assets of a major corporation. The firm paid taxes of 40% on capital gains.

Asset	Purchase price	Sale price
A	$ 3,000	$ 3,400
B	12,000	12,000
C	62,000	80,000
D	41,000	45,000
E	16,500	18,000

a. Determine the amount of capital gain realized on each of the five assets.

b. Calculate the amount of tax paid on each of the assets.

  3–21 **Tax loss carryback and carryforward**   Ordway Shipbuilding Company had pretax earnings and associated tax liabilities for the period 1991 to 2000 as follows:

Year	Pretax earnings	Tax liability
1991	$600,000	$240,000
1992	450,000	180,000
1993	200,000	80,000
1994	300,000	120,000
1995		
1996	400,000	160,000
1997	300,000	120,000
1998	500,000	200,000
1999	600,000	240,000
2000	300,000	120,000

The firm pays taxes at a 40% rate. For each of the following cases, (1) calculate the pretax earnings and taxes after adjustments for any allowable carryback/carryforward for each year, and (2) indicate the *total* change in taxes, if any, resulting from these actions.

a. In 1995, Ordway had an operating loss of $1.8 million.

b. In 1995, Ordway had pretax earnings of $350,000.

c. In 1995, Ordway had an operating loss of $400,000.

d. In 1995, Ordway had pretax earnings of exactly $0.

  3–22 **Cash flow**   A firm had earnings after taxes of $50,000 in 2000. Depreciation charges were $28,000, and a $2,000 charge for amortization of a bond discount was incurred. What was the firm's *cash flow from operations* during 2000?

  3–23 **Depreciation**   On January 1, 2000, Norton Systems acquired two new assets. Asset A was research equipment costing $17,000 and having a 3-year recovery period. Asset B was duplicating equipment having an installed cost of $45,000 and a 5-year recovery period. Using the MACRS depreciation percentages in Table 3.8 on page 96, prepare a depreciation schedule for each of these assets.

  3–24 **MACRS depreciation expense, taxes, and cash flow**   Pavlovich Instruments, Inc., a maker of precision telescopes, expects to report per-tax income of $430,000 this year. The company's financial manager is considering the timing

Required

a. Use the financial data presented to prepare Cline Custom Bicycles' statement of cash flows for the year ended December 31, 2000.

b. Evaluate the statement prepared in **a** in light of Cline's current cash flow difficulties.

c. On the basis of your evaluation in **b**, what recommendations might you offer Darin Cline?

WEB EXERCISE

GOTO web site www.yahoo.com. On the left side of the Yahoo home page screen, click Business & Economy. On the right side of the next screen click Y! Finance.

Using this Yahoo screen, find the symbol for Southwest Airlines. Click on this symbol to find the latest trading data for Southwest Airlines.

1. What was the selling price for the last sale of Southwest's common stock? How much in dollars per share was the change?

2. What was the number of shares sold in this trade?

By the information about Southwest Airlines, you will see Profile. Click on it.

3. What was Southwest Airlines' sales? Its after-tax income?

4. What were Southwest's earnings per share? Its book value per share?

5. How many shares does Southwest Airlines have outstanding?

Click on Highlights.

6. What were Southwest's earnings per share for each of the last four years?

7. What is the company's 5-year growth rate for EPS?

Financial Statement Analysis

LEARNING GOALS

LG1 Understand the parties interested in performing financial ratio analysis and the common types of ratio comparisons.

LG2 Describe some of the cautions that should be considered in performing financial ratio analysis.

LG3 Use popular ratios to analyze a firm's liquidity and the activity of inventory, accounts receivable, accounts payable, and total assets.

LG4 Discuss the relationship between debt and financial leverage and the ratios that can be used to assess the firm's degree of indebtedness and its ability to meet the payments associated with debt.

LG5 Evaluate a firm's profitability relative to its sales, asset investment, owners' equity investment, and share value.

LG6 Use the DuPont system and a summary of financial ratios to perform a complete ratio analysis of a firm.

LG1 **LG2** **4.1 Using Financial Ratios**

ratio analysis
Involves the methods of calculating and interpreting financial ratios to assess the firm's performance.

In the preceding chapter, we reviewed the firm's four basic financial statements. The information contained in these statements is of major significance to various interested parties who regularly need to have relative measures of the company's operating efficiency. *Relative* is the key word here, because the analysis of financial statements is based on the knowledge and use of *ratios* or *relative values*.

Ratio analysis involves methods of calculating and interpreting financial ratios to assess the firm's performance. The basic inputs to ratio analysis are the firm's income statement and balance sheet. Before we look at those inputs,

Apples and Oranges

You've been told many times that you can't compare apples and oranges. Does that old adage mean you can't make comparisons between companies? The answer depends on how you define apples and oranges! If you look at two companies as wholes— one the apple and one the orange— comparison would be difficult, if not impossible. Instead, you must break

the comparison into smaller segments. You *can* compare individual performance categories of the apple and the orange—say, the amount of debt that each company has in proportion to its assets. Such performance comparisons between companies in the same industry can be made by analyzing pieces of data in published financial statements. This chapter will show you how to use financial statements to make comparisons between firms and over time.

though, we need to describe the parties interested in financial ratios and the general types of ratio comparisons.

Interested Parties

Ratio analysis of a firm's financial statements is of interest to shareholders, creditors, and the firm's own management. Both present and prospective shareholders are interested in the firm's current and future level of risk and return, which directly affect share price. The firm's creditors are primarily interested in the short-term liquidity of the company and its ability to make interest and principal payments. A secondary concern of creditors is the firm's profitability; they want assurance that the business is healthy and will continue to be successful. Management, like stockholders, is concerned with all aspects of the firm's financial situation. Thus, it attempts to produce financial ratios that will be considered favorable by both owners and creditors. In addition, management uses ratios to monitor the firm's performance from period to period. Any unexpected changes are examined, to isolate developing problems.

Types of Ratio Comparisons

Ratio analysis is not merely the application of a formula to financial data to calculate a given ratio. More important is the *interpretation* of the ratio value. To answer such questions as, Is it too high or too low? Is it good or bad?, a meaningful basis for comparison is needed. Two types of ratio comparisons can be made: cross-sectional and time-series.

Cross-Sectional Analysis

cross-sectional analysis
Comparison of different firms' financial ratios at the same point in time; involves comparing the firm's ratios to those of other firms in its industry or to industry averages.

benchmarking
A type of *cross-sectional analysis* in which the firm's ratio values are compared to those of a key competitor or group of competitors, primarily to identify areas for improvement.

Cross-sectional analysis involves the comparison of different firms' financial ratios at the same point in time. The typical business is interested in how well it has performed in relation to other firms in its industry. Often, the reported financial statements of competing firms will be available for analysis. Frequently, a firm will compare its ratio values to those of a key competitor or group of competitors that it wishes to emulate. This type of cross-sectional analysis, called **benchmarking,** has become very popular. By comparing the firm's ratios to those of the *benchmark company* (or *companies*), it can identify areas in which it excels and, more importantly, areas for improvement.

Another popular type of comparison is to industry averages. These figures can be found in the *Almanac of Business and Industrial Financial Ratios, Dun & Bradstreet's Industry Norms and Key Business Ratios, Business Month, FTC Quarterly Reports, Robert Morris Associates Statement Studies,* and other sources such as industry association publications.[1] A sample from one available source of industry averages is given in Table 4.1.

Comparing a particular ratio to the standard should uncover any *deviations from the norm.* Many people mistakenly believe that as long as the firm being analyzed has a value "better than" the industry average, it can be viewed favorably. However, this "better than average" viewpoint can be misleading. Quite often a ratio value that is far better than the norm can indicate problems. These may, on more careful analysis, be more severe than had the ratio been worse than the industry average. It is therefore important to investigate *significant deviations to either side* of the industry standard.

The analyst must also recognize that ratios with large deviations from the norm are only the *symptoms* of a problem. Further analysis is typically required to isolate the *causes* of the problem. Once the reason for the problem is known,

Hint   Industry averages are not particularly useful when analyzing firms with multiproduct lines. In the case of multiproduct firms, it is difficult to select the appropriate benchmark industry.

---

1. Cross-sectional comparisons of firms operating in several lines of business are difficult to perform. The use of weighted-average industry average ratios based on the firm's product-line mix or, if data are available, analysis of the firm on a product-line basis can be performed to evaluate a multiproduct firm.

Firm A

Cash	$ 0	Accounts payable	$ 0
Marketable securities	0	Notes payable	10,000
Accounts receivable	0	Accruals	0
Inventories	20,000	Total current liabilities	$10,000
Total current assets	$20,000		

Firm B

Cash	$ 5,000	Accounts payable	$ 5,000
Marketable securities	5,000	Notes payable	3,000
Accounts receivable	5,000	Accruals	2,000
Inventories	5,000	Total current liabilities	$10,000
Total current assets	$20,000		

Both firms appear to be equally liquid, because their current ratios are both 2.0 ($20,000 ÷ $10,000). However, a closer look at the differences in the composition of current assets and liabilities suggests that *firm B is more liquid than firm A*. This is true for two reasons: (1) Firm B has more liquid assets in the form of cash and marketable securities than firm A, which has only a single, relatively illiquid asset in the form of inventories, and (2) firm B's current liabilities are in general more flexible than the single current liability—notes payable—of firm A.

It is therefore important to look beyond measures of overall liquidity to assess the activity (liquidity) of specific current accounts. A number of ratios are available for measuring the activity of the most important current accounts, which include inventory, accounts receivable, and accounts payable.[5] The activity (efficiency of utilization) of total assets can also be assessed.

Inventory Turnover

inventory turnover
Measures the activity, or liquidity, of a firm's inventory.

Inventory turnover commonly measures the activity, or liquidity, of a firm's inventory. It is calculated as follows:

$$\text{Inventory turnover} = \frac{\text{cost of goods sold}}{\text{inventory}}$$

Applying this relationship to Bartlett Company in 2000 yields

$$\text{Inventory turnover} = \frac{\$2,088,000}{\$289,000} = 7.2$$

5. For convenience, the activity ratios involving these current accounts assume that their end-of-period values are good approximations of the average account balance during the period—typically 1 year. Technically, when the month-end balances of inventory, accounts receivable, or accounts payable vary during the year, the average balance, calculated by summing the 12 month-end account balances and dividing the total by 12, should be used instead of the year-end value. If month-end balances are unavailable, the average can be approximated by dividing the sum of the beginning-of-year and end-of-year balances by 2. These approaches ensure a ratio that on the average better reflects the firm's circumstances. Because the data needed to find averages are generally unavailable to the external analyst, year-end values are frequently used to calculate activity ratios for current accounts.

average age of inventory
Average length of time inventory is
held by the firm.

The resulting turnover is meaningful only when it is compared with that of other firms in the same industry or to the firm's past inventory turnover. An inventory turnover of 20.0 would not be unusual for a grocery store, whereas a common inventory turnover for an aircraft manufacturer would be 4.0.

Inventory turnover can easily be converted into an **average age of inventory** by dividing it into 360—the number of days in a year.[6] For Bartlett Company, the average age of inventory would be 50.0 days (360 ÷ 7.2). This value can also be viewed as the average number of days' sales in inventory.

Average Collection Period

average collection period
The average amount of time needed to
collect accounts receivable.

The **average collection period,** or average age of accounts receivable, is useful in evaluating credit and collection policies.[7] It is arrived at by dividing the average daily sales[8] into the accounts receivable balance:

$$\text{Average collection period} = \frac{\text{accounts receivable}}{\text{average sales per day}}$$

$$= \frac{\text{accounts receivable}}{\dfrac{\text{annual sales}}{360}}$$

The average collection period for Bartlett Company in 2000 is

$$\frac{\$503,000}{\dfrac{\$3,074,000}{360}} = \frac{\$503,000}{\$8,539} = 58.9 \text{ days}$$

On the average it takes the firm 58.9 days to collect an account receivable.

The average collection period is meaningful only in relation to the firm's credit terms. If Bartlett Company extends 30-day credit terms to customers, an average collection period of 58.9 days may indicate a poorly managed credit or collection department, or both. Or, the lengthened collection period could be the result of an intentional relaxation of credit-term enforcement in response to competitive pressures. If the firm had extended 60-day credit terms, the 58.9-day average collection period would be quite acceptable. Clearly, additional information would be required to draw definitive conclusions about the effectiveness of the firm's credit and collection policies.

---

6. Unless otherwise specified, a 360-day year consisting of twelve 30-day months is assumed throughout this textbook. This assumption allows some simplification of the calculations used to illustrate key concepts.

7. The average collection period is sometimes called the *days' sales outstanding (DSO)*. A discussion of the evaluation and establishment of credit and collection policies is presented in Chapter 17.

8. The formula as presented assumes, for simplicity, that all sales are made on a credit basis. If such is not the case, *average credit sales per day* should be substituted for average sales per day.

Average Payment Period

The **average payment period,** or average age of accounts payable, is calculated in the same manner as the average collection period:

$$\text{Average payment period} = \frac{\text{accounts payable}}{\text{average purchases per day}}$$

$$= \frac{\text{accounts payable}}{\dfrac{\text{annual purchases}}{360}}$$

The difficulty in calculating this ratio stems from the need to find annual purchases[9]—a value not available in published financial statements. Ordinarily, purchases are estimated as a given percentage of cost of goods sold. If we assume that Bartlett Company's purchases equaled 70 percent of its cost of goods sold in 2000, its average payment period is

$$\frac{\$382,000}{\dfrac{.70 \times \$2,088,000}{360}} = \frac{\$382,000}{\$4,060} = 94.1 \text{ days}$$

This figure is meaningful only in relation to the average credit terms extended to the firm. If Bartlett Company's suppliers, on the average, have extended 30-day credit terms, an analyst would give it a low credit rating. If the firm has been generally extended 90-day credit terms, its credit would be acceptable. Prospective lenders and suppliers of trade credit are especially interested in the average payment period, because it provides them with a sense of the bill-paying patterns of the firm.

Total Asset Turnover

The **total asset turnover** indicates the efficiency with which the firm uses its assets to generate sales. Generally, the higher a firm's total asset turnover, the more efficiently its assets have been used. This measure is probably of greatest interest to management, because it indicates whether the firm's operations have been financially efficient. Total asset turnover is calculated as follows:

$$\text{Total asset turnover} = \frac{\text{sales}}{\text{total assets}}$$

The value of Bartlett Company's total asset turnover in 2000 is

$$\frac{\$3,074,000}{\$3,597,000} = .85$$

The company therefore turns an amount equal to its total assets .85 times a year.

---

9. Technically, annual *credit* purchases—rather than annual purchases—should be used in calculating this ratio. For simplicity, this refinement is ignored here.

One caution with respect to use of this ratio: It uses the *historical costs* of total assets. Because some firms have significantly newer or older assets than others, comparing total asset turnovers of those firms can be misleading. Because of inflation and the use of historical costs, firms with newer assets will tend to have lower turnovers than those with older assets.[10] The differences in these turnovers could therefore result from more costly assets rather than from differing operating efficiencies. The financial manager should be cautious when using this ratio for cross-sectional comparisons.

? Review Question

4–6   To assess the reasonableness of the firm's average collection period and average payment period ratios, what additional information is needed? Explain.

4.4 Analyzing Debt

financial leverage
The magnification of risk and return introduced through the use of fixed-cost financing such as debt and preferred stock.

The *debt position* of a firm indicates the amount of other people's money being used in attempting to generate profits. In general, the financial analyst is most concerned with long-term debts, because these commit the firm to paying interest, and eventually the principal, over the long run. Because creditors' claims must be satisfied before earnings can be distributed to shareholders, present and prospective shareholders pay close attention to degree of indebtedness and ability to repay debts. Lenders are also concerned about the firm's indebtedness, because the more indebted the firm, the more likely it will be unable to satisfy the creditors' claims. Management obviously must be concerned with indebtedness.

In general, the more debt a firm uses in relation to its total assets, the greater its *financial leverage.* **Financial leverage** is the magnification of risk and return introduced through the use of fixed-cost financing such as debt and preferred stock. The more fixed-cost debt, or financial leverage, a firm uses, the greater will be its risk and its expected return.

Example ▼   Michael Karp and Amy Parsons are incorporating a new business venture they have formed. After much analysis they have determined that an initial investment of $50,000—current assets of $20,000 and fixed assets of $30,000—is necessary. These funds can be obtained in either of two ways. The first is the *no-debt plan,* under which they would together invest the full $50,000 without borrowing. The

---

10. This problem would not exist if firms were required to use current-cost accounting. Financial Accounting Standards Board (FASB) Standard No. 33, *Financial Reporting and Changing Prices,* issued in 1979 and amended by FASB Standard No. 82, *Financial Reporting and Price Changes: Elimination of Certain Disclosures,* issued in 1984, prescribes procedures for inflation accounting. The standard currently requires only large publicly held corporations to include such reporting as *supplementary information* in their stockholders' reports. For a discussion of these and other FASB statements, see a current edition of an intermediate accounting textbook.

TABLE 4.4	Financial Statements Associated with Michael and Amy's Alternatives

Balance Sheets	No-debt plan	Debt plan
Current assets	$20,000	$20,000
Fixed assets	30,000	30,000
Total assets	$50,000	$50,000
Debt (12% interest)	$ 0	$25,000
(1) Equity	50,000	25,000
Total liabilities and equity	$50,000	$50,000

Income Statements		
Sales	$30,000	$30,000
Less: Costs and operating expenses	18,000	18,000
Operating profits	$12,000	$12,000
Less: Interest expense	0	$.12 \times \$25,000 =$ 3,000
Net profit before taxes	$12,000	$ 9,000
Less: Taxes (rate = 40%)	4,800	3,600
(2) Net profit after taxes	$ 7,200	$ 5,400
Return on equity [(2) ÷ (1)]	$\dfrac{\$7,200}{\$50,000} = 14.4\%$	$\dfrac{\$5,400}{\$25,000} = 21.6\%$

other alternative, the *debt plan,* involves making a combined investment of $25,000 and borrowing the balance of $25,000 at 12% annual interest. Regardless of which alternative they choose, Michael and Amy expect sales to average $30,000, costs and operating expenses to average $18,000, and earnings to be taxed at a 40% rate. The balance sheets and income statements associated with the no-debt and debt plans are summarized in Table 4.4.

The no-debt plan results in after-tax profits of $7,200, which represent a 14.4% rate of return on the partners' $50,000 investment. The debt plan results in $5,400 of after-tax profits, which represent a 21.6% rate of return on their combined investment of $25,000. The debt plan provides Michael and Amy with a higher rate of return; but the risk of this plan is also greater, because the annual $3,000 of interest must be paid before receipt of earnings.

This example makes it clear that *with increased debt comes greater risk as well as higher potential return.* Therefore, the greater the financial leverage, the greater the potential risk and return. A detailed discussion of the impact of debt on the firm's risk, return, and value is included in Chapter 12. Here, we emphasize the use of financial debt ratios to assess externally the degree of a firm's indebtedness and its ability to meet fixed payments associated with debt.

Measures of Debt

degree of indebtedness
Measures amount of debt relative to other significant balance sheet amounts.

ability to service debts
The ability of a firm to make the contractual payments required on a scheduled basis over the life of a debt.

coverage ratios
Ratios that measure the firm's ability to pay certain fixed charges.

There are two general types of debt measures: measures of the degree of indebtedness and measures of the ability to service debts. The **degree of indebtedness** measures the amount of debt relative to other significant balance sheet amounts. One of the most commonly used measures is the debt ratio, which is discussed in what follows.

The second type of debt measure, the **ability to service debts,** assesses a firm's ability to make the contractual payments required on a scheduled basis over the life of a debt.[11] Lease payments as well as preferred stock dividend payments also represent scheduled obligations. The firm's ability to pay certain fixed charges is measured using **coverage ratios.** Typically, higher coverage ratios are preferred, but too high a ratio (above industry norms) may indicate unnecessarily low risk and returns. Alternatively, the lower the firm's coverage ratios, the more risky the firm is considered to be. "Riskiness" here refers to the firm's ability to pay fixed obligations. If a firm is unable to pay these obligations, it will be in default, and its creditors may seek immediate repayment. In most instances this would force a firm into bankruptcy. Two coverage ratios—the times interest earned ratio and the fixed-payment coverage ratio—are discussed in this section.[12]

Debt Ratio

debt ratio
Measures the proportion of total assets financed by the firm's creditors.

The **debt ratio** measures the proportion of total assets financed by the firm's creditors. The higher this ratio, the greater the amount of other people's money being used in an attempt to generate profits. The ratio is calculated as follows:

$$\text{Debt ratio} = \frac{\text{total liabilities}}{\text{total assets}}$$

The debt ratio for Bartlett Company in 2000 is

$$\frac{\$1,643,000}{\$3,597,000} = .457 = 45.7\%$$

This indicates that the company has financed close to half of its assets with debt. The higher this ratio, the greater the firm's degree of indebtedness and the more financial leverage it has.

---

11. The term *service* refers to the payment of interest and repayment of principal associated with a firm's debt obligations. When a firm services its debts, it pays—or fulfills—these obligations.

12. Coverage ratios use data that is derived on an *accrual basis* (discussed in Chapter 1) to measure what in a strict sense should be measured on a *cash basis.* This occurs because debts are serviced by using cash flows, not the accounting values shown on the firm's financial statements. But because it is difficult to determine cash flows available for debt service from the firm's financial statements, the calculation of coverage ratios as presented here is quite common due to the ready availability of financial statement data.

Times Interest Earned Ratio

times interest earned ratio
Sometimes called the *interest coverage ratio,* it measures the firm's ability to make contractual interest payments.

The **times interest earned ratio,** sometimes called the *interest coverage ratio,* measures the firm's ability to make contractual interest payments. The higher the value of this ratio, the better able the firm is to fulfill its interest obligations. The times interest earned ratio is calculated as follows:

$$\text{Times interest earned} = \frac{\text{earnings before interest and taxes}}{\text{interest}}$$

Applying this ratio to Bartlett Company yields the following 2000 value:

$$\text{Times interest earned} = \frac{\$418,000}{\$93,000} = 4.5$$

The value of *earnings before interest and taxes* is the same as the figure for *operating profits* shown in Bartlett's income statement. The firm's times interest earned ratio seems acceptable. As a rule, a value of at least 3.0—and preferably closer to 5.0—is suggested. If the firm's earnings before interest and taxes were to shrink by 78 percent [$(4.5 - 1.0) \div 4.5$], the firm would still be able to pay the $93,000 in interest it owes. Thus, it has a good margin of safety.

Fixed-Payment Coverage Ratio

fixed-payment coverage ratio
Measures the firm's ability to meet all fixed-payment obligations.

The **fixed-payment coverage ratio** measures the firm's ability to meet all fixed-payment obligations. Like the times interest earned ratio, the higher this value, the better. Loan interest, principal payments on debt, scheduled lease payments, and preferred stock dividends[13] are commonly included in this ratio. The formula for the fixed-payment coverage ratio is as follows:

$$\frac{\text{earnings before interest and taxes + lease payments}}{\text{interest + lease payments} + \{(\text{principal payments} + \text{preferred stock dividends}) \times [1/(1 - T)]\}}$$

where T is the corporate tax rate applicable to the firm's income. The term $1/(1 - T)$ is included to adjust the after-tax principal and preferred stock dividend payments back to a before-tax equivalent that is consistent with the before-tax values of all other terms. Applying the formula to Bartlett Company's 2000 data yields:

Fixed-payment coverage ratio =

$$\frac{\$418,000 + \$35,000}{\$93,000 + \$35,000 + \{(\$71,000 + \$10,000) \times [1/(1 - 0.29)]\}}$$

$$= \frac{\$453,000}{\$242,000} = 1.9$$

Earnings available are nearly twice as large as its fixed-payment obligations. Thus, the firm appears able to safely meet its fixed payments.

---

13. Although preferred stock dividends, which are stated at the time of issue, can be "passed" (not paid) at the option of the firm's directors, it is generally believed that the payment of such dividends is necessary. *This text therefore treats the preferred stock dividend as a contractual obligation, to be paid as a fixed amount, as scheduled.*

Like the times interest earned ratio, the fixed-payment coverage ratio measures the risk of the firm being unable to meet scheduled fixed payments and thus be driven into bankruptcy. The lower the ratio, the greater the risk to both lenders and owners, and the greater the ratio, the lower the risk. This ratio therefore allows owners, creditors, and managers to assess the firm's ability to handle additional fixed-payment obligations such as debt.

? Review Question

4–7   What is *financial leverage?* What ratio can be used to measure the firm's *degree of indebtedness?* What ratios are used to assess the firm's *ability to service debts?*

4.5 Analyzing Profitability

There are many measures of profitability. As a group, these measures evaluate the firm's earnings with respect to a given level of sales, a certain level of assets, the owners' investment, or share value. Without profits, a firm could not attract outside capital. Moreover, present owners and creditors would become concerned about the company's future and attempt to recover their funds. Owners, creditors, and management pay close attention to boosting profits due to the great importance placed on earnings in the marketplace.

Common-Size Income Statements

common-size income statement
An income statement in which each item is expressed as a percentage of sales.

A popular tool for evaluating profitability in relation to sales is the **common-size income statement.**[14] On this statement, each item is expressed as a percentage of sales, thus highlighting the relationship between sales and specific costs, expenses, and forms of income. Common-size income statements are especially useful in comparing performance across years. Three frequently cited ratios of profitability that can be read directly from the common-size income statement are (1) the gross profit margin, (2) the operating profit margin, and (3) the net profit margin.

Common-size income statements for 2000 and 1999 for Bartlett Company are presented and evaluated in Table 4.5. The statements reveal that the firm's cost of goods sold increased from 66.7 percent of sales in 1999 to 67.9 percent in 2000, resulting in a worsening gross profit margin. However, thanks to a decrease in total operating expenses, the firm's net profit margin rose from 5.8 percent of sales in 1999 to 7.5 percent in 2000. The decrease in expenses more than compensated for the increase in the cost of goods sold. A decrease in the

---

14. This statement is sometimes called a *percent income statement.* The same treatment is often applied to the firm's balance sheet to make it easier to evaluate changes in the asset and financial structures of the firm. In addition to measuring profitability, these statements in effect can be used as an alternative or supplement to liquidity, activity, and debt-ratio analysis.

TABLE 4.5	Bartlett Company Common-Size Income Statements		
	For the years ended December 31		Evaluation[a]
	2000	1999	1999–2000
Sales revenue	100.0%	100.0%	same
Less: Cost of goods sold	67.9	66.7	worse
(1) Gross profit margin	32.1%	33.3%	worse
Less: Operating expenses			
Selling expense	3.3%	4.2%	better
General and administrative expenses	6.3	7.3	better
Lease expense	1.1	1.3	better
Depreciation expense	7.8	8.7	better
Total operating expense	18.5%	21.5%	better
(2) Operating profit margin	13.6%	11.8%	better
Less: Interest expense	3.0	3.5	better
Net profits before taxes	10.6%	8.3%	better
Less: Taxes	3.1	2.5	worse[b]
(3) Net profit margin	7.5%	5.8%	better

[a]Subjective assessments based on data provided.

[b]Taxes as a percent of sales increased noticeably between 1999 and 2000 due to differing costs and expenses, whereas the average tax rates (taxes ÷ net profits before taxes) for 1999 and 2000 remained about the same—30% and 29%, respectively.

firm's 2000 interest expense (3.0 percent of sales versus 3.5 percent in 1999) added to the increase in 2000 profits.

Gross Profit Margin

gross profit margin
Measures the percentage of each sales dollar remaining after the firm has paid for its goods.

Hint   This is a very significant ratio for small retailers, especially during times of inflationary prices. If the owner of the firm does not raise prices when the cost of sales is rising, the gross profit margin will erode.

The **gross profit margin** measures the percentage of each sales dollar remaining after the firm has paid for its goods. The higher the gross profit margin, the better, and the lower the relative cost of merchandise sold. Of course, the opposite case is also true, as the Bartlett Company example shows. The gross profit margin is calculated as follows:

$$\text{Gross profit margin} = \frac{\text{sales} - \text{cost of goods sold}}{\text{sales}} = \frac{\text{gross profits}}{\text{sales}}$$

The value for Bartlett Company's gross profit margin for 2000 is

$$\frac{\$3,074,000 - \$2,088,000}{\$3,074,000} = \frac{\$986,000}{\$3,074,000} = 32.1\%$$

This value is labeled (1) on the common-size income statement in Table 4.5.

Operating Profit Margin

operating profit margin
Measures the percentage of each sales dollar remaining after all costs and expenses *other than* interest and taxes are deducted; the *pure profits* earned on each sales dollar.

The **operating profit margin** measures the percentage of each sales dollar remaining after all costs and expenses *other than* interest and taxes are deducted. It represents the *pure profits* earned on each sales dollar. Operating profits are "pure" because they measure only the profits earned on operations and ignore any financial and government charges (interest and taxes). A high operating profit margin is preferred. The operating profit margin is calculated as follows:

$$\text{Operating profit margin} = \frac{\text{operating profits}}{\text{sales}}$$

The value for Bartlett Company's operating profit margin for 2000 is

$$\frac{\$418,000}{\$3,074,000} = 13.6\%$$

This value is labeled (2) on the common-size income statement in Table 4.5.

Net Profit Margin

net profit margin
Measures the percentage of each sales dollar remaining after all costs and expenses, *including* interest and taxes, have been deducted.

The **net profit margin** measures the percentage of each sales dollar remaining after all costs and expenses, *including* interest and taxes, have been deducted. The higher the firm's net profit margin, the better. The net profit margin is a commonly cited measure of the firm's success with respect to earnings on sales. "Good" net profit margins differ considerably across industries. A net profit margin of 1 percent or less would not be unusual for a grocery store, whereas a net profit margin of 10 percent would be low for a retail jewelry store. The net profit margin is calculated as follows:

$$\text{Net profit margin} = \frac{\text{net profits after taxes}}{\text{sales}}$$

Bartlett Company's net profit margin for 2000 is

$$\frac{\$231,000}{\$3,074,000} = 7.5\%$$

This value is labeled (3) on the common-size income statement in Table 4.5.

Return on Total Assets (ROA)

return on total assets (ROA)
Measures the firm's overall effectiveness in generating profits with its available assets; also called the *return on investment (ROI)*.

The **return on total assets (ROA)**, also called the *return on investment (ROI)*, measures the firm's overall effectiveness in generating profits with its available assets. The higher the firm's return on total assets, the better. The return on total assets is calculated as follows:

$$\text{Return on total assets} = \frac{\text{net profits after taxes}}{\text{total assets}}$$

Bartlett Company's return on total assets in 2000 is

$$\frac{\$231,000}{\$3,597,000} = 6.4\%$$

To assess Bartlett's 6.4 percent return on total assets, appropriate cross-sectional and time-series data would be needed.

Return on Equity (ROE)

return on equity (ROE)
Measures the return earned on the owners' investment in the firm.

The **return on equity (ROE)** measures the return earned on the owners' investment in the firm.[15] Generally, the higher this return, the better off are the owners. Return on equity is calculated as follows:

$$\text{Return on equity} = \frac{\text{net profits after taxes}}{\text{stockholders' equity}}$$

This ratio for Bartlett Company in 2000 is

$$\frac{\$231,000}{\$1,954,000} = 11.8\%$$

To evaluate Bartlett's 11.8 percent return on equity, appropriate cross-sectional and time-series data would be needed.

Earnings Per Share (EPS)

Hint EPS represents the dollar amount earned *on behalf of* each share—not the amount of earnings *actually distributed* to shareholders.

The firm's *earnings per share (EPS)* are generally of interest to present or prospective stockholders and to management. The earnings per share represent the number of dollars earned on behalf of each outstanding share of common stock. Earnings per share are calculated as follows:

$$\text{Earnings per share} = \frac{\text{earnings available for common stockholders}}{\text{number of shares of common stock outstanding}}$$

The value of Bartlett Company's earnings per share in 2000 is

$$\frac{\$221,000}{76,262} = \$2.90$$

This measure is closely watched by the investing public and is considered an important indicator of corporate success.

Price/Earnings (P/E) Ratio

price/earnings (P/E) ratio
Measures the amount investors are willing to pay for each dollar of the firm's earnings; the higher the P/E ratio, the greater the investor confidence.

Though not a true measure of profitability, the **price/earnings (P/E) ratio** is commonly used to assess the owners' appraisal of share value.[16] The P/E ratio measures the amount investors are willing to pay for each dollar of the firm's earnings. This ratio indicates the degree of confidence that investors have in the firm's future performance. The higher the P/E ratio, the greater the investor confidence.[17] The P/E ratio is calculated as follows:

$$\text{Price/earnings (P/E) ratio} = \frac{\text{market price per share of common stock}}{\text{earnings per share}}$$

---

15. This ratio includes preferred stock dividends in the profit figure and preferred stock in the equity value, but because the amount of preferred stock and its impact on a firm are generally quite small or nonexistent, this formula is a reasonably good approximation of the true owners'—that is, the common stockholders'—return.

16. Use of the price/earnings ratio to estimate the value of the firm is part of the discussion of "Other approaches to common stock valuation" in Chapter 7.

17. Another popular measure of investor confidence is the *market/book (M/B) ratio*, calculated by dividing the current common stock price per share by the per share book (accounting) value of stockholders' equity. The M/B ratio reflects the level of return on equity and the degree of investor confidence. Typically, relatively high M/B ratios are associated with good equity returns and investor optimism. Relatively low M/B ratios are associated with generally poor equity returns and investor pessimism. This ratio is of greatest interest to investors.

In Practice

For Bankers, Cash Flow Upstages Earnings

For company treasurers, traditional earnings-focused ratio analysis provides an objective historical view of a company's financial condition. Bankers, however, emphasize cash flow–based measures *to evaluate whether a company can generate enough cash, first, to repay a loan, and, second, to grow the company. "Cash flow tends to be more dynamic," says Cris Stone, executive vice president for corporate banking at Regions Bank, Birmingham, Alabama. Another reason to use cash flow ratios is the number of service companies in the economy. Because they have fewer tangible assets to liquidate, cash flow is a more useful measure of service companies' ability to meet debt payments.*

One of the most popular measures of cash flow is earnings before interest, taxes, depreciation, and amortization (EBITDA). *Many banks now look at the ratio of debt to EBITDA rather than a balance sheet–derived debt ratio. Some banks also use multiples of cash flow to determine how much to lend to a company. For example, BankBoston will lend manufacturing companies up to about five times cash flow, but has a higher limit of 7.5 to 10.5 times cash flow for fast-growing cellular companies.*

Banks take different approaches to loan analysis and ratios, so financial managers who take the time to learn which ratios are most important—and how they are calculated—increase their chance of qualifying for a loan. For example, one bank may use EBITDA to evaluate cash flow from operations; another may use free cash flow, *which is cash flow less dividend payments. In addition, lenders consider nonfinancial factors such as quality of management, its vision for the business, and in the case of small businesses, the owner's integrity, as critical elements in lending decisions.*

If Bartlett Company's common stock at the end of 2000 was selling at 32¼ (i.e., $32.25), using the *earnings per share (EPS)* of $2.90 from the income statement in Table 4.2, the P/E ratio at year-end 2000 is

$$\frac{\$32.25}{\$2.90} = 11.1$$

Thus, investors were paying $11.10 for each $1.00 of earnings.

? Review Questions

4–8   What is a *common-size income statement?* Which three ratios of profitability are found on this statement?

4–9   What would explain a firm's having a high gross profit margin and a low net profit margin?

4–10   Define and differentiate between return on total assets (ROA), return on equity (ROE), and earnings per share (EPS). Which measure is probably of greatest interest to owners? Why?

4–11   What is the *price/earnings (P/E) ratio?* How does it relate to investor confidence in the firm's future? Is the P/E ratio a true measure of profitability?

4.6 A Complete Ratio Analysis

Analysts frequently wish to take a global look at a firm's financial performance. As noted earlier, no single ratio is adequate for assessing all aspects of a firm's financial condition. Here we consider two popular approaches to a complete ratio analysis: (1) the DuPont system of analysis, and (2) the summary analysis of a large number of ratios. Each of these approaches has merit. The DuPont system acts as a *diagnostic tool* with which to assess the key areas responsible for the firm's financial condition. The summary analysis approach tends to view *all aspects* of the firm's financial activities to isolate key areas of responsibility.

DuPont System of Analysis

DuPont system of analysis
System used by management to dissect the firm's financial statements and to assess its financial condition.

The **DuPont system of analysis** is named for the DuPont Corporation, which originally popularized its use. It is used by financial managers to dissect the firm's financial statements and to assess its financial condition. The DuPont system merges the income statement and balance sheet into two summary measures of profitability: return on total assets (ROA) and return on equity (ROE). Figure 4.2 depicts the basic DuPont system with Bartlett Company's 2000 monetary and ratio values. The upper portion of the chart summarizes the income statement activities; the lower portion summarizes the balance sheet activities.

The DuPont system links the *net profit margin* (which measures the firm's profitability on sales) with its *total asset turnover* (which indicates how efficiently the firm has used its assets to generate sales). The **DuPont formula** then multiplies these two ratios to find the firm's *return on total assets (ROA)*:

DuPont formula
Multiplies the firm's *net profit margin* by its *total asset turnover* to calculate the firm's *return on total assets (ROA).*

$$\text{ROA} = \text{net profit margin} \times \text{total asset turnover}$$

Substituting the appropriate formulas into the equation and simplifying produces the formula given earlier:

$$\text{ROA} = \frac{\text{net profits after taxes}}{\text{sales}} \times \frac{\text{sales}}{\text{total assets}} = \frac{\text{net profits after taxes}}{\text{total assets}}$$

If the 2000 values of the net profit margin and total asset turnover for Bartlett Company, calculated earlier, are substituted into the DuPont formula, the result is

$$\text{ROA} = 7.5\% \times .85 = 6.4\%$$

As expected, this value is the same as that calculated directly in an earlier section. The DuPont formula allows the firm to break down its return on total assets into a profit-on-sales and an efficiency-of-asset-use component. Typically, a firm with a low net profit margin has a high total asset turnover, which results in a reasonably good return on total assets. Often, the opposite situation exists.

FIGURE 4.2   DuPont System
The DuPont system of analysis with application to Bartlett Company (2000)

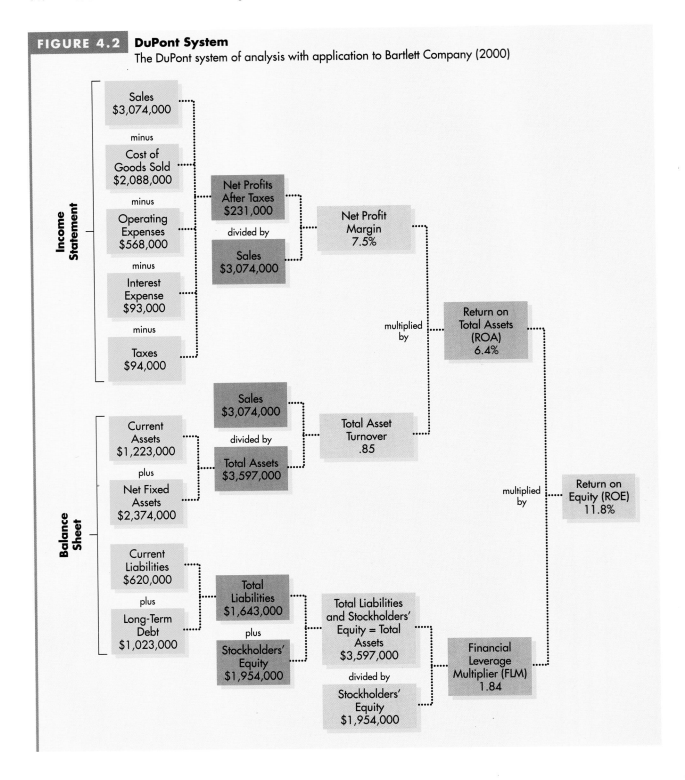

In Practice	
DuPont Withstands the Test of Time	*For over 80 years, financial managers have relied on the DuPont system of financial analysis to evaluate the various components that make up return on total assets and return on equity. "The DuPont model is a way of visualizing the information so that everyone can see it," says Stephen Jablonsky, accounting and MIS professor at Penn State University. "Where financial people are integrated into the business, they use traditional measures of evaluating performance, such as profit margins, return on total assets, and return on equity, all contained in the DuPont model."*

Heavy equipment manufacturer Caterpillar Inc. praises DuPont analysis for its ability to improve performance. "[DuPont] is a good tool for getting people started in understanding how they can have an impact on results," explains Doug McCallen, budgets and forecasts manager. Caterpillar uses return on total assets as a key performance measure and gives each unit a goal. When problems arise, managers can track down the cause to either operating efficiency (the income statement portion of the chart) or asset utilization (balance sheet ratios). Since implementing this companywide system, Caterpillar's return on total assets (ROA) soared, as did profits.

Another proponent of the DuPont model is Nucor, a steel manufacturer. Explains Sam Siegel, Vice Chairman and CFO, "It's simple. All of our people understand it." And because they understand it, employees at each Nucor facility strive to meet the company's target return on assets employed, the performance measure that also forms the basis for Nucor's incentives program. Although from time to time Nucor has considered alternative models, Siegel has stayed with the pragmatic DuPont system. "I don't say it's the best way," he comments. "All I say is that it has worked for us."

modified DuPont formula
Relates the firm's return on total assets (ROA) to its return on equity (ROE) using the *financial leverage multiplier (FLM)*.

financial leverage multiplier (FLM)
The ratio of the firm's total assets to stockholders' equity.

The second step in the DuPont system employs the **modified DuPont formula**. This formula relates the firm's return on total assets (ROA) to the return on equity (ROE). The latter is calculated by multiplying the ROA by the **financial leverage multiplier (FLM),** which is the ratio of total assets to stockholders' equity:[18]

$$ROE = ROA \times FLM$$

Substituting the appropriate formulas into the equation and simplifying produces the formula given earlier:

$$ROE = \frac{\text{net profits after taxes}}{\text{total assets}} \times \frac{\text{total assets}}{\text{stockholders' equity}} = \frac{\text{net profits after taxes}}{\text{stockholders' equity}}$$

---

18. The financial leverage multiplier is equivalent to $1/(1 - \text{debt ratio})$ and represents 1 divided by the percentage of total financing raised with equity. For computational convenience, the financial leverage multiplier is utilized here rather than the seemingly more descriptive debt ratio.

Use of the financial leverage multiplier (FLM) to convert the ROA to the ROE reflects the impact of leverage (use of debt) on owners' return. Substituting the values for Bartlett Company's ROA of 6.4 percent, calculated earlier, and Bartlett's FLM of 1.84 ($3,597,000 total assets ÷ $1,954,000 stockholders' equity) into the modified DuPont formula yields

$$ROE = 6.4\% \times 1.84 = 11.8\%$$

The 11.8 percent ROE calculated by using the modified DuPont formula is the same as that calculated directly.

The considerable advantage of the DuPont system is that it allows the firm to break its return on equity into three parts: a profit-on-sales component (net profit margin), an efficiency-of-asset-use component (total asset turnover), and a use-of-leverage component (financial leverage multiplier). The total return to the owners therefore can be analyzed in light of these important dimensions.

As an illustration, look at the ratio values summarized in Table 4.6. Bartlett Company's net profit margin and total asset turnover increased between 1999 and 2000 to levels above the industry average. In combination, improved profit on sales and better use of assets resulted in an improved ROA. Increased asset return coupled with the increased use of debt reflected in the increased financial leverage multiplier (not shown) caused the owners' return (ROE) to increase. Simply stated, the DuPont system of analysis shows that the improvement in Bartlett Company's 2000 ROE resulted from greater profit on sales, better use of assets, and increased leverage. Of course, it is important to recognize that the increased return reflected in the ROE may be due to the increased risk caused by the higher leverage. In other words, the use of more financial leverage increases *both* return and risk.

Summarizing All Ratios

Ratio values calculated for 1998 through 2000 for Bartlett Company, along with the industry average ratios for 2000, are summarized in Table 4.6 on pages 152 and 153. The table shows the formula for each ratio. Using these data, we can discuss the four key aspects of Bartlett's performance—(1) liquidity, (2) activity, (3) debt, and (4) profitability—on a cross-sectional and time-series basis.

Liquidity

The overall liquidity of the firm seems to exhibit a reasonably stable trend, having been maintained at a level that is relatively consistent with the industry average in 2000. The firm's liquidity seems to be good.

Activity

Bartlett Company's inventory appears to be in good shape. Its inventory management seems to have improved, and in 2000 it performed at a level above that of the industry. The firm may be experiencing some problems with accounts receivable. The average collection period seems to have crept up above that of the industry. Bartlett also appears to be slow in paying its bills—nearly 30 days later than the industry average. Payment procedures should be examined to ensure that the company's credit standing is not adversely affected. Although overall liquidity appears good, some attention should be given to the management of receivables and payables. Bartlett's total asset turnover reflects a sizable decline in the efficiency of asset utilization between 1998 and 1999. Although in 2000 the total asset turnover rose to a level considerably above the industry average, it appears that the pre-1999 level of efficiency has not yet been achieved.

Debt

Bartlett Company's indebtedness increased over the 1998–2000 period and is currently at a level above the industry average. Although the increase in the debt ratio could be cause for alarm, the firm's ability to meet interest and fixed-payment obligations improved from 1999 to 2000 to a level that outperforms the industry. The firm's increased indebtedness in 1999 apparently caused a deterioration in its ability to pay debt adequately, but improved income in 2000 enabled the firm to meet its fixed-payment obligations consistent with the average firm in the industry. In summary, it appears that although 1999 was an off year, the company's ability to service debts in 2000 adequately compensates for the increased degree of indebtedness.

Profitability

Bartlett's profitability relative to sales in 2000 was better than the average company in the industry, although it did not match the firm's 1998 performance. Although the *gross* profit margin in 1999 and 2000 was better than in 1998, higher levels of operating and interest expenses in 1999 and 2000 caused the 2000 *net* profit margin to fall below that of 1998. However, Bartlett's 2000 net profit margin is favorable compared to the industry average. The firm's ROA, ROE, and EPS behaved similar to its net profit margin over the 1998–2000 period. Bartlett appears to have experienced either a sizable drop in sales or a rapid expansion in assets between 1998 and 1999. The owners' return, as evidenced by the high 2000 ROE, suggests that the firm is performing well. Of course, as noted in the DuPont system of analysis of Bartlett's 2000 results, the increased ROE actually resulted from increased returns and increased risk. This can be seen in the firm's increased debt ratios and financial leverage multiplier (FLM). In addition, although the price/earnings (P/E) ratio is below that of the industry, some improvement occurred between 1999 and 2000. The firm's above-average returns—net profit margin, ROA, ROE, and EPS—may be due to its above-average risk, as reflected in its below-industry-average P/E ratio.

In summary, the firm appears to be growing and has recently expanded its assets, primarily through the use of debt. The 1999–2000 period seems to reflect a phase of adjustment and recovery from the rapid growth in assets. Bartlett's sales, profits, and other performance factors seem to be growing with the increase in the size of the operation. In short, the firm appears to have done quite well in 2000.

TABLE 4.6   **Summary of Bartlett Company Ratios (1998–2000, Including 2000 Industry Averages)**

| Ratio | Formula | Year | | | Industry average 2000[c] | Evaluation[d] | | |
		1998[a]	1999[b]	2000[b]		Cross-sectional 2000	Time-series 1998–2000	Overall
Liquidity								
Net working capital	current assets − current liabilities	$583,000	$521,000	$603,000	$427,000	good	good	good
Current ratio	$\dfrac{\text{current assets}}{\text{current liabilities}}$	2.04	2.08	1.97	2.05	OK	OK	OK
Quick (acid-test) ratio	$\dfrac{\text{current assets − inventory}}{\text{current liabilities}}$	1.32	1.46	1.51	1.43	OK	good	good
Activity								
Inventory turnover	$\dfrac{\text{cost of goods sold}}{\text{inventory}}$	5.1	5.7	7.2	6.6	good	good	good
Average collection period	$\dfrac{\text{accounts receivable}}{\text{average sales per day}}$	43.9 days	51.2 days	58.9 days	44.3 days	poor	poor	poor
Average payment period	$\dfrac{\text{accounts payable}}{\text{average purchases per day}}$	75.8 days	81.2 days	94.1 days	66.5 days	poor	poor	poor
Total asset turnover	$\dfrac{\text{sales}}{\text{total assets}}$	.94	.79	.85	.75	OK	OK	OK
Debt								
Degree of indebtedness:								
Debt ratio	$\dfrac{\text{total liabilities}}{\text{total assets}}$	36.8%	44.3%	45.7%	40.0%	OK	OK	OK

Ratio	Formula	Year 1998[a]	Year 1999[b]	Year 2000[b]	Industry average 2000[c]	Evaluation[d] Cross-sectional 2000	Evaluation[d] Time series 1998–2000	Evaluation[d] Overall
Debt (continued)								
Ability to service debts:								
Times interest earned ratio	$\dfrac{\text{earnings before interest and taxes}}{\text{interest}}$	5.6	3.3	4.5	4.3	good	OK	OK
Fixed-payment coverage ratio	$\dfrac{\text{earnings before interest and taxes + lease payments}}{\text{int. + lease pay. + \{(prin. + pref. div.)} \times [1/(1 - T)]\}}$	2.4	1.4	1.9	1.5	good	OK	good
Profitability								
Gross profit margin	$\dfrac{\text{gross profits}}{\text{sales}}$	31.4%	33.3%	32.1%	30.0%	OK	OK	OK
Operating profit margin	$\dfrac{\text{operating profits}}{\text{sales}}$	14.6%	11.8%	13.6%	11.0%	good	OK	good
Net profit margin	$\dfrac{\text{net profits after taxes}}{\text{sales}}$	8.8%	5.8%	7.5%	6.4%	good	OK	good
Return on total assets (ROA)	$\dfrac{\text{net profits after taxes}}{\text{total assets}}$	8.3%	4.5%	6.4%	4.8%	good	OK	good
Return on equity (ROE)	$\dfrac{\text{net profits after taxes}}{\text{stockholders' equity}}$	13.1%	8.1%	11.8%	8.0%	good	OK	good
Earnings per share (EPS)	$\dfrac{\text{earnings available for common stockholders}}{\text{number of shares of common stock outstanding}}$	$3.26	$1.81	$2.90	$2.26	good	OK	good
Price/earnings (P/E) ratio	$\dfrac{\text{market price per share of common stock}}{\text{earnings per share}}$	10.5	10.0	11.1	12.5	OK	OK	OK

[a] Calculated from data not included in the chapter.
[b] Calculated by using the financial statements presented in Tables 4.2 and 4.3.
[c] Obtained from sources not included in this chapter.
[d] Subjective assessments based on data provided.

? Review Questions

4–12 Financial ratio analysis is often divided into four areas: *liquidity, activity, debt,* and *profitability* ratios. Differentiate each of these areas of analysis from the others. Which is of the greatest relative concern to creditors?

4–13 What three areas of analysis are combined in using the *modified DuPont formula*? How are they combined to explain the firm's return on equity (ROE)? How is risk from financial leverage captured in this system?

4–14 Describe how you would approach a complete ratio analysis of the firm by summarizing a large number of ratios.

SUMMARY

 Understand the parties interested in performing financial ratio analysis and the common types of ratio comparisons. Ratio analysis allows present and prospective stockholders and lenders and the firm's management to evaluate the firm's financial performance. It can be performed on a cross-sectional or a time-series basis. Benchmarking is a popular type of cross-sectional analysis.

 Describe some of the cautions that should be considered in performing financial ratio analysis. (1) A single ratio does not generally provide sufficient information. (2) Financial statements being compared should be dated at the same point in time during the year. (3) Audited financial statements should be used. (4) Data should be checked for consistency of accounting treatment. (5) Inflation and different asset ages can distort ratio comparisons.

 Use popular ratios to analyze a firm's liquidity and the activity of inventory, accounts receivable, accounts payable, and total assets. The liquidity, or ability of the firm to pay its bills as they come due, can be measured by net working capital, the current ratio, or the quick (acid-test) ratio. Activity ratios measure the speed with which accounts are converted into sales or cash. Inventory activity can be measured by turnover, accounts receivable by the average collection period, and accounts payable by the average payment period. Total asset turnover measures the efficiency with which the firm uses its assets to generate sales. Formulas for these liquidity and activity ratios are summarized in Table 4.6.

 Discuss the relationship between debt and financial leverage and the ratios that can be used to assess the firm's degree of indebtedness and its ability to meet the payments associated with debt. The more debt a firm uses, the greater its financial leverage, which magnifies both risk and return. Financial debt ratios measure both the degree of indebtedness and the ability to service debts. A common measure of indebtedness is the debt ratio. The ability to pay fixed charges can be measured by times interest earned and fixed-payment coverage ratios. Formulas for these debt ratios are summarized in Table 4.6.

 Evaluate a firm's profitability relative to its sales, asset investment, owners' equity investment, and share value. The common-size income statement, which shows all items as a percentage of sales, can be used to determine gross profit margin, operating profit margin, and net profit margin. Other measures of profitability include return on total assets, return on equity, earnings per share, and the price/earnings ratio. Formulas for these profitability ratios are summarized in Table 4.6.

and Creek's recent financial statements (which follow), evaluate and recommend appropriate action on the loan request.

Income Statement
Creek Enterprises
for the year ended December 31, 2000

Sales revenue		$30,000,000
Less: Cost of goods sold		21,000,000
Gross profits		$ 9,000,000
Less: Operating expenses		
Selling expense	$3,000,000	
General and administrative expenses	1,800,000	
Lease expense	200,000	
Depreciation expense	1,000,000	
Total operating expense		6,000,000
Operating profits		$ 3,000,000
Less: Interest expense		1,000,000
Net profits before taxes		$ 2,000,000
Less: Taxes (rate = 40%)		800,000
Net profits after taxes		$ 1,200,000

Balance Sheet
Creek Enterprises
December 31, 2000

Assets		Liabilities and stockholders' equity	
Current assets		Current liabilities	
Cash	$ 1,000,000	Accounts payable	$ 8,000,000
Marketable securities	3,000,000	Notes payable	8,000,000
Accounts receivable	12,000,000	Accruals	500,000
Inventories	7,500,000	Total current liabilities	$16,500,000
Total current assets	$23,500,000	Long-term debt (includes financial leases)[b]	$20,000,000
Gross fixed assets (at cost)[a]		Stockholders' equity	
Land and buildings	$11,000,000	Preferred stock (25,000 shares,	
Machinery and equipment	20,500,000	$4 dividend)	$ 2,500,000
Furniture and fixtures	8,000,000	Common stock (1 million shares at $5 par)	5,000,000
Gross fixed assets	$39,500,000	Paid-in capital in excess of par value	4,000,000
Less: Accumulated depreciation	13,000,000	Retained earnings	2,000,000
Net fixed assets	$26,500,000	Total stockholders' equity	$13,500,000
Total assets	$50,000,000	Total liabilities and stockholders' equity	$50,000,000

[a]The firm has a 4-year financial lease requiring annual beginning-of-year payments of $200,000. Three years of the lease have yet to run.
[b]Required annual principal payments are $800,000.

Industry averages

Debt ratio	.51
Times interest earned ratio	7.30
Fixed-payment coverage ratio	1.85

INTERMEDIATE   **4–7   Common-size statement analysis**   A common-size income statement for Creek Enterprises' 1999 operations follows. Using the firm's 2000 income statement presented in Problem 4–6, develop the 2000 common-size income statement and compare it to the 1999 statement. Which areas require further analysis and investigation?

Common-size Income Statement
Creek Enterprises
for the year ended December 31, 1999

Sales revenue ($35,000,000)		100.0%
Less: Cost of goods sold		65.9
Gross profits		34.1%
Less: Operating expenses		
Selling expense	12.7%	
General and administrative expenses	6.3	
Lease expense	.6	
Depreciation expense	3.6	
Total operating expense		23.2
Operating profits		10.9%
Less: Interest expense		1.5
Net profits before taxes		9.4%
Less: Taxes (rate = 40%)		3.8
Net profits after taxes		5.6%

  4–8   The relationship between financial leverage and profitability   Pelican Paper, Inc., and Timberland Forest, Inc., are rivals in the manufacture of craft papers. Some financial statement values for each company are listed. Use them in a ratio analysis that compares their financial leverage and profitability.

CHALLENGE

	Pelican Paper, Inc.	Timberland Forest, Inc.
Total assets	$10,000,000	$10,000,000
Total equity	9,000,000	5,000,000
Total debt	1,000,000	5,000,000
Annual interest	100,000	500,000
Total sales	$25,000,000	$25,000,000
EBIT	6,250,000	6,250,000
Net income	3,690,000	3,450,000

a. Calculate the following debt and coverage ratios for the two companies. Discuss their financial risk and ability to cover the costs in relation to each other.
(1) Debt ratio.
(2) Times interest earned.
b. Calculate the following profitability ratios for the two companies. Discuss their profitability relative to each other.
(1) Operating profit margin.
(2) Net profit margin.
(3) Return on assets.
(4) Return on equity.
c. In what way has the larger debt of Timberland Forest made it more profitable than Pelican Paper? What are the risks that Timberland's investors undertake when they choose to purchase its stock instead of Pelican's?

4–9 Ratio proficiency MacDougal Printing, Inc., had sales totaling $40,000,000 in fiscal year 2000. Some ratios for the company are listed. Use this information to determine the dollar values of various income statement and balance sheet accounts as requested.

MacDougal Printing, Inc.	
year ended December 31, 2000	
Sales	$40,000,000
Gross profit margin	80%
Operating profit margin	35%
Net profit margin	8%
Return on total assets	16%
Return on equity	20%
Total asset turnover	2
Average collection period	62.2 days

Calculate values for the following:
a. Gross profits.
b. Cost of goods sold.
c. Operating profits.
d. Operating expenses.
e. Net profit.
f. Total assets.
g. Total equity.
h. Accounts receivable.

4–10 Dupont system of analysis Use the following ratio information for Johnson International and the industry averages for Johnson's line of business to:
a. Construct the DuPont system of analysis for both Johnson and the industry.
b. Evaluate Johnson (and the industry) over the 3-year period.
c. In which areas does Johnson require further analysis? Why?

Johnson	1998	1999	2000
Financial leverage multiplier	1.75	1.75	1.85
Net profit margin	.059	.058	.049
Total asset turnover	2.11	2.18	2.34
Industry averages			
Financial leverage multiplier	1.67	1.69	1.64
Net profit margin	.054	.047	.041
Total asset turnover	2.05	2.13	2.15

INTERMEDIATE

4–11   Cross-sectional ratio analysis   Use the following financial statements for Fox Manufacturing Company for the year ended December 31, 2000, along with the industry average ratios also given in what follows, to:
a. Prepare and interpret a ratio analysis of the firm's 2000 operations.
b. Summarize your findings and make recommendations.

Income Statement
Fox Manufacturing Company
for the year ended December 31, 2000

Sales revenue		$600,000
Less: Cost of goods sold		460,000
Gross profits		$140,000
Less: Operating expenses		
General and administrative expenses	$30,000	
Depreciation expense	30,000	
Total operating expense		60,000
Operating profits		$ 80,000
Less: Interest expense		10,000
Net profits before taxes		$ 70,000
Less: Taxes		27,100
Net profits after taxes (earnings available for common stockholders)		$ 42,900
Earnings per share (EPS)		$ 2.15

INTERMEDIATE   **4–14** Complete ratio analysis, recognizing significant differences   Home Health, Inc., has come to Jane Ross for a yearly financial checkup. As a first step, Jane has prepared a complete set of ratios for fiscal years 1999 and 2000. She will use them to look for significant changes in the company's situation from one year to the next.

Home Health, Inc.		
	1999	**2000**
Net working capital	$55,000	$58,000
Current ratio	3.25	3.00
Quick ratio	2.50	2.20
Inventory turnover	12.80	10.30
Average collection period	42 days	31 days
Total asset turnover	1.40	2.00
Debt ratio	.45	.62
Times interest earned	4.00	3.85
Gross profit margin	68%	65%
Operating profit margin	14%	16%
Net profit margin	8.3%	8.1%
Return on total assets	11.6%	16.2%
Return on equity	21.1%	42.6%

a. In order to focus on the degree of change, calculate the year-to-year proportional change by subtracting the year 2000 ratio from the year 1999 ratio, then dividing the difference by the year 1999 ratio. Multiply the result by 100. Preserve the positive or negative sign. The result is the percentage change in the ratio from 1999 to 2000. Calculate the proportional change for the ratios shown here.

b. For any ratio that shows a year-to-year difference of 10% or more, state whether the difference is in the company's favor or not.

CHALLENGE **c.** For the most significant changes (25% or more), look at the other ratios and name at least one other change that may have contributed to the change in the ratio that you are discussing.

CASE   CHAPTER 4   **Assessing Martin Manufacturing's Current Financial Position**

Terri Spiro, an experienced budget analyst at Martin Manufacturing Company, has been charged with assessing the firm's financial performance during 2000 and its financial position at year-end 2000. To complete this assignment, she gathered the firm's 2000 financial statements, shown on the next page. In addition, Terri obtained the firm's ratio values for 1998 and 1999, along with the 2000 industry average ratios (also applicable to 1998 and 1999). These are presented in the table on page 169.

Income Statement
Martin Manufacturing Company
for the year ended December 31, 2000

Sales revenue		$5,075,000
Less: Cost of goods sold		3,704,000
Gross profits		$1,371,000
Less: Operating expenses		
Selling expense	$650,000	
General and administrative expenses	416,000	
Depreciation expense	152,000	
Total operating expense		1,218,000
Operating profits		$ 153,000
Less: Interest expense		93,000
Net profits before taxes		$ 60,000
Less: Taxes (rate = 40%)		24,000
Net profits after taxes		$ 36,000

Balance Sheets
Martin Manufacturing Company

	December 31	
Assets	**2000**	**1999**
Current assets		
Cash	$ 25,000	$ 24,100
Accounts receivable	805,556	763,900
Inventories	700,625	763,445
Total current assets	$1,531,181	$1,551,445
Gross fixed assets (at cost)	$2,093,819	$1,691,707
Less: Accumulated depreciation	500,000	348,000
Net fixed assets	$1,593,819	$1,343,707
Total assets	$3,125,000	$2,895,152
Liabilities and stockholders' equity		
Current liabilities		
Accounts payable	$ 230,000	$ 400,500
Notes payable	311,000	370,000
Accruals	75,000	100,902
Total current liabilities	$ 616,000	$ 871,402
Long-term debt	$1,165,250	$ 700,000
Total liabilities	$1,781,250	$1,571,402
Stockholders' equity		
Preferred stock	$ 50,000	$ 50,000
Common stock (at par)	100,000	100,000
Paid-in capital in excess of par value	193,750	193,750
Retained earnings	1,000,000	980,000
Total stockholders' equity	$1,343,750	$1,323,750
Total liabilities and stockholders' equity	$3,125,000	$2,895,152

Historical ratios
Martin Manufacturing Company

Ratio	Actual 1998	Actual 1999	Actual 2000	Industry average 2000
Current ratio	1.7	1.8	_____	1.5
Quick ratio	1.0	.9	_____	1.2
Inventory turnover (times)	5.2	5.0	_____	10.2
Average collection period	50 days	55 days	_____	46 days
Total asset turnover (times)	1.5	1.5	_____	2.0
Debt ratio	45.8%	54.3%	_____	24.5%
Times interest earned ratio	2.2	1.9	_____	2.5
Gross profit margin	27.5%	28.0%	_____	26.0%
Net profit margin	1.1%	1.0%	_____	1.2%
Return on total assets (ROA)	1.7%	1.5%	_____	2.4%
Return on equity (ROE)	3.1%	3.3%	_____	3.2%

Required

a. Calculate the firm's 2000 financial ratios, and then fill in the preceding table.
b. Analyze the firm's current financial position from both a cross-sectional and a time-series viewpoint. Break your analysis into an evaluation of the firm's liquidity, activity, debt, and profitability.
c. Summarize the firm's overall financial position based on your findings in **b**.

WEB EXERCISE

GOTO web site www.yahoo.com. On the left side of the Yahoo home page screen, click Business & Economy. On the right side of the next screen, click Y! Finance. Enter the stock symbol LUV in the QUOTES box. Click on Ratio Comparisons.

1. Whose are the three groups of standards to which Southwest Airlines ratios are compared?
2. Which of the financial ratios that were covered in this chapter are given for Southwest Airlines Companies, Inc.?
3. When compared to the industry standards, which two ratios does Southwest Airlines seem to be doing very well? Which two ratios does Southwest Airlines seem to be doing *not* so well?
4. Where does LUV rank in the airline industry in total market capitalization?

Now GOTO web site www.hoovers.com. In the toolbox in the left column, click ticker symbol and enter LUV into the search box; then click GO>>.

5. Who are the top competitors to Southwest Airlines?
6. Who is the CFO of Southwest Airlines?

At the top of the page, click Financials.

7. Which two financial statements are data given for Southwest Airlines?
8. How many years of data are given here?

INTEGRATIVE CASE 1

TRACK SOFTWARE, INC.

Seven years ago, after 15 years in public accounting, Stanley Booker, CPA, resigned his position as Manager of Cost Systems for Davis, Cohen, and O'Brien Public Accountants and started Track Software, Inc. In the 2 years preceding his departure from Davis, Cohen, and O'Brien, Stanley had spent nights and weekends developing a sophisticated cost accounting software program that became Track's initial product offering. As the firm grew, Stanley planned to develop and expand the software product offerings—all of which would be related to streamlining the accounting processes of medium- to large-sized manufacturers.

Although Track experienced losses during its first 2 years of operation—1994 and 1995—its profit has increased steadily from 1996 to the present (2000). The firm's profit history, including dividend payments and contributions to retained earnings, is summarized in Table 1.

Stanley started the firm with a $100,000 investment—his savings of $50,000 as equity and a $50,000 long-term loan from the bank. He had hoped to maintain his initial 100 percent ownership in the corporation, but after experiencing a $50,000 loss during the first year of operation (1994), he sold 60 percent of the stock to a group of investors to obtain needed funds. Since then, no other stock transactions have taken place. Although he owns only 40 percent of the firm, Stanley actively manages all aspects of its activities; the other stockholders are not active in management of the firm.

Stanley has just prepared the firm's 2000 income statement, balance sheet, and statement of retained earnings, shown in Tables 2, 3, and 4 (on pages 171–73), along with the 1999 balance sheet. In addition, he compiled the 1999 ratio values and industry average ratio values, which are applicable to both 1999 and 2000 and summarized in Table 5 (on page 173). He is quite pleased to have achieved record earnings of $48,000 in 2000, but he is concerned about the firm's cash flows.

TABLE 1

	Profit, dividend, and retained earnings, 1994–2000 Track Software, Inc.		
Year	Net profits after taxes (1)	Dividends paid (2)	Contribution to retained earnings [(1)−(2)] (3)
1994	($50,000)	$ 0	($50,000)
1995	(20,000)	0	(20,000)
1996	15,000	0	15,000
1997	35,000	0	35,000
1998	40,000	1,000	39,000
1999	43,000	3,000	40,000
2000	48,000	5,000	43,000

Specifically, he is finding it more and more difficult to pay the firm's bills in a timely manner. To gain insight into these cash flow problems, Stanley is planning to prepare the firm's 2000 statement of cash flows.

Stanley is further frustrated by the firm's inability to afford to hire a software developer to complete development of a cost estimation package that is believed to have "blockbuster" sales potential. Stanley began development of this package 2 years ago, but the firm's growing complexity has forced him to devote more of his time to administrative duties, thereby halting the development of this product. Stanley's reluctance to fill this position stems from his concern that the added $80,000 per year in salary and benefits for the position would certainly lower the firm's earnings per share (EPS) over the next couple of years. Although the project's success is in no way guaranteed, Stanley believes that if the money were spent to hire the software developer, the firm's sales and earnings would significantly rise once the 2- to 3-year development, production, and marketing process was completed.

Another of Stanley's concerns is the firm's rising interest expense. Because the firm relies heavily on short-term borrowing to maintain financial flexibility, recent rises in interest rates have resulted in rapid rises in Track's interest expense. In an attempt to get a feel for interest rates, Stanley researched the rates of interest on loans of varying maturities. These are shown in Table 6 (on page 174).

Table 2

Income Statement ($000) Track Software, Inc. for the year ended December 31, 2000		
Sales revenue		$1,550
Less: Cost of goods sold		1,030
Gross profits		$ 520
Less: Operating expenses		
Selling expense	$150	
General and administrative expense	270	
Depreciation expense	11	
Total operating expense		431
Operating profits		$ 89
Less: Interest expense		29
Net profits before taxes		$ 60
Less: Taxes (20%)		12
Net profits after taxes		$ 48

Table 3

Balance Sheets ($000) Track Software, Inc.		
	December 31	
Assets	**2000**	**1999**
Current assets		
Cash	$ 12	$ 31
Marketable securities	66	82
Accounts receivable	152	104
Inventories	191	145
Total current assets	$421	$362
Gross fixed assets	$195	$180
Less: Accumulated depreciation	63	52
Net fixed assets	$132	$128
Total assets	$553	$490
Liabilities and stockholders' equity		
Current liabilities		
Accounts payable	$136	$126
Notes payable	200	190
Accruals	27	25
Total current liabilities	$363	$341
Long-term debt	$ 38	$ 40
Total liabilities	$401	$381
Stockholders' equity		
Common stock (100,000 shares at		
$.20 par value)	$ 20	$ 20
Paid-in capital in excess of par	30	30
Retained earnings	102	59
Total stockholders' equity	$152	$109
Total liabilities and stockholders' equity	$553	$490

Table 4

Statement of Retained Earnings ($000) Track Software, Inc. for the year ended December 31, 2000	
Retained earnings balance (January 1, 2000)	$ 59
Plus: Net profits after taxes (for 2000)	48
Less: Cash dividends on common stock (paid during 2000)	(5)
Retained earnings balance (December 31, 2000)	$102

Table 5

Ratio	Actual 1999	Industry Average 2000
Net working capital	$21,000	$96,000
Current ratio	1.06	1.82
Quick ratio	.63	1.10
Inventory turnover	10.40	12.45
Average collection period	29.6 days	20.2 days
Total asset turnover	2.66	3.92
Debt ratio	.78	.55
Times interest earned ratio	3.0	5.6
Gross profit margin	32.1%	42.3%
Operating profit margin	5.5%	12.4%
Net profit margin	3.0%	4.0%
Return on total assets	8.0%	15.6%
Return on equity	36.4%	34.7%

With all of these concerns in mind, Stanley set out to review the various data to develop strategies that would help to ensure a bright future for Track Software. As part of this process, Stanley believed that a thorough ratio analysis of the firm's 2000 results would provide important additional insights.

TABLE 6 Interest Rates for Various Loan Maturities

Loan maturity	Interest rate
3 months	12.0%
6 months	11.7
1 year	11.5
3 years	11.0
5 years	10.4
10 years	9.9
20 years	9.5

REQUIRED

a. (1) Upon what financial goal does Stanley seem to be focusing? Is it the correct goal? Why or why not?

(2) Could a potential agency problem exist in this firm? Explain.

b. Calculate the firm's earnings per share (EPS) for each year, recognizing that the number of shares of common stock outstanding has remained *unchanged* since the firm's inception. Comment on the EPS performance in view of your response in **a**.

c. Use the financial data presented to prepare a statement of cash flows for the year ended December 31, 2000. Evaluate the statement in light of Track's current cash flow difficulties.

d. (1) Use the interest rate data provided to draw the current yield curve facing the firm.

(2) Describe the shape of the yield curve drawn in (1).

(3) In view of the yield curve and other facts given in the case, what financing strategy might be advisable for Track?

e. Analyze the firm's financial condition in 2000 as it relates to (1) liquidity, (2) activity, (3) debt, and (4) profitability using the financial statements provided in Tables 2 and 3 and the ratio data included in Table 5. Be sure to *evaluate* the firm on both a cross-sectional and a time-series basis.

f. What recommendation would you give to Stanley regarding hiring a new software developer? Relate your recommendation here to your responses in **a**.

Money Time

Time and money are inextricably related. We regularly pay for time, from parking meters, to video rentals, to overnight package delivery services. One of the principal ideas in finance is the relationship between time and money. Called the *time value of money,* this economic principle recognizes that the passage of time affects the value of money. It advises you that if offered a dollar either today or next

month, you'd be better off to take the dollar today. You'll have the use of the dollar now, which you can put to some productive use for the whole month. (Also, you're more likely to *get* the dollar today; the person making the offer may not actually come through with the payment next month!) This chapter explores the concept and various applications of the time value of money.

two views of time value—future value and present value—and the computational aids used to streamline time value calculations.

Future Versus Present Value

Financial values and decisions can be assessed by using either future value or present value techniques. Although these techniques will result in the same decisions, they view the decision differently. Future value techniques typically measure cash flows at the *end* of a project's life; present value techniques measure

FIGURE 5.1

Time Line
Time line depicting an investment's cash flows

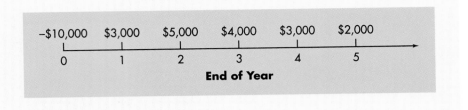

time line
A horizontal line on which time zero appears at the leftmost end and future periods are marked from left to right; can be used to depict investment cash flows.

cash flows at the *start* of a project's life (time zero). *Future value* is cash you will receive at a given future date, and *present value* is just like cash in hand today.

A **time line** can be used to depict the cash flows associated with a given investment. It is a horizontal line on which time zero appears at the leftmost end and future periods are marked from left to right. A time line covering five periods (in this case, years) is given in Figure 5.1. The cash flow occurring at time zero and at the end of each year is shown above the line; the negative values represent *cash outflows* ($10,000 at time zero) and the positive values represent *cash inflows* ($3,000 inflow at the end of year 1, $5,000 inflow at the end of year 2, and so on). Time lines allow the analyst to fully understand the cash flows associated with a given investment.

Because money has a time value, all of the cash flows associated with an investment, such as those in Figure 5.1, must be measured at the same point in time. Typically, that point is either the end or the beginning of the investment's life. The future value technique uses *compounding* to find the future value of each cash flow at the end of the investment's life and then sums those values to find the investment's future value. This approach is depicted above the time line in Figure 5.2, which shows that the future value of each cash flow is measured at the end of the investment's 5-year life. Alternatively, the present value technique

FIGURE 5.2

Compounding and Discounting
Time line showing compounding to find future value and discounting to find present value

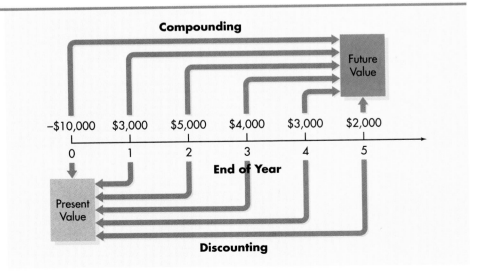

uses *discounting* to find the present value of each cash flow at time zero and then sums these values to find the investment's value today. Application of this approach is depicted below the time line in Figure 5.2.

The meaning and mechanics of both compounding to find future value and discounting to find present value are covered later in this chapter. Although future value and present value result in the same decisions, *financial managers—because they make decisions at time zero—tend to rely primarily on present value techniques.*

Career Key

The time value of money is of great concern to *management*. They plan the firm's cash collections and disbursements so that the firm will get maximum benefit from its money.

Computational Aids

Time-consuming calculations are often involved in finding future and present values. Although you should understand the concepts and mathematics underlying these calculations, the practical application of these important time value techniques can be streamlined. Here we focus on the use of financial tables and hand-held financial calculators as computational aids. Personal computers can also be used to simplify time value calculations.

Financial Tables

Financial tables, easily developed from formulas, include various future and present value interest factors that simplify time value calculations. Although the degree of decimal precision (rounding) varies, the tables are typically indexed by the interest rate (in columns) and the number of periods (in rows). Figure 5.3 shows this general layout. If we wished to find the interest factor at a 20 percent interest rate for 10 years, its value would be found at the intersection of the 20% column and the 10-year row as shown by the dark blue box. A full set of the four basic financial tables is included in Appendix A, at the end of the book. These

FIGURE 5.3

Financial Tables
Layout and use of a financial table

Period	1%	2%	...	10%	...	20%	...	50%
1			...		...	:	...	
2			...		...	:	...	
3			...		...	:	...	
:	:	:	...	:	...	:	...	:
10	...	...	...	...	...	X.XXX	...	...
:	:	:	...	:	...	:	...	:
20			...		...		...	
:	:	:	...	:	...	:	...	:
50			...		...		...	

Interest Rate (column heading spanning, arrow pointing to 20%)

tables are described more fully later in the chapter and are used to demonstrate the application of time value techniques.

Financial Calculators

During the past 15 years, the power of the financial calculator has improved dramatically, and its cost has declined. Today, a powerful financial calculator can be purchased for $20 to $30. Generally, *financial calculators* include numerous preprogrammed, often menu-driven financial routines. This chapter and those that follow show the keystrokes for calculating interest factors and making other financial computations. For convenience, we use the important financial keys, labeled in a fashion consistent with most major financial calculators.

We focus primary attention on the keys pictured and defined in Figure 5.4. We typically use the compute (**CPT**) key and four of the five keys in the second row, with one of the four keys representing the unknown value being calculated. (Occasionally, all five of the keys, with one representing the unknown value, are used.) The keystrokes on some of the more sophisticated calculators are menu-driven, so that after you select the appropriate routine, the calculator prompts you to input each value; on these calculators, a compute key is not needed to obtain a solution. Regardless, any calculator with the basic future and present value functions can be used in lieu of financial tables. The keystrokes of other financial calculators are explained in the reference guides that accompany them.

Hint   Anyone familiar with electronic spreadsheets, such as Lotus, Excel, and Quattro Pro, realizes that most of the time value of money calculations can be done expeditiously by using the special functions contained in the spreadsheet.

Although this text demonstrates the use of both financial tables and financial calculators, you are strongly urged to use a calculator to streamline routine financial calculations *once you understand the basic underlying concepts*. With a little practice, both the speed and accuracy of financial computations using a calculator can be greatly enhanced. Note that because of a calculator's greater precision, slight differences are likely to exist between values calculated by using financial tables and those found with a financial calculator. Remember, conceptual understanding of the material is the objective. An ability to solve problems with the aid of a calculator does not necessarily reflect such an understanding, so don't settle just for answers. Work with the material until you are sure you also understand the concepts.

FIGURE 5.4

Calculator Keys
Important financial keys on the typical financial calculator

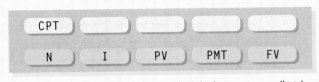

CPT — Compute Key Used to Initiate Financial Calculation Once All Values Are Input
N — Number of Periods
I — Interest Rate per Period
PV — Present Value
PMT — Amount of Payment; Used Only for Annuities
FV — Future Value

? Review Questions

5–1   Why does the timing of cash flows have economic consequences? What is a *time line,* and how does it depict cash flows?

5–2   What is the difference between *future value* and *present value?* Which approach is preferred by financial managers? Why?

5–3   How are financial tables laid out and accessed? Does an ability to solve problems on a financial calculator reflect conceptual understanding?

5.2 Future Value of a Single Amount

Imagine that at age 25 you begin making annual cash deposits of $2,000 into a savings account that pays 5 percent annual interest. At the end of 40 years, at age 65, you would have made deposits totaling $80,000 (40 years × $2,000 per year). Assuming that you have made no withdrawals, what do you think your account balance would be? $100,000? $150,000? $200,000? No, your $80,000 would have grown to $242,000! Why? Because the time value of money allowed the deposits to earn interest, and interest on interest, over the 40 years.

The Concept of Future Value

compound interest
Interest earned on a given deposit that has become part of the principal at the end of a specified period.

principal
The amount of money on which interest is paid.

future value
The value of a present amount at a future date found by applying *compound interest* over a specified period of time.

We speak of **compound interest** to indicate that the amount of interest earned on a given deposit has become part of the principal at the end of a specified period. The term **principal** refers to the amount of money on which the interest is paid. Annual compounding is the most common type.

The **future value** of a present amount is found by applying *compound interest* over a specified period of time. Savings institutions advertise compound interest returns at a rate of x percent or x percent interest compounded annually, semiannually, quarterly, monthly, weekly, daily, or even continuously. The concept of future value with annual compounding can be illustrated by a simple example.

Example ▼   If Fred Moreno places $100 in a savings account paying 8% interest compounded annually, at the end of 1 year he will have $108 in the account—the initial principal of $100 plus 8% ($8) in interest. The future value at the end of the first year is calculated by using Equation 5.1:

$$\text{Future value at end of year 1} = \$100 \times (1 + .08) = \$108 \qquad (5.1)$$

If Fred were to leave this money in the account for another year, he would be paid interest at the rate of 8% on the new principal of $108. At the end of this second year there would be $116.64 in the account—the principal at the beginning of year 2 ($108) plus 8% of the $108 ($8.64) in interest. The future value at the end of the second year is calculated by using Equation 5.2:

$$\text{Future value at end of year 2} = \$108 \times (1 + .08) \qquad (5.2)$$
$$= \$116.64$$

Substituting the expression between the equal signs in Equation 5.1 for the $108 figure in Equation 5.2 gives us Equation 5.3:

$$\text{Future value at end of year 2} = \$100 \times (1 + .08) \times (1 + .08) \qquad (5.3)$$
$$= \$100 \times (1 + .08)^2$$
$$= \$116.64$$

▲ This equation leads to a more general formula for calculating future value.

The Equation for Future Value

The basic relationship in Equation 5.3 can be generalized to find the future value after any number of periods. Let

FV_n = future value at the end of period n
PV = initial principal, or present value
k = annual rate of interest paid. (*Note:* On financial calculators, I is typically used to represent this rate.)
n = number of periods—typically years—the money is left on deposit

By using this notation, a general equation for the future value at the end of period n can be formulated:

$$FV_n = PV \times (1 + k)^n \qquad (5.4)$$

The application of Equation 5.4 can be illustrated by a simple example.

Example ▼ Jane Farber placed $800 in a savings account paying 6% interest compounded annually and wonders how much money will be in the account at the end of 5 years. Substituting $PV = \$800$, $k = .06$, and $n = 5$ into Equation 5.4 gives the amount at the end of year 5:

$$FV_5 = \$800 \times (1 + .06)^5 = \$800 \times (1.338) = \$1,070.40$$

Jane will have $1,070.40 in the account at the end of the fifth year.

Time-Line Use This analysis can be depicted on a time line as shown:

Time line for future value of a single amount ($800 initial principal, earning 6%, at the end of 5 years)

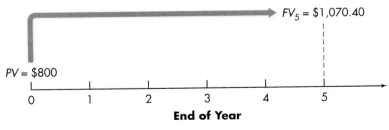

Using Tables and Calculators to Find Future Value

Solving the equation in the preceding example is time-consuming, because one must raise 1.06 to the fifth power. Using a future value interest table or a financial calculator greatly simplifies the calculation, as we will demonstrate in this section. A table that provides values for $(1 + k)^n$ in Equation 5.4 is included near the back of the book, in Appendix Table A–1.[1] The value in each cell of the table is called the **future value interest factor.** This factor is the multiplier used to calculate at a specified interest rate the future value of a present amount as of a given time. The future value interest factor for an initial principal of $1 compounded at k percent for n periods is referred to as $FVIF_{k,n}$:

future value interest factor
The multiplier used to calculate at a specified interest rate the future value of a present amount as of a given time.

$$\text{Future value interest factor} = FVIF_{k,n} = (1 + k)^n \tag{5.5}$$

By finding the intersection of the annual interest rate, k, and the appropriate periods, n, you will find the future value interest factor relevant to a particular problem.[2] By letting $FVIF_{k,n}$ represent the appropriate factor, we can rewrite Equation 5.4 as follows:

$$FV_n = PV \times (FVIF_{k,n}) \tag{5.6}$$

That expression indicates that to find the future value at the end of period n of an initial deposit, we have merely to multiply the initial deposit, PV, by the appropriate future value interest factor.[3]

Example ▼ In the preceding example, Jane Farber placed $800 in her savings account at 6% interest compounded annually and wishes to find out how much will be in the account at the end of 5 years.

Table Use The future value interest factor for an initial principal of $1 on deposit for 5 years at 6% interest compounded annually, $FVIF_{6\%,5yrs}$, found in Table A–1, is 1.338. Multiplying the initial principal of $800 by this factor results in a future value at the end of year 5 of $1,070.40.

Calculator Use[4] The preprogrammed financial functions in the financial calculator can be used to calculate the future value directly.[5] First, punch in $800 and depress **PV**; next, punch in 5 and depress **N**; then, punch in 6 and depress **I** (which is equivalent to "k" in our notation)[6]; finally, to calculate the future

---

1. This table is commonly referred to as a "compound interest table" or a "table of the future value of one dollar." As long as you understand the source of the table values, the various names attached to it should not create confusion; you can always make a trial calculation of a value for one factor, as a check.

2. Although we commonly deal with years rather than periods, financial tables are frequently presented in terms of periods to provide maximum flexibility.

3. Occasionally, you may want to roughly estimate how long a given sum must earn at a given annual rate to double the amount. The *Rule of 72* is used to make this estimate; dividing the annual rate of interest into 72 results in the approximate number of periods it will take to double one's money at the given rate. For example, to double one's money at a 10% annual rate of interest will take about 7.2 years (72 ÷ 10 = 7.2). Looking at Table A–1, we can see that the future value interest factor for 10% and 7 years is slightly below 2 (1.949); this approximation therefore appears to be reasonably accurate.

4. Many calculators allow the user to set the number of payments per year. Most of these calculators are preset for monthly payments—12 payments per year. Because we work primarily with annual payments—one payment per year—it is important to *make sure that your calculator is set for one payment per year*. Although most calculators are preset to recognize that all payments occur at the end of the period, it is also important to *make sure that your calculator is correctly set on the* END *mode*. Consult the reference guide that accompanies your calculator for instructions for setting this value.

5. To avoid including previous data in current calculations, *always clear all registers of your calculator before inputting values and making each computation.*

6. The known values *can be punched into the calculator in any order*; the order specified in this as well as other calculator use demonstrations included in this text results merely from convenience and personal preference.

value, depress **CPT** and then **FV**. The future value of $1,070.58 should appear on the calculator display. On many calculators, this value will be preceded by a minus sign (i.e., −1,070.58). *If a minus sign appears on your calculator, ignore it here, as well as in all other "Calculator Use" illustrations in this text.*[7]

Inputs: 800   5   6

Functions: PV   N   I   CPT   FV

Outputs: 1070.58

Because the calculator is more accurate than the future value of factors, which have been rounded to the nearest .001, a slight difference—in this case, $.18—will frequently exist between the values found by these alternative methods. Clearly, the improved accuracy and ease of calculation tend to favor the use of the calculator. *Note: In future examples of calculator use, we will use only a display similar to that shown above. If you need a reminder of the procedures involved, go back and review the paragraph just before the display.*

A Graphic View of Future Value

Remember that we measure future value at the *end* of the given period. The relationship between various interest rates, the number of periods interest is earned, and the future value of one dollar is illustrated in Figure 5.5. It clearly shows that

FIGURE 5.5

Future Value Relationship
Interest rates, time periods, and future value of one dollar

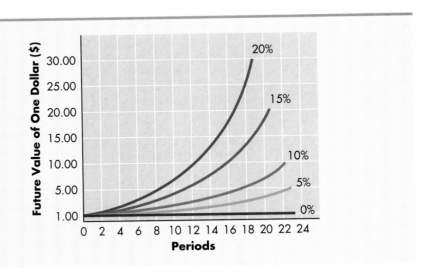

---

7. The calculator differentiates inflows from the outflows by preceding outflows with a negative sign. For example, in the problem just demonstrated, the $800 present value (PV), because it was keyed as a positive number (i.e., 800) is considered an inflow or deposit. Therefore, the calculated future value (FV) of −1070.58 is preceded by a minus sign to show that it is the resulting outflow or withdrawal. Had the $800 present value been keyed in as a negative number (i.e., −800), the future value of $1,070.58 would be displayed as a positive number (i.e., 1070.58). Simply stated, *the cash flows—present value (PV) and future value (FV)—will have opposite signs.*

(1) the higher the interest rate, the higher the future value, and (2) the longer the period of time, the higher the future value. Note that for an interest rate of 0 percent, the future value always equals the present value ($1.00). But for any interest rate greater than zero, the future value is greater than the present value of $1.00.

Compounding More Frequently Than Annually

Interest is often compounded more frequently than once a year. Savings institutions compound interest semiannually, quarterly, monthly, weekly, daily, or even continuously. This section discusses various issues and techniques related to compounding more frequently than annually.

Semiannual Compounding

semiannual compounding
Compounding of interest over two periods within the year.

Semiannual compounding of interest involves two compounding periods within the year. Instead of the stated interest rate being paid once a year, one-half of the stated interest rate is paid twice a year.

Example ▼

Fred Moreno has decided to invest $100 in a savings account paying 8% interest *compounded semiannually.* If he leaves his money in the account for 2 years, he will be paid 4% interest compounded over four periods, each of which is 6 months long. Table 5.1 uses interest factors to show that at the end of 1 year, with 8% semiannual compounding, Fred will have $108.16; at the end of 2 years, he will have $116.99.
▲

Quarterly Compounding

quarterly compounding
Compounding of interest over four periods within the year.

Quarterly compounding of interest involves four compounding periods within the year. One-fourth of the stated interest rate is paid four times a year.

Example ▼

Fred Moreno has found an institution that will pay him 8% interest *compounded quarterly.* If he leaves his money in this account for 2 years, he will be paid 2% interest compounded over eight periods, each of which is 3 months long. Table 5.2 uses interest factors to show the amount Fred will have at the end of 2

TABLE 5.1 The Future Value from Investing $100 at 8% Interest Compounded Semiannually Over 2 Years

Period	Beginning principal (1)	Future value interest factor (2)	Future value at end of period [(1) × (2)] (3)
6 months	$100.00	1.04	$104.00
1 year	104.00	1.04	108.16
18 months	108.16	1.04	112.49
2 years	112.49	1.04	116.99

TABLE 5.2	The Future Value from Investing $100 at 8% Interest Compounded Quarterly Over 2 Years		
Period	Beginning principal (1)	Future value interest factor (2)	Future value at end of period [(1) × (2)] (3)
3 months	$100.00	1.02	$102.00
6 months	102.00	1.02	104.04
9 months	104.04	1.02	106.12
1 year	106.12	1.02	108.24
15 months	108.24	1.02	110.40
18 months	110.40	1.02	112.61
21 months	112.61	1.02	114.86
2 years	114.86	1.02	117.16

▲ years. At the end of 1 year, with 8% quarterly compounding, Fred will have $108.24; at the end of 2 years, he will have $117.16.

Table 5.3 compares values for Fred Moreno's $100 at the end of years 1 and 2 given annual, semiannual, and quarterly compounding at the 8 percent rate. As shown, *the more frequently interest is compounded, the greater the amount of money accumulated.* This is true for any interest rate for any period of time.

A General Equation for Compounding More Frequently Than Annually

It should be clear from the preceding examples that if m equals the number of times per year interest is compounded, Equation 5.4 (our formula for annual compounding) can be rewritten as

Hint If $m = 1$, Equation 5.7 reduces to Equation 5.4. Thus, if interest is compounded annually, Equation 5.7 will provide the same result as Equation 5.4.

$$FV_n = PV \times \left(1 + \frac{k}{m}\right)^{m \times n} \tag{5.7}$$

The general use of Equation 5.7 can be illustrated with a simple example.

TABLE 5.3	The Future Value from Investing $100 at 8% Interest for Years 1 and 2 Given Various Compounding Periods		
	Compounding period		
End of year	Annual	Semiannual	Quarterly
1	$108.00	$108.16	$108.24
2	116.64	116.99	117.16

Example ▼ The preceding examples calculated the amount that Fred Moreno would have at the end of 2 years if he deposited $100 at 8% interest compounded semiannually and quarterly. For semiannual compounding, m would equal 2 in Equation 5.7; for quarterly compounding, m would equal 4. Substituting the appropriate values for semiannual and quarterly compounding into Equation 5.7:

1. *For semiannual compounding:*

$$FV_2 = \$100 \times \left(1 + \frac{.08}{2}\right)^{2 \times 2} = \$100 \times (1 + .04)^4 = \$116.99$$

2. *For quarterly compounding:*

$$FV_2 = \$100 \times \left(1 + \frac{.08}{4}\right)^{4 \times 2} = \$100 \times (1 + .02)^8 = \$117.16$$

▲ These results agree with the values for FV_2 in Tables 5.1 and 5.2.

If the interest were compounded monthly, weekly, or daily, m would equal 12, 52, or 365, respectively.

Using Tables and Calculators

We can use the future value interest factors for one dollar, given in Table A–1, when interest is compounded m times each year. Instead of indexing the table for k percent and n years, as we do when interest is compounded annually, we index it for $(k \div m)$ percent and $(m \times n)$ periods. However, the table is less useful, because it includes only selected rates for a limited number of periods. Instead, a financial calculator or personal computer is typically required.

Example ▼ Fred Moreno wished to find the future value of $100 invested at 8% compounded both semiannually and quarterly for 2 years. The number of compounding periods, m, the interest rate, and number of periods used in each case, along with the future value interest factor, are:

Compounding period	m	Interest rate $(k \div m)$	Periods $(m \times n)$	Future value interest factor from Table A–1
Semiannual	2	8% ÷ 2 = 4%	2 × 2 = 4	1.170
Quarterly	4	8% ÷ 4 = 2%	4 × 2 = 8	1.172

Table Use   Multiplying each of the factors by the initial $100 deposit results in a value of $117.00 (1.170 × $100) for semiannual compounding and a value of $117.20 (1.172 × $100) for quarterly compounding.

Calculator Use If the calculator were used for the semiannual compounding calculation, the number of periods would be 4 and the interest rate would be 4%. The future value of $116.99 should appear on the calculator display.

Inputs:	100	4	4		
Functions:	PV	N	I	CPT	FV
Outputs:					116.99

For the quarterly compounding case, the number of periods would be 8 and the interest rate would be 2%. The future value of $117.17 should appear on the calculator display.

Inputs:	100	8	2		
Functions:	PV	N	I	CPT	FV
Outputs:					117.17

Comparing the calculator and table values, we can see that the calculator values generally agree with those values given in Table 5.3 but are more precise because the table factors have been rounded.

Continuous Compounding

continuous compounding
Compounding of interest an infinite number of times per year at intervals of microseconds.

In the extreme case, interest can be compounded continuously. **Continuous compounding** involves compounding over every microsecond—the smallest time period imaginable. In this case, m in Equation 5.7 would approach infinity, and through the use of calculus, the equation would become:

$$FV_n \text{ (continuous compounding)} = PV \times (e^{k \times n}) \tag{5.8}$$

where e is the exponential function, which has a value of 2.7183.[8] The future value interest factor for continuous compounding is therefore

$$FVIF_{k,n} \text{ (continuous compounding)} = e^{k \times n} \tag{5.9}$$

Example ▼ To find the value at the end of 2 years ($n = 2$) of Fred Moreno's $100 deposit ($PV = \$100$) in an account paying 8% annual interest ($k = .08$), compounded continuously, we can substitute into Equation 5.8:

$$FV_2 \text{ (continuous compounding)} = \$100 \times e^{.08 \times 2} = \$100 \times 2.7183^{.16}$$
$$= \$100 \times 1.1735 = \$117.35$$

Calculator Use To find this value using the calculator, first, find the value of $e^{.16}$ by punching in .16 and then pressing **2nd** and then **e^x** to get 1.1735. Next multi-

---

8. Most calculators have the exponential function, typically noted by e^x, built into them. The use of this key is especially helpful in calculating future value when interest is compounded continuously.

ply this value by $100 to get the future value of $117.35. (*Note:* On some calculators, **2nd** may not have to be pressed before pressing eˣ.)

Inputs:	.16		100

Functions:	2nd	eˣ	X	=

Outputs:	1.1735		117.35

The future value with continuous compounding therefore equals $117.35, which, as expected, is larger than the future value of interest compounded semiannually ($116.99) or quarterly ($117.16). As was noted earlier, $117.35 is the largest amount that would result from compounding the 8% interest more frequently than annually, given an initial deposit of $100 and a 2-year time horizon.

Nominal and Effective Annual Rates of Interest

nominal (stated) annual rate
Contractual annual rate of interest charged by a lender or promised by a borrower.

effective (true) annual rate (EAR)
The annual rate of interest actually paid or earned.

Both consumers and businesses need to make objective comparisons of loan costs or investment returns over different compounding periods. In order to put interest rates on a common basis, to allow comparison, we distinguish between nominal and effective annual rates. The **nominal,** or **stated, annual rate** is the contractual annual rate charged by a lender or promised by a borrower. The **effective,** or **true, annual rate** (**EAR**) is the annual rate of interest actually paid or earned.

The effective annual rate reflects the impact of compounding frequency, whereas the nominal annual rate does not. In terms of interest earnings, the EAR is probably best viewed as the *annual* interest rate that would result in the same future value as that resulting from application of the nominal annual rate using the stated compounding frequency. It increases with increased compounding frequency.

Using the notation introduced earlier, we can calculate the effective annual rate, EAR, by substituting values for the nominal annual rate, k, and the compounding frequency, m, into Equation 5.10.

$$EAR = \left(1 + \frac{k}{m}\right)^{m} - 1 \qquad (5.10)$$

We can apply this equation using data from preceding examples.

Example ▼ Fred Moreno wishes to find the effective annual rate associated with an 8% nominal annual rate ($k = .08$) when interest is compounded (1) annually ($m = 1$); (2) semiannually ($m = 2$); and (3) quarterly ($m = 4$). Substituting these values into Equation 5.10, we get the following:

1. *For annual compounding:*

$$EAR = \left(1 + \frac{.08}{1}\right)^{1} - 1 = (1 + .08)^{1} - 1 = 1 + .08 - 1 = .08 = 8\%$$

2. *For semiannual compounding:*

$$EAR = \left(1 + \frac{.08}{2}\right)^{2} - 1 = (1 + .04)^{2} - 1 = 1.0816 - 1 = .0816 = 8.16\%$$

3. *For quarterly compounding:*

$$EAR = \left(1 + \frac{.08}{4}\right)^4 - 1 = (1 + .02)^4 - 1 = 1.0824 - 1 = .0824 = 8.24\%$$

These values demonstrate two important points: (1) The nominal and effective rates are equivalent for annual compounding, and (2) the effective annual rate increases with increasing compounding frequency.[9]

▲

annual percentage rate (APR)
The *nominal annual rate* of interest, found by multiplying the periodic rate by the number of periods in 1 year, that must be disclosed to consumers on credit cards and on other loans as a result of "truth-in-lending laws."

annual percentage yield (APY)
The *effective annual rate* of interest that must be disclosed to consumers by banks on their savings products as a result of "truth-in-savings laws."

At the consumer level, "truth-in-lending laws" require disclosure on credit cards and loans of the **annual percentage rate** (APR). The APR is the *nominal annual rate* found by multiplying the periodic rate by the number of periods in 1 year. For example, a bank credit card that charges 1½ percent per month would have an APR of 18 percent (1.5% per month × 12 months per year). "Truth-in-savings laws," on the other hand, require banks to quote the **annual percentage yield** (APY). The APY is the *effective annual rate* a savings product pays. For example, a savings account that pays .5 percent per month would have an APY of 6.17 percent $[(1.005)^{12} - 1]$. Quoting loan interest rates at their lower nominal annual rate (the APR) and savings interest rates at the higher effective annual rate (the APY) offers two advantages: It tends to standardize disclosure to consumers, and allows financial institutions to quote the most attractive interest rates—low loan rates and high savings rates.

? Review Questions

5–4   How is the *compounding process* related to the payment of interest on savings? What is the general equation for the future value, FV_n, in period n if PV dollars are deposited in an account paying k percent annual interest?

5–5   What effect would (**a**) a *decrease* in the interest rate or (**b**) an *increase* in the holding period of a deposit have on its future value? Why?

5–6   What effect does compounding interest more frequently than annually have on (**a**) the future value generated by a beginning principal and (**b**) the *effective annual rate (EAR)?* Why?

5–7   What is *continuous compounding?* How does the magnitude of the future value of a given deposit at a given rate of interest obtained by using continuous compounding compare to the value obtained by using annual or any other compounding period?

---

9. The *maximum* effective annual rate for a given nominal annual rate occurs when interest is compounded *continuously*. The effective annual rate for this extreme case can be found by using the following equation:

$$EAR \text{ (continuous compounding)} = e^k - 1 \qquad (5.10a)$$

For the 8% nominal annual rate ($k = .08$), substitution into Equation 5.10a results in an effective annual rate of

$$e^{.08} - 1 = 1.0833 - 1 = .0833 = 8.33\%$$

in the case of continuous compounding. This is the highest effective annual rate attainable with an 8% nominal rate.

5–8   Differentiate between a *nominal annual rate* and an *effective annual rate (EAR)*. Define *annual percentage rate* (APR) and *annual percentage yield* (APY). Under what compounding period are they equivalent?

5.3 Future Value of an Annuity

annuity
A stream of equal annual cash flows. These cash flows can be *inflows* of returns earned on investments or *outflows* of funds invested to earn future returns.

ordinary annuity
An annuity for which the cash flow occurs at the *end* of each period.

annuity due
An annuity for which the cash flow occurs at the *beginning* of each period.

An **annuity** is a stream of equal annual cash flows. These cash flows can be *inflows* of returns earned on investments or *outflows* of funds invested to earn future returns. Before looking at how to calculate the future value of annuities, we should distinguish between the two basic types of annuities.

Types of Annuities

The two basic types of annuities are the *ordinary annuity* and the *annuity due*. For an **ordinary annuity,** the *cash flow occurs at the end of each period*. For an **annuity due,** the *cash flow occurs at the beginning of each period*.

Example ▼

Fran Abrams is choosing which of two annuities to receive. Both are 5-year, $1,000 annuities; annuity A is an ordinary annuity, and annuity B is an annuity due. To better understand the difference between these annuities, she has listed their cash flows in Table 5.4. Note that the amount of each annuity totals $5,000; the two annuities differ in the timing of their cash flows: The cash flows are received sooner with the annuity due than with the ordinary annuity.

▲

Although the cash flows of both annuities in Table 5.4 total $5,000, the annuity due would have a higher future value than the ordinary annuity because

TABLE 5.4	Comparison of Ordinary Annuity and Annuity Due Cash Flows ($1,000, 5 Years)	
	Annual cash flows	
End of year[a]	Annuity A *(ordinary)*	Annuity B *(annuity due)*
0	$ 0	$1,000
1	1,000	1,000
2	1,000	1,000
3	1,000	1,000
4	1,000	1,000
5	1,000	0
Totals	$5,000	$5,000

[a]The ends of years 0, 1, 2, 3, 4, and 5 are equivalent to the beginnings of years 1, 2, 3, 4, 5, and 6, respectively.

Hint   The most common occurrences of annuities in business are fixed loan payments, the interest on corporate bonds, and the dividends paid to preferred stockholders. In all three of these examples, the amount of payment at the end of each time period is the same.

each of its five annual cash flows can earn interest for one year more than each of the ordinary annuity's cash flows. In general, as will be demonstrated later in this chapter, *the future value of an annuity due is always greater than the future value of an otherwise identical ordinary annuity.*

Because ordinary annuities are more frequently used in finance, *unless otherwise specified, the term "annuity" is used throughout this book to refer to ordinary annuities.*

Finding the Future Value of an Ordinary Annuity

The calculations required to find the future value of an ordinary annuity can be illustrated by the following example.

Example ▼   Fran Abrams wishes to determine how much money she will have at the end of 5 years if she deposits $1,000 annually at the *end of each* of the next 5 years into a savings account paying 7% annual interest. (Her cash flows are represented by annuity A—the ordinary annuity—in Table 5.4.) Table 5.5 presents the calculations required to find the future value of this annuity at the end of year 5.

Time-Line Use   This situation is depicted on the following time line:

Time line for future value of an ordinary annuity ($1,000 end-of-year deposit, earning 7%, at the end of 5 years)

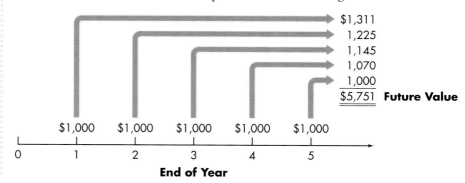

| TABLE 5.5 | The Future Value of a $1,000 5-Year Ordinary Annuity Compounded at 7% |

End of year	Amount deposited (1)	Number of years compounded (2)	Future value interest factors from Table A–1 (3)	Future value at end of year [(1) × (3)] (4)
1	$1,000	4	1.311	$1,311
2	1,000	3	1.225	1,225
3	1,000	2	1.145	1,145
4	1,000	1	1.070	1,070
5	1,000	0	1.000	1,000
			Future value of ordinary annuity at end of year 5	$5,751

As the table and figure show, at the end of year 5, Fran will have $5,751 in her account. Column 2 of the table indicates that because the deposits are made at the end of the year, the first deposit will earn interest for 4 years, the second for 3 years, and so on. The future value interest factors in column 3 correspond to these interest-earning periods and the 7% rate of interest.

Simplifying the Future Value of an Annuity Calculation

Hint   This is true only in the case of an annuity, because only with an annuity are the payments equal.

The calculations in the preceding example can be simplified somewhat, because each of the factors is multiplied by the same dollar amount. The calculations can be expressed as follows:

$$
\begin{aligned}
\text{Future value of annuity at end of year 5} = &[\$1{,}000 \times (1.311)] \\
&+ [\$1{,}000 \times (1.225)] \\
&+ [\$1{,}000 \times (1.145)] \\
&+ [\$1{,}000 \times (1.070)] \\
&+ [\$1{,}000 \times (1.000)] \\
&= \$5{,}751
\end{aligned}
\tag{5.11}
$$

Factoring out the $1,000, we can rewrite Equation 5.11 as:

$$
\begin{aligned}
\text{Future value of annuity at end of year 5} = \$1{,}000 \times (&1.311 + 1.225 \\
&+ 1.145 + 1.070 \\
&+ 1.000) = \$5{,}751
\end{aligned}
\tag{5.12}
$$

Equation 5.12 indicates that to find the future value of the annuity, the annual cash flow must be multiplied by the sum of the appropriate future value interest factors. This equation leads to a more general formula, introduced in what follows.

Using Tables and Calculators to Find Future Value of an Annuity

Annuity calculations can be simplified by using an interest table or a financial calculator. A table for the future value of a $1 *ordinary annuity* is given in Appendix Table A–2. The factors in the table are derived by summing the future value interest factors for the appropriate number of years. In the case of Equation 5.12, summing these factors (the terms in parentheses) results in Equation 5.13:

$$
\begin{aligned}
\text{Future value of annuity at end of year 5} &= \$1{,}000 \times (5.751) \\
&= \$5{,}751
\end{aligned}
\tag{5.13}
$$

future value interest factor for an annuity
The multiplier used to calculate the future value of an *ordinary annuity* at a specified interest rate over a given period of time.

The formula for the **future value interest factor for an annuity** when interest is compounded annually at k percent for n periods, $FVIFA_{k,n}$, is

$$
FVIFA_{k,n} = \sum_{t=1}^{n} (1 + k)^{t-1}
\tag{5.14}
$$

This factor is the multiplier used to calculate the future value of an *ordinary annuity* at a specified interest rate over a given period of time. The formula merely states that the future value interest factor for an n-year ordinary annuity is found by adding the sum of the first $(n - 1)$ future value interest factors to 1.000 (i.e., $FVIFA_{k,n} = 1.000 + \sum_{t=1}^{n-1} FVIF_{k,t}$). This relationship can be easily verified by reviewing the terms in Equation 5.12.[10]

Now that we know how $FVIFA_{k,n}$ is calculated, let's put it to use to find the future value of an annuity. Using FVA_n for the future value of an n-year annuity, PMT for the amount to be deposited annually at the end of each year, and $FVIFA_{k, n}$ for the appropriate *future value interest factor for a one-dollar annuity compounded at* k *percent for* n *years*, the relationship among these variables can be expressed as follows:

$$FVA_n = PMT \times (FVIFA_{k,n}) \tag{5.15}$$

An example will illustrate this calculation for both a table and a financial calculator.

Example ▼ As noted earlier, Fran Abrams wishes to find the future value (FVA_n) at the end of 5 years (n) of an annual *end-of-year deposit* of \$1,000 *(PMT)* into an account paying 7% annual interest (k) during the next 5 years.

Table Use   The appropriate future value interest factor for an ordinary 5-year annuity at 7% $(FVIFA_{7\%,5 \text{ yrs}})$ found in Table A–2, is 5.751. Using Equation 5.15, the \$1,000 deposit × 5.751 results in a future value for the annuity of \$5,751.

Calculator Use   Using the calculator inputs shown, you should find the future value of the ordinary annuity to be \$5,750.74—a slightly more precise answer than that found using the table.

Inputs: 1000   5   7

Functions: PMT   N   I   CPT   FV

▲ **Outputs:**   5750.74

Finding the Future Value of an Annuity Due

The calculations to find the future value of the less common form of an annuity—an annuity due—can be demonstrated by the following example.

Example ▼ Fran Abrams wishes to find out how much money she would have at the end of 5 years if she deposits \$1,000 annually at the *beginning of each* of the next 5 years into a savings account paying 7% annual interest. Her cash flows in this case are

---

10. A mathematical expression that can be applied to calculate the future value interest factor for an ordinary annuity more efficiently is

$$FVIFA_{k,n} = [(1/k) \times ((1 + k)^n - 1)] \tag{5.14a}$$

The use of this expression is especially attractive in the absence of the appropriate financial tables or a financial calculator or personal computer.

TABLE 5.6 **The Future Value of a $1,000 5-Year Annuity Due Compounded at 7%**

End of year[a]	Amount deposited (1)	Number of years compounded (2)	Future value interest factors from Table A–1 (3)	Future value at end of year [(1) × (3)] (4)
0	$1,000	5	1.403	$1,403
1	1,000	4	1.311	1,311
2	1,000	3	1.225	1,225
3	1,000	2	1.145	1,145
4	1,000	1	1.070	1,070
			Future value of annuity due at end of year	$6,154

[a]The ends of years 0, 1, 2, 3, and 4 are equivalent to the beginnings of years 1, 2, 3, 4, and 5, respectively.

represented by annuity B—the annuity due—in Table 5.4. Table 5.6 demonstrates the calculations required.

Time-Line Use This situation is depicted on the following time line:

Time line for future value of an annuity due ($1,000 beginning-of-year deposit, earning 7%, at the end of 5 years)

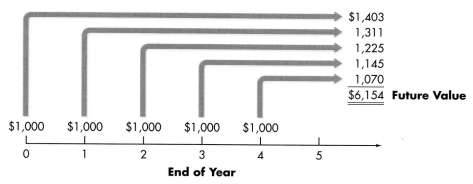

As the table and figure show, at the end of year 5, Fran will have $6,154 in her account. Column 2 of the table indicates that because the deposits are made at the beginning of each year, the first deposit earns interest for 5 years, the second for 4 years, and so on. The future value interest factors in column 3 correspond to those interest-earning periods and the 7% rate of interest.

Using Tables and Calculators to Find Future Value of an Annuity Due

A simple conversion can be applied to use the future value interest factors for an ordinary annuity in Table A–2 with annuities due. Equation 5.16 presents this conversion:

$$FVIFA_{k,n} \text{ (annuity due)} = FVIFA_{k,n} \times (1 + k) \tag{5.16}$$

This equation says that the future value interest factor for an n-year annuity due at k percent can be found merely by multiplying the future value interest factor for an ordinary annuity at k percent for n years by $(1 + k)$. Why is this adjustment necessary? Because each cash flow of an annuity due earns interest for 1 year more than an ordinary annuity (from the start to the end of the year). Multiplying $FVIFA_{k,n}$ by $(1 + k)$ simply adds an additional year's interest to *each* annuity cash flow. An example will demonstrate how to use Equation 5.16 and a financial calculator to find the future value of an annuity due.

Example ▼ As noted, Fran Abrams wishes to find the future value (FVA_n) at the end of 5 years *(n)* of an annual *beginning-of-year deposit* of $1,000 *(PMT)* into an account paying 7% annual interest *(k)* during the next 5 years.

Table Use   Substituting $k = 7\%$ and $n = 5$ years into Equation 5.16, with the aid of the appropriate interest factor from Table A–2, we get:

$$FVIFA_{7\%, 5 \text{ yrs}} \text{ (annuity due)} = FVIFA_{7\%, 5 \text{ yrs}} \times (1 + .07) = 5.751 \times 1.07 = 6.154$$

Then, substituting $PMT = \$1,000$ and $FVIFA_{7\%, 5 \text{ yrs}}$ (annuity due) = 6.154 into Equation 5.15, we get a future value for the annuity due:

$$FVA_5 = \$1,000 \times 6.154 = \$6,154$$

Calculator Use   Before using your calculator to find the future value of an annuity due, depending upon the specific calculator, you must either switch it to BEGIN mode or use the DUE key. Then, using the inputs shown, you should find the future value of the annuity due to be $6,153.29.
   Note: Switch calculator to BEGIN mode.

Inputs:	1000	5	7		
Functions:	PMT	N	I	CPT	FV
Outputs:					6153.29

   Note: Because we almost always assume end of period cash flows, *be sure to switch your calculator back to* END *mode when you have completed your annuity due calculations.*

Comparison with an Ordinary Annuity

As noted earlier, the future value of an annuity due is always greater than the future value of an otherwise identical ordinary annuity. We saw this in comparing the future values at the end of year 5 of Fran Abrams's two annuities:

Ordinary annuity $5,751 (from Table 5.5)
Annuity due $6,154 (from Table 5.6)

Because the annuity due's cash flow occurs at the beginning of the period rather than at the end, its future value is greater. In the example, Fran would earn about $400 more with the annuity due.

In spite of their superior earning power, annuities due are much less frequently encountered. Throughout the remainder of this text we therefore emphasize ordinary annuities. To reiterate, *unless otherwise specified, the term "annuity" refers to ordinary annuities, to which the* FVIFA *factors in Table A–2 directly apply and which financial calculators view as standard.*

? Review Questions

5–9   Differentiate between (a) an *ordinary annuity* and (b) an *annuity due.* Which always has greater future value for otherwise identical annuities and interest rates? Why? Which form is more common?

5–10   Explain how to conveniently determine the future value of an ordinary annuity. How can the future value interest factors for an ordinary annuity be conveniently modified to find the future value of an annuity due?

5.4 Present Value of a Single Amount

present value
The current dollar value of a future amount; the amount of money that would have to be invested today at a given interest rate over a specified period to equal the future amount.

It is often useful to determine the value today of a future amount of money. **Present value** is the current dollar value of a future amount—the amount of money that would have to be invested today at a given interest rate over a specified period to equal the future amount. Present value depends largely on the investment opportunities of the recipient and the point in time at which the amount is to be received. This section explores the present value of a single amount.

The Concept of Present Value

discounting cash flows
The process of finding present values; the inverse of compounding interest.

The process of finding present values is often referred to as **discounting cash flows.** It is concerned with answering the question: "If I can earn k percent on my money, what is the most I would be willing to pay now for an opportunity to receive FV_n dollars n periods from today?" This process is actually the inverse of compounding interest. Instead of finding the future value of present dollars invested at a given rate discounting determines the present value of a future amount, assuming the opportunity to earn a certain return, k, on the money. This annual rate of return is variously referred to as the *discount rate, required return, cost of capital,* or *opportunity cost.*[11] These terms will be used interchangeably in this text.

Career Key

Present value is an area of particular interest to the *marketing* department, which will need to justify funding for new programs and products by using *PV* techniques. *Accounting* personnel will also frequently use such techniques in calculating loan amortization schedules and bond discount and premium values.

Example ▼ Paul Shorter has an opportunity to receive $300 one year from now. If he can earn 6% on his investments in the normal course of events, what is the most he

---

11. The theoretical underpinning of this "required return" is introduced in Chapter 6 and further refined in subsequent chapters.

should pay now for this opportunity? To answer this question, he must determine how many dollars would have to be invested at 6% today to have $300 one year from now. By letting PV equal this unknown amount and using the same notation as in the future value discussion:

$$PV \times (1 + .06) = \$300 \tag{5.17}$$

Solving Equation 5.17 for PV gives us Equation 5.18:

$$PV = \frac{\$300}{(1 + .06)} \tag{5.18}$$
$$= \$283.02$$

The "present value" of $300 received one year from today, given an opportunity cost of 6%, is $283.02. That is, investment of $283.02 today at the 6% opportunity cost would result in $300 at the end of one year.

The Equation for Present Value

The present value of a future amount can be found mathematically by solving Equation 5.4 for PV. In other words, the present value, PV, of some future amount, FV_n, to be received n periods from now, assuming an opportunity cost of k, is calculated as:

$$PV = \frac{FV_n}{(1 + k)^n} = FV_n \times \left[\frac{1}{(1 + k)^n} \right] \tag{5.19}$$

Note the similarity between this general equation for present value and the equation in the preceding example (Equation 5.18). The use of this equation can be illustrated by a simple example.

Example ▼ Pam Valenti wishes to find the present value of $1,700 that will be received 8 years from now. Pam's opportunity cost is 8%. Substituting $FV_8 = \$1,700$, $n = 8$, and $k = .08$ into Equation 5.19 yields:

$$PV = \frac{\$1,700}{(1 + .08)^8} = \frac{\$1,700}{1.851} = \$918.42 \tag{5.20}$$

Time-Line Use   This analysis can be depicted on the following time line:

Time line for present value of a single amount ($1,700 future amount, discounted at 8%, from the end of 8 years)

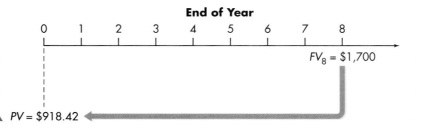

Using Tables and Calculators to Find Present Value

present value interest factor
The multiplier used to calculate at a specified discount rate the present value of an amount to be received in a future period.

The present value calculation can be simplified by using a **present value interest factor.** This factor is the multiplier used to calculate at a specified discount rate the present value of an amount to be received in a future period. The present value interest factor for the present value of $1 discounted at k percent for n periods is referred to as $PVIF_{k,n}$:

$$\text{Present value interest factor} = PVIF_{k,n} = \frac{1}{(1 + k)^n} \qquad (5.21)$$

Appendix Table A–3 presents present value interest factors for $1. By letting $PVIF_{k,n}$ represent the appropriate factor, we can rewrite Equation 5.19:

$$PV = FV_n \times (PVIF_{k,n}) \qquad (5.22)$$

This expression indicates that to find the present value of an amount to be received in a future period, n, we have merely to multiply the future amount, FV_n, by the appropriate present value interest factor.

Example ▼ As noted, Pam Valenti wishes to find the present value of $1,700 to be received 8 years from now, assuming an 8% opportunity cost.

Table Use   The present value interest factor for 8% and 8 years, $PVIF_{8\%,8\text{ yrs}}$, found in Table A–3, is .540. Multiplying the $1,700 future value by this factor results in a present value of $918.

Calculator Use   Using the calculator's financial functions and the inputs shown below, you should find the present value to be $918.46.

Inputs:	1700	8	8		
Functions:	FV	N	I	CPT	PV
Outputs:				918.46	

The value obtained with the calculator—$918.46—is more accurate than the values found using the equation or the table, although for purposes of this text, these differences are insignificant. ▲

A Graphic View of Present Value

Remember that present value calculations assume that the future values are measured at the *end* of the given period. The relationship among various discount rates, time periods, and the present value of one dollar is illustrated in Figure 5.6. Everything else being equal, the figure clearly shows that: (1) the higher the discount rate, the lower the present value, and (2) the longer the period of time, the

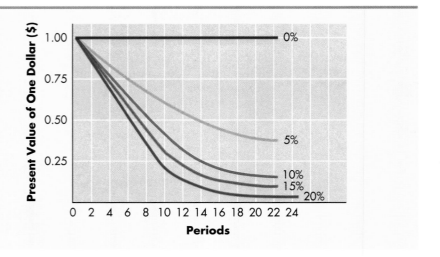

FIGURE 5.6

Present Value Relationship

Discount rates, time periods, and present value of one dollar

lower the present value. Also note that given a discount rate of 0 percent, the present value always equals the future value ($1.00). But for any discount rate greater than zero, the present value is less than the future value of $1.00.

Comparing Present Value and Future Value

We will close this section with a couple of important observations about present values. One is that the expression for the present value interest factor for k percent and n periods, $1/(1 + k)^n$, is the inverse of the future value interest factor for k percent and n periods, $(1 + k)^n$. This fact can be confirmed by dividing a present value interest factor for k percent and n periods, $PVIF_{k,n}$, into 1.0 and comparing the resulting value to the future value interest factor given in Table A–1 for k percent and n periods, $FVIF_{k,n}$. The two values should be equivalent.

Second, because of the relationship between present value interest factors and future value interest factors, we can find the present value interest factors given a table of future value interest factors, and vice versa. For example, the future value interest factor from Table A–1 for 10 percent and five periods is 1.611. Dividing this value into 1.0 yields .621, which is the present value interest factor given in Table A–3 for 10 percent and five periods.

? Review Questions

5–11 What is meant by "the present value of a future amount"? What is the equation for the present value, PV, of a future amount, FV_n, to be received in period n, assuming that the firm requires a minimum return of k percent? How are present value and future value calculations related?

5–12 What effect does *increasing* (**a**) the required return and (**b**) the time period have on the present value of a future amount? Why?

**It All Starts with
Time Value**

*How much will an investment earn over its life? What's the monthly payment
on a loan to buy equipment, and will this machinery result in sufficient cost
savings to warrant the investment? How does the compound growth rate of
our company's earnings per share compare to those of competitors? Time
value of money calculations make it possible to answer questions like these.*

*Financial managers are using traditional time value techniques in new
ways. Lexus and credit card issuer MBNA determine the value of a new customer or an existing one by calculating the present value of profits generated
by customers in the future. With this information, companies can decide
whether to spend to acquire new customers or increase repeat purchases and
to target groups that warrant larger investments. Research shows that increasing customer retention by 5 percent raised the value of the average customer
by 25 to 95 percent, depending on the industry.*

*CFOs also apply similar techniques to value company brands. Interbrand
Corp., a pioneer in brand valuation, applies present value to forecasts of brand
earnings, choosing the present value rate based on the brand's strength. Once
the primary responsibility of marketing managers, brand management is now
coming to the attention of many CFOs. "A CFO is the company's ultimate risk
manager.... A misdefined or misdirected brand is a tremendous risk, and,
therefore, must be analyzed, quantified, and managed," says Bob Hiebeler,
managing director of Arthur Anderson Knowledge Space. Valuing a brand
helps the company make better resource allocation decisions. Wall Street analysts also want to know how companies value their brands. They look at brand
strategy as an indication of how a company positions itself for the future. In
fact, a Corporate Branding Partnership survey revealed that companies with
strong brands are better able to ride out today's volatile stock markets.*

  ## 5.5 Present Value of Cash Flow Streams

mixed stream
A stream of cash flows that reflects no
particular pattern.

Quite often in finance there is a need to find the present value of a *stream* of cash
flows to be received in various future periods. Two basic types of cash flow
streams are possible: the mixed stream and the annuity. A **mixed stream** of cash
flows reflects no particular pattern; an *annuity*, as stated earlier, is a pattern of
equal annual cash flows. Because certain shortcuts are possible in finding the
present value of an annuity, we will discuss mixed streams and annuities separately. In addition, the present value of mixed streams with embedded annuities
and perpetuities are considered in this section.

Present Value of a Mixed Stream

To find the present value of a mixed stream of cash flows, we determine the present value of each future amount, as described in the preceding section, and then
add together all the individual present values.

Example ▼ Frey Company, a shoe manufacturer, has been offered an opportunity to receive the following mixed stream of cash flows over the next 5 years:

Year	Cash flow
1	$400
2	800
3	500
4	400
5	300

If the firm must earn at least 9% on its investments, what is the most it should pay for this opportunity?

Table Use   To solve this problem, determine the present value of each cash flow discounted at 9% for the appropriate number of years. The sum of these individual values is the present value of the total stream. The present value interest factors required are those shown in Table A–3. Table 5.7 presents the calculations needed to find the present value of the cash flow stream, which turns out to be $1,904.60.

Calculator Use   You can use a calculator to find the present value of each individual cash flow, as demonstrated earlier; then add the present values, to get the present value of the stream. However, most financial calculators have a function that allows you to punch in *all cash flows*, specify the discount rate, and then directly calculate the present value of the entire cash flow stream. Because calculators provide more precise solutions than those based on rounded table factors,

---

TABLE 5.7   The Present Value of a Mixed Stream of Cash Flows

Year (n)	Cash flow (1)	$PVIF_{9\%,n}$[a] (2)	Present value $[(1) \times (2)]$ (3)
1	$400	.917	$ 366.80
2	800	.842	673.60
3	500	.772	386.00
4	400	.708	283.20
5	300	.650	195.00
		Present value of mixed stream	$1,904.60

[a]Present value interest factors at 9% are from Table A–3.

the present value of Frey Company's cash flow stream found using a calculator will be close, but not precisely equal, to the $1,904.60 value calculated before.

Paying $1,904.60 would provide exactly a 9% return. Frey should not pay more than that amount for the opportunity to receive these cash flows.

Time-Line Use This situation is depicted on the following time line:

Time line for present value of a mixed stream (end-of-year cash flows, discounted at 9%, over the corresponding number of years)

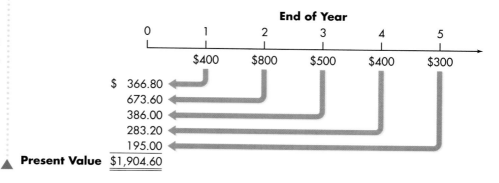

Present Value of an Annuity[12]

The method for finding the present value of an annuity is similar to that used for a mixed stream, but can be simplified somewhat.

E x a m p l e ▼ Braden Company, a small producer of plastic toys, wants to determine the most it should pay to purchase a particular annuity. The firm requires a minimum return of 8% on all investments, and the annuity consists of cash flows of $700 per year for 5 years. Table 5.8 shows the long method for finding the present value of the annuity—which is the same as the method used for the mixed stream. This procedure yields a present value of $2,795.10.

Time-Line Use Similarly, this situation is depicted on the following time line:

Time line for present value of an annuity ($700 end-of-year cash flows, discounted at 8%, over 5 years)

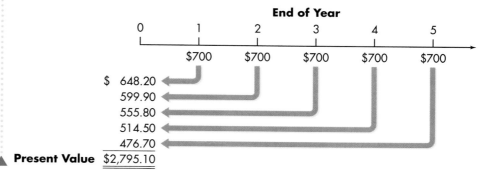

---

12. Consistent with the discussions of future value, our concern here is only with *ordinary annuities*—those with cash flows occurring at the *end* of each period.

TABLE 5.8	The Long Method for Finding the Present Value of an Annuity

Year (n)	Cash flow (1)	$PVIF_{8\%,n}{}^{a}$ (2)	Present value [(1) × (2)] (3)
1	$700	.926	$ 648.20
2	700	.857	599.90
3	700	.794	555.80
4	700	.735	514.50
5	700	.681	476.70
		Present value of annuity	$2,795.10

^{a}Present value interest factors at 8% are from Table A–3.

Simplifying the Present Value of an Annuity Calculation

The calculations in the preceding example can be simplified by recognizing that each of the five present value interest factors was multiplied by the same annual amount ($700). This calculation can be expressed as follows:

$$\text{Present value of annuity} = [\$700 \times (.926)] + [\$700 \times (.857)] \qquad (5.23)$$
$$+ [\$700 \times (.794)] + [\$700 \times (.735)]$$
$$+ [\$700 \times (.681)] = \$2,795.10$$

Hint The simplification in the present value of an annuity calculation here is similar to that made in Equation 5.11 for the future value of an annuity.

Simplifying Equation 5.23 by factoring out the $700 yields Equation 5.24:

$$\text{Present value of annuity} = \$700 \times (.926 + .857 + .794 + .735 + .681) \qquad (5.24)$$
$$= \$2,795.10$$

Thus, the present value of an annuity can be found by multiplying the annual cash flow by the sum of the appropriate present value interest factors. This equation leads to a more general formula, introduced in what follows.

Using Tables and Calculators to Find Present Value of an Annuity

Annuity calculations can be simplified by using an interest table for the present value of an annuity or a financial calculator. The values for the present value of a $1 annuity are given in Appendix Table A–4. The factors in the table are derived by summing the present value interest factors for the appropriate number of years. In the case of Equation 5.24, summing these factors results in Equation 5.25:

$$\text{Present value of annuity} = \$700 \times (3.993) = \$2,795.10 \qquad (5.25)$$

The interest factors in Table A–4 actually represent the sum of the first n present value interest factors in Table A–3 for a given discount rate. The formula

present value interest factor for an annuity
The multiplier used to calculate the present value of an annuity at a specified discount rate over a given period of time.

for the **present value interest factor for an annuity** with end-of-year cash flows that are discounted at k percent for n periods, $PVIFA_{k,n}$, is:[13]

$$PVIFA_{k,n} = \sum_{t=1}^{n} \frac{1}{(1 + k)^{t}}$$ (5.26)

This factor is the multiplier used to calculate the present value of an annuity at a specified discount rate over a given period of time. The formula merely states that the present value interest factor for an n-year annuity is found by summing the first n present value interest factors at the given rate (i.e., $PVIFA_{k,n} = \Sigma_{t=1}^{n} PVIF_{k,t}$). This relationship can be verified by reviewing the terms in Equation 5.24.[14]

By letting PVA_n equal the present value of an n-year annuity, PMT equal the amount to be received annually at the end of each year, and $PVIFA_{k,n}$ represent the appropriate value for the *present value interest factor for a one-dollar annuity discounted at* k *percent for* n *years*, the relationship among these variables can be expressed as follows:

$$PVA_n = PMT \times (PVIFA_{k,n})$$ (5.27)

An example will illustrate this calculation for both a table and a financial calculator.

Example ▼ Braden Company, as noted, wants to find the present value of a 5-year annuity of $700 assuming an 8% opportunity cost.

Table Use The present value interest factor for an annuity at 8% for 5 years ($PVIFA_{8\%,5yrs}$) found in Table A–4, is 3.993. Using Equation 5.27, $700 $\times$ 3.993 results in a present value of $2,795.10.

Calculator Use Using the calculator's financial functions and the inputs shown below, you should find the present value of the annuity to be $2,794.90.

Inputs: 700   5   8

Functions: PMT   N   I   CPT   PV

Outputs: 2794.90

---

13. The formula for the present value interest factor for an *annuity due* is $\sum_{t=1}^{n} 1/(1 + k)^{t-1}$, because in this case, all cash flows occur at the beginning of each period. The factor therefore merely represents 1.0 plus the sum of the first $(n - 1)$ present value interest factors. The present value interest factor for an annuity due can be found by multiplying the present value interest factor for an ordinary annuity, $PVIFA_{k,n}$, by $(1 + k)$.

14. A mathematical expression that can be applied to calculate the present value interest factor for an ordinary annuity more efficiently is

$$PVIFA_{k,n} = \frac{1}{k} \times \left[1 - \frac{1}{(1 + k)^{n}} \right]$$ (5.26a)

The use of this expression is especially attractive in the absence of the appropriate financial tables or a financial calculator or personal computer.

The value obtained with the calculator—$2,794.90—is more accurate than those found using the equation or the table, although for purposes of this text these differences are insignificant.

Present Value of a Mixed Stream with an Embedded Annuity

Occasionally, a mixed stream of cash flows will have an annuity embedded within it. In such a case, the computations can be streamlined by the following three-step procedure:

Step 1   Find the present value of the annuity at the specified discount rate using the regular procedure. (*Note:* The resulting present value is measured at the beginning of the annuity, which is equivalent to the end of the period immediately preceding the start of the annuity.)

Step 2   Add the present value calculated in Step 1 to any other cash flow occurring in the period just before the start of that annuity, and eliminate the individual annuity cash flows, to determine the revised cash flows.

Step 3   Discount the revised cash flows found in Step 2 back to time zero in the normal fashion at the specified discount rate.

An example will illustrate this three-step procedure.

Example ▼ Powell Products expects an investment to generate the cash flows shown in column 1 of Table 5.9. If the firm must earn 9% on its investments, what is the present value of the expected cash flow stream?

TABLE 5.9   The Present Value of a Mixed Stream with an Embedded Annuity

		Step 1	Step 2		Step 3
Year (n)	Cash flow (1)	Present value of annuity (2)	Revised cash flow [(1) + (2)] (3)	$PVIF_{9\%,n}$ (4)	Present value [(3) × (4)] (5)
1	$5,000		$ 5,000	.917	$ 4,585.00
2	6,000	22,680	28,680	.842	24,148.56
3	7,000	↑	0	.772	0
4	7,000	$PVIFA_{9\%,4yrs}$	0	.708	0
5	7,000	× 3.240	0	.650	0
6	7,000		0	.596	0
7	8,000		8,000	.547	4,376.00
8	9,000		9,000	.502	4,518.00
			Present value of mixed stream		$37,627.56

Table Use The three-step procedure is applied to Powell's cash flows in Table 5.9, because it has a 4-year $7,000 annuity embedded in its cash flows.

Step 1 As noted in column 2 of Table 5.9, the present value of the embedded $7,000 annuity is calculated by multiplying the $7,000 by the present value of an annuity interest factor at 9% for 4 years ($PVIFA_{9\%,4yrs.}$). Its present value at the end of year 2 (i.e., the beginning of year 3) is $22,680.

Step 2 The end-of-year-2 value of the annuity, from Step 1, is added to the end-of-year-2 cash flow of $6,000 to determine the revised cash flow noted in column 3 of Table 5.9. This results in total cash flow of $28,680 in year 2 and the elimination of the annuity cash flow for years 3 through 6.

Step 3 Multiplying the revised cash flows in column 3 of Table 5.9 by the appropriate present value interest factors at 9% in column 4 results in the present values shown in column 5 of the table. The present value of this mixed stream, found by summing column 5, is $37,627.56.

The present value calculation has been simplified by first finding the present value of the embedded $7,000 annuity.

Calculator Use A similar procedure to that just demonstrated would be applied in using a calculator. The resulting answer would be $37,617.96, which is close to, but more precise than, the value calculated in Table 5.9.[15]

Time-Line Use The computation used in this situation is presented on the following time line:

Time line for present value of a mixed stream with an embedded annuity (end-of-year cash flows, discounted at 9%, over the corresponding number of years)

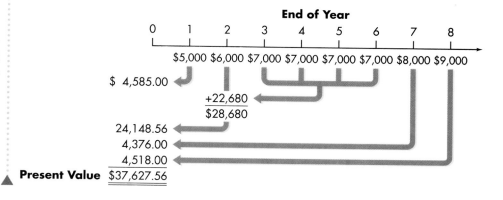

---

15. Most financial calculators have a frequency function that allows easy input of cash flow streams that have annuities embedded in them. The use of this feature, if it is available, is explained in the calculator's reference guide.

Present Value of a Perpetuity

perpetuity
An annuity with an infinite life, providing continual annual cash flow.

A **perpetuity** is an annuity with an infinite life—in other words, an annuity that never stops providing its holder with a cash flow at the end of each year. It is sometimes necessary to find the present value of a perpetuity. The present value interest factor for a perpetuity discounted at the rate k is

$$PVIFA_{k,\infty} = \frac{1}{k} \qquad (5.28)$$

As the equation shows, the appropriate factor, $PVIFA_{k,\infty}$, is found merely by dividing the discount rate, k (stated as a decimal), into 1. The validity of this method can be seen by looking at the factors in Table A–4 for 8, 10, 20, and 40 percent: As the number of periods (typically years) approaches 50, the values of these factors approach 12.500 (1 ÷ .08), 10.000 (1 ÷ .10), 5.000 (1 ÷ .20), and 2.500 (1 ÷ .40), respectively.

Example ▼ Ross Clark wishes to determine the present value of a $1,000 perpetuity discounted at 10%. The appropriate present value interest factor can be found by dividing 1 by .10, as noted in Equation 5.28. Substituting the resulting factor, 10, and the amount of the perpetuity, PMT = $1,000, into Equation 5.27 results in a present value of $10,000 for the perpetuity. In other words, the receipt of $1,000 every year for an indefinite period is worth only $10,000 today if Ross can earn 10% on his investments. If he had $10,000 and earned 10% interest on it each year, $1,000 a year could be withdrawn indefinitely without touching the ▲ initial $10,000, which would never be drawn upon.

? Review Questions

5–13   How is the present value of a mixed stream of cash flows calculated? How can the calculations required to find the present value of an annuity be simplified? How can the calculation of the present value of a mixed stream with an embedded annuity be streamlined?

5–14   What is a *perpetuity?* How might the present value interest factor for such a stream of cash flows be determined?

5.6 Special Applications of Time Value

Future value and present value techniques have a number of important applications. We'll study three of them in this section: (1) the calculation of the deposits needed to accumulate a future sum, (2) the calculation of amortization on loans, and (3) the determination of interest or growth rates.

Deposits to Accumulate a Future Sum

Suppose you want to buy a house 5 years from now and estimate that an initial down payment of $20,000 will be required at that time. You wish to make equal annual end-of-year deposits in an account paying annual interest of 6 percent, so you must determine what size annuity will result in a lump sum equal to $20,000 at the end of year 5. The solution to this problem is closely related to the process of finding the future value of an annuity.

Earlier in the chapter, we found the future value of an n-year annuity, FVA_n, by multiplying the annual deposit, PMT, by the appropriate interest factor, $FVIFA_{k,n}$. The relationship of the three variables has been defined by Equation 5.15, which is rewritten here as Equation 5.29:

$$FVA_n = PMT \times (FVIFA_{k,n}) \tag{5.29}$$

We can find the annual deposit required to accumulate FVA_n dollars, given a specified interest rate, k, and a certain number of years, n, by solving Equation 5.29 for PMT. Isolating PMT on the left side of the equation gives us

$$PMT = \frac{FVA_n}{FVIFA_{k,n}} \tag{5.30}$$

Once this is done, we have only to substitute the known values of FVA_n and $FVIFA_{k,n}$ into the right side of the equation to find the annual deposit required.

Example ▼ As just stated, you want to determine the equal annual end-of-year deposits required to accumulate $20,000 at the end of 5 years given an interest rate of 6%.

Table Use   Table A–2 indicates that the future value interest factor for an annuity at 6% for 5 years ($FVIFA_{6\%,5yrs}$) is 5.637. Substituting $FVA_5 = \$20,000$ and $FVIFA_{6\%,5yrs} = 5.637$ into Equation 5.30 yields an annual required deposit, PMT, of $3,547.99. Thus, if that amount is deposited at the end of each year for 5 years, at 6% interest, there will be $20,000 in the account at the end of the 5 years.

Calculator Use   Using the calculator inputs shown, you should find the annual deposit amount to be $3,547.93. Note that this value, except for a slight rounding difference, agrees with the value found by using Table A–2.

Inputs: 20000   5   6

Functions: FV   N   I   CPT   PMT

Outputs: 3547.93

Loan Amortization

loan amortization
The determination of the equal annual loan payments necessary to provide a lender with a specified interest return and to repay the loan principal over a specified period.

The term **loan amortization** refers to the determination of the equal annual loan payments necessary to provide a lender with a specified interest return and repay the loan principal over a specified period. The loan amortization process involves finding the future payments (over the term of the loan) whose present value at the loan interest rate equals the amount of initial principal borrowed. Lenders

loan amortization schedule
A schedule of equal payments to repay a loan. It shows the allocation of each loan payment to interest and principal.

use a **loan amortization schedule** to determine these payment amounts and the allocation of each payment to interest and principal. In the case of home mortgages, these tables are used to find the equal *monthly* payments necessary to *amortize*, or pay off, the mortgage at a specified interest rate over a 15- to 30-year period.

Amortizing a loan actually involves creating an annuity out of a present amount. For example, say you borrow $6,000 at 10 percent and agree to make equal annual end-of-year payments over 4 years. To find the size of the payments, the lender determines the amount of a 4-year annuity discounted at 10 percent that has a present value of $6,000. This process is actually the inverse of finding the present value of an annuity.

Earlier in this chapter, we found the present value, PVA_n, of an n-year annuity by multiplying the annual amount, PMT, by the present value interest factor for an annuity, $PVIFA_{k,n}$. This relationship, which was originally expressed as Equation 5.27, is rewritten here as Equation 5.31:

$$PVA_n = PMT \times (PVIFA_{k,n}) \tag{5.31}$$

To find the equal annual payment required to amortize the loan, PVA_n, over a certain number of years at a specified interest rate, we need to solve Equation 5.31 for PMT. Isolating PMT on the left side of the equation gives

$$PMT = \frac{PVA_n}{PVIFA_{k,n}} \tag{5.32}$$

Once this is done, we have only to substitute the known values into the right side of the equation to find the annual payment required.

E x a m p l e ▼ As just stated, you want to determine the equal annual end-of-year payments necessary to amortize fully a $6,000, 10% loan over 4 years.

Table Use   Table A–4 indicates that the present value interest factor for an annuity corresponding to 10% and 4 years ($PVIFA_{10\%,4yrs}$) is 3.170. Substituting $PVA_4 = \$6,000$ and $PVIFA_{10\%,4yrs} = 3.170$ into Equation 5.32 and solving for PMT yields an annual loan payment of $1,892.74. Thus, to repay the interest and principal on a $6,000, 10%, 4-year loan, equal annual end-of-year payments of $1,892.74 are necessary.

Calculator Use   Using the calculator inputs shown, you should find the annual payment amount to be $1,892.82. Except for a slight rounding difference, this value agrees with the one found using Table A–4.

Inputs: 6000   4   10

Functions: PV   N   I   CPT   PMT

Outputs: 1892.82

The allocation of each loan payment to interest and principal can be seen in columns 3 and 4 of the *loan amortization schedule* in Table 5.10. The portion of

TABLE 5.10 Loan Amortization Schedule ($6,000 Principal, 10% Interest, 4-Year Repayment Period)

End of year	Loan payment (1)	Beginning-of-year principal (2)	Payments		End-of-year principal [(2) − (4)] (5)
			Interest [.10 × (2)] (3)	Principal [(1) − (3)] (4)	
1	$1,892.74	$6,000.00	$600.00	$1,292.74	$4,707.26
2	1,892.74	4,707.26	470.73	1,422.01	3,285.25
3	1,892.74	3,285.25	328.53	1,564.21	1,721.04
4	1,892.74	1,721.04	172.10	1,720.64	—[a]

[a]Due to rounding, a slight difference ($.40) exists between the beginning-of-year-4 principal (in column 2) and the year-4 principal payment (in column 4).

each payment representing interest (column 3) declines over the repayment period, and the portion going to principal repayment (column 4) increases. This pattern is typical of amortized loans; with level payments, as the principal is reduced, the interest component declines, leaving a larger portion of each subsequent payment to repay principal.

Interest or Growth Rates

It is often necessary to calculate the compound annual interest or *growth rate* (i.e., annual rate of change in values) of a series of cash flows. In doing this, either future value or present value interest factors can be used. The approach using present value interest factors is described in this section. The simplest situation is one in which a person wishes to find the rate of interest or growth in a *series of cash flows.*[16]

Example ▼ Ray Noble wishes to find the rate of interest or growth of the following series of cash flows:

Year	Cash flow	
2000	$1,520	4
1999	1,440	3
1998	1,370	2
1997	1,300	1
1996	1,250	

16. Because the calculations required for finding interest rates and growth rates, given certain cash flows, are the same, this section refers to the calculations as those required to find interest *or* growth rates.

In Practice

Personal Finance

Time Is on Your Side

For many years, the 30-year, fixed-rate mortgage has been the traditional choice of homebuyers. Recently, fixed-rate mortgages with a 15-year term have gained in popularity. Many homeowners are pleasantly surprised to discover that the monthly payment has to increase by only about 25% to pay off the loan in half the time. Not only would you own your home sooner, but you'd pay considerably less interest over the life of the loan.

For example, assume you need a $200,000 mortgage and can borrow at fixed rates. The shorter loan would carry a lower rate because it presents less interest rate risk for the lender. Here's how the two mortgages compare:

Term	Rate	Monthly Principal and Interest	Total Interest Paid over Loan Term
15 year	6.5%	$1,742	$113,625
30 year	6.85	1,311	271,390

The extra $431 a month, or a total of $77,580, saves $157,765 in interest payments over the life of the loan, for net savings of $80,185!

Why isn't everyone rushing to take out a shorter mortgage? Many homeowners can't afford the higher monthly payment, or would rather have the extra spending money now. Others hope to do even better by investing the difference themselves. Suppose you invested $431 each month in a mutual fund with an average annual return of 7 percent. At the end of 15 years, your $77,580 investment would have grown to $136,611—or $59,031 more than you contributed! However, many people lack the self-discipline to save rather than spend that money. For them, the 15-year mortgage represents forced savings.

Yet another option is to make additional principal payments whenever possible. This shortens the life of the loan without committing you to the higher payments. By paying an extra $100 each month, you can shorten the life of a 30-year mortgage to 24¼ years, with attendant interest savings.

By using the first year (1996) as a base year, we see that interest has been earned (or growth experienced) for 4 years.

Table Use   The first step in finding the interest or growth rate is to divide the amount received in the earliest year by the amount received in the latest year. This gives the present value interest factor for a *single amount* for 4 years, $PVIF_{k,4yrs}$, which is .822 ($1,250 ÷ $1,520). The interest rate in Table A–3 associated with the factor closest to .822 for 4 years is the interest or growth rate of Ray's cash flows. In the row for year 4 in Table A–3, the factor for 5% is .823—

almost exactly the .822 value. Therefore, the interest or growth rate of the given cash flows is approximately (to the nearest whole percent) 5%.[17]

Calculator Use   Using the calculator, we treat the earliest value as a present value, PV, and the latest value as a future value, FV_n. (*Note:* Most calculators require *either* the PV or FV value to be input as a negative number in order to calculate an unknown interest or growth rate. That approach is used here.) Using the inputs shown below, you should find the interest or growth rate to be 5.01%, which is consistent with, but more precise than, the value found using Table A–3.

Inputs: 1250   -1520   4

Functions: PV   FV   N   CPT   I

▲ **Outputs:**   5.01

   Another type of problem involving interest rates involves finding the interest rate associated with an *annuity,* or equal-payment loan.

E x a m p l e ▼ Jan Jacobs can borrow $2,000 to be repaid in equal annual end-of-year amounts of $514.14 for the next 5 years. She wants to find the interest rate on this loan.

Table Use   Substituting $PVA_5 = \$2,000$ and $PMT = \$514.14$ into Equation 5.31 and rearranging the equation to solve for $PVIFA_{k,5yrs}$, we get

$$PVIFA_{k,5yrs} = \frac{PVA_5}{PMT} = \frac{\$2,000}{\$514.14} = 3.890 \qquad (5.33)$$

The interest rate for 5 years associated with the annuity factor closest to 3.890 in Table A–4 is 9%. Therefore, the interest rate on the loan is approximately (to the nearest whole percent) 9%.

Calculator Use   (*Note:* Most calculators require *either* the PMT or PV value to be input as a negative number in order to calculate an unknown interest rate on an equal-payment loan. That approach is used here.) Using the inputs shown, you should find the interest rate to be 9.00%, which is consistent with, but more precise than, the approximate value found using Table A–4.

Inputs: 514.14   -2000   5

Functions: PMT   PV   N   CPT   I

▲ **Outputs:**   9.00

---

17. To obtain more precise estimates of interest or growth rates, *interpolation*—a mathematical technique for estimating unknown intermediate values—can be applied. For information on how to interpolate a more precise answer in this example, see the book's home page at www.awlonline.com/gitman.

A final type of interest-rate problem involves finding the interest rate associated with a mixed stream of payments expected to result from a given initial investment. For example, assume that in exchange for an initial $1,000 investment, you will receive annual cash flows over years 1 through 5 of $200, $400, $300, $500, and $200, respectively. What interest rate would you earn on this investment? This rate is often called the *internal rate of return (IRR)*. Because of the relatively complex nature of this computation, which can be greatly simplified using a financial calculator, we will defer discussion of it until it is applied in Chapter 9.

? Review Questions

5–15   How can you determine the size of the equal annual end-of-year deposits necessary to accumulate a certain future sum in a specified future period?

5–16   Describe the procedure used to amortize a loan into a series of equal annual payments. What is a *loan amortization schedule?*

5–17   Which present value interest factors would be used to find (a) the growth rate associated with a series of cash flows and (b) the interest rate associated with an equal-payment loan?

SUMMARY

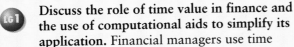 **Discuss the role of time value in finance and the use of computational aids to simplify its application.** Financial managers use time value of money techniques when assessing the value of the expected cash flow streams associated with decision alternatives. Alternatives can be assessed by either compounding to find future value or discounting to find present value. Because they are at time zero when making decisions, financial managers rely primarily on present value techniques. Both financial tables and financial calculators can streamline the application of time value techniques.

Understand the concept of future value, its calculation for a single amount, and the effects of compounding interest more frequently than annually. Future value relies on compound interest to measure future amounts: The initial principal or deposit in one period, along with the interest earned on it, becomes the beginning principal of the following period. Interest can be compounded at intervals ranging from annually to daily, and even continuously. The more frequently interest is compounded, the larger the future amount that will be accumulated and the higher the effective annual rate (EAR). The annual percentage rate (APR)—a nominal annual rate—is quoted on credit cards and loans, and the annual percentage yield (APY)—an effective annual rate—is quoted on savings products. The interest factor formulas and basic equation for the future value of a single amount are given in Table 5.11.

Find the future value of an ordinary annuity and an annuity due and compare these two types of annuities. An annuity is a pattern of equal annual cash flows. For an ordinary annuity, cash flows occur at the end of the period. For an annuity due, cash flows occur at the beginning of the period. The future value of an ordinary annuity can be found by using the future value interest factor for an annuity; an adjustment is required to find the future value of an annuity due. The interest factor formulas and basic equation for the future value of an annuity are given in Table 5.11.

TABLE 5.11 Summary of Key Definitions, Formulas, and Equations for Time Value of Money

---

Variable definitions

---

e = exponential function = 2.7183
EAR = effective annual rate
FV_n = future value or amount at the end of period n
FVA_n = future value of an n-year annuity
k = annual rate of interest
m = number of times per year interest is compounded
n = number of periods—typically, years—over which money earns a return
PMT = amount deposited or received annually at the end of each year
PV = initial principal or present value
PVA_n = present value of an n-year annuity
t = period number index

Interest factor formulas

Future value of a single amount:

$$FVIF_{k,n} = \left(1 + \frac{k}{m}\right)^{m \times n}$$ [Eq. 5.7]

for annual compounding, $m = 1$,

$$FVIF_{k,n} = (1 + k)^n$$ [Eq. 5.5; factors in Table A–1]

for continuous compounding, $m = \infty$,

$$FVIF_{k,n} = e^{k \times n}$$ [Eq. 5.9]

to find the effective annual rate,

$$EAR = \left(1 + \frac{k}{m}\right)^m - 1$$ [Eq. 5.10]

Future value of an (ordinary) annuity:

$$FVIFA_{k,n} = \sum_{t=1}^{n} (1 + k)^{t-1}$$ [Eq. 5.14; factors in Table A–2]

Future value of an annuity due:

$$FVIFA_{k,n} \text{ (annuity due)} = FVIFA_{k,n} \times (1 + k)$$ [Eq. 5.16]

Present value of a single amount:

$$PVIF_{k,n} = \frac{1}{(1 + k)^n}$$ [Eq. 5.21; factors in Table A–3]

Present value of an annuity:

$$PVIFA_{k,n} = \sum_{t=1}^{n} \frac{1}{(1 + k)^t}$$ [Eq. 5.26; factors in Table A–4]

Present value of a perpetuity:

$$PVIFA_{k,\infty} = \frac{1}{k}$$ [Eq. 5.28]

Basic equations

Future value (single amount):	$FV_n = PV \times (FVIF_{k,n})$	[Eq. 5.6]
Future value (annuity):	$FVA_n = PMT \times (FVIFA_{k,n})$	[Eq. 5.15]
Present value (single amount):	$PV = FV_n \times (PVIF_{k,n})$	[Eq. 5.22]
Present value (annuity):	$PVA_n = PMT \times (PVIFA_{k,n})$	[Eq. 5.27]

Understand the concept of present value, its calculation for a single amount, and the relationship of present to future value. Present value is the inverse of future value. The present value of a future amount is the amount of money today that is equivalent to the given future amount, considering the return that can be earned on the current money. The interest factor formula and basic equation for the present value of a single amount are given in Table 5.11.

 Calculate the present value of a mixed stream of cash flows, an annuity, a mixed stream with an embedded annuity, and a perpetuity. The present value of a mixed stream of cash flows is the sum of the present values of each individual cash flow in the stream. The present value of an annuity can be found by using the present value interest factor for an annuity. For a mixed stream with an embedded annuity, the present value of the annuity is found, then used to replace the annuity flows, and the new mixed stream's present value is calculated. The present value of a perpetuity—an infinite-lived annuity—is found using 1 divided by the discount rate to represent the present value interest factor. The interest factor formulas and basic equation for the present value of an annuity are given in Table 5.11.

 Describe the procedures involved in (1) determining deposits to accumulate a future sum, (2) loan amortization, and (3) finding interest or growth rates. The annual deposit to accumulate a given future sum can be found by solving the equation for the future value of an annuity for the annual payment. A loan can be amortized into equal annual payments by solving the equation for the present value of an annuity for the annual payment. Interest or growth rates can be estimated by finding the unknown interest rate in the equation for the present value of a single amount, an annuity, or a mixed stream.

SELF-TEST PROBLEMS   (Solutions in Appendix B)

ST 5–1   Future values   Delia Martin has $10,000 that she can deposit in any of three savings accounts for a 3-year period. Bank A compounds interest on an annual basis, bank B compounds interest twice each year, and bank C compounds interest each quarter. All three banks have a stated annual interest rate of 4%.
   a. What amount would Ms. Martin have at the end of the third year, leaving all interest paid on deposit, in each bank?
   b. What effective annual rate (EAR) would she earn in each of the banks?
   c. On the basis of your findings in **a** and **b,** which bank should Ms. Martin deal with? Why?
   d. If a fourth bank—Bank D, also with a 4% stated interest rate—compounds interest continuously, how much would Ms. Martin have at the end of the third year? Does this alternative change your recommendation in **c?** Explain why or why not.

ST 5–2   Future values of annuities   Ramesh Abdul wishes to choose the better of two equally costly cash flow streams—annuity X and annuity Y. X is an *annuity due* with a cash inflow of $9,000 for each of 6 years. Y is an *ordinary annuity* with a cash inflow of $10,000 for each of 6 years. Assume that Ramesh can earn 15% on his investments.

a. On a purely intuitive basis, which annuity do you think is more attractive? Why?

b. Find the future value at the end of year 6, FVA_6, for both annuities—X and Y.

c. Use your finding in **b** to indicate which annuity is more attractive. Why? Compare your finding to your intuitive response in **a.**

ST 5–3   **Present values**   You have a choice of accepting either of two 5-year cash flow streams or lump-sum amounts. One cash flow stream is an annuity, and the other is a mixed stream. You may accept alternative A or B—either as a cash flow stream or as a lump sum. Given the cash flow stream and lump-sum amounts associated with each, and assuming a 9% opportunity cost, which alternative (A or B) and in which form (cash flow stream or lump-sum amount) would you prefer?

	Cash flow stream	
End of year	Alternative A	Alternative B
1	$700	$1,100
2	700	900
3	700	700
4	700	500
5	700	300
	Lump-sum amount	
At time zero	$2,825	$2,800

ST 5–4   **Deposits to accumulate a future sum**   Judi Jordan wishes to accumulate $8,000 by the end of 5 years by making equal annual end-of-year deposits over the next 5 years. If Judi can earn 7% on her investments, how much must she deposit at the *end of each year* to meet this goal?

PROBLEMS

WARM-UP

5–1   **Using a time line**   The financial manager at Starbuck Industries is considering an investment that requires an initial outlay of $25,000 and is expected to result in cash inflows of $3,000 at the end of year 1, $6,000 at the end of years 2 and 3, $10,000 at the end of year 4, $8,000 at the end of year 5, and $7,000 at the end of year 6.

a. Draw and label a time line depicting the cash flows associated with Starbuck Industries' proposed investment.

b. Use arrows to demonstrate, on the time line in **a,** how compounding to find future value can be used to measure all cash flows at the end of year 6.

c. Use arrows to demonstrate, on the time line in **b,** how discounting to find present value can be used to measure all cash flows at time zero.

d. Which of the approaches—future value or present value—is most often relied on by the financial manager for decision-making purposes? Why?

  5–2 Future value calculation *Without referring to tables or the preprogrammed function on your financial calculator,* use the basic formula for future value along with the given interest rate, k, and number of periods, n, to calculate the future value interest factor in each of the cases shown in the following table. Compare the calculated value to the table value in Appendix Table A–1.

Case	Interest rate, k	Number of periods, n
A	12%	2
B	6	3
C	9	2
D	3	4

  5–3 Future value tables Use the future value interest factors in Appendix Table A–1 in each of the cases shown in the following table to estimate, to the nearest year, how long it would take an initial deposit, assuming no withdrawals,

a. To double.

b. To quadruple.

Case	Interest rate
A	7%
B	40
C	20
D	10

 **5–4 Future values** For each of the cases shown in the table below, calculate the future value of the single cash flow deposited today that will be available at the end of the deposit period if the interest is compounded annually at the rate specified over the given period.

Case	Single cash flow	Interest rate	Deposit period (years)
A	$ 200	5%	20
B	4,500	8	7
C	10,000	9	10
D	25,000	10	12
E	37,000	11	5
F	40,000	12	9

INTERMEDIATE

5–5   Future value   You have $1,500 to invest today at 7% interest compounded annually.

    a. How much will you have accumulated in the account at the end of
        (1) 3 years?
        (2) 6 years?
        (3) 9 years?
    b. Use your findings in **a** to calculate the amount of interest earned in
        (1) the first 3 years (years 1 to 3).
        (2) the second 3 years (years 4 to 6).
        (3) the third 3 years (years 7 to 9).
    c. Compare and contrast your findings in **b**. Explain why the amount of interest earned increases in each succeeding 3-year period.

CHALLENGE

5–6   Inflation and future value   As part of your financial planning you wish to purchase a new car exactly 5 years from today. The car you wish to purchase costs $14,000 today, and your research indicates that its price will increase by 2% to 4% per year over the next 5 years.

    a. Estimate the price of the car at the end of 5 years if inflation is
        (1) 2% per year.
        (2) 4% per year.
    b. How much more expensive will the car be if the rate of inflation is 4% rather than 2%?

CHALLENGE

5–7   Future value and time   You can deposit $10,000 into an account paying 9% annual interest either today or exactly 10 years from today. How much better off will you be at the end of 40 years if you decide to make the initial deposit today rather than 10 years from today?

CHALLENGE

5–8   Future value calculation   Misty needs to have $15,000 at the end of 5 years in order to fulfill her goal of purchasing a small sailboat. She is willing to invest the funds as a single amount today but wonders what sort of investment return she will need to earn. Use your calculator or the time value tables to figure out the approximate annually compounded rate of return needed in each of these cases:

    a. Misty can invest $10,200 today.
    b. Misty can invest $8,150 today.
    c. Misty can invest $7,150 today.

INTERMEDIATE

5–9   Single-payment loan repayment   A person borrows $200 to be repaid in 8 years with 14% annually compounded interest. The loan may be repaid at the end of any earlier year with no prepayment penalty.

    a. What amount would be due if the loan is repaid at the end of year 1?
    b. What is the repayment at the end of year 4?
    c. What amount is due at the end of the eighth year?

INTERMEDIATE

5–10   Changing compounding frequency   Using annual, semiannual, and quarterly compounding periods, for each of the following: (1) calculate the future value if $5,000 is initially deposited, and (2) determine the effective annual rate (EAR):

    a. At 12% annual interest for 5 years.

   b. At 16% annual interest for 6 years.
   c. At 20% annual interest for 10 years.

INTERMEDIATE

5–11   Compounding frequency, future value, and effective annual rates   For each of the following cases:

Case	Amount of initial deposit	Nominal annual rate, k	Compounding frequency, m (times/year)	Deposit period (years)
A	$ 2,500	6%	2	5
B	50,000	12	6	3
C	1,000	5	1	10
D	20,000	16	4	6

   a. Calculate the future value at the end of the specified deposit period.
   b. Determine the effective annual rate, EAR.
   c. Compare the nominal annual rate, k, to the effective annual rate, EAR. What relationship exists between compounding frequency and the nominal and effective annual rates?

INTERMEDIATE

5–12   Continuous compounding   For each of the following cases, find the future value at the end of the deposit period, assuming that interest is compounded continuously at the given nominal annual rate.

Case	Amount of initial deposit	Nominal annual rate, k	Deposit period (years)
A	$1,000	9%	2
B	600	10	10
C	4,000	8	7
D	2,500	12	4

CHALLENGE

5–13   Compounding frequency and future value   You plan to invest $2,000 in an individual retirement arrangement (IRA) today at a *nominal annual rate* of 8%, which is expected to apply to all future years.
   a. How much will you have in the account at the end of 10 years if interest is compounded
   (1) annually?
   (2) semiannually?
   (3) daily? (assume a 360-day year)
   (4) continuously?
   b. What is the *effective annual rate, EAR*, for each compounding period in **a**?
   c. How much greater will your IRA account balance be at the end of 10 years if interest is compounded continuously rather than annually?

d. How does the compounding frequency affect the future value and effective annual rate for a given deposit? Explain in terms of your findings in **a** through **c.**

CHALLENGE

5–14   Comparing compounding periods   René Levin wishes to determine the future value at the end of 2 years of a $15,000 deposit made today into an account paying a nominal annual rate of 12%.

 a. Find the future value of René's deposit assuming that interest is compounded
   (1) annually.
   (2) quarterly.
   (3) monthly.
   (4) continuously.
 b. Compare your findings in **a,** and use them to demonstrate the relationship between compounding frequency and future value.
 c. What is the maximum future value obtainable given the $15,000 deposit, 2-year time period, and 12% nominal annual rate? Use your findings in **a** to explain.

INTERMEDIATE

5–15   Future value of an annuity   For each of the following cases:

Case	Amount of annuity	Interest rate	Deposit period (years)
A	$ 2,500	8%	10
B	500	12	6
C	30,000	20	5
D	11,500	9	8
E	6,000	14	30

 a. Calculate the future value of the annuity assuming that it is an
   (1) ordinary annuity.
   (2) annuity due.
 b. Compare your findings in **a**(1) and **a**(2). All else being identical, which type of annuity—ordinary or annuity due—is preferable? Explain why.

CHALLENGE

5–16   Ordinary annuity versus annuity due   Marian Kirk wishes to select the better of two 10-year annuities—C and D—as described.

   Annuity C   An ordinary annuity of $2,500 per year for 10 years.
   Annuity D   An annuity due of $2,200 per year for 10 years.

 a. Find the future value of both annuities at the end of year 10 assuming that Marian can earn
   (1) 10% annual interest.
   (2) 20% annual interest.
 b. Use your findings in **a** to indicate which annuity has the greater future value at the end of year 10 for both the (1) 10% and (2) 20% interest rates.

c. Briefly compare, contrast, and explain any differences between your findings using the 10% and 20% interest rates in **b.**

5–17　**Future value of a retirement annuity**　Cal Thomas, a 25-year-old college graduate, wishes to retire at age 65. To supplement other sources of retirement income, he can deposit $2,000 each year into a tax-deferred individual retirement arrangement (IRA). The IRA will be invested to earn an annual return of 10%, which is assumed attainable over the next 40 years.

a. If Cal makes annual end-of-year $2,000 deposits into the IRA, how much would he have accumulated by the end of his 65th year?

b. If Cal decides to wait until age 35 to begin making annual end-of-year $2,000 deposits into the IRA, how much would he have accumulated by the end of his 65th year?

c. Using your findings in **a** and **b,** discuss the impact of delaying making deposits into the IRA for 10 years (age 25 to age 35) on the amount accumulated by the end of Cal's 65th year.

d. Rework parts **a, b,** and **c** assuming that Cal makes all deposits at the beginning rather than at the end of each year. Discuss the effect of beginning-of-year deposits on the future value accumulated by the end of Cal's 65th year.

5–18　**Annuities and compounding**　Janet Boyle intends to deposit $300 per year in a credit union for the next 10 years, and the credit union pays an annual interest rate of 8%.

a. Determine the future value that Janet will have at the end of 10 years given that end-of-period deposits are made and no interest is withdrawn if
(1) $300 is deposited annually and the credit union pays interest annually.
(2) $150 is deposited semiannually and the credit union pays interest semiannually.
(3) $75 is deposited quarterly and the credit union pays interest quarterly.

b. Use your finding in **a** to discuss the effect of more frequent deposits and compounding of interest on the future value of an annuity.

5–19　**Future value of a mixed stream**　For each of the mixed streams of cash flows shown in the following table, determine the future value at the end of the final year if deposits are made at the *beginning of each year* into an account paying annual interest of 12%, assuming that no withdrawals are made during the period.

	Cash flow stream		
Year	A	B	C
1	$ 900	$30,000	$1,200
2	1,000	25,000	1,200
3	1,200	20,000	1,000
4		10,000	1,900
5		5,000	

INTERMEDIATE

5-20 Future value of lump sum versus a mixed stream Gina Vitale has just contracted to sell a small parcel of land that she inherited a few years ago. The buyer is willing to pay $24,000 at closing of the transaction or will pay the amounts shown in the following table at the *beginning* of each of the next 5 years. Because Gina doesn't really need the money today, she plans to let it accumulate in an account that earns 7% annual interest. Given her desire to buy a house at the end of 5 years after closing on the sale of the lot, she decides to choose the payment alternative—$24,000 lump sum or mixed stream of payments in the following table—that provides the higher future value at the end of 5 years.

Mixed stream	
Beginning of year	Cash flow
1	$ 2,000
2	4,000
3	6,000
4	8,000
5	10,000

a. What is the future value of the lump sum at the end of year 5?
b. What is the future value of the mixed stream at the end of year 5?
c. Based on your findings in **a** and **b,** which alternative should Gina take?
d. If Gina could earn 10% rather than 7% on the funds, would your recommendation in **c** change? Explain.

WARM-UP

5-21 Present value calculation *Without referring to tables or the preprogrammed function on your financial calculator,* use the basic formula for present value along with the given opportunity cost, k, and number of periods, n, to calculate the present value interest factor in each of the cases shown in the following table. Compare the calculated value to the table value.

Case	Opportunity cost, k	Number of periods, n
A	2%	4
B	10	2
C	5	3
D	13	2

WARM-UP

5-22 Present values For each of the cases shown in the following table, calculate the present value of the cash flow, discounting at the rate given and assuming that the cash flow is received at the end of the period noted.

Case	Single cash flow	Discount rate	End of period (years)
A	$ 7,000	12%	4
B	28,000	8	20
C	10,000	14	12
D	150,000	11	6
E	45,000	20	8

5–23 Present value concept   Answer each of the following questions.
  a. What single investment, made today, earning 12% annual interest, will be worth $6,000 at the end of 6 years?
  b. What is the present value of $6,000 to be received at the end of 6 years if the discount rate is 12%?
  c. What is the most you would pay today for a promise to repay you $6,000 at the end of 6 years if your opportunity cost is 12%?
  d. Compare, contrast, and discuss your findings in **a** through **c**.

5–24 Present value   Jim Nance has been offered a future payment of $500 three years from today. If his opportunity cost is 7% compounded annually, what value should he place on this opportunity today? What is the most he should pay to purchase this payment today?

5–25 Present value   An Iowa state savings bond can be converted to $100 at maturity 6 years from purchase. If the state bonds are to be competitive with U.S. Savings Bonds, which pay 8% annual interest (compounded annually), at what price must the state sell its bonds? Assume no cash payments on savings bonds prior to redemption.

5–26 Present value and discount rates   You just won a lottery that promises to pay you $1,000,000 exactly 10 years from today. Because the $1,000,000 payment is guaranteed by the state in which you live, opportunities exist to sell the claim today for an immediate lump-sum cash payment.
  a. What is the least you will sell your claim for if you could earn the following rates of return on similar-risk investments during the 10-year period?
    (1) 6%
    (2) 9%
    (3) 12%
  b. Rework **a** under the assumption that the $1,000,000 payment will be received in 15 rather than 10 years.
  c. Based on your findings in **a** and **b,** discuss the effect of both the size of the rate of return and the time until receipt of payment on the present value of a future sum.

5–27 Present value comparisons of lump sums   In exchange for a $20,000 payment today, a well-known company will allow you to choose *one* of the alternatives shown in the following table. Your opportunity cost is 11%.

Alternative	Lump-sum amount
A	$28,500 at end of 3 years
B	$54,000 at end of 9 years
C	$160,000 at end of 20 years

a. Find the value today of each alternative.
b. Are all the alternatives acceptable, i.e., worth $20,000 today?
c. Which alternative, if any, would you take?

5–28 **Cash flow investment decision** Tom Alexander has an opportunity to purchase any of the investments shown in the following table. The purchase price, the amount of the single cash inflow, and its year of receipt are given for each investment. Which purchase recommendations would you make, assuming that Tom can earn 10% on his investments?

INTERMEDIATE

Investment	Price	Single cash inflow	Year of receipt
A	$18,000	$30,000	5
B	600	3,000	20
C	3,500	10,000	10
D	1,000	15,000	40

5–29 **Relationship between future value and present value** Using *only* the information in the following table:

INTERMEDIATE

Year (t)	Cash flow	Future value interest factor at 5% ($FVIF_{5\%,t}$)
1	$ 800	1.050
2	900	1.102
3	1,000	1.158
4	1,500	1.216
5	2,000	1.276

a. Determine the *present value* of the mixed stream of cash flows using a 5% discount rate.
b. How much would you be willing to pay for an opportunity to buy this stream, assuming that you can at best earn 5% on your investments?
c. What effect, if any, would a 7% rather than a 5% opportunity cost have on your analysis? (Explain verbally.)

INTERMEDIATE   5–30   **Present value of an annuity**   Anna Waldheim was seriously injured in an industrial accident. She sued the responsible parties and was awarded a judgment of $2,000,000. Today, she and her attorney are attending a settlement conference with the defendants. The defendants have made an initial offer of $156,000 per year for 25 years. Anna plans to counteroffer at $255,000 per year for 25 years. Both offer and counteroffer have a present value of $2,000,000, the amount of the judgment. Both assume payments at the end of each year.
   a. What interest rate assumption have the defendants used in their offer (rounded to the nearest whole percent)?
   b. What interest rate assumption have Anna and her lawyer used in their counteroffer (rounded to the nearest whole percent)?
   c. Anna is willing to settle for an annuity that carries an interest rate assumption of 9%. What annual payment would be acceptable to her?

CHALLENGE   5–31   **Present value of an annuity**   Tim Smith is shopping for a used car. He has found one priced at $4,500. The dealer has told Tim that if he can come up with a down payment of $500, the dealer will finance the balance of the price at a 12% annual rate over 2 years (24 months).
   a. Assuming that Tim accepts the dealer's offer, what will his *monthly* (end-of-month) payment amount be?
   b. Use a financial calculator or Equation 5.26a found in footnote 14 to help you figure out what Tim's *monthly* payment would be if the dealer was willing to finance the balance of the car price at a 9% yearly rate.

WARM-UP   5–32   **Present value—Mixed streams**   Find the present value of the streams of cash flows shown in the following table. Assume that the firm's opportunity cost is 12%.

A		B		C	
Year	Cash flow	Year	Cash flow	Year	Cash flow
1	−$2,000	1	$10,000	1–5	$10,000/yr
2	3,000	2–5	5,000/yr	6–10	8,000/yr
3	4,000	6	7,000		
4	6,000				
5	8,000				

5–33   **Present value—Mixed streams**   Given the mixed streams of cash flows shown in the following table:

INTERMEDIATE

	Cash flow stream	
Year	A	B
1	$ 50,000	$ 10,000
2	40,000	20,000
3	30,000	30,000
4	20,000	40,000
5	10,000	50,000
Totals	$150,000	$150,000

a. Find the present value of each stream using a 15% discount rate.
b. Compare the calculated present values and discuss them in light of the fact that the undiscounted total cash flows total $150,000 in each case.

5–34 **Present value of a mixed stream** Harte Systems, Inc., a maker of electronic surveillance equipment, is considering selling to a well-known hardware chain the rights to market its home security system. The proposed deal calls for payments of $30,000 and $25,000 at the end of years 1 and 2 and annual year-end payments of $15,000 in years 3 through 9. A final payment of $10,000 would be due at the end of year 10.

INTERMEDIATE

a. Lay out the cash flows involved in the offer on a time line.
b. If Harte applies a required rate of return of 12% to them, what is the present value of this series of payments?
c. A second company has offered Harte a one-time payment of $100,000 for the rights to market the home security system. Which offer should Harte accept?

5–35 **Funding budget shortfalls** As part of your personal budgeting process, you have determined that in each of the next 5 years you will have budget shortfalls. In other words, you will need the amounts shown in the following table at the end of the given year to balance your budget, that is, inflows = outflows. You expect to be able to earn 8% on your investments during the next 5 years and wish to fund the budget shortfalls over the next 5 years with a single lump sum.

INTERMEDIATE

End of year	Budget shortfall
1	$ 5,000
2	4,000
3	6,000
4	10,000
5	3,000

a. How large must the lump-sum deposit today into an account paying 8% annual interest be to provide for full coverage of the anticipated budget shortfalls?

b. What effect would an increase in your earnings rate have on the amount calculated in **a**? Explain.

5–36 **Present value of an annuity**   For each of the cases shown in the following table, calculate the present value of the annuity, assuming that the annuity cash flows occur at the end of each year.

Case	Amount of annuity	Interest rate	Period (years)
A	$ 12,000	7%	3
B	55,000	12	15
C	700	20	9
D	140,000	5	7
E	22,500	10	5

5–37 **Present value of a retirement annuity**   An insurance agent is trying to sell you an immediate retirement annuity, which for a lump-sum fee paid today will provide you with $12,000 per year for the next 25 years. You currently earn 9% on low-risk investments comparable to the retirement annuity. Ignoring taxes, what is the most you would pay for this annuity?

5–38 **Funding your retirement**   You plan to retire in exactly 20 years. Your goal is to create a fund that will allow you to receive $20,000 per year for the 30 years between retirement and death (a psychic told you would die after 30 years). You know that you will be able to earn 11% per year during the 30-year retirement period.

a. How large a fund will you need *when you retire* in 20 years to provide the 30-year, $20,000 retirement annuity?

b. How much would you need *today* as a lump sum to provide the amount calculated in **a** if you earn only 9% per year during the 20 years preceding retirement?

c. What effect would an increase in the rate you can earn both during and prior to retirement have on the values found in **a** and **b**? Explain.

5–39 **Present value of an annuity versus a lump sum**   Assume that you just won the state lottery. Your prize can be taken either in the form of $40,000 at the end of each of the next 25 years (i.e., $1,000,000 over 25 years) or as a lump sum of $500,000 paid immediately.

a. If you expect to be able to earn 5% annually on your investments over the next 25 years, ignoring taxes and other considerations, which alternative should you take? Why?

b. Would your decision in **a** be altered if you could earn 7% rather than 5% on your investments over the next 25 years? Why?

c. On a strict economic basis, at approximately what earnings rate would you be indifferent in choosing between the two plans?

5–40 **Present value of a mixed stream with an embedded annuity**   In each of the cases shown in the following table, the mixed cash flow stream has an annuity embedded within it. Use the three-step procedure presented in the text to streamline the calculation of the present value of each of these streams, assuming a 12% discount rate in each case.

A		B		C	
Year	Cash flow	Year	Cash flow	Year	Cash flow
1	$12,000	1	$15,000	1–5	$ 1,000/yr
2	10,000	2–10	20,000/yr	6	6,000
3	8,000	11–30	25,000/yr	7	7,000
4	8,000			8	8,000
5	8,000			9–15	10,000/yr
6	8,000				
7	8,000				
8	5,000				

5–41 **Perpetuities**   Given the data in the following table, determine for each of the perpetuities:

Perpetuity	Annual amount	Discount rate
A	$ 20,000	8%
B	100,000	10
C	3,000	6
D	60,000	5

a. The appropriate present value interest factor.
b. The present value.

5–42 **Creating an endowment**   On completion of her introductory finance course, Marla Lee was so pleased with the amount of useful and interesting knowledge she gained that she convinced her parents, who were wealthy alums of the university she was attending, to create an endowment. The endowment would allow three needy students to take the introductory finance course each year into perpetuity. The guaranteed annual cost of tuition and books for the course was $600 per student. The endowment would be created by making a lump-sum payment to the university. The university expected to earn exactly 6% per year on these funds.

a. How large an initial lump-sum payment must Marla's parents make to the university to fund the endowment?

b. What amount would be needed to fund the endowment if the university could earn 9% rather than 6% per year on the funds?

WARM-UP

5–43 Deposits to accumulate future sums   For each of the cases shown in the following table, determine the amount of the equal annual end-of-year deposit required to accumulate the given sum at the end of the specified period, assuming the stated annual interest rate.

Case	Sum to be accumulated	Accumulation period (years)	Interest rate
A	$ 5,000	3	12%
B	100,000	20	7
C	30,000	8	10
D	15,000	12	8

INTERMEDIATE

5–44 Creating a retirement fund   To supplement your planned retirement in exactly 42 years, you estimate that you need to accumulate $220,000 by the end of 42 years from today. You plan to make equal annual end-of-year deposits into an account paying 8% annual interest.

a. How large must the annual deposits be to create the $220,000 fund by the end of 42 years?

b. If you can afford to deposit only $600 per year into the account, how much will you have accumulated by the end of the 42nd year?

INTERMEDIATE

5–45 Accumulating a growing future sum   A retirement home at Deer Trail Estates now costs $85,000. Inflation is expected to cause this price to increase at 6% per year over the 20 years before C. L. Donovan retires. How large an equal annual end-of-year deposit must be made each year into an account paying an annual interest rate of 10% for Donovan to have the cash to purchase a home at retirement?

INTERMEDIATE

5–46 Deposits to create a perpetuity   You have decided to endow your favorite university with a scholarship. It is expected to cost $6,000 per year to attend the university into perpetuity. You expect to give the university the endowment in 10 years and will accumulate it by making annual (end-of-year) deposits into an account. The rate of interest is expected to be 10% for all future time periods.

a. How large must the endowment be?

b. How much must you deposit at the end of each of the next 10 years to accumulate the required amount?

CHALLENGE

5–47 Inflation, future value, and annual deposits   While vacationing in Florida, John Kelley saw the vacation home of his dreams. It was listed with a sale price of $200,000. The only catch is that John is 40 years old and plans to continue working until he is 65. Still, he has decided prices generally increase at the overall rate of inflation. John believes that he can earn 9% annually after taxes on his investments. He is willing to invest a fixed amount at the end of each of the next 25 years to fund the cash purchase of such a house when he retires.

a. Inflation is expected to average 5% a year for the next 25 years. What will John's dream house cost when he retires?

b. How much must John invest at the end of each of the next 25 years in order to have the cash purchase price of the house when he retires?

c. If John invests at the beginning instead of at the end of each of the next 25 years, how much must he invest each year?

WARM-UP

5–48   Loan amortization   Determine the equal annual end-of-year payment required each year over the life of the loans shown in the following table to repay them fully during the stated term of the loan.

Loan	Principal	Interest rate	Term of loan (years)
A	$12,000	8%	3
B	60,000	12	10
C	75,000	10	30
D	4,000	15	5

INTERMEDIATE

5–49   Loan amortization schedule   Joan Messineo borrowed $15,000 at a 14% annual rate of interest to be repaid over 3 years. The loan is amortized into three equal annual end-of-year payments.

a. Calculate the annual end-of-year loan payment.

b. Prepare a loan amortization schedule showing the interest and principal breakdown of each of the three loan payments.

c. Explain why the interest portion of each payment declines with the passage of time.

CHALLENGE

5–50   Loan interest deductions   Liz Rogers just closed a $10,000 business loan that is to be repaid in three equal annual end-of-year payments. The interest rate on the loan is 13%. As part of her firm's detailed financial planning, Liz wishes to determine the annual interest deduction attributable to the loan. (Because it is a business loan, the interest portion of each loan payment is tax-deductible to the business.)

a. Determine the firm's annual loan payment.

b. Prepare an amortization schedule for the loan.

c. How much interest expense will Liz's firm have in *each* of the next 3 years as a result of this loan?

WARM-UP **5–51   Growth rates**   You are given the series of cash flows shown in the following table:

	Cash flows		
Year	A	B	C
1	$500	$1,500	$2,500
2	560	1,550	2,600
3	640	1,610	2,650
4	720	1,680	2,650
5	800	1,760	2,800
6		1,850	2,850
7		1,950	2,900
8		2,060	
9		2,170	
10		2,280	

a. Calculate the compound annual growth rate associated with each cash flow stream.
b. If year 1 values represent initial deposits in a savings account paying annual interest, what is the annual rate of interest earned on each account?
c. Compare and discuss the growth rate and interest rate found in **a** and **b**, respectively.

INTERMEDIATE

5–52   Rate of return   Rishi Singh has $1,500 to invest. His investment counselor suggests an investment that pays no stated interest but will return $2,000 at the end of 3 years.
a. What annual rate of return will Mr. Singh earn with this investment?
b. Mr. Singh is considering another investment, of equal risk, which earns an annual return of 8%. Which investment should he take, and why?

INTERMEDIATE

5–53   Rate of return and investment choice   Clare Jaccard has $5,000 to invest. Because she is only 25 years old, she is not concerned about the length of the investment's life. What she is sensitive to is the rate of return she will earn on the investment. With the help of her financial adviser Clare has isolated the four equally risky investments, each providing a lump-sum return, shown in the following table. All of the investments require an initial $5,000 payment.

Investment	Lump-sum return	Investment life (years)
A	$ 8,400	6
B	15,900	15
C	7,600	4
D	13,000	10

a. Calculate to the nearest 1% the rate of return on each of the four investments available to Clare.

b. Which investment would you recommend to Clare given her goal of maximizing the rate of return?

INTERMEDIATE

5–54 **Rate of return—Annuity**   What is the rate of return on an investment of $10,606 if the company expects to receive $2,000 each year for the next 10 years?

INTERMEDIATE

5–55 **Choosing the best annuity**   Raina Herzig wishes to choose the best of four immediate retirement annuities available to her. In each case, in exchange for paying a single premium today, she will receive equal annual end-of-year cash benefits for a specified number of years. She considers the annuities to be equally risky and is not concerned about their differing lives. Her decision will be based solely on the rate of return she will earn on each annuity. The key terms of each of the four annuities are shown in the following table.

Annuity	Premium paid today	Annual benefit	Life (years)
A	$30,000	$3,100	20
B	25,000	3,900	10
C	40,000	4,200	15
D	35,000	4,000	12

a. Calculate to the nearest 1% the rate of return on each of the four annuities being considered by Raina.
b. Given Raina's stated decision criterion, which annuity would you recommend?

INTERMEDIATE

5–56 **Loan rates of interest**   John Fleming has been shopping for a loan to finance the purchase of a used car. He has found three possibilities that seem attractive and wishes to select the one having the lowest interest rate. The information available with respect to each of the three $5,000 loans is shown in the following table:

Loan	Principal	Annual payment	Term (years)
A	$5,000	$1,352.81	5
B	5,000	1,543.21	4
C	5,000	2,010.45	3

a. Determine the interest rate associated with each of the loans.
b. Which loan should Mr. Fleming take?

CASE CHAPTER 5	Finding Jill Moran's Retirement Annuity

Sunrise Industries wishes to accumulate funds to provide a retirement annuity for its vice president of research, Jill Moran. Ms. Moran by contract will retire at the end of exactly 12 years. Upon retirement, she is entitled to receive an annual end-of-year payment of $42,000 for exactly 20 years. If she dies prior to the end of the 20-year period, the annual payments will pass to her heirs. During the 12-year "accumulation period" Sunrise wishes to fund the annuity by making equal annual end-of-year deposits into an account earning 9% interest. Once the 20-year "distribution period" begins, Sunrise plans to move the accumulated monies into an account earning a guaranteed 12% per year. At the end of the distribution period, the account balance will equal zero. Note that the first deposit will be made at the end of year 1 and the first distribution payment will be received at the end of year 13.

Required

a. Draw a time line depicting all of the cash flows associated with Sunrise's view of the retirement annuity.

b. How large a sum must Sunrise accumulate by the end of year 12 to provide the 20-year, $42,000 annuity?

c. How large must Sunrise's equal annual end-of-year deposits into the account be over the 12-year accumulation period to fund fully Ms. Moran's retirement annuity?

d. How much would Sunrise have to deposit annually during the accumulation period if it could earn 10% rather than 9% during the accumulation period?

e. How much would Sunrise have to deposit annually during the accumulation period if Ms. Moran's retirement annuity was a perpetuity and all other terms were the same as initially described?

WEB EXERCISE

GOTO web site www.arachnoid.com/lutusp/finance_old.html. Page down to the portion of this screen that contains the financial calculator.

1. To determine the FV of a fixed amount enter the following:

Into PV, enter −1000; into np, enter 1; into pmt, enter 0; and, into ir, enter 8.

Now click on Calculate FV, and 1080.00 should appear in the FV window.

2. Determine FV for each of the following compounding periods by changing *only* the following:

   a. np to 2, and ir to 8/2
   b. np to 12, and ir to 8/12
   c. np to 52, and ir to 8/52

3. To determine the PV of a fixed amount enter the following:

   Into FV, 1080; into np, 1; into pmt, 0; and, into ir, 8. Now click on Calculate PV. What is the PV?

4. To determine the FV of an annuity enter the following:

   Into PV, 0; into FV, 0; into np, 12; into pmt, 1000; and, into ir, 8. Now click on Calculate FV. What is the FV?

5. To determine the PV of an annuity, change only the FV setting to 0; keep the other entries the same as in question 4. Click on Calculate PV. What is the PV?

6. Check your answers for questions 4 and 5 by using the techniques discussed in this chapter.

GOTO web site www.homeowners.com/. Click Calculators in the left column. Click Mortgage Calculator.

7. Enter the following into the mortgage calculator: Loan amount, 100000; duration in years, 30; and interest rate, 10. Click on compute payment. What is the monthly payment?

8. Calculate the monthly payment for $100,000 loans for 30 years at 8%, 6%, 4%, and 2%.

9. Calculate the monthly payment for $100,000 loans at 8% for 30 years, 20 years, 10 years, and 5 years.

Risk and Return

LEARNING GOALS

LG1 Understand the meaning and fundamentals of risk, return, and risk preferences.

LG2 Describe procedures for measuring the risk of a single asset.

LG3 Discuss the measurement of return and standard deviation for a portfolio and the various types of correlation that can exist between series of numbers.

LG4 Understand the risk and return characteristics of a portfolio in terms of correlation and diversification, and the impact of international assets on a portfolio.

LG5 Review the two types of risk and the derivation and role of beta in measuring the relevant risk of both an individual security and a portfolio.

LG6 Explain the capital asset pricing model (CAPM), its relationship to the security market line (SML), and shifts in the SML caused by changes in inflationary expectations and risk aversion.

LG1

6.1 Risk and Return Fundamentals

To maximize share price, the financial manager must learn to assess two key determinants: risk and return.[1] Each financial decision presents certain risk and return characteristics, and the unique combination of these characteristics has an impact on share price. Risk can be viewed as it relates either to a single asset or

---

1. Two important points should be recognized here: (1) Although for convenience the publicly traded corporation is being discussed, the risk and return concepts presented apply equally well to all firms; and (2) concern centers only on the wealth of common stockholders, because they are the "residual owners" whose returns are in no way specified in advance.

"Not for a Million Bucks!"

Expressions like this one and "Make it worth my while" touch on one of the key concepts of finance—that risk and return are linked. The idea that return should increase if risk increases is fundamental in finance. Of course, people, as well as firms, have different views of risk, depending on who they are and what they know how to do. Also, some people and some firms are simply more willing to take risks than are others—and for some, the mere thrill of risk is almost enough return in itself. Generally, though, most financial managers, like most people, shy away from undue risk and so must be compensated for taking on risk. As this chapter will show, firms can quantify and assess the risk and return for individual assets and for groups of assets, using various tools and techniques.

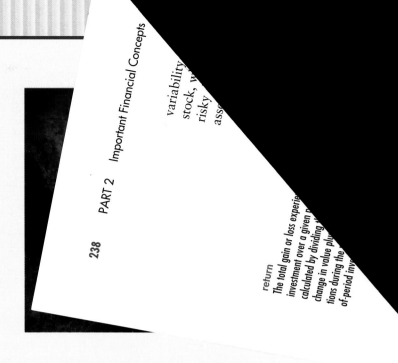

variability, with stock, risky asset

return
The total gain or loss experienced over a given [investment over a given] period, calculated by dividing the [asset's] change in value plus [any cash] tions during the [period by] of-period inv[estment]

---

portfolio
A collection, or group, of assets.

risk
The chance of financial loss or, more formally, the variability of returns associated with a given asset.

to a **portfolio**—a collection, or group, of assets. We will look at both, beginning with the risk of a single asset. First, though, it is important to introduce some fundamental concepts about risk, return, and risk preferences.

Risk Defined

In the most basic sense, **risk** is the chance of financial loss. Assets having greater chances of loss are viewed as more risky than those with lesser chances of loss. More formally, the term *risk* is used interchangeably with *uncertainty* to refer to the *variability of returns associated with a given asset*. A government bond that guarantees its holder $100 interest after 30 days has no risk, because there is no associated with the return. A $100 investment in a firm's common ~~which~~ over the same period may earn anywhere from $0 to $200, is very ~~due~~ to the high variability of return. The more certain the return from an ~~asset~~, the less variability and therefore the less risk.

Return Defined

Obviously, if we are going to assess risk based on variability of return, we need to be certain we know what *return* is, and how to measure it. The **return** is the total gain or loss experienced on an investment over a given period of time. It is commonly measured as the change in value plus any cash distributions during the period, expressed as a percentage of the beginning-of-period investment value. The expression for calculating the rate of return earned on any asset over period t, k_t, is commonly defined as:

$$k_t = \frac{P_t - P_{t-1} + C_t}{P_{t-1}} \qquad (6.1)$$

where

k_t = actual, expected, or required rate of return[2] during period t
P_t = price (value) of asset at time t
P_{t-1} = price (value) of asset at time $t - 1$
C_t = cash (flow) received from the asset investment in the time period $t - 1$ to t

The return, k_t, reflects the combined effect of changes in value, $P_t - P_{t-1}$, and cash flow, C_t, over period t.[3]

Equation 6.1 is used to determine the rate of return over a time period as short as 1 day or as long as 10 years or more. However, in most cases, t is 1 year, and k therefore represents an annual rate of return.

E x a m p l e ▼ Robin's Gameroom, a high-traffic video arcade, wishes to determine the return on two of its video machines, Conqueror and Demolition. Conqueror was purchased 1 year ago for $20,000 and currently has a market value of $21,500. During the year, it generated $800 of after-tax cash receipts. Demolition was purchased 4 years ago; its value in the year just completed declined from $12,000 to $11,800. During the year, it generated $1,700 of after-tax cash receipts. Substituting into Equation 6.1, we can calculate the annual rate of return, k, for each video machine:

Conqueror (C):

$$k_C = \frac{\$21,500 - \$20,000 + \$800}{\$20,000} = \frac{\$2,300}{\$20,000} = \underline{\underline{11.5\%}}$$

2. The terms *expected return* and *required return* are used interchangeably throughout this text, because in an efficient market (discussed later) they would be expected to be equal. The actual return is an *ex post* value, whereas expected and required returns are *ex ante* values. Therefore, the actual return may be greater than, equal to, or less than the expected/required return.

3. The beginning-of-period value, P_{t-1}, and the end-of-period value, P_t, are not necessarily *realized values*. They are often *unrealized*, which means that although the asset was *not* actually purchased at time $t - 1$ and sold at time t, values P_{t-1} and P_t *could* have been realized had those transactions been made.

Demolition (D):

$$k_D = \frac{\$11,800 - \$12,000 + \$1,700}{\$12,000} = \frac{\$1,500}{\$12,000} = \underline{\underline{12.5\%}}$$

Although the market value of Demolition declined during the year, its cash flow caused it to earn a higher rate of return than that earned by Conqueror during the same period. Clearly, the combined impact of changes in value and cash flow measured by the rate of return is important.

Risk Preferences

Feelings about risk differ among managers (and firms).[4] Thus, it is important to specify a generally acceptable level of risk. The three basic risk preference behaviors—risk-averse, risk-indifferent, and risk-seeking—are depicted graphically in Figure 6.1.

risk-indifferent
The attitude toward risk in which no change in return would be required for an increase in risk.

risk-averse
The attitude toward risk in which an increased return would be required for an increase in risk.

- For the **risk-indifferent** manager, the required return does not change as risk goes from x_1 to x_2. In essence, no change in return would be required for the increase in risk. Clearly, this attitude is nonsensical in almost any business context.
- For the **risk-averse** manager, the required return increases for an increase in risk. Because they shy away from risk, these managers require higher expected returns to compensate them for taking greater risk.

FIGURE 6.1

Risk Preferences
Risk preference behaviors

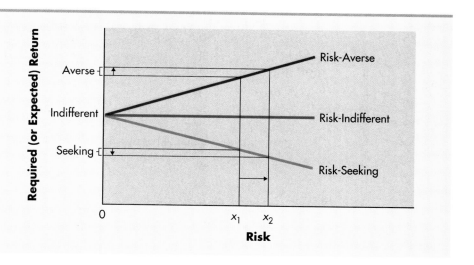

---

risk-seeking
The attitude toward risk in which a decreased return would be accepted for an increase in risk.

- For the **risk-seeking** manager, the required return decreases for an increase in risk. Theoretically, because they enjoy risk, these managers are willing to give up some return to take more risk. However, such behavior would not be likely to benefit the firm.

Most managers are risk-averse; for a given increase in risk, they require an increase in return. They generally tend to be conservative rather than aggressive when accepting risk for their firm. Accordingly, a *risk-averse financial manager requiring higher returns for greater risk is assumed throughout this text.*

Hint   Remember that most *investors* are also risk-averse. Like risk-averse managers, for a given increase in risk, they also require an increase in return for their investment in that firm.

? Review Questions

6–1   Define *risk* as it relates to financial decision making. Do any assets have perfectly certain returns?

6–2   Define *return*. Describe the basic calculation involved in finding the return on an investment.

6–3   Compare the following risk preferences: (**a**) risk-averse, (**b**) risk-indifferent, and (**c**) risk-seeking. Which is most common among financial managers?

6.2 Risk of a Single Asset

The concept of risk is best developed by first considering a single asset held in isolation. Although you will later see that the risk of a portfolio of assets is measured in much the same way as the risk of a single asset, certain benefits accrue to holders of portfolios. For both single assets and for portfolios, we can assess risk by looking at the expected return behavior of assets, and we can measure the risk using statistics.

Risk Assessment

Risk can be assessed using sensitivity analysis and probability distributions, which provide a feel for the level of risk embodied in a given asset.

Sensitivity Analysis

sensitivity analysis
An approach for assessing risk that uses a number of possible return estimates to obtain a sense of the variability among outcomes.

Sensitivity analysis uses a number of possible return estimates to obtain a sense of the variability among outcomes.[5] One common method involves estimating the pessimistic (worst), the most likely (expected), and the optimistic (best) returns associated with a given asset. In this case, the asset's risk can be measured

---

5. The term "sensitivity analysis" is intentionally used in a general rather than technically correct fashion here to simplify this discussion. A more technical and precise definition and discussion of this technique and "scenario analysis" is presented in Chapter 10.

TABLE 6.1	Assets A and B	
	Asset A	Asset B
Initial investment	$10,000	$10,000
Annual rate of return		
Pessimistic	13%	7%
Most likely	15%	15%
Optimistic	17%	23%
Range	4%	16%

range
A measure of an asset's risk, which is found by subtracting the pessimistic (worst) outcome from the optimistic (best) outcome.

by the **range,** which is found by subtracting the pessimistic outcome from the optimistic outcome. The greater the range for a given asset, the more variability, or risk, it is said to have.

Example ▼ Norman Company, a custom golf equipment manufacturer, wants to choose the better of two investments, A and B. Each requires an initial outlay of $10,000 and each has a *most likely* annual rate of return of 15%. Management has made *pessimistic* and *optimistic* estimates of the returns associated with each. The three estimates for each asset, along with its range, are given in Table 6.1. Asset A appears to be less risky than asset B; its range of 4% (17% − 13%) is less than the range of 16% (23% − 7%) for asset B. The risk-averse decision maker would prefer asset A over asset B, because A offers the same most likely return as **▲** B (15%) but with lower risk (smaller range).

Although the use of sensitivity analysis and the range is rather crude, it does provide the decision maker with a feel for the behavior of returns that can be used to assess roughly the risk involved.

Probability Distributions

probability
The *chance* that a given outcome will occur.

Probability distributions provide a more quantitative insight into an asset's risk. The **probability** of a given outcome is its *chance* of occurring. If an outcome has an 80 percent probability of occurrence, the given outcome would be expected to occur 8 out of 10 times. If an outcome has a probability of 100 percent, it is certain to occur. Outcomes having a probability of zero will never occur.

Example ▼

probability distribution
A model that relates probabilities to the associated outcomes.

Norman Company's past estimates indicate that the probabilities of the pessimistic, most likely, and optimistic outcomes are 25%, 50%, and 25%, respectively. The sum of these probabilities must equal 100%; that is, they must be **▲** based on all the alternatives considered.

bar chart
The simplest type of probability distribution; shows only a limited number of outcomes and associated probabilities for a given event.

A **probability distribution** is a model that relates probabilities to the associated outcomes. The simplest type of probability distribution is the **bar chart,** which shows only a limited number of outcome–probability coordinates. The bar charts for Norman Company's assets A and B are shown in Figure 6.2. Although both

FIGURE 6.2

Bar Charts

Bar charts for asset A's and asset B's returns

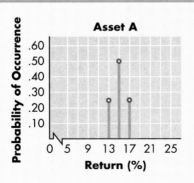
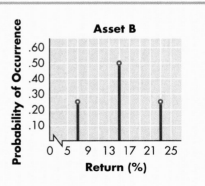

FIGURE 6.3

Continuous Probability Distributions

Continuous probability distributions for asset A's and asset B's returns

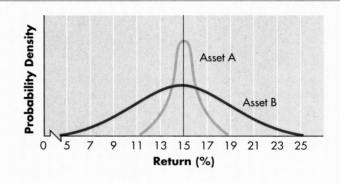

assets have the same most likely return, the range of return is much more dispersed for asset B than for asset A—16 versus 4 percent.

If we knew all the possible outcomes and associated probabilities, we could develop a **continuous probability distribution.** This type of distribution can be thought of as a bar chart for a very large number of outcomes.[6] Figure 6.3 presents continuous probability distributions for assets A and B.[7] Note in Figure 6.3 that although as A and B have the same most likely return (15 percent), the distribution of returns for asset B has much greater *dispersion* than the distribution for asset A. Clearly, asset B is more risky than asset A.

continuous probability distribution
A probability distribution showing all the possible outcomes and associated probabilities for a given event.

Risk Measurement

In addition to its *range,* the risk of an asset can be measured quantitatively using statistics. Here we consider two statistics—the standard deviation and the coefficient of variation—that can be used to measure the variability of asset returns.

---

6. To develop a continuous probability distribution, one must have data on a large number of historical occurrences for a given event. Then, by developing a frequency distribution indicating how many times each outcome has occurred over the given time horizon, one can convert these data into a probability distribution. Probability distributions for risky events can also be developed by using *simulation*—a process discussed briefly in Chapter 10.

7. The continuous distribution's probabilities change due to the large number of additional outcomes considered. The area under each of the curves is equal to 1, which means that 100% of the outcomes, or all the possible outcomes, are considered.

Standard Deviation

standard deviation (σ_k)
The most common statistical indicator of an asset's risk; it measures the dispersion around the *expected value*.

expected value of a return ($\bar{k}$)
The most likely return on a given asset.

The most common statistical indicator of an asset's risk is the **standard deviation**, σ_k, which measures the dispersion around the *expected value*.[8] The **expected value of a return**, $\bar{k}$, is the most likely return on an asset, which is calculated as:[9]

$$\bar{k} = \sum_{i=1}^{n} k_i \times Pr_i \tag{6.2}$$

where

$$k_i = \text{return for the } i\text{th outcome}$$
$$Pr_i = \text{probability of occurrence of the } i\text{th outcome}$$
$$n = \text{number of outcomes considered}$$

Example ▼ The expected values for Norman Company's assets A and B are presented in Table 6.2. Column 1 gives the Pr_i's and column 2 gives the k_i's. In each case n equals 3. The expected value for each asset's return is 15%.

| TABLE 6.2 | **Expected Values of Returns for Assets A and B** | | |

Possible outcomes	Probability (1)	Returns (2)	Weighted value [(1) × (2)] (3)
		Asset A	
Pessimistic	.25	13%	3.25%
Most likely	.50	15	7.50
Optimistic	.25	17	4.25
Total	1.00	Expected return	15.00%
		Asset B	
Pessimistic	.25	7%	1.75%
Most likely	.50	15	7.50
Optimistic	.25	23	5.75
Total	1.00	Expected return	15.00%

---

8. Although risk is typically viewed as determined by the dispersion of outcomes around an expected value, many people believe that risk exists only when outcomes are below the expected value, because only returns below the expected value are considered bad. Nevertheless, the common approach is to view risk as determined by the variability on either side of the expected value, because the greater this variability, the less confident one can be of the outcomes associated with an investment.

9. The formula for finding the expected value of return, $\bar{k}$, when all of the outcomes, k_i, are known *and* their related probabilities are assumed to be equal, is a simple arithmetic average:

$$k = \frac{\sum_{i=1}^{n} k_i}{n} \tag{6.2a}$$

where n is the number of observations. Equation 6.2 is emphasized in this chapter because returns and related probabilities are often available.

TABLE 6.3	The Calculation of the Standard Deviation of the Returns for Assets A and B[a]

Asset A

i	k_i	$\overline{k}$	$k_i - \overline{k}$	$(k_i - \overline{k})^2$	Pr_i	$(k_i - \overline{k})^2 \times Pr_i$
1	13%	15%	−2%	4%	.25	1%
2	15	15	0	0	.50	0
3	17	15	2	4	.25	1

$$\sum_{i=1}^{3} (k_i - \overline{k})^2 \times Pr_i = 2\%$$

$$\sigma_{k_A} = \sqrt{\sum_{i=1}^{3} (k_i - \overline{k})^2 \times Pr_i} = \sqrt{2}\% = \underline{1.41\%}$$

Asset B

i	k_i	$\overline{k}$	$k_i - \overline{k}$	$(k_i - \overline{k})^2$	Pr_i	$(k_i - \overline{k})^2 \times Pr_i$
1	7%	15%	−8%	64%	.25	16%
2	15	15	0	0	.50	0
3	23	15	8	64	.25	16

$$\sum_{i=1}^{3} (k_i - \overline{k})^2 \times Pr_i = 32\%$$

$$\sigma_{k_B} = \sqrt{\sum_{i=1}^{3} (k_i - \overline{k})^2 \times Pr_i} = \sqrt{32}\% = \underline{5.66\%}$$

[a]Calculations in this table are made in percentage form rather than decimal form—e.g., 13% rather than .13. As a result, some of the intermediate computations may appear to be inconsistent with those that would result from using decimal form. Regardless, the resulting standard deviations are correct and identical to those that would result from using decimal rather than percentage form.

Career Key

The *marketing* department considers standard deviation when deciding to add or delete product lines. The addition and/or deletion of product lines might produce an erratic earnings pattern that would increase the risk of the firm. And the standard deviation can be influenced by the *operations* department, which can help stabilize earnings by entering into long-term contracts with suppliers that will reduce the fluctuations in raw material prices and subsequently in earnings.

The expression for the *standard deviation of returns*, σ_k, is:[10]

$$\sigma_k = \sqrt{\sum_{i=1}^{n} (k_i - \overline{k})^2 \times Pr_i} \tag{6.3}$$

In general, the higher the standard deviation, the greater the risk.

Example ▼ Table 6.3 presents the standard deviations for Norman Company's assets A and B, based on the earlier data. The standard deviation for asset A is 1.41%, and the

---

10. The formula that is commonly used to find the standard deviation of returns, σ_k, in a situation in which *all* outcomes are known *and* their related probabilities are assumed equal, is

$$\sigma_k = \sqrt{\frac{\sum_{i=1}^{n} (k_i - k)^2}{n - 1}} \tag{6.3a}$$

where n is the number of observations. Equation 6.3 is emphasized in this chapter because returns and related probabilities are often available.

FIGURE 6.4

Bell-Shaped Curve
Normal probability distribution, with ranges

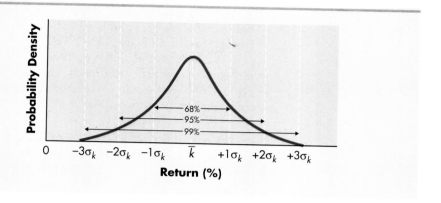

standard deviation for asset B is 5.66%. The higher risk of asset B is clearly
reflected in its higher standard deviation.

normal probability distribution
A symmetrical probability distribution
whose shape resembles a "bell-shaped"
curve.

A **normal probability distribution,** depicted in Figure 6.4, always resembles a
"bell-shaped" curve. It is symmetrical: From the peak of the graph, the curve's
extensions are mirror images (reflections) of each other. The symmetry of the
curve means that half the probability is associated with the values to the left of
the peak and half with values to the right. As noted on the figure, for normal
probability distributions, 68 percent of the possible outcomes will lie between
±1 standard deviation from the expected value, 95 percent of all outcomes will
lie between ±2 standard deviations from the expected value, and 99 percent of
all outcomes will lie between ±3 standard deviations from the expected value.[11]

Example ▼

If we assume that the probability distribution of returns for the Norman Company
is normal, 68% of the possible outcomes would have a return ranging between
13.59 and 16.41% for asset A and between 9.34 and 20.66% for asset B; 95% of
the possible return outcomes would range between 12.18 and 17.82% for asset A
and between 3.68 and 26.32% for asset B; and 99% of the possible return outcomes would range between 10.77 and 19.23% for asset A and between −1.98 and
31.98% for asset B. The greater risk of asset B is clearly reflected by its much wider
range of possible returns for each level of confidence (68%, 95%, etc.).

Coefficient of Variation

coefficient of variation (CV)
A measure of relative dispersion that is
useful in comparing the risk of assets
with differing expected returns.

The **coefficient of variation, CV,** is a measure of relative dispersion that is useful
in comparing the risk of assets with differing expected returns. Equation 6.4
gives the expression for the coefficient of variation:

$$CV = \frac{\sigma_k}{\bar{k}}$$

(6.4)

The higher the coefficient of variation, the greater the risk.

---

11. Tables of values indicating the probabilities associated with various deviations from the expected value of a
normal distribution can be found in any basic statistics text. These values can be used to establish confidence limits
and make inferences about possible outcomes. Such applications may be found in most basic statistics and upper-
level managerial finance textbooks.

E x a m p l e ▼ When the standard deviation (from Table 6.3) and the expected returns (from Table 6.2) for assets A and B are substituted into Equation 6.4, the coefficients of variation for A and B are .094 (1.41% ÷ 15%) and .377 (5.66% ÷ 15%), respectively. Asset B has the higher coefficient of variation and is therefore more risky than asset A—which we already know from the standard deviation. Because both assets have the same expected return, the coefficient of variation has not
▲ provided any new information.

The real utility of the coefficient of variation comes in comparing the risk of assets that have *different* expected returns.

E x a m p l e ▼ A firm wants to select the less risky of two alternative assets—X and Y. The expected return, standard deviation, and coefficient of variation for each of these assets' returns are

Statistics	Asset X	Asset Y
(1) Expected return	12%	20%
(2) Standard deviation	9%[a]	10%
(3) Coefficient of variation [(2) ÷ (1)]	.75	.50[a]

[a]Preferred asset using the given risk measure.

Based solely on their standard deviations, the firm would prefer asset X, which has a lower standard deviation than asset Y (9% versus 10%). However, management would be making a serious error in choosing asset X over asset Y, because the relative dispersion—the risk—of the assets as reflected in the coefficient of variation is lower for Y than for X (.50 versus .75). Clearly, the use of the coefficient of variation to compare asset risk is effective because it also con-
▲ siders the relative size, or expected return, of the assets.

? Review Questions

6–4   How can *sensitivity analysis* be used to assess asset risk? Define and describe the role of the *range* in sensitivity analysis.

6–5   What does a plot of the *probability distribution* of outcomes show a decision maker about an asset's risk? What is the difference between a *bar chart* and a *continuous probability distribution?*

6–6   What does the *standard deviation* of asset returns indicate? What relationship exists between the size of the standard deviation and the degree of asset risk?

6–7   What is the *coefficient of variation?* How is it calculated? When is it preferred over the standard deviation for comparing asset risk?

6.3 Risk of a Portfolio

efficient portfolio
A portfolio that maximizes return for a given level of risk or minimizes risk for a given level of return.

The risk of any single proposed asset investment should not be viewed independent of other assets. New investments must be considered in light of their impact on the risk and return of the *portfolio* of assets.[12] The financial manager's goal is to create an **efficient portfolio,** one that maximizes return for a given level of risk or minimizes risk for a given level of return. We therefore need a way to measure the return of a portfolio of assets. Once we can do that, we will look at the statistical concept of *correlation,* which underlies the process of diversification that is used to develop an efficient portfolio.

Portfolio Return and Standard Deviation

The *return on a portfolio* is a weighted average of the returns on the individual assets from which it is formed. We can use Equation 6.5 to find the portfolio return, k_p:

$$k_p = (w_1 \times k_1) + (w_2 \times k_2) + \cdots + (w_n \times k_n) = \sum_{j=1}^{n} w_j \times k_j \qquad (6.5)$$

where

w_j = proportion of the portfolio's total dollar value represented by asset j
k_j = return on asset j

Of course, $\sum_{j=1}^{n} w_j = 1$, which means that 100 percent of the portfolio's assets must be included in this computation.

The *standard deviation of a portfolio's returns* is found by applying the formula for the standard deviation of a single asset. Specifically, Equation 6.3 would be used when the probabilities of the returns are known, and Equation 6.3a (from footnote 10) would be applied when the outcomes are known and their related probabilities of occurrence are assumed to be equal.

Example ▼ Assume that we wish to determine the expected value and standard deviation of returns for portfolio XY, created by combining equal portions (50%) of assets X and Y. The expected returns of assets X and Y for each of the next 5 years (2001–2005) are given in columns 1 and 2, respectively, in part A of Table 6.4. In column 3, the weights of 50% for both assets X and Y along with their respective returns from columns 1 and 2 are substituted into Equation 6.5. Column 4 shows the results of the calculation—an expected portfolio return of 12% for each year, 2001 to 2005.

Furthermore, as shown in part B of Table 6.4, the expected value of these portfolio returns over the 5-year period is also 12% (calculated by using Equation 6.2a, in footnote 9). In part C of Table 6.4, portfolio XY's standard deviation is calculated to be 0% (using Equation 6.3a, in footnote 10). This value should not be surprising because the expected return each year is the same—12%. No variability is exhibited in the expected returns from year to
▲ year.

---

12. The portfolio of a firm, which would consist of its total assets, is not differentiated from the portfolio of an owner, which would likely contain a variety of different investment vehicles (i.e., assets). The differing characteristics of these two types of portfolios should become clear upon completion of Chapter 10.

TABLE 6.4 Expected Return, Expected Value, and Standard Deviation of Returns for Portfolio XY

A. Expected portfolio returns

	Expected return			Expected portfolio
	Asset X	Asset Y	Portfolio return calculation[a]	return, k_p
Year	(1)	(2)	(3)	(4)
2001	8%	16%	$(.50 \times 8\%) + (.50 \times 16\%) =$	12%
2002	10	14	$(.50 \times 10\%) + (.50 \times 14\%) =$	12
2003	12	12	$(.50 \times 12\%) + (.50 \times 12\%) =$	12
2004	14	10	$(.50 \times 14\%) + (.50 \times 10\%) =$	12
2005	16	8	$(.50 \times 16\%) + (.50 \times 8\%) =$	12

B. Expected value of portfolio returns, 2001–2005[b]

$$\bar{k}_p = \frac{12\% + 12\% + 12\% + 12\% + 12\%}{5} = \frac{60\%}{5} = \underline{\underline{12\%}}$$

C. Standard deviation of expected portfolio returns[c]

$$\sigma_{k_p} =$$

$$\sqrt{\frac{(12\% - 12\%)^2 + (12\% - 12\%)^2 + (12\% - 12\%)^2 + (12\% - 12\%)^2 + (12\% - 12\%)^2}{5-1}}$$

$$= \sqrt{\frac{0\% + 0\% + 0\% + 0\% + 0\%}{4}} = \sqrt{\frac{0}{4}}\% = \underline{\underline{0\%}}$$

[a]Using Equation 6.5.
[b]Using Equation 6.2a found in footnote 9.
[c]Using Equation 6.3a found in footnote 10.

correlation
A statistical measure of the relationship, if any, between series of numbers representing data of any kind.

positively correlated
Descriptive of two series that move in the same direction.

negatively correlated
Descriptive of two series that move in opposite directions.

correlation coefficient
A measure of the degree of correlation between two series.

perfectly positively correlated
Describes two *positively correlated* series that have a *correlation coefficient* of +1.

Correlation

Correlation is a statistical measure of the relationship, if any, between series of numbers representing data of any kind, from returns to test scores. If two series move in the same direction, they are **positively correlated;** if the series move in opposite directions, they are **negatively correlated.**[13]

The degree of correlation is measured by the **correlation coefficient,** which ranges from +1 for **perfectly positively correlated** series to −1 for **perfectly nega-**

---

13. The general *long-term trend* of two series could be the same (both increasing or both decreasing) or different (one increasing, the other decreasing), and the correlation of their *short-term (point-to-point) movements* in both situations could be either positive or negative. In other words, the pattern of movement around the trends could be correlated independent of the actual relationship between the trends. Further clarification of this seemingly inconsistent behavior can be found in most basic statistics texts.

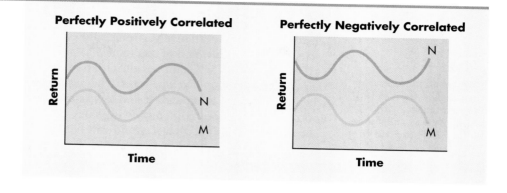

FIGURE 6.5

Correlations
The correlation between series M and N

perfectly negatively correlated
Describes two *negatively correlated* series that have a *correlation coefficient* of −1.

tively correlated series. These two extremes are depicted for series M and N in Figure 6.5. The perfectly positively correlated series move exactly together; the perfectly negatively correlated series move in exactly opposite directions.

Diversification

The concept of correlation is essential to developing an efficient portfolio. To reduce overall risk, it is best to combine or add to the portfolio assets that have a negative (or a low positive) correlation. Combining negatively correlated assets can reduce the overall variability of returns. Figure 6.6 shows that a portfolio containing the negatively correlated assets F and G, both having the same expected return, $\bar{k}$, also has the return $\bar{k}$ but has less risk (variability) than either of the individual assets. Even if assets are not negatively correlated, the lower the positive correlation between them, the lower the resulting risk.

uncorrelated
Describes two series that lack any interaction and therefore have a *correlation coefficient* close to zero.

Some assets are **uncorrelated**—that is, there is no interaction between their returns. Combining uncorrelated assets can reduce risk—not as effectively as combining negatively correlated assets, but more effectively than combining positively correlated assets. The correlation coefficient for uncorrelated assets is close to zero and acts as the midpoint between perfect positive and perfect negative correlation.

FIGURE 6.6

Diversification
Combining negatively correlated assets to diversify risk

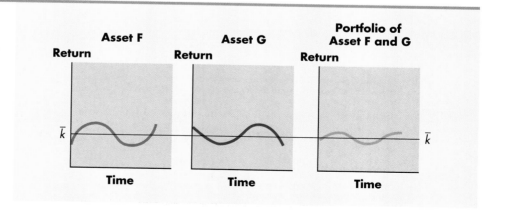

The creation of a portfolio by combining two assets with perfectly positively correlated returns *cannot* reduce the portfolio's overall risk below the risk of the least risky asset. Alternatively, a portfolio combining two assets with less than perfectly positive correlation *can* reduce total risk to a level below that of either of the components, which in certain situations may be zero. For example, assume that you manufacture machine tools. The business is very *cyclical,* with high sales when the economy is expanding and low sales during a recession. If you acquired another machine-tool company, with sales positively correlated with those of your firm, the combined sales would still be cyclical, and risk would remain the same. Alternatively, however, you could acquire a sewing-machine manufacturer, which is *countercyclical.* It typically has low sales during economic expansion and high sales during recession (when consumers are more likely to make their own clothes). Combination with the sewing-machine manufacturer, which has negatively correlated sales, should reduce risk.

Career Key

Management is concerned about the effect on its risk level of its product diversification decisions. Adding and/or deleting product groups will affect the firm's portfolio of products and the level of risk that is associated with it.

E x a m p l e ▼ Table 6.5 presents the anticipated returns from three different assets—X, Y, and Z—over the next 5 years, along with their expected values and standard devia-

| TABLE 6.5 | **Returns, Expected Values, and Standard Deviations for Assets X, Y, and Z and Portfolios XY and XZ** |

	Assets			Portfolios	
Year	X	Y	Z	XY[a] (50%X + 50%Y)	XZ[b] (50%X + 50%Z)
2001	8%	16%	8%	12%	8%
2002	10	14	10	12	10
2003	12	12	12	12	12
2004	14	10	14	12	14
2005	16	8	16	12	16
Statistics:[c]					
Expected value	12%	12%	12%	12%	12%
Standard deviation[d]	3.16%	3.16%	3.16%	0%	3.16%

[a]Portfolio XY, which consists of 50% of asset X and 50% of asset Y, illustrates *perfect negative correlation,* because these two return streams behave in completely opposite fashion over the 5-year period. The return values shown here were calculated in part A of Table 6.4.

[b]Portfolio XZ, which consists of 50% of asset X and 50% of asset Z, illustrates *perfect positive correlation,* because these two return streams behave identically over the 5-year period. These return values were calculated by using the same method demonstrated for portfolio XY in part A of Table 6.4.

[c]Because the probabilities associated with the returns are not given, the general equations, Equation 6.2a in footnote 9 and Equation 6.3a in footnote 10, were used to calculate expected values and standard deviations, respectively. Calculation of the expected value and standard deviation for portfolio XY is demonstrated in parts B and C, respectively, of Table 6.4.

[d]The portfolio standard deviations can be directly calculated from the standard deviations of the component assets using the following formula:

$$\sigma_{k_p} = \sqrt{w_1^2\sigma_1^2 + w_2^2\sigma_2^2 + 2w_1w_2r_{1,2}\sigma_1\sigma_2}$$

where w_1 and w_2 are the proportions of component assets 1 and 2, σ_1 and σ_2 are the standard deviations of component assets 1 and 2, and $r_{1,2}$ is the correlation coefficient between the returns of component assets 1 and 2.

tions. Each of the assets has an expected value of return of 12% and a standard deviation of 3.16%. The assets therefore have equal return and equal risk. The return patterns of assets X and Y are perfectly negatively correlated. They move in exactly opposite directions over time. The returns of assets X and Z are perfectly positively correlated. They move in precisely the same direction. (*Note:* The returns for X and Z are identical.)[14]

Portfolio XY   Portfolio XY (shown in Table 6.5) is created by combining equal portions of assets X and Y—the perfectly negatively correlated assets.[15] (Calculation of portfolio XY's annual expected returns, their expected value, and the standard deviation of expected portfolio returns was demonstrated in Table 6.4.) The risk in this portfolio, as reflected by its standard deviation, is reduced to 0%, while the expected return remains at 12%. Thus, the combination results in the complete elimination of risk. Whenever assets are perfectly negatively correlated, an optimum combination (similar to the 50–50 mix in the case of assets X and Y) exists for which the resulting standard deviation will equal 0.

Portfolio XZ   Portfolio XZ (shown in Table 6.5) is created by combining equal portions of assets X and Z—the perfectly positively correlated assets. The risk in this portfolio, as reflected by its standard deviation, is unaffected by this combination. Risk remains at 3.16%, and the expected return value remains at 12%. Whenever perfectly positively correlated assets such as X and Z are combined, the standard deviation of the resulting portfolio cannot be reduced *below that of the least risky asset*; the maximum portfolio standard deviation will be that of the riskiest asset. Because assets X and Z have the same standard deviation, the minimum and maximum standard deviations are the same (3.16%). This result can be attributed to the unlikely situation that X and Z are identical assets.

Correlation, Diversification, Risk, and Return

In general, the lower the correlation between asset returns, the greater the potential diversification of risk. (This should be clear from the behaviors illustrated in Table 6.5.) For each pair of assets, there is a combination that will result in the lowest risk (standard deviation) possible. How much risk can be reduced by this combination depends on the degree of correlation. Many potential combinations (assuming divisibility) could be made, but only one combination of the infinite number of possibilities will minimize risk.

Hint   Remember, low correlation between two series of numbers is less positive and more negative—indicating greater dissimilarity of behavior of the two series.

Three possible correlations—perfect positive, uncorrelated, and perfect negative—illustrate the effect of correlation on the diversification of risk and return. Table 6.6 summarizes the impact of correlation on the range of return and risk for various two-asset portfolio combinations. The table shows that as we move

---

14. Identical return streams are used in this example to permit clear illustration of the concepts, but it is *not* necessary for return streams to be identical for them to be perfectly positively correlated. Any return streams that move (i.e., vary) exactly together—regardless of the relative magnitude of the returns—are perfectly positively correlated.

15. For illustrative purposes it has been assumed that each of the assets—X, Y, and Z—can be divided up and combined with other assets to create portfolios. This assumption is made only to permit clear illustration of the concepts. The assets are not actually divisible.

TABLE 6.6	Correlation, Return, and Risk for Various Two-Asset Portfolio Combinations	
Correlation coefficient	Range of return	Range of risk
+1 (perfect positive)	Between returns of two assets held in isolation	Between risk of two assets held in isolation
0 (uncorrelated)	Between returns of two assets held in isolation	Between risk of most risky asset and an amount less than risk of least risky asset but greater than 0
−1 (perfect negative)	Between returns of two assets held in isolation	Between risk of most risky asset and 0

from perfect positive correlation to uncorrelated assets to perfect negative correlation, the ability to reduce risk is improved. Note that in no case will a portfolio of assets be riskier than the riskiest asset included in the portfolio.

Example ▼ A firm has calculated the expected return and the risk for each of two assets—R and S.

Asset	Expected return, $\bar{k}$	Risk (standard deviation), σ
R	6%	3%
S	8	8

Clearly, asset R is a lower-return, lower-risk asset than asset S.

To evaluate possible combinations, the firm considered three possible correlations—perfect positive, uncorrelated, and perfect negative. The results of the analysis are shown in Figure 6.7, using the ranges of return and risk noted above. In all cases, the return will range between the 6% return of R and the 8% return of S. The risk, on the other hand, ranges between the individual risks of R and S (from 3 to 8%) in the case of perfect positive correlation, from below 3% (the risk of R) and greater than 0% to 8% (the risk of S) in the uncorrelated case, and between 0 and 8% (the risk of S) in the perfectly negatively correlated case.

Note that *only in the case of perfect negative correlation can the risk be reduced to 0.* Also note that as the correlation becomes less positive and more negative (moving from the top of the figure down), the ability to reduce risk improves. The amount of risk reduction achieved depends on the proportions in which the assets are combined. Although determining the risk-minimizing combination is beyond the scope of this discussion, it is an important issue in developing portfolios of assets.

▲

FIGURE 6.7

Possible Correlations
Range of portfolio return ($\bar{k}_p$) and risk (σ_{k_p}) for combinations of assets R and S for various correlation coefficients

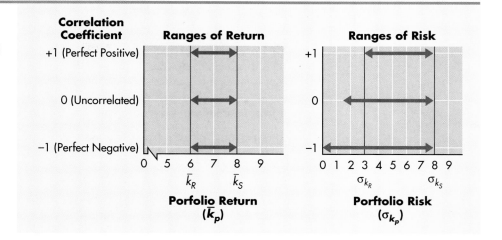

In Practice

Less Risk through Diversification

At first glance, GE Capital Corp.'s unusual combination of businesses might seem like a recipe for disaster. Its 28 separate business lines fall into five major product groups: specialty insurance; consumer services such as private-label credit card operations for retailers, plus auto and home financing; equipment leasing and management, ranging from aircraft and automotive to railcars, satellites, and portable toilets; commercial financing; and financing for smaller businesses. Recently it also entered the rapidly growing information technology services market. However, such diversity is a primary reason for the success of GE Capital, the financial unit of General Electric Co. With annual compound growth of almost 20% for the past 5 years, the company has contributed about 40% of profit and 60% of earnings growth to its parent.

Much of this growth has been in Europe. Since 1994, GE Capital has bought 30 to 40 European companies each year, often in mundane niche markets—portable toilets and pet insurance, to name two—that other financial institutions ignore. With no other bidders, GE Capital buys these firms at a bargain price.

While some observers have labeled GE Capital's acquisitions "weird," the underlying strategy is anything but. The firm spreads risk through diversification, looking for growth in one area to compensate for losses or flat earnings in others. It blends riskier companies whose performance is tied to fluctuations in financial markets with ones that service financial assets and perform consistently regardless of market conditions. Next, GE Capital will take its diversification strategy to Asia. First stop: Japan, where financial restructuring presents opportunities for foreign companies.

International Diversification

The ultimate example of portfolio diversification involves including foreign assets in a portfolio. The inclusion of assets from countries that are less sensitive to the U.S. business cycle (i.e., that are negatively correlated) reduces the portfolio's responsiveness to market movements and to foreign currency fluctuations.

Returns from International Diversification

Over long periods, returns from internationally diversified portfolios tend to be superior to those of purely domestic ones. This is particularly so if the U.S. economy is performing relatively poorly and the dollar is depreciating in value against most foreign currencies. At such times the dollar returns to U.S. investors on a portfolio of foreign assets can be very attractive indeed. However, over any single short or intermediate period, international diversification can yield subpar returns—particularly during periods when the dollar is appreciating in value relative to other currencies. When the U.S. currency gains in value, the dollar value of a foreign-currency-denominated portfolio of assets declines. Even if this portfolio yields a satisfactory return in local currency, the return to U.S. investors will be reduced when translated into dollars. Subpar local currency portfolio returns, coupled with an appreciating dollar, can yield truly dismal dollar returns to U.S. investors.

Overall, though, the logic of international portfolio diversification assumes that these fluctuations in currency values and relative performance will average out over long periods and that an internationally diversified portfolio will tend to yield a comparable return at a lower level of risk than will similar purely domestic portfolios.

Risks of International Diversification

political risk
Risk that arises from the possibility that a host government might take actions harmful to foreign investors or that political turmoil in a country might endanger investments made in that country by foreign nationals.

U.S. investors should, however, also be aware of the potential dangers of international investing. In addition to the risk induced by currency fluctuations, several other financial risks are unique to international investing. The most important of these fall in the category of political risk. **Political risk** arises from the possibility that a host government might take actions harmful to foreign investors or that political turmoil in a country might endanger investments made in that country by foreign nationals. Political risks are particularly acute in developing countries, where unstable or ideologically motivated governments may attempt to block return of profits by foreign investors or even seize (nationalize) their assets in the host country. An example of political risk was the concern after Desert Storm in the early 1990s that Saudi Arabian fundamentalists would take over and nationalize the U.S. oil facilities located there. This concern was caused by the decline in Saudi oil revenues and the poor health of pro-American King Fahd.

Even where governments do not impose exchange controls or seize assets, international investors may suffer if a shortage of hard currency prevents payment of dividends or interest to foreigners. When governments are forced to allocate scarce foreign exchange, they rarely give top priority to the interests of foreign investors. Instead, hard currency reserves are typically used to pay for necessary imports such as food and industrial materials and to pay interest on the government's own debts. Because most of the debt of developing countries is held by banks rather than individuals, foreign investors are often badly harmed when a country experiences political or economic problems.

? Review Questions

6–8   Why must assets be evaluated in a portfolio context? What is an *efficient portfolio?* How can the return and standard deviation of a portfolio be determined?

6–9   Why is the *correlation* between asset returns important? How does diversification allow risky assets to be combined so that the risk of the portfolio is less than the risk of the individual assets in it?

6–10   How does international diversification enhance risk reduction? When might international diversification result in subpar returns? What are *political risks,* and how do they affect international diversification?

6.4 Risk and Return: The Capital Asset Pricing Model (CAPM)

capital asset pricing model (CAPM)
The basic theory that links together risk and return for all assets.

The most important aspect of risk is the *overall risk* of the firm as viewed by investors in the marketplace. Overall risk significantly affects investment opportunities—and even more important, the owners' wealth. The basic theory that links together risk and return for all assets is the **capital asset pricing model (CAPM)**.[16] We will use CAPM to understand the basic risk-return trade-offs involved in all types of financial decisions.

Types of Risk

To understand the basic types of risk, consider what happens to the risk of a portfolio consisting of a single security (asset), to which we add securities randomly selected from, say, the population of all actively traded securities. Using the standard deviation of return, σ_{k_p}, to measure the total portfolio risk, Figure 6.8 depicts the behavior of the total portfolio risk (*y* axis) as more securities are added (*x* axis). With the addition of securities, the total portfolio risk declines, due to the effects of diversification, and tends to approach a limit. Research has shown that, on average, most of the risk-reduction benefits of diversification can

---

16. The initial development of this theory is generally attributed to William F. Sharpe, "Capital Asset Prices: A Theory of Market Equilibrium Under Conditions of Risk," *Journal of Finance* 19 (September 1964), pp. 425–442, and John Lintner, "The Valuation of Risk Assets and the Selection of Risky Investments in Stock Portfolios and Capital Budgets," *Review of Economics and Statistics* 47 (February 1965), pp 13–37. A number of authors subsequently advanced, refined, and tested this now widely accepted theory.

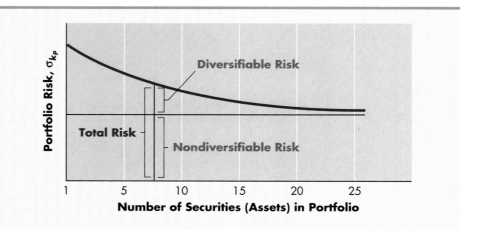

FIGURE 6.8

Risk Reduction
Portfolio risk and diversification

total risk
The combination of a security's nondiversifiable and diversifiable risk.

diversifiable risk
The portion of an asset's risk that is attributable to firm-specific, random causes; can be eliminated through diversification.

nondiversifiable risk
The relevant portion of an asset's risk attributable to market factors that affect all firms; cannot be eliminated through diversification.

be gained by forming portfolios containing 15 to 20 randomly selected securities.[17]

The **total risk** of a security can be viewed as consisting of two parts:

$$\text{Total security risk} = \text{nondiversifiable risk} + \text{diversifiable risk} \qquad (6.6)$$

Diversifiable risk, sometimes called *unsystematic risk,* represents the portion of an asset's risk that is associated with random causes that can be eliminated through diversification. It is attributable to firm-specific events, such as strikes, lawsuits, regulatory actions, and loss of a key account. **Nondiversifiable risk,** also called *systematic risk,* is attributable to market factors that affect all firms; it cannot be eliminated through diversification. Factors such as war, inflation, international incidents, and political events account for nondiversifiable risk.

Because any investor can create a portfolio of assets that will eliminate virtually all diversifiable risk, *the only relevant risk is nondiversifiable risk.* Any investor or firm therefore must be concerned solely with nondiversifiable risk. The measurement of nondiversifiable risk is thus of primary importance in selecting assets with the most desired risk-return characteristics.

The Model: CAPM

The capital asset pricing model (CAPM) links together nondiversifiable risk and return for all assets. We will discuss the model in five sections. The first defines, derives, and describes the beta coefficient, which is a measure of nondiversifiable risk. The second section presents an equation of the model itself, and the third

---

17. See, for example, W. H. Wagner and S. C. Lau, "The Effect of Diversification on Risk," *Financial Analysts Journal* 26 (November–December 1971), pp. 48–53, and Jack Evans and Stephen H. Archer, "Diversification and the Reduction of Dispersion: An Empirical Analysis," *Journal of Finance* 23 (December 1968), pp. 761–767. A more recent study, Gerald D. Newbould and Percy S. Poon, "The Minimum Number of Stocks Needed for Diversification," *Financial Practice and Education* (Fall 1993), pp. 85–87, shows that because an investor holds but one of a large number of possible *x*-security portfolios, it is unlikely that he or she will experience the average outcome. As a consequence, the study suggests that a minimum of 40 stocks is needed to fully diversify a portfolio. This study tends to support the widespread popularity of mutual fund investments.

graphically describes the relationship between risk and return. The fourth section discusses the effects of changes in inflationary expectations and risk aversion on the relationship between risk and return. The final section offers some general comments on CAPM.

Beta Coefficient

beta coefficient (*b*)
A measure of nondiversifiable risk. An *index* of the degree of movement of an asset's return in response to a change in the *market return*.

market return
The return on the market portfolio of all traded securities.

The **beta coefficient, *b*,** measures nondiversifiable risk. It is an *index* of the degree of movement of an asset's return in response to a change in the *market return*. An asset's historical returns are used in finding the asset's beta coefficient. The **market return** is the return on the market portfolio of all traded securities. The *Standard & Poor's 500 Stock Composite Index* or some similar stock index is commonly used as the market return. Although betas for actively traded stocks can be obtained from a variety of sources, you should understand how they are derived and interpreted and how they are applied to portfolios.

Deriving Beta from Return Data   The relationship between an asset's return and the market return and its use in deriving beta can be demonstrated graphically. Figure 6.9 plots the relationship between the returns of two assets— R and S—and the market return. Note that the horizontal (*x*) axis measures the market returns and the vertical (*y*) axis measures the individual asset's returns.

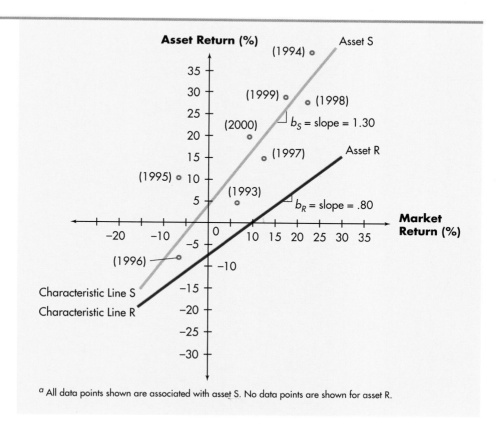

FIGURE 6.9

Beta Derivation[a]
Graphic derivation of beta for assets R and S

[a] All data points shown are associated with asset S. No data points are shown for asset R.

The first step in deriving beta involves plotting the coordinates for the market return and asset returns from various points in time. Such annual market return–asset return coordinates are shown *for asset S only* for the years 1993 through 2000. For example, in 2000, asset S's return was 20 percent when the market return was 10 percent. By use of statistical techniques, the "characteristic line" that best explains the relationship between the asset return and the market return coordinates is fit to the data points.[18] The slope of this line is beta. The beta for asset R is about .80 and that for asset S is about 1.30. Clearly, asset S's higher beta (steeper characteristic line slope) indicates that its return is more responsive to changing market returns. Therefore it is more risky than asset R.[19]

Interpreting Betas   The beta coefficient for the market is considered to be equal to 1.0; all other betas are viewed in relation to this value. Asset betas may take on values that are either positive or negative, but positive betas are the norm. The majority of beta coefficients fall between .5 and 2.0. The return of a stock that is half as responsive as the market ($b = .5$) is expected to change by 1/2 percent for each 1 percent change in the return of the market portfolio. A stock that is twice as responsive as the market ($b = 2.0$) is expected to experience a 2 percent change in its return for each 1 percent change in the return of the market portfolio. Table 6.7 provides some selected beta values and their interpretations. Beta coefficients for actively traded stocks can be obtained from published sources, such as *Value Line Investment Survey,* or through brokerage firms. Betas for some selected stocks are given in Table 6.8.

Portfolio Betas   The beta of a portfolio can be easily estimated using the betas of the individual assets it includes. Letting w_j represent the proportion of the portfolio's total dollar value represented by asset j and b_j equal the beta of asset j, we can use Equation 6.7 to find the portfolio beta, b_p:

Hint   Remember that published and calculated betas are based on historical data. When investors use beta for decision making, they should recognize that past performance relative to the market average may not predict future performance.

---

18. The empirical measurement of beta is approached by using *least-squares regression analysis* to find the regression coefficient (b_j) in the equation for the "characteristic line":

$$k_j = a_j + b_j k_m + e_j$$

where

k_j = return on asset j

a_j = intercept

b_j = beta coefficient, which equals $\dfrac{Cov\ (k_j,\ k_m)}{\sigma_m^2}$

where

$Cov\ (k_j,\ k_m)$ = covariance of the return on asset j, k_j, and the market portfolio, k_m

σ_m^2 = variance of the return on the market portfolio

k_m = required rate of return on the market portfolio of securities

e_j = random error term, which reflects the diversifiable, or unsystematic, risk of asset j

The calculations involved in finding betas are somewhat rigorous. If you want to know more about these calculations, consult an advanced managerial finance or investments text.

19. The values of beta also depend on the time interval used for return calculations and the number of returns used in the regression analysis. In other words, betas calculated using monthly returns would not necessarily be comparable to those calculated using a similar number of daily returns.

TABLE 6.7   Selected Beta Coefficients and Their Interpretations

Beta	Comment	Interpretation
2.0	Move in same direction as market	Twice as responsive, or risky, as the market
1.0		Same response or risk as the market (i.e., average risk)
.5		Only half as responsive, or risky, as the market
0		Unaffected by market movement
− .5	Move in opposite direction to market	Only half as responsive, or risky, as the market
−1.0		Same response or risk as the market (i.e., average risk)
−2.0		Twice as responsive, or risky, as the market

TABLE 6.8   Beta Coefficients for Selected Stocks (April 9, 1999)

Stock	Beta	Stock	Beta
Anheuser-Busch	.70	Merrill Lynch & Company	2.00
Apple Computer	.95	Microsoft Corp.	1.10
Callaway Golf	1.75	Occidental Petroleum	.85
Cascade Natural Gas	.55	Procter & Gamble	.90
Delta Air Lines	1.25	Seagram Company	1.05
Exxon Corporation	.80	Sempra Energy	.60
General Motors	1.10	Sony Corporation	.90
Harley-Davidson	1.20	Tandy Corporation	1.35
Intel Corp.	1.00	Universal Foods	.75
IBM	1.10	Xerox Corporation	1.00

Source: Value Line Investment Survey (New York: Value Line Publishing, April 9, 1999).

$$b_p = (w_1 \times b_1) + (w_2 \times b_2) + \ldots + (w_n \times b_n) = \sum_{j=1}^{n} w_j \times b_j \qquad (6.7)$$

Of course, $\sum_{j=1}^{n} w_j = 1$, which means that 100 percent of the portfolio's assets must be included in this computation.

Portfolio betas are interpreted in the same way as individual asset betas. They indicate the degree of responsiveness of the *portfolio's* return to changes in the market return. For example, when the market return increases by 10 percent, a portfolio with a beta of .75 will experience a 7.5 percent increase in its return (.75 × 10%); a portfolio with a beta of 1.25 will experience a 12.5 percent increase in its return (1.25 × 10%). Clearly, a portfolio containing mostly low-beta assets will have a low beta, and one containing mostly high-beta assets will have a high beta.

Hint Mutual fund managers are key users of the portfolio beta and return concepts. They are continually evaluating what would happen to the fund's beta and return if the securities of a particular firm are added or deleted from the fund's portfolio.

Example ▼ The Austin Fund, a large investment company, wishes to assess the risk of two portfolios—V and W. Both portfolios contain five assets, with the proportions

TABLE 6.9	Austin Fund's Portfolios V and W				
	Portfolio V			Portfolio W	
Asset	Proportion	Beta		Proportion	Beta
1	.10	1.65		.10	.80
2	.30	1.00		.10	1.00
3	.20	1.30		.20	.65
4	.20	1.10		.10	.75
5	.20	1.25		.50	1.05
Totals	1.00			1.00	

and betas shown in Table 6.9. The betas for the two portfolios, b_v and b_w, can be calculated by substituting data from the table into Equation 6.7:

$$b_v = (.10 \times 1.65) + (.30 \times 1.00) + (.20 \times 1.30) + (.20 \times 1.10) + (.20 \times 1.25)$$
$$= .165 + .300 + .260 + .220 + .250 = 1.195 \approx \underline{\underline{1.20}}$$

$$b_w = (.10 \times .80) + (.10 \times 1.00) + (.20 \times .65) + (.10 \times .75) + (.50 \times 1.05)$$
$$= .080 + .100 + .130 + .075 + .525 = \underline{\underline{.91}}$$

Portfolio V's beta is 1.20, and portfolio W's is .91. These values make sense, because portfolio V contains relatively high-beta assets and portfolio W contains relatively low-beta assets. Clearly, portfolio V's returns are more responsive to changes in market returns and are therefore more risky than portfolio W's.

The Equation

By using the beta coefficient to measure nondiversifiable risk, the *capital asset pricing model (CAPM)* is given in Equation 6.8:

$$k_j = R_F + [b_j \times (k_m - R_F)] \tag{6.8}$$

where

k_j = required return on asset j

R_F = risk-free rate of return, commonly measured by the return on a U.S. Treasury bill

b_j = beta coefficient or index of nondiversifiable risk for asset j

k_m = market return; return on the market portfolio of assets

The required return on an asset, k_j, is an increasing function of beta, b_j, which measures nondiversifiable risk. In other words, *the higher the risk, the higher the required return, and the lower the risk, the lower the required return.*

The model can be divided into two parts: (1) the *risk-free rate,* and (2) the *risk premium.* These are, respectively, the two elements on either side of the addition sign in Equation 6.8. The $(k_m - R_F)$ portion of the risk premium is called the *market risk premium,* because it represents the premium the investor must receive for taking the average amount of risk associated with holding the market portfolio of assets.[20]

E x a m p l e ▼ Benjamin Corporation, a growing computer-software developer, wishes to determine the required return on an asset Z, which has a beta of 1.5. The risk-free rate of return is found to be 7%; the return on the market portfolio of assets is 11%. Substituting $b_z = 1.5$, $R_F = 7\%$, and $k_m = 11\%$ into the capital asset pricing model given in Equation 6.8 yields a required return:

$$k_z = 7\% + [1.5 \times (11\% - 7\%)] = 7\% + 6\% = \underline{\underline{13\%}}$$

The market risk premium of 4% (11% − 7%), when adjusted for the asset's index of risk (beta) of 1.5, results in a risk premium of 6% (1.5 × 4%). That risk premium, when added to the 7% risk-free rate, results in a 13% required return. Other things being equal, the higher the beta, the higher the required return, and
▲ the lower the beta, the lower the required return.

The Graph: The Security Market Line (SML)

security market line (SML)
The depiction of the *capital asset pricing model (CAPM)* as a graph that reflects the required return in the marketplace for each level of nondiversifiable risk (beta).

When the capital asset pricing model (Equation 6.8) is depicted graphically, it is called the **security market line (SML).** The SML will, in fact, be a straight line. It reflects the required return in the marketplace for each level of nondiversifiable risk (beta). In the graph, risk as measured by beta, b, is plotted on the x axis, and required returns, k, are plotted on the y axis. The risk-return trade-off is clearly represented by the SML.

E x a m p l e ▼ In the preceding example for Benjamin Corporation, the risk-free rate, R_F, was 7%, and the market return, k_m, was 11%. The SML can be plotted by using the two sets of coordinates for the betas associated with R_F and k_m, b_{R_F} and b_m (i.e., $b_{R_F} = 0$,[21] $R_F = 7\%$; and $b_m = 1.0$, $k_m = 11\%$). Figure 6.10 presents the resulting security market line. As traditionally shown, the security market line in Figure 6.10 presents the required return associated with all positive betas. The market risk premium of 4% (k_m of 11% − R_F of 7%) has been highlighted. For a beta for asset Z, b_z, of 1.5, its corresponding required return, k_z, is 13%. Also shown in the figure is asset Z's risk premium of 6% (k_z of 13% − R_F of 7%). It should

---

20. Although CAPM has been widely accepted, a broader theory, *arbitrage pricing theory (APT),* first described by Stephen A. Ross, "The Arbitrage Theory of Capital Asset Pricing," *Journal of Economic Theory* (December 1976), pp. 341–360, has in recent years received a great deal of attention in the financial literature. The theory suggests that the risk premium on securities may be better explained by a number of factors underlying and in place of the market return used in CAPM. The CAPM in effect can be viewed as being derived from APT. Although testing of APT theory confirms the importance of the market return, it has thus far failed to clearly identify other risk factors. As a result of this failure as well as APT's lack of practical acceptance and usage, we concentrate our attention here on CAPM.

21. Because R_F is the rate of return on a risk-free asset, the beta associated with the risk-free asset, b_{R_F}, would equal 0. The 0 beta on the risk-free asset reflects not only its absence of risk but also that the asset's return is unaffected by movements in the market return.

FIGURE 6.10

Security Market Line
Security market line (SML) with Benjamin Corporation's asset Z data shown

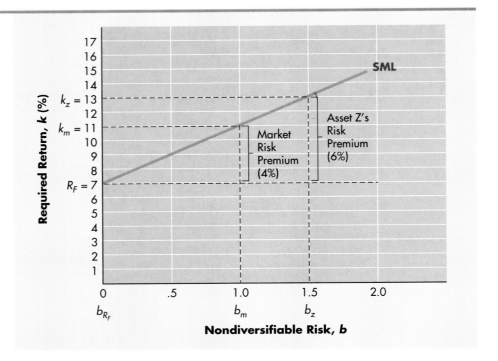

be clear that for assets with betas greater than 1, the risk premium is greater than that for the market; for assets with betas less than 1, the risk premium is less than that for the market.

Shifts in the Security Market Line

The security market line is not stable over time, and shifts in the security market line can result in a change in required return. The position and slope of the SML is affected by two major forces—inflationary expectations and risk aversion—which are separately analyzed next.[22]

Changes in Inflationary Expectations   Changes in inflationary expectations, as noted in Chapter 2, affect the risk-free rate of return, R_F. The equation for the risk-free rate of return (Equation 2.3) is rewritten as Equation 6.9:

$$R_F = k^* + IP \tag{6.9}$$

This equation shows that assuming a constant real rate of interest, k^*, changes in inflationary expectations, reflected in an inflation premium, IP, will result in corresponding changes in the risk-free rate. Therefore, a change in inflationary expec-

---

22. A firm's beta can change over time as a result of changes in the firm's asset mix, in its financing mix, or in external factors not within management's control, such as earthquakes, toxic spills, and so on. The impacts of changes in beta on value are discussed in Chapter 7.

tations resulting from events such as international trade embargoes or major changes in Federal Reserve policy will result in a shift in the SML. Because the risk-free rate is a basic component of all rates of return (see Equation 2.2 in Chapter 2), any change in R_F will be reflected in *all* required rates of return.

Changes in inflationary expectations result in parallel shifts in the SML in direct response to the magnitude and direction of the change. This effect can best be illustrated by an example.

Example ▼   In the preceding example, using CAPM, the required return for asset Z, k_Z, was found to be 13%. Assuming that the risk-free rate of 7% includes a 2% real rate of interest, k^*, and a 5% inflation premium, *IP*, then Equation 6.9 confirms that

$$R_F = 2\% + 5\% = 7\%$$

Now assume that recent economic events have resulted in an *increase of 3% in inflationary expectations, raising the inflation premium* to 8% (IP_1). As a result, all returns would likewise rise by 3%. In this case, the new returns (noted by subscript 1) are

$$R_{F_1} = 10\% \text{ (rises from 7\% to 10\%)}$$
$$k_{m_1} = 14\% \text{ (rises from 11\% to 14\%)}$$

Substituting these values, along with asset Z's beta (b_Z) of 1.5, into the CAPM (Equation 6.8), we find that asset Z's new required return (k_{Z_1}) can be calculated:

$$k_{Z_1} = 10\% + [1.5 \times (14\% - 10\%)] = 10\% + 6\% = \underline{\underline{16\%}}$$

Comparing k_{Z_1} of 16% to k_Z of 13%, we see that the change of 3% in asset Z's required return exactly equals the change in the inflation premium. The same 3% increase would result for all assets.

Figure 6.11 depicts the situation just described. It shows that the 3% increase in inflationary expectations results in a parallel shift upward of 3% in the SML. Clearly, the required returns on all assets rise by 3%. Note that the rise in the inflation premium from 5 to 8% (*IP* to IP_1) causes the risk-free rate to rise from 7 to 10% (R_F to R_{F_1}) and the market return to increase from 11 to 14% (k_m to k_{m_1}). The security market line therefore shifts upward by 3% (SML to SML_1), causing the required return on all risky assets, such as asset Z, to rise by 3%. It should now be clear that *a given change in inflationary expectations will be fully reflected in a corresponding change in the returns of all assets, as reflect-*
▲ *ed graphically in a parallel shift of the SML.*

Changes in Risk Aversion   The slope of the security market line reflects the general risk preferences of investors in the marketplace. As discussed earlier and shown in Figure 6.1, most investors are risk-averse—they require increased returns for increased risk. This positive relationship between risk and return is graphically represented by the SML, which depicts the relationship between non-diversifiable risk as measured by beta (*x* axis), and the required return (*y* axis).

FIGURE 6.11

Inflation Shifts SML
Impact of increased inflationary expectations on the SML

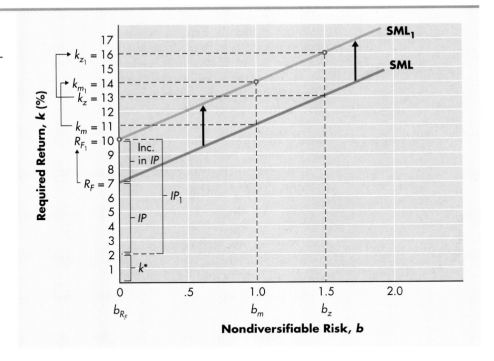

The slope of the SML reflects the degree of risk aversion: *the steeper its slope, the greater the degree of risk aversion,* because a higher level of return would be required for each level of risk as measured by beta. In other words, *risk premiums increase with increasing risk avoidance.*

Changes in risk aversion, and therefore shifts in the SML, result from changing preferences of investors, which generally result from economic, political, and social events. Examples of events that *increase* risk aversion would be a stock market crash, assassination of a key political leader, the outbreak of war, and so forth. In general, widely accepted expectations of hard times ahead tend to cause investors to become more risk-averse, requiring higher returns as compensation for accepting a given level of risk. The impact of increased risk aversion on the SML can best be demonstrated by an example.

Example ▼ In the preceding examples, the SML in Figure 6.10 reflected a risk-free rate (R_F) of 7%, a market return (k_m) of 11%, a market risk premium ($k_m - R_F$) of 4%, and a required return on asset Z (k_Z) of 13% with a beta (b_Z) of 1.5. Assume that recent economic events have made investors more risk-averse, causing a new higher market return (k_{m_1}) of 14%. Graphically, this change would cause the SML to shift upward as shown in Figure 6.12, causing a new market risk premium ($k_{m_1} - R_F$) of 7%. As a result, the required return on all risky assets will increase. For asset Z, with a beta of 1.5, the new required return (k_{Z_1}) can be calculated by using CAPM (Equation 6.8):

$$k_{Z_1} = 7\% + [1.5 \times (14\% - 7\%)] = 7\% + 10.5\% = \underline{\underline{17.5\%}}$$

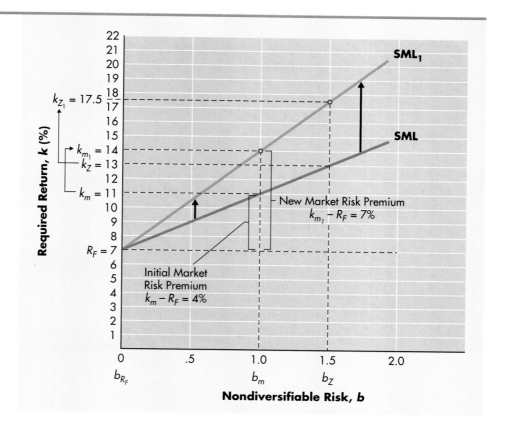

FIGURE 6.12

Risk Aversion Shifts SML

Impact of increased risk aversion on the SML

This value can be seen on the new security market line (SML_1) in Figure 6.12. Note that although asset Z's risk, as measured by beta, did not change, its required return has increased due to the increased risk aversion reflected in the market risk premium. It should now be clear that *greater risk aversion results in higher required returns for each level of risk. Similarly, a reduction in risk aversion would cause the required return for each level of risk to decline.*

Some Comments on CAPM

The capital asset pricing model generally relies on historical data to estimate required returns. The betas, which are developed using data for the given asset as well as for the market, may or may not actually reflect the *future* variability of returns. Therefore the required returns specified by the model can be viewed only as rough approximations. Other users of betas commonly make subjective adjustments to reflect their expectations of the future when such expectations differ from the actual risk-return behaviors of the past.

The CAPM was actually developed to explain the behavior of security prices and provide a mechanism whereby investors could assess the impact of a proposed security investment on their portfolio's overall risk and return. It is based on an assumed **efficient market**—a market in which there are many small

efficient market
An assumed "perfect" market in which there are many small investors, each having the same information and expectations with respect to securities; there are no restrictions on investment, no taxes, and no transaction costs; and all investors are rational, view securities similarly, and are risk-averse, preferring higher returns and lower risk.

In Practice

What's at Risk? VAR Has the Answer

Financial managers, always on the lookout for new ways to measure and manage risk, are adding value-at-risk (VAR) techniques to their repertoire. VAR predicts the drop in a company's net worth if things go wrong, by calculating the financial risk in the future market value of a portfolio of assets, liabilities, and equity. First used by banks and brokerage firms to measure the risk of market movements, VAR now has proponents among nonfinancial companies like Xerox, General Motors, and GTE.

How does VAR work? A bank could take a diverse portfolio of financial assets and calculate price swings by measuring performance on specific days in the past. Plotting the percentage gain or loss for hundreds of days would reveal the value at risk of that portfolio. If it was riskier than previously thought, traders could take corrective action—selling a particular type of security, for example—to reduce risk.

BMW Financial Services of North America developed its own VAR technique to measure interest-rate risk using the standard deviation of historical interest rate movement. The firm uses two types of VAR calculations. Equity-at-risk tells shareholders how much of their investment is at risk. Earnings-at-risk is also important, because earnings growth is important to increasing shareholder wealth.

Like any quantitative model, VAR has its limitations. Perhaps its biggest drawback is the reliance on historical patterns that may not hold true in the future. However, VAR also can show companies whether they are properly diversified and whether they have sufficient capital. Among its other benefits: it tells managers if their actions are too cautious, identifies potential risk trouble spots, and provides a way to compare business units that measure performance differently for internal reporting.

investors, each having the same information and expectations with respect to securities; there are no restrictions on investment, no taxes, and no transaction costs; and all investors are rational, view securities similarly, and are risk-averse, preferring higher returns and lower risk.

Although the perfect world of the efficient market appears to be unrealistic, empirical studies have provided support for the existence of the expectational relationship described by CAPM in active markets such as the New York Stock Exchange.[23] In the case of real corporate assets, such as plant and equipment, research thus far has failed to prove the general applicability of CAPM because

---

23. A study by Eugene F. Fama and Kenneth R. French, "The Cross-Section of Expected Stock Returns," *Journal of Finance* 47 (June 1992), pp. 427–465, raised serious questions about the validity of CAPM. The study failed to find a significant relationship between the *historic* betas and *historic* returns on over 2,000 stocks during 1963–1990. In other words, they found that the magnitude of a stock's *historical* beta had no relationship to the level of its *historical* return. Although Fama and French's study continues to receive attention, CAPM has not been abandoned because its rejection as a *historical* model fails to reject its validity as an *expectational* model. Therefore, in spite of this challenge, CAPM continues to be viewed as a logical and useful framework—both conceptually and operationally—for linking *expected* nondiversifiable risk and return.

of indivisibility, relatively large size, limited number of transactions, and absence of an efficient market for such assets.

In spite of the fact that the risk-return trade-off described by CAPM is not generally applicable to all assets, it provides a useful conceptual framework for evaluating and linking risk and return. An awareness of this trade-off and an attempt to consider risk as well as return in financial decision making should aid the financial manager in achieving the goal of owner wealth maximization.

? Review Questions

6–11   What is the relationship of total risk, nondiversifiable risk, and diversifiable risk? Why is nondiversifiable risk the *only relevant risk?*

6–12   What is *beta* and what does it measure? How are asset betas derived, and where can they be obtained? How can you find the beta of a portfolio?

6–13   What is the equation for the *capital asset pricing model (CAPM)?* Explain the meaning of each variable. Assuming a risk-free rate of 8 percent and a market return of 12 percent, draw the *security market line (SML).*

6–14   What impact would the following changes have on the security market line and therefore on the required return for a given level of risk? (**a**) An increase in inflationary expectations. (**b**) Investors become less risk-averse.

6–15   Why do financial managers have difficulty applying CAPM in decision making? Generally, what benefit does CAPM provide them?

SUMMARY

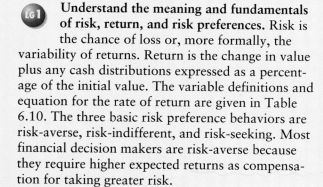

Understand the meaning and fundamentals of risk, return, and risk preferences. Risk is the chance of loss or, more formally, the variability of returns. Return is the change in value plus any cash distributions expressed as a percentage of the initial value. The variable definitions and equation for the rate of return are given in Table 6.10. The three basic risk preference behaviors are risk-averse, risk-indifferent, and risk-seeking. Most financial decision makers are risk-averse because they require higher expected returns as compensation for taking greater risk.

Describe procedures for measuring the risk of a single asset. The risk of a single asset is measured in much the same way as the risk of a portfolio, or collection, of assets. Sensitivity analysis and probability distributions can be used to assess risk. In addition to the range, the standard deviation and the coefficient of variation are statistics that can be used to measure risk quantitatively. The key variable definitions and equations for the expected value of a return, standard deviation of return, and the coefficient of variation are summarized in Table 6.10.

Discuss the measurement of return and standard deviation for a portfolio and the various types of correlation that can exist between series of numbers. The return of a portfolio is calculated as the weighted average of returns on the individual assets from which it is formed. The variable definitions and equation for portfolio return are given in Table 6.10. The portfolio standard deviation is found by using the formula for the standard deviation of a single asset. Correlation, the statistical relationship between series of numbers,

TABLE 6.10 **Summary of Key Definitions and Formulas for Risk and Return**

Variable definitions

b_j = beta coefficient or index of nondiversifiable risk for asset j

b_p = portfolio beta

C_t = cash received from the asset investment in the time period $t-1$ to t

CV = coefficient of variation

$\bar{k}$ = expected value of a return

k_i = return for the ith outcome

k_j = required return on asset j

k_m = market return; the return on the market portfolio of assets

k_p = portfolio return

k_t = actual, expected, or required rate of return during period t

n = number of outcomes considered

P_t = price (value) of asset at time t

P_{t-1} = price (value) of asset at time $t-1$

Pr_i = probability of occurrence of the ith outcome

R_F = risk-free rate of return

σ_k = standard deviation of returns

w_j = proportion of total portfolio dollar value represented by asset j

Risk and return formulas

Rate of return during period t:

$$k_t = \frac{P_t - P_{t-1} + C_t}{P_{t-1}}$$ [Eq. 6.1]

Expected value of a return:
for probabilistic data,

$$\bar{k} = \sum_{i=1}^{n} k_i \times Pr_i$$ [Eq. 6.2]

general formula,

$$\bar{k} = \frac{\sum_{i=1}^{n} k_i}{n}$$ [Eq. 6.2a]

Standard deviation of return:
for probabilistic data,

$$\sigma_k = \sqrt{\sum_{i=1}^{n} (k_i - \bar{k})^2 \times Pr_i}$$ [Eq. 6.3]

general formula,

$$\sigma_k = \sqrt{\frac{\sum_{i=1}^{n}(k_1 - \bar{k})^2}{n-1}}$$ [Eq. 6.3a]

Coefficient of variation:

$$CV = \frac{\sigma_k}{\bar{k}}$$ [Eq. 6.4]

Portfolio return:

$$k_p = \sum_{j=1}^{n} w_j \times k_j$$ [Eq. 6.5]

Total security risk = nondiversifiable
risk + diversifiable risk [Eq. 6.6]

Portfolio beta:

$$b_p = \sum_{j=1}^{n} w_j \times b_j$$ [Eq. 6.7]

Capital asset pricing model
(CAPM):

$$k_j = R_F + [b_j \times (k_m - R_F)]$$ [Eq. 6.8]

can be positive (the series move in the same direction), negative (the series move in opposite directions), or uncorrelated (the series exhibit no discernible relationship). At the extremes, the series can be perfectly positively correlated (have a correlation coefficient of +1) or perfectly negatively correlated (have a correlation coefficient of −1).

 Understand the risk and return characteristics of a portfolio in terms of correlation and diversification, and the impact of international assets on a portfolio. Diversification involves combining assets with low (less positive and more negative) correlation to reduce the risk of the portfolio. Although the return on a two-asset portfolio will lie between the returns of the two assets held in isolation, the range of risk depends on the correlation between the two assets. If they are perfectly positively correlated, the portfolio's risk will be between the individual asset's risks. If uncorrelated, the portfolio's risk will be between the risk of the most risky asset and an amount less than the risk of the least risky asset but greater than zero. If negatively correlated, the portfolio's risk will be between the risk of the most risky asset and zero. International diversification, which involves including foreign assets in a portfolio, can be used to further reduce a portfolio's risk.

 Review the two types of risk and the derivation and role of beta in measuring the relevant risk of both an individual security and a **portfolio.** The total risk of a security consists of nondiversifiable and diversifiable risk. Nondiversifiable risk is the only relevant risk because diversifiable risk can be easily eliminated through diversification. Nondiversifiable risk can be measured by the beta coefficient, which reflects the relationship between an asset's return and the market return. Beta is derived by using statistical techniques to find the slope of the "characteristic line" that best explains the historic relationship between the asset's return and the market return. The beta of a portfolio is a weighted average of the betas of the individual assets that it includes.

 Explain the capital asset pricing model (CAPM), its relationship to the security market line (SML), and shifts in the SML caused by changes in inflationary expectations and risk aversion. The capital asset pricing model (CAPM) uses beta to relate an asset's risk relative to the market to the asset's required return. The variable definitions and equation for CAPM are given in Table 6.10. The graphic depiction of CAPM is the security market line (SML), which shifts over time in response to changing inflationary expectations and/or changes in investor risk aversion. Changes in inflationary expectations result in parallel shifts in the SML in direct response to the magnitude and direction of change. Increasing risk aversion results in a steepening in the slope of the SML, and decreasing risk aversion reduces the slope of the SML.

SELF-TEST PROBLEMS   **(Solutions in Appendix B)**

ST 6–1   Portfolio analysis   You have been asked for your advice in selecting a portfolio of assets and have been supplied with the following data:

	Expected return		
Year	Asset A	Asset B	Asset C
2001	12%	16%	12%
2002	14	14	14
2003	16	12	16

No probabilities have been supplied. You have been told that you can create two portfolios—one consisting of assets A and B and the other consisting of assets A and C—by investing equal proportions (i.e., 50%) in each of the two component assets.

a. What is the expected return for each asset over the 3-year period?
b. What is the standard deviation for each asset's return?
c. What is the expected return for each of the two portfolios?
d. How would you characterize the correlations of returns of the two assets making up each of the two portfolios identified in **c**?
e. What is the standard deviation for each portfolio?
f. Which portfolio do you recommend? Why?

ST 6–2 **Beta and CAPM** Currently under consideration is a project with a beta, b, of 1.50. At this time, the risk-free rate of return, R_F, is 7%, and the return on the market portfolio of assets, k_m, is 10%. The project is actually *expected* to earn an annual rate of return of 11%.

a. If the return on the market portfolio were to increase by 10%, what would be expected to happen to the project's *required return?* What if the market return were to decline by 10%?
b. Use the capital asset pricing model (CAPM) to find the *required return* on this investment.
c. On the basis of your calculation in **b**, would you recommend this investment? Why or why not?
d. Assume that as a result of investors becoming less risk-averse, the market return drops by 1% to 9%. What impact would this change have on your responses in **b** and **c**?

PROBLEMS

WARM-UP

6–1 **Rate of return** Douglas Keel, a financial analyst for Orange Industries, wishes to estimate the rate of return for two similar-risk investments—X and Y. Keel's research indicates that the immediate past returns will act as reasonable estimates of future returns. A year earlier, investment X had a market value of $20,000 and investment Y, of $55,000. During the year, investment X generated cash flow of $1,500 and investment Y generated cash flow of $6,800. The current market values of investments X and Y are $21,000 and $55,000, respectively.

a. Calculate the expected rate of return on investments X and Y using the most recent year's data.
b. Assuming that the two investments are equally risky, which one should Keel recommend? Why?

WARM-UP

6–2 **Return calculations** For each of the investments shown in the following table, calculate the rate of return earned over the unspecified time period.

Investment	Beginning-of-period value	End-of-period value	Cash flow during period
A	$ 800	$ 1,100	$ −100
B	120,000	118,000	15,000
C	45,000	48,000	7,000
D	600	500	80
E	12,500	12,400	1,500

INTERMEDIATE **6–3** **Risk preferences**   Sharon Smith, the financial manager for Barnett Corporation, wishes to evaluate three prospective investments—X, Y, and Z. Currently, the firm earns 12% on its investments, which have a risk index of 6%. The expected return and expected risk of the investments are as follows:

Investment	Expected return	Expected risk index
X	14%	7%
Y	12	8
Z	10	9

a. If Sharon Smith were *risk-indifferent,* which investments would she select? Explain why.
b. If she were *risk-averse,* which investments would she select? Why?
c. If she were *risk-seeking,* which investments would she select? Why?
d. Given the traditional risk preference behavior exhibited by financial managers, which investment would be preferred? Why?

INTERMEDIATE **6–4** **Risk analysis**   Solar Designs is considering two possible types of expansion to its product line. After investigating the possible outcomes, the company made the estimates shown in the following table:

	Expansion A	Expansion B
Initial investment	$12,000	$12,000
Annual rate of return		
Pessimistic	16%	10%
Most likely	20%	20%
Optimistic	24%	30%

a. Determine the range of the rates of return for each of the two projects.
b. Which project is less risky? Why?
c. If you were making the investment decision, which one would you choose? Why? What does this imply about your feelings toward risk?
d. Assume that expansion B's most likely outcome is 21% per year and all other facts remain the same. Does this change your answer to part **c**? Why?

6–5   **Risk and probability**   Micro-Pub, Inc., is considering the purchase of one of two microfilm cameras—R or S. Both should provide benefits over a 10-year period, and each requires an initial investment of $4,000. Management has constructed the following table of estimates of probabilities and rates of return for pessimistic, most likely, and optimistic results:

	Camera R		Camera S	
	Amount	Probability	Amount	Probability
Initial investment	$4,000	1.00	$4,000	1.00
Annual rate of return				
Pessimistic	20%	.25	15%	.20
Most likely	25%	.50	25%	.55
Optimistic	30%	.25	35%	.25

a. Determine the range for the rate of return for each of the two cameras.
b. Determine the expected value of return for each camera.
c. Which camera is riskier? Why?

  6–6   **Bar charts and risk**   Swan's Sportswear is considering bringing out a line of designer jeans. Currently, it is negotiating with two different well-known designers. Because of the highly competitive nature of the industry, the two designs have been given code names. After market research, the firm has established the expectations shown in the following table about the annual rates of return:

		Annual rate of return	
Market acceptance	Probability	Line J	Line K
Very poor	.05	.0075	.010
Poor	.15	.0125	.025
Average	.60	.0850	.080
Good	.15	.1475	.135
Excellent	.05	.1625	.150

Use the table to:
a. Construct a bar chart for each line's annual rate of return.
b. Calculate the expected value of return for each line.
c. Evaluate the relative riskiness for each jean line's rate of return using the bar charts.

WARM-UP

6–7   Coefficient of variation   Metal Manufacturing has isolated four alternatives for meeting its need for increased production capacity. The data gathered relative to each of these alternatives is summarized in the following table.

Alternative	Expected return	Standard deviation of return
A	20%	7.0%
B	22	9.5
C	19	6.0
D	16	5.5

a.   Calculate the coefficient of variation for each alternative.
b.   If the firm wishes to minimize risk, which alternative do you recommend? Why?

WARM-UP

6–8   Standard deviation versus coefficient of variation as measures of risk   Greengage, Inc., a successful nursery, is considering several expansion opportunities. All of the alternatives promise to produce an acceptable return. The owners are extremely risk-averse; therefore, they will choose the least risky of the alternatives. Data on four possible projects are as follows.

Project	Expected Return	Range	Standard Deviation
A	12.0%	.040	.029
B	12.5	.050	.032
C	13.0	.060	.035
D	12.8	.045	.030

a.   Which alternative is least risky based on range?
b.   Which alternative has the lowest standard deviation? Explain why standard deviation is not an appropriate measure of risk for purposes of this comparison.
c.   Calculate the coefficient of variation for each alternative. What alternative will Greengage's owners choose? Explain why this may be the best measure of risk for comparing this set of opportunities.

CHALLENGE

6–9   Assessing return and risk   Swift Manufacturing must choose between two asset purchases. The annual rate of return and the related probabilities given in the following table summarize the firm's analysis to this point.

Project 257		Project 432	
Rate of return	Probability	Rate of return	Probability
−10%	.01	10%	.05
10	.04	15	.10
20	.05	20	.10
30	.10	25	.15
40	.15	30	.20
45	.30	35	.15
50	.15	40	.10
60	.10	45	.10
70	.05	50	.05
80	.04		
100	.01		

a. For each project, compute:
   (1) The range of possible rates of return.
   (2) The expected value of return.
   (3) The standard deviation of the returns.
   (4) The coefficient of variation.
b. Construct a bar chart of each distribution of rates of return.
c. Which project would you consider less risky? Why?

CHALLENGE 6–10 **Integrative—Expected return, standard deviation, and coefficient of variation**
Three assets—F, G, and H—are currently being considered by Perth Industries.
The probability distributions of expected returns for these assets are shown in
the following table.

	Asset F		Asset G		Asset H	
i	Pr_i	Return, k_i	Pr_i	Return, k_i	Pr_i	Return, k_i
1	.10	40%	.40	35%	.10	40%
2	.20	10	.30	10	.20	20
3	.40	0	.30	−20	.40	10
4	.20	−5			.20	0
5	.10	−10			.10	−20

a. Calculate the expected value of return, $\bar{k}$, for each of the three assets. Which
   provides the largest expected return?
b. Calculate the standard deviation, σ_k, for each of the three assets' returns.
   Which appears to have the greatest risk?
c. Calculate the coefficient of variation, CV, for each of the three assets. Which
   appears to have the largest *relative* risk?

CHALLENGE 6–11 **Normal probability distribution**   Assuming that the rates of return associated
with a given asset investment are normally distributed and that the expected

return, $\bar{k}$, is 18.9% and the coefficient of variation, CV, is .75, answer the following questions.

a. Find the standard deviation of returns, σ_k.

b. Calculate the range of expected return outcomes associated with the following probabilities of occurrence.

    (1) 68%

    (2) 95%

    (3) 99%

c. Draw the probability distribution associated with your findings in **a** and **b**.

CHALLENGE **6–12 Portfolio return and standard deviation** Jamie Wong is considering building a portfolio containing two assets, L and M. Asset L will represent 40% of the dollar value of the portfolio, and asset M will account for the other 60%. The expected returns over the next 6 years, 2001–2006, for each of these assets, are shown in the following table.

	Expected return	
Year	Asset L	Asset M
2001	14%	20%
2002	14	18
2003	16	16
2004	17	14
2005	17	12
2006	19	10

a. Calculate the expected portfolio return, k_p, for *each* of the 6 years.

b. Calculate the expected value of portfolio returns, $\bar{k}_p$, over the 6-year period.

c. Calculate the standard deviation of expected portfolio returns, σ_{k_p}, over the 6-year period.

d. How would you characterize the correlation of returns of the two assets L and M?

e. Discuss any benefits of diversification achieved through creation of the portfolio.

CHALLENGE **6–13 Portfolio analysis** You have been given the return data shown in the first table on three assets—F, G, and H—over the period 2001–2004.

	Expected return		
Year	Asset F	Asset G	Asset H
2001	16%	17%	14%
2002	17	16	15
2003	18	15	16
2004	19	14	17

Using these assets, you have isolated the three investment alternatives shown in the following table:

Alternative	Investment
1	100% of asset F
2	50% of asset F and 50% of asset G
3	50% of asset F and 50% of asset H

a. Calculate the expected return over the 4-year period for each of the three alternatives.
b. Calculate the standard deviation of returns over the 4-year period for each of the three alternatives.
c. Use your findings in a and b to calculate the coefficient of variation for each of the three alternatives.
d. On the basis of your findings, which of the three investment alternatives do you recommend? Why?

6–14   **Correlation, risk, and return**   Matt Peters wishes to evaluate the risk and return behaviors associated with various combinations of assets V and W under three assumed degrees of correlation—perfect positive, uncorrelated, and perfect negative. The expected return and risk values calculated for each of the assets are shown in the following table:

INTERMEDIATE

Asset	Expected return, $\bar{k}$	Risk (standard deviation), σ_k
V	8%	5%
W	13	10

a. If the returns of assets V and W are *perfectly positively correlated* (correlation coefficient = +1), describe the *range* of (1) expected return and (2) risk associated with all possible portfolio combinations.
b. If the returns of assets V and W are *uncorrelated* (correlation coefficient = 0), describe the *approximate range* of (1) expected return and (2) risk associated with all possible portfolio combinations.
c. If the returns of assets V and W are *perfectly negatively correlated* (correlation coefficient = −1), describe the *range* of (1) expected return and (2) risk associated with all possible portfolio combinations.

6–15   **International investment returns**   Joe Martinez, a U.S. citizen living in Brownsville, Texas, invested in the common stock of Telmex, a Mexican corporation. He purchased 1,000 shares at 20.50 pesos per share. Twelve months

INTERMEDIATE

later, he sold them at 24.75 pesos per share. He received no dividends during that time.

a. What was Joe's investment return (in percentage terms) for the year, based on the peso value of the shares?

b. The exchange rate for pesos was 9.21 pesos per $US1.00 at the time of the purchase. At the time of the sale, the exchange rate was 9.85 pesos per $US1.00. Translate the purchase and sale prices into $US.

c. Calculate Joe's investment return based on the $US value of the shares.

d. Explain why the two returns are different. Which one is more important to Joe? Why?

INTERMEDIATE 6–16   **Total, nondiversifiable, and diversifiable risk**   David Talbot randomly selected securities from all those listed on the New York Stock Exchange for his portfolio. He began with one security and added securities one by one until a total of 20 securities were held in the portfolio. After each security was added, David calculated the portfolio standard deviation, σ_{k_p}. The calculated values are shown in the following table:

Number of securities	Portfolio risk, σ_{k_p}	Number of securities	Portfolio risk, σ_{k_p}
1	14.50%	11	7.00%
2	13.30	12	6.80
3	12.20	13	6.70
4	11.20	14	6.65
5	10.30	15	6.60
6	9.50	16	6.56
7	8.80	17	6.52
8	8.20	18	6.50
9	7.70	19	6.48
10	7.30	20	6.47

a. On a set of number of securities in portfolio (x axis)–portfolio risk (y axis) axes, plot the portfolio risk data given in the preceding table.

b. Divide the total portfolio risk in the graph into its *nondiversifiable* and *diversifiable* risk components and label each of these on the graph.

c. Describe which of the two risk components is the *relevant risk,* and explain why it is relevant. How much of this risk exists in David Talbot's portfolio?

INTERMEDIATE 6–17   **Graphic derivation of beta**   A firm wishes to graphically estimate the betas for two assets—A and B. It has gathered the following return data for the market portfolio and both assets over the last ten years, 1991–2000.

	Actual return		
Year	Market portfolio	Asset A	Asset B
1991	6%	11%	16%
1992	2	8	11
1993	−13	−4	−10
1994	−4	3	3
1995	−8	0	−3
1996	16	19	30
1997	10	14	22
1998	15	18	29
1999	8	12	19
2000	13	17	26

a. On a set of market return (x axis)–asset return (y axis) axes, use the data given to draw the characteristic line for asset A and for asset B (on the same set of axes).
b. Use the characteristic lines from **a** to estimate the betas for assets A and B.
c. Use the betas found in **b** to comment on the relative risks of assets A and B.

WARM-UP 6–18 **Interpreting beta** A firm wishes to assess the impact of changes in the market return on an asset that has a beta of 1.20.
a. If the market return increased by 15%, what impact would this change be expected to have on the asset's return?
b. If the market return decreased by 8%, what impact would this change be expected to have on the asset's return?
c. If the market return did not change, what impact, if any, would be expected on the asset's return?
d. Would this asset be considered more or less risky than the market? Explain.

WARM-UP 6–19 **Betas** Answer the following questions for assets A to D shown in the table.

Asset	Beta
A	.50
B	1.60
C	−.20
D	.90

a. What impact would a *10% increase* in the market return be expected to have on each asset's return?
b. What impact would a *10% decrease* in the market return be expected to have on each asset's return?
c. If you were certain that the market return would *increase* in the near future, which asset would you prefer? Why?
d. If you were certain that the market return would *decrease* in the near future, which asset would you prefer? Why?

INTERMEDIATE 6-20   **Betas and risk rankings**   Stock A has a beta of .80, stock B has a beta of 1.40, and stock C has a beta of −.30.

    a. Rank these stocks from the most risky to the least risky.

    b. If the return on the market portfolio increases by 12%, what change would you expect in the return for each of the stocks?

    c. If the return on the market portfolio declines by 5%, what change would you expect in the return for each of the stocks?

    d. If you felt that the stock market was just ready to experience a significant decline, which stock would you likely add to your portfolio? Why?

    e. If you anticipated a major stock market rally, which stock would you add to your portfolio? Why?

INTERMEDIATE 6-21   **Portfolio betas**   Rose Berry is attempting to evaluate two possible portfolios—both consisting of the same five assets but held in different proportions. She is particularly interested in using beta to compare the risk of the portfolios and in this regard has gathered the data shown in the following table.

Asset	Asset beta	Portfolio weights	
		Portfolio A	**Portfolio B**
1	1.30	10%	30%
2	.70	30	10
3	1.25	10	20
4	1.10	10	20
5	.90	40	20
Totals		100%	100%

    a. Calculate the betas for portfolios A and B.

    b. Compare the risk of each portfolio to the market as well as to each other. Which portfolio is more risky?

WARM-UP 6-22   **Capital asset pricing model (CAPM)**   For each of the cases shown in the following table, use the capital asset pricing model to find the required return.

Case	Risk-free rate, R_F	Market return, k_m	Beta, b
A	5%	8%	1.30
B	8	13	.90
C	9	12	−.20
D	10	15	1.00
E	6	10	.60

6–23   **Beta coefficients and the capital asset pricing model**   Katherine Wilson is wondering how much risk she must undertake in order to generate an acceptable return on her portfolio. The risk-free return currently is 5%. The return on the average stock (market return) is 16%. Use the CAPM to calculate the beta coefficient associated with each of the following portfolio returns.

INTERMEDIATE

a. 10%
b. 15%
c. 18%
d. 20%
e. Katherine is risk-averse. What is the highest return she can expect if she is unwilling to take more than an average risk?

INTERMEDIATE 6–24   **Manipulating CAPM**   Use the basic equation for the capital asset pricing model (CAPM) to work each of the following:

a. Find the *required return* for an asset with a beta of .90 when the risk-free rate and market return are 8 and 12%, respectively.
b. Find the *risk-free rate* for a firm with a required return of 15% and a beta of 1.25 when the market return is 14%.
c. Find the *market return* for an asset with a required return of 16% and a beta of 1.10 when the risk-free rate is 9%.
d. Find the *beta* for an asset with a required return of 15% when the risk-free rate and market return are 10 and 12.5%, respectively.

   6–25   **Portfolio return and beta**   Jamie Peters invested $100,000 to set up the following portfolio one year ago:

 CHALLENGE

Asset	Cost	Beta at purchase	Yearly income	Value today
A	$20,000	.80	$1,600	$20,000
B	35,000	.95	1,400	36,000
C	30,000	1.50	—	34,500
D	15,000	1.25	375	16,500

a. Calculate the portfolio beta based on the original cost figures.
b. Calculate the percentage return of each position in the portfolio for the year.
c. Calculate the percentage return of the portfolio based on original cost using income and gains during the year.
d. At the time Jamie made his investments, investors were estimating the market return for the coming year would be 10%. The estimate of the risk-free rate of return averaged 4% for the coming year. Calculate an expected rate of return for each stock based on its beta and the expectations of market and risk-free returns.
e. Based on the actual results, explain how each stock in the portfolio performed relative to those CAPM-generated expectations of performance. What factors could explain these differences?

  6–26   **Security market line, SML**   Assume that the risk-free rate, R_F, is currently 9% and that the market return, k_m, is currently 13%.

INTERMEDIATE

a. Draw the security market line (SML) on a set of nondiversifiable risk (x axis)–required return (y axis) axes.

b. Calculate and label the *market risk premium* on the axes in a.

c. Given the previous data, calculate the required return on asset A having a beta of .80 and asset B having a beta of 1.30.

d. Draw in the betas and required returns from c for assets A and B on the axes in a. Label the *risk premium* associated with each of these assets, and discuss them.

CHALLENGE 6–27 **Shifts in the security market line**   Assume that the risk-free rate, R_F, is currently 8%, the market return, k_m, is 12%, and asset A has a beta, b_A, of 1.10.

a. Draw the security market line (SML) on a set of nondiversifiable risk (x axis)–required return (y axis) axes.

b. Use the CAPM to calculate the required return, k_A, on asset A, and depict asset A's beta and required return on the SML drawn in a.

c. Assume that as a result of recent economic events, inflationary expectations have declined by 2%, lowering R_F and k_m to 6 and 10%, respectively. Draw the new SML on the axes in a, and calculate and show the new required return for asset A.

d. Assume that as a result of recent events, investors have become more risk-averse, causing the market return to rise by 1% to 13%. Ignoring the shift in part c, draw the new SML on the same set of axes as used before, and calculate and show the new required return for asset A.

e. From the previous changes, what conclusions can be drawn about the impact of (1) decreased inflationary expectations and (2) increased risk aversion on the required returns of risky assets?

  6–28 **Integrative—Risk, return, and CAPM**   Wolff Enterprises must consider several investment projects, A through E, using the capital asset pricing model (CAPM) and its graphic representation, the security market line (SML). Relevant information is presented in the following table.

CHALLENGE

Item	Rate of return	Beta, b
Risk-free asset	9%	0
Market portfolio	14	1.00
Project A	—	1.50
Project B	—	.75
Project C	—	2.00
Project D	—	0
Project E	—	−.50

a. Calculate the required return and risk premium for each project, given its level of nondiversifiable risk.

b. Use your findings in a to draw the security market line (required return relative to nondiversifiable risk).

c. Discuss the relative nondiversifiable risk of projects A through E.

d. Assume that recent economic events have caused investors to become less risk-averse, causing the market return to decline by 2%, to 12%. Calculate the new required returns for assets A through E, and draw the new security market line on the same set of axes as used in **b.**

e. Compare your findings in **a** and **b** with those in **d.** What conclusion can you draw about the impact of a decline in investor risk aversion on the required returns of risky assets?

CASE CHAPTER 6	Analyzing Risk and Return on Chargers Products' Investments

Junior Sayou, a financial analyst for Chargers Products, a manufacturer of stadium benches, must evaluate the risk and return of two assets—X and Y. The firm is considering adding these assets to its diversified asset portfolio. To assess the return and risk of each asset, Junior gathered data on the annual cash flow and beginning- and end-of-year values of each asset over the immediately preceding 10 years, 1991–2000. These data are summarized in the following table. Junior's investigation suggests that both assets, on average, will tend to perform in the future just as they have during the past 10 years. He therefore believes that the expected annual return can be estimated by finding the average annual return for each asset over the past 10 years.

Junior believes that each asset's risk can be assessed in two ways: in isolation and as part of the firm's diversified portfolio of assets. The risk of the assets in isolation can be found by using the standard deviation and coefficient of variation of returns over the past 10 years. The capital asset pricing model (CAPM) can be used to assess the asset's risk as part of the firm's portfolio of assets. Applying some sophisticated quantitative techniques, Junior estimated betas for assets X and Y of 1.60 and 1.10, respectively. In addition, he found that the risk-free rate is currently 7% and the market return is 10%.

Return Data for Assets X and Y, 1991–2000

	Asset X			Asset Y		
		Value			Value	
Year	Cash flow	Beginning	Ending	Cash flow	Beginning	Ending
1991	$1,000	$20,000	$22,000	$1,500	$20,000	$20,000
1992	1,500	22,000	21,000	1,600	20,000	20,000
1993	1,400	21,000	24,000	1,700	20,000	21,000
1994	1,700	24,000	22,000	1,800	21,000	21,000
1995	1,900	22,000	23,000	1,900	21,000	22,000
1996	1,600	23,000	26,000	2,000	22,000	23,000
1997	1,700	26,000	25,000	2,100	23,000	23,000
1998	2,000	25,000	24,000	2,200	23,000	24,000
1999	2,100	24,000	27,000	2,300	24,000	25,000
2000	2,200	27,000	30,000	2,400	25,000	25,000

Required

a. Calculate the annual rate of return for each asset in *each* of the 10 preceding years, and use those values to find the average annual return for each asset over the 10-year period.

b. Use the returns calculated in **a** to find (1) the standard deviation and (2) the coefficient of variation of the returns for each asset over the 10-year period 1991–2000.

c. Use your findings in **a** and **b** to evaluate and discuss the return and risk associated with each asset. Which asset appears to be preferable? Explain.

d. Use the CAPM to find the required return for each asset. Compare this value with the average annual returns calculated in **a**.

e. Compare and contrast your findings in **c** and **d**. What recommendations would you give Junior with regard to investing in either of the two assets? Explain to Junior why he is better off using beta rather than the standard deviation and coefficient of variation to assess the risk of each asset.

f. Rework **d** and **e** under each of the following circumstances:
   (1) A rise of 1% in inflationary expectations causes the risk-free rate to rise to 8% and the market return to rise to 11%.
   (2) As a result of favorable political events, investors suddenly become less risk-averse, causing the market return to drop by 1%, to 9%.

WEB EXERCISE

GOTO web site www.stern.nyu.edu/~adamodar/New_Home_Page/datafile/histret.html.

1. Compute the arithmetic average for the annual return for stocks, T-bills, and T-bonds for the last 10 years of data.
2. Compute the standard deviation for the averages calculated in Question 1.
3. Which has the highest arithmetic average—stocks, T-bills, or T-bonds?
4. Which has the largest standard deviation?
5. How much money would you have if you had invested $100 into stocks in 1926? If you had invested $100 in T-bills in 1926? And, if you had invested $100 in T-bonds in 1926?
6. Using the arithmetic average data given on this web site, what is the risk premium of stocks versus T-bills for the shortest time period given in the charts?
7. Using the arithmetic average data given on this web site, what is the risk premium of stocks versus T-bonds for the shortest time period given in the charts?
8. Explain the difference between your answer to Question 6 and your answer to Question 7.

Bond and Stock Valuation

LEARNING GOALS

LG1 Describe the key inputs and basic model used in the valuation process.

LG2 Apply the basic valuation model to bonds and describe the impact of required return and time to maturity on bond values.

LG3 Explain yield to maturity (YTM), its calculation, and the procedure used to value bonds that pay interest semiannually.

LG4 Understand the concept of market efficiency and basic common stock valuation under each of three cases: zero growth, constant growth, and variable growth.

LG5 Discuss the use of book value, liquidation value, and price/earnings (P/E) multiples to estimate common stock values.

LG6 Understand the relationships among financial decisions, return, risk, and the firm's value.

7.1 Valuation Fundamentals

valuation
The process that links risk and return to determine the worth of an asset.

As was noted in Chapter 6, all major financial decisions must be viewed in terms of expected risk, expected return, and their combined impact on share price. **Valuation** is the process that links risk and return to determine the worth of an asset. It is a relatively simple process that can be applied to *expected* streams of benefits from bonds, stocks, income properties, oil wells, and so on. To determine their worth at a given point in time, the manager uses the time-value-of-money techniques presented in Chapter 5 and the concepts of risk and return developed in Chapter 6.

What's Baking?

With just three basic ingredients—flour, butter, and eggs—an experienced baker can create a variety of treats. The proportions he or she uses, plus the choice of other ingredients, give each creation its particular character. So, too, do three basic ingredients—returns, timing, and risk—determine the value of the projects that firms undertake. The choice of the other ingredients, and the market's taste for those other ingredients, determines the financial success of the firm's projects and of the firm. Just as nutritionists have found ways to measure the nutritional value of food, so, too, have financial analysts devised ways, broadly called *valuation,* to measure the value of any asset. This chapter explains valuation and how the value of a firm's bonds and stocks can be measured.

Key Inputs

The key inputs to the valuation process include cash flows (returns), timing, and the required return (risk). Each is described next.

Cash Flows (Returns)

The value of any asset depends on the cash flow(s) it is *expected* to provide over the ownership period. To have value, an asset does not have to provide an annual cash flow; it can provide an intermittent cash flow or even a single cash flow over the period.

Example ▼ Celia Sargent, financial analyst for Groton Corporation, a diversified holding company, wishes to estimate the value of three of its assets—common stock in Michaels Enterprises, an interest in an oil well, and an original painting by a well-known artist. Her cash flow estimates for each were as follows.

Stock in Michaels Enterprises *Expect* to receive cash dividends of $300 per year indefinitely.

Oil well *Expect* to receive cash flow of $2,000 at the end of 1 year, $4,000 at the end of 2 years, and $10,000 at the end of 4 years, when the well is to be sold.

Original painting *Expect* to be able to sell the painting in 5 years for $85,000.

▲ With these cash flow estimates, Celia has taken the first step toward placing a value on each of these assets.

Timing

In addition to making cash flow estimates, we must know the timing of the cash flows.[1] For example, Celia expected the cash flows of $2,000, $4,000, and $10,000 for the oil well to occur at the end of years 1, 2, and 4, respectively. In combination, the cash flow and its timing fully define the return expected from the asset.

Required Return (Risk)

Hint   The required rate of return is the result of investors being risk-averse. In order for the risk-averse investor to purchase a given asset, the investor *must have* at least enough return to compensate for the asset's perceived risk.

The level of risk associated with a given cash flow can significantly affect its value. In general, the greater the risk of (or the less certain) a cash flow, the lower its value. Greater risk can be incorporated into an analysis by using a higher required return or discount rate. In the valuation process, just as in present value and CAPM calculations, the required return is used to incorporate risk into the analysis: The higher the risk, the greater the required return; the lower the risk, the less the required return.

Example ▼ Let's return to Celia Sargent's task of placing a value on Groton Corporation's original painting and consider two scenarios.

Scenario 1—Certainty A major art gallery has contracted to buy the painting for $85,000 at the end of 5 years. Because this is considered a certain situation, Celia views this asset as "money in the bank." She thus would use the prevailing risk-free rate, R_F, of 9% as the required return when calculating the value of the painting.

Scenario 2—High Risk The value of original paintings by this artist has fluctuated widely over the past 10 years. Although Celia expects to be able to get

---

1. Although cash flows can occur at any time during a year, for computational convenience as well as custom, we will assume they occur at the end of the year unless otherwise noted.

Valuing the American Dream

For many people, owning their own business represents the dream of a lifetime. But how much should this dream cost? To get an idea of how to value a small business, check out the "Business for Sale" column in Inc., *a magazine focused on smaller emerging businesses. Each month, the column describes the operations, financial situation, industry outlook, price rationale, and pros and cons of a small business offered for sale. For example, 1998 columns featured such diverse companies as a rodeo event marketing company, an equipment rental company, an Internet service provider, and a credit-reporting agency. Prices for these businesses ranged from $200,000 to several million dollars.*

The $1.2 million asking price for the credit-reporting agency was in line with the price rationale suggested by Inc.'s *valuation experts. Because service companies typically sell for 4 to 5 times recast earnings (defined as earnings before interest, taxes, depreciation, and owner's compensation), the agency's 1998 recast earnings of $231,000 translate into a price range of $924,000 to $1,155,000. What pushed the price toward the higher number? Although the agency is only 4 years old, its gross revenues tripled between 1996 and 1998. It has no debt and a growing, well-diversified customer base. The company has already diversified, providing tenant and employment screening reports as well as selling consumers their credit reports with advice on how to improve their credit rating. The industry outlook is good; rising consumer expenditures and home buying create the need for credit reports. The downside? The experts caution the new owner not to pay too much for the business. The key to success is continued growth, and that will require substantial outlays for new technology.*

$85,000 for the painting, she realizes that its sale price in 5 years could range between $30,000 and $140,000. Due to the high uncertainty surrounding the painting's value, Celia believes that a 15% required return is appropriate.

These two estimates of the appropriate required return illustrate how this rate captures risk. The often subjective nature of such estimates is also clear.

The Basic Valuation Model

Simply stated, the value of any asset is *the present value of all future cash flows it is expected to provide over the relevant time period.* The time period can be as short as 1 year or as long as infinity. The value of an asset is therefore determined by discounting the expected cash flows back to their present value, using the required return commensurate with the asset's risk as the appropriate discount rate. Utilizing the present value techniques presented in Chapter 5, we can express the value of any asset at time zero, V_0, as

$$V_0 = \frac{CF_1}{(1+k)^1} + \frac{CF_2}{(1+k)^2} + \cdots + \frac{CF_n}{(1+k)^n} \tag{7.1}$$

where

$$V_0 = \text{value of the asset at time zero}$$
$$CF_t = \text{cash flow } expected \text{ at the end of year } t$$
$$k = \text{appropriate required return (discount rate)}$$
$$n = \text{relevant time period}$$

Using present value interest factor notation, $PVIF_{k,n}$ from Chapter 5, Equation 7.1 can be rewritten as

$$V_0 = [CF_1 \times (PVIF_{k,1})] + [CF_2 \times (PVIF_{k,2})] + \cdots + [CF_n \times (PVIF_{k,n})] \qquad (7.2)$$

Substituting the expected cash flows, CF_t, over the relevant time period, n, and the appropriate required return, k, into Equation 7.2, we can determine the value of any asset.

E x a m p l e ▼ Celia Sargent, using appropriate required returns and Equation 7.2, calculated the value of each asset (using present value interest factors from Table A–3), as shown in Table 7.1. Michaels Enterprises stock has a value of $2,500, the oil well's value is $9,262, and the original painting has a value of $42,245. Had she instead used a calculator, the values of the oil well and original painting would have been $9,266.98 and $42,260.03, respectively. Note that regardless of the pattern of the expected cash flow from an asset, the basic valuation equation can
▲ be used to determine its value.

? Review Questions

7–1 Define *valuation* and explain why it is important for the financial manager to understand the valuation process.

7–2 Briefly describe the three key inputs to the valuation process. Does the valuation process apply only to assets providing an annual cash flow? Explain.

7–3 Define and specify the general equation for the value of any asset, V_0, in terms of its *expected* cash flow in each year and the appropriate required return.

7.2 Bond Valuation

The basic valuation equation can be customized for use in valuing specific securities—bonds, preferred stock, and common stock. Bonds and preferred stock are similar, because they have stated contractual interest and dividend cash flows. The dividends on common stock, on the other hand, are not known in advance. Bond valuation is described in this section, and common stock valuation is discussed in the following section. Because the procedures are identical, the valuation of preferred stock is demonstrated as a special case in the discussion of valuing common stock.

TABLE 7.1	Valuation of Groton Corporation's Assets by Celia Sargent

Asset	Cash flow, CF	Appropriate required return	Valuation
Michaels Enterprises stock[a]	$300/year indefinitely	12%	$V_0 = \$300 \times (PVIFA_{12\%,\infty})$ $= \$300 \times \dfrac{1}{.12} = \underline{\underline{\$2,500}}$

Oil well[b]

Year (t)	CF_t
1	$ 2,000
2	4,000
3	0
4	10,000

20%

$V_0 = [\$2,000 \times (PVIF_{20\%,1})]$
$+ [\$4,000 \times (PVIF_{20\%,2})]$
$+ [\$0 \times (PVIF_{20\%,3})]$
$+ [\$10,000 \times (PVIF_{20\%,4})]$
$= [\$2,000 \times (.833)]$
$+ [\$4,000 \times (.694)]$
$+ [\$0 \times (.579)]$
$+ [\$10,000 \times (.482)]$
$= \$1,666 + \$2,776$
$+ \$0 + \$4,820$
$= \underline{\underline{\$9,262}}$

Original painting[c]	$85,000 at end of year 5	15%	$V_0 = \$85,000 \times (PVIF_{15\%,5})$ $= \$85,000 \times (.497)$ $= \underline{\underline{\$42,245}}$

[a]This is a perpetuity (infinite-lived annuity), and therefore the present value interest factor given in Equation 5.28 is applied.
[b]This is a mixed stream of cash flows and therefore requires a number of PVIFs, as noted.
[c]This is a lump-sum cash flow and therefore requires a single PVIF.

Bond Fundamentals

Hint A bondholder receives two cash flows from a bond if held to maturity—interest and the bond's face value. For valuation purposes, the interest is an annuity and the face value is a single payment received at a specified future date.

As discussed in Chapter 2, *bonds* are long-term debt instruments used by business and government to raise large sums of money, typically from a diverse group of lenders. Most corporate bonds pay interest *semiannually* (every 6 months) at a stated *coupon interest rate,* have an initial *maturity* of 10 to 30 years, and have a *par,* or *face, value* of $1,000 that must be repaid at maturity.[2] An example will illustrate the terms of a corporate bond.

Example ▼ Mills Company, a large defense contractor, on January 1, 2001, issued a 10% coupon interest rate, 10-year bond with a $1,000 par value that pays interest semiannually. Investors who buy this bond receive the contractual right to two

2. Bonds often have features that allow them to be retired by the issuer prior to maturity; these *call* and *conversion* features were presented in Chapter 2. For the purpose of the current discussion, these features are ignored.

cash flows: (1) $100 annual interest (10% coupon interest rate $\times$ $1,000 par value) distributed as $50 ($\frac{1}{2}$ $\times$ $100) at the end of each 6 months, and (2) the $1,000 par value at the end of the tenth year.

We will use data for Mills's bond issue to look at basic bond valuation.

Basic Bond Valuation

The value of a bond is the present value of the payments its issuer is contractual-ly obligated to make, from the current time until it matures. The basic equation for the value, B_0, of a bond is given by Equation 7.3:

$$B_0 = I \times \left[\sum_{t=1}^{n} \frac{1}{(1 + k_d)^t} \right] + M \times \left[\frac{1}{(1 + k_d)^n} \right] \tag{7.3}$$

$$= I \times (PVIFA_{k_d,n}) + M \times (PVIF_{k_d,n}) \tag{7.3a}$$

where

B_0 = value of the bond at time zero
I = *annual* interest paid in dollars[3]
n = number of years to maturity
M = par value in dollars
k_d = required return on a bond

We can calculate bond value using Equation 7.3a and the appropriate financial tables (A–3 and A–4) or by using a financial calculator.

Example ▼ *Assuming that interest on the Mills Company bond issue is paid annually* and that the required return is equal to the bond's coupon interest rate, I = $100, k_d = 10%, M = $1,000, and n = 10 years.

Table Use   Substituting the values noted above into Equation 7.3a yields

$$B_0 = \$100 \times (PVIFA_{10\%,10yrs}) + \$1,000 \times (PVIF_{10\%,10yrs})$$
$$= \$100 \times (6.145) + \$1,000 \times (.386)$$
$$= \$614.50 + \$386.00 = \underline{\$1,000.50}$$

The bond therefore has a value of approximately $1,000.[4]

---

3. The payment of annual rather than semiannual bond interest is assumed throughout the following discussion. This assumption simplifies the calculations involved while maintaining the conceptual accuracy of the valuation procedures presented.

4. Note that a slight rounding error ($.50) results here due to the use of the table factors, which are rounded to the nearest thousandth.

Calculator Use   Using the Mills Company's inputs shown, you should find the bond value to be exactly $1,000.

Inputs: 10   10   100   1000

Functions: N   I   PMT   FV   CPT   PV

Outputs: 1000

Note that *the bond value calculated in the example is equal to its par value; this will always be the case when the required return is equal to the coupon interest rate.*[5]

Time-Line Use   The computations involved in finding the bond value are depicted graphically on the following time line.

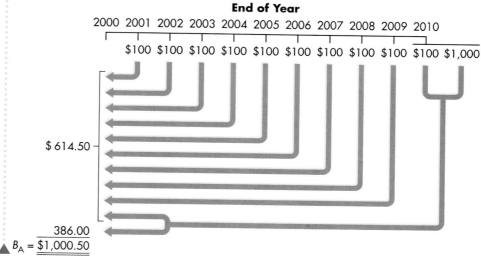

Graphic depiction of bond valuation (Mills Company's 10% coupon interest rate, 10-year maturity, $1,000 par, January 1, 2001, issue paying annual interest; required return = 10%)

End of Year

2000 2001 2002 2003 2004 2005 2006 2007 2008 2009 2010

$100 $100 $100 $100 $100 $100 $100 $100 $100 $100 $1,000

$614.50

386.00

B_A = $\underline{\$1,000.50}$

Bond Value Behavior

In practice, the value of a bond in the marketplace is rarely equal to its par value. As was seen in the bond quotations in Figure 2.3, part A on page 54, the closing prices of bonds differ from their par values of 100 (100 percent of par). Some are valued below par (quoted below 100), and others are valued above par (quoted above 100). A variety of forces in the economy as well as the passage of time tend to affect value. Because these external forces are in no way controlled by

5. Note that because bonds pay interest in arrears, the prices at which they are quoted and traded reflect their value *plus* any accrued interest. For example, a $1,000 par value, 10% coupon bond paying interest semiannually and having a calculated value of $900 would pay interest of $50 at the end of each 6-month period. If it is now 3 months since the beginning of the interest period, three-sixths of the $50 interest, or $25 (i.e., 3/6 × $50), would be accrued. The bond would therefore be quoted at $925—its $900 value plus the $25 in accrued interest. For convenience, *throughout this book, bond values will always be assumed to be calculated at the beginning of the interest period*, thereby avoiding the need to consider accrued interest.

bond issuers or investors, it is useful to understand the impact that required return and time to maturity have on bond value.

Required Returns and Bond Values

Whenever the required return on a bond differs from the bond's coupon interest rate, the bond's value will differ from its par value. The required return on the bond is likely to differ from the coupon interest rate because either (1) economic conditions have changed, causing a shift in the basic cost of long-term funds, or (2) the firm's risk has changed. Increases in the basic cost of long-term funds or in risk will raise the required return; decreases in the cost of funds or in risk will lower the required return.

discount
The amount by which a bond sells at a value that is less than its par value.

premium
The amount by which a bond sells at a value that is greater than its par value.

Regardless of the exact cause, what is important is the relationship between the required return and the coupon interest rate: When the required return is greater than the coupon interest rate, the bond value, B_0, will be less than its par value, M. In this case, the bond is said to sell at a **discount**, which will equal $M - B_0$. On the other hand, when the required return falls below the coupon interest rate, the bond value will be greater than par. In this situation the bond is said to sell at a **premium**, which will equal $B_0 - M$.

E x a m p l e ▼ In the preceding example, we saw that when the required return equaled the coupon interest rate, the bond's value equaled its $1,000 par value. If for the same bond the required return were to rise to 12%, its value would be found as follows (using Equation 7.3a):

Table Use

$$B_0 = \$100 \times (PVIFA_{12\%,10\text{yrs}}) + \$1,000 \times (PVIF_{12\%,10\text{yrs}})$$
$$= \$100 \times (5.650) + \$1,000 \times (.322) = \underline{\underline{\$887.00}}$$

Calculator Use Using the inputs shown, you should find the value of the bond, with a 12% required return, to be $887.00.

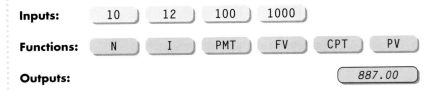

The bond would therefore sell at a *discount* of $113.00 ($1,000 par value − $887.00 value).

If, on the other hand, the required return fell to, say, 8%, the bond's value would be found as follows:

Table Use

$$B_0 = \$100 \times (PVIFA_{8\%, 10\text{yrs}}) + \$1,000 \times (PVIF_{8\%, 10\text{yrs}})$$
$$= \$100 \times (6.710) + \$1,000 \times (.463) = \underline{\underline{\$1,134.00}}$$

Calculator Use Using the inputs shown, you should find the value of the bond, with an 8% required return, to be $1,134.20. Note that this value is more precise than the $1,134 value calculated using the rounded financial table factors.

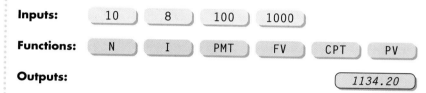

Inputs:	10	8	100	1000		
Functions:	N	I	PMT	FV	CPT	PV
Outputs:					1134.20	

The bond would therefore sell for a *premium* of about $134.00 ($1,134.00 value − $1,000 par value). The results of this and earlier calculations for Mills Company's bond values are summarized in Table 7.2 and graphically depicted in ▲ Figure 7.1.

Time to Maturity and Bond Values

Whenever the required return is different from the coupon interest rate, the amount of time to maturity affects bond value. An additional factor is whether required returns are constant or changing over the life of the bond.

Constant Required Returns When the required return is different from the coupon interest rate and is assumed to be *constant until maturity*, the value of the bond will approach its par value as the passage of time moves the bond's value closer to maturity. (Of course, when the required return *equals* the coupon interest rate, the bond's value will remain at par until it matures.)

TABLE 7.2 Bond Values for Various Required Returns (Mills Company's 10% Coupon Interest Rate, 10-Year Maturity, $1,000 Par, January 1, 2001, Issue Paying Annual Interest)

Required return, k_d	Bond value, B_0	Status
12%	$ 887.00	Discount
10	1,000.00	Par value
8	1,134.00	Premium

FIGURE 7.1

Bond Values and Required Returns

Bond value and required returns (Mills Company's 10% coupon interest rate, 10-year maturity, $1,000 par, January 1, 2001, issue paying annual interest)

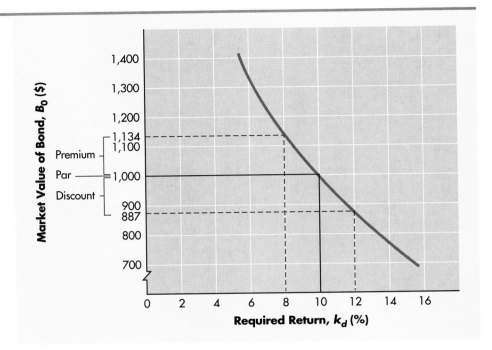

FIGURE 7.2

Time to Maturity and Bond Values

Relationship between time to maturity, required returns, and bond values (Mills Company's 10% coupon interest rate, 10-year maturity, $1,000 par, January 1, 2001, issue paying annual interest)

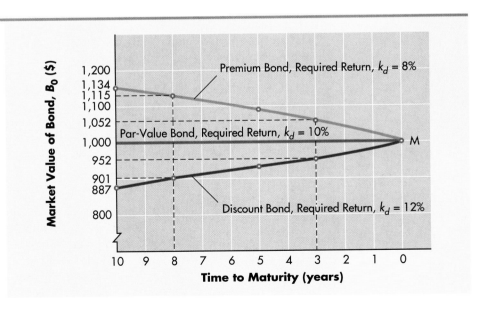

Example ▼ Figure 7.2 depicts the behavior of the bond values calculated earlier and presented in Table 7.2 for Mills Company's 10% coupon interest rate bond paying annual interest and having 10 years to maturity. Each of the three required returns—12, 10, and 8%—is assumed to remain constant over the 10 years to the bond's maturity. The bond's value in each case approaches and ultimately equals the bond's $1,000 par value at its maturity.

At the 12% required return, the bond's discount declines with the passage of time, as the bond's value increases from $887 to $1,000. When the 10% required return equals the bond's coupon interest rate, its value remains unchanged at $1,000 over its maturity. Finally, at the 8% required return, the bond's premium will decline as its value drops from $1,134 to $1,000 at maturity. With the required return assumed to be constant to maturity, the bond's value approaches its $1,000 par or maturity value as the time to maturity declines.

Changing Required Returns   The chance that interest rates will change and thereby change the required return and bond value is called **interest-rate risk.** Bondholders are typically more concerned with rising rates, which decrease bond value. The shorter the amount of time until a bond's maturity, the less responsive is its market value to a given change in the required return. In other words, short maturities have less interest-rate risk than do long maturities when all other features—coupon interest rate, par value, and interest-payment frequency—are the same.

interest-rate risk
The chance that interest rates will change and thereby change the required return and bond value. Rising rates, which result in decreasing bond values, are of greatest concern.

E x a m p l e ▼   The effect of changing required returns on bonds of differing maturity can be illustrated by using Mills Company's bond and Figure 7.2. If, as denoted by the dashed line at 8 years to maturity, the required return rises from 10% to 12%, the bond's value decreases from $1,000 to $901—a 9.9% increase. If the same change in required return had occurred with only 3 years to maturity, as denoted by the dashed line, the bond's value would have dropped to just $952—only a 4.8% decrease. Similar types of responses can be seen in terms of the change in bond value associated with decreases in required returns. The shorter the time to maturity, the smaller the impact on bond value caused by a given change in the required return. ▲

Yield to Maturity (YTM)

When investors evaluate and trade bonds, they commonly consider **yield to maturity (YTM),** which is the rate of return investors earn if they buy the bond at a specific price and hold it until maturity. The measure assumes, of course, that the issuer makes all scheduled interest and principal payments as promised. The yield to maturity on a bond with a current price equal to its par value (i.e., $B_0 = M$) will always equal the coupon interest rate. When the bond value differs from par, the yield to maturity will differ from the coupon interest rate.

yield to maturity (YTM)
The rate of return investors earn if they buy a bond at a specific price and hold it until maturity. Assumes that issuer makes all scheduled interest and principal payments as promised.

Assuming that interest is paid annually, the yield to maturity on a bond can be found by solving Equation 7.3 for k_d. In other words, the current value, B_0, the annual interest, I, the par value, M, and the years to maturity, n, are known, and the required return must be found. The required return is the bond's yield to maturity. The YTM can be found by trial and error or by use of a financial calculator. The calculator provides accurate YTM values with minimum effort. Finding YTM is demonstrated in the following example.

E x a m p l e ▼   The Mills Company bond, which currently sells for $1,080, has a 10% coupon interest rate and $1,000 par value, pays interest annually, and has 10 years to

In Practice

The Value of a Zero

Many investors buy bonds to get a steady stream of interest payments. So why would anyone buy a zero-coupon bond? One reason is their cost. Because they pay no interest, zeros sell at a deep discount from par value: A $1,000 30-year government agency zero-coupon bond might cost about $175. At maturity, the investor receives the $1,000 par value. The difference between the price of the bond and its par value is the return to the investor. Stated as an annual yield, the return represents compounding, just as if the issuer had paid interest during the bond term. In this example, the bond yields 6%.

Even though a corporate issuer of a zero-coupon bond makes no cash interest payments, for tax purposes it can take an interest deduction. To calculate the annual implicit interest expense, the issuer must first determine the bond's value at the beginning of each year using the formula $M/(1 + k_d)^n$, where M is the par value in dollars, k_d is the required return, and n is number of years to maturity. The difference in the bond's value from year to year is the implicit interest.

Assume that a corporation issues a 5-year zero-coupon bond with a $1,000 par value and a required yield of 6.5%. Applying the preceding formula, we find that the initial price of this bond is $729.88 [$1,000/(1 + .065)^5 = $1,000/1.3700867]. Total implicit interest over the 5 years is $270.12 ($1,000 − $729.88). The following table uses the formula to calculate the bond's value at the end of each year and the implicit interest expense that the corporation can deduct each year:

Year	Beginning Value	Ending Value	Implicit Interest Expense
1	$729.88	$ 777.32	$ 47.44
2	777.32	827.84	50.53
3	827.84	881.66	53.82
4	881.66	938.97	57.31
5	938.97	1,000.00	61.03
Total			$270.13 (difference due to rounding)

maturity. Because $B_0 = \$1,080$, $I = \$100$ (.10 × $1,000), $M = \$1,000$, and $n = 10$ years, substituting into Equation 7.3a, we get

$$\$1,080 = \$100 \times (PVIFA_{k_d,10\text{yrs}}) + \$1,000 \times (PVIF_{k_d,10\text{yrs}})$$

Our objective is to solve the equation for k_d—the YTM.

Trial and Error   Because we know that a required return, k_d, of 10% (which equals the bond's 10% coupon interest rate) would result in a value of $1,000, the discount rate that would result in $1,080 must be less than 10%. (Remember that the lower the discount rate, the higher the present value, and the higher the discount rate, the lower the present value.) Trying 9%, we get

$$\$100 \times (PVIFA_{9\%,10\text{yrs}}) + \$1,000 \times (PVIF_{9\%,10\text{yrs}}) = \$100 \times (6.418) + \$1,000 \times (.422)$$
$$= \$641.80 + \$422.00 = \$1,063.80$$

Because the 9% rate is not quite low enough to bring the value up to $1,080, we next try 8% and get

$$\$100 \times (PVIFA_{8\%,10\text{yrs}}) + \$1,000 \times (PVIF_{8\%,10\text{yrs}}) = \$100 \times (6.710) + \$1,000 \times (.463)$$
$$= \$671.00 + \$463.00 = \$1,134.00$$

Because the value at the 8% rate is higher than $1,080 and the value at the 9% rate is lower than $1,080, the bond's yield to maturity must be between 8 and 9%. Because the $1,063.80 is closer to $1,080, the YTM to the nearest whole percent is 9%. (By using *interpolation*, we could eventually find the more precise YTM value to be 8.77%.)[6]

Calculator Use   [*Note:* Most calculators require *either* the present (B_0 in this case) or future (I and M in this case) values to be input as a negative number to calculate yield to maturity. That approach is used here.] Using the inputs shown, you should find the YTM to be 8.766%. Note that this number is more precise than the YTM value found before by using the trial-and-error approach.

Inputs: | 10 | | -1080 | | 100 | | 1000 |

Functions: | N | | PV | | PMT | | FV | | CPT | | I |

▲ **Outputs:** | 8.766 |

Semiannual Interest and Bond Values

The procedure used to value bonds paying interest semiannually is similar to that shown in Chapter 5 for compounding interest more frequently than annually—except that here we need to find present value instead of future value. It involves

1. Converting annual interest, I, to semiannual interest by dividing I by 2.
2. Converting the number of years to maturity, n, to the number of 6-month periods to maturity by multiplying n by 2.
3. Converting the required stated (rather than effective)[7] return for similar-risk bonds that also pay semiannual interest from an annual rate, k_d, to a semiannual rate by dividing k_d by 2.

---

6. For information on how to interpolate a more precise answer, see the book's home page at www.awlonline.com/gitman

7. As was noted in Chapter 5, the effective annual rate of interest, EAR, for stated interest rate k, when interest is paid semiannually ($m = 2$), can be found by using Equation 5.10:

$$\text{EAR} = \left(1 + \frac{k}{2}\right)^2 - 1$$

For example, a bond with a 12% required stated return, k_d, that pays semiannual interest would have an effective annual rate of

$$\text{EAR} = \left(1 + \frac{.12}{2}\right)^2 - 1 = (1.06)^2 - 1 = 1.1236 - 1 = .1236 = \underline{12.36\%}$$

Because most bonds pay semiannual interest at semiannual rates equal to 50% of the stated annual rate, their effective annual rates are generally higher than their stated rates.

Substituting these three changes into Equation 7.3 yields

$$B_0 = \frac{I}{2} \times \left[\sum_{i=1}^{2n} \frac{1}{\left(1 + \frac{k_d}{2}\right)^t} \right] + M \times \left[\frac{1}{\left(1 + \frac{k_d}{2}\right)^{2n}} \right] \qquad (7.4)[8]$$

$$= \frac{I}{2} \times \left(PVIFA_{\frac{k_d}{2},2n} \right) + M \times \left(PVIF_{\frac{k_d}{2},2n} \right) \qquad (7.4a)$$

An example will illustrate the application of this equation.

Example ▼ Assuming that the Mills Company bond pays interest semiannually and that the required stated return, k_d, is 12% for similar-risk bonds that also pay semiannual interest, substituting these values into Equation 7.4a yields

$$B_0 = \frac{\$100}{2} \times \left(PVIFA_{\frac{12\%}{2},2 \times 10\text{yrs}} \right) + \$1,000 \times \left(PVIF_{\frac{12\%}{2},2 \times 10\text{yrs}} \right)$$

Table Use

$$B_0 = \$50 \times (PVIFA_{6\%,20 \text{ periods}}) + \$1,000 \times (PVIF_{6\%,20 \text{ periods}})$$
$$= \$50 \times (11.470) + \$1,000 \times (.312) = \underline{\underline{\$885.50}}$$

Calculator Use   When using a calculator to find bond value when interest is paid semiannually, we must double the number of periods and divide both the required stated return and the annual interest by 2. For the Mills Company bond, we would use 20 periods (2 × 10 years), a required return of 6% (12% ÷ 2), and an interest payment of $50 ($100 ÷ 2). Using these inputs, you should find the bond value with semiannual interest to be $885.30. Note that this value is more precise than the value calculated using the rounded financial table factors.

Comparing this result with the $887.00 value found earlier for annual compounding (see Table 7.2), we can see that the bond's value is lower when semian-

---

8. Although it may appear inappropriate to use the semiannual discounting procedure on the maturity value, M, this technique is necessary to find the correct bond value. One way to confirm the accuracy of this approach is to calculate the bond value for the case where the required stated return and coupon interest rate are equal; for B_0 to equal M, as would be expected in such a case, the maturity value must be discounted on a semiannual basis.

nual interest is paid. *This will always occur when the bond sells at a discount.* For bonds selling at a premium, the opposite will occur: The value with semiannual interest will be greater than with annual interest.

? Review Questions

7–4   Describe the basic procedure used to value a bond that pays annual interest. What procedure is used to value bonds paying interest semiannually?

7–5   What relationship between the required return and coupon interest rate will cause a bond to sell (a) at a discount? (b) at a premium? and (c) at its par value? Explain.

7–6   If the required return on a bond differs from its coupon interest rate and is assumed to be constant until maturity, describe the behavior of the bond value over the passage of time as the bond moves toward maturity.

7–7   As a risk-averse investor, to protect against the potential impact of rising interest rates on bond value, would you prefer bonds with short or long periods until maturity? Explain why.

7–8   What is meant by a bond's *yield to maturity (YTM)*? Briefly describe both the trial-and-error approach and the use of a financial calculator for finding YTM.

7.3 Common Stock Valuation

Common stockholders expect to be rewarded through periodic cash dividends and an increasing—or at least nondeclining—share value. Like current owners, prospective owners and security analysts frequently estimate the firm's value. They purchase the stock when they believe that it is *undervalued*—that its true value is greater than its market price. They sell the stock when they feel that it is *overvalued*—that its market price is greater than its true value.

In this section, we will describe specific stock valuation techniques. First, though, we will look at the concept of an efficient market, which questions whether that the prices of actively traded stocks can differ from their true values.

Market Efficiency[9]

Economically rational buyers and sellers use their assessment of an asset's risk and return to determine its value. To a buyer, the asset's value represents the maximum price that he or she would pay to acquire it; a seller views the asset's

---

9. A great deal of theoretical and empirical research has been performed in the area of market efficiency. For purposes of this discussion, generally accepted beliefs about market efficiency are described rather than the technical aspects of the various forms of market efficiency and their theoretical implications. For a good discussion of the theory and evidence relative to market efficiency, see William L. Megginson, *Corporate Finance Theory* (Reading, MA: Addison Wesley Longman, 1997), Chapter 3.

value as a minimum sale price. In competitive markets with many active participants, such as the New York Stock Exchange, the interactions of many buyers and sellers result in an equilibrium price—the *market value*—for each security. This price reflects the collective actions of buyers and sellers based on all available information. Buyers and sellers are assumed to immediately digest new information as it becomes available, and through their purchase and sale activities to quickly create a new market equilibrium price.

Market Adjustment to New Information

Hint   Be sure to clarify in your own mind the difference between the required return and the expected return. *Required return* is what an investor *has to have* to invest in a specific asset, and *expected return* is the return an investor *thinks she will get* if the asset is purchased.

expected return, $\hat{k}$
The return that is expected to be earned on a given asset each period over an infinite time horizon.

Hint   This relationship between the expected return and the required return can be seen in Equation 7.5, where a decrease in asset price will result in an increase in the expected return.

The process of market adjustment to new information can be viewed in terms of rates of return. From Chapter 6, we know that for a given level of risk, investors require a specified periodic return—the *required return, k*—which can be estimated by using beta and CAPM. At each point in time, investors estimate the **expected return, $\hat{k}$**—the return that is expected to be earned on a given asset each period over an infinite time horizon. The expected return can be estimated by using a simplified form of Equation 6.1:

$$\hat{k} = \frac{\text{expected benefit during each period}}{\text{current price of asset}} \tag{7.5}$$

Whenever investors find that the expected return is not equal to the required return ($\hat{k} \neq k$), a market price adjustment will occur. If the expected return is less than the required return ($\hat{k} < k$), investors will sell the asset, because they do not expect it to earn a return commensurate with its risk. Such action would drive the price down, which (assuming no change in expected benefits) will cause the expected return to rise to the level of the required return. If the expected return were above the required return ($\hat{k} > k$), investors would buy the asset, driving its price up and its expected return down to the point that it equals the required return.

Example ▼ The common stock of Alton Industries (AI) is currently selling for $50 per share, and market participants expect it to generate benefits of $6.50 per share during each coming period. In addition, the risk-free rate, R_F, is currently 7%; the market return, k_m, is 12%; and the stock's beta, b_{AI}, is 1.20. When these values are substituted into Equation 7.5, the firm's current expected return, $\hat{k}_0$, is

$$\hat{k}_0 = \frac{\$6.50}{\$50.00} = \underline{\underline{13\%}}$$

When the appropriate values are substituted into the CAPM (Equation 6.8), the current required return, k_0, is

$$k_0 = 7\% + [1.20 \times (12\% - 7\%)] = 7\% + 6\% = \underline{13\%}$$

Because $\hat{k}_0 = k_0$, the market is currently in equilibrium, and the stock is fairly priced at $50 per share.

Assume that a press release announces that a major product liability suit has been filed against Alton Industries. As a result, investors immediately adjust their risk assessment upward, raising the firm's beta from 1.20 to 1.40. The new required return, k_1, becomes

$$k_1 = 7\% + [1.40 \times (12\% - 7\%)] = 7\% + 7\% = \underline{\underline{14\%}}$$

Because the expected return of 13% is now below the required return of 14%, many investors would sell the stock—driving its price down to about $46.43—the price that would result in a 14% expected return, $\hat{k}_1$.

$$\hat{k}_1 = \frac{\$6.50}{\$46.43} = \underline{\underline{14\%}}$$

The new price of $46.43 brings the market back into equilibrium, because the expected return now equals the required return.

The Efficient Market Hypothesis

As noted in Chapter 6, active markets such as the New York Stock Exchange are efficient—they are made up of many rational investors who react quickly and objectively to new information. The **efficient market hypothesis,** which is the basic theory describing the behavior of such a "perfect" market, specifically states:

efficient market hypothesis
Theory describing the behavior of an assumed "perfect" market in which (1) securities are typically in equilibrium, (2) security prices fully reflect all public information available and react swiftly to new information, and, (3) because stocks are fairly priced, investors need not waste time looking for mispriced securities.

1. Securities are typically in equilibrium, meaning that they are fairly priced and their expected returns equal their required returns.
2. At any point in time, security prices fully reflect all public information available about the firm and its securities,[10] and these prices react swiftly to new information.
3. Because stocks are fully and fairly priced, investors need not waste their time trying to find and capitalize on mispriced (undervalued or overvalued) securities.

Not all market participants are believers in the efficient market hypothesis. Some feel that it is worthwhile to search for undervalued or overvalued securities and to trade them to profit from market inefficiencies. Others argue that it is mere luck that would allow market participants to correctly anticipate new information and as a result earn *excess returns*—that is, actual returns > required returns. They believe that it is unlikely that market participants can *over the long run* earn excess returns. Contrary to this belief, some well-known investors such as Warren Buffett and Peter Lynch *have* over the long run consistently earned excess returns on their portfolios. It is unclear whether their performance is the result of their superior ability to anticipate new information or some form of market inefficiency.

---

10. Those market participants who have nonpublic—*inside*—information may have an unfair advantage that permits them to earn an excess return. Since the mid-1980s with the disclosure of the insider-trading activities of a number of well-known financiers and investors, major national attention has been focused on the "problem" of insider trading and its resolution. Clearly, those who trade securities based on inside information have an unfair and illegal advantage. Empirical research has confirmed that those with inside information do indeed have an opportunity to earn an excess return. Here we ignore this possibility, given its illegality and that enhanced surveillance and enforcement by the securities industry and the government have in recent years (it appears) significantly reduced insider trading. We, in effect, assume that all relevant information is public, and therefore the market is efficient.

Throughout this text we ignore the disbelievers and continue to assume market efficiency. This means that *the terms "expected return" and "required return" are used interchangeably,* because they should be equal in an efficient market. This also means that stock prices accurately reflect true value based on risk and return. In other words, we will operate under the assumption that the market price at any point in time is the best estimate of value. We're now ready to look closely at the mechanics of stock valuation.

The Basic Stock Valuation Equation

Like bonds, the value of a share of common stock is equal to the present value of all future benefits (dividends) it is expected to provide. In other words, *the value of a share of common stock is equal to the present value of all future dividends it is expected to provide over an infinite time horizon.*[11] Although a stockholder can earn capital gains by selling stock at a price above that originally paid, what is really sold is the right to all future dividends. What about stocks that are not expected to pay dividends in the foreseeable future? Such stocks have a value attributable to a distant dividend expected to result from sale of the company or liquidation of its assets. Therefore, *from a valuation viewpoint, only dividends are relevant.* Redefining terms, the basic valuation model in Equation 7.1 can be specified for common stock as given in Equation 7.6:

Career Key

Management must be very conscious of the relationship between their dividend policy and the market price of the firm. Investors' expectations that a firm's dividend will be low or unpredictable will reduce the value of the firm's stock.

$$P_0 = \frac{D_1}{(1+k_s)^1} + \frac{D_2}{(1+k_s)^2} + \cdots + \frac{D_\infty}{(1+k_s)^\infty} \qquad (7.6)$$

where

$$P_0 = \text{value of common stock}$$
$$D_t = \text{per share dividend expected at the end of year } t$$
$$k_s = \text{required return on common stock}$$

The equation can be simplified somewhat by redefining each year's dividend, D_t, in terms of anticipated growth. We will consider three cases here—zero growth, constant growth, and variable growth.

Zero Growth

zero-growth model
An approach to dividend valuation that assumes a constant, nongrowing dividend stream.

The simplest approach to dividend valuation, the **zero-growth model,** assumes a constant, nongrowing dividend stream. In terms of the notation already introduced,

$$D_1 = D_2 = \cdots = D_\infty$$

Letting D_1 represent the amount of the annual dividend, Equation 7.6 under zero growth would reduce to

$$P_0 = D_1 \times \sum_{t=1}^{\infty} \frac{1}{(1+k_s)^t} = D_1 \times (PVIFA_{k_s,\infty}) = D_1 \times \frac{1}{k_s} = \frac{D_1}{k_s} \qquad (7.7)$$

The equation shows that with zero growth, the value of a share of stock would equal the present value of a perpetuity of D_1 dollars discounted at a rate k_s.

---

11. The need to consider an infinite time horizon is not critical, because a sufficiently long period, say, 50 years, will result in about the same present value as an infinite period for moderate-sized required returns. For example, at 15%, a dollar to be received 50 years from now, $PVIF_{15\%,50yrs}$, is worth only about $.001 today.

Example ▼ The dividend of Denham Company, an established textile producer, is expected
to remain constant at $3 per share indefinitely. If the required return on its stock
▲ is 15%, the stock's value is $20 ($3 ÷ .15).

Preferred Stock Valuation   Because preferred stock typically provides its
holders with a fixed annual dividend over its assumed infinite life, *Equation 7.7
can be used to find the value of preferred stock*. The value of preferred stock can
be estimated by substituting the stated dividend on the preferred stock for D_1
and the required return for k_s, in Equation 7.7. For example, a preferred stock
paying a $5 stated annual dividend and having a required return of 13 percent
would have a value of $38.46 ($5 ÷ .13). Detailed discussion of preferred stock
was included in Chapter 2.

Constant Growth

constant-growth model
A widely cited dividend valuation approach that assumes that dividends will grow at a constant rate that is less than the required return.

The most widely cited dividend valuation approach, the **constant-growth model,**
assumes that dividends will grow at a constant rate, g, that is less than the
required return, k_s. The assumption that $k_s > g$ is a necessary mathematical condition for deriving this model.[12] By letting D_0 represent the most recent dividend,
Equation 7.6 can be rewritten as follows:

$$P_0 = \frac{D_0 \times (1+g)^1}{(1+k_s)^1} + \frac{D_0 \times (1+g)^2}{(1+k_s)^2} + \cdots + \frac{D_0 \times (1+g)^\infty}{(1+k_s)^\infty} \tag{7.8}$$

If we simplify Equation 7.8, it can be rewritten as follows:[13]

$$P_0 = \frac{D_1}{k_s - g} \tag{7.9}$$

---

12. Another assumption of the constant-growth model as presented is that earnings and dividends grow at the same
rate. This assumption is true only in cases in which a firm pays out a fixed percentage of its earnings each year (has
a fixed payout ratio). In the case of a declining industry, a negative growth rate ($g < 0\%$) might exist. In such a case,
the constant growth model, as well as the variable-growth model presented in the next section, remains fully applicable to the valuation process.

13. For the interested reader, the calculations necessary to derive Equation 7.9 from Equation 7.8 follow. The first
step is to multiply each side of Equation 7.8 by $(1 + k_s)/(1 + g)$ and subtract Equation 7.8 from the resulting expression. This yields

$$\frac{P_0 \times (1+k_s)}{1+g} - P_0 = D_0 - \frac{D_0 \times (1+g)^\infty}{(1+k_s)^\infty} \tag{1}$$

Because k_s is assumed to be greater than g, the second term on the right side of Equation 1 should be zero. Thus,

$$P_0 \times \left(\frac{1+k_s}{1+g} - 1\right) = D_0 \tag{2}$$

Equation 2 is simplified as follows:

$$P_0 \times \left[\frac{(1+k_s) - (1+g)}{1+g}\right] = D_0 \tag{3}$$

$$P_0 \times (k_s - g) = D_0 \times (1+g) \tag{4}$$

$$P_0 = \frac{D_1}{k_s - g} \tag{5}$$

Equation 5 equals Equation 7.9.

Gordon model
A common name for the *constant-growth model* that is widely cited in dividend valuation.

The constant-growth model in Equation 7.9 is commonly called the **Gordon model.** An example will show how it works.

Example ▼ Lamar Company, a small cosmetics company, from 1995 through 2000 paid the following per-share dividends:

Year	Dividend per share
2000	$1.40
1999	1.29
1998	1.20
1997	1.12
1996	1.05
1995	1.00

The annual growth rate of dividends is assumed to equal the expected constant rate of dividend growth, g. Using Appendix Table A–3 for the present value interest factor, $PVIF$, or a financial calculator in conjunction with the technique described for finding growth rates in Chapter 5, we find that the annual growth rate of dividends equals 7%.[14] The company estimates that its dividend in 2001, D_1, will equal $1.50. The required return, k_s, is assumed to be 15%. By substituting these values into Equation 7.9, the value of the stock is

$$P_0 = \frac{\$1.50}{.15 - .07} = \frac{\$1.50}{.08} = \underline{\underline{\$18.75 \text{ per share}}}$$

Assuming that the values of D_1, k_s, and g are accurately estimated, Lamar
▲ Company's stock value is $18.75 per share.

---

14. The technique involves solving the following equation for g:

$$D_{2000} = D_{1995} \times (1 + g)^5$$

$$\frac{D_{1995}}{D_{2000}} = \frac{1}{(1 + g)^5} = PVIF_{g,5}$$

Two basic steps can be followed using the present value table. First, by dividing the earliest dividend (D_{1995} = $1.00) by the most recent dividend (D_{2000} = $1.40), a factor for the present value of one dollar, $PVIF$, of .714 ($1.00 ÷ $1.40) results. Although six dividends are shown, *they reflect only 5 years of growth.* The number of years of growth can alternatively be found by subtracting the earliest year from the most recent year, i.e., 2000 − 1995 = *5 years of growth.* By looking across the table at the present value interest factors, $PVIF$, for 5 years, the factor closest to .714 occurs at 7% (.713). Therefore, the growth rate of the dividends, rounded to the nearest whole percentage, is 7%.

Alternatively, a financial calculator can be used. (*Note:* Most calculators require *either* the PV or FV value to be input as a negative number to calculate an unknown interest or growth rate. That approach is used here.) Using the inputs shown, you should find the growth rate to be 6.96%, which we round to 7%.

Inputs: 1.00   -1.40   5

Functions: PV   FV   N   CPT   I

Outputs: 6.96

Variable Growth

variable-growth model
A dividend valuation approach that allows for a change in the dividend growth rate.

The zero- and constant-growth common stock models do not allow for any shift in expected growth rates. Because future growth rates might shift up or down due to changing expectations, it is useful to consider a **variable-growth model** that allows for a change in the dividend growth rate.[15] Letting g_1 equal the initial growth rate and g_2 equal the subsequent growth rate and assuming a single shift in growth rates occurs at the end of year N, we can use the following four-step procedure to determine the value of a share of stock.

Step 1   Find the value of the cash dividends at the end of *each year*, D_t, during the initial growth period—years 1 through N. This step may require adjusting the most recent dividend, D_0, using the initial growth rate, g_1, to calculate the dividend amount for each year. Therefore, for the first N years:

$$D_t = D_0 \times (1 + g_1)^t = D_0 \times FVIF_{g_1,t}$$

Step 2   Find the present value of the dividends expected during the initial growth period. By using the notation presented earlier, this value can be given as

$$\sum_{t=1}^{N} \frac{D_0 \times (1+g_1)^t}{(1+k_s)^t} = \sum_{t=1}^{N} \frac{D_t}{(1+k_s)^t} = \sum_{t=1}^{N} (D_t \times PVIF_{k_s,t})$$

Step 3   Find the value of the stock *at the end of the initial growth period*, $P_N = (D_{N+1})/(k_s - g_2)$, which is the present value of all dividends expected from year $N + 1$ to infinity—assuming a constant dividend growth rate, g_2. This value is found by applying the constant-growth model (presented as Equation 7.9 in the preceding section) to the dividends expected from year $N + 1$ to infinity. The present value of P_N would represent the value *today* of all dividends that are expected to be received from year $N + 1$ to infinity. This value can be represented by

$$\frac{1}{(1+k_s)^N} \times \frac{D_{N+1}}{k_s - g_2} = PVIF_{k_s,N} \times P_N$$

Step 4   Add the present value components found in Steps 2 and 3 to find the value of the stock, P_0, given in Equation 7.10:

$$P_0 = \underbrace{\sum_{t=1}^{N} \frac{D_0 \times (1+g_1)^t}{(1+k_s)^t}}_{\substack{\text{Present value} \\ \text{of dividends} \\ \text{during initial} \\ \text{growth period}}} + \underbrace{\left[\frac{1}{(1+k_s)^N} \times \frac{D_{N+1}}{k_s - g_2} \right]}_{\substack{\text{Present value of} \\ \text{price of stock at} \\ \text{end of initial} \\ \text{growth period}}} \tag{7.10}$$

The following example illustrates the application of these steps to a variable-growth situation with only one growth rate change.

---

15. Although more than one change in the growth rate can be incorporated in the model, to simplify the discussion we will consider only a single growth-rate change. The number of variable-growth valuation models is technically unlimited, but concern over all likely shifts in growth is unlikely to yield much more accuracy than a simpler model.

E x a m p l e ▼ The most recent (2000) annual dividend payment of Warren Industries, a rapidly growing boat manufacturer, was $1.50 per share. The firm's financial manager expects that these dividends will increase at a 10% annual rate, g_1, over the next 3 years (2001, 2002, and 2003) due to the introduction of a hot new boat. At the end of the 3 years (end of 2003), the firm's mature product line is expected to result in a slowing of the dividend growth rate to 5% per year for the foreseeable future (noted as g_2). The firm's required return is 15%. To estimate the current (end of 2000) value of Warren's common stock, $P_0 = P_{2000}$, the four-step procedure presented before must be applied to these data.

Step 1   The value of the cash dividends in each of the next 3 years is calculated in columns 1, 2, and 3 of Table 7.3. The 2001, 2002, and 2003 dividends are $1.65, $1.82, and $2.00, respectively.

Step 2   The present value of the three dividends expected during the 2001–2003 initial growth period is calculated in columns 3, 4, and 5 of Table 7.3. The sum of the present values of the three dividends is $4.14.

Step 3   The value of the stock at the end of the initial growth period ($N = 2003$) can be found by first calculating $D_{N+1} = D_{2004}$:

$$D_{2004} = D_{2003} \times (1 + .05) = \$2.00 \times (1.05) = \$2.10$$

By using $D_{2004} = \$2.10$, a 15% required return, and a 5% dividend growth rate, we can calculate the value of the stock at the end of 2003 as follows:

$$P_{2003} = \frac{D_{2004}}{k_s - g_2} = \frac{\$2.10}{.15 - .05} = \frac{\$2.10}{.10} = \$21.00$$

Finally, in Step 3, the share value of $21 at the end of 2003 must be converted into a present (end-of–2000) value. Using the 15% required return, we get

$$PVIF_{k_s,N} \times P_N = PVIF_{15\%,3} \times P_{2003} = .658 \times \$21.00 = \$13.82$$

TABLE 7.3	**Calculation of Present Value of Warren Industries' Dividends (2001–2003)**

t	End of year	$D_0 = D_{2000}$ (1)	$FVIF_{10\%,t}$ (2)	D_t $[(1) \times (2)]$ (3)	$PVIF_{15\%,t}$ (4)	Present value of dividends $[(3) \times (4)]$ (5)
1	2001	$1.50	1.100	$1.65	.870	$1.44
2	2002	1.50	1.210	1.82	.756	1.38
3	2003	1.50	1.331	2.00	.658	1.32

$$\text{Sum of present value of dividends} = \sum_{t=1}^{3} \frac{D_0 \times (1+g_1)^t}{(1+k_s)^t} = \$4.14$$

Step 4   Adding the present value of the initial dividend stream (found in Step 2) to the present value of the stock at the end of the initial growth period (found in Step 3) as specified in Equation 7.10, we get the current (end-of-2000) value of Warren Industries' stock:

$$P_{2000} = \$4.14 + \$13.82 = \underline{\$17.96 \text{ per share}}$$

The stock is currently worth $17.96 per share.

Time-Line Use   The calculation of this value is summarized diagrammatically:

Finding Warren Industries' current (end-of-2000) value with variable growth

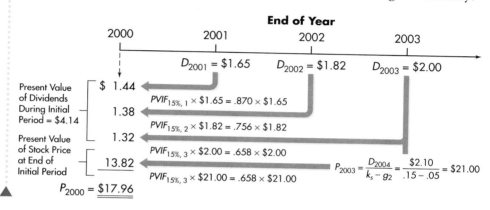

It is important to recognize that the zero-, constant-, and variable-growth valuation models provide useful frameworks for estimating stock value. Clearly, the estimates produced cannot be very precise, given that the forecasts of future growth and discount rates are themselves necessarily approximate. Looked at another way, a great deal of rounding error can be introduced into the stock price estimate as a result of rounding growth and discount rate estimates to the nearest whole percent. When applying valuation models, it is therefore advisable to carefully estimate these rates and conservatively round them, probably to the nearest tenth of a percent.

Other Approaches to Common Stock Valuation

Many other approaches to common stock valuation exist. The more popular approaches include book value, liquidation value, and some type of a price/earnings multiple.

Book Value

book value per share
The amount per share of common stock that would be received if all of the firm's assets were *sold for their exact book (accounting) value* and the proceeds remaining after paying all liabilities (including preferred stock) were divided among the common stockholders.

Book value per share is simply the amount per share of common stock that would be received if all of the firm's assets were *sold for their exact book (accounting) value* and the proceeds remaining after paying all liabilities (including preferred stock) were divided among the common stockholders. This method lacks sophistication and can be criticized on the basis of its reliance on historical balance sheet data. It ignores the firm's expected earnings potential and generally lacks any true relationship to the firm's value in the marketplace. Let us look at an example.

Example ▼ At year-end 2000, Lamar Company's balance sheet shows total assets of $6 million, total liabilities including preferred stock of $4.5 million, and 100,000 shares of common stock outstanding. Its book value per share therefore would be

$$\frac{\$6,000,000 - \$4,500,000}{100,000 \text{ shares}} = \$15 \text{ per share}$$

Career Key

This is an area that can be influenced by the *accounting* personnel. Their accounting practices will affect the book value of the firm and thus may change the investors' valuation of the firm.

Because this value assumes that assets could be sold for their book value, it may not represent the minimum price at which shares are valued in the marketplace. As a matter of fact, although most stocks sell above book value, it is not unusual to find stocks selling below book value when investors believe either that assets are overvalued or the firm's liabilities are understated. ▲

Liquidation Value

liquidation value per share
The *actual amount* per share of common stock that would be received if all of the firm's assets were *sold for their market value*, liabilities (including preferred stock) are paid, and any remaining money were divided among the common stockholders.

Liquidation value per share is the *actual amount* per share of common stock that would be received if all of the firm's assets were *sold for their market value*, liabilities (including preferred stock) were paid, and any remaining money were divided among the common stockholders.[16] This measure is more realistic than book value—because it is based on current market value of the firm's assets—but it still fails to consider the earning power of those assets. An example will illustrate.

Example ▼ Lamar Company found upon investigation that it could obtain only $5.25 million if it sold its assets today. The firm's liquidation value per share therefore would be

$$\frac{\$5,250,000 - \$4,500,000}{100,000 \text{ shares}} = \$7.50 \text{ per share}$$

▲ Ignoring liquidation expenses, this amount would be the firm's minimum value.

Price/Earnings (P/E) Multiples

price/earnings multiple approach
A technique to estimate the firm's share value; calculated by multiplying the firm's expected earnings per share (EPS) by the average price/earnings (P/E) ratio for the industry.

The *price/earnings (P/E) ratio*, introduced in Chapter 4, reflects the amount investors are willing to pay for each dollar of earnings. The average P/E ratio in a particular industry can be used as the guide to a firm's value—if it is assumed that investors value the earnings of that firm in the same way they do the "average" firm in the industry. The **price/earnings multiple approach** is a popular technique to estimate the firm's share value, by multiplying the firm's expected earnings per share (EPS) by the average price/earnings (P/E) ratio for the industry. The average P/E ratio for the industry can be obtained from a source such as *Standard & Poor's Industrial Ratios.*

---

16. In the event of liquidation, creditors' claims must be satisfied first, then those of the preferred stockholders. Anything left goes to common stockholders. A more detailed discussion of liquidation procedures is presented in Chapter 19.

The use of P/E multiples is especially helpful in valuing firms that are not publicly traded, whereas market price quotations can be used to value publicly traded firms.[17] In any case, the price/earnings multiple approach is considered superior to the use of book or liquidation values because it considers *expected* earnings.[18] An example will demonstrate the use of price/earnings multiples.

Example ▼ Lamar Company is expected to earn $2.60 per share next year (2001). This expectation is based on an analysis of the firm's historical earnings trend and expected economic and industry conditions. The average price/earnings (P/E) ratio for firms in the same industry is 7. Multiplying Lamar's expected earnings per share (EPS) of $2.60 by this ratio gives us a value for the firm's shares of $18.20, assuming that investors will continue to measure the value of the average ▲ firm at 7 times its earnings.

So, how much is Lamar Company's stock really worth? That's a trick question, because there's no one right answer. It is important to recognize that the answer depends on the assumptions made and the techniques used. Professional securities analysts typically use a variety of models and techniques to value stocks. For example, an analyst might use the constant-growth model, liquidation value, and price/earnings (P/E) multiples to estimate the worth of a given stock. If the analyst feels comfortable with his or her estimates, the stock would be valued at no more than the largest estimate. Of course, should the firm's estimated liquidation value per share exceed its "going concern" value per share, estimated by using one of the valuation models (zero-, constant-, or variable-growth) or the P/E multiple approach, the firm would be viewed as being "worth more dead than alive." In such an event, the firm would lack sufficient earning power to justify its existence and should probably be liquidated.

Hint   From an investor's perspective, the stock in this situation would be an attractive investment only if it could be purchased at a price below its liquidation value—which in an efficient market could never occur.

? Review Questions

7–9   In an *efficient market,* describe the events that occur in response to new information that causes the expected return to exceed the required return. What happens to the market value?

7–10   What does the *efficient market hypothesis* say about (**a**) securities prices, (**b**) their reaction to new information, and (**c**) investor opportunities to profit?

7–11   Describe, compare, and contrast the following common stock valuation models: (**a**) zero-growth, (**b**) constant-growth, and (**c**) variable-growth.

---

17. Generally, when the P/E ratio is used to value *privately owned* or *closely owned* corporations, a premium is added to adjust for the issue of control. This adjustment is necessary, because the P/E ratio implicitly reflects minority interests of noncontrolling investors in *publicly owned* companies—a condition that does not exist in privately or closely owned corporations.

18. The price/earnings multiple approach to valuation does have a theoretical explanation. If we view 1 divided by the price/earnings ratio, or the *earnings/price ratio,* as the rate at which investors discount the firm's earnings and if we assume that the projected earnings per share will be earned indefinitely (i.e., no growth in earnings per share), the price/earnings multiple approach can be looked on as a method of finding the present value of a perpetuity of projected earnings per share at a rate equal to the earnings/price ratio. This method is in effect a form of the zero-growth model presented in Equation 7.7 on page 302.

7–12 Explain each of the three other approaches to common stock valuation: (a) book value, (b) liquidation value, and (c) price/earnings (P/E) multiples. Which of these is considered the best?

7.4 Decision Making and Common Stock Value

Valuation equations measure the stock value at a point in time based on expected return (D_1, g) and risk (k_s) data. Any decisions of the financial manager that affect these variables can cause the value of the firm, P_0, to change. Figure 7.3 depicts the relationship among financial decisions, return, risk, and stock value.

Changes in Expected Return

Career Key

The *marketing* department can greatly influence the value of a firm. Through product development, promotion, and sales strategies, marketing personnel can influence investors' expectations of cash flows, risks, and, consequently, value.

Assuming that economic conditions remain stable, any management action that would cause current and prospective stockholders to raise their dividend expectations should increase the firm's value. In Equation 7.9,[19] we can see that P_0 will increase for any increase in D_1 or g. Any action of the financial manager that will increase the level of expected returns without changing risk (the required return) should be undertaken, because it will positively affect owners' wealth.

Example ▼ Using the constant-growth model, Lamar Company was found to have a share value of $18.75. On the following day, the firm announced a major technological breakthrough that would revolutionize its industry. Current and prospective stockholders would not be expected to adjust their required return of 15% as a result, but they would expect future dividends to increase. Specifically, they would feel that although the dividend next year, D_1, will remain at $1.50, the expected rate of growth thereafter will increase from 7 to 9%. If we substitute $D_1 = \$1.50$, $k_s = .15$, and $g = .09$ into Equation 7.9, the resulting value equals $25 [i.e., $1.50 ÷ (.15 − .09)]. The increased value therefore resulted from the
▲ higher expected future dividends reflected in the increase in the growth rate.

FIGURE 7.3

Decision Making and Stock Value

Financial decisions, return, risk, and stock value

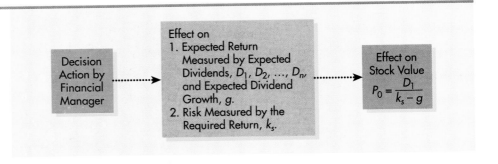

---

19. To convey the interrelationship among financial decisions, return, risk, and stock value, the constant-growth dividend-valuation model is used. Other models—zero-growth or variable-growth—could be used, but the simplicity of exposition using the constant-growth model justifies its use here.

Changes in Risk

Although k_s is defined as the required return it is (as pointed out in Chapter 6) directly related to the nondiversifiable risk, which can be measured by beta. The *capital asset pricing model (CAPM)* given in Equation 6.8 is restated as Equation 7.11:

$$k_s = R_F + [b \times (k_m - R_F)] \tag{7.11}$$

With the risk-free rate, R_F, and the market return, k_m, held constant, the required return, k_s, depends directly on beta. In other words, any action taken by the financial manager that increases risk will also increase the required return. In Equation 7.9, we can see that with all else constant, an increase in the required return, k_s, will reduce share value, P_0. Likewise, a decrease in the required return will increase share value. Thus, any action of the financial manager that increases risk contributes toward a reduction in value, and any action that decreases risk contributes toward an increase in value.

Example ▼   Assume that Lamar Company's 15% required return resulted from a risk-free rate of 9%, a market return of 13%, and a beta of 1.50. Substituting into the capital asset pricing model, Equation 7.11, we get a required return, k_s, of 15%:

$$k_s = 9\% + [1.50 \times (13\% - 9\%)] = \underline{\underline{15\%}}$$

With this return, the value of the firm was calculated to be $18.75 in the earlier example (page 304).

Now imagine that the financial manager makes a decision that, without changing expected dividends, increases the firm's beta to 1.75. Assuming that R_F and k_m remain at 9 and 13%, respectively, the required return will increase to 16% (i.e., 9% + [1.75 × (13% − 9%)]) to compensate stockholders for the increased risk. Substituting $D_1 = \$1.50$, $k_s = .16$, and $g = .07$ into the valuation equation, Equation 7.9, results in a share value of $16.67 [i.e., $1.50 ÷ (.16 − .07)]. As expected, raising the required return (without any corresponding increase in expected return) causes the firm's stock value to decline. Clearly, the ▲ financial manager's action was not in the owners' best interest.

Combined Effect

A financial decision rarely affects return and risk independently; most decisions affect both factors. In terms of the measures presented, with an increase in risk (beta, b) one would expect an increase in return (D_1 or g, or both), assuming that R_F and k_m remain unchanged. The net effect on value depends on the size of the changes in these variables.

Example ▼   If we assume that the two changes illustrated for Lamar Company in the preceding examples occur simultaneously as a result of an action of the financial decision maker, key variable values would be $D_1 = \$1.50$, $k_s = .16$, and $g = .09$. Substituting into the valuation model, we obtain a share price of $21.43 [$1.50 ÷ (.16 − .09)]. The net result of the decision, which increased return (g from 7 to 9%) as well as risk (b from 1.50 to 1.75 and therefore k_s from 15 to 16%), is positive: The share price increased from $18.75 to $21.43. Assuming that the key variables are accurately measured, the decision appears to be in the best interest of the firm's owners, because it increases their wealth.

? Review Questions

7–13 Explain the linkages among financial decisions, return, risk, and stock value. How do the *capital asset pricing model (CAPM)* and the *Gordon model* fit into this basic framework? Explain.

7–14 Assuming that all other variables remain unchanged, what impact would *each* of the following have on stock price? (a) The firm's beta increases. (b) The firm's required return decreases. (c) The dividend expected next year decreases. (d) The rate of growth in dividends is expected to increase. Explain your answers.

SUMMARY

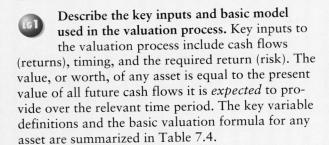 **Describe the key inputs and basic model used in the valuation process.** Key inputs to the valuation process include cash flows (returns), timing, and the required return (risk). The value, or worth, of any asset is equal to the present value of all future cash flows it is *expected* to provide over the relevant time period. The key variable definitions and the basic valuation formula for any asset are summarized in Table 7.4.

Apply the basic valuation model to bonds and describe the impact of required return and time to maturity on bond values. The value of a bond is the present value of its interest payments plus the present value of its par value. The key variable definitions and the basic valuation formula for a bond are summarized in Table 7.4. The discount rate used to determine bond value is the required return, which may differ from the bond's coupon interest rate. A bond can sell at a discount, at par, or at a premium, depending upon whether the required return is respectively greater than, equal to, or less than its coupon interest rate. The amount of time to maturity affects bond values even if required return remains constant. When required return is constant, the value of a bond will approach its par value as the passage of time moves the bond closer to maturity. The shorter the amount of time until a bond's maturity, the less responsive is its market value to a given change in the required return.

Explain yield to maturity (YTM), its calculation, and the procedure used to value bonds that pay interest semiannually. Yield to maturity (YTM) is the rate of return investors earn if they buy a bond at a specific price and hold it until maturity, assuming that the issuer makes all scheduled interest and principal payments as promised. YTM can be calculated by trial and error or financial calculator. Bonds that pay interest semiannually are valued by using the same procedure that is used to value bonds paying annual interest except that the interest payments are one-half of the annual interest payments, the number of periods is twice the number of years to maturity, and the required return used is one-half of the stated annual required return on similar-risk bonds.

Understand the concept of market efficiency and basic common stock valuation under each of three cases: zero growth, constant growth, and variable growth. Market efficiency, which is assumed throughout the text, suggests that there are many rational investors whose quick reactions to new information cause the market value of common stock to adjust upward or downward depending upon whether the expected return is above or below, respectively, the required return for

TABLE 7.4	**Summary of Key Valuation Definitions and Formulas**

Variable definitions

B_0 = bond value

CF_t = cash flow *expected* at the end of year t

D_0 = most recent per-share dividend

D_t = per-share dividend expected at the end of year t

g = constant rate of growth in dividends

g_1 = initial dividend growth rate (in variable growth model)

g_2 = subsequent dividend growth rate (in variable growth model)

I = annual interest on a bond

k = appropriate required return (discount rate)

k_d = required return on a bond

k_s = required return on common stock

M = par, or face, value of a bond

n = relevant time period, or number of years to maturity

N = last year of initial growth period (in variable growth model)

P_0 = value of common stock

V_0 = value of the asset at time zero

Valuation formulas

Value of any asset:

$$V_0 = \frac{CF_1}{(1+k)^1} + \frac{CF_2}{(1+k)^2} + \cdots + \frac{CF_n}{(1+k)^n}$$ [Eq. 7.1]

$$= [CF_1 \times (PVIF_{k,1}) + [CF_2 \times (PVIF_{k,2})] + \ldots + [CF_n \times (PVIF_{k,n})]$$ [Eq. 7.2]

Bond value:

$$B_0 = I \times \left[\sum_{t=1}^{n} \frac{1}{(1+k_d)^t} \right] + M \times \left[\frac{1}{(1+k_d)^n} \right]$$ [Eq. 7.3]

$$= I \times (PVIFA_{k_d,n}) + M \times (PVIF_{k_d,n})$$ [Eq. 7.3a]

Common stock value:

Zero growth: $P_0 = \dfrac{D_1}{k_s}$ (also used to value preferred stock)   [Eq. 7.7]

Constant growth: $P_0 = \dfrac{D_1}{k_s - g}$ [Eq. 7.9]

Variable growth: $P_0 = \displaystyle\sum_{t=1}^{N} \frac{D_0 \times (1+g_1)^t}{(1+k_s)^t} + \left[\frac{1}{(1+k_s)^N} \times \frac{D_{N+1}}{k_s - g_2} \right]$ [Eq. 7.10]

the period. The efficient market hypothesis suggests that securities are fairly priced, they reflect fully all publicly available information, and investors should therefore not waste time trying to find and capital- ize on mispriced securities. The value of a share of common stock is the present value of all future divi- dends it is expected to provide over an infinite time horizon. Three cases of dividend growth—zero growth, constant growth, and variable growth—can be considered in common stock valuation. The key variable definitions and the basic valuation formulas for each of these cases are summarized in Table 7.4. The most widely cited model is the constant-growth model.

 Discuss the use of book value, liquidation value, and price/earnings (P/E) multiples to estimate common stock values. Book value per share is the amount per share of common stock that would be received if all of the firm's assets were *sold for their book (accounting) value* and the proceeds remaining after paying all liabilities (including preferred stock) were divided among the common stockholders. Liquidation value per share is the *actual amount* per share of common stock that would be received if all of the firm's assets were *sold for their market value,* liabilities (including preferred stock) were paid, and the remaining money were divided among the common stockholders. The price/earnings (P/E) multiples approach estimates stock value by multiplying the firm's expected earnings per share (EPS) by the average

price/earnings (P/E) ratio for the industry. Of these three approaches, P/E multiples are the most popular in practice because, unlike book and liquidation value, they view the firm as a going concern whose value lies in its earning power rather than its asset values.

 Understand the relationships among financial decisions, return, risk, and the firm's value. In a stable economy, any action of the financial manager that increases the level of expected return without changing risk should increase share value, and any action that reduces the level of expected return without changing risk should reduce share value. Similarly, any action that increases risk (required return) will reduce share value, and any action that reduces risk will increase share value. In the constant-growth model, returns are measured by next year's dividend (D_1) and its growth rate (g), and risk is measured by the required return (k_s). Because most financial decisions affect both return and risk, an assessment of their combined effect on value must be part of the financial decision-making process.

SELF-TEST PROBLEMS   (Solutions in Appendix B)

   ST 7–1 Bond valuation Lahey Industries has a $1,000 par value bond with an 8% coupon interest rate outstanding. The bond has 12 years remaining to its maturity date.
    a. If interest is paid *annually,* what is the value of the bond when the required return is (1) 7%, (2) 8%, and (3) 10%?
    b. Indicate for each case in **a** whether the bond is selling at a discount, at a premium, or at its par value.
    c. Using the 10% required return, find the bond's value when interest is paid *semiannually.*

   ST 7–2 Yield to maturity Elliot Enterprises' bonds currently sell for $1,150, have an 11% coupon interest rate and a $1,000 par value, pay interest *annually,* and have 18 years to maturity.
    a. Calculate the bonds' yield to maturity (YTM).
    b. Compare the YTM calculated in **a** to the bonds' coupon interest rate, and use a comparison of the bonds' current price and their par value to explain this difference.

   ST 7–3 Common stock valuation Perry Motors' common stock currently pays an annual dividend of $1.80 per share. The required return on the common stock is 12%. Estimate the value of the common stock under each of the following dividend-growth-rate assumptions.

a. Dividends are expected to grow at an annual rate of 0% to infinity.
b. Dividends are expected to grow at a constant annual rate of 5% to infinity.
c. Dividends are expected to grow at an annual rate of 5% for each of the next 3 years followed by a constant annual growth rate of 4% in years 4 to infinity.

PROBLEMS

WARM-UP   LG1   **7–1   Valuation fundamentals**   Imagine that you are trying to evaluate the economics of purchasing an automobile. You expect the car to provide annual after-tax cash benefits of $1,200 and that you can sell the car for after-tax proceeds of $5,000 at the end of the planned 5-year ownership period. All funds for purchasing the car will be drawn from your savings, which are currently earning 6% after taxes.
a. Identify the cash flows, their timing, and the required return applicable to valuing the car.
b. What is the maximum price you would be willing to pay to acquire the car? Explain.

WARM-UP   LG1   **7–2   Valuation of assets**   Using the information provided in the following table, find the value of each asset.

Asset	Cash flow End of year	Cash flow Amount	Appropriate required return
A	1	$ 5,000	18%
	2	5,000	
	3	5,000	
B	1 through ∞	$ 300	15%
C	1	$ 0	16%
	2	0	
	3	0	
	4	0	
	5	35,000	
D	1 through 5	$ 1,500	12%
	6	8,500	
E	1	$ 2,000	14%
	2	3,000	
	3	5,000	
	4	7,000	
	5	4,000	
	6	1,000	

INTERMEDIATE

7–3 Asset valuation and risk   Laura Drake wishes to estimate the value of an asset expected to provide cash inflows of $3,000 per year at the end of years 1 through 4 and $15,000 at the end of year 5. Her research indicates that she must earn 10% on low-risk assets, 15% on average-risk assets, and 22% on high-risk assets.

a. What is the most Laura should pay for the asset if it is classified as (1) low risk, (2) average risk, and (3) high risk?

b. If Laura is unable to assess the risk of the asset and wants to be certain she's making a good deal, based on your findings in **a,** what is the most she should pay? Why?

c. All else being the same, what effect does increasing risk have on the value of an asset? Explain in light of your findings in **a.**

INTERMEDIATE

7–4 Basic bond valuation   Complex Systems has an issue of $1,000-par-value bonds with a 12% coupon interest rate outstanding. The issue pays interest *annually* and has 16 years remaining to its maturity date.

a. If bonds of similar risk are currently earning a 10% rate of return, how much should the Complex Systems bond sell for today?

b. Describe the *two* possible reasons that similar-risk bonds are currently earning a return below the coupon interest rate on the Complex Systems bond.

c. If the required return were at 12% instead of 10%, what would the current value of Complex Systems' bond be? Contrast this finding with your findings in **a** and discuss.

WARM-UP

7–5 Bond valuation—Annual interest   Calculate the value of each of the bonds shown in the following table, all of which pay interest *annually.*

Bond	Par value	Coupon interest rate	Years to maturity	Required return
A	$1,000	14%	20	12%
B	1,000	8	16	8
C	100	10	8	13
D	500	16	13	18
E	1,000	12	10	10

INTERMEDIATE

7–6 Bond value and changing required returns   Midland Utilities has outstanding a bond issue that will mature to its $1,000 par value in 12 years. The bond has a coupon interest rate of 11% and pays interest *annually.*

a. Find the value of the bond if the required return is (1) 11%, (2) 15%, and (3) 8%.

b. Plot your findings in **a** on a set of required return (x axis)–market value of bond (y axis) axes.

c. Use your findings in **a** and **b** to discuss the relationship between the coupon interest rate on a bond and the required return and the market value of the bond relative to its par value.

d. What two reasons cause the required return to differ from the coupon interest rate?

INTERMEDIATE

7–7   Bond value and time—Constant required returns   Pecos Manufacturing has just issued a 15-year, 12% coupon interest rate, $1,000-par bond that pays interest *annually*. The required return is currently 14%, and the company is certain it will remain at 14% until the bond matures in 15 years.

a. Assuming that the required return does remain at 14% until maturity, find the value of the bond with (1) 15 years, (2) 12 years, (3) 9 years, (4) 6 years, (5) 3 years, and (6) 1 year to maturity.

b. Plot your findings on a set of time to maturity (*x* axis)–market value of bond (*y* axis) axes constructed similarly to Figure 7.2.

c. All else remaining the same, when the required return differs from the coupon interest rate and is assumed to be constant to maturity, what happens to the bond value as time moves toward maturity? Explain in light of the graph in **b**.

CHALLENGE

7–8   Bond value and time—Changing required returns   Lynn Parsons is considering investing in either of two outstanding bonds. The bonds both have $1,000 par values and 11% coupon interest rates and pay *annual* interest. Bond A has exactly 5 years to maturity, and bond B has 15 years to maturity.

a. Calculate the value of bond A if the required return is (1) 8%, (2) 11%, and (3) 14%.

b. Calculate the value of bond B if the required return is (1) 8%, (2) 11%, and (3) 14%.

c. From your findings in **a** and **b,** complete the following table, and discuss the relationship between time to maturity and changing required returns.

Required return	Value of bond A	Value of bond B
8%	?	?
11	?	?
14	?	?

d. If Lynn wanted to minimize *interest-rate risk,* which bond should she purchase? Why?

WARM-UP

7–9   Yield to maturity   The relationship between a bond's yield to maturity and coupon rate can be used to predict its pricing level. For each of the bonds listed, state whether the price of the bond will be at a premium to par, at par, or at a discount to par.

Bond	Coupon rate	Yield to maturity	Price
A	6%	10%	
B	8	8	
C	9	7	
D	7	9	
E	12	10	

INTERMEDIATE

7–10   Yield to maturity   The Salem Company bond currently sells for $955, has a 12% coupon interest rate and $1,000 par value, pays interest *annually,* and has 15 years to maturity.
a. Calculate the yield to maturity (YTM) on this bond.
b. Explain the relationship that exists between the coupon interest rate and yield to maturity and the par value and market value of a bond.

INTERMEDIATE

7–11   Yield to maturity   Each of the bonds shown in the following table pays interest *annually.*

Bond	Par value	Coupon interest rate	Years to maturity	Current value
A	$1,000	9%	8	$ 820
B	1,000	12	16	1,000
C	500	12	12	560
D	1,000	15	10	1,120
E	1,000	5	3	900

a. Calculate the yield to maturity (YTM) for each bond.
b. What relationship exists between the coupon interest rate and yield to maturity and the par value and market value of a bond? Explain.

CHALLENGE

7–12   Bond valuation and yield to maturity   Mark Goldsmith's broker has shown him two bonds. Each has a maturity of 5 years, a par value of $1,000, and a yield to maturity of 12%. Bond A has a coupon rate of 6% paid annually. Bond B has a coupon rate of 14% paid annually.
a. Calculate the selling price for each of the bonds.
b. Mark has $20,000 to invest. Based on the price of the bonds, how many of either one could Mark purchase if he were to choose it over the other? (Mark cannot really purchase a fraction of a bond, but for purposes of this question, pretend that he can.)

c. Calculate the yearly interest income of each bond based on its coupon rate and the number of bonds that Mark could buy with his $20,000.

d. Assume that Mark will reinvest the interest payments as they are paid (at the end of each year) and that his rate of return on the reinvestment is only 10%. For each bond, calculate the value of the principal payment plus the value of Mark's reinvestment account at the end of the 5 years.

e. Why are the two values calculated in **d** different? If Mark were worried that he would earn less than the 12% yield to maturity rate on the reinvested interest payments, which of these two bonds would be a better choice?

INTERMEDIATE

**7–13   Bond valuation—Semiannual interest   Find the value of a bond maturing in 6 years, with a $1,000 par value and a coupon interest rate of 10% (5% paid semiannually) if the required return on similar-risk bonds is 14% annual interest (7% paid semiannually).

INTERMEDIATE

**7–14   Bond valuation—Semiannual interest   Calculate the value of each of the bonds shown in the following table, all of which pay interest *semiannually*.

Bond	Par value	Coupon interest rate	Years to maturity	Required stated return
A	$1,000	10%	12%	8%
B	1,000	12	20	12
C	500	12	5	14
D	1,000	14	10	10
E	100	6	4	14

CHALLENGE

**7–15   Bond valuation—Quarterly interest   Calculate the value of a $5,000-par-value bond paying quarterly interest at an annual coupon interest rate of 10% and having 10 years until maturity if the required return on similar-risk bonds is currently a 12% annual rate paid *quarterly*.

WARM-UP

**7–16   Common stock valuation—Zero growth   Scotto Manufacturing is a mature firm in the machine-tool-component industry. The firm's most recent common stock dividend was $2.40 per share. Due to its maturity as well as stable sales and earnings, the firm's management feels that dividends will remain at the current level for the foreseeable future.

a. If the required return is 12%, what will be the value of Scotto's common stock?

b. If the firm's risk as perceived by market participants suddenly increases, causing the required return to rise to 20%, what will be the common stock value?

c. Based on your findings in **a** and **b**, what impact does risk have on value? Explain.

INTERMEDIATE

**7–17   Common stock value—Zero growth   Kelsey Drums, Inc., is a well-established supplier of fine percussion instruments to orchestras all over the United States.

The company's class A common stock has paid a dividend of $5.00 per share per year for the last 15 years. Management expects to continue to pay at that rate for the foreseeable future. Sally Talbot purchased 100 shares of Kelsey class A common 10 years ago at a time when the required rate of return for the stock was 16%. She wants to sell her shares today. The current required rate of return for the stock is 12%. How much capital gain or loss will she have on her shares?

INTERMEDIATE **7–18 Preferred stock valuation**   Jones Design wishes to estimate the value of its outstanding preferred stock. The preferred issue has an $80 par value and pays an annual dividend of $6.40 per share. Similar-risk preferred stocks are currently earning a 9.3% annual rate of return.
a. What is the market value of the outstanding preferred stock?
b. If an investor purchases the preferred stock at the value calculated in a, how much does she gain or lose per share if she sells the stock when the required return on similar-risk preferreds has risen to 10.5%? Explain.

WARM-UP
7–19 Common stock value—Constant growth   Use the constant-growth model (Gordon model) to find the value of each of the firms shown in the following table.

Firm	Dividend expected next year	Dividend growth rate	Required return
A	$1.20	8%	13%
B	4.00	5	15
C	.65	10	14
D	6.00	8	9
E	2.25	8	20

INTERMEDIATE **7–20 Common stock value—Constant growth**   McCracken Roofing, Inc., common stock paid a dividend of $1.20 per share last year. The company expects earnings and dividends to grow at a rate of 5% per year for the foreseeable future.
a. What required rate of return for this stock would result in a price per share of $28?
b. If McCracken had an earnings and dividend growth rate of 10%, what required rate of return would result in a price per share of $28?

7–21 Common stock value—Constant growth   Elk County Telephone has paid the dividends shown in the following table over the past 6 years:

Year	Dividend per share
2000	$2.87
1999	2.76
1998	2.60
1997	2.46
1996	2.37
1995	2.25

The firm's dividend per share next year is expected to be $3.02.

a. If you can earn 13% on similar-risk investments, what is the most you would pay per share for this firm?

b. If you can earn only 10% on similar-risk investments, what is the most you would be willing to pay per share?

c. Compare and contrast your findings in **a** and **b**, and discuss the impact of changing risk on share value.

CHALLENGE

7–22   **Common stock value—Variable growth**   Newman Manufacturing is considering a cash purchase of the stock of Grips Tool. During the year just completed, Grips earned $4.25 per share and paid cash dividends of $2.55 per share ($D_0 = $2.55). Grips' earnings and dividends are expected to grow at 25% per year for the next 3 years, after which they are expected to grow at 10% per year to infinity. What is the maximum price per share Newman should pay for Grips if it has a required return of 15% on investments with risk characteristics similar to those of Grips?

CHALLENGE

7–23   **Common stock value—Variable growth**   Home Place Hotels, Inc., is entering into a 3-year remodeling and expansion project. The construction will have a limiting effect on earnings during that time but should allow the company to enjoy much improved growth in earnings and dividends when it is complete. Last year, the company paid a dividend of $3.40. It expects zero growth in the next year. In years 2 and 3, 5% growth is expected, and in year 4, 15% growth. In year 5 and thereafter, growth should be a constant 10% per year. What is the maximum price per share that an investor who requires a return of 14% should pay for Home Place Hotels common stock?

CHALLENGE

7–24   **Common stock value—Variable growth**   Lawrence Industries' most recent annual dividend was $1.80 per share ($D_0 = $1.80), and the firm's required return is 11%. Find the market value of Lawrence's shares when:

a. Dividends are expected to grow at 8% annually for 3 years followed by a 5% constant annual growth rate in years 4 to infinity.

b. Dividends are expected to grow at 8% annually for 3 years followed by 0% annual growth in years 4 to infinity.

c. Dividends are expected to grow at 8% annually for 3 years followed by a 10% constant annual growth rate in years 4 to infinity.

CHALLENGE **LG4**

7–25   **Common stock value—All growth models**   You are evaluating the potential purchase of a small business currently generating $42,500 of after-tax cash flow ($D_0 = \$42,500$). Based on a review of similar-risk investment opportunities, you must earn an 18% rate of return on the proposed purchase. Because you are relatively uncertain about future cash flows, you decide to estimate the firm's value using several possible cash flow, growth rate assumptions.

a.   What is the firm's value if cash flows are expected to grow at an annual rate of 0% to infinity?

b.   What is the firm's value if cash flows are expected to grow at a constant annual rate of 7% to infinity?

c.   What is the firm's value if cash flows are expected to grow at an annual rate of 12% for the first 2 years followed by a constant annual rate of 7% in years 3 to infinity?

INTERMEDIATE **LG5**

7–26   **Book and liquidation value**   The balance sheet for Gallinas Industries is as follows.

		Balance Sheet Gallinas Industries December 31	
Assets		**Liabilities and stockholders' equity**	
Cash	$ 40,000	Accounts payable	$ 100,000
Marketable securities	60,000	Notes payable	30,000
Accounts receivable	120,000	Accrued wages	30,000
Inventories	160,000	Total current liabilities	$160,000
Total current assets	$380,000	Long-term debt	$180,000
Land and buildings (net)	$150,000	Preferred stock	$ 80,000
Machinery and equipment	250,000	Common stock (10,000 shares)	360,000
Total fixed assets (net)	$400,000	Total liabilities and stockholders' equity	$780,000
Total assets	$780,000		

Additional information with respect to the firm is available:

(1)   Preferred stock can be liquidated at book value.

(2)   Accounts receivable and inventories can be liquidated at 90% of book value.

(3)   The firm has 10,000 shares of common stock outstanding.

(4)   All interest and dividends are currently paid up.

(5)   Land and buildings can be liquidated at 130% of book value.

(6)   Machinery and equipment can be liquidated at 70% of book value.

(7)   Cash and marketable securities can be liquidated at book value.

Given this information, answer the following:
a. What is Gallinas Industries' book value per share?
b. What is its liquidation value per share?
c. Compare, contrast, and discuss the values found in **a** and **b**.

WARM-UP   **7–27   Valuation with price/earnings multiples**   For each of the firms shown in the following table, use the data given to estimate their common stock value employing price/earnings (P/E) multiples.

Firm	Expected EPS	Price/earnings multiple
A	$3.00	6.2
B	4.50	10.0
C	1.80	12.6
D	2.40	8.9
E	5.10	15.0

INTERMEDIATE   **7–28   Management action and stock value**   REH Corporation's most recent dividend was $3 per share, its expected annual rate of dividend growth is 5%, and the required return is now 15%. A variety of proposals are being considered by management to redirect the firm's activities. For each of the following proposed actions, determine the impact on share price and indicate the best alternative.
a. Do nothing, which will leave the key financial variables unchanged.
b. Invest in a new machine that will increase the dividend growth rate to 6% and lower the required return to 14%.
c. Eliminate an unprofitable product line, which will increase the dividend growth rate to 7% and raise the required return to 17%.
d. Merge with another firm, which will reduce the growth rate to 4% and raise the required return to 16%.
e. Acquire a subsidiary operation from another manufacturer. The acquisition should increase the dividend growth rate to 8% and increase the required return to 17%.

     7–29   Integrative—Valuation and CAPM formulas   Given the following information for the stock of Foster Company, calculate its beta.

INTERMEDIATE

Current price per share of common	$50.00
Expected dividend per share next year	$ 3.00
Constant annual dividend growth rate	9%
Risk-free rate of return	7%
Return on market portfolio	10%

      7–30   Integrative—Risk and valuation   Giant Enterprises has a beta of 1.20, the risk-free rate of return is currently 10%, and the market return is 14%. The company, which plans to pay a dividend of $2.60 per share in the coming year, anticipates that its future dividends will increase at an annual rate consistent

CHALLENGE

with that experienced over the 1994–2000 period, when the following dividends were paid:

Year	Dividend per share	Year	Dividend per share
2000	$2.45	1996	$1.82
1999	2.28	1995	1.80
1998	2.10	1994	1.73
1997	1.95		

a. Use the capital asset pricing model (CAPM) to determine the required return on Giant Enterprises' stock.
b. Using the constant-growth model and your finding in **a**, estimate the value of Giant Enterprises' stock.
c. Explain what effect, if any, a decrease in beta would have on the value of Giant's stock.

CHALLENGE

7–31   **Integrative—Valuation and CAPM**   Hamlin Steel Company wishes to determine the value of Craft Foundry, a firm that it is considering acquiring for cash. Hamlin wishes to use the capital asset pricing model (CAPM) to determine the applicable discount rate to use as an input to the constant-growth valuation model. Craft's stock is not publicly traded. After studying the betas of firms similar to Craft that are publicly traded, Hamlin believes that an appropriate beta for Craft's stock would be 1.25. The risk-free rate is currently 9%, and the market return is 13%. Craft's historic dividend per share for each of the past 6 years is shown in the following table.

Year	Dividend per share
2000	$3.44
1999	3.28
1998	3.15
1997	2.90
1996	2.75
1995	2.45

a. Given that Craft is expected to pay a dividend of $3.68 next year, determine the maximum cash price Hamlin should pay for each share of Craft.

b. Discuss the use of the CAPM for estimating the value of common stock, and describe the effect on the resulting value of Craft of:

(1) A decrease in its dividend growth rate of 2% from that exhibited over the 1995–2000 period.

(2) A decrease in its beta to 1.

Assessing the Impact of Suarez Manufacturing's Proposed Risky Investment on Its Bond and Stock Values

Early in 2001, Inez Marcus, the chief financial officer for Suarez Manufacturing, was given the task of assessing the impact of a proposed risky investment on the firm's bond and stock values. To perform the necessary analysis, Inez gathered the following relevant data on the firm's bonds and stock.

Bonds The firm has one bond issue currently outstanding. It has a $1,000 par value, a 9% coupon interest rate, and 18 years remaining to maturity. Interest on the bond is paid *annually,* and the bond's required return is currently 8%. After a great deal of research and consultation, Inez concluded that the proposed investment would not violate any of the bond's numerous provisions. Because the proposed investment will increase the overall risk of the firm, she expects that if it is undertaken, the required return on these bonds will increase to 10%.

Stock During the immediate past 5 years (1996–2000) the annual dividends paid on the firm's common stock were as follows:

Year	Dividend per share
2000	$1.90
1999	1.70
1998	1.55
1997	1.40
1996	1.30

The firm expects that without the proposed investment the dividend in 2001 will be $2.09 per share and the historic annual rate of growth (rounded to the nearest whole percent) will continue in the future. Currently, the required return on the common stock is 14%. Inez's research indicates that if the proposed investment is undertaken, the 2001 dividend will rise to $2.15 per share and the annual rate of dividend growth will increase to 13%. She feels that in the *best case,* the dividend would continue to grow at this rate each year into the future, and in the *worst case,* the 13% annual rate of growth in dividends would continue only through 2003, and then at the beginning of 2004, the rate of growth would return to the rate that was experienced between 1996 and 2000. As a result of the increased risk associated with the proposed risky investment, the required return on the common stock is expected to increase by 2% to an annual rate of 16%, regardless of which dividend-growth outcome occurs.

Armed with the preceding data, Inez must now assess the impact of the proposed risky investment on the market value of Suarez's bonds and stock. To simplify her calculations, she plans to round the historic growth rate in common stock dividends to the nearest whole percent.

Required

a. Find the *current* value of each of Suarez Manufacturing's bonds.
b. Find the *current* value per share of Suarez Manufacturing's common stock.
c. Find the value of Suarez's bonds in the event that it *undertakes the proposed risky investment*. Compare this value to that found in **a**. What effect would the proposed investment have on the firm's bondholders? Explain.
d. Find the value of Suarez's common stock in the event that it *undertakes the proposed risky investment* and assuming that the dividend growth rate stays at 13% forever. Compare this value to that found in **b**. What effect would the proposed investment have on the firm's stockholders? Explain.
e. On the basis of your findings in **c** and **d**, who wins and who loses as a result of undertaking the proposed risky investment? Should the firm do it? Why?
f. Rework parts **d** and **e** assuming that at the beginning of 2004, the annual dividend growth rate returns to the rate experienced between 1996 and 2000.

WEB EXERCISE

GOTO web site www.smartmoney.com. In the left column Click on BOND INVESTING. Then click on BOND CALCULATOR which is located down the page under the column "UNDERSTANDING BONDS." Read the instructions on how to use the bond calculator. Using the bond calculator:

1. Calculate the yield to maturity (YTM) for a bond whose coupon rate is 7.5% with maturity date of July 31, 2090, which you bought for 95.
2. What is the YTM of the above bond if you bought it for 105? For 100?
3. Change the yield % box to 8.5. What would be the price of this bond?
4. Change the yield. What is this bond's price?
5. Change the maturity date to 2003 and reset yield % to 6.5. What is the price of this bond?
6. Why is the price of the bond in Question 5 lower than the price of the bond in Question 4?

Now GOTO www.marketguide.com. Click on RESEARCH at the top of the page. Enter LUV, and click on PRICE CHARTS.

1. What was Southwest Airlines' highest price in this 12-month period? What was its lowest price? Has its price been stable or dynamic? Increasing or decreasing?

Click on PERFORMANCE.

2. What has been the price performance YTD for Southwest Airlines? For the S&P 500?

ENCORE INTERNATIONAL

In the world of trendsetting fashion, instinct and marketing savvy are prerequisites to success. Jordan Ellis had both. During 2000, his international casual-wear company, Encore, rocketed to $300 million in sales after 10 years in business. His fashion line covered the young woman from head to toe with hats, sweaters, dresses, blouses, skirts, pants, sweatshirts, socks, and shoes. In Manhattan, there was an Encore shop every five or six blocks, each featuring a different color. Some shops showed the entire line in mauve, and others featured it in canary yellow.

Encore had made it. The company's historical growth was so spectacular that no one could have predicted it. However, securities analysts speculated that Encore could not keep up the pace. They warned that competition is fierce in the fashion industry and that the firm might encounter little or no growth in the future. They estimated that stockholders also should expect no growth in future dividends.

Contrary to the conservative security analysts, Jordan Ellis felt that the company could maintain a constant annual growth rate in dividends per share of 6% in the future, or possibly 8% for the next 2 years and 6% thereafter. Ellis based his estimates on an established long-term expansion plan into European and Latin American markets. By venturing into these markets the risk of the firm as measured by beta was expected to immediately increase from 1.10 to 1.25.

In preparing the long-term financial plan, Encore's chief financial officer has assigned a junior financial analyst, Marc Scott, to evaluate the firm's current stock price. He has asked Marc to consider the conservative predictions of the securities analysts and the aggressive predictions of the company founder, Jordan Ellis.

Marc has compiled these 2000 financial data to aid his analysis.

Data item	2000 value
Earnings per share (EPS)	$6.25
Price per share of common stock	$40.00
Book value of common stock equity	$60,000,000
Total common shares outstanding	2,500,000
Common stock dividend per share	$4.00

REQUIRED

a. What is the firm's current book value per share?

b. What is the firm's current P/E ratio?

c. (1) What are the required return and risk premium for Encore stock using the capital asset pricing model, assuming a beta of 1.10? (*Hint:* Use the security market line— with data points noted—given in the following figure to find the market return.)

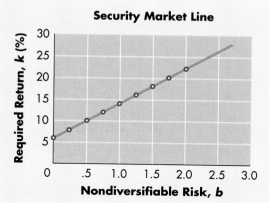

Security Market Line

Data Points	
b	**k**
0.00	6.00%
0.25	8.00
0.50	10.00
0.75	12.00
1.00	14.00
1.25	16.00
1.50	18.00
1.75	20.00
2.00	22.00

(2) What are the required return and risk premium for Encore stock using the capital asset pricing model, assuming a beta of 1.25?

(3) What is the effect on the required return if the beta rises as expected?

d. If the securities analysts are correct and there is no growth in future dividends, what is the value per share of the Encore stock? (*Note:* Beta = 1.25.)

e. (1) If Jordan Ellis's predictions are correct, what is the value per share of Encore stock if the firm maintains a constant annual 6% growth rate in future dividends? (*Note:* Beta = 1.25.)

(2) If Jordan Ellis's predictions are correct, what is the value per share of Encore stock if the firm maintains a constant annual 8% growth rate in dividends per share over the next 2 years and 6% thereafter? (*Note:* Beta = 1.25.)

f. Compare the current (2000) price of the stock and the stock values found in **a, d,** and **e.** Discuss why these values may differ. Which valuation method do you believe most clearly represents the true value of the Encore stock?

PART

3

Long-Term Investment Decisions

Capital Budgeting and Cash Flow Principles

LEARNING GOALS

LG1 Understand the key capital expenditure motives and the steps in the capital budgeting process.

LG2 Define the basic terminology used to describe projects, funds availability, decision approaches, and cash flow patterns.

LG3 Discuss the major components of relevant cash flows, expansion versus replacement cash flows, sunk costs and opportunity costs, and international capital budgeting and long-term investments.

LG4 Calculate the initial investment associated with a proposed capital expenditure, given relevant data.

LG5 Determine relevant operating cash inflows using the income statement format.

LG6 Find the terminal cash flow, given relevant data.

8.1 The Capital Budgeting Decision Process

capital budgeting
The process of evaluating and selecting long-term investments consistent with the firm's goal of owner wealth maximization.

Long-term investments represent sizable outlays of funds that commit a firm to some course of action. Consequently, the firm needs procedures to analyze and properly select those investments. It must be able to measure relevant cash flows and apply appropriate decision techniques. As time passes, fixed assets may become obsolete or may require an overhaul; at these points, too, financial decisions may be required. **Capital budgeting** is the process of evaluating and selecting long-term investments consistent with the firm's goal of owner wealth

Such Stuff as Dreams Are Made of

Every year, with great hope and expectations, businesspeople dream up new plans for expanding, replacing, or renewing the long-term assets they use to run their businesses. These dreams often are the stuff that success is made of, yet they can turn into nightmares for the firm and its managers if they fail to produce the necessary financial returns. Therefore, besides dreams, companies also need some very down-to-earth consideration of the costs of implementing their dreams and the returns they are likely to reap from these expenditures. This process is called *capital budgeting*. It is an important topic in finance, so much so that the next three chapters of this book are devoted to it. This chapter explains how to identify the cash outflows and inflows that are relevant to capital budgeting decisions.

maximization. Firms typically make a variety of long-term investments, but the most common for the manufacturing firm is in *fixed assets*, which include property (land), plant, and equipment. These assets, often referred to as *earning assets*, generally provide the basis for the firm's earning power and value.

Capital budgeting (investment) and financing decisions are treated *separately*. Typically, once a proposed investment has been determined to be acceptable, the financial manager then chooses the best financing method. Therefore, in Chapters 8 through 10 we concentrate on fixed asset acquisition. (In later chapters we'll address the financing of fixed assets.) We begin by discussing the motives for capital expenditure.

Capital Expenditure Motives

capital expenditure
An outlay of funds by the firm that is expected to produce benefits over a period of time *greater than* 1 year.

operating expenditure
An outlay of funds by the firm resulting in benefits received *within* 1 year.

A **capital expenditure** is an outlay of funds by the firm that is expected to produce benefits over a period of time *greater than* 1 year. An **operating expenditure** is an outlay resulting in benefits received *within* 1 year. Fixed asset outlays are capital expenditures, but not all capital expenditures are classified as fixed assets. A $60,000 outlay for a new machine with a usable life of 15 years is a capital expenditure that would appear as a fixed asset on the firm's balance sheet. A $60,000 outlay for advertising that produces benefits over a long period is also a capital expenditure, but advertising would rarely be shown as a fixed asset.[1]

Capital expenditures are made for many reasons. The basic motives for capital expenditures are to expand, replace, or renew fixed assets or to obtain some other less tangible benefit over a long period. Table 8.1 briefly describes the key motives for making capital expenditures.

Steps in the Process

capital budgeting process
Consists of five distinct but interrelated steps beginning with *proposal generation*, followed by *review and analysis*, *decision making*, *implementation*, and *follow-up*.

The **capital budgeting process** consists of five distinct but interrelated steps. It begins with *proposal generation*, followed by *review and analysis, decision making, implementation*, and *follow-up*. Table 8.2 describes these steps. Each

TABLE 8.1	**Key Motives for Making Capital Expenditures**
Motive	Description
Expansion	The most common motive for a capital expenditure is to expand the level of operations—usually through acquisition of fixed assets. A growing firm often needs to acquire new fixed assets rapidly, such as the purchase of property and plant facilities.
Replacement	As a firm's growth slows and it reaches maturity, most capital expenditures will be made to replace or renew obsolete or worn-out assets. Each time a machine requires a major repair, the outlay for the repair should be compared to the outlay to replace the machine and the benefits of replacement.
Renewal	Renewal, an alternative to replacement, may involve rebuilding, overhauling, or retrofitting an existing fixed asset. For example, an existing drill press could be renewed by replacing its motor and adding a numeric control system, or a physical facility could be renewed by rewiring and adding air conditioning. To improve efficiency, both replacement and renewal of existing machinery may be suitable solutions.
Other purposes	Some capital expenditures do not result in the acquisition or transformation of tangible fixed assets. Instead, they involve a long-term commitment of funds in expectation of a future return. These expenditures include outlays for advertising, research and development, management consulting, and new products. Other capital expenditure proposals—such as the installation of pollution-control and safety devices mandated by the government—are difficult to evaluate because they provide intangible returns rather than clearly measurable cash flows.

---

1. Some firms do, in effect, capitalize advertising outlays if there is reason to believe that the benefit of the outlay will be received at some future date. The capitalized advertising may appear as a deferred charge such as "deferred advertising expense," which is then amortized over the future. Expenses of this type are often deferred for reporting purposes to increase reported earnings, whereas for tax purposes, the entire amount will be expensed to reduce tax liability.

TABLE 8.2   Steps in the Capital Budgeting Process

Steps (listed in order)	Description
1. Proposal generation	Proposals for capital expenditures are made at all levels within a business organization. To stimulate a flow of ideas, many firms offer cash rewards for proposals that are ultimately adopted. Capital expenditure proposals typically travel from the originator to a reviewer at a higher level in the organization. Clearly, proposals that require large outlays will be much more carefully scrutinized than less costly ones.
2. Review and analysis	Capital expenditure proposals are formally reviewed (1) to assess their appropriateness in light of the firm's overall objectives and plans and, more important, (2) to evaluate their economic validity. The proposed costs and benefits are estimated and then converted into a series of relevant cash flows. Various capital budgeting techniques are applied to these cash flows to measure the investment merit of the potential outlay. In addition, various aspects of the *risk* associated with the proposal are evaluated. Once the economic analysis is completed, a summary report, often with a recommendation, is submitted to the decision maker(s).
3. Decision making	The actual dollar outlay and the importance of a capital expenditure determine the organizational level at which the expenditure decision is made. Firms typically delegate capital expenditure authority on the basis of certain dollar limits. Generally, the board of directors reserves the right to make final decisions on capital expenditures requiring outlays beyond a certain amount. Inexpensive capital expenditures, such as the purchase of a hammer for $15, are treated as operating outlays not requiring formal analysis.[a] Generally, firms operating under critical time constraints with respect to production often give the plant manager the power to make decisions necessary to keep the production line moving.
4. Implementation	Once a proposal has been approved and funding has been made available,[b] the implementation phase begins. For minor outlays, the expenditure is made and payment is rendered. For major expenditures, greater control is required. Often the expenditures for a single proposal may occur in phases, each outlay requiring the signed approval of company officers.
5. Follow-up	Involves monitoring the results during the operating phase of a project. Comparison of actual costs and benefits with those expected and those of previous projects is vital. When actual outcomes deviate from projected outcomes, action may be required to cut the costs, improve benefits, or possibly terminate the project. Analysis of deviations of actual from forecast values provides data that can be used to improve the capital budgeting process, particularly the accuracy of cash flow estimates.

[a]There is a certain dollar limit beyond which outlays are *capitalized* (i.e., treated as a fixed asset) and *depreciated* rather than *expensed*. This dollar limit depends largely on what the U.S. Internal Revenue Service will permit. In accounting, the issue of whether to capitalize or expense an outlay is resolved by using the *principle of materiality*, which suggests that any outlays deemed material (i.e., large) relative to the firm's scale of operations should be capitalized, whereas others should be expensed in the current period.

[b]Capital expenditures are often approved as part of the annual budgeting process, although funding will not be made available until the budget is implemented—frequently as long as 6 months after approval.

step in the process is important. Review and analysis and decision making—steps 2 and 3—consume the majority of time and effort in the process, however. Follow-up (Step 5) is an important, but often ignored, step aimed at allowing the firm to keep improving the accuracy of its cash flow estimates.

Because of their fundamental importance, primary attention in this and the following chapters is given to review and analysis and decision making.

In Practice

Information Technology's Big Byte

In the rapidly changing information technology (IT) environment, managers clamor for the latest hardware and software upgrades. Financial managers, on the other hand, struggle with a major dilemma: how to control costs yet spend enough to maintain efficient IT operations and remain competitive in the marketplace. It's a difficult but critical issue. IT is now the single largest capital expense category for U.S. companies. By one estimate, it accounts for over 40 percent of total capital equipment expenditures. Although projects involving the latest technology make the headlines, for most companies, the everyday operational infrastructure, such as data centers, networks, desktop computers, software, and maintenance, comprises the majority of IT spending.

The absence of sound capital budgeting procedures to evaluate proposed IT expenditures can be disastrous. Boston Chicken, the chain of home-style fast-food restaurants based in Golden, Colorado, poured millions of dollars into cutting-edge computer systems for its Boston Market restaurants. One analyst commented, "Their technology motto was, 'The more it costs, the more we need it.'" Rather than improved productivity, the company found itself with soaring food costs and inefficient sales and operations.

Unlike Boston Chicken, Pink Jeep Tours, a Sedona, Arizona, company that runs guided jeep tours, got its money's worth when it replaced an inefficient manual reservations system with a $200,000 state-of-the-art computerized system in 1995. Although this outlay would be small potatoes to Boston Chicken, this major capital expense for Pink Jeep required rebudgeting long-term expenses and cutting other costs. The rewards were big, however. Reservation time was cut from 10 minutes to under a minute, so that Pink Jeep could cut its reservations staff in half while increasing sales 50 percent and increasing average rate of seats filled on tours from 72 to 94 percent.

Basic Terminology

Before we develop the concepts, techniques, and practices related to the capital budgeting process, it will be useful to explain some basic terminology. In addition, we present some key assumptions that are used to simplify the discussion in this chapter and in Chapters 9 and 10.

Independent Versus Mutually Exclusive Projects

independent projects
Projects whose cash flows are unrelated or independent of one another; the acceptance of one *does not eliminate* the others from further consideration.

The two most common project types are (1) independent projects and (2) mutually exclusive projects. **Independent projects** are those whose cash flows are unrelated or independent of one another; the acceptance of one *does not eliminate* the others from further consideration. If a firm has unlimited funds to invest, all the independent projects that meet its minimum acceptance criterion can be implemented. For example, a firm with unlimited funds may be faced with three acceptable independent projects—(1) installing air conditioning in the plant, (2) acquiring a small supplier, and (3) purchasing a new computer system. Clearly, the acceptance of any one of these projects does not eliminate the others from further consideration; all three could be undertaken.

mutually exclusive projects
Projects that compete with one another, so that the acceptance of one *eliminates* the others from further consideration.

Mutually exclusive projects are those that have the same function and therefore compete with one another. The acceptance of one *eliminates* from further consideration all other similar-function projects. For example, a firm in need of increased production capacity could obtain it by (1) expanding its plant, (2) acquiring another company, or (3) contracting with another company for production. Clearly, the acceptance of one eliminates the need for either of the others.

Unlimited Funds Versus Capital Rationing

unlimited funds
The financial situation in which a firm is able to accept all independent projects that provide an acceptable return.

capital rationing
The financial situation in which a firm has only a fixed number of dollars to allocate among competing capital expenditures.

The availability of funds for capital expenditures affects the firm's decisions. If a firm has **unlimited funds** for investment, making capital budgeting decisions is quite simple: All independent projects that will provide returns greater than some predetermined level can be accepted.

Typically, though, firms are not in such a situation; they instead operate under **capital rationing**. This means that they have only a fixed number of dollars available for capital expenditures and that numerous projects will compete for these dollars. Therefore the firm must ration its funds by allocating them to projects that will maximize share value. Procedures for dealing with capital rationing are presented in Chapter 10. The discussions that follow in this chapter assume unlimited funds.

Accept–Reject Versus Ranking Approaches

accept–reject approach
The evaluation of capital expenditure proposals to determine whether they meet the firm's minimum acceptance criterion.

ranking approach
The ranking of capital expenditure projects on the basis of some predetermined measure, such as the rate of return.

Two basic approaches to capital budgeting decisions are available. The **accept–reject approach** involves evaluating capital expenditure proposals to determine whether they meet the firm's minimum acceptance criterion. This approach can be used when the firm has unlimited funds, as a preliminary step when evaluating mutually exclusive projects, or in a situation in which capital must be rationed. In these cases, only acceptable projects should be considered.

The second method, the **ranking approach,** involves ranking projects on the basis of some predetermined measure, such as the rate of return. The project with the highest return is ranked first, and the project with the lowest return is ranked last. Only acceptable projects should be ranked. Ranking is useful in selecting the "best" of a group of mutually exclusive projects and in evaluating projects with a view to capital rationing.

Conventional Versus Nonconventional Cash Flow Patterns

conventional cash flow pattern
An initial outflow followed by only a series of inflows.

Cash flow patterns associated with capital investment projects can be classified as *conventional* or *nonconventional*. A **conventional cash flow pattern** consists of an initial outflow followed by only a series of inflows. For example, a firm may spend $10,000 today and as a result expect to receive equal annual cash inflows of $2,000 each year for the next 8 years, as depicted on the time line in

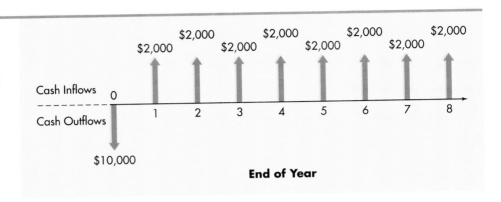

FIGURE 8.1

Conventional Cash Flow

Time line for a conventional cash flow pattern

Figure 8.1.[2] Another conventional cash flow pattern that provides unequal annual cash inflows is depicted in Figure 8.3 on page 340.

A **nonconventional cash flow pattern** is one in which an initial outflow is *not* followed by only a series of inflows. For example, the purchase of a machine may require an initial cash outflow of $20,000 and may generate cash inflows of $5,000 each year for 4 years. In the fifth year after purchase, an outflow of $8,000 may be required to overhaul the machine, after which it generates inflows of $5,000 each year for 5 more years. This nonconventional pattern is illustrated on the time line in Figure 8.2.

Difficulties often arise in evaluating projects with nonconventional patterns of cash flow. *The discussions in the remainder of this chapter and in Chapters 9 and 10 are therefore limited to the evaluation of conventional patterns.*

nonconventional cash flow pattern
A pattern in which an initial outflow is *not* followed by only a series of inflows.

Annuity Versus Mixed Stream Cash Flows

As pointed out in Chapter 5, an **annuity** is a stream of equal annual cash flows. A series of cash flows exhibiting any pattern other than that of an annuity is a **mixed stream** of cash flows. The cash inflows of $2,000 per year (for 8 years) in

annuity
A stream of equal annual cash flows.

mixed stream
A series of cash flows exhibiting any pattern other than that of an annuity.

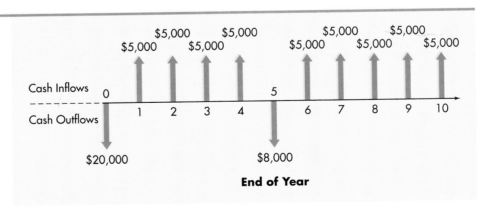

FIGURE 8.2

Nonconventional Cash Flow

Time line for a nonconventional cash flow pattern

2. Arrows rather than plus or minus signs are frequently used on time lines to distinguish between cash inflows and cash outflows. Upward-pointing arrows represent cash inflows (positive cash flows), and downward-pointing arrows represent cash outflows (negative cash flows).

Figure 8.1 are inflows from an annuity, whereas the unequal pattern of inflows in Figure 8.3 (page 340) represents a mixed stream. As you observed in Chapter 5, time value of money techniques are much simpler to apply when the pattern of cash flows is an annuity.

? Review Questions

8–1   What is *capital budgeting?* How do capital expenditures relate to the capital budgeting process? Do all capital expenditures involve fixed assets? Explain.

8–2   What are the key motives described in the chapter for making capital expenditures? Discuss, compare, and contrast them.

8–3   Briefly describe each of the five steps involved in the capital budgeting process.

8–4   Define and differentiate between each of the following sets of capital budgeting terms: **(a)** independent versus mutually exclusive projects; **(b)** unlimited funds versus capital rationing; **(c)** accept–reject versus ranking approaches; **(d)** conventional versus nonconventional cash flow patterns; and **(e)** annuity versus mixed stream cash flows.

8.2 The Relevant Cash Flows

relevant cash flows
The incremental after-tax cash outflow (investment) and resulting subsequent inflows associated with a proposed capital expenditure.

incremental cash flows
The *additional* cash flows—outflows or inflows—expected to result from a proposed capital expenditure.

To evaluate capital expenditure alternatives, the firm must determine the **relevant cash flows,** which are the *incremental after-tax cash outflow (investment) and resulting subsequent inflows.* The **incremental cash flows** represent the *additional* cash flows—outflows or inflows—expected to result from a proposed capital expenditure. As noted in Chapter 3, cash flows, rather than accounting figures, are used because cash flows directly affect the firm's ability to pay bills and purchase assets.

The remainder of this chapter is devoted to the procedures for measuring the relevant cash flows associated with proposed capital expenditures.

Major Cash Flow Components

initial investment
The relevant cash outflow for a proposed project at time zero.

operating cash inflows
The incremental after-tax cash inflows resulting from use of a project during its life.

The cash flows of any project having the *conventional pattern* can include three basic components: (1) an initial investment, (2) operating cash inflows, and (3) terminal cash flow. All projects—whether for expansion, replacement, renewal, or some other purpose—have the first two components. Some, however, lack the final component, terminal cash flow.

Figure 8.3 depicts on a time line the cash flows for a project. Each of the cash flow components is labeled. The **initial investment** is $50,000 for the proposed project. This is the relevant cash outflow at time zero. The **operating cash inflows,** which are the incremental after-tax cash inflows resulting from use of the project during its life, gradually increase from $4,000 in the first year to

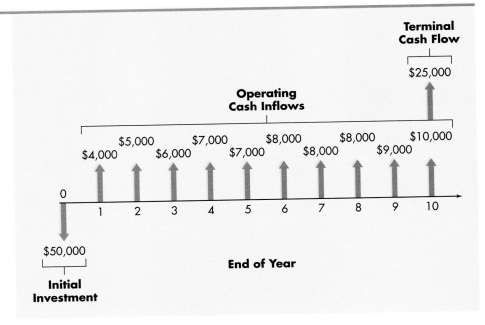

FIGURE 8.3

Cash Flow Components
Time line for major cash flow components

$10,000 in its tenth and final year. The **terminal cash flow** of $25,000, received at the end of the project's 10-year life, is the after-tax nonoperating cash flow occurring in the final year of the project. It is usually attributable to liquidation of the project. Note that the terminal cash flow does *not* include the $10,000 operating cash inflow for year 10.

Expansion Versus Replacement Cash Flows

Developing relevant cash flows is most straightforward in the case of *expansion decisions*. In this case, the initial investment, operating cash inflows, and terminal cash flow are merely the after-tax cash outflow and inflows associated with the proposed outlay.

The development of relevant cash flows for *replacement decisions* is more complicated; the firm must find the *incremental* cash outflows and inflows that will result from the proposed replacement. The initial investment in this case is the difference between the initial investment needed to acquire the new asset and any after-tax cash inflows expected from liquidation today of the old asset (asset being replaced). The operating cash inflows are the difference between the operating cash inflows from the new asset and those from the old asset. The terminal cash flow is the difference between the after-tax cash flows expected upon termination of the new and the old assets. These relationships are shown in Figure 8.4.

Actually, all capital budgeting decisions can be viewed as replacement decisions. Expansion decisions are merely replacement decisions in which all cash flows from the old asset are zero. In light of this fact, the following discussions emphasize the more general replacement decisions.

FIGURE 8.4

Relevant Cash Flows for Replacement Decisions

Calculation of the three components of relevant cash flow for a replacement decision

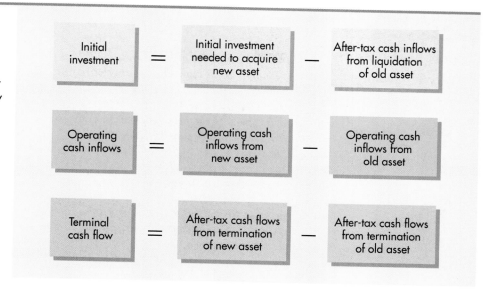

Sunk Costs and Opportunity Costs

When estimating the relevant cash flows associated with a proposed capital expenditure, the firm must recognize any *sunk costs* and *opportunity costs*. These costs are easy to mishandle or ignore, particularly when determining a project's incremental cash flows. **Sunk costs** are cash outlays that have already been made (i.e., past outlays) and therefore have no effect on the cash flows relevant to the current decision. As a result, *sunk costs should not be included in a project's incremental cash flows*. **Opportunity costs** are cash flows that could be realized from the best alternative use of an owned asset. They therefore represent cash flows that will *not be realized* as a result of employing that asset in the proposed project. Because of this, any *opportunity costs should be included as cash outflows when determining a project's incremental cash flows*.

sunk costs
Cash outlays that have already been made (i.e., past outlays) and therefore have no effect on the cash flows relevant to a current decision.

opportunity costs
Cash flows that could be realized from the best alternative use of an owned asset.

E x a m p l e ▼

Hint   Sunk costs and opportunity costs are concepts you must fully understand. Funds already spent are irrelevant to future decisions, but funds given to one project that eliminates the investment returns of another project *are* considered a relevant cost.

Jankow Equipment is considering renewing its drill press X12, which it purchased 3 years earlier for $237,000, by retrofitting it with the computerized control system from an obsolete piece of equipment it owns. The obsolete equipment could be sold today for a high bid of $42,000, but without its computerized control system, it would be worth nothing. Jankow is in the process of estimating the labor and material costs of retrofitting the system to drill press X12 and the benefits expected from the retrofit. The $237,000 cost of drill press X12 is a *sunk cost* because it represents an earlier cash outlay. It *would not be included* as a cash outflow when determining the cash flows relevant to the retrofit decision. Although Jankow owns the obsolete piece of equipment, the proposed use of its computerized control system represents an *opportunity cost* of $42,000—the highest price at which it could be sold today. This opportunity cost *would be included* as a cash outflow associated with using the computerized control system. ▲

In Practice

Coors Brews Better Financial Performance

As Coors Brewing Co. grew from a local brewer to the number three national brand, it went on a capital spending spree to add capacity. The firm needed better planning however: Managers did not prepare project cost reports, the company bought the top-of-the-line equipment, and top management approved projects despite unattractive returns. By the early 1990s, Coors' financial performance was suffering.

This changed in 1995 when seasoned financial executive Tim Wolf joined Coors as CFO. Wolf quickly identified the need for greater financial discipline in planning and capital budgeting. He implemented more stringent guidelines for capital spending and required business unit managers to develop a sound business case to justify proposed capital expenditures. He also created a partnership between finance and operating departments, who now recognized the key role finance played.

The first project to use Wolf's new capital budgeting procedures was a facility to wash and sanitize returnable bottles. Wanting to replace the outdated equipment, managers analyzed the financial implications of six operating scenarios to determine the best alternative, which turned out to be moving the plant to Virginia. Every department that would be affected had input into design and operating cost estimates. The project team presented the complete case to Wolf, who spent 6 months asking questions that cut over 25 percent from the initial cost estimates. "I think the extra time was well spent," says Wolf. "If you can reduce your capital costs, leverage the benefits, and get them faster, that's the way to run your capital process."

In Wolf's first 3 years at Coors, capital spending dropped significantly, return on invested capital rose nearly 3 percent (from 5.9 to 8.8 percent), and cash flow went from a negative $26 million to a positive $138 million. The result was improved shareholder value as the stock price climbed from $19 in early 1997 to almost $60 in early 1999.

International Capital Budgeting and Long-Term Investments

Although the same basic capital budgeting principles are used for domestic and international projects, several additional factors must be addressed in evaluating foreign investment opportunities. International capital budgeting differs from the domestic version because (1) cash inflows and outflows occur in a foreign currency, and (2) foreign investments potentially face significant political risk, including the risk that the company's assets may be seized. Both of these risks can be minimized through careful planning.

Companies face both long- and short-term *currency risks* relating to both the invested capital and the cash flows resulting from it. Long-term currency risk can be minimized by at least partly financing the foreign investment in the local capital markets rather than with dollar-denominated capital from the parent company. This step ensures that the project's revenues, operating costs, and financing costs will be in the local currency. Likewise, the dollar value of short-term, local currency cash flows can be protected by using special securities and strategies such as futures, forwards, and options market instruments.

Political risks can be minimized by using both financial and operating strategies. For example, by structuring the investment as a joint venture and selecting a well-connected local partner, the U.S. company can minimize the risk that its operations will be seized or harassed. Companies also can protect themselves from having their investment returns blocked by local governments by structuring the financing of such investments as debt rather than as equity. Debt-service payments are legally enforceable claims, whereas equity returns (such as dividends) are not. Even if local courts do not support the claims of the U.S. company, the company can threaten to pursue its case in U.S. courts.

foreign direct investment
The transfer of capital, managerial, and technical assets to a foreign country.

In spite of the preceding difficulties, **foreign direct investment,** which involves the transfer of capital, managerial, and technical assets to a foreign country, has surged in recent years. This is evident in the growing market values of both foreign assets owned by U.S.-based companies and foreign direct investment in the United States, particularly by British, Canadian, Dutch, German, and Japanese companies. Furthermore, foreign direct investment by U.S. companies seems to be accelerating, particularly in East Asia and Latin America.

❓ Review Questions

8–5   Why is it important to evaluate capital budgeting projects on the basis of *incremental after-tax cash flows?* How can expansion decisions be treated as replacement decisions? Explain.

8–6   What are *sunk costs?* What are *opportunity costs?* What effect do each of these types of costs have on a project's incremental cash flows?

8–7   How does international capital budgeting differ from the domestic version? How can *currency risk* and *political risk* be minimized when making *foreign direct investment?*

8.3 Finding the Initial Investment

The term *initial investment* as used here refers to the relevant cash outflows to be considered when evaluating a prospective capital expenditure. Because our discussion of capital budgeting is concerned only with investments that exhibit conventional cash flows, the initial investment occurs at *time zero*—the time at which the expenditure is made. The initial investment is calculated by subtracting all cash inflows occurring at time zero from all cash outflows occurring at time zero.

The basic format for determining the initial investment is given in Table 8.3. The cash flows that must be considered when determining the initial investment associated with a capital expenditure are the installed cost of the new asset, the after-tax proceeds (if any) from the sale of an old asset, and the change (if any) in net working capital. Note that if there are no installation costs and the firm is not

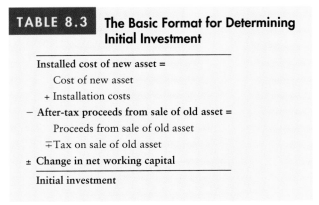

TABLE 8.3   **The Basic Format for Determining Initial Investment**

Installed cost of new asset =
    Cost of new asset
    + Installation costs
− After-tax proceeds from sale of old asset =
    Proceeds from sale of old asset
    ∓Tax on sale of old asset
± Change in net working capital

Initial investment

replacing an existing asset, the purchase price of the asset adjusted for any change in net working capital is equal to the initial investment.

Installed Cost of New Asset

As shown in Table 8.3, the installed cost of the new asset is found by adding the cost of the new asset to its installation costs. The **cost of new asset** is the net outflow its acquisition requires. Usually, we are concerned with the acquisition of a fixed asset for which a definite purchase price is paid. **Installation costs** are any added costs necessary to place an asset into operation. They are considered part of the firm's capital expenditure. The Internal Revenue Service (IRS) requires the firm to add installation costs to the purchase price of an asset to determine its depreciable value, which is expensed over a period of years. The **installed cost of new asset,** calculated by adding the cost of the asset to its installation costs, equals its depreciable value.

After-Tax Proceeds from Sale of Old Asset

Table 8.3 shows that the **after-tax proceeds from sale of old asset** decrease the firm's initial investment in the new asset. These proceeds are the difference between the old asset's sale proceeds and any applicable taxes or tax refunds relating to its sale. The **proceeds from sale of old asset** are the net cash inflows it provides. This amount is net of any costs incurred in the process of removing the asset. Included in these *removal costs* are *cleanup costs,* such as those related to removal and disposal of chemical and nuclear wastes. These costs may not be trivial.

The proceeds from the sale of an old asset are normally subject to some type of tax.[3] This **tax on sale of old asset** depends on the relationship between its sale price, initial purchase price, and *book value.* The actual tax treatment is dictated by government tax laws, procedures, and forms, all of which are periodically revised. An understanding of (1) book value and (2) basic tax rules is necessary to determine the tax on sale of an asset.

cost of new asset
The net outflow required to acquire a new asset.

installation costs
Any added costs necessary to place an asset into operation.

installed cost of new asset
The cost of the asset plus its installation costs; equals the asset's depreciable value.

after-tax proceeds from sale of old asset
The difference between the old asset's sale proceeds and any applicable taxes or tax refunds relating to its sale.

proceeds from sale of old asset
The cash inflows, net of any *removal* or *cleanup costs,* resulting from the sale of an existing asset.

tax on sale of old asset
Tax that depends upon the relationship between the old asset's sale price, initial purchase price, and *book value.*

---

3. A brief discussion of the tax treatment of ordinary and capital gains income was presented in Chapter 3.

Book Value

book value
The strict accounting value of an asset, calculated by subtracting its accumulated depreciation from installed cost.

The **book value** of an asset is its strict accounting value. It can be calculated using the following equation:

$$\text{Book value} = \text{installed cost of asset} - \text{accumulated depreciation} \qquad (8.1)$$

Example ▼ Hudson Industries, a small electronics company, 2 years ago acquired a machine tool with an installed cost of $100,000. The asset was being depreciated under MACRS using a 5-year recovery period.[4] Table 3.8 (page 96) shows that 20 and 32% of the installed cost would be depreciated in years 1 and 2, respectively. In other words, 52% (20% + 32%) of the $100,000 cost, or $52,000 (.52 × $100,000), would represent the accumulated depreciation at the end of year 2. Substituting into Equation 8.1, we get

$$\text{Book value} = \$100,000 - \$52,000 = \underline{\$48,000}$$

▲ The book value of Hudson's asset at the end of year 2 is therefore $48,000.

Basic Tax Rules

Career Key

Accounting personnel will provide revenue, cost, depreciation, and tax data for use in developing cash flow projections for proposed projects. In many firms, they will prepare the complete cash flow analysis because of their objectivity and their familiarity with much of the data.

Four potential tax situations can occur when selling an asset. These situations depend on the relationship between the asset's sale price, its initial purchase price, and its book value. The three key forms of taxable income and their associated tax treatments are defined and summarized in Table 8.4. The assumed tax rates used throughout this text are noted in the final column. The four possible tax situations, which result in one or more forms of taxable income, are the following: the asset is sold (1) for more than its initial purchase price; (2) for more than its book value but less than its initial purchase price; (3) for its book value; and (4) for less than its book value.

Example ▼ The old asset purchased 2 years ago for $100,000 by Hudson Industries has a current book value of $48,000. What will happen if the firm now decides to sell the asset and replace it? The tax consequences depend on the sale price. Figure 8.5 on page 347 depicts the taxable income resulting from four possible sale prices in light of the asset's original purchase price of $100,000 and its current book value of $48,000. The taxable consequences of each of these sale prices is described separately in what follows.

recaptured depreciation
The portion of an asset's sale price that is above its book value and below its initial purchase price.

The sale of the asset for more than its initial purchase price   If Hudson sells the old asset for $110,000, it realizes a capital gain of $10,000, which is taxed as ordinary income.[5] The firm also experiences ordinary income in the form of **recaptured depreciation**, which is the portion of the sale price that is above book

---

4. For a review of MACRS, see Chapter 3. Under current tax law, most manufacturing equipment has a 7-year recovery period, as noted in Table 3.7. Using this recovery period results in 8 years of depreciation, which unnecessarily complicates examples and problems. To simplify, *manufacturing equipment is treated as 5-year assets in this and the following chapters.*

5. Although the current tax law requires corporate capital gains to be treated as ordinary income, the structure for corporate capital gains is retained under the law to facilitate a rate differential in the likely event of future tax revisions. Therefore, this distinction is made throughout the text discussions.

| TABLE 8.4 | **Tax Treatment on Sales of Assets** |

Form of taxable income	Definition	Tax treatment	Assumed tax rate
Capital gain	Portion of the sale price that is in excess of the initial purchase price.	Regardless of how long the asset has been held, the total capital gain is taxed as ordinary income.	40%
Recaptured depreciation	Portion of the sale price that is in excess of book value and represents a recovery of previously taken depreciation.	All recaptured depreciation is taxed as ordinary income.	40%
Loss on sale of asset	Amount by which sale price is *less than* book value.	If asset is depreciable and used in business, loss is deducted from ordinary income.	40% of loss is a tax savings
		If asset is *not* depreciable or is *not* used in business, loss is deductible only against capital gains.	40% of loss is a tax savings

value and below the initial purchase price. In this case there is recaptured depreciation of $52,000 ($100,000 − $48,000). Both the $10,000 capital gain and the $52,000 recaptured depreciation are shown under the $110,000 sale price in Figure 8.5. The taxes on the total gain of $62,000 are calculated as follows:

	Amount (1)	Rate (2)	Tax [(1) × (2)] (3)
Capital gain	$10,000	.40	$ 4,000
Recaptured depreciation	52,000	.40	20,800
Totals	$62,000		$24,800

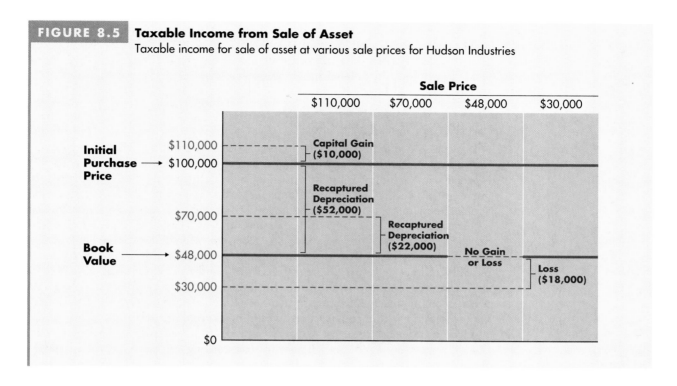

FIGURE 8.5   **Taxable Income from Sale of Asset**
Taxable income for sale of asset at various sale prices for Hudson Industries

These taxes should be used in calculating the initial investment in the new asset, using the format in Table 8.3. In effect, the taxes raise the amount of the initial investment in the new asset by reducing the proceeds from sale of the old asset.

The sale of the asset for more than its book value but less than its initial purchase price   If Hudson sells the old asset for $70,000, there is no capital gain. However, the firm still experiences a gain in the form of recaptured depreciation of $22,000 ($70,000 − $48,000), as shown under the $70,000 sale price in Figure 8.5. This amount is taxed as ordinary income. Because the firm is assumed to be in the 40% tax bracket, the taxes on the $22,000 gain are $8,800. This amount in taxes should be used in calculating the initial investment in the new asset.

The sale of the asset for its book value   If the asset is sold for $48,000, its book value, the firm breaks even. There is no gain or loss, as shown under the $48,000 sale price in Figure 8.5. Because *no tax results from selling an asset for its book value,* there is no effect on the initial investment in the new asset.

The sale of the asset for less than its book value   If Hudson sells the asset for $30,000, it experiences a loss of $18,000 ($48,000 − $30,000), as shown under the $30,000 sale price in Figure 8.5. If this is a depreciable asset used in the business, the loss may be used to offset ordinary operating income. If the asset is *not* depreciable or *not* used in the business, the loss can be used only to offset capital gains. In either case, the loss will save the firm $7,200 ($18,000 × .40) in taxes. And, if current operating earnings or capital gains are not sufficient to offset the loss, the firm may be able to apply these losses to prior or future years' taxes.[6]

Change in Net Working Capital[7]

Net working capital, as noted in Chapter 4, is the amount by which a firm's current assets exceed its current liabilities. This topic is treated in depth in Part 5, especially in Chapter 15, but at this point it is important to note that changes in net working capital often accompany capital expenditure decisions. If a firm acquires new machinery to expand its level of operations, levels of cash, accounts receivable, inventories, accounts payable, and accruals will increase. As was noted in Chapter 3, increases in cash, accounts receivable, and inventories are *uses of cash* (cash outflows or investments), whereas increases in accounts payable and accruals are *sources of cash* (cash inflows or financing). As long as the expanded operations continue, the increased investment in current assets (cash, accounts receivable, and inventories) and increased current liability financing (accounts payable and accruals) would be expected to continue.

change in net working capital
The difference between a change in current assets and a change in current liabilities.

The difference between the change in current assets and the change in current liabilities would be the **change in net working capital.** Generally, current assets increase by more than current liabilities, resulting in increased net working capital, which would be treated as an initial outflow.[8] If the change in net working capital were negative, it would be shown as an initial inflow. The change in net working capital—whether an increase or a decrease—*is not taxable* because it merely involves a net buildup or reduction of current accounts.

E x a m p l e ▼ Danson Company, a metal products manufacturer, is contemplating expanding its operations. In addition to Danson's acquiring a variety of new capital equipment, financial analysts expect that the changes in current accounts summarized in Table 8.5 will occur and be maintained over the life of the expansion. Current assets are expected to increase by $22,000, and current liabilities are expected to increase by $9,000, resulting in a $13,000 increase in net working capital. In this case, the increase would represent an increased net working capital investment ▲ and be treated as a cash outflow in calculating the initial investment.

---

6. As noted in Chapter 3, the tax law provides detailed procedures for using *tax loss carrybacks/carryforwards.* Application of such procedures to capital budgeting is beyond the scope of this text, and they are therefore ignored in subsequent discussions.

7. Occasionally, this cash outflow is intentionally ignored to enhance the attractiveness of a proposed investment and thereby improve its likelihood of acceptance. Similar intentional omissions and/or overly optimistic estimates are sometimes made to enhance project acceptance. The presence of formal review and analysis procedures should help the firm to ensure that capital budgeting cash flow estimates are realistic and unbiased and that the "best" projects—those making the maximum contribution to owner wealth—are accepted.

8. When net working capital changes apply to the initial investment associated with a proposed capital expenditure, they are for convenience assumed to be instantaneous and thereby occurring at time zero. In practice, the change in net working capital will frequently occur over a period of months as the capital expenditure is implemented.

TABLE 8.5	Calculation of Change in Net Working Capital for Danson Company

Current account	Change in balance	
Cash	+ $ 4,000	
Accounts receivable	+ 10,000	
Inventories	+ 8,000	
(1) **Current assets**		+ $22,000
Accounts payable	+ $ 7,000	
Accruals	+ 2,000	
(2) **Current liabilities**		+ 9,000
Change in net working capital [(1) − (2)]		+ $13,000

Calculating the Initial Investment

A variety of tax and other considerations enter into the initial investment calculation. The following example illustrates calculation of the initial investment according to the format in Table 8.3.[9]

Example ▼ Powell Corporation, a large diversified manufacturer of aircraft components, is trying to determine the initial investment required to replace an old machine with a new, more sophisticated model. The machine's purchase price is $380,000, and an additional $20,000 will be required to install it. It will be depreciated under MACRS using a 5-year recovery period. The present (old) machine was purchased 3 years ago at a cost of $240,000 and was being depreciated under MACRS using a 5-year recovery period. The firm has found a buyer willing to pay $280,000 for the present machine and remove it at the buyer's expense. The firm expects that a $35,000 increase in current assets and an $18,000 increase in current liabilities will accompany the replacement; these changes will result in a $17,000 ($35,000 − $18,000) *increase* in net working capital. Both ordinary income and capital gains are taxed at a rate of 40%.

The only component of the initial investment calculation that is difficult to obtain is taxes. Because the firm is planning to sell the present machine for $40,000 more than its initial purchase price, it will realize a *capital gain of $40,000*. The book value of the present machine can be found by using the depreciation percentages from Table 3.8 (page 96) of 20, 32, and 19% for years 1, 2, and 3, respectively. The resulting book value is $69,600 ($240,000 − [(.20 + .32 + .19) × $240,000]). An *ordinary gain* of $170,400 ($240,000 − $69,600)

---

9. Throughout the discussions of capital budgeting, all assets evaluated as candidates for replacement are assumed to be depreciable assets that are directly used in the business, so any losses on the sale of these assets can be applied against ordinary operating income. The decisions are also structured to ensure that the usable life remaining on the old asset is just equal to the life of the new asset; this assumption permits the avoidance of the problem of unequal lives, which is discussed in Chapter 10.

in recaptured depreciation is also realized on the sale. The total taxes on the gain are $84,160 [($40,000 + $170,400) × .40]. Substituting these amounts into the format in Table 8.3 results in an initial investment of $221,160, which represents the net cash outflow required at time zero:

Installed cost of proposed machine		
Cost of proposed machine	$380,000	
+ Installation costs	20,000	
Total installed cost—proposed		
(depreciable value)		$400,000
− **After-tax proceeds from sale of present machine**		
Proceeds from sale of present machine	$280,000	
− Tax on sale of present machine	84,160	
Total after-tax proceeds—present		195,840
+ **Change in net working capital**		17,000
Initial investment		$221,160

? Review Questions

8–8   Describe each of the following inputs to the initial investment, and use the basic format presented in this chapter to explain how the initial investment is calculated by using them: (**a**) cost of new asset; (**b**) installation costs; (**c**) proceeds from sale of old asset; (**d**) tax on sale of old asset; and (**e**) change in net working capital.

8–9   What is the *book value* of an asset, and how is it calculated? Describe the three key forms of taxable income and their associated tax treatments.

8–10   What four tax situations may result from the sale of an asset that is being replaced? Describe the tax treatment in each situation.

8–11   Referring to the basic format for calculating initial investment, explain how a firm would determine the *depreciable value* of the new asset.

8.4 Finding the Operating Cash Inflows

The benefits expected from a capital expenditure are measured by its *operating cash inflows*, which are *incremental after-tax cash inflows*. In this section we use the income statement format to develop clear definitions of the terms *after-tax*, *cash inflows*, and *incremental*.

Interpreting the Term *After-Tax*

Benefits expected to result from proposed capital expenditures must be measured on an *after-tax basis*, because the firm will not have the use of any benefits until it has satisfied the government's tax claims. These claims depend on the firm's taxable income, so the deduction of taxes *prior to* making comparisons between proposed investments is necessary for consistency when evaluating capital expenditure alternatives.

Interpreting the Term *Cash Inflows*

All benefits expected from a proposed project must be measured on a *cash flow basis.* Cash inflows represent dollars that can be spent, not merely "accounting profits." A simple technique for converting after-tax net profits into operating cash inflows was illustrated in Chapter 3. The basic calculation requires adding any *noncash charges* deducted as expenses on the firm's income statement back to net profits after taxes. Probably the most common noncash charge found on income statements is depreciation. It is the only noncash charge that will be considered in this section.

Example ▼ Powell Corporation's estimates of its revenue and expenses (excluding depreciation), with and without the proposed new machine described in the preceding example, are given in Table 8.6. Note that both the expected usable life of the proposed machine and the remaining usable life of the present machine is 5 years. The amount to be depreciated with the proposed machine is calculated by summing the purchase price of $380,000 and the installation costs of $20,000.

TABLE 8.6	Powell Corporation's Revenue and Expenses (Excluding Depreciation) for Proposed and Present Machines

Year	Revenue (1)	Expenses (excl. depr.) (2)
With proposed machine		
1	$2,520,000	$2,300,000
2	2,520,000	2,300,000
3	2,520,000	2,300,000
4	2,520,000	2,300,000
5	2,520,000	2,300,000
With present machine		
1	$2,200,000	$1,990,000
2	2,300,000	2,110,000
3	2,400,000	2,230,000
4	2,400,000	2,250,000
5	2,250,000	2,120,000

TABLE 8.7	Depreciation Expense for Proposed and Present Machines for Powell Corporation

Year	Cost (1)	Applicable MACRS depreciation percentages (from Table 3.8) (2)	Depreciation [(1) × (2)] (3)
With proposed machine			
1	$400,000	20%	$ 80,000
2	400,000	32	128,000
3	400,000	19	76,000
4	400,000	12	48,000
5	400,000	12	48,000
6	400,000	5	20,000
Totals		100%	$400,000
With present machine			
1	$240,000	12% (year-4 depreciation)	$ 28,800
2	240,000	12 (year-5 depreciation)	28,800
3	240,000	5 (year-6 depreciation)	12,000
4	Because the present machine is at the end of the third year of its cost		0
5	recovery at the time the analysis is performed, it has only the final		0
6	3 years of depreciation (as noted above) yet applicable.		0
Total			$69,600[a]

[a]The total $69,600 represents the book value of the present machine at the end of the third year, as calculated in the preceding example.

The proposed machine is to be depreciated under MACRS using a 5-year recovery period. (See Chapter 3 and Table 3.8 on page 96 for more detail.)[10] The resulting depreciation on this machine for each of the 6 years, as well as the remaining 3 years of depreciation on the present machine, are calculated in Table 8.7.[11]

The operating cash inflows in each year can be calculated using the income statement format shown in Table 8.8. Substituting the data from Tables 8.6 and 8.7 into this format and assuming a 40% tax rate, we get Table 8.9. It demonstrates the calculation of operating cash inflows for each year for both the proposed and the present machine. Because the proposed machine is depreciated over 6 years, the analysis must be performed over the 6-year period to fully cap-

10. As noted in Chapter 3, it takes $n + 1$ years to depreciate an n-year class asset under current tax law. Therefore, MACRS percentages are given for each of 6 years for use in depreciating an asset with a 5-year recovery period.

11. It is important to recognize that although both machines will provide 5 years of use, the proposed new machine will be depreciated over the 6-year period, whereas the present machine—as noted in the preceding example—has been depreciated over 3 years and therefore has only its final 3 years (years 4, 5, and 6) of depreciation (i.e., 12, 12, and 5%, respectively, under MACRS) remaining.

TABLE 8.8	Calculation of Operating Cash Inflows Using the Income Statement Format

Revenue
− Expenses (excluding depreciation)
Profits before depreciation and taxes
− Depreciation
Net profits before taxes
− Taxes
Net profits after taxes
+ Depreciation
Operating cash inflows

TABLE 8.9	Calculation of Operating Cash Inflows for Powell Corporation's Proposed and Present Machines

	Year					
	1	2	3	4	5	6
With proposed machine						
Revenue[a]	$2,520,000	$2,520,000	$2,520,000	$2,520,000	$2,520,000	$ 0
− Expenses (excl. depr.)[b]	2,300,000	2,300,000	2,300,000	2,300,000	2,300,000	0
Profits before depr. and taxes	$ 220,000	$ 220,000	$ 220,000	$ 220,000	$ 220,000	$ 0
− Depreciation[c]	80,000	128,000	76,000	48,000	48,000	20,000
Net profits before taxes	$ 140,000	$ 92,000	$ 144,000	$ 172,000	$ 172,000	−$20,000
− Taxes (rate = 40%)	56,000	36,800	57,600	68,800	68,800	− 8,000
Net profits after taxes	$ 84,000	$ 55,200	$ 86,400	$ 103,200	$ 103,200	−$12,000
+ Depreciation[c]	80,000	128,000	76,000	48,000	48,000	20,000
Operating cash inflows	$ 164,000	$ 183,200	$ 162,400	$ 151,200	$ 151,200	$ 8,000
With present machine						
Revenue[a]	$2,200,000	$2,300,000	$2,400,000	$2,400,000	$2,250,000	$ 0
− Expenses (excl. depr.)[b]	1,990,000	2,110,000	2,230,000	2,250,000	2,120,000	0
Profits before depr. and taxes	$ 210,000	$ 190,000	$ 170,000	$ 150,000	$ 130,000	$ 0
− Depreciation[c]	28,800	28,800	12,000	0	0	0
Net profits before taxes	$ 181,200	$ 161,200	$ 158,000	$ 150,000	$ 130,000	$ 0
− Taxes (rate = 40%)	72,480	64,480	63,200	60,000	52,000	0
Net profits after taxes	$ 108,720	$ 96,720	$ 94,800	$ 90,000	$ 78,000	$ 0
+ Depreciation[c]	28,800	28,800	12,000	0	0	0
Operating cash inflows	$ 137,520	$ 125,520	$ 106,800	$ 90,000	$ 78,000	$ 0

[a]From column 1 of Table 8.6.
[b]From column 2 of Table 8.6.
[c]From column 3 of Table 8.7.

ture the tax effect of its year-6 depreciation. The resulting operating cash inflows are shown in the final row of Table 8.9 for each machine. The $8,000 year-6 cash inflow for the proposed machine results solely from the tax benefit of its ▲ year-6 depreciation deduction.

Interpreting the Term *Incremental*

The final step in estimating the operating cash inflows for a proposed project is to calculate the *incremental (relevant)* cash inflows. Incremental operating cash inflows are needed, because our concern is *only* with the change in operating cash flows as a result of the proposed project.

Example ▼ Table 8.10 demonstrates the calculation of Powell Corporation's incremental (relevant) operating cash inflows for each year. The estimates of operating cash inflows developed in Table 8.9 are given in columns 1 and 2. Column 2 values represent the amount of operating cash inflows that Powell Corporation will receive if it does not replace the present machine. If the proposed machine replaces the present machine, the firm's operating cash inflows for each year will be those shown in column 1. Subtracting the present machine's operating cash inflows from the proposed machine's operating cash inflows results in the incremental operating cash inflows for each year, shown in column 3 of Table 8.10. These cash flows represent the amounts by which each respective year's cash inflows will increase as a result of the replacement. For example, in year 1, Powell Corporation's cash inflows would increase by $26,480 if the proposed project were undertaken. Clearly, these are the relevant inflows to be considered

| **TABLE 8.10** | **Incremental (Relevant) Operating Cash Inflows for Powell Corporation** |

	Operating cash inflows		
Year	Proposed machine[a] (1)	Present machine[a] (2)	Incremental (relevant) [(1) − (2)] (3)
1	$164,000	$137,520	$26,480
2	183,200	125,520	57,680
3	162,400	106,800	55,600
4	151,200	90,000	61,200
5	151,200	78,000	73,200
6	8,000	0	8,000

[a]From final row for respective machine in Table 8.9.

ed funds for capital investments and must ration them among carefully selected projects. To make investment decisions when proposals are mutually exclusive or when capital must be rationed, projects must be ranked; otherwise, accept–reject decisions must be made. Conventional cash flow patterns consist of an initial outflow followed by a series of inflows; any other pattern is nonconventional. These patterns can be either annuities or mixed streams.

 Discuss the major components of relevant cash flows, expansion versus replacement cash flows, sunk costs and opportunity costs, and international capital budgeting and long-term investments. The relevant cash flows for capital budgeting decisions are the initial investment, the operating cash inflows, and the terminal cash flow for a given project. For replacement decisions, these flows are found by determining the difference between the cash flows of the new asset and the old asset. Expansion decisions are viewed as replacement decisions in which all cash flows from the old asset are zero. When estimating relevant cash flows, sunk costs should be ignored, and opportunity costs should be included as cash outflows. In international capital budgeting, currency risk and political risk can be minimized through careful planning.

 Calculate the initial investment associated with a proposed capital expenditure, given relevant data. The initial investment is the initial outflow required, including the installed cost of the new asset, the after-tax proceeds from the sale of the old asset, and any change in net working capital. Finding the after-tax proceeds from sale of the old asset, which reduces the initial investment, involves cost, depreciation, and tax data. The book value of an asset is its strict accounting value, which is used to determine what taxes are owed as a result of selling an asset. Any of three forms of taxable income—capital gain, recaptured depreciation, or a loss—can result from sale of an asset. The form of taxable income that applies depends on whether the asset is sold for (1) more than its initial purchase price, (2) more than book value but less than initially paid, (3) book value, or (4) less than book value. The change in net working capital is the difference between the change in current assets (cash outflows or investments) and the change in current liabilities (cash inflows or financing) expected from a given capital expenditure.

 Determine relevant operating cash inflows using the income statement format. The operating cash inflows are the incremental after-tax cash inflows expected to result from a project. The income statement format, which involves adding depreciation back to net profits after taxes, gives the operating cash inflows associated with the proposed and present projects. The relevant (incremental) cash inflows, which are used to evaluate the proposed project, are the differences between the operating cash inflows of the proposed project and those of the present project.

Find the terminal cash flow, given relevant data. The terminal cash flow represents the after-tax cash flow, exclusive of operating cash inflows, expected from liquidation of a project at the end of its life. It is found by calculating and then finding the difference between the after-tax proceeds from sale of the new and the old asset at project termination and then adjusting this difference for any change in net working capital. Sale price and depreciation data are used to find the taxes and therefore the after-tax sale proceeds on the new and old assets. The change in net working capital typically represents the recovery of the net working capital investment included in the initial investment.

SELF-TEST PROBLEMS   (Solutions in Appendix B)

  ST 8–1   Book value, taxes, and initial investment   Irvin Enterprises is considering the purchase of a new piece of equipment to replace the current equipment. The new equipment costs $75,000 and requires $5,000 in installation costs. It will

be depreciated under MACRS using a 5-year recovery period. The old piece of equipment was purchased for an installed cost of $50,000 4 years ago; it was being depreciated under MACRS using a 5-year recovery period. The old equipment can be sold today for $55,000 net of any removal or cleanup costs. As a result of the proposed replacement, the firm's investment in net working capital is expected to increase by $15,000. The firm pays taxes at a rate of 40% on both ordinary income and capital gains. (Table 3.8 on page 96 contains the applicable MACRS depreciation percentages.)

a. Calculate the book value of the old piece of equipment.

b. Determine the taxes, if any, attributable to the sale of the old equipment.

c. Find the initial investment associated with the proposed equipment replacement.

ST 8–2   Determining relevant cash flows   A machine currently in use was originally purchased 2 years ago for $40,000. The machine is being depreciated under MACRS using a 5-year recovery period; it has 3 years of usable life remaining. The current machine can be sold today to net $42,000 after removal and cleanup costs. A new machine, using a 3-year MACRS recovery period, can be purchased at a price of $140,000. It requires $10,000 to install and has a 3-year usable life. If the new machine were acquired, the investment in accounts receivable would be expected to rise by $10,000, the inventory investment will increase by $25,000, and accounts payable will increase by $15,000. *Profits before depreciation and taxes* are expected to be $70,000 for each of the next 3 years with the old machine and $120,000 in the first year and $130,000 in the second and third years with the new machine. At the end of 3 years, the market value of the old machine will equal zero, but the new machine could be sold to net $35,000 before taxes. Both ordinary corporate income and capital gains are subject to a 40% tax. (Table 3.8 on page 96 contains the applicable MACRS depreciation percentages.)

a. Determine the initial investment associated with the proposed replacement decision.

b. Calculate the incremental operating cash inflows for years 1 to 4 associated with the proposed replacement. (*Note:* Only depreciation cash flows must be considered in year 4.)

c. Calculate the terminal cash flow associated with the proposed replacement decision. (*Note:* This is at the end of year 3.)

d. Depict on a time line the relevant cash flows found in **a, b,** and **c** associated with the proposed replacement decision assuming that it is terminated at the end of year 3.

PROBLEMS

WARM-UP   **8–1   Classification of expenditures**   Given the following list of outlays, indicate whether each is normally considered a *capital* or an *operating expenditure*. Explain your answers.

a. An initial lease payment of $5,000 for electronic point-of-sale cash register systems.
b. An outlay of $20,000 to purchase patent rights from an inventor.
c. An outlay of $80,000 for a major research and development program.
d. An $80,000 investment in a portfolio of marketable securities.
e. A $300 outlay for an office machine.
f. An outlay of $2,000 for a new machine tool.
g. An outlay of $240,000 for a new building.
h. An outlay of $1,000 for a marketing research report.

  8–2   Basic terminology   A firm is considering the following three separate situations.

Situation A   Build either a small office building or a convenience store on a parcel of land located in a high-traffic area. Adequate funding is available, and both projects are known to be acceptable. The office building requires an initial investment of $620,000 and is expected to provide operating cash inflows of $40,000 per year for 20 years. The convenience store is expected to cost $500,000 and to provide a growing stream of operating cash inflows over its 20-year life. The initial operating cash inflow is $20,000 and will increase by 5% each year.

Situation B   Replace a machine with a new one requiring a $60,000 initial investment and providing operating cash inflows of $10,000 per year for the first 5 years. At the end of year 5, a machine overhaul costing $20,000 is required. After it is completed, expected operating cash inflows are $10,000 in year 6; $7,000 in year 7; $4,000 in year 8; and $1,000 in year 9, at the end of which the machine will be scrapped.

Situation C   Invest in any or all of the four machines whose relevant cash flows are given in the following table. The firm has $500,000 budgeted to fund these machines, all of which are known to be acceptable. Initial investment for each machine is $250,000.

	Operating cash inflows			
Year	Machine 1	Machine 2	Machine 3	Machine 4
1	$ 50,000	$70,000	$65,000	$90,000
2	70,000	70,000	65,000	80,000
3	90,000	70,000	80,000	70,000
4	−30,000	70,000	80,000	60,000
5	100,000	70,000	−20,000	50,000

For each situation or project, indicate
a. Whether the *situation* is independent or mutually exclusive.
b. Whether the availability of funds is unlimited or if capital rationing exists.
c. Whether accept–reject or ranking decisions are required.

d. Whether each *project's* cash flows are conventional or nonconventional.
e. Whether each *project's* cash flow pattern is an annuity or a mixed stream.

INTERMEDIATE 8–3 **Relevant cash flow pattern fundamentals**   For each of the following projects, determine the *relevant cash flows,* classify the cash flow pattern, and depict the cash flows on a time line.

a. A project requiring an initial investment of $120,000 that generates annual operating cash inflows of $25,000 for the next 18 years. In each of the 18 years, maintenance of the project will require a $5,000 cash outflow.

b. A new machine having an installed cost of $85,000. Sale of the old machine will yield $30,000 after taxes. Operating cash inflows generated by the replacement will exceed the operating cash inflows of the old machine by $20,000 in each year of a 6-year period. At the end of year 6, liquidation of the new machine will yield $20,000 after taxes, which is $10,000 greater than the after-tax proceeds expected from the old machine had it been retained and liquidated at the end of year 6.

c. An asset requiring an initial investment of $2 million that will yield annual operating cash inflows of $300,000 for each of the next 10 years. Operating cash outlays will be $20,000 for each year except year 6, when an overhaul requiring an additional cash outlay of $500,000 will be required. The asset's liquidation value at the end of year 10 is expected to be $0.

INTERMEDIATE 8–4 **Expansion versus replacement cash flows**   Edison Systems has estimated the cash flows over the 5-year lives for two projects, A and B. These cash flows are summarized in the following table.

	Project A	Project B
Initial investment	$40,000	$12,000[a]
Year	Operating cash inflows	
1	$10,000	$ 6,000
2	12,000	6,000
3	14,000	6,000
4	16,000	6,000
5	10,000	6,000

[a]After-tax cash inflow expected from liquidation.

a. If project A were actually a *replacement* for project B and if the $12,000 initial investment shown for B were the after-tax cash inflow expected from liquidating it, what would be the relevant cash flow for this replacement decision?

b. How can an *expansion decision* such as project A be viewed as a special form of a replacement decision? Explain.

WARM-UP 8–5 **Sunk costs and opportunity costs**   Masters Golf Products, Inc., spent 3 years and $1,000,000 to develop its new line of club heads to replace a line that is becoming obsolete. In order to begin manufacturing them, the company will have to invest $1,800,000 in new equipment. The new clubs are expected to generate an increase in operating cash inflows of $750,000 per year for the next 10 years. The company has determined that the existing line could be sold to a competitor for $250,000.

a. How should the $1,000,000 in development costs be classified?

b. How should the $250,000 sale price for the existing line be classified?

c. Depict all of the known relevant cash flows on a time line.

INTERMEDIATE

8–6   Sunk costs and opportunity costs   Covol Industries is developing the relevant cash flows associated with the proposed replacement of an existing machine tool with a new technologically advanced one. Given the following costs related to the proposed project, explain whether each would be treated as a *sunk cost* or an *opportunity cost* in developing the relevant cash flows associated with the proposed replacement decision.

a. Covol would be able to use the same tooling, which had a book value of $40,000, on the new machine tool as it had used on the old one.

b. Covol would be able to use its existing computer system to develop programs for operating the new machine tool. The old machine tool did not require these programs. Although the firm's computer has excess capacity available, the capacity could be leased to another firm for an annual fee of $17,000.

c. Covol would have to obtain additional floor space to accommodate the larger new machine tool. The space that would be used is currently being leased to another company for $10,000 per year.

d. Covol would use a small storage facility to store the increased output of the new machine tool. The storage facility was built by Covol at a cost of $120,000 3 years earlier. Because of its unique configuration and location, it is currently of no use to either Covol or any other firm.

e. Covol would retain an existing overhead crane, which it had planned to sell for its $180,000 market value. Although the crane was not needed with the old machine tool, it would be used to position raw materials on the new machine tool.

WARM-UP

8–7   Book value   Find the book value for each of the assets shown in the following table, assuming that MACRS depreciation is being used. (*Note:* See Table 3.8 on page 96 for the applicable depreciation percentages.)

Asset	Installed cost	Recovery period	Elapsed time since purchase
A	$ 950,000	5 years	3 years
B	40,000	3	1
C	96,000	5	4
D	350,000	5	1
E	1,500,000	7	5

INTERMEDIATE 8–8   **Book value and taxes on sale of assets**   Troy Industries purchased a new machine 3 years ago for $80,000. It is being depreciated under MACRS with a 5-year recovery period using the percentages given in Table 3.8 on page 96. Assume 40% ordinary and capital gains tax rates.
a. What is the book value of the machine?
b. Calculate the firm's tax liability if it sold the machine for the following amounts: $100,000; $56,000; $23,200; and $15,000.

INTERMEDIATE 8–9   **Tax calculations**   For each of the following cases, describe the various taxable components of the funds received through sale of the asset, and determine the total taxes resulting from the transaction. Assume 40% ordinary and capital gains tax rates. The asset was purchased for $200,000 2 years ago and is being depreciated under MACRS using a 5-year recovery period. (See Table 3.8 on page 96 for the applicable depreciation percentages.)
a. The asset is sold for $220,000.
b. The asset is sold for $150,000.
c. The asset is sold for $96,000.
d. The asset is sold for $80,000.

WARM-UP 8–10   **Change in net working capital calculation**   Samuels Manufacturing is considering the purchase of a new machine to replace one they feel is obsolete. The firm has total current assets of $920,000 and total current liabilities of $640,000. As a result of the proposed replacement, the following *changes* are anticipated in the levels of the current asset and current liability accounts noted.

Account	Change
Accruals	+ $ 40,000
Marketable securities	0
Inventories	− 10,000
Accounts payable	+ 90,000
Notes payable	0
Accounts receivable	+ 150,000
Cash	+ 15,000

a. Using the information given, calculate the change, if any, in net working capital that is expected to result from the proposed replacement action.
b. Explain why a change in these current accounts would be relevant in determining the initial investment for the proposed capital expenditure.
c. Would the change in net working capital enter into any of the other cash flow components comprising the relevant cash flows? Explain.

INTERMEDIATE 8–11   **Calculating initial investment**   Vastine Medical, Inc., is considering replacing its existing computer system which was purchased 2 years ago for a cost of $325,000. The system can be sold today for $200,000. It is being depreciating using MACRS and a 5-year recovery period (see Table 3.8, page 96). A new computer system will cost $500,000 to purchase and install. Replacement of the computer system would not involve any change in net working capital. Assume a 40% tax rate on capital gains and ordinary income.

a. Calculate the book value of the existing computer system.
b. Calculate the after-tax proceeds of its sale at $200,000.
c. Calculate the initial investment associated with the replacement project.

8–12 **Initial investment—Basic calculation**   Cushing Corporation is considering the purchase of a new grading machine to replace the existing one. The existing machine was purchased 3 years ago at an installed cost of $20,000; it was being depreciated under MACRS using a 5-year recovery period. (See Table 3.8 on page 96 for the applicable depreciation percentages.) The existing machine is expected to have a usable life of at least 5 more years. The new machine costs $35,000 and requires $5,000 in installation costs; it will be depreciated using a 5-year recovery period under MACRS. The existing machine can currently be sold for $25,000 without incurring any removal or cleanup costs. The firm pays 40% taxes on both ordinary income and capital gains. Calculate the *initial investment* associated with the proposed purchase of a new grading machine.

INTERMEDIATE

8–13 **Initial investment at various sale prices**   Edwards Manufacturing Company is considering replacing one machine with another. The old machine was purchased 3 years ago for an installed cost of $10,000. The firm is depreciating the machine under MACRS using a 5-year recovery period. (See Table 3.8 on page 96 for the applicable depreciation percentages.) The new machine costs $24,000 and requires $2,000 in installation costs. Assume the firm is subject to a 40% tax rate on both ordinary income and capital gains. In each of the following cases, calculate the initial investment for the replacement.
a. Edwards Manufacturing Company (EMC) sells the old machine for $11,000.
b. EMC sells the old machine for $7,000.
c. EMC sells the old machine for $2,900.
d. EMC sells the old machine for $1,500.

INTERMEDIATE

CHALLENGE   8–14 **Calculating initial investment**   DuPree Coffee Roasters, Inc., wishes to expand and modernize its facilities. A computer controlled automatic-feed roaster will cost them $130,000 to install. The firm has a chance to sell its 4-year old roaster for $35,000. The existing roaster originally cost $60,000 and was being depreciated using MACRS and a 7-year recovery period (see Table 3.8 on page 96). DuPree pays taxes at a rate of 40% on capital gains and ordinary income.
a. What is the book value of the existing roaster?
b. Calculate the after-tax proceeds of the sale of the existing roaster.
c. Calculate the net change in working capital using the following figures:

Anticipated changes in current assets and current liabilities	
Accruals	−$20,000
Inventory	+50,000
Accounts payable	+40,000
Accounts receivable	+70,000
Cash	0
Notes payable	+15,000

d. Calculate the initial investment associated with the proposed new roaster.

8–15   **Depreciation**   A firm is evaluating the acquisition of an asset that costs $64,000 and requires $4,000 in installation costs. If the firm depreciates the asset under MACRS using a 5-year recovery period (see Table 3.8 on page 96 for the applicable depreciation percentages), determine the depreciation charge for each year.

8–16   **Incremental operating cash inflows**   A firm is considering renewing its equipment to meet increased demand for its product. The cost of equipment modifications is $1.9 million plus $100,000 in installation costs. The firm will depreciate the equipment modifications under MACRS using a 5-year recovery period. (See Table 3.8 on page 96 for the applicable depreciation percentages.) Additional sales revenue from the renewal should amount to $1.2 million per year, and additional operating expenses and other costs (excluding depreciation) will amount to 40% of the additional sales. The firm has an ordinary tax rate of 40%. (*Note:* Answer the following questions for each of the next 6 *years.*)
a. What incremental earnings before depreciation and taxes will result from the renewal?
b. What incremental earnings after taxes will result from the renewal?
c. What incremental operating cash inflows will result from the renewal?

8–17   **Incremental operating cash inflows—Expense reduction**   Miller Corporation is considering replacing a machine. The replacement will reduce operating expenses (i.e., increase revenues) by $16,000 per year for each of the 5 years the new machine is expected to last. Although the old machine has zero book value, it can be used for 5 more years. The depreciable value of the new machine is $48,000. The firm will depreciate the machine under MACRS using a 5-year recovery period (see Table 3.8 on page 96 for the applicable depreciation percentages) and is subject to a 40% tax rate on ordinary income. Estimate the incremental operating cash inflows generated by the replacement. (*Note:* Be sure to consider the depreciation in year 6.)

8–18   **Incremental operating cash inflows**   Strong Tool Company has been considering purchasing a new lathe to replace a fully depreciated lathe that will last 5 more years. The new lathe is expected to have a 5-year life and depreciation charges of $2,000 in year 1; $3,200 in year 2; $1,900 in year 3; $1,200 in both year 4 and year 5; and $500 in year 6. The firm estimates the revenues and expenses (excluding depreciation) for the new and the old lathes as shown in the following table. The firm is subject to a 40% tax rate on ordinary income.
a. Calculate the operating cash inflows associated with each lathe. (*Note:* Be sure to consider the depreciation in year 6.)

	New lathe		Old lathe	
Year	Revenue	Expenses (excl. depr.)	Revenue	Expenses (excl. depr.)
1	$40,000	$30,000	$35,000	$25,000
2	41,000	30,000	35,000	25,000
3	42,000	30,000	35,000	25,000
4	43,000	30,000	35,000	25,000
5	44,000	30,000	35,000	25,000

b. Calculate the incremental (relevant) operating cash inflows resulting from the proposed lathe replacement.

c. Depict on a time line the incremental operating cash inflows calculated in **b.**

 8–19 **Determining operating cash flows**   Scenic Tours, Inc., is a provider of bus tours throughout the New England area. The corporation is considering the replacement of 10 of its older buses. The existing buses were purchased 4 years ago at a total cost of $2,700,000 and are being depreciated using MACRS and a 5-year recovery period (see Table 3.8, page 96). The new buses would have larger passenger capacity and better fuel efficiency as well as lower maintenance costs. The total cost for 10 new buses is $3,000,000. Like the older buses, the new ones would be depreciated using MACRS and a 5-year recovery period. Scenic is taxed at a rate of 40% on ordinary income and capital gains. The following table presents revenues and cash expenses for the proposed purchase as well as the present fleet. Use all of the information given to calculate operating cash inflows for the proposed and present buses.

	Year					
	1	2	3	4	5	6
With the proposed new buses						
Revenue	$1,850,000	$1,850,000	$1,830,000	$1,825,000	$1,815,000	$1,800,000
−Expenses (excl. depreciation)	460,000	460,000	468,000	472,000	485,000	500,000
With the present buses						
Revenue	$1,800,000	$1,800,000	$1,790,000	$1,785,000	$1,775,000	$1,750,000
−Expenses (excl. depreciation)	500,000	510,000	520,000	520,000	530,000	535,000

 8–20 **Terminal cash flows—Various lives and sale prices**   Looner Industries is currently analyzing the purchase of a new machine costing $160,000 and requiring $20,000 in installation costs. Purchase of this machine is expected to result in an increase in net working capital of $30,000 to support the expanded level of operations. The firm plans to depreciate the asset under MACRS using a 5-year recovery period (see Table 3.8 on page 96 for the applicable depreciation percentages) and expects to sell the machine to net $10,000 before taxes at the end of its usable life. The firm is subject to a 40% tax rate on both ordinary and capital gains income.

a. Calculate the terminal cash flow for a usable life of (1) 3 years, (2) 5 years, and (3) 7 years.

b. Discuss the effect of usable life on terminal cash flows using your findings in **a.**

c. Assuming a 5-year usable life, calculate the terminal cash flow if the machine were sold to net (1) $9,000 or (2) $170,000 (before taxes) at the end of 5 years.

d. Discuss the effect of sale price on terminal cash flows using your findings in **c.**

8–21 **Terminal cash flow—Replacement decision**   Russell Industries is considering replacing a fully depreciated machine having a remaining useful life of 10 years with a newer, more sophisticated machine. The new machine will cost $200,000 and will require $30,000 in installation costs. It will be depreciated under MACRS using a 5-year recovery period (see Table 3.8 on page 96 for the applicable depreciation percentages). A $25,000 increase in net working capital will be required to support the new machine. The firm plans to evaluate the potential replacement over a 4-year period. They estimate that the old machine could be sold at the end of 4 years to net $15,000 before taxes; the new machine at the end of 4 years will be worth $75,000 before taxes. Calculate the terminal cash flow at the end of year 4 that is relevant to the proposed purchase of the new machine. The firm is subject to a 40% tax rate on both ordinary and capital gains income.

8–22 **Relevant cash flows for a marketing campaign**   Marcus Tube, a manufacturer of high-quality aluminum tubing, has maintained stable sales and profits over the past 10 years. Although the market for aluminum tubing has been expanding by 3% per year, Marcus has been unsuccessful in sharing this growth. To increase its sales, the firm is considering an aggressive marketing campaign that centers on regularly running ads in all relevant trade journals and exhibiting products at all major regional and national trade shows. The campaign is expected to require an *annual* tax-deductible expenditure of $150,000 over the next 5 years. Sales revenue, as noted in the income statement for 2000 shown in what follows, totaled $20,000,000. If the proposed marketing campaign is not initiated, sales are expected to remain at this level in each of the next 5 years, 2001–2005. With the marketing campaign, sales are expected to rise to the levels shown in the second table for each of the next 5 years; cost of goods sold is expected to remain at 80% of sales; general and administrative expense (exclusive of any marketing campaign outlays) is expected to remain at 10% of sales; and annual depreciation expense is expected to remain at $500,000. Assuming a 40% tax rate, find the relevant cash flows over the next 5 years associated with the proposed marketing campaign.

Income Statement
Marcus Tube
for the year ended December 31, 2000

Sales revenue		$20,000,000
Less: Cost of goods sold (80%)		16,000,000
Gross profits		$ 4,000,000
Less: Operating expenses		
General and administrative expense (10%)	$2,000,000	
Depreciation expense	500,000	
Total operating expense		2,500,000
Net profits before taxes		$ 1,500,000
Less: Taxes (rate = 40%)		600,000
Net profits after taxes		$ 900,000

Sales Forecast Marcus Tube	
Year	Sales revenue
2001	$20,500,000
2002	21,000,000
2003	21,500,000
2004	22,500,000
2005	23,500,000

CHALLENGE

8–23 **Relevant cash flows—No terminal value**   Central Laundry and Cleaners is considering replacing an existing piece of machinery with a more sophisticated machine. The old machine was purchased 3 years ago at a cost of $50,000, and this amount was being depreciated under MACRS using a 5-year recovery period. The machine has 5 years of usable life remaining. The new machine being considered costs $76,000 and requires $4,000 in installation costs. The new machine would be depreciated under MACRS using a 5-year recovery period. The old machine can currently be sold for $55,000 without incurring any removal or cleanup costs. The firm pays 40% taxes on both ordinary income and capital gains. The revenues and expenses (excluding depreciation) associated with the new and the old machine for the next 5 years are given in the table below. (Table 3.8 on page 96 contains the applicable MACRS depreciation percentages.)

a. Calculate the initial investment associated with replacement of the old machine by the new one.

b. Determine the incremental operating cash inflows associated with the proposed replacement. (*Note:* Be sure to consider the depreciation in year 6.)

	New machine		Old machine	
Year	Revenue	Expenses (excl. depr.)	Revenue	Expenses (excl. depr.)
1	$750,000	$720,000	$674,000	$660,000
2	750,000	720,000	676,000	660,000
3	750,000	720,000	680,000	660,000
4	750,000	720,000	678,000	660,000
5	750,000	720,000	674,000	660,000

c. Depict on a time line the relevant cash flows found in a and b associated with the proposed replacement decision.

CHALLENGE

8–24 **Integrative—Determining relevant cash flows**   Lombard Company is contemplating the purchase of a new high-speed widget grinder to replace the existing grinder. The existing grinder was purchased 2 years ago at an installed cost of $60,000; it was being depreciated under MACRS using a 5-year recovery period. The existing grinder is expected to have a usable life of 5 more years. The new grinder costs $105,000 and requires $5,000 in installation costs; it has a 5-year usable life and would be depreciated under MACRS using a 5-year recovery period. The existing grinder can currently be sold for $70,000 without incurring any removal or cleanup costs. To support the increased business resulting from purchase of the new grinder, accounts receivable would increase by $40,000, inventories by $30,000, and accounts payable by $58,000. At the end of 5 years, the existing grinder is expected to have a market value of zero; the new grinder would be sold to net $29,000 after removal and cleanup costs and before taxes. The firm pays 40% taxes on both ordinary income and capital gains. The estimated *profits before depreciation and taxes* over the 5 years for both the new and existing grinder are shown in the following table. (Table 3.8 on page 96 contains the applicable MACRS depreciation percentages.)

	Profits before depreciation and taxes	
Year	New grinder	Existing grinder
1	$43,000	$26,000
2	43,000	24,000
3	43,000	22,000
4	43,000	20,000
5	43,000	18,000

a. Calculate the initial investment associated with the replacement of the existing grinder by the new one.
b. Determine the incremental operating cash inflows associated with the proposed grinder replacement. (*Note:* Be sure to consider the depreciation in year 6.)
c. Determine the terminal cash flow expected at the end of year 5 from the proposed grinder replacement.
d. Depict on a time line the relevant cash flows associated with the proposed grinder replacement decision.

8–25   Integrative—Determining relevant cash flows   Atlantic Drydock is considering replacing an existing hoist with one of two newer, more efficient pieces of equipment. The existing hoist is 3 years old, cost $32,000, and is being depreciated under MACRS using a 5-year recovery period. Although the existing hoist has only 3 years (years 4, 5, and 6) of depreciation remaining under MACRS, it has a remaining usable life of 5 years. Hoist A, one of the two possible replacement hoists, costs $40,000 to purchase and $8,000 to install. It has a 5-year usable life and will be depreciated under MACRS using a 5-year recovery period. The other hoist, B, costs $54,000 to purchase and $6,000 to install. It also has a 5-year usable life and will be depreciated under MACRS using a 5-year recovery period.

Increased investments in net working capital will accompany the decision to acquire hoist A or hoist B. Purchase of hoist A would result in a $4,000 increase in net working capital; hoist B would result in a $6,000 increase in net working capital. The projected *profits before depreciation and taxes* with each alternative hoist and the existing hoist are given in the following table.

| Year | Profits before depreciation and taxes | | |
	With hoist A	With hoist B	With existing hoist
1	$21,000	$22,000	$14,000
2	21,000	24,000	14,000
3	21,000	26,000	14,000
4	21,000	26,000	14,000
5	21,000	26,000	14,000

The existing hoist can currently be sold for $18,000 and will not incur any removal or cleanup costs. At the end of 5 years, the existing hoist can be sold to net $1,000 before taxes. Hoists A and B can be sold to net $12,000 and $20,000 before taxes, respectively, at the end of the 5-year period. The firm is subject to a 40% tax rate on both ordinary income and capital gains. (Table 3.8 on page 96 contains the applicable MACRS depreciation percentages.)

a. Calculate the initial investment associated with each alternative.
b. Calculate the incremental operating cash inflows associated with each alternative. *(Note:* Be sure to consider the depreciation in year 6.)
c. Calculate the terminal cash flow at the end of year 5 associated with each alternative.
d. Depict on a time line the relevant cash flows associated with each alternative.

CASE   CHAPTER 8   **Developing Relevant Cash Flows for Clark Upholstery Company's Machine Renewal or Replacement Decision**

Bo Humphries, chief financial officer of Clark Upholstery Company, expects the firm's *net profits after taxes* for the next 5 years to be as shown in the following table.

Year	Net profits after taxes
1	$100,000
2	150,000
3	200,000
4	250,000
5	320,000

Bo is beginning to develop the relevant cash flows needed to analyze whether to renew or replace Clark's *only* depreciable asset, a machine that originally cost $30,000, has a current book value of zero, and can now be sold for $20,000. *(Note:* Because the firm's only depreciable asset is fully depreciated—its book value is zero—its expected net profits after taxes equal its operating cash inflows.) He estimates that at the end of 5 years, the existing machine can be sold to net $2,000 before taxes. Bo plans to use the following information to develop the relevant cash flows for each of the alternatives.

Alternative 1   Renew the existing machine at a total depreciable cost of $90,000. The renewed machine would have a 5-year usable life and be depreciated under MACRS using a 5-year recovery period. Renewing the machine would result in the following projected revenues and expenses (excluding depreciation):

Year	Revenue	Expenses (excluding depreciation)
1	$1,000,000	$801,500
2	1,175,000	884,200
3	1,300,000	918,100
4	1,425,000	943,100
5	1,550,000	968,100

The renewed machine would result in an increased investment of $15,000 in net working capital. At the end of 5 years, the machine could be sold to net $8,000 before taxes.

Alternative 2   Replace the existing machine with a new machine costing $100,000 and requiring installation costs of $10,000. The new machine would have a 5-year usable life and be depreciated under MACRS using a 5-year recovery period. The firm's projected revenues and expenses (excluding depreciation), if it acquires the machine, would be as follows:

Year	Revenue	Expenses (excluding depreciation)
1	$1,000,000	$764,500
2	1,175,000	839,800
3	1,300,000	914,900
4	1,425,000	989,900
5	1,550,000	998,900

The new machine would result in an increased investment of $22,000 in net working capital. At the end of 5 years, the new machine could be sold to net $25,000 before taxes.

The firm is subject to a 40% tax on both ordinary income and capital gains. As noted, the company uses MACRS depreciation. (See Table 3.8 on page 96 for the applicable depreciation percentages.)

Required

a. Calculate the initial investment associated with each of Clark Upholstery's alternatives.

b. Calculate the incremental operating cash inflows associated with each of Clark's alternatives. (*Note:* Be sure to consider the depreciation in year 6.)

c. Calculate the terminal cash flow at the end of year 5 associated with each of Clark's alternatives.

d. Use your findings in **a, b,** and **c** to depict on a time line the relevant cash flows associated with each of Clark Upholstery's alternatives.

e. Based solely upon your comparison of their relevant cash flows, which alternative appears to be better? Why?

WEB EXERCISE

GOTO web site www.reportgallery.com. Click ANNUAL REPORT at the top of the page. Scroll down to Alcoa and click on ANNUAL REPORT. In the left column click on Liquidity and Capital Resources. Scroll down to the Investing Activities and click on Capital expenditures.

1. How much did Alcoa spend on capital expenditures for each of the last 5 years?
2. Were their capital expenditures increasing or decreasing?
3. Is their capital spending consistent or erratic?
4. What were their major uses of capital spending for the most recent year?

Click on Consolidated Balance Sheets in the left column.

5. What are the account balances for Properties, Plant, and Equipment for the 2 most recent years?
6. What percent of Properties, Plant, and Equipment does Alcoa replace every year? (*Hint:* For a rough estimate, divide the capital expenditures for a year by that year's balance in Properties, Plant, and Equipment.)

CHAPTER 9

Capital Budgeting Techniques

LEARNING GOALS

LG1 Understand the role of capital budgeting techniques in the capital budgeting process.

LG2 Calculate, interpret, and evaluate the payback period.

LG3 Calculate, interpret, and evaluate the net present value (NPV).

LG4 Calculate, interpret, and evaluate the internal rate of return (IRR).

LG5 Use net present value profiles to compare net present value and internal rate of return techniques.

LG6 Discuss NPV and IRR in terms of conflicting rankings and the theoretical and practical strengths of each approach.

LG1

9.1 Overview of Capital Budgeting Techniques

When firms have developed relevant cash flows, as demonstrated in Chapter 8, they then analyze them to assess whether a project is acceptable or to rank projects. A number of techniques are available for performing such analyses. The preferred approaches integrate time value procedures (Chapter 5), risk and return considerations (Chapter 6), and valuation concepts (Chapter 7) to select capital expenditures that are consistent with the firm's goal of maximizing owners' wealth. This chapter focuses on the use of these techniques in a certain environment to evaluate capital expenditure proposals for decision-making purposes; Chapter 10 introduces risk and other refinements in capital budgeting.

Which Will It Be?

Any time you make a decision, you employ decision-making criteria of some sort. When you chose a college, for example, you considered the size, location, reputation, and cost of your various choices. Looking over the multitude of schools, you undoubtedly rejected many and put others on a list of "possibles." Eventually, you probably came up with a ranked list of your choices and applied to some number of those schools—at which point the schools undertook a comparable evaluation of your academic record. So, too, do companies use decision-making criteria in evaluating capital budgeting projects. Chapter 8 laid out the cash inflows and outflows that companies consider relevant in making such decisions. This chapter focuses on the techniques that companies use to accept or reject and to rank possible projects.

Career Key

Accounting personnel will help determine the after-tax cash flows for capital expenditure proposals. They are more familiar with the tax code and have access to much of the cost data.

We will use one basic problem to illustrate all the techniques described in this chapter. The problem concerns Bennett Company, a medium-sized metal fabricator that is currently contemplating two projects: project A requires an initial investment of $42,000, and project B requires an initial investment of $45,000. The projected relevant operating cash inflows for the two projects are presented in Table 9.1 and depicted on the time lines in Figure 9.1.[1] The projects

---

1. For simplification, these 5-year-lived projects with 5 years of cash inflows are used throughout this chapter. Projects with usable lives equal to the number of years of cash inflows are also included in the end-of-chapter problems. Recall from Chapter 8 that under current tax law, MACRS depreciation results in $n + 1$ years of depreciation for an n-year class asset. This means that projects will commonly have at least 1 year of cash flow beyond their recovery period. In actual practice, usable lives of projects (and the associated cash inflows) may differ significantly from their depreciable lives. Generally, under MACRS, usable lives are longer than depreciable lives.

TABLE 9.1	Capital Expenditure Data for Bennett Company	
	Project A	Project B
Initial investment	$42,000	$45,000
Year	Operating cash inflows	
1	$14,000	$28,000
2	14,000	12,000
3	14,000	10,000
4	14,000	10,000
5	14,000	10,000
Average	$14,000	$14,000

Hint Remember, the initial investment is an *outflow* occurring at time
zero.

exhibit *conventional cash flow patterns*, which are assumed throughout the text. In addition, at this point we continue to assume that all projects' cash flows have the same level of risk, that projects being compared have equal usable lives, and that the firm has unlimited funds. Because very few decisions are actually made

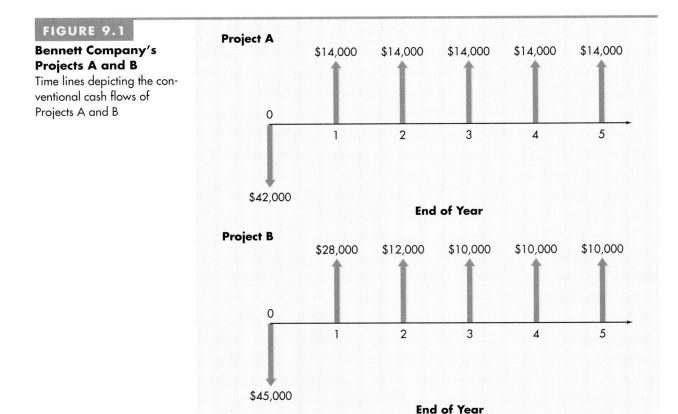

FIGURE 9.1

Bennett Company's Projects A and B
Time lines depicting the conventional cash flows of Projects A and B

under such conditions, some of these simplifying assumptions are relaxed in Chapter 10. In the next three sections we begin with a look at the three most popular capital budgeting techniques—payback period, net present value, and internal rate of return.[2]

? Review Question

9–1   Once the firm has determined its projects' relevant cash flows, what must it do next? What is its goal in selecting projects?

9.2 Payback Period

payback period
The exact amount of time required for a firm to recover its initial investment in a project as calculated from *cash inflows.*

Payback periods are commonly used to evaluate proposed investments. The **payback period** is the exact amount of time required for the firm to recover its initial investment in a project as calculated from *cash inflows.* In the case of an *annuity,* the payback period can be found by dividing the initial investment by the annual cash inflow. For a *mixed stream* of cash inflows, the yearly cash inflows must be accumulated until the initial investment is recovered. Although popular, the payback period is generally viewed as an *unsophisticated capital budgeting technique,* because it does *not* explicitly consider the time value of money by discounting cash flows to find present value.

The Decision Criteria

When the payback period is used to make accept–reject decisions, the decision criteria are as follows:

- If the payback period is *less than* the maximum acceptable payback period, *accept* the project.
- If the payback period is *greater than* the maximum acceptable payback period, *reject* the project.

The length of the maximum acceptable payback period is determined by management. This value is set *subjectively,* based on a number of factors including, but not limited to, the type of project (expansion, replacement, renewal, etc.), the perceived risk of the project, and the perceived relationship between the payback period and share value. It is simply a value that management feels that on average will result in good—that is, value-creating—investment decisions.

---

2. Two other closely related techniques that are sometimes used to evaluate capital budgeting projects are the *average (or accounting) rate of return (ARR)* and the *profitability index (PI).* The ARR is an unsophisticated technique that is calculated by dividing a project's average profits after taxes by its average investment. Because it fails to consider cash flows and the time value of money, it is ignored here. The PI, sometimes called the *benefit–cost ratio,* is calculated by dividing the present value of cash inflows by the initial investment. This technique, which does consider the time value of money, is sometimes used as a starting point in the selection of projects under capital rationing; the more popular NPV and IRR methods are discussed here.

Example ▼ We can calculate the payback period for Bennett Company's projects A and B using the data in Table 9.1. For project A, which is an annuity, the payback period is 3.0 years ($42,000 initial investment ÷ $14,000 annual cash inflow). Because project B generates a mixed stream of cash inflows, the calculation of its payback period is not as clear-cut. In year 1, the firm will recover $28,000 of its $45,000 initial investment. By the end of year 2, $40,000 ($28,000 from year 1 + $12,000 from year 2) will be recovered. At the end of year 3, $50,000 ($40,000 from years 1 and 2 + $10,000 from year 3) will be recovered. Because the amount received by the end of year 3 is greater than the initial investment of $45,000, the payback period is somewhere between 2 and 3 years. Only 50% of the year 3 cash inflow of $10,000 is needed to complete the payback of the initial $45,000. The payback period for project B is therefore 2.5 years (2 years + 50% of year 3).

If Bennett's maximum acceptable payback period were 2.75 years, project A would be rejected and project B would be accepted. If the maximum payback were 2.25 years, both projects would be rejected. If the projects were being ranked, project B would be preferred over project A, because it has a shorter payback period. ▲

Pros and Cons of Payback Periods

The payback period is widely used by (1) large firms to evaluate small projects and (2) small firms to evaluate most projects. Its popularity in these instances results from its computational simplicity and intuitive appeal. It is also appealing in that it considers cash flows rather than accounting profits. By measuring how quickly the firm recovers its initial investment, it also gives *some* implicit consideration to the timing of cash flows and therefore to the time value of money. Because it can be viewed as a measure of *risk exposure,* many firms use the payback period as a decision criterion or as a supplement to sophisticated decision techniques. The longer the firm must wait to recover its invested funds, the greater the possibility of a calamity. Therefore, the shorter the payback period, the lower the firm's exposure to such risk.

The major weakness of the payback period is that the appropriate payback period is merely a subjectively determined number. It cannot be specified in light of the wealth maximization goal because it is not based on discounting cash flows to determine whether they add to the firm's value. Instead, the appropriate payback period is simply the maximum acceptable period of time over which management decides that a project's cash flows must break even (i.e., just equal the initial investment). A second weakness is that this approach fails to take *fully* into account the time factor in the value of money.[3] This weakness can be illustrated by an example.

> **Hint** In *all three* of the decision methods presented in this text, the relevant data are *after-tax cash flows.* The only relevance of accounting profit is to help determine the after-tax cash flow.

> **Hint** The payback period indicates to firms taking on projects of high risk how quickly they can recover their investment. In addition, it tells firms with limited sources of capital how quickly the funds invested in a given project will become available for future projects.

Example ▼ DeYarman Enterprises, a small medical appliance manufacturer, is considering two mutually exclusive projects, which it has named projects Gold and Silver. The firm uses only the payback period to choose projects. The relevant cash

---

3. To consider differences in timing *explicitly* in applying the payback method, the *present value payback period* is sometimes used. It is found by first calculating the present value of the cash inflows at the appropriate discount rate and then finding the payback period by using the present value of the cash inflows.

TABLE 9.2	Relevant Cash Flows and Payback Periods for DeYarman Enterprises' Projects	
	Project Gold	Project Silver
Initial investment	$50,000	$50,000
Year	Cash inflows	
1	$ 5,000	$40,000
2	5,000	2,000
3	40,000	8,000
4	10,000	10,000
5	10,000	10,000
Payback period	3 years	3 years

flows and payback period for each project are given in Table 9.2. Both projects have 3-year payback periods, which would suggest that they are equally desirable. But comparison of the pattern of cash inflows over the first 3 years shows that more of the $50,000 initial investment in project Silver is recovered sooner than is recovered for project Gold. For example, in year 1, $40,000 of the $50,000 invested in project Silver is recovered, whereas only $5,000 of the $50,000 investment in project Gold is recovered. Given the time value of money, project Silver would clearly be preferred over project Gold, in spite of the fact

In Practice

Limits of Payback Analysis

The high labor component of U.S. textile manufacturers creates a cost disadvantage that makes it hard for them to compete in global markets. They lag behind other U.S. industries and foreign textile producers in terms of plant automation. One key hurdle is payback period. The industry standard for capital expenditure projects for machinery is 3 years. Because few major automation projects have such a short payback period, the pace of automation has been very slow. For example, the payback period for materials transport automation—moving material from one point to another with minimum labor—averages 5 to 6 years.

This situation underscores a major limitation of payback period analysis. Companies that rely only on the payback period may not give fair consideration to technology that can greatly improve their long-term manufacturing effectiveness. Whereas Japanese managers will invest $1 million to replace one job, U.S. managers invest about $250,000. At prevailing wage rates, the Japanese accept a 5- to 6-year payback, compared to a period of 3 to 4 years in the United States. These differences demonstrate the linkages that exist between a firm's operations and finance.

TABLE 9.3	Calculation of the Payback Period for Rashid Company's Two Alternative Investment Projects	
	Project X	Project Y
Initial investment	$10,000	$10,000
Year	Cash inflows	
1	$5,000	$3,000
2	5,000	4,000
3	1,000	3,000
4	100	4,000
5	100	3,000
Payback period	2 years	3 years

that they both have identical 3-year payback periods. The payback approach does not fully account for the time value of money, which if recognized, would ▲ cause project Silver to be preferred over project Gold.

A third weakness of payback is its failure to recognize cash flows that occur after the payback period.

Example ▼ Data for two investment opportunities—X and Y—of Rashid Company, a software developer, are given in Table 9.3. The payback period for project X is 2 years; for project Y, it is 3 years. Strict adherence to the payback approach suggests that project X is preferable to project Y. However, if we look beyond the payback period, we see that project X returns only an additional $1,200 ($1,000 in year 3 + $100 in year 4 + $100 in year 5), whereas project Y returns an additional $7,000 ($4,000 in year 4 + $3,000 in year 5). On the basis of this information, project Y appears preferable to X. The payback approach ignored the cash ▲ inflows past the end of the payback period.[4]

? Review Questions

9–2   What is the *payback period?* How is it calculated?

9–3   What weaknesses are commonly associated with the use of the payback period to evaluate a proposed investment?

---

4. To get around this weakness, some analysts add a desired dollar return to the initial investment and then calculate the payback period for the increased amount. For example, if the analyst wished to pay back the initial investment plus 20% for projects X and Y in Table 9.3, the amount to be recovered would be $12,000 [$10,000 + (.20 × $10,000)]. For project X, the payback period would be infinite because the $12,000 would never be recovered; for project Y, the payback period would be 3.50 years [3 years + ($2,000 ÷ $4,000) years]. Clearly, project Y would be preferred.

9.3 Net Present Value (NPV)

Because *net present value (NPV)* gives explicit consideration to the time value of money, it is considered a *sophisticated capital budgeting technique.* All such techniques in one way or another discount the firm's cash flows at a specified rate. This rate—often called the *discount rate, required return, cost of capital,* or *opportunity cost*—refers to the minimum return that must be earned on a project to leave the firm's market value unchanged. In this chapter, we take this rate as a "given." In a later chapter (Chapter 11) we will explain how it is calculated.

The **net present value (NPV)** is found by subtracting a project's initial investment (*II*) from the present value of its cash inflows (CF_t) discounted at a rate equal to the firm's cost of capital (*k*):

net present value (NPV)
A sophisticated capital budgeting technique; found by subtracting a project's initial investment from the present value of its cash inflows discounted at a rate equal to the firm's cost of capital.

$$\text{NPV} = \text{present value of cash inflows} - \text{initial investment}$$

$$\text{NPV} = \sum_{t=1}^{n} \frac{CF_t}{(1+k)^t} - II \tag{9.1}$$

$$= \sum_{t=1}^{n} (CF_t \times PVIF_{k,t}) - II \tag{9.1a}$$

By using NPV, both inflows and outflows are measured in terms of present dollars. Because we are dealing only with investments that have *conventional cash flow patterns,* the initial investment is automatically stated in terms of today's dollars. If it were not, the present value of a project would be found by subtracting the present value of outflows from the present value of inflows.

The Decision Criteria

When NPV is used to make accept–reject decisions, the decision criteria are as follows:

- If the NPV is *greater than* $0, *accept* the project.
- If the NPV is *less than* $0, *reject* the project.

If the NPV is greater than $0, the firm will earn a return greater than its cost of capital. Such action should enhance the market value of the firm and therefore the wealth of its owners.

Example ▼ The net present value (NPV) approach can be illustrated by using Bennett Company data presented in Table 9.1. If the firm has a 10% cost of capital, the net present values for projects A (an annuity) and B (a mixed stream) can be calculated as in Table 9.4. These calculations are based on the techniques presented in Chapter 5 using present value table factors.[5] The results show that the net present values of projects A and B are $11,074 and $10,914, respectively. Both projects are acceptable, because the net present value of each is greater than $0. If the projects were being ranked, however, project A would be considered ▲ superior to B, because it has a higher net present value ($11,074 versus $10,914).

---

5. Alternatively, a financial calculator could have been used to streamline these calculations as described in Chapter 5. Most of the more sophisticated financial calculators are preprogrammed to find NPVs. With these calculators, you merely punch in all cash flows along with the cost of capital or discount rate and depress **NPV** to find the net present value. Using such a calculator, the resulting values for projects A and B are $11,071 and $10,924, respectively.

TABLE 9.4	The Calculation of NPVs for Bennett Company's Capital Expenditure Alternatives

Project A

Annual cash inflow	$14,000
× Present value annuity interest factor, $PVIFA^a$	3.791
Present value of cash inflows	$53,074
− Initial investment	42,000
Net present value (NPV)	$11,074

Project B

Year	Cash inflows (1)	Present value interest factor, $PVIF^b$ (2)	Present value $[(1) \times (2)]$ (3)
1	$28,000	.909	$25,452
2	12,000	.826	9,912
3	10,000	.751	7,510
4	10,000	.683	6,830
5	10,000	.621	6,210
		Present value of cash inflows	$55,914
		− Initial investment	45,000
		Net present value (NPV)	$10,914

[a]From Table A-4, for 5 years and 10%.
[b]From Table A-3, for given year and 10%.

❓ Review Questions

9–4   What is the *net present value (NPV)?* How is it calculated for a project with a *conventional cash flow pattern?*

9–5   What are the acceptance criteria for NPV? How do they relate to the firm's market value?

9.4 Internal Rate of Return (IRR)

internal rate of return (IRR)
A sophisticated capital budgeting technique; the discount rate that equates the present value of cash inflows with the initial investment associated with a project, thereby causing NPV = $0; the compound annual rate of return the firm will earn if it invests in the project and receives the given cash inflows.

The *internal rate of return (IRR)* is probably the most used *sophisticated capital budgeting technique* for evaluating investment alternatives. However, it is considerably more difficult than NPV to calculate by hand. The **internal rate of return (IRR)** is the discount rate that equates the present value of cash inflows with the initial investment associated with a project. The IRR, in other words, is the discount rate that equates the NPV of an investment opportunity with $0 (because the present value of cash inflows equals the initial investment). It is the compound annual rate of return that the firm will earn if it invests in the project and receives the given cash inflows. Mathematically, the IRR is found by solving Equation 9.1 for the value of k that causes NPV to equal $0.

$$\$0 = \sum_{t=1}^{n} \frac{CF_t}{(1 + IRR)^t} - II$$

$$\sum_{t=1}^{n} \frac{CF_t}{(1 + IRR)^t} = II \qquad (9.2)$$

The actual calculation by hand of the IRR from Equation 9.2 is no easy chore.

The Decision Criteria

When IRR is used to make accept–reject decisions, the decision criteria are as follows:

- If the IRR is *greater than* the cost of capital, *accept* the project.
- If the IRR is *less than* the cost of capital, *reject* the project.

These criteria guarantee that the firm earns at least its required return. Such an outcome should enhance the market value of the firm and therefore the wealth of its owners.

Career Key

Information systems analysts will design decision modules that help reduce the amount of work required to analyze proposed capital expenditures. With their help, techniques such as sensitivity analysis are easier to apply.

Calculating the IRR

The IRR can be found either by using trial-and-error techniques or with the aid of a sophisticated financial calculator or a computer.[6] Here we demonstrate the trial-and-error approach. Calculating the IRR for an annuity is considerably easier than calculating it for a mixed stream of operating cash inflows.[7] The steps

---

6. Nearly all inexpensive financial calculators can be used to find the IRR of an annuity, but they lack a function for finding the IRR of a mixed stream of cash flows. Most more sophisticated (and more expensive) financial calculators are preprogrammed to find IRRs. With these calculators, you merely punch in all cash flows and depress **IRR** to find the internal rate of return. Computer software, like the *PMF CD-ROM* that accompanies this text, is also available for calculating IRRs.

7. The ease of calculating the IRR for an annuity as well as the steps in the process results from an ability to simplify Equation 9.2. Because for annuities, $CF_1 = CF_2 = \cdots = CF_n$, the CF_t term can be factored from Equation 9.2. Doing this, we get

$$CF_t \sum_{t=1}^{n} \frac{1}{(1 + IRR)^t} = II$$

Dividing both sides of the equation by CF_t, we get

$$\sum_{t=1}^{n} \frac{1}{(1 + IRR)^t} = \frac{II}{CF_t}$$

Because the left side of the equation is equal to $PVIFA_{IRR,n}$ and the right side equals the payback period—the initial investment divided by the annual cash inflow—it is not difficult to estimate the IRR for annuities.

involved in calculating the IRR in each case are given in Table 9.5. These steps are illustrated by the following example.

Example ▼ The two-step procedure given in Table 9.5 for finding the IRR of an *annuity* can be demonstrated by using Bennett Company's project A cash flows given in Table 9.1.

Step 1   Dividing the initial investment of $42,000 by the annual cash inflow of $14,000 results in a payback period of 3.000 years ($42,000 ÷ $14,000 = 3.000).

Step 2   According to Table A–4, the *PVIFA* factors closest to 3.000 for 5 years are 3.058 (for 19%) and 2.991 (for 20%). The value closest to 3.000 is 2.991; therefore, the IRR for project A, to the nearest 1%, is 20%. The actual value, which is between 19 and 20%, could be found by using a calculator[8] or computer or by interpolation[9]; it is 19.86%. (*Note:* For our purposes, values rounded to the nearest 1% will suffice.) Project A with an IRR of 20% is quite acceptable, because this IRR is above the firm's 10% cost of capital.

The seven-step procedure given in Table 9.5 for finding the internal rate of return of a *mixed stream* of cash inflows can be illustrated by using Bennett Company's project B cash flows given in Table 9.1.

Step 1   Summing the cash inflows for years 1 through 5 results in total cash inflows of $70,000. That amount, when divided by the number of years in the project's life, results in an average annual cash inflow of $14,000 [($28,000 + $12,000 + $10,000 + $10,000 + $10,000) ÷ 5].

Step 2   Dividing the initial outlay of $45,000 by the average annual cash inflow of $14,000 results in an "average payback period" (or present value of an annuity factor, *PVIFA*) of 3.214 years.

Step 3   In Table A–4, the factor closest to 3.214 for 5 years is 3.199, the factor for a discount rate of 17%. The starting estimate of the IRR is therefore 17%.

Step 4   Because the actual early-year cash inflows are greater than the average annual cash inflows of $14,000, a *subjective* increase of 2% is made in the discount rate. This makes the estimated IRR 19%.

---

8. The procedure for using a financial calculator to find the unknown interest rate on an equal-payment loan described in Chapter 5 can be used to find the IRR for an annuity. When applying this procedure, we treat the life of the annuity the same as the term of the loan, the initial investment the same as the loan principal, and the annual cash inflows the same as the annual loan payments. The resulting solution is the IRR for the annuity rather than the interest rate on the loan.

9. *Interpolation* is a mathematical technique used to find intermediate or fractional values when only integer data are provided. Because interest factors for whole percentages are included in the financial tables in Appendix A, interpolation is required to calculate more precisely the internal rate of return. For information on how to interpolate a more precise answer, see the book's homepage at www.awlonline.com/gitman.

TABLE 9.5   Steps for Calculating the Internal Rates of Return (IRRs) of Annuities and Mixed Streams

FOR AN ANNUITY

Step 1: Calculate the payback period for the project.[a]

Step 2: Find, for the life of the project, the present value interest factor closest to the payback value. (Use Table A-4, which shows the present value interest factors for a $1 annuity, *PVIFA*.) The discount rate associated with that factor is the internal rate of return (IRR) to the nearest 1%.

FOR A MIXED STREAM[b]

Step 1: Find the average annual cash inflow by dividing the sum of the annual cash inflows by the number of years in the project's life.

Step 2: Divide the average annual cash inflow into the initial investment to get an "average payback period" (or present value interest factor for a $1 annuity, *PVIFA*). The average payback is needed to estimate the IRR for the average annual cash inflow.

Step 3: Find the discount rate associated with the present value interest factor in Table A-4 (*PVIFA*) for the life of the project that is closest to the average payback period (as described in Step 2 for finding the IRR of an annuity). The result will be a *very rough* approximation of the IRR based on the assumption that the mixed stream of cash inflows is an annuity.

Step 4:[c] Adjust subjectively the IRR obtained in Step 3 by comparing the pattern of average annual cash inflows (calculated in Step 1) to the actual mixed stream of cash inflows. If the actual cash flow stream seems to have higher inflows in the earlier years than the average stream, adjust the IRR up. If the actual cash inflows in the earlier years are below the average, adjust the IRR down. The amount of adjustment up or down typically ranges from 1 to 3 percentage points, depending upon how much the actual cash inflow stream's pattern deviates from the average annual cash inflows. For small deviations, an adjustment of around 1 percentage point may be best, whereas for large deviations, adjustments of around 3 percentage points are generally appropriate. If the average cash inflows seem fairly close to the actual pattern, make no adjustment in the IRR.

Step 5: Calculate the net present value of the mixed stream project using the IRR from Step 4. Be sure to use Table A-3 (the present value interest factors for $1, *PVIF*), treating the estimated IRR as the discount rate.

Step 6: If the resulting NPV is greater than zero, subjectively raise the discount rate; if the resulting NPV is less than zero, subjectively lower the discount rate. The greater the deviation of the resulting NPV from zero, the larger the subjective adjustment. Typically, adjustments of 1 to 3 percentage points are used for relatively small deviations, whereas larger adjustments are required for relatively large deviations.

Step 7: Calculate the NPV using the new discount rate. Repeat Step 6. Stop as soon as two *consecutive* discount rates that cause the NPV to be positive and negative, respectively, have been found.[d] Whichever of these rates causes the NPV to be closer to zero is the IRR to the nearest 1%.

---

[a]The payback period calculated actually represents the interest factor for the present value of an annuity (*PVIFA*) for the given life discounted at an unknown rate, which, once determined, represents the IRR for the project.

[b]Note that subjective estimates are suggested in Steps 4 and 6. After working a number of these problems, a "feel" for the appropriate subjective adjustment, or "educated guess," may result.

[c]The purpose of this step is to provide a more accurate first estimate of the IRR. This step can be skipped.

[d]A shortcut method is to find a discount rate that results in a positive NPV and another that results in a negative NPV. Using only these two values, one can interpolate between the two discount rates to find the IRR. This approach, which may be nearly as accurate as that described before, can guarantee an answer after only two NPV calculations. Of course, because interpolation involves a straight-line approximation to an exponential function, the wider the interpolation interval, the less accurate the estimate.

Step 5 By using the present value interest factors (*PVIF*) for 19% and the correct year from Table A–3, we calculate the net present value of the mixed stream as follows:

Year (*t*)	Cash inflows (1)	$PVIF_{19\%,t}$ (2)	Present value at 19% [(1) × (2)] (3)
1	$28,000	.840	$23,520
2	12,000	.706	8,472
3	10,000	.593	5,930
4	10,000	.499	4,990
5	10,000	.419	4,190
	Present value of cash inflows		$47,102
	− Initial investment		45,000
	Net present value (NPV)		$ 2,102

Steps 6 and 7 Because the net present value of $2,102, calculated in Step 5, is greater than zero, the discount rate should be subjectively increased. Because the NPV deviates by only about 5% from the $45,000 initial investment, let's try a 2 percentage point increase, to 21%.

Year (*t*)	Cash inflows (1)	$PVIF_{21\%,t}$ (2)	Present value at 21% [(1) × (2)] (3)
1	$28,000	.826	$23,128
2	12,000	.683	8,196
3	10,000	.564	5,640
4	10,000	.467	4,670
5	10,000	.386	3,860
	Present value of cash inflows		$45,494
	− Initial investment		45,000
	Net present value (NPV)		$ 494

These calculations indicate that the NPV of $494 for an IRR of 21% is reasonably close to, but still greater than, zero. Thus a higher discount rate should be tried. Because we are so close, let's try a 1 percentage point increase, to 22%. As the following calculations show, the net present value using a discount rate of 22% is −$256.

Year (t)	Cash inflows (1)	$PVIF_{22\%,t}$ (2)	Present value at 22% [(1) × (2)] (3)
1	$28,000	.820	$22,960
2	12,000	.672	8,064
3	10,000	.551	5,510
4	10,000	.451	4,510
5	10,000	.370	3,700
	Present value of cash inflows		$44,744
	− Initial investment		45,000
	Net present value (NPV)		−$ 256

Because 21 and 22% are consecutive discount rates that give positive and negative net present values, we can stop the trial-and-error process here. The IRR that we are seeking is the discount rate for which the NPV is closest to $0. For project B, 22% causes the NPV to be closer to $0 than 21%, so we will use 22% as the IRR. If we had used a financial calculator or a computer or interpolation, the exact IRR would be 21.65%; as indicated earlier, for our purposes the IRR rounded to the nearest 1% will suffice.

Project B is acceptable, because its IRR of approximately 22% is greater than Bennett Company's 10% cost of capital. This is the same conclusion reached by using the NPV criterion.

It is interesting to note in the example that the IRR suggests that project B, which has an IRR of approximately 22 percent, is preferable to project A, which has an IRR of approximately 20 percent. This conflicts with the rankings of the projects obtained in an earlier example by using NPV. Such conflicts are not unusual. *There is no guarantee that these two techniques—NPV and IRR—will rank projects in the same order. However, both methods should reach the same conclusion about the acceptability or nonacceptability of projects.*

? Review Questions

9–6 What is the *internal rate of return (IRR)* on an investment? How is it determined?

9–7 What are the acceptance criteria for IRR? How do they relate to the firm's market value?

9–8 Do the net present value (NPV) and internal rate of return (IRR) always agree with respect to accept–reject decisions? With respect to ranking decisions? Explain.

In Practice

Creating Value with EVA®

Answering the question, "Does the company use investors' money wisely?" is one of the financial manager's chief responsibilities and biggest challenges. At many firms—from Fortune 500 companies and investment firms to community hospitals—economic value added (EVA)® is the tool of choice for making capital budgeting and other investment decisions, measuring overall financial performance, and motivating management.

Developed in 1983 and trademarked by financial consultants Stern Stewart, EVA (defined in Chapter 1) is the difference between a project's net operating profits after taxes and the cost of funds used to finance the project (the amount of capital times the company's cost of capital). In addition, EVA treats research and development (R&D) outlays as investments in future products or processes and capitalizes instead of expensing them. An investment with a positive EVA earns more than the firm's cost of capital and therefore creates wealth. It is similar to internal rate of return calculations, except that it states the results in dollars rather than percentages. The EVA calculation can be applied to specific long-term investments such as new facilities or equipment as well as to the company as a whole.

Companies that use EVA believe that it leads to better overall performance. Managers focus on allocating and managing assets, not just on accounting profits. "We're much more attentive to the use of capital and the amount of capital in each business," says Warren Posey, Armstrong World Industries Inc. assistant treasurer and director of investor relations.

EVA is not a panacea, however. Its critics say it's just another accounting measure and may not be the right one for many companies. Because it favors big projects in big companies, they claim it doesn't do a good job on capital allocation. Companies in capital-intensive industries are big supporters of EVA, though. Pharmaceutical company Eli Lilly was an early adopter. "[EVA] really highlights the fact that once you've invested in an asset like a lab or new drug, you're required on an ongoing basis to command a shareholder return on that asset," explains CEO Randall Tobias.

Engine manufacturer Briggs & Stratton also praises EVA. Jim Weir, the company's executive vice president of operations, calls EVA the "single best measurement tool that we could find for our business ... because it provided a common language ... among all our different operating divisions." Based on an EVA analysis, Briggs & Stratton decided to outsource the manufacture of molded plastic components and some engines. As a result, capital requirements fell and operating profits rose sharply.

Millennium Chemicals Inc., based in Iselin, New Jersey, also credits EVA with improved financial performance. Its former planning and incentive compensation system was based on return on capital and operating profit, not on increasing shareholder value. Executives chose projects that increased profits over those with satisfactory returns that lowered their unit's average return on assets. With EVA, managers evaluate projects over a longer period of time to see if the investment maximizes long-term cash flows. They take a new approach to capital spending that emphasizes long-term growth for the company and for its shareholders.

9.5 Comparing NPV and IRR Techniques

For conventional projects, *net present value (NPV) and internal rate of return (IRR) will always generate the same accept–reject decision, but differences in their underlying assumptions can cause them to rank projects differently.* To understand the differences and preferences surrounding these techniques, we need to look at net present value profiles, conflicting rankings, and the question of which approach is better.

Net Present Value Profiles

net present value profile
Graph that depicts the net present value of a project for various discount rates.

Projects can be compared graphically by constructing **net present value profiles** that depict their net present values for various discount rates. These profiles are useful in evaluating and comparing projects, especially when conflicting rankings exist.

E x a m p l e ▼ To prepare net present value profiles for Bennett Company's two projects, A and B, the first step is to develop a number of discount-rate–net-present-value coordinates. Three coordinates can be easily obtained for each project; they are at discount rates of 0%, 10% (the cost of capital, k), and the IRR. The net present value at a 0% discount rate is found by merely adding all the cash inflows and subtracting the initial investment. Using the data in Table 9.1 and Figure 9.1, for project A we get

$$(\$14,000 + \$14,000 + \$14,000 + \$14,000 + \$14,000) - \$42,000 = \$28,000$$

and for project B we get

$$(\$28,000 + \$12,000 + \$10,000 + \$10,000 + \$10,000) - \$45,000 = \$25,000$$

The net present values for projects A and B at the 10% cost of capital were found to be $11,074 and $10,914, respectively (in Table 9.4). Because the IRR is the discount rate for which net present value equals zero, the IRRs of 20% for project A and 22% for project B result in $0 NPVs. The three sets of coordinates for each of the projects are summarized in Table 9.6.

Plotting the data from Table 9.6 on a set of discount-rate–NPV axes results in the net present value profiles for projects A and B shown in Figure 9.2. An analysis of Figure 9.2 indicates that for any discount rate less than approximately 10.7%, the NPV for project A is greater than the NPV for project B. Beyond this point, the NPV for project B is greater than that for project A. Because the net present value profiles for projects A and B cross at a positive NPV, the IRRs for the projects cause conflicting rankings whenever they are compared to NPVs ▲ calculated at discount rates below 10.7%.

The NPV profiles for the Bennett Company example demonstrate that *conflicting rankings* of projects by NPV and IRR can occur.

TABLE 9.6	Discount-Rate–NPV Coordinates for Projects A and B

Discount rate	Net present value	
	Project A	Project B
0%	$28,000	$25,000
10	11,074	10,914
20	0	—
22	—	0

FIGURE 9.2

NPV Profiles

Net present value profiles for Bennett Company's projects A and B

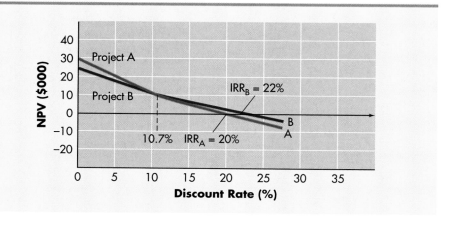

Conflicting Rankings

Ranking is an important consideration when projects are mutually exclusive or when capital rationing is necessary. When projects are mutually exclusive, ranking enables the firm to determine the best project from a financial viewpoint. When capital rationing is necessary, ranking projects will provide a logical starting point for determining the group of projects to accept. As we'll see, **conflicting rankings** using NPV and IRR result from *differences in the magnitude and timing of cash flows.*

The underlying cause of conflicting rankings is the implicit assumption concerning the *reinvestment* of **intermediate cash inflows**—cash inflows received prior to the termination of a project. NPV assumes that intermediate cash inflows are reinvested at the cost of capital, whereas IRR assumes that intermedi-

conflicting rankings
Conflicts in the ranking given a project by NPV and IRR, resulting from *differences in the magnitude and timing of cash flows.*

intermediate cash inflows
Cash inflows received prior to the termination of a project.

ate cash inflows are invested at a rate equal to the project's IRR.[10] These differing assumptions can be demonstrated with an example.

Example ▼ A project requiring a $170,000 initial investment is expected to provide operating cash inflows of $52,000, $78,000, and $100,000 at the end of each of the next 3 years. The NPV of the project (at the firm's 10% cost of capital) is $16,867 and its IRR is 15%. Clearly, the project is acceptable (NPV = $16,867 > $0 and IRR = 15% > 10% cost of capital). Table 9.7 demonstrates calculation of the project's future value at the end of its 3-year life, assuming both a 10% (its cost of capital) and a 15% (its IRR) rate of return. A future value of $248,720 results from reinvestment at the 10% cost of capital (total in column 5) and a future value of $258,496 results from reinvestment at the 15% IRR (total in column 7).

If the future value in each case in Table 9.7 were viewed as the return received 3 years from today from the $170,000 initial investment, the cash flows would be those given in Table 9.8. The NPVs and IRRs in each case are shown

TABLE 9.7	**Reinvestment Rate Comparisons for a Project**[a]						
				Reinvestment rate			
		Number of years earning		10%		15%	
Year (1)	Cash inflows (2)	interest (*t*) [3 − (1)] (3)	$FVIF_{10\%,t}$ (4)	Future value [(2) × (4)] (5)	$FVIF_{15\%,t}$ (6)	Future value [(2) × (6)] (7)
1	$ 52,000	2	1.210	$ 62,920	1.323	$ 68,796
2	78,000	1	1.100	85,800	1.150	89,700
3	100,000	0	1.000	100,000	1.000	100,000
		Future value end of year 3		$248,720		$258,496

NPV @ 10% = $16,867

IRR = 15%

[a]Initial investment in this project is $170,000.

---

10. To eliminate the reinvestment rate assumption of the IRR, some practitioners calculate the *modified internal rate of return (MIRR)*. The MIRR is found by converting each operating cash inflow to its future value measured at the end of the project's life and then summing the future values of all inflows to get the project's *terminal value*. Each future value is found by using the cost of capital, thereby eliminating the reinvestment rate criticism of the traditional IRR. The MIRR represents the discount rate that causes the terminal value to just equal the initial investment. Because it uses the cost of capital as the reinvestment rate, the MIRR is generally viewed as a better measure of a project's true profitability than the IRR. Although this technique is frequently used in commercial real estate valuation and is a preprogrammed function on some sophisticated financial calculators, its failure to resolve the issue of conflicting rankings and its theoretical inferiority to NPV have resulted in the MIRR's receiving only limited attention and acceptance in the financial literature. For a thorough analysis of the arguments surrounding IRR and MIRR, see D. Anthony Plath and William F. Kennedy, "Teaching Return-Based Measures of Project Evaluation," *Financial Practice and Education* (Spring/Summer 1994), pp. 77–86.

TABLE 9.8	Project Cash Flows After Reinvestment	
	Reinvestment rate	
	10%	15%
Initial investment	$170,000	
Year	Operating cash inflows	
1	$ 0	$ 0
2	0	0
3	248,720	258,496
NPV @ 10%	$ 16,867	$ 24,213
IRR	13.5%	15.0%

below the cash flows in Table 9.8. You can see that at the 10% reinvestment rate, the NPV remains at $16,867; reinvestment at the 15% IRR produces an NPV of $24,213.

From this result, it should be clear that the NPV technique assumes reinvestment at the cost of capital (10% in this example). (Note that with reinvestment at 10%, the IRR would be 13.5%.) On the other hand, the IRR technique assumes an ability to reinvest intermediate cash inflows at the IRR. If reinvestment does not occur at this rate, the IRR will differ from 15%. Reinvestment at a rate below the IRR would result in an IRR below that calculated (at 13.5%, for example, if the reinvestment rate were only 10%). Reinvestment at a rate above the IRR would result in an IRR above that calculated.

In general, projects with similar-sized investments and lower cash inflows in the early years tend to be preferred at lower discount rates.[11] Projects having higher cash inflows in the early years tend to be preferred at higher discount rates. Why? Because at high discount rates, later-year cash inflows tend to be severely penalized in present value terms. For example, at a high discount rate, say, 20 percent, the present value of $1 received at the end of 5 years is about 40 cents, whereas the present value of $1 received at the end of 15 years is less than 7 cents. Clearly, at high discount rates a project's early year cash inflows count most in terms of its NPV. Table 9.9 summarizes the preferences associated with extreme discount rates and dissimilar cash inflow patterns.

---

11. Because differences in the relative sizes of initial investments can also affect conflicts in rankings, the initial investments are assumed to be similar. This permits isolation of the effect of differences in the magnitude and timing of cash inflows on project rankings.

TABLE 9.9	Preferences Associated with Extreme Discount Rates and Dissimilar Cash Inflow Patterns

	Cash inflow pattern	
Discount rate	Lower early year cash inflows	Higher early year cash inflows
Low	Preferred	Not preferred
High	Not preferred	Preferred

Example ▼

In an earlier example, Bennett Company's projects A and B were found to have conflicting rankings at the firm's 10% cost of capital. This finding was depicted in Figure 9.2. If we review each project's cash inflow pattern as presented in Table 9.1 and Figure 9.1, we see that although the projects require similar initial investments, they have dissimilar cash inflow patterns—project A has level cash inflows and project B has higher early-year cash inflows. Table 9.9 indicates that project B would be preferred over project A at higher discount rates. Figure 9.2 shows that this is in fact the case. At a discount rate in excess of 10.7%, project B's NPV is above that of project A. Clearly, the magnitude and timing of the projects' cash inflows do affect their rankings. ▲

Although the classification of cash inflow patterns in Table 9.9 is useful in explaining conflicting rankings, differences in the magnitude and timing of cash inflows do not guarantee conflicts in ranking. In general, the greater the difference between the magnitude and timing of cash inflows, the greater the likelihood of conflicting rankings. Conflicts based on NPV and IRR can be reconciled computationally; to do so, one creates and analyzes an incremental project reflecting the difference in cash flows between the two mutually exclusive projects. Because a detailed description of this procedure is beyond the scope of an introductory text, suffice it to say that IRR techniques can be used to generate consistently the same project rankings as those obtained by using NPV.

Which Approach Is Better?

It is difficult to choose one approach over the other because the theoretical and practical strengths of the approaches differ. It is therefore wise to view both NPV and IRR techniques in light of each of those dimensions.

Theoretical View

On a purely theoretical basis, NPV is the better approach to capital budgeting. Its theoretical superiority is attributed to a number of factors. Most important is that the use of NPV implicitly assumes that any intermediate cash inflows generated by an investment are *reinvested at the firm's cost of capital.* The use of IRR assumes *reinvestment at the often high rate specified by the IRR.* Because the cost of capital tends to be a reasonable estimate of the rate at which the firm could *actually reinvest* intermediate cash inflows, the use of NPV with its more conservative and realistic reinvestment rate is in theory preferable.

In addition, certain mathematical properties may cause a project with a nonconventional cash flow pattern to have zero or more than one IRR; this problem does not occur with the NPV approach.

Practical View

Evidence suggests that in spite of the theoretical superiority of NPV, *financial managers prefer to use IRR.*[12] The preference for IRR is attributable to the general disposition of businesspeople toward *rates of return* rather than actual *dollar returns.* Because interest rates, profitability, and so on are most often expressed as annual rates of return, the use of IRR makes sense to financial decision makers. They tend to find NPV more difficult to use because it does not measure benefits *relative to the amount invested.* Because a variety of methods and techniques are available for avoiding the pitfalls of the IRR, its widespread use should not be viewed as reflecting a lack of sophistication on the part of financial decision makers.

? Review Questions

9–9   How can a *net present value profile* be used to compare projects when conflicting rankings exist? What causes conflicts in the ranking of projects using net present value and internal rate of return?

9–10 Explain how, on a purely theoretical basis, the assumption concerning the reinvestment of intermediate cash inflows tends to favor the use of NPV over IRR. In practice, which technique is preferred? Why?

SUMMARY

LG1 **Understand role of capital budgeting techniques in the capital budgeting process.**
Capital budgeting techniques are used to analyze and assess project acceptability and ranking. They are applied to each project's relevant cash flows to select capital expenditures that are consistent with the firm's goal of maximizing owners' wealth.

LG2 **Calculate, interpret, and evaluate the payback period.** The payback period measures the exact amount of time required for the firm to recover its initial investment from cash inflows. The formula and decision criteria for the payback period are summarized in Table 9.10. Shorter payback periods are preferred. In addition to its ease of calculation and simple intuitive

---

12. For example, see Harold Bierman, Jr., "Capital Budgeting in 1992: A Survey," *Financial Management* (Autumn 1993), p. 24, and Lawrence J. Gitman and Charles E. Maxwell, "A Longitudinal Comparison of Capital Budgeting Techniques Used by Major U.S. Firms: 1986 versus 1976," *Journal of Applied Business Research* (Fall 1987), pp. 41–50, for discussions of evidence with respect to capital budgeting decision-making practices in major U.S. firms.

TABLE 9.10	Summary of Key Formulas/Definitions and Decision Criteria for Capital Budgeting Techniques	
Technique	**Formula/Definition**	**Decision criteria**
Payback period[a]	*For annuity:* $$\frac{\text{initial investment}}{\text{annual cash inflow}}$$ *For mixed stream:* Calculate cumulative cash inflows on year-to-year basis until the initial investment is recovered.	*Accept* if < maximum acceptable payback period; *reject* if > maximum acceptable payback period.
Net present value (NPV)[b]	Present value of cash inflows − initial investment.	*Accept* if > $0; *reject* if < $0.
Internal rate of return (IRR)[b]	The discount rate that equates the present value of cash inflows with the initial investment, thereby causing NPV = $0.	*Accept* if > the cost of capital; *reject* if < the cost of capital.

[a]Unsophisticated technique, because it does not give explicit consideration to the time value of money.

[b]Sophisticated technique, because it gives explicit consideration to the time value of money.

appeal, the payback period's appeal lies in its consideration of cash flows, the implicit consideration given to timing, and its ability to measure risk exposure. Its weaknesses include its lack of linkage to the wealth maximization goal, failure to explicitly consider time value, and the fact that it ignores cash flows that occur after the payback period.

 Calculate, interpret, and evaluate the net present value (NPV). Because it gives explicit consideration to the time value of money, NPV is considered a sophisticated capital budgeting technique. The basic formula and decision criteria for NPV are summarized in Table 9.10. When calculating NPV, the rate at which cash flows are discounted is often called the discount rate, required return, cost of capital, or opportunity cost. By whatever name, this rate represents the minimum return that must be earned on a project to leave the firm's market value unchanged.

 Calculate, interpret, and evaluate the internal rate of return (IRR). Like NPV, IRR is a sophisticated capital budgeting technique because it explicitly considers the time value of money. The basic formula and decision criteria for

IRR are summarized in Table 9.10. IRR can be viewed as the compound annual rate of return the firm will earn if it invests in a project and receives the given cash inflows. By accepting only those projects with IRRs in excess of the firm's cost of capital, the firm should enhance its market value and the wealth of its owners. Both NPV and IRR provide the same accept–reject decisions for a given project but often conflict when ranking projects.

 Use net present value profiles to compare net present value and internal rate of return techniques. A net present value profile is a graph that depicts the net present value of a project for various discount rates. It is useful in comparing projects, especially when conflicting rankings exist between NPV and IRR. The NPV profile is prepared by developing a number of discount rate–net present value coordinates, often using discount rates of 0 percent, the cost of capital, and the IRR for each project, and then plotting them on the same set of discount rate–NPV axes.

 Discuss NPV and IRR in terms of conflicting rankings and the theoretical and practical strengths of each approach. Conflicting

rankings of projects frequently occur when using NPV and IRR, as a result of differences in the magnitude and timing of each project's cash flows. The underlying cause is the differing implicit assumptions of NPV and IRR with regard to the reinvestment of intermediate cash inflows—cash inflows received prior to termination of a project. NPV assumes that intermediate cash inflows are reinvested at the more conservative cost of capital, whereas IRR assumes reinvestment at the project's IRR. NPV is theoretically preferable to IRR because it assumes the more conservative reinvestment rate and does not exhibit the mathematical problems that can occur when calculating IRRs for nonconventional cash flows. In practice, the IRR is more commonly used because it is consistent with the general preference toward rates of return.

SELF-TEST PROBLEM   (Solution in Appendix B)

ST 9–1   **All techniques with NPV profile—Mutually exclusive projects**   Fitch Industries is in the process of choosing the better of two equal-risk, mutually exclusive, capital expenditure projects—M and N. The relevant cash flows for each project are shown in the following table. The firm's cost of capital is 14%.

	Project M	Project N
Initial investment (II)	$28,500	$27,000
Year (t)	Cash inflows (CF_t)	
1	$10,000	$11,000
2	10,000	10,000
3	10,000	9,000
4	10,000	8,000

a. Calculate each project's payback period.
b. Calculate the net present value (NPV) for each project.
c. Calculate the internal rate of return (IRR) for each project.
d. Summarize the preferences dictated by each measure calculated above, and indicate which project you would recommend. Explain why.
e. Draw the net present value profiles for each project on the same set of axes, and explain the circumstances under which a conflict in rankings might exist.

PROBLEMS

WARM-UP

9–1   **Payback period**   Jordan Enterprises is considering a capital expenditure that requires an initial investment of $42,000 and returns after-tax cash inflows of $7,000 per year for 10 years. The firm has a maximum acceptable payback period of 8 years.
a. Determine the payback period for this project.
b. Should the company accept the project? Why or why not?

9–2 **Payback comparisons**   Nova Products has a 5-year maximum acceptable payback period. The firm is considering the purchase of a new machine and must choose between two alternative ones. The first machine requires an initial investment of $14,000 and generates annual after-tax cash inflows of $3,000 for each of the next 7 years. The second machine requires an initial investment of $21,000 and provides an annual cash inflow after taxes of $4,000 for 20 years.

a. Determine the payback period for each machine.

b. Comment on the acceptability of the machines, assuming they are independent projects.

c. Which machine should the firm accept? Why?

d. Do the machines in this problem illustrate any of the criticisms of using payback? Discuss.

9–3 **Choosing between two projects with acceptable payback periods**   Shell Camping Gear, Inc., is considering two mutually exclusive projects. Each requires an initial investment of $100,000. John Shell, president of the company, has set a maximum payback period of 4 years. The after-tax cash inflows associated with each project are as follows:

| Year | Cash inflows (CF_t) | |
	Project A	Project B
1	$10,000	$40,000
2	20,000	30,000
3	30,000	20,000
4	40,000	10,000
5	20,000	20,000

a. Determine the payback period of each project.

b. Because they are mutually exclusive, Shell must choose one. Which one should the company invest in?

c. Explain why one of the projects is a better choice than the other one.

9–4 **NPV**   Calculate the net present value (NPV) for the following 20-year projects. Comment on the acceptability of each. Assume that the firm has an opportunity cost of 14%.

a. Initial investment is $10,000; cash inflows are $2,000 per year.

b. Initial investment is $25,000; cash inflows are $3,000 per year.

c. Initial investment is $30,000; cash inflows are $5,000 per year.

9–5 **NPV for varying costs of capital**   Dane Cosmetics is evaluating a new fragrance-mixing machine. The machine requires an initial investment of $24,000 and will generate after-tax cash inflows of $5,000 per year for 8 years. For each of the costs of capital listed, (1) calculate the net present value (NPV), (2) indicate whether to accept or reject the machine, and (3) explain your decision.

a. The cost of capital is 10%.

b. The cost of capital is 12%.

c. The cost of capital is 14%.

9–6   Net present value—Independent projects   Using a 14% cost of capital, calculate the net present value for each of the independent projects shown in the following table and indicate whether or not each is acceptable.

	Project A	Project B	Project C	Project D	Project E
Initial investment (*II*)	$26,000	$500,000	$170,000	$950,000	$80,000
Year (*t*)			Cash inflows (*CF$_t$*)		
1	$4,000	$100,000	$20,000	$230,000	$ 0
2	4,000	120,000	19,000	230,000	0
3	4,000	140,000	18,000	230,000	0
4	4,000	160,000	17,000	230,000	20,000
5	4,000	180,000	16,000	230,000	30,000
6	4,000	200,000	15,000	230,000	0
7	4,000		14,000	230,000	50,000
8	4,000		13,000	230,000	60,000
9	4,000		12,000		70,000
10	4,000		11,000		

9–7   NPV   Simes Innovations, Inc., is negotiating to purchase exclusive rights to manufacture and market a solar-powered toy car. The car's inventor has offered Simes the choice of either a one-time payment of $1,500,000 today or a series of 5 year-end payments of $385,000.

a. If Simes has a cost of capital of 9%, which form of payment should the company choose?

b. What yearly payment would make the two offers identical in value at a cost of capital of 9%?

c. Would your answer to part **a** of this problem be different if the yearly payments were made at the beginning of each year? Show what difference, if any, that change in timing would make to the present value calculation.

d. The after-tax cash inflows associated with this purchase are projected to amount to $250,000 per year for 15 years. Will this factor change the firm's decision as to how to fund the initial investment?

9–8   NPV and maximum return   A firm can purchase a fixed asset for a $13,000 initial investment. If the asset generates an annual after-tax cash inflow of $4,000 for 4 years:

a. Determine the net present value (NPV) of the asset, assuming that the firm has a 10% cost of capital. Is the project acceptable?

b. Determine the maximum required rate of return (closest whole-percentage rate) that the firm can have and still accept the asset. Discuss this finding in light of your response in **a**.

9–9   NPV—Mutually exclusive projects   Hook Industries is considering the replacement of one of its old drill presses. Three alternative replacement presses are under consideration. The relevant cash flows associated with each are shown in the following table. The firm's cost of capital is 15%.

	Press A	Press B	Press C
Initial investment *(II)*	$85,000	$60,000	$130,000
Year *(t)*		Cash inflows *(CF$_t$)*	
1	$18,000	$12,000	$50,000
2	18,000	14,000	30,000
3	18,000	16,000	20,000
4	18,000	18,000	20,000
5	18,000	20,000	20,000
6	18,000	25,000	30,000
7	18,000	—	40,000
8	18,000	—	50,000

a. Calculate the net present value (NPV) of each press.
b. Using NPV, evaluate the acceptability of each press.
c. Rank the presses from best to worst using NPV.

9–10 Payback and NPV Neil Corporation has three projects under consideration.
The cash flows for each of them are shown in the following table. The firm has
a 16% cost of capital.

INTERMEDIATE

	Project A	Project B	Project C
Initial investment *(II)*	$40,000	$40,000	$40,000
Year *(t)*		Cash inflows *(CF$_t$)*	
1	$13,000	$ 7,000	$19,000
2	13,000	10,000	16,000
3	13,000	13,000	13,000
4	13,000	16,000	10,000
5	13,000	19,000	7,000

a. Calculate each project's payback period. Which project is preferred according to this method?
b. Calculate each project's net present value (NPV). Which project is preferred according to this method?
c. Comment on your findings in **a** and **b**, and recommend the best project. Explain your recommendation.

9–11 Internal rate of return For each of the projects shown in the following table,
calculate the internal rate of return (IRR), and indicate for each project the maximum cost of capital that the firm could have and find the IRR acceptable.

INTERMEDIATE

	Project A	Project B	Project C	Project D
Initial investment (*II*)	$90,000	$490,000	$20,000	$240,000
Year (*t*)	Cash inflows (*CF_t*)			
1	$20,000	$150,000	$7,500	$120,000
2	25,000	150,000	7,500	100,000
3	30,000	150,000	7,500	80,000
4	35,000	150,000	7,500	60,000
5	40,000	—	7,500	—

INTERMEDIATE

9–12   IRR—Mutually exclusive projects   Bell Manufacturing is attempting to choose the better of two mutually exclusive projects for expanding the firm's warehouse capacity. The relevant cash flows for the projects are shown in the following table. The firm's cost of capital is 15%.

	Project X	Project Y
Initial investment (*II*)	$500,000	$325,000
Year (*t*)	Cash inflows (*CF_t*)	
1	$100,000	$140,000
2	120,000	120,000
3	150,000	95,000
4	190,000	70,000
5	250,000	50,000

a. Calculate the IRR to the nearest whole percent for each of the projects.
b. Assess the acceptability of each project based on the IRRs found in a.
c. Which project is preferred, based on the IRRs found in a?

CHALLENGE

9–13   IRR, investment life, and cash inflows   Oak Enterprises accepts projects earning more than the firm's 15% cost of capital. Oak is currently considering a 10-year project that provides annual cash inflows of $10,000 and requires an initial investment of $61,450. (*Note:* All amounts are after taxes.)
a. Determine the IRR of this project. Is it acceptable?
b. Assuming that the cash inflows continue to be $10,000 per year, how many *additional years* would the flows have to continue to make the project acceptable (i.e., have an IRR of 15%)?
c. With the given life, initial investment, and cost of capital, what is the minimum annual cash inflow the firm should accept?

INTERMEDIATE

9–14   NPV and IRR   Benson Designs has prepared the following estimates for a long-term project it is considering. The initial investment is $18,250, and the project is expected to yield after-tax cash inflows of $4,000 per year for 7 years. The firm has a 10% cost of capital.
a. Determine the net present value (NPV) for the project.
b. Determine the internal rate of return (IRR) for the project.

c. Would you recommend that the firm accept or reject the project? Explain your answer.

INTERMEDIATE 9–15 **NPV, with rankings**   Botany Bay, Inc., a maker of casual clothing, is considering four projects. Because of past financial difficulties, the company has a high cost of capital at 15%. Which of these projects would be acceptable under those cost circumstances?

	Project A	Project B	Project C	Project D
Initial investment	$50,000	$100,000	$80,000	$180,000
Year (t)		Cash inflows (CF_t)		
1	$20,000	$35,000	$20,000	$100,000
2	20,000	50,000	40,000	80,000
3	20,000	50,000	60,000	60,000

a. Calculate the NPV of each project using a cost of capital of 15%.
b. Rank acceptable projects by NPV.
c. At what approximate cost of capital would all of the projects be acceptable?

   9–16 **All techniques, conflicting rankings**   Nicholson Roofing Materials, Inc., is considering two mutually exclusive projects, each with an initial investment of $150,000. The company's board of directors has set a 4-year payback requirement and sets cost of capital at 9%. The cash inflows associated with the two projects are as follows:

INTERMEDIATE

	Cash inflows (CF_t)	
Year	Project A	Project B
1	$45,000	$75,000
2	45,000	60,000
3	45,000	30,000
4	45,000	30,000
5	45,000	30,000
6	45,000	30,000

a. Calculate the payback period for each project.
b. Calculate the NPV of each project at 0%.
c. Calculate the NPV of each project at 9%.
d. Derive the IRR of each project.
e. Rank them by each of the techniques used. Make and justify a recommendation.

   9–17 **Payback, NPV, and IRR**   Rieger International is attempting to evaluate the feasibility of investing $95,000 in a piece of equipment having a 5-year life. The firm has estimated the *cash inflows* associated with the proposal as shown in the following table. The firm has a 12% cost of capital.

 INTERMEDIATE

Year (*t*)	Cash inflows (CF_t)
1	$20,000
2	25,000
3	30,000
4	35,000
5	40,000

a. Calculate the payback period for the proposed investment.
b. Calculate the net present value (NPV) for the proposed investment.
c. Calculate the internal rate of return (IRR), rounded to the nearest whole percent, for the proposed investment.
d. Evaluate the acceptability of the proposed investment using NPV and IRR. What recommendation would you make relative to implementation of the project? Why?

CHALLENGE

9–18   NPV, IRR, and NPV profiles   Thomas Company is considering two mutually exclusive projects. The firm, which has a 12% cost of capital, has estimated its cash flows as shown in the following table.

	Project A	Project B
Initial investment (*II*)	$130,000	$85,000
Year (*t*)	Cash inflows (CF_t)	
1	$ 25,000	$40,000
2	35,000	35,000
3	45,000	30,000
4	50,000	10,000
5	55,000	5,000

a. Calculate the NPV of each project, and assess its acceptability.
b. Calculate the IRR for each project, and assess its acceptability.
c. Draw the NPV profile for each project on the same set of axes.
d. Evaluate and discuss the rankings of the two projects based on your findings in **a, b,** and **c.**
e. Explain your findings in **d** in light of the pattern of cash inflows associated with each project.

CHALLENGE

9–19   All techniques—Mutually exclusive investment decision   Pound Industries is attempting to select the best of three mutually exclusive projects. The initial investment and after-tax cash inflows associated with each project are shown in the following table.

Cash flows	Project A	Project B	Project C
Initial investment (*II*)	$60,000	$100,000	$110,000
Cash inflows (*CF*), years 1–5	$20,000	$ 31,500	$ 32,500

a. Calculate the payback period for each project.
b. Calculate the net present value (NPV) of each project, assuming that the firm has a cost of capital equal to 13%.
c. Calculate the internal rate of return (IRR) for each project.
d. Draw the net present value profile for each project on the same set of axes, and discuss any conflict in ranking that may exist between NPV and IRR.
e. Summarize the preferences dictated by each measure, and indicate which project you would recommend. Explain why.

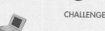

CHALLENGE

9–20 **All techniques with NPV profile—Mutually exclusive projects**   The following two projects of equal risk are alternatives for expanding the firm's capacity. The firm's cost of capital is 13%. The cash flows for each project are shown in the following table.

	Project A	Project B
Initial investment (*II*)	$80,000	$50,000
Year (*t*)	Cash inflows (*CF$_t$*)	
1	$15,000	$15,000
2	20,000	15,000
3	25,000	15,000
4	30,000	15,000
5	35,000	15,000

a. Calculate each project's payback period.
b. Calculate the net present value (NPV) for each project.
c. Calculate the internal rate of return (IRR) for each project.
d. Draw a net present value profile for each project on the same set of axes, and discuss any conflict in ranking that may exist between NPV and IRR.
e. Summarize the preferences dictated by each measure, and indicate which project you would recommend. Explain why.

9–21 **Integrative—Complete investment decision**   Wells Printing is considering the purchase of a new printing press. The total installed cost of the press is $2.2 million. This outlay would be partially offset by the sale of an existing press. The old press has zero book value, cost $1 million 10 years ago, and can be sold currently for $1.2 million before taxes. As a result of the new press, sales in each of the next 5 years are expected to increase by $1.6 million, but product costs (excluding depreciation) will represent 50% of sales. The new press will not affect the firm's net working capital requirements. The new press will be depreciated under MACRS using a 5-year recovery period (see Table 3.8 on page 96). The firm is subject to a 40% tax rate on both ordinary income and capital gains. Wells Printing's cost of capital is 11%. (*Note*: Assume that both the old and new press will have terminal values of $0 at the end of year 6.)
a. Determine the initial investment required by the new press.
b. Determine the operating cash inflows attributable to the new press. (*Note*: Be sure to consider the depreciation in year 6.)
c. Determine the payback period.

CHALLENGE

d. Determine the net present value (NPV) and the internal rate of return (IRR) related to the proposed new press.

e. Make a recommendation to accept or reject the new press, and justify your answer.

CHALLENGE

9–22   Integrative—Investment decision   Holliday Manufacturing is considering the replacement of an existing machine. The new machine costs $1.2 million and requires installation costs of $150,000. The existing machine can be sold currently for $185,000 before taxes. It is 2 years old, cost $800,000 new, and has a $384,000 book value and a remaining useful life of 5 years. It was being depreciated under MACRS using a 5-year recovery period (see Table 3.8 on page 96) and therefore has the final 4 years of depreciation remaining. If held until the end of 5 years, the machine's market value would be $0. Over its 5-year life, the new machine should reduce operating costs by $350,000 per year. The new machine will be depreciated under MACRS using a 5-year recovery period (see Table 3.8 on page 96). The new machine can be sold for $200,000 net of removal and clean up costs at the end of 5 years. An increased investment in net working capital of $25,000 will be needed to support operations if the new machine is acquired. Assume that the firm has adequate operating income against which to deduct any loss experienced on the sale of the existing machine. The firm has a 9% cost of capital and is subject to a 40% tax rate on both ordinary income and capital gains.

a. Develop the relevant cash flows needed to analyze the proposed replacement.

b. Determine the net present value (NPV) of the proposal.

c. Determine the internal rate of return (IRR) of the proposal.

d. Make a recommendation to accept or reject the replacement proposal, and justify your answer.

e. What is the highest cost of capital the firm could have and still accept the proposal? Explain.

CASE   CHAPTER 9

Making Norwich Tool's Lathe Investment Decision

Norwich Tool, a large machine shop, is considering replacing one of its lathes with either of two new lathes—lathe A or lathe B. Lathe A is a highly automated, computer-controlled lathe; lathe B is a less expensive lathe that uses standard technology. To analyze these alternatives, Mario Jackson, a financial analyst, prepared estimates of the initial investment and incremental (relevant) cash inflows associated with each lathe. These are shown in the following table.

	Lathe A	Lathe B
Initial investment (II)	$660,000	$360,000
Year (t)	Cash inflows (CF_t)	
1	$128,000	$ 88,000
2	182,000	120,000
3	166,000	96,000
4	168,000	86,000
5	450,000	207,000

Note that Mario plans to analyze both lathes over a 5-year period. At the end of that time, the lathes would be sold, thus accounting for the large fifth-year cash inflows.

Mario feels the two lathes are equally risky and the acceptance of either of them will not change the firm's overall risk. He therefore decides to apply the firm's 13% cost of capital when analyzing the lathes. Norwich Tool requires all projects to have a maximum payback period of 4.0 years.

Required

a. Use the payback period to assess the acceptability and relative ranking of each lathe.
b. Assuming equal risk, use the following sophisticated capital budgeting techniques to assess the acceptability and relative ranking of each lathe:
   (1) Net present value (NPV).
   (2) Internal rate of return (IRR).
c. Summarize the preferences indicated by the techniques used in **a** and **b**. Do the projects have conflicting rankings?
d. Draw a net present value profile for each project on the same set of axes, and discuss any conflict in rankings that may exist between NPV and IRR. Explain any observed conflict in terms of the relative differences in the magnitude and timing of each project's cash flows.
e. Use your findings in **a** through **d** to indicate on both a (1) theoretical and (2) practical basis which lathe would be preferred. Explain any difference in recommendations.

WEB EXERCISE   www

GOTO web site www.arachnoid.com/lutusp/finance_old.html. Page down to the portions of this screen that contains the financial calculator.

1. To determine the internal rate of return (IRR) of a project whose initial investment was $5,000 and its cash flows are $1,000/year for the next 10 years, perform the steps outlined below. By entering various interest rates you will eventually get a present value of $5,000. When this happens you have determined the IRR of the project.

   To get started, into PV, enter 0; into FV, enter 0; into np, enter 1000; into pmt, enter 10; and to start, into ir, enter 8. Click Calculate PV. This gives you a number much greater than $5,000. Now change ir to 20 and then click Calculate PV. Keeping changing the ir until PV = $5,000, the same as the initial investment.

2. Try another problem. The initial investment is $10,000. The time of the cash flows is 6 years, and the cash flow per year is $2,500. What is its IRR?

3. To calculate the IRR of an investment of $3,000 with a single cash flow of $4,800 in 3 years from the investment, do the following: Into FV, enter 4800; into np, enter 3; into pmt, enter 0; and then into ir, enter 8. Then click Calculate PV. As above, keep changing ir until the PV is equal to the initial investment of $3,000. What is this investment's IRR?

10 Risk and Refinements in Capital Budgeting

LEARNING GOALS

LG1 Understand the importance of explicitly recognizing risk in the analysis of capital budgeting projects.

LG2 Discuss breakeven cash flow, sensitivity and scenario analysis, and simulation as behavioral approaches for dealing with risk, and the unique risks facing multinational companies.

LG3 Describe the two basic risk-adjustment techniques in terms of NPV and the procedures for applying the certainty equivalent (CE) approach.

LG4 Review the use of risk-adjusted discount rates (RADRs), portfolio effects, and the practical aspects of RADRs relative to CEs.

LG5 Recognize the problem caused by unequal-lived mutually exclusive projects and the use of annualized net present values (ANPVs) to resolve it.

LG6 Explain the objective of capital rationing and the two basic approaches to project selection under it.

LG1

10.1 Introduction to Risk in Capital Budgeting

The capital budgeting techniques introduced in Chapter 9 were applied in an environment we assumed to be certain. All of the projects' relevant cash flows, developed using techniques presented in Chapter 8, were assumed to have the same level of risk as the firm. In other words, all mutually exclusive projects were equally risky and the acceptance of any project would not change the firm's overall risk. In actuality, these situations are rare—project cash flows typically have different levels of risk, and the acceptance of a project generally does impact the

Getting a Handle on Risk

Every year, millions of visitors pour into U.S. casinos, looking for big—or even modest—returns on their gambling dollars. Two key features of gambling, of course, are *uncertainty* and *hope*—the uncertainty of when, if ever, there will be a payoff, and the ongoing hope that it will come with the next quarter, or dollar, or twenty "invested." Although most business investments are not gambles, a similar uncertainty does exist. Managers do all they can to ensure the outcomes of their investments, but despite their best planning and analysis, risk remains because of events outside the company's immediate control. In the two preceding chapters, we looked at capital budgeting decisions in the face of certain outcomes. Here we turn to the question of how to incorporate the issue of risk into capital budgeting decisions.

firm's overall risk, though often in a minor way. We begin this chapter by relaxing the assumptions of a certain environment and equal-risk projects, in order to focus on the incorporation of risk into the capital budgeting decision process.

For convenience, in this chapter, we continue the Bennett Company example that was used in Chapter 9. The relevant cash flows and NPVs for Bennett Company's two mutually exclusive projects—A and B—are summarized in Table 10.1.

In the following two sections, we use the basic risk concepts presented in Chapter 6 to demonstrate both behavioral and quantitative approaches for explicitly recognizing risk in the analysis of capital budgeting projects.

TABLE 10.1	Relevant Cash Flows and NPVs for Bennett Company's Projects	
	Project A	Project B
A. Relevant Cash Flows		
Initial investment	$42,000	$45,000
Year	Operating cash flows	
1	$14,000	$28,000
2	14,000	12,000
3	14,000	10,000
4	14,000	10,000
5	14,000	10,000
B. Decision Technique		
NPV @ 10% cost of capital[a]	$11,074	$10,914

[a]From Table 9.4 on page 382; calculated using present value interest factors from tables.

? Review Question

10–1   Are capital budgeting decisions typically made in an environment of certainty? Are most mutually exclusive projects equally risky? Can the acceptance of a project change a firm's overall risk?

10.2 Behavioral Approaches for Dealing with Risk

Behavioral approaches can be used to get a "feel" for the level of project risk, whereas *quantitative approaches* allow explicit adjustment of projects for risk. Here we present a few behavioral approaches for dealing with risk in capital budgeting: risk and cash inflows, sensitivity and scenario analysis, and simulation. In addition, some international risk considerations are discussed. We consider quantitative approaches in a later section.

Risk and Cash Inflows

risk (in capital budgeting)
The chance that a project will prove unacceptable or, more formally, the degree of variability of cash flows.

In the discussion of capital budgeting, **risk** refers to the chance that a project will prove unacceptable—that is, NPV < $0 or IRR < cost of capital. More formally, risk in capital budgeting refers to the degree of variability of cash flows. Projects with a small chance of acceptability and a broad range of expected cash flows are more risky than projects having a high chance of acceptability and a narrow range of expected cash flows.

Career Key

The *marketing* department will be very involved in this part of the analysis of capital expenditure proposals. It will provide the revenue estimates for the various proposals.

In the conventional capital budgeting projects assumed here, risk stems almost entirely from *cash inflows,* because the initial investment is generally known with relative certainty. These inflows, of course, derive from a number of variables related to revenues, expenditures, and taxes. Examples would include the level of sales, cost of raw materials, labor rates, utility costs, and tax rates. We will concentrate on the risk in the cash inflows, but remember that this risk actually results from the interaction of these underlying variables. Therefore, to assess the risk of a proposed capital expenditure, the analyst needs to evaluate the probability that the cash inflows will be large enough to provide for project acceptance.

Example ▼ Treadwell Tire Company, a tire retailer with a 10% cost of capital, is considering investing in either of two mutually exclusive projects, A and B, each requiring a $10,000 initial investment and expected to provide equal annual cash inflows over their 15-year lives. For either project to be acceptable according to the net present value technique, its NPV must be greater than zero. If we let *CF* equal the annual cash inflow and *II* equal the initial investment, the following condition must be met for projects with annuity cash inflows, such as A and B, to be acceptable:

$$NPV = [CF \times (PVIFA_{k,n})] - II > \$0 \tag{10.1}$$

breakeven cash inflow
The minimum level of cash inflow necessary for a project to be acceptable, i.e., NPV > $0.

By substituting $k = 10\%$, $n = 15$ years, and $II = \$10,000$, we can find the **breakeven cash inflow**—the minimum level of cash inflow necessary for Treadwell's projects to be acceptable:

$$[CF \times (PVIFA_{10\%,15yrs})] - \$10,000 > \$0$$
$$CF \times (7.606) > \$10,000$$
$$CF > \frac{\$10,000}{7.606} = \underline{\underline{\$1,315}}$$

In other words, for the projects to be acceptable, they must have annual cash inflows of at least $1,315.

Given this breakeven level of cash inflows, the risk of each project could be assessed by determining the probability that the project's cash inflows will equal or exceed this breakeven level. The various statistical techniques that would determine that probability are covered in more advanced courses.[1] For now, we can simply assume that such a statistical analysis results in the following:

Probability of $CF_A > \$1,315 \rightarrow 100\%$
Probability of $CF_B > \$1,315 \rightarrow 65\%$

---

1. Normal distributions are commonly used to develop the concept of the probability of success, i.e., of a project having a positive NPV. The reader interested in learning more about this technique should see any second- or MBA-level managerial finance text.

Because project A is certain (100% probability) to have a positive net present value, whereas there is only a 65% chance that project B will have a positive NPV, project A is less risky than project B. Of course, the potential level of returns associated with each project must be evaluated in view of the firm's risk preference before the preferred project is selected.

The example clearly identifies risk as it relates to the chance that a project is acceptable, but it does not address the issue of cash flow variability. Even though project B has a greater chance of loss than project A, it might result in higher potential NPVs. Recall from Chapters 6 and 7 that it is the *combination* of risk and return that determines value. Similarly, the worth of a capital expenditure and its impact on the firm's value must be viewed in light of both risk and return. The analyst must therefore consider the *variability* of cash inflows and NPVs to assess project risk and return fully.

Sensitivity and Scenario Analysis

sensitivity analysis
A behavioral approach that uses a number of possible values for a given variable to assess its impact on a firm's return.

Two approaches for dealing with project risk to capture the variability of cash inflows and NPVs are sensitivity analysis and scenario analysis. **Sensitivity analysis**, as noted in Chapter 6, is a behavioral approach that uses a number of possible values for a given variable, such as cash inflows, to assess its impact on the firm's return, measured here by NPV. This technique is often useful in getting a feel for the variability of return in response to changes in a key variable. In capital budgeting, one of the most common sensitivity approaches is to estimate the NPVs associated with pessimistic (worst), most likely (expected), and optimistic (best) cash inflow estimates. The *range* can be determined by subtracting the pessimistic-outcome NPV from the optimistic-outcome NPV.

E x a m p l e ▼

Continuing with Treadwell Tire Company, assume that the financial manager made pessimistic, most likely, and optimistic estimates of the cash inflows for each project. The cash inflow estimates and resulting NPVs in each case are summarized in Table 10.2. Comparing the ranges of cash inflows ($1,000 for project A and $4,000 for B) and, more important, the ranges of NPVs ($7,606 for project A and $30,424 for B) makes it clear that project A is less risky than project B. Given that both projects have the same most likely NPV of $5,212, the assumed risk-averse decision maker will take project A because it has less risk and no possibility of loss.

scenario analysis
A behavioral approach that evaluates the impact on return of simultaneous changes in a number of variables.

Scenario analysis, which is a behavioral approach similar to sensitivity analysis but broader in scope, is used to evaluate the impact of various circumstances on the firm's return. Rather than isolating the effect of a change in a single variable, scenario analysis evaluates the impact of simultaneous changes in a number of variables, such as cash inflows, cash outflows, and the cost of capital. For example, the firm could evaluate the impact of both high inflation (scenario 1) and low inflation (scenario 2) on a project's NPV. Each scenario will affect the firm's cash inflows, cash outflows, and cost of capital, thereby resulting in different levels of NPV. The decision maker can use these NPV estimates to roughly assess the risk involved with respect to the level of inflation. The widespread

Career Key

Information systems analysts will be key to this part of the capital expenditure analysis process. They will design the systems to help complete the sensitivity and scenario analysis and the simulation approach.

TABLE 10.2	Sensitivity Analysis of Treadwell's Projects A and B	
	Project A	Project B
Initial investment	$10,000	$10,000
	Annual cash inflows	
Outcome		
Pessimistic	$ 1,500	$ 0
Most likely	2,000	2,000
Optimistic	2,500	4,000
Range	$ 1,000	$ 4,000
	Net present values[a]	
Outcome		
Pessimistic	$ 1,409	−$10,000
Most likely	5,212	5,212
Optimistic	9,015	20,424
Range	$ 7,606	$30,424

[a]These values were calculated by using the corresponding annual cash inflows. A 10% cost of capital and a 15-year life for the annual cash inflows were used.

availability of computer-based spreadsheet programs (such as *Excel* and *Lotus 1–2–3*) has greatly enhanced the use of both scenario and sensitivity analysis.

Simulation

simulation
A statistically based behavioral approach that applies predetermined probability distributions and random numbers to estimate risky outcomes.

Simulation is a statistically based behavioral approach that applies predetermined probability distributions and random numbers to estimate risky outcomes. By tying the various cash flow components together in a mathematical model and repeating the process numerous times, the financial manager can develop a probability distribution of project returns. Figure 10.1 presents a flowchart of the simulation of the net present value of a project. The process of generating random numbers and using the probability distributions for cash inflows and outflows allows the financial manager to determine values for each of these variables. Substituting these values into the mathematical model results in an NPV. By repeating this process perhaps a thousand times, a probability distribution of net present values is created.

Hint   These behavioral approaches may seem a bit imprecise to one who has not used them. But, repeated use and an "after-the-fact" review of previous analyses improve the accuracy of the users.

Although only gross cash inflows and outflows are simulated in Figure 10.1, more sophisticated simulations using individual inflow and outflow components, such as sales volume, sale price, raw material cost, labor cost, maintenance expense, and so on, are quite common. From the distribution of returns, regardless of how they are measured (NPV, IRR, and so on), the decision maker can

FIGURE 10.1

NPV Simulation
Flowchart of a net present value simulation

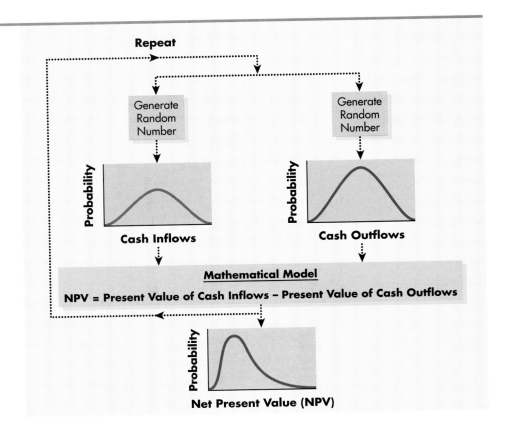

determine not only the expected value of the return but also the probability of achieving or surpassing a given return. The use of computers has made the simulation approach feasible. The output of simulation provides an excellent basis for decision making, because it allows the decision maker to view a continuum of risk-return trade-offs rather than a single-point estimate.

International Risk Considerations

Although the basic techniques of capital budgeting are the same for purely domestic firms as for multinational companies (MNCs), firms that operate in several countries face risks that are unique to the international arena. Two types of risk are particularly important and have been discussed briefly in earlier chapters: exchange rate risk and political risk—including, in the extreme, the risk that assets in foreign countries will be seized by the host government.

Exchange rate risk refers to the danger that an unexpected change in the exchange rate between the dollar and the currency in which a project's cash flows are denominated can reduce the market value of that project's cash flow. Although a project's initial investment can usually be predicted with some certainty, the dollar value of future cash inflows can be dramatically altered if the

exchange rate risk
The danger that an unexpected change in the exchange rate between the dollar and the currency in which a project's cash flows are denominated can reduce the market value of that project's cash flow.

In Practice

Net Payoffs

Do investments in the latest Internet-based technology—from hardware and software to web page content and design and training—pay off? So far, the results are mixed. According to International Data Corporation (IDC), a major information technology research firm, through 1998 for every $1.50 companies invested, companies got back only $1.00.

One exception to this rule is Loanshop.com, the first company to offer mortgages online. The company gets over half of its loan inquiries via e-mail, and quick response to serious leads is its key to higher sales. Its success in converting leads to sales is greatest within an hour of receipt and drops quickly, to less than 1% after 24 hours. Loanshop.com had two options to speed up the process of separating serious leads from routine questions: Hire more staff or invest in e-mail technology to automatically read and answer routine e-mail and route high-priority inquiries to mortgage counselors. But what were the relevant financial, operating, or process measurements that showed whether the new technology added value? While many of its rivals focused on the number of visitors to the web site, Loanshop.com President Jack Rodgers disagreed: "It's a meaningless number if no one buys our product."

Loanshop.com's managers knew that one person could process 100 e-mail messages in an 8-hour day. An e-mail automation system could perform this task in just 15 minutes—a 96% reduction. Armed with this data, managers developed the relevant cash flow scenarios for each option and determined that the technology solution was the better choice. The results speak for themselves: Loanshop.com doubled its mortgage counselors' sales, reduced the number of employees handling e-mail by over one-third, and earned a 40% return on investment in 14 months.

---

local currency depreciates against the dollar. In the short term, specific cash flows can be hedged by using financial instruments such as currency futures and options. Long-term exchange rate risk can best be minimized by financing the project, in whole or in part, in local currency.

Political risk is much harder to protect against. Once a foreign project is accepted, the foreign government can block the return of profits, seize the firm's assets, or otherwise interfere with a project's operation. The inability to manage political risk after the fact makes it even more important that managers account for political risks before making an investment. They can do so either by adjusting a project's expected cash inflows to account for the probability of political interference or by using risk-adjusted discount rates (discussed later in this chapter) in capital budgeting formulas. In general, it is much better to subjectively adjust individual project cash flows for political risk than to use a blanket adjustment for all projects.

In addition to unique risks that MNCs must face, several other special issues are relevant only for international capital budgeting. These include tax law differences, the importance of *transfer pricing* in evaluating projects, and the need to analyze international projects from a strategic as well as a financial perspective. Because only after-tax cash flows are relevant for capital budgeting, financial managers must carefully account for taxes paid to foreign governments on profits earned within their borders. They must also assess the impact of these tax payments on the parent company's U.S. tax liability, because full or partial credit is generally allowed for foreign tax payments.

transfer prices
Prices that subsidiaries charge each other for the goods and services traded between them.

Much of the international trade involving MNCs is, in reality, simply the shipment of goods and services from one of a parent company's wholly owned subsidiaries to another subsidiary located abroad. The parent company therefore has great discretion in setting the **transfer prices,** the prices that subsidiaries charge each other for the goods and services traded between them. The widespread use of transfer pricing in international trade makes capital budgeting in MNCs very difficult unless the transfer prices accurately reflect actual costs and incremental cash flows.

Finally, MNCs often must approach international capital projects from a strategic point of view, rather than from a strictly financial perspective. For example, an MNC may feel compelled to invest in a country to ensure continued access, even if the project itself may not have a positive net present value. This motivation was important for Japanese automakers who set up assembly plants in the United States in the early 1980s. For much the same reason, U.S. investment in Europe surged during the years before the market integration of the European Community in 1992. MNCs often will invest in production facilities in the home country of major rivals to deny these competitors an uncontested home market. Finally, MNCs may feel compelled to invest in certain industries or countries to achieve a broad corporate objective such as completing a product line or diversifying raw material sources, even when the project's cash flows may not be sufficiently profitable.

? Review Questions

10–2   Define *risk* in terms of the cash inflows from a capital budgeting project. How can determination of the *breakeven cash inflow* be used to gauge project risk? Explain.

10–3   Briefly describe, compare, and explain how each of the following behavioral approaches can be used to deal with project risk: (a) sensitivity analysis; (b) scenario analysis; and (c) simulation.

10–4   Briefly define and explain how each of the following items that are unique to multinational companies affect their capital budgeting decisions: (a) exchange rate risk; (b) political risk; (c) tax law differences; (d) transfer pricing; and (e) strategic rather than financial viewpoint.

10.3 Risk-Adjustment Techniques

The approaches for dealing with risk that have been presented so far allow the financial manager to get a "feel" for project risk. Unfortunately, they do not provide a quantitative basis for evaluating risky projects. We will now illustrate the two major risk-adjustment techniques using the net present value (NPV) decision method.[2] The NPV decision rule of accepting only those projects with NPVs > $0 will continue to hold. The basic equation for NPV, first presented in Equation 9.1, is restated below:

$$\text{NPV} = \sum_{t=1}^{n} \frac{CF_t}{(1+k)^t} - II \tag{10.2}$$

where

$$CF_t = \text{cash inflow in year } t$$
$$II = \text{initial investment}$$
$$k = \text{cost of capital or discount rate}$$
$$n = \text{life of project (in years)}$$

Close examination of Equation 10.2 reveals that because the initial investment (II), which occurs at time zero, is known with certainty, a project's risk is embodied in the present value of its cash inflows:

$$\sum_{t=1}^{n} \frac{CF_t}{(1+k)^t} \tag{10.3}$$

Two opportunities to adjust the present value of cash inflows for risk exist: (1) the cash inflows, CF_t, can be adjusted, or (2) the discount rate, k, can be adjusted. Here we describe and compare two techniques—the cash inflow adjustment process, using *certainty equivalents*, and the discount rate adjustment process, using *risk-adjusted discount rates*. In addition, we consider the portfolio effects of project analysis as well as the practical aspects of certainty equivalents and risk-adjusted discount rates.

Certainty Equivalents (CEs)

certainty equivalents (CEs)
Risk-adjustment factors that represent the percent of estimated cash inflow that investors would be satisfied to receive *for certain* rather than the cash inflows that are *possible* for each year.

One of the most direct and theoretically preferred approaches for risk adjustment is the use of **certainty equivalents** **(CEs),** which represent the percent of estimated cash inflow that investors would be satisfied to receive *for certain* rather than the cash inflows that are *possible* for each year. Equation 10.4 presents the basic expression for NPV when certainty equivalents are used for risk adjustment:

$$\text{NPV} = \sum_{t=1}^{n} \frac{\alpha_t \times CF_t}{(1+R_F)^t} - II \tag{10.4}$$

where

$$\alpha_t = \text{certainty equivalent factor in year } t \ (0 \leq \alpha_t \leq 1)$$
$$CF_t = \text{relevant cash inflow in year } t$$
$$R_F = \text{risk-free rate of return}$$

The equation shows that a project's cash inflows are first adjusted for risk by converting the expected cash inflows to certain amounts, $\alpha_t \times CF_t$. These certain

---

2. The IRR could just as well have been used, but because NPV is theoretically preferable, it is used instead.

risk-free rate, R_F
The rate of return that one would earn on a virtually riskless investment such as a U.S. Treasury bill.

cash inflows are, in effect, equivalent to "cash in hand," but not at time zero. The second part of the calculation adjusts the certain cash inflows for the time value of money by discounting them at the risk-free rate, R_F.[3] The **risk-free rate, R_F**, is the rate of return that one would earn on a virtually riskless investment such as a U.S. Treasury bill. It is used to discount the certain cash inflows and should not be confused with a risk-adjusted discount rate. (If a risk-adjusted rate were used, the risk would in effect be counted twice.) Although the process described here of converting risky cash inflows to certain cash inflows is somewhat subjective, the technique is theoretically sound.

Example ▼   Bennett Company wishes to consider risk in the analysis of two projects, A and B. The relevant cash flows for these projects are presented in part A of Table 10.1, and the NPVs, assuming that the projects had equivalent risks, are presented in part B of Table 10.1. Ignoring risk differences and using net present value, calculated using the firm's 10% cost of capital, project A was preferred over project B, because its NPV of $11,074 was greater than B's NPV of $10,914.

Now let's assume, however, that on further analysis the firm found that project A was actually more risky than project B. To consider the differing risks, the firm estimated the certainty equivalent factors for each project's cash inflows for each year. Columns 2 and 7 of Table 10.3 show the estimated values for projects A and B, respectively. Multiplying the risky cash inflows (in columns 1 and 6) by the corresponding certainty equivalent factors (in columns 2 and 7, respectively) gives the certain cash inflows for projects A and B shown in columns 3 and 8, respectively.

Upon investigation, Bennett's management estimated the prevailing risk-free rate of return, R_F, to be 6%. Using that rate to discount the certain cash inflows for each of the projects results in the net present values of $4,541 for project A and $10,141 for B, as shown at the bottom of columns 5 and 10, respectively. (The calculated values using a financial calculator are $4,544 and $10,151 for projects A and B, respectively.) Note that as a result of the risk adjustment, project B is now preferred. The usefulness of the certainty equivalent approach for risk adjustment should be quite clear. The only difficulty lies in the need to make ▲ subjective estimates of the certainty equivalent factors.

Risk-Adjusted Discount Rates (RADRs)

A more practical approach for risk adjustment involves the use of *risk-adjusted discount rates (RADRs)*. Instead of adjusting the cash inflows for risk, as the certainty equivalent approach does, this approach adjusts the discount rate.[4] Equation 10.5 presents the basic expression for NPV when risk-adjusted discount rates are used:

$$NPV = \sum_{t=1}^{n} \frac{CF_t}{(1 + RADR)^t} - II \qquad (10.5)$$

---

3. Alternatively, the internal rate of return could be calculated for certain cash inflows and then compared to the risk-free rate to make the accept–reject decision.

4. The risk-adjusted discount rate approach can be applied in using the internal rate of return as well as the net present value. If the IRR is used, the risk-adjusted discount rate becomes the cutoff rate that must be exceeded by the IRR for the project to be accepted. In using NPV, the projected cash inflows are merely discounted at the risk-adjusted discount rate.

TABLE 10.3 Analysis of Bennett Company's Projects A and B Using Certainty Equivalents

Project A

Year (t)	Cash inflows (1)	Certainty equivalent factors[a] (2)	Certain cash inflows [(1) × (2)] (3)	$PVIF_{6\%,t}$ (4)	Present value [(3) × (4)] (5)
1	$14,000	.90	$12,600	.943	$11,882
2	14,000	.90	12,600	.890	11,214
3	14,000	.80	11,200	.840	9,408
4	14,000	.70	9,800	.792	7,762
5	14,000	.60	8,400	.747	6,275
			Present value of cash inflows		$46,541
			− Initial investment		42,000
			Net present value (NPV)		$ 4,541

Project B

Year (t)	Cash inflows (6)	Certainty equivalent factors[a] (7)	Certain cash inflows [(6) × (7)] (8)	$PVIF_{6\%,t}$ (9)	Present value [(8) × (9)] (10)
1	$28,000	1.00	$28,000	.943	$26,404
2	12,000	.90	10,800	.890	9,612
3	10,000	.90	9,000	.840	7,560
4	10,000	.80	8,000	.792	6,336
5	10,000	.70	7,000	.747	5,229
			Present value of cash inflows		$55,141
			− Initial investment		45,000
			Net present value (NPV)		$10,141

Note: The relevant cash flows for these projects were presented in Table 10.1, and the analysis of the projects using NPV and assuming equal risk was presented in Table 9.4 and summarized in Table 10.1.

[a] These values were estimated by management; they reflect the risk that managers perceive in the cash inflows.

risk-adjusted discount rate (RADR)
The rate of return that must be earned on a given project to compensate the firm's owners adequately—that is, to maintain or improve the firm's share price.

The **risk-adjusted discount rate (RADR)** is the rate of return that must be earned on a given project to compensate the firm's owners adequately—that is, to maintain or improve the firm's share price. The higher the risk of a project, the higher the RADR and therefore the lower the net present value for a given stream of cash inflows. Because the logic underlying the use of RADRs is closely linked to the capital asset pricing model (CAPM) developed in Chapter 6, here we review CAPM, discuss its use in finding RADRs, and describe the application of RADRs.

Review of CAPM

In Chapter 6, the *capital asset pricing model (CAPM)* was used to link the *relevant* risk and return for all assets traded in *efficient markets*. In the development of the CAPM, the *total risk* of an asset was defined as

$$\text{Total risk} = \text{nondiversifiable risk} + \text{diversifiable risk} \qquad (10.6)$$

For assets traded in an efficient market, the *diversifiable risk*, which results from uncontrollable or random events, can be eliminated through diversification. The relevant risk is therefore the *nondiversifiable risk*—the risk for which owners of these assets are rewarded. Nondiversifiable risk for securities is commonly measured by using *beta*, which is an index of the degree of movement of an asset's return in response to a change in the market return.

Using beta, b_j, to measure the relevant risk of any asset j, the CAPM is

$$k_j = R_F + [b_j \times (k_m - R_F)] \qquad (10.7)$$

where

$$k_j = \text{required return on asset } j$$
$$R_F = \text{risk-free rate of return}$$
$$b_j = \text{beta coefficient for asset } j$$
$$k_m = \text{return on the market portfolio of assets}$$

In Chapter 6, we demonstrated that the required return on any asset could be determined by substituting values of R_F, b_j, and k_m into the CAPM—Equation 10.7. Any security that is expected to earn in excess of its required return would be acceptable, and those that are expected to earn an inferior return would be rejected.

Using CAPM to Find RADRs

If we assume for a moment that real corporate assets such as computers, machine tools, and special-purpose machinery are traded in efficient markets, the CAPM could be redefined as noted in Equation 10.8:

$$k_{\text{project } j} = R_F + [b_{\text{project } j} \times (k_m - R_F)] \qquad (10.8)$$

The *security market line* (SML)—the graphic depiction of the CAPM—is shown for Equation 10.8 in Figure 10.2. Any project having an IRR falling above the SML would be acceptable, because its IRR would exceed the required return, k_{project}; any project with an IRR below k_{project} would be rejected. In terms of

CAPM and SML
CAPM and SML in capital
budgeting decision making

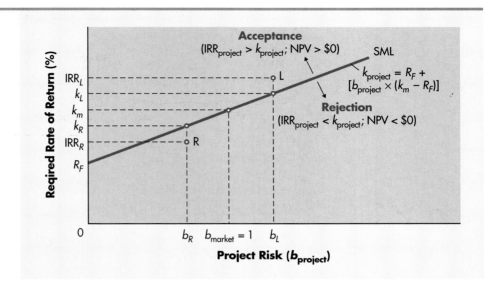

Project Risk ($b_{project}$)

NPV, any project falling above the SML would have a positive NPV, and any project falling below the SML would have a negative NPV.[5]

Example ▼ Two projects, L and R, are shown in Figure 10.2. Project L has a beta, b_L, and generates an internal rate of return, IRR_L. The required return for a project with risk b_L is k_L. Because project L generates a return greater than that required ($IRR_L > k_L$), project L would be acceptable. Project L would have a positive NPV when its cash inflows are discounted at its required return, k_L. Project R, on the other hand, generates an IRR below that required for its risk, b_R ($IRR_R < k_R$). This project would have a negative NPV when its cash inflows are discounted at its required return, k_R. Project R should be rejected. ▲

Applying RADRs

Because the CAPM is based upon an assumed efficient market, which does *not* exist for real corporate assets such as plant and equipment, the CAPM is not directly applicable in making capital budgeting decisions. Attention is therefore typically devoted to assessing the *total risk* of a project and using it to determine the risk-adjusted discount rate (RADR), which can be used in Equation 10.5 to find the NPV.

In order not to damage the firm's market value, it must use the correct discount rate when evaluating a project. If a firm discounts a risky project's cash inflows at too low a rate and accepts the project, the firm's market price may drop as investors recognize that the firm itself has become more risky. On the

---

5. As noted earlier, whenever the IRR is above the cost of capital or required return (IRR > k), the NPV is positive, and whenever the IRR is below the cost of capital or required return (IRR < k), the NPV is negative. Because by definition the IRR is the discount rate that causes NPV to equal zero and the IRR and NPV always agree on accept–reject decisions, the relationship noted in Figure 10.2 logically follows.

other hand, if the firm discounts a project's cash inflows at too high a rate, it will reject acceptable projects. Eventually, the firm's market price may drop because investors, believing that the firm is being overly conservative, will sell their stock, putting downward pressure on the firm's market value.

Unfortunately, there is no formal mechanism for linking total project risk to the level of required return. As a result, most firms subjectively determine the RADR by adjusting their existing required return up or down depending on whether the proposed project is more or less risky, respectively, than the average risk of the firm. Although some firms use a CAPM-type of approach to link project risk and return, such an approach provides merely a "rough estimate" because both (1) the project risk measure and (2) the linkage between risk and return are estimates. The following example will demonstrate a CAPM-type approach that relies on subjectively determined data linking project risk and return.

Example ▼   Bennett Company wishes to use the risk-adjusted discount rate approach to determine, according to NPV, whether to implement project A or project B. In addition to the data presented earlier, Bennett's management, after a great deal of analysis, assigned a "risk index" of 1.6 to project A and 1.0 to B. The risk index is merely a numerical scale used to classify project risk—higher index values are assigned to higher-risk projects, and vice versa. The CAPM-type relationship used by the firm to link risk, measured by the risk index, and the required return (RADR) is shown in the following table.

	Risk index	Required return (RADR)
	0.0	6% (risk-free rate, R_F)
	0.2	7
	0.4	8
	0.6	9
	0.8	10
Project B →	1.0	11
	1.2	12
	1.4	13
Project A →	1.6	14
	1.8	16
	2.0	18

Because project A is riskier than project B (index of 1.6 for A versus 1.0 for B), its RADR of 14% is greater than B's RADR of 11%. The net present value of each project, using its RADR, is calculated in Table 10.4. (The calculated values using a financial calculator are $6,063 and $9,798 for projects A and B, respectively.) The results clearly show that project B is preferable, because its risk-adjusted NPV of $9,802 is greater than the $6,062 risk-adjusted NPV for project A. This is the same conclusion that resulted from using certainty equivalents in the preceding example. As noted by the NPVs in part B of Table 10.1, when the discount rates are not adjusted for risk, project A would be preferred to project B.

	Project X	Project Y
Initial investment	$70,000	$78,000
Year (t)	Cash inflows (CF_t)	
1	$30,000	$22,000
2	30,000	32,000
3	30,000	38,000
4	30,000	46,000

a. Use a certainty equivalent approach to calculate the net present value of each project given the following certainty equivalent factors:

Year	Project X	Project Y
1	.85	.95
2	.90	.90
3	.95	.85
4	.95	.80

b. Use a risk-adjusted rate of return approach to calculate the net present value of each project given that Project X has a RADR factor of 1.20 and Project Y has a RADR factor of 1.40. (Use Equation 10.8 to calculate the required project return for each.)

c. Explain why the results of the two approaches may differ from one another. Which project would you choose? Justify your choice.

WARM-UP   LG4 10–12 **Risk classes and RADR**   Moses Manufacturing is attempting to select the best of three mutually exclusive projects, X, Y, and Z. Though all the projects have 5-year lives, they possess differing degrees of risk. Project X is in Class V, the highest-risk class; project Y is in Class II, the below-average-risk class; and project Z is in Class III, the average-risk class. The basic cash flow data for each project and the risk classes and risk-adjusted discount rates (RADRs) used by the firm are shown in the following tables.

	Project X	Project Y	Project Z
Initial investment (II)	$180,000	$235,000	$310,000
Year (t)	Cash inflows (CF_t)		
1	$ 80,000	$ 50,000	$ 90,000
2	70,000	60,000	90,000
3	60,000	70,000	90,000
4	60,000	80,000	90,000
5	60,000	90,000	90,000

Risk Classes and RADRs

Risk Class	Description	Risk-adjusted discount rate (RADR)
I	Lowest risk	10%
II	Below-average risk	13
III	Average risk	15
IV	Above-average risk	19
V	Highest risk	22

a. Find the risk-adjusted NPV for each project.
b. Which, if any, project would you recommend that the firm undertake?

10–13   Unequal lives—ANPV approach   Evans Industries wishes to select the best of three possible machines, each expected to fulfill the firm's ongoing need for additional aluminum-extrusion capacity. The three machines—A, B, and C—are equally risky. The firm plans to use a 12% cost of capital to evaluate each of them. The initial investment and annual cash inflows over the life of each machine are shown in the following table.

INTERMEDIATE

	Machine A	Machine B	Machine C
Initial investment (*II*)	$92,000	$65,000	$100,500
Year(*t*)		Cash inflows (*CF$_t$*)	
1	$12,000	$10,000	$ 30,000
2	12,000	20,000	30,000
3	12,000	30,000	30,000
4	12,000	40,000	30,000
5	12,000	—	30,000
6	12,000	—	—

a. Calculate the NPV for each machine over its life. Rank the machines in descending order based on NPV.
b. Use the *annualized net present value (ANPV)* approach to evaluate and rank the machines in descending order based on the ANPV.
c. Compare and contrast your findings in **a** and **b**. Which machine would you recommend that the firm acquire? Why?

10–14   Unequal lives—ANPV approach   Portland Products is considering the purchase of one of three mutually exclusive projects for increasing production efficiency.

INTERMEDIATE

The firm plans to use a 14% cost of capital to evaluate these equal-risk projects. The initial investment and annual cash inflows over the life of each project are shown in the following table.

	Project X	Project Y	Project Z
Initial investment (*II*)	$78,000	$52,000	$66,000
Year (*t*)		Cash inflows (*CF*$_t$)	
1	$17,000	$28,000	$15,000
2	25,000	38,000	15,000
3	33,000	—	15,000
4	41,000	—	15,000
5	—	—	15,000
6	—	—	15,000
7	—	—	15,000
8	—	—	15,000

a. Calculate the NPV for each project over its life. Rank the projects in descending order based on NPV.
b. Use the *annualized net present value (ANPV)* approach to evaluate and rank the projects in descending order based on the ANPV.
c. Compare and contrast your findings in a and b. Which project would you recommend that the firm purchase? Why?

INTERMEDIATE 10–15   **Unequal lives—ANPV approach**   JBL Co. has designed a new product sampling system. Management must choose among three alternative courses of action: (1) The firm can sell the design outright to another corporation with payment over 2 years. (2) It can license the design to another manufacturer for a period of 5 years, its likely product life. (3) It can manufacture and market the system itself. The company has a cost of capital of 12%. Cash flows associated with each alternative are as follows:

Alternative	Sell	License	Manufacture
Initial investment	$200,000	$200,000	$450,000
Year (*t*)		Cash inflows (*CF*$_t$)	
1	$200,000	$250,000	$200,000
2	250,000	100,000	250,000
3		80,000	200,000
4		60,000	200,000
5		40,000	200,000
6			200,000

a. Calculate the net present value of each alternative and rank the alternatives according to NPV.
b. Calculate the *annualized net present value (ANPV)* of each alternative and rank them accordingly.
c. Why is ANPV preferred over NPV when ranking projects with unequal lives?

INTERMEDIATE 10–16 **Capital rationing—IRR and NPV approaches** Valley Corporation is attempting to select the best of a group of independent projects competing for the firm's fixed capital budget of $4.5 million. The firm recognizes that any unused portion of this budget will earn less than its 15% cost of capital, thereby resulting in a present value of inflows that is less than the initial investment. The firm has summarized the key data to be used in selecting the best group of projects in the following table.

Project	Initial investment	IRR	Present value of inflows at 15%
A	$5,000,000	17%	$5,400,000
B	800,000	18	1,100,000
C	2,000,000	19	2,300,000
D	1,500,000	16	1,600,000
E	800,000	22	900,000
F	2,500,000	23	3,000,000
G	1,200,000	20	1,300,000

a. Use the *internal rate of return (IRR) approach* to select the best group of projects.
b. Use the *net present value (NPV) approach* to select the best group of projects.
c. Compare, contrast, and discuss your findings in **a** and **b**.
d. Which projects should the firm implement? Why?

INTERMEDIATE 10–17 **Capital rationing—NPV approach** A firm with a 13% cost of capital must select the optimal group of projects from those shown in the following table, given its capital budget of $1 million.

Project	Initial investment	NPV at 13% cost of capital
A	$300,000	$ 84,000
B	200,000	10,000
C	100,000	25,000
D	900,000	90,000
E	500,000	70,000
F	100,000	50,000
G	800,000	160,000

a. Calculate the *present value of cash inflows* associated with each project.
b. Select the optimal group of projects, keeping in mind that unused funds are costly.

CASE   CHAPTER 10

Evaluating Cherone Equipment's Risky Plans for Increasing Its Production Capacity

Cherone Equipment, a manufacturer of electronic fitness equipment, wishes to evaluate two alternative plans for increasing its production capacity to meet the rapidly growing demand for its key product—the Cardiocycle. After months of investigation and analysis, the firm culled the list of alternatives down to the following two plans that would allow it to meet the forecast product demand.

Plan X   Use current proven technology to expand the existing plant and semi-automated production line. This plan is viewed as only slightly more risky than the firm's current average level of risk.

Plan Y   Install new, just-developed automatic production equipment in the existing plant to replace the current semiautomated production line. Because this plan eliminates the need to expand the plant, it is less expensive than Plan X but is believed to be far more risky due to the unproven nature of the technology.

Cherone, which routinely uses NPV to evaluate capital budgeting projects, has a cost of capital of 12%. Currently the risk-free rate of interest, R_F, is 9%. The firm decided to evaluate the two plans over a 5-year time period, at the end of which each plan would be liquidated. The relevant cash flows associated with each plan are summarized in the following table:

	Plan X	Plan Y
Initial investment (*II*)	$2,700,000	$2,100,000
Year (*t*)	Cash inflows (*CF_t*)	
1	$ 470,000	$ 380,000
2	610,000	700,000
3	950,000	800,000
4	970,000	600,000
5	1,500,000	1,200,000

The firm developed additional data that can be used to adjust the two plans for risk. The data, given in the following table, can be used to adjust either the cash inflows using certainty equivalents (CEs) or the discount rate using risk-adjusted discount rates (RADRs).

	Plan X	Plan Y
Year (t)	Certainty equivalent factors (α_t)	
1	1.00	.90
2	1.00	.80
3	.90	.80
4	.90	.70
5	.80	.80
	Risk-adjusted discount rate (RADR)	
	13%	15%

Required

a. Assuming the two plans have the same risk as the firm, use the following capital budgeting techniques and the firm's cost of capital to evaluate their acceptability and relative ranking.
   (1) Net present value (NPV).
   (2) Internal rate of return (IRR).
b. Recognizing the differences in plan risk, use the NPV method and each of the following risk-adjustment techniques and the data given earlier to evaluate the acceptability and relative ranking of the two plans.
   (1) Certainty equivalents (CEs).
   (2) Risk-adjusted discount rates (RADRs).
c. Compare and contrast your finding in **a** and **b.** Which plan would you recommend? Did explicit recognition of the risk differences of the plans affect this recommendation?
d. Would your recommendations in **a** and **b** be changed if the firm were operating under capital rationing? Explain.

WEB EXERCISE

GOTO web site www.contingencyanalysis.com. Scroll down the page and click Fundamentals. Scroll down the next page and click Risk Measures.

1. What are the three categories of risk measures? Scroll down the left column and click 9. Beta.
2. What are the two components of equity risks in the CAPM?
3. Which of these two risks can be diversified away?
4. Which risk does beta measure?
5. Can beta be used to measure a portfolio's systematic risk?
6. In which type of portfolios can beta be a misleading measure of total risk?

LASTING IMPRESSIONS COMPANY

Lasting Impressions (LI) Company is a medium-sized commercial printer of promotional advertising brochures, booklets, and other direct-mail pieces. The firm's major clients are New York– and Chicago-based ad agencies. The typical job is characterized by high quality and production runs of over 50,000 units. LI has not been able to compete effectively with larger printers because of its existing older, inefficient presses. The firm is currently having problems cost effectively meeting run length requirements as well as meeting quality standards.

The general manager has proposed the purchase of one of two large six-color presses designed for long, high-quality runs. The purchase of a new press would enable LI to reduce its cost of labor and therefore the price to the client, putting the firm in a more competitive position. The key financial characteristics of the old press and the two proposed presses are summarized in what follows.

Old press   Originally purchased 3 years ago at an installed cost of $400,000, it is being depreciated under MACRS using a 5-year recovery period. The old press has a remaining economic life of 5 years. It can be sold today to net $420,000 before taxes; if it is retained, it can be sold to net $150,000 before taxes at the end of 5 years.

Press A   This highly automated press can be purchased for $830,000 and will require $40,000 in installation costs. It will be depreciated under MACRS using a 5-year recovery period. At the end of the 5 years, the machine could be sold to net $400,000 before taxes. If this machine is acquired, it is anticipated that the following current account changes would result.

Cash	+ $ 25,400
Accounts receivable	+ 120,000
Inventories	– 20,000
Accounts payable	+ 35,000

Press B   This press is not as sophisticated as press A. It costs $640,000 and requires $20,000 in installation costs. It will be depreciated under MACRS using a 5-year recovery period. At the end of 5 years, it can be sold to net $330,000 before taxes. Acquisition of this press will have no effect on the firm's net working capital investment.

The firm estimates that its profits before depreciation and taxes with the old press and with press A or press B for each of the 5 years would be as shown in Table 1. The firm is subject to a 40% tax rate on both ordinary income and capital gains. The firm's cost of capital, k, applicable to the proposed replacement is 14%.

TABLE 1 Profits Before Depreciation and Taxes for Lasting Impressions Company's Presses

Year	Old press	Press A	Press B
1	$120,000	$250,000	$210,000
2	120,000	270,000	210,000
3	120,000	300,000	210,000
4	120,000	330,000	210,000
5	120,000	370,000	210,000

REQUIRED

a. For each of the two proposed replacement presses, determine:
   (1) Initial investment.
   (2) Operating cash inflows. (*Note:* Be sure to consider the depreciation in year 6.)
   (3) Terminal cash flow. (*Note:* This is at the end of year 5.)
b. Using the data developed in **a,** find and depict on a time line the relevant cash flow stream associated with each of the two proposed replacement presses assuming that each is terminated at the end of 5 years.
c. Using the data developed in **b,** apply each of the following decision techniques:
   (1) Payback period. (*Note:* For year 5, use only the operating cash inflows—exclude terminal cash flow—when making this calculation.)
   (2) Net present value (NPV).
   (3) Internal rate of return (IRR).
d. Draw net present value profiles for the two replacement presses on the same set of axes, and discuss conflicting rankings of the two presses, if any, resulting from use of NPV and IRR decision techniques.
e. Recommend which, if either, of the presses the firm should acquire if the firm has (1) unlimited funds or (2) capital rationing.
f. What is the impact on your recommendation of the fact that the operating cash inflows associated with press A are characterized as very risky in contrast to the low-risk operating cash inflows of press B?

PART 4

Long-Term Financial Decisions

11

The Cost of Capital

11.1 An Overview of the Cost of Capital

The cost of capital is an extremely important financial concept. It acts as a major link between the firm's long-term investment decisions (discussed in Part 3) and the wealth of the owners as determined by investors in the marketplace. It is in effect the "magic number" that is used to decide whether a proposed corporate investment will increase or decrease the firm's stock price. Clearly, only those investments that are expected to increase stock price (NPV > $0, or IRR > cost of

The Right Mix

If you and a friend each bought a pound of jelly beans, mixed from among your favorite flavors, would you each buy the same mix? Probably not. It's the same with two companies' choices of financing sources—each will choose proportions of debt and equity financing to suit its particular tastes. The success of any firm will depend in large part on the difference between the cost of the firm's funding from various sources and its earnings on project investments. In previous chapters we simply assumed a reasonable cost of capital. This chapter will demonstrate how to calculate the cost of specific sources of capital—long-term debt, preferred stock, common stock, and retained earnings. It also will show how to combine the various costs for a target financing mix that reflects the firm's desired capital structure proportions.

cost of capital
The rate of return that a firm must earn on its project investments to maintain its market value and attract funds.

capital) would be recommended. Due to its key role in financial decision making, the importance of the cost of capital cannot be overemphasized.

The **cost of capital** is the rate of return that a firm must earn on its project investments to maintain the market value of its stock. It can also be thought of as the rate of return required by the market suppliers of capital to attract their funds to the firm. If risk is held constant, projects with a rate of return above the cost of capital will increase the value of the firm, and projects with a rate of return below the cost of capital will decrease the value of the firm.

Basic Assumptions

The cost of capital is a dynamic concept affected by a variety of economic and firm factors. To isolate the basic structure of the cost of capital, we make some key assumptions relative to risk and taxes:

1. **Business risk**—the risk to the firm of being unable to cover operating costs— *is assumed to be unchanged.* This assumption means that the firm's acceptance of a given project does not affect its ability to meet operating costs.
2. **Financial risk**—the risk to the firm of being unable to cover required financial obligations (interest, lease payments, preferred stock dividends)—*is assumed to be unchanged.* This assumption means that projects are financed in such a way that the firm's ability to meet required financing costs is unchanged.
3. After-tax costs are considered relevant. In other words, *the cost of capital is measured on an after-tax basis.* This assumption is consistent with the framework used to make capital budgeting decisions.

Risk and Financing Costs

Regardless of the type of financing employed, the following equation explains the general relationship between risk and financing costs:

$$k_l = r_l + bp + fp \qquad (11.1)$$

where

$$k_l = \text{specific (or nominal) cost of the various types of}$$
$$\text{long-term financing, } l$$
$$r_l = \text{risk-free cost of the given type of financing, } l$$
$$bp = \text{business risk premium}$$
$$fp = \text{financial risk premium}$$

Equation 11.1 is merely another form of the nominal interest equation— Equation 2.2 presented in Chapter 2—where r_l equals R_F and $bp + fp$ equals RP_1, the factor for issuer and issue characteristics. It indicates that the cost of each type of capital depends on the risk-free cost of that type of funds, the business risk of the firm, and the financial risk of the firm.[1] We can evaluate the equation in either of two ways:

1. *Time-series comparisons* are made by comparing the firm's cost of each type of financing *over time.* Here the differentiating factor is the risk-free cost of the given type of financing.

---

1. Although the relationship between r_l, bp, and fp is presented as linear in Equation 11.1, this is only for simplicity; the actual relationship is likely to be much more complex mathematically. The only definite conclusion that can be drawn is that the cost of a specific type of financing for a firm is somehow functionally related to the risk-free cost of that type of financing adjusted for the firm's business and financial risks [i.e., that $k_l = f(r_l, bp, fp)$].

2. *Comparisons between firms* are made at a single point in time by comparing a firm's cost of each type of capital with its cost *to another firm*. In this case, the risk-free cost of the given type of financing would remain constant,[2] and the cost differences would be attributable to the differing business and financial risks of each firm.

Example ▼ Hobson Company, a midwestern meat packer, had a cost of long-term debt 2 years ago of 8%. This 8% represented a 4% risk-free cost of long-term debt, a 2% business risk premium, and a 2% financial risk premium. Currently, the risk-free cost of long-term debt is 6%. How much would you expect the company's cost of long-term debt to be today, assuming that its business and financial risk have remained unchanged? The previous business risk premium of 2% and financial risk premium of 2% will still prevail, because neither has changed. Adding that 4% total risk premium to the 6% risk-free cost of long-term debt results in a cost of long-term debt to Hobson Company of 10%. In this *time-series comparison,* in which business and financial risk are assumed to be constant, the cost of the long-term funds changes only in response to changes in the risk-free cost of the given type of funds.

Another company, Raj Company, which has a 2% business risk premium and a 4% financial risk premium, can be used to demonstrate *comparisons between firms.* Although Raj and Hobson are both in the meat-packing business (and thus have the same business risk premium of 2%), the cost of long-term debt to Raj Company is currently 12% (the 6% risk-free cost plus a 2% business risk premium plus a 4% financial risk premium). This is greater than the 10% cost of long-term debt for Hobson. The difference is attributable to the greater
▲ financial risk associated with Raj.

The Basic Concept

The cost of capital is estimated at a given point in time. It reflects the expected average future cost of funds over the long run, based on the best information available. Although firms typically raise money in lumps, the cost of capital should reflect the interrelatedness of financing activities. For example, if a firm raises funds with debt (borrowing) today, it is likely that some form of equity, such as common stock, will have to be used next time. Most firms maintain a deliberate, optimal mix of debt and equity financing. This mix is commonly called a **target capital structure**—a topic that will be discussed in greater detail in Chapter 12. It is sufficient here to say that although firms raise money in lumps, they tend toward some desired *mix of financing.*

To capture the interrelatedness of financing assuming the presence of a target capital structure, we need to look at the *overall cost of capital* rather than the cost of the specific source of funds used to finance a given expenditure.

target capital structure
The desired optimal mix of debt and equity financing that most firms attempt to achieve and maintain.

Career Key
Management will use the cost of capital when assessing the acceptability and relative ranking of capital expenditure projects. The firm's target capital structure policy will go a long way to determining what the firm's cost of capital will be.

---

2. The risk-free cost of each type of financing, r_f, may differ considerably. In other words, at a given point in time, the risk-free cost of long-term debt may be 6% while the risk-free cost of common stock may be 9%. The risk-free cost is expected to be different for each type of financing, *l.* The risk-free cost of different *maturities* of the same type of debt may differ, because, as discussed in Chapter 2, long-term issues are generally viewed as more risky than short-term issues.

Example ▼ A firm is *currently* faced with an investment opportunity. Assume the following:

Best project available today

> Cost = $100,000
> Life = 20 years
> IRR = 7%

Cost of least-cost financing source available

> Debt = 6%

Because it can earn 7% on the investment of funds costing only 6%, the firm undertakes the opportunity. Imagine that *1 week later* a new investment opportunity is available:

Best project available 1 week later

> Cost = $100,000
> Life = 20 years
> IRR = 12%

Cost of least-cost financing source available

> Equity = 14%

In this instance, the firm rejects the opportunity, because the 14% financing cost is greater than the 12% expected return.

Were the firm's actions in the best interests of its owners? No—it accepted a project yielding a 7% return and rejected one with a 12% return. Clearly, there should be a better way, and there is: The firm can use a combined cost, which over the long run would provide for better decisions. By weighting the cost of each source of financing by its target proportion in the firm's capital structure, the firm can obtain a *weighted average cost* that reflects the interrelationship of financing decisions. Assuming that a 50–50 mix of debt and equity is targeted, the weighted average cost above would be 10% [(.50 × 6% debt) + (.50 × 14% equity)]. With this cost, the first opportunity would have been rejected (7% IRR < 10% weighted average cost), and the second one would have been accepted (12% IRR > 10% weighted average cost). Such an outcome would clearly be more desirable. ▲

The Cost of Specific Sources of Capital

This chapter focuses on finding the costs of specific sources of capital and combining them to determine and apply the weighted average cost of capital. Our concern is only with the *long-term* sources of funds available to a business firm, because these sources supply the permanent financing. Long-term financing supports the firm's fixed asset investments.[3] We assume throughout the chapter that such investments are selected by using appropriate capital budgeting techniques.

There are four basic sources of long-term funds for the business firm: long-term debt, preferred stock, common stock, and retained earnings. The right-hand side of a balance sheet can be used to illustrate these sources:

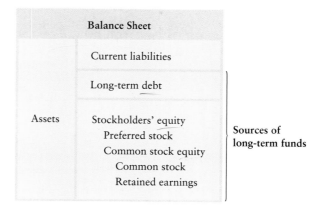

Although not all firms will use each of these methods of financing, each firm is expected to have funds from some of these sources in its capital structure. The *specific cost* of each source of financing is the *after-tax* cost of obtaining the financing *today*, not the historically based cost reflected by the existing financing on the firm's books. Techniques for determining the specific cost of each source of long-term funds are presented on the following pages. Although these techniques tend to develop precisely calculated values, the resulting values are at best *rough approximations* because of the numerous assumptions and forecasts that underlie them. Although we round calculated costs to the nearest .1 percent throughout this chapter, it is not unusual for practicing financial managers to use costs rounded to the nearest 1 percent because these values are merely estimates.

❓ Review Questions

11–1   What is the *cost of capital?* What role does it play in making long-term investment decisions? Why is use of a weighted average cost rather than the specific cost recommended?

11–2   Why are business and financial risk assumed to be unchanged when evaluating the cost of capital? Discuss the implications of these assumptions on the acceptance and financing of new projects.

11–3   Why is the cost of capital most appropriately measured on an after-tax basis?

---

3. The role of both long-term and short-term financing in supporting both fixed and current asset investments is addressed in Chapter 15. Suffice it to say that long-term funds are at minimum used to finance fixed assets.

11–4   You have just been told, "Because we are going to finance this project with debt, its required rate of return must exceed the cost of debt." Do you agree or disagree? Explain.

11.2 The Cost of Long-Term Debt

cost of long-term debt, k_i
The after-tax cost today of raising long-term funds through borrowing.

The **cost of long-term debt,** k_i, is the after-tax cost today of raising long-term funds through borrowing. For convenience, we typically assume that the funds are raised through the sale of bonds. In addition, consistent with Chapter 7, we assume that the bonds pay *annual*—rather than *semiannual*—interest.

Net Proceeds

net proceeds
Funds actually received from the sale of a security.

flotation costs
The total costs of issuing and selling a security.

Most corporate long-term debts are incurred through the sale of bonds. The **net proceeds** from the sale of a bond, or any security, are the funds that are actually received from the sale. **Flotation costs**—the total costs of issuing and selling a security—reduce the net proceeds from the sale. These costs apply to all public offerings of securities—debt, preferred stock, and common stock. They include two components: (1) *underwriting costs*—compensation earned by investment bankers for selling the security, and (2) *administrative costs*—issuer expenses such as legal, accounting, printing, and other expenses.

Example ▼

Duchess Corporation, a major hardware manufacturer, is contemplating selling $10 million worth of 20-year, 9% coupon (stated *annual* interest rate) bonds, each with a par value of $1,000. Because similar-risk bonds earn returns greater than 9%, the firm must sell the bonds for $980 to compensate for the lower coupon interest rate. The flotation costs are 2% of the par value of the bond (2% × $1,000), or $20. The net proceeds to the firm from the sale of each bond are

▲ therefore $960 ($980 − $20).

Before-Tax Cost of Debt

The before-tax cost of debt, k_d, for a bond can be obtained in any of three ways—quotation, calculation, or approximation.

Using Cost Quotations

Hint From the issuer's perspective, the IRR on a bond's cash flows is its *cost to maturity;* from the investor's perspective, the IRR on a bond's cash flows is its *yield to maturity (YTM),* as explained in Chapter 7. These two measures are conceptually similarly, although their point of view is different.

When the net proceeds from sale of a bond equal its par value, the before-tax cost would just equal the coupon interest rate. For example, a 10 percent coupon interest rate bond that nets proceeds equal to the bond's $1,000 par value would have a before-tax cost, k_d, of 10 percent.

A second quotation that is sometimes used is the *yield to maturity (YTM)* (see Chapter 7) on a similar-risk bond.[4] For example, if a similar-risk bond has a YTM of 9.7 percent, this value can be used as the before-tax cost of debt, k_d.

---

4. Generally, the yield to maturity of bonds with a similar "rating" is used. Bond ratings, which are published by independent agencies, were discussed in Chapter 2.

Calculating the Cost

This approach finds the before-tax cost of debt by calculating the *internal rate of return (IRR)* on the bond cash flows. From the issuer's point of view, this value can be referred to as the *cost to maturity* of the cash flows associated with the debt. The cost to maturity can be calculated by using either the trial-and-error techniques for finding IRR demonstrated in Chapter 9 or a financial calculator. It represents the annual before-tax percentage cost of the debt.

E x a m p l e ▼ In the preceding example, the net proceeds of a $1,000, 9% coupon interest rate, 20-year bond were found to be $960. The calculation of the annual cost is quite simple. The cash flow pattern is exactly the opposite of a conventional pattern; it consists of an initial inflow (the net proceeds) followed by a series of annual outlays (the interest payments). In the final year, when the debt is retired, an outlay representing the repayment of the principal also occurs. The cash flows associated with the Duchess Corporation's bond issue are as follows:

End of year(s)	Cash flow
0	$ 960
1–20	−$ 90
20	−$1,000

The initial $960 inflow is followed by annual interest outflows of $90 (9% coupon interest rate × $1,000 par value) over the 20-year life of the bond. In year 20, an outflow of $1,000 (the repayment of the principal) occurs. The before-tax cost of debt can be determined by finding the IRR—the discount rate that equates the present value of the outflows with the initial inflow.

Trial and Error   We know from the discussions in Chapter 7 that discounting a bond's future cash flows at its coupon interest rate will result in its $1,000 par value. Therefore, the discount rate necessary to cause Duchess Corporation's bond value to equal $960 must be greater than its 9% coupon interest rate. (Remember that the higher the discount rate, the lower the present value, and the lower the discount rate, the higher the present value.) Applying a 10% discount rate to the bond's future cash flows, we get

$$\$90 \times (PVIFA_{10\%,20yrs}) + \$1,000 \times (PVIF_{10\%,20yrs})$$
$$= \$90 \times (8.514) + \$1,000 \times (.149)$$
$$= \$766.26 + \$149.00 = \$915.26$$

Because the bond's value of $1,000 at its 9% coupon interest rate is higher than $960 and the $915.26 value at the 10% discount rate is lower than $960, the bond's before-tax cost must be between 9 and 10%. Because the $1,000 value is closer to $960, the before-tax cost of the bond rounded to the nearest whole percent would be 9%. By using *interpolation* (as described on the book's homepage at www.awlonline.com/gitman) the more precise value for the bond's before-tax cost is 9.47%.

Calculator Use [*Note:* Most calculators require either the present (net proceeds) or future (annual interest payments and repayment of principal) values to be input as a negative number to calculate cost to maturity. That approach is used here.] By using the calculator and the inputs shown, the before-tax cost (cost to maturity) of 9.452% should appear on the calculator display. Note that this number is the precise value of the bond's cost to maturity, which is closely approximated by the interpolated value of 9.47% found using the trial-and-error approach.

Inputs: 20   -960   90   1000

Functions: N   PV   PMT   FV   CPT   I

▲ **Outputs:**   9.452

Approximating the Cost

The before-tax cost of debt, k_d, for a bond with a $1,000 par value can be approximated by using the following equation:

$$k_d = \frac{I + \frac{\$1,000 - N_d}{n}}{\frac{N_d + \$1,000}{2}} \qquad (11.2)$$

where

$$I = \text{annual interest in dollars}$$
$$N_d = \text{net proceeds from the sale of debt (bond)}$$
$$n = \text{number of years to the bond's maturity}$$

Example ▼ Substituting the appropriate values from the Duchess Corporation example into the approximation formula given in Equation 11.2, we get

$$k_d = \frac{\$90 + \frac{\$1,000 - \$960}{20}}{\frac{\$960 + \$1,000}{2}} = \frac{\$90 + \$2}{\$980}$$

$$= \frac{\$92}{\$980} = \underline{\underline{9.4\%}}$$

This approximate before-tax cost of debt does not differ greatly from the
▲ 9.452% value calculated precisely in the preceding example.

After-Tax Cost of Debt

As indicated earlier, the *specific cost* of financing must be stated on an after-tax basis. Because interest on debt is tax deductible, it reduces the firm's taxable income. The interest deduction therefore reduces taxes by an amount equal to the product of the deductible interest and the firm's tax rate. In light of this, the after-tax cost of debt, k_i, can be found by multiplying the before-tax cost, k_d, by 1 minus the tax rate, T, as stated in the following equation:

$$k_i = k_d \times (1 - T) \tag{11.3}$$

Example ▼ We can demonstrate the after-tax debt cost calculation using the 9.4% before-tax debt cost approximation for Duchess Corporation, which has a 40% tax rate. Applying Equation 11.3 results in an after-tax cost of debt of 5.6% [9.4% × (1 − .40)]. Typically, the explicit cost of long-term debt is less than the explicit cost of any of the alternative forms of long-term financing, primarily because
▲ of the tax deductibility of interest.

In Practice

Flying High at Continental Airlines

Larry Kellner, CFO of Continental Airlines, took over the financial pilot's seat in 1995, when the airline was about to crash into bankruptcy for the third time. He inherited a company that had almost no credibility with external stakeholders from investors to creditors, more than $500 million in debt, a billion dollars of aircraft leases in default, and essentially no cash—yet needed billions of dollars in additional financing to survive.

To convince Continental's external stakeholders that the airline would not only take off but keep on flying this time, Kellner had to negotiate with lenders and aircraft manufacturers for better financing terms. His candor about Continental's current situation and where the firm was going was a distinct change from earlier times. "I believe in underpromising and overdelivering," Kellner explains. "My approach is to be blunt, direct, honest, and to make sense. You go to stakeholders with what you want to do—not some crazy idea—tell them why, listen, compromise, and move on."

Navigating through turbulent financial skies, Kellner significantly reduced the amount of both Continental's outstanding debt and its interest expense. He approached his creditors as partners, not adversaries, and was able to restructure high-interest debt on more favorable terms. In addition, Kellner raised over $6 billion in new financing in about 18 months at advantageous rates—within 85 basis points over Treasuries—and increased cash reserves to $1 billion. With this lower cost of debt, Continental operated more efficiently and had the resources to weather a future economic downturn. Operational performance and customer service also improved, and Continental's reputation with the investment community soared.

? Review Questions

11–5   What is meant by the *net proceeds* from the sale of a bond? What are flotation costs and how do they affect a bond's net proceeds?

11–6   Describe the trial-and-error approach used to calculate the before-tax cost of debt. How does this calculation relate to a bond's *cost to maturity* and IRR? How can this value be found more efficiently and accurately?

11–7   What sort of general approximation can be used to find the before-tax cost of debt? How is the before-tax cost of debt converted into the after-tax cost?

11.3   The Cost of Preferred Stock

Preferred stock represents a special type of ownership interest in the firm. It gives preferred stockholders the right to receive their *stated* dividends before any earnings can be distributed to common stockholders. Because preferred stock is a form of ownership, the proceeds from its sale are expected to be held for an infinite period of time. The key characteristics of preferred stock were described in Chapter 2. However, the one aspect of preferred stock that requires clarification at this point is dividends.

Preferred Stock Dividends

Most preferred stock dividends are stated as a *dollar amount*—"x dollars per year." When dividends are stated this way, the stock is often referred to as "x-dollar preferred stock." Thus, a $4 preferred stock is expected to pay preferred stockholders $4 in dividends each year on each share of preferred stock owned.

Sometimes preferred stock dividends are stated as an *annual percentage rate*. This rate represents the percentage of the stock's par, or face, value that equals the annual dividend. For instance, an 8 percent preferred stock with a $50 par value would be expected to pay an annual dividend of $4 a share (.08 × $50 par = $4). Before the cost of preferred stock is calculated, any dividends stated as percentages should be converted to annual dollar dividends.

Calculating the Cost of Preferred Stock

cost of preferred stock, k_p
The relationship between the cost of the preferred stock and the amount of funds provided by the preferred stock issue; found by dividing the annual dividend, D_p, by the net proceeds from the sale of the preferred stock, N_p.

The **cost of preferred stock, k_p,** is the ratio of the preferred stock dividend to the firm's net proceeds from the sale of the preferred stock—that is, the relationship between the "cost" of the preferred stock, in the form of its annual dividend, and the amount of funds provided by the preferred stock issue. The net proceeds represent the amount of money to be received minus any flotation costs. Equation 11.4 gives the cost of preferred stock, k_p, in terms of the annual dollar dividend, D_p, and the net proceeds from the sale of the stock, N_p:

$$k_p = \frac{D_p}{N_p}$$

(11.4)

Because preferred stock dividends are paid out of the firm's *after-tax* cash flows, a tax adjustment is not required.

Example ▼ Duchess Corporation is contemplating issuance of a 10% (annual dividend) preferred stock that is expected to sell for its $87 per share par value.[5] The cost of issuing and selling the stock is expected to be $5 per share. The first step in finding the cost of the stock is to calculate the dollar amount of the annual preferred dividend, which is $8.70 (.10 × $87). The net proceeds from the proposed sale of stock can be found by subtracting the flotation costs from the sale price. This gives a value of $82 per share. Substituting the annual dividend, D_p, of $8.70 and the net proceeds, N_p, of $82 into Equation 11.4 gives the cost of preferred ▲ stock, 10.6% ($8.70 ÷ $82).

The cost of preferred stock (10.6%) is more expensive than the cost of long-term debt (5.6%). This difference results primarily because the cost of long-term debt—interest—is tax deductible.

? Review Question

11–8   How would you calculate the cost of preferred stock? Why do we concern ourselves with the net proceeds from the sale of the stock instead of its sale price?

11.4 The Cost of Common Stock

The *cost of common stock* is the return required on the stock by investors in the marketplace. There are two forms of common stock financing: (1) retained earnings and (2) new issues of common stock. As a first step in finding each of these costs, we must estimate the cost of common stock equity.

Finding the Cost of Common Stock Equity

cost of common stock equity,
k_s
The rate at which investors discount the expected dividends of the firm to determine its share value.

The **cost of common stock equity, k_s,** is the rate at which investors discount the expected dividends of the firm to determine its share value. Two techniques measure the cost of common stock equity capital.[6] One uses the constant-growth valuation model; the other relies on the capital asset pricing model (CAPM).

---

5. For simplicity, the preferred stock in this example is assumed to be sold for its par value. In practice, particularly for subsequent issues of already outstanding preferred stock, it is typically sold at a price that differs from its par value.

6. Other more subjective techniques are available for estimating the cost of common stock equity. One popular technique is the *bond yield plus a premium;* it estimates the cost of common stock equity by adding a premium, typically between 3 and 5%, to the firm's current cost of long-term debt. Another even more subjective technique uses the firm's *expected return on equity (ROE)* as a measure of its cost of common stock equity. Here we focus only on the more theoretically based techniques.

Using the Constant-Growth Valuation (Gordon) Model

constant-growth valuation (Gordon) model
Assumes that the value of a share of stock equals the present value of all future dividends (assumed to grow at a constant rate) that it is expected to provide over an infinite time horizon.

The **constant-growth valuation model**—the **Gordon model**—was presented in Chapter 7. It is based on the widely accepted premise that the value of a share of stock is equal to the present value of all future dividends (assumed to grow at a constant rate) over an infinite time horizon. The key expression derived in Chapter 7 and presented as Equation 7.9 is restated in Equation 11.5:

$$P_0 = \frac{D_1}{k_s - g} \tag{11.5}$$

where

P_0 = value of common stock
D_1 = per share dividend expected at the end of year 1
k_s = required return on common stock
g = constant rate of growth in dividends

Solving Equation 11.5 for k_s results in the following expression for the *cost of common stock equity:*

$$k_s = \frac{D_1}{P_0} + g \tag{11.6}$$

Equation 11.6 indicates that the cost of common stock equity can be found by dividing the dividend expected at the end of year 1 by the current price of the stock and adding the expected growth rate. Because common stock dividends are paid from *after-tax* income, no tax adjustment is required.

Example ▼ Duchess Corporation wishes to determine its cost of common stock equity, k_s. The market price, P_0, of its common stock is $50 per share. The firm expects to pay a dividend, D_1, of $4 at the end of the coming year, 2001. The dividends paid on the outstanding stock over the past 6 years (1995–2000) were as follows:

Year	Dividend
2000	$3.80
1999	3.62
1998	3.47
1997	3.33
1996	3.12
1995	2.97

Using the table for the present value interest factors, *PVIF* (Table A–3), or a financial calculator in conjunction with the technique described for finding growth rates in Chapter 5, we can calculate the annual growth rate of dividends, *g*. It turns out to be approximately 5% (more precisely, it is 5.05%). Substituting $D_1 = \$4$, $P_0 = \$50$, and $g = 5\%$ into Equation 11.6 results in the cost of common stock equity:

$$k_s = \frac{\$4}{\$50} + 5.0\% = 8.0\% + 5.0\% = \underline{\underline{13.0\%}}$$

The 13.0% cost of common stock equity represents the return required by *existing* shareholders to leave the market price of the firm's outstanding shares ▲ unchanged.

Using the Capital Asset Pricing Model (CAPM)

capital asset pricing model (CAPM)
Describes the relationship between the required return, or cost of common stock equity, k_s, and the nondiversifiable risk of the firm as measured by the beta coefficient, b.

The **capital asset pricing model (CAPM)** was developed and discussed in Chapter 6. It describes the relationship between the required return, or cost of common stock equity, k_s, and the nondiversifiable risk of the firm as measured by the beta coefficient, b. The basic CAPM is given in Equation 11.7:

$$k_s = R_F + [b \times (k_m - R_F)] \tag{11.7}$$

where

R_F = risk-free rate of return
k_m = market return; return on the market portfolio of assets

By using CAPM, the cost of common stock equity is the return required by investors as compensation for the firm's nondiversifiable risk, measured by beta.

E x a m p l e ▼ Duchess Corporation now wishes to calculate its cost of common stock equity, k_s, by using the capital asset pricing model. The firm's investment advisers and its own analyses indicate that the risk-free rate, R_F, equals 7%; the firm's beta, b, equals 1.5; and the market return, k_m, equals 11%. Substituting these values into Equation 11.7, the company estimates the cost of common stock equity, k_s, as follows:

$$k_s = 7.0\% + [1.5 \times (11.0\% - 7.0\%)] = 7.0\% + 6.0\% = \underline{\underline{13.0\%}}$$

The 13.0% cost of common stock equity, which is the same as that found by using the constant growth valuation model, represents the required return of ▲ investors in Duchess Corporation common stock.

Comparing the Constant-Growth and CAPM Techniques

Use of CAPM differs from the constant-growth valuation model in that it directly considers the firm's risk, as reflected by beta, in determining the *required* return or cost of common stock equity. The constant-growth model does not look at risk; it uses the market price, P_0, as a reflection of the *expected* risk-return preference of investors in the marketplace. The constant-growth valuation model and CAPM techniques for finding k_s are, in a practical sense, theoretically equivalent. But it is difficult to demonstrate that equivalency, due to measurement problems associated with growth, beta, the risk-free rate (what maturity of government security to use), and the market return. The use of the constant-growth valuation model is often preferred because the data required are more readily available.

Another difference is that when the constant-growth valuation model is used to find the cost of common stock equity, it can easily be adjusted for flotation costs to find the cost of new common stock; the CAPM does not provide a simple adjustment mechanism. The difficulty in adjusting the cost of common stock equity calculated by using CAPM occurs because in its common form the model does not include the market price, P_0, a variable needed to make such an adjustment. Although CAPM has a stronger theoretical foundation, the computational appeal of the traditional constant-growth valuation model justifies its use throughout this text to measure common stock costs.

The Cost of Retained Earnings

cost of retained earnings, k_r
The same as the cost of an *equivalent fully subscribed issue of additional common stock*, which is measured by the cost of common stock equity, k_s.

Dividends are paid out of a firm's earnings. Their payment, made in cash to the common stockholders, reduces the firm's retained earnings. If a firm needed common stock equity financing of a certain amount, it could issue additional common stock in that amount and still pay dividends to its stockholders. Alternatively, the firm could increase common stock equity by retaining the earnings (not paying the cash dividends) in the needed amount. In a strict accounting sense, the retention of earnings increases common stock equity in the same way that the sale of additional shares of common stock does. Thus, the **cost of retained earnings, k_r**, to the firm is the same as the cost of an *equivalent fully subscribed issue of additional common stock*. Stockholders therefore find the firm's retention of earnings acceptable only if they expect that it will earn at least their required return on the reinvested funds.

Hint   Using retained earnings as a major source of financing for capital expenditures does not give away control of the firm and does not dilute present earnings per share, as would occur if new common stock were issued. However, the firm must effectively manage retained earnings, in order to produce profits that increase future retained earnings.

Viewing retained earnings as a fully subscribed issue of additional common stock, we can set the firm's cost of retained earnings, k_r, equal to the cost of common stock equity as given by Equations 11.6 and 11.7.[7]

$$k_r = k_s \tag{11.8}$$

It is not necessary to adjust the cost of retained earnings for flotation costs, because by retaining earnings, the firm "raises" equity capital without incurring these costs.

E x a m p l e ▼   The cost of retained earnings for Duchess Corporation was actually calculated in the preceding examples: It is equal to the cost of common stock equity. Thus, k_r equals 13.0%. As we will show in the next section, the cost of retained earnings is always lower than the cost of a new issue of common stock, due to the absence ▲ of flotation costs when financing projects with retained earnings.

The Cost of New Issues of Common Stock

Our purpose in finding the firm's overall cost of capital is to determine the after-tax cost of *new* funds required for financing projects. Attention must therefore be given to the cost of a new issue of common stock, k_n. As will be explained later, this cost is important only when sufficient retained earnings are unavailable.

---

7. Technically, if a stockholder received dividends and wished to invest them in additional shares of the firm's stock, he or she would have to first pay personal taxes on the dividends and then pay brokerage fees before acquiring additional shares. By using pt as the average stockholder's personal tax rate and bf as the average brokerage fees stated as a percentage, the cost of retained earnings, k_r, can be specified as: $k_r = k_s \times (1 - pt) \times (1 - bf)$. Due to the difficulty in estimating pt and bf, only the simpler definition of k_r given in Equation 11.8 is used here.

cost of a new issue of common stock, k_n
The cost of common stock, net of underpricing and associated flotation costs.

underpriced
Stock sold at a price below its current market price, P_0.

The **cost of a new issue of common stock, k_n**, is determined by calculating the cost of common stock, net of underpricing and associated flotation costs. Normally, to sell a new issue, it will have to be **underpriced**—sold at a price below the current market price, P_0. Firms underprice new issues for a variety of reasons. First, when the market is in equilibrium (i.e., the demand for shares equals the supply of shares), additional demand for shares can be achieved only at a lower price. Second, when additional shares are issued, each share's percent of ownership in the firm is diluted, thereby justifying a lower share value. Finally, many investors view the issuance of additional shares as a signal that management is using common stock equity financing because it believes that the shares are currently overpriced. Recognizing this information, they will buy shares only at a price below the current market price. Clearly, these and other factors necessitate underpricing of new offerings of common stock. Flotation costs paid for issuing and selling the new issue will further reduce proceeds.

The cost of new issues can be calculated using the constant-growth valuation model expression for the cost of existing common stock, k_s, as a starting point. If we let N_n represent the net proceeds from the sale of new common stock after subtracting underpricing and flotation costs, the cost of the new issue, k_n, can be expressed as follows:[8]

$$k_n = \frac{D_1}{N_n} + g \qquad (11.9)$$

The net proceeds from sale of new common stock, N_n, will be less than the current market price, P_0. Therefore, the cost of new issues, k_n, will always be greater than the cost of existing issues, k_s, which, as noted before, is equal to the cost of retained earnings, k_r. *The cost of new common stock is normally greater than any other long-term financing cost.* Because common stock dividends are paid from after-tax cash flows, no tax adjustment is required.

Example ▼ In the constant-growth valuation model example, we found Duchess Corporation's cost of common stock equity, k_s, to be 13%, using the following values: an expected dividend, D_1, of $4; a current market price, P_0, of $50; and an expected growth rate of dividends, g, of 5%.

To determine its cost of *new* common stock, k_n, Duchess Corporation has estimated that, on the average, new shares can be sold for $47. The $3 per share underpricing is necessary because of the competitive nature of the market. A second cost associated with a new issue is flotation costs of $2.50 per share that would be paid to issue and sell the new issue. The total underpricing and flotation costs per share are therefore expected to be $5.50.

Subtracting the $5.50 per share underpricing and flotation cost from the current $50 share price, P_0, results in expected net proceeds, N_n, of $44.50 per share

---

8. An alternative, but computationally less straightforward, form of this equation is

$$k_n = \frac{D_1}{P_0 \times (1 - f)} + g \qquad (11.9a)$$

where f represents the *percentage* reduction in current market price expected as a result of underpricing and flotation costs. Simply stated, N_n in Equation 11.9 is equivalent to $P_0 \times (1 - f)$ in Equation 11.9a. For convenience, Equation 11.9 is used to define the cost of a new issue of common stock, k_n.

($50.00 − $5.50). Substituting $D_1 = \$4$, $N_n = \$44.50$, and $g = 5\%$ into Equation 11.9 results in a cost of new common stock, k_n, as follows:

$$k_n = \frac{\$4.00}{\$44.50} + 5.0\% = 9.0\% + 5.0\% = \underline{\underline{14.0\%}}$$

Duchess Corporation's cost of new common stock, k_n, is therefore 14.0%. This is the value to be used in subsequent calculations of the firm's overall cost of capital.

▲

？ Review Questions

11–9   What premise about share value underlies the constant-growth valuation (Gordon) model that is used to measure the cost of common stock equity, k_s? What does each component of the equation represent?

11–10   If retained earnings are viewed as an *equivalent fully subscribed issue of additional common stock,* why is the cost of financing a project with retained earnings less than the cost of using a new issue of common stock?

11.5 The Weighted Average Cost of Capital (WACC)

weighted average cost of capital (WACC), k_a
Reflects the expected average future cost of funds over the long run; found by weighting the cost of each specific type of capital by its proportion in the firm's capital structure.

Now that we have reviewed methods for calculating the cost of specific sources of financing, we can present techniques for determining the overall cost of capital. As noted earlier, the **weighted average cost of capital (WACC)**, k_a, reflects the expected average future cost of funds over the long run. It is found by weighting the cost of each specific type of capital by its proportion in the firm's capital structure.

Calculating the Weighted Average Cost of Capital (WACC)

The calculation of the weighted average cost of capital (WACC) is performed by multiplying the specific cost of each form of financing by its proportion in the firm's capital structure and summing the weighted values. As an equation, the weighted average cost of capital, k_a, can be specified as follows:

$$k_a = (w_i \times k_i) + (w_p \times k_p) + (w_s \times k_{r\ or\ n}) \tag{11.10}$$

where

w_i = proportion of long-term debt in capital structure
w_p = proportion of preferred stock in capital structure
w_s = proportion of common stock equity in capital structure
$w_i + w_p + w_s = 1.0$

Three important points should be noted in Equation 11.10:

1. For computational convenience, it is best to convert the weights to decimal form and leave the specific costs in percentage terms.
2. *The sum of weights must equal 1.0.* Simply stated, all capital structure components must be accounted for.
3. The firm's common stock equity weight, w_s, is multiplied by either the cost of retained earnings, k_r, or the cost of new common stock, k_n. Which cost is used depends on whether the firm's common stock equity will be financed using retained earnings, k_r, or new common stock, k_n.

Example ▼ In earlier examples, we found the costs of the various types of capital for Duchess Corporation to be as follows:

Cost of debt, k_i = 5.6%
Cost of preferred stock, k_p = 10.6%
Cost of retained earnings, k_r = 13.0%
Cost of new common stock, k_n = 14.0%

The company uses the following weights in calculating its weighted average cost of capital:

Source of capital	Weight
Long-term debt	40%
Preferred stock	10
Common stock equity	50
Total	100%

Because the firm expects to have a sizable amount of retained earnings available ($300,000), it plans to use its cost of retained earnings, k_r, as the cost of common stock equity. Duchess Corporation's weighted average cost of capital is calculated in Table 11.1. The resulting weighted average cost of capital for Duchess is 9.8%. Assuming an unchanged risk level, the firm should accept all ▲ projects that will earn a return greater than or equal to 9.8%.

TABLE 11.1   Calculation of the Weighted Average Cost of Capital for Duchess Corporation

Hint For computational convenience, the financing proportion weights are listed in decimal form in column 1 and the specific costs are shown in percentage terms in column 2.

Source of capital	Weight (1)	Cost (2)	Weighted cost $[(1) \times (2)]$ (3)
Long-term debt	.40	5.6%	2.2%
Preferred stock	.10	10.6	1.1
Common stock equity	.50	13.0	6.5
Totals	1.00		9.8%

Weighted average cost of capital = 9.8%

Weighting Schemes

Weights can be calculated based on *book value* or on *market value* and using *historic* or *target* proportions.

Book Value Versus Market Value

book value weights
Weights that use accounting values to measure the proportion of each type of capital in the firm's financial structure.

market value weights
Weights that use market values to measure the proportion of each type of capital in the firm's financial structure.

Book value weights use accounting values to measure the proportion of each type of capital in the firm's financial structure. **Market value weights** measure the proportion of each type of capital at its market value. Market value weights are appealing, because the market values of securities closely approximate the actual dollars to be received from their sale. Moreover, because the costs of the various types of capital are calculated by using prevailing market prices, it seems reasonable to use market value weights. In addition, the long-term investment cash flows to which the cost of capital is applied are estimated in terms of current as well as future market values. *Market value weights are clearly preferred over book value weights.*

Historic Versus Target

historic weights
Either book or market value weights based on *actual* capital structure proportions.

target weights
Either book or market value weights based on *desired* capital structure proportions.

Historic weights can be either book or market value weights based on *actual* capital structure proportions. For example, past or current book value proportions would constitute a form of historic weighting, as would past or current market value proportions. Such a weighting scheme would therefore be based on real—rather than desired—proportions.

    Target weights, which can also be based on either book or market values, reflect the firm's *desired* capital structure proportions. Firms using target weights establish such proportions on the basis of the "optimal" capital structure they wish to achieve. (The development of these proportions and the optimal structure are discussed in detail in Chapter 12.)

    When one considers the somewhat approximate nature of the weighted average cost of capital calculation, the choice of weights may not be critical. However, from a strictly theoretical point of view, the *preferred weighting scheme is target market value proportions,* and these are assumed throughout this chapter.

Career Key

The *marketing* department will be concerned with the weighted average cost of capital because acceptance of its proposed projects will depend on whether its IRRs are greater than the WACC.

> ## ? Review Question
>
> 11–11   What is the *weighted average cost of capital (WACC),* and how is it calculated? Describe the logic underlying the use of *target capital structure weights,* and compare and contrast this approach with the use of *historic weights.*

LG5 LG6   11.6 The Marginal Cost and Investment Decisions

The firm's weighted average cost of capital is a key input to the investment decision-making process. As demonstrated earlier in the chapter, the firm should make only those investments for which the expected return is greater than the weighted average cost of capital. Of course, at any given time, the firm's financing costs and investment returns will be affected by the volume of financing and investment undertaken. The concepts of a *weighted marginal cost of capital* and an *investment opportunities schedule* provide the mechanisms whereby financing and investment decisions can be made simultaneously.

The Weighted Marginal Cost of Capital (WMCC)

weighted marginal cost of capital (WMCC)
The firm's weighted average cost of capital associated with its *next dollar* of total new financing.

The weighted average cost of capital may vary at any time depending on the volume of financing the firm plans to raise. *As the volume of financing increases, the costs of the various types of financing will increase, raising the firm's weighted average cost of capital.* Therefore, it is useful to calculate the **weighted marginal cost of capital (WMCC)**, which is simply the firm's weighted average cost of capital associated with its *next dollar* of total new financing. This marginal cost is relevant to current decisions.

Because the costs of the financing components—debt, preferred stock, and common stock—rise as larger amounts are raised, the WMCC is an increasing function of the level of total new financing. Increases in the component financing costs occur because the larger the amount of new financing, the greater the risk to the funds supplier. Funds suppliers require greater returns in the form of interest, dividends, or growth as compensation for the increased risk introduced as larger volumes of *new* financing are incurred.

Another factor that causes the weighted average cost of capital to increase is the use of common stock equity financing. New financing provided by common stock equity will be taken from available retained earnings until exhausted and then will be obtained through new common stock financing. Because retained earnings are a less expensive form of common stock equity financing than the sale of new common stock, once retained earnings have been exhausted, the weighted average cost of capital will rise with the addition of more expensive new common stock.

Finding Breaking Points

breaking point
The level of *total* new financing at which the cost of one of the financing components rises, thereby causing an upward shift in the *weighted marginal cost of capital (WMCC)*.

To calculate the WMCC, we must calculate the **breaking points**, which reflect the level of *total* new financing at which the cost of one of the financing components rises. The following general equation can be used to find breaking points:

$$BP_j = \frac{AF_j}{w_j} \tag{11.11}$$

where

BP_j = breaking point for financing source j
AF_j = amount of funds available from financing source j at a given cost
w_j = capital structure weight (historic or target, stated in decimal form) for financing source j

E x a m p l e ▼ When Duchess Corporation exhausts its $300,000 of available retained earnings (k_r = 13.0%), it must use the more expensive new common stock financing (k_n = 14.0%) to meet its common stock equity needs. In addition, the firm expects that it can borrow only $400,000 of debt at the 5.6% cost; additional debt will have an after-tax cost (k_i) of 8.4%. Two breaking points therefore exist—(1) when the $300,000 of retained earnings costing 13.0% is exhausted and (2) when the $400,000 of long-term debt costing 5.6% is exhausted.

The breaking points can be found by substituting these values and the corresponding capital structure weights given earlier into Equation 11.11. We get

$$BP_{\text{common equity}} = \frac{\$300,000}{.50} = \$600,000$$

$$BP_{\text{long-term debt}} = \frac{\$400,000}{.40} = \$1,000,000$$

Calculating the WMCC

Once the breaking points have been determined, the next step is to calculate the weighted average cost of capital over the range of total new financing between breaking points. First, we find the WACC for a level of total new financing between zero and the first breaking point. Next, we find the WACC for a level of total new financing between the first and second breaking points, and so on. By definition, for each of the ranges of total new financing between breaking points, certain component capital costs will increase, causing the weighted average cost of capital to increase to a higher level than that over the preceding range.

weighted marginal cost of capital (WMCC) schedule
Graph that relates the firm's weighted average cost of capital to the level of total new financing.

Together, these data can be used to prepare the **weighted marginal cost of capital (WMCC) schedule,** which is a graph that relates the firm's weighted average cost of capital to the level of total new financing.

E x a m p l e ▼ Table 11.2 summarizes the calculation of the WACC for Duchess Corporation over the three total new financing ranges created by the two breaking points—$600,000 and $1,000,000. Comparing the costs in column 3 of the table for each of the three ranges, we can see that the costs in the first range ($0 to $600,000) are those calculated in earlier examples and used in Table 11.1. The second range ($600,000 to $1,000,000) reflects the increase in the common stock equity cost to 14.0%. In the final range, the increase in the long-term debt cost to 8.4% is introduced.

The weighted average costs of capital (WACC) for the three ranges created by the two breaking points are summarized in the table shown at the bottom of Figure 11.1. These data describe the weighted marginal cost of capital (WMCC), which increases as levels of total new financing increase. Figure 11.1 presents the WMCC schedule. Again, it is clear that the WMCC is an increasing function of ▲ the amount of total new financing raised.

The Investment Opportunities Schedule (IOS)

investment opportunities schedule (IOS)
A ranking of investment possibilities from best (highest return) to worst (lowest return).

At any given time, a firm has certain investment opportunities available to it. These opportunities differ with respect to the size of investment, risk, and return.[9] The firm's **investment opportunities schedule (IOS)** is a ranking of investment

---

9. Because the calculated weighted average cost of capital does not apply to risk-changing investments, we assume that all opportunities have equal risk similar to the firm's risk.

TABLE 11.2   Weighted Average Cost of Capital for Ranges of Total New Financing for Duchess Corporation

Range of total new financing	Source of capital (1)	Weight (2)	Cost (3)	Weighted cost [(2) × (3)] (4)
$0 to $600,000	Debt	.40	5.6%	2.2%
	Preferred	.10	10.6	1.1
	Common	.50	13.0	6.5
			Weighted average cost of capital	9.8%
$600,000 to $1,000,000	Debt	.40	5.6%	2.2%
	Preferred	.10	10.6	1.1
	Common	.50	14.0	7.0
			Weighted average cost of capital	10.3%
$1,000,000 and above	Debt	.40	8.4%	3.4%
	Preferred	.10	10.6	1.1
	Common	.50	14.0	7.0
			Weighted average cost of capital	11.5%

FIGURE 11.1

WMCC Schedule
Weighted marginal cost of capital (WMCC) schedule for Duchess Corporation

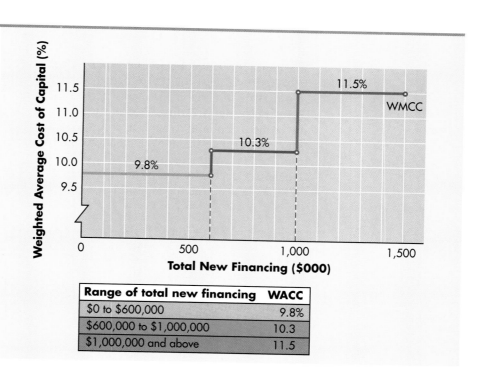

Range of total new financing	WACC
$0 to $600,000	9.8%
$600,000 to $1,000,000	10.3
$1,000,000 and above	11.5

| TABLE 11.3 | Investment Opportunities Schedule (IOS) for Duchess Corporation | | |

Investment opportunity	Internal rate of return (IRR) (1)	Initial investment (2)	Cumulative investment*ᵃ* (3)
A	15.0%	$100,000	$ 100,000
B	14.5	200,000	300,000
C	14.0	400,000	700,000
D	13.0	100,000	800,000
E	12.0	300,000	1,100,000
F	11.0	200,000	1,300,000
G	10.0	100,000	1,400,000

*ᵃ*The cumulative investment represents the total amount invested in projects with higher returns plus the investment required for the given investment opportunity.

possibilities from best (highest return) to worst (lowest return). As the cumulative amount of money invested in a firm's capital projects increases, its return (IRR) on the projects will decrease; generally, the first project selected will have the highest return, the next project the second highest, and so on. In other words, the return on investments will *decrease* as the firm accepts additional projects.

Example ▼ Duchess Corporation's current investment opportunities schedule (IOS) lists the best (highest return) to the worst (lowest return) investment possibilities in column 1 of Table 11.3. Column 2 of the table shows the initial investment required by each project. Column 3 shows the cumulative total invested funds required to finance all projects better than and including the corresponding investment opportunity. Plotting the project returns against the cumulative investment (column 1 against column 3 in Table 11.3) on a set of total new financing or investment–weighted average cost of capital and IRR axes results in the firm's investment opportunities schedule (IOS). A graph of the IOS for Duchess Corporation is given in Figure 11.2. Use of the IOS along with the **▲** WMCC in decision making is discussed in the following section.

Using the WMCC and IOS to Make Financing/Investment Decisions

As long as a project's internal rate of return is greater than the weighted marginal cost of new financing, the firm should accept the project.[10] The return will decrease with the acceptance of more projects, and the weighted marginal cost of capital will increase because greater amounts of financing will be required. The firm would therefore *accept projects up to the point at which the marginal return*

---

10. Although net present value could be used to make these decisions, the internal rate of return is used here because of the ease of comparison it offers.

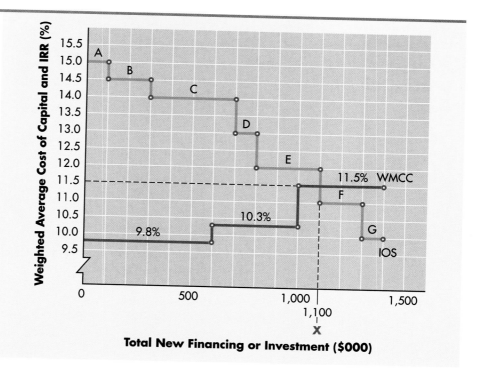

FIGURE 11.2

IOS and WMCC Schedules

Using the IOS and WMCC to select projects

---

on its investment equals its weighted marginal cost of capital. Beyond that point, its investment return will be less than its capital cost.[11]

This approach is consistent with the maximization of net present value (NPV), because for conventional projects (1) the NPV is positive as long as the IRR exceeds the weighted average cost of capital, k_a, and (2) the larger the difference between the IRR and k_a, the larger the resulting NPV. Therefore, the acceptance of projects beginning with those having the greatest positive difference between IRR and k_a down to the point at which IRR just equals k_a should result in the maximum total NPV for all independent projects accepted. Such an outcome is completely consistent with the firm's goal of owner wealth maximization. Returning to the Duchess Corporation example, we can demonstrate this procedure.

Example ▼ Figure 11.2 shows the Duchess Corporation's WMCC schedule and IOS on the same set of axes. By using these two functions in combination, the firm's optimal capital budget ("X" in the figure) is determined. By raising $1.1 million of new financing and investing these funds in projects A, B, C, D, and E, the firm should maximize the wealth of its owners, because these projects result in the maximum total net present value. Note that the 12.0% return on the last dollar invested (in project E) *exceeds* its 11.5% weighted average cost; investment in project F is not

---

11. So as not to confuse the discussion presented here, the fact that the use of the IRR for selecting projects may not provide optimum decisions is ignored. The problems associated with the IRR and its use in capital rationing were discussed in greater detail in Chapter 10.

In Practice

Clearing International Hurdles

Finance managers at General Motors (GM) headquarters in Detroit base hurdle rates (minimum rates of return) for both domestic and international investment decisions on the company's cost of capital. Timothy Smith, director of capital and business planning for GM's Latin American, African, and Middle Eastern operations, wondered if those rates accurately measured the costs and risks of operating overseas or if they relied mostly on past performance of foreign capital markets. Smith wanted a more rigorous approach than the common practice at most multinational corporations, which is to adjust the firm's U.S. cost of capital for the perceived risk of a particular country.

Smith worked with financial consultants Applied Finance Group (AFG) to create a model that included the return on equity (ROE) investors required in those foreign markets. AFG developed a formula for a "market-derived discount rate" (MDDR), the discount rate (IRR) that equated a company's projected cash flows to its market value (equity plus book value of debt). AFG analyzed MDDRs of industrial companies in eight countries and calculated median rates. Assigning the United States a benchmark of 1.0, AFG derived multiples based on the median MDDRs for each country. Brazil had the highest MDDR multiple, 2.21 times that of the United States, and Singapore's was 0.78. According to this model, a company with a 10 percent U.S. hurdle rate would require a 22.1 percent return on a Brazilian investment but only 7.8 percent in Singapore. GM is testing this approach and monitoring the results. One advantage is that it provides numerical data in place of educated guesses about international risk.

feasible because its 11.0% return is *less than* the 11.5% cost of funds available for investment.

Note that at the point at which the IRR equals the weighted average cost of capital, k_a—the optimal capital budget of $1,100,000 at point X in Figure 11.2—the firm's size as well as its shareholder value will be optimized. In a sense, the size of the firm is determined by the market—the availability of and returns on investment opportunities, and the availability and cost of financing.

Of course, as noted in Chapter 10, most firms operate under *capital rationing* because management imposes an internal capital expenditure (and therefore financing) budget constraint that is below the optimum capital budget (where IRR = k_a). Suffice it to say that due to capital rationing, a gap frequently exists between the theoretically optimal capital budget and the firm's actual level of financing/investment.

? Review Questions

11–12 What is the *weighted marginal cost of capital (WMCC)?* What does the *WMCC schedule* represent? Why does this schedule increase?

11–13 What is the *investment opportunities schedule (IOS)?* Is it typically depicted as an increasing or decreasing function of the level of investment at a given point in time? Why?

11–14 Use a graph to show how the WMCC schedule and the IOS can be used to find the level of financing/investment that maximizes owner wealth. Why, on a practical basis, do many firms finance/invest at a level below this optimum?

SUMMARY

(LG1) Understand the basic assumptions, concept, and specific sources of capital underlying the cost of capital. The cost of capital is the rate of return that a firm must earn on its investments to maintain its market value and attract needed funds. The specific costs of the basic sources of capital (long-term debt, preferred stock, retained earnings, and common stock) can be calculated individually. Only the cost of debt must be adjusted for taxes. The cost of each is affected by business and financial risks, which are assumed to be unchanged, and by the risk-free cost of the type of financing. To capture the interrelatedness of financing, a weighted average cost of capital should be used.

(LG2) Determine the cost of long-term debt and the cost of preferred stock. The cost of long-term debt is the after-tax cost today of raising long-term funds through borrowing. Cost quotations, calculation using either trial-and-error techniques or a financial calculator, or an approximation can be used to find the before-tax cost of debt, which must then be tax-adjusted. The cost of preferred stock is the stated annual dividend expressed as a percentage of the net proceeds from the sale of preferred shares. The key variable definitions and formulas for the before- and after-tax cost of debt and the cost of preferred stock are given in Table 11.4.

(LG3) Calculate the cost of common stock equity and convert it into the cost of retained earnings and the cost of new issues of common stock. The cost of common stock equity can be calculated by using the constant-growth valuation model or the capital asset pricing model (CAPM). The cost of retained earnings is equal to the cost of common stock equity. An adjustment in the cost of common stock equity to reflect underpricing and flotation cost is required to find the cost of new issues of common stock. The key variable defini-

tions and formulas for the cost of common stock equity, the cost of retained earnings, and the cost of new issues of common stock are given in Table 11.4.

(LG4) Find the weighted average cost of capital (WACC) and discuss the alternative weighting schemes. The firm's WACC reflects the expected average future cost of funds over the long run. It can be determined by combining the costs of specific types of capital after weighting each cost using historical book or market value weights, or target book or market value weights. The theoretically preferred approach uses target weights based on market values. The key variable definitions and formula for WACC are given in Table 11.4.

(LG5) Describe the rationale for and procedures used to determine breaking points and the weighted marginal cost of capital (WMCC). A firm's WMCC reflects the fact that as the volume of total new financing increases, the costs of the various types of financing will increase, raising the firm's WACC. Breaking points, which are found by dividing the amount of funds available from a given financing source by its capital structure weight, represent the level of total new financing at which the cost of one of the financing components rises, causing an upward shift in the WMCC. The WMCC is the firm's WACC associated with its next dollar of total new financing. The WMCC schedule relates the WACC to each level of total new financing.

(LG6) Explain how the weighted marginal cost of capital (WMCC) can be used with the investment opportunities schedule (IOS) to make the firm's financing/investment decisions. The IOS presents a ranking of currently available investments from those with the highest returns to those with the lowest returns. It is used in combination with the WMCC to find the level of financing/

TABLE 11.4	**Summary of Key Definitions and Formulas for Cost of Capital**

Variable definitions

AF_j = amount of funds available from financing source j at a given cost

b = beta coefficient or measure of nondiversifiable risk

BP_j = breaking point for financing source j

D_1 = per share dividend expected at the end of year 1

D_p = annual preferred stock dividend (in dollars)

g = constant rate of growth in dividends

I = annual interest in dollars

k_a = weighted average cost of capital

k_d = before-tax cost of debt

k_i = after-tax cost of debt

k_m = required return on the market portfolio

k_n = cost of a new issue of common stock

k_p = cost of preferred stock

k_r = cost of retained earnings

k_s = required return on common stock

n = number of years to the bond's maturity

N_d = net proceeds from the sale of debt (bond)

N_n = net proceeds from the sale of new common stock

N_p = net proceeds from the sale of preferred stock

P_0 = value of common stock

R_F = risk-free rate of return

T = firm's tax rate

w_i = proportion of long-term debt in capital structure

w_j = capital structure proportion (historic or target, stated in decimal form) for financing source j

w_p = proportion of preferred stock in capital structure

w_s = proportion of common stock equity in capital structure

Cost of capital formulas

Before-tax cost of debt:

$$k_d = \frac{I + \dfrac{\$1,000 - N_d}{n}}{\dfrac{N_d + \$1,000}{2}} \qquad \text{[Eq. 11.2]}$$

After-tax cost of debt:

$$k_i = k_d \times (1 - T) \qquad \text{[Eq. 11.3]}$$

Cost of preferred stock:

$$k_p = \frac{D_p}{N_p} \qquad \text{[Eq. 11.4]}$$

Cost of common stock equity:

Using constant-growth valuation model:

$$k_s = \frac{D_1}{P_0} + g \qquad \text{[Eq. 11.6]}$$

Using CAPM:

$$k_s = R_F + [b \times (k_m - R_F)] \qquad \text{[Eq. 11.7]}$$

Cost of retained earnings:

$$k_r = k_s \qquad \text{[Eq. 11.8]}$$

Cost of new issues of common stock:

$$k_n = \frac{D_1}{N_n} + g \qquad \text{[Eq. 11.9]}$$

Weighted average cost of capital (WACC):

$$k_a = (w_i \times k_i) + (w_p \times k_p) + (w_s \times k_{r \text{ or } n}) \qquad \text{[Eq. 11.10]}$$

Breaking point:

$$BP_j = \frac{AF_j}{w_j} \qquad \text{[Eq. 11.11]}$$

investment that maximizes owner wealth. With this approach, the firm accepts projects up to the point at which the marginal return on its investment equals its weighted marginal cost of capital.

SELF-TEST PROBLEM   (Solution in Appendix B)

ST 11–1 **Specific costs, WACC, WMCC, and IOS**   Humble Manufacturing is interested in measuring its overall cost of capital. Current investigation has gathered the following data. The firm is in the 40% tax bracket.

Debt   The firm can raise an unlimited amount of debt by selling $1,000 par value, 10% coupon interest rate, 10-year bonds on which *annual interest* payments will be made. To sell the issue, an average discount of $30 per bond must be given. The firm must also pay flotation costs of $20 per bond.

Preferred stock   The firm can sell 11% (annual dividend) preferred stock at its $100-per-share par value. The cost of issuing and selling the preferred stock is expected to be $4 per share. An unlimited amount of preferred stock can be sold under these terms.

Common stock   The firm's common stock is currently selling for $80 per share. The firm expects to pay cash dividends of $6 per share next year. The firm's dividends have been growing at an annual rate of 6%, and this rate is expected to continue in the future. The stock will have to be underpriced by $4 per share, and flotation costs are expected to amount to $4 per share. The firm can sell an unlimited amount of new common stock under these terms.

Retained earnings   The firm expects to have $225,000 of retained earnings available in the coming year. Once these retained earnings are exhausted, the firm will use new common stock as the form of common stock equity financing.

a. Calculate the specific cost of each source of financing. (Round to the nearest .1%.)
b. The firm uses the weights shown in the following table, which are based on target capital structure proportions, to calculate its weighted average cost of capital. (Round to the nearest .1%.)

Source of capital	Weight
Long-term debt	40%
Preferred stock	15
Common stock equity	45
Total	100%

(1) Calculate the single breaking point associated with the firm's financial situation. (*Hint:* This point results from the exhaustion of the firm's retained earnings.)

(2) Calculate the weighted average cost of capital associated with total new financing below the breaking point calculated in (1).

(3) Calculate the weighted average cost of capital associated with total new financing above the breaking point calculated in (1).

c. Using the results of **b** along with the information shown in the following table on the available investment opportunities, draw the firm's weighted marginal cost of capital (WMCC) schedule and investment opportunities schedule (IOS) on the same set of total new financing or investment (x axis)–weighted average cost of capital and IRR (y axis) axes.

Investment opportunity	Internal rate of return (IRR)	Initial investment
A	11.2%	$100,000
B	9.7	500,000
C	12.9	150,000
D	16.5	200,000
E	11.8	450,000
F	10.1	600,000
G	10.5	300,000

d. Which, if any, of the available investments do you recommend that the firm accept? Explain your answer. How much total new financing is required?

PROBLEMS

WARM-UP   **11–1   Cost of debt—Risk premiums**   Mulberry Printing's cost of long-term debt last year was 10%. This rate was attributable to a 7% risk-free cost of long-term debt, a 2% business risk premium, and a 1% financial risk premium. The firm currently wishes to obtain a long-term loan.

a. If the firm's business and financial risk are unchanged from the previous period and the risk-free cost of long-term debt is now 8%, at what rate would you expect the firm to obtain a long-term loan?

b. If, as a result of borrowing, the firm's financial risk will increase enough to raise the financial risk premium to 3%, how much would you expect the firm's borrowing cost to be?

c. One of the firm's competitors has a 1% business risk premium and a 2% financial risk premium. What is that firm's cost of long-term debt likely to be?

WARM-UP   **11–2   Concept of cost of capital**   Wren Manufacturing is in the process of analyzing its investment decision-making procedures. The two projects evaluated by the firm during the past month were projects 263 and 264. The basic variables surrounding each project analysis using the IRR decision technique and the resulting decision actions are summarized in the following table.

Basic variables	Project 263	Project 264
Cost	$64,000	$58,000
Life	15 years	15 years
IRR	8%	15%
Least-cost financing		
Source	Debt	Equity
Cost (after-tax)	7%	16%
Decision		
Action	Accept	Reject
Reason	8% IRR > 7% cost	15% IRR < 16% cost

a. Evaluate the firm's decision-making procedures, and explain why the acceptance of project 263 and rejection of project 264 may not be in the owners' best interest.

b. If the firm maintains a capital structure containing 40% debt and 60% equity, find its weighted average cost using the data in the table.

c. Had the firm used the weighted average cost calculated in **b,** what actions would have been taken relative to projects 263 and 264?

d. Compare and contrast the firm's actions with your findings in **c.** Which decision method seems more appropriate? Explain why.

INTERMEDIATE

11–3 **Cost of debt using both methods**   Currently, Warren Industries can sell 15-year, $1,000 par-value bonds paying *annual interest* at a 12% coupon rate. As a result of current interest rates, the bonds can be sold for $1,010 each; flotation costs of $30 per bond will be incurred in this process. The firm is in the 40% tax bracket.

a. Find the net proceeds from sale of the bond, N_d.

b. Show the cash flows from the firm's point of view over the maturity of the bond.

c. Use the *IRR approach* with interpolation or a financial calculator to calculate the before-tax and after-tax cost of debt.

d. Use the *approximation formula* to estimate the before-tax and after-tax cost of debt.

e. Compare and contrast the cost of debt calculated in **c** and **d.** Which approach do you prefer? Why?

WARM-UP

11–4 **Cost of debt using the approximation formula**   For each of the following $1,000 par-value bonds, assuming *annual interest* payment and a 40% tax rate, calculate the *after-tax* cost to maturity using the *approximation formula*.

Bond	Life	Underwriting fee	Discount (−) or premium (+)	Coupon intest rate
A	20 years	$25	−$20	9%
B	16	40	+ 10	10
C	15	30	− 15	12
D	25	15	Par	9
E	22	20	− 60	11

INTERMEDIATE   **11–5** **The cost of debt using the approximation formula**   Gronseth Drywall Systems, Inc., is in discussions with its investment bankers regarding the issuance of new bonds. The investment banker has informed the firm that different maturities will carry different coupon rates and sell at different prices. The firm must choose among several alternatives. In each case, the bonds will have a $1,000 par value and flotation costs will be $30 per bond. The company is taxed at 40%. Calculate the after-tax cost of financing with each of the following alternatives.

Alternative	Coupon rate	Time to maturity	Premium or discount
A	9%	16 years	$250
B	7	5	50
C	6	7	par
D	5	10	−75

WARM-UP   **11–6** **Cost of preferred stock**   Taylor Systems has just issued preferred stock. The stock has a 12% annual dividend and a $100 par value and was sold at $97.50 per share. In addition, flotation costs of $2.50 per share must be paid.
a. Calculate the cost of the preferred stock.
b. If the firm sells the preferred stock with a 10% annual dividend and nets $90.00 after flotation costs, what is its cost?

WARM-UP   **11–7** **Cost of preferred stock**   Determine the cost for each of the following preferred stocks.

Preferred stock	Par value	Sale price	Flotation cost	Annual dividend
A	$100	$101	$9.00	11%
B	40	38	$3.50	8%
C	35	37	$4.00	$5.00
D	30	26	5% of par	$3.00
E	20	20	$2.50	9%

11–8   **Cost of common stock equity—CAPM**   J&M Corporation common stock has a beta, *b*, of 1.2. The risk-free rate is 6%, and the market return is 11%.
a. Determine the risk premium on J&M common stock.
b. Determine the required return that J&M common stock should provide.
c. Determine J&M's cost of common stock equity using the CAPM.

INTERMEDIATE

11–9   **Cost of common stock equity**   Ross Textiles wishes to measure its cost of common stock equity. The firm's stock is currently selling for $57.50. The firm expects to pay a $3.40 dividend at the end of the year (2001). The dividends for the past 5 years are shown in the following table.

INTERMEDIATE

Year	Dividend
2000	$3.10
1999	2.92
1998	2.60
1997	2.30
1996	2.12

After underpricing and flotation costs, the firm expects to net $52 per share on a new issue.
a. Determine the growth rate of dividends.
b. Determine the net proceeds, N_n, that the firm actually receives.
c. Using the constant-growth valuation model, determine the cost of retained earnings, k_r.
d. Using the constant-growth valuation model, determine the cost of new common stock, k_n.

11–10   **Retained earnings versus new common stock**   Using the data for each firm shown in the following table, calculate the cost of retained earnings and the cost of new common stock using the constant-growth valuation model.

INTERMEDIATE

Firm	Current market price per share	Dividend growth rate	Projected dividend per share next year	Underpricing per share	Flotation cost per share
A	$50.00	8%	$2.25	$2.00	$1.00
B	20.00	4	1.00	.50	1.50
C	42.50	6	2.00	1.00	2.00
D	19.00	2	2.10	1.30	1.70

11–11   **The effect of tax rate on WACC**   Equity Lighting Corp. wishes to explore the effect on its cost of capital of the rate at which the company pays taxes. The

INTERMEDIATE

firm wishes to maintain a capital structure of 30% debt, 10% preferred stock, and 60% common stock. The cost of financing with retained earnings is 14%, the cost of preferred stock financing is 9%, and the before-tax cost of debt financing is 11%. Calculate the weighted average cost of capital (WACC) given the tax rate assumptions in parts **a** to **c**.

a. Tax rate = 40%
b. Tax rate = 35%
c. Tax rate = 25%
d. Describe the relationship between changes in the rate of taxation and the weighted average cost of capital.

11–12   WACC—Book weights   Ridge Tool has on its books the amounts and specific (after-tax) costs shown in the following table for each source of capital.

WARM-UP

Source of capital	Book value	Specific cost
Long-term debt	$700,000	5.3%
Preferred stock	50,000	12.0
Common stock equity	650,000	16.0

a. Calculate the firm's weighted average cost of capital using book value weights.
b. Explain how the firm can use this cost in the investment decision-making process.

11–13   WACC—Book weights and market weights   Webster Company has compiled the information shown in the following table.

INTERMEDIATE

Source of capital	Book value	Market value	After-tax cost
Long-term debt	$4,000,000	$3,840,000	6.0%
Preferred stock	40,000	60,000	13.0
Common stock equity	1,060,000	3,000,000	17.0
Totals	$5,100,000	$6,900,000	

a. Calculate the weighted average cost of capital using book value weights.
b. Calculate the weighted average cost of capital using market value weights.
c. Compare the answers obtained in **a** and **b**. Explain the differences.

11–14   **WACC and target weights**   After careful analysis, Dexter Brothers has determined that its optimal capital structure is composed of the sources and target market value weights shown in the following table.

INTERMEDIATE

Source of capital	Target market value weight
Long-term debt	30%
Preferred stock	15
Common stock equity	55
Total	100%

The cost of debt is estimated to be 7.2%; the cost of preferred stock is estimated to be 13.5%; the cost of retained earnings is estimated to be 16.0%; and the cost of new common stock is estimated to be 18.0%. All of these are after-tax rates. Currently, the company's debt represents 25%, the preferred stock represents 10%, and the common stock equity represents 65% of total capital based on the market values of the three components. The company expects to have a significant amount of retained earnings available and does not expect to sell any new common stock.

a. Calculate the weighted average cost of capital based on historic market value weights.

b. Calculate the weighted average cost of capital based on target market value weights.

  11–15   **Cost of capital and break point**   Edna Recording Studios, Inc., reported earnings available to common stock of $4,200,000 last year. From that, the company paid a dividend of $1.26 on each of its 1,000,000 common shares outstanding. The capital structure of the company includes 40% debt, 10% preferred stock, and 50% common stock. It is taxed at a rate of 40%.

CHALLENGE

a. If the market price of common stock is $40 and dividends are expected to grow at a rate of 6% a year for the foreseeable future, what is the company's cost of financing with retained earnings?

b. If flotation costs on new shares of common stock amount to $1.00 per share, what is the company's cost of new common stock financing?

c. The company can issue $2.00 dividend preferred stock for a market price of $25.00 per share. Flotation costs would amount to $3.00 per share. What is the cost of preferred stock financing?

d. The company can issue $1,000 par, 10% coupon, 5-year bonds that can be sold for $1,200 each. Flotation costs would amount to $25.00 per bond. Use the estimation formula to figure the approximate cost of new debt financing.

e. What is the maximum investment that Edna Recording can make in new projects before it must issue new common stock?

f. What is the WACC for projects with a cost at or below the amount calculated in part e?

g. What is the WMCC for projects with a cost above the amount calculated in part e (assuming that debt across all ranges remains at the percentage cost calculated in part d)?

11–16   **Calculation of specific costs, WACC, and WMCC**   Dillon Labs has asked its financial manager to measure the cost of each specific type of capital as well as the weighted average cost of capital. The weighted average cost is to be measured by using the following weights: 40% long-term debt, 10% preferred stock, and 50% common stock equity (retained earnings, new common stock, or both). The firm's tax rate is 40%.

Debt   The firm can sell for $980 a 10-year, $1,000-par-value bond paying *annual interest* at a 10% coupon rate. A flotation cost of 3% of the par value is required in addition to the discount of $20 per bond.

Preferred stock   Eight percent (annual dividend) preferred stock having a par value of $100 can be sold for $65. An additional fee of $2 per share must be paid to the underwriters.

Common stock   The firm's common stock is currently selling for $50 per share. The dividend expected to be paid at the end of the coming year (2001) is $4. Its dividend payments, which have been approximately 60% of earnings per share in each of the past 5 years, were as shown in the following table.

Year	Dividend
2000	$3.75
1999	3.50
1998	3.30
1997	3.15
1996	2.85

It is expected that, to sell, new common stock must be underpriced $5 per share and the firm must also pay $3 per share in flotation costs. Dividend payments are expected to continue at 60% of earnings.

a. Calculate the specific cost of each source of financing. (Assume that $k_r = k_s$.)
b. If earnings available to common shareholders are expected to be $7 million, what is the breaking point associated with the exhaustion of retained earnings?
c. Determine the weighted average cost of capital between zero and the breaking point calculated in **b**.
d. Determine the weighted average cost of capital just beyond the breaking point calculated in **b**.

11–17   **Calculation of specific costs, WACC, and WMCC**   Lang Enterprises is interested in measuring its overall cost of capital. Current investigation has gathered the following data. The firm is in the 40% tax bracket.

Debt   The firm can raise an unlimited amount of debt by selling $1,000 par-value, 8% coupon interest rate, 20-year bonds on which *annual interest* payments will be made. To sell the issue, an average discount of $30 per bond would have to be given. The firm also must pay flotation costs of $30 per bond.

Preferred stock   The firm can sell 8% preferred stock at its $95-per-share par value. The cost of issuing and selling the preferred stock is expected to be $5 per share. An unlimited amount of preferred stock can be sold under these terms.

Common stock   The firm's common stock is currently selling for $90 per share. The firm expects to pay cash dividends of $7 per share next year. The firm's dividends have been growing at an annual rate of 6%, and this is expected to continue into the future. The stock must be underpriced by $7 per share, and flotation costs are expected to amount to $5 per share. The firm can sell an unlimited amount of new common stock under these terms.

Retained earnings   When measuring this cost, the firm does not concern itself with the tax bracket or brokerage fees of owners. It expects to have available $100,000 of retained earnings in the coming year; once these retained earnings are exhausted, the firm will use new common stock as the form of common stock equity financing.

a. Calculate the specific cost of each source of financing. (Round answers to the nearest .1%.)

Source of capital	Weight
Long-term debt	30%
Preferred stock	20
Common stock equity	50
Total	100%

b. The firm's capital structure weights used in calculating its weighted average cost of capital are shown in the table above. (Round answer to the nearest .1%.)
   (1) Calculate the single breaking point associated with the firm's financial situation. (*Hint:* This point results from exhaustion of the firm's retained earnings.)
   (2) Calculate the weighted average cost of capital associated with total new financing below the breaking point calculated in (1).
   (3) Calculate the weighted average cost of capital associated with total new financing above the breaking point calculated in (1).

  11–18   Integrative—WACC, WMCC, and IOS   Cartwell Products has compiled the data shown in the following table for the current costs of its three basic sources of capital—long-term debt, preferred stock, and common stock equity—for various ranges of new financing.

Source of capital	Range of new financing	After-tax cost
Long-term debt	$0 to $320,000	6%
	$320,000 and above	8
Preferred stock	$0 and above	17%
Common stock equity	$0 to $200,000	20%
	$200,000 and above	24

The company's capital structure weights used in calculating its weighted average cost of capital are shown in the following table.

Source of capital	Weight
Long-term debt	40%
Preferred stock	20
Common stock equity	40
Total	100%

a. Determine the breaking points and ranges of *total* new financing associated with each source of capital.
b. Using the data developed in **a**, determine the breaking points (levels of *total* new financing) at which the firm's weighted average cost of capital will change.
c. Calculate the weighted average cost of capital for each range of total new financing found in **b**. (*Hint:* There are three ranges.)
d. Using the results of **c** along with the following information on the available investment opportunities, draw the firm's weighted marginal cost of capital (WMCC) schedule and investment opportunities schedule (IOS) on the same set of total new financing or investment (*x* axis)–weighted average cost of capital and IRR (*y* axis) axes.

Investment opportunity	Internal rate of return (IRR)	Initial investment
A	19%	$200,000
B	15	300,000
C	22	100,000
D	14	600,000
E	23	200,000
F	13	100,000
G	21	300,000
H	17	100,000
I	16	400,000

e. Which, if any, of the available investments do you recommend that the firm accept? Explain your answer.

CHALLENGE

11–19   **Integrative—WACC, WMCC, and IOC**   Grainger Corp., a supplier of fitness equipment, is trying to decide whether to undertake any or all of the proposed projects in its investment opportunities schedule (IOS). The firm's cost of capital schedule and investment opportunities schedule are presented as follows:

Cost of Capital Schedule			
Range of new financing	Source	Weight	After-tax cost
0–$600,000	Debt	.50	6.3%
	Preferred stock	.10	12.5
	Common stock	.40	15.3
$600,000–$1,000,000	Debt	.50	6.3%
	Preferred stock	.10	12.5
	Common stock	.40	16.4
$1,000,000 and above	Debt	.50	7.8%
	Preferred stock	.10	12.5
	Common stock	.40	16.4

Investment Opportunities Schedule		
Investment opportunity	Internal rate of return	Cost
Project H	14.5%	$200,000
Project G	13.0	700,000
Project K	12.8	500,000
Project M	11.4	600,000

a. Complete the cost of capital schedule by calculating the WACC and WMCC for the various ranges of new financing.
b. Identify those projects that you recommend Grainger Corp. undertake in the next year.
c. Illustrate your recommendations by drawing a graph of Grainger's costs and opportunities similar to Figure 11.2.
d. Explain why certain projects are recommended and other(s) are not.

CASE   CHAPTER 11   **Making Star Products' Financing/Investment Decision**

Star Products Company is a growing manufacturer of automobile accessories whose stock is actively traded on the over-the-counter exchange. During 2000, the Dallas-based company experienced sharp increases in both sales and earnings. Because of this recent growth, Melissa Jen, the company's treasurer, wants to make sure that available funds are being used to their fullest. Management policy is to maintain the current capital structure proportions of 30% long-term debt, 10% preferred stock, and 60% common stock equity for at least the next 3 years. The firm is in the 40% tax bracket.

Star's division and product managers have presented several competing investment opportunities to Ms. Jen. However, because funds are limited, choices of which projects to accept must be made. The investment opportunities schedule (IOS) is shown in the following table.

Investment Opportunities Schedule (IOS) for Star Products Company

Investment opportunity	Internal rate of return (IRR)	Initial investment
A	15%	$400,000
B	22	200,000
C	25	700,000
D	23	400,000
E	17	500,000
F	19	600,000
G	14	500,000

To estimate the firm's weighted average cost of capital (WACC), Ms. Jen contacted a leading investment banking firm, which provided the financing cost data shown in the following table.

Financing Cost Data Star Products Company

Long-term debt: The firm can raise $450,000 of additional debt by selling 15-year, $1,000 par-value, 9% coupon interest rate bonds that pay *annual interest*. It expects to net $960 per bond after flotation costs. Any debt in excess of $450,000 will have a before-tax cost, k_d, of 13%.

Preferred stock: Preferred stock, regardless of the amount sold, can be issued with a $70 par-value, 14% annual dividend rate, and will net $65 per share after flotation costs.

Common stock equity: The firm expects dividends and earnings per share to be $.96 and $3.20, respectively, in 2001 and to continue to grow at a constant rate of 11% per year. The firm's stock currently sells for $12 per share. Star expects to have $1,500,000 of retained earnings available in the coming year. Once the retained earnings have been exhausted, the firm can raise additional funds by selling new common stock, netting $9 per share after underpricing and flotation costs.

Required

a. Calculate the cost of each source of financing, as specified:
   (1) Long-term debt, first $450,000.
   (2) Long-term debt, greater than $450,000.

(3) Preferred stock, all amounts.

(4) Common stock equity, first $1,500,000.

(5) Common stock equity, greater than $1,500,000.

b. Find the breaking points associated with each source of capital, and use them to specify each of the ranges of total new financing over which the firm's weighted average cost of capital (WACC) remains constant.

c. Calculate the weighted average cost of capital (WACC) over each of the ranges of total new financing specified in **b**.

d. Using your findings in **c** along with the investment opportunities schedule (IOS), draw the firm's weighted marginal cost of capital (WMCC) and IOS on the same set of total new financing or investment (*x* axis)–weighted average cost of capital and IRR (*y* axis) axes.

e. Which, if any, of the available investments would you recommend that the firm accept? Explain your answer.

WEB EXERCISE

GOTO web site www.stls.frb.org. Click on ECONOMIC RESEARCH; click on FRED; click on MONTHLY INTEREST RATES; and then click on BANK PRIME LOAN RATE CHANGES—HISTORIC DATES OF CHANGES AND RATES—1929.

1. What was the prime interest rate in 1934?
2. What was the highest the prime interest rate has been? When was that?
3. What was the highest prime interest rate since you've been born?
4. What is the present prime interest rate?
5. Between the years of 1987 and the present, what was the lowest prime interest rate? The highest prime interest rate?

Now GOTO web site www.stern.nyu.edu/~adamodar/New_Home_Page/datafile/histret.html.

6. What was the arithmetic average for stock returns during the same time period as in Question 5? How does this return compare to your answers to Question 5?

CHAPTER

12

Leverage and Capital Structure

ⓁEARNING ⒼOALS

LG1 Discuss the role of breakeven analysis, how to determine the operating breakeven point, and the effect of changing costs on the breakeven point.

LG2 Understand operating, financial, and total leverage and the relationships among them.

LG3 Describe the basic types of capital, external assessment of capital structure, capital structure of non-U.S. firms, and capital structure theory.

LG4 Explain the optimal capital structure using a graphic view of the firm's debt, equity, and weighted average cost of capital functions, and a modified form of the zero-growth valuation model.

LG5 Discuss the graphic presentation, risk considerations, and basic shortcomings of using the EBIT–EPS approach to compare alternative capital structures.

LG6 Review the return and risk of alternative capital structures and their linkage to market value, and other important capital structure considerations.

12.1 Leverage

leverage
Results from the use of fixed-cost assets or funds to magnify returns to the firm's owners.

capital structure
The mix of long-term debt and equity maintained by the firm.

Leverage results from the use of fixed-cost assets or funds to magnify returns to the firm's owners. Generally, increases in leverage result in increased return and risk, whereas decreases in leverage result in decreased return and risk. The amount of leverage in the firm's **capital structure**—the mix of long-term debt and equity maintained by the firm—can significantly affect its value by affecting return and risk. Unlike some causes of risk, management has almost complete control over the risk introduced through the use of leverage. Because of its effect

Jacking Up Owners' Wealth

Remember from your science class that a lever is a simple instrument that gives you more power. Although we think of levers being used principally to lift weights in various situations, the principle of leverage also is demonstrated in instruments such as scissors, nutcrackers, crowbars, and catapults. Leverage in finance involves the use of fixed costs (the lever) to magnify returns (lifting the car). Leverage is desirable to stockholders because it produces more earning power per share of stock. However, the use of leverage in the firm's capital structure has the potential also to increase the firm's risk. This chapter will show that leverage and capital structure are closely related concepts that can be used to minimize the firm's cost of capital and to maximize owners' wealth.

on value, the financial manager must understand how to measure and evaluate leverage, particularly when making capital structure decisions.

The three basic types of leverage can best be defined with reference to the firm's income statement, as shown in the general income statement format in Table 12.1:

- *Operating leverage* is concerned with the relationship between the firm's sales revenue and its earnings before interest and taxes, or EBIT. (EBIT is a descriptive label for *operating profits.*)
- *Financial leverage* is concerned with the relationship between the firm's EBIT and its common stock earnings per share (EPS).

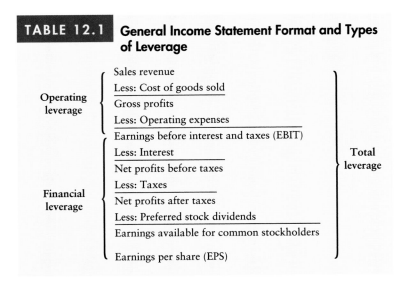

TABLE 12.1 General Income Statement Format and Types of Leverage

Operating leverage {
Sales revenue
Less: Cost of goods sold
Gross profits
Less: Operating expenses

Financial leverage {
Earnings before interest and taxes (EBIT)
Less: Interest
Net profits before taxes
Less: Taxes
Net profits after taxes
Less: Preferred stock dividends
Earnings available for common stockholders

Earnings per share (EPS)

} Total leverage

- *Total leverage* is concerned with the relationship between the firm's sales revenue and EPS.

We will examine the three types of leverage concepts in detail in sections that follow. First, though, we will look at breakeven analysis, which lays the foundation for leverage concepts by demonstrating the effects of fixed costs on the firm's operations.

Breakeven Analysis

Breakeven analysis, sometimes called **cost-volume-profit analysis,** is used by the firm (1) to determine the level of operations necessary to cover all operating costs and (2) to evaluate the profitability associated with various levels of sales. The firm's **operating breakeven point** is the level of sales necessary to cover all *operating costs.* At that point, earnings before interest and taxes equals $0.[1]

The first step in finding the operating breakeven point is to divide the cost of goods sold and operating expenses into fixed and variable operating costs. *Fixed costs* are a function of time, not sales volume, and are typically contractual; rent, for example, is a fixed cost. *Variable costs* vary directly with sales and are a function of volume, not time; shipping costs, for example, are a variable cost.[2]

breakeven analysis
Indicates the level of operations necessary to cover all operating costs and the profitability associated with various levels of sales.

operating breakeven point
The level of sales necessary to cover all *operating costs;* the point at which EBIT = $0.

Career Key
The *marketing* department uses breakeven analysis in pricing and new product decisions.

---

1. Quite often, the breakeven point is calculated so that it represents the point at which *all operating and financial costs* are covered. Our concern in this chapter is not with this overall breakeven point.

2. Some costs, commonly called *semifixed* or *semivariable,* are partly fixed and partly variable. One example would be sales commissions that are fixed for a certain volume of sales and then increase to higher levels for higher volumes. For convenience and clarity, we assume that all costs can be classified as either fixed or variable.

TABLE 12.2   **Operating Leverage, Costs, and Breakeven Analysis**

	Item	Algebraic representation
Operating leverage	Sales revenue	$(P \times Q)$
	Less: Fixed operating costs	$-\quad FC$
	Less: Variable operating costs	$-(VC \times Q)$
	Earnings before interest and taxes	EBIT

The Algebraic Approach

Using the following variables, we can recast the operating portion of the firm's income statement given in Table 12.1 into the algebraic representation shown in Table 12.2.

$$P = \text{sale price per unit}$$
$$Q = \text{sales quantity in units}$$
$$FC = \text{fixed operating cost per period}$$
$$VC = \text{variable operating cost per unit}$$

Rewriting the algebraic calculations in Table 12.2 as a formula for earnings before interest and taxes yields Equation 12.1:

$$\text{EBIT} = (P \times Q) - FC - (VC \times Q) \tag{12.1}$$

Simplifying Equation 12.1 yields

$$\text{EBIT} = Q \times (P - VC) - FC \tag{12.2}$$

As noted above, the operating breakeven point is the level of sales at which all fixed and variable *operating costs* are covered—the level at which EBIT equals $0. Setting EBIT equal to $0 and solving Equation 12.2 for Q yields:

$$Q = \frac{FC}{P - VC} \tag{12.3}$$

Q is the firm's operating breakeven point.[3]

---

3. Because the firm is assumed to be a single-product firm, its operating breakeven point is found in terms of unit sales, Q. For multiproduct firms, the operating breakeven point is generally found in terms of dollar sales, S. This is done by substituting the contribution margin, which is 100% minus total variable operating costs as a percentage of total sales, noted $VC\%$, into the denominator of Equation 12.3. The result is Equation 12.3a:

$$S = \frac{FC}{1 - VC\%} \tag{12.3a}$$

This multiproduct-firm breakeven point assumes that the firm's product mix remains the same at all levels of sales.

Example ▼ Assume that Cheryl's Posters, a small poster retailer, has fixed operating costs of $2,500, its sale price per unit (poster) is $10, and its variable operating cost per unit is $5. Applying Equation 12.3 to these data yields:

$$Q = \frac{\$2,500}{\$10 - \$5} = \frac{\$2,500}{\$5} = 500 \text{ units}$$

At sales of 500 units, the firm's EBIT should just equal $0. The firm will have positive EBIT for sales greater than 500 units and negative EBIT, or a loss, for sales less than 500 units. We can confirm this by substituting values above ▲ and below 500 units, along with the other values given, into Equation 12.1.

The Graphic Approach

Figure 12.1 presents in graph form the breakeven analysis of the data in the preceding example. The firm's operating breakeven point is the point at which its *total operating cost*—the sum of its fixed and variable operating costs—equals sales revenue. At this point, EBIT equals $0. The figure shows that for sales *below* 500 units, total operating cost exceeds sales revenue, and EBIT is less than $0 (a loss). For sales *above* the breakeven point of 500 units, sales revenue exceeds total operating cost, and EBIT is greater than $0.

FIGURE 12.1

Breakeven Analysis
Graphic operating
breakeven analysis

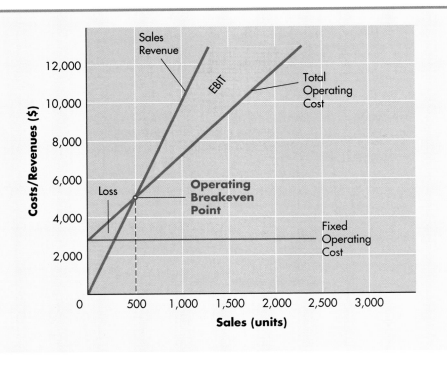

TABLE 12.3	Sensitivity of Operating Breakeven Point to Increases in Key Breakeven Variables

Increase in variable	Effect on operating breakeven point
Fixed operating cost *(FC)*	Increase
Sale price per unit *(P)*	Decrease
Variable operating cost per unit *(VC)*	Increase

Note: Decreases in each of the variables shown would have the opposite effect from that indicated on the breakeven point.

Changing Costs and the Operating Breakeven Point

A firm's operating breakeven point is sensitive to a number of variables: fixed operating cost (FC), the sale price per unit (P), and the variable operating cost per unit (VC). The effects of increases or decreases in these variables can be readily seen by referring to Equation 12.3. The sensitivity of the breakeven sales volume (Q) to an *increase* in each of these variables is summarized in Table 12.3. As might be expected, an increase in cost (FC or VC) tends to increase the operating breakeven point, whereas an increase in the sale price per unit (P) will decrease the operating breakeven point.

Example ▼ Assume that Cheryl's Posters wishes to evaluate the impact of several options: (1) increasing fixed operating costs to $3,000, (2) increasing the sale price per unit to $12.50, (3) increasing the variable operating cost per unit to $7.50, and (4) simultaneously implementing all three of these changes. Substituting the appropriate data into Equation 12.3 yields the following results:

$$(1) \text{ Operating breakeven point} = \frac{\$3,000}{\$10 - \$5} = 600 \text{ units}$$

$$(2) \text{ Operating breakeven point} = \frac{\$2,500}{\$12.50 - \$5} = 333\frac{1}{3} \text{ units}$$

$$(3) \text{ Operating breakeven point} = \frac{\$2,500}{\$10 - \$7.50} = 1,000 \text{ units}$$

$$(4) \text{ Operating breakeven point} = \frac{\$3,000}{\$12.50 - \$7.50} = 600 \text{ units}$$

Comparing the resulting operating breakeven points to the initial value of 500 units, we can see that the cost increases (actions 1 and 3) raise the breakeven point, whereas the revenue increase (action 2) lowers the breakeven point. The combined effect of increasing all three variables (action 4) also results in an ▲ increased operating breakeven point.

We now turn our attention to the three types of leverage. It is important to recognize that the demonstrations of leverage that follow are conceptual in nature and that the measures presented are *not* routinely used by financial managers for decision-making purposes.

Operating Leverage

Operating leverage results from the existence of *fixed operating costs* in the firm's income stream. Using the structure presented in Table 12.2, we can define **operating leverage** as the potential use of *fixed operating costs* to magnify the effects of changes in sales on the firm's earnings before interest and taxes.

operating leverage
The potential use of *fixed operating costs* to magnify the effects of changes in sales on the firm's earnings before interest and taxes.

Example ▼ Using the data for Cheryl's Posters (sale price, $P = \$10$ per unit; variable operating cost, $VC = \$5$ per unit; fixed operating cost, $FC = \$2,500$), Figure 12.2 presents the operating breakeven graph originally shown in Figure 12.1. The additional notations on the graph indicate that as the firm's sales increase from 1,000 to 1,500 units (Q_1 to Q_2), its EBIT increases from \$2,500 to \$5,000 ($EBIT_1$ to $EBIT_2$). In other words, a 50% increase in sales (1,000 to 1,500 units) results in a 100% increase in EBIT. Table 12.4 includes the data for Figure 12.2

FIGURE 12.2

Operating Leverage
Breakeven analysis and operating leverage

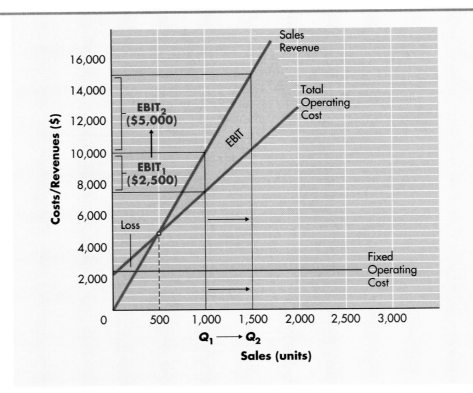

Career Key
The *operations* department will be concerned with the firm's operating leverage. The actions the firm takes and how it structures its operating costs will have a major impact on the firm's operating leverage.

TABLE 12.4	**The EBIT for Various Sales Levels**		
		Case 2	Case 1
		−50%	+50%
Sales (in units)	500	1,000	1,500
Sales revenue[a]	$5,000	$10,000	$15,000
Less: Variable operating costs[b]	2,500	5,000	7,500
Less: Fixed operating costs	2,500	2,500	2,500
Earnings before interest and taxes (EBIT)	$ 0	$ 2,500	$ 5,000
		−100%	+100%

[a]Sales revenue = $10/unit × sales in units.
[b]Variable operating costs = $5/unit × sales in units.

as well as relevant data for a 500-unit sales level. We can illustrate two cases using the 1,000-unit sales level as a reference point:

Case 1   A 50% *increase* in sales (from 1,000 to 1,500 units) results in a 100% *increase* in earnings before interest and taxes (from $2,500 to $5,000).

Case 2   A 50% *decrease* in sales (from 1,000 to 500 units) results in a 100% *decrease* in earnings before interest and taxes (from $2,500 to $0).

From the preceding example, we see that operating leverage works in *both directions*. When a firm has fixed operating costs, operating leverage is present. An increase in sales results in a more-than-proportional increase in EBIT; a decrease in sales results in a more-than-proportional decrease in EBIT.

Measuring the Degree of Operating Leverage (DOL)

degree of operating leverage (DOL)
The numerical measure of the firm's operating leverage.

The **degree of operating leverage (DOL)** is the numerical measure of the firm's operating leverage. It can be derived using the following equation:[4]

$$DOL = \frac{\text{percentage change in EBIT}}{\text{percentage change in sales}} \qquad (12.4)$$

Whenever the percentage change in EBIT resulting from a given percentage change in sales is greater than the percentage change in sales, operating leverage

---

4. The degree of operating leverage also depends on the base level of sales used as a point of reference. The closer the base sales level used is to the operating breakeven point, the greater the operating leverage. *Comparison of the degree of operating leverage of two firms is valid only when the base level of sales used for each firm is the same.*

exists. This means that as long as DOL is greater than 1, there is operating leverage.

Example ▼ Applying Equation 12.4 to cases 1 and 2 in Table 12.4 yields the following results:[5]

$$\text{Case 1:} \quad \frac{+100\%}{+50\%} = 2.0$$

$$\text{Case 2:} \quad \frac{-100\%}{-50\%} = 2.0$$

Because the result is greater than 1, operating leverage exists. For a given base level of sales, the higher the value resulting from applying Equation 12.4, the ▲ greater the degree of operating leverage.

A more direct formula for calculating the degree of operating leverage at a base sales level, Q, is shown in Equation 12.5.[6]

$$\text{DOL at base sales level } Q = \frac{Q \times (P - VC)}{Q \times (P - VC) - FC} \qquad (12.5)$$

Example ▼ Substituting $Q = 1{,}000$, $P = \$10$, $VC = \$5$, and $FC = \$2{,}500$ into Equation 12.5 yields the following result:

$$\text{DOL at 1,000 units} = \frac{1{,}000 \times (\$10 - \$5)}{1{,}000 \times (\$10 - \$5) - \$2{,}500} = \frac{\$5{,}000}{\$2{,}500} = 2.0$$

The use of the formula results in the same value for DOL (2.0) as that found by ▲ using Table 12.4 and Equation 12.4.[7]

Fixed Costs and Operating Leverage

Changes in fixed operating costs affect operating leverage significantly. Firms can sometimes incur fixed operating costs rather than variable operating costs and at other times may be able to substitute one type of cost for the other. For example, a firm could make fixed-dollar lease payments rather than payments equal to a specified percentage of sales. Or it could compensate sales representa-

---

5. Because the concept of leverage is *linear*, positive and negative changes of equal magnitude will always result in equal degrees of leverage when the same base sales level is used as a point of reference. This relationship holds for all types of leverage discussed in this chapter.

6. Technically, the formula for DOL given in Equation 12.5 should include absolute value signs because it is possible to get a negative DOL when the EBIT for the base sales level is negative. Because we assume that the EBIT for the base level of sales is positive, we do not use the absolute value signs.

7. When total sales in dollars—instead of unit sales—are available, the following equation in which TR = dollar level of base sales and TVC = total variable operating costs in dollars can be used:

$$\text{DOL at base dollar sales } TR = \frac{TR - TVC}{TR - TVC - FC}$$

This formula is especially useful for finding the DOL for multiproduct firms. It should be clear that because in the case of a single-product firm, $TR = P \times Q$ and $TVC = VC \times Q$, substitution of these values into Equation 12.5 results in the equation given here.

tives with a fixed salary and bonus rather than on a pure percent-of-sales commission basis. The effects of changes in fixed operating costs on operating leverage can best be illustrated by continuing our example.

Example ▼ Assume that Cheryl's Posters exchanges a portion of its variable operating costs for fixed operating costs by eliminating sales commissions and increasing sales salaries. This exchange results in a reduction in the variable operating cost per unit from $5 to $4.50 and an increase in the fixed operating costs from $2,500 to $3,000. Table 12.5 presents an analysis like that in Table 12.4, but using new costs. Although the EBIT of $2,500 at the 1,000-unit sales level is the same as before the shift in operating cost structure, Table 12.5 shows that the firm has increased its operating leverage by shifting to greater fixed operating costs.

With the substitution of the appropriate values into Equation 12.5, the degree of operating leverage at the 1,000-unit base level of sales becomes

$$\text{DOL at 1,000 units} = \frac{1,000 \times (\$10 - \$4.50)}{1,000 \times (\$10 - \$4.50) - \$3,000} = \frac{\$5,500}{\$2,500} = 2.2$$

By comparing this value to the DOL of 2.0 before the shift to more fixed costs, it is clear that the higher the firm's fixed operating costs relative to variable operating costs, the greater the degree of operating leverage. ▲

Financial Leverage

financial leverage
The potential use of *fixed financial costs* to magnify the effects of changes in earnings before interest and taxes on the firm's earnings per share.

Financial leverage results from the presence of *fixed financial costs* in the firm's income stream. Using the framework in Table 12.1, we can define **financial leverage** as the potential use of *fixed financial costs* to magnify the effects of changes in earnings before interest and taxes on the firm's earnings per share. The two fixed financial costs that may be found on the firm's income statement

TABLE 12.5	**Operating Leverage and Increased Fixed Costs**		
		Case 2	Case 1
		−50%	+50%
Sales (in units)	500	1,000	1,500
Sales revenue[a]	$5,000	$10,000	$15,000
Less: Variable operating costs[b]	2,250	4,500	6,750
Less: Fixed operating costs	3,000	3,000	3,000
Earnings before interest and taxes (EBIT)	−$ 250	$ 2,500	$ 5,250
		−110%	+110%

[a]Sales revenue was calculated as indicated in Table 12.4.
[b]Variable operating costs = $4.50/unit × sales in units.

are (1) interest on debt and (2) preferred stock dividends. These charges must be paid regardless of the amount of EBIT available to pay them.[8]

Example ▼ Chen Foods, a small Oriental food company, expects EBIT of $10,000 in the current year. It has a $20,000 bond with a 10% (annual) coupon rate of interest and an issue of 600 shares of $4 (annual dividend per share) preferred stock outstanding. It also has 1,000 shares of common stock outstanding. The annual interest on the bond issue is $2,000 (.10 × $20,000). The annual dividends on the preferred stock are $2,400 ($4.00/share × 600 shares). Table 12.6 presents the EPS corresponding to levels of EBIT of $6,000, $10,000, and $14,000, assuming that the firm is in the 40% tax bracket. Two situations are shown:

Case 1   A 40% *increase* in EBIT (from $10,000 to $14,000) results in a 100% *increase* in earnings per share (from $2.40 to $4.80).

Case 2   A 40% *decrease* in EBIT (from $10,000 to $6,000) results in a 100% *decrease* in earnings per share (from $2.40 to $0).

The effect of financial leverage is such that an increase in the firm's EBIT results in a more-than-proportional increase in the firm's earnings per share, whereas a decrease in the firm's EBIT results in a more-than-proportional decrease in EPS.

Career Key

Management will have to decide how much financial leverage the firm will have. Increasing financial leverage may increase the EPS, but at some point, investors will feel that the additional risk is not adequately compensated for by the increased EPS. At that point, the stock price will decline.

TABLE 12.6   The EPS for Various EBIT Levels[a]

	Case 2		Case 1
	−40%		+40%
EBIT	$6,000	$10,000	$14,000
Less: Interest (*I*)	2,000	2,000	2,000
Net profits before taxes	$4,000	$ 8,000	$12,000
Less: Taxes (*T* = .40)	1,600	3,200	4,800
Net profits after taxes	$2,400	$ 4,800	$ 7,200
Less: Preferred stock dividends (*PD*)	2,400	2,400	2,400
Earnings available for common (EAC)	$ 0	$ 2,400	$ 4,800
Earnings per share (EPS)	$\frac{\$0}{1,000} = \$0$	$\frac{\$2,400}{1,000} = \$2.40$	$\frac{\$4,800}{1,000} = \$4.80$
	−100%		+100%

[a]As noted in Chapter 3, for accounting and tax purposes, interest is a *tax-deductible expense*, whereas dividends must be paid from after-tax cash flows.

8. As noted in Chapter 2, although preferred stock dividends can be "passed" (not paid) at the option of the firm's directors, it is generally believed that payment of such dividends is necessary. *This text treats the preferred stock dividend as a contractual obligation, not only to be paid as a fixed amount, but also to be paid as scheduled.* Although failure to pay preferred dividends cannot force the firm into bankruptcy, it increases the common stockholders' risk because they cannot be paid dividends until the claims of preferred stockholders are satisfied.

Measuring the Degree of Financial Leverage (DFL)

The **degree of financial leverage** (DFL) is the numerical measure of the firm's financial leverage. It can be computed much like the degree of operating leverage. The following equation presents one approach for obtaining the DFL:[9]

$$DFL = \frac{\text{percentage change in EPS}}{\text{percentage change in EBIT}} \qquad (12.6)$$

Whenever the percentage change in EPS resulting from a given percentage change in EBIT is greater than the percentage change in EBIT, financial leverage exists. This means that whenever DFL is greater than 1, there is financial leverage.

Example ▼ Applying Equation 12.6 to cases 1 and 2 in Table 12.6 yields:

$$\text{Case 1:} \quad \frac{+100\%}{+40\%} = 2.5$$

$$\text{Case 2:} \quad \frac{-100\%}{-40\%} = 2.5$$

In both cases, the quotient is greater than 1, so financial leverage exists. The ▲ higher this value, the greater the degree of financial leverage.

A more direct formula for calculating the degree of financial leverage at a base level of EBIT is given by Equation 12.7, using the notation from Table 12.6.[10] Note that in the denominator, the term $1/(1 - T)$ converts the after-tax preferred stock dividend to a before-tax amount for consistency with the other terms in the equation.

$$DFL \text{ at base level EBIT} = \frac{EBIT}{EBIT - I - \left(PD \times \dfrac{1}{1 - T}\right)} \qquad (12.7)$$

Example ▼ Substituting EBIT = \$10,000, I = \$2,000, PD = \$2,400, and the tax rate (T = .40) into Equation 12.7 yields the following result:

$$DFL \text{ at } \$10,000 \text{ EBIT} = \frac{\$10,000}{\$10,000 - \$2,000 - \left(\$2,400 \times \dfrac{1}{1 - .40}\right)}$$

$$= \frac{\$10,000}{\$4,000} = 2.5$$

---

9. This approach is valid only when the base level of EBIT used to calculate and compare these values is the same. In other words, *the base level of EBIT must be held constant to compare the financial leverage associated with different levels of fixed financial costs.*

10. By using the formula for DFL in Equation 12.7, it is possible to get a negative value for the DFL if the EPS for the base level of EBIT is negative. Rather than show absolute value signs in the equation, it is instead assumed that the base-level EPS is positive.

Notice that the formula given in Equation 12.7 provides a more direct method for calculating the degree of financial leverage than the approach illustrated using Table 12.6 and Equation 12.6.

Total Leverage

total leverage
The potential use of *fixed costs, both operating and financial,* to magnify the effect of changes in sales on the firm's earnings per share.

We also can assess the combined effect of operating and financial leverage on the firm's risk using a framework similar to that used to develop the individual concepts of leverage. This combined effect, or **total leverage,** can be defined as the potential use of *fixed costs, both operating and financial,* to magnify the effect of changes in sales on the firm's earnings per share. Total leverage can therefore be viewed as the *total impact of the fixed costs* in the firm's operating and financial structure.

Example ▼ Cables Inc., a computer cable manufacturer, expects sales of 20,000 units at $5 per unit in the coming year and must meet the following: variable operating costs of $2 per unit, fixed operating costs of $10,000, interest of $20,000, and preferred stock dividends of $12,000. The firm is in the 40% tax bracket and has 5,000 shares of common stock outstanding. Table 12.7 presents the levels of earnings per share associated with the expected sales of 20,000 units and with sales of 30,000 units.

The table illustrates that as a result of a 50% increase in sales (from 20,000 to 30,000 units), the firm would experience a 300% increase in earnings per share (from $1.20 to $4.80). Although not shown in the table, a 50% decrease in sales would, conversely, result in a 300% decrease in earnings per share. The linear nature of the leverage relationship accounts for the fact that sales changes of equal magnitude in opposite directions result in EPS changes of equal magnitude in the corresponding direction. At this point, it should be clear that whenever a firm has fixed costs—operating or financial—in its structure, total leverage ▲ will exist.

Measuring the Degree of Total Leverage (DTL)

degree of total leverage (DTL)
The numerical measure of the firm's total leverage.

The **degree of total leverage (DTL)** is the numerical measure of the firm's total leverage. It can be computed much like operating and financial leverage. The following equation presents one approach for measuring DTL:[11]

$$DTL = \frac{\text{percentage change in EPS}}{\text{percentage change in sales}} \tag{12.8}$$

Whenever the percentage change in EPS resulting from a given percentage change in sales is greater than the percentage change in sales, total leverage exists. This means that as long as the DTL is greater than 1, there is total leverage.

---

11. This approach is valid only when the base level of sales used to calculate and compare these values is the same. In other words, *the base level of sales must be held constant to compare the total leverage associated with different levels of fixed costs.*

TABLE 12.7	The Total Leverage Effect			
		+50%		
Sales (in units)		20,000	30,000	
Sales revenue[a]		$100,000	$150,000	DOL =
Less: Variable operating costs[b]		40,000	60,000	
Less: Fixed operating costs		10,000	10,000	$\frac{+60\%}{+50\%} = 1.2$
Earnings before interest and taxes (EBIT)		$ 50,000	$ 80,000	
		+60%		
Less: Interest		20,000	20,000	DFL =
Net profits before taxes		$ 30,000	$ 60,000	
Less: Taxes (T = .40)		12,000	24,000	$\frac{+300\%}{+60\%} = 5.0$
Net profits after taxes		$ 18,000	$ 36,000	
Less: Preferred stock dividends		12,000	12,000	
Earnings available for common		$ 6,000	$ 24,000	
Earnings per share (EPS)		$\frac{\$6000}{5,000} = \$1.20$	$\frac{\$24,000}{5,000} = \$4.80$	
		+300%		

DTL = $\frac{+300\%}{+50\%} = 6.0$

[a]Sales revenue = $5/unit × sales in units.
[b]Variable operating costs = $2/unit × sales in units.

Example ▼ Applying Equation 12.8 to the data in Table 12.7 yields:

$$DTL = \frac{+300\%}{+50\%} = 6.0$$

Because this result is greater than 1, total leverage exists. The higher the value, the greater the degree of total leverage. ▲

A more direct formula for calculating the degree of total leverage at a given base level of sales, Q, is given by Equation 12.9,[12] which uses the same notation presented earlier:

$$DTL \text{ at base sales level } Q = \frac{Q \times (P - VC)}{Q \times (P - VC) - FC - I - \left(PD \times \frac{1}{1 - T}\right)} \qquad (12.9)$$

---

12. By using the formula for DTL in Equation 12.9, it is possible to get a negative value for the DTL if the EPS for the base level of sales is negative. For our purposes, rather than show absolute value signs in the equation, we instead assume that the base-level EPS is positive.

E x a m p l e ▼ Substituting Q = 20,000, P = \$5, VC = \$2, FC = \$10,000, I = \$20,000, PD = \$12,000, and the tax rate (T = .40) into Equation 12.9 yields the following result:

$$\text{DTL at 20,000 units} = \frac{20,000 \times (\$5 - \$2)}{20,000 \times (\$5 - \$2) - \$10,000 - \$20,000 - \left(\$12,000 \times \dfrac{1}{1 - .40}\right)}$$

$$= \frac{\$60,000}{\$10,000} = 6.0$$

Clearly, the formula used in Equation 12.9 provides a more direct method for calculating the degree of total leverage than the approach illustrated using Table
▲ 12.7 and Equation 12.8.

The Relationship of Operating, Financial, and Total Leverage

Total leverage reflects the *combined impact* of operating and financial leverage on the firm. High operating leverage and high financial leverage will cause total leverage to be high. The opposite will also be true. The relationship between operating leverage and financial leverage is *multiplicative* rather than *additive*. The relationship between the degree of total leverage (DTL) and the degrees of operating leverage (DOL) and financial leverage (DFL) is given by Equation 12.10.

$$DTL = DOL \times DFL \tag{12.10}$$

E x a m p l e ▼ Substituting the values calculated for DOL and DFL, shown on the right-hand side of Table 12.7, into Equation 12.10 yields

$$DTL = 1.2 \times 5.0 = 6.0$$

The resulting degree of total leverage is the same value calculated directly in the
▲ preceding examples.

❓ R e v i e w   Q u e s t i o n s

12–1 What is meant by the term *leverage*? How do operating leverage, financial leverage, and total leverage relate to the income statement?

12–2 What is the *operating breakeven point*? How do changes in fixed operating costs, the sale price per unit, and the variable operating cost per unit affect it?

12–3 What is *operating leverage*? What causes it? How is the *degree of operating leverage (DOL)* measured?

12–4 What is *financial leverage*? What causes it? How is the *degree of financial leverage (DFL)* measured?

In Practice

Leverage by the Books

Barnes & Noble sells one of every eight books sold in the U.S.—in over 1,000 stores (Barnes & Noble, Bookstop, Bookstar, B. Dalton, Doubleday, and Scribner's), through direct mail, and on the World Wide Web. Likewise, Borders Group operates 250 book and music superstores plus another 900 Waldenbooks stores and sells its products online. It pioneered the concept of including cafés in its superstores, a practice that Barnes & Noble has copied in some locations. Spun off from Kmart in 1990, Borders is the country's most profitable bookseller.

How do these two seemingly similar companies compare in degrees of operating, financial, and total leverage? The following table summarizes the key data for these measures for the fiscal year ending January 1998.

	Barnes & Noble		Borders	
	FY 98	FY 97	FY 98	FY 97
Sales (millions)	$2,797	$2,448	$2,266	$1,957
EBIT (millions)	$147	$120	$138	$10
EPS	$0.96*	$0.77	$1.06	$0.77
(1) % chg.—sales	14.3		15.8	
(2) % chg.—EBIT	22.5		34.0	
(3) % chg.—EPS	24.7		37.7	
DOL [(2) ÷ (1)]	1.6		2.2	
DFL [(3) ÷ (2)]	1.1		1.1	
DTL [(3) ÷ (1)]	1.8		2.4	

*before extraordinary charge

The key difference between the companies is operating leverage. The numbers indicate that on a relative basis Borders must have greater fixed costs in its operating structure than does Barnes & Noble. This is not surprising if you consider that Borders has 1,150 individual stores, each with fixed costs like rent and utilities, compared to about 1,000 for Barnes & Noble, and also that most of Borders' stores are mall stores, which are likely to have higher fixed costs. Because both companies are profitable, we would expect that Borders, with its higher fixed costs, will see its profits grow much faster beyond its breakeven point, as seems to be the case. (It's important to remember that this example represents one year only, and the degree of operating, financial, and total leverage may change in the future.)

12–5   What is the general relationship among operating leverage, financial leverage, and the total leverage of the firm? Do these types of leverage complement each other? Why or why not?

12.2 The Firm's Capital Structure

Capital structure is one of the most complex areas of financial decision making due to its interrelationship with other financial decision variables.[13] Poor capital structure decisions can result in a high cost of capital, thereby lowering project NPVs and making more of them unacceptable. Effective decisions can lower the cost of capital, resulting in higher NPVs and more acceptable projects, thereby increasing the value of the firm. This section links together the concepts presented in Chapters 5, 6, 7, and 11 and the discussion of leverage in this chapter.

Types of Capital

All of the items on the right-hand side of the firm's balance sheet, excluding current liabilities, are sources of capital. The following simplified balance sheet illustrates the basic breakdown of total capital into its two components—*debt capital* and *equity capital.*

	Balance Sheet		
	Current liabilities		
	Long-term debt	Debt capital	
Assets	Stockholders' equity		Total capital
	Preferred stock	Equity capital	
	Common stock equity		
	Common stock		
	Retained earnings		

The various types and characteristics of *corporate bonds,* a major source of *debt capital,* were discussed in detail in Chapter 2. In Chapter 11, the cost of debt was found to be less than the cost of other forms of financing. Lenders demand relatively lower returns because they take the least risk of any long-term contributors of capital: (1) They have a higher priority of claim against any earnings or assets available for payment. (2) They have a far stronger legal pressure against the company to make payment than do preferred or common stockholders. And (3) the tax deductibility of interest payments lowers the debt cost to the firm substantially.

Unlike borrowed funds that must be repaid at a specified future date, *equity capital* is expected to remain in the firm for an indefinite period of time. The two basic sources of equity capital are (1) preferred stock and (2) common stock

---

13. Of course, although capital structure is financially important, it, like many business decisions, is generally not as important as the firm's products or services. In a practical sense, a firm can probably more readily increase its value by improving quality and reducing costs rather than by fine-tuning its capital structure.

equity, which includes common stock and retained earnings. As was demonstrated in Chapter 11, common stock is typically the most expensive form of equity, followed by retained earnings and preferred stock, respectively. Our concern here is the relationship between debt and equity capital. Key differences between these two types of capital, relative to voice in management, claims on income and assets, maturity, and tax treatment, were summarized in Chapter 2, Table 2.5. Due to its secondary position relative to debt, suppliers of equity capital take greater risk and therefore must be compensated with higher expected returns than suppliers of debt capital.

External Assessment of Capital Structure

Earlier it was shown that *financial leverage* results from the use of fixed-payment financing, such as debt and preferred stock, to magnify return and risk. Debt ratios, which measure the firm's degree of financial leverage, were presented in Chapter 4. A direct measure of the degree of indebtedness is the *debt ratio*. The higher this ratio, the greater the firm's financial leverage. Measures of the firm's ability to meet fixed payments associated with debt include the *times interest earned ratio* and the *fixed-payment coverage ratio*. These ratios provide indirect information on financial leverage. The smaller these ratios, the less able the firm is to meet payments as they come due. In general, low debt-payment ratios are associated with high degrees of financial leverage. The more risk a firm is willing to take, the greater its financial leverage. In theory, the firm should maintain financial leverage consistent with a capital structure that maximizes owners' wealth.

An *acceptable degree of financial leverage for one industry or line of business can be highly risky in another,* due to differing operating characteristics between industries or lines of business. Table 12.8 presents the debt and times interest earned ratios for selected industries and lines of business. Significant industry differences can be seen in these data. For example, the debt ratio for electronic computer manufacturers is 52.6 percent, whereas for auto retailers it is 78.4 percent. Differences in debt positions are also likely to exist *within* an industry or line of business.

Capital Structure of Non-U.S. Firms

Modern capital structure theory has developed largely within the framework of the U.S. financial system, and most empirical studies of these theories have employed data from U.S. companies. In recent years, however, both corporate executives and academic researchers have focused greater attention on financing patterns of European, Japanese, Canadian, and other non-U.S. companies. They have found important differences as well as striking similarities between U.S. and non-U.S. companies.

In general, non-U.S. companies have much higher degrees of indebtedness than their U.S. counterparts. Most of the reasons for this relate to the more developed capital markets in the United States, which have played a greater role in corporate financing than has been the case in other countries. In most European countries and especially in Japan and other Pacific Rim nations, large

TABLE 12.8 Debt Ratios for Selected Industries and Lines of Business (Fiscal Years Ended 4/1/97 Through 3/31/98)

Industry or line business	Debt ratio	Times interest earned ratio
Manufacturing industries		
Books	63.9%	3.6
Dairy products	59.2	3.5
Electronic computers	52.6	5.1
Fertilizers	61.0	2.7
Iron and steel foundries	62.1	4.1
Jewelry and precious metals	61.1	2.0
Machine tools and metalworking equipment	57.8	4.0
Wines, distilled liquors, liqueurs	55.0	4.1
Women's dresses	55.1	4.0
Wholesaling industries		
Furniture	66.1	3.2
General groceries	66.5	2.5
Hardware and paints	58.1	3.1
Men's and boys' clothing	60.4	2.5
Petroleum products	66.1	2.4
Retailing industries		
Autos, new and used	78.4	2.0
Department stores	54.9	2.8
Radios, TV, consumer electronics	64.8	1.9
Restaurants	71.1	2.8
Shoes	58.1	2.2
Service industries		
Accounting, auditing, bookkeeping	53.4	5.7
Advertising agencies	72.9	6.0
Auto repair—general	65.8	2.7
Insurance agents and brokers	73.6	3.6
Physicians	72.7	2.7
Travel agencies	70.5	3.2

(*Source: RMA Annual Statement Studies, 1998* (fiscal years ended 4/1/97 through 3/31/98) (Philadelphia: Robert Morris Associates, 1995). Copyright © 1998 by Robert Morris Associates.)

Note: Robert Morris Associates recommends that these ratios be regarded only as general guidelines and not as absolute industry norms. No claim is made as to the representativeness of their figures.

commercial banks are more actively involved in the financing of corporate activity than has been true in the United States. Furthermore, in many of these countries, banks are allowed to make large equity investments in nonfinancial corporations—a practice that is prohibited for U.S. banks. Finally, share ownership tends to be much more tightly controlled among founding family, institutional, and even public investors in Europe and Asia than it is for most large U.S. corporations, many of which have up to a million individual shareholders. The tight ownership structure of non-U.S. firms helps to resolve many agency problems that affect large U.S. companies, thus allowing non-U.S. firms to tolerate a higher degree of indebtedness.

On the other hand, similarities exist between U.S. and non-U.S. corporations. First, the same industry patterns of capital structure tend to be found around the world. For example, in almost all countries, pharmaceutical and other high-growth industrial firms tend to have lower debt ratios than do steel companies, airlines, and electric utility companies. Second, the capital structures of the largest U.S.-based multinational companies, which have access to many different capital markets around the world, typically resemble the capital structures of multinational companies from other countries more than they resemble those of smaller national companies. Finally, the worldwide trend is away from reliance on banks for corporate financing and toward greater reliance on security issuance. Over time the differences in the capital structures of U.S. and non-U.S. firms will probably lessen.

Capital Structure Theory

Scholarly research suggests that there is an optimal capital structure range. However, *the understanding of capital structure at this point does not provide financial managers with a specified methodology for use in determining a firm's optimal capital structure.* Nevertheless, financial theory does provide help in understanding how a firm's chosen financing mix affects the firm's value.

In 1958, Franco Modigliani and Merton H. Miller[14] (commonly known as "M and M"),[15] the capital structure that a firm chooses does not affect its value. Many researchers, including M and M, have examined the effects of less restrictive assumptions on the relationship between capital structure and the firm's value. The result is a theoretical *optimal* capital structure based on balancing the benefits and costs of debt financing. The major benefit of debt financing is the tax shield, which allows interest payments to be deducted in calculating taxable income. The cost of debt financing results from (1) the increased probability of bankruptcy caused by debt obligations, (2) the *agency costs* of the lender's monitoring the firm's actions, and (3) the costs associated with managers having more information about the firm's prospects than do investors.

Tax Benefits

Allowing firms to deduct interest payments on debt when calculating taxable income reduces the amount of the firm's earnings paid in taxes, thereby making more earnings available for bondholders and stockholders. The deductibility of

14. Franco Modigliani and Merton H. Miller, "The Cost of Capital, Corporation Finance, and the Theory of Investment," *American Economic Review* (June 1958), pp. 261–297.

15. Perfect market assumptions include (1) no taxes, (2) no brokerage or flotation costs for securities, (3) symmetrical information—investors and managers have the same information about the firm's investment prospects, and (4) investors can borrow at the same rate as corporations.

interest means the cost of debt, k_i, to the firm is subsidized by the government. Letting k_d equal the before-tax cost of debt and T equal the tax rate, from Chapter 11 (Equation 11.3), we have $k_i = k_d \times (1 - T)$.

Probability of Bankruptcy

The chance that a firm will become bankrupt due to an inability to meet its obligations as they come due depends largely on its level of both business risk and financial risk.

Business Risk   In Chapter 11, we defined *business risk* as the risk to the firm of being unable to cover its operating costs. In general, the greater the firm's *operating leverage*—the use of fixed operating costs—the higher its business risk. Although operating leverage is an important factor affecting business risk, two other factors—revenue stability and cost stability—also affect it. *Revenue stability* refers to the relative variability of the firm's sales revenues. Firms with reasonably stable levels of demand and with products that have stable prices have stable revenues. The result is low levels of business risk. Firms with highly volatile product demand and prices have unstable revenues that result in high levels of business risk. *Cost stability* refers to the relative predictability of input prices such as those for labor and materials. The more predictable and stable these input prices are, the lower the business risk; the less predictable and stable they are, the higher the business risk.

Business risk varies among firms, regardless of their lines of business, and is not affected by capital structure decisions. The level of business risk must be taken as a "given." The higher a firm's business risk, the more cautious the firm must be in establishing its capital structure. Firms with high business risk therefore tend toward less highly leveraged capital structures, and firms with low business risk tend toward more highly leveraged capital structures. We will hold business risk constant throughout the discussions that follow.

Example ▼   Cooke Company, a soft drink manufacturer, is preparing to make a capital structure decision. It has obtained estimates of sales and the associated levels of earnings before interest and taxes (EBIT) from its forecasting group: There is a 25% chance that sales will total $400,000, a 50% chance that sales will total $600,000, and a 25% chance that sales will total $800,000. Fixed operating costs total $200,000, and variable operating costs equal 50% of sales. These data are summarized and the resulting EBIT calculated in Table 12.9.

TABLE 12.9   Sales and Associated EBIT Calculations for Cooke Company ($000)

Probability of sales	.25	.50	.25
Sales revenue	$400	$600	$800
Less: Fixed operating costs	200	200	200
Less: Variable operating costs (50% of sales)	200	300	400
Earnings before interest and taxes (EBIT)	$ 0	$100	$200

The table shows that there is a 25% chance that the EBIT will be $0, a 50% chance that it will be $100,000, and a 25% chance that it will be $200,000. The financial manager must accept as given these levels of EBIT and their associated probabilities when developing the firm's capital structure. These EBIT data effectively reflect a certain level of business risk that captures the firm's operating leverage, sales revenue variability, and cost predictability.

Financial Risk   The firm's capital structure directly affects its *financial risk*, which is the risk to the firm of being unable to cover required financial obligations. The penalty for not meeting financial obligations is bankruptcy. The more fixed cost financing—debt (including financial leases) and preferred stock—a firm has in its capital structure, the greater its financial leverage and risk. Financial risk depends on the capital structure decision made by the management, and that decision is affected by the business risk the firm faces.

The *total risk* of a firm—business and financial risk combined—determines its probability of bankruptcy. Financial risk, its relationship to business risk, and their combined impact can be demonstrated by continuing the Cooke Company example.

Hint   The cash flows to investors from bonds are less risky than the dividends from preferred stock, which are less risky than dividends from common stock. Only with bonds is the issuer contractually obligated to pay the scheduled interest, and the amounts due to bondholders and preferred stockholders are usually fixed. Therefore, the required return for bonds is generally lower than for preferred stock, which is lower than for common stock.

Example ▼   Cooke Company's current capital structure is as shown:

Current capital structure	
Long-term debt	$ 0
Common stock equity (25,000 shares at $20)	500,000
Total capital	$500,000

Hint   As you learned in Chapter 4, the debt ratio is equal to the amount of total debt divided by the total assets. The higher this ratio, the more financial leverage a firm is using.

Let us assume that the firm is considering seven alternative capital structures. If we measure these structures using the debt ratio, they are associated with ratios of 0, 10, 20, 30, 40, 50, and 60%. Assuming (1) the firm has no current liabilities, (2) its capital structure currently contains all equity as shown, and (3) the total amount of capital remains constant[16] at $500,000, the mix of debt and equity associated with the seven debt ratios would be as shown in Table 12.10. Also shown in the table is the number of shares of common stock outstanding under each alternative.

Associated with each of the debt levels in column 3 of Table 12.10 (on page 510) would be an interest rate that would be expected to increase with increases in financial leverage. The level of debt, the associated interest rate (assumed to apply to *all* debt), and the dollar amount of annual interest associated with each of the alternative capital structures are summarized in Table 12.11 (on page 510). Because both the level of debt and the interest rate increase with increasing financial leverage (debt ratios), the annual interest increases as well.

---

16. This assumption is needed to permit the assessment of alternative capital structures without having to consider the returns associated with the investment of additional funds raised. Attention here is given only to the *mix* of capital rather than to its investment.

TABLE 12.10	Capital Structures Associated with Alternative Debt Ratios for Cooke Company

| | Capital structure ($000) | | | Shares of common stock |
Debt ratio (1)	Total assets[a] (2)	Debt [(1) × (2)] (3)	Equity [(2) − (3)] (4)	outstanding (000) [(4) ÷ $20][b] (5)
0%	$500	$ 0	$500	25.00
10	500	50	450	22.50
20	500	100	400	20.00
30	500	150	350	17.50
40	500	200	300	15.00
50	500	250	250	12.50
60	500	300	200	10.00

[a]Because the firm, for convenience, is assumed to have no current liabilities, its total assets equal its total capital of $500,000.

[b]The $20 value represents the book value per share of common stock equity noted earlier.

Table 12.12, on the next page, uses the levels of EBIT and associated probabilities developed in Table 12.9, the number of shares of common stock found in column 5 of Table 12.10, and the annual interest values calculated in column 3 of Table 12.11 to calculate the earnings per share (EPS) for debt ratios of 0, 30, and 60%. A 40% tax rate is assumed. Also shown are the resulting expected

TABLE 12.11	Level of Debt, Interest Rate, and Dollar Amount of Annual Interest Associated with Cooke Company's Alternative Capital Structures

Capital structure debt ratio	Debt ($000) (1)	Interest rate on *all* debt (2)	Interest ($000) [(1) × (2)] (3)
0%	$ 0	0.0%	$ 0.00
10	50	9.0	4.50
20	100	9.5	9.50
30	150	10.0	15.00
40	200	11.0	22.00
50	250	13.5	33.75
60	300	16.5	49.50

TABLE 12.12	Calculation of EPS for Selected Debt Ratios ($000) for Cooke Company

Debt Ratio = 0%

Probability of EBIT	.25	.50	.25
EBIT (Table 12.9)	$ 0.00	$100.00	$200.00
Less: Interest (Table 12.11)	0.00	0.00	0.00
Net profits before taxes	$ 0.00	$100.00	$200.00
Less: Taxes ($T = .40$)	0.00	40.00	80.00
Net profits after taxes	$ 0.00	$ 60.00	$120.00
EPS (25.0 shares, Table 12.10)	$ 0.00	$ 2.40	$ 4.80
Expected EPS[a]		$ 2.40	
Standard deviation of EPS[a]		$ 1.70	
Coefficient of variation of EPS[a]		0.71	

Debt Ratio = 30%

Probability of EBIT	.25	.50	.25
EBIT (Table 12.9)	$ 0.00	$100.00	$200.00
Less: Interest (Table 12.11)	15.00	15.00	15.00
Net profits before taxes	($15.00)	$ 85.00	$185.00
Less: Taxes ($T = .40$)	(6.00)[b]	34.00	74.00
Net profits after taxes	($ 9.00)	$ 51.00	$111.00
EPS (17.50 shares, Table 12.10)	($ 0.51)	$ 2.91	$ 6.34
Expected EPS[a]		$ 2.91	
Standard deviation of EPS[a]		$ 2.42	
Coefficient of variation of EPS[a]		0.83	

Debt Ratio = 60%

Probability of EBIT	.25	.50	.25
EBIT (Table 12.9)	$ 0.00	$100.00	$200.00
Less: Interest (Table 12.11)	49.50	49.50	49.50
Net profits before taxes	($49.50)	$ 50.50	$150.50
Less: Taxes ($T = .40$)	(19.80)[b]	20.20	60.20
Net profits after taxes	($29.70)	$ 30.30	$ 90.30
EPS (10.00 shares, Table 12.10)	($ 2.97)	$ 3.03	$ 9.03
Expected EPS[a]		$ 3.03	
Standard deviation of EPS[a]		$ 4.24	
Coefficient of variation of EPS[a]		1.40	

[a]The procedures used to calculate the expected value, standard deviation, and coefficient of variation were presented in Equations 6.2, 6.3, and 6.4, respectively, in Chapter 6.

[b]It is assumed that the firm receives the tax benefit from its loss in the current period as a result of applying the tax loss carryback procedures specified in the tax law (see Chapter 3).

| TABLE 12.13 | Expected EPS, Standard Deviation, and Coefficient of Variation for Alternative Capital Structures for Cooke Company |

Capital structure debt ratio	Expected EPS (1)	Standard deviation of EPS (2)	Coefficient of variation of EPS [(2) ÷ (1)] (3)
0%	$2.40	$1.70	0.71
10	2.55	1.88	0.74
20	2.72	2.13	0.78
30	2.91	2.42	0.83
40	3.12	2.83	0.91
50	3.18	3.39	1.07
60	3.03	4.24	1.40

EPS, the standard deviation of EPS, and the coefficient of variation of EPS associated with each debt ratio.[17]

Table 12.13 summarizes the pertinent data for the seven alternative capital structures. The values shown for 0, 30, and 60% debt ratios were developed in Table 12.12, whereas calculations of similar values for the other debt ratios (10, 20, 40 and 50%) are not shown. Because the coefficient of variation measures the risk relative to the expected EPS, it is the preferred risk measure for use in comparing capital structures. As the firm's financial leverage increases, so does its coefficient of variation of EPS. As expected, an increasing level of risk is associated with increased levels of financial leverage.

The relative risk of the two extremes of the capital structures evaluated in Table 12.12 (debt ratios = 0% and 60%) can be illustrated by showing the probability distribution of EPS associated with each of them. Figure 12.3 shows these two distributions. The expected level of EPS increases with increasing financial leverage, and so does risk, as reflected in the relative dispersion of each of the distributions. Clearly, the uncertainty of the expected EPS, as well as the chance of experiencing negative EPS, is greater when higher degrees of financial leverage are employed.

Further, the nature of the risk-return trade-off associated with the seven capital structures under consideration can be clearly observed by plotting the expected EPS and coefficient of variation relative to the debt ratio. Plotting the data from Table 12.13 results in Figure 12.4. The figure shows that as debt is substituted for equity (as the debt ratio increases), the level of EPS rises and then begins to fall (graph *a*). The graph demonstrates that the peak earnings per share

---

17. For explanatory convenience, the coefficient of variation of EPS, which measures total (nondiversifiable and diversifiable) risk, is used throughout this chapter as a proxy for beta, which measures the relevant nondiversifiable risk.

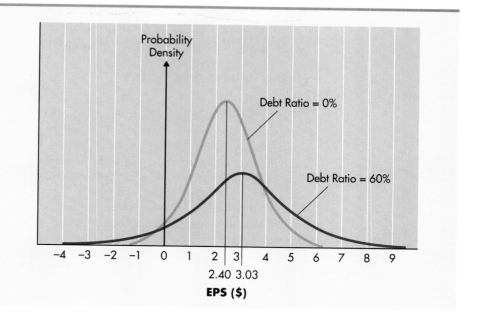

FIGURE 12.3

Probability Distributions

Probability distributions of EPS for debt ratios of 0 and 60% for Cooke Company

occurs at a debt ratio of 50%. The decline in earnings per share beyond that ratio results from the fact that the significant increases in interest are not fully offset by the reduction in the number of shares of common stock outstanding.

If we look at the risk behavior as measured by the coefficient of variation (graph *b*), we can see that risk increases with increasing leverage. A portion of the risk can be attributed to business risk, but that portion changing in response to increasing financial leverage would be attributed to financial risk.

Clearly, a risk-return trade-off exists relative to the use of financial leverage. How to combine these risk-return factors into a valuation framework will be

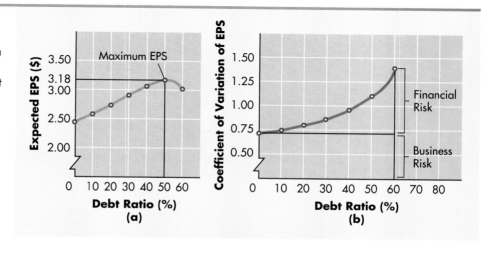

FIGURE 12.4

Expected EPS and Coefficient of Variation of EPS

Expected EPS and coefficient of variation of EPS for alternative capital structures for Cooke Company

addressed later in the chapter. The key point to recognize here is that as a firm introduces more leverage into its capital structure, it will experience increases in both the expected level of return and the associated risk.

Agency Costs Imposed by Lenders

As noted in Chapter 1, the managers of firms typically act as *agents* of the owners (stockholders). The owners give the managers the authority to manage the firm for the owners' benefit. The *agency problem* created by this relationship extends not only to the relationship between owners and managers, but also to the relationship between owners and lenders.

When a lender provides funds to a firm, the interest rate charged is based on the lender's assessment of the firm's risk. The lender-borrower relationship, therefore, depends on the lender's expectations for the firm's subsequent behavior. The borrowing rates are, in effect, locked in when the loans are negotiated. After obtaining a loan at a certain rate, the firm could increase its risk by investing in risky projects or by incurring additional debt. Such action could weaken the lender's position in terms of its claim on the cash flow of the firm. From another point of view, if these risky investment strategies paid off, the stockholders would benefit. Because payment obligations to the lender remain unchanged, the excess cash flows generated by a positive outcome from the riskier action would enhance the value of the firm to its owners. In other words, if the risky investments pay off, the owners receive all the benefits; but if the risky investments do not pay off, the lenders share in the costs.

Clearly, an incentive exists for the managers acting on behalf of the stockholders to "take advantage" of lenders. To avoid this situation, lenders impose certain monitoring techniques on borrowers, who as a result incur *agency costs*. The most obvious strategy is to deny subsequent loan requests or to increase the cost of future loans to the firm. Because this strategy is an after-the-fact approach, other controls must be included in the loan agreement. Lenders typically protect themselves by including provisions that limit the firm's ability to significantly alter its business and financial risk. These loan provisions tend to center on issues such as the minimum level of liquidity, asset acquisitions, executive salaries, and dividend payments.

Hint Typical loan provisions included in corporate bonds are discussed in Chapter 2.

By including appropriate provisions in the loan agreement, the lender can control the firm's risk and thus protect itself against the adverse consequences of this agency problem. Of course, in exchange for incurring agency costs by agreeing to the operating and financial constraints placed on it by the loan provisions, the firm should benefit by obtaining funds at a lower cost.

Asymmetric Information

Two relatively recent surveys examined capital structure decisions.[18] Financial executives were asked which of two major criteria determined their financing decisions: (1) maintaining a *target capital structure* or (2) following a hierarchy

---

18. The results of the survey of Fortune 500 firms are reported in J. Michael Pinegar and Lisa Wilbricht, "What Managers Think of Capital Structure Theory: A Survey," *Financial Management* (Winter 1989), pp. 82–91, and the results of a similar survey of the 500 largest OTC firms are reported in Linda C. Hittle, Kamal Haddad, and Lawrence J. Gitman, "Over-the-Counter Firms, Asymmetric Information, and Financing Preferences," *Review of Financial Economics* (Fall 1992), pp. 81–92.

pecking order
A hierarchy of financing beginning with retained earnings followed by debt financing and finally external equity financing.

asymmetric information
The situation in which managers of a firm have more information about operations and future prospects than do investors.

signal
A financing action by management that is believed to reflect its view of the firm's stock value; generally, debt financing is viewed as a *positive signal* that management believes that the stock is "undervalued," and a stock issue is viewed as a *negative signal* that management believes that the stock is "overvalued."

of financing. This hierarchy, called a **pecking order,** begins with retained earnings followed by debt financing and finally external equity financing. Respondents from 31 percent of Fortune 500 firms and from 11 percent of the (smaller) 500 largest over-the-counter firms answered target capital structure. Respondents from 69 percent of the Fortune 500 firms and 89 percent of the 500 largest OTC firms chose the pecking order.

At first glance, on the basis of financial theory, this choice appears to be inconsistent with wealth maximizing goals. However, Stewart Myers explained how "asymmetric information" could account for the pecking order financing preferences of financial managers.[19] **Asymmetric information** results when managers of a firm have more information about operations and future prospects than do investors. Assuming that managers make decisions with the goal of maximizing the wealth of existing stockholders, then asymmetric information can affect the capital structure decisions that managers make.

Suppose, for example, that management has found a valuable investment that will require additional financing. Management believes that the prospects for the firm's future are very good and that the market, as indicated by the firm's current stock price, does not fully appreciate the firm's value. In this case, it would be advantageous to current stockholders if management raised the required funds using debt rather than issuing new stock. Using debt to raise funds is frequently viewed as a **signal** that reflects management's view of the firm's stock value. Debt financing is a *positive signal* suggesting that management believes that the stock is "undervalued" and therefore a bargain. When the firm's positive future outlook becomes known to the market, the increased value would be fully captured by existing owners, rather than having to be shared with new stockholders.

If, however, the outlook for the firm is poor, management may believe that the firm's stock is "overvalued." In that case, it would be in the best interest of existing stockholders for the firm to issue new stock. Therefore investors often interpret the announcement of a stock issue as a *negative signal*—bad news concerning the firm's prospects—and the stock price declines. This decrease in stock value, along with high underwriting costs for stock issues (compared to debt issues), make new stock financing very expensive. When the negative future outlook becomes known to the market, the decreased value would be shared with new stockholders, rather than be fully captured by existing owners.

Because asymmetric information conditions exist from time to time, firms should maintain some reserve borrowing capacity, by keeping debt levels low. This reserve allows the firm to take advantage of good investment opportunities without having to sell stock at a low value or send signals that unduly influence the stock price.

The Optimal Capital Structure

So, what *is* an optimal capital structure, even if it exists (so far) only in theory? To provide some insight into an answer, we will examine some basic financial relationships. It is generally believed that *the value of the firm is maximized*

19. Stewart C. Myers, "The Capital Structure Puzzle," *Journal of Finance* (July 1984), pp. 575–592.

when the cost of capital is minimized. By using a modification of the simple zero-growth valuation model (see Equation 7.7 in Chapter 7), we can define the value of the firm, V, by Equation 12.11:

$$V = \frac{\text{EBIT} \times (1 - T)}{k_a} \qquad (12.11)$$

where

$$\text{EBIT} = \text{earnings before interest and taxes}$$
$$T = \text{tax rate}$$
$$k_a = \text{weighted average cost of capital}$$

Clearly, if we assume that EBIT is constant, the value of the firm, V, is maximized by minimizing the weighted average cost of capital, k_a.

Cost Functions

Figure 12.5(a) plots three cost functions—the after-tax cost of debt, k_i; the cost of equity, k_s; and the weighted average cost of capital, k_a—as a function of financial leverage measured by the debt ratio (debt to total assets). The *cost of debt,* k_i, remains low due to the tax shield but slowly increases with increasing leverage to compensate lenders for increasing risk. The *cost of equity,* k_s, is above the cost of debt and increases with increasing financial leverage, but generally increases more rapidly than the cost of debt. The increase in the cost of equity occurs because the stockholders require a higher return as leverage increases, to compensate for the higher degree of financial risk.

The *weighted average cost of capital,* k_a, results from a weighted average of the firm's debt and equity capital costs. At a debt ratio of zero, the firm is 100 percent equity financed. As debt is substituted for equity and as the debt ratio increases, the weighted average cost of capital declines because the debt cost is less than the equity cost ($k_i < k_s$). As the debt ratio continues to increase, the increased debt and equity costs eventually cause the weighted average cost of capital to rise (after point M in Figure 12.5(a)). This behavior results in a U-shaped, or saucer-shaped, weighted average cost of capital function, k_a.

A Graphic View of the Optimal Structure

optimal capital structure
The capital structure at which the weighted average cost of capital is minimized, thereby maximizing the firm's value.

Because the maximization of value, V, is achieved when the overall cost of capital, k_a, is at a minimum (see Equation 12.11), the **optimal capital structure** is therefore that at which the weighted average cost of capital, k_a, is minimized. In Figure 12.5(a), point M represents the *minimum weighted average cost of capital*—the point of optimal financial leverage and hence of optimal capital structure for the firm.

Figure 12.5(b) plots the value of the firm resulting from substitution of k_a in Figure 12.5(a) for various levels of financial leverage into the zero-growth valuation model in Equation 12.11. As shown in Figure 12.5(b), at the optimal capital structure, point M, the value of the firm is maximized at V^*.

FIGURE 12.5

Cost Functions and Value
Capital costs and the optimal capital structure

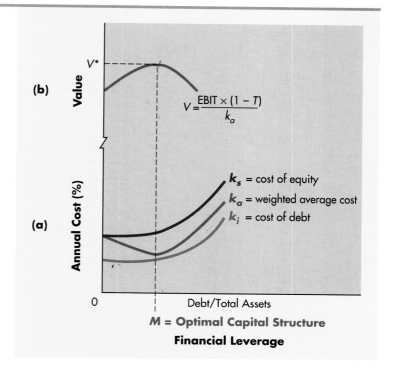

Generally, the lower the firm's weighted average cost of capital, the greater the difference between the return on a project and this cost, and therefore the greater the owners' return. Simply stated, minimizing the weighted average cost of capital allows management to undertake a larger number of profitable projects, thereby further increasing the value of the firm.

As a practical matter, there is no way to calculate the optimal capital structure implied by Figure 12.5. Because it is impossible either to know or remain at the precise optimal capital structure, firms generally try to operate in a range that places them near what they believe to be the optimal capital structure. The fact that retained earnings and other new financings will cause the firm's actual capital structure to change further justifies the focus on a capital structure range rather than a single optimum point.

? Review Questions

12–6   What is a firm's *capital structure?* What ratios assess the degree of financial leverage in a firm's capital structure?

12–7   Discuss the differences, and the reasons for them, in the capital structures of U.S. and non-U.S. corporations. In what ways are the capital structures of U.S. and non-U.S. firms similar?

12–8   What is the major benefit of debt financing? How does it affect the firm's cost of debt?

In Practice

USG Builds a New Capital Structure

In 1988 USG Corp., the world leader in gypsum wallboard products and the number two producer of ceiling grid and ceiling tile, was threatened with a hostile takeover. To remain independent, the board of directors over-leveraged the company, bringing total debt to $3 billion. With interest payments of $1 million a day, USG was in poor shape to ride out the 1990 recession in the housing market. Sales fell as the price of wallboard took a nose dive, and that same year the 88-year-old USG posted its first loss.

Over the next three years, treasurer Rick Fleming and CFO J. Bradford James reduced total debt to $1.6 billion. But USG still had problems servicing its heavy debt load, and in 1993 the firm filed for bankruptcy. Its stock price collapsed to under $1 a share.

Fleming announced that the company would rebuild its financial house: By May 1998, USG would reduce its debt to $650 million and regain its investment grade debt rating (BBB/Baa or better). He developed a formula, based on the company's credit rating, to allocate free cash flow. The lower the rating, the higher the percentage that would go to debt repayment as opposed to capital expenditures. Fleming, who became CFO in 1994, also raised equity to pay down debt more quickly and improve the company's debt ratio. By 1995 he had restructured the remaining debt to lengthen maturities.

While Fleming was rigorously managing USG's capital structure, the housing markets recovered. High demand for USG's products boosted sales, helping Fleming reach his goals ahead of schedule. By December 1997, the firm's debt was $620 million, and Standard & Poor's upgraded USG's debt rating to BBB; Moody's followed suit in early 1998. In recent years USG's stock price has outperformed its industry, and the company resumed paying dividends in mid-1998.

12–9   Define *business risk,* and discuss the three factors that affect it. What influence does business risk have on the firm's capital structure decisions? Define *financial risk,* and explain its relationship to the firm's capital structure.

12–10   Briefly describe the *agency problem* that exists between owners and lenders. Explain how the firm must incur *agency costs* for the lender to resolve this problem.

12–11   How does *asymmetric information* affect the firm's capital structure decisions? Explain how and why investors may view the firm's financing actions as *signals.*

12–12   Describe the generally accepted theory concerning the behavior of the cost of debt, the cost of equity, and the weighted average cost of capital as the firm's financial leverage increases from zero. Where is the *optimal capital structure* under this theory? What is its relationship to the firm's value at that point?

12.3 The EBIT–EPS Approach to Capital Structure

EBIT–EPS approach
An approach for selecting the capital structure that maximizes earnings per share over the expected range of earnings before interest and taxes.

The **EBIT–EPS approach** to capital structure involves selecting the capital structure that maximizes earnings per share over the expected range of earnings before interest and taxes. Here the main emphasis is on the effects of various capital structures on *owners' returns*. Because one of the key variables affecting the market value of the firm's shares is its earnings, EPS can be conveniently used to analyze alternative capital structures.

Presenting a Financing Plan Graphically

To analyze the effects of a firm's capital structure on the owners' returns, we consider the relationship between earnings before interest and taxes (EBIT) and earnings per share (EPS). A constant level of EBIT—constant *business risk*—is assumed, to isolate the effect on returns of the financing costs associated with alternative capital structures. EPS is used to measure the owners' returns, which are expected to be closely related to share price.[20]

The Data Required

To graph a financing plan, we need to know at least two EBIT–EPS coordinates. The approach for obtaining coordinates can be illustrated by an example.

Example ▼

EBIT–EPS coordinates can be found by assuming two EBIT values and calculating the EPS associated with them.[21] Such calculations for three capital structures—debt ratios of 0, 30, and 60%—for Cooke Company were presented in Table 12.12. By using the EBIT values of $100,000 and $200,000, the associated EPS values calculated there are summarized in the table within Figure 12.6 on
▲ page 520.

Plotting the Data

The Cooke Company data can be plotted on a set of EBIT–EPS axes, as shown in Figure 12.6. The figure shows the level of EPS expected for each level of EBIT. For levels of EBIT below the *x*-axis intercept, a loss (negative EPS) results. Each

---

20. The relationship that is expected to exist between EPS and owner wealth is not one of cause and effect. As indicated in Chapter 1, the maximization of profits does not necessarily assure the firm that owners' wealth is also being maximized. Nevertheless, it is expected that the movement of earnings per share will have some effect on owners' wealth, because EPS data constitute one of the few pieces of information investors receive, and they often bid the firm's share price up or down in response to the level of these earnings.

21. A convenient method for finding one EBIT–EPS coordinate is to calculate the *financial breakeven point,* the level of EBIT for which the firm's EPS just equals $0. It is the level of EBIT needed just to cover all fixed financial costs—annual interest (I) and preferred stock dividends (PD). The equation for the financial breakeven point is

$$\text{Financial breakeven point} = I + \frac{PD}{1 - T}$$

where T is the tax rate. It can be seen that when $PD = \$0$, the financial breakeven point is equal to I, the annual interest payment.

FIGURE 12.6

EBIT–EPS Approach
A comparison of selected capital structures for Cooke Company (data from Table 12.12)

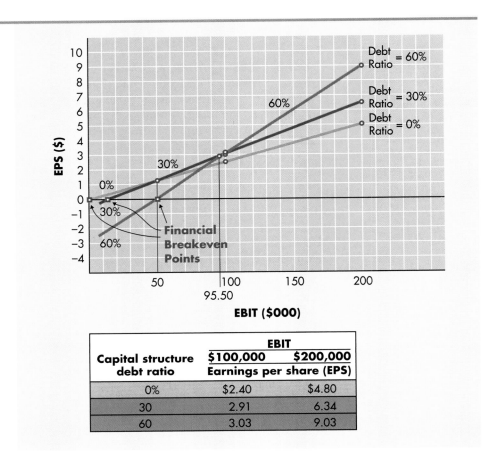

Capital structure debt ratio	EBIT	
	$100,000	**$200,000**
	Earnings per share (EPS)	
0%	$2.40	$4.80
30	2.91	6.34
60	3.03	9.03

financial breakeven point
The level of EBIT necessary just to cover all fixed financial costs; the level of EBIT for which EPS = $0.

of the *x*-axis intercepts is a **financial breakeven point,** where EBIT just covers all fixed financial costs (EPS = $0).

Comparing Alternative Capital Structures

We can compare alternative capital structures by graphing financing plans as shown in Figure 12.6. The following example illustrates this procedure.

E x a m p l e ▼ Cooke Company's capital structure alternatives were plotted on the EBIT–EPS axes in Figure 12.6. This figure discloses that over certain ranges of EBIT, each capital structure is superior to the others in terms of maximizing EPS. The zero-leverage capital structure (debt ratio = 0%) is superior to either of the other capital structures for levels of EBIT between $0 and $50,000; between $50,000 and $95,500 of EBIT, the capital structure associated with a debt ratio of 30% is preferred. At a level of EBIT in excess of $95,500, the capital structure associated with a debt ratio of 60% provides the highest earnings per share.[22]

Considering Risk in EBIT–EPS Analysis

When interpreting EBIT–EPS analysis, it is important to consider the risk of each capital structure alternative. Graphically, the risk of each capital structure can be viewed in light of the *financial breakeven point* (EBIT-axis intercept) and the *degree of financial leverage* reflected in the slope of the capital structure line: *The higher the financial breakeven point and the steeper the slope of the capital structure line, the greater the financial risk.*[23]

Further assessment of risk can be performed by using ratios. With increased financial leverage, as measured by the debt ratio, we expect a corresponding decline in the firm's ability to make scheduled interest payments, as measured by the times interest earned ratio.

Example ▼ Reviewing the three capital structures plotted for Cooke Company in Figure 12.6, we can see that as the debt ratio increases, so does the financial risk of each alternative. Both the financial breakeven point and the slope of the capital structure lines increase with increasing debt ratios. If we use the $100,000 EBIT value, the times interest earned ratio (EBIT ÷ interest) for the zero-leverage capital structure is infinity ($100,000 ÷ $0); for the 30% debt case, it is 6.67 ($100,000 ÷ $15,000); and for the 60% debt case, it is 2.02 ($100,000 ÷ $49,500). Because lower times interest earned ratios reflect higher risk, these ratios support the earlier conclusion that the risk of the capital structures increases with increasing financial leverage. The capital structure for a debt ratio of 60% is riskier than

---

22. An algebraic technique can be used to find the *indifference points* between the capital structure alternatives. This technique involves expressing each capital structure as an equation stated in terms of earnings per share, setting the equations for two capital structures equal to each other, and solving for the level of EBIT that causes the equations to be equal. By using the notation from footnote 21 and letting n equal the number of shares of common stock outstanding, the general equation for the earnings per share from a financing plan is

$$\text{EPS} = \frac{(1 - T) \times (\text{EBIT} - I) - PD}{n}$$

Comparing Cooke Company's 0 and 30% capital structures, we get

$$\frac{(1 - .40) \times (\text{EBIT} - \$0) - \$0}{25.00} = \frac{(1 - .40) \times (\text{EBIT} - \$15.00) - \$0}{17.50}$$

$$\frac{.60 \times \text{EBIT}}{25.00} = \frac{.60 \times \text{EBIT} - \$9.00}{17.50}$$

$$10.50 \times \text{EBIT} = 15.00 \times \text{EBIT} - \$225.00$$

$$\$225.00 = 4.50 \times \text{EBIT}$$

$$\text{EBIT} = \$50$$

The calculated value of the indifference point between the 0 and 30% capital structures is therefore $50,000, as can be seen in Figure 12.6.

23. The degree of financial leverage (DFL) is reflected in the slope of the EBIT–EPS function. The steeper the slope, the greater the degree of financial leverage, because the change in EPS (*y* axis) resulting from a given change in EBIT (*x* axis) will increase with increasing slope and will decrease with decreasing slope.

that for a debt ratio of 30%, which in turn is riskier than the capital structure for a debt ratio of 0%.

Basic Shortcoming of EBIT–EPS Analysis

The most important point to recognize when using EBIT–EPS analysis is that this technique tends to concentrate on *maximizing earnings* rather than maximizing owner wealth. The use of an EPS-maximizing approach generally ignores risk. If investors did not require risk premiums (additional returns) as the firm increased the proportion of debt in its capital structure, a strategy involving maximizing EPS would also maximize owner wealth. Because risk premiums increase with increases in financial leverage, the maximization of EPS *does not* ensure owner wealth maximization. To select the best capital structure, both return (EPS) and risk (via the required return, k_s) must be integrated into a valuation framework consistent with the capital structure theory presented earlier.

? Review Question

12–13 Explain the *EBIT–EPS approach* to capital structure. Include in your explanation a graph indicating the *financial breakeven point;* label the axes. Is this approach consistent with maximization of value? Explain.

12.4 Choosing the Optimal Capital Structure

Creating a wealth maximization framework for use in making capital structure decisions is not easy. Although the two key factors—return and risk—can be used separately to make capital structure decisions, integration of them into a market value context provides the best results. This section describes the procedures for linking the return and risk associated with alternative capital structures to market value to select the best capital structure.

Linkage

To determine its value under alternative capital structures, the firm must find the level of return that must be earned to compensate investors and owners for the risk being incurred. That is, the risk associated with each structure must be linked to the required rate of return. Such a framework is consistent with the overall valuation framework developed in Chapter 7 and applied to capital budgeting decisions in Chapters 9 and 10.

The required return associated with a given level of financial risk can be estimated in a number of ways. Theoretically, the preferred approach would be to first estimate the beta associated with each alternative capital structure and then use the CAPM (see Equation 6.8) to calculate the required return, k_s. A more operational approach involves linking the financial risk associated with each capital structure alternative directly to the required return. Such an approach is similar to the CAPM-type approach demonstrated in Chapter 10 for linking project risk and required return (RADR). Here it involves estimating the required return associated with each level of financial risk, as measured by a statistic such as the coefficient of variation of EPS. Regardless of the approach used, one would expect that the required return would increase as the financial risk increases.

Example ▼ Cooke Company, using the coefficients of variation of EPS associated with each of the seven alternative capital structures as a risk measure, estimated the associated required returns. These are shown in Table 12.14. As expected, the estimated required return, k_s, increases with increasing risk, as measured by the ▲ coefficient of variation of EPS.

Estimating Value

The value of the firm associated with alternative capital structures can be estimated by using one of the standard valuation models. If, for simplicity, we assume that all earnings are paid out as dividends, we can use a zero-growth valuation model such as that developed in Chapter 7. The model, originally stated in Equation 7.7, is restated here with EPS substituted for dividends, because in each year the dividends would equal EPS:

$$P_0 = \frac{\text{EPS}}{k_s}$$

(12.12)

By substituting the estimated level of EPS and the associated required return, k_s, into Equation 12.12, we can estimate the per share value of the firm, P_0.

Example ▼ Returning again to Cooke Company, we can now estimate the value of its stock under each of the alternative capital structures. Substituting the expected EPS

TABLE 12.14	Required Returns for Cooke Company's Alternative Capital Structures	
Capital structure debt ratio	Coefficient of variation of EPS (from column 3 of Table 12.13) (1)	Estimated required return, k_s (2)
0%	0.71	11.5%
10	0.74	11.7
20	0.78	12.1
30	0.83	12.5
40	0.91	14.0
50	1.07	16.5
60	1.40	19.0

TABLE 12.15	Calculation of Share Value Estimates Associated with Alternative Capital Structures for Cooke Company		
Capital structure debt ratio	Expectd EPS (from column 1 of Table 12.13) (1)	Estimated required return, k_s (from column 2 of Table 12.14) (2)	Estimated share value [(1) ÷ (2)] (3)
0%	$2.40	.115	$20.87
10	2.55	.117	21.79
20	2.72	.121	22.48
30	2.91	.125	23.28
40	3.12	.140	22.29
50	3.18	.165	19.27
60	3.03	.190	15.95

(from column 1 of Table 12.13) and the required returns, k_s (from column 2 of Table 12.14), into Equation 12.12 for each of the alternative capital structures, we obtain the share values given in column 3 of Table 12.15. Plotting the resulting share values against the associated debt ratios, as shown in Figure 12.7, clearly illustrates that the maximum share value occurs at the capital structure associated with a debt ratio of 30%.

FIGURE 12.7

Estimating Value
Estimated share value and EPS for alternative capital structures for Cooke Company

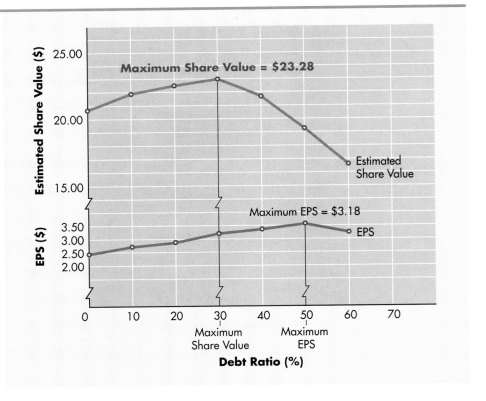

Maximizing Value Versus Maximizing EPS

Throughout this text, the goal of the financial manager has been specified as maximizing owner wealth, not profit. Although there is some relationship between the level of expected profit and value, there is no reason to believe that profit-maximizing strategies necessarily result in wealth maximization. It is therefore the wealth of the owners as reflected in the estimated share value that should serve as the criterion for selecting the best capital structure. A final look at Cooke Company will help to highlight this point.

Example ▼   Further analysis of Figure 12.7 clearly shows that although the firm's profits (EPS) are maximized at a debt ratio of 50%, share value is maximized at a 30% debt ratio. In this case, the preferred capital structure would be the 30% debt ratio. The EPS-maximization approach does not provide a similar conclusion because it does not consider risk. Therefore, to maximize owner wealth, Cooke
▲   Company should employ the capital structure that results in a 30% debt ratio.

Some Other Important Considerations

Because there is really no practical way to calculate the optimal capital structure, any quantitative analysis of capital structure must be tempered with other important considerations. Numerous additional factors relative to capital structure decisions could be listed; some of the more important factors, categorized by broad area of concern, are summarized in Table 12.16 on page 526.

? Review Questions

12–14   Do *maximizing value* and *maximizing EPS* lead to the same conclusion about the optimal capital structure? If not, what is the cause?

12–15   How might a firm go about determining its optimal capital structure? In addition to quantitative considerations, what other important factors should a firm consider when it is making a capital structure decision?

SUMMARY

 Discuss the role of breakeven analysis, how to determine the operating breakeven point, and the effect of changing costs on the breakeven point. Breakeven analysis measures the level of sales necessary to cover total operating costs. The operating breakeven point may be calculated algebraically, by dividing fixed operating costs by the difference between the sale price per unit and variable operating cost per unit, or it may be determined graphically. The operating breakeven point increases with increased fixed and variable operat-

ing costs and decreases with an increase in sale price, and vice versa.

 Understand operating, financial, and total leverage and the relationships among them. Operating leverage is the use of fixed operating costs by the firm to magnify the effects of changes in sales on EBIT. The higher the fixed operating costs, the greater the operating leverage. Financial leverage is the use of fixed financial costs by the firm to magnify the effects of changes in

TABLE 12.16   Important Factors to Consider in Making Capital Structure Decisions

Concern	Factor	Description
Business risk	Revenue stability	Firms having stable and predictable revenues can more safely undertake highly levered capital structures than can firms with volatile patterns of sales revenue. Firms with growing sales tend to be in the best position to benefit from added debt because they can reap the positive benefits of leverage, which magnifies the effect of these increases.
	Cash flow	When considering a new capital structure the firm must focus on its ability to generate the necessary cash flows to meet obligations. Cash forecasts reflecting an ability to service debts (and preferred stock) must support any capital structure shift.
Agency costs	Contractual obligations	A firm may be contractually constrained with respect to the type of funds that it can raise. For example, a firm might be prohibited from selling additional debt except when the claims of holders of such debt are made subordinate to the existing debt. Contractual constraints on the sale of additional stock as well as the ability to distribute dividends on stock might also exist.
	Management preferences	Occasionally, a firm will impose an internal constraint on the use of debt to limit its risk exposure to a level deemed acceptable to management. In other words, due to risk aversion, the firm's management constrains the firm's capital structure at a level that may or may not be the true optimum.
	Control	A management concerned about control may prefer to issue debt rather than (voting) common stock. Under favorable market conditions, a firm that wanted to sell equity could issue *nonvoting shares* or make a *preemptive offering* (see Chapter 2), allowing each shareholder to maintain proportionate ownership. Generally, only in closely held firms or firms threatened by takeover does control become a major concern in the capital structure decision.
Asymmetric information	External risk assessment	The firm's ability to raise funds quickly and at favorable rates depends on the external risk assessments of lenders and bond raters. The firm must therefore consider the potential impact of capital structure decisions both on share value and on published financial statements from which lenders and raters tend to assess the firm's risk.
	Timing	At times when interest rates are low, debt financing might be more attractive; when interest rates are high, the sale of stock may be more appealing. Sometimes both debt and equity capital become unavailable at what would be viewed as reasonable terms. General economic conditions—especially those of the capital market—can thus significantly affect capital structure decisions.

EBIT on EPS. The higher the fixed financial costs—typically, interest on debt and preferred stock dividends—the greater the financial leverage. The total leverage of the firm is the use of fixed costs—both operating and financial—to magnify the effects of changes in sales on EPS. Total leverage reflects the combined effect of operating and financial leverage.

LG3 **Describe the basic types of capital, external assessment of capital structure, capital structure of non-U.S. firms, and capital structure theory.** The two basic types of capital—debt and equity—that make up a firm's capital structure differ with respect to voice in management, claims on income and assets, maturity, and tax treatment. Capital structure can be externally assessed by using financial ratios—debt ratio, times interest earned ratio, and fixed-payment coverage ratio. Non-U.S. companies tend to have much higher leverage ratios than do their U.S. counterparts, primarily because U.S. capital markets are much better developed. Similarities between U.S. corporations and those of other countries include industry patterns of capital structure, large multinational company capital structures, and the trend toward greater reliance on securities issuance and less reliance on banks for financing.

Research suggests that there is an optimal capital structure that balances the firm's benefits and costs of debt financing. The major benefit of debt financing is the tax shield. The costs of debt financing include the probability of bankruptcy, caused by business and financial risk; agency costs imposed by lenders; and asymmetric information, which typically causes firms to raise funds in a pecking order of retained earnings, then debt, and finally external equity financing, to send positive signals to the market and thereby enhance the wealth of shareholders.

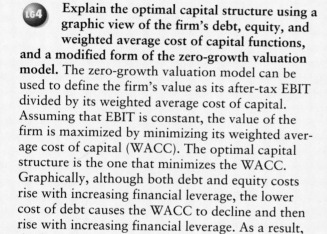

Explain the optimal capital structure using a graphic view of the firm's debt, equity, and weighted average cost of capital functions, and a modified form of the zero-growth valuation model. The zero-growth valuation model can be used to define the firm's value as its after-tax EBIT divided by its weighted average cost of capital. Assuming that EBIT is constant, the value of the firm is maximized by minimizing its weighted average cost of capital (WACC). The optimal capital structure is the one that minimizes the WACC. Graphically, although both debt and equity costs rise with increasing financial leverage, the lower cost of debt causes the WACC to decline and then rise with increasing financial leverage. As a result, the firm's WACC exhibits a U-shape having a minimum value, which defines the optimum capital structure—the one that maximizes owner wealth.

 Discuss the graphic presentation, risk considerations, and basic shortcomings of using the EBIT–EPS approach to compare alternative capital structures. The EBIT–EPS approach can be used to evaluate capital structures in light of the returns they provide the firm's owners and their degree of financial risk. Under the EBIT–EPS approach, the preferred capital structure is the one that is expected to provide maximum EPS over the firm's expected range of EBIT. Graphically, this approach reflects risk in terms of the financial breakeven point and the slope of the capital structure line. The major shortcoming of EBIT–EPS analysis is that by ignoring risk, it concentrates on maximizing earnings rather than owners' wealth.

 Review the return and risk of alternative capital structures and their linkage to market value, and other important capital structure considerations. The best capital structure can be selected from various alternatives by using a valuation model to link return and risk factors. The preferred capital structure would be the one that results in the highest estimated share value—not the highest profits (EPS). Other important nonquantitative factors, such as revenue stability, cash flow, contractual obligations, management preferences, control, external risk assessment, and timing, must also be considered when making capital structure decisions.

SELF-TEST PROBLEMS   (Solutions in Appendix B)

    ST 12–1   Breakeven point and all forms of leverage   TOR most recently sold 100,000 units at $7.50 each; its variable operating costs are $3.00 per unit, and its fixed operating costs are $250,000. Annual interest charges total $80,000, and the firm has 8,000 shares of $5 (annual dividend) preferred stock outstanding. It currently has 20,000 shares of common stock outstanding. Assume that the firm has a 40% tax rate.

  a. At what level of sales (in units) would the firm break even on operations (i.e., EBIT = $0)?

  b. Calculate the firm's earnings per share (EPS) in tabular form at (1) the current level of sales and (2) a 120,000-unit sales level.

  c. Using the current *$750,000 level of sales as a base,* calculate the firm's degree of operating leverage (DOL).

d. Using the EBIT *associated with the $750,000 level of sales as a base,* calculate the firm's degree of financial leverage (DFL).
e. Use the degree of total leverage (DTL) concept to determine the effect (in percentage terms) of a 50% increase in TOR's sales *from the $750,000 base level* on its earnings per share.

 ST 12–2 **EBIT–EPS analysis** Newlin Electronics is considering additional financing of $10,000. It currently has $50,000 of 12% (annual interest) bonds and 10,000 shares of common stock outstanding. The firm can obtain the financing through a 12% (annual interest) bond issue or the sale of 1,000 shares of common stock. The firm has a 40% tax rate.
a. Calculate two EBIT–EPS coordinates for each plan by selecting any two EBIT values and finding their associated EPS.
b. Plot the two financing plans on a set of EBIT–EPS axes.
c. On the basis of your graph in **b,** at what level of EBIT does the bond plan become superior to the stock plan?

  ST 12–3 **Optimal capital structure** Hawaiian Macadamia Nut Company has collected the following data with respect to its capital structure, expected earnings per share, and required return.

Capital structure debt ratio	Expected earnings per share	Required return, k_s
0%	$3.12	13%
10	3.90	15
20	4.80	16
30	5.44	17
40	5.51	19
50	5.00	20
60	4.40	22

a. Compute the estimated share value associated with each of the capital structures using the simplified method described in this chapter (see Equation 12.12).
b. Determine the optimal capital structure based on (1) maximization of expected earnings per share and (2) maximization of share value.
c. Which capital structure do you recommend? Why?

PROBLEMS

WARM-UP 12–1 **Breakeven point—Algebraic** Kate Rowland wishes to estimate the number of flower arrangements she must sell at $24.95 to break even. She has estimated fixed operating costs of $12,350 per year and variable operating costs of $15.45

per arrangement. How many flower arrangements must Kate sell to break even on operating costs?

12–2 Breakeven comparisons—Algebraic   Given the price and cost data shown in the following table for each of the three firms, F, G, and H, answer the following questions.

WARM-UP

Firm	F	G	H
Sale price per unit	$ 18.00	$ 21.00	$ 30.00
Variable operating cost per unit	6.75	13.50	12.00
Fixed operating cost	45,000	30,000	90,000

a. What is the operating breakeven point in units for each firm?

b. How would you rank these firms in terms of their risk?

INTERMEDIATE **12–3 Breakeven point—Algebraic and graphic**   Fine Leather Enterprises sells its single product for $129.00 per unit. The firm's fixed operating costs are $473,000 annually, and its variable operating costs are $86.00 per unit.

a. Find the firm's operating breakeven point in units.

b. Label the *x* axis "Sales (units)" and the *y* axis "Costs/Revenues ($)," and then graph the firm's sales revenue, total operating cost, and fixed operating cost functions on these axes. In addition, label the operating breakeven point and the areas of loss and profit (EBIT).

INTERMEDIATE **12–4 Breakeven analysis**   Barry Carter is considering opening a record store. He wants to estimate the number of CDs he must sell to break even. The CDs will be sold for $13.98 each, variable operating costs are $10.48 per CD, and annual fixed operating costs are $73,500.

a. Find the operating breakeven point in CDs.

b. Calculate the total operating costs at the breakeven volume found in **a.**

c. If Barry estimates that at a minimum he can sell 2,000 CDs *per month*, should he go into the record business?

d. How much EBIT would Barry realize if he sells the minimum 2,000 CDs per month noted in **c**?

INTERMEDIATE **12–5 Breakeven point—Changing costs/revenues**   JWG Company publishes *Creative Crosswords*. Last year the book of puzzles sold for $10 with variable operating cost per book of $8 and fixed operating costs of $40,000. How many books must be sold this year to achieve the breakeven point for the stated operating costs, given the following different circumstances?

a. All figures remain the same as last year.

b. Fixed operating costs increase to $44,000; all other figures remain the same.

c. The selling price increases to $10.50; all costs remain the same as last year.

d. Variable operating cost per book increases to $8.50; all other figures remain the same.

e. What conclusions about the operating breakeven point can be drawn from your answers?

12–6   **Breakeven analysis**   Molly Jasper and her sister, Caitlin Peters, got into the novelties business almost by accident. Molly, a talented sculptor, would make little figurines as gifts for friends. Occasionally, she and Caitlin would set up a booth at a crafts fair and sell a few of the figurines along with jewelry that Caitlin made. Little by little, demand for the figurines, now called Mollycaits, grew, and the sisters began to reproduce some of the favorites in resin using molds of the originals. The day came when a buyer for a major department store offered them a contract to produce 1,500 figurines of various designs for $10,000. Molly and Caitlin realized that it was time to get down to business. To make bookkeeping simpler, Molly had priced all of the figurines at $8.00. Variable operating costs amounted to an average of $6.00 per unit. In order to produce the order, Molly and Caitlin would have to rent industrial facilities for a month, which would cost them $4,000.

   a. Calculate Mollycait's operating breakeven point.
   b. Calculate Mollycait's EBIT on the department store order.
   c. If Molly renegotiates the contract at a price of $10.00, what will the EBIT be?
   d. If the store refuses to pay more than $8.00 per unit, but is willing to negotiate quantity, what quantity of figurines would result in an EBIT of $4,000?
   e. At this time, Mollycaits come in 15 different varieties. Whereas the average variable cost per unit is $6.00, the actual cost varies from unit to unit. What recommendation would you have for Molly and Caitlin with regard to pricing and/or the number and type of units that they offer for sale?

  12–7   **EBIT sensitivity**   Stewart Industries sells its finished product for $9 per unit. Its fixed operating costs are $20,000, and the variable operating cost per unit is $5.

   a. Calculate the firm's earnings before interest and taxes (EBIT) for sales of 10,000 units.
   b. Calculate the firm's EBIT for sales of 8,000 and 12,000 units, respectively.
   c. Calculate the percentage changes in sales (from the 10,000-unit base level) and associated percentage changes in EBIT for the shifts in sales indicated in **b.**
   d. On the basis of your findings in **c,** comment on the sensitivity of changes in EBIT in response to changes in sales.

  12–8   **Degree of operating leverage**   Grey Products has fixed operating costs of $380,000, variable operating costs per unit of $16, and a selling price of $63.50 per unit.

   a. Calculate the operating breakeven point in units.
   b. Calculate the firm's EBIT at 9,000, 10,000, and 11,000 units, respectively.
   c. By using 10,000 units as a base, what are the percentage changes in units sold and EBIT as sales move from the base to the other sales levels used in **b?**
   d. Use the percentages computed in **c** to determine the degree of operating leverage (DOL).
   e. Use the formula for degree of operating leverage to determine the DOL at 10,000 units.

INTERMEDIATE   **12–9   Degree of operating leverage—Graphic**   Levin Corporation has fixed operating costs of $72,000, variable operating costs of $6.75 per unit, and a selling price of $9.75 per unit.

a. Calculate the operating breakeven point in units.

b. Compute the degree of operating leverage (DOL) for the following unit sales levels: 25,000, 30,000, 40,000. Use the formula given in the chapter.

c. Graph the DOL figures that you computed in **b** (on the *y* axis) against sales levels (on the *x* axis).

d. Compute the degree of operating leverage at 24,000 units; add this point to your graph.

e. What principle is illustrated by your graph and figures?

 INTERMEDIATE   **12–10   EPS calculations**   Southland Industries has $60,000 of 16% (annual interest) bonds outstanding, 1,500 shares of preferred stock paying an annual dividend of $5 per share, and 4,000 shares of common stock outstanding. Assuming that the firm has a 40% tax rate, compute earnings per share (EPS) for the following levels of EBIT:

a. $24,600

b. $30,600

c. $35,000

 INTERMEDIATE   **12–11   Degree of financial leverage**   Northwestern Savings and Loan has a current capital structure consisting of $250,000 of 16% (annual interest) debt and 2,000 shares of common stock. The firm pays taxes at the rate of 40%.

a. Using EBIT values of $80,000 and $120,000, determine the associated earnings per share (EPS).

b. Using $80,000 of EBIT as a base, calculate the degree of financial leverage (DFL).

c. Rework parts **a** and **b** assuming that the firm has $100,000 of 16% (annual interest) debt and 3,000 shares of common stock.

 INTERMEDIATE   **12–12   DFL and graphic display of financing plans**   Wells and Associates has EBIT of $67,500. Interest costs are $22,500, and the firm has 15,000 shares of common stock outstanding. Assume a 40% tax rate.

a. Use the degree of financial leverage (DFL) formula to calculate the DFL for the firm.

b. Using a set of EBIT–EPS axes, plot Wells and Associates' financing plan.

c. Assuming that the firm also has 1,000 shares of preferred stock paying a $6.00 annual dividend per share, what is the DFL?

d. Plot the financing plan including the 1,000 shares of $6.00 preferred stock on the axes used in **b**.

e. Briefly discuss the graph of the two financing plans.

 INTERMEDIATE   **12–13   Integrative—Multiple leverage measures**   Play-More Toys produces inflatable beach balls, selling 400,000 balls a year. Each ball produced has a variable operating cost of $.84 and sells for $1.00. Fixed operating costs are $28,000. The firm has annual interest charges of $6,000, preferred dividends of $2,000, and a 40% tax rate.

a. Calculate the operating breakeven point in units.

b. Use the degree of operating leverage (DOL) formula to calculate DOL.
c. Use the degree of financial leverage (DFL) formula to calculate DFL.
d. Use the degree of total leverage (DTL) formula to calculate DTL. Compare this to the product of DOL and DFL calculated in **b** and **c**.

12–14   Integrative—Leverage and risk   Firm R has sales of 100,000 units at $2.00 per unit, variable operating costs of $1.70 per unit, and fixed operating costs of $6,000. Interest is $10,000 per year. Firm W has sales of 100,000 units at $2.50 per unit, variable operating costs of $1.00 per unit, and fixed operating costs of $62,500. Interest is $17,500 per year. Assume that both firms are in the 40% tax bracket.
a. Compute the degree of operating, financial, and total leverage for firm R.
b. Compute the degree of operating, financial, and total leverage for firm W.
c. Compare the relative risks of the two firms.
d. Discuss the principles of leverage illustrated in your answers.

12–15   Integrative—Multiple leverage measures and prediction   Carolina Fastener, Inc., makes a patented marine bulkhead latch that wholesales for $6.00. Each latch has variable operating costs of $3.50. Fixed operating costs are $50,000 per year. The firm pays $13,000 interest and preferred dividends of $7,000 per year. At this point, the firm is selling 30,000 latches a year and is taxed at 40%.
a. Calculate Carolina Fastener's operating breakeven point.
b. Based on the firm's current sales of 40,000 units per year and its interest and preferred dividend costs, calculate its EBIT and net profits.
c. Calculate the firm's degree of operating leverage (DOL).
d. Calculate the firm's degree of financial leverage (DFL).
e. Calculate the firm's degree of total leverage (DTL).
f. Carolina Fastener has entered into a contract to produce and sell an additional 15,000 latches in the coming year. Use the DOL, DFL, and DTL to predict and calculate the changes in EBIT and net profit. Check your work by a simple calculation of Carolina Fastener's EBIT and net profit using the basic information given.

12–16   Various capital structures   Charter Enterprises currently has $1 million in total assets and is totally equity financed. It is contemplating a change in capital structure. Compute the amount of debt and equity that would be outstanding if the firm were to shift to one of the following debt ratios: 10, 20, 30, 40, 50, 60, and 90%. (*Note:* The amount of total assets would not change.) Is there a limit to the debt ratio's value?

12–17   Debt and financial risk   Tower Interiors has made the forecast of sales shown in the following table. Also given is the probability of each level of sales.

Sales	Probability
$200,000	.20
300,000	.60
400,000	.20

The firm has fixed operating costs of $75,000 and variable operating costs equal to 70% of the sales level. The company pays $12,000 in interest per period. The tax rate is 40%.

a. Compute the earnings before interest and taxes (EBIT) for each level of sales.

b. Compute the earnings per share (EPS) for each level of sales, the expected EPS, the standard deviation of the EPS, and the coefficient of variation of EPS, assuming that there are 10,000 shares of common stock outstanding.

c. Tower has the opportunity to reduce leverage to zero and pay no interest. This will require that the number of shares outstanding be increased to 15,000. Repeat **b** under this assumption.

d. Compare your findings in **b** and **c**, and comment on the effect of the reduction of debt to zero on the firm's financial risk.

INTERMEDIATE   12–18 **EPS and optimal debt ratio**   Williams Glassware has estimated, at various debt ratios, the expected earnings per share and the standard deviation of the earnings per share as shown in the following table.

Debt ratio	Earnings per share (EPS)	Standard deviation of EPS
0%	$2.30	$1.15
20	3.00	1.80
40	3.50	2.80
60	3.95	3.95
80	3.80	5.53

a. Estimate the optimal debt ratio based on the relationship between earnings per share and the debt ratio. You will probably find it helpful to graph the relationship.

b. Graph the relationship between the coefficient of variation and the debt ratio. Label the areas associated with business risk and financial risk.

INTERMEDIATE 12–19 **EBIT–EPS and capital structure**   Data-Check is considering two capital structures. The key information is shown in the following table. Assume a 40% tax rate.

Source of capital	Structure A	Structure B
Long-term debt	$100,000 at 16% coupon rate	$200,000 at 17% coupon rate
Common stock	4,000 shares	2,000 shares

a. Calculate two EBIT–EPS coordinates for each of the structures by selecting any two EBIT values and finding their associated EPS.

b. Plot the two capital structures on a set of EBIT–EPS axes.

c. Indicate over what EBIT range, if any, each structure is preferred.

d. Discuss the leverage and risk aspects of each structure.

e. If the firm is fairly certain that its EBIT will exceed $75,000, which structure would you recommend? Why?

12–20 **EBIT–EPS and preferred stock**   Litho-Print is considering two possible capital structures, A and B, shown in the following table. Assume a 40% tax rate.

Source of capital	Structure A	Structure B
Long-term debt	$75,000 at 16% coupon rate	$50,000 at 15% coupon rate
Preferred stock	$10,000 with an 18% annual dividend	$15,000 with an 18% annual dividend
Common stock	8,000 shares	10,000 shares

a. Calculate two EBIT–EPS coordinates for each of the structures by selecting any two EBIT values and finding their associated EPS.
b. Graph the two capital structures on the same set of EBIT–EPS axes.
c. Discuss the leverage and risk associated with each of the structures.
d. Over what range of EBIT is each structure preferred?
e. Which structure do you recommend if the firm expects its EBIT to be $35,000? Explain.

   12–21 **Integrative—Optimal capital structure**   Medallion Cooling Systems, Inc., has

total assets of $10,000,000, EBIT of $2,000,000, preferred dividends of $200,000 and is taxed at a rate of 40%. In an effort to determine the optimal capital structure, the firm has assembled data on the cost of debt, the number of common shares for various levels of indebtedness, and the overall required return on investment:

Capital structure debt ratio	Cost of debt, k_d	Number of common shares	Required return, k_s
0%	0%	200,000	12%
15	8	170,000	13
30	9	140,000	14
45	12	110,000	16
60	15	80,000	20

a. Calculate earnings per share for each level of indebtedness.
b. Use Equation 12.12 and the earnings per share calculated in part a to calculate a price per share for each level of indebtedness.
c. Choose the optimal capital structure. Justify your choice.

   12–22 **Integrative—Optimal capital structure**   Nelson Corporation has made the following forecast of sales, with the associated probability of occurrence noted.

Sales	Probability
$200,000	.20
300,000	.60
400,000	.20

The company has fixed operating costs of $100,000 per year, and variable operating costs represent 40% of sales. The existing capital structure consists of 25,000 shares of common stock that have a $10 per share book value. No other capital items are outstanding. The marketplace has assigned the following discount rates to risky earnings per share.

Coefficient of variation of EPS	Estimated required return, k_s
.43	15%
.47	16
.51	17
.56	18
.60	22
.64	24

The company is contemplating *shifting its capital structure* by substituting debt in the capital structure for common stock. The three different debt ratios under consideration are shown in the following table, along with an estimate of the corresponding required interest rate on *all* debt.

Debt ratio	Interest rate on *all* debt
20%	10%
40	12
60	14

The tax rate is 40%. The market value of the equity for a levered firm can be found by using the simplified method (see Equation 12.12).
a. Calculate the expected earnings per share (EPS), the standard deviation of EPS, and the coefficient of variation of EPS for the three proposed capital structures.
b. Determine the optimal capital structure, assuming (1) maximization of earnings per share and (2) maximization of share value.
c. Construct a graph (similar to Figure 12.7) showing the relationships in **b**. (*Note:* You will probably have to sketch the lines, because you have only three data points.)

   12–23 **Integrative—Optimal capital structure**   The board of directors of Morales Publishing, Inc., has commissioned a capital structure study. The company has
  CHALLENGE   total assets of $40,000,000. It has earnings before interest and taxes of $8,000,000 and is taxed at 40%.
a. Create a spreadsheet like the one in Table 12.10 showing values of debt and equity as well as the total number of shares, assuming a book value of $25 per share.

% Debt	Total assets	$ Debt	$ Equity	No. of shares @ $25
0%	$40,000,000	$	$	
10	40,000,000			
20	40,000,000			
30	40,000,000			
40	40,000,000			
50	40,000,000			
60	40,000,000			

b. Given the before-tax cost of debt at various levels of indebtedness, calculate the yearly interest expenses.

% Debt	$ Total debt	Before tax cost of debt, k_d	$ Interest expense
0%	$	0.0%	$
10		7.5	
20		8.0	
30		9.0	
40		11.0	
50		12.5	
60		15.5	

c. Using EBIT of $8,000,000, a 40% tax rate, and information developed in parts **a** and **b,** calculate the most likely earnings per share for the firm at various levels of indebtedness. Mark the level of indebtedness that maximizes EPS.

% Debt	EBIT	Interest expense	EBT	Taxes	Net income	No. of shares	EPS
0%	$8,000,000						
10	8,000,000						
20	8,000,000						
30	8,000,000						
40	8,000,000						
50	8,000,000						
60	8,000,000						

d. Using the EPS developed in part **c,** the estimates of required return, k_s, and Equation 12.12, estimate the value per share at various levels of indebtedness. Mark the level of indebtedness that results in the maximum price per share, P_0.

Debt	EPS	k_s	P_0
0%	—	10.0%	—
10	—	10.3	—
20	—	10.9	—
30	—	11.4	—
40	—	12.6	—
50	—	14.8	—
60	—	17.5	—

e. Prepare a recommendation to the board of directors of Morales Publishing, Inc., that specifies the degree of indebtedness that will accomplish the firm's goal of optimizing shareholder wealth. Use your findings in parts **a** through **d** to justify your recommendation.

CHALLENGE

12–24 Integrative—Optimal capital structure Country Textiles, which has fixed operating costs of $300,000 and variable operating costs equal to 40% of sales, has made the following three sales estimates, with their probabilities noted.

Sales	Probability
$ 600,000	.30
900,000	.40
1,200,000	.30

The firm wishes to analyze five possible capital structures—0, 15, 30, 45, and 60% debt ratios. The firm's total assets of $1 million are assumed to be constant. Its common stock has a book value of $25 per share, and the firm is in the 40% tax bracket. The following additional data have been gathered for use in analyzing the five capital structures under consideration.

Capital structure debt ratio	Before-tax cost of debt, k_d	Required return, k_s
0%	.0%	10.0%
15	8.0	10.5
30	10.0	11.6
45	13.0	14.0
60	17.0	20.0

a. Calculate the level of EBIT associated with each of the three levels of sales.
b. Calculate the amount of debt, the amount of equity, and the number of shares of common stock outstanding for each of the capital structures being considered.
c. Calculate the annual interest on the debt under each of the capital structures being considered. (*Note:* The before-tax cost of debt, k_d, is the interest rate applicable to *all* debt associated with the corresponding debt ratio.)

d. Calculate the EPS associated with each of the three levels of EBIT calculated in **a** for each of the five capital structures being considered.

e. Calculate the (1) expected EPS, (2) standard deviation of EPS, and (3) coefficient of variation of EPS for each of the capital structures, using your findings in **d**.

f. Plot the expected EPS and coefficient of variation of EPS against the capital structures (x axis) on separate sets of axes, and comment on the return and risk relative to capital structure.

g. Using the EBIT–EPS data developed in **d**, plot the 0, 30, and 60% capital structures on the same set of EBIT-EPS axes, and discuss the ranges over which each is preferred. What is the major problem with the use of this approach?

h. Using the valuation model given in Equation 12.12 and your findings in **e**, estimate the share value for each of the capital structures being considered.

i. Compare and contrast your findings in **f** and **h**. Which structure is preferred if the goal is to maximize EPS? Which structure is preferred if the goal is to maximize share value? Which capital structure do you recommend? Explain.

CASE   CHAPTER 12   **Evaluating Tampa Manufacturing's Capital Structure**

Tampa Manufacturing, an established producer of printing equipment, expects its sales to remain flat for the next 3 to 5 years due to both a weak economic outlook and an expectation of little new printing technology development over that period. On the basis of this scenario, the firm's management has been instructed by its board to institute programs that will allow it to operate more efficiently, earn higher profits, and, most important, maximize share value. In this regard, the firm's chief financial officer (CFO), Jon Lawson, has been charged with evaluating the firm's capital structure. Lawson believes that the current capital structure, which contains 10% debt and 90% equity, may lack adequate financial leverage. To evaluate the firm's capital structure, Lawson has gathered the data summarized in the following table on the current capital structure (10% debt ratio) and two alternative capital structures—A (30% debt ratio) and B (50% debt ratio)—that he would like to consider.

| | Capital structure[a] | | |
Source of capital	Current (10% debt)	A (30% debt)	B (50% debt)
Long-term debt	$1,000,000	$3,000,000	$5,000,000
Coupon interest rate[b]	9%	10%	12%
Common stock	100,000 shares	70,000 shares	40,000 shares
Required return on equity, k_s[c]	12%	13%	18%

[a]These structures are based on maintaining the firm's current level of $10,000,000 of total financing.

[b]Interest rate applicable to *all* debt.

[c]Market-based return for the given level of risk.

Lawson expects the firm's earnings before interest and taxes (EBIT) to remain at its current level of $1,200,000. The firm has a 40% tax rate.

Required

a. Use the current level of EBIT to calculate the times interest earned ratio for each capital structure. Evaluate the current and two alternative capital structures using the times interest earned and debt ratios.

b. Prepare a single EBIT–EPS graph showing the current and two alternative capital structures.

c. On the basis of the graph in **b,** which capital structure will maximize Tampa's earnings per share (EPS) at its expected level of EBIT of $1,200,000? Why might this *not* be the best capital structure?

d. Using the zero-growth valuation model given in Equation 12.12, find the market value of Tampa's equity under each of the three capital structures at the $1,200,000 level of expected EBIT.

e. On the basis of your findings in **c** and **d,** which capital structure would you recommend? Why?

WEB EXERCISE

GOTO web site www.smartmoney.com. In the column on the right under Quotes & Research enter the symbol DIS; click Stock Snapshot; and then click GO.

1. What is the name of the company? Click on Financials.
2. What is the 5-year high and the 5-year low for the company's debt/equity ratio (the ratio of long-term debt to stockholders' equity)?

At the bottom of this page under Stock Search, enter the next stock symbol from the list below and then click Submit. Enter the name of the company in the matrix below and then click Financials. Enter the 5-year high and low for the debt/equity ratios in the matrix for each of the stock symbols.

Symbol	Company name	Debt/equity ratio	
		5-yr. low	5-yr. high
DIS			
AIT			
MRK			
LG			
LUV			
IBM			
GE			
BUD			
PFE			
INTC			

3. Which of the companies have high debt/equity ratios?
4. Which of the companies have low debt/equity ratios?
5. Why do the companies that have a low debt/equity ratio use more equity even though it is more expensive than debt?

13 Dividend Policy

LEARNING GOALS

LG1 Understand cash dividend payment procedures and the role of dividend reinvestment plans.

LG2 Describe the residual theory of dividends and the key arguments with regard to dividend irrelevance and relevance.

LG3 Discuss the key factors involved in formulating a dividend policy.

LG4 Review and evaluate the three basic types of dividend policies.

LG5 Evaluate stock dividends from accounting, shareholder, and company points of view.

LG6 Explain stock splits and stock repurchases and the firm's motivation for undertaking each of them.

13.1 Dividend Fundamentals

Expected cash dividends are the key return variable from which owners and investors determine share value. They represent a source of cash flow to stockholders and provide information about the firm's current and future performance. Because **retained earnings**—earnings not distributed as dividends—are a form of *internal* financing, the dividend decision can significantly affect the firm's *external* financing requirements. In other words, if the firm needs financ-

retained earnings
Earnings not distributed as dividends; a form of *internal* financing.

Relishing the Leftovers

After the guests go home, are you glad to see some leftovers in the kitchen (and especially when most of what is left over is the dessert, rather than the vegetables)? If so, you'll understand immediately one of the dividend theories presented in this chapter—the residual theory of dividends, which views dividends as the cash flows remaining available to stockholders after all acceptable investment

opportunities have been undertaken. The size and pattern of the dividends provide information about the firm's current and future performance. Some stockholders want and expect to receive dividends, whereas others are content to see an increase in stock price without receiving dividends. This chapter addresses the issue of whether dividends matter to stockholders and discusses the key aspects of dividend policy.

ing, the larger the cash dividend paid, the greater the amount of financing that must be raised externally through borrowing or through the sale of common or preferred stock. (Remember that although dividends are charged to retained earnings, they are actually paid out of cash.) To understand the fundamentals of dividend policy, you first need to understand the procedures for paying cash dividends and how dividend reinvestment plans work.

Cash Dividend Payment Procedures

The payment of cash dividends to corporate stockholders is decided by the firm's board of directors. The directors normally meet quarterly or semiannually to determine whether and in what amount dividends should be paid. The past period's financial performance and future outlook, as well as recent dividends paid, are key inputs to the dividend decision. The payment date of the cash dividend, if one is declared, must also be established.

Amount of Dividends

Whether dividends should be paid and, if so, how large they should be are important decisions that depend primarily on the firm's dividend policy. Many firms pay some cash dividends each period. Most firms have a set policy with respect to the amount of the periodic dividend, but the firm's directors can change this amount at the dividend meeting, based largely on significant increases or decreases in earnings.

Relevant Dates

If the directors of the firm declare a dividend, they also indicate the record and payment dates associated with the dividend. Typically, the directors issue a statement indicating their dividend decision, the record date, and the payment date. This statement is generally quoted in the *Wall Street Journal, Barron's,* and other financial news media.

Record Date   All persons whose names are recorded as stockholders on the **date of record,** which is set by the directors, receive a declared dividend at a specified future time. These stockholders are often referred to as *holders of record.*

Due to the time needed to make bookkeeping entries when a stock is traded, the stock begins selling **ex dividend** 4 *business days* prior to the date of record. Purchasers of a stock selling ex dividend do not receive the current dividend. A simple way to determine the first day on which the stock sells ex dividend is to subtract 4 days from the date of record; if a weekend intervenes, subtract 6 days. Ignoring general market fluctuations, the stock's price is expected to drop by the amount of the declared dividend on the ex dividend date.

date of record (dividends)
Set by the firm's directors, the date on which all persons whose names are recorded as stockholders receive a declared dividend at a specified future time.

ex dividend
Period beginning 4 *business days* prior to the date of record during which a stock is sold without the right to receive the current dividend.

Payment Date   The payment date is also set by the directors and is generally a few weeks after the record date. The **payment date** is the actual date on which the firm mails the dividend payment to the holders of record. An example will clarify the various dates and the accounting effects.

payment date
The actual date on which the firm mails the dividend payment to the holders of record.

Example ▼   At the quarterly dividend meeting of Rudolf Company, a distributor of office products, held June 10, the directors declared an $.80-per-share cash dividend for holders of record on Monday, July 1. The firm had 100,000 shares of common stock outstanding. The payment date for the dividend was August 1. Before the dividend was declared, the key accounts of the firm were as follows:

Cash	$200,000	Dividends payable	$ 0
		Retained earnings	1,000,000

When the dividend was announced by the directors, $80,000 of the retained earnings ($.80 per share × 100,000 shares) was transferred to the dividends payable account. The key accounts thus became

Cash	$200,000	Dividends payable	$ 80,000
		Retained earnings	920,000

Rudolf Company's stock began selling ex dividend 4 *business days* prior to the date of record, which was June 25. This date was found by subtracting 6 days (because a weekend intervened) from the July 1 date of record. Purchasers of Rudolf's stock on June 24 or earlier received the rights to the dividends; those purchasing the stock on or after June 25 did not. Assuming a stable market, Rudolf's stock price was expected to drop by approximately $.80 per share when it began selling ex dividend on June 25. When the August 1 payment date arrived, the firm mailed dividend checks to the holders of record as of July 1. This produced the following balances in the key accounts of the firm:

Cash	$120,000	Dividends payable	$ 0
		Retained earnings	920,000

The net effect of declaring and paying the dividend was to reduce the firm's total assets (and stockholders' equity) by $80,000.

Dividend Reinvestment Plans   (DRP)

dividend reinvestment plans (DRPs)
Plans that enable stockholders to use dividends received on the firm's stock to acquire additional full or fractional shares at little or no transaction (brokerage) cost.

Today many firms offer **dividend reinvestment plans (DRPs),** which enable stockholders to use dividends received on the firm's stock to acquire additional shares—even fractional shares—at little or no transaction (brokerage) cost. A small number of these companies, such as Exxon, Texaco, and W. R. Grace, even allow investors to make their *initial purchases* of the firm's stock directly from the company without going through a broker. Under current tax law, cash dividends from all plans (or the value of the stocks received through a DRP) are taxed as ordinary income. In addition, when the acquired shares are sold, if the proceeds are in excess of the original purchase price, the capital gain is taxed at the applicable capital gains tax rate.

Dividend reinvestment plans can be handled by a company in either of two ways. Both allow the stockholder to elect to have dividends reinvested in the firm's shares. In one approach, a third-party trustee is paid a fee to buy the firm's *outstanding shares* in the open market on behalf of the shareholders who wish to reinvest their dividends. This type of plan benefits participating shareholders by allowing them to use their dividends to purchase shares generally at a lower transaction cost than they would otherwise pay.

The second approach involves buying *newly issued shares* directly from the firm without paying any transaction costs. This approach allows the firm to raise new capital while permitting owners to reinvest their dividends, frequently at about 5 percent below the current market price. The firm can justify the below-market sale price economically because it saves the underpricing and flotation costs that would accompany the public sale of new shares. Clearly, the existence of a DRP may enhance the appeal of a firm's shares.

? Review Questions

13–1   How do the *date of record* and the *holders of record* relate to the payment of cash dividends? What does the term *ex dividend* mean?

13–2   What is a *dividend reinvestment plan?* What benefit is available to plan participants? Describe the two ways in which companies can handle such plans.

13.2 The Relevance of Dividend Policy

Numerous theories and empirical findings concerning dividend policy have been reported in the financial literature. Although this research provides some interesting insights about dividend policy, capital budgeting and capital structure decisions are generally considered far more important than dividend decisions. In other words, good investment and financing decisions should not be sacrificed for a dividend policy of questionable importance.

A number of key questions have yet to be resolved: Does dividend policy matter? What effect does dividend policy have on share price? Is there a model that can be used to evaluate alternative dividend policies in view of share value? Here we begin by describing the residual theory of dividends, which is used as a backdrop for discussion of the key arguments in support of dividend irrelevance and then those in support of dividend relevance.

The Residual Theory of Dividends

residual theory of dividends
A theory that the dividend paid by a firm should be the amount left over after all acceptable investment opportunities have been undertaken.

One school of thought—the **residual theory of dividends**—suggests that the dividend paid by a firm should be viewed as a *residual*—the amount left over after all acceptable investment opportunities have been undertaken. Using this approach, the firm would treat the dividend decision in three steps as follows:

Step 1   Determine its optimum level of capital expenditures, which would be the level generated by the point of intersection of the investment opportunities schedule (IOS) and weighted marginal cost of capital (WMCC) schedule (see Chapter 11).

Step 2   Using the optimal capital structure proportions (see Chapter 12), estimate the total amount of equity financing needed to support the expenditures generated in Step 1.

Step 3 Because the cost of retained earnings, k_r, is less than the cost of new common stock, k_n, use retained earnings to meet the equity requirement determined in Step 2. If retained earnings are inadequate to meet this need, sell new common stock. If the available retained earnings are in excess of this need, distribute the surplus amount—the residual—as dividends.

In this approach, no cash dividend is paid as long as the firm's equity need is in excess of the amount of retained earnings. The argument supporting this approach is that it is sound management to be certain that the company has the money it needs to compete effectively and therefore increase share price. This view of dividends tends to suggest that the required return of investors, k_s, is *not* influenced by the firm's dividend policy—a premise that in turn suggests that dividend policy is irrelevant.

Example ▼ Overbrook Industries, a manufacturer of canoes and other small watercraft, has available from the current period's operations $1.8 million that can be retained or paid out in dividends. The firm's optimal capital structure is at a debt ratio of 30%, which represents 30% debt and 70% equity. Figure 13.1 depicts the firm's weighted marginal cost of capital (WMCC) schedule along with three investment opportunities schedules. For each IOS, the level of total new financing or investment determined by the point of intersection of the IOS and the WMCC has been noted. For IOS_1, it is $1.5 million; for IOS_2, $2.4 million; and for IOS_3, $3.2 million. Although only one IOS will exist in practice, it is useful to look at the possible dividend decisions generated by applying the residual theory in each of the three cases. Table 13.1 summarizes this analysis.

FIGURE 13.1

WMCC and IOSs
WMCC and IOSs for Overbrook Industries

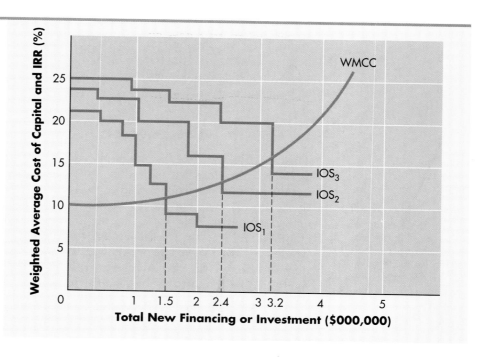

TABLE 13.1	Applying the Residual Theory of Dividends to Overbrook Industries for Each of Three IOSs (Shown in Figure 13.1)

| | Investment opportunities schedules | | |
Item	IOS_1	IOS_2	IOS_3
(1) New financing or investment (Fig. 13.1)	$1,500,000	$2,400,000	$3,200,000
(2) Retained earnings available (given)	$1,800,000	$1,800,000	$1,800,000
(3) Equity needed [70% × (1)]	1,050,000	1,680,000	2,240,000
(4) Dividends [(2) − (3)]	$ 750,000	$ 120,000	$ 0[a]
(5) Dividend payout ratio [(4) ÷ (2)]	41.7%	6.7%	0%

[a]In this case, additional new common stock in the amount of $440,000 ($2,240,000 needed − $1,800,000 available) would have to be sold; no dividends would be paid.

Table 13.1 shows that if IOS_1 exists, the firm will pay out $750,000 in dividends, because only $1,050,000 of the $1,800,000 of available earnings is needed. A 41.7% payout ratio results. For IOS_2, dividends of $120,000 (a payout ratio of 6.7%) result. Should IOS_3 exist, the firm would pay no dividends (a 0% payout ratio), because its retained earnings of $1,800,000 would be less than the $2,240,000 of equity needed. In this case, the firm would have to obtain additional new common stock financing to meet the new requirements generated by the intersection of the IOS_3 and WMCC. Depending on which IOS exists, the firm's dividend would in effect be the residual, if any, remaining after financing all acceptable investments.

Dividend Irrelevance Arguments

dividend irrelevance theory
A theory put forth by Miller and Modigliani that, in a perfect world, the value of a firm is unaffected by the distribution of dividends and is determined solely by the earning power and risk of its assets.

The residual theory of dividends implies that if the firm cannot earn a return (IRR) from investment of its earnings that is in excess of cost (WMCC), it should distribute the earnings by paying dividends to stockholders. This approach suggests that dividends are irrelevant—that they represent an earnings residual rather than an active decision variable that affects the firm's value. Such a view is consistent with the **dividend irrelevance theory** put forth by Merton H. Miller and Franco Modigliani.[1] M and M's theory shows that in a perfect world (certainty, no taxes, no transactions costs, and no other market imperfections), the value of the firm is unaffected by the distribution of dividends. They argue that the firm's value is determined solely by the earning power and risk of its assets (investments) and

1. Merton H. Miller and Franco Modigliani, "Dividend Policy, Growth and the Valuation of Shares," *Journal of Business* 34 (October 1961), pp. 411–433.

that the manner in which it splits its earnings stream between dividends and internally retained (and reinvested) funds does not affect this value.

However, studies have shown that large dividend changes affect share price in the same direction—increases in dividends result in increased share price, and decreases in dividends result in decreased share price. In response, M and M argue that these effects are attributable not to the dividend itself but rather to the **informational content** of dividends with respect to future earnings. In other words, it is not the preference of shareholders for current dividends (rather than future capital gains) that is responsible for this behavior. Instead, a change in dividends, up or down, is viewed as a *signal* that management expects future earnings to change in the same direction. An increase in dividends is viewed as a

informational content
The information provided by the dividends of a firm with respect to future earnings, which causes owners to bid up or down the price of the firm's stock.

In Practice

Comcast Broadcasts a New Dividend Policy

"Simply put, dividends are out of style—and rightly so," claims Edward M. Kerschner of Wall Street's PaineWebber. *"Dividends are a terribly tax-inefficient way of delivering returns to investors,"* he says, because they are taxed twice, at the corporate and individual levels. Kerschner notes that industries that traditionally pay large dividends—telecommunications and utilities, for example—are now tending to allocate funds to acquisitions, investment, debt paydown, share buybacks, and other uses, and to raise dividends more slowly as they face intensified competition.

Philadelphia-based Comcast, one of the nation's largest cable system operators, agrees with Kerschner. In March 1999, Comcast eliminated its quarterly cash dividend of around 2 cents a share. Comcast management determined that reinvesting the $35 million cash per year would add more value than paying the small dividend. Also, the administrative costs associated with processing the dividend were often greater than the actual dividend.

Another reason for Comcast's decision is its changing ownership profile. Only about 10 percent of the company's stock is in the hands of smaller individual investors. Institutional investors own about three-quarters of the company's shares, with another 15 percent held by three large investors. According to senior vice president and treasurer John R. Alchin, the dividend is essentially irrelevant to the company's institutional investors. *"This [dividend policy] is long overdue,"* he commented. *"Nobody has bought the stock for the dividend since 1986."*

Comcast is now in a position where capital appreciation, not dividends, attracts investors. Between 1997 and early 1999, its share price rose from $20 to $65 a share—an annual growth rate of 80.3 percent, significantly above the market averages.

Not everyone agrees with Kerschner and Comcast. Gregory Linus Weiss, editor of dividend-monitoring newsletter Investment Quality Trends, *reminds companies that when the upward trend in stock prices grinds to a halt or prices begin to fall, they may need to reconsider their dividend policies. At that point, dividends may come to matter more to investors.*

positive signal that causes investors to bid up the share price; a decrease in dividends is a *negative signal* that causes a decrease in share price.

M and M further argue that a **clientele effect** exists: A firm attracts shareholders whose preferences with respect to the payment and stability of dividends correspond to the payment pattern and stability of the firm itself. Investors desiring stable dividends as a source of income hold the stock of firms that pay about the same dividend amount each period. Investors preferring to earn capital gains are more attracted to growing firms that reinvest a large portion of their earnings, resulting in a fairly unstable pattern of dividends. Because the shareholders get what they expect, M and M argue that the value of their firm's stock is unaffected by dividend policy.

In summary, M and M and other dividend irrelevance proponents argue that, all else being equal, an investor's required return—and therefore the value of the firm—is unaffected by dividend policy for three reasons:

1. The firm's value is determined solely by the earning power and risk of its assets.
2. If dividends do affect value, they do so solely because of their informational content, which signals management's earnings expectations.
3. A clientele effect exists that causes a firm's shareholders to receive the dividends they expect.

These views of M and M with respect to dividend irrelevance are consistent with the residual theory, which focuses on making the best investment decisions to maximize share value. The proponents of dividend irrelevance conclude that because dividends are irrelevant to a firm's value, the firm does not need to have a dividend policy. Although many research studies have been performed to validate or refute the dividend irrelevance theory, none has been successful in providing irrefutable evidence.

Dividend Relevance Arguments

The key argument in support of **dividend relevance theory** is attributed to Myron J. Gordon and John Lintner,[2] who suggest that there is, in fact, a direct relationship between the firm's dividend policy and its market value. Fundamental to this proposition is their **bird-in-the-hand argument,** which suggests that investors are generally risk-averse and attach less risk to current dividends than to future dividends or capital gains. Simply stated, "a bird in the hand is worth two in the bush." Current dividend payments are therefore believed to reduce investor uncertainty, causing investors to discount the firm's earnings at a lower rate and, all else being equal, to place a higher value on the firm's stock. Conversely, if dividends are reduced or not paid, investor uncertainty will increase, raising the required return and lowering the stock's value.

Although many other arguments relating to dividend relevance have been put forward, *numerous empirical studies fail to provide conclusive evidence in support of the intuitively appealing dividend relevance argument.* In practice, however, the actions of financial managers and stockholders alike often tend to

clientele effect
The argument that a firm attracts shareholders whose preferences with respect to the payment and stability of dividends correspond to the payment pattern and stability of the firm itself.

dividend relevance theory
The theory, attributed to Gordon and Lintner, that there is a direct relationship between a firm's dividend policy and its market value.

bird-in-the-hand argument
The belief, in support of *dividend relevance theory*, that current dividend payments ("a bird in the hand") reduce investor uncertainty and result in a higher value for the firm's stock.

---

2. Myron J. Gordon, "Optimal Investment and Financing Policy," *Journal of Finance* 18 (May 1963), pp. 264–272, and John Lintner, "Dividends, Earnings, Leverage, Stock Prices, and the Supply of Capital to Corporations," *Review of Economics and Statistics* 44 (August 1962), pp. 243–269.

support the belief that dividend policy does affect
cern centers on the day-to-day behavior of busin
chapter is consistent with the belief that *divider*
must develop a dividend policy that fulfills the g
their wealth as reflected in the firm's share pric

? Review Questions

13–3 Describe the *residual theory of dividends*. Does following this
lead to a stable dividend? Is this approach consistent with dividend rev
vance? Explain.

13–4 Describe, compare, and contrast the basic arguments relative to the irrelevance or relevance of dividend policy given by: (**a**) Miller and
Modigliani (M and M), and (**b**) Gordon and Lintner.

13.3 Factors Affecting Dividend Policy

Before discussing the basic types of dividend policies, we should consider the factors involved in formulating dividend policy. These include legal constraints,
contractual constraints, internal constraints, the firm's growth prospects, owner
considerations, and market considerations.

Legal Constraints

Most states prohibit corporations from paying out as cash dividends any portion
of the firm's "legal capital," which is measured by the par value of common stock.
Other states define legal capital to include not only the par value of the common
stock, but also any paid-in capital in excess of par. These *capital impairment
restrictions* are generally established to provide a sufficient equity base to protect
creditors' claims. An example will clarify the differing definitions of capital.

Example ▼ The stockholders' equity account of Miller Flour Company, a large grain processor, is presented in the following table.

Miller Flour Company
Stockholders' Equity

Common stock at par	$100,000
Paid-in capital in excess of par	200,000
Retained earnings	140,000
Total stockholders' equity	$440,000

---

3. A common exception is small firms, because they frequently treat dividends as a residual remaining after all
acceptable investments have been initiated. This course of action occurs because small firms usually do not have
ready access to capital markets. The use of retained earnings therefore acts as a key source of financing for growth,
which is generally an important goal of a small firm.

In states where the firm's legal capital is defined as the par value of its common stock, the firm could pay out $340,000 ($200,000 + $140,000) in cash dividends without impairing its capital. In states where the firm's legal capital includes all ▲ paid-in capital, the firm could pay out only $140,000 in cash dividends.

An earnings requirement limiting the amount of dividends to the sum of the firm's present and past earnings is sometimes imposed. In other words, the firm cannot pay more in cash dividends than the sum of its most recent and past retained earnings. However, *the firm is not prohibited from paying more in dividends than its current earnings.*[4]

Example ▼ Assume Miller Flour Company, from the preceding example, in the year just ended has $30,000 in earnings available for common stock dividends. As the preceding table indicates, the firm has past retained earnings of $140,000. Thus, it ▲ can legally pay dividends of up to $170,000.

If a firm has overdue liabilities or is legally insolvent or bankrupt (if the fair market value of its assets is less than its liabilities), most states prohibit its payment of cash dividends. In addition, the Internal Revenue Service prohibits firms from accumulating earnings to reduce the owners' taxes. A firm's owners must pay income taxes on dividends when received, but the owners are not taxed on capital gains in market value until the stock is sold. If the IRS can determine that a firm has accumulated an excess of earnings to allow owners to delay paying ordinary income taxes, it may levy an **excess earnings accumulation tax** on any retained earnings above $250,000—the amount that is currently exempt from this tax for all firms except personal service corporations.

excess earnings accumulation tax
The tax levied by the IRS on retained earnings above $250,000, when it has determined that the firm has accumulated an excess of earnings to allow owners to delay paying ordinary income taxes.

Contractual Constraints

Often, the firm's ability to pay cash dividends is constrained by restrictive provisions in a loan agreement. Generally, these constraints prohibit the payment of cash dividends until a certain level of earnings has been achieved, or they may limit dividends to a certain dollar amount or percentage of earnings. Constraints on dividends help to protect creditors from losses due to the firm's insolvency. The violation of a contractual constraint is generally grounds for a demand of immediate payment by the funds supplier.

Internal Constraints

The firm's ability to pay cash dividends is generally constrained by the amount of excess cash available rather than the level of retained earnings against which to charge them. Although it is possible for a firm to borrow funds to pay dividends, lenders are generally reluctant to make such loans because they produce no tangible or operating benefits that will help the firm repay the loan. Although a firm

---

4. A firm having an operating loss in the current period can still pay cash dividends as long as sufficient retained earnings against which to charge the dividend are available and, of course, as long as it has the cash with which to make the payments.

may have high earnings, its ability to pay dividends may be constrained by a low level of liquid assets (cash and marketable securities).

Example ▼ Miller Flour Company's stockholders' equity account presented earlier indicates that if the firm's legal capital is defined as all paid-in capital, the firm can pay $140,000 in dividends. If the firm has total liquid assets of $50,000 ($20,000 in cash plus marketable securities worth $30,000) and $35,000 of this is needed for operations, the maximum cash dividend the firm can pay is $15,000 ($50,000 − ▲ $35,000).

Growth Prospects

Hint   Firms that grow very rapidly, such as high-tech firms, cannot afford to pay dividends. Their stockholders are influenced by the possibility of exceptionally higher share price and dividend levels in the future.

The firm's financial requirements are directly related to the anticipated degree of asset expansion. If the firm is in a growth stage, it may need all its funds to finance capital expenditures. Firms exhibiting little or no growth may nevertheless periodically need funds to replace or renew assets.

A firm must evaluate its financial position from the standpoint of profitability and risk to develop insight into its ability to raise capital externally. It must determine not only its ability to raise funds, but also the cost and speed with which financing can be obtained. Generally, a large, mature firm has adequate access to new capital, whereas a rapidly growing firm may not have sufficient funds available to support its numerous acceptable projects. A growth firm is likely to have to depend heavily on internal financing through retained earnings; it is likely to pay out only a very small percentage of its earnings as dividends. A more stable firm that needs long-term funds only for planned outlays is in a better position to pay out a large proportion of its earnings, particularly if it has ready sources of financing.

Owner Considerations[5]

In establishing a dividend policy, the firm's primary concern should be to maximize owner wealth. Although it is impossible to establish a policy that maximizes each owner's wealth, the firm must establish a policy that has a favorable effect on the wealth of the *majority* of owners.

One consideration is the *tax status of a firm's owners*. If a firm has a large percentage of wealthy stockholders who are in a high tax bracket, it may decide to pay out a *lower* percentage of its earnings to allow the owners to delay the payment of taxes until they sell the stock.[6] Of course, when the stock is sold, if

---

5. Theoretically, in an *efficient market,* owner considerations are automatically handled by the pricing mechanism. The logic is as follows. A firm that pays a dividend that is smaller than required by a large number of owners will experience a decline in price because the dissatisfied shareholders will sell their shares. The resulting drop in share price will (as explained in Chapter 7) raise the expected return to investors, which will cause the firm's WMCC to rise. As a result—all else being equal—the firm's optimal capital budget will become smaller and the demand for retained earnings will fall. This decrease should allow the firm to satisfy shareholders by paying the larger dividends that they demand. In spite of this logic, it is helpful to understand some of the important considerations underlying owner behavior.

6. The consideration of the owners' tax status in making dividend policy decisions is illegal, although it is difficult for the IRS to enforce this law. Rather, the IRS will look for high retained earnings and high liquidity. Firms in this situation are penalized through the *excess earnings accumulation tax.* It is quite difficult, if not impossible, to determine the extent to which the tax status of a firm's owners affects dividend policy decisions.

the proceeds are in excess of the original purchase price, the capital gain will be taxed, possibly at a more favorable rate than the one applied to ordinary income. Lower-income shareholders, however, who need dividend income, will prefer a *higher* payout of earnings.

A second consideration is the *owners' investment opportunities.* A firm should not retain funds for investment in projects yielding lower returns than the owners could obtain from external investments of equal risk. The firm should evaluate the returns that are expected on its own investment opportunities and, using present value techniques, determine whether greater returns are obtainable from external investments such as government securities or other corporate stocks. If it appears that the owners have better opportunities externally, the firm should pay out a higher percentage of its earnings. If the firm's investment opportunities are at least as good as similar-risk external investments, a lower payout would be justifiable.

A final consideration is the *potential dilution of ownership.* If a firm pays out a higher percentage of earnings, new equity capital will have to be raised with common stock, which may result in the dilution of both control and earnings for the existing owners. By paying out a low percentage of its earnings, the firm can minimize such possibility of dilution.

Market Considerations

An awareness of the market's probable response to certain types of policies is helpful in formulating a suitable dividend policy. Stockholders are believed to value a *fixed or increasing level of dividends* as opposed to a fluctuating pattern of dividends. This belief is supported by the research of John Lintner, who found that corporate managers are averse to changing the dollar amount of dividends in response to changes in earnings, particularly when earnings decline.[7] In addition, stockholders are believed to value a policy of *continuous dividend payment.* Because regularly paying a fixed or increasing dividend eliminates uncertainty about the frequency and magnitude of dividends, the earnings of the firm are likely to be discounted at a lower rate. This should result in an increase in the market value of the stock and therefore increased owners' wealth.

A final market consideration is the *informational content* of dividends. As indicated earlier, shareholders often view the firm's dividend payment as a *signal* relative to its future success. A stable and continuous dividend is a *positive signal* that conveys to the owners that the firm is in good health. If the firm skips a dividend payment in a given period due to a loss or to very low earnings, shareholders are likely to interpret this as a *negative signal.* The nonpayment of the dividend creates uncertainty about the future, and this uncertainty is likely to result in lower stock value. Owners and investors generally construe a dividend payment during a period of losses as an indication that the loss is merely temporary.

Hint The risk-return concept also applies to the firm's dividend policy. A firm that lets its dividends fluctuate from period to period will be viewed as risky, and investors will require a higher rate of return, which will increase the firm's cost of capital.

---

7. John Lintner, "Distribution of Income of Corporations among Dividends, Retained Earnings, and Taxes," *American Economic Review* 46 (May 1956), pp. 97–113.

? Review Question

12–6   Briefly describe each of the following factors affecting dividend policy: (a) legal constraints; (b) contractual constraints; (c) internal constraints; (d) growth prospects; (e) owner considerations; and (f) market considerations.

13.4 Types of Dividend Policies

dividend policy
The firm's plan of action to be followed whenever a dividend decision must be made.

The firm's **dividend policy** represents a plan of action to be followed whenever the dividend decision must be made. The dividend policy must be formulated with two basic objectives in mind: maximizing the wealth of the firm's owners and providing for sufficient financing. These two interrelated objectives must be fulfilled in light of a number of factors—legal, contractual, internal, growth, owner-related, and market-related—that limit the policy alternatives. Three of the more commonly used dividend policies are described in the following sections. A particular firm's cash dividend policy may incorporate elements of each.

Constant-Payout-Ratio Dividend Policy

dividend payout ratio
Indicates the percentage of each dollar earned that is distributed to the owners in the form of cash; calculated by dividing the firm's cash dividend per share by its earnings per share.

constant-payout-ratio dividend policy
A dividend policy based on the payment of a certain percentage of earnings to owners in each dividend period.

One type of dividend policy occasionally adopted by firms is the use of a constant payout ratio. The **dividend payout ratio**, calculated by dividing the firm's cash dividend per share by its earnings per share, indicates the percentage of each dollar earned that is distributed to the owners in the form of cash. With a **constant-payout-ratio dividend policy,** the firm establishes that a certain percentage of earnings is paid to owners in each dividend period.

The problem with this policy is that if the firm's earnings drop or if a loss occurs in a given period, the dividends may be low or even nonexistent. Because dividends are often considered an indicator of the firm's future condition and status, the firm's stock price may thus be adversely affected by this type of action.

Example ▼   Peachtree Industries, a miner of potassium, has a policy of paying out 40% of earnings in cash dividends. In periods when a loss occurs, the firm's policy is to pay no cash dividends. Peachtree's earnings per share, dividends per share, and average price per share for the past 6 years are shown in the following table.

Year	Earnings/share	Dividends/share	Average price/share
2000	−$ .50	$ .00	$42.00
1999	3.00	1.20	52.00
1998	1.75	.70	48.00
1997	− 1.50	.00	38.00
1996	2.00	.80	46.00
1995	4.50	1.80	50.00

Dividends increased in 1997–1998 and in 1998–1999 and decreased in the other years. The data show that in years of decreasing dividends, the firm's stock price dropped; when dividends increased, the price of the stock increased. Peachtree's sporadic dividend payments appear to make its owners uncertain about the returns they can expect from their investment in the firm and therefore ▲ tend to generally depress the stock's price.

Hint Regulated utilities in low-growth areas can use a constant-payout-ratio dividend policy. Their capital requirements are usually low and their earnings are more certain than most firms.

Although a constant-payout-ratio dividend policy is used by some firms, it is *not* recommended.

Regular Dividend Policy

regular dividend policy
A dividend policy based on the payment of a fixed-dollar dividend in each period.

Another type of dividend policy, the **regular dividend policy,** is based on the payment of a fixed-dollar dividend in each period. The regular dividend policy provides the owners with generally positive information, indicating that the firm is okay and thereby minimizing their uncertainty. Often, firms using this policy increase the regular dividend once a *proven* increase in earnings has occurred. Under this policy, dividends are almost never decreased.

Example ▼ The dividend policy of Woodward Laboratories, a producer of a popular artificial sweetener, is to pay annual dividends of $1.00 per share until per-share earnings have exceeded $4.00 for three consecutive years, at which time the annual dividend is raised to $1.50 per share and a new earnings plateau is established. The firm does not anticipate decreasing its dividend unless its liquidity is in jeopardy. Woodward's earnings per share, dividends per share, and average price per share for the past 12 years are shown in the following table.

Year	Earnings/share	Dividends/share	Average price/share
2000	$4.50	$1.50	$47.50
1999	3.90	1.50	46.50
1998	4.60	1.50	45.00
1997	4.20	1.00	43.00
1996	5.00	1.00	42.00
1995	2.00	1.00	38.50
1994	6.00	1.00	38.00
1993	3.00	1.00	36.00
1992	.75	1.00	33.00
1991	.50	1.00	33.00
1990	2.70	1.00	33.50
1989	2.85	1.00	35.00

Whatever the level of earnings, Woodward Laboratories paid dividends of $1.00 per share through 1997. In 1998, the dividend was raised to $1.50 per share because earnings in excess of $4.00 per share had been achieved for 3 years. In 1998, the firm also had to establish a new earnings plateau for further dividend increases. Woodward Laboratories' average price per share exhibited a stable, increasing behavior in spite of a somewhat volatile pattern of earnings.

target dividend-payout ratio
A policy under which the firm attempts to pay out a certain percentage of earnings as a stated dollar dividend, which it adjusts toward a target payout as proven earnings increases occur.

Often, a regular dividend policy is built around a **target dividend-payout ratio**. Under this policy, the firm attempts to pay out a certain percentage of earnings, but rather than let dividends fluctuate, it pays a stated dollar dividend and adjusts it toward the target payout as proven earnings increases occur. For instance, Woodward Laboratories appears to have a target payout ratio of around 35 percent. The payout was about 35 percent ($1.00 ÷ $2.85) when the dividend policy was set in 1989, and when the dividend was raised to $1.50 in 1998, the payout ratio was about 33 percent ($1.50 ÷ $4.60).

Low-Regular-and-Extra Dividend Policy

low-regular-and-extra dividend policy
A dividend policy based on paying a low regular dividend, supplemented by an additional dividend when earnings warrant it.

extra dividend
An additional dividend optionally paid by the firm if earnings are higher than normal in a given period.

Some firms establish a **low-regular-and-extra dividend policy**, paying a low regular dividend, supplemented by an additional dividend when earnings warrant it. When earnings are higher than normal in a given period, the firm may pay this additional dividend, which is designated an **extra dividend**. By calling the additional dividend an extra dividend, the firm avoids giving shareholders false hopes. The use of the "extra" designation is especially common among companies that experience cyclical shifts in earnings.

By establishing a low regular dividend that is paid each period, the firm gives investors the stable income necessary to build confidence in the firm, and the extra dividend permits them to share in the earnings from an especially good period. Firms using this policy must raise the level of the regular dividend once proven increases in earnings have been achieved. The extra dividend should not be a regular event, or it becomes meaningless. The use of a target dividend-payout ratio in establishing the regular dividend level is advisable.

> **? Review Question**
>
> 12–6   What are: (**a**) a constant-payout-ratio dividend policy; (**b**) a regular dividend policy; and (**c**) a low-regular-and-extra dividend policy? What are the effects of these policies?

13.5 Other Forms of Dividends

A number of other forms of dividends are available to the firm. In this section, we discuss two other methods of paying dividends—stock dividends and stock repurchases—as well as a closely related topic, stock splits.

Stock Dividends

stock dividend
The payment to existing owners of a dividend in the form of stock.

A **stock dividend** is the payment to existing owners of a dividend in the form of stock. Often, firms pay stock dividends as a replacement for or a supplement to cash dividends. Although stock dividends do not have a real value, stockholders may perceive them to represent something they did not have before and therefore to have value.

Accounting Aspects

small (ordinary) stock dividend
A stock dividend that represents less than 20 to 25 percent of the common stock outstanding at the time the dividend is declared.

In an accounting sense, the payment of a stock dividend is a shifting of funds between capital accounts rather than a use of funds. When a firm declares a stock dividend, the procedures for announcement and distribution are the same as those described earlier for a cash dividend. The accounting entries associated with the payment of stock dividends vary depending on whether it is a **small (ordinary) stock dividend,** which is generally a stock dividend representing less than 20 to 25 percent of the common stock outstanding at the time the dividend is declared. Because small stock dividends are most common, the accounting entries associated with them are illustrated in the following example.

E x a m p l e ▼ The current stockholders' equity on the balance sheet of Garrison Corporation, a distributor of prefabricated cabinets, is as shown in the following accounts.

Preferred stock	$ 300,000
Common stock (100,000 shares at $4 par)	400,000
Paid-in capital in excess of par	600,000
Retained earnings	700,000
Total stockholders' equity	$2,000,000

If Garrison declares a 10% stock dividend and the market price of its stock is $15 per share, $150,000 of retained earnings (10% × 100,000 shares × $15 per share) will be capitalized. The $150,000 will be distributed between common stock and paid-in capital in excess of par accounts based on the par value of the common stock. The resulting account balances are as follows:

Preferred stock	$ 300,000
Common stock (110,000 shares at $4 par)	440,000
Paid-in capital in excess of par	710,000
Retained earnings	550,000
Total stockholders' equity	$2,000,000

Because 10,000 new shares (10% of 100,000) have been issued and the prevailing market price is $15 per share, $150,000 ($15 per share × 10,000 shares) is shifted from retained earnings to the common stock and paid-in capital accounts. A total of $40,000 ($4 par × 10,000 shares) is added to common stock, and the remaining $110,000 [($15 − $4) × 10,000 shares] is added to the paid-in capital in excess of par. The firm's total stockholders' equity has not changed; funds have only been *redistributed* among stockholders' equity ▲ accounts.

The Shareholder's Viewpoint

The shareholder receiving a stock dividend typically receives nothing of value. After the dividend is paid, the per-share value of the shareholder's stock decreases in proportion to the dividend in such a way that the market value of his or her total holdings in the firm remains unchanged. The shareholder's proportion of ownership in the firm also remains the same, and *as long as the firm's earnings remain unchanged,* so does his or her share of total earnings. (Clearly, if the firm's earnings and cash dividends increase at the time the stock dividend is issued, an increase in share value is likely to result.) A continuation of the preceding example will clarify this point.

Example ▼ Ms. X owned 10,000 shares of Garrison Corporation's stock. The company's most recent earnings were $220,000, and earnings are not expected to change in the near future. Before the stock dividend, Ms. X owned 10% (10,000 shares ÷ 100,000 shares) of the firm's stock, which was selling for $15 per share. Earnings per share were $2.20 ($220,000 ÷ 100,000 shares). Because Ms. X owned 10,000 shares, her earnings were $22,000 ($2.20 per share × 10,000 shares). After receiving the 10% stock dividend, Ms. X has 11,000 shares, which again is 10% of the ownership (11,000 shares ÷ 110,000 shares). The market price of the stock can be expected to drop to $13.64 per share [$15 × (1.00 ÷ 1.10)], which means that the market value of Ms. X's holdings is $150,000 (11,000 shares × $13.64 per share). This is the same as the initial value of her holdings (10,000 shares × $15 per share). The future earnings per share drops to $2 ($220,000 ÷ 110,000 shares) because the same $220,000 in earnings must now be divided among 110,000 shares. Because Ms. X still owns 10% of the

▲ stock, her share of total earnings is still $22,000 ($2 per share × 11,000 shares).

In summary, if the firm's earnings remain constant and total cash dividends do not increase, a stock dividend results in a lower per-share market value for the firm's stock.

The Company's Viewpoint

Although stock dividends are more costly to issue than cash dividends, certain advantages may outweigh these costs. Firms find the stock dividend a way to give owners something without having to use cash. Generally, when a firm needs to preserve cash to finance rapid growth, a stock dividend is used. As long as the stockholders recognize that the firm is reinvesting the cash flow generated from earnings so as to maximize future earnings, the market value of the firm should at least remain unchanged. However, if the stock dividend is paid so that cash can be retained to satisfy past-due bills, a decline in market value may result.

Stock Splits

stock split
A method commonly used to lower the market price of a firm's stock by increasing the number of shares belonging to each shareholder.

Although not a type of dividend, *stock splits* have an effect on a firm's share price similar to that of stock dividends. A **stock split** is a method commonly used to lower the market price of a firm's stock by increasing the number of shares belonging to each shareholder. Quite often, a firm believes that its stock is priced too high and that lowering the market price will enhance trading activity. Stock splits are often made prior to issuing additional stock to enhance its marketability and stimulate market activity.

A stock split has no effect on the firm's capital structure. It commonly increases the number of shares outstanding and reduces the stock's per-share par value. In a 2-for-1 split, for example, two new shares are exchanged for each old share, with each new share worth half the value of each old share.

Example ▼ Delphi Company, a forest products concern, had 200,000 shares of $2 par-value common stock and no preferred stock outstanding. Because the stock is selling at a high market price, the firm has declared a 2-for-1 stock split. The total before- and after-split stockholders' equity is shown in the following table.

Before split	
Common stock (200,000 shares at $2 par)	$ 400,000
Paid-in capital in excess of par	4,000,000
Retained earnings	2,000,000
Total stockholders' equity	$6,400,000

After 2-for-1 split	
Common stock (400,000 shares at $1 par)	$ 400,000
Paid-in capital in excess of par	4,000,000
Retained earnings	2,000,000
Total stockholders' equity	$6,400,000

▲ The insignificant effect of the stock split on the firm's books is obvious.

reverse stock split
A method used to raise the market price of a firm's stock by exchanging a certain number of outstanding shares for one new share of stock.

Stock can be split in any way desired. Sometimes a **reverse stock split** is made: A certain number of outstanding shares are exchanged for one new share. For example, in a 2-for-3 split, two new shares are exchanged for three old shares, and so on. Reverse stock splits are initiated when a stock is selling at too low a price to appear respectable.[8]

It is not unusual for a stock split to cause a slight increase in the market value of the stock. This is attributable to the informational content of stock splits and the fact that *total* dividends paid commonly increase slightly after a split.[9]

Stock Repurchases

stock repurchase
The repurchasing by the firm of outstanding shares of its common stock in the marketplace; desired effects of stock repurchases are that they either enhance shareholder value or help to discourage unfriendly takeovers.

Over the past 15 or so years, firms have increased their repurchasing of outstanding common stock in the marketplace. The practical motives for **stock repurchases** include obtaining shares to be used in acquisitions, having shares available for employee stock option plans, or retiring shares. The recent increase in frequency and importance of stock repurchases is due to the fact that they either enhance shareholder value or help to discourage an unfriendly takeover.

---

8. If a firm's stock is selling at a low price—possibly less than a few dollars—many investors are hesitant to purchase it because they believe it is "cheap." These somewhat unsophisticated investors correlate cheapness and quality, and they feel that a low-priced stock is a low-quality investment. A reverse stock split raises the stock price and increases per-share earnings.

9. Eugene F. Fama, Lawrence Fisher, Michael C. Jensen, and Richard Roll, "The Adjustment of Stock Prices to New Information," *International Economic Review* 10 (February 1969), pp. 1–21, found that the stock price increases before the split announcement, and the increase in stock price is maintained if dividends per share are increased but is lost if dividends per share are *not* increased following the split.

In Practice

Investors Head to Splitsville

Typically, companies announce stock splits when their shares reach a point—often $50 or $100—at which investors consider the stock expensive. Dividing a high-priced stock into two or three lower-priced shares can increase its marketability by attracting more investors.

"Splits are very important to individual investors, even though you're essentially getting two fives for a 10," explains Zach Wagner, an analyst at Edward Jones in St. Louis. Generally, stocks that split have performed very well in the past, so that many investors believe splits indicate that good performance may continue. There is some evidence that this is indeed true. One study showed that over 15 years, a portfolio of 1,275 stocks that split yielded an average return of 19 percent in the first year after the split and 65 percent over 3 years, compared to returns of 11 and 53 percent, respectively, for a similar group of stocks that did not split. In the short term, stock prices tend to rise between the time the split is announced and the date of the split. For example, in mid-February 1999, athletic shoe company K-Swiss reported healthy earnings and a 2-for-1 split—pushing its shares up 23 percent.

However, some analysts point out that stocks that split have already risen in price, so that the above-average performance simply reflects an increase in the company's growth and earnings. Splits also signal management's confidence that the upward trend will continue. Companies don't want to split a $50 stock into two shares at $25 and then see the price drop.

Financial advisers remind investors that a stock split, by itself, is not a reason to buy a stock. As with any stock purchase, you should evaluate the fundamentals of the company, including key ratios, its price/earnings multiple, profit outlook, and industry factors. In terms of a company's underlying value, a stock split is essentially a nonevent.

Stock repurchases enhance shareholder value by (1) reducing the number of shares outstanding and thereby raising earnings per share, (2) sending a *positive signal* to investors in the marketplace that management believes that the stock is undervalued, and (3) providing a temporary floor for the stock price, which may have been declining. The use of repurchases to discourage unfriendly takeovers is predicated on the belief that a corporate raider is less likely to gain control of the firm if there are fewer publicly traded shares available. Here we focus on retiring shares through repurchase, because this motive for repurchase is similar to the payment of cash dividends.

Stock Repurchases Viewed as a Cash Dividend

When common stock is repurchased for retirement, the underlying motive is to distribute excess cash to the owners. As a result of any repurchase, the owners receive cash for their shares. Generally, as long as earnings remain constant, the repurchase reduces the number of outstanding shares, raising the earnings per share and therefore the market price per share. In addition, certain owner tax benefits may result. The repurchase of common stock results in a type of *reverse dilution,* because the earnings per share and the market price of stock are increased by reducing the number of shares outstanding. The net effect of the repurchase is similar to the payment of a cash dividend.

Example ▼   Benton Company, a national sportswear chain, has released the following financial data:

Earnings available for common stockholders	$1,000,000
Number of shares of common stock outstanding	400,000
Earnings per share ($1,000,000 ÷ 400,000)	$2.50
Market price per share	$50
Price/earnings (P/E) ratio ($50 ÷ $2.50)	20

The firm is contemplating using $800,000 of its earnings either to pay cash dividends or to repurchase shares. If the firm pays cash dividends, the amount of the dividend would be $2 per share ($800,000 ÷ 400,000 shares). If the firm pays $52 per share to repurchase stock, it could repurchase approximately 15,385 shares ($800,000 ÷ $52 per share). As a result of this repurchase, 384,615 shares (400,000 shares − 15,385 shares) of common stock remain outstanding. Earnings per share (EPS) rise to $2.60 ($1,000,000 ÷ 384,615). If the stock still sold at 20 times earnings (P/E = 20), applying the *price/earnings multiple approach* presented in Chapter 7, its market price would rise to $52 per share ($2.60 × 20). In both cases, the stockholders would receive $2 per share—a $2 cash dividend in the dividend case or a $2 increase in share price ($50 per share ▲ to $52 per share) in the repurchase case.

The advantages of stock repurchases are an increase in per-share earnings and certain owner tax benefits. The tax advantage occurs because if the cash dividend were paid, the owners would have to pay ordinary income taxes on it, whereas the $2 increase in the market value of the stock due to the repurchase will not be taxed until the owner sells the stock. Of course, when the stock is sold, and the proceeds are in excess of the original purchase price, the capital gain is taxed, possibly at a more favorable rate than the one applied to ordinary income. The IRS allegedly watches firms that regularly repurchase stock and levies a penalty if it believes repurchases have been made to delay the payment of taxes by stockholders.

Accounting Entries

The accounting entries that result when common stock is repurchased are a reduction in cash and the establishment of a contra capital account called "treasury stock," which is shown as a deduction from stockholders' equity. The label *treasury stock* is used on the balance sheet to indicate the presence of repurchased shares.

The Repurchase Process

When a company intends to repurchase a block of outstanding shares, it should make shareholders aware of its intentions. Specifically, it should advise them of the purpose of the repurchase (acquisition, stock options, retirement) and the disposition (if any) planned for the repurchased shares (traded for shares of another firm, distribution to executives, or held in the treasury).

Three basic methods of repurchase are commonly used. One is to purchase shares on the *open market*. This places upward pressure on the price of shares if

tender offer
A formal offer to purchase a given number of shares of a firm's stock at a specified price.

the number of shares being repurchased is reasonably large in comparison with the total number outstanding. The second method is through tender offers. A **tender offer** is a formal offer to purchase a given number of shares of a firm's stock at a specified price. The price at which a tender offer is made is set above the current market price to attract sellers. If the number of shares desired cannot be repurchased through the tender offer, open-market purchases can be used to obtain the additional shares. Tender offers are preferred when large numbers of shares are repurchased, because the company's intentions are clearly stated and each stockholder has an opportunity to sell shares at the tendered price. A third method that is sometimes used involves the purchase on a *negotiated basis* of a large block of shares from one or more major stockholders. Again, in this case, the firm would have to state its intentions and make certain that the purchase price is fair and equitable in view of the interests and opportunities of the remaining shareholders.

? Review Questions

13-7 What is a *stock dividend?* Why do firms issue stock dividends? Comment on the following statement: "I have a stock that promises to pay a 20 percent stock dividend every year, and therefore it guarantees that I will break even in 5 years."

13-8 What is a *stock split?* What is a *reverse stock split?* Compare a stock split with a stock dividend.

13-9 What is the logic behind *repurchasing shares* of common stock to distribute excess cash to the firm's owners? How might this raise the per-share earnings and market price of outstanding shares?

SUMMARY

 Understand cash dividend payment procedures and the role of dividend reinvestment plans. The cash dividend decision is normally a quarterly decision made by the board of directors that establishes the record date and payment date. Generally, the larger the dividend charged to retained earnings and paid in cash, the greater the amount of financing that must be raised externally. Some firms offer dividend reinvestment plans that allow stockholders to acquire shares in lieu of cash dividends, often at an attractive price. A company offering such a plan can either have a trustee buy outstanding shares on behalf of participating shareholders, or it can issue new shares to participants.

 Describe the residual theory of dividends and the key arguments with regard to dividend irrelevance and relevance. The residual theory suggests that dividends should be viewed as the earnings left after all acceptable investment opportunities have been undertaken. Dividend irrelevance, which is implied by the residual theory, is argued by Miller and Modigliani using a perfect world wherein information content and clientele effects exist. Gordon and Lintner argue dividend relevance based on the uncertainty-reducing effect of dividends, supported by their bird-in-the-hand argument. Although intuitively appealing, empirical studies fail to provide clear support of dividend relevance. The actions of financial managers and stockholders alike, however, tend to support the belief that dividend policy does affect stock value.

 Discuss the key factors involved in formulating a dividend policy. A firm's dividend policy should maximize the wealth of its owners while providing for sufficient financing. Dividend policy is affected by certain legal, contractual, and internal constraints as well as growth prospects, owner considerations, and market considerations. Legal constraints prohibit corporations from paying out as cash dividends any portion of the firm's "legal capital"; they also constrain firms with overdue liabilities or legally insolvent or bankrupt firms from paying cash dividends. Contractual constraints result from restrictive provisions in the firm's loan agreements. Internal constraints tend to result from a firm's limited excess cash availability. Growth prospects affect the relative importance of retaining earnings rather than paying them out in dividends. The tax status of owners, the owners' investment opportunities, and the potential dilution of ownership are important owner considerations. Finally, market considerations relate to stockholders' preference for the continuous payment of fixed or increasing streams of dividends and the perceived informational content of dividends.

 Review and evaluate the three basic types of dividend policies. With a constant-payout ratio dividend policy, the firm pays a fixed percentage of earnings out to the owners each period. With this policy, dividends move up and down with earnings, and no dividend is paid when a loss occurs. Under a regular dividend policy, the firm pays a fixed-dollar dividend each period; it increases the amount of dividends only after a proven increase in earnings has occurred. The low-regular-and-extra dividend policy is similar to the regular dividend policy, except that it pays an "extra dividend" in periods when the firm's earnings are higher than normal. The regular and the low-regular-and-extra dividend policies are generally preferred over the constant-payout-ratio dividend policy because their stable patterns of dividends reduce uncertainty.

 Evaluate stock dividends from accounting, shareholder, and company points of view. Occasionally, firms pay stock dividends as a replacement for or supplement to cash dividends. The payment of stock dividends involves a shifting of funds between capital accounts rather than a use of funds. Shareholders receiving stock dividends typically receive nothing of value—the market value of their holdings, their proportion of ownership, and their share of total earnings remain unchanged. Although more costly than cash dividends to issue, the firm may be able to use stock dividends to satisfy owners and therefore retain its market value without having to use cash.

 Explain stock splits and stock repurchases and the firm's motivation for undertaking each of them. Stock splits are sometimes used to enhance trading activity of a firm's shares by lowering or raising the market price of its stock. A stock split merely involves accounting adjustments—it has no effect on either the firm's cash or its capital structure. Stock repurchases can be made in lieu of cash dividend payments to retire outstanding shares and delay the payment of taxes. They involve the actual outflow of cash to reduce the number of outstanding shares and thereby increase earnings per share and the market price per share. Whereas stock repurchases can be viewed as dividend alternatives, stock splits are used to deliberately adjust the market price of shares.

SELF-TEST PROBLEM   (Solution in Appendix B)

ST 13–1 **Stock repurchase** The Off-Shore Steel Company has earnings available for common stockholders of $2 million and 500,000 shares of common stock outstanding at $60 per share. The firm is currently contemplating the payment of $2 per share in cash dividends.
a. Calculate the firm's current earnings per share (EPS) and price/earnings (P/E) ratio.

b. If the firm can repurchase stock at $62 per share, how many shares can be purchased in lieu of making the proposed cash dividend payment?

c. How much will the EPS be after the proposed repurchase? Why?

d. If the stock sells at the old P/E ratio, what will the market price be after repurchase?

e. Compare and contrast the EPS before and after the proposed repurchase.

f. Compare and contrast the stockholders' position under the dividend and repurchase alternatives.

PROBLEMS

WARM-UP   **13–1   Dividend payment procedures**   Wood Shoes, at the quarterly dividend meeting, declared a cash dividend of $1.10 per share for holders of record on Monday, July 10. The firm has 300,000 shares of common stock outstanding and has set a payment date of July 31. Prior to the dividend declaration, the firm's key accounts were as follows:

| Cash | $500,000 | Dividends payable | $ 0 |
| | | Retained earnings | 2,500,000 |

a. Show the entries after the meeting adjourned.

b. When is the *ex dividend* date?

c. After the July 31 payment date, what values would the key accounts have?

d. What effect, if any, will the dividend have on the firm's total assets?

e. Ignoring general market fluctuations, what effect, if any, will the dividend have on the firm's stock price on the ex dividend date?

INTERMEDIATE **13–2   Dividend payment**   Kathy Snow wishes to purchase shares of Countdown Computing, Inc. The company's board of directors has declared a cash dividend of $.80 to be paid to holders of record on Wednesday, May 12.

a. What is the last day that Kathy can purchase the stock (trade date) in order to receive the dividend?

b. What day does this stock begin trading "ex dividend"?

c. What change, if any, would you expect in the price per share when the stock begins trading on ex dividend day?

d. If Kathy held the stock for less than one quarter and then sold it for $39 per share, would she achieve a higher investment return by (1) buying the stock *prior to* the ex dividend date at $35 per share and collecting the $.80 dividend, or (2) buying it *on* the ex dividend date at $34.20 per share but not receiving the dividend?

INTERMEDIATE **13–3   Residual dividend policy**   As president of Young's of California, a large clothing chain, you have just received a letter from a major stockholder. The stockholder asks about the company's dividend policy. In fact, the stockholder has asked you to estimate the amount of the dividend that you are likely to pay next year. You have not yet collected all the information about the expected dividend payment, but you do know the following:

(1) The company follows a residual dividend policy.
(2) The total capital budget for next year is likely to be one of three amounts, depending on the results of capital budgeting studies that are currently under way. The capital expenditure amounts are $2 million, $3 million, and $4 million.
(3) The forecasted level of potential retained earnings next year is $2 million.
(4) The target or optimal capital structure is a debt ratio of 40%.

You have decided to respond by sending the stockholder the best information available to you.
a. Describe a *residual dividend policy*.
b. Compute the amount of the dividend (or the amount of new common stock needed) and the dividend payout ratio for each of the three capital expenditure amounts.
c. Compare, contrast, and discuss the amount of dividends (calculated in **b**) associated with each of the three capital expenditure amounts.

  13–4   **Dividend constraints**   The Howe Company's stockholders' equity account is as follows:

Common stock (400,000 shares at $4 par)	$1,600,000
Paid-in capital in excess of par	1,000,000
Retained earnings	1,900,000
Total stockholders' equity	$4,500,000

The earnings available for common stockholders from this period's operations are $100,000, which have been included as part of the $1.9 million retained earnings.
a. What is the maximum dividend per share that the firm can pay? (Assume that legal capital includes *all* paid-in capital.)
b. If the firm has $160,000 in cash, what is the largest per-share dividend it can pay without borrowing?
c. Indicate the accounts and changes, if any, that will result if the firm pays the dividends indicated in **a** and **b**.
d. Indicate the effects of an $80,000 cash dividend on stockholders' equity.

 13–5   **Dividend payment procedures**   A firm has $800,000 in paid-in capital, retained earnings of $40,000 (including the current year's earnings), and 25,000 shares of common stock outstanding. In the current year, it has $29,000 of earnings available for the common stockholders.
a. What is the most the firm can pay in cash dividends to each common stockholder? (Assume that legal capital includes *all* paid-in capital.)
b. What effect would a cash dividend of $.80 per share have on the firm's balance sheet entries?
c. If the firm cannot raise any new funds from external sources, what do you consider the key constraint with respect to the magnitude of the firm's dividend payments? Why?

INTERMEDIATE **13–6** **Low-regular-and-extra dividend policy** Bennett Farm Equipment Sales, Inc., is in a highly cyclic business. While the firm has a target payout ratio of 25%, its board realizes that strict adherence to that ratio would result in a fluctuating dividend and create uncertainty for the firm's stockholders. Therefore, the firm has declared a regular dividend of $.50 per share per year with extra cash dividends to be paid when earnings justify them. Earnings per share for the last several years are as follows:

Year	EPS
1995	$1.97
1996	$2.15
1997	$2.80
1998	$2.20
1999	$2.40
2000	$3.00

a. Calculate the payout ratio for each year based on the regular $.50 dividend and the cited EPS.
b. Calculate the difference between the regular $.50 dividend and a 25% payout for each year.
c. Bennett has established a policy of paying an extra dividend only when the difference between the regular dividend and a 25% payout amounts to $1.00 or more. Show the regular and extra dividends in those years when an extra dividend would be paid. What would be done with the "extra" in years when an extra dividend is not paid?
d. The firm expects that future earnings per share will continue to cycle but remain above $2.20 per share in most years. What factors should be considered in making a revision to the amount paid as a regular dividend? If the firm revises the regular dividend, what new amount should it pay?

INTERMEDIATE **13–7** **Alternative dividend policies** A firm has had the earnings per share over the last 10 years shown in the following table.

Year	Earnings per share
2000	$4.00
1999	3.80
1998	3.20
1997	2.80
1996	3.20
1995	2.40
1994	1.20
1993	1.80
1992	− .50
1991	.25

a. If the firm's dividend policy were based on a constant payout ratio of 40% for all years with positive earnings and 0% otherwise, what would be the annual dividend for each year?

b. If the firm had a dividend payout of $1.00 per share, increasing by $.10 per share whenever the dividend payout fell below 50% for two consecutive years, what annual dividend would the firm pay each year?

c. If the firm's policy were to pay $.50 per share each period except when earnings per share exceed $3.00, when an extra dividend equal to 80% of earnings beyond $3.00 would be paid, what annual dividend would the firm pay each year?

d. Discuss the pros and cons of each dividend policy described in **a** through **c**.

CHALLENGE  13–8 **Alternative dividend policies**   Given the earnings per share over the period 1993–2000 shown in the following table, determine the annual dividend per share under each of the policies set forth in **a** through **d**.

Year	Earnings per share
2000	$1.40
1999	1.56
1998	1.20
1997	– .85
1996	1.05
1995	.60
1994	1.00
1993	.44

a. Pay out 50% of earnings in all years with positive earnings.

b. Pay $.50 per share and increase to $.60 per share whenever earnings per share rise above $.90 per share for two consecutive years.

c. Pay $.50 per share except when earnings exceed $1.00 per share, in which case an extra dividend of 60% of earnings above $1.00 per share is paid.

d. Combine policies in **b** and **c**. When the dividend is raised (in **b**), raise the excess dividend base (in **c**) from $1.00 to $1.10 per share.

e. Compare and contrast each of the dividend policies described in **a** through **d**.

INTERMEDIATE 13–9 **Stock dividend—Firm**   Columbia Paper has the stockholders' equity account given below. The firm's common stock has a current market price of $30 per share.

Preferred stock	$100,000
Common stock (10,000 shares at $2 par)	20,000
Paid-in capital in excess of par	280,000
Retained earnings	100,000
Total stockholders' equity	$500,000

a. Show the effects on Columbia of a 5% stock dividend.

b. Show the effects of (1) a 10% and (2) a 20% stock dividend.

c. In light of your answers to **a** and **b**, discuss the effects of stock dividends on stockholders' equity.

INTERMEDIATE **13–10   Cash versus stock dividend**   Milwaukee Tool has the stockholders' equity account given below. The firm's common stock currently sells for $4 per share.

Preferred stock	$ 100,000
Common stock (400,000 shares at $1 par)	400,000
Paid-in capital in excess of par	200,000
Retained earnings	320,000
Total stockholders' equity	$1,020,000

a. Show the effects on the firm of a $.01, $.05, $.10, and $.20 per-share *cash* dividend.

b. Show the effects on the firm of a 1, 5, 10, and 20% *stock* dividend.

c. Compare the effects in **a** and **b**. What are the significant differences in the two methods of paying dividends?

 **13–11   Stock dividend—Investor**   Sarah Warren currently holds 400 shares of Nutri-Foods. The firm has 40,000 shares outstanding. The firm most recently had earnings available for common stockholders of $80,000, and its stock has been selling for $22 per share. The firm intends to retain its earnings and pay a 10% stock dividend.

a. How much does the firm currently earn per share?

b. What proportion of the firm does Sarah Warren currently own?

c. What proportion of the firm will Ms. Warren own after the stock dividend? Explain your answer.

d. At what market price would you expect the stock to sell after the stock dividend?

e. Discuss what effect, if any, the payment of stock dividends will have on Ms. Warren's share of the ownership and earnings of Nutri-Foods.

CHALLENGE **13–12   Stock dividend—Investor**   Security Data Company has outstanding 50,000 shares of common stock currently selling at $40 per share. The firm most recently had earnings available for common stockholders of $120,000, but it has decided to retain these funds and is considering either a 5 or 10% stock dividend in lieu of a cash dividend.

a. Determine the firm's current earnings per share.

b. If Sam Waller currently owns 500 shares of the firm's stock, determine his proportion of ownership currently and under each of the proposed stock dividend plans. Explain your findings.

c. Calculate and explain the market price per share under each of the stock dividend plans.

d. For each of the proposed stock dividends, calculate the earnings per share after payment of the stock dividend.

e. What is the value of Sam Waller's holdings under each of the plans? Explain.

f. Should Mr. Waller have any preference with respect to the proposed stock dividends? Why or why not?

INTERMEDIATE **13–13   Stock split—Firm**   Growth Industries' current stockholders' equity account is as follows:

Preferred stock	$ 400,000
Common stock (600,000 shares at $3 par)	1,800,000
Paid-in capital in excess of par	200,000
Retained earnings	800,000
Total stockholders' equity	$3,200,000

a. Indicate the change, if any, expected if the firm declares a 2-for-1 stock split.
b. Indicate the change, if any, expected if the firm declares a 1-for-1$\frac{1}{2}$ *reverse* stock split.
c. Indicate the change, if any, expected if the firm declares a 3-for-1 stock split.
d. Indicate the change, if any, expected if the firm declares a 6-for-1 stock split.
e. Indicate the change, if any, expected if the firm declares a 1-for-4 *reverse* stock split.

  13–14   Stock split versus stock dividend—Firm   Mammoth Corporation is considering a 3-for-2 stock split. It currently has the stockholders' equity position shown. The current stock price is $120 per share. The most recent period's earnings available for common stock is included in retained earnings.

CHALLENGE

Preferred stock	$ 1,000,000
Common stock (100,000 shares at $3 par)	300,000
Paid-in capital in excess of par	1,700,000
Retained earnings	10,000,000
Total stockholders' equity	$13,000,000

a. What effects on Mammoth would result from the stock split?
b. What change in stock price would you expect to result from the stock split?
c. What is the maximum cash dividend per share that the firm could pay on common stock before and after the stock split? (Assume that legal capital includes *all* paid-in capital.)
d. Contrast your answers to a through c with the circumstances surrounding a 50% stock dividend.
e. Explain the differences between stock splits and stock dividends.

  13–15   Stock dividend versus stock split—Firm   The board of Wicker Home Health Care, Inc., is exploring ways to expand the number of shares outstanding in order to reduce the market price per share to a level that the firm considers more appealing to investors. The options under consideration are a 20% stock

CHALLENGE

dividend or a 5-for-4 stock split. At the present time, the firm's equity account and other per share information are as follows:

Preferred stock	$ 0
Common stock (100,000 shares at $1 par)	100,000
Paid-in capital in excess of par	900,000
Retained earnings	700,000
Total stockholders' equity	$1,700,000
Price per share	$30.00
Earnings per share	$3.60
Dividend per share	$1.08

a. Show the effect on the equity accounts and per share data of a 20% stock dividend.

b. Show the effect on the equity accounts and per share data of a 5-for-4 stock split.

c. Which option will accomplish Wicker's goal of reducing current stock price while maintaining a stable level of retained earnings?

d. What legal constraints might encourage the firm to choose a split over a stock dividend?

INTERMEDIATE 13–16   **Stock repurchase**   The following financial data on the Bond Recording Company are available:

Earnings available for common stockholders	$800,000
Number of shares of common stock outstanding	400,000
Earnings per share ($800,000 ÷ 400,000)	$2
Market price per share	$20
Price/earnings (P/E) ratio ($20 ÷ $2)	10

The firm is currently contemplating using $400,000 of its earnings to pay cash dividends of $1 per share or repurchasing stock at $21 per share.

a. Approximately how many shares of stock can the firm repurchase at the $21-per-share price using the funds that would have gone to pay the cash dividend?

b. Calculate EPS after the repurchase. Explain your calculations.

c. If the stock still sells at 10 times earnings, how much will the market price be after the repurchase?

d. Compare and contrast the pre- and post-repurchase earnings per share.

e. Compare and contrast the stockholders' position under the dividend and repurchase alternatives. What are the tax implications under each alternative?

CHALLENGE 13–17   **Stock repurchase**   Harte Textiles, Inc., a maker of custom upholstery fabrics, is concerned about preserving the wealth of its stockholders during a cyclical downturn in the home furnishings business. The company has maintained a constant dividend payout of $2.00 tied to a target payout ratio of 40%.

Management is preparing a share repurchase recommendation to present to the firm's board of directors. The following data have been gathered from the last two years:

	1999	2000
Earnings available for common stockholders	$1,260,000	$1,200,000
Number of shares outstanding	300,000	300,000
Earnings per share	$4.20	$4.00
Market price per share	$23.50	$20.00
Price/earnings ratio	5.6	5.0

a. How many shares should the company have outstanding in order to combine the earnings available for common stockholders of $1,200,000 in the year 2000 and a dividend of $2.00 to produce the desired payout ratio of 40%?
b. How many shares would have to be repurchased to have the level of shares outstanding calculated in a?

CASE CHAPTER 13	Establishing General Access Company's Dividend Policy and Initial Dividend

General Access Company (GAC) is a fast-growing Internet access provider that initially went public in early 1994. Its revenue growth and profitability have steadily risen since the firm's inception in late 1992. GAC's growth has been financed through the initial common stock offering, the sale of bonds in 1997, and the retention of all earnings. Because of its rapid growth in revenue and profits, with only short-term earnings declines, GAC's common stockholders have been content to let the firm reinvest earnings to expand capacity to meet the growing demand for its services. This strategy has benefited most stockholders in terms of stock splits and capital gains. Since the company's initial public offering in 1994, GAC's stock twice has been split 2-for-1. In terms of total growth, the market price of GAC's stock, after adjustment for stock splits, has increased by 800 percent during the six-year period, 1994–2000.

Because GAC's rapid growth is beginning to slow, the firm's CEO, Marilyn McNeely, believes that its shares are becoming less attractive to investors. Ms. McNeely has had discussions with her CFO, Bobby Joe Rook, who believes that the firm must begin to pay cash dividends. He argues that many investors value regular dividends, and that by beginning to pay them, GAC would increase the demand—and therefore price—for its shares. Ms. McNeely decided that at the next board meeting she would propose that the firm begin to pay dividends on a regular basis.

Ms. McNeely realized that if the board approved her recommendation, it would have to (1) establish a dividend policy and (2) set the amount of the initial annual dividend. She had Mr. Rook prepare the summary of the firm's annual EPS given in the following table.

Year	EPS	Year	EPS
2000	$3.70	1996	$2.20
1999	4.10	1995	.83
1998	3.90	1994	.55
1997	3.30		

Mr. Rook indicated that he expects EPS to remain within 10% (plus or minus) of the most recent (2000) value during the next three years. His most likely estimate is an annual increase of about 5%.

After much discussion, Ms. McNeely and Mr. Rook agreed that she would recommend to the board one of the following types of dividend policies:

1. Constant-payout-ratio dividend policy
2. Regular dividend policy
3. Low-regular-and-extra dividend policy

Ms. McNeely realizes that her dividend proposal would significantly affect the firm's share price and future financing opportunities and costs. She also knows that she must be sure her proposal is complete and that it fully educates the board with regard to the long-run implications of each policy.

Required

a. Analyze each of the three dividend policies in light of GAC's financial position.
b. Which dividend policy would you recommend? Justify your recommendation.
c. What are the key factors to consider when setting the amount of a firm's initial annual dividend?
d. How should Ms. McNeely go about setting the initial annual dividend she will recommend to the board?
e. In view of your dividend policy recommendation in **b,** how large an initial dividend would you recommend? Justify your recommendation.

WEB EXERCISE

GOTO web site www.smartmoney.com. In the column on the right under Quotes & Research enter the symbol DIS; click Stock Snapshot; and then click GO.

1. What is the name of the company?
2. What is its dividend amount? Its dividend frequency? Its dividend yield?

Enter that data into the matrix below. Enter the next stock symbol into the box on the bottom of the page under Stock Search and then click Submit. Complete the following matrix in that manner.

Symbol	Company name	$ Amount	Dividend frequency	Yield %
DIS	_____	_____	_____	_____
AIT	_____	_____	_____	_____
MRK	_____	_____	_____	_____
LG	_____	_____	_____	_____
LUV	_____	_____	_____	_____
IBM	_____	_____	_____	_____
GE	_____	_____	_____	_____
BUD	_____	_____	_____	_____
PFE	_____	_____	_____	_____
INTC	_____	_____	_____	_____

3. Which of the companies have the lowest dividend yields?
4. Which of the companies have the highest dividend yields?

INTEGRATIVE CASE 4

O'GRADY APPAREL COMPANY

O'Grady Apparel Company was founded nearly 150 years ago when an Irish merchant named Garrett O'Grady landed in Los Angeles with an inventory of heavy canvas, which he hoped to sell for tents and wagon covers to miners headed for the California goldfields. Instead, he turned to the sale of harder-wearing clothing.

Today, the O'Grady Apparel Company is a small manufacturer of fabrics and clothing whose stock is traded on the over-the-counter exchange. In 2000, the Los Angeles–based company experienced sharp increases in both domestic and European markets resulting in record earnings. Sales rose from $15.9 million in 1999 to $18.3 million in 2000 with earnings per share of $3.28 and $3.84, respectively.

The European sales represented 29% of total sales in 2000, up from 24% the year before and only 3% in 1995, 1 year after foreign operations were launched. Although foreign sales represent nearly one-third of total sales, the growth in the domestic market is expected to affect the company most markedly. In 2001, management expects sales to surpass $21 million, and earnings per share are expected to rise to $4.40. (Selected income statement items are presented in Table 1.)

Because of the recent growth, Margaret Jennings, the corporate treasurer, is concerned that available funds are not being used to their fullest. The projected $1,300,000 of internally generated 2001 funds are expected to be insufficient to meet the company's expansion needs. Management has set a policy to maintain the current capital structure proportions of 25% long-term debt, 10% preferred stock, and 65% common stock equity for at least the next 3 years. In addition, it plans to continue paying out 40% of its earnings as dividends. Total capital expenditures are yet to be determined.

TABLE 1   Selected Income Statement Items

	1998	1999	2000	Projected 2001
Net sales	$13,860,000	$15,940,000	$18,330,000	$21,080,000
Net profits after taxes	1,520,000	1,750,000	2,020,000	2,323,000
Earnings per share (EPS)	2.88	3.28	3.84	4.40
Dividends per share	1.15	1.31	1.54	1.76

Ms. Jennings has been presented with several competing investment opportunities by division and product managers. However, because funds are limited, choices of which projects to accept must be made. The investment opportunities schedule (IOS) is shown in Table 2. To analyze the effect of the increased financing requirements on the weighted average cost of capital (WACC), Ms. Jennings contacted a leading investment banking firm that provided the financing cost data given in Table 3. O'Grady is in the 40% tax bracket.

TABLE 2 Investment Opportunities Schedule (IOS)

Investment opportunity	Internal rate of return (IRR)	Initial investment
A	21%	$400,000
B	19	200,000
C	24	700,000
D	27	500,000
E	18	300,000
F	22	600,000
G	17	500,000

TABLE 3 Financing Cost Data

Long-term debt: The firm can raise $700,000 of additional debt by selling 10-year, $1,000, 12% annual interest rate bonds to net $970 after flotation costs. Any debt in excess of $700,000 will have a before-tax cost, k_d, of 18%.

Preferred stock: Preferred stock, regardless of the amount sold, can be issued with a $60 par value, 17% annual dividend rate, and will net $57 per share after flotation costs.

Common stock equity: The firm expects its dividends and earnings to continue to grow at a constant rate of 15% per year. The firm's stock is currently selling for $20 per share. The firm expects to have $1,300,000 of available retained earnings. Once the retained earnings have been exhausted, the firm can raise additional funds by selling new common stock, netting $16 per share after underpricing and flotation costs.

REQUIRED

a. Over the relevant ranges noted in the following table, calculate the after-tax cost of each source of financing needed to complete the table.

Source of capital	Range of new financing	After-tax cost (%)
Long-term debt	$0–$700,000	_____
	$700,000 and above	_____
Preferred stock	$0 and above	_____
Common stock equity	$0–$1,300,000	_____
	$1,300,000 and above	_____

b. (1) Determine the breaking points associated with each source of capital.
   (2) Using the breaking points developed in (1), determine each of the ranges of *total* new financing over which the firm's weighted average cost of capital (WACC) remains constant.
   (3) Calculate the weighted average cost of capital for each range of total new financing.

c. (1) Using your findings in **b**(3) with the investment opportunities schedule (IOS), draw the firm's weighted marginal cost of capital (WMCC) schedule and IOS on the same set of total new financing or investment (x axis)–weighted average cost of capital and IRR (y axis) axes.
   (2) Which, if any, of the available investments would you recommend that the firm accept? Explain your answer.

d. (1) Assuming that the specific financing costs do not change, what effect would a shift to a more highly levered capital structure consisting of 50% long-term debt, 10% preferred stock, and 40% common stock have on your previous findings? (*Note:* Rework **b** and **c** using these capital structure weights.)
   (2) Which capital structure—the original one or this one—seems better? Why?

e. (1) What type of dividend policy does the firm appear to employ? Does it seem appropriate given the firm's recent growth in sales and profits, and its current investment opportunities?
   (2) Would you recommend an alternative dividend policy? Explain. How would this policy impact the investments recommended in **c** (2)?

PART

5

Short-Term Financial Decisions

Financial Planning

14

LG1 Understand the financial planning process, including long-term (strategic) financial plans and short-term (operating) plans.

LG2 Discuss the cash planning process, the role of sales forecasts, and the procedures for preparing the cash budget.

LG3 Describe the cash budget evaluation process, procedures for coping with uncertainty, and the issue of cash flow within the month.

LG4 Prepare a pro forma income statement using both the percent-of-sales method and a breakdown of costs and expenses into their fixed and variable components.

LG5 Explain the procedures used to develop a pro forma balance sheet using the judgmental approach and the use of the plug figure—external financing required—in this process.

LG6 Describe the weaknesses of the simplified approaches to pro forma preparation and the common uses of pro forma financial statements.

LG1

14.1 The Financial Planning Process

Financial planning is an important aspect of the firm's operations because it provides road maps for guiding, coordinating, and controlling the firm's actions to achieve its objectives. Two key aspects of the financial planning process are *cash planning* and *profit planning*. Cash planning involves the preparation of the firm's cash budget; profit planning is usually done by means of pro forma financial statements. These statements not only are useful for internal financial planning, but also are routinely required by existing and prospective lenders.

"If Only I'd Known..."

If you knew or could accurately predict what was in your future, you could make decisions today that would help bring about the results you want. Some outcomes are pretty much within your control (your grades, for example). For other outcomes, you can't do much more than make plans based on what you currently know, and hope for the best. (A good sense of humor—the ability to laugh at absurdity—will help you deal with whatever comes along.) Companies are pretty much in the same position. Because there is much in the business environment that is beyond their control, they try to control their future by careful and extensive planning, for both the long term and the short term. This chapter outlines the financial planning process, with particular attention to short-term planning focused on the firm's cash and its profits.

financial planning process
Planning that begins with long-term (strategic) financial plans that in turn guide the formulation of short-term (operating) plans and budgets.

The **financial planning process** begins with long-term, or strategic, financial plans that in turn guide the formulation of short-term, or operating, plans and budgets. Generally, the short-term plans and budgets implement the firm's long-term strategic objectives. The major emphasis in this chapter is on short-term financial plans and budgets. The following three chapters focus on the financial decisions involved in implementation of the firm's short-term financial plans. First, though, we begin with a few comments on long-term financial plans.

Long-Term (Strategic) Financial Plans

Long-term (strategic) financial plans lay out a company's planned financial actions and the anticipated financial impact of those actions over periods ranging from 2 to 10 years. The use of 5-year strategic plans, which are revised as significant new information becomes available, is common. Generally, firms that are subject to high degrees of operating uncertainty, relatively short production cycles, or both, tend to use shorter planning horizons.

Long-term financial plans are part of an integrated strategy that, along with production and marketing plans, guides the firm toward achievement of its strategic goals. Those long-term plans consider proposed fixed asset outlays, research and development activities, marketing and product development actions, capital structure, and major sources of financing. Also included would be termination of existing projects, product lines, or lines of business; repayment or retirement of outstanding debts; and any planned acquisitions. Such plans tend to be supported by a series of annual budgets and profit plans.

Short-Term (Operating) Financial Plans

Short-term (operating) financial plans specify short-term financial actions and the anticipated impact of those actions. These plans most often cover a 1- to 2-year period. Key inputs include the sales forecast and various forms of operating and financial data. Key outputs include a number of operating budgets, the cash budget, and pro forma financial statements. The entire short-term financial planning process is outlined in the flow diagram of Figure 14.1.

Short-term financial planning begins with the sales forecast. From it production plans are developed that take into account lead (preparation) times and include estimates of the required types and quantities of raw materials. Using the production plans, the firm can estimate direct labor requirements, factory overhead outlays, and operating expenses. Once these estimates have been made, the firm's pro forma income statement and cash budget can be prepared. With the basic inputs—pro forma income statement, cash budget, fixed asset outlay plan, long-term financing plan, and current-period balance sheet—the pro forma balance sheet can finally be developed. Throughout the remainder of this chapter, we will concentrate on the key outputs of the short-term financial planning process: the cash budget, the pro forma income statement, and the pro forma balance sheet.

? Review Questions

14–1 What is the *financial planning process?* Define and contrast *long-term (strategic) financial plans* and *short-term (operating) financial plans*.

14–2 Which three statements result as part of the short-term (operating) financial planning process? Describe the flow of information from the sales forecast through the preparation of these statements.

FIGURE 14.1 **Short-Term Financial Planning**
The short-term (operating) financial planning process

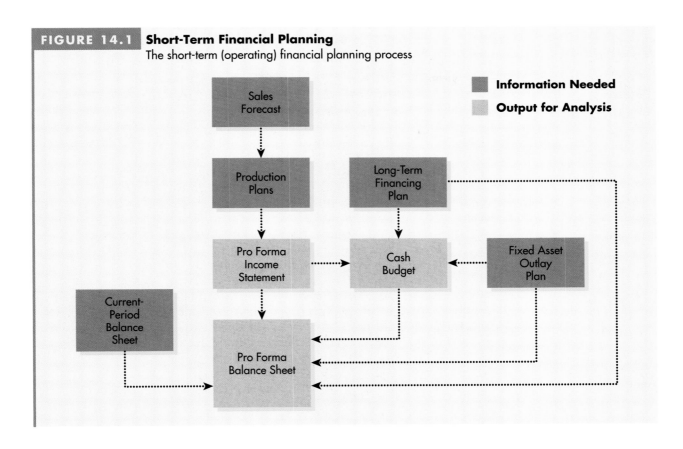

14.2 Cash Planning: Cash Budgets

cash budget (cash forecast)
A statement of the firm's planned inflows and outflows of cash that is used to estimate its short-term cash requirements.

The **cash budget,** or **cash forecast,** is a statement of the firm's planned inflows and outflows of cash. It is used by the firm to estimate its short-term cash requirements, with particular attention to planning for surplus cash and for cash shortages. A firm expecting a cash surplus can plan short-term investments (marketable securities), whereas a firm expecting shortages in cash must arrange for short-term financing (notes payable). The cash budget gives the financial manager a clear view of the timing of the firm's expected cash inflows and outflows over a given period.

Typically, the cash budget is designed to cover a 1-year period, divided into smaller time intervals. The number and type of intervals depend on the nature of the business. The more seasonal and uncertain a firm's cash flows, the greater the number of intervals. Because many firms are confronted with a seasonal cash flow pattern, the cash budget is quite often presented on a monthly basis. Firms with stable patterns of cash flow may use quarterly or annual time intervals.

In Practice

Insuring Planning Success at Nationwide

Ask managers to name their least favorite task, and financial planning is likely to be near the top of the list. Many complain of weak linkages between strategic planning and performance measurement.

To overcome these and other problems, Nationwide Financial Services (NFS), a division of Nationwide Insurance Enterprises, revamped its planning procedures in anticipation of going public in 1997. Like many companies, NFS's planning data were mostly financially oriented. However, these traditional performance measures were no longer sufficient for the company, which faced greater competition in the insurance industry and whose customers wanted more individualized financial solutions.

"We really had no linkage to nonfinancial attributes—customer satisfaction, employee satisfaction," explains Holly Snyder, NFS director of planning and management reporting. In addition, the emphasis on financial measures meant that nonfinancial employees didn't take ownership of the planning or budget process. The solution was a planning tool called the "balanced scorecard," developed by a team of managers from all disciplines. In addition to traditional financial measures such as net operating income and return on equity, the NFS scorecard included nonfinancial measures—for example, customer retention, customer service, and operational goals like back office productivity.

The scorecard became another step in NFS's planning process and the mechanism to link planning to strategic decisions. "The scorecard model is the tool we use to outline necessary changes," says Snyder. If a forecast shows 23 percent premium growth but the scorecard goal is 27 percent, managers look for strategies to close the gap. Another benefit of the scorecard: It states in simple terms the parameters for success, so that employees at all levels can understand how their achievements contribute to the overall success of the company.

sales forecast
The prediction of the firm's sales over a given period, based on external and/or internal data, and used as the key input to the short-term financial planning process.

Career Key
The *marketing* department will provide key input into the sales forecast. Marketing personnel will need, especially, to inform the financial planners of new-product introductions and the significant changes in promotion that will occur.

The Sales Forecast

The key input to the short-term financial planning process, and therefore the cash budget, is the firm's **sales forecast.** This is the prediction of the firm's sales over a given period and is ordinarily furnished to the financial manager by the marketing department. On the basis of this forecast, the financial manager estimates the monthly cash flows that will result from projected sales receipts and from outlays related to production, inventory, and sales. The manager also determines the level of fixed assets required and the amount of financing, if any, needed to support the forecast level of production and sales. In practice, obtaining good data is the most difficult aspect of forecasting.[1] The sales forecast may

---

1. A discussion of the calculation of the various forecasting techniques, such as regression, moving averages, and exponential smoothing, is not included in this text. For a description of the technical side of forecasting, refer to a basic statistics, econometrics, or management science text.

be based on an analysis of external data, of internal data, or on a combination of the two.

external forecast
A sales forecast based on the relationships observed between the firm's sales and certain key external economic indicators.

An **external forecast** is based on the relationships observed between the firm's sales and certain key external economic indicators such as the gross domestic product (GDP), new housing starts, and disposable personal income. Forecasts containing these indicators are readily available. The rationale for this approach is that because the firm's sales are often closely related to some aspect of overall national economic activity, a forecast of economic activity should provide insight into future sales.

internal forecast
A sales forecast based on a buildup, or consensus, of forecasts through the firm's own sales channels.

Internal forecasts are based on a buildup, or consensus, of sales forecasts through the firm's own sales channels. Typically, the firm's salespeople in the field are asked to estimate the number of units of each type of product that they expect to sell in the coming year. These forecasts are collected and totaled by the sales manager, who may adjust the figures using knowledge of specific markets or of the salesperson's forecasting ability. Finally, adjustments may be made for additional internal factors, such as production capabilities.

Hint The firm needs to spend a great deal of time and effort to make the sales forecast as precise as possible. An "after-the-fact" analysis of the prior year's forecast will help the firm determine which approach or combination of approaches will give it the most accurate forecasts.

Firms generally use a combination of external and internal forecast data to make the final sales forecast. The internal data provide insight into sales expectations, and the external data provide a means of adjusting these expectations to take into account general economic factors. The nature of the firm's product also often affects the mix and types of forecasting methods used.

Preparing the Cash Budget

The general format of the cash budget is presented in Table 14.1. We will discuss each of its components individually.

Cash Receipts

cash receipts
All of a firm's inflows of cash in a given financial period.

Cash receipts include all of a firm's inflows of cash in a given financial period. The most common components of cash receipts are cash sales, collections of accounts receivable, and other cash receipts.

TABLE 14.1 **The General Format of the Cash Budget**

	Jan.	Feb.	. . .	Nov.	Dec.
Cash receipts	$XXX	$XXG		$XXM	$XXT
Less: Cash disbursements	XXA	XXH	. . .	XXN	XXU
Net cash flow	XXB	XXI		XXO	XXV
Add: Beginning cash	XXC	XXD	XXJ	XXP	XXQ
Ending cash	XXD	XXJ		XXQ	XXW
Less: Minimum cash balance	XXE	XXK	. . .	XXR	XXY
Required total financing	$XXX	$XXL		$XXS	$XXX
Excess cash balance	$XXF				$XXZ

Example ▼ Coulson Industries, a defense contractor, is developing a cash budget for October, November, and December. Coulson's sales in August and September were $100,000 and $200,000, respectively. Sales of $400,000, $300,000, and $200,000 have been forecast for October, November, and December, respectively. Historically, 20% of the firm's sales have been for cash, 50% have generated accounts receivable collected after 1 month, and the remaining 30% have generated accounts receivable collected after 2 months. Bad debt expenses (uncollectible accounts) have been negligible.[2] In December, the firm will receive a $30,000 dividend from stock in a subsidiary. The schedule of expected cash receipts for the company is presented in Table 14.2. It contains the following items:

Forecast sales   This initial entry is *merely informational*. It is provided as an aid in calculating other sales-related items.

Cash sales   The cash sales shown for each month represent 20% of the total sales forecast for that month.

Collections of A/R   These entries represent the collection of accounts receivable (A/R) resulting from sales in earlier months.

Lagged 1 month   These figures represent sales made in the preceding month that generated accounts receivable collected in the current month. Because 50% of the current month's sales are collected 1 month later, the collections of A/R with a 1-month lag shown for September represent 50% of the sales in August, collections for October represent 50% of September sales, and so on.

Lagged 2 months   These figures represent sales made 2 months earlier that generated accounts receivable collected in the current month. Because 30% of

TABLE 14.2	A Schedule of Projected Cash Receipts for Coulson Industries ($000)				
Forecast sales	Aug. $100	Sept. $200	Oct. $400	Nov. $300	Dec. $200
Cash sales (.20)	$ 20	$ 40	$ 80	$ 60	$ 40
Collections of A/R:					
Lagged 1 month (.50)		50	100	200	150
Lagged 2 months (.30)			30	60	120
Other cash receipts					30
Total cash receipts			$210	$320	$340

---

2. Normally, it would be expected that the collection percentages would total slightly less than 100%, because some of the accounts receivable would be uncollectible. In this example, the sum of the collection percentages is 100% (20% + 50% + 30%), which reflects the fact that all sales are assumed to be collected.

sales are collected 2 months later, the collections with a 2-month lag shown for October represent 30% of the sales in August, and so on.

Other cash receipts   These are cash receipts expected from sources other than sales. Interest received, dividends received, proceeds from the sale of equipment, stock and bond sale proceeds, and lease receipts may show up here. For Coulson Industries, the only other cash receipt is the $30,000 dividend due in December.

Total cash receipts   This figure represents the total of all the cash receipts listed for each month. For Coulson Industries, we are concerned only with October, ▲ November, and December, as shown in Table 14.2.

Cash Disbursements

cash disbursements
All outlays of cash by the firm during a given financial period.

Cash disbursements include all outlays of cash by the firm during a given financial period. The most common cash disbursements are

Cash purchases	Fixed asset outlays
Payments of accounts payable	Interest payments
Rent (and lease) payments	Cash dividend payments
Wages and salaries	Principal payments (loans)
Tax payments	Repurchases or retirements of stock

It is important to recognize that *depreciation and other noncash charges are NOT included in the cash budget,* because they merely represent a scheduled write-off of an earlier cash outflow. The impact of depreciation, as noted in Chapter 3, is reflected in the cash outflow for the tax payments.

E x a m p l e ▼ Coulson Industries has gathered the following data needed for the preparation of a cash disbursements schedule for October, November, and December.

Purchases   The firm's purchases represent 70% of sales. Of this amount, 10% is paid in cash, 70% is paid in the month immediately following the month of purchase, and the remaining 20% is paid 2 months following the month of purchase.[3]

Rent payments   Rent of $5,000 will be paid each month.

Wages and salaries   The firm's wages and salaries are estimated by adding 10% of its monthly sales to the $8,000 fixed cost figure.

Tax payments   Taxes of $25,000 must be paid in December.

Fixed asset outlays   New machinery costing $130,000 will be purchased and paid for in November.

---

3. Unlike the collection percentages for sales, the total of the payment percentages should equal 100%, because it is expected that the firm will pay off all of its accounts payable.

TABLE 14.3 A Schedule of Projected Cash Disbursements for Coulson Industries ($000)

	Aug. $70	Sept. $140	Oct. $280	Nov. $210	Dec. $140
Purchases (.70 × sales)					
Cash purchases (.10)	$ 7	$ 14	$ 28	$ 21	$ 14
Payments of A/P:					
Lagged 1 month (.70)		49	98	196	147
Lagged 2 months (.20)			14	28	56
Rent payments			5	5	5
Wages and salaries			48	38	28
Tax payments					25
Fixed asset outlays				130	
Interest payments					10
Cash dividend payments			20		
Principal payments					20
Total cash disbursements			$213	$418	$305

Interest payments   An interest payment of $10,000 is due in December.

Cash dividend payments   Cash dividends of $20,000 will be paid in October.

Principal payments (loans)   A $20,000 principal payment is due in December.

Repurchases or retirements of stock   No repurchase or retirement of stock is expected during the October–December period.

The firm's cash disbursements schedule is presented in Table 14.3. Some items in the table are explained in greater detail below.

Purchases   This entry is *merely informational*. The figures represent 70% of the forecast sales for each month. They have been included to facilitate the calculation of the cash purchases and related payments.

Cash purchases   The cash purchases represent 10% of each month's purchases.

Payments of A/P   These entries represent the payment of accounts payable (A/P) resulting from purchases in earlier months.

Lagged 1 month   These figures represent purchases made in the preceding month that are paid for in the current month. Because 70% of the firm's purchases are paid for 1 month later, the payments with a 1-month lag shown for September represent 70% of the August purchases, payments for October represent 70% of September purchases, and so on.

Lagged 2 months   These figures represent purchases made 2 months earlier that are paid for in the current month. Because 20% of the firm's purchases are paid for 2 months later, the payments with a 2-month lag for October represent 20% of the August purchases, and so on.

Wages and salaries   These amounts were obtained by adding $8,000 to 10% of the *sales* in each month. The $8,000 represents the salary component; the rest represents wages.

▲ The remaining items on the cash disbursements schedule are self-explanatory.

Net Cash Flow, Ending Cash, Financing, and Excess Cash

Now look back at the general-format cash budget in Table 14.1. We have inputs for the first two entries and now continue calculating the firm's cash needs. The firm's **net cash flow** is found by subtracting the cash disbursements from cash receipts in each period. Then, by adding beginning cash to the firm's net cash flow, the **ending cash** for each period can be found. Finally, subtracting the desired minimum cash balance from ending cash yields the **required total financing** or the **excess cash balance.** If the ending cash is less than the minimum cash balance, *financing* is required. Such financing is typically viewed as short-term and therefore represented by notes payable. If the ending cash is greater than the minimum cash balance, *excess cash* exists. Any excess cash is assumed to be invested in a liquid, short-term, interest-paying vehicle—that is, in marketable securities.

net cash flow
The mathematical difference between the firm's cash receipts and its cash disbursements in each period.

ending cash
The sum of the firm's beginning cash and its net cash flow for the period.

required total financing
Amount of funds needed by the firm if the ending cash for the period is less than the desired minimum cash balance; typically represented by notes payable.

excess cash balance
The (excess) amount available for investment by the firm if the period's ending cash is greater than the desired minimum cash balance; assumed to be invested in marketable securities.

E x a m p l e ▼   Table 14.4 presents Coulson Industries' cash budget, based on the cash receipt and cash disbursement data already developed. At the end of September,

TABLE 14.4   **A Cash Budget for Coulson Industries ($000)**

	Oct.	Nov.	Dec.
Total cash receipts[a]	$210	$320	$340
Less: Total cash disbursements[b]	213	418	305
Net cash flow	$ (3)	$ (98)	$ 35
Add: Beginning cash	50	47	(51)
Ending cash	$ 47	$ (51)	$ (16)
Less: Minimum cash balance	25	25	25
Required total financing (notes payable)[c]	—	$ 76	$ 41
Excess cash balance (marketable securities)[d]	$ 22	—	—

[a]From Table 14.2.

[b]From Table 14.3.

[c]Values are placed in this line when the ending cash is less than the desired minimum cash balance. These amounts are typically financed short-term and therefore are represented by notes payable.

[d]Values are placed in this line when the ending cash is greater than the desired minimum cash balance. These amounts are typically assumed to be invested short-term and therefore are represented by marketable securities.

Coulson's cash balance was $50,000 and its notes payable and marketable securities equaled $0.[4] The company wishes to maintain as a reserve for unexpected needs a minimum cash balance of $25,000.

For Coulson Industries to maintain its required $25,000 ending cash balance, it will need to have borrowed $76,000 in November and $41,000 in December. In October, the firm will have an excess cash balance of $22,000, which can be held in an interest-earning marketable security. The required total financing figures in the cash budget refer to *how much will be owed at the end of the month;* they do *not* represent the monthly changes in borrowing.

The monthly changes in borrowing and in excess cash can be found by further analyzing the cash budget. In October, the $50,000 beginning cash, which becomes $47,000 after the $3,000 net cash outflow, results in a $22,000 excess cash balance once the $25,000 minimum cash is deducted. In November, the $76,000 of required total financing resulted from the $98,000 net cash outflow less the $22,000 of excess cash from October. The $41,000 of required total financing in December resulted from reducing November's $76,000 of required total financing by the $35,000 of net cash inflow during December. Summarizing, the financial actions for each month would be as follows:

October: Invest $22,000 of excess cash.
November: Liquidate $22,000 of excess cash and borrow $76,000.
December: Repay $35,000 of amount borrowed.

Evaluating the Cash Budget

Hint The cash budget is not only a great tool to let management know when it has cash shortages or excesses, but it may be a required document by potential creditors. It communicates to them what the money is going to be used for, and how and when they will get their loan paid back.

The cash budget provides the firm with figures indicating whether a cash shortage or surplus is expected to result in each of the months covered by the forecast. Each month's figure is based on the internally imposed requirement of a minimum cash balance and *represents the total balance at the end of the month.*

At the end of each of the 3 months, Coulson expects the following balances in cash, marketable securities, and notes payable:

Account	End-of-month balance ($000)		
	Oct.	Nov.	Dec.
Cash	$25	$25	$25
Marketable securities	22	0	0
Notes payable	0	76	41

---

4. If Coulson had either outstanding notes payable or held marketable securities at the end of September, its "beginning cash" value would be misleading. It could be either overstated or understated, depending on whether the firm had notes payable or marketable securities, respectively, on its books at that time. For simplicity, the cash budget discussions and problems presented in this chapter assume that the firm's notes payable and marketable securities equal $0 at the beginning of the period of concern.

Note that the firm is assumed to first liquidate its marketable securities to meet deficits and then borrow with notes payable if additional financing is needed. As a result, it will not have marketable securities and notes payable on its books at the same time.

Because it may be necessary for the firm to borrow up to $76,000 for the 3-month period, the financial manager should be sure that a line of credit is established or some other arrangement made to ensure the availability of these funds.

Coping with Uncertainty in the Cash Budget

Hint The manager will usually arrange to borrow more than the maximum financing indicated in the cash budget, because of the uncertainty of the ending cash values, which are derived from various forecasts.

Aside from careful estimating of the inputs to the cash budget, there are two ways of coping with the uncertainty of the cash budget.[5] One is to prepare several cash budgets—based on pessimistic, most likely, and optimistic forecasts. From this range of cash flows, the financial manager can determine the amount of financing needed to cover the most adverse situation. The use of several cash budgets based on differing assumptions also should give the financial manager a sense of the riskiness of alternatives so that he or she can make more intelligent short-term financial decisions. This sensitivity analysis, or "what if" approach, is often used to analyze cash flows under a variety of possible circumstances. Computers and electronic spreadsheets are commonly used to simplify the process of sensitivity analysis.

E x a m p l e ▼ Table 14.5 presents the summary of Coulson Industries' cash budget prepared for each month of concern using pessimistic, most likely, and optimistic estimates

TABLE 14.5 A Sensitivity Analysis of Coulson Industries' Cash Budget ($000)

	October			November			December		
	Pessi-mistic	Most likely	Opti-mistic	Pessi-mistic	Most likely	Opti-mistic	Pessi-mistic	Most likely	Opti-mistic
Total cash receipts	$160	$210	$285	$ 210	$320	$ 410	$ 275	$340	$422
Less: Total cash disbursements	200	213	248	380	418	467	280	305	320
Net cash flow	$ (40)	$ (3)	$ 37	$(170)	$ (98)	$ (57)	$ (5)	$ 35	$102
Add: Beginning cash	50	50	50	10	47	87	(160)	(51)	30
Ending cash	$ 10	$ 47	$ 87	$(160)	$ (51)	$ 30	$(165)	$(16)	$132
Less: Minimum cash balance	25	25	25	25	25	25	25	25	25
Required total financing	$ 15	—	—	$ 185	$ 76	—	$ 190	$ 41	—
Excess cash balance	—	$ 22	$ 62	—	—	$ 5	—	—	$107

---

5. The term *uncertainty* is used here to refer to the variability of the cash flow outcomes that may actually occur.

of cash receipts and disbursements. The most likely estimate is based on the expected outcomes presented earlier in Tables 14.2 through 14.4.

During the month of October, Coulson will at worst need a maximum of $15,000 of financing, and at best it will have a $62,000 excess cash balance available for short-term investment. During November, its financing requirement will be between $0 and $185,000, or it could experience an excess cash balance of $5,000 during November. The December projections show maximum borrowing of $190,000 with a possible excess cash balance of $107,000. By considering the extreme values reflected in the pessimistic and optimistic outcomes, Coulson Industries should be better able to plan cash requirements. For the 3-month period, the peak borrowing requirement under the worst circumstances would be $190,000, which happens to be considerably greater than the most likely estimate of $76,000 for this period.

Career Key

Information systems analysts will design financial planning and budgeting modules within the financial information system. They will also help design forecasting systems and will assist in sensitivity analysis.

A second and much more sophisticated way of coping with uncertainty in the cash budget is *simulation*.[6] By simulating the occurrence of sales and other uncertain events, the firm can develop a probability distribution of its ending cash flows for each month. The financial decision maker can then use the probability distribution to determine the amount of financing necessary to provide a desired degree of protection against a cash shortage.

Cash Flow Within the Month

Because the cash budget shows cash flows only on a total monthly basis, the information provided by the cash budget is not necessarily adequate for ensuring solvency. A firm must look more closely at its pattern of daily cash receipts and cash disbursements to ensure that adequate cash is available for paying bills as they come due. For an example related to this topic, see the book's web site at **www.awlonline.com/gitman.**

The synchronization of cash flows in the cash budget at month-end does not ensure that the firm will be able to meet daily cash requirements. Because a firm's cash flows are generally quite variable when viewed on a daily basis, effective cash planning requires a look *beyond* the cash budget. The financial manager must therefore plan and monitor cash flow more frequently than on a monthly basis. The greater the variability of cash flows from day to day, the greater the attention required.

? Review Questions

14–3   What is the purpose of the *cash budget?* The key input to the cash budget is the sales forecast. What is the difference between *external* and *internal* forecast data?

---

6. A more detailed discussion of the use of simulation is included among the approaches for dealing with risk in capital budgeting in Chapter 10.

14–4   Briefly describe the basic format of the cash budget, beginning with forecast sales and ending with *required total financing* or *excess cash balance.*

14–5   How can the two "bottom lines" of the cash budget be used to determine the firm's short-term borrowing and investment requirements?

14–6   What is the cause of uncertainty in the cash budget? What two techniques can be used to cope with this uncertainty?

14–7   What actions or analysis beyond preparation of the cash budget should the financial manager undertake to ensure that cash is available when needed? Why?

14.3 Profit Planning: Pro Forma Statement Fundamentals

pro forma statements
Projected, or forecast, financial statements—income statements and balance sheets.

Whereas cash planning focuses on forecasting cash flows to assure the firm's solvency, *profit planning* relies on accrual concepts to project the firm's profit and overall financial position. Shareholders, creditors, and the firm's management, therefore, pay close attention to the **pro forma statements,** which are projected, or forecast, financial statements—income statements and balance sheets. The preparation of these statements requires a careful blending of a number of procedures to account for the revenues, costs, expenses, assets, liabilities, and equity resulting from the firm's anticipated level of operations. The basic steps in this process were shown in the flow diagram of Figure 14.1. The financial manager frequently uses one of a number of simplified approaches to estimate the pro forma statements. The most popular approaches are based on the belief that the financial relationships reflected in the firm's financial statements will not change in the coming period. The commonly used approaches are presented in subsequent discussions.

Hint   A key point in understanding pro forma statements is that these are the goals and objectives of the firm for the planning period. In order for these goals and objectives to be achieved, operational plans will have to be developed. Financial plans can be realized only if the correct actions are implemented.

Two inputs are required for preparing pro forma statements using the simplified approaches: (1) financial statements for the preceding year and (2) the sales forecast for the coming year. A variety of assumptions must also be made. The company that we will use to illustrate the simplified approaches to pro forma preparation is Vectra Manufacturing, which manufactures and sells one product. It has two basic models—model X and model Y—which are produced by the same process but require different amounts of raw material and labor.

Preceding Year's Financial Statements

The income statement for the firm's 2000 operations is given in Table 14.6. It indicates that Vectra had sales of $100,000, total cost of goods sold of $80,000, net profits before taxes of $9,000, and net profits after taxes of $7,650. The firm paid $4,000 in cash dividends, leaving $3,650 to be transferred to retained earnings. The firm's balance sheet for 2000 is given in Table 14.7.

Sales Forecast

Like the cash budget, the key input for the development of pro forma statements is the sales forecast. The sales forecast for the coming year for Vectra Manufacturing is given in Table 14.8 on page 593. This forecast is based on both

TABLE 14.6	An Income Statement for Vectra Manufacturing for the Year Ended December 31, 2000

Sales revenue		
Model X (1,000 units at $20/unit)	$20,000	
Model Y (2,000 units at $40/unit)	80,000	
Total sales		$100,000
Less: Cost of goods sold		
Labor	$28,500	
Material A	8,000	
Material B	5,500	
Overhead	38,000	
Total cost of goods sold		80,000
Gross profits		$ 20,000
Less: Operating expenses		10,000
Operating profits		$ 10,000
Less: Interest expense		1,000
Net profits before taxes		$ 9,000
Less: Taxes (.15 × $9,000)		1,350
Net profits after taxes		$ 7,650
Less: Common stock dividends		4,000
To retained earnings		$ 3,650

TABLE 14.7	A Balance Sheet for Vectra Manufacturing (December 31, 2000)

Assets		Liabilities and equities	
Cash	$ 6,000	Accounts payable	$ 7,000
Marketable securities	4,000	Taxes payable	300
Accounts receivable	13,000	Notes payable	8,300
Inventories	16,000	Other current liabilities	3,400
Total current assets	$39,000	Total current liabilities	$19,000
Net fixed assets	$51,000	Long-term debt	$18,000
Total assets	$90,000	Stockholders' equity	
		Common stock	$30,000
		Retained earnings	$23,000
		Total liabilities and	
		stockholders' equity	$90,000

TABLE 14.8	2001 Sales Forecast for Vectra Manufacturing
Unit sales	
Model X	1,500
Model Y	1,950
Dollar sales	
Model X ($25/unit)	$ 37,500
Model Y ($50/unit)	97,500
Total	$135,000

external and internal data. The unit sale prices of the products reflect an increase from $20 to $25 for model X and from $40 to $50 for model Y. These increases are required to cover anticipated increases in the costs of labor, material, overhead, and operating expenses.

? Review Question

14–8   What is the purpose of *pro forma statements?* What inputs are required for preparing them using the simplified approaches?

14.4 Preparing the Pro Forma Income Statement

percent-of-sales method
A method for developing the pro forma income statement that expresses the cost of goods sold, operating expenses, and interest expense as a percentage of projected sales.

A simple method for developing a pro forma income statement is to use the **percent-of-sales method.** It forecasts sales and then expresses the cost of goods sold, operating expenses, and interest expense as percentages of projected sales. For Vectra Manufacturing, these percentages are as follows:

$$\frac{\text{Cost of goods sold}}{\text{Sales}} = \frac{\$80,000}{\$100,000} = 80.0\%$$

$$\frac{\text{Operating expenses}}{\text{Sales}} = \frac{\$10,000}{\$100,000} = 10.0\%$$

$$\frac{\text{Interest expense}}{\text{Sales}} = \frac{\$1,000}{\$100,000} = 1.0\%$$

The dollar values used are taken from the 2000 income statement (Table 14.6).

Applying these percentages to the firm's forecast sales of $135,000, developed in Table 14.8, and assuming that the firm will pay $4,000 in common stock dividends in 2001, results in the pro forma income statement in Table 14.9.

TABLE 14.9 A Pro Forma Income Statement, Using the Percent-of-Sales Method, for Vectra Manufacturing for the Year Ended December 31, 2001

Sales revenue	$135,000
Less: Cost of goods sold (.80)	108,000
Gross profits	$ 27,000
Less: Operating expenses (.10)	13,500
Operating profits	$ 13,500
Less: Interest expense (.01)	1,350
Net profits before taxes	$ 12,150
Less: Taxes (.15 × $12,150)	1,823
Net profits after taxes	$ 10,327
Less: Common stock dividends	4,000
To retained earnings	$ 6,327

Considering Types of Costs and Expenses

The technique that is used to prepare the pro forma income statement in Table 14.9 assumes that all the firm's costs and expenses are *variable*. This means that the use of the historical (2000) ratios of cost of goods sold, operating expenses, and interest expense to sales assumes that for a given percentage increase in sales, the same percentage increase in each of these components results. For example, as Vectra's sales increased by 35 percent (from $100,000 in 2000 to $135,000 projected for 2001), its cost of goods sold also increased by 35 percent (from $80,000 in 2000 to $108,000 projected for 2001). On the basis of this assumption, the firm's net profits before taxes also increased by 35 percent (from $9,000 in 2000 to $12,150 projected for 2001).

A broad implication of this approach is that because the firm has no fixed costs, it will not receive the benefits that often result from them.[7] Therefore, the use of past cost and expense ratios generally *tends to understate profits when sales are increasing and overstate profits when sales are decreasing.* Clearly, if the firm has fixed costs, these costs do not change when sales increase; the result is increased profits. By remaining unchanged when sales decline, these costs tend to lower profits. The best way to adjust for the presence of fixed costs in pro forma

---

7. The potential returns as well as risks resulting from use of fixed (operating and financial) costs to create "leverage" are discussed in Chapter 12. The key point to recognize here is that when the firm's revenue is *increasing*, fixed costs can magnify returns.

income statement preparation is to break the firm's historical costs and expenses into *fixed* and *variable components*.[8]

Example ▼ Vectra Manufacturing's 2000 actual and 2001 pro forma income statements, broken into fixed and variable cost components, are shown:

Income Statements Vectra Manufacturing	2000 Actual	2001 Pro forma
Sales revenue	$100,000	$135,000
Less: Cost of good sold		
Fixed cost	40,000	40,000
Variable cost (.40 × sales)	40,000	54,000
Gross profits	$ 20,000	$ 41,000
Less: Operating expenses		
Fixed expense	5,000	5,000
Variable expense (.05 × sales)	5,000	6,750
Operating profits	$ 10,000	$ 29,250
Less: Interest expense (all fixed)	1,000	1,000
Net profits before taxes	$ 9,000	$ 28,250
Less: Taxes (.15 × net profits before taxes)	1,350	4,238
Net profits after taxes	$ 7,650	$ 24,012

Breaking Vectra's costs and expenses into fixed and variable components provides a more accurate projection of its pro forma profit. Had the firm treated all costs as variable, its pro forma net profits before taxes would equal 9% of sales, just as was the case in 2000 ($9,000 net profits before taxes ÷ $100,000 sales). As shown in Table 14.9, by assuming that *all* costs are variable, the net profits before taxes would have been $12,150 (.09 × $135,000 projected sales) instead of the $28,250 of net profits before taxes obtained before by using the ▲ firm's fixed cost–variable cost breakdown.

This example should make it clear that ignoring fixed costs in the pro forma income statement preparation process typically results in misstatement of the firm's forecast profit. Therefore, when using a simplified approach to pro forma

8. The application of *regression analysis*—a statistically based technique for measuring the relationship between variables—to past cost data as they relate to past sales could be used to develop equations that recognize the fixed and variable nature of each cost. Such equations could be employed when preparing the pro forma income statement from the sales forecast. The use of the regression approach in pro forma income statement preparation is widespread, and many computer software packages for use in pro forma preparation rely on this technique. Expanded discussions of the application of this technique can be found in most second-level managerial finance texts.

income statement preparation, it is advisable to consider first breaking down costs and expenses into fixed and variable components.

? Review Questions

14–9 Briefly describe the pro forma income statement preparation process using the *percent-of-sales method*. What are the strengths and weaknesses of this simplified approach?

14–10 Comment on the following statement: "Because nearly all firms have fixed costs, ignoring them in the pro forma income statement preparation process typically results in misstatement of the firm's forecast profit." How can such a "misstatement" be avoided?

14.5 Preparing the Pro Forma Balance Sheet

judgmental approach
A method for developing the pro forma balance sheet in which the values of certain balance sheet accounts are estimated, and others are calculated, using the firm's external financing as a balancing, or "plug," figure.

A number of simplified approaches are available for preparing the pro forma balance sheet. Probably the best and most popular is the judgmental approach.[9] Under the **judgmental approach,** the values of certain balance sheet accounts are estimated and others are calculated. The firm's external financing is used as a balancing, or "plug," figure. To apply the judgmental approach to prepare Vectra Manufacturing's 2001 pro forma balance sheet, a number of assumptions must be made:

1. A minimum cash balance of $6,000 is desired.
2. Marketable securities are assumed to remain unchanged from their current level of $4,000.
3. Accounts receivable on average represents 45 days of sales. Because Vectra's annual sales are projected to be $135,000, accounts receivable should average $16,875 ($\frac{1}{8} \times$ $135,000). (Forty-five days expressed fractionally is one-eighth of a year: $45/360 = \frac{1}{8}$.)
4. The ending inventory should remain at a level of about $16,000, of which 25 percent (approximately $4,000) should be raw materials and the remaining 75 percent (approximately $12,000) should consist of finished goods.
5. A new machine costing $20,000 will be purchased. Total depreciation for the year is $8,000. Adding the $20,000 acquisition to the existing net fixed assets of $51,000 and subtracting the depreciation of $8,000 yields net fixed assets of $63,000.
6. Purchases are expected to represent approximately 30% of annual sales, which in this case is approximately $40,500 (.30 × $135,000). The firm estimates that it can take 72 days on average to satisfy its accounts payable.

9. The judgmental approach represents an improved version of the often discussed *percent-of-sales approach* to pro forma balance sheet preparation. Because the judgmental approach requires only slightly more information and should yield better estimates than the somewhat naive percent-of-sales approach, it is presented here.

Thus, accounts payable should equal one-fifth (72 days ÷ 360 days) of the firm's purchases, or $8,100 (⅕ × $40,500).

7. Taxes payable are expected to equal one-fourth of the current year's tax liability, which equals $455 (one-fourth of the tax liability of $1,823 shown in the pro forma income statement in Table 14.9).

8. Notes payable are assumed to remain unchanged from their current level of $8,300.

9. No change in other current liabilities is expected. They remain at the level of the previous year: $3,400.

10. The firm's long-term debt and its common stock are expected to remain unchanged at $18,000 and $30,000, respectively; no issues, retirements, or repurchases of bonds or stocks are planned.

11. Retained earnings will increase from the beginning level of $23,000 (from the balance sheet dated December 31, 2000, in Table 14.7) to $29,327. The increase of $6,327 represents the amount of retained earnings calculated in the year-end 2001 pro forma income statement in Table 14.9.

external financing required ("plug" figure)
Under the judgmental approach for developing a pro forma balance sheet, the amount of external financing needed to bring the statement into balance.

A 2001 pro forma balance sheet for Vectra Manufacturing based on these assumptions is presented in Table 14.10. A **"plug" figure**—called the **external financing required**—of $8,293 is needed to bring the statement into balance. This means that the firm will have to obtain about $8,293 of additional external financing to support the increased sales level of $135,000 for 2001.

A *positive* value for "external financing required," like that shown in Table 14.10, means that to support the forecast level of operation, the firm must raise

TABLE 14.10 A Pro Forma Balance Sheet, Using the Judgmental Approach, for Vectra Manufacturing (December 31, 2001)

Assets			Liabilities and equities	
Cash		$ 6,000	Accounts payable	$ 8,100
Marketable securities		4,000	Taxes payable	455
Accounts receivable		16,875	Notes payable	8,300
Inventories			Other current liabilities	3,400
Raw materials	$ 4,000		Total current liabilities	$ 20,255
Finished goods	12,000		Long-term debt	$ 18,000
Total inventory		16,000	Stockholders' equity	
Total current assets		$ 42,875	Common stock	$ 30,000
Net fixed assets		$ 63,000	Retained earnings	$ 29,327
Total assets		$ 105,875	Total	$ 97,582
			External financing required[a]	$ 8,293
			Total liabilities and stockholders' equity	$105,875

[a]The amount of external financing needed to force the firm's balance sheet to balance. Due to the nature of the judgmental approach, the balance sheet is not expected to balance without some type of adjustment.

funds externally using debt and/or equity financing. Once the form of financing is determined, the pro forma balance sheet is modified to replace "external financing required" with the planned increases in the debt and/or equity accounts.

A *negative* value for external financing required indicates that the firm's forecast financing is in excess of its needs. In this case, funds would be available for use in repaying debt, repurchasing stock, or increasing dividends. Once the specific actions are determined, "external financing required" is replaced in the pro forma balance sheet with the planned reductions in the debt and/or equity accounts. Obviously, besides being used to prepare the pro forma balance sheet, the judgmental approach also is frequently used specifically to estimate the firm's financing requirements.

? Review Questions

14–11 Describe the *judgmental approach* for simplified preparation of the pro forma balance sheet. Contrast this with the more detailed approach shown in Figure 14.1.

14–12 What is the significance of the "plug" figure, *external financing required,* used with the judgmental approach for preparing the pro forma balance sheet? Differentiate between the interpretation and strategy associated with positive and negative values for *external financing required.*

14.6 Evaluation of Pro Forma Statements

Analysts—including investors, lenders, and managers—frequently use the techniques presented here to make rough estimates of pro forma financial statements. Simplified approaches to pro forma preparation are expected to remain popular despite the growing use of computers to streamline financial planning. An understanding of the basic weaknesses of these simplified approaches is therefore important. Equally important is the ability to effectively use pro forma statements to make financial decisions.

Weaknesses of Simplified Approaches

The basic weaknesses of the simplified pro forma approaches shown in the chapter lie in two assumptions: (1) that the firm's past financial condition is an accurate indicator of its future, and (2) that certain variables, such as cash, accounts receivable, and inventories, can be forced to take on certain "desired" values. These assumptions cannot be justified solely on the basis of their ability to simplify the calculations involved. Good financial analysts do not generally assume that simplification of the forecasting model and assumptions enhances insight into what's going to happen. Because the quality of pro forma statements depends on the quality of the forecasting model and its assumptions, practicing analysts seek out the models and assumptions that best suit their particular situation.

Other simplified approaches exist. Most are based on the assumption that certain relationships among revenues, costs, expenses, assets, liabilities, and equity will prevail in the future. For example, in preparing the pro forma balance sheet, all assets, liabilities, *and* equity are sometimes increased by the percentage increase expected in sales. The financial analyst must know the techniques used in preparing pro forma statements to judge the quality of the estimated values and thus the degree of confidence he or she can have in them.

Using Pro Forma Statements

In addition to estimating the amount of external financing that is required to support a given level of sales, pro forma statements also provide a basis for analyzing in advance the level of profitability and overall financial performance of the firm in the coming year. Using pro forma statements, both financial managers and lenders can analyze the firm's sources and uses of cash as well as its liquidity, activity, debt, and profitability. Sources and uses can be evaluated by preparing a pro forma statement of cash flows. Various ratios can be calculated from the pro forma income statement and balance sheet to evaluate performance.

After analyzing the pro forma statements, the financial manager can take steps to adjust planned operations to achieve short-term financial goals. For

---

In Practice

Small Business

A Daily Dose of Results

Managers in large companies may not have a choice in how often they get management reports they need for comparison to the firm's financial plans. Small business owners, however, can set their own reporting schedules based on the needs of their particular business. For some, this means monitoring results daily.

Ron Friedman takes the pulse of Santa Monica, California, accounting firm Stonefield Josephson Inc. every morning. Friedman, the firm's CEO, reviews the previous day's key indicators. A firm believer in the value of daily reports, he recommends that his clients do the same. "Think of all the time and money you lose when you find out about problems only at the end of the week or the month," he says.

Ray Finch, president of Emerald Dunes golf course in West Palm Beach, Florida, agrees. He insisted that daily reporting capability be part of the golf club's customized financial software package. Watching daily revenue figures in June 1996, he discovered that business was tapering off as summer approached. To keep sales on track with forecasts, he decided to start his advertising campaign promoting special off-season summer rates earlier than originally planned. By timing newspaper and television ads to coincide with the U.S. Open Golf Tournament, he caught the attention of a prime audience and increased sales 28 percent the following week—a window of opportunity he would have missed by relying on monthly reports.

Clearly, daily management reports have to be tailored to the type of business. No manager has time to wade through stacks of statistics. But a summary of important numbers, presented in an easy-to-read format, can be a valuable management tool that helps small business owners track operating results and implement changes when actual results lag behind forecasts.

example, if profits on the pro forma income statement are too low, a variety of pricing or cost-cutting actions, or both, might be initiated. If the projected level of accounts receivable on the pro forma balance sheet is too high, changes in credit or collection policy may be called for. Pro forma statements are therefore of key importance in solidifying the firm's financial plans for the coming year.

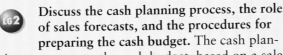

? Review Questions

14–13 What are the two key weaknesses of the simplified approaches to pro forma statement preparation?

14–14 What is the financial manager's objective in evaluating pro forma statements?

SUMMARY

LG1 **Understand the financial planning process, including long-term (strategic) financial plans and short-term (operating) plans.** The two key aspects of the financial planning process are cash planning and profit planning. Cash planning involves the cash budget or cash forecast. Profit planning relies on the pro forma income statement and balance sheet. Long-term (strategic) financial plans act as a guide for preparing short-term (operating) financial plans. Long-term plans tend to cover periods ranging from 2 to 10 years and are updated periodically. Short-term plans most often cover a 1- to 2-year period.

LG2 **Discuss the cash planning process, the role of sales forecasts, and the procedures for preparing the cash budget.** The cash planning process uses the cash budget, based on a sales forecast, to estimate short-term cash surpluses and shortages. The sales forecast may be based on external or internal data or on a combination of the two. The cash budget is typically prepared for a 1-year period divided into months. It nets cash receipts and disbursements for each period to calculate net cash flow. Ending cash is estimated by adding beginning cash to the net cash flow. By subtracting the desired minimum cash balance from the ending cash, the financial manager can determine required total financing (typically notes payable) or the excess cash balance (typically held as marketable securities).

LG3 **Describe the cash budget evaluation process, procedures for coping with uncertainty, and the issue of cash flow within the month.** The cash budget allows the firm to plan investment of cash surpluses and to arrange for adequate borrowing to meet forecast cash shortages. To cope with uncertainty in the cash budget, sensitivity analysis (preparation of several cash budgets) or computer simulation can be used. A firm must also consider its pattern of daily cash receipts and cash disbursements to ensure that adequate cash is available to meet bills as they come due.

LG4 **Prepare a pro forma income statement using both the percent-of-sales method and a breakdown of costs and expenses into their fixed and variable components.** A pro forma income statement can be developed by calculating past percentage relationships between certain cost and expense items and the firm's sales and then applying these percentages to forecasts. Because this approach implies that all costs and expenses are variable, it tends to understate profits when sales are increasing and overstate profits when sales are decreasing. This problem can be avoided by breaking down costs and expenses into fixed and variable components. In this case, the fixed components remain unchanged from the most recent year, and the variable costs and expenses are forecast on a percent-of-sales basis.

Explain the procedures used to develop a pro forma balance sheet using the judgmental approach and the use of the plug figure—external financing required—in this process. Under the judgmental approach, the values of certain balance sheet accounts are estimated and others are calculated, frequently on the basis of their relationship to sales. The firm's external financing is used as a balancing, or "plug," figure. A positive value for "external financing required" means that the firm must raise funds externally; a negative value indicates that funds are available for use in repaying debt, repurchasing stock, or increasing dividends.

Describe the weaknesses of the simplified approaches to pro forma preparation and the common uses of pro forma financial statements. Simplified approaches for pro forma statement preparation, although popular, can be criticized for assuming that the firm's past condition is an accurate predictor of the future and that certain variables can be forced to take on desired values. Pro forma statements are commonly used to analyze the firm's level of profitability and overall financial performance so that adjustments can be made to planned operations to achieve short-term financial goals.

SELF-TEST PROBLEMS   (Solutions in Appendix B)

ST 14–1 **Cash budget and pro forma balance sheet inputs** Jane McDonald, a financial analyst for Carroll Company, has prepared the following sales and cash disbursement estimates for the period February–June of the current year.

Month	Sales	Cash disbursements
February	$500	$400
March	600	300
April	400	600
May	200	500
June	200	200

Ms. McDonald notes that historically, 30% of sales have been for cash. Of *credit sales,* 70% are collected 1 month after the sale, and the remaining 30% are collected 2 months after the sale. The firm wishes to maintain a minimum ending balance in its cash account of $25. Balances above this amount would be invested in short-term government securities (marketable securities), whereas any deficits would be financed through short-term bank borrowing (notes payable). The beginning cash balance at April 1 is $115.

a. Prepare a cash budget for April, May, and June.
b. How much financing, if any, at a maximum would Carroll Company need to meet its obligations during this 3-month period?
c. If a pro forma balance sheet dated at the end of June were prepared from the information presented, give the size of each of the following: cash, notes payable, marketable securities, and accounts receivable.

 ST 14–2 **Pro forma income statement** Euro Designs, Inc., expects sales during 2001 to rise from the 2000 level of $3.5 million to $3.9 million. Due to a scheduled large loan payment, the interest expense in 2001 is expected to drop to

$325,000. The firm plans to increase its cash dividend payments during 2001 to $320,000. The company's year-end 2000 income statement follows.

Income Statement Euro Designs, Inc. for the year ended December 31, 2000	
Sales revenue	$3,500,000
Less: Cost of goods sold	1,925,000
Gross profits	$1,575,000
Less: Operating expenses	420,000
Operating profits	$1,155,000
Less: Interest expense	400,000
Net profits before taxes	$ 755,000
Less: Taxes (rate = 40%)	302,000
Net profits after taxes	$ 453,000
Less: Cash dividends	250,000
To retained earnings	$ 203,000

a. Use the *percent-of-sales method* to prepare a 2001 pro forma income statement for Euro Designs, Inc.
b. Explain why the statement may underestimate the company's actual 2001 pro forma income.

PROBLEMS

WARM-UP **14–1   Cash receipts**   A firm has actual sales of $65,000 in April and $60,000 in May. It expects sales of $70,000 in June and $100,000 in July and in August. Assuming that sales are the only source of cash inflows and that half of these are for cash and the remainder are collected evenly over the following 2 months, what are the firm's expected cash receipts for June, July, and August?

WARM-UP **14–2   Cash disbursements schedule**   Maris Brothers, Inc., needs a cash disbursement schedule for the months of April, May, and June. Use the format of Table 14.3 and the following information in its preparation.

Sales: February = $500,000; March = $500,000; April = $560,000; May = $610,000; June = $650,000; July = $650,000

Purchases: Purchases are calculated as 60% of the next month's sales, 10% of purchases are made in cash, 50% of purchases are paid for 1 month after purchase, and the remaining 40% of purchases are paid for 2 months after purchase.

Rent: The firm pays rent of $8,000 per month.

Wages and salaries: Base wage and salary costs are fixed at $6,000 per month plus a variable cost of 7% of the current month's sales.

Taxes: A tax payment of $54,500 is due in June.

Fixed asset outlays: New equipment costing $75,000 will be bought and paid for in April.

Interest payments: An interest payment of $30,000 is due in June.

Cash dividends: Dividends of $12,500 will be paid in April.

Principal repayments and retirements: No principal repayments or retirements are due during these months.

14–3 Cash budget—Basic   Grenoble Enterprises had sales of $50,000 in March and $60,000 in April. Forecast sales for May, June, and July are $70,000, $80,000, and $100,000, respectively. The firm has a cash balance of $5,000 on May 1 and wishes to maintain a minimum cash balance of $5,000. Given the following data, prepare and interpret a cash budget for the months of May, June, and July.

INTERMEDIATE

(1) The firm makes 20% of sales for cash, 60% are collected in the next month, and the remaining 20% are collected in the second month following sale.
(2) The firm receives other income of $2,000 per month.
(3) The firm's actual or expected purchases, all made for cash, are $50,000, $70,000, and $80,000 for the months of May through July, respectively.
(4) Rent is $3,000 per month.
(5) Wages and salaries are 10% of the previous month's sales.
(6) Cash dividends of $3,000 will be paid in June.
(7) Payment of principal and interest of $4,000 is due in June.
(8) A cash purchase of equipment costing $6,000 is scheduled in July.
(9) Taxes of $6,000 are due in June.

14–4 Cash budget—Advanced   The actual sales and purchases for Xenocore, Inc., for September and October 2000, along with its forecast sales and purchases for the period November 2000 through April 2001, follow.

CHALLENGE

Year	Month	Sales	Purchases
2000	September	$210,000	$120,000
2000	October	250,000	150,000
2000	November	170,000	140,000
2000	December	160,000	100,000
2001	January	140,000	80,000
2001	February	180,000	110,000
2001	March	200,000	100,000
2001	April	250,000	90,000

The firm makes 20% of all sales for cash and collects on 40% of its sales in each of the 2 months following the sale. Other cash inflows are expected to be $12,000 in September and April, $15,000 in January and March, and $27,000 in February. The firm pays cash for 10% of its purchases. It pays for 50% of its purchases in the following month and for 40% of its purchases 2 months later.

Wages and salaries amount to 20% of the preceding month's sales. Rent of $20,000 per month must be paid. Interest payments of $10,000 are due in January and April. A principal payment of $30,000 is also due in April. The firm expects to pay cash dividends of $20,000 in January and April. Taxes of $80,000 are due in April. The firm also intends to make a $25,000 cash purchase of fixed assets in December.

a. Assuming that the firm has a cash balance of $22,000 at the beginning of November, determine the end-of-month cash balances for each month, November through April.

b. Assuming that the firm wishes to maintain a $15,000 minimum cash balance, determine the required total financing or excess cash balance for each month, November through April.

c. If the firm were requesting a line of credit to cover needed financing for the period November to April, how large would this line have to be? Explain your answer.

WARM-UP   **14–5 Cash flow concepts** The following represent financial transactions that Johnsfield & Co. will be undertaking in the next planning period. For each transaction, check the statement or statements that will be affected immediately.

| | Statement | | |
Transaction	Cash budget	Pro forma income statement	Pro forma balance sheet
Cash sale			
Credit sale			
Accounts receivable are collected			
Asset with 5-year life is purchased			
Depreciation is taken			
Amortization of goodwill is taken			
Sale of common stock			
Retirement of outstanding bonds			
Fire insurance premium is paid for the next 3 years			

INTERMEDIATE   **14–6 Cash budget—Sensitivity analysis** Trotter Enterprises, Inc., has gathered the following data in order to plan for its cash requirements and short-term investment opportunities for October, November, and December. All amounts are shown in thousands of dollars.

| | October | | | November | | | December | | |
	Pessi-mistic	Most likely	Opti-mistic	Pessi-mistic	Most likely	Opti-mistic	Pessi-mistic	Most likely	Opti-mistic
Total cash receipts	$260	$342	$462	$200	$287	$366	$191	$294	$353
Total cash disbursements	285	326	421	203	261	313	287	332	315

a. Prepare a sensitivity analysis of Trotter's cash budget using −$20,000 as the beginning cash balance for October and a minimum required cash balance of $18,000.

b. Use the analysis prepared in part **a** to predict Trotter's financing needs and investment opportunities over the months of October, November, and December. Discuss how the knowledge of the timing and amounts involved can aid the planning process.

INTERMEDIATE 14–7 **Multiple cash budgets—Sensitivity analysis** Brownstein, Inc., expects sales of $100,000 during each of the next 3 months. It will make monthly purchases of $60,000 during this time. Wages and salaries are $10,000 per month plus 5% of sales. Brownstein expects to make a tax payment of $20,000 in the next month and a $15,000 purchase of fixed assets in the second month and to receive $8,000 in cash from the sale of an asset in the third month. All sales and purchases are for cash. Beginning cash and the minimum cash balance are assumed to be zero.

a. Construct a cash budget for the next 3 months.

b. Brownstein is unsure of the sales levels, but all other figures are certain. If the most pessimistic sales figure is $80,000 per month and the most optimistic is $120,000 per month, what are the monthly minimum and maximum ending cash balances that the firm can expect for each of the 1-month periods?

c. Briefly discuss how the financial manager can use the data in **a** and **b** to plan for financing needs.

INTERMEDIATE 14–8 **Pro forma income statement** The marketing department of Metroline Manufacturing estimates that its sales in 2001 will be $1.5 million. Interest expense is expected to remain unchanged at $35,000, and the firm plans to pay $70,000 in cash dividends during 2001. Metroline Manufacturing's income statement for the year ended December 31, 2000, is given below, followed (on page 606) by a breakdown of the firm's cost of goods sold and operating expenses into their fixed and variable cost components.

Income Statement Metroline Manufacturing for the year ended December 31, 2000	
Sales revenue	$1,400,000
Less: Cost of goods sold	910,000
Gross profits	$ 490,000
Less: Operating expenses	120,000
Operating profits	$ 370,000
Less: Interest expense	35,000
Net profits before taxes	$ 335,000
Less: Taxes (rate = 40%)	134,000
Net profits after taxes	$ 201,000
Less: Cash dividends	66,000
To retained earnings	$ 135,000

Fixed and Variable Cost Breakdown Metroline Manufacturing for the year ended December 31, 2000	
Cost of goods sold	
Fixed cost	$210,000
Variable cost	700,000
Total cost	$910,000
Operating expenses	
Fixed expenses	$ 36,000
Variable expenses	84,000
Total expenses	$120,000

a. Use the *percent-of-sales method* to prepare a pro forma income statement for the year ended December 31, 2001.
b. Use *fixed and variable cost data* to develop a pro forma income statement for the year ended December 31, 2001.
c. Compare and contrast the statements developed in **a** and **b**. Which statement will likely provide the better estimates of 2001 income? Explain why.

CHALLENGE   **14–9** Pro forma income statement—Sensitivity analysis   Allen Products, Inc., wants to do a sensitivity analysis for the coming year. The pessimistic prediction for sales is $900,000; the most likely amount of sales is $1,125,000; and the optimistic prediction is $1,280,000. Allen's income statement for the most recent year is as follows.

Income Statement Allen Products, Inc. for the year ended December 31, 2000	
Sales revenue	$937,500
Less: Cost of goods sold	421,875
Gross profits	$515,625
Less: Operating expenses	234,375
Operating profits	$281,250
Less: Interest expense	30,000
Net profits before taxes	$251,250
Less: Taxes (rate = .25)	62,813
Net profits after taxes	$188,437

a. Use the *percent-of-sales method,* the income statement for December 31, 2000, and the sales revenue estimates to develop pessimistic, most likely, and optimistic pro forma income statements for the coming year.

b. Explain how the percent-of-sales method could result in an overstatement of profits for the pessimistic case and an understatement of profits for the most likely and optimistic cases.

c. Restate the pro forma income statements prepared in part **a** to incorporate the following assumptions about costs:

$250,000 of the cost of goods sold is fixed; the rest is variable.
$180,000 of the operating expenses is fixed; the rest is variable.
All of the interest expense is fixed.

d. Compare your findings in part **c** to your findings in part **a**. Do your observations confirm your explanation in part **b**?

INTERMEDIATE 14–10 **Pro forma balance sheet—Basic**   Leonard Industries wishes to prepare a pro forma balance sheet for December 31, 2001. The firm expects 2001 sales to total $3,000,000. The following information has been gathered.

(1) A minimum cash balance of $50,000 is desired.
(2) Marketable securities are expected to remain unchanged.
(3) Accounts receivable represent 10% of sales.
(4) Inventories represent 12% of sales.
(5) A new machine costing $90,000 will be acquired during 2001. Total depreciation for the year will be $32,000.
(6) Accounts payable represent 14% of sales.
(7) Accruals, other current liabilities, long-term debt, and common stock are expected to remain unchanged.
(8) The firm's net profit margin is 4%, and it expects to pay out $70,000 in cash dividends during 2001.
(9) The December 31, 2000, balance sheet follows.

	Balance Sheet Leonard Industries December 31, 2000		
Assets		**Liabilities and equities**	
Cash	$ 45,000	Accounts payable	$ 395,000
Marketable securities	15,000	Accruals	60,000
Accounts receivable	255,000	Other current liabilities	30,000
Inventories	340,000	Total current liabilities	$ 485,000
Total current assets	$ 655,000	Long-term debt	$ 350,000
Net fixed assets	$ 600,000	Common stock	$ 200,000
Total assets	$1,255,000	Retained earnings	$ 220,000
		Total liabilities and stockholders' equity	$1,255,000

a. Use the *judgmental approach* to prepare a pro forma balance sheet dated December 31, 2001, for Leonard Industries.

b. How much, if any, additional financing will Leonard Industries require in 2001? Discuss.

c. Could Leonard Industries adjust its planned 2001 dividend to avoid the situation described in **b**? Explain how.

INTERMEDIATE 14–11   **Pro forma balance sheet**   Peabody & Peabody has 2000 sales of $10 million. It wishes to analyze expected performance and financing needs for 2002—2 years ahead. Given the following information, answer questions **a** and **b**.

(1) The percent of sales for items that vary directly with sales are as follows:
   Accounts receivable, 12%
   Inventory, 18%
   Accounts payable, 14%
   Net profit margin, 3%
(2) Marketable securities and other current liabilities are expected to remain unchanged.
(3) A minimum cash balance of $480,000 is desired.
(4) A new machine costing $650,000 will be acquired in 2001, and equipment costing $850,000 will be purchased in 2002. Total depreciation in 2001 is forecast as $290,000, and in 2002 $390,000 of depreciation will be taken.
(5) Accruals are expected to rise to $500,000 by the end of 2002.
(6) No sale or retirement of long-term debt is expected.
(7) No sale or repurchase of common stock is expected.
(8) The dividend payout of 50% of net profits is expected to continue.
(9) Sales are expected to be $11 million in 2001 and $12 million in 2002.
(10) The December 31, 2000, balance sheet follows.

Balance Sheet
Peabody & Peabody
December 31, 2000
($000)

Assets		Liabilities and equities	
Cash	$ 400	Accounts payable	$1,400
Marketable securities	200	Accruals	400
Accounts receivable	1,200	Other current liabilities	80
Inventories	1,800	Total current liabilities	$1,880
Total current assets	$3,600	Long-term debt	$2,000
Net fixed assets	$4,000	Common equity	$3,720
Total assets	$7,600	Total liabilities and stockholders' equity	$7,600

a. Prepare a pro forma balance sheet dated December 31, 1999.
b. Discuss the financing changes suggested by the statement prepared in **a**.

   14–12   **Integrative—Pro forma statements**   Red Queen Restaurants wishes to prepare financial plans. Use the financial statements and the other information provided in what follows on page 609 to prepare the financial plans.

CHALLENGE

Income Statement
Red Queen Restaurants
for the year ended December 31, 2000

Sales revenue	$800,000
Less: Cost of goods sold	600,000
Gross profits	$200,000
Less: Operating expenses	100,000
Net profits before taxes	$100,000
Less: Taxes (rate = 40%)	40,000
Net profits after taxes	$ 60,000
Less: Cash dividends	20,000
To retained earnings	$ 40,000

Balance Sheet
Red Queen Restaurants
December 31, 2000

Assets		Liabilities and equities	
Cash	$ 32,000	Accounts payable	$100,000
Marketable securities	18,000	Taxes payable	20,000
Accounts receivable	150,000	Other current liabilities	5,000
Inventories	100,000	Total current liabilities	$125,000
Total current assets	$300,000	Long-term debt	$200,000
Net fixed assets	$350,000	Common stock	$150,000
Total assets	$650,000	Retained earnings	$175,000
		Total liabilities and stockholders' equity	$650,000

The following financial data are also available:
(1) The firm has estimated that its sales for 2001 will be $900,000.
(2) The firm expects to pay $35,000 in cash dividends in 2001.
(3) The firm wishes to maintain a minimum cash balance of $30,000.
(4) Accounts receivable represent approximately 18% of annual sales.
(5) The firm's ending inventory will change directly with changes in sales in 2001.
(6) A new machine costing $42,000 will be purchased in 2001. Total depreciation for 2001 will be $17,000.
(7) Accounts payable will change directly in response to changes in sales in 2001.
(8) Taxes payable will equal one-fourth of the tax liability on the pro forma income statement.
(9) Marketable securities, other current liabilities, long-term debt, and common stock will remain unchanged.

a. Prepare a pro forma income statement for the year ended December 31, 2001, using the *percent-of-sales method.*
b. Prepare a pro forma balance sheet dated December 31, 2001, using the *judgmental approach.*
c. Analyze these statements, and discuss the resulting *external financing required.*

   14–13 **Integrative—Pro forma statements** Provincial Imports, Inc., has assembled statements and information to prepare financial plans for the coming year.

CHALLENGE

Income Statement
Provincial Imports, Inc.
for the year ended December 31, 2000

Sales revenue	$5,000,000
Less: Cost of goods sold	2,750,000
Gross profits	$2,250,000
Less: Operating expenses	850,000
Operating profits	$1,400,000
Less: Interest expense	200,000
Net profits before taxes	$1,200,000
Less: Taxes (rate = 40%)	480,000
Net profits after taxes	$ 720,000
Less: Cash dividends	288,000
To retained earnings	$ 432,000

Balance Sheet
Provincial Imports, Inc.
December 31, 2000

Assets		Liabilities and equities	
Cash	$ 200,000	Accounts payable	$ 700,000
Marketable securities	275,000	Taxes payable	95,000
Accounts receivable	625,000	Notes payable	200,000
Inventories	500,000	Other current liabilities	5,000
Total current assets	$1,600,000	Total current liabilities	$1,000,000
Net fixed assets	$1,400,000	Long-term debt	$ 550,000
Total assets	$3,000,000	Common stock	$ 75,000
		Retained earnings	$1,375,000
		Total liabilities and equity	$3,000,000

Information related to financial projections for the year 2001:
(1) Projected sales are $6,000,000.
(2) Cost of goods sold includes $1,000,000 in fixed costs.
(3) Operating expense includes $250,000 in fixed costs.
(4) Interest expense will remain unchanged.
(5) The firm will pay cash dividends amounting to 40% of net profits after taxes.
(6) Cash and inventories will double.
(7) Marketable securities, notes payable, long-term debt, and common stock will remain unchanged.
(8) Accounts receivable, accounts payable, and other current liabilities will change in direct response to the change in sales.
(9) A new computer system costing $356,000 will be purchased during the year. Total depreciation expense for the year will be $110,000.

a. Prepare a pro forma income statement for the year ending December 31, 2001, using the information given and the *percent-of-sales method*.
b. Prepare a pro forma balance sheet as of December 31, 2001, using the information given and the *judgmental approach*. Include a reconciliation of the retained earnings account.
c. Analyze these statements, and discuss the resulting *external financing required*.

CASE CHAPTER 14	**Preparing Martin Manufacturing's 2001 Pro Forma Financial Statements**

To improve its competitive position, Martin Manufacturing is planning to implement a major plant-modernization program. Included will be construction of a state-of-the-art manufacturing facility that will cost $400 million in 2001 and is expected to lower the variable cost per ton of steel. Terri Spiro, an experienced budget analyst, has been charged with preparing a forecast of the firm's 2001 financial position assuming construction of the proposed new facility. She plans to use the 2000 financial statements presented on page 168, along with the key projected financial data summarized in the following table.

Key Projected Financial Data (2001) Martin Manufacturing Company ($000)	
Data item	Value
Sales revenue	$6,500,000
Minimum cash balance	$25,000
Inventory turnover (times)	7.0
Average collection period	50 days
Fixed asset purchases	$400,000
Dividend payments	$20,000
Depreciation expense	$185,000
Interest expense	$97,000
Accounts payable increase	20%
Accruals and long-term debt	Unchanged
Notes payable, preferred and common stock	Unchanged

Required

a. Use the historic and projected financial data provided to prepare a pro forma income statement for the year ended December 31, 2001. (*Hint:* Use the *percent-of-sales method* to estimate all values *except* for depreciation expense and interest expense, which have been estimated by management and included in the table.)

b. Use the projected financial data along with relevant data from the pro forma income statement prepared in **a** to prepare the pro forma balance sheet at December 31, 2001. (*Hint:* Use the *judgmental approach*.)

c. Will Martin Manufacturing Company need to obtain *external financing* to fund construction of the proposed facility? Explain.

WEB EXERCISE

GOTO web site metalab.unc.edu/reference/moss/usbus. Under INDUSTRY RESEARCH click on Key Industry Overviews.

1. What are the printed sources of Multi-Industry Overviews?
2. What are the Related Internet Links listed on this screen?

GOTO web site www.edgeonline.com.

3. What tools are available in the INTERACTIVE TOOLBOX?

Select Profit and Loss Statement from the menu in the INTERACTIVE TOOLBOX.

4. Enter the following account balances into the Profit and Loss Statement.

Net sales	$5,000,000
Salaries and wages	2,000,000
Rent	1,000,000
Light, heat, and power	500,000
Other expenses	100,000
Provision for income tax	100,000
In all other blanks, enter a	0

Click CALCULATE. What is the net profit after income tax?

To gather information useful for sales forecasting, financial managers need data that relate to the market for their products. To see some data sources that could be useful for sales forecasting, GOTO web site www.census.gov.

5. What is the U.S. population?

Select the state in which you live or go to school. Click GET STATE PROFILE. Double click on *the county in which your home or school is located.* Click on the 19xx Economic Census. (Choose the latest available year.)

6. In the country data, how many manufacturing establishments are there?
7. In the state data, how many manufacturing establishments are there?
8. In the United States data, how many manufacturing establishments are there?
9. Which is the largest city in your county? What is its population?

CHAPTER

15

Working Capital and Short-Term Financing

LEARNING GOALS

LG1 Understand the two definitions of net working capital and the trade-off between profitability and risk as it relates to changing levels of current assets and current liabilities.

LG2 Discuss, in terms of profitability and risk, the aggressive financing strategy and the conservative financing strategy for meeting the firm's financing requirement.

LG3 Review the key characteristics of the two major sources of spontaneous short-term financing—accounts payable and accruals.

LG4 Analyze credit terms offered by suppliers to determine whether to take or give up cash discounts and whether to stretch accounts payable.

LG5 Describe the interest rates and basic types of unsecured bank sources of short-term loans, commercial paper, and short-term international loans.

LG6 Explain the characteristics of secured short-term loans and the use of accounts receivable and inventory as short-term loan collateral.

LG1

15.1 Net Working Capital Fundamentals

The firm's balance sheet provides information about the structure of a firm's investments on the one hand and the structure of its financing sources on the other. The structures chosen should consistently lead to the maximization of the value of the owners' investment in the firm.

Important components of the firm's structure include the level of investment in current assets and the extent of current liability financing. In U.S. manufacturing firms, current assets currently account for about 40 percent of total assets;

Short and Sweet Financing

In the last decade alone, New England Confectionery Company (NECCO®) has sold more than 72 *billion* Sweethearts® Conversation Hearts. During peak production periods, 100,000 pounds of the famous candies are made each day, and the majority are sold during the 6 weeks from January 1 to February 14 each year. Firms that depend heavily on seasonal items—valentine candies or snowshoes, for example—need effective strategies with which to manage buildups of inventory and accounts receivable before they can turn these back into cash. Indeed, all firms have a similar need, though to a lesser degree. Various strategies exist for managing the financing of the firm's recurring operations, using both short-term and long-term financing. This chapter explains these key short-term financing strategies.

short-term financial management
Management of current assets and current liabilities.

current liabilities represent about 26 percent of total financing. Therefore, it should not be surprising to learn that **short-term financial management**—managing current assets and current liabilities—is one of the financial manager's most important and time-consuming activities. A study of Fortune 1000 firms found that more than one-third of financial management time is spent managing current assets and about one-fourth of financial management time is spent managing current liabilities.[1]

1. Lawrence J. Gitman and Charles E. Maxwell, "Financial Activities of Major U.S. Firms: Survey and Analysis of Fortune's 1000," *Financial Management* (Winter 1985), pp. 57–65.

The goal of short-term financial management is to manage each of the firm's current assets and current liabilities to achieve a balance between profitability and risk that contributes positively to the firm's value. Too much investment in current assets reduces profitability, whereas too little investment increases the risk of not being able to pay debts as they come due. Too little current liability financing also reduces profitability, whereas too much of this financing increases the risk of not being able to pay debts as they come due. Any of these situations generally leads to lower firm value.

This chapter does not discuss the optimal level of current assets and current liabilities that a firm should have. That issue is unresolved in the financial literature. Here we first consider the basic relationship between current assets and current liabilities, and then look at the key features of the major sources of short-term (current liability) financing. Subsequent chapters address the management of current assets.

Net Working Capital

working capital
Current assets, which represent the portion of investment that circulates from one form to another in the ordinary conduct of business.

Current assets, commonly called **working capital,** represent the portion of investment that circulates from one form to another in the ordinary conduct of business. This idea embraces the recurring transition from cash to inventories to receivables and back to cash that forms the **operating cycle** of the firm. As cash substitutes, *marketable securities* are considered part of working capital. Similarly, *prepaid expenses* are included as working capital because they represent services owed to the company, thereby eliminating the need for later cash outlays.

operating cycle
The recurring transition of a firm's working capital from cash to inventories to receivables and back to cash.

Current liabilities represent the firm's short-term financing, because they include all debts of the firm that come due (must be paid) in 1 year or less. These debts usually include amounts owed to suppliers (accounts payable), banks (notes payable), and employees and governments (accruals), among others.

Hint   A firm can lower its working capital if it can speed up its operating cycle. For example, if a firm accepts bank credit (like a Visa card), it will receive cash sooner after the sale is transacted than if it has to wait until the customer pays its accounts receivable.

As noted in Chapter 4, **net working capital** is commonly defined as the difference between the firm's current assets and its current liabilities. When the current assets exceed the current liabilities, the firm has *positive net working capital.* In this most common case, net working capital is alternatively defined as *the portion of the firm's current assets financed with long-term funds* (the sum of long-term debt and stockholders' equity). Because current liabilities represent the firm's sources of short-term funds, the amount by which current assets exceed current liabilities must be financed with long-term funds. When current assets are less than current liabilities, the firm has *negative net working capital.* In this less common case, net working capital is the portion of the firm's fixed assets financed with current liabilities. This conclusion follows from the balance sheet equation: assets equal liabilities plus equity.

net working capital
The difference between the firm's current assets and its current liabilities, or, alternatively, the portion of current assets financed with long-term funds; can be *positive* or *negative.*

The conversion of current assets from inventory to receivables to cash provides the source of cash used to pay the current liabilities. The cash outlays for current liabilities are relatively predictable. When an obligation is incurred, the firm generally knows when the corresponding payment will be due. What is difficult to predict are the cash inflows—the conversion of the current assets to more liquid forms. The more predictable its cash inflows, the less net working capital a firm needs. Because most firms are unable to match cash inflows to outflows

Hint   Stated differently, some portion of current assets is usually financed with long-term funds.

with certainty, current assets that more than cover outflows for current liabilities are usually necessary. In general, the greater the margin by which a firm's current assets cover its current liabilities, the better able it will be to pay its bills as they come due.

The Trade-off Between Profitability and Risk

profitability
The relationship between revenues and costs generated by using the firm's assets—both current and fixed—in productive activities.

risk (of technical insolvency)
The probability that a firm will be unable to pay its bills as they come due.

technically insolvent
Describes a firm that is unable to pay its bills as they come due.

A trade-off exists between a firm's profitability and its risk. **Profitability,** in this context, is the relationship between revenues and costs generated by using the firm's assets—both current and fixed—in productive activities. A firm's profits can be increased by (1) increasing revenues or (2) decreasing costs. **Risk,** in the context of short-term financial management, is the probability that a firm will be unable to pay its bills as they come due. A firm that cannot pay its bills as they come due is said to be **technically insolvent.** It is generally assumed that the greater the firm's net working capital, the lower its risk. In other words, the more net working capital, the more liquid the firm and therefore the lower its risk of becoming technically insolvent. Using these definitions of profitability and risk, we can demonstrate the trade-off between them by considering separately changes in current assets and current liabilities.

Changes in Current Assets

How changing the level of the firm's current assets affects its profitability–risk trade-off can be demonstrated using the ratio of current assets to total assets. This ratio indicates the *percentage of total assets* that is current. For purposes of illustration, we will assume that the level of total assets remains unchanged.[2] The effects on both profitability and risk of an increase or decrease in this ratio are summarized in the upper portion of Table 15.1. When the ratio increases—that is, when current assets increase—profitability decreases. Why? Because current assets are less profitable than fixed assets. Fixed assets are more profitable

TABLE 15.1   **Effects of Changing Ratios on Profits and Risk**

Ratio	Change in ratio	Effect on profit	Effect on risk
Current assets / Total assets	Increase	Decrease	Decrease
	Decrease	Increase	Increase
Current liabilities / Total assets	Increase	Increase	Increase
	Decrease	Decrease	Decrease

---

2. The level of total assets is assumed to be *constant* in this and the following discussion to isolate the effect of changing asset and financing mixes on the firm's profitability and risk.

Hint   It is generally easier to turn receivables into the more liquid asset cash than it is to turn inventory into cash. As we will see later in this chapter, the firm can sell its receivables for cash. Inventory has to be sold and then converted to a receivable before it becomes cash.

because they add more value to the product than that provided by current assets. Without fixed assets, the firm could not produce the product.

The risk effect, however, decreases as the ratio of current assets to total assets increases. The increase in current assets increases net working capital, thereby reducing the risk of technical insolvency. In addition, as you go down the asset side of the balance sheet, the risk associated with the assets increases: Investment in cash and marketable securities is less risky than investment in accounts receivable, inventories, and fixed assets. Accounts receivable investment is less risky than investment in inventories and fixed assets. Investment in inventories is less risky than investment in fixed assets. The nearer an asset is to cash, the less risky it is. The opposite effects on profit and risk result from a decrease in the ratio of current assets to total assets.

Changes in Current Liabilities

How changing the level of the firm' s current liabilities affects its profitability–risk trade-off can be demonstrated by using the ratio of current liabilities to total assets. This ratio indicates the percentage of total assets that has been financed with current liabilities. Again, assuming that total assets remain unchanged, the effects on both profitability and risk of an increase or decrease in the ratio are summarized in the lower portion of Table 15.1. When the ratio increases, profitability increases. Why? Because the firm uses more of the less expensive current-liability financing and less long-term financing. Current liabilities are less expensive because only notes payable, which represent about 20 percent of the typical manufacturer's current liabilities, have a cost. The other current liabilities are basically debts on which the firm pays no charge or interest. However, when the ratio of current liabilities to total assets increases, the risk of technical insolvency also increases, because the increase in current liabilities in turn decreases net working capital. The opposite effects on profit and risk result from a decrease in the ratio of current liabilities to total assets.

? Review Questions

15–1   Why is *short-term financial management* one of the most important and time-consuming activities of the financial manager? What are the two most common definitions of *net working capital?*

15–2   What relationship would you expect between the predictability of a firm's cash inflows and the firm's required level of net working capital? How are net working capital, liquidity, and *risk of technical insolvency* related?

15–3   Why does an increase in the ratio of current to total assets decrease both profits and risk as measured by net working capital? How do changes in the ratio of current liabilities to total assets affect profitability and risk?

15.2 Net Working Capital Strategies

One of the most important decisions that must be made with respect to current assets and liabilities is how current liabilities will be used to finance current assets. The amount of current liabilities that is available is limited by the dollar amount of purchases in the case of accounts payable, by the dollar amount of accrued liabilities in the case of accruals, and by the amount of seasonal borrowing considered acceptable by lenders in the case of notes payable and commercial paper. Lenders make short-term loans to allow a firm to finance seasonal buildups of accounts receivable or inventory. *They generally do not lend short-term money for long-term uses.*[3]

There are two basic strategies for determining an appropriate mix of short-term (current liability) and long-term financing—the aggressive strategy and the conservative strategy. Before discussing the cost and risk considerations of these strategies, we will consider the permanent and seasonal components of the firm's financing need. In these discussions, we use the alternative definition that defines net working capital as *the portion of current assets financed with long-term funds.*

permanent need
Financing requirements for the firm's fixed assets plus the permanent portion of the firm's current assets; these requirements remain unchanged over the year.

seasonal need
Financing requirements for the temporary portion of current assets, which vary over the year.

The Firm's Financing Need

The firm's financing requirements can be separated into a permanent and a seasonal need. The **permanent need,** which consists of fixed assets plus the permanent portion of the firm's current assets, remains unchanged over the year. The **seasonal need,** which consists of the temporary portion of current assets, varies over the year.

Example ▼ Nicholson Company's estimate of current, fixed, and total asset requirements on a monthly basis for the coming year is given in columns 1, 2, and 3 of Table 15.2. Note that the relatively stable level of total assets over the year reflects, for convenience, an absence of growth by the firm. Columns 4 and 5 break down the total requirement into permanent and seasonal components. The permanent component (column 4) is the lowest level of total assets during the period; the seasonal portion is the difference between the total funds requirement for each month and the permanent funds requirement.

By comparing the firm's fixed assets (column 2) to its permanent funds requirement (column 4), we see that the permanent funds requirement exceeds the firm's level of fixed assets. That is, *a portion of the firm's current assets is permanent,* because they are apparently always being replaced. The size of Nicholson's permanent component of current assets is $800. This value represents the base level of current assets that remains on the firm's books throughout the entire year. This value can also be found by subtracting the level of fixed

---

3. The rationale for, techniques of, and parties to short-term business loans are discussed in detail later in this chapter. The primary source of short-term loans to businesses—commercial banks—make these loans *only for seasonal or self-liquidating purposes* such as temporary buildups of accounts receivable or inventory.

TABLE 15.2   Estimated Funds Requirements for Nicholson Company

Month	Current assets (1)	Fixed assets (2)	Total assets[a] [(1) + (2)] (3)	Permanent funds requirement[b] (4)	Seasonal funds requirement [(3) − (4)] (5)
January	$4,000	$13,000	$17,000	$13,800	$3,200
February	3,000	13,000	16,000	13,800	2,200
March	2,000	13,000	15,000	13,800	1,200
April	1,000	13,000	14,000	13,800	200
May	800	13,000	13,800	13,800	0
June	1,500	13,000	14,500	13,800	700
July	3,000	13,000	16,000	13,800	2,200
August	3,700	13,000	16,700	13,800	2,900
September	4,000	13,000	17,000	13,800	3,200
October	5,000	13,000	18,000	13,800	4,200
November	3,000	13,000	16,000	13,800	2,200
December	2,000	13,000	15,000	13,800	1,200
Monthly average[c]				$13,800	$1,950

[a]This represents the firm's total funds requirement.
[b]This represents the minimum total asset requirement.
[c]Found by summing the monthly amounts for the 12 months and dividing the resulting totals by 12.

assets from the permanent funds requirement ($13,800 − $13,000 = $800). The relationships presented in Table 15.2 are depicted graphically in Figure 15.1.

An Aggressive Financing Strategy

aggressive financing strategy
Strategy by which the firm finances at least its seasonal requirements, and possibly some of its permanent requirements, with short-term funds and the balance of its permanent requirements with long-term funds.

An **aggressive financing strategy** is one by which the firm finances at least its seasonal requirements, and possibly some of its permanent requirements, with short-term funds. The balance is financed with long-term funds.

Example ▼ Nicholson Company's permanent and seasonal funds requirements were shown in Table 15.2. An aggressive strategy would finance the permanent portion of the firm's funds requirement ($13,800) with long-term funds and the seasonal portion (ranging from $0 in May to $4,200 in October) with short-term funds. Much of the short-term financing would likely be in the form of *trade credit* (i.e., accounts payable). The application of this financing strategy to the firm's total funds requirement is illustrated graphically in Figure 15.2.

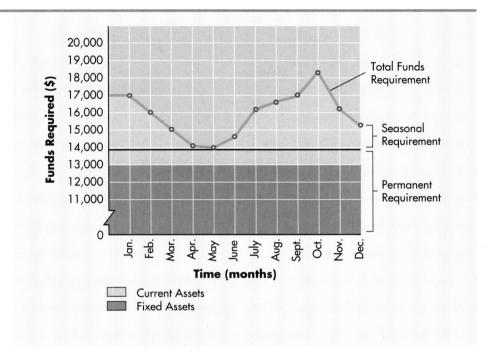

FIGURE 15.1

Funds Requirements
Nicholson Company's estimated funds requirements

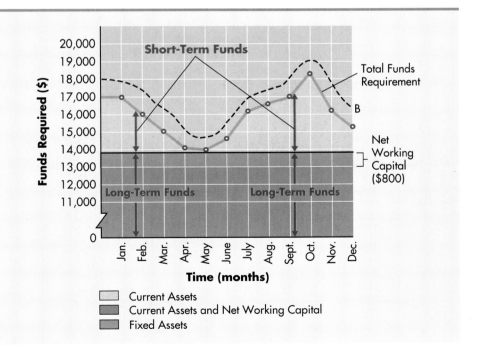

FIGURE 15.2

Aggressive Strategy
Applying the aggressive strategy to Nicholson Company's funds requirements

Cost Considerations

Under the aggressive strategy, Nicholson's average short-term borrowing (seasonal funds requirement) is $1,950, and average long-term borrowing (permanent funds requirement) is $13,800 (see columns 4 and 5 of Table 15.2). If the annual cost of short-term funds needed by Nicholson is 3 percent and the annual cost of long-term financing is 11 percent, the total cost of the financing strategy is estimated as follows:

$$
\begin{aligned}
\text{Cost of short-term financing} &= 3\% \times \$ 1,950 = \$ 58.50 \\
\text{Cost of long-term financing} &= 11\% \times 13,800 = \underline{1,518.00} \\
\text{Total cost} & \underline{\$1,576.50}
\end{aligned}
$$

The relatively low cost of short-term financing (3 percent) results from using a high amount of free trade credit (a topic discussed later in the chapter).

Risk Considerations

The aggressive strategy operates with minimum net working capital, because only the permanent portion of the firm's current assets is shown financed with long-term funds. For Nicholson Company, as shown in Figure 15.2, the level of net working capital is $800, which is the amount of permanent current assets ($13,800 permanent funds requirement − $13,000 fixed assets = $800).

The aggressive financing strategy is risky not only from the standpoint of low net working capital, but also because it forces the firm to draw as heavily as possible on its short-term sources of funds to meet seasonal fluctuations in its requirements. If the total requirement turns out to be, say, the level represented by dashed line B in Figure 15.2, the firm may find it difficult to obtain longer-term funds quickly enough to satisfy short-term needs. This risk associated with the aggressive strategy results because a firm has only a limited amount of short-term borrowing capacity. If it draws too heavily on this capacity, unexpected needs for funds may become difficult to satisfy.

A Conservative Financing Strategy

conservative financing strategy
Strategy by which the firm finances all projected funds requirements with long-term funds and uses short-term financing only for emergencies or unexpected outflows.

The most **conservative financing strategy** should be to finance all projected funds requirements with long-term funds and use short-term financing only for emergencies or unexpected outflows of funds. It is difficult to imagine how this strategy could actually be implemented, because the use of short-term financing tools, such as accounts payable and accruals, is virtually unavoidable. In illustrating this strategy, however, the spontaneous short-term financing provided by payables and accruals is ignored.

Example ▼ Figure 15.3 shows the application of the conservative strategy to the total funds requirement for Nicholson Company. Long-term financing of $18,000, which equals the firm's peak need (during October), is used under this strategy. Therefore, all the funds required over the 1-year period, including the entire ▲ $18,000 forecast for October, are financed with long-term funds.

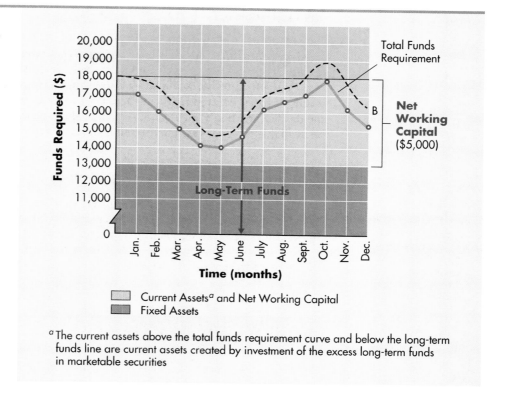

FIGURE 15.3

Conservative Strategy
Applying the conservative strategy to Nicholson Company's funds requirements

*The current assets above the total funds requirement curve and below the long-term funds line are current assets created by investment of the excess long-term funds in marketable securities

Cost Considerations

Here, as in the preceding example, we use 11 percent as the annual cost of long-term funds. Because the average long-term financing balance under the conservative financing strategy is $18,000, the total cost of this strategy is $1,980 (11% × $18,000). Compared to the total cost of $1,576.50 for the aggressive strategy, the conservative strategy is more expensive. The reason for this higher expense is apparent in Figure 15.3. The area above the total funds requirement curve and below the long-term funds, or borrowing, line represents the level of funds that are not actually needed but for which the firm is paying interest. Although the financial manager invests these excess available funds in marketable securities so as partially to offset their borrowing cost, it is unlikely that the firm can earn a large enough return on these funds to cause the cost of this strategy to fall below the cost of the aggressive strategy.[4]

---

4. For example, assume that under the conservative strategy, Nicholson Company can earn 2% per year, after transaction costs, on its average investable balance of $2,250—the $18,000 long-term financing − $13,800 average permanent funds requirement (from bottom of column 4 of Table 15.2) − $1,950 average seasonal funds requirement (from bottom of column 5 of Table 15.2). The firm would earn $45 (2% × $2,250), which reduces its cost of the conservative strategy to $1,935 ($1,980 cost − $45 investment return)—an amount still well above the $1,576.50 cost of the aggressive strategy. Although the return on the investable balance does reduce the cost of the conservative strategy, for conceptual clarity this small effect is ignored throughout the chapter.

Risk Considerations

The $5,000 of net working capital ($18,000 long-term financing − $13,000 fixed assets) associated with the conservative strategy should mean a very low level of risk.[5] The firm's risk should also be lowered because the strategy does not require the firm to use any of its limited short-term borrowing capacity. In other words, if total required financing actually turns out to be the level represented by the dashed line B in Figure 15.3, sufficient short-term borrowing capacity should be available to cover the unexpected needs and avoid technical insolvency.

Conservative Versus Aggressive Strategy

Career Key

Management will decide whether to aggressively or conservatively finance the firm's funds requirements. This decision is, again, made using the risk-return concept. Management will decide how much risk they are willing to live with in order to get a higher return.

Unlike the aggressive strategy, the conservative strategy requires the firm to pay interest on unneeded funds. The lower cost of the aggressive strategy therefore makes it more profitable than the conservative strategy. However, the aggressive strategy involves much more risk. For most firms, a trade-off between the extremes represented by these two strategies should result in an acceptable financing strategy.

? Review Question

15–4   Describe both the *aggressive financing strategy* and the *conservative financing strategy* for meeting a firm's funds requirements. Compare and contrast the effects of each of these strategies on the firm's profitability and risk.

15.3 Spontaneous Sources of Short-Term Financing

spontaneous financing
Financing that arises from the normal operations of the firm, the two major short-term sources of which are accounts payable and accruals.

unsecured short-term financing
Short-term financing obtained without pledging specific assets as collateral.

Spontaneous financing arises from the normal operations of the firm. The two major spontaneous sources of short-term financing are accounts payable and accruals. As the firm's sales increase, accounts payable increase in response to the increased purchases required to produce at higher levels. Also in response to increasing sales, the firm's accruals increase as wages and taxes rise due to greater labor requirements and the increased taxes on the firm's increased earnings. There is normally no explicit cost attached to either of these current liabilities, although they do have certain implicit costs. In addition, both are forms of **unsecured short-term financing**—short-term financing obtained without pledging specific assets as collateral. The firm should take advantage of these "interest-free" sources of unsecured short-term financing whenever possible.

---

5. The level of net working capital is constant throughout the year, because the firm has $5,000 in current assets that are fully financed with long-term funds. Because the portion of the $5,000 in excess of the scheduled level of current assets is assumed to be held as marketable securities, the firm's current asset balance increases to this level.

Accounts Payable

Hint
An account payable of a purchaser is an account receivable on the supplier's books. Chapter 17 highlights the key strategies and considerations involved in extending credit to customers.

Accounts payable are the major source of unsecured short-term financing for business firms. They result from transactions in which merchandise is purchased but no formal note is signed to show the purchaser's liability to the seller. The purchaser in effect agrees to pay the supplier the amount required in accordance with credit terms normally stated on the supplier's invoice. The discussion of accounts payable here is presented from the viewpoint of the purchaser.

Credit Terms

The supplier's credit terms state the credit period, the size of the cash discount offered (if any), the cash discount period, and the date the credit period begins. Each of these aspects of a firm's credit terms is concisely stated in such expressions as "2/10 net 30 EOM." These expressions are a shorthand containing the key information about the length of the credit period (30 days), the cash discount (2 percent), the cash discount period (10 days), and the date the credit period begins, which is the end of each month (EOM).

credit period
The number of days until full payment of an account payable is required.

Credit Period   The **credit period** of an account payable is the number of days until full payment is required. Regardless of whether a cash discount is offered, the credit period associated with any transaction must always be indicated. Credit periods usually range from zero to 120 days. Most credit terms refer to the credit period as the "net period." The word *net* indicates that the full amount of the purchase must be paid within the number of days indicated from the beginning of the credit period. For example, "net 30 days" means that the firm must make *full payment* within 30 days of the beginning of the credit period.

cash discount
A percentage deduction from the purchase price if the buyer pays within a specified time.

Cash Discount   A **cash discount,** if offered as part of the credit terms, is a percentage deduction from the purchase price if the buyer pays within a specified time. Cash discounts normally range from between 1 and 5 percent. A 2 percent cash discount indicates that the purchaser of $100 of merchandise need pay only $98 if payment is made within the specified shorter interval.

cash discount period
The number of days after the beginning of the credit period during which the cash discount is available.

Cash Discount Period   The **cash discount period** is the number of days after the beginning of the credit period during which the cash discount is available. Typically, the cash discount period is between 5 and 20 days. Often, large customers of smaller firms use their position as key customers as a form of leverage, enabling them to take cash discounts far beyond the end of the cash discount period. This strategy, although ethically questionable, is not uncommon.

date of invoice
Indicates that the beginning of the credit period is the date on the invoice for the purchase.

Beginning of the Credit Period   The beginning of the credit period is stated as part of the supplier's credit terms. One of the most common designations for the beginning of the credit period is the **date of invoice.**[6] Both the cash discount

---

6. Occasionally, firms receive invoices before receiving the actual merchandise purchased. In these situations the beginning of the credit period is not tied to the invoice date, which could be 30 days prior to the receipt of goods.

end of month (EOM)
Indicates that the credit period for all purchases made within a given month begins on the first day of the month immediately following.

period and the net period are then measured from the invoice date. **End of month (EOM)** indicates that the credit period for all purchases made within a given month begins on the first day of the month immediately following. These terms simplify record keeping on the part of the firm extending credit. For an example comparing these two credit period beginnings, see the book's web site at **www.awlonline.com/gitman.**

To maintain their competitive position, firms within an industry generally offer the same terms. In many cases, stated credit terms are not the terms that are actually given to a customer. Special arrangements, or "deals," are made to provide certain customers with more favorable terms. The prospective purchaser is wise to look closely at the credit terms of suppliers when making a purchase decision. In many instances, concessions may be available.

Analyzing Credit Terms

The credit terms that a firm is offered by its suppliers allow it to delay payments for its purchases. Because the supplier's cost of having its money tied up in merchandise after it is sold is probably reflected in the purchase price, the purchaser is already indirectly paying for this benefit. The purchaser should therefore carefully analyze credit terms to determine the best trade credit strategy. If a firm is extended credit terms that include a cash discount, it has two options—to take the cash discount or to give it up.

Taking the Cash Discount If a firm intends to take a cash discount, it should pay on the last day of the discount period. There is no cost associated with taking a cash discount.

Example ▼ Lawrence Industries, operator of a small chain of video stores, purchased $1,000 worth of merchandise on February 27 from a supplier extending terms of 2/10 net 30 EOM. If the firm takes the cash discount, it must pay $980 [$1,000 − (.02 × $1,000)] by March 10, thereby saving $20. **▲**

cost of giving up a cash discount
The implied rate of interest paid to delay payment of an account payable for an additional number of days.

Giving Up the Cash Discount If the firm chooses to give up the cash discount, it should pay on the final day of the credit period. There is an implicit cost associated with giving up a cash discount. The **cost of giving up a cash discount** is the implied rate of interest paid to delay payment of an account payable for an additional number of days. In other words, the amount is the interest being paid by the firm to keep its money for a number of days. This cost can be illustrated by a simple example. The example assumes that payment will be made on the last possible day (either the final day of the cash discount period or the final day of the credit period).

Example ▼ In the preceding example, we saw that Lawrence Industries could take the cash discount on its February 27 purchase by paying $980 on March 10. If Lawrence gives up the cash discount, payment can be made on March 30. To keep its money for an extra 20 days, the firm must give up an opportunity to pay $980 for its $1,000 purchase. In other words, it will cost the firm $20 to delay payment for 20 days.

To calculate the cost of giving up the cash discount, the *true purchase price* must be viewed as the *discounted cost of the merchandise,* which is $980 for Lawrence Industries. The annual percentage cost of giving up the cash discount can be calculated using Equation 15.1:[7]

where

$$\text{Cost of giving up cash discount} = \frac{CD}{100\% - CD} \times \frac{360}{N} \qquad (15.1)$$

CD = stated cash discount in percentage terms
N = number of days payment can be delayed by giving up the cash discount

Substituting the values for CD (2%) and N (20 days) into Equation 15.1 results in an annualized cost of giving up the cash discount of 36.73% [(2% ÷ 98%) × (360 ÷ 20)]. A 360-day year is assumed.[8]

A simple way to *approximate* the cost of giving up a cash discount is to use the stated cash discount percentage, CD, in place of the first term of Equation 15.1:

$$\text{Approximate cost of giving up cash discount} = CD \times \frac{360}{N} \qquad (15.2)$$

The smaller the cash discount, the closer the approximation to the actual cost of giving it up. Using this approximation, the cost of giving up the cash discount for Lawrence Industries is 36% [2% × (360 ÷ 20)].

Using the Cost of Giving Up a Cash Discount in Decision Making   The financial manager must determine whether it is advisable to take a cash discount. It is important to recognize that taking cash discounts may represent an important source of additional profitability.

E x a m p l e ▼   Mason Products, a large building supply company, has four possible suppliers, each offering different credit terms. Otherwise, their products and services are identical. Table 15.3 presents the credit terms offered by suppliers A, B, C, and D, and the cost of giving up the cash discounts in each transaction. The approximation method of calculating the cost of giving up a cash discount (Equation 15.2) has been used. The cost of giving up the cash discount from supplier A is 36%; from supplier B, 8%; from supplier C, 21.6%; and from supplier D, 28.8%.

---

7. Equation 15.1 and the related discussions are based on the assumption that only one discount is offered. In the event that multiple discounts are offered, calculation of the cost of giving up the discount must be made for each alternative.

8. This example assumes that Lawrence Industries gives up only one discount during the year, which costs it 2.04% for 20 days (i.e., 2% ÷ 98%) or 36.73% when annualized. However, if Lawrence Industries *continually* gives up the 2% cash discounts, the effect of compounding will cause the annualized cost to rise to 43.84%:

Annualized cost when discounts are *continually* given up

$$= \left(1 + \frac{CD}{100\% - CD}\right)^{360/N} - 1 \qquad (15.1a)$$

$$= \left(1 + \frac{2\%}{100\% - 2\%}\right)^{360/20} - 1 = \underline{\underline{43.84\%}}$$

TABLE 15.3	Cash Discounts and Associated Costs for Mason Products	
Supplier	Credit terms	Approximate cost of giving up a cash discount
A	2/10 net 30 EOM	36.0%
B	1/10 net 55 EOM	8.0
C	3/20 net 70 EOM	21.6
D	4/10 net 60 EOM	28.8

If the firm needs short-term funds, which it can borrow from its bank at an interest rate of 13%, and if each of the suppliers is viewed *separately,* which (if any) of the suppliers' cash discounts will the firm give up? In dealing with supplier A, the firm takes the cash discount, because the cost of giving it up is 36%, and then borrows the funds it requires from its bank at 13% interest. With supplier B, the firm would do better to give up the cash discount because the cost of this action is less than the cost of borrowing money from the bank (8% versus 13%). With either supplier C or supplier D, the firm should take the cash discount because in both cases the cost of giving up the discount is greater than the ▲ 13% cost of borrowing from the bank.

Career Key

Accounting personnel will analyze credit terms from suppliers and will decide whether to take or give up cash discounts offered for early payment. Accountants look at cash discounts as finance charges. They will need to determine if it is cheaper to take the supplier's financing or use another source of financing.

The example shows that the cost of giving up a cash discount is relevant when evaluating a single supplier's credit terms in light of certain *bank borrowing costs.* However, other factors relative to payment strategies may also need to be considered. For example, some firms, particularly small firms and poorly managed firms, routinely give up *all* discounts because they either lack alternative sources of unsecured short-term financing or fail to recognize the implicit costs of their actions.

Effects of Stretching Accounts Payable

stretching accounts payable
Paying bills as late as possible without damaging the firm's credit rating.

A strategy that is often employed by a firm is **stretching accounts payable**—that is, paying bills as late as possible without damaging its credit rating. Such a strategy can reduce the cost of giving up a cash discount.

Example ▼ Lawrence Industries was extended credit terms of 2/10 net 30 EOM. The cost of giving up the cash discount, assuming payment on the last day of the credit period, was found to be approximately 36% [2% × (360 ÷ 20)]. If the firm were able to stretch its account payable to 70 days without damaging its credit rating, the cost of giving up the cash discount would be only 12% [2% × (360 ÷ 60)]. ▲ Stretching accounts payable reduces the implicit cost of giving up a cash discount.

Although stretching accounts payable may be financially attractive, it raises an important ethical issue: It may cause the firm to violate the agreement it

In Practice

Mastering
Working Capital
Management

In 1997, CFO Magazine and REL Consultancy Group introduced their first Working Capital Survey. This annual study is based on working capital performance of about 1,000 public companies with sales over $500 million. Designed to help companies manage working capital more efficiently, the survey identifies quantitative working capital benchmarks. Overall results combine cash conversion efficiency (CCE)—how well companies convert revenue to cash flow—and days of working capital (DWC)—a summary of unweighted days' sales outstanding, payables, and inventory. The companies that rank first within their industries have the highest CCE and the fewest DWC, weighted equally. Top-ranked companies don't usually capture first place in all categories, however, and may even be far below average in some areas.

For example, USX-US Steel placed first in the metals industry in 1997. The company collected its accounts receivable in 37 days, 4 days faster than its rivals. However, it stretched payables to 65 days, twice the average in its group. This lowered DWC significantly, earning it the top rank even though at 3.3 percent its CCE was well below the 6.0 percent industry average.

Nucor, another steel company, prides itself on tight collections policies. It has the highest CCE ratio in the metals group—12.6 percent. Nucor is not tempted to match the longer terms its competitors give. "We believe we are in a manufacturing business, not the banking business," says CFO Sam Siegel. "Our terms are 30 days after shipment of goods. If someone wants to pay in 60 days, we're not interested. It can happen once. But after that they're going to have to borrow from the banks—we're not in the lending business."

Contrast this approach to the textile industry, which ranks very low in the CFO/REL survey. Why? Textiles companies operate in a very different environment. Retailers don't want to hold inventory themselves, so textiles manufacturers themselves typically carry large inventories. In addition, industry practice is to grant long payment terms to retailers.

entered into with its supplier when it purchased merchandise. Clearly, a supplier would not look kindly on a customer who regularly and purposely postponed paying for purchases.

Accruals

The second spontaneous source of short-term business financing is accruals. **Accruals** are liabilities for services received for which payment has yet to be made. The most common items accrued by a firm are wages and taxes. Because taxes are payments to the government, their accrual cannot be manipulated by the firm. However, the accrual of wages can be manipulated to some extent. This is accomplished by delaying payment of wages, thereby receiving an interest-free

accruals
Liabilities for services received for which payment has yet to be made.

loan from employees who are paid sometime after they have performed the work. The pay period for employees who earn an hourly rate is often governed by union regulations or by state or federal law. However, in other cases, the frequency of payment is at the discretion of the company's management.

Example ▼ Tenney Company, a large janitorial service company, currently pays its employees at the end of each work week. The weekly payroll totals $400,000. If the firm were to extend the pay period so as to pay its employees 1 week later throughout an entire year, the employees would in effect be loaning the firm $400,000 for a year. If the firm could earn 10% annually on invested funds, such a strategy ▲ would be worth $40,000 per year (.10 × $400,000).

? Review Questions

15–5 What are the two key sources of spontaneous short-term financing for a firm? Why are these sources considered *spontaneous,* and how are they related to the firm's sales? Do they normally have a stated cost?

15–6 Is there a cost associated with *taking a cash discount?* Is there any cost associated with *giving up a cash discount?* How is the decision to take a cash discount affected by the firm's cost of borrowing short-term funds?

15.4 Unsecured Sources of Short-Term Loans

Businesses obtain unsecured short-term loans from two major sources—banks and commercial paper. Unlike the spontaneous sources of unsecured short-term financing, these sources are negotiated and result from deliberate actions taken by the financial manager. Bank loans are more popular because they are available to firms of all sizes; commercial paper tends to be available only to large firms. In addition, international loans can be used to finance international transactions.

short-term, self-liquidating loan
An unsecured short-term loan in which the use to which the borrowed money is put provides the mechanism through which the loan is repaid.

Bank Loans

The major type of loan made by banks to businesses is the **short-term, self-liquidating loan.** Self-liquidating loans are intended merely to carry the firm through seasonal peaks in financing needs that are due primarily to buildups of accounts receivable and inventory. As receivables and inventories are converted into cash, the funds needed to retire these loans are generated. In other words, the use to which the borrowed money is put provides the mechanism through which the loan is repaid—hence the term *self-liquidating.* Banks lend unsecured, short-term funds in three basic ways: through single-payment notes, lines of credit, and revolving credit agreements. Before we look at these types of loans, we need to lay some groundwork about loan interest rates.

Career Key

The *marketing* department will be concerned with the availability of credit to customers, which may depend on the firm's ability to acquire short-term financing. If the firm cannot offer financing to customers, sales will definitely be lower than if it could offer financing.

Loan Interest Rates

prime rate of interest (prime rate)
The lowest rate of interest charged by the nation's leading banks on business loans to their most important and reliable business borrowers.

The interest rate on a bank loan can be a fixed or a floating rate, typically based on the prime rate of interest. The **prime rate of interest (prime rate)** is the lowest rate of interest charged by the nation's leading banks on business loans to their most important and reliable business borrowers.[9] The prime rate fluctuates with changing supply-and-demand relationships for short-term funds.[10] Banks generally determine the rate to be charged on loans to various borrowers by adding a premium to the prime rate to adjust it for the borrower's "riskiness." The premium may amount to 4 percent or more, although most unsecured short-term loans carry premiums of less than 2 percent.[11]

fixed-rate loan
A loan with a rate of interest determined at a set increment above the prime rate at which it remains fixed until maturity.

floating-rate loan
A loan with a rate of interest initially set at an increment above the prime rate and allowed to "float," or vary, above prime *as the prime rate varies* until maturity.

Fixed- and Floating-Rate Loans   Loans can have either fixed or floating interest rates. On a **fixed-rate loan,** the rate of interest is determined at a set increment above the prime rate on the date of the loan and remains unvarying at that fixed rate until maturity. On a **floating-rate loan,** the increment above the prime rate is initially established, and the rate of interest is allowed to "float," or vary, above prime *as the prime rate varies* until maturity. Generally, the increment above the prime rate on a floating-rate loan will be *lower* than on a fixed-rate loan of equivalent risk because the lender bears less risk with a floating-rate loan. The sometimes volatile nature of the prime rate, coupled with the widespread use of computers by banks to monitor and calculate loan interest, has been responsible for popularity of floating-rate loans.

Method of Computing Interest   Once the *nominal (or stated) annual rate* is established, the method of computing interest is determined. Interest can be paid either when a loan matures or in advance. If interest is paid *at maturity,* the *effective (or true) annual rate*—the actual rate of interest paid—for an assumed 1-year period[12] is equal to:

$$\frac{\text{Interest}}{\text{Amount borrowed}} \qquad (15.3)$$

Most bank loans to businesses require the interest payment at maturity.

When interest is paid *in advance,* it is deducted from the loan so that the borrower actually receives less money than is requested. Loans on which interest is

9. A trend away from using the prime rate as a benchmark has begun in the United States in response to various borrower lawsuits against banks. Some banks now use the term "base rate" or "reference rate" rather than "prime rate" for pricing corporate and other loans. In fact, the use of the *London Interbank Offered Rate (LIBOR)* is gaining momentum as a base lending rate in the United States.

10. During the past 25 years, the prime rate has varied from a record high of 21.5% (December 1980) to a low of 6.0% (mid-1992 through early 1994). Since 1995, it has fluctuated in the range of 8 to 9%, and in April 1999 was 7.75%.

11. Some, generally very large, firms can borrow from their banks at an interest rate slightly below the prime rate. This typically occurs when the borrowing firm either maintains high deposit balances at the bank over time or agrees to pay an upfront fee to "buy down" the interest rate. Below-prime-rate loans are clearly the exception rather than the rule.

12. Effective annual rates (EARs) for loans with maturities of less than 1 year can be found by using the technique presented in Chapter 5 for finding EARs when interest is compounded more frequently than annually. See Equation 5.10.

discount loans
Loans on which interest is paid in advance by deducting it from the amount borrowed.

paid in advance are called **discount loans.** The *effective annual rate for a discount loan* assuming a 1-year period is calculated as

$$\frac{\text{Interest}}{\text{Amount borrowed} - \text{interest}} \qquad (15.4)$$

Paying interest in advance raises the effective annual rate above the stated annual rate.

E x a m p l e ▼   Wooster Company, a manufacturer of athletic apparel, wants to borrow $10,000 at a stated annual rate of 10% interest for 1 year. If the interest on the loan is paid at maturity, the firm will pay $1,000 (.10 × $10,000) for the use of the $10,000 for the year. Substituting into Equation 15.3, the effective annual rate is therefore

$$\frac{\$1,000}{\$10,000} = 10.0\%$$

If the money is borrowed at the same *stated* annual rate for 1 year but interest is paid in advance, the firm still pays $1,000 in interest, but it receives only $9,000 ($10,000 − $1,000). Thus, the effective annual rate in this case is

$$\frac{\$1,000}{\$10,000 - \$1,000} = \frac{\$1,000}{\$9,000} = 11.1\%$$

Paying interest in advance thus makes the effective annual rate (11.1%) greater
▲   than the stated annual rate (10.0%).

Single-Payment Notes

single-payment note
A short-term, one-time loan, payable as a single amount at its maturity.

A **single-payment note** can be obtained from a commercial bank by a creditworthy business borrower. This type of loan is usually a "one-shot" deal made when a borrower needs additional funds for a short period. The resulting instrument is a *note,* which must be signed by the borrower. The note states the terms of the loan, which include the length of the loan and the interest rate. This type of short-term note generally has a maturity of 30 days to 9 months or more. The interest charged is generally tied in some way to the prime rate of interest and may have either a fixed or a floating rate.

E x a m p l e ▼   Gordon Manufacturing, a producer of rotary mower blades, recently borrowed $100,000 from each of two banks—bank A and bank B. The loans were incurred on the same day, when the prime rate of interest was 9%. Each loan involved a 90-day note with interest to be paid at the end of 90 days. The interest rate was set at 1½% above the prime rate on bank A's fixed-rate note. Over the 90-day period, the rate of interest on this note will remain at 10½% (9% prime rate + 1½% increment) regardless of fluctuations in the prime rate. The total interest cost on this loan is $2,625 [$100,000 × (10½% × 90/360)]. The effective 90-day rate on this loan is 2.625% ($2,625/$100,000).

Assuming that the loan from bank A is rolled over each 90 days throughout the year under the same terms and circumstances, its effective *annual* interest rate is found by using Equation 5.10. Because the loan costs 2.625% for 90 days, it is necessary to compound $(1 + 0.02625)$ for four periods in the year (i.e., 360/90) and then subtract 1:

$$\text{Effective annual rate} = (1 + 0.02625)^4 - 1$$
$$= 1.1092 - 1 = 0.1092 = \underline{10.92\%}$$

The effective annual rate of interest on the fixed-rate, 90-day note is 10.92%.

Bank B set the interest rate at 1% above the prime rate on its floating-rate note. The rate charged over the 90 days will vary directly with the prime rate. Initially, the rate will be 10% (9% + 1%), but when the prime rate changes, so will the rate of interest on the note. For instance, if after 30 days, the prime rate rises to 9.5%, and after another 30 days, it drops to 9.25%, the firm would be paying .833% for the first 30 days (10% × 30/360), .875% for the next 30 days (10.5% × 30/360), and .854 percent for the last 30 days (10.25% × 30/360). Its total interest cost would be $2,562 [$100,000 × (.833% + .875% + .854%)], resulting in an effective 90-day rate of 2.562% ($2,562/$100,000).

Again, assuming the loan is rolled over each 90 days throughout the year under the same terms and circumstances, its effective annual rate is 10.65%:

$$\text{Effective annual rate} = (1 + 0.02562)^4 - 1$$
$$= 1.1065 - 1 = 0.1065 = \underline{10.65\%}$$

▲ Clearly, in this case the floating-rate loan would have been less expensive than the fixed-rate loan due to its generally lower effective annual rate.

Lines of Credit

line of credit
An agreement between a commercial bank and a business specifying the amount of unsecured short-term borrowing the bank will make available to the firm over a given period of time.

A **line of credit** is an agreement between a commercial bank and a business specifying the amount of unsecured short-term borrowing the bank will make available to the firm over a given period of time. It is similar to the agreement under which issuers of bank credit cards, such as MasterCard, Visa, and Discover, extend preapproved credit to cardholders. A line of credit agreement is typically made for a period of 1 year and often places certain constraints on the borrower. It is *not a guaranteed loan* but indicates that if the bank has sufficient funds available, it will allow the borrower to owe it *up to* a certain amount of money. The amount of a line of credit is *the maximum the firm can owe the bank* at any point in time.

When applying for a line of credit, the borrower may be required to submit such documents as its cash budget, its pro forma income statement, its pro forma balance sheet, and its recent financial statements. If the bank finds the customer acceptable, the line of credit will be extended. The major attraction of a line of credit from the bank's point of view is that it eliminates the need to examine the creditworthiness of a customer each time it borrows money.

Interest Rates   The interest rate on a line of credit is normally stated as a floating rate—the *prime rate plus a percentage*. If the prime rate changes, the interest rate charged on new *as well as outstanding* borrowing automatically changes. The amount a borrower is charged in excess of the prime rate depends on its creditworthiness. The more creditworthy the borrower, the lower the interest increment above prime, and vice versa.

operating change restrictions
Contractual restrictions that a bank may impose on a firm's financial condition or operations as part of a line of credit agreement.

Operating Change Restrictions   In a line of credit agreement, a bank may impose **operating change restrictions,** which give it the right to revoke the line if any major changes occur in the firm's financial condition or operations. The firm is usually required to submit for periodic review up-to-date and, preferably, audited financial statements. In addition, the bank typically needs to be informed of shifts in key managerial personnel or in the firm's operations prior to changes taking place. Such changes may affect the future success and debt-paying ability of the firm and thus could alter its credit status. If the bank does not agree with the proposed changes and the firm makes them anyway, the bank has the right to revoke the line of credit.

compensating balance
A required checking account balance equal to a certain percentage of the amount borrowed.

Compensating Balances   To ensure that the borrower will be a good customer, many short-term unsecured bank loans—single-payment notes and lines of credit—often require the borrower to maintain a **compensating balance** in a checking account equal to a certain percentage of the amount borrowed. Compensating balances of 10 to 20 percent are frequently required. A compensating balance not only forces the borrower to be a good customer of the bank, but may also raise the interest cost to the borrower.

Example ▼

Hint   Sometimes the compensating balance is stated as a percentage of the amount of the line of credit. In other cases, it is linked to both the amount borrowed and the amount of the line of credit.

Estrada Graphics, a graphic design firm, has borrowed $1 million under a line of credit agreement. It must pay a stated interest rate of 10% and maintain in its checking account a compensating balance equal to 20% of the amount borrowed, or $200,000. Thus, it actually receives the use of only $800,000. To use that amount for a year, the firm pays interest of $100,000 ($.10 \times $1,000,000$). The effective annual rate on the funds is therefore 12.5% ($100,000 ÷ $800,000), 2.5% more than the stated rate of 10%.

If the firm normally maintains a balance of $200,000 or more in its checking account, the effective annual rate equals the stated annual rate of 10% because none of the $1 million borrowed is needed to satisfy the compensating balance requirement. If the firm normally maintains a $100,000 balance in its checking account, only an additional $100,000 will have to be tied up, leaving it with $900,000 of usable funds. The effective annual rate in this case would be 11.1% ($100,000 ÷ $900,000). Thus, a compensating balance raises the cost of borrowing *only if* it is larger than the firm's normal cash balance.

▲

annual cleanup
The requirement that for a certain number of days during the year borrowers under a line of credit carry a zero loan balance (i.e., owe the bank nothing).

Annual Cleanups   To ensure that money lent under a line of credit agreement is actually being used to finance seasonal needs, many banks require an **annual cleanup.** This means that the borrower must have a loan balance of zero—that is, owe the bank nothing—for a certain number of days during the year. Forcing the borrower to carry a zero loan balance for a certain period ensures that short-term loans do not turn into long-term loans.

All the characteristics of a line of credit agreement are negotiable to some extent. Today, banks bid competitively to attract large, well-known firms. A prospective borrower should attempt to negotiate a line of credit with the most favorable interest rate, for an optimal amount of funds, and with a minimum of restrictions. Borrowers today frequently pay fees to lenders instead of maintaining deposit balances as compensation for loans and other services. The lender attempts to get a good return with maximum safety. These negotiations should produce a line of credit that is suitable to both borrower and lender.

Revolving Credit Agreements

revolving credit agreement
A line of credit *guaranteed* to a borrower by a bank for a stated period regardless of the scarcity of money.

A **revolving credit agreement** is nothing more than a *guaranteed line of credit*. It is guaranteed in the sense that the commercial bank making the arrangement assures the borrower that a specified amount of funds will be made available regardless of the scarcity of money. The interest rate and other requirements are similar to those for a line of credit. It is not uncommon for a revolving credit agreement to be for a period greater than 1 year.[13] Because the bank guarantees the availability of funds, a **commitment fee** is normally charged on a revolving credit agreement.[14] This fee often applies to the average unused balance of the credit line. It is normally about .5 percent of the *average unused portion* of the funds.

commitment fee
The fee that is normally charged on a *revolving credit agreement;* it often applies to the average unused balance of the credit line.

Example ▼

REH Company, a major real estate developer, has a $2 million revolving credit agreement with its bank. Its average borrowing under the agreement for the past year was $1.5 million. The bank charges a commitment fee of .5%. Because the average unused portion of the committed funds was $500,000 ($2 million − $1.5 million), the commitment fee for the year was $2,500 (.005 × $500,000). Of course, REH also had to pay interest on the actual $1.5 million borrowed under the agreement. Assuming that $160,000 interest was paid on the $1.5 million borrowed, the effective cost of the agreement is 10.83% [($160,000 + $2,500)/$1,500,000]. Although more expensive than a line of credit, a revolving credit agreement can be less risky from the borrower's viewpoint, because the availability of funds is guaranteed.

▲

Commercial Paper

commercial paper
A form of financing consisting of short-term, unsecured promissory notes issued by firms with a high credit standing.

Commercial paper is a form of financing that consists of short-term, unsecured promissory notes issued by firms with a high credit standing. Generally, only quite large firms of unquestionable financial soundness are able to issue commercial paper. Most commercial paper has maturities ranging from 3 to 270 days. Although there is no set denomination, it is generally issued in multiples of $100,000 or more. A large portion of the commercial paper today is issued by finance companies; manufacturing firms account for a smaller portion of this type of financing. Businesses often purchase commercial paper, which they hold as marketable securities, to provide an interest-earning reserve of liquidity.

---

13. Many authors classify the revolving credit agreement as a form of *intermediate-term financing,* defined as having a maturity of 1 to 7 years. In this text, the intermediate-term financing classification is not used; only short-term and long-term classifications are made. Because many revolving credit agreements are for more than 1 year, they can be classified as a form of long-term financing; however, they are discussed here because of their similarity to line of credit agreements.

14. Some banks not only require payment of the commitment fee, but also require the borrower to maintain, in addition to a compensating balance against actual borrowings, a compensating balance of 10% or so against the unused portion of the commitment.

**Banking on
Small Business**

Prasad Rao, CEO of Cybertech International Corp., an Illinois computer systems consulting company, sought a bank loan for his small business. Although he pledged collateral of greater value than the loan amount and presented solid projected financial statements, bankers turned down his request. He finally received approval a year later, after he had actual sales to show bankers.

Rao's experience is not unusual. As Mike James, Wells Fargo Bank executive vice president explains, banks work on very thin margins and don't have much room for error. They want to keep their default rate under 5 percent, and startups fail at much higher rates than that. Why isn't collateral enough for loan approval? "We don't want to be in the liquidation business," he says.

Young companies like Cybertech International that can repay loans from revenues, not collateral, stand a better chance of success in the banking marketplace. Providing good information is another way to win over bankers. That means having financial statements from a certified public accountant and bringing the banker on-site to see how the company operates. At Uni-Dial Communications, a telecommunications products reseller in Louisville, Kentucky, CEO J. Sherman Henderson rolled out the red carpet for the lending officer's visit. He also included a group of key employees in his presentation, which impressed the banker.

Bonita Schwartz suspected that being a woman cost her a loan from one bank. She sought a loan from another bank, which used a different, less personal approval method: a computer program that reviewed her short application and assigned a score. It considered such factors as the age of her business and how quickly she paid bills. "It no longer mattered whether I was a man or a woman. What mattered now was that I worked hard and my credit was good," says Schwartz, who used the $450,000 loan to build a new headquarters for her research services company.

Interest on Commercial Paper

Commercial paper is sold at a discount from its *par,* or *face, value.* The interest paid by the issuer of commercial paper is determined by the size of the discount and the length of time to maturity. The actual interest earned by the purchaser is determined by certain calculations, illustrated by the following example.

Example ▼ Bertram Corporation, a large shipbuilder, has just issued $1 million worth of commercial paper that has a 90-day maturity and sells for $980,000. At the end of 90 days, the purchaser of this paper will receive $1 million for its $980,000 investment. The interest paid on the financing is therefore $20,000 on a principal of $980,000. The effective 90-day rate on the paper is 2.04% ($20,000/$980,000). Assuming the paper is rolled over each 90 days throughout the year, the effective annual rate for Bertram's commercial paper, found by using Equation 5.10, is 8.41% [$(1 + 0.0204)^4 - 1$].

An interesting characteristic of commercial paper is that it *normally* has a yield of 2 to 4 percent below the prime rate. In other words, firms are able to raise funds more cheaply through the sale of commercial paper than by borrowing from a commercial bank. The reason is that many suppliers of short-term funds do not have the option, as banks do, of making low-risk business loans at the prime rate.[15] They can invest only in marketable securities such as Treasury bills and commercial paper. The yields on these marketable securities on January 22, 1999, when the prime rate of interest was 7.75 percent, were about 4.3 percent for 3-month Treasury bills and about 4.9 percent for 3-month commercial paper.

Although the stated interest cost of borrowing through the sale of commercial paper is normally lower than the prime rate, the *overall cost* of commercial paper may not be cheaper than a bank loan. Additional costs include the fees paid by most issuers to obtain the bank line of credit used to back the paper, fees paid to obtain third-party ratings used to make the paper more salable, and flotation costs. In addition, even if it is slightly more expensive to borrow from a commercial bank, it may at times be advisable to do so to establish a good working relationship with a bank. This strategy ensures that when money is tight, funds can be obtained promptly and at a reasonable interest rate.

Hint Commercial paper is directly placed with investors by the issuer or is sold by commercial paper dealers. Most of it is purchased by other businesses and financial institutions.

International Loans

In some ways, arranging short-term financing for international trade is no different from financing purely domestic operations. In both cases, producers must finance the production and storage of goods for sale and then continue to finance accounts receivable before collecting any cash payments from sales. In other ways, however, the short-term financing of international sales and purchases is fundamentally different from strictly domestic trade.

International Transactions

The important difference between international and domestic transactions is that payments are often made or received in a foreign currency. Not only must a U.S. company pay the costs of doing business in the foreign exchange market, it also is exposed to *exchange rate risk* if there is a delay between the date that a foreign-currency invoice is created and the date it is paid. A U.S.-based company that exports goods and has accounts receivable denominated in a foreign currency faces the risk that the U.S. dollar will appreciate in value relative to the foreign currency. The risk to a U.S. importer with foreign-currency-denominated accounts payable is that the dollar will depreciate. Although exchange rate risk

---

15. Commercial banks are legally prohibited from loaning amounts in excess of 15% (plus an additional 10% for loans secured by readily marketable collateral) of the bank's unimpaired capital and surplus to any one borrower. This restriction is intended to protect depositors by forcing the commercial bank to spread its risk across a number of borrowers. In addition, smaller commercial banks do not have many opportunities to lend to large, high-quality business borrowers.

can often be *hedged* by using currency forward, futures, or options markets, doing so is costly and is not possible for all foreign currencies.

Typical international transactions are large in size and have long maturity dates. Therefore, companies that are involved in international trade generally have to finance larger dollar amounts for longer time periods than companies who operate domestically. Furthermore, because foreign companies are rarely well known in the United States, some financial institutions are reluctant to lend to U.S. exporters or importers, particularly smaller firms.

Financing International Trade

letter of credit
A letter written by a company's bank to the company's foreign supplier, stating that the bank guarantees payment of an invoiced amount if all the underlying agreements are met.

Several specialized techniques have evolved for financing international trade. Perhaps the most important financing vehicle is the **letter of credit,** a letter written by a company's bank to the company's foreign supplier, stating that the bank guarantees payment of an invoiced amount if all the underlying agreements are met. The letter of credit essentially substitutes the bank's reputation and creditworthiness for that of its commercial customer, increasing the likelihood that foreign suppliers will sell to a U.S. importer. Likewise, a U.S. exporter is more willing to sell goods to a foreign buyer if the transaction is covered by a letter of credit issued by a well-known bank in the buyer's home country.

Firms that do business in foreign countries on an ongoing basis often finance their operations, at least in part, in the local market. A company that has an assembly plant in Mexico, for example, might choose to finance its purchases of Mexican goods and services with peso funds borrowed from a Mexican bank. This not only minimizes exchange rate risk, but also improves the company's business ties to the host community. Multinational companies, however, sometimes finance their international transactions through dollar-denominated loans from international banks. The *Eurocurrency loan markets* allow creditworthy borrowers to obtain financing on very attractive terms.

Transactions Between Subsidiaries

Much international trade involves transactions between corporate subsidiaries. A U.S. company might, for example, manufacture one part in an Asian plant and another part in the United States, assemble the product in Brazil, and sell it in Europe. The shipment of goods back and forth between subsidiaries creates accounts receivable and accounts payable, but the parent company has considerable discretion about how and when payments are made. In particular, the parent can minimize foreign exchange fees and other transaction costs by "netting" what affiliates owe each other and paying only the net amount due, rather than having both subsidiaries pay each other the gross amounts due.

❓ Review Questions

15–7 What is the *prime rate of interest,* and how is it relevant to the cost of short-term bank borrowing? What is a *floating-rate loan?* How does the *effective annual rate* differ between a loan requiring interest payments *at maturity* and another similar loan requiring interest *in advance?*

15–8   What are the basic terms and characteristics of a *single-payment note?* How is the *effective annual rate* on such a note found?

15–9   What is a *line of credit?* Describe each of the following features that are often included in these agreements: (**a**) operating change restrictions; (**b**) compensating balance; and (**c**) annual cleanup

15–10   What is a *revolving credit agreement?* How does this arrangement differ from the line of credit agreement? What is a *commitment fee?*

15–11   How is *commercial paper* used to raise short-term funds? Who can issue commercial paper? Who buys commercial paper?

15–12   What is the important difference between international and domestic transactions? How is a *letter of credit* used in financing international trade transactions? How is "netting" used in transactions between subsidiaries?

15.5 Secured Sources of Short-Term Loans

secured short-term financing
Short-term financing (loans) obtained by pledging specific assets as collateral.

security agreement
The agreement between the borrower and the lender that specifies the collateral held against a secured loan.

When a firm has exhausted its unsecured sources of short-term financing, it may be able to obtain additional short-term loans on a secured basis. **Secured short-term financing** has specific assets pledged as collateral. The *collateral* commonly takes the form of an asset, such as accounts receivable or inventory. The lender obtains a security interest in the collateral through a **security agreement** with the borrower that specifies the collateral held against the loan. In addition, the terms of the loan against which the security is held form part of the security agreement. They specify the conditions required for the security interest to be removed, along with the interest rate on the loan, repayment dates, and other loan provisions. A copy of the security agreement is filed in a public office within the state—typically, a county or state court. Filing provides subsequent lenders with information about which assets of a prospective borrower are unavailable for use as collateral. The filing requirement protects the lender by legally establishing the lender's security interest.

Characteristics of Secured Short-Term Loans

Although many people believe that holding collateral as security reduces the risk of a loan, lenders do not usually view loans in this way. Lenders recognize that holding collateral can reduce losses if the borrower defaults, but *the presence of collateral has no impact on the risk of default.* A lender requires collateral to ensure recovery of some portion of the loan in the event of default. What the lender wants above all, however, is to be repaid as scheduled. In general, lenders prefer to make less risky loans at lower rates of interest than to be in a position in which they must liquidate collateral.

Collateral and Terms

Lenders of secured short-term funds prefer collateral that has a duration closely matched to the term of the loan. Current assets—accounts receivable and inventories—are the most desirable short-term loan collateral, because they normally

percentage advance
The percent of the book value of the collateral that constitutes the principal of a secured loan.

convert into cash much sooner than do fixed assets. Thus, the short-term lender of secured funds generally accepts only liquid current assets as collateral.

Typically, the lender determines the desirable **percentage advance** to make against the collateral. This percentage advance constitutes the principal of the secured loan and is normally between 30 and 100 percent of the book value of the collateral. It varies according to the type and liquidity of collateral.

The interest rate charged on secured short-term loans is typically *higher* than the rate on unsecured short-term loans. Commercial banks and other institutions do not normally consider secured loans less risky than unsecured loans. In addition, negotiating and administering secured loans is more troublesome for the lender than negotiating and administering unsecured loans. The lender therefore normally requires added compensation in the form of a service charge, a higher interest rate, or both.

Hint Remember that firms typically borrow on a secured basis only after exhausting less costly unsecured sources of short-term funds.

Institutions Extending Secured Short-Term Loans

The primary sources of secured short-term loans to businesses are commercial banks and finance companies. Both institutions deal in short-term loans secured primarily by accounts receivable and inventory. The operations of commercial banks have already been described. **Commercial finance companies** are lending institutions that make *only* secured loans—both short-term and long-term—to businesses. Unlike banks, finance companies are not permitted to hold deposits.

commercial finance companies
Lending institutions that make *only* secured loans—both short-term and long-term—to businesses.

Only when its unsecured and secured short-term borrowing power from the commercial bank is exhausted will a borrower turn to the commercial finance company for additional secured borrowing. Because the finance company generally ends up with higher-risk borrowers, its interest charges on secured short-term loans are usually higher than those of commercial banks. The leading U.S. commercial finance companies include the CIT Group and GE Capital.

The Use of Accounts Receivable as Collateral

Two commonly used means of obtaining short-term financing with accounts receivable are pledging accounts receivable and factoring accounts receivable. Actually, only a pledge of accounts receivable creates a secured short-term loan; factoring really entails the *sale* of accounts receivable at a discount. Although factoring is not actually a form of secured short-term borrowing, it does involve the use of accounts receivable to obtain needed short-term funds.

Pledging Accounts Receivable

pledge of accounts receivable
The use of a firm's accounts receivable as security, or collateral, to obtain a short-term loan.

A **pledge of accounts receivable** is often used to secure a short-term loan. Because accounts receivable are normally quite liquid, they are an attractive form of short-term loan collateral.

The Pledging Process When a firm requests a loan against accounts receivable, the lender first evaluates the firm's accounts receivable to determine their desirability as collateral. The lender makes a list of the acceptable accounts, along with the billing dates and amounts. If the borrowing firm requests a loan for a fixed amount, the lender needs to select only enough accounts to secure the funds requested. If the borrower wants the maximum loan available, the lender evaluates all the accounts to select the maximum amount of acceptable collateral.

After selecting the acceptable accounts, the lender normally adjusts the dollar value of these accounts for expected returns on sales and other allowances. If a customer whose account has been pledged returns merchandise or receives some type of allowance, such as a cash discount for early payment, the amount of the collateral is automatically reduced. For protection from such occurrences, the lender normally reduces the value of the acceptable collateral by a fixed percentage.

Next, the percentage to be advanced against the collateral must be determined. The lender evaluates the quality of the acceptable receivables and the expected cost of their liquidation. This percentage represents the principal of the loan and typically ranges between 50 and 90 percent of the face value of acceptable accounts receivable. To protect its interest in the collateral, the lender files a **lien,** which is a publicly disclosed legal claim on the collateral. For an example of the complete pledging process, see the book's web site at **www.awlonline.com/gitman.**

lien
A publicly disclosed legal claim on collateral.

Notification Pledges of accounts receivable are normally made on a **nonnotification basis,** meaning that a customer whose account has been pledged as collateral is not notified. Under the nonnotification arrangement, the borrower still collects the pledged account receivable, and the lender trusts the borrower to remit these payments as they are received. If a pledge of accounts receivable is made on a **notification basis,** the customer is notified to remit payment directly to the lender.

nonnotification basis
The basis on which a borrower, having pledged an account receivable, continues to collect the account payments without notifying the account customer.

notification basis
The basis on which an account customer whose account has been pledged (or factored) is notified to remit payment directly to the lender (or factor).

Pledging Cost The stated cost of a pledge of accounts receivable is normally 2 to 5 percent above the prime rate. In addition to the stated interest rate, a service charge of up to 3 percent may be levied by the lender to cover its administrative costs. Clearly, pledges of accounts receivable are a high-cost source of short-term financing.

Factoring Accounts Receivable

Factoring accounts receivable involves their outright sale at a discount to a financial institution. A **factor** is a financial institution that specializes in purchasing accounts receivable from businesses. Some commercial banks and commercial finance companies also factor accounts receivable. Although not the same as obtaining a short-term loan, factoring accounts receivable is similar to borrowing with accounts receivable as collateral.

factoring accounts receivable
The outright sale of accounts receivable at a discount to a *factor* or other financial institution to obtain funds.

factor
A financial institution that specializes in purchasing accounts receivable from businesses.

Factoring Agreement A factoring agreement normally states the exact conditions and procedures for the purchase of an account. The factor, like a lender against a pledge of accounts receivable, chooses accounts for purchase, selecting only those that appear to be acceptable credit risks. Where factoring is to be on a continuing basis, the factor will actually make the firm's credit decisions, because

nonrecourse basis
The basis on which accounts receivable are sold to a factor with the understanding that the factor accepts all credit risks on the purchased accounts.

this will guarantee the acceptability of accounts.[16] Factoring is normally done on a *notification basis,* and the factor receives payment of the account directly from the customer. In addition, most sales of accounts receivable to a factor are made on a **nonrecourse basis.** This means that the factor agrees to accept all credit risks. Thus, if a purchased account turns out to be uncollectible, the factor must absorb the loss.

Typically, the factor is not required to pay the firm until the account is collected or until the last day of the credit period, whichever occurs first. The factor sets up an account similar to a bank deposit account for each customer. As payment is received or as due dates arrive, the factor deposits money into the seller's account, from which the seller is free to make withdrawals as needed.

In many cases, if the firm leaves the money in the account, a *surplus* will exist on which the factor will pay interest. In other instances, the factor may make *advances* to the firm against uncollected accounts that are not yet due. These advances represent a negative balance in the firm's account, on which interest is charged.

Factoring Cost   Factoring costs include commissions, interest levied on advances, and interest earned on surpluses. The factor deposits in the firm's account the book value of the collected or due accounts purchased by the factor, less the commissions. The commissions are typically stated as a 1 to 3 percent discount from the book value of factored accounts receivable. The *interest levied on advances* is generally 2 to 4 percent above the prime rate. It is levied on the actual amount advanced. The *interest paid on surpluses* is generally around .5 percent per month. An example of the factoring process is included on the book's web site at **www.awlonline.com/gitman.**

Although its costs may seem high, factoring has certain advantages that make it attractive to many firms. One is the ability it gives the firm to *turn accounts receivable immediately into cash* without having to worry about repayment. Another advantage of factoring is that it ensures a *known pattern of cash flows.* In addition, if factoring is undertaken on a continuous basis, the firm *can eliminate its credit and collection departments.*

The Use of Inventory as Collateral

Inventory is generally second to accounts receivable in desirability as short-term loan collateral. Inventory normally has a market value that is greater than its book value, which is used to establish its value as collateral. A lender securing a loan with inventory will probably be able to sell it for at least book value if the borrower defaults on its obligations.

The most important characteristic of inventory being evaluated as loan collateral is *marketability,* which must be considered in light of its physical properties. A

---

16. The use of credit cards such as MasterCard, Visa, and Discover by consumers has some similarity to factoring, because the vendor accepting the card is reimbursed at a discount for purchases made by using the card. The difference between factoring and credit cards is that cards are nothing more than a line of credit extended by the issuer, which charges the vendors a fee for accepting the cards. In factoring, the factor does not analyze credit until after the sale has been made; in many cases (except when factoring is done on a continuous basis), the initial credit decision is the responsibility of the vendor, not the factor who purchases the account.

warehouse of *perishable* items, such as fresh peaches, may be quite marketable, but if the cost of storing and selling the peaches is high, they may not be desirable collateral. *Specialized items,* such as moon-roving vehicles, are not desirable collateral either, because finding a buyer for them could be difficult. When evaluating inventory as possible loan collateral, the lender looks for items with very stable market prices that have ready markets and that lack undesirable physical properties.

Floating Inventory Liens

floating inventory lien
A lender's claim on the borrower's general inventory as collateral for a secured loan.

A lender may be willing to secure a loan under a **floating inventory lien,** which is a claim on inventory in general. This arrangement is most attractive when the firm has a stable level of inventory that consists of a diversified group of relatively inexpensive merchandise. Inventories of items such as auto tires, screws and bolts, and shoes are candidates for floating-lien loans. Because it is difficult for a lender to verify the presence of the inventory, the lender will generally advance less than 50 percent of the book value of the average inventory. The interest charge on a floating lien is 3 to 5 percent above the prime rate. Commercial banks often require floating liens as extra security on what would otherwise be an unsecured loan. Floating-lien inventory loans may also be available from commercial finance companies. An example of a floating lien is included on the book's web site at **www.awlonline.com/gitman.**

Trust Receipt Inventory Loans

trust receipt inventory loan
An agreement under which the lender advances 80 to 100 percent of the cost of the borrower's relatively expensive inventory items in exchange for the borrower's promise to immediately repay the loan, with accrued interest, on the sale of each item.

A **trust receipt inventory loan** often can be made against relatively expensive automotive, consumer durable, and industrial goods that can be identified by serial number. Under this agreement, the borrower keeps the inventory and the lender may advance 80 to 100 percent of its cost. The lender files a *lien* on all the items financed. The borrower is free to sell the merchandise but is trusted to remit the amount lent against each item, along with accrued interest, to the lender immediately after the sale. The lender then releases the lien on the item. The lender makes periodic checks of the borrower's inventory to make sure that the required amount of collateral remains in the hands of the borrower. The interest charge to the borrower is normally 2 percent or more above the prime rate. Trust receipt loans are often made by manufacturers' wholly owned financing subsidiaries, known as *captive finance companies,* to their customers. Captive finance companies are especially popular in industries that manufacture consumer durable goods because they provide the manufacturer with a useful sales tool. For example, General Motors Acceptance Corporation (GMAC), the financing subsidiary of General Motors, grants these types of loans to its dealers. Trust receipt loans are also available through commercial banks and commercial finance companies.

warehouse receipt loan
An arrangement in which the lender receives control of the pledged inventory collateral, which is stored by a designated warehousing company on the lender's behalf.

Warehouse Receipt Loans

A **warehouse receipt loan** is an arrangement whereby the lender, who may be a commercial bank or commercial finance company, receives control of the pledged inventory collateral, which is stored by a designated agent on the lender's behalf. After selecting acceptable collateral, the lender hires a warehousing company to act as its agent and take possession of the inventory.

Two types of warehousing arrangements are possible. A *terminal warehouse* is a central warehouse that is used to store the merchandise of various customers. The lender normally uses such a warehouse when the inventory is easily transported and can be delivered to the warehouse relatively inexpensively. Under a *field warehouse* arrangement the lender hires a field warehousing company to set up a warehouse on the borrower's premises or to lease part of the borrower's warehouse to store the pledged collateral. Regardless of which type of warehouse is used, the warehousing company places a guard over the inventory. Only on written approval of the lender can any portion of the secured inventory be released.

The actual lending agreement specifically states the requirements for the release of inventory. As in the case of other secured loans, the lender accepts only collateral that is believed to be readily marketable and advances only a portion—generally 75 to 90 percent—of the collateral's value. The specific costs of warehouse receipt loans are generally higher than those of any other secured lending arrangements due to the need to hire and pay a third party (the warehousing company) to guard and supervise the collateral. The basic interest charged on warehouse receipt loans is higher than that charged on unsecured loans, generally ranging from 3 to 5 percent above the prime rate. In addition to the interest charge, the borrower must absorb the costs of warehousing by paying the warehouse fee, which is generally between 1 and 3 percent of the amount of the loan. The borrower is normally also required to pay the insurance costs on the warehoused merchandise. An example of the procedures and costs of a warehouse receipt loan is included on the book's web site at **www.awlonline.com/gitman.**

⁇ Review Questions

15–13   In general, what interest rates and fees are levied on secured short-term loans? Why are these rates generally *higher* than the rates on unsecured short-term loans?

15–14   Describe and compare the basic features of the following methods of using accounts receivable to obtain short-term financing: (a) pledging accounts receivable, and (b) factoring accounts receivable. Be sure to mention the institutions offering each of them.

15–15   Describe the basic features and compare each of the following methods of using *inventory* as short-term loan collateral: (a) floating lien; (b) trust receipt loan; and (c) warehouse receipt loan.

SUMMARY

 Understand the two definitions of net working capital and the trade-off between profitability and risk as it relates to changing levels of current assets and current liabilities. Net working capital is the difference between current assets and current liabilities or, alternatively, the portion of a firm's current assets financed with long-term funds. Profitability is the relationship between revenues and costs. Risk, in the context of short-term financial decisions, is the probability that a firm will become technically insolvent—unable to pay its bills as they come due. By assuming a constant level of total assets, the higher a firm's ratio of current assets to total assets, the less profitable the firm, and the less risky it is. The converse is also true. With constant total assets, the higher a firm's ratio of current liabilities to total assets, the more profitable and more risky the firm is. The converse of this statement is also true.

 Discuss, in terms of profitability and risk, the aggressive financing strategy and the conservative financing strategy for meeting the firm's total financing requirement. The aggressive strategy for determining the appropriate financing mix is a high-profit, high-risk strategy under which the firm finances at least its seasonal needs, and possibly some of its permanent needs, with short-term funds and the majority of its permanent needs with long-term funds. The conservative strategy is a low-profit, low-risk strategy under which all funds requirements—both permanent and seasonal—are financed with long-term funds. Short-term funds are saved for emergencies or unexpected outflows.

Review the key characteristics of the two major sources of spontaneous short-term financing—accounts payable and accruals. Spontaneous sources of short-term financing include accounts payable, which are the primary source of short-term funds, and accruals. Accounts payable result from credit purchases of merchandise, and accruals result primarily from wage and tax obligations. The key features of these forms of financing are summarized in part I of Table 15.4.

Analyze credit terms offered by suppliers to determine whether to take or give up cash discounts and whether to stretch accounts payable. Credit terms may differ with respect to the credit period, cash discount, cash discount period, and beginning of the credit period. The cost of giving up cash discounts is a factor in deciding whether to take or give up a cash discount. Cash

discounts should be given up only when a firm in need of short-term funds must pay an interest rate on borrowing that is greater than the cost of giving up the cash discount. Stretching accounts payable can lower the cost of giving up a cash discount.

 Describe the interest rates and basic types of unsecured bank sources of short-term loans, commercial paper, and short-term international loans. Banks are the major source of unsecured short-term loans to businesses. The interest rate on these loans is tied to the prime rate of interest by a risk premium and may be fixed or floating. It should be evaluated by using the effective annual rate. This rate is calculated differently depending on whether interest is paid when the loan matures or in advance. Bank loans may take the form of a single-payment note, a line of credit, or a revolving credit agreement. Commercial paper is an unsecured IOU issued by firms with a high credit standing. The key features of the various types of bank loans as well as commercial paper are summarized in part II of Table 15.4.

International sales and purchases expose firms to exchange rate risk. They are larger and of longer maturity than typical transactions, and can be financed using a letter of credit, by borrowing in the local market, or through dollar-denominated loans from international banks. On transactions between subsidiaries, "netting" can be used to minimize foreign exchange fees and other transaction costs.

Explain the characteristics of secured short-term loans and the use of accounts receivable and inventory as short-term loan collateral. Secured short-term loans are those for which the lender requires collateral—typically, current assets such as accounts receivable or inventory. Only a percentage of the book value of acceptable collateral is advanced by the lender. These loans are more expensive than unsecured loans; collateral does not lower the risk of default, and increased administrative costs result. Both commercial banks and commercial finance companies make secured short-term loans. Both pledging, which is the use of accounts receivable as loan collateral, and factoring, which is the outright sale of accounts receivable at a discount, involve the use of accounts receivable

TABLE 15.4 Summary of Key Features of Common Sources of Short-Term Financing

Type of short-term financing	Source	Cost or conditions	Characteristics
I. Spontaneous sources of short-term financing			
Accounts payable	Suppliers of merchandise	No stated cost except when a cash discount is offered for early payment.	Credit extended on open account for 0 to 120 days. The largest source of short-term financing.
Accruals	Employees and government	Free.	Result because wages (employees) and taxes (government) are paid at discrete points in time after the service has been rendered. Hard to manipulate this source of financing.
II. Unsecured sources of short-term loans			
Bank sources			
(1) Single-payment notes	Commercial banks	Prime plus 0% to 4% risk premium—fixed or floating rate.	A single-payment loan used to meet a funds shortage expected to last only a short period of time.
(2) Lines of credit	Commercial banks	Prime plus 0% to 4% risk premium—fixed or floating rate. Often must maintain 10% to 20% compensating balance and clean up the line.	A prearranged borrowing limit under which funds, if available, will be lent to allow the borrower to meet seasonal needs.
(3) Revolving credit agreements	Commercial banks	Prime plus 0% to 4% risk premium—fixed or floating rate. Often must maintain 10% to 20% compensating balance and pay a commitment fee of approximately .5% of the average unused balance.	A line of credit agreement under which the availability of funds is guaranteed. Often for a period greater than 1 year.
Commercial paper	Other businesses, banks, life insurance companies, pension funds, and money market	Generally 2% to 4% below the prime rate of interest.	An unsecured short-term promissory note issued by the most financially sound firms.

(continued)

2. What is the complete financial package of factoring?

At the end of that screen, click "Why do companies use factoring?"

3. Why use factoring?

At the end of that screen, click "How does factoring work?"

4. What are the four steps in factoring?

On the BUSINESS FINANCING SOLUTIONS menu, select RECEIVABLES OUTSOURCING SERVICE. Then click GO.

5. What are the commercial services options available?

Click on BULK PURCHASE OF ACCOUNTS RECEIVABLE. Then click GO.

6. When do companies take advantage of bulk purchases of accounts receivable?

CHAPTER 16

Cash and Marketable Securities

LEARNING GOALS

LG1 Discuss the motives for holding cash and marketable securities, estimation of cash balances, and the level of marketable securities investment.

LG2 Demonstrate the three basic strategies for the efficient management of cash, using the firm's operating and cash conversion cycles.

LG3 Explain *float*, including its three basic components, and the firm's major objective with respect to the levels of collection float and disbursement float.

LG4 Review popular techniques for speeding up collections and slowing down disbursements, the role of banking relationships in cash management, and international cash management.

LG5 Understand the basic characteristics of marketable securities and the key features of popular government and nongovernment issues.

LG6 Describe the Baumol model and the Miller-Orr model and how they can be used to determine the optimum quantity in which to convert marketable securities and cash.

16.1 Cash and Marketable Security Balances

cash
The ready currency to which all liquid assets can be reduced.

Cash and marketable securities are the most liquid of the firm's assets. **Cash** is the ready currency to which all liquid assets can be reduced. **Marketable securities** are short-term, interest-earning, money market instruments that are used by the firm to obtain a return on temporarily idle funds. Together, cash and marketable securities serve as a pool of funds that can be used to pay bills as they

660

for raw materials and labor is 35 days, which represents the average payment period (APP). Substituting MAX Company's 155-day operating cycle (OC), found in the preceding example, and its 35-day average payment period into Equation 16.2 results in its cash conversion cycle (CCC):

$$CCC = OC - APP$$
$$= 155 - 35 = 120 \text{ days}$$

MAX Company's cash conversion cycle is shown below the time line in Figure 16.1. There are 120 days between the cash *outflow* to pay the account payable (on day 35) and the cash *inflow* from the collection of the account receivable (on day 155). During this period—the cash conversion cycle—the firm's money is tied up.

Managing the Cash Conversion Cycle

A *positive* cash conversion cycle, like that of MAX Company, means that the firm must use negotiated forms of financing, such as unsecured short-term loans or secured sources of financing, to support the cash conversion cycle.

Ideally, a firm would like to have a *negative* cash conversion cycle. A negative CCC means the average payment period exceeds the operating cycle. Manufacturing firms usually will *not* have negative cash conversion cycles unless they extend their average payment periods an unreasonable length of time. Nonmanufacturing firms are more likely to have negative cash conversion cycles because they generally carry smaller, faster-moving inventories and often sell their products or services for cash. As a result, these firms have shorter operating cycles, which may be exceeded in length by the firm's average payment periods. When a firm's cash conversion cycle is negative, the firm should benefit by being able to use spontaneous financing to help support aspects of the business other than just the operating cycle.

In the more common case of a positive cash conversion cycle, the firm needs to pursue strategies to minimize the CCC without losing sales or damaging its credit rating. Basic strategies for managing the cash conversion cycle are as follows:

1. Turn over inventory as quickly as possible, avoiding stockouts (depletions of stock) that might result in a loss of sales.
2. Collect accounts receivable as quickly as possible without losing future sales due to high-pressure collection techniques. Cash discounts, if they are economically justifiable, may be used to accomplish this objective.
3. Pay accounts payable as late as possible without damaging the firm's credit rating, but take advantage of any favorable cash discounts.[2]

The effects of implementing these strategies are described in the following paragraphs using MAX Company data. We ignore the costs of implementing each

Career Key

Operations will be required to reduce the operating cycle by more efficiently managing inventory and production. This may require them to adopt new systems, such as a just-in-time (JIT) inventory system, or to decide to have someone else make component parts for them.

---

2. A discussion of the variables to consider when determining whether to take cash discounts appears in Chapter 15. A cash discount is often an enticement to pay accounts payable early to effectively reduce the purchase price of goods. Strategies for the use of accruals as a free source of short-term financing are also discussed in Chapter 15.

proposed strategy; in practice, these costs would be measured against the calculated savings in order to make the appropriate strategic decision.

Efficient Inventory-Production Management

One strategy available to MAX is to increase inventory turnover. To do so, the firm can increase raw materials turnover, shorten the production cycle, or increase finished goods turnover. Each of these approaches will result in a reduction in the amount of negotiated financing required—that is, the cash conversion cycle will be shortened.

E x a m p l e ▼ If MAX Company increases inventory turnover by reducing the average age of inventory from the current level of 85 days to 70 days, it will reduce its cash conversion cycle by 15 days, to 105 days (CCC = 120 days − 15 days). The effect of this change on the firm can be estimated as follows: Suppose MAX currently spends $12 million annually on operating cycle investments. The daily expenditure is $33,333 ($12 million ÷ 360 days). Because the cash conversion cycle is reduced 15 days, $500,000 of financing ($33,333 × 15) can be repaid. If MAX pays 10% for its negotiated financing, the firm will reduce financing costs and thereby increase profit by $50,000 (.10 × $500,000) as a result of managing ▲ inventory more efficiently.

Hint As discussed in Chapter 15, one method of accelerating the collection of accounts receivable is to let someone else do the financing for you, such as by using bank credit cards or a factor. Another method is to change the credit terms: increase the cash discount or shorten the required payment period.

Accelerating the Collection of Accounts Receivable

Another means of reducing the cash conversion cycle is to speed up—accelerate—the collection of accounts receivable. Accounts receivable, like inventory, tie up dollars that could otherwise be used to reduce financing or be invested in earning assets.

E x a m p l e ▼ If MAX Company is able to reduce the average collection period from the current level of 70 days to 50 days, it will reduce its cash conversion cycle by 20 days, to 100 days (CCC = 120 days − 20 days = 100 days). Again, assume that $12 million is spent annually—$33,333 daily—to support the operating cycle. By improving the management of accounts receivable by 20 days, the firm will require $666,666 less in negotiated financing (i.e., $33,333 × 20). With an interest rate of 10%, the firm is able to reduce financing costs and thereby increase ▲ profits by $66,666 (.10 × $666,666).

Stretching Accounts Payable

A third strategy is to *stretch accounts payable*—that is, to pay bills as late as possible without damaging the firm's credit rating. Although this approach is financially attractive, it involves an ethical issue: Clearly, a supplier would not look favorably on a customer that purposely postponed payment.[3]

---

3. The resolution of this ethical issue is not further addressed in this text. Suffice it to say that although the use of various techniques to slow down payments is widespread due to its financial appeal, it may not be justifiable on purely ethical grounds.

Example ▼ If MAX Company can stretch the payment period from the current average of 35 days to an average of 45 days, its cash conversion cycle will be reduced to 110 days (CCC = 85 days + 70 days − 45 days = 110 days). Once more, if operating cycle expenditures total $12 million annually, stretching accounts payable 10 additional days will reduce the firm's negotiated financing need by $333,333 [($12 million ÷ 360) × 10 days]. With an interest rate of 10%, the firm can reduce its financing costs and thereby increase profits by $33,333 (.10 × ▲ $333,333).

Combining Cash Management Strategies

Firms typically do not attempt to implement just one cash management strategy; rather they attempt to use them all to reduce their reliance on negotiated financing. Of course, when implementing these strategies, firms should take care to avoid repeated inventory stockouts, to avoid losing sales because of the use of high-pressure collection techniques, and not to damage the firm's credit rating by overstretching accounts payable. A combination of these strategies would have the following effects on MAX Company.

Example ▼ If MAX simultaneously decreased the average age of inventory by 15 days, sped the collection of accounts receivable by 20 days, and increased the average payment period by 10 days, its cash conversion cycle would be reduced to 75 days, as shown here:

Initial cash conversion cycle		120 days
Reduction due to:		
1. Decreased inventory age		
85 days to 70 days =	15 days	
2. Decreased collection period		
70 days to 50 days =	20 days	
3. Increased payment period		
35 days to 45 days =	10 days	
Less: Total reduction in cash conversion cycle		45 days
New cash conversion cycle		75 days

The 45-day reduction in the cash conversion cycle means that MAX Company can reduce its reliance on negotiated financing. If annual expenditures for operations are $12 million, then interest-bearing financing can be reduced by $1.5 million [($12 million ÷ 360 days) × 45 days]. If the company pays 10% interest on its financing, it can save $150,000 (i.e., .10 × $1,500,000) through improved ▲ management of the cash conversion cycle.

? Review Questions

16–3   Compare and contrast the firm's *operating cycle* and its *cash conversion cycle*. What is the firm's objective with respect to each of them?

16–4   What are the *key strategies* with respect to inventory, accounts receivable, and accounts payable for the firm that wants to manage its cash conversion cycle efficiently?

In Practice

Dell Computer Upgrades Its Cash Management Program

As its revenues grew at record rates, Dell Computer discovered that the rate at which it converted those sales to cash wasn't keeping pace. By late 1996, the company's accounts receivable and inventory levels were too high, for one thing. To solve Dell's problem, CFO Tom Meredith made liquidity reengineering a companywide priority, not just a finance department concern, and included not only all Dell's employees, but also its vendors, suppliers, and customers.

Dell used the components of its cash conversion cycle (CCC)—average collection period (ACP), average age of inventory (AAI), and average payment period (APP)—to develop internal benchmarks to measure liquidity. "These were metrics we felt people at the line level could understand and act upon," says Danny Caswell, manager of Dell's asset management department. It made significant changes in all three areas. Analyzing inventory procedures revealed that Dell was holding inventory that could be held by its vendors instead. Convincing those vendors to hold the inventory reduced AAI from over 30 days to 13 days. In addition, Dell stretched its APP from 33 to 54 days. "We were often paying our bills before the negotiated terms," notes Caswell. "We've maximized the time difference now."

To cope with the meteoric rise in sales and ACP, Dell implemented an automated receivables collection system. Customized software improved order processing and collection methods. The new system also took over labor-intensive tasks such as sending letters to overdue accounts at specified times and creating activity reports with current account status. ACP dropped from 50 to 37 days, freeing up a significant amount of cash for Dell.

One year after implementing the liquidity improvement program, Dell's CCC had dropped from a respectable 40 days to an "ideal" minus 5 days—rare for a manufacturing company like Dell.

16–5   If a firm reduces the average age of its inventory, what effect might this action have on the cash conversion cycle? On the firm's total sales? Is there a trade-off between average inventory and sales? Give reasons for your answers.

16.3 Cash Management Techniques

Financial managers have available a variety of cash management techniques aimed at minimizing the firm's negotiated financing requirements. Assuming that the firm has done all that it can to stimulate customers to pay promptly and to select vendors offering the most attractive and flexible credit terms, the firm can further speed collections and slow disbursements by taking advantage of the "float" existing in the collection and payment systems.

Float

float
Funds dispatched by a payer that are not yet in a form that can be spent by the payee.

In the broadest sense, **float** refers to funds that have been dispatched by a payer (the firm or individual *making* payment) but are not yet in a form that can be spent by the payee (the firm or individual *receiving* payment). Float also exists when a payee has received funds in a spendable form but these funds have not been withdrawn from the account of the payer. Delays in the collection–payment system resulting from the transportation and processing of checks are responsible for float. However, with electronic payment systems, as well as changes being put in place by the Federal Reserve System, in the foreseeable future float will virtually disappear. Until that time, financial managers will continue to take advantage of float.

Types of Float

collection float
The delay between the time when a payer or customer deducts a payment from its checking account ledger and the time when the payee or vendor actually receives these funds in a spendable form.

disbursement float
The lapse between the time when a firm deducts a payment from its checking account ledger (disburses it) and the time when funds are actually withdrawn from its account.

Currently, business firms and individuals can experience both collection and disbursement float in the process of making financial transactions. **Collection float** results from the delay between the time when a payer or customer deducts a payment from its checking account ledger and the time when the payee actually receives the funds in a spendable form. Thus, collection float is experienced by the payee and is a delay in the receipt of funds.

Disbursement float results from the lapse between the time when a firm deducts a payment from its checking account ledger (disburses it) and the time when funds are actually withdrawn from its account. Disbursement float is experienced by the payer and is a delay in the actual withdrawal of funds.

Components of Float

mail float
The delay between the time when a payer mails a payment and the time when the payee receives it.

processing float
The delay between the receipt of a check by the payee and its deposit in the firm's account.

clearing float
The delay between the deposit of a check by the payee and the actual availability of the funds.

Both collection float and disbursement float have the same three basic components:

1. **Mail float:** The delay between the time when a payer places payment in the mail and the time when it is received by the payee.
2. **Processing float:** The delay between the receipt of a check by the payee and the deposit of it in the firm's account.
3. **Clearing float:** The delay between the deposit of a check by the payee and the actual availability of the funds. This component of float is attributable to the time required for a check to clear the banking system.[4] The use of electronic methods to process checks within the banking system continues to reduce clearing float.

Figure 16.2 illustrates the key components of float resulting from the issuance and mailing of a check by the payer company to the payee company on day zero. The entire process required a total of 9 days: 3 days' mail float, 2 days'

---

4. Currently, on checks cleared through the Federal Reserve banking system, clearing time of less than 2 days is guaranteed to the collecting bank, but, of course, this does not assure the depositor (payee) that the bank will make the money available within 2 days. With the passage of the *Expedited Funds Availability Act of 1987*, banks are required to make funds available to payees within 2 business days of deposit on local (same Federal Reserve processing region) checks and within 5 business days on out-of-town checks.

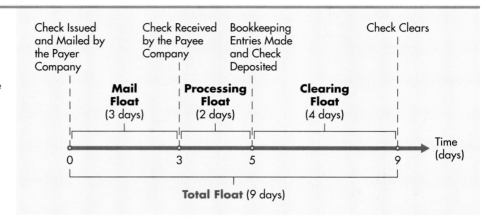

FIGURE 16.2

Float Time Line
Float resulting from a check issued and mailed by the payer company to the payee company

processing float, and 4 days' clearing float. To the payer company, the delay is disbursement float; to the payee company, the delay is collection float.

Speeding Up Collections

Firms want not only to stimulate customers to pay accounts as promptly as possible but also to convert their payments into a spendable form as quickly as possible—in other words, to *minimize collection float*. A variety of techniques are aimed at *speeding up collections*, and thereby reducing collection float.

Concentration Banking

Firms with numerous sales outlets throughout the country often designate certain offices as collection centers for given geographic areas. Customers in these areas remit their payments to these offices, which in turn deposit the receipts in local banks. At certain times, or when needed, funds are transferred by wire from these regional banks to a concentration, or disbursing, bank, from which bill payments are dispatched.[5]

concentration banking
A collection procedure in which payments are made to regional collection centers, then deposited in local banks for quick clearing. Shortens mail and clearing float.

    Concentration banking is used to reduce collection float by shortening the mail and clearing float components. Mail float is reduced because regional collection centers are closer to the point from which the check is sent. Clearing float may also be reduced, because the payee's regional bank is likely to be in the same Federal Reserve district or the same city as the bank on which the check is drawn; it may even be the same bank. A reduction in clearing float will, of course, make funds available to the firm more quickly.

Example ▼

Suppose Erich, Inc., a hair products manufacturer, could change to concentration banking and reduce its collection period by 3 days. If the company normally carried $10 million in receivables and that level represented 30 days of sales, cut-

---

5. Most large firms disburse funds, or pay bills, only from certain banks. Normally, separate payroll and general expense accounts are maintained.

ting 3 days from the collection process would result in a $1 million decline in receivables [(3 ÷ 30) × $10,000,000]. Given a 10% opportunity cost, the gross annual benefits of concentration banking would amount to $100,000 (.10 × $1,000,000). Clearly, assuming no change in risk, as long as total annual costs—*incremental* administrative costs and bank service fees and the opportunity cost of holding specified minimum bank balances—are less than the expected annual benefits of $100,000, Erich, Inc.'s proposed program of concentration banking should be implemented.

Lockboxes

lockbox system
A collection procedure in which payers send their payments to a nearby post office box that is emptied by the firm's bank several times daily; the bank deposits the payment checks in the firm's account. Shortens processing, mail, and clearing float.

Another method used to reduce collection float is the **lockbox system,** which differs from concentration banking in several important ways. Instead of mailing payment to a collection center, the payer sends it to a post office box that is emptied by the firm's bank several times daily. The bank deposits the checks in the firm's account and sends to the collecting firm a deposit slip (or a computer file) indicating the payments received. Lockboxes normally are geographically dispersed, and the funds, when collected, are wired from each lockbox bank to the firm's disbursing bank.

The lockbox system is superior to concentration banking because it reduces processing float as well as mail and clearing float. The bank immediately deposits the receipts in the firm's account, so that processing occurs *after* funds are deposited. This allows the firm to use the funds almost immediately for disbursing payments. Additional reductions in mail float may also result, because payments do not have to be delivered but are picked up by the bank at the post office.

Example ▼ Dennison Group, a manufacturer of disposable razors, has annual credit sales of $6 million, which are billed at a constant rate each day. It takes about 4 days to receive customers' payments at corporate headquarters. It takes another day for the credit department to process receipts and deposit them in the bank. A cash management consultant has told Dennison that a lockbox system would shorten the mail float from 4 days to 1 ½ days and completely eliminate the processing float. The lockbox system would cost the firm $8,000 per year. Dennison currently earns 12% on investments of comparable risk. The lockbox system would free $58,333 of cash [($6 million ÷ 360 days) × (4 days mail float + 1 day processing float − 1 ½ days mail float)] that is currently tied up in mail and processing float. The gross annual benefit would be $7,000 (.12 × $58,333). Because the $7,000 gross annual benefit is less than the $8,000 annual cost, Dennison ▲ should *not* use the lockbox.

Direct Sends

direct send
A collection procedure in which the payee presents checks for payment directly to the banks on which they are drawn, reducing clearing float.

To reduce clearing float, firms that have received large checks drawn on distant banks or a large number of checks drawn on banks in a given city may arrange to present these checks directly for payment to the bank on which they are drawn. Such a procedure is called a **direct send.** Rather than depositing these checks in its collection account, the firm arranges to present the checks to the bank on which they are drawn and receive immediate payment. The firm can use Express

Mail or private express services to get the checks into a bank in the same city or to a sales office where an employee can take the checks to the bank and present them for payment. In most cases, the funds will be transferred via wire into the firm's disbursement account.

Deciding whether to use direct sends is relatively straightforward. If the benefits from the reduced clearing time are greater than the cost, the checks should be sent directly for payment rather than cleared through normal banking channels.

Example ▼

If a firm with an opportunity to earn 10% on its idle balances can, through a direct send, make available $1.2 million 3 days earlier than would otherwise be the case, the benefit of this direct send would be $1,000 [.10 × (3 days ÷ 360 days) × $1,200,000]. If the cost of achieving this 3-day reduction in float is less than $1,000, the direct send would be recommended. ▲

Other Techniques

A number of other techniques can be used to reduce collection float. One method that is commonly used by firms that collect a fixed amount from customers on a regular basis is the preauthorized check. A **preauthorized check (PAC)** is a check written against a customer's checking account for a previously agreed-upon amount by the firm to which it is payable. Because the check has been legally authorized by the customer, it does not require the customer's signature. The payee merely issues and then deposits the PAC in its account. The check then clears through the banking system in the usual way.

Firms with multiple collection points use depository transfer checks to speed up the transfer of funds. A **depository transfer check (DTC)** is an unsigned check drawn on one of the firm's bank accounts and deposited into its account at another bank—typically, a concentration or major disbursing bank. Once the DTC has cleared the bank on which it is drawn, the actual transfer of funds is completed. Most firms currently transmit deposit information via telephone rather than by mail to their concentration banks, which then prepare and deposit DTCs into the firm's accounts.

Firms also frequently use wire transfers to reduce collection float. **Wire transfers** are telegraphic communications that, via bookkeeping entries, remove funds from the payer's bank and deposit them into the payee's bank. Wire transfers can eliminate mail and clearing float and may reduce processing float as well. They are sometimes used instead of DTCs to move funds into key disbursing accounts, although a wire transfer is more expensive than a DTC.

Another popular method of accelerating cash inflows is the use of **ACH (automated clearinghouse) debits.** These are preauthorized electronic withdrawals from the payer's account. A computerized clearing facility (called an automated clearinghouse, or ACH) makes a paperless transfer of funds between the payer and payee banks and settles accounts among participating banks. Individual depositor accounts are settled by respective bank balance adjustments. ACH transfers clear in 1 day, in most cases reducing mail, processing, and clearing float.

preauthorized check (PAC)
A check written by the payee against a customer's checking account for a previously agreed-upon amount.

depository transfer check (DTC)
An unsigned check drawn on one of the firm's bank accounts and deposited into its account at a concentration or major disbursement bank.

wire transfers
Telegraphic communications that, via bookkeeping entries, remove funds from the payer's bank and deposit them into the payee's bank.

ACH (automated clearinghouse) debits
Preauthorized electronic withdrawals from the payer's account that are transferred to the payee's account via a settlement among banks by the automated clearinghouse.

Slowing Down Disbursements

In terms of accounts payable, the firm wants not only to pay its accounts as late as possible but also to slow down the availability of funds to suppliers and employees once the payment has been dispatched. In other words, it wants to *maximize disbursement float*. A variety of techniques aimed at *slowing down disbursements* and thereby increasing disbursement float are available.

Controlled Disbursing

controlled disbursing
The strategic use of mailing points and bank accounts to lengthen mail float and clearing float, respectively.

Controlled disbursing involves the strategic use of mailing points and bank accounts to lengthen mail float and clearing float, respectively. When the date of postmark is considered the effective date of payment by the supplier, the firm may be able to lengthen the mail time associated with disbursements.[6] It can place payments in the mail at locations from which they will take a considerable amount of time to reach the supplier. Typically, small towns that are not close to major highways or cities provide opportunities to increase mail float. Of course, the benefits of using selected mailing points may not justify the costs of this strategy, particularly because the U.S. Postal Service gives rate reductions on mail that is presorted by ZIP Code and sent from designated major post offices.

Hint   Data on clearing time among banks located in various cities can be developed by the firm itself. It also can be obtained from a major bank's cash management service department or purchased from a firm that sells such information.

Availability of data on check-clearing times allows firms to develop disbursement schemes that maximize clearing float on their payments. These methods involve assigning payments going to vendors in certain geographic areas to be drawn on specific banks from which maximum clearing float will result.

Playing the Float

playing the float
A method of consciously anticipating the resulting float, or delay, associated with the payment process and using it to keep funds in an interest-earning form for as long as possible.

Playing the float is a method of consciously anticipating the resulting float, or delay, associated with the payment process. Firms often play the float by writing checks against funds that are not currently in their checking accounts. They can do this because they know that a delay will occur between the receipt and the deposit of checks by suppliers and the actual withdrawal of funds from their checking accounts. Although the ineffective use of this practice could result in problems associated with "bounced checks," many firms use float to stretch out their accounts payable.[7]

Firms play the float in a variety of ways—all of which are aimed at keeping funds in an interest-earning form for as long as possible. For example, one way of playing the float is to deposit a certain proportion of a payroll into the firm's checking account on several successive days *following* the issuance of a group of

---

6. A supplier's credit terms as well as any penalties associated with late payment are typically stated in the invoice that accompanies the shipment of merchandise. Of course, depending on the supplier, the terms of the invoice may or may not be enforced. Knowledge of the strictness of suppliers' credit terms is often useful for developing the firm's accounts payable strategies.

7. Issuing checks against nonexistent funds can be prosecuted only if the check is drawn on insufficient funds. The fact that a check bounces is viewed as prima facie—but not irrefutable—evidence of fraud. The burden of proof that the act causing insufficient funds was not willful is placed on the issuer. If such proof cannot be given, the issuer will be convicted of fraud. Prosecution rarely results, because the issuer usually obtains sufficient funds to satisfy the obligation prior to the filing of any criminal charges. Nevertheless, issuing checks against nonexistent funds is unethical.

staggered funding
A way to *play the float* by depositing a certain proportion of a payroll into the firm's checking account on several successive days *following* the issuance of a group of checks.

checks. This technique is commonly referred to as **staggered funding.** If the firm can determine from historic data that only 25 percent of its payroll checks are cashed on the day immediately following the issuance of the checks, then only 25 percent of the value of the payroll needs to be in its checking account 1 day later. The amount of checks cashed on each of several succeeding days can also be estimated until the entire payroll is accounted for. Normally, however, to protect itself against any irregularities, a firm will place slightly more money in its account than is needed to cover the expected withdrawals.

payable-through draft
A draft drawn on the payer's checking account, payable to a given payee but not payable on demand; approval of the draft by the payer is required before the bank pays the draft.

Another way of playing the float is to use payable-through drafts, rather than checks, to pay large sums of money. A **payable-through draft** is similar to a check in that it is drawn on the payer's checking account and is payable to a given payee. Unlike a check, however, it is not payable on demand; approval of the draft by the payer is required before the bank pays the draft. The advantage to the payer is that money does not have to be placed on deposit until the draft clears the bank; instead, the firm can invest it in short-term money market vehicles. As the drafts are cleared for payment by the payer, the investments can be liquidated and the funds used to cover the drafts. Banks may charge a modest fee for processing the drafts, but this technique enables the firm to keep its money more fully invested for a longer period of time.

Example ▼ Assume that by using payable-through drafts in place of checks to meet its payroll, Mardon Manufacturing, a producer of chain link fencing, can increase its disbursement float by 5 days. By keeping its monthly payroll of $12 million invested at 10% for 5 additional days each month for an entire year, the firm will realize profits of $200,000 from this increase in float [.10 × (5 days ÷ 360
▲ days) × $12,000,000 × (12 months/year) = $200,000].

But note that many vendors will not accept payable-through drafts as payment for the goods or services provided, and in some states the use of these drafts is prohibited by law.

Overdraft Systems, Zero-Balance Accounts, and ACH Credits

Firms that aggressively manage cash disbursements will often arrange for some type of overdraft system or a zero-balance account. In an **overdraft system,** if the firm's checking account balance is insufficient to cover all checks presented against the account, the bank will automatically lend the firm enough money to cover the amount of the overdraft. The bank, of course, will charge the firm interest on the funds lent and will limit the amount of overdraft coverage. Such an arrangement is important for a business that actively plays the float.

overdraft system
Automatic coverage by the bank of all checks presented against the firm's account, regardless of the account balance.

zero-balance account
A checking account in which a zero balance is maintained and the firm is required to deposit funds to cover checks drawn on the account only as they are presented for payment.

Firms can also establish **zero-balance accounts**—checking accounts in which zero balances are maintained. Under this arrangement, each day the bank will notify the firm of the total amount of checks presented against the account. The firm then transfers only that amount—typically, from a master account or through liquidation of a portion of its marketable securities—into the account. Once the corresponding checks have been paid, the account balance reverts to zero. The bank, of course, must be compensated for this service.

The Bank Branch in Your PC

It's 9 P.M. and you are worried. Did the big check you wrote yesterday clear today and overdraw your checking account? There's no need to spend a sleepless night until the bank opens. With online banking, you can check your account status right away from your computer, via the Internet or through direct phone lines that work with personal finance software. If necessary, you can transfer funds from your savings account. While you are at it, you may as well pay some bills electronically. It's easy: no need to write checks or spend money on postage.

Online banking is finally catching on with consumers. Mercer Management, a national consulting firm, estimates that about 20 percent of U.S. households will bank via computer by 2003. In addition to account management and bill-paying services, online programs at many banks allow you to apply for a loan, purchase securities, and get financial advice.

Banks also benefit from the cost savings of electronic banking. According to Richard Herrington, president of Franklin Financial Corp., it costs $1.80 for a teller to handle a transaction, compared to 26 cents for an online transaction.

Some banks give customers free Internet access and charge from $6 to $10 per month for bill-paying services, and others charge monthly fees for both Internet access and bill paying. But monthly charges aren't the only thing to consider before switching to online banking. With electronic payments, you may lose your ability to play the float because the bank withdraws funds on the payment date. When you pay a bill by writing a check and mailing it, 4 to 6 days may pass before the money is actually withdrawn from your account, so you keep the float. If you opt for electronic banking, you'd be wise to monitor your account balances closely—an easy enough task from your in-home bank branch!

ACH (automated clearinghouse) credits
Deposits of payroll directly into the payees' (employees') accounts. Sacrifices disbursement float but may generate goodwill for the employer.

ACH (automated clearinghouse) credits are frequently used by corporations for making direct bank deposits of payroll into the payees' (employees') accounts. Disbursement float is sacrificed with this technique because ACH transactions immediately draw down the company's payroll account on payday, whereas in check-based payroll systems, not all employees cash their checks on payday, thus allowing the firm to use *staggered funding* as discussed earlier. The benefit of ACH credits is that employees enjoy convenience, which may generate enough goodwill to justify the firm's loss of float.

The Role of Banking Relationships

Maintaining strong banking relations is one of the most important elements in an effective cash management system. Banks have become keenly aware of the profitability of corporate accounts and in recent years have developed a number of

Hint The financial manager of a small business must have a very strong relationship with a commercial banker. Since the small firm cannot afford to hire someone strictly as a cash manager, the financial manager, who is probably a generalist, needs to rely on the expertise of the commercial banker for the firm's most cost-effective means of managing cash.

innovative services to attract businesses. No longer are banks simply places to establish checking accounts and secure loans; instead, they have become the source of a wide variety of cash management services. For example, banks now sell to commercial clients sophisticated information-processing packages that deal with everything from basic accounting and budgeting to complex multinational disbursement and centralized cash control. All are designed to help financial managers maximize day-to-day cash availability and facilitate short-term investing. Of course, bank services should be used only when the benefits derived from them are greater than their costs.

Example ▼

Clear, Inc., an optical lens manufacturer, has been offered a cash management service that should eliminate "excess" cash on deposit and reduce certain administrative and clerical costs. The service, which costs $50,000 per year, involves the collection, movement, and reporting of corporate cash. The purported benefits are these: (1) Tighter control over the cash flow should reduce the negotiated financing required to support operations by some $600,000 and (2) administrative and clerical costs should drop by about $1,000 per month (because the bank will be taking on administrative and clerical duties as part of the service). By using a 10% opportunity cost, the benefits and costs would be as follows:

Benefits (annual)	
Savings from reduced financing (.10 × $600,000)	$60,000
Reduced administrative and clerical costs ($1,000 × 12)	12,000
Total annual benefits	$72,000
Less: Costs (annual)	
Bank service charge	50,000
Net annual benefits	$22,000

From a benefit–cost perspective, the proposal looks promising. The major risk, of course, is that the purported benefits will fall far short of the mark. Management, however, can get at least an idea of such risk by estimating the minimum reduction in financing or opportunity cost required to generate a sufficient level of total benefits. **▲**

International Cash Management

Although the motivations for holding cash and the basic concepts underlying cash management are the same worldwide, there are dramatic differences in practical cash management techniques for international versus strictly domestic business transactions. In fact, the differences between U.S. and international banking and payment systems are so great that only an elementary comparison is made here. More detailed information about payments and cash management systems abroad can be found in textbooks on international finance or short-term financial (working capital) management.

Differences in Banking Systems

Banking systems outside the United States differ fundamentally from the U.S. model in several key aspects. First, foreign banks are generally far less restricted either geographically or in the services they are allowed to offer. Second, retail transactions are typically routed through a **Giro system** that is usually operated by, or in association with, the national postal system. Because of this direct payment system, checks are used much less frequently than in the United States. Third, banks in other countries are allowed to pay interest on corporate demand deposits, and they also routinely provide overdraft protection.

To recoup the cost of these services, however, non-U.S. banks generally charge more and higher fees for services and also engage in the practice of **value dating.** This involves delaying, often for days or even weeks, the availability of funds deposited with the bank. This lag between the date funds are deposited and when they are usable obviously complicates cash management procedures. If a transaction involves collecting on a foreign-currency–denominated check drawn on a bank outside of the host country, the delay in availability of good funds can be very long indeed.

Cash Management Practices

The cash management practices of multinational corporations are complicated by the need both to maintain local currency deposit balances in banks in every country in which the firm operates and to retain centralized control over cash balances and cash flows that, in total, can be quite large. The largest multinational corporations have honed their treasury operations to such an extent that they can balance these conflicting objectives efficiently and even profitably. To do so, they rely on the cash collection, disbursement, and foreign exchange trading expertise of large international banks, all of which operate very sophisticated computerized treasury services.

Multinational firms can also minimize their cash requirements by using **intracompany netting.** As described in Chapter 15, when two subsidiaries in different countries trade with each other—thereby generating payment obligations to each other—only the net amount of payment owed will be transferred across national boundaries. In fact, it may be possible to handle many of these transactions strictly internally—on the books of the parent company—without having to resort to the international payment system at all.

Large international cash payments are almost invariably handled by one of the wire transfer services operated by international banking consortia. The most important of these networks is the **Clearing House Interbank Payment System,** called **CHIPS.** Hundreds of billions of dollars worth of payments are settled *every day* using wire transfer and settlement services. Although the bulk of these transactions result from foreign exchange trading, many are also due to settlement of international payment obligations.

Multinational companies with excess funds to invest benefit from having access to a wide variety of government and corporate investment vehicles. Companies naturally have access to all of the marketable securities offered to

Giro system
System through which retail transactions are handled in association with a foreign country's national postal system.

value dating
A procedure used by non-U.S. banks to delay, often for days or even weeks, the availability of funds deposited with them.

intracompany netting
A technique used by subsidiaries of multinational firms to minimize their cash requirements by transferring across national boundaries only the net amount of payments owed between them.

Clearing House Interbank Payment System (CHIPS)
The most important wire transfer service; operated by international banking consortia.

U.S. investors (described in the following section). Multinational companies can also invest funds in foreign government securities, or they can invest directly in the *Eurocurrency market* either in dollars or in other convertible currencies. This financial flexibility often provides multinational corporations with a key competitive advantage, particularly if they need to transfer funds into or out of countries experiencing political or financial difficulties.

❓ Review Questions

16–6 Define *float* and describe its three basic components. Compare and contrast collection and disbursement float, and state the financial manager's goal with respect to each of these types of float.

16–7 Briefly describe the key features of each of the following techniques for *speeding up collections*: (**a**) concentration banking, (**b**) lockboxes, (**c**) direct sends, (**d**) preauthorized checks (PACs), (**e**) depository transfer checks (DTCs), (**f**) wire transfers, and (**g**) ACH (automated clearinghouse) debits.

16–8 Briefly describe the key features of each of the following techniques for *slowing down disbursements*: (**a**) controlled disbursing, (**b**) playing the float, (**c**) overdraft systems, (**d**) zero-balance accounts, and (**e**) ACH (automated clearinghouse) credits.

16–9 How should available bank services used in the cash management process be evaluated?

16–10 Describe the key differences between banking systems outside the United States and the U.S. model. What is *value dating* and how does it affect international cash management?

16–11 What is *intracompany netting* and what is its purpose? What is *CHIPS* and what role does it play in the international payment system?

16.4 Marketable Securities

Marketable securities are short-term, interest-earning, money market instruments that can easily be converted into cash.[8] Marketable securities are classified as part of the firm's liquid assets. The securities that are most commonly held as part of the firm's marketable securities portfolio are divided into two groups: (1) government issues and (2) nongovernment issues. Before describing both of these types of marketable securities, we discuss the basic characteristics of marketable securities. Table 16.1 summarizes the key features and recent (April 7, 1999) yields for the marketable securities described in the sections that follow.

---

8. As explained in Chapter 2, the *money market* results from a financial relationship between the suppliers and demanders of short-term funds, that is, marketable securities.

TABLE 16.1	Features and Recent Yields on Popular Marketable Securities[a]

Government Issues

Security	Issuer	Description	Initial maturity	Risk and return	Yield on April 7, 1999[b]
Treasury bills	U.S. Treasury	Issued weekly at auction; sold at a discount; strong secondary market	91 and 182 days, occasionally 1 year	Lowest, virtually risk-free	4.38%
Treasury notes	U.S. Treasury	Stated interest rate; interest paid semiannually; strong secondary market	1 to 10 years	Low, but slightly higher than U.S. Treasury bills	4.49%
Federal agency issues	Agencies of federal government	Not an obligation of U.S. Treasury; strong secondary market	9 months to 30 years	Slightly higher than U.S. Treasury issues	4.64%[c]

Nongovernment Issues

Security	Issuer	Description	Initial maturity	Risk and return	Yield on April 7, 1999[b]
Negotiable certificates of deposit (CDs)	Commercial banks	Represent specific cash deposits in commercial banks; amounts and maturities tailored to investor needs; large denominations; good secondary market	1 month to 3 years	Higher than U.S. Treasury issues and comparable to commercial paper	4.90%
Commercial paper	Corporation with a high credit standing	Unsecured note of issuer; large denominations	3 to 270 days	Higher than U.S. Treasury issues and comparable to negotiable CDs	4.83%
Banker's acceptances	Banks	Results from a bank guarantee of a business transaction; sold at discount from maturity value	30 to 180 days	Slightly lower than negotiable CDs and commercial paper but higher than U.S. Treasury issues	4.76%
Eurodollar deposits	Foreign banks	Deposits of currency not native to the country in which the bank is located; large denominations; active secondary market	1 day to 3 years	Highest, due to less regulation of depository banks and some foreign exchange risk	4.93%
Money market mutual funds	Professional portfolio management companies	Professionally managed portfolios of marketable securities; provide instant liquidity	None— depends on wishes of investor	Vary, but generally higher than U.S. Treasury issues and comparable to negotiable CDs and commercial paper	4.27%[d]
Repurchase agreements	Bank or security dealer	Bank or security dealer sells specific securities to firm and agrees to repurchase them at a specific price and time	Customized to purchaser's needs	Generally slightly below that associated with the outright purchase of the security	—

[a]The prime rate of interest at this time was 7.75%.

[b]Yields obtained for 3-month maturities of each security.

[c]A Federal National Mortgage Association (FNMA) issue maturing in July 1999 is used here in the absence of any average-yield data.

[d]The Schwab Money Market Fund with an average maturity of 71 days is used here in the absence of any average-yield data.

Source: Wall Street Journal, April 8, 1999, pp. C13, C18, C20.

Characteristics of Marketable Securities

The basic characteristics of marketable securities affect the degree of their salability. To be truly marketable, a security must have two basic characteristics: (1) a ready market and (2) safety of principal (no likelihood of loss in value).

A Ready Market

breadth of a market
A characteristic of a ready market, determined by the number of participants (buyers) in the market.

depth of a market
A characteristic of a ready market, determined by its ability to absorb the purchase or sale of a large dollar amount of a particular security.

The market for a security should have both breadth and depth to minimize the amount of time required to convert it into cash. The **breadth of a market** is determined by the number of participants (buyers). A broad market is one that has many participants. The **depth of a market** is determined by its ability to absorb the purchase or sale of a large dollar amount of a particular security. It is therefore possible to have a broad market that has no depth. Thus 100,000 participants each willing to purchase one share of a security is less desirable than 1,000 participants each willing to purchase 2,000 shares. Although both breadth and depth are needed to make a security salable, it is much more important for a market to have depth.

Safety of Principal

safety of principal
The ease of salability of a security for close to its initial value.

There should be little or no loss in the value of a marketable security over time. Consider a security that was recently purchased for $1,000. If it can be sold quickly for $500, does that make it marketable? No. According to the definition of marketability, the security not only must be salable quickly, but also must be salable for close to the amount initially invested. This aspect of marketability is referred to as **safety of principal.** Only securities that can be easily converted into cash without experiencing any appreciable reduction in principal are candidates for short-term investment.

Government Issues

The short-term obligations issued by the federal government and available as marketable security investments are Treasury bills, Treasury notes, and federal agency issues. These securities have relatively low yields due to their low risk and because the interest income on all Treasury issues and most federal agency issues, although taxable at the federal level, is exempt from state and local taxes.

Treasury Bills

Treasury bills
U.S. Treasury obligations issued weekly on an auction basis, having varying maturities, generally under 1 year, and virtually no risk.

Treasury bills are obligations of the U.S. Treasury that are issued weekly on an auction basis. The most common maturities are 91 and 182 days, although bills with 1-year maturities are occasionally sold. Treasury bills are sold by competitive bidding. Because they are issued in bearer form, there is a strong *secondary (resale) market.* The bills are sold at a discount from their face value, the face value being received at maturity. The smallest denomination of a Treasury bill currently available is $1,000. Because Treasury bills are issues of the United States government, they are considered to be virtually risk-free. For this reason, and because of the strong secondary market for them, Treasury bills are one of the most popular marketable securities. The yields on Treasury bills are generally lower than those on any other marketable securities due to their virtually risk-free nature and favorable tax status.

Treasury Notes

Treasury notes
U.S. Treasury obligations with initial maturities of between 1 and 10 years, paying interest at a stated rate semiannually, and having virtually no risk.

Treasury notes have initial maturities of between 1 and 10 years; due to the existence of a strong secondary market, they are quite attractive marketable security investments. They are generally issued in minimum denominations of either $1,000 or $5,000, carry a coupon interest rate, and pay interest semiannually. Because of their virtually risk-free nature and favorable tax status, Treasury notes generally have a low yield relative to other securities with similar maturities.

Federal Agency Issues

federal agency issues
Low-risk securities issued by government agencies but not guaranteed by the U.S. Treasury, having generally short maturities, and offering slightly higher yields than comparable U.S. Treasury issues.

Certain agencies of the federal government issue their own debt. These **federal agency issues** are not part of the public debt, are not a legal obligation of the U.S. Treasury, and are not guaranteed by the U.S. Treasury. Regardless of their lack of direct government backing, the issues of government agencies are readily accepted as low-risk securities, because most purchasers feel that they are implicitly guaranteed by the federal government. Agency issues generally have minimum denominations of $1,000 or more and are issued either with a stated interest rate or at a discount. Agencies commonly issuing short-term instruments include the Federal Farm Credit Bank (FFCB), the Federal Home Loan Bank (FHLB), and the Federal National Mortgage Association (FNMA). Of course, instead of agency issues with short initial maturities, other longer-term agency issues with less than 1 year to maturity could be purchased. Most agency issues offer slightly higher yields than U.S. Treasury issues having similar maturities. Agency issues have a strong secondary market, which is most easily reached through government securities dealers.

Nongovernment Issues

Additional marketable securities are issued by banks or businesses. These nongovernment issues typically have slightly higher yields than government issues with similar maturities due to the slightly higher risks associated with them and the fact that their interest income is taxable at all levels—federal, state, and local. The principal nongovernment marketable securities are described in what follows.

Negotiable Certificates of Deposit (CDs)

negotiable certificates of deposit (CDs)
Legally transferable instruments that represent specific cash deposits in commercial banks and have varying maturities and yields based on size, maturity, and prevailing money market conditions. Yields are generally above those on U.S. Treasury issues and comparable to those on commercial paper with similar maturities.

Negotiable certificates of deposit (CDs) are legally transferable instruments that represent the deposit of a certain number of dollars in a commercial bank. The amounts and maturities are normally tailored to the investor's needs. Average maturities of 30 days are common. A good secondary market for CDs exists. Normally, the smallest denomination for a negotiable CD is $100,000. The yields on CDs are initially set on the basis of size, maturity, and prevailing money market conditions. They are typically above those on U.S. Treasury issues and comparable to the yields on commercial paper with similar maturities.

Commercial Paper

commercial paper
A short-term, unsecured promissory note issued by a corporation that has a very high credit standing, having a yield above that paid on U.S. Treasury issues and comparable to that available on negotiable CDs with similar maturities.

Commercial paper is a short-term, unsecured promissory note issued by a corporation that has a very high credit standing.[9] These notes are generally issued in multiples of $100,000 and have initial maturities of anywhere from 3 to 270 days.[10] They can be sold directly by the issuer or through dealers. The yield on commercial paper typically is above that paid on U.S. Treasury issues and comparable to that on negotiable CDs with similar maturities.

Banker's Acceptances

banker's acceptances
Short-term, low-risk marketable securities arising from bank guarantees of business transactions; are sold by banks at a discount from their maturity value and provide yields slightly below those on negotiable CDs and commercial paper, but higher than those on U.S. Treasury issues.

Banker's acceptances arise from a short-term credit arrangement used by businesses to finance transactions, especially those involving firms in foreign countries or firms with unknown credit capacities. The purchaser requests its bank to issue a *letter of credit* on its behalf, authorizing the seller to draw a *time draft*—an order to pay a specified amount at a specified time—in payment for the goods. Once the goods are shipped, the seller presents the time draft along with proof of shipment to its bank. The seller's bank then forwards the draft to the buyer's bank for acceptance and receives payment. The buyer's bank may either hold the acceptance to maturity or sell it at a discount in the money market. If it is sold, the size of the discount from the acceptance's maturity value and the amount of time until the acceptance is paid determine the purchaser's yield.

As a result of its sale, the banker's acceptance becomes a marketable security that can be traded in the marketplace. The initial maturities of banker's acceptances are typically between 30 and 180 days, 90 days being most common. A banker's acceptance is a low-risk security because at least two, and sometimes three, parties may be liable for its payment at maturity. The yields on banker's acceptances are generally slightly below those on negotiable CDs and commercial paper, but higher than those on U.S. Treasury issues.

Eurodollar Deposits

Eurodollar deposits
Deposits of currency not native to the country in which the bank is located; legally transferable, usually pay interest at maturity, and typically denominated in units of $1 million. Provide yields above nearly all other marketable securities with similar maturities.

Eurodollar deposits are deposits of currency that are not native to the country in which the bank is located. London is the center of the Eurodollar market. Other important centers are Paris, Frankfurt, Zurich, Nassau (Bahamas), Singapore, and Hong Kong. Nearly 75 percent of these deposits are in the form of U.S. dollars. The deposits are legally transferable, usually pay interest at maturity, and are typically denominated in units of $1 million. Maturities range from overnight to several years, with most being in the 1-week to 6-month maturity range.

Eurodollar deposits tend to provide yields above nearly all other marketable securities, government or nongovernment, with similar maturities. These higher

---

9. The role of commercial paper from the point of view of the issuer is included in the discussion in Chapter 15 of the various sources of short-term financing available to business.

10. The maximum maturity is 270 days because the Securities and Exchange Commission (SEC) requires formal registration of corporate issues having maturities greater than 270 days.

yields are attributable to (1) the fact that the depository banks are generally less closely regulated than U.S. banks and are therefore more risky, and (2) some foreign exchange risk may be present. An active secondary market allows Eurodollar deposits to be used to meet all three motives for holding cash and near-cash balances.

Money Market Mutual Funds

money market mutual funds
Professionally managed portfolios of various popular marketable securities, having instant liquidity, competitive yields, and often-low transactions costs.

Money market mutual funds, often called *money funds,* are professionally managed portfolios of marketable securities. Shares in these funds can be easily acquired. A minimum initial investment of as low as $500, but generally $1,000 or more, is required. Money funds provide instant liquidity in much the same way as a checking or savings account. By investing in these funds, investors often earn returns that are comparable to or higher than those from negotiable CDs and commercial paper—especially during periods of high interest rates. In recent years, generally low interest rates have caused money fund returns to fall below those on most other marketable securities. Nevertheless, due to the high liquidity, competitive yields, and often-low transactions costs, these funds have achieved significant growth in size and popularity.

Repurchase Agreements

repurchase agreement
An arrangement whereby a bank or securities dealer sells specific marketable securities to a firm and agrees to buy them back at a specific price and time.

A **repurchase agreement** is not a specific security. It is an arrangement whereby a bank or securities dealer sells specific marketable securities to a firm and agrees to buy them back at a specific price at a specified point in time. In exchange for the tailor-made maturity date provided by this arrangement, the seller provides the purchaser with a return slightly below that obtainable through outright purchase of similar marketable securities. The benefit to the purchaser is the guaranteed repurchase, and the tailor-made maturity date ensures that the purchaser will have cash at a specified point in time. The actual securities involved may be government or nongovernment issues. Repurchase agreements are ideal for marketable securities investments made to satisfy the transactions motive.

? Review Questions

16–12 What two characteristics make a security marketable? Which aspect of a market for a security is more important—breadth or depth? Why?

16–13 Discuss the two reasons why government issues of marketable securities have generally lower yields than nongovernment issues with similar maturities.

16–14 For each of the following government-based marketable securities, give a brief description emphasizing issuer, initial maturity, liquidity, risk, and return: (a) Treasury bill, (b) Treasury note, and (c) federal agency issue.

16–15 Describe the basic features—including issuer, initial maturity, liquidity, risk, and return—of each of the following nongovernment marketable securities: (a) negotiable certificate of deposit (CD), (b) commercial paper, (c) banker's acceptance, and (d) Eurodollar deposit.

16–16   Briefly describe the basic features of the following marketable securities, and explain how they both involve other marketable securities: (**a**) money market mutual fund and (**b**) repurchase agreement

16.5 Cash Conversion Models

An important responsibility of the financial manager is to determine the optimum quantity of marketable securities to convert into cash when additional cash is needed, and, conversely, the optimum quantity of cash to convert to marketable securities when a buildup of surplus cash occurs. The cash conversion quantity depends on a number of factors, including the fixed cost of transferring funds between cash and marketable securities, the rate of interest that can be earned on marketable securities, and the firm's demand for cash. Because of the number of factors, reasonably sophisticated models are required to determine the *optimum* cash conversion quantity. These **cash conversion models** balance the relevant costs and benefits of holding cash versus investing in marketable securities to determine the economically optimum quantity of each. Here we consider two of the best-known cash conversion models—the Baumol model and the Miller-Orr model.

cash conversion models
Models that balance the relevant costs and benefits of holding cash versus investing in marketable securities, to determine the economically optimum quantity of each.

Baumol Model

The **Baumol model**[11] is a simple approach that provides for cost-efficient cash balances by determining the optimal cash conversion quantity. Much like the process of determining optimal order quantities of inventory, which we'll discuss in the next chapter, the Baumol model treats cash as an inventory item whose inflows and outflows can be predicted with *certainty*. A portfolio of marketable securities acts as a backup reservoir of funds, from which cash balances can be replenished or to which excess cash can be moved in order to earn a return.

The firm manages its cash "inventory" by calculating two costs: (1) the cost of converting marketable securities to cash and vice versa and (2) the cost of holding cash rather than marketable securities. The first of these is called the *conversion cost*; the second is the *opportunity cost*. The conversion cost includes the fixed cost of placing an order for cash or marketable securities. It includes the cost of communicating the need to transfer funds to or from the cash account, paperwork costs, brokerage fees, and the cost of any follow-up action. The conversion cost is stated as dollars per conversion. The opportunity cost is simply the rate of interest that can be earned on marketable securities. Alternatively, it can be viewed as the interest earnings per dollar given up as a result of holding funds in a noninterest-earning cash account.

---

11. William J. Baumol, "The Transactions Demand for Cash: An Inventory Theoretic Approach," *Quarterly Journal of Economics* (November 1952), pp. 545–556.

Economic Conversion Quantity (ECQ)

Using the conversion and the opportunity costs, the model calculates the **economic conversion quantity (ECQ)**. This amount is the cost-minimizing quantity in which the firm should convert marketable securities to cash or cash to marketable securities. By using the inventory analogy, it is the optimum size, in dollar terms, of the firm's "order" for cash or marketable securities. The ECQ is calculated by the following formula:[12]

$$ECQ = \sqrt{\frac{2 \times \text{conversion cost} \times \text{demand for cash}}{\text{opportunity cost (in decimal form)}}} \qquad (16.3)$$

Total Cost

The firm's *total cost* of cash is the sum of the total conversion and total opportunity costs. *Total conversion cost* equals the cost per conversion times the number of conversions per period. The *number of conversions* per period can be found by dividing the period's cash demand by the economic conversion quantity (ECQ). The *total opportunity cost* equals the opportunity cost (in decimal form) times the average cash balance; this cost is expressed as a dollar amount. The *average cash balance* is found by dividing ECQ by 2. The total cost equation is

$$\text{Total cost} = (\text{cost per conversion} \times \text{number of conversions}) \qquad (16.4)$$
$$+ [\text{opportunity cost (in decimal form)} \times \text{average cash balance}]$$

The objective of the Baumol model is to determine the economic conversion quantity (ECQ) of cash that *minimizes total cost*. Cash transfers that are larger or smaller than ECQ result in higher total cost.

Graphically, the Baumol model can be depicted as a sawtooth pattern of cash holdings, as shown in Figure 16.3 (on page 686). The initial ECQ-dollar cash balance calculated by the equation decreases steadily to zero as the firm spends the cash. When the cash account reaches a zero balance, an additional "order" of ECQ dollars is transferred from marketable securities to cash. The entire model can be demonstrated with a simple example.

Example ▼ The management of JanCo, a small distributor of sporting goods, anticipates $1,500,000 in cash outlays (demand) during the coming year. The firm has determined that it costs $30 to convert marketable securities to cash and vice versa. The marketable securities portfolio currently earns an 8% annual rate of return. Substituting into Equation 16.3 results in the economic conversion quantity of cash:

$$ECQ = \sqrt{\frac{2 \times \$30 \times \$1,500,000}{.08}} = \underline{\underline{\$33,541}}$$

---

12. Baumol's model is symmetrical in the sense that the *economic conversion quantity (ECQ)* is the cost-minimizing quantity for conversion of *either* marketable securities to cash *or* cash to marketable securities. Although the marketable-security-to-cash conversion is demonstrated here, the ECQ applies equally well to cash-to-marketable-security conversions.

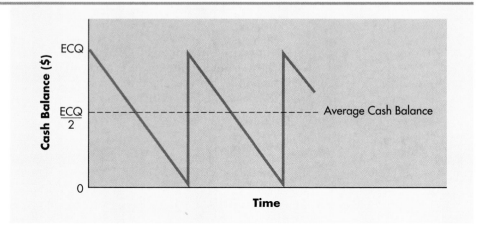

FIGURE 16.3

Baumol Model
Cash balance under Baumol model

JanCo receives $33,541 each time it replenishes the cash account. During the year the firm will make 45 conversions to replenish the cash account— $1,500,000/$33,541 = 44.7. The average cash balance is $16,770.50 ($33,541/2). The total cost of managing the cash is found by substituting the appropriate values into Equation 16.4:

$$\text{Total cost} = (\$30 \times 45) + (.08 \times \$16,770.50) = \underline{\$2,692}$$

Cash transfers that are either larger or smaller than $33,541 will result in higher total cost of managing JanCo's cash holdings. ▲

Miller-Orr Model

The Baumol model is based on the assumption of certain cash flows. However, when future cash flows are *uncertain*, the Miller-Orr model[13] is generally more realistic and appropriate than the Baumol model. The **Miller-Orr model** provides for cost-efficient cash balances by determining an *upper limit* (maximum amount) and a *return point* for them. The return point represents the target cash balance level. Cash balances are allowed to fluctuate between the upper limit and a lower limit, which we assume to be a zero balance.

Miller-Orr model
A model that provides for cost-efficient cash balances by determining an *upper limit* and *return point* for cash balances; assumes *uncertain* cash flows.

Setting the Return Point and Upper Limit

The value the firm selects for the return point depends on (1) conversion costs, (2) the daily opportunity cost of funds, and (3) the variance of daily net cash flows. The variance is estimated by using daily net cash flows (inflows minus outflows for the day). The equation for determining the return point is

$$\text{Return point} = \sqrt[3]{\frac{3 \times \text{conversion cost} \times \text{variance of daily net cash flows}}{4 \times \text{daily opportunity cost (in decimal form)}}} \qquad (16.5)$$

13. Merton H. Miller and Daniel Orr, "A Model of the Demand for Money by Firms," *Quarterly Journal of Economics* (August 1966), pp. 413–435.

where $\sqrt[3]{\ }$ means to take the cube root of the solution under the $\sqrt{\ }$ sign.

In the Miller-Orr model, the *upper limit for the cash balance* is always set at three times the return point.

When Cash Balance Reaches the Upper Limit

When the cash balance reaches the upper limit, an amount equal to the *upper limit minus the return point* is converted to marketable securities:

$$\text{Cash converted to marketable securities} = \text{upper limit} - \text{return point} \qquad (16.6)$$

When Cash Balance Falls to Zero (the Lower Limit)

When the cash balance falls to zero (the lower limit), the amount converted from marketable securities to cash is the amount represented by the *return point:*

$$\text{Marketable securities converted to cash} = \text{return point} - \text{zero balance} \qquad (16.7)$$

Figure 16.4 depicts this model.

E x a m p l e ▼ Continuing with the prior example, it costs JanCo $30 to convert marketable securities to cash and vice versa; the firm's marketable securities portfolio earns an 8% annual return, which is 0.0222% daily (8%/360 days). The variance of JanCo's daily net cash flows is estimated to be $27,000. Substituting into Equation 16.5 yields the return point:

$$\text{Return point} = \sqrt[3]{\frac{3 \times \$30 \times \$27,000}{4 \times 0.000222}} = \underline{\underline{\$1,399}}$$

The upper limit is $3 \times$ return point:

$$\text{Upper limit} = 3 \times \$1,399 = \underline{\underline{\$4,197}}$$

FIGURE 16.4

Miller-Orr Model
Cash balance under Miller-Orr model

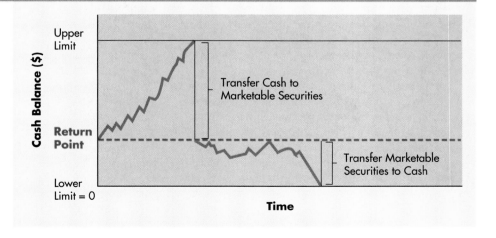

The firm's cash balance will be allowed to vary between $0 and $4,197. When the upper limit is reached, $2,798 ($4,197 − $1,399) is converted from cash to marketable securities (see Equation 16.6). When the cash balance falls to zero (the lower limit), $1,399 ($1,399 − $0) is converted from marketable securities ▲ to cash (see Equation 16.7).

? Review Question

16–17 What purpose do the *Baumol* and *Miller-Orr models* serve? Briefly describe their similarities and differences.

SUMMARY

 Discuss the motives for holding cash and marketable securities, estimation of cash balances, and the level of marketable securities investment. The three motives for holding cash and near-cash (marketable securities) are (1) the transactions motive, (2) the safety motive, and (3) the speculative motive. Management's goal should be to maintain levels of cash balances and marketable securities that contribute to improving the value of the firm. Cash balances satisfy transactional needs; marketable securities provide a safety stock of liquid resources and, possibly, the ability to profit from unexpected events that may arise.

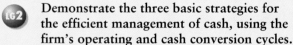 **Demonstrate the three basic strategies for the efficient management of cash, using the firm's operating and cash conversion cycles.** The efficient management of cash is affected by the firm's operating and cash conversion cycles. Management wants to minimize the length of these cycles without jeopardizing profitability. Three basic strategies for managing the cash conversion cycle are (1) turning over inventory as quickly as possible, (2) collecting accounts receivable as quickly as possible, and (3) paying accounts payable as late as possible without damaging the firm's credit rating. These strategies should reduce the firm's cash conversion cycle and negotiated financing need, thereby improving profitability.

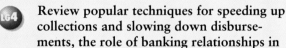 **Explain *float*, including its three basic components, and the firm's major objective with respect to the levels of collection float and disbursement float.** Float refers to funds that have been dispatched by a payer but are not yet in a form that can be spent by the payee. Both collection and disbursement float have the same three components: (1) mail float, (2) processing float, and (3) clearing float. The firm's major objective with respect to float is to minimize collection float and maximize disbursement float within reasonable limits.

Review popular techniques for speeding up collections and slowing down disbursements, the role of banking relationships in cash management, and international cash management. Popular techniques for speeding up collections include concentration banking, lockboxes, direct sends, preauthorized checks (PACs), depository transfer checks (DTCs), wire transfers, and ACH (automated clearinghouse) debits. Techniques for slowing down disbursements include controlled disbursing, playing the float, overdraft systems, zero-balance accounts, and ACH (automated clearinghouse) credits. Banks now offer many cash management services, and strong banking relationships are crucial for effective cash management. Dramatic differences between foreign and domestic banking systems result in more complex cash management practices for international firms.

LG5 **Understand the basic characteristics of marketable securities and the key features of popular government and nongovernment issues.** Marketable securities allow the firm to earn a return on temporarily idle funds. To be considered marketable, a security must have a ready market with both breadth and depth. Furthermore, the risk associated with the safety of the principal must be quite low. The key features and recent yields for each of the three key government issues were summarized in the upper portion of Table 16.1. These securities have relatively low yields due to their low risk and because interest income on all Treasury issues and most federal agency issues is exempt from state and local taxes.

The key features and recent yields for each of the principal nongovernment marketable securities were summarized in the lower portion of Table 16.1. These securities have slightly higher yields than government issues with similar maturities due to the slightly higher risks associated with them and because their interest income is taxable at all levels—federal, state, and local.

LG6 **Describe the Baumol model and the Miller-Orr model and how they can be used to determine the optimum quantity in which to convert marketable securities and cash.** Cash conversion models balance the relevant costs and benefits of holding cash versus marketable securities, to determine the economically optimum cash conversion quantity. This quantity is the cost-efficient amount to transfer from marketable securities to cash and vice versa. The two best-known cash conversion models are the Baumol model and the Miller-Orr model. The Baumol model assumes that the future demand for cash is known with certainty, whereas the Miller-Orr model incorporates the more realistic assumption of uncertain cash flows.

SELF-TEST PROBLEMS   (Solutions in Appendix B)

 ST 16–1   Cash conversion cycle   Hurkin Manufacturing Company pays accounts payable on the tenth day after purchase. The average collection period is 30 days, and the average age of inventory is 40 days. The firm currently spends about $18 million on operating cycle investments. The firm is considering a plan that would stretch its accounts payable by 20 days. If the firm pays 12% per year for its financing, what annual savings can it realize by this plan? Assume no discount for early payment of trade credit and a 360-day year.

 ST 16–2   Lockbox decision   A firm that has an annual opportunity cost of 9% is contemplating installation of a lockbox system at an annual cost of $90,000. The system is expected to reduce mailing time by $1\frac{1}{2}$ days, reduce processing time by $1\frac{1}{2}$ days, and reduce check clearing time by 1 day. If the firm collects $300,000 per day, would you recommend the system? Explain.

PROBLEMS

 WARM-UP **16–1   Cash conversion cycle**   American Products is concerned about managing cash efficiently. On the average, inventories have an average age of 90 days, and accounts receivable are collected in 60 days. Accounts payable are paid approximately 30 days after they arise. The firm spends $30 million on operating cycle investments each year, at a constant rate. Assuming a 360-day year:

   a. Calculate the firm's operating cycle.
   b. Calculate the firm's cash conversion cycle.
   c. Calculate the amount of negotiated financing required to support the firm's cash conversion cycle.
   d. Discuss how management might be able to reduce the cash conversion cycle.

 16–2   Cash conversion cycle   Harris & Company has an inventory turnover of 12 times each year, an average collection period of 45 days, and an average payment period of 40 days. The firm spends $1 million on operating cycle investments each year. Assuming a 360-day year:
   a. Calculate the firm's operating cycle.
   b. Calculate the firm's cash conversion cycle.
   c. Calculate the amount of negotiated financing required to support the firm's cash conversion cycle.
   d. If the firm's operating cycle were lengthened, without any change in its average payment period (APP), how would this affect its cash conversion cycle and negotiated financing need?

 16–3   Comparison of cash conversion cycles   A firm turns its inventory, on average, every 105 days. Its accounts receivable are collected, on the average, after 75 days, and accounts payable are paid an average of 60 days after they arise. Assuming a 360-day year, what changes will occur in the cash conversion cycle under each of the following circumstances?
   a. The average age of inventory changes to 90 days.
   b. The average collection period changes to 60 days.
   c. The average payment period changes to 105 days.
   d. The circumstances in **a, b,** and **c** occur simultaneously.

 16–4   Changes in cash conversion cycles   A firm is considering several plans that affect its current accounts. Given the five plans and their probable results shown in the following table, which one would you favor? Explain.

| | Change | | |
| | Average age of inventory | Average collection period | Average payment period |
Plan			
A	+30 days	+20 days	+5 days
B	+20 days	−10 days	+15 days
C	−10 days	0 days	−5 days
D	−15 days	+15 days	+10 days
E	+5 days	−10 days	+15 days

 16–5   Changing cash conversion cycle   Camp Manufacturing turns its inventory 8 times each year, has an average payment period of 35 days, and has an average collection period of 60 days. The firm's total annual outlays for operating cycle investments are $3.5 million. Assuming a 360-day year:

a. Calculate the firm's operating and cash conversion cycles.
b. Calculate the firm's daily cash operating expenditure. How much negotiated financing is required to support its cash conversion cycle?
c. Assuming the firm pays 14% for its financing, by how much would it increase its annual profits by *favorably* changing its current cash conversion cycle by 20 days?

INTERMEDIATE 16–6 **Changing the cash conversion cycle**   Aspen Jeans, Inc., has collected data about its current operations. The average age of inventory is 55 days; the average collection period is 42 days; and the average payment period is 46 days. The firm has an opportunity cost of short-term financing equal to 9%. Annual investments in the operating cycle amount to $4,800,000. Aspen has been offered a contract to produce private label jeans for a large retailer. If the firm takes the contract it will increase operating profits by $35,000 and reduce the average age of inventory to 50 days. However, it will increase the length of the collection period to 65 days. No changes will occur in the payment period or the amount of operating cycle investments. In all calculations assume a 360-day year.
a. Calculate Aspen Jean's current operating and cash conversion cycles.
b. Recalculate the firm's cycles for the effects that the new contract will produce.
c. Calculate the change in the cost of financing operating cycle investments.
d. Compare your results in c to the promised additional operating profits. Should the firm accept the contract or not?

INTERMEDIATE 16–7 **Multiple changes in cash conversion cycle**   Garrett Industries turns its inventory six times each year; it has an average collection period of 45 days and an average payment period of 30 days. The firm's annual operating cycle investment is $3 million. Assuming a 360-day year:
a. Calculate the firm's cash conversion cycle, its daily cash operating expenditure, and the amount of negotiated financing required to support its cash conversion cycle.
b. Find the firm's cash conversion cycle and negotiated financing requirement if it makes the following changes simultaneously.
(1) Shortens the average age of inventory by 5 days.
(2) Speeds the collection of accounts receivable by an average of 10 days.
(3) Extends the average payment period by 10 days.
c. If the firm pays 13% for its negotiated financing, by how much, if anything, could it increase its annual profit as a result of the changes in b?
d. If the annual cost of achieving the profit in c is $35,000, what action would you recommend to the firm? Why?

WARM-UP 16–8 **Float**   Simon Corporation has daily cash receipts of $65,000. A recent analysis of its collections indicated that customers' payments were in the mail an average of 2½ days. Once received, the payments are processed in 1½ days. After payments are deposited, it takes an average of 3 days for these receipts to clear the banking system.
a. How much collection float (in days) does the firm currently have?

    b. If the firm's opportunity cost is 11%, would it be economically advisable for the firm to pay an annual fee of $16,500 to reduce collection float by 3 days? Explain why or why not.

INTERMEDIATE 16–9 **Accounts receivable collection float** Simmons Express, Inc., is a long-haul trucking company serving customers all over the continental U.S. and parts of Canada. At present, all billing activities, from preparation to collection, are handled by staff at corporate headquarters in Peoria, Illlinois. Payments are recorded and deposits are made once a day in the firm's bank, Peoria National. You have been hired to study ways to reduce collection float and thereby create savings.

    a. Suggest and explain at least three specific ways that Simmons could reduce its collection float.

    b. Your best suggestion will cut the collection float by 3 days. Simmons bills $5,400,000 per year. Assuming evenly distributed collections throughout a 360-day year and an 8% cost of short-term financing, what savings could be achieved by implementing the suggestion? If the suggestion will cost $3,000 to implement, should it be done?

INTERMEDIATE 16–10 **Concentration banking** Mead Enterprises sells to a national market and bills all credit customers from the New York City office. Using a continuous billing system, the firm has collections of $1.2 million per day. Under consideration is a concentration banking system that would require customers to mail payments to the nearest regional office to be deposited in local banks.

    Mead estimates that the collection period for accounts will be shortened an average of $2\frac{1}{2}$ days under this system. The firm also estimates that *annual* service charges and administrative costs of $300,000 will result from the proposed system. The firm can earn 14% on equal-risk investments.

    a. How much cash will be made available for other uses if the firm accepts the proposed concentration banking system?

    b. What savings will the firm realize on the $2\frac{1}{2}$-day reduction in the collection period?

    c. Would you recommend the change? Explain your answer.

CHALLENGE 16–11 **Concentration banking—Range of outcomes** Pet-Care Company markets its products through widely dispersed distributors in the United States. It currently takes between 6 and 9 days for cash-receipt checks to become available to the firm once they are mailed. Through use of a concentration banking system, the firm estimates that the collection float can be reduced to between 2 and 4 days. Daily cash receipts currently average $10,000. The firm's minimum opportunity cost is 5.5%.

    a. Use the data given to determine the minimum and maximum annual savings from implementing the proposed system.

    b. If the annual cost of the concentration banking system is $7,500, what recommendation would you make?

    c. What impact, if any, would the fact that the firm's opportunity cost is 12% have on your analysis? Explain.

WARM-UP 16–12 **Lockbox system** Eagle Industries feels that a lockbox system can shorten its accounts receivable collection period by 3 days. Credit sales are $3,240,000 per year, billed on a continuous basis. The firm has other equally risky investments with a return of 15%. The cost of the lockbox system is $9,000 per year.

a. What amount of cash will be made available for other uses under the lock-box system?

b. What net benefit (cost) will the firm receive if it adopts the lockbox system? Should it adopt the proposed lockbox system?

 WARM-UP LG4 **16–13** **Direct send—Single**   Ocean Research of San Diego, California, just received a check in the amount of $800,000 from a customer in Bangor, Maine. If the firm processes the check in the normal manner, the funds will become available in 6 days. To speed up this process, the firm could send an employee to the bank in Bangor on which the check is drawn to present it for payment. Such action will cause the funds to become available after 2 days. If the cost of the direct send is $650 and the firm can earn 11% on these funds, what recommendation would you make? Explain.

 INTERMEDIATE LG4 **16–14** **Direct sends—Multiple**   Delta Company just received four sizable checks drawn on various distant banks throughout the United States. The data on these checks are summarized in the table below. The firm, which has a 12% opportunity cost, can lease a small business jet with pilot to fly the checks to the cities of the banks on which they are drawn and present them for immediate payment. This task can be accomplished in a single day—thereby reducing to 1 day the funds availability from each of the four checks. The total cost of leasing the jet with pilot and other incidental expenditures is $4,500. Analyze the proposed action and make a recommendation.

Check	Amount	Number of days until funds are available
1	$ 600,000	7 days
2	2,000,000	5
3	1,300,000	4
4	400,000	6

 WARM-UP LG4 **16–15** **Controlled disbursing**   A large Texas firm has annual cash disbursements of $360 million made continuously over the year. Although annual service and administrative costs would increase by $100,000, the firm is considering writing all disbursement checks on a small bank in Oregon. The firm estimates that this will allow an additional $1\frac{1}{2}$ days of cash usage. If the firm earns a return on other equally risky investments of 12%, should it change to the distant bank? Why or why not?

 WARM-UP LG4 **16–16** **Playing the float**   Clay Travel, Inc., routinely funds its checking account to cover all checks when written. A thorough analysis of its checking account discloses that the firm could maintain an average account balance that is 25% below the current level and adequately cover all checks presented. The average account balance is currently $900,000. If the firm can earn 10% on short-term investments, what, if any, annual savings would result from maintaining the lower average account balance?

 INTERMEDIATE   **16–17   Payroll account management**   Cord Products has a weekly payroll of $250,000. The payroll checks are issued on Friday afternoon each week. In examining the check-cashing behavior of its employees, it has found the pattern shown in the following table.

Number of business days[a] since issue of check	Percentage of checks cleared
1	20%
2	40
3	30
4	10

[a]Excludes Saturday and Sunday.

Given this information, what recommendation would you make to the firm with respect to managing its payroll account? Explain.

 WARM-UP   **16–18   Zero-balance account**   Union Company is considering establishment of a zero-balance account. The firm currently maintains an average balance of $420,000 in its disbursement account. As compensation to the bank for maintaining the zero-balance account, the firm will have to pay a monthly fee of $1,000 and maintain a $300,000 noninterest-earning deposit in the bank. The firm currently has no other deposits in the bank. Evaluate the proposed zero-balance account, and make a recommendation to the firm assuming that it has a 12% opportunity cost.

 INTERMEDIATE   **16–19   International collections—Value dating**   International Mining Machinery, Inc. (IMM) has contracted to sell equipment valued at $10,000,000 to a German mining company. The contract specifies that the German buyer must deposit the funds due in U.S. currency in a Munich bank as of April 1. Because of the banking practice known as value dating, IMM will not be able to access the funds until April 15, 14 days after the deposit. The Munich bank will pay interest at a 4% annual rate on the deposited funds for the 14 days. IMM has a short-term financing cost of 7%. Assuming a 360-day year, what will the 14-day delay cost IMM?

 INTERMEDIATE   **16–20   Baumol model**   Namtig Industries forecasts cash outlays of $1.8 million for its next fiscal year. To minimize investment in the cash account, management intends to apply the Baumol model. A financial analyst for the company has estimated the conversion cost of converting marketable securities to cash (or cash to marketable securities) to be $45 per conversion transaction and the annual opportunity cost of holding cash instead of marketable securities to be 8%.

a. Calculate the optimal amount of cash to transfer from marketable securities to cash (i.e., the economic conversion quantity, ECQ). What will be the average cash balance?

b. How many transactions will be required for the year?

c. Calculate the total cost resulting from use of the ECQ calculated in **a**.

d. If management makes 12 equal conversions (i.e., one per month), what will be (1) the total conversion cost, (2) the total opportunity cost, and (3) the total cost? Contrast and discuss this value in light of your finding in **c**.

INTERMEDIATE  16–21 **Miller-Orr model**   STIC Corporation uses the Miller-Orr model to manage its cash account. Recently, someone asked how sensitive is the solution for the return point and upper limit to changes in the conversion cost, the variance of daily net cash flows, and the *daily* opportunity cost rate. The values that are currently being used are a $50 conversion cost, a $2 million daily net cash flow variance, and a 10% *annual* opportunity cost.

a. Calculate the return point and upper limit using the current values.

b. Simultaneously increase each of the three variable values used in **a** by 50% and recalculate the return point and upper limit.

c. Discuss the sensitivity of the model to changes in the values of the input variables.

CHALLENGE   16–22 **Miller-Orr model**   The financial manager of YARL Corporation recently learned that application of the Miller-Orr cash-balance model has resulted in significant savings to another company in the industry. Eager to see whether it could provide savings to YARL, she studied YARL's cash system and found:

(1) Currently, about $100,000 is maintained in a noninterest-earning cash account.

(2) Conversion costs to transfer marketable securities to cash, and vice versa, average $30 per conversion.

(3) The variance of daily net cash flows is $1.5 million.

(4) Marketable securities can earn 9% *annually*, assuming a 360-day year.

The financial manager has asked you to do the following:

a. Calculate the return point and upper limit using the Miller-Orr model.

b. Determine how much additional profit YARL can earn by using the Miller-Orr model instead of maintaining its current cash balance. The average cash balance for the Miller-Orr model is: Return point × ⁴⁄₃.

c. Recommend whether YARL should rely on the Miller-Orr model or continue to use its current system of maintaining a large cash balance if YARL's variance of daily net cash flows rises to $3 million.

CASE   CHAPTER 16   **Assessing Roche Publishing Company's Cash Management Efficiency**

Lisa Pinto, vice president of finance at Roche Publishing Company, a rapidly growing publisher of college texts, is concerned about the firm's high level of short-term negotiated financing. She feels that the firm can improve the management of its cash and, as a result, reduce its heavy reliance on negotiated financing. In this regard, she charged Arlene Bessenoff, the treasurer, with assessing the firm's cash management efficiency. Arlene decided to begin her investigation by studying the firm's operating and cash conversion cycles.

Arlene found that Roche's average payment period was 25 days. She consulted industry data, which showed that the average payment period for the industry was 40 days. Investigation of three similar publishing companies revealed that their average payment period was also 40 days.

Next, Arlene studied the production cycle and inventory policies. The average age of inventory was 120 days. She determined that the industry standard as reported in a survey done by *Publishing World,* the trade association journal, was 85 days.

Further analysis showed Arlene that the firm's average collection period was 60 days. The industry average, derived from the trade association data and information on three similar publishing companies, was found to be 42 days—30% lower than Roche's.

Roche Publishing Company was spending an estimated $14,400,000 per year on its operating cycle investments. Arlene considered this expenditure level to be the minimum that she could expect the firm to disburse during the coming year. Her concern was whether the firm's cash management was as efficient as it could be. She estimated that the firm could achieve the industry standards in managing its payables, inventory, and receivables by incurring an annual cost of $120,000. Arlene knew that the company paid 12% annual interest for its negotiated financing. For this reason, she was concerned about the financing cost resulting from any inefficiencies in the management of Roche's cash conversion cycle.

Required

a. Assuming a constant rate for purchases, production, and sales throughout the year, what are Roche's existing operating cycle (OC), cash conversion cycle (CCC), and negotiated financing need?

b. If Roche can optimize operations according to industry standards, what would its operating cycle (OC), cash conversion cycle (CCC), and negotiated financing need be under these more efficient conditions?

c. In terms of negotiated financing requirements, what is the annual cost of Roche Publishing Company's operational inefficiency?

d. Should the firm incur the $120,000 annual cost to achieve the industry level of operational efficiency? Explain why or why not.

WEB EXERCISE

GOTO web site www.mercantile.com. Click BUSINESS BANKING in the left column.

1. What are the business services offered in the left column?

Click CASH MANAGEMENT.

2. What are the services offered in the cash management area?

Click RECEIPTS.

3. What are the areas of service involving receipts?
4. What are the three types of lockbox services?

GOTO web site www.national-city.com. Click BUSINESS BANKING.

5. Under the MORE INFO menu, what are the services available for small businesses?
6. Under the MORE INFO menu, what are the services available for Treasury Management?
7. Under the MORE INFO menu, what are the services available for International Services?

GOTO web site www.firstmerchants.com. Click on COMMERCIAL BANKING SERVICES.

8. What are the services available to businesses?

Accounts Receivable and Inventory

LEARNING GOALS

LG1 Discuss credit selection, including the five C's of credit, obtaining and analyzing credit information, credit scoring, and managing international credit.

LG2 Use the key variables to evaluate quantitatively the effects of either relaxing or tightening a firm's credit standards.

LG3 Review the effects of changes in each of the three components of credit terms on key financial variables and profits, and the procedure for quantitatively evaluating cash discount changes.

LG4 Explain the key features of collection policy, including aging accounts receivable, the effects of changes in collection efforts, and the popular collection techniques.

LG5 Understand inventory fundamentals, the relationship between inventory and accounts receivable, and international inventory management.

LG6 Describe the common techniques for managing inventory, including the ABC system, the basic economic order quantity model, the reorder point, the materials requirement planning system, and the just-in-time system.

LG1

17.1 Credit Selection

Accounts receivable represent the firm's extension of credit to its customers. For the average manufacturer, accounts receivable account for about 37 percent of *current assets* and about 16 percent of *total assets*. For most manufacturers, extending credit to customers is a cost of doing business. By keeping its money tied up in accounts receivable, the firm loses the time value of the money and runs the risk of not being paid the amounts owed. In return for incurring these costs, the firm can be competitive, attract and retain customers, and maintain and improve sales and profits.

"The Check's in the Mail"

Like "the dog ate my homework," the promise that the check is in the mail often is used as an excuse. But, in truth, an awful lot of checks *are* in the mail every day. (Just think how many accounts you and your family pay each month.) Accounts receivable and inventory typically represent a firm's largest investment in *current* assets. For small manufacturing firms and most retail firms it is not unusual to find over half of the total assets invested in receivables and inventory. Wise management of these accounts can affect the firm's costs in a big way, as well as impact the firm's competitive position. This chapter demonstrates the effects that credit and collection policies can have on the firm's investment in accounts receivable, and it presents basic information on inventory management.

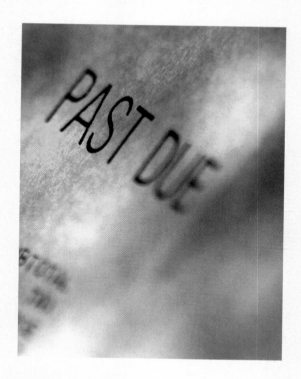

credit policy
The determination of credit selection, credit standards, and credit terms.

Generally, the firm's financial manager controls accounts receivable through the establishment and management of (1) **credit policy**, which includes determining credit selection, credit standards, and credit terms, and (2) *collection policy*. The firm's approach to managing these aspects of accounts receivable is heavily influenced by competitive conditions—typically, greater leniency enhances competition, and less leniency hinders competition. Here we discuss credit selection; in later sections, we look at credit standards, credit terms, and collection policy.

credit selection
The decision whether to extend credit to a customer and how much credit to extend.

A firm's **credit selection** involves deciding whether to extend credit to a customer and how much credit to extend. First, we look at the five C's of credit, which are the traditional focus of credit investigation.

The Five C's of Credit

Credit analysts often use the **five C's of credit** to focus their analysis on the key dimensions of an applicant's creditworthiness—character, capacity, capital, collateral, and conditions.

1. *Character:* The applicant's record of meeting past obligations—financial, contractual, and moral. Past payment history as well as any pending or resolved legal judgments against the applicant would be used.
2. *Capacity:* The applicant's ability to repay the requested credit. Financial statement analysis (see Chapter 4), with particular emphasis on liquidity and debt ratios, is typically used to assess the applicant's capacity.
3. *Capital:* The financial strength of the applicant as reflected by its ownership position. Analysis of the applicant's debt relative to equity and its profitability ratios are frequently used to assess its capital.
4. *Collateral:* The amount of assets the applicant has available for use in securing the credit. The larger the amount of available assets, the greater the chance that a firm will recover its funds if the applicant defaults. A review of the applicant's balance sheet, asset-value appraisals, and any legal claims filed against the applicant's assets can be used to evaluate its collateral.
5. *Conditions:* The current economic and business climate as well as any unique circumstances affecting either party to the credit transaction. For example, if the firm has excess inventory of the items the applicant wishes to purchase on credit, the firm may be willing to sell on more favorable terms or to less creditworthy applicants. General economic and business conditions, as well as special circumstances, are considered in assessing conditions.

The credit analyst typically gives primary attention to the first two C's—character and capacity—because they represent the most basic requirements for extending credit to an applicant. The last three C's—capital, collateral, and conditions—are important in structuring the credit arrangement and making the final credit decision, which is also affected by the credit analyst's experience and judgment.

Obtaining Credit Information

When a business is approached by a customer desiring credit terms, the credit department typically begins the evaluation process by requiring the applicant to fill out forms that request financial and credit information and references. Working from the application, the firm obtains additional information from other sources. If the firm has previously extended credit to the applicant, it will have its own information on the applicant's payment history. The major external sources of credit information are as follows:

1. **Financial Statements.** By requiring the credit applicant to provide financial statements for the past few years, the firm can analyze the applicant firm's liquidity, activity, debt, and profitability positions.

2. **Dun & Bradstreet. Dun & Bradstreet (D&B)** is the largest mercantile credit-reporting agency in the United States. It provides subscribers with a copy of

its *Reference Book,* which contains credit ratings and keyed estimates of overall financial strength for virtually millions of U.S. and international companies. An example of the D&B Key to Ratings is included on the text's web site at **www.awlonline.com/gitman.** D&B subscribers can also purchase detailed reports on specific companies and electronic access to D&B's database of business information through its *Electronic Access Systems.*

3. **Credit Interchange Bureaus.** The National Credit Interchange System is a national network of local credit bureaus that exchange information. Reports obtained through these exchanges contain factual data rather than analyses. A fee is usually levied for each inquiry.

4. **Direct Credit Information Exchanges.** Often, local, regional, or national trade associations serve as clearinghouses for credit information that is supplied by and made available to their member companies. Another approach is to contact other suppliers selling to the applicant and request information on the applicant's payment history.

5. **Bank Checking.** It may be possible for the firm's bank to obtain credit information from the applicant's bank. However, the type of information obtained will most likely be vague unless the applicant helps the firm obtain it. Typically, an estimate of the firm's cash balance is provided. For instance, the bank may indicate that the applicant normally maintains a "high-five-figure" balance in its checking account.

Analyzing Credit Information

credit analysis
The evaluation of credit applicants.

line of credit
The maximum amount a credit customer can owe the selling firm at any one time.

Firms typically establish procedures for use in **credit analysis**—the evaluation of credit applicants. Often the firm not only must determine the creditworthiness of a customer, but also must estimate the maximum amount of credit the customer is capable of supporting. Once this is done, the firm can establish a **line of credit,** the maximum amount the customer can owe the firm at any one time. The line of credit extended by a firm to its customer is similar to a line of credit extended by a bank to a short-term borrower, as described in Chapter 15. Lines of credit eliminate the necessity of checking a major customer's credit each time a large purchase is made.

We now consider procedures for analyzing credit information, the economic considerations involved in such analyses, and the small business problem.

Procedures

A credit applicant's financial statements and accounts payable ledger can be used to calculate its "average payment period." This can be compared to the credit terms currently extended to the applicant by others. For customers requesting large amounts of credit or lines of credit, a thorough ratio analysis of the firm's liquidity, activity, debt, and profitability should be performed by using the relevant financial statements. A time-series comparison (discussed in Chapter 4) of similar ratios for various years should uncover any developing trends. The *Dun & Bradstreet Reference Book* can be used for estimating the maximum line of credit to extend. Dun & Bradstreet suggests no more than 10 percent of the amount it assigns as a customer's "estimated financial strength."

One of the key inputs to the final credit decision is the credit analyst's *subjective judgment* of a firm's creditworthiness. Experience provides a "feel" for the nonquantifiable aspects of the quality of a firm's operations. The analyst will add his or her knowledge of the character of the applicant's management, references from other suppliers, and the firm's historic payment patterns to any quantitative figures developed to determine creditworthiness. The analyst will then make the final decision as to whether to extend credit to the applicant and in what amount.

Economic Considerations

Regardless of whether the firm's credit department is evaluating the creditworthiness of a customer desiring credit for a specific transaction or that of a regular customer to establish a line of credit, the basic procedures are the same. The only difference is the depth of the analysis. A firm would be unwise to spend $100 to investigate the creditworthiness of a customer making a one-time $40 purchase, but $100 for a credit investigation may be a good investment in the case of a customer that is expected to make credit purchases of $60,000 annually. Clearly, the firm's credit selection procedures consider the benefits and costs of obtaining and analyzing credit information.

The Small Business Problem

Managing accounts receivable is one of the biggest financial problems facing small businesses. Small firms typically lack the personnel and processes needed to make informed credit decisions. In addition, they are eager to increase sales volumes through the extension of credit, sometimes incurring bad debts in the process. Frequently, the credit customers of small firms are local businesses managed by personal friends, which makes denying credit particularly difficult. However, the credit decision must be made on the basis of sound financial and business principles. Clearly, it is better to have a potential credit customer get upset than for excessive uncollectible receivables to jeopardize the firm.

Credit Scoring

Consumer credit decisions involve a large group of similar applicants, each representing a small part of the firm's total business. These can be handled by using impersonal, computer-based, credit decision techniques. One popular technique is **credit scoring**—a procedure resulting in a score that measures an applicant's overall credit strength. The credit score is derived as a weighted average of the scores obtained on key financial and credit characteristics. Credit scoring is often used by large credit card operations such as oil companies and department stores.

Example ▼ Haller's Stores, a major regional department store chain, uses a credit scoring model to make its consumer credit decisions. Each credit applicant fills out a credit application. The application is reviewed and scored by one of the company's credit analysts, and the relevant information is entered into computer pro-

TABLE 17.1   Credit Scoring of Barb Baxter by Haller's Stores

Financial and credit characteristics	Score (0 to 100) (1)	Predetermined weight (2)	Weighted score [(1) × (2)] (3)
Credit references	80	.15	12.00
Home ownership	100	.15	15.00
Income range	70	.25	17.50
Payment history	75	.25	18.75
Years at address	90	.10	9.00
Years on job	80	.10	8.00
Total		1.00	Credit score 80.25

Key: Column 1: Scores assigned by analyst or computer using company guidelines on the basis of data presented in credit application. Scores range from 0 (lowest) to 100 (highest). Column 2: Weights based on the company's analysis of the relative importance of each financial and credit characteristic in predicting whether or not a customer will pay its account. The sum of these weights must equal 1.00.

grams. The rest of the process, including making the credit decision, generating a letter of acceptance or rejection, and mailing a credit card, is automated.

Table 17.1 demonstrates the calculation of Barb Baxter's credit score. The firm's predetermined credit standards are summarized in Table 17.2. The cutoff credit scores were developed by Haller's Stores to accept the group of credit applicants that will result in a positive contribution to the firm's share value. Evaluating Barb Baxter's credit score of 80.25 in light of the firm's credit standards, Haller's would decide to *extend standard credit terms* to her (because 80.25 > 75).

The attractiveness of credit scoring should be clear from the preceding example. Unfortunately, most manufacturers sell to a diversified group of different-sized businesses, not to individuals. The statistical characteristics necessary for applying credit scoring to decisions regarding *mercantile credit*—credit extended

TABLE 17.2   Credit Standards for Haller's Stores

Credit score	Action
Greater than 75	Extend standard credit terms.
65 to 75	Extend limited credit; if account is properly maintained, convert to standard credit terms after 1 year.
Less than 65	Reject application.

Personal Finance

Learning Credit Lessons the Hard Way

For college students, getting a first credit card is easy. Card issuers run major promotions on campuses, offering gifts just for applying. And the approval process is also simple. All that students at a 4-year accredited university need is some source of income: a part- or full-time job, a grant or scholarship or loan, or money from their parents. After the first card, students get inundated with offers from other banks; before long, you may have several cards—and large unpaid balances. If you skip payments, the card issuer will report you to credit agencies. The result is a poor credit history, which can affect your ability to rent an apartment, get a job, or get credit in the future.

If your credit history leaves something to be desired, you might be tempted to use a credit repair service that claims to improve a poor credit record. In most cases, however, these services are scams that can cost you $1,000 or more in fees but do nothing to change your record. "Although there are legitimate, not-for-profit credit counseling services, the Federal Trade Commission (FTC) has never seen a legitimate credit repair company," warns Jodie Bernstein, the FTC's director of consumer protection.

*The best defense against a poor credit history is to limit your use of credit cards in the first place. But if you do run into problems meeting your monthly payments, look for a nonprofit credit counseling service like the National Foundation for Consumer Credit (**www.nfcc.org**), Debt Counselors of America (**www.getoutofdebt.org**), or Genus (**www.genus.org**). These services provide budget counseling and help you develop a repayment plan and learn to control future spending. When debts are very large, the counselor can negotiate a formal repayment plan with creditors, which may lower the monthly payments and waive late fees. Budget help should be free or cost very little. There is a monthly charge for debt repayment plans; some firms charge only a few dollars per creditor. If the fees sound high, look for another counselor.*

by business firms to other business firms—rarely exist. In the following discussions, we concentrate on the basic concepts of mercantile credit decisions, which cannot be expressed easily in quantifiable terms.

Managing International Credit

Whereas credit management is difficult enough for managers of purely domestic companies, these tasks become much more complex for companies that operate internationally. This is partly because (as we have seen before) international operations typically expose a firm to *exchange rate risk*. It is also due to the dangers and delays involved in shipping goods long distances and having to cross at least two international borders.

Exports of finished goods are usually denominated in the currency of the importer's local market; most commodities, on the other hand, are denominated in dollars. Therefore, a U.S. company that sells a product in France, for example, would have to price that product in French francs and extend credit to a French wholesaler in the local currency (francs). If the franc *depreciates* against the dollar before the U.S. exporter collects on its account receivable, the U.S. company experiences an exchange rate loss; the francs collected are worth fewer dollars than expected at the time the sale was made. Of course, the dollar could just as easily depreciate against the franc, yielding an exchange rate gain to the U.S. exporter. Most companies fear the loss more than they welcome the gain.

For a major currency like the French franc, the exporter can *hedge* against this risk by using the currency futures, forward, or options markets, but it is costly to do so, particularly for relatively small amounts. If the exporter is selling to a customer in a developing country—where 40 percent of U.S. exports are now sold—there will probably be no effective instrument available for protecting against exchange rate risk at any price. This risk may be further magnified because credit standards (and acceptable collection techniques) may be much lower in developing countries than in the United States. Although it may seem tempting to just "not bother" with exporting, U.S. companies no longer can concede foreign markets to international rivals. These export sales, if carefully monitored and, where possible, effectively hedged against exchange rate risk, often prove to be very profitable. Novice or infrequent exporters may choose to rely on *factors* (see Chapter 15) to manage their international export (credit) sales. Although expensive, these firms are typically much better at evaluating the creditworthiness of foreign customers and are better able to bear credit risk than are most small exporters.

? Review Questions

17–1   What do the *accounts receivable* of a firm represent? What is meant by a firm's *credit policy*?

17–2   Briefly list the *five C's of credit* and discuss their role in the *credit selection* process.

17–3   Summarize the basic sources of credit information. What procedures are commonly used to analyze credit information?

17–4   How do economic considerations affect the depth of credit analysis performed by a firm? Explain why managing accounts receivable is one of the biggest financial problems facing small firms.

17–5   Describe *credit scoring* and explain why this technique is typically applied to consumer credit decisions rather than to mercantile credit decisions.

17–6   Why are the risks involved in international credit management more complex than those associated with purely domestic credit sales?

17.2 Changing Credit Standards

credit standards
The minimum requirements for extending credit to a customer.

The firm's **credit standards** are the minimum requirements for extending credit to a customer. Understanding the key variables that must be considered when a firm is contemplating relaxing or tightening its credit standards will give a general idea of the kinds of decisions involved.

Key Variables

The major variables to be considered when evaluating proposed changes in credit standards are (1) sales volume, (2) the investment in accounts receivable, and (3) bad debt expenses.[1] Let us examine each in more detail.

Sales Volume

Career Key
The *marketing* department will be significantly affected by the firm's credit policy. The level of sales can be greatly altered by changes in the firm's credit standards and credit terms.

Changing credit standards can be expected to change the volume of sales. If credit standards are relaxed, sales are expected to increase; if credit standards are tightened, sales are expected to decrease. Generally, increases in sales affect profits positively, whereas decreases in sales affect profits negatively.

Investment in Accounts Receivable

Accounts receivable involve a cost to the firm, attributable to the forgone earnings opportunities from the funds tied up in accounts receivable. The higher the firm's investment in accounts receivable, the greater the carrying cost; the lower the firm's investment in accounts receivable, the lower the carrying cost. If the firm relaxes its credit standards, the volume of accounts receivable increases, and so does the carrying cost. This change results from increased sales and longer collection periods due to slower payment.[2] The opposite occurs if credit standards are tightened. Thus, a relaxation of credit standards is expected to affect profits negatively because of higher carrying costs, whereas tightening credit standards would affect profits positively as a result of lower carrying costs.

Bad Debt Expenses

Hint Relaxing the credit standards and/or credit terms will increase the risk of the firm, but it may also increase the return to the firm. Bad debts and the average collection period will both increase with more lenient credit standards and/or credit terms, but the increased revenue may produce profits that exceed these costs.

The probability, or risk, of acquiring a bad debt increases as credit standards are relaxed. The increase in bad debts associated with relaxation of credit standards raises bad debt expenses and affects profits negatively. The opposite effects on bad debt expenses and profits result from a tightening of credit standards.

---

1. A relaxation of credit standards would be expected to add to the *clerical costs* as a result of the need for a larger credit department, whereas a tightening of credit standards might save clerical costs. Because these costs are assumed to be included in the variable cost per unit, they are not explicitly isolated in the analyses presented in this chapter.

2. Because of the forward-looking nature of accounts receivable analysis, certain items such as sales, collections, and bad debts resulting from changes in the management of accounts receivable must be estimated. The need to estimate these future values may introduce a great deal of uncertainty into the decision process. Some of the techniques discussed in Chapter 10, such as sensitivity and scenario analysis and simulation, can be applied to these estimates to adjust them for uncertainty.

The basic changes and effects on profits expected to result from the *relaxation* of credit standards are summarized as follows:

Effects of Relaxation of Credit Standards		
Variable	Direction of change	Effect on profits
Sales volume	Increase	Positive
Investment in accounts receivable	Increase	Negative
Bad debt expenses	Increase	Negative

If credit standards were tightened, the opposite effects would be expected.

Determining Values of Key Variables

Determining the key credit standard variables can be illustrated by the following example.[3]

Example ▼ Dodd Tool, a manufacturer of lathe tools, is currently selling a product for $10 per unit. Sales (all on credit) for last year were 60,000 units. The variable cost per unit is $6. The firm's total fixed costs are $120,000.

The firm is currently contemplating a *relaxation of credit standards* that is expected to result in a 5% increase in unit sales, to 63,000 units, an increase in the average collection period from its current level of 30 days to 45 days, and an increase in bad debt expenses from the current level of 1% of sales to 2%. The firm's required return on equal-risk investments, which is the opportunity cost of tying up funds in accounts receivable, is 15%.

To determine whether to implement the proposed relaxation of credit standards, Dodd Tool must calculate the effect on the firm's additional profit contribution from sales, the cost of the marginal investment in accounts receivable, and the cost of marginal bad debts.

Additional Profit Contribution from Sales   Because fixed costs are "sunk" and thereby unaffected by a change in the sales level, the only cost relevant to a change in sales would be out-of-pocket or variable costs. Sales are expected to increase by 5%, or 3,000 units. The profit contribution per unit will equal the difference between the sale price per unit ($10) and the variable cost per unit ($6). The profit contribution per unit therefore will be $4. The total additional profit contribution from sales will be $12,000 (3,000 units × $4 per unit).

---

3. Because various credit policy decisions tend to commit the firm to long-run behaviors, a number of authors have suggested that credit policy decisions should be made by using a present value framework. See Yong H. Kim and Joseph C. Atkins, "Evaluating Investments in Accounts Receivable: A Maximizing Framework," *Journal of Finance* 33 (May 1978), pp. 402–412. Although their suggestions are valid, an article by Kanwal S. Sachdeva and Lawrence J. Gitman, "Accounts Receivable Decisions in a Capital Budgeting Framework," *Financial Management* 10 (Winter 1981), pp. 45–49, has shown that single-period decision rules similar to those applied throughout this chapter will provide correct accept–reject decisions without the computational rigor of the present value approach.

Cost of the Marginal Investment in Accounts Receivable   The cost of the marginal investment in accounts receivable can be calculated by finding the difference between the cost of carrying receivables before and after the introduction of the relaxed credit standards. Because our concern is only with the out-of-pocket costs, *the relevant cost in this analysis is the variable cost*. The average investment in accounts receivable can be calculated by using the following formula:

$$\text{Average investment in accounts receivable} = \frac{\text{total variable cost of annual sales}}{\text{turnover of accounts receivable}} \tag{17.1}$$

where

$$\text{Turnover of accounts receivable}[4] = \frac{360}{\text{average collection period}}$$

The total variable cost of annual sales under the proposed and present plans can be found as follows, using the variable cost per unit of $6:

Total variable cost of annual sales:

Under proposed plan: ($6 × 63,000 units) = $378,000
Under present plan: ($6 × 60,000 units) = $360,000

Implementation of the proposed plan will cause the total variable cost of annual sales to increase from $360,000 to $378,000.

The turnover of accounts receivable refers to the number of times each year the firm's accounts receivable are actually turned into cash. In each case, it is found by dividing the average collection period into 360—the number of days in a year.

Turnover of accounts receivable:

Under proposed plan: $\dfrac{360}{45} = 8$

Under present plan: $\dfrac{360}{30} = 12$

With implementation of the proposed plan, the accounts receivable turnover would slow from 12 to 8 times per year.

By substituting the cost and turnover data just calculated into Equation 17.1 for each case, we get the following average investments in accounts receivable:

---

4. The turnover of accounts receivable can also be calculated by *dividing annual sales by accounts receivable*. For the purposes of this chapter, only the formula transforming the average collection period to a turnover of accounts receivable is emphasized.

Average investment in accounts receivable:

$$\text{Under proposed plan: } \frac{\$378,000}{8} = \$47,250$$

$$\text{Under present plan: } \frac{\$360,000}{12} = \$30,000$$

The marginal investment in accounts receivable as well as its cost are calculated as follows:

Cost of marginal investment in accounts receivable:

	Average investment under proposed plan	$47,250
−	Average investment under present plan	30,000
	Marginal investment in accounts receivable	$17,250
×	Required return on investment	.15
	Cost of marginal investment in A/R[5]	$ 2,588

The resulting value of $2,588 is considered a cost because it represents the maximum amount that could have been earned on the $17,250 had it been placed in the best equal-risk investment alternative available at the firm's required return on investment of 15%.

Cost of Marginal Bad Debts   The cost of marginal bad debts is found by taking the difference between the level of bad debts before and after the relaxation of credit standards.

Cost of marginal bad debts:

Under proposed plan: (.02 × $10/unit × 63,000 units) =	$12,600
Under present plan: (.01 × $10/unit × 60,000 units) =	6,000
Cost of marginal bad debts	$ 6,600

The bad debt costs are calculated by using the sale price per unit ($10) to back out not just the true loss of variable cost ($6) that results when a customer fails to pay its account, but also the profit contribution per unit—in this case $4—that is included in the "additional profit contribution from sales." Thus, the resulting cost of marginal bad debts is $6,600.

Making the Credit Standard Decision

To decide whether to relax its credit standards, the firm must compare the additional profit contribution from sales to the added costs of the marginal investment in accounts receivable and the cost of marginal bad debts. If the additional

---

5. Throughout the text, *A/R* will frequently be used interchangeably with *accounts receivable.*

TABLE 17.3   The Effects on Dodd Tool of a Relaxation of Credit Standards

Additional profit contribution from sales		
[3,000 units × ($10 − $6)]		$12,000
Cost of marginal investment in A/R[a]		
Average investment under proposed plan:		
$\dfrac{\$6 \times 63,000}{8} = \dfrac{\$378,000}{8}$	$47,250	
Average investment under present plan:		
$\dfrac{\$6 \times 60,000}{12} = \dfrac{\$360,000}{12}$	30,000	
Marginal investment in A/R	$17,250	
Cost of marginal investment in A/R (.15 × $17,250)		($ 2,588)
Cost of marginal bad debts		
Bad debts under proposed plan (.02 × $10 × 63,000)	$12,600	
Bad debts under present plan (.01 × $10 × 60,000)	6,000	
Cost of marginal bad debts		($ 6,600)
Net profit from implementation of proposed plan		$ 2,812

[a]The denominators 8 and 12 in the calculation of the average investment in accounts receivable under the proposed and present plans are the accounts receivable turnovers for each of these plans (360/45 = 8 and 360/30 = 12).

profit contribution is greater than marginal costs, credit standards should be relaxed; otherwise, present standards should remain unchanged.

Example ▼ The results and key calculations relating to Dodd Tool's decision to relax its credit standards are summarized in Table 17.3. The additional profit contribution from the increased sales would be $12,000, which exceeds the sum of the costs of the marginal investment in accounts receivable and marginal bad debts. Therefore, the firm *should* relax its credits standards as proposed. The net addition to total profits resulting from such an action will be $2,812 per year. ▲

The procedure described here for making a credit standard decision is also commonly used for evaluating other changes in the management of accounts receivable. If Dodd Tool had been contemplating tightening its credit standards, for example, the cost would have been a reduction in the profit contribution from sales, and the return would have been from reductions in the cost of the marginal investment in accounts receivable and in the cost of bad debts. Another application of this procedure is demonstrated later in the chapter.

? Review Question

17–7   What key variables should be considered when evaluating possible changes in a firm's *credit standards?* What are the basic trade-offs in a *tightening* of credit standards?

17.3 Changing Credit Terms

credit terms
Specify the repayment terms required of a firm's credit customers.

A firm's **credit terms** specify the repayment terms required of all its credit cus- tomers.[6] A type of shorthand is used to indicate the terms. For example, credit terms stated as *2/10 net 30* mean that the purchaser receives a 2 percent cash dis- count if the bill is paid within 10 days after the beginning of the credit period; if the customer does not take the cash discount, the full amount must be paid within 30 days after the beginning of the credit period. Credit terms cover three things: (1) the cash discount, if any (in this case, 2 percent); (2) the cash discount period (in this case, 10 days); and (3) the credit period (in this case, 30 days). Changes in any aspect of the firm's credit terms may have an effect on its overall profitability. This section discusses the positive and negative factors associated with such changes and quantitative procedures for evaluating them.

Cash Discount

When a firm initiates or *increases* a cash discount, the changes and effects on profits shown in the following table can be expected:

Effects of Increase in Cash Discount		
Variable	**Direction of change**	**Effect on profits**
Sales volume	Increase	Positive
Investment in accounts receivable due to nondiscount takers paying earlier	Decrease	Positive
Investment in accounts receivable due to new customers	Increase	Negative
Bad debt expenses	Decrease	Positive
Profit per unit	Decrease	Negative

---

6. An in-depth discussion of credit terms as viewed by the *customer*—that is, *accounts payable*—is presented in Chapter 15. In this chapter, our concern is with *accounts receivable*—credit terms from the point of view of the *seller*.

The sales volume should increase because, if the buyer is willing to pay by day 10, the unit price decreases, making the product more competitive. The net effect on accounts receivable is difficult to determine: the nondiscount takers paying earlier will reduce accounts receivable, but the new customers will increase accounts receivable. The bad debt expenses should decline: as customers on the average will pay earlier, the probability of their not paying at all will decrease.[7] Both the decrease in the receivables investment and the decrease in bad debt expenses should result in increased profits. The negative aspect of an increased cash discount is a decreased profit per unit as more customers take the discount and pay the reduced price.

Decreasing or eliminating a cash discount would have opposite effects. The quantitative effects of changes in cash discounts can be evaluated by a procedure similar to that used earlier to evaluate changes in credit standards.

Example ▼ Assume that Dodd Tool is considering initiating a cash discount of 2% for payment within 10 days after a purchase. The firm's current average collection period is 30 days (turnover = 360/30 = 12), credit sales of 60,000 units are made at $10 per unit, and the variable cost per unit is $6. The firm expects that if the cash discount is initiated, 60% of its sales will be on discount, and sales will increase by 5% to 63,000 units. The average collection period is expected to drop to 15 days (turnover = 360/15 = 24). Bad debt expenses are expected to drop from the current level of 1% of sales to .5% of sales. The firm's required return on equal-risk investments remains at 15%.

The analysis of this decision is presented in Table 17.4. The calculations are similar to those presented for Dodd's credit standard decision in Table 17.3[8] except for the final entry, "Cost of cash discount." This cost of $7,560 reflects the fact that *profits will be reduced* as a result of a 2% cash discount being taken on 60% of the new level of sales. Even with that cost of the cash discount, Dodd Tool can increase profit by $9,428 by initiating the proposed discount. Such an action therefore seems advisable. This type of analysis can also be applied to ▲ decisions concerning the elimination or reduction of cash discounts.

Cash Discount Period

The net effect of changes in the cash discount period is difficult to analyze because of the nature of the forces involved. If the cash discount period were *increased*, the changes noted in the unnumbered table on page 713 could be expected:

---

7. This contention is based on the fact that the longer a person has to pay, the less likely it is that the person will pay. The more time that elapses, the more opportunities there are for a customer to become technically insolvent or fail. Therefore, the probability of a bad debt is expected to increase directly with increases in the credit period.

8. The calculation of the average investment in accounts receivable presented for both the present and proposed plans is not entirely correct. Whenever a change in credit terms or some other aspect of accounts receivable is expected to change the payment pattern of existing customers, formal analysis should recognize that the firm's pattern of receipt of both cost *and* profit from these customers is being altered. Therefore, the average investment in receivables for existing customers whose payment patterns have been altered should be measured at the sale price, not at cost. For an excellent discussion of this point, see Edward A. Dyl, "Another Look at the Investment in Accounts Receivable," *Financial Management* 6 (Winter 1977), pp. 67–70. To convey the key concepts throughout the remainder of this chapter without confusing the reader, the average accounts receivable investment is calculated at cost regardless of whether or not existing customers' payment patterns are altered by the proposed action.

TABLE 17.4	The Effects on Dodd Tool of Initiating a Cash Discount

Additional profit contribution from sales
  [3,000 units × ($10 − $6)] $12,000

Cost of marginal investment in A/R
  Average investment under proposed plan:

$$\frac{\$6 \times 63{,}000}{24} = \frac{\$378{,}000}{24} \qquad \$15{,}750$$

  Average investment under present plan:

$$\frac{\$6 \times 60{,}000}{12} = \frac{\$360{,}000}{12} \qquad 30{,}000$$

  Marginal investment in A/R   ($14,250)
    Cost of marginal investment in A/R (.15 × $14,250) $ 2,138[a]

Cost of marginal bad debts
  Bad debts under proposed plan (.005 × $10 × 63,000) $ 3,150
  Bad debts under present plan (.01 × $10 × 60,000)   6,000
    Cost of marginal bad debts $ 2,850[a]

Cost of cash discount[b] (.02 × .60 × $10 × 63,000)   ($ 7,560)

Net profit from implementation of proposed plan $ 9,428

[a]This value is positive, because it represents a savings rather than a cost.

[b]This calculation reflects the fact that a 2% cash discount will be taken on 60% of the new level of sales—63,000 units at $10 each.

	Effects of Increase in Cash Discount Period	
Variable	**Direction of change**	**Effect on profits**
Sales volume	Increase	Positive
Investment in accounts receivable due to nondiscount takers paying earlier	Decrease	Positive
Investment in accounts receivable due to discount takers still getting cash discount but paying later	Increase	Negative
Investment in accounts receivable due to new customers	Increase	Negative
Bad debt expenses	Decrease	Positive
Profit per unit	Decrease	Negative

The problems in determining the exact results of changes in the cash discount period are directly attributable to the three forces affecting the firm's *investment in accounts receivable*. If the firm were to shorten the cash discount period, the effects would be the opposite of those just described.

Credit Period

Changes in the credit period also affect the firm's profitability. The following effects on profits can be expected from an *increase* in the length of the credit period:

Effects of Increase in Length of Credit Period		
Variable	**Direction of change**	**Effect on profits**
Sales volume	Increase	Positive
Investment in accounts receivable	Increase	Negative
Bad debt expenses	Increase	Negative

Increasing the length of the credit period should increase sales, but both accounts receivable and bad debt expenses are likely to increase as well. Thus, the sales increase will have a positive net effect on profits, whereas the increases in accounts receivable investment and bad debt expenses will negatively affect profits. A decrease in the length of the credit period is likely to have the opposite effect. The credit period decision is analyzed in the same ways as the credit standard decision illustrated in Table 17.3.

? Review Questions

17–8   What is meant by *credit terms?* What are the three components of credit terms? How do credit terms affect the firm's accounts receivable?

17–9   What are the expected effects of a *decrease* in the firm's cash discount? In such a case, what is likely to happen to sales volume, accounts receivable, bad debt expenses, and per-unit profits?

17–10   What are the expected effects of a *decrease* in the firm's credit period? What is likely to happen to sales volume, accounts receivable, and bad debt expenses?

17.4 Collection Policy

collection policy
The procedures for collecting a firm's accounts receivable when they are due.

The firm's **collection policy** is its procedures for collecting accounts receivable when they are due. The effectiveness of this policy can be partly evaluated by looking at the level of bad debt expenses. This level depends not only on collection policy, but also on the firm's credit policy. If the level of bad debts attributable to *credit policy* is relatively constant, increasing collection expenditures can be expected to reduce bad debts. This relationship is depicted in Figure 17.1. As the figure indicates, up to point A, additional collection expenditures will reduce bad debt losses. Beyond that point, additional collection expenditures will not reduce bad debt losses sufficiently to justify the outlay of funds. Popular

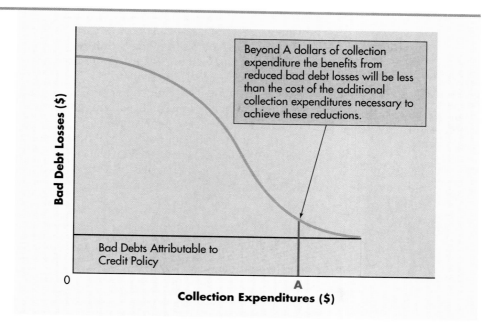

FIGURE 17.1

**Collection Policy
Relationship**
Collection expenditures and
bad debt losses

approaches used to evaluate credit and collection policies include the *average
collection period ratio* (presented in Chapter 4) and *aging accounts receivable.*

Aging Accounts Receivable

aging
A technique used to evaluate credit or
collection policies by indicating the proportion of the accounts receivable balance that has been outstanding for a
specified period of time.

Aging is a technique that indicates the proportion of the accounts receivable balance that has been outstanding for a specified period of time. It requires that the
firm's accounts receivable be broken down into groups based on the time of
origin. This breakdown is typically made on a month-by-month basis, going
back 3 or 4 months.

E x a m p l e ▼

Assume that Dodd Tool extends 30-day EOM credit terms to its customers. The
firm's December 31, 2000, balance sheet shows $200,000 of accounts receivable.
An evaluation of those accounts receivable results in the following breakdown:

Days	Current	0–30	31–60	61–90	Over 90	
Month	December	November	October	September	August	Total
Accounts receivable	$60,000	$40,000	$66,000	$26,000	$8,000	$200,000
Percentage of total	30	20	33	13	4	100

Because it is assumed that Dodd Tool gives its customers 30 days after the
end of the month in which the sale is made to pay off their accounts, any

December receivables that are still on the firm's books are considered current. November receivables are between zero and 30 days overdue, October receivables still unpaid are 31 to 60 days overdue, and so on.

The table shows that 30% of the firm's receivables are current, 20% are 1 month late, 33% are 2 months late, 13% are 3 months late, and 4% are more than 3 months late. Although payment seems generally slow, a noticeable irregularity in these data is the high percentage represented by October receivables. This indicates that some problem may have occurred in October. Investigation may find that the problem can be attributed to the hiring of a new credit manager, the acceptance of a new account that has made a large credit purchase it has not yet paid for, or ineffective collection policy. When such a discrepancy is found, the analyst should determine its cause.

Effects of Changes in Collection Efforts

The changes and effects on profits that are expected to result from an *increase* in collection efforts are as follows:

Effects of Changes in Collection Efforts		
Variable	Direction of change	Effect on profits
Sales volume	None or decrease	None or negative
Investment in accounts receivable	Decrease	Positive
Bad debt expenses	Decrease	Positive
Collection expenditures	Increase	Negative

Increased collection efforts should reduce accounts receivable and bad debt expenses, increasing profits. If the level of collection effort is too intense, the cost of this strategy may include lost sales in addition to increased collection expenditures. In other words, if the firm pushes its customers too hard to pay their accounts, they may take their business elsewhere. The firm should therefore be careful not to be overly aggressive. The quantitative effects of changes in collection policy expenditures can be evaluated in a way similar to that used to evaluate changes in credit standards and cash discounts.

Popular Collection Techniques

A number of collection techniques are employed. As an account becomes more and more overdue, the collection effort becomes more personal and more intense. Use of computers in collection of accounts is common. Computers can monitor accounts receivable and send collection letters at certain predetermined points if payment has not been received. After a prescribed number of these letters have been sent without any receipt of payment, a special notice will be generated, probably as part of a report to the credit manager. At this point, the collection efforts become more directly personal. Actions such as telephone calls, personal visits,

In Practice

Small Business

Credit Checkups a Must for Small Firms

It's easy to become complacent about credit and collection policies when the economy is strong—and pay the price when recession hits. Yantis Construction, a company in San Antonio, Texas, with annual revenues of $26 million, learned this lesson the hard way. When recession hit the Texas economy in the 1980s, one of the firm's top customers, who had always paid promptly, fell behind on multimillion dollar payments. The customer told president Tom Yantis that it was arranging financing and would pay soon. Yantis trusted the customer's word about the financing—and ended up losing money. "People act differently during a recession than you would ever expect," says Yantis. "It's not really their fault. It's your fault for failing to anticipate what might happen in the worst of situations."

To avoid getting caught in the same position again, Yantis revamped the company's credit and collection policies. He now gives customers sizable discounts for making up-front payments. "When times are good, we try to build relationships with our major customers that encourage them to make early payments," says Yantis. A customer's failure to take an attractive discount can be a warning signal that something is wrong, especially if the customer usually takes the discount. Calling promptly to find out why can minimize the risk of losses. Companies that don't stay on top of their credit and accounts receivable collection policies risk the ultimate price—failure—for another company's problems.

and use of a collection agency will then be taken. Legal action is also a possibility. The popular collection techniques are briefly described in Table 17.5 (page 718), listed in the order typically followed in the collection process.

? Review Questions

17–11   What is meant by a firm's *collection policy?* Explain how *aging* accounts receivable can be used to evaluate the effectiveness of both the credit policy and the collection policy.

17–12   What effects on profits are expected to result from a *decrease* in collection efforts? Describe the popular collection techniques.

17.5 Inventory Management

Inventory is a necessary current asset that permits the production–sale process to operate with a minimum of disturbance. Like accounts receivable, inventory represents a significant investment for most firms. For the average manufacturer, it

TABLE 17.5	Popular Collection Techniques
Technique[a]	Brief description
Letters	After a certain number of days, the firm sends a polite letter reminding the customer of its overdue account. If the account is not paid within a certain period after the letter has been sent, a second, more demanding letter is sent. This letter may be followed by yet another letter, if necessary.
Telephone calls	If letters prove unsuccessful, a telephone call may be made to the customer to personally request immediate payment. Such a call is typically directed to the customer's accounts payable department. If the customer has a reasonable excuse, arrangements may be made to extend the payment period. A call from the seller's attorney may be used if all other discussions seem to fail.
Personal visits	This technique is much more common at the consumer credit level, but it may also be effectively employed by industrial suppliers. Sending a local salesperson or a collection person to confront the customer can be very effective. Payment may be made on the spot.
Collection agencies	A firm can turn uncollectible accounts over to a collection agency or an attorney for collection. The fees for this service are typically quite high; the firm may receive less than 50 cents on the dollar from accounts collected in this way.
Legal action	Legal action is the most stringent step in the collection process. It is an alternative to the use of a collection agency. Not only is direct legal action expensive, but it may force the debtor into bankruptcy, thereby reducing the possibility of future business without guaranteeing the ultimate receipt of the overdue amount.

[a]Techniques are listed in the order typically followed in the collection process.

Career Key

Operations will design and implement the inventory management system. The standards of the system may be established by upper management, but the process to achieve those standards will be created by the people in operations.

accounts for about 42 percent of *current assets* and about 18 percent of *total assets*. Chapter 16 illustrated the importance of turning over inventory quickly to reduce financing costs. The financial manager may act as a "watchdog" and adviser in matters concerning inventory; he or she does not have direct control over inventory, but does provide input into the inventory management process.

Inventory Fundamentals

Two aspects of inventory require some elaboration. One is the *types of inventory;* the other concerns differing viewpoints as to the *appropriate level of inventory.*

Types of Inventory

The three basic types of inventory are raw materials, work in process, and finished goods. **Raw materials inventory** consists of items purchased by the firm—usually, basic materials such as screws, plastic, raw steel, or rivets—for use in the manufacture of a finished product. If a firm manufactures complex products with numerous parts, its raw materials inventory may consist of manufactured

raw materials inventory
Items purchased by the firm for use in the manufacture of a finished product.

work-in-process inventory
All items that are currently in production.

finished goods inventory
Items that have been produced but not yet sold.

items that have been purchased from another company or from another division of the same firm. **Work-in-process inventory** consists of all items that are currently in production. These are normally partially finished goods at some intermediate stage of completion. **Finished goods inventory** consists of items that have been produced but not yet sold.

Differing Viewpoints About Inventory Level

Differing viewpoints about appropriate inventory levels commonly exist among a firm's finance, marketing, manufacturing, and purchasing managers. Each views inventory levels in light of its own objectives. The *financial manager's* general disposition toward inventory levels is to keep them low, to ensure that the firm's money is not being unwisely invested in excess resources. The *marketing manager,* on the other hand, would like to have large inventories of the firm's finished products. This would ensure that all orders could be filled quickly, eliminating the need for backorders due to stockouts.

The *manufacturing manager's* major responsibility is to correctly implement the production plan, so that it results in the desired amount of finished goods of acceptable quality at a low cost. In fulfilling this role, the manufacturing manager would keep raw materials inventories high to avoid production delays and would favor high finished goods inventories by making large production runs for the sake of lower unit production costs. The *purchasing manager* is concerned solely with the raw materials inventories. He or she is responsible for seeing that whatever raw materials are required by production are available in the correct quantities at the desired times and at a favorable price. Without proper control, the purchasing manager may purchase larger quantities of resources than are actually needed in order to get quantity discounts or in anticipation of rising prices or a shortage of certain materials.

Inventory as an Investment

Inventory is an investment in the sense that it requires that the firm tie up its money, thereby giving up certain other earning opportunities. In general, the higher a firm's average inventories, the larger the dollar investment and cost required; the lower its average inventories, the smaller the dollar investment and cost required. When evaluating planned changes in inventory levels, the financial manager should consider such changes from a benefit-versus-cost standpoint.

Example ▼ Ultimate Manufacturing is contemplating making larger production runs to reduce the high setup costs associated with the production of its only product, industrial hoists. The total *annual* reduction in setup costs that can be obtained has been estimated to be $10,000. As a result of the larger production runs, the average inventory investment is expected to increase from $200,000 to $300,000. If the firm can earn 15% per year on equal-risk investments, the *annual* cost of the additional $100,000 inventory investment will be $15,000 (.15 × $100,000). Comparing the annual $15,000 cost of the system with the annual savings of $10,000 shows that the *proposal should be rejected* because it results in a net annual *loss* of $5,000. ▲

The Relationship Between Inventory and Accounts Receivable

The level and the management of inventory and accounts receivable are closely related.[9] Generally, in manufacturing firms, when an item is sold, it moves from inventory to accounts receivable and ultimately to cash. Because of the close relationship between inventory and accounts receivable, their management should not be viewed independently. For example, the decision to extend credit to a customer can result in an increased level of sales, which can be supported only by higher levels of inventory and accounts receivable. The credit terms extended will also affect the investment in inventory and receivables, because longer credit terms may allow a firm to move items from inventory to accounts receivable. Generally, such a strategy is advantageous, because *the cost of carrying an item in inventory is greater than the cost of carrying an account receivable.* The cost of carrying inventory includes, in addition to the required return on the invested funds, the costs of storing, insuring, and otherwise maintaining the physical inventory.

Example ▼ Mills Industries, a producer of PVC pipe, estimates that the annual cost of carrying $1 of merchandise in inventory for a 1-year period is 25 cents, whereas the annual cost of carrying $1 of receivables is 15 cents. The firm currently maintains average inventories of $300,000 and an average *investment* in accounts receivable of $200,000. The firm believes that by altering its credit terms, it can cause its customers to purchase in larger quantities, thereby reducing its average inventories to $150,000 and increasing the average investment in accounts receivable to $350,000. The altered credit terms are not expected to generate new business but to result in a shift in purchasing and payment patterns. The costs of the present and proposed inventory–accounts receivable systems are calculated in Table 17.6.

Table 17.6 shows that by shifting $150,000 of inventory to accounts receivable, Mills Industries is able to lower the cost of carrying inventory and accounts receivable from $105,000 to $90,000—a $15,000 addition to profits. This profit

TABLE 17.6 Analysis of Inventory–Accounts Receivable Systems for Mills Industries

Variable	Cost/return (1)	Present Average investment (2)	Present Cost [(1) × (2)] (3)	Proposed Average investment (4)	Proposed Cost [(1) × (4)] (5)
Average inventory	25%	$300,000	$ 75,000	$150,000	$37,500
Average receivables	15	200,000	30,000	350,000	52,500
Totals		$500,000	$105,000	$500,000	$90,000

9. Although this chapter emphasizes the financial considerations in accounts receivable and inventory decisions, other nonfinancial considerations may significantly influence a firm's decisions in these areas.

is achieved without changing the level of average inventory and accounts receivable investment from its $500,000 total. Rather, the profit is attributed to a shift in the mix of these current assets so that a larger portion of them is held in the less costly form of accounts receivable.

The inventory–accounts receivable relationship is affected by decisions made in all areas of the firm—finance, marketing, manufacturing, and purchasing. The financial manager should consider the interaction between inventory and accounts receivable when developing strategies and making decisions related to the production-sale process. This interaction is especially important when making credit decisions, because the required as well as actual levels of inventory will be directly affected.

International Inventory Management

International inventory management is typically much more complicated for exporters in general, and for multinational companies in particular, than for purely domestic companies. The production and manufacturing economies of scale that might be expected from selling products globally may prove elusive if products must be tailored for individual local markets, as very frequently happens, or if actual production of goods takes place in factories around the world. When raw materials, intermediate goods, or finished products must be transported long distances—particularly by ocean shipping—there will inevitably be more delays, confusion, damage, theft, and other difficulties to overcome than occur in a one-country operation. The international inventory manager therefore puts a premium on flexibility, and he or she is usually less concerned about ordering the economically optimal quantity of inventory than about making sure that sufficient quantities of inventory are delivered where they are needed, when they are needed, and in a condition to be used as planned.

❓ Review Questions

17–13 What is the financial manager's role with respect to the management of inventory? What are likely to be the viewpoints of each of the following managers about the levels of the various types of inventory: (a) finance, (b) marketing, (c) manufacturing, and (d) purchasing?

17–14 Explain the relationship between inventory and accounts receivable. Assuming that the total investment in inventory and accounts receivable remains constant, what impact would lengthening the credit terms have on the firm's profits? Why?

17–15 What factors make managing inventory more difficult for exporters and multinational companies?

17.6 Techniques for Managing Inventory

Although the techniques that are commonly used in managing inventory are not strictly financial, it is helpful for the financial manager to understand them. In this section we will examine five common inventory management techniques.

The ABC System

ABC system
Inventory management technique that divides inventory into three categories of descending importance based on the dollar investment in each.

A firm using the **ABC system** divides its inventory into three groups, A, B, and C. The *A group* includes those items that require the largest dollar investment. In the typical distribution of inventory items, this group consists of the 20 percent of inventory items that account for 80 percent of the firm's dollar investment. The *B group* consists of the items accounting for the next largest investment. The *C group* typically consists of a large number of items accounting for a relatively small dollar investment.

Dividing inventory into A, B, and C items allows the firm to determine the level and types of inventory control procedures needed. Control of the A items should be most intensive because of the high dollar investment involved. The use of *perpetual inventory record keeping* that allows daily monitoring of these inventory levels is appropriate. B items are frequently controlled through *periodic checking*—possibly weekly—of their levels. C items could be controlled by using unsophisticated procedures such as a **red-line method,** in which a reorder is placed when enough inventory has been removed from a bin containing the inventory item to expose a red line drawn around the inside of the bin. The economic order quantity (EOQ) model, discussed next, is appropriate for use in monitoring A and B items.

red-line method
Unsophisticated inventory management technique in which a reorder is placed when sufficient use of inventory items from a bin exposes a red line drawn around the inside of the bin.

The Basic Economic Order Quantity (EOQ) Model

economic order quantity (EOQ) model
Inventory management technique for determining an item's optimal order quantity, which is the one that minimizes the total of its order and carrying costs.

One of the most commonly cited sophisticated tools for determining the optimal order quantity for an item of inventory is the **economic order quantity (EOQ) model.** It takes into account various operating and financial costs and determines the order quantity that minimizes total inventory cost.[10]

Basic Costs

Excluding the actual cost of the merchandise, the costs associated with inventory can be divided into three broad groups: order costs, carrying costs, and total cost. Each has certain key components and characteristics.

order costs
The fixed clerical costs of placing and receiving an inventory order.

Order Costs Order costs include the fixed clerical costs of placing and receiving an order—the cost of writing a purchase order, of processing the resulting paperwork, and of receiving an order and checking it against the invoice. Order costs are normally stated as dollars per order.

carrying costs
The variable costs per unit of holding an item in inventory for a specified time period.

Carrying Costs Carrying costs are the variable costs per unit of holding an item in inventory for a specified time period. These costs are typically stated as dollars per unit per period. Carrying costs include costs for storage, insurance, deterioration and obsolescence, and most important, the opportunity cost of tying up funds in inventory. A commonly cited rule of thumb suggests that the

10. The EOQ methodology is also applied to situations in which the firm wishes to minimize a total cost with fixed and variable components. It is commonly used to determine optimal production quantities when there is a fixed setup cost and a variable operating cost. The EOQ methodology, referred to as the *Baumol model,* was applied in Chapter 16 to determine the economic conversion quantity (ECQ) for converting marketable securities to cash and vice versa.

cost of carrying an item in inventory for 1 year is between 20 and 30 percent of the cost (value) of the item.

total cost (of inventory)
The sum of the *order costs* and *carrying costs* of inventory.

Total Cost   The **total cost** of inventory is defined as the sum of the order and carrying costs. Total cost is important in the EOQ model, because the model's objective is to determine the order quantity that minimizes it.

A Graphic Approach

The stated objective of the EOQ model is to find the order quantity that minimizes the firm's total inventory cost. The economic order quantity can be found graphically by plotting order quantities on the *x*, or horizontal, axis and costs on the *y*, or vertical, axis. Figure 17.2 shows the general behavior of these costs. The total cost line represents the sum of the order costs and carrying costs for each order quantity. The minimum total cost occurs at the point labeled EOQ, where the order cost line and the carrying cost line intersect.

A Mathematical Approach

A formula can be developed for determining the firm's EOQ for a given inventory item. We can develop the firm's total cost equation where

$$S = \text{usage in units per period}$$
$$O = \text{order cost per order}$$
$$C = \text{carrying cost per unit per period}$$
$$Q = \text{order quantity in units}$$

The first step in deriving the total cost equation is to develop an expression for the order cost function and the carrying cost function. The order cost can be

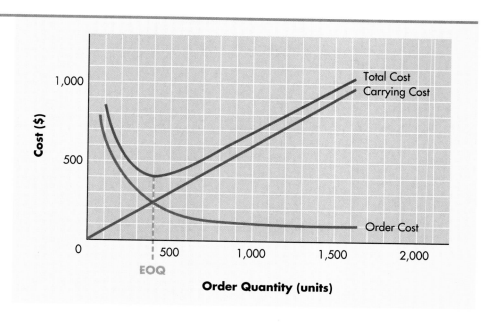

FIGURE 17.2

EOQ
A graphic presentation of an EOQ

expressed as the product of the cost per order and the number of orders. Because the number of orders equals the usage during the period divided by the order quantity (S/Q), the order cost can be expressed as

$$\text{Order cost} = O \times S/Q \tag{17.2}$$

The carrying cost is defined as the cost of carrying a unit per period multiplied by the firm's average inventory. The average inventory is defined as the order quantity divided by 2 $(Q/2)$, because inventory is assumed to be depleted at a constant rate. Thus, the carrying cost can be expressed as

$$\text{Carrying cost} = C \times Q/2 \tag{17.3}$$

Hint   The EOQ calculation helps management minimize the total cost of inventory. Lowering order costs will cause an increase in carrying costs, and may increase total cost. Likewise, an increase in total cost may result from reduced carrying costs. The goal, facilitated by using the EOQ calculation, is to lower total cost.

Analyzing Equations 17.2 and 17.3 shows that as the order quantity, Q, increases, the order cost will decrease and the carrying cost will increase proportionately.

The total cost equation is obtained by combining the order cost and carrying cost expressions in Equations 17.2 and 17.3, as follows:

$$\text{Total cost} = (O \times S/Q) + (C \times Q/2) \tag{17.4}$$

Because the EOQ is defined as the order quantity that minimizes the total cost function, Equation 17.4 must be solved for the EOQ.[11] The following formula results:

$$\text{EOQ} = \sqrt{\frac{2 \times S \times O}{C}} \tag{17.5}$$

Example ▼ Assume that RSP, Inc., a manufacturer of electronic test equipment, uses 1,600 units of an item annually. Its order cost is $50 per order, and the carrying cost is $1 per unit per year. Substituting $S = 1,600$, $O = \$50$, and $C = \$1$ into Equation 17.5 yields an EOQ of 400 units:

$$\text{EOQ} = \sqrt{\frac{2 \times 1,600 \times \$50}{\$1}} = \sqrt{160,000} = \underline{400 \text{ units}}$$

---

11. The solution can be found by either (1) taking the first derivative of Equation 17.4 with respect to Q, setting it equal to zero, and solving for Q, the EOQ, or (2) setting the order cost equal to the carrying cost and solving for Q, the EOQ, as follows:

$$O \times \frac{S}{Q} = C \times \frac{Q}{2}$$

(1) Multiply both sides by Q

$$O \times S = C \times \frac{Q^2}{2}$$

(2) Multiply both sides by 2

$$2 \times O \times S = C \times Q^2$$

(3) Divide both sides by C

$$\frac{2 \times O \times S}{C} = Q^2$$

(4) Take the square root of both sides

$$\sqrt{\frac{2 \times S \times O}{C}} = Q = \text{EOQ}$$

If the firm orders in quantities of 400 units, it will minimize its total inventory cost. This solution is depicted in Figure 17.2.

Although even the simple EOQ model has weaknesses, it certainly provides decision makers with better grounds for a decision than subjective observations. Despite the fact that the financial manager is normally not directly associated with the use of the EOQ model, he or she must be aware of its utility, and must also provide certain financial inputs, specifically with respect to inventory carrying costs.

The Reorder Point

reorder point
The point at which to reorder inventory, expressed equationally as: lead time in days × daily usage.

Once the firm has calculated its economic order quantity, it must determine *when* to place orders. A reorder point is required that considers the lead time needed to place and receive orders. Assuming a constant usage rate for inventory, the **reorder point** can be determined by the following equation:

$$\text{Reorder point} = \text{lead time in days} \times \text{daily usage} \qquad (17.6)$$

safety stocks
Extra inventories that can be drawn down when actual lead times and/or usage rates are greater than expected.

For example, if a firm knows that it requires 10 days to place and receive an order, and if it uses five units of inventory daily, the reorder point would be 50 units (10 days × 5 units per day). Thus, when the firm's inventory level reaches 50 units, an order will be placed for an amount equal to the economic order quantity. If the estimates of lead time and daily usage are correct, the order will be received exactly when the inventory level reaches zero. Because of the difficulty in precisely predicting lead times and daily usage rates, many firms typically maintain **safety stocks,** which are extra inventories that can be drawn down if needed.

Materials Requirement Planning (MRP) System

materials requirement planning (MRP) system
Inventory management system that uses EOQ concepts and a computer to compare production needs to available inventory balances and determine when orders should be placed for various items on a product's *bill of materials.*

Many companies use a **materials requirement planning (MRP) system** to determine what to order, when to order, and what priorities to assign to ordering materials. MRP uses EOQ concepts to determine how much to order. Using a computer, it simulates each product's bill of materials structure, inventory status, and manufacturing process. The *bill of materials* structure simply refers to every part or material that goes into making the finished product. For a given production plan, the computer simulates needed materials requirements by comparing production needs to available inventory balances. On the basis of the time it takes for a product that is in process to move through the various production stages and the lead time required to get materials, the MRP system determines when orders should be placed for the various items on the bill of materials.

The advantage of the MRP system is that it forces the firm to more thoughtfully consider its inventory needs and plan accordingly. The objective is to lower the firm's inventory investment without impairing production. If the firm's opportunity cost of capital for investments of equal risk is 15 percent, every dollar of investment released from inventory increases before-tax profits by $.15.

Just-in-Time (JIT) System

just-in-time (JIT) system
Inventory management system that minimizes inventory investment by having material inputs arrive at exactly the time they are needed for production.

The **just-in-time (JIT) system** is used to minimize inventory investment. The philosophy is that materials should arrive at exactly the time they are needed for production. Ideally, the firm would have only work-in-process inventory. Because its objective is to minimize inventory investment, a JIT system uses no, or very little, safety stocks. Extensive coordination must exist between the firm, its suppliers, and shipping companies to ensure that material inputs arrive on time. Failure of materials to arrive on time results in a shutdown of the production line until the materials arrive. Likewise, a JIT system requires high-quality parts from suppliers. When quality problems arise, production must be stopped until the problems are resolved.

The goal of the JIT system is manufacturing efficiency. It uses inventory as a tool for attaining efficiency by emphasizing quality in terms of both the materials used and their timely delivery. When JIT is working properly, it forces process inefficiencies to surface and be resolved. A JIT system requires cooperation among all parties involved in the process—suppliers, shipping companies, and the firm's employees.

? Review Questions

17–16   Briefly describe each of the following techniques for managing inventory: (a) ABC system, (b) reorder point, (c) materials requirement planning (MRP) system, and (d) just-in-time (JIT) system.

17–17   What is the *EOQ model?* To which group of inventory items is it most applicable? What costs does it consider? What financial cost is involved?

SUMMARY

 Discuss credit selection, including the five C's of credit, obtaining and analyzing credit information, credit scoring, and managing international credit. Credit selection includes deciding whether to extend credit to a customer and how much credit to extend. The five C's of credit—character, capacity, capital, collateral, and conditions—guide credit investigation. Credit information can be obtained from a variety of external sources and analyzed in a number of ways. An analyst's subjective judgment is an important input to the final decision. Impersonal credit decision techniques, such as credit scoring, are often used at the consumer level. Credit management is difficult for companies that operate internationally due to the presence of exchange rate risk, difficulties in shipping across international borders, and the need to assess and bear the credit risks of foreign customers.

 Use the key variables to evaluate quantitatively the effects of either relaxing or tightening a firm's credit standards. At the mercantile level, credit standards must be set by considering the trade-offs between the key variables—the profit contribution from sales, the cost of investment in accounts receivable, and the cost of bad debts. Generally, when credit standards are relaxed, the profit contribution from sales increases, as do the costs of investment in accounts receivable and bad debts. If the increased profit contribution exceeds the increased costs, the credit standards should be relaxed. A tightening of credit standards would result in decreases in each of the key variables; if the cost reductions exceed the reduced profit contribution, credit standards should be tightened.

LG3 **Review the effects in changes in each of the three components of credit terms on key financial variables and profits, and the procedure for quantitatively evaluating cash discount changes.** Credit terms have three components: (1) the cash discount, (2) the cash discount period, and (3) the credit period. Changes in these variables affect the firm's sales, investment in accounts receivable, bad debt expenses, and profit per unit. Quantitatively, a proposed increase of a cash discount is evaluated by comparing the profit increases attributable to the added sales, the reduction in accounts receivable investment, and the reduction in bad debts to the cost of the cash discount. If the profit increases exceed the cost, the discount increase should be undertaken. The proposed decrease of a cash discount would be analyzed similarly, except that the profit and cost factors would be reversed.

LG4 **Explain the key features of collection policy, including aging accounts receivable, the effects of changes in collection efforts, and the popular collection techniques.** Collection policy determines the type and degree of effort exercised to collect overdue accounts. Firms look at the average collection period ratio and also often age accounts receivable to evaluate the effectiveness of the firm's credit and collection policies. The procedures used to evaluate changes in collection efforts are similar to those for credit standards and credit terms. Generally, increased collection expenditures will have little effect on sales volume and will reduce the investment in accounts receivable and bad debt expenses. The popular collection techniques include letters, telephone calls, personal visits, collection agencies, and legal action.

LG5 **Understand inventory fundamentals, the relationship between inventory and accounts receivable, and international inventory management.** The viewpoints held by marketing, manufacturing, and purchasing managers regarding the appropriate levels of types of inventory (raw materials, work in process, and finished goods) tend to conflict with that of the financial manager. The financial manager views inventory as an investment that consumes dollars and should be maintained at a low level. Because it is more expensive to carry an item in inventory than to carry an account receivable, the financial manager must consider the relationship between inventory and accounts receivable when making related decisions. International inventory managers place greater emphasis on making sure that sufficient quantities of inventory are delivered where they are needed, when they are needed, and in the right condition than on ordering the economically optimal quantities.

LG6 **Describe the common techniques for managing inventory, including the ABC system, the basic economic order quantity model, the reorder point, the materials requirement planning system, and the just-in-time system.** The ABC system determines which inventories require the most attention according to dollar investment. One of the most common techniques for determining optimal order quantities is the economic order quantity (EOQ) model. Once the optimal order quantity has been determined, the firm can set the reorder point, the level of inventory at which an order will be placed. A materials requirement planning (MRP) system can be used to determine when orders should be placed for various items on a firm's bill of materials. Just-in-time (JIT) systems are used to minimize inventory investment by having materials arrive at exactly the time they are needed for production.

SELF-TEST PROBLEMS   (Solutions in Appendix B)

 ST 17–1 **Easing collection efforts** Regency Rug Repair Company is attempting to evaluate whether it should ease collection efforts. The firm repairs 72,000 rugs per year at an average price of $32 each. Bad debt expenses are 1% of sales, and

collection expenditures are $60,000. The average collection period is 40 days, and the variable cost per unit is $28. By easing the collection efforts, Regency expects to save $40,000 per year in collection expense. Bad debts will increase to 2% of sales, and the average collection period will increase to 58 days. Sales will increase by 1,000 repairs per year. If the firm has a required rate of return on equal-risk investments of 24%, what recommendation would you give the firm? Use your analysis to justify your answer.

ST 17–2   EOQ analysis   Thompson Paint Company uses 60,000 gallons of pigment per year. The cost of ordering pigment is $200 per order, and the cost of carrying the pigment in inventory is $1 per gallon per year. The firm uses pigment at a constant rate every day throughout the year.

a. Calculate the EOQ.
b. Calculate the total cost of the plan suggested by the EOQ.
c. Determine the total number of orders suggested by this plan.
d. Assuming that it takes 20 days to receive an order once it has been placed, determine the reorder point in terms of gallons of pigment. (*Note:* Use a 360-day year.)

PROBLEMS

INTERMEDIATE   **17–1   Credit scoring**   Clemens Department Store uses credit scoring to evaluate retail credit applications. The financial and credit characteristics considered and weights indicating their relative importance in the credit decision are given in the table that follows. The firm's credit standards are to accept all applicants with credit scores of 80 or more, to extend limited credit on a probationary basis to applicants with scores of greater than 70 and less than 80, and to reject all applicants with scores below 70.

Financial and credit characteristics	Predetermined weight
Credit references	.25
Education	.15
Home ownership	.10
Income range	.10
Payment history	.30
Years on job	.10

The firm currently needs to process three applications that were recently received and scored by one of its credit analysts. The scores for each of the applicants on each of the financial and credit characteristics are summarized in the following table:

	Applicant		
Financial and credit characteristics	**A**	**B**	**C**
	Score (0 to 100)		
Credit references	60	90	80
Education	70	70	80
Home ownership	100	90	60
Income range	75	80	80
Payment history	60	85	70
Years on job	50	60	90

a. Use the data presented to find the credit score for each of the applicants.
b. Recommend the appropriate action for each of the three applicants.

WARM-UP

17–2 **Accounts receivable and costs** Randolph Company currently has an average collection period of 45 days and annual credit sales of $1 million. Assume a 360-day year.
a. What is the firm's average accounts receivable balance?
b. If the variable cost of each product is 60% of sales, what is the average *investment* in accounts receivable?
c. If the equal-risk opportunity cost of the investment in accounts receivable is 12%, what is the total opportunity cost of the investment in accounts receivable?

INTERMEDIATE

17–3 **Accounts receivable changes without bad debts** Tara's Textiles currently has credit sales of $360 million per year and an average collection period of 60 days. Assume that the price of Tara's products is $60 per unit and the variable costs are $55 per unit. The firm is considering an account receivable change that will result in a 20% increase in sales and an equal 20% increase in the average collection period. No change in bad debts is expected. The firm's equal-risk opportunity cost on its investment in accounts receivable is 14%.
a. Calculate the additional profit contribution from new sales that the firm will realize if it makes the proposed change.
b. What marginal investment in accounts receivable will result?
c. Calculate the cost of the marginal investment in accounts receivable.
d. Should the firm implement the proposed change? What other information would be helpful in your analysis?

CHALLENGE

17–4 **Accounts receivable changes and bad debts** A firm is evaluating an account receivable change that would increase bad debts from 2 to 4% of sales. Sales are currently 50,000 units, the selling price is $20 per unit, and the variable cost per unit is $15. As a result of the proposed change, sales are forecast to increase to 60,000 units.
a. What are bad debts in dollars currently and under the proposed change?
b. Calculate the cost of the marginal bad debts to the firm.

c. Ignoring the additional profit contribution from increased sales, if the proposed change saves $3,500 and causes no change in the average investment in accounts receivable, would you recommend it? Explain.

d. Considering *all* changes in costs and benefits, would you recommend the proposed change? Explain.

e. Compare and discuss your answers in **c** and **d**.

INTERMEDIATE

17–5   Tightening credit standards—Sales and bad debt effects only   Michael's Menswear feels that its credit costs are too high. By tightening its credit standards, bad debts will fall from 5% of sales to 2%. However, sales will fall from $100,000 to $90,000 per year. The variable cost per unit is 50% of the sale price, and the average investment in receivables is expected to remain unchanged.

a. What cost will the firm face in a reduced contribution to profits from sales?

b. Should the firm tighten its credit standards? Explain your answer.

CHALLENGE

17–6   Relaxation of credit standards   Lewis Enterprises is considering relaxing its credit standards to increase its currently sagging sales. As a result of the proposed relaxation, sales are expected to increase by 10% from 10,000 to 11,000 units during the coming year, the average collection period is expected to increase from 45 to 60 days, and bad debts are expected to increase from 1 to 3% of sales. The sale price per unit is $40, and the variable cost per unit is $31. If the firm's required return on equal-risk investments is 25%, evaluate the proposed relaxation, and make a recommendation to the firm.

CHALLENGE

17–7   Initiating a cash discount   Gardner Company currently makes all sales on credit and offers no cash discount. The firm is considering a 2% cash discount for payment within 15 days. The firm's current average collection period is 60 days, sales are 40,000 units, selling price is $45 per unit, and variable cost per unit is $36. The firm expects that the change in credit terms will result in an increase in sales to 42,000 units, that 70% of the sales will take the discount, and that the average collection period will fall to 30 days. If the firm's required rate of return on equal-risk investments is 25%, should the proposed discount be offered?

CHALLENGE

17–8   Shortening the credit period   A firm is contemplating *shortening* its credit period from 40 to 30 days and believes that as a result of this change, its average collection period will decline from 45 to 36 days. Bad debt expenses are expected to decrease from 1.5 to 1% of sales. The firm is currently selling 12,000 units but believes that as a result of the proposed change, sales will decline to 10,000 units. The sale price per unit is $56, and its variable cost per unit is $45. The firm has a required return on equal-risk investments of 25%. Evaluate this decision, and make a recommendation to the firm.

CHALLENGE

17–9   Lengthening the credit period   Parker Tool is considering lengthening its credit period from 30 to 60 days. All customers will continue to pay on the net date. The firm currently bills $450,000 for sales and has $345,000 in variable costs. The change in credit terms is expected to increase sales to $510,000. Bad debt expense will increase from 1 to 1.5% of sales. The firm has a required rate of return on equal-risk investments of 20%.

a. What additional profit contribution from sales will be realized from the proposed change?
b. What is the cost of the marginal investment in accounts receivable?
c. What is the cost of the marginal bad debts?
d. Do you recommend this change in credit terms? Why or why not?

INTERMEDIATE   17–10   **Aging accounts receivable**   Burnham Services' accounts receivable totaled $874,000 on August 31, 2000. A breakdown of these outstanding accounts on the basis of the month in which the credit sale was initially made follows. The firm extends 30-day EOM credit terms to its credit customers.

Month of credit sale	Accounts receivable
August 2000	$320,000
July 2000	250,000
June 2000	81,000
May 2000	195,000
April 2000 or before	28,000
Total (August 31, 2000)	$874,000

a. Prepare an aging schedule for Burnham Services' August 31, 2000, accounts receivable balance.
b. Using your findings in **a,** evaluate the firm's credit and collection activities.
c. What are some probable causes of the situation discussed in **b?**

   17–11   **Inventory investment**   Paterson Products is considering leasing a computerized inventory control system to reduce its average inventories. The annual cost of the system is $46,000. It is expected that with the system the firm's average inventory will decline by 50% from its current level of $980,000. The level of stockouts is expected to be unaffected by this system. The firm can earn 20% per year on equal-risk investments.

WARM-UP

a. How much of a reduction in average inventory will result from the proposed installation of the computerized inventory control system?
b. How much, if any, annual savings will the firm realize on the reduced level of average inventory?
c. Should the firm lease the computerized inventory control system? Explain why or why not.

INTERMEDIATE   17–12   **Inventory versus accounts receivable costs**   Hamilton Supply estimates the annual cost of carrying a dollar of inventory is $.27, and the annual carrying cost of an equal investment in accounts receivable is $.17. The firm's current balance sheet reflects its average inventory of $400,000 and average investment in accounts receivable of $100,000. If the firm can convince its customers to purchase in large quantities, the average level of inventory can be reduced by $200,000, and the average investment in receivables can be increased by the same amount. Assuming no change in annual sales, what addition to profits will be generated from this shift? Explain your answer.

17–13   Inventory—The ABC system   Newton, Inc., has 16 different items in its inventory. The average number of units held in inventory and the average unit cost for each item are listed in the following table. The firm wishes to introduce the ABC system of inventory management. Suggest a breakdown of the items into classifications of A, B, and C. Justify your selection and point out items that could be considered borderline cases.

Item	Average number of units in inventory	Average cost per unit
1	1,800	$ 0.54
2	1,000	8.20
3	100	6.00
4	250	1.20
5	8	94.50
6	400	3.00
7	80	45.00
8	1,600	1.45
9	600	0.95
10	3,000	0.18
11	900	15.00
12	65	1.35
13	2,200	4.75
14	1,800	1.30
15	60	18.00
16	200	17.50

17–14   Graphic EOQ analysis   Knoll Manufacturing uses 10,000 units of raw material per year on a continuous basis. Placing and processing an order for additional inventory cost $200 per order. The firm estimates the cost of carrying one unit in inventory at $.25 per year.

a. What are the annual order costs, carrying costs, and total costs of inventory if the firm orders in quantities of 1,000; 2,000; 3,000; 4,000; 5,000; 6,000; and 7,000 units?

b. Graph the order cost, carrying cost, and total cost (y axis) relative to order quantity (x axis). Label the EOQ.

c. On the basis of your graph, in what quantity would you order? Is this consistent with the EOQ equation? Explain why or why not.

INTERMEDIATE  **17–15** **EOQ analysis**   Tiger Corporation purchases 1,200,000 units per year of one component. The fixed cost per order is $25. The annual carrying cost of the item is 27% of its $2 cost.

   a. Determine the EOQ under the following conditions: (1) no changes, (2) order cost of zero, and (3) carrying cost of zero.

   b. What do your answers illustrate about the EOQ model? Explain.

WARM-UP **17–16** **Reorder point**   Beeman Gas and Electric (BG&E) is required to carry a minimum of 20 days' average coal usage, which is 100 tons of coal. It takes 10 days between order and delivery. At what level of coal would BG&E reorder?

INTERMEDIATE **17–17** **EOQ, reorder point, and safety stock**   A firm uses 800 units of a product per year on a continuous basis. The product has a fixed cost of $50 per order, and its carrying cost is $2 per unit per year. It takes 5 days to receive a shipment after an order is placed, and the firm wishes to hold in inventory 10 days' usage as a safety stock.

   a. Calculate the EOQ.

   b. Determine the average level of inventory. (*Note:* Use a 360-day year to calculate daily usage.)

   c. Determine the reorder point.

   d. Which of the following variables change if the firm does not hold the safety stock: (1) order cost, (2) carrying cost, (3) reorder point, (4) total inventory cost, (5) average level of inventory, (6) number of orders per year, (7) economic order quantity? Explain.

CASE   CHAPTER 17

Evaluating Global Textiles' Proposed Change in Credit Terms

Ken Steinbacher, a financial analyst for Global Textiles, has been asked to investigate a proposed change in the firm's credit terms. The company's founder and president believes that by increasing the credit period from 30 to 65 days, two important benefits will result: (1) sales will increase as a result of attracting *new customers,* and (2) some *existing customers* will purchase merchandise sooner to ensure its availability, given the unpredictable timing of the selling seasons. Annual sales are estimated to increase from the current level of $4,000,000 to $4,800,000. Eighty percent of this increase is expected to be attributable to new customers, and the other 20% is expected to result from existing customers. Because some existing customers will be making their purchases earlier than in the past, their actions will merely result in a shifting of inventory to accounts receivable. Ken estimated that the decline in inventory investment attributable to the actions of existing customers would just equal the additional accounts receivable investment associated with their actions.

Ken's investigation indicates that with the extended credit period, the firm's average collection period will increase from 45 to 90 days. In addition, bad debts will increase from 1 to 2 1/2% of sales. The firm's variable costs are expected to continue to amount to 80% of each $1 of sales. Global currently requires a 16% rate of return on equal-risk accounts receivable investments, and its cost of carrying $1 of inventory for 1 year is 26 cents.

Required

a. Find the additional annual profit contribution expected from the increased credit period.
b. Determine the increase in Global's average investment in accounts receivable and the resulting annual cost attributable to the proposed increase in the credit period.
c. Calculate the annual savings resulting from the reduced inventory investment attributable to the existing customers' earlier purchases.
d. Calculate the annual cost expected to result from the increase in bad debt expenses attributable to the proposed lengthening of the credit period.
e. Use your findings in **a** through **d** to advise Ken on whether or not the proposed increase in the credit period can be financially justified. Explain your recommendation.
f. What impact, if any, would ignoring the effect of the proposed increase in the credit period on the level of inventory investment found in **c** have on your recommendation in **e**? Explain.

WEB EXERCISE

GOTO web site www.inc.com/virtualconsult/. Click on WORKSHEETS at the top of the screen. Scroll down the page and click on Check your Z-Score: How's your Fiscal Fitness.

1. What does the Z-score indicate?
2. What are the five ratios that are used in calculating the Altman's Z-score? Which ratio is the most significant in determining the Z-score?
3. What is the score for a healthy company? For a company in fiscal danger?

4. Using the Z-score worksheet, enter the following account balances and determine these two companies' Z-scores:

	(in millions)	
	Company A	**Company B**
Earnings before interest and taxes	−$ 251	$ 1,602
Total assets	761	13,071
Net sales	1,389	13,319
Market value of equity	18	6,440
Total liabilities	621	7,212
Working capital	341	3,964
Retained earnings	41	8,717

After entering these account balances, click CALCULATE Z-SCORE.

5. Would you give credit to either of these two companies? Why or why not?

INTEGRATIVE CASE 5

CASA DE DISEÑO

In January 2001, Teresa Leal was named treasurer of Casa de Diseño. She decided that she could best orient herself by systematically examining each area of the company's financial operations. She began by studying the firm's short-term financial activities.

Casa de Diseño is located in southern California and specializes in a furniture line called "Ligne Moderna." Of high quality and contemporary design, the furniture appeals to the customer who wants something unique for his or her home or apartment. Most Ligne Moderna furniture is built by special order, because a wide variety of upholstery, accent trimming, and colors are available. The product line is distributed through exclusive dealership arrangements with well-established retail stores. Casa de Diseño's manufacturing process virtually eliminates the use of wood. Plastic and metal provide the basic framework, and wood is used only for decorative purposes.

Casa de Diseño entered the plastic furniture market in late 1995. The company markets its plastic furniture products as indoor–outdoor items under the brand name "Futuro." Futuro plastic furniture emphasizes comfort, durability, and practicality, and is distributed through wholesalers. The Futuro line has been very successful, accounting for nearly 40 percent of the firm's sales and profits in 2000. Casa de Diseño anticipates some additions to the Futuro line and also some limited change of direction in its promotion in an effort to expand the applications of the plastic furniture.

Ms. Leal has decided to study the firm's cash management practices. To determine the effects of these practices, she must first determine the current operating and cash conversion cycles. In her investigations, she found that Casa de Diseño purchases all of its raw materials and production supplies on open account. The company is operating at production levels that preclude volume discounts. Most suppliers do not offer cash discounts, and Casa de Diseño usually receives credit terms of net 30. An analysis of Casa de Diseño's accounts payable showed that its average payment period is 30 days. Leal consulted industry data and found that the industry average payment period was 39 days. Investigation of six California furniture manufacturers revealed that their average payment period was also 39 days.

Next, Leal studied the production cycle and inventory policies. Casa de Diseño tries not to hold any more inventory than necessary in either raw materials or finished goods. The average inventory age was 110 days. Leal determined that the industry standard as reported in a survey done by *Furniture Age,* the trade association journal, was 83 days.

Casa de Diseño sells to all of its customers on a net 60 basis, in line with the industry trend to grant such credit terms on specialty furniture. Leal discovered, by aging the accounts receivable, that the average collection period for the firm was 75 days. Investigation of the trade association's and California manufacturers' averages showed that the same collection period existed where net 60 credit terms were given. Where cash discounts were offered, the collection period was significantly shortened. Leal believed that if Casa de Diseño were to offer credit terms of 3/10 net 60, the average collection period could be reduced by 40 percent.

Casa de Diseño was spending an estimated $26,500,000 per year on operating cycle investments. Leal considered this expenditure level to be the minimum she could expect the firm to disburse during 2001. Her concern was whether the firm's cash management was as efficient as it could be. She knew that the company paid 15 percent for its negotiated financing. For this reason, she was concerned about the financing cost resulting from any inefficiencies in the management of Casa de Diseño's cash conversion cycle.

REQUIRED

a. Assuming a constant rate for purchases, production, and sales throughout the year, what are Casa de Diseño's existing operating cycle (OC), cash conversion cycle (CCC), and negotiated financing needs?

b. If Leal can optimize Casa de Diseño's operations according to industry standards, what would Casa de Diseño's operating cycle (OC), cash conversion cycle (CCC), and negotiated financing need be under these more efficient conditions?

c. In terms of negotiated financing requirements, what is the cost of Casa de Diseño's operational inefficiency?

d. (1) If in addition to achieving industry standards for payables and inventory, the firm can reduce the average collection period by offering 3/10 net 60 credit terms, what additional savings in negotiated financing costs would result from the shortened cash conversion cycle, assuming that the level of sales remains constant?

(2) If the firm's sales (all on credit) are $40,000,000 and 45 percent of the customers are expected to take the cash discount, by how much will the firm's annual revenues be reduced as a result of the discount?

(3) If the firm's variable cost of the $40,000,000 in sales is 80 percent, determine the reduction in the average investment in accounts receivable and the annual savings resulting from this reduced investment assuming that sales remain constant. (Assume a 360-day year.)

(4) If the firm's bad debt expenses decline from 2 to 1.5 percent of sales, what annual savings would result, assuming that sales remain constant?

(5) Use your findings in (2) through (4) to assess whether offering the cash discount can be justified financially. Explain why or why not.

e. On the basis of your analysis in **a** through **d**, what recommendations would you offer Teresa Leal?

PART

6

Special Topics in Managerial Finance

18

Hybrid and Derivative Securities

LEARNING GOALS

LG1 Differentiate between hybrid and derivative securities and their roles in the corporation.

LG2 Review the basic types of leases, leasing arrangements, the lease-versus-purchase decision, the effects of leasing on future financing, and the advantages and disadvantages of leasing.

LG3 Describe the basic types of convertible securities, their general features, and financing with convertibles.

LG4 Demonstrate the procedures for determining the straight bond value, conversion (or stock) value, and market value of a convertible bond.

LG5 Explain the basic characteristics of stock purchase warrants, the implied price of an attached warrant, and the values of warrants.

LG6 Define options and discuss the basics of calls and puts, options markets, options trading, the role of call and put options in fund raising, and hedging foreign currency exposures with options.

18.1 An Overview of Hybrids and Derivatives

Chapter 2 described the characteristics of the key securities—corporate bonds, common stock, and preferred stock—used by corporations to raise long-term funds. In their simplest form, bonds are pure debt and common stock is pure equity. Preferred stock, on the other hand, is a form of equity that promises to pay fixed periodic dividends that are similar to the fixed contractual interest payments on bonds. Because it blends the characteristics of *both* debt (a fixed divi-

Outstanding in Their Field

Hybrid corn, which is the dominant type planted in the United States since the 1940s, is the result of crossing two varieties of seed to produce plants with improved quality. Hybrids are common in modern-day agriculture and besides corn, include varieties of sugar beets, alfalfa, barley, rice, wheat, tomatoes, melons, squash, pears, plums, and many flowers. The point of breeding hybrids is to produce offspring that include the best characteristics of the two parent plants. Although you won't find them in fields inspecting their crops, financial engineers are also interested in hybridization, and they have produced securities that combine desirable characteristics of debt and equity. This chapter will look at the various hybrid securities and also at options, a security that is neither debt nor equity.

hybrid security
A form of debt or equity financing that possesses characteristics of *both* debt and equity financing.

derivative security
A security that is neither debt nor equity but derives its value from an underlying asset that is often another security; called "derivatives," for short.

dend payment) and equity (ownership), preferred stock is considered a **hybrid security.** Other popular hybrid securities include financial leases, convertible securities, and stock purchase warrants. Each of these hybrid securities is described in the following pages.

In addition to hybrid securities, this chapter, in the final section, focuses on *options,* a popular **derivative security**—a security that is neither debt nor equity but derives its value from an underlying asset that is often another security. As you'll learn, *derivatives* are not used by corporations to raise funds, but rather serve as a useful tool for managing certain aspects of the firm's risk.

? Review Question

18–1 Differentiate between a *hybrid security* and a *derivative security*. How does their use by the corporation differ?

18.2 Leasing

leasing
The process by which a firm can obtain the use of certain fixed assets for which it must make a series of contractual, periodic, tax-deductible payments.

lessee
The receiver of the services of the assets under a lease contract.

lessor
The owner of assets that are being leased.

Leasing allows the firm to obtain the use of certain fixed assets for which it must make a series of contractual, periodic, tax-deductible payments. The **lessee** is the receiver of the services of the assets under the lease contract; the **lessor** is the owner of the assets. Leasing can take a number of forms.

Basic Types of Leases

The two basic types of leases that are available to a business are *operating* and *financial* leases (often called *capital leases* by accountants).

Operating Leases

operating lease
A *cancelable* contractual arrangement whereby the lessee agrees to make periodic payments to the lessor, often for 5 or fewer years, to obtain an asset's services; generally, the total payments over the term of the lease are *less* than the lessor's initial cost of the leased asset.

An **operating lease** is normally a contractual arrangement whereby the lessee agrees to make periodic payments to the lessor, often for 5 or fewer years, to obtain an asset's services. Such leases are generally *cancelable* at the option of the lessee, who may be required to pay a penalty for cancellation. Assets that are leased under operating leases have a usable life that is *longer* than the term of the lease. Usually, however, they would become less efficient and technologically obsolete if leased for a longer period. Computer systems are prime examples of assets whose relative efficiency is expected to diminish as the technology changes. The operating lease is therefore a common arrangement for obtaining such systems, as well as for other relatively short-lived assets such as automobiles.

If an operating lease is held to maturity, the lessee at that time returns the leased asset to the lessor, who may lease it again or sell the asset. Normally, the asset still has a positive market value at the termination of the lease. In some instances, the lease contract will give the lessee the opportunity to purchase the leased asset. Generally, the total payments made by the lessee to the lessor are *less* than the lessor's initial cost of the leased asset.

Financial (or Capital) Leases

financial (or capital) lease
A *longer-term* lease than an operating lease that is *noncancelable* and obligates the lessee to make payments for the use of an asset over a predefined period of time; the total payments over the term of the lease are *greater* than the lessor's initial cost of the leased asset.

A **financial (or capital) lease** is a *longer-term* lease than an operating lease. Financial leases are *noncancelable* and obligate the lessee to make payments for the use of an asset over a predefined period of time. Financial leases are commonly used for leasing land, buildings, and large pieces of equipment. The non-cancelable feature of the financial lease makes it similar to certain types of long-term debt. The lease payment becomes a fixed, tax-deductible expenditure that must be paid at predefined dates. Like debt, failure to make the contractual lease payments can result in bankruptcy for the lessee.

With a financial lease, the total payments over the lease period are *greater* than the lessor's initial cost of the leased asset. In other words, the lessor must receive more than the asset's purchase price to earn its required return on the investment. Technically, under Financial Accounting Standards Board (FASB) Standard No. 13, "Accounting for Leases," a financial (or capital) lease is defined as one having *any* of the following elements:

1. The lease transfers ownership of the property to the lessee by the end of the lease term.
2. The lease contains an option to purchase the property at a "bargain price." Such an option must be exercisable at a "fair market value."
3. The lease term is equal to 75 percent or more of the estimated economic life of the property (exceptions exist for property leased toward the end of its usable economic life).
4. At the beginning of the lease, the present value of the lease payments is equal to 90 percent or more of the fair market value of the leased property.

The emphasis in this chapter is on financial leases because they result in inescapable long-term financial commitments by the firm.

Leasing Arrangements

Lessors use three primary techniques for obtaining assets to be leased. The method depends largely on the desires of the prospective lessee.

direct lease
A lease under which a lessor owns or acquires the assets that are leased to a given lessee.

sale-leaseback arrangement
A lease under which the lessee sells an asset for cash to a prospective lessor and then leases back the same asset, making fixed periodic payments for its use.

leveraged lease
A lease under which the lessor acts as an equity participant, supplying only about 20 percent of the cost of the asset, while a lender supplies the balance.

maintenance clauses
Provisions normally included in an operating lease that require the lessor to maintain the assets and to make insurance and tax payments.

renewal options
Provisions especially common in operating leases that grant the lessee the option to re-lease assets at the expiration of the lease.

1. A **direct lease** results when a lessor owns or acquires the assets that are leased to a given lessee. In other words, the lessee did not previously own the assets that it is leasing.
2. In a **sale-leaseback arrangement,** lessors acquire leased assets by purchasing assets already owned by the lessee and leasing them back. This technique is normally initiated by a firm that needs funds for operations. By selling an existing asset to a lessor and then *leasing it back,* the lessee receives cash for the asset immediately while obligating itself to make fixed periodic payments for use of the leased asset.
3. Leasing arrangements that include one or more third-party lenders are **leveraged leases.** Under a leveraged lease, the lessor acts as an equity participant, supplying only about 20 percent of the cost of the asset, and a lender supplies the balance. Leveraged leases have become especially popular in structuring leases of very expensive assets.

A lease agreement normally specifies whether the lessee is responsible for maintenance of the leased assets. Operating leases normally include **maintenance clauses** requiring the lessor to maintain the assets and to make insurance and tax payments. Financial leases almost always require the lessee to pay maintenance and other costs.

The lessee is usually given the option to renew a lease at its expiration. **Renewal options,** which grant lessees the right to re-lease assets at expiration, are especially common in operating leases, because their term is generally shorter

purchase options
Provisions frequently included in both operating and financial leases that allow the lessee to purchase the leased asset at maturity, typically for a pre-specified price.

than the usable life of the leased assets. **Purchase options** allowing the lessee to purchase the leased asset at maturity, typically for a prespecified price, are frequently included in both operating and financial leases.

The lessor can be one of a number of parties. In operating leases, the lessor is likely to be the manufacturer's leasing subsidiary or an independent leasing company. Financial leases are frequently handled by independent leasing companies or by the leasing subsidiaries of large financial institutions such as commercial banks and life insurance companies. Life insurance companies are especially active in real estate leasing. Pension funds, like commercial banks, have also been increasing their leasing activities.

The Lease-Versus-Purchase Decision

lease-versus-purchase (or lease-versus-buy) decision
The decision facing firms needing to acquire new fixed assets: whether to lease the assets or to purchase them, using borrowed funds or available liquid resources.

Firms that are contemplating the acquisition of new fixed assets commonly confront the **lease-versus-purchase (or lease-versus-buy) decision.** The alternatives available are (1) lease the assets, (2) borrow funds to purchase the assets, or (3) purchase the assets using available liquid resources. Alternatives 2 and 3, although they differ, are analyzed in a similar fashion; even if the firm has the liquid resources with which to purchase the assets, the use of these funds is viewed as equivalent to borrowing. Therefore, we need to compare only the leasing and purchasing alternatives.

Hint Although, for clarity, the approach demonstrated here compares the present values of the cash flows for the lease and the purchase, a more direct approach would calculate the NPV of the *incremental* cash flows.

The lease-versus-purchase decision involves application of the capital budgeting methods presented in Chapters 8 through 10. First, we determine the relevant cash flows and then apply present value techniques. The following steps are involved in the analysis:

Step 1 Find the *after-tax cash outflows for each year under the lease alternative.* This step generally involves a fairly simple tax adjustment of the annual lease payments. In addition, the cost of exercising a purchase option in the final year of the lease term must frequently be included.[1]

Career Key

Accounting personnel will provide important data and tax insights to the lease-vs.-purchase decision. These analyses will be important to both the purchasing and selling functions of the firm.

Step 2 Find the *after-tax cash outflows for each year under the purchase alternative.* This step involves adjusting the sum of the scheduled loan payment and maintenance cost outlay for the tax shields resulting from the tax deductions attributable to maintenance, depreciation, and interest.

Step 3 Calculate the *present value of the cash outflows* associated with the lease (from Step 1) and purchase (from Step 2) alternatives using the *after-tax cost of debt* as the discount rate. The after-tax cost of debt is used to evaluate the lease-versus-purchase decision because the decision itself involves the choice between two *financing* techniques—leasing or borrowing—having very low risk.

---

1. Including the cost of exercising a purchase option in the lease alternative cash flows ensures that under both the lease and purchase alternatives the firm owns the asset at the end of the relevant time horizon. The alternative would be to include the cash flows from sale of the asset in the purchase alternative cash flows at the end of the lease term. These approaches guarantee avoidance of unequal lives, which were discussed in Chapter 10. In addition, they make any subsequent cash flows irrelevant because they would either be identical or nonexistent, respectively, under each alternative.

Step 4   Choose the alternative with the *lower present value* of cash outflows from Step 3. This will be the *least-cost* financing alternative.

The application of each of these steps is demonstrated in the following example.

E x a m p l e ▼   Roberts Company, a small machine shop, is contemplating acquiring a new machine tool costing $24,000. Arrangements can be made to lease or purchase the machine. The firm is in the 40% tax bracket.

Lease The firm would obtain a 5-year lease requiring annual end-of-year lease payments of $6,000.[2] All maintenance costs would be paid by the lessor, and insurance and other costs would be borne by the lessee. The lessee would exercise its option to purchase the machine for $4,000 at termination of the lease.

Purchase The firm would finance the purchase of the machine with a 9%, 5-year loan requiring end-of-year installment payments of $6,170.[3] The machine would be depreciated under MACRS using a 5-year recovery period. The firm would pay $1,500 per year for a service contract that covers all maintenance costs; insurance and other costs would be borne by the firm. The firm plans to keep the machine and use it beyond its 5-year recovery period.

Using these data, we can apply the steps presented earlier.

Step 1   The after-tax cash outflow from the lease payments can be found by multiplying the before-tax payment of $6,000 by 1 minus the tax rate, *T*, of 40%.

$$\text{After-tax cash outflow from lease} = \$6,000 \times (1 - T)$$
$$= \$6,000 \times (1 - .40) = \$3,600$$

Therefore, the lease alternative results in annual cash outflows over the 5-year lease of $3,600. In the final year, the $4,000 cost of the purchase option would be added to the $3,600 lease outflow to get a total cash outflow in year 5 of $7,600 ($3,600 + $4,000).

Step 2   The after-tax cash outflow from the purchase alternative is a bit more difficult to find. First, the interest component of each annual loan payment must be determined, because the Internal Revenue Service allows the deduction of interest only—not principal—from income

---

2. Lease payments are generally made at the beginning of the year. To simplify the following discussions, end-of-year lease payments are assumed.

3. The annual loan payment on the 9%, 5-year loan of $24,000 is calculated by using the loan amortization technique described in Chapter 5. Dividing the present value interest factor for an annuity, *PVIFA*, from Table A–4 at 9% for 5 years (3.890) into the loan principal of $24,000 results in the annual loan payment of $6,170. (*Note:* By using a financial calculator, the annual loan payment would be $6,170.22.) For a more detailed discussion of loan amortization, see Chapter 5.

TABLE 18.1   Determining the Interest and Principal Components of the Roberts Company Loan Payments

| End of year | Loan payments (1) | Beginning-of-year principal (2) | Payments | | End-of-year principal [(2) − (4)] (5) |
			Interest [.09 × (2)] (3)	Principal [(1) − (3)] (4)	
1	$6,170	$24,000	$2,160	$4,010	$19,990
2	6,170	19,990	1,799	4,371	15,619
3	6,170	15,619	1,406	4,764	10,855
4	6,170	10,855	977	5,193	5,662
5	6,170	5,662	510	5,660	—[a]

[a]The values in this table have been rounded to the nearest dollar, which results in a slight difference ($2) between the beginning-of-year-5 principal (in column 2) and the year-5 principal payment (in column 4).

for tax purposes.[4] Table 18.1 presents the calculations required to split the loan payments into their interest and principal components. Columns 3 and 4 show the annual interest and principal paid.

In Table 18.2, the annual loan payment is shown in column 1, and the annual maintenance cost, which is a tax-deductible expense,

TABLE 18.2   After-Tax Cash Outflows Associated with Purchasing for Roberts Company

End of year	Loan payments (1)	Maintenance costs (2)	Depreciation (3)	Interest[a] (4)	Total deductions [(2) + (3) + (4)] (5)	Tax shields [(.40 × (5)] (6)	After-tax cash outflows [(1) + (2) − (6)] (7)
1	$6,170	$1,500	$4,800	$2,160	$ 8,460	$3,384	$4,286
2	6,170	1,500	7,680	1,799	10,979	4,392	3,278
3	6,170	1,500	4,560	1,406	7,466	2,986	4,684
4	6,170	1,500	2,880	977	5,357	2,143	5,527
5	6,170	1,500	2,880	510	4,890	1,956	5,714

[a]From Table 18.1, column 3.

4. When the rate of interest on the loan used to finance the purchase just equals the cost of debt, the present value of the after-tax loan payments (annual principal payments − interest tax shields) discounted at the after-tax cost of debt would just equal the initial loan principal. In such a case, it is unnecessary to amortize the loan to determine the payment amount and the amounts of interest when finding after-tax cash outflows. The loan payments and interest payments (columns 1 and 4 in Table 18.2) could be ignored, and in their place, the initial loan principal ($24,000) would be shown as an outflow occurring at time zero. To allow for a loan interest rate that is different from the firm's cost of debt and for easier understanding, here we isolate the loan payments and interest payments rather than use this computationally more efficient approach.

is shown in column 2. Next, we find the annual depreciation write-off resulting from the $24,000 machine. Using the applicable MACRS 5-year recovery period depreciation percentages—20% in year 1, 32% in year 2, 19% in year 3, and 12% in years 4 and 5—given in Table 3.8 on page 96 results in the annual depreciation for years 1 through 5 given in column 3 of Table 18.2.[5]

Table 18.2 presents the calculations required to determine the cash outflows[6] associated with borrowing to purchase the new machine. Column 7 of the table presents the after-tax cash outflows associated with the purchase alternative. A few points should be clarified with respect to the calculations in Table 18.2. The major cash outflows are the total loan payment for each year given in column 1 and the annual maintenance cost in column 2. The sum of these two outflows is reduced by the tax savings from writing off the maintenance, depreciation, and interest expenses associated with the new machine and its financing. The resulting cash outflows are the after-tax cash outflows associated with the purchase alternative.

Step 3   The present values of the cash outflows associated with the lease (from Step 1) and purchase (from Step 2) alternatives are calculated in Table 18.3 using the firm's 6% after-tax cost of debt.[7] Applying the appropriate present value interest factors given in columns 2 and 5 to the after-tax cash outflows in columns 1 and 4 results in the present values of lease and purchase cash outflows in columns 3 and 6, respectively. The sum of the present values of the cash outflows for the leasing alternative is given in column 3 of Table 18.3, and the sum for the purchasing alternative is given in column 6.

Step 4   Because the present value of cash outflows for leasing ($18,151) is lower than that for purchasing ($19,539), *the leasing alternative is preferred*. Leasing results in an incremental savings of $1,388 ($19,539 − $18,151) and is therefore the less costly alternative.[8]

The techniques described here for comparing lease and purchase alternatives may be applied in different ways. The approach illustrated by the Roberts Company data is one of the most straightforward. It is important to recognize that the lower cost of one alternative over the other results from factors such as the differing tax brackets of the lessor and lessee, different tax treatments of leases versus purchases, and differing risks and borrowing costs for lessor and

---

5. The year-6 depreciation is ignored, because we are considering the cash flows solely over a 5-year time horizon. Similarly, depreciation on the leased asset when purchased at the end of the lease for $4,000 is ignored. The tax benefits resulting from this depreciation would make the lease alternative even more attractive. Clearly, the analysis would become both more precise and more complex if we chose to look beyond the 5-year time horizon.

6. Although other cash outflows such as insurance and operating expenses may be relevant here, they would be the same under the lease and purchase alternatives and therefore would cancel out in the final analysis.

7. If we ignore any flotation costs, the firm's after-tax cost of debt would be 5.4% [9% debt cost × (1 − .40 tax rate)]. To reflect both the flotation costs associated with selling new debt and the possible need to sell the debt at a discount, an after-tax debt cost of 6% is used as the applicable discount rate. A more detailed discussion of techniques for calculating the after-tax cost of debt is found in Chapter 11.

8. By using a financial calculator, the present value of the cash outflows for the lease would be $18,154, and that for the purchase would be $19,541, resulting in an incremental savings of $1,387.

| TABLE 18.3 | A Comparison of the Cash Outflows Associated with Leasing Versus Purchasing for Roberts Company |

	Leasing			Purchasing		
End of year	After-tax cash outflows (1)	Present value factors[a] (2)	Present value of outflows [(1) × (2)] (3)	After-tax cash outflows[b] (4)	Present value factors[a] (5)	Present value of outflows [(4) × (5)] (6)
1	$3,600	.943	$ 3,395	$4,286	.943	$ 4,042
2	3,600	.890	3,204	3,278	.890	2,917
3	3,600	.840	3,024	4,684	.840	3,935
4	3,600	.792	2,851	5,527	.792	4,377
5	7,600[c]	.747	5,677	5,714	.747	4,268
	PV of cash outflows		$18,151	PV of cash outflows		$19,539

[a]From Table A-3, *PVIF,* for 6% and the corresponding year.
[b]From column 7 of Table 18.2.
[c]After-tax lease payment outflow of $3,600 plus the $4,000 cost of exercising the purchase option.

lessee. Therefore, when making a lease-versus-purchase decision, the firm will find that inexpensive borrowing opportunities, high required lessor returns, and a low risk of obsolescence increase the attractiveness of purchasing. Subjective factors must also be included in the decision-making process. Like most financial decisions, the lease-versus-purchase decision requires some judgment or intuition.

Effects of Leasing on Future Financing

Because leasing is considered a type of financing, it affects the firm's future financing. Lease payments are shown as a tax-deductible expense on the firm's income statement. Anyone analyzing the firm's income statement would probably recognize that an asset is being leased, although the actual details of the amount and term of the lease would be unclear.

The Financial Accounting Standards Board (FASB), in Standard No. 13, "Accounting for Leases," requires explicit disclosure of *financial (capital) lease* obligations on the firm's balance sheet. Such a lease must be shown as a **capitalized lease,** meaning that the present value of all its payments is included as an asset and corresponding liability on the firm's balance sheet. An *operating lease,* on the other hand, need not be capitalized, but its basic features must be disclosed in a footnote to the financial statements. Standard No. 13, of course, establishes detailed guidelines to be used in capitalizing leases. Subsequent standards have further refined lease capitalization and disclosure procedures.

capitalized lease
A *financial (capital) lease* that has the present value of all its payments included as an asset and corresponding liability on the firm's balance sheet, as required by Financial Accounting Standards Board (FASB) Standard No. 13.

In Practice

Driving a Lease
Deal Home

Personal Finance

The ads are tempting: Lease a new Toyota Camry for $198 a month for 3 years with no down payment. It's no wonder about one-third of all car buyers today choose to lease rather than buy. But is leasing really as good as it sounds?

When you lease a car, you don't own the car but only pay for a portion of the car's value. Your lease payment is based on the difference between the cap-italized cost (the car's purchase price including sales tax) and its estimated market (residual) value at the end of the lease (usually 2 to 4 years). Then a money factor, *or financing rate, is applied to this amount. At the end of the lease term, you can turn in the car or buy it at the residual value.*

To get a good lease deal, you need to know three figures: the capitalized cost (the car's purchase price), the residual value, and the money factor. The dealer should be willing to provide these costs, list all other fees, and give a mathematical breakdown of how the payment is calculated.

Many consumers don't realize they can negotiate a lower capitalized cost and a higher residual value. Leasing agents often increase the price of leased vehicles, so research the dealer invoice cost, taking into account rebates and other incentives, and drive a hard bargain.

To analyze whether you should lease or buy, you will need to compare the total costs of each option over the lease or loan term. For leasing, this includes the down payment, security deposit, total of monthly payments, other fees, and opportunity cost of savings that could be earned on the initial payment. If you purchase the car with a loan, total cost includes the down payment (which is usually higher than with a lease), the opportunity cost of savings on the down payment, sales tax, and total of monthly payments. However, because you own the car after repaying the loan, you subtract the car's esti-mated value at the end of the loan term from the total cost. In most cases, leasing is the more expensive alternative.

Example ▼ Lawrence Company, a manufacturer of water purifiers, is leasing an asset under a 10-year lease requiring annual end-of-year payments of $15,000. The lease can be capitalized merely by calculating the present value of the lease payments over the life of the lease. However, the rate at which the payments should be discount-ed is difficult to determine.[9] If 10% were used, the present, or capitalized, value of the lease would be $92,175 ($15,000 × 6.145). (The value calculated by using a financial calculator is $92,169.) This value would be shown as an asset and corresponding liability on the firm's balance sheet, which should result in an ▲ accurate reflection of the firm's true financial position.

---

9. The Financial Accounting Standards Board in Standard No. 13 established certain guidelines for the appropriate discount rate to use when capitalizing leases. Most commonly, the rate that the lessee would have incurred to borrow the funds to buy the asset with a secured loan under terms similar to the lease repayment schedule would be used. This simply represents the *before-tax cost of a secured debt.*

Because the consequences of missing a financial lease payment are the same as those of missing an interest or principal payment on debt, a financial analyst must view the lease as a long-term financial commitment of the lessee. With FASB No. 13, the inclusion of each financial (capital) lease as an asset and corresponding liability (i.e., long-term debt) provides for a balance sheet that more accurately reflects the firm's financial status. It thereby permits various types of financial ratio analyses to be performed directly on the statement by any interested party.

Advantages and Disadvantages of Leasing

Leasing has a number of commonly cited advantages and disadvantages that should be considered when making a lease-versus-purchase decision. It is not unusual for a number of them to apply in a given situation.

Advantages

The commonly cited advantages of leasing are as follows:

1. In a lease arrangement, the firm may *avoid the cost of obsolescence* if the lessor fails to accurately anticipate the obsolescence of assets and sets the lease payment too low. This is especially true in the case of operating leases, which generally have relatively short lives.
2. A lessee *avoids many of the restrictive covenants* that are normally included as part of a long-term loan. Requirements with respect to minimum net working capital, subsequent borrowing, changes in management, and so on are *not* normally found in a lease agreement.
3. In the case of low-cost assets that are infrequently acquired, leasing—especially operating leases—may provide the firm with needed *financing flexibility*. That is, the firm does not have to arrange other financing for these assets.
4. Sale-leaseback arrangements may permit the firm to *increase its liquidity* by converting an *existing* asset into cash, which can then be used as working capital. This can be advantageous for a firm short of working capital or in a liquidity bind.
5. Leasing allows the lessee, in effect, to *depreciate land,* which is prohibited if the land were purchased. Because the lessee who leases land is permitted to deduct the *total lease payment* as an expense for tax purposes, the effect is the same as if the firm had purchased the land and then depreciated it.
6. Because it results in the receipt of service from an asset possibly without increasing the assets or liabilities on the firm's balance sheet, leasing may result in misleading *financial ratios*. Understating assets and liabilities can cause certain ratios, such as the total asset turnover, to look better than they might be. With the passage of FASB No. 13, this advantage no longer applies to financial leases, although in the case of operating leases, it remains a potential advantage.
7. Leasing provides *100 percent financing*. Most loan agreements for the purchase of fixed assets require the borrower to pay a portion of the purchase

price as a down payment. As a result, the borrower is able to borrow only 90 to 95 percent of the purchase price of the asset.

8. When a *firm becomes bankrupt* or is reorganized, the maximum claim of lessors against the corporation is 3 years of lease payments, and the lessor of course gets the asset back. If debt is used to purchase an asset, the creditors have a claim that is equal to the total outstanding loan balance.

Disadvantages

The commonly cited disadvantages of leasing are as follows:

1. A lease does not have a stated interest cost. Thus, in many leases the *return to the lessor is quite high,* so the firm might be better off borrowing to purchase the asset.
2. At the end of the term of the lease agreement, the *salvage value* of an asset, if any, is realized by the lessor. If the lessee had purchased the asset, it could have claimed its salvage value. Of course, an expected salvage value when recognized by the lessor results in lower lease payments.
3. Under a lease, the lessee is generally *prohibited from making improvements* on the leased property or asset without the approval of the lessor. If the property were owned outright, this difficulty would not arise. Of course, lessors generally encourage leasehold improvements when they are expected to enhance the asset's salvage value.
4. If a lessee leases an *asset that subsequently becomes obsolete,* it still must make lease payments over the remaining term of the lease. This is true even if the asset is unusable.

? Review Questions

18–2 What is *leasing?* Define, compare, and contrast *operating leases* and *financial (or capital) leases.* How does the Financial Accounting Standards Board (FASB) Standard No. 13 define a financial (or capital) lease? Describe three methods used by lessors to acquire assets to be leased.

18–3 Describe the four basic steps involved in the *lease-versus-purchase decision* process. How are capital budgeting methods applied in this process?

18–4 What type of lease must be treated as a *capitalized lease* on the balance sheet? How does the financial manager capitalize a lease?

18–5 List and discuss the commonly cited advantages and disadvantages that should be considered when making a lease-versus-purchase decision.

conversion feature
An option that is included as part of a bond or a preferred stock issue that allows its holder to change the security into a stated number of shares of common stock.

18.3 Convertible Securities

A **conversion feature** is an option that is included as part of a bond or a preferred stock issue that allows its holder to change the security into a stated number of shares of common stock. The conversion feature typically enhances the marketability of an issue.

Types of Convertible Securities

Corporate bonds and preferred stocks may be convertible into common stock. The most common type of convertible security is the bond. Convertibles normally have an accompanying *call feature*. This feature permits the issuer to retire or encourage conversion of outstanding convertibles when appropriate.

Convertible Bonds

convertible bond
A bond that can be changed into a specified number of shares of common stock.

A **convertible bond** can be changed into a specified number of shares of common stock. It is almost always a *debenture*—an unsecured bond—with a call feature. Because the conversion feature provides the purchaser with the possibility of becoming a stockholder on favorable terms, convertible bonds are generally a less expensive form of financing than similar-risk nonconvertible or **straight bonds.** The conversion feature adds a degree of speculation to a bond issue, although the issue still maintains its value as a bond.

straight bond
A bond that is nonconvertible, having no conversion feature.

Convertible Preferred Stock

convertible preferred stock
Preferred stock that can be changed into a specified number of shares of common stock.

straight preferred stock
Preferred stock that is nonconvertible, having no conversion feature.

Convertible preferred stock is preferred stock that can be changed into a specified number of shares of common stock. It can normally be sold with a lower stated dividend than a similar-risk nonconvertible or **straight preferred stock.** The reason is that the convertible preferred holder is assured of the fixed dividend payment associated with a preferred stock and also may receive the appreciation resulting from increases in the market price of the underlying common stock. Convertible preferred stock behaves much like convertible bonds. The following discussions will concentrate on the more popular convertible bonds.

General Features of Convertibles

Convertible securities are almost always convertible anytime during the life of the security. Occasionally, conversion is permitted only for a limited number of years, say, for 5 or 10 years after issuance of the convertible.

Conversion Ratio

conversion ratio
The ratio at which a convertible security can be exchanged for common stock.

The **conversion ratio** is the ratio at which a convertible security can be exchanged for common stock. The conversion ratio can be stated in two ways.

conversion price
The per-share price that is effectively paid for common stock as the result of conversion of a convertible security.

1. Sometimes the conversion ratio is stated in terms of a given number of shares of common stock. To find the **conversion price,** which is the per-share price that is effectively paid for common stock as the result of conversion, the *par value* (not the market value) of the convertible security must be divided by the conversion ratio.

Example ▼ Western Wear Company, a manufacturer of denim products, has outstanding a bond with a $1,000 par value and convertible into 25 shares of common stock. The bond's conversion ratio is 25. The conversion price for the bond is $40 per
▲ share ($1,000 ÷ 25).

2. Sometimes, instead of the conversion ratio, the conversion price is given. The conversion ratio can be obtained by dividing the *par value* of the convertible by the conversion price.

Example ▼

Mosher Company, a franchiser of seafood restaurants, has outstanding a convertible 20-year bond with a par value of $1,000. The bond is convertible at $50 **▲** per share into common stock. The conversion ratio is 20 ($1,000 ÷ $50).

The issuer of a convertible security normally establishes a conversion ratio or conversion price that sets the conversion price per share at the time of issuance above the current market price of the firm's stock. If the prospective purchasers do not expect conversion ever to be feasible, they will purchase a straight security or some other convertible issue.

Conversion (or Stock) Value

conversion (or stock) value
The value of a convertible security measured in terms of the market price of the common stock into which it can be converted.

The **conversion (or stock) value** is the value of the convertible measured in terms of the market price of the common stock into which it can be converted. The conversion value can be found simply by multiplying the conversion ratio by the current market price of the firm's common stock.

Example ▼

McNamara Industries, a petroleum processor, has outstanding a $1,000 bond that is convertible into common stock at $62.50 a share. The conversion ratio is therefore 16 ($1,000 ÷ $62.50). Because the current market price of the common stock is $65 per share, the conversion value is $1,040 (16 × $65). Because the conversion value is above the bond value of $1,000, conversion is a viable option **▲** for the owner of the convertible security.

Effect on Earnings

contingent securities
Convertibles, warrants, and stock options. Their presence affects the reporting of a firm's earnings per share (EPS).

The presence of **contingent securities,** which include convertibles as well as warrants (described later in this chapter) and stock options (described in Chapter 1 and later in this chapter), affects the reporting of the firm's earnings per share (EPS). Firms with contingent securities that if converted or exercised would dilute (i.e., lower) earnings per share are required to report earnings in two ways—*basic EPS* and *diluted EPS*.

basic EPS
Earnings per share (EPS) calculated without regard to any contingent securities.

Basic EPS are calculated without regard to any contingent securities. They are found by dividing earnings available for common stockholders by the number of shares of common stock outstanding. This is the standard method of calculating EPS that has been used throughout this textbook.

diluted EPS
Earnings per share (EPS) calculated under the assumption that *all* contingent securities that would have dilutive effects are converted and exercised, and are therefore common stock.

Diluted EPS are calculated under the assumption that all contingent securities that would have dilutive effects are converted and exercised, and are therefore common stock. They are found by adjusting basic EPS for the impact of converting all convertibles and exercising all warrants and options that would have dilutive effects on the firm's earnings. This approach treats as common stock *all* contingent securities. It is calculated by dividing earnings available for common stockholders (adjusted for interest and preferred stock dividends that would *not* be paid given assumed conversion of *all* outstanding contingent securities that would have dilutive effects) by the number of shares of common stock that would be outstanding if *all* contingent securities that would have dilutive effects are converted and exercised. Rather than demonstrate these accounting calculations,[10] suffice it to say that firms with outstanding convertibles, warrants, and/or stock options must report basic and diluted EPS on their income statements.

Financing with Convertibles

Using convertible securities to raise long-term funds can help the firm achieve its cost of capital and capital structure goals. There also are a number of more specific motives and considerations involved in evaluating convertible financing.

Motives for Convertible Financing

Convertibles can be used for a variety of reasons. One popular motive is their use as a form of *deferred common stock financing*. When a convertible security is issued, both issuer and purchaser expect the security to be converted into common stock at some future point. Because the security is first sold with a conversion price above the current market price of the firm's stock, conversion is initially not attractive. The issuer of a convertible could alternatively sell common stock, but only at or below its current market price. By selling the convertible, the issuer in effect makes a *deferred sale* of common stock. As the market price of the firm's common stock rises to a higher level, conversion may occur. By deferring the issuance of new common stock until the market price of the stock has increased, fewer shares will have to be issued, thereby decreasing the dilution of both ownership and earnings.

Another motive for convertible financing is its *use as a "sweetener" for financing*. Because the purchaser of the convertible is given the opportunity to become a common stockholder and share in the firm's future success, *convertibles can be normally sold with lower interest rates than nonconvertibles*. Therefore, from the firm's viewpoint, including a conversion feature reduces the interest cost of debt. The purchaser of the issue sacrifices a portion of interest return for the potential opportunity to become a common stockholder. Another important motive for issuing convertibles is that, generally speaking, *convertible securities can be issued with far fewer restrictive covenants than nonconvertibles*. Because many investors view convertibles as equity, the covenant issue is not important to them.

> **Hint**   Convertible securities are advantageous to both the issuer and the holder. The issuer does not have to give up immediate control as it would have to if it were issuing common stock. The holder of a convertible security has the possibility of a future speculative gain.

---

10. For excellent discussions and demonstrations of the two methods of reporting EPS, see Donald A. Kieso and Jerry J. Weygandt, *Intermediate Accounting,* 9th ed. (New York: John Wiley, 1998), pp. 860–870.

A final motive for using convertibles is to *raise cheap funds temporarily*. By using convertible bonds, the firm can temporarily raise debt, which is typically less expensive than common stock, to finance projects. Once such projects are on line, the firm may wish to shift its capital structure to a less highly levered position. A conversion feature gives the issuer the opportunity, through actions of convertible holders, to shift its capital structure at a future point in time.

Other Considerations

When the price of the firm's common stock rises above the conversion price, the market price of the convertible security will normally rise to a level close to its conversion value. When this happens, many convertible holders will not convert, because they already have the market price benefit obtainable from conversion and can still receive fixed periodic interest payments. Because of this behavior, virtually all convertible securities have a *call feature* that enables the issuer to encourage or *"force"* conversion. The call price of the security generally exceeds the security's par value by an amount equal to 1 year's stated interest on the security. Although the issuer must pay a premium for calling a security, the call privilege is generally not exercised until the conversion value of the security is 10 to 15 percent *above the call price*. This type of premium above the call price helps to assure the issuer that the holders of the convertible will convert it when the call is made, instead of accepting the call price.

Unfortunately, there are instances when the market price of a security does not reach a level sufficient to stimulate the conversion of associated convertibles. A convertible security that cannot be forced into conversion by using the call feature is called an **overhanging issue**. An overhanging issue can be quite detrimental to a firm. If the firm were to call the issue, the bondholders would accept the call price rather than convert the bonds. In this case, the firm not only would have to pay the call premium, but would require additional financing to pay off the bonds at their par value. If the firm raised these funds through the sale of equity, a large number of shares would have to be issued due to their low market price. This, in turn, could result in the dilution of existing ownership. Another source of financing the call would be the use of debt or preferred stock, but this use would leave the firm's capital structure no less levered than before the call.

overhanging issue
A convertible security that cannot be forced into conversion by using the call feature.

Determining the Value of a Convertible Bond

The key characteristic of convertible securities that enhances their marketability is their ability to minimize the possibility of a loss while providing a possibility of capital gains. Here we discuss the three values of a convertible bond: (1) the straight bond value, (2) the conversion value, and (3) the market value.

Straight Bond Value

straight bond value
The price at which a convertible bond would sell in the market without the conversion feature.

The **straight bond value** of a convertible bond is the price at which it would sell in the market without the conversion feature. This value is found by determining the value of a nonconvertible bond with similar payments issued by a firm with the same risk. The straight bond value is typically the *floor*, or minimum, price at which the convertible bond would be traded. The straight bond value equals the present value of the bond's interest and principal payments discounted at the interest rate the firm would have to pay on a nonconvertible bond.

Example ▼ Duncan Company, a southeastern discount store chain, has just sold a $1,000-par-value, 20-year convertible bond with a 12% coupon interest rate. The bond interest will be paid at the end of each year, and the principal will be repaid at maturity.[11] A straight bond could have been sold with a 14% coupon interest rate, but the conversion feature compensates for the lower rate on the convertible. The straight bond value of the convertible is calculated as shown:

Year(s)	Payments (1)	Present value interest factor at 14% (2)	Present value [(1) × (2)] (3)
1–20	$ 120[a]	6.623[b]	$794.76
20	1,000	.073[c]	73.00
		Straight bond value	$867.76

[a]$1,000 at 12% = $120 interest per year.

[b]Present value interest factor for an annuity, *PVIFA*, discounted at 14% for 20 years, from Table A-4.

[c]Present value interest factor for $1, *PVIF*, discounted at 14% for year 20, from Table A-3.

This value, $867.76, is the minimum price at which the convertible bond is expected to sell. (The value calculated using a financial calculator is $867.54.) Generally, only in certain instances in which the stock's market price is below the ▲ conversion price will the bond be expected to sell at this level.

Conversion (or Stock) Value

Recall that the *conversion (or stock) value* of a convertible security is the value of the convertible measured in terms of the market price of the common stock into which the security can be converted. When the market price of the common stock exceeds the conversion price, the conversion (or stock) value exceeds the par value. An example will clarify the point.

Example ▼ Duncan Company's convertible bond described earlier is convertible at $50 per share. Each bond can be converted into 20 shares, because each bond has a

---

11. Consistent with Chapter 7, we continue to assume the payment of annual rather than semiannual bond interest. This assumption simplifies the calculations involved while maintaining the conceptual accuracy of the procedures presented.

$1,000 par value. The conversion values of the bond when the stock is selling at $30, $40, $50, $60, $70, and $80 per share are shown in the following table.

Market price of stock	Conversion value
$30	$ 600
40	800
50 (conversion price)	1,000 (par value)
60	1,200
70	1,400
80	1,600

When the market price of the common stock exceeds the $50 conversion price, the conversion value exceeds the $1,000 par value. Because the straight bond value (calculated in the preceding example) is $867.76, the bond will, in a stable environment, never sell for less than this amount, regardless of how low its conversion value is. If the market price per share were $30, the bond would still sell for $867.76—not $600—because its value as a bond would dominate.

Market Value

The market value of a convertible is likely to be greater than its straight value or its conversion value. The amount by which the market value exceeds its straight or conversion value is called the **market premium.** The general relationship of the straight bond value, conversion value, market value, and market premium for Duncan Company's convertible bond is shown in Figure 18.1 (on page 758). The straight bond value acts as a floor for the security's value up to the point X, where the stock price is high enough to cause the conversion value to exceed the straight bond value. The market premium is attributed to the fact that the convertible gives investors a chance to experience attractive capital gains from increases in the stock price while taking less risk. The floor (straight bond value) provides protection against losses resulting from a decline in the stock price caused by falling profits or other factors. The market premium tends to be greatest when the straight bond value and conversion (or stock) value are nearly equal. Investors perceive the benefits of these two sources of value to be greatest at this point. (See the In Practice box on page 759 for an example of convertible debt.)

? Review Questions

18–6   What is the *conversion feature?* What is a *conversion ratio?* How do convertibles and other *contingent securities* affect EPS? Briefly describe the motives for convertible financing.

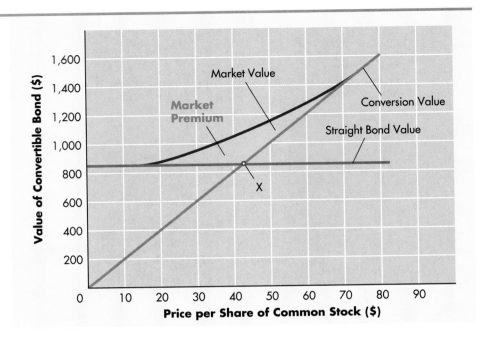

FIGURE 18.1

Values and Market Premium

The values and market premium for Duncan Company's convertible bond

18–7   When the market price of the stock rises above the conversion price, why may a convertible security *not* be converted? How can the *call feature* be used to force conversion in this situation? What is an *overhanging issue?*

18–8   Define the *straight bond value, conversion (or stock) value, market value,* and *market premium* associated with a convertible bond, and describe the general relationships among them.

18.4 Stock Purchase Warrants

stock purchase warrant
An instrument that gives its holder the right to purchase a certain number of shares of common stock at a specified price over a certain period of time.

Stock purchase warrants are similar to stock *rights,* which were briefly described in Chapter 2. A **stock purchase warrant** gives the holder the right to purchase a certain number of shares of common stock at a specified price over a certain period of time. (Of course, holders of warrants earn no income from them until the warrants are exercised or sold.) Warrants also bear some similarity to convertibles in that they provide for the injection of additional equity capital into the firm at some future date.

Hint   One of the major reasons for tying a warrant or offering a security as a convertible is that, with either of these features, the investor will not require the issuing firm to pay an interest rate that is as high as a security without these features.

Basic Characteristics

Warrants are often attached to debt issues as "sweeteners." When a firm makes a large bond issue, the attachment of stock purchase warrants may add to the marketability of the issue and lower the required interest rate. As sweeteners, war-

In Practice

Amazon Takes a Ride with Convertible Debt

Why would an investor buy a bond with unattractive terms and a poor rating—Caa3, well below investment grade (Baa)? If the bond issuer is high-flying online bookseller Amazon.com, even conservative institutional investors will stand in line to buy its high-yield (junk) bonds. Demand for its January 1999 issue of convertible bonds was so high that Amazon raised the size from $500 million to $1.25 billion, the largest U.S. convertible offering. The 10-year subordinated bonds carried a 4.75 percent coupon and were convertible to common stock at a conversion price of $156.05 a share, 27 percent over the share price on the issue date. The company can call the bonds during years 1 through 3 if the share price rises above $234 (50 percent above the conversion price) and at any time after year 3. Amazon.com plans to use the proceeds for marketing and building improved distribution facilities, as well as to have cash on hand to make acquisitions using a mix of stock and cash.

What's unusual about this issue is its low coupon. Typically, the lower the credit rating, the higher the yield has to be to compensate investors for the greater risk. Comments Steve Seefeld, president of online analysis service Convertbond.com, "It's a great deal if Amazon keeps going up, but 4.75 percent isn't much to be paid for a crummy credit." The addition of so much debt, even at this bargain rate, weakens Amazon's already shaky balance sheet even more. And like many electronic commerce businesses, the company was not yet profitable, with a loss of 84 cents a share at December 31, 1998.

Yet bond investors were willing to ignore the increased risk for the chance to participate in the Internet mania that has made many equity investors rich. They are betting that the pioneering Internet retailer's phenomenal growth will continue to send Amazon.com's stock soaring even higher.

---

rants are similar to conversion features. Often, when a new firm is raising its initial capital, suppliers of debt will require warrants to permit them to share in whatever success the firm achieves. In addition, established companies sometimes offer warrants with debt to compensate for risk and thereby lower the interest rate and/or provide for fewer *restrictive covenants*.

Exercise Prices

exercise (or option) price
The price at which holders of warrants can purchase a specified number of shares of common stock.

The price at which holders of warrants can purchase a specified number of shares of common stock is normally referred to as the **exercise (or option) price.** This price is normally set at 10 to 20 percent above the market price of the firm's stock at the time of issuance. Until the market price of the stock exceeds the exercise price, holders of warrants would not exercise them, because they could purchase the stock more inexpensively in the marketplace.

Warrants normally have a life of no more than 10 years, although some have infinite lives. Although, unlike convertible securities, warrants cannot be called, their limited life stimulates holders to exercise them when the exercise price is below the market price of the firm's stock.

Warrant Trading

A warrant is usually *detachable,* which means that the bondholder may sell the warrant without selling the security to which it is attached. Many detachable warrants are listed and actively traded on organized securities exchanges and on the over-the-counter exchange. The majority of actively traded warrants are listed on the American Stock Exchange. Warrants often provide investors with better opportunities for gain (with increased risk) than the underlying common stock.

Comparison of Warrants to Rights and Convertibles

The similarity between a warrant and a right should be clear. Both result in new equity capital, although the warrant provides for *deferred* equity financing. The life of a right is typically not more than a few months; a warrant is generally exercisable for a period of years. Rights are issued at a subscription price below the prevailing market price of the stock; warrants are generally issued at an exercise price 10 to 20 percent above the prevailing market price.

Warrants and convertibles also have similarities. The exercise of a warrant shifts the firm's capital structure to a less highly levered position because new common stock is issued without any change in debt. If a convertible bond were converted, the reduction in leverage would be even more pronounced, because common stock would be issued in exchange for a reduction in debt. In addition, the exercise of a warrant provides an influx of new capital; with convertibles, the new capital is raised when the securities are originally issued rather than when converted. The influx of new equity capital resulting from the exercise of a warrant does not occur until the firm has achieved a certain degree of success that is reflected in an increased price for its stock. In this instance, the firm conveniently obtains needed funds.

The Implied Price of an Attached Warrant

implied price of a warrant
The price effectively paid for each warrant attached to a bond.

When attached to a bond, the **implied price of a warrant**—the price that is effectively paid for each attached warrant—can be found by first using Equation 18.1:

$$\text{Implied price of } all \text{ warrants} = \text{price of bond with warrants attached} - \text{straight bond value} \tag{18.1}$$

The straight bond value is found in a fashion similar to that used in valuing convertible bonds. Dividing the implied price of *all* warrants by the number of warrants attached to each bond results in the implied price of *each* warrant.

Example ▼ Martin Marine Products, a manufacturer of marine drive shafts and propellers, just issued a 10.5% coupon interest rate, $1,000-par, 20-year bond paying annual interest and having 20 warrants attached for the purchase of the firm's stock. The bonds were initially sold for their $1,000 par value. When issued, similar-risk straight bonds were selling to yield a 12% rate of return. The straight value of the bond would be the present value of its payments discounted at the 12% yield on similar-risk straight bonds.

Year(s)	Payments (1)	Present value interest factor at 12% (2)	Present value[a] [(1) × (2)] (3)
1–20	$ 105[b]	7.469[c]	$784
20	1,000	.104[d]	104
		Straight bond value[e]	$888

[a]For convenience, these values have been rounded to the nearest $1.
[b]$1,000 at 10.5% = $105 interest per year.
[c]Present value interest factor for an annuity, *PVIFA*, discounted at 12% for 20 years, from Table A-4.
[d]Present value interest factor for $1, *PVIF*, discounted at 12% for year 20, from Table A-3.
[e]The value calculated by using a financial calculator and rounding to the nearest $1 is also $888.

Substituting the $1,000 price of the bond with warrants attached and the $888 straight bond value into Equation 18.1, we get an implied price of *all* warrants of $112:

$$\text{Implied price of } all \text{ warrants} = \$1,000 - \$888 = \underline{\$112}$$

Dividing the implied price of *all* warrants by the number of warrants attached to each bond—20 in this case—we find the implied price of *each* warrant:

$$\text{Implied price of } each \text{ warrant} = \frac{\$112}{20} = \underline{\$5.60}$$

▲ Therefore, by purchasing Martin Marine Products' bond with warrants attached for $1,000, one is effectively paying $5.60 for each warrant.

The implied price of each warrant is meaningful only when compared to the specific features of the warrant—the number of shares that can be purchased and the specified exercise price. These features can be analyzed in light of the prevailing common stock price to estimate the true *market value* of each warrant. Clearly, if the implied price is above the estimated market value, the price of the bond with warrants attached may be too high. If the implied price is below the estimated market value, the bond may be quite attractive. Firms must therefore price their bonds with warrants attached in a way that causes the implied price of its warrants to fall slightly below their estimated market value. Such an approach allows the firm to more easily sell the bonds at a lower coupon interest rate than would apply to straight debt, thereby reducing its debt service costs.

The Value of Warrants

warrant premium
The difference between the actual market value and theoretical value of a warrant.

Like a convertible security, a warrant has both a market and a theoretical value. The difference between these values, or the **warrant premium**, depends largely on investor expectations and the ability of investors to get more leverage from the warrants than from the underlying stock.

Theoretical Value of a Warrant

The *theoretical value* of a stock purchase warrant is the amount one would expect the warrant to sell for in the marketplace. Equation 18.2 gives the theoretical value of a warrant:

$$TVW = (P_0 - E) \times N \tag{18.2}$$

where

$$TVW = \text{theoretical value of a warrant}$$
$$P_0 = \text{current market price of a share of common stock}$$
$$E = \text{exercise price of the warrant}$$
$$N = \text{number of shares of common stock obtainable with}$$
$$\text{one warrant}$$

The use of Equation 18.2 can be illustrated by the following example.

E x a m p l e ▼ Dustin Electronics, a major producer of transistors, has outstanding warrants that are exercisable at $40 per share and entitle holders to purchase three shares of common stock. The warrants were initially attached to a bond issue to sweeten the bond. The common stock of the firm is currently selling for $45 per share. Substituting P_0 = $45, E = $40, and N = 3 into Equation 18.2 yields a theoretical warrant value of $15 [($45 − $40) × 3]. Therefore, Dustin's warrants should **▲** sell for $15 in the marketplace.

Market Value of a Warrant

The market value of a stock purchase warrant is generally above the theoretical value of the warrant. Only when the theoretical value of the warrant is very high or the warrant is near its expiration date are the market and theoretical values close. The general relationship between the theoretical and market values of Dustin Electronics' warrants is presented graphically in Figure 18.2. The market value of warrants generally exceeds the theoretical value by the greatest amount when the stock's market price is close to the warrant exercise price per share. In addition, the amount of time until expiration also affects the market value of the warrant. Generally speaking, the closer the warrant is to its expiration date, the more likely that its market value will equal its theoretical value.

Warrant Premium

The *warrant premium,* or amount by which the market value of Dustin Electronics' warrants exceeds the theoretical value of these warrants, is also shown in Figure 18.2. This premium results from a combination of positive investor expectations and the ability of the investor with a fixed sum to invest to obtain much larger potential returns (and risk) by trading in warrants rather than the underlying stock.

FIGURE 18.2

Values and Warrant Premium

The values and warrant premium for Dustin Electronics' stock purchase warrants

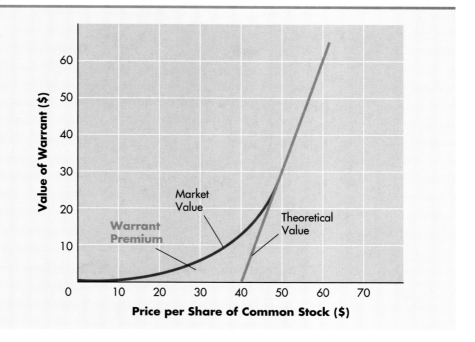

E x a m p l e ▼ Stan Buyer has $2,430, which he is interested in investing in Dustin Electronics. The firm's stock is currently selling for $45 per share, and its warrants are selling for $18 per warrant. Each warrant entitles the holder to purchase three shares of Dustin's common stock at $40 per share. Because the stock is selling for $45 per share, the theoretical warrant value, calculated in the preceding example, is $15 [($45 − $40) × 3].

The warrant premium results from positive investor expectations and leverage opportunities. Stan Buyer could spend his $2,430 in either of two ways: He could purchase 54 shares of common stock at $45 per share, or 135 warrants at $18 per warrant, ignoring brokerage fees. If Mr. Buyer purchases the stock and its price rises to $48, he will gain $162 ($3 per share × 54 shares) by selling the stock. If instead, he purchases the 135 warrants and the stock price increases by $3 per share, Mr. Buyer will gain approximately $1,215. Because the price of a share of stock rises by $3, the price of each warrant can be expected to rise by $9 (because each warrant can be used to purchase three shares of common stock). A gain of $9 per warrant on 135 warrants means a total goal gain of $1,215 on the
▲ warrants.

The greater leverage associated with trading warrants should be clear from the example. Of course, because leverage works both ways, it results in greater risk. If the market price fell by $3, the loss on the stock would be $162, whereas the loss on the warrants would be close to $1,215. Clearly, investing in warrants is more risky than investing in the underlying stock.

? Review Questions

18–9   What are *stock purchase warrants?* What are the similarities and key differences between the effects of warrants and those of convertibles on the firm's capital structure and its ability to raise new capital?

18–10   What is the *implied price of a warrant?* How is it estimated? To be effective, how should it relate to the estimated *market value* of a warrant?

18–11   What is the general relationship between the theoretical and market values of a warrant? In what circumstances are these values quite close? What is a *warrant premium?*

18.5 Options

option
An instrument that provides its holder with an opportunity to purchase or sell a specified asset at a stated price on or before a set *expiration date.*

In the most general sense, an **option** can be viewed as an instrument that provides its holder with an opportunity to purchase or sell a specified asset at a stated price on or before a set *expiration date.* Options are probably the most popular type of *derivative security.* Today, the interest in options centers on options on common stock. The development of organized options exchanges has created markets in which to trade these options, which themselves are securities. Three basic forms of options are rights, warrants, and calls and puts. Rights are discussed in Chapter 2, and warrants were described in the preceding section.

Calls and Puts

call option
An option to *purchase* a specified number of shares of a stock (typically, 100) on or before a specified future date at a stated price.

striking price
The price at which the holder of a call option can buy (or the holder of a put option can sell) a specified amount of stock at any time prior to the option's expiration date.

put option
An option to *sell* a given number of shares of a stock (typically, 100) on or before a specified future date at a stated price.

The two most common types of options are calls and puts. A **call option** is an option to *purchase* a specified number of shares of a stock (typically, 100) on or before a specified future date at a stated price. Call options usually have initial lives of 1 to 9 months, occasionally 1 year. The **striking price** is the price at which the holder of the option can buy the stock at any time prior to the option's expiration date; it is generally set at or near the prevailing market price of the stock at the time the option is issued. For example, if a firm's stock is currently selling for $50 per share, a call option on the stock initiated today would likely have a striking price set at $50 per share. To purchase a call option, a specified price of normally a few hundred dollars must be paid.

A **put option** is an option to *sell* a given number of shares of a stock (typically, 100) on or before a specified future date at a stated striking price. Like the call option, the striking price of the put is set close to the market price of the underlying stock at the time of issuance. The lives and costs of puts are similar to those of calls.

Options Markets

There are two ways of making options transactions. The first involves making a transaction through one of 20 or so call and put options dealers with the help of a stockbroker. The other, more popular mechanism is the organized options exchanges. The dominant exchange is the *Chicago Board Options Exchange (CBOE)*, which was established in 1973. Other exchanges on which options are traded include the American Stock Exchange, the New York Stock Exchange, and several regional stock exchanges. The options traded on these exchanges are standardized and thus are considered registered securities. Each option is for 100 shares of the underlying stock. The price at which options transactions can be made is determined by the forces of supply and demand.

Options Trading

The most common motive for purchasing call options is the expectation that the market price of the underlying stock will *rise* by more than enough to cover the cost of the option and thereby allow the purchaser of the call to profit.

Example ▼ Assume that Cindy Peters pays $250 for a 3-month *call option* on Wing Enterprises, a maker of aircraft components, at a striking price of $50. This means that by paying $250, Cindy is guaranteed that she can purchase 100 shares of Wing at $50 per share at any time during the next 3 months. The stock price must climb $2.50 per share ($250 ÷ 100 shares) to $52.50 per share to cover the cost of the option (ignoring any brokerage fees or dividends). If the stock price were to rise to $60 per share during the period, Cindy's net profit would be $750 [(100 shares × $60/share) − (100 shares × $50/share) − $250].

Because this return would be earned on a $250 investment, it illustrates the high potential return on investment that options offer. Of course, had the stock price not risen above $50 per share, Cindy would have lost the $250 because there would have been no reason to exercise the option. Had the stock price risen to between $50 and $52.50 per share, Cindy probably would have exercised the
▲ option to reduce her loss to an amount less than $250.

Hint Put and call options are created by *individuals and other firms*. The firm has nothing to do with the creation of these options. Warrants and the convertible features are created by the issuing firm.

Put options are purchased in the expectation that the share price of a given security will *decline* over the life of the option. Purchasers of puts commonly own the shares and wish to protect a gain they have realized since their initial purchase. Buying a put locks in the gain because it enables them to sell their shares at a known price during the life of the option. Investors gain from put options when the price of the underlying stock declines by more than the per-share cost of the option. The logic underlying the purchase of a put is exactly the opposite of that underlying the use of call options.

Example ▼ Assume that Don Kelly pays $325 for a 6-month *put option* on Dante United, a baked goods manufacturer, at a striking price of $40. Don purchased the put option in expectation that the stock price would drop due to the introduction of a new product line by Dante's chief competitor. By paying $325, Don is assured that he can sell 100 shares of Dante at $40 per share at any time during the next 6 months. The stock price must drop by $3.25 per share ($325 ÷ 100 shares) to $36.75 per share to cover the cost of the option (ignoring any brokerage fees or dividends). If the stock price were to drop to $30 per share during the period, Don's net profit would be $675 [(100 shares × $40/share) − (100 shares × $30/share) − $325].

Because the return would be earned on a $325 investment, it again illustrates the high potential return on investment that options offer. Of course, had the stock price risen above $40 per share, Don would have lost the $325 because there would have been no reason to exercise the option. Had the stock price fallen to between $36.75 and $40.00 per share, Don probably would have exercised the option to reduce his loss to an amount less than $325.

The Role of Call and Put Options in Fund Raising

Although call and put options are extremely popular investment vehicles, they play *no* direct role in the fund-raising activities of the financial manager. These options are issued by investors, not businesses. *They are not a source of financing to the firm.* Corporate pension managers, whose job it is to invest and manage corporate pension funds, may use call and put options as part of their investment activities to earn a return or to protect or lock in returns already earned on securities. The presence of options trading in the firm's stock could—by increasing trading activity—stabilize the firm's share price in the marketplace, but the financial manager has no direct control over this. Buyers of options have neither any say in the firm's management nor any voting rights; only stockholders are given these privileges. Despite the popularity of call and put options as an investment vehicle, the financial manager has very little need to deal with them, especially as part of fund-raising activities.

Hedging Foreign Currency Exposures with Options

hedging
Offsetting or protecting against the risk of adverse price movements.

Since 1983, the Philadelphia Stock Exchange (PHLX) has offered exchange-traded options contracts on the Canadian dollar, the Japanese yen, and several important European currencies. *Currency options* proved to be an immediate hit and today are used by a wide range of traders—from the largest multinational companies to small exporters and importers, as well as by individual investors and speculators. Unlike futures and forward contracts, options offer the key benefit of **hedging,** which involves offsetting or protecting against the risk of adverse price movements, while simultaneously preserving the possibility of profiting from favorable price movements. The key drawback to using options to hedge foreign currency exposures is its high cost relative to using more traditional futures or forward contracts.

E x a m p l e ▼ Assume that a U.S. exporter just booked a sale denominated in Swiss francs with payment due upon delivery in 3 months. The company could hedge the risk of depreciation in the dollar by purchasing a Swiss franc put option. This would give the company the right to sell Swiss francs at a fixed price (say, $.70/Sf). This option would become valuable if the Swiss franc were to depreciate from today's $.72/Sf to, say, $.65/Sf before the exporter receives payment in Swiss francs. On the other hand, if the Swiss franc were to appreciate from $.72/Sf to, say, $.79/Sf, the U.S. exporter would allow the put option to expire unexercised and would instead convert the Swiss francs received in payment into dollars at the new, higher dollar price. The exporter would be protected from adverse price risk but ▲ would still be able to profit from favorable price movements.

? Review Questions

18–12 What is an *option?* Define *calls* and *puts*. What role, if any, do call and put options play in the fund-raising activities of the financial manager?

18–13 How can the firm use currency options to *hedge* foreign currency exposures resulting from international transactions? Describe the key benefit and drawback of using currency options rather than futures and forward contracts.

SUMMARY

LG1 Differentiate between hybrid and derivative securities and their roles in the corporation. Hybrid securities are forms of debt or equity financing that possess characteristics of both debt and equity financing. Popular hybrid securities include preferred stock, financial leases, convertible securities, and stock purchase warrants. Derivative securities are neither debt nor equity and derive their value from an underlying asset that is often another security. Options, which are sometimes used by corporations to manage risk, are a popular derivative security.

LG2 Review the basic types of leases, leasing arrangements, the lease-versus-purchase decision, the effects of leasing on future financing, and the advantages and disadvantages of leasing. A lease allows the firm to make contractual, tax-deductible payments to obtain the use of fixed assets. Operating leases are generally 5 or fewer years in term, cancelable, and renewable, and they provide for maintenance by the lessor. Financial leases are longer-term, noncancelable, and not renewable, and they require the lessee to maintain the asset. FASB Standard No. 13 provides specific guidelines for defining a financial (or capital) lease. A lessor can obtain assets to be leased through a direct lease, a sale-leaseback arrangement, or a leveraged lease. The lease-versus-purchase decision can be evaluated by calculating the after-tax cash outflows associated with the leasing and purchasing alternatives. The more desirable alternative is the one that has the lower present value of after-tax cash outflows. FASB Standard No. 13 requires firms to show financial (or capital) leases as assets and corresponding liabilities on their balance sheets; operating leases must be shown in footnotes to the financial statements. A number of commonly cited advantages and disadvantages should be considered when making lease-versus-purchase decisions.

LG3 Describe the basic types of convertible securities, their general features, and financing with convertibles. Corporate bonds and preferred stock may both be convertible into common stock. The conversion ratio indicates the number of shares for which a convertible can be exchanged and determines the conversion price. A conversion privilege is almost always available anytime during the life of the security. The conversion (or stock) value is the value of the convertible measured in terms of the market price of the common stock into which it can be converted. The presence of convertibles and other contingent securities (warrants and stock options) often requires the firm to report both basic and diluted earnings per share (EPS). Convertibles are used to obtain deferred common stock financing, to "sweeten" bond issues, to minimize restrictive covenants, and to raise cheap funds temporarily. The call feature is sometimes used to encourage or "force" conversion; occasionally, an overhanging issue results.

LG4 Demonstrate the procedures for determining the straight bond value, conversion (or stock) value, and market value of a convertible bond. The straight bond value of a convertible is the price at which it would sell in the market without the conversion feature. It typically represents the minimum value at which a convertible bond trades. The conversion (or stock) value of the convertible is found by multiplying the conversion ratio by the current market price of the underlying common stock. The market value of a convertible generally exceeds both its straight and conversion values, thus resulting in a market premium. The premium, which is largest when the straight and conversion values are nearly equal, is due to the attractive gains potential from the stock and the risk protection provided by the straight value of the convertible.

 Explain the basic characteristics of stock purchase warrants, the implied price of an attached warrant, and the values of warrants. Stock purchase warrants allow their holders to purchase a certain number of shares of common stock at the specified exercise price. Warrants are often attached to debt issues as "sweeteners," generally have limited lives, are detachable, and may be listed and traded on securities exchanges. Warrants are similar to stock rights, except that the life of a warrant is generally longer than that of a right, and the exercise price of a warrant is initially set above the underlying stock's current market price. Warrants are similar to convertibles, but exercising them has a less pronounced effect on the firm's leverage and brings in new funds. The implied price of an attached warrant can be found by dividing the difference between the bond price with warrants

attached and the straight bond value by the number of warrants attached to each bond. The market value of a warrant usually exceeds its theoretical value, creating a warrant premium. The premium results from positive investor expectations and the ability of investors to get more leverage from trading warrants than from trading the underlying stock.

Define options and discuss the basics of calls and puts, options markets, options trading, the role of call and put options in fund raising, and hedging foreign currency exposures with options. An option provides its holder with an opportunity to purchase or sell a specified asset at a stated price on or before a set expiration date. Rights, warrants, and calls and puts are all options. Calls are options to purchase common stock, and puts are options to sell common stock. Options exchanges, such as the Chicago Board Options Exchange (CBOE), provide organized marketplaces in which purchases and sales of both call and put options can be made in an orderly fashion. The options traded on the exchanges are standardized, and the price at which they trade is determined by the forces of supply and demand. Call and put options do not play a direct role in the fund-raising activities of the financial manager. On the other hand, currency options can be used to hedge the firm's foreign currency exposures resulting from international transactions.

SELF-TEST PROBLEMS   (Solutions in Appendix B)

ST 18–1   Lease versus purchase   The Hot Bagel Shop wishes to evaluate two plans, leasing and borrowing to purchase, for financing an oven. The firm is in the 40% tax bracket.

Lease   The shop can lease the oven under a 5-year lease requiring annual end-of-year payments of $5,000. All maintenance costs will be paid by the lessor, and insurance and other costs will be borne by the lessee. The lessee will exercise its option to purchase the asset for $4,000 at termination of the lease.

Purchase   The oven costs $20,000 and will have a 5-year life. It will be depreciated under MACRS using a 5-year recovery period. (See Table 3.8 on page 96 for the applicable depreciation percentages.) The total purchase price will be financed by a 5-year, 15% loan requiring equal annual end-of-year payments of

$5,967. The firm will pay $1,000 per year for a service contract that covers all maintenance costs; insurance and other costs will be borne by the firm. The firm plans to keep the equipment and use it beyond its 5-year recovery period.

a. For the leasing plan, calculate the following:
   (1) The after-tax cash outflow each year.
   (2) The present value of the cash outflows, using a 9% *discount rate*.
b. For the purchasing plan, calculate the following:
   (1) The annual interest expense deductible for tax purposes for each of the 5 years.
   (2) The after-tax cash outflow resulting from the purchase for each of the 5 years.
   (3) The present value of the cash outflows, using a 9% *discount rate*.
c. Compare the present value of the cash outflow streams from each plan, and determine which would be preferable. Explain your answer.

 ST 18–2   **Finding convertible bond values**   Mountain Mining Company has an outstanding issue of convertible bonds with a $1,000 par value. These bonds are convertible into 40 shares of common stock. They have an 11% annual coupon interest rate and a 25-year maturity. The interest rate on a straight bond of similar risk is currently 13%.
a. Calculate the *straight bond value* of the bond.
b. Calculate the *conversion (or stock) values* of the bond when the market price of the common stock is $20, $25, $28, $35, and $50 per share.
c. For each of the stock prices given in **b** at what price would you expect the bond to sell? Why?
d. What is the least you would expect the bond to sell for, regardless of the common stock price behavior?

PROBLEMS

WARM-UP   18–1   **Lease cash flows**   Given the lease payments and terms shown in the following table, determine the yearly after-tax cash outflows for each firm, assuming that lease payments are made at the end of each year and that the firm is in the 40% tax bracket. Assume that no purchase option exists.

Firm	Annual lease payment	Term of lease
A	$100,000	4 years
B	80,000	14
C	150,000	8
D	60,000	25
E	20,000	10

INTERMEDIATE   **LG2**   18–2   **Loan interest**   For each of the loan amounts, interest rates, annual payments, and loan terms shown in the following table, calculate the annual interest paid each year over the term of the loan, assuming that the payments are made at the end of each year.

Loan	Amount	Interest rate	Annual payment	Term
A	$14,000	10%	$ 4,416	4 years
B	17,500	12	10,355	2
C	2,400	13	1,017	3
D	49,000	14	14,273	5
E	26,500	16	7,191	6

 INTERMEDIATE   **LG2**   18–3   **Loan payments and interest**   Schuyler Company wishes to purchase an asset costing $117,000. The full amount needed to finance the asset can be borrowed at 14% interest. The terms of the loan require equal end-of-year payments for the next 6 years. Determine the total annual loan payment, and break it into the amount of interest and the amount of principal paid for each year. (*Hint:* Use techniques presented in Chapter 5 to find the loan payment.)

  LG2   18–4   **Lease versus purchase**   JLB Corporation is attempting to determine whether to lease or purchase research equipment. The firm is in the 40% tax bracket, and its after-tax cost of debt is currently 8%. The terms of the lease and the purchase are as follows:

CHALLENGE

Lease   Annual end-of-year lease payments of $25,200 are required over the 3-year life of the lease. All maintenance costs will be paid by the lessor; insurance and other costs will be borne by the lessee. The lessee will exercise its option to purchase the asset for $5,000 at termination of the lease.

Purchase   The research equipment, costing $60,000, can be financed entirely with a 14% loan requiring annual end-of-year payments of $25,844 for 3 years. The firm in this case will depreciate the truck under MACRS using a 3-year recovery period. (See Table 3.8 on page 96 for the applicable depreciation percentages.) The firm will pay $1,800 per year for a service contract that covers all maintenance costs; insurance and other costs will be borne by the firm. The firm plans to keep the equipment and use it beyond its 3-year recovery period.

a. Calculate the after-tax cash outflows associated with each alternative.
b. Calculate the present value of each cash outflow stream using the after-tax cost of debt.
c. Which alternative, lease or purchase, would you recommend? Why?

 CHALLENGE   **LG2**   18–5   **Lease versus purchase**   Northwest Lumber Company needs to expand its facilities. To do so, the firm must acquire a machine costing $80,000. The machine can be leased or purchased. The firm is in the 40% tax bracket, and its after-tax cost of debt is 9%. The terms of the lease and purchase plans are as follows:

Lease   The leasing arrangement requires end-of-year payments of $19,800 over 5 years. All maintenance costs will be paid by the lessor; insurance and other costs will be borne by the lessee. The lessee will exercise its option to purchase the asset for $24,000 at termination of the lease.

Purchase   If the firm purchases the machine, its cost of $80,000 will be financed with a 5-year, 14% loan requiring equal end-of-year payments of $23,302. The machine will be depreciated under MACRS using a 5-year recovery period. (See Table 3.8 on page 96 for the applicable depreciation percentages.) The firm will pay $2,000 per year for a service contract that covers all maintenance costs; insurance and other costs will be borne by the firm. The firm plans to keep the equipment and use it beyond its 5-year recovery period.

a. Determine the after-tax cash outflows of Northwest Lumber under each alternative.
b. Find the present value of the after-tax cash outflows using the after-tax cost of debt.
c. Which alternative, lease or purchase, would you recommend? Why?

 INTERMEDIATE   **18–6   Capitalized lease values**   Given the lease payments, terms remaining until the leases expire, and discount rates shown in the following table, calculate the capitalized value of each lease, assuming that lease payments are made annually at the end of each year.

Lease	Lease payment	Remaining term	Discount rate
A	$ 40,000	12 years	10%
B	120,000	8	12
C	9,000	18	14
D	16,000	3	9
E	47,000	20	11

 WARM-UP   **18–7   Conversion price**   Calculate the conversion price for each of the following convertible bonds:
a. A $1,000-par-value bond that is convertible into 20 shares of common stock.
b. A $500-par-value bond that is convertible into 25 shares of common stock.
c. A $1,000-par-value bond that is convertible into 50 shares of common stock.

 WARM-UP   **18–8   Conversion ratio**   What is the conversion ratio for each of the following bonds?
a. A $1,000-par-value bond that is convertible into common stock at $43.75 per share.
b. A $1,000-par-value bond that is convertible into common stock at $25 per share.
c. A $600-par-value bond that is convertible into common stock at $30 per share.

WARM-UP LG3 **18–9 Conversion (or stock) value**   What is the conversion (or stock) value of each of the following convertible bonds?
a. A $1,000-par-value bond that is convertible into 25 shares of common stock. The common stock is currently selling at $50 per share.
b. A $1,000-par-value bond that is convertible into 12.5 shares of common stock. The common stock is currently selling for $42 per share.
c. A $1,000-par-value bond that is convertible into 100 shares of common stock. The common stock is currently selling for $10.50 per share.

WARM-UP LG3 **18–10 Conversion (or stock) value**   Find the conversion (or stock) value for each of the convertible bonds described in the following table.

Convertible	Conversion ratio	Current market price of stock
A	25	$42.25
B	16	50.00
C	20	44.00
D	5	19.50

INTERMEDIATE LG4 **18–11 Straight bond value**   Calculate the straight bond value for each of the bonds shown in the following table.

Bond	Par value	Coupon interest rate (paid annually)	Interest rate on equal-risk straight bond	Years to maturity
A	$1,000	10%	14%	20
B	800	12	15	14
C	1,000	13	16	30
D	1,000	14	17	25

CHALLENGE LG4 **18–12 Determining values—Convertible bond**   Eastern Clock Company has an outstanding issue of convertible bonds with a $1,000 par value. These bonds are convertible into 50 shares of common stock. They have a 10% annual coupon interest rate and a 20-year maturity. The interest rate on a straight bond of similar risk is currently 12%.
a. Calculate the *straight bond value* of the bond.
b. Calculate the *conversion (or stock) values* of the bond when the market price of the common stock is $15, $20, $23, $30, and $45 per share.
c. For each of the stock prices given in **b**, at what price would you expect the bond to sell? Why?
d. What is the least you would expect the bond to sell for, regardless of the common stock price behavior?

CHALLENGE 18–13 **Determining values—Convertible bond**   Craig's Cake Company has an outstanding issue of 15-year convertible bonds with a $1,000 par value. These bonds are convertible into 80 shares of common stock. They have a 13% annual coupon interest rate, whereas the interest rate on straight bonds of similar risk is 16%.

a. Calculate the *straight bond value* of this bond.

b. Calculate the *conversion (or stock) values* of the bond when the market price is $9, $12, $13, $15, and $20 per share of common stock.

c. For each of the common stock prices given in **b,** at what price would you expect the bond to sell? Why?

d. Graph the straight value and conversion value of the bond for each common stock price given. Plot the per-share common stock prices on the *x* axis and the bond values on the *y* axis. Use this graph to indicate the minimum market value of the bond associated with each common stock price.

INTERMEDIATE 18–14 **Implied prices of attached warrants**   Calculate the implied price of *each* warrant for each of the bonds shown in the following table.

Bond	Price of bond with warrants attached	Par value	Coupon interest rate (paid annually)	Interest rate on equal-risk straight bond	Years to maturity	Number of warrants attached to bond
A	$1,000	$1,000	12%	13%	15	10
B	1,100	1,000	9.5	12	10	30
C	500	500	10	11	20	5
D	1,000	1,000	11	12	20	20

CHALLENGE  18–15 **Evaluation of the implied price of an attached warrant**   Dinoo Mathur wishes to determine whether the $1,000 price asked for Stanco Manufacturing's bond is fair in light of the theoretical value of the attached warrants. The $1,000-par, 30-year, 11.5%-coupon-interest-rate bond pays annual interest and has 10 warrants attached for purchase of common stock. The theoretical value of each warrant is $12.50. The interest rate on an equal-risk straight bond is currently 13%.

a. Find the straight value of Stanco Manufacturing's bond.

b. Calculate the implied price of *all* warrants attached to Stanco's bond.

c. Calculate the implied price of *each* warrant attached to Stanco's bond.

d. Compare the implied price for each warrant calculated in **c** to its theoretical value. On the basis of this comparison, what recommendation would you give Dinoo with respect to the fairness of Stanco's bond price? Explain.

CHALLENGE  18–16 **Warrant values**   Kent Hotels has warrants that allow the purchase of three shares of its outstanding common stock at $50 per share. The common stock price per share and the market value of the warrant associated with that stock price are shown in the table at the top of page 774.

Common stock price per share	Market value of warrant
$42	$ 2
46	8
48	9
54	18
58	28
62	38
66	48

a. For each of the common stock prices given, calculate the theoretical warrant value.
b. Graph the theoretical and market values of the warrant on a set of per-share common stock price (*x* axis)–warrant value (*y* axis) axes.
c. If the warrant value is $12 when the market price of common stock is $50, does this contradict or support the graph you have constructed? Explain.
d. Specify the area of *warrant premium*. Why does this premium exist?
e. If the expiration date of the warrants is quite close, would you expect your graph to look different? Explain.

CHALLENGE 18–17 **Common stock versus warrant investment** Susan Michaels is evaluating the Burton Tool Company's common stock and warrants to choose the better investment. The firm's stock is currently selling for $50 per share; its warrants to purchase three shares of common stock at $45 per share are selling for $20. Ignoring transactions costs, Ms. Michaels has $8,000 to invest. She is quite optimistic with respect to Burton because she has certain "inside information" about the firm's prospects with respect to a large government contract.
a. How many shares of stock and how many warrants can Ms. Michaels purchase?
b. Suppose Ms. Michaels purchased the stock, held it 1 year, then sold it for $60 per share. What total gain would she realize, ignoring brokerage fees and taxes?
c. Suppose Ms. Michaels purchased warrants and held them for 1 year and the market price of the stock increased to $60 per share. What would be her total gain if the market value of warrants increased to $45 and she sold out, ignoring brokerage fees and taxes?
d. What benefit, if any, would the warrants provide? Are there any differences in the risk of these two alternative investments? Explain.

CHALLENGE 18–18 **Common stock versus warrant investment** Tom Baldwin can invest $6,300 in the common stock or the warrants of Lexington Life Insurance. The common stock is currently selling for $30 per share. Its warrants, which provide for the purchase of two shares of common stock at $28 per share, are currently selling for $7. The stock is expected to rise to a market price of $32 within the next year, so the expected theoretical value of a warrant over the next year is $8. The expiration date of the warrant is 1 year from the present.

a. If Mr. Baldwin purchases the stock, holds it for 1 year, and then sells it for $32, what is his total gain? (Ignore brokerage fees and taxes.)
b. If Mr. Baldwin purchases the warrants and converts them to common stock in 1 year, what is his total gain if the market price of common shares is actually $32? (Ignore brokerage fees and taxes.)
c. Repeat **a** and **b** assuming that the market price of the stock in 1 year is (1) $30 and (2) $28.
d. Discuss the two alternatives and the tradeoffs associated with them.

  18–19   **Options profits and losses**   For each of the *100-share options* shown in the following table, use the underlying stock price at expiration and other information to determine the amount of profit or loss an investor would have had, ignoring brokerage fees.

Option	Type of option	Cost of option	Striking price per share	Underlying stock price per share at expiration
A	Call	$200	$50	$55
B	Call	350	42	45
C	Put	500	60	50
D	Put	300	35	40
E	Call	450	28	26

  18–20   **Call option**   Carol Krebs is considering buying 100 shares of Sooner Products, Inc., at $62 per share. Because she has read that the firm will likely soon receive certain large orders from abroad, she expects the price of Sooner to increase to $70 per share. As an alternative, Carol is considering purchase of a call option for 100 shares of Sooner at a striking price of $60. The 90-day option will cost $600. Ignore any brokerage fees or dividends.
a. What will Carol's profit be on the stock transaction if its price does rise to $70 and she sells?
b. How much will Carol earn on the option transaction if the underlying stock price rises to $70?
c. How high must the stock price rise for Carol to break even on the option transaction?
d. Compare, contrast, and discuss the relative profit and risk from the stock and the option transactions.

  18–21   **Put option**   Ed Martin, the pension fund manager for Stark Corporation, is considering purchase of a put option in anticipation of a price decline in the stock of Carlisle, Inc. The option to sell 100 shares of Carlisle, Inc., at any time during the next 90 days at a striking price of $45 can be purchased for $380. The stock of Carlisle is currently selling for $46 per share.
a. Ignoring any brokerage fees or dividends, what profit or loss will Ed make if he buys the option, and the lowest price of Carlisle, Inc., stock during the 90 days is $46, $44, $40, and $35?

b. What effect would the fact that the price of Carlisle's stock slowly rose from its initial $46 level to $55 at the end of 90 days have on Ed's purchase?

c. In light of your findings, discuss the potential risks and returns from using put options to attempt to profit from an anticipated decline in share price.

CASE CHAPTER 18

Financing L. Rashid Company's Chemical-Waste-Disposal System

L. Rashid Company, a rapidly growing chemical processor, needs to raise $3 million in external funds to finance the acquisition of a new chemical-waste-disposal system. After carefully analyzing alternative financing sources, Denise McMahon, the firm's vice-president of finance, reduced the financing possibilities to three alternatives: (1) debt, (2) debt with warrants, and (3) a financial lease. The key terms of each of these financing alternatives follow.

Debt The firm can borrow the full $3 million from First Shreveport Bank. The bank will charge 12% annual interest and require annual end-of-year payments of $1,249,050 over the next 3 years. The disposal system will be depreciated under MACRS using a 3-year recovery period. (See Table 3.8 on page 96 for the applicable depreciation percentages.) The firm will pay $45,000 at the end of each year for a service contract that covers all maintenance costs; insurance and other costs will be borne by the firm. The firm plans to keep the equipment and use it beyond its 3-year recovery period.

Debt with Warrants The firm can borrow the full $3 million from Southern National Bank. The bank will charge 10% annual interest and will, in addition, require a grant of 50,000 warrants, each allowing the purchase of two shares of the firm's stock for $30 per share any time during the next 10 years. The stock is currently selling for $28 per share, and the warrants are estimated to have a market value of $1 each. The price (market value) of the debt with the warrants attached is estimated to equal the $3 million initial loan principal. The annual end-of-year payments on this loan will be $1,206,345 over the next 3 years. Depreciation, maintenance, and insurance and other costs will have the same costs and treatments under this alternative, as those described before for the straight debt financing alternative.

Financial Lease The waste-disposal system can be leased from First International Capital. The lease will require annual end-of-year payments of $1,200,000 over the next 3 years. All maintenance costs will be paid by the lessor; insurance and other costs will be borne by the lessee. The lessee will exercise its option to purchase the system for $220,000 at termination of the lease at the end of 3 years.

Denise decided to first determine which of the debt financing alternatives—debt or debt with warrants—would least burden the firm's cash flows over the next 3 years. In this regard, she felt that very few, if any, warrants would be exercised during this period. Once the best debt financing alternative was found, Denise planned to use lease-versus-purchase analysis to evaluate it in light of the lease alternative. The firm is in the 40% bracket, and its after-tax cost of debt would be 7% under the debt alternative and 6% under the debt with warrants alternative.

Required

a. Under the debt with warrants alternative, find the following:
  (1) Straight debt value.
  (2) Implied price of *all* warrants.
  (3) Implied price of *each* warrant.
  (4) Theoretical value of a warrant.
b. On the basis of your findings in **a,** do you think the price of the debt with warrants is too high or too low? Explain.
c. Assuming that the firm can raise the needed funds under the specified terms, which debt financing alternative—debt or debt with warrants—would you recommend in view of your findings above? Explain.
d. For the purchase alternative, financed as recommended in **c,** calculate the following:
  (1) The annual interest expense deductible for tax purposes for each of the next 3 years.
  (2) The after-tax cash outflow for each of the next 3 years.
  (3) The present value of the cash outflows using the appropriate discount rate.
e. For the lease alternative, calculate the following:
  (1) The after-tax cash outflow for each of the next 3 years.
  (2) The present value of the cash outflows using the appropriate discount rate applied in **d(3)**.
f. Compare the present values of the cash outflow streams for the purchase [in **d(3)**] and lease [in **e(2)**] alternatives, and determine which would be preferable. Explain and discuss your recommendation.

 WEB EXERCISE

GOTO web site www.cboe.com Click on EDUCATION.

1. What are the five benefits of options?
2. What are LEAPS?

GOTO web site www.adtrading.com. In the "REGULAR ARTICLES" section, click on The ADT guide. Then click on 1. Futures.

3. What are financial futures?
4. Where are they traded? Who can trade there?
5. What are the characteristics of a contract?

GOTO web site www.pacificex.com. Click OPTIONS. Click glossary. Scroll down to the "OPTIONS TRADING TERMS" section.

6. What are the classes of options?

19

Mergers, LBOs, Divestitures, and Business Failure

ᒪEARNING ᏀOALS

LG1 Understand merger fundamentals, including basic terminology, motives for merging, and types of mergers.

LG2 Describe the objectives and procedures used in leveraged buyouts (LBOs) and divestitures.

LG3 Demonstrate the procedures used to value the target company and discuss the effect of stock swap transactions on earnings per share.

LG4 Discuss the merger negotiation process, the role of holding companies, and international mergers.

LG5 Understand the types and major causes of business failure and the use of voluntary settlements to sustain or liquidate the failed firm.

LG6 Explain bankruptcy legislation and the procedures involved in reorganizing or liquidating a bankrupt firm.

19.1 Merger Fundamentals

Firms sometimes use mergers to expand externally by acquiring control of another firm. Whereas the overriding objective for a merger should be to improve the firm's share value, a number of more immediate motivations such as diversification, tax considerations, and increasing owner liquidity frequently exist. Sometimes mergers are pursued to acquire needed assets rather than the going concern. Here we discuss merger fundamentals—terminology, motives, and types. In the following sections, we will describe the related topics of leveraged

'Til Death or Mismanagement Do Us Part

Most mergers are entered into with hopes, dreams, fanfare, and the expectation of future success. Many mergers, both marital and corporate, meet or exceed those hopes and expectations. As in marital mergers, the successful business mergers are typically those in which each party knows and appreciates the strengths of the other party and believes that the weaknesses (if any) can be overcome or dealt with. Careful evaluation of the target firm and a clear-eyed understanding of the motives for the

merger are also important. Sadly for those involved, though, not all mergers prove successful, and disappointing outcomes demand action of one sort or another. This chapter looks at the topic of business mergers and at the alternatives in the case of business failure.

buyouts and divestitures and will review the procedures used to analyze and negotiate mergers.

Basic Terminology

corporate restructuring
The activities involving expansion or contraction of a firm's operations or changes in its asset or financial (ownership) structure.

In the broadest sense, activities involving expansion or contraction of a firm's operations or changes in its asset or financial (ownership) structure are called **corporate restructuring**. The topics addressed in this chapter—mergers, LBOs, and divestitures—are some of the most common forms of corporate restructuring;

there are many others, which are beyond the scope of this text.[1] Here, we define some basic merger terminology; other terms are introduced and defined as needed in subsequent discussions.

Mergers, Consolidations, and Holding Companies

merger
The combination of two or more firms, in which the resulting firm maintains the identity of one of the firms, usually the larger one.

consolidation
The combination of two or more firms to form a completely new corporation.

holding company
A corporation that has voting control of one or more other corporations.

subsidiaries
The companies controlled by a holding company.

A **merger** occurs when two or more firms are combined and the resulting firm maintains the identity of one of the firms. Usually, the assets and liabilities of the smaller firm are merged into those of the larger firm. **Consolidation,** on the other hand, involves the combination of two or more firms to form a completely new corporation. The new corporation normally absorbs the assets and liabilities of the companies from which it is formed. Because of the similarity of mergers and consolidations, the term *merger* is used throughout this chapter to refer to both.

A **holding company** is a corporation that has voting control of one or more other corporations. Having control in large, widely held companies generally requires ownership of between 10 and 20 percent of the outstanding stock. The companies controlled by a holding company are normally referred to as its **subsidiaries.** Control of a subsidiary is typically obtained by purchasing a sufficient number of shares of its stock.

Acquiring Versus Target Companies

acquiring company
The firm in a merger transaction that attempts to acquire another firm.

target company
The firm in a merger transaction that the acquiring company is pursuing.

The firm in a merger transaction that attempts to acquire another firm is commonly called the **acquiring company.** The firm that the acquiring company is pursuing is referred to as the **target company.** Generally, the acquiring company identifies, evaluates, and negotiates with the management and/or shareholders of the target company. Occasionally, the management of a target company initiates its acquisition by seeking to be acquired.

Friendly Versus Hostile Takeovers

friendly merger
A merger transaction endorsed by the target firm's management, approved by its stockholders, and easily consummated.

Mergers can occur on either a friendly or a hostile basis. Typically, after identifying the target company, the acquirer initiates discussions. If the target management is receptive to the acquirer's proposal, it may endorse the merger and recommend shareholder approval. If the stockholders approve the merger, the transaction is typically consummated either through a cash purchase of shares by the acquirer or through an exchange of the acquirer's stock, bonds, or some combination for the target firm's shares. This type of negotiated transaction is known as a **friendly merger.**

If, on the other hand, the takeover target's management does not support the proposed takeover, it can fight the acquirer's actions. In this case, the acquirer can attempt to gain control of the firm by buying sufficient shares of the target firm in the marketplace. This is typically accomplished by using *tender offers,* which, as noted in Chapter 13, are formal offers to purchase a given number of shares at a specified price. This type of unfriendly transaction is commonly

---

1. For comprehensive coverage of the many aspects of corporate restructuring, see J. Fred Weston, Kwang S. Chung, and Susan E. Hoag, *Takeovers, Restructuring, and Corporate Governance,* 2nd ed. (Upper Saddle River, NJ: Prentice Hall, 1998).

hostile merger
A merger transaction not supported by the target firm's management, forcing the acquiring company to try to gain control of the firm by buying shares in the marketplace.

referred to as a **hostile merger.** Clearly, hostile mergers are more difficult to consummate because the target firm's management acts to deter rather than facilitate the acquisition. Regardless, hostile takeovers are sometimes successful.

Strategic Versus Financial Mergers

strategic merger
A merger transaction undertaken to achieve economies of scale.

Mergers are undertaken for either strategic or financial reasons. **Strategic mergers** seek to achieve various economies of scale by eliminating redundant functions, increasing market share, improving raw material sourcing and finished product distribution, and so on.[2] In these mergers, the operations of the acquiring and target firms are somehow combined to achieve economies and thereby cause the performance of the merged firm to exceed that of the premerged firms. The mergers of Daimler-Benz and Chrysler (both auto manufacturers) and Norwest and Wells Fargo (both banks) are examples of strategic mergers. An interesting variation of the strategic merger involves the purchase of specific product lines (rather than the whole company) for strategic reasons. The purchase of Simon and Schuster (textbook publishing) from Paramount (global media) by Pearson PLC (global conglomerate), which owns Addison Wesley Longman (textbook publishing), is an example of such a merger.

financial merger
A merger transaction undertaken with the goal of restructuring the acquired company to improve its cash flow and unlock its hidden value.

Financial mergers, on the other hand, are based on the acquisition of companies that can be restructured to improve their cash flow. These mergers involve the acquisition of the target firm by an acquirer, which may be another company or a group of investors—often the firm's existing management. The objective of the acquirer is to drastically cut costs and sell off certain unproductive or noncompatible assets in order to increase the firm's cash flow. The increased cash flow is used to service the sizable debt that is typically incurred to finance these transactions. Financial mergers are based, not on the firm's ability to achieve economies of scale, but on the acquirer's belief that through restructuring, the firm's hidden value can be unlocked.

The ready availability of *junk bond* financing throughout the 1980s fueled the financial merger mania during that period. Examples of financial mergers include the takeover of RJR Nabisco by Kohlberg Kravis Roberts (KKR), Campeau Corporation's (real estate) acquisition of Allied Stores and Federated Department Stores, and Merv Griffin's acquisition of Resorts International (hotels/casinos) from Donald Trump. With the collapse of the junk bond market in the early 1990s, the bankruptcy filings of a number of prominent financial mergers of the 1980s, and the rising stock market of the later 1990s, financial mergers have lost their luster. As a result, the strategic merger, which does not rely as heavily on debt, tends to dominate today.

Motives for Merging

Firms merge to fulfill certain objectives. The overriding goal for merging is the maximization of the owners' wealth as reflected in the acquirer's share price. More specific motives include growth or diversification, synergy, fund

2. A somewhat similar nonmerger arrangement is the *strategic alliance,* an agreement typically between a large company with established products and channels of distribution and an emerging technology company with a promising research and development program in areas of interest to the larger company. In exchange for its financial support, the larger, established company obtains a stake in the technology being developed by the emerging company. Today, strategic alliances are commonplace in the biotechnology, information technology, and software industries.

raising, increased managerial skill or technology, tax considerations, increased ownership liquidity, and defense against takeover. These motives should be pursued when they are believed to be consistent with owner wealth maximization.

Growth or Diversification

Career Key

The *marketing* department will be very involved in the analysis of potential mergers and acquisitions. The firm's mix of product and service offerings could be significantly altered by these actions. Personnel assignments might also be at issue after the merger has been consummated.

Companies that desire rapid growth in *size* or *market share* or diversification in *the range of their products* may find that a merger can be used to fulfill this objective. Instead of going through the time-consuming process of internal growth or diversification, the firm may achieve the same objective in a short period of time by merging with an existing firm. Such a strategy is often less costly than the alternative of developing the necessary production capacity. If a firm that wants to expand operations can find a suitable going concern, it may avoid many of the risks associated with the design, manufacture, and sale of additional or new products. Moreover, when a firm expands or extends its product line by acquiring another firm, it also removes a potential competitor.[3]

Synergy

Hint   Synergy is said to be present when a whole is greater than the sum of the parts—when "1 + 1 = 3."

The *synergy* of mergers is the economies of scale resulting from the merged firms' lower overhead. These economies of scale from lowering the combined overhead increase earnings to a level greater than the sum of the earnings of each of the independent firms. Synergy is most obvious when firms merge with other firms in the same line of business, because many redundant functions and employees can thereby be eliminated. Staff functions, such as purchasing and sales, are probably most greatly affected by this type of combination.

Fund Raising

Often, firms combine to enhance their fund-raising ability. A firm may be unable to obtain funds for its own internal expansion but able to obtain funds for external business combinations. Quite often, one firm may combine with another that has high liquid assets and low levels of liabilities. The acquisition of this type of "cash-rich" company immediately increases the firm's borrowing power by decreasing its financial leverage. This should allow funds to be raised externally at lower cost.

Increased Managerial Skill or Technology

Career Key

Mergers and acquisitions are important to *management* not only because of their effects on the firm, but also because of their effects on managers' jobs. In addition to having more responsibilities, managers may have to manage a business in which they have little or no experience. Besides their personal concerns, they need to understand how compatible the merging company's corporate cultures are.

Occasionally, a firm will have good potential that it finds itself unable to develop fully because of deficiencies in certain areas of management or an absence of needed product or production technology. If the firm cannot hire the manage-

---

3. Certain legal constraints on growth exist—especially when the elimination of competition is expected. The various antitrust laws, which are closely enforced by the Federal Trade Commission (FTC) and the Justice Department, prohibit business combinations that eliminate competition, particularly when the resulting enterprise would be a monopoly.

In Practice

PhotoDisc's
Future Picture
Sharpens

While headlines spread the news about multibillion-dollar megamergers between giants in such industries as oil and telecommunications, small companies also are merging at record rates. According to Richard Peterson of Securities Data, a firm that tracks merger and acquisition activity, deals involving companies with sales under $100 million skyrocketed from $17.3 billion in 1992 to $62.5 billion in 1997, rising 66 percent from 1996 to 1997. Small-company owners are more likely than ever to find themselves in the position of evaluating an offer to buy their company or making an offer to acquire another firm.

PhotoDisc, a Seattle company founded in 1991, was one of the first companies to sell digital photographs to a wide range of professional users such as advertising agencies, newspapers, magazines, and publishing companies. As the business expanded and PhotoDisc became one of the largest providers of graphics via CD-ROM and the Internet, founder and CEO Mark Torrance considered taking the company public but was concerned that the relatively small $100 million company would be overshadowed in 1997's IPO boom. A better option appeared when Mark Getty, grandson of oil billionaire J. Paul Getty and head of London-based Getty Communications PLC, contacted him. Although both companies sold stock photography, PhotoDisc's strengths were in technology and distributing images on CD-ROMs and over the Web, whereas Getty focused on quality images sold for limited or exclusive use. In February 1998, the two companies completed a stock and cash transaction valued at about $240 million that created a new U.S. company called Getty Images Inc. With PhotoDisc's distribution technology, Getty Images will be able to use electronic commerce to deliver its image library, which after its acquisition of other visual content providers includes 30 million images and about 13,000 hours of film footage.

ment or develop the technology it needs, it might combine with a compatible firm that has the needed managerial personnel or technical expertise. Of course, any merger should contribute to the maximization of owners' wealth.

Tax Considerations

tax loss carryforward
In a merger, the tax loss of one of the firms that can be applied against a limited amount of future income of the merged firm over the shorter of either 15 years or until the total tax loss has been fully recovered.

Quite often, tax considerations are a key motive for merging. In such a case, the tax benefit generally stems from the fact that one of the firms has a **tax loss carryforward**. This means that the company's tax loss can be applied against a limited amount of future income of the merged firm over the shorter of either 15 years or until the total tax loss has been fully recovered.[4] Two situations could

---

4. The *Tax Reform Act of 1986*, to deter firms from combining solely to take advantage of tax loss carryforwards, initiated an annual limit on the amount of taxable income against which such losses can be applied. The annual limit is determined by formula and is tied to the value of the loss corporation before the combination. Although not fully eliminating this motive for combination, the act makes it more difficult for firms to justify combinations solely on the basis of tax loss carryforwards.

actually exist. A company with a tax loss could acquire a profitable company to utilize the tax loss. In this case, the acquiring firm would boost the combination's after-tax earnings by reducing the taxable income of the acquired firm. A tax loss may also be useful when a profitable firm acquires a firm that has such a loss. In either situation, however, the merger must be justified not only on the basis of the tax benefits but also on grounds consistent with the goal of owner wealth maximization. Moreover, the tax benefits described can be used only in mergers—not in the formation of holding companies—because only in the case of mergers are operating results reported on a consolidated basis. An example will clarify the use of the tax loss carryforward.

Example ▼ Bergen Company, a wheel bearing manufacturer, has a total of $450,000 in tax loss carryforwards resulting from operating tax losses of $150,000 a year in each of the past 3 years. To use these losses and to diversify its operations, Hudson Company, a molder of plastics, has acquired Bergen through a merger. Hudson expects to have *earnings before taxes* of $300,000 per year. We assume that these earnings are realized, that they fall within the annual limit that is legally allowed for application of the tax loss carryforward resulting from the merger (see footnote 4), that the Bergen portion of the merged firm just breaks even, and that Hudson is in the 40% tax bracket. The total taxes paid by the two firms and their after-tax earnings without and with the merger are as shown in Table 19.1.

With the merger the total tax payments are less—$180,000 (total of line 7) versus $360,000 (total of line 2). With the merger the total after-tax earnings are more—$720,000 (total of line 8) versus $540,000 (total of line 3). The merged firm is able to deduct the tax loss over the shorter of either 15 years or until the

TABLE 19.1 Total Taxes and After-Tax Earnings for Hudson Company Without and With Merger

	Year 1	Year 2	Year 3	Total for 3 years
Total taxes and after-tax earnings without merger				
(1) Earnings before taxes	$300,000	$300,000	$300,000	$900,000
(2) Taxes [.40 × (1)]	120,000	120,000	120,000	360,000
(3) Earnings after taxes [(1) −(2)]	$180,000	$180,000	$180,000	$540,000
Total taxes and after-tax earnings with merger				
(4) Earnings before losses	$300,000	$300,000	$300,000	$900,000
(5) Tax loss carryforward	300,000	150,000	0	450,000
(6) Earnings before taxes [(4) − (5)]	$ 0	$150,000	$300,000	$450,000
(7) Taxes [.40 × (6)]	0	60,000	120,000	180,000
(8) Earnings after taxes [(4) − (7)]	$300,000	$240,000	$180,000	$720,000

total tax loss has been fully recovered. In this example, the shorter is at the end of year 2.

Increased Ownership Liquidity

The merger of two small firms or a small and a larger firm may provide the owners of the small firm(s) with greater liquidity. This is due to the higher marketability associated with the shares of larger firms. Instead of holding shares in a small firm that has a very "thin" market, the owners will receive shares that are traded in a broader market and can thus be liquidated more readily. Also, owning shares for which market price quotations are readily available provides owners with a better sense of the value of their holdings. Especially in the case of small, closely held firms, the improved liquidity of ownership obtainable through merger with an acceptable firm may have considerable appeal.

Defense Against Takeover

Hint   An unfriendly takeover refers to the fact that top management and/or the major stockholders would *not* like to become a part of another firm. In some cases, many of the stockholders do not feel the same about the impending takeover.

Occasionally, when a firm becomes the target of an unfriendly takeover, it will as a defense acquire another company. Such a strategy typically works like this: The original target firm takes on additional debt to finance its defensive acquisition; because of the debt load, the target firm becomes too highly levered financially to be of any further interest to its suitor.

To be effective, a defensive takeover must create greater value for shareholders than they would have realized had the firm been merged with its suitor. An example of such a defense was the 1988 incurrence of about $2.5 billion in debt a year after Harcourt Brace Jovanovich's (HBJ's) (publishing, insurance, theme parks) acquisition of Holt, Rinehart and Winston (publishing) from CBS, Inc., to ward off its suitor, Robert Maxwell (British takeover specialist, now deceased). To service the huge debt incurred in this transaction, HBJ subsequently sold its Sea World theme parks to Anheuser-Busch Co. (alcoholic beverages) but subsequently defaulted on many of its debts. After much negotiation, HBJ (now called Harcourt Brace) was acquired by General Cinema in 1991. In retrospect, it appears that HBJ's defense may have been its downfall. Clearly, the use of a merger with a large amount of debt financing as a takeover defense, although effectively deterring the takeover, can result in subsequent financial difficulty and possibly failure. The movement away from highly debt-financed mergers in favor of cash and stock financial transactions during the 1990s has nearly eliminated use of this strategy as a defense against an unfriendly takeover.

Types of Mergers

Hint   A merger undertaken to obtain the synergy benefit is usually a horizontal merger. Diversification can be either a vertical or congeneric merger. The other benefits of merging can be achieved by any one of the four types of mergers.

horizontal merger
A merger of two firms *in the same line of business.*

vertical merger
A merger in which a firm acquires *a supplier or a customer.*

The four types of mergers are the (1) horizontal merger, (2) vertical merger, (3) congeneric merger, and (4) conglomerate merger. A **horizontal merger** results when two firms *in the same line of business* are merged. An example would be the merger of two machine-tool manufacturers. This form of merger results in the expansion of a firm's operations in a given product line and at the same time eliminates a competitor. A **vertical merger** occurs when a firm acquires *a supplier or a customer.* For example, the merger of a machine-tool manufacturer with its

congeneric merger
A merger in which one firm acquires another firm that is *in the same general industry* but neither in the same line of business nor a supplier or customer.

conglomerate merger
A merger combining firms in *unrelated businesses*.

supplier of castings would be a vertical merger. The economic benefit of a vertical merger stems from the firm's increased control over the acquisition of raw materials or the distribution of finished goods.

A **congeneric merger** is achieved by acquiring a firm that is *in the same general industry* but neither in the same line of business nor a supplier or customer. An example is the merger of a machine-tool manufacturer with the manufacturer of industrial conveyor systems. The benefit of a congeneric merger is the resulting ability to use the same sales and distribution channels to reach customers of both businesses. A **conglomerate merger** involves the combination of firms in *unrelated businesses*. The merger of a machine-tool manufacturer with a chain of fast-food restaurants would be an example of this kind of merger. The key benefit of the conglomerate merger is its ability to *reduce risk* by merging firms with different seasonal or cyclical patterns of sales and earnings.[5]

? Review Questions

19–1   Define and differentiate each of the following sets of terms: (**a**) mergers, consolidations, and holding companies; (**b**) acquiring versus target company; (**c**) friendly versus hostile mergers; and (**d**) strategic versus financial mergers.

19–2   Briefly describe each of the following motives for merging: (**a**) growth or diversification, (**b**) synergy, (**c**) fund raising, (**d**) increased managerial skill or technology, (**e**) tax considerations, (**f**) increased ownership liquidity, and (**g**) defense against takeover.

19–3   Briefly describe each of the following types of mergers: (**a**) horizontal, (**b**) vertical, (**c**) congeneric, and (**d**) conglomerate.

19.2 LBOs and Divestitures

Before we address the mechanics of merger analysis and negotiation, you need to understand two topics that are closely related to mergers—LBOs and divestitures. An LBO is a method of structuring an acquisition, and divestitures involve the sale of a firm's assets.

leveraged buyout (LBO)
An acquisition technique involving the use of a large amount of debt to purchase a firm; an example of a *financial merger.*

Hint   The acquirers in LBOs are other firms or groups of investors that frequently include key members of the firm's existing management.

Leveraged Buyouts (LBOs)

A popular technique that was widely used during the 1980s to make acquisitions is the **leveraged buyout (LBO)**, which involves the use of a large amount of debt to purchase a firm. LBOs are a clear-cut example of a *financial merger* undertaken to create a high-debt private corporation with improved cash flow and value. Typically, in an LBO, 90 percent or more of the purchase price is financed with debt. A large part of the borrowing is secured by the acquired firm's assets, and the lenders, because of the high risk, take a portion of the firm's equity. *Junk*

---

5. A discussion of the key concepts underlying the portfolio approach to the diversification of risk was presented in Chapter 6. In the theoretical literature, some questions exist relating to whether diversification by the firm is a proper motive consistent with shareholder wealth maximization. Many scholars argue that by buying shares in different firms, investors can obtain the same benefits as they would realize from owning stock in the merged firm. It appears that other benefits need to be available to justify mergers.

bonds have been routinely used to raise the large amounts of debt needed to finance LBO transactions. Of course, the purchasers in an LBO expect to use the improved cash flow to service the large amount of junk bond and other debt incurred in the buyout.

An attractive candidate for acquisition through leveraged buyout should possess three basic attributes:

1. It must have a good position in its industry with a solid profit history and reasonable expectations of growth.
2. The firm should have a relatively low level of debt and a high level of "bankable" assets that can be used as loan collateral.
3. It must have stable and predictable cash flows that are adequate to meet interest and principal payments on the debt and provide adequate working capital.

Of course, a willingness on the part of existing ownership and management to sell the company on a leveraged basis is also needed.

The leveraged buyout of Gibson Greeting Cards by a group of investors headed by William Simon, former secretary of the Treasury, is the classic example of a highly successful LBO. In the early 1980s, Simon's group, Wesray, purchased Gibson from RCA for $81 million. The group put up $1 million and borrowed the remaining $80 million, using the firm's assets as collateral. Within 3 years after Gibson had been acquired, Wesray had publicly sold 50 percent of the company for $87 million. Wesray still owned 50 percent of Gibson and had earned $87 million on a $1 million investment. Although success of this magnitude is not typical, it does point out the potential rewards from the use of LBOs to finance acquisitions. Another successful LBO was the management buyout of Topps Co. (baseball cards, Bazooka bubble gum), which was subsequently taken public, resulting in sizable profits for the buyout group.

Many LBOs did not live up to original expectations. The largest ever was the late-1988, $24.5 billion buyout of RJR Nabisco by KKR, mentioned earlier. In 1991, RJR was taken public and the firm continued to struggle under the heavy debt of the LBO for a few years before improving its debt position and credit rating. Campeau Corporation's buyouts of Allied Stores and Federated Department Stores resulted in its later filing for bankruptcy protection, from which reorganized companies later emerged. In recent years, other highly publicized LBOs have defaulted on the high yield debt incurred to finance the buyout. Although the LBO remains a viable financing technique under the right circumstances, its use is greatly diminished from the frenzied pace of the 1980s. Whereas the LBOs of the 1980s were used, often indiscriminately, for hostile takeovers, today LBOs are most often used to finance management buyouts.

Divestitures

operating unit
A part of a business, such as a plant, division, product line, or subsidiary, that contributes to the actual operations of the firm.

divestiture
The selling of some of a firm's assets for various strategic motives.

Companies often achieve external expansion by acquiring an **operating unit**—plant, division, product line, subsidiary, and so on—of another company. In such a case, the seller generally believes that the value of the firm will be enhanced by converting the unit into cash or some other more productive asset. The selling of some of a firm's assets is called **divestiture**. Unlike business failure, the motive for divestiture is often positive: to generate cash for expansion of other product lines, to get rid of a poorly performing operation, to streamline the corporation, or to restructure the corporation's business consistent with its strategic goals.

Firms divest themselves of operating units by a variety of methods. One involves the *sale of a product line to another firm.* An example, noted earlier, is Paramount's sale of Simon and Schuster to Pearson PLC to free up cash and allow Paramount to better focus its business on global mass consumer markets. Outright sales of operating units can be accomplished on a cash or stock swap basis using the procedures described later in this chapter. A second method that has become popular involves the *sale of the unit to existing management.* This sale is often achieved through the use of a *leveraged buyout (LBO).* Sometimes divestiture is achieved through a **spin-off,** which results in an operating unit becoming an independent company. A spin-off is accomplished by issuing shares in the divested operating unit on a pro rata basis to the parent company's shareholders. Such an action allows the unit to be separated from the corporation and to trade as a separate entity. An example was the decision by AT&T to spin off its Global Information Solutions unit (formerly and now NCR, which produces electronic terminals and computers), to allow AT&T to better focus on its core communications business. Like outright sale, this approach achieves the divestiture objective, although it does not bring additional cash or stock to the parent company. The final and least popular approach to divestiture involves *liquidation of the operating unit's individual assets.*

Regardless of the method used to divest a firm of an unwanted operating unit, the goal typically is to create a more lean and focused operation that will enhance the efficiency as well as the profitability of the enterprise and create maximum value for shareholders. Recent divestitures seem to suggest that many operating units are worth much more to others than to the firm itself. Comparisons of postdivestiture and predivestiture market values have shown that the **breakup value**—the sum of the values of a firm's operating units if each is sold separately—of many firms is significantly greater than their combined value. As a result of market valuations, divestiture often creates value in excess of the cash or stock received in the transaction. Although these outcomes frequently occur, financial theory has been unable to fully and satisfactorily explain them.[6]

spin-off
A form of divestiture in which an operating unit becomes an independent company by issuing shares in it on a pro rata basis to the parent company's shareholders.

breakup value
The value of a firm measured as the sum of the values of its operating units if each is sold separately.

? Review Questions

19–4   What is a *leveraged buyout (LBO)?* What are the three key attributes of an attractive candidate for acquisition using an LBO?

19–5   What is a *divestiture?* What is an *operating unit?* What are four common methods used by firms to divest themselves of operating units? What is *breakup value?*

19.3 Analyzing and Negotiating Mergers

We now turn to the procedures that are used to analyze and negotiate mergers. Initially, we will consider how to value the target company and how to use stock swap transactions to acquire companies. Next, we will look at the merger negoti-

---

6. For an excellent discussion and theoretical explanation of *breakup value,* see Edward M. Miller, "Why the Break-up of Conglomerate Business Enterprises Often Increases Value," *The Journal of Social, Political & Economic Studies* (Fall 1995), pp. 317–341.

ation process. Then, we will review the major advantages and disadvantages of holding companies. Finally, we will discuss international mergers.

Valuing the Target Company

Once the acquiring company isolates a target company that it wishes to acquire, it must estimate the target's value. The value would then be used, along with a proposed financing scheme, to negotiate the transaction—on a friendly or hostile basis. The value of the target would be estimated by using the valuation techniques presented in Chapter 7 and applied to long-term investment decisions in Chapters 8, 9, and 10. Similar capital budgeting techniques would be applied whether the target firm is being acquired for its assets or as a going concern.

Acquisitions of Assets

Occasionally, a firm is acquired not for its income-earning potential but as a collection of assets (generally fixed assets) that the acquiring company needs. The price paid for this type of acquisition depends largely on which assets are being acquired; consideration must also be given to the value of any tax losses. To determine whether the purchase of assets is financially justified, the acquirer must estimate both the costs and benefits of the target assets. This is a capital budgeting problem (see Chapters 8, 9, and 10), because an initial cash outlay is made to acquire assets and, as a result, future cash inflows are expected.

Example ▼ Clark Company, a major manufacturer of electrical transformers, is interested in acquiring certain fixed assets of Noble Company, an industrial electronics company. Noble, which has tax loss carryforwards from losses over the past 5 years, is interested in selling out, but it wishes to sell out entirely, not just get rid of certain fixed assets. A condensed balance sheet for Noble Company follows.

Balance Sheet Noble Company			
Assets		**Liabilities and stockholders' equity**	
Cash	$ 2,000	Total liabilities	$ 80,000
Marketable securities	0	Stockholders' equity	120,000
Accounts receivable	8,000	Total liabilities and	
Inventories	10,000	stockholders' equity	$200,000
Machine A	10,000		
Machine B	30,000		
Machine C	25,000		
Land and buildings	115,000		
Total assets	$200,000		

Clark Company needs only machines B and C and the land and buildings. However, it has made some inquiries and has arranged to sell the accounts receivable, inventories, and machine A for $23,000. Because there is also $2,000 in cash, Clark will get $25,000 for the excess assets. Noble wants $100,000 for the entire company, which means that Clark will have to pay the firm's creditors $80,000 and its owners $20,000. The actual outlay required of Clark after liquidating the unneeded assets will be $75,000 [($80,000 + $20,000) − $25,000]. In other words, to obtain the use of the desired assets (machines B and C and the land and buildings) and the benefits of Noble's tax losses, Clark must pay $75,000. The *after-tax cash inflows* that are expected to result from the new assets and applicable tax losses are $14,000 per year for the next 5 years and $12,000 per year for the following 5 years. The desirability of this asset acquisition can be determined by calculating the net present value of this outlay using Clark Company's 11% cost of capital, as shown in Table 19.2. *Because the net present value of $3,072 is greater than zero, Clark's value should be increased by* ▲ *acquiring Noble Company's assets.*

Acquisitions of Going Concerns

Acquisitions of target companies that are going concerns are best analyzed by using capital budgeting techniques similar to those described for asset acquisitions. The methods of estimating expected cash flows from an acquisition are similar to those used in estimating capital budgeting cash flows. Typically, *pro forma income statements* reflecting the postmerger revenues and costs attributable to the target company are prepared (see Chapter 14). They are then adjusted to reflect the expected cash flows over the relevant time period. Whenever a firm considers acquiring a target company that has different risk behaviors, it should adjust the cost of capital appropriately before applying the appropriate capital budgeting techniques (see Chapter 10).

TABLE 19.2	**Net Present Value of Noble Company's Assets**		
Year(s)	Cash inflows (1)	Present value factor at 11% (2)	Present value [(1) × (2)] (3)
1–5	$14,000	3.696[a]	$51,744
6	12,000	.535[b]	6,420
7	12,000	.482[b]	5,784
8	12,000	.434[b]	5,208
9	12,000	.391[b]	4,692
10	12,000	.352[b]	4,224
		Present value of inflows	$78,072
		Less: Cash outlay required	75,000
		Net present value[c]	$ 3,072

[a]The present value interest factor for an annuity, *PVIFA*, with a 5-year life discounted at 11% obtained from Table A-4.

[b]The present value interest factor, *PVIF*, for $1 discounted at 11% percent for the corresponding year obtained from Table A-3.

[c]Using a financial calculator, the net present value is $3,063.

Example ▼ Square Company, a major media company, is contemplating the acquisition of Circle Company, a small independent film producer that can be purchased for $60,000. Square currently has a high degree of financial leverage, which is reflected in its 13% cost of capital. Because of the low financial leverage of Circle Company, Square estimates that its overall cost of capital will drop to 10% after the acquisition. Because the effect of the less risky capital structure cannot be reflected in the expected cash flows, the postmerger cost of capital (10%) must be used to evaluate the cash flows that are expected from the acquisition. The postmerger cash flows attributable to the target company are forecast over a 30-year time horizon. These estimated cash flows (all inflows) and the resulting net present value of the target company, Circle Company, are shown in Table 19.3.

Because the $2,357 net present value of the target company is greater than zero, the merger is acceptable. Note that, had the effect of the changed capital structure on the cost of capital not been considered, the acquisition would have been found unacceptable, because the net present value *at a 13% cost of capital*
▲ is negative $11,864 (or −$11,868 using a financial calculator).

Stock Swap Transactions

Once the value of the target company is determined, the acquirer must develop a proposed financing package. The simplest, but probably least common, case would be a pure cash purchase. Beyond this extreme case, there are virtually an infinite number of financing packages that use various combinations of cash, debt, preferred stock, and common stock.

stock swap transaction
An acquisition method in which the acquiring firm exchanges its shares for shares of the target company according to a predetermined ratio.

Here we look at the other extreme—**stock swap transactions,** in which the acquisition is paid for using an exchange of common stock. The acquiring firm

TABLE 19.3	**Net Present Value of the Circle Company Acquisition**		
Year(s)	Cash inflows (1)	Present value factor at 10%[a] (2)	Present value [(1) × (2)] (3)
1–10	$ 5,000	6.145	$30,725
11–18	13,000	(8.201 − 6.145)[b]	26,728
19–30	4,000	(9.427 − 8.201)[b]	4,904
		Present value of inflows	$62,357
		Less: Cash purchase price	60,000
		Net present value[c]	$ 2,357

[a]Present value interest factors for annuities, *PVIFA*, obtained from Table A-4.

[b]These factors are found by using a shortcut technique that can be applied to annuities for periods of years beginning at some point in the future. By finding the appropriate interest factor for the present value of an annuity given for the last year of the annuity and subtracting the present value interest factor of an annuity for the year immediately preceding the beginning of the annuity, the appropriate interest factor for the present value of an annuity beginning sometime in the future can be obtained. You can check this shortcut by using the long approach and comparing the results.

[c]Using a financial calculator, the net present value is $2,364.

exchanges its shares for shares of the target company according to a predetermined ratio. The *ratio of exchange* of shares is determined in the merger negotiations. This ratio affects the various financial yardsticks that are used by existing and prospective shareholders to value the merged firm's shares. With the demise of LBOs, the use of stock swaps to finance mergers has grown in popularity during recent years.

Ratio of Exchange

ratio of exchange
The ratio of the amount *paid* per share of the target company to the market price per share of the acquiring firm.

When one firm swaps its stock for the shares of another firm, the firms must determine the number of shares of the acquiring firm to be exchanged for each share of the target firm. The first requirement, of course, is that the acquiring company have sufficient shares available to complete the transaction. Often, a firm's repurchase of shares (discussed in Chapter 13) is necessary to obtain sufficient shares for such a transaction. The acquiring firm generally offers more for each share of the target company than the current market price of its publicly traded shares. The actual **ratio of exchange** is merely the ratio of the amount *paid* per share of the target company to the market price per share of the acquiring firm. It is calculated in this manner because the acquiring firm pays the target firm in stock, which has a value equal to its market price.

Example ▼ Grand Company, a leather products concern, whose stock is currently selling for $80 per share, is interested in acquiring Small Company, a producer of belts. To prepare for the acquisition, Grand has been repurchasing its own shares over the past 3 years. Small's stock is currently selling for $75 per share, but in the merger negotiations, Grand has found it necessary to offer Small $110 per share. Because Grand does not have sufficient financial resources to purchase the firm for cash and it does not wish to raise these funds, Small has agreed to accept Grand's stock in exchange for its shares. As stated, Grand's stock currently sells for $80 per share, and it must pay $110 per share for Small's stock. Therefore, the ratio of exchange is 1.375 ($110 ÷ $80). This means that Grand Company ▲ must exchange 1.375 shares of its stock for each share of Small's stock.

Effect on Earnings Per Share

Although cash flows and value are the primary focus, it is useful to consider the effects of a proposed merger on earnings per share—the accounting returns that are related to cash flows and value (see Chapter 7). Ordinarily, the resulting earnings per share differ from the premerger earnings per share for both the acquiring firm and the target firm. They depend largely on the ratio of exchange and the premerger earnings per share of each firm. It is best to view the initial and long-run effects of the ratio of exchange on earnings per share separately.

Initial Effect   When the ratio of exchange is equal to 1 and both the acquiring firm and the target firm have the *same* premerger earnings per share, the merged firm's earnings per share will initially remain constant. In this rare instance, both the acquiring and target firms would also have equal price/earnings (P/E) ratios. In actuality, the earnings per share of the merged firm are gen-

	TABLE 19.4	**Grand Company's and Small Company's Financial Data**	

Item	Grand Company	Small Company
(1) Earnings available for common stock	$500,000	$100,000
(2) Number of shares of common stock outstanding	125,000	20,000
(3) Earnings per share [(1) ÷ (2)]	$4	$5
(4) Market price per share	$80	$75
(5) Price/earnings (P/E) ratio [(4) ÷ (3)]	20	15

erally above the premerger earnings per share of one firm and below the premerger earnings per share of the other, after the necessary adjustment has been made for the ratio of exchange.

Example ▼ As seen in the preceding example, Grand Company is contemplating acquiring Small Company by swapping 1.375 shares of its stock for each share of Small's stock. The current financial data related to the earnings and market price for each of these companies are given in Table 19.4.

To complete the merger and retire the 20,000 shares of Small Company stock outstanding, Grand will have to issue and (or) use treasury stock totaling 27,500 shares (1.375 × 20,000 shares). Once the merger is completed, Grand will have 152,500 shares of common stock (125,000 + 27,500) outstanding. If the earnings of each of the firms remain constant, the merged company will be expected to have earnings available for the common stockholders of $600,000 ($500,000 + $100,000). The earnings per share of the merged company therefore should equal approximately $3.93 ($600,000 ÷ 152,500 shares).

It would appear at first that Small Company's shareholders have sustained a decrease in per-share earnings from $5 to $3.93, but because each share of Small Company's original stock is equivalent to 1.375 shares of the merged company, the equivalent earnings per share are actually $5.40 ($3.93 × 1.375). In other words, as a result of the merger, Grand Company's original shareholders experience a decrease in earnings per share from $4 to $3.93 to the benefit of Small Company's shareholders, whose earnings per share increase from $5 to $5.40.

▲ These results are summarized in Table 19.5.

The postmerger earnings per share for owners of the acquiring and target companies can be explained by comparing the price/earnings ratio paid by the acquiring company with its initial P/E ratio. This relationship is summarized in Table 19.6. By paying more than its current value per dollar of earnings to acquire each dollar of earnings (P/E paid > P/E of acquiring company), the acquiring firm transfers the claim on a portion of its premerger earnings to the owners of the target firm. Therefore, on a postmerger basis *the target firm's EPS increases, and the acquiring firm's EPS decreases*. Note that this outcome is *almost always* the case, because the acquirer typically pays, on average, a 50 percent premium above the target firm's market price, thereby resulting in the P/E

Hint If the acquiring company were to pay less than its current value per dollar of earnings to acquire each dollar of earnings (P/E paid < P/E of acquiring company), the opposite effects would result.

TABLE 19.5	Summary of the Effects on Earnings Per Share of a Merger Between Grand Company and Small Company at $110 Per Share

	Earnings per share	
Stockholders	Before merger	After merger
Grand Company	$4.00	$3.93[a]
Small Company	5.00	5.40[b]

$$[a]\frac{\$500,000 + \$100,000}{125,000 + (1.375 \times 20,000)} = \$3.93$$

[b]$\$3.93 \times 1.375 = \$5.40$

TABLE 19.6	Effect of Price/Earnings (P/E) Ratios on Earnings Per Share (EPS)

	Effect on EPS	
Relationship between P/E paid and P/E of acquiring company	Acquiring company	Target company
P/E paid > P/E of acquiring company	Decrease	Increase
P/E paid = P/E of acquiring company	Constant	Constant
P/E paid < P/E of acquiring company	Increase	Decrease

paid being much above its own P/E. The P/E ratios associated with the Grand–Small merger demonstrate the effect of the merger on EPS.

Example ▼ Grand Company's P/E ratio is 20, and the P/E ratio paid for Small Company's earnings was 22 ($110 ÷ $5). Because the P/E paid for Small Company was greater than the P/E for Grand Company (22 versus 20), the effect of the merger was to decrease the EPS for original holders of shares in Grand Company (from $4.00 to $3.93) and to increase the effective EPS of original holders of shares in ▲ Small Company (from $5.00 to $5.40).

Long-Run Effect   The long-run effect of a merger on the earnings per share of the merged company depends largely on whether the earnings of the merged firm grow. Often, although a decrease in the per-share earnings of the stock held by the original owners of the acquiring firm is expected initially, the long-run effects of the merger on earnings per share are quite favorable. Because firms generally expect growth in earnings, the key factor enabling the acquiring company to experience higher future EPS than it would have without the merger is that the earnings attributable to the target company's assets grow at a faster rate than those resulting from the acquiring company's premerger assets. An example will clarify this point.

Example ▼ In 2000, Grand Company acquired Small Company by swapping 1.375 shares of its common stock for each share of Small Company. Other key financial data and the effects of this exchange ratio were discussed in preceding examples. The total earnings of Grand Company were expected to grow at an annual rate of 3% without the merger; Small Company's earnings were expected to grow at a 7% annual rate without the merger. The same growth rates are expected to apply to the component earnings streams with the merger.[7] The table in Figure 19.1 below shows the future effects on EPS for Grand Company without and with the proposed Small Company merger, based on these growth rates.

FIGURE 19.1

Future EPS
Future EPS without and with the Grand–Small merger

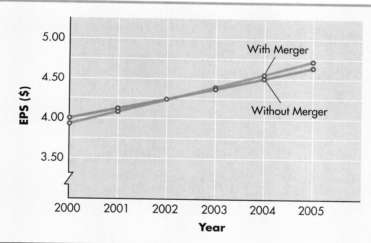

Year	Without Merger		With Merger	
	Total earnigs[a]	Earnings per share[b]	Total earnings[c]	Earnings per share[d]
2000	$500,000	$4.00	$600,000	$3.93
2001	515,000	4.12	622,000	4.08
2002	530,450	4.24	644,940	4.23
2003	546,364	4.37	668,868	4.39
2004	562,755	4.50	693,835	4.55
2005	579,638	4.64	719,893	4.72

[a]Based on a 3% annual growth rate.
[b]Based on 125,000 shares outstanding.
[c]Based on a 3% annual growth in the Grand Company's earnings and a 7% annual growth in the Small Company's earnings.
[d]Based on 152,500 shares outstanding [125,000 shares + (1.375 × 20,000 shares)].

7. Frequently, because of synergy, the combined earnings stream is greater than the sum of the individual earnings streams. This possibility is ignored here.

The table indicates that the earnings per share without the merger will be greater than the EPS with the merger for the years 2000 through 2002. After 2002, however, the EPS will be higher than they would have been without the merger as a result of the faster earnings growth rate of Small Company (7% versus 3%). Although a few years are required for this difference in the growth rate of earnings to pay off, in the future Grand Company will receive an earnings benefit as a result of merging with Small Company at a 1.375 ratio of exchange. The long-run earnings advantage of the merger is clearly depicted in ▲ Figure 19.1.[8]

Effect on Market Price Per Share

ratio of exchange in market price
Indicates the market price per share of the acquiring firm *paid* for each dollar of market price per share of the target firm.

The market price per share does not necessarily remain constant after the acquisition of one firm by another. Adjustments occur in the marketplace in response to changes in expected earnings, the dilution of ownership, changes in risk, and certain other operating and financial changes. By using the ratio of exchange, a **ratio of exchange in market price** can be calculated. It indicates the market price per share of the acquiring firm *paid* for each dollar of market price per share of the target firm. This ratio, the *MPR*, is defined by Equation 19.1:

$$MPR = \frac{MP_{\text{acquiring}} \times RE}{MP_{\text{target}}} \tag{19.1}$$

where

$$
\begin{aligned}
MPR &= \text{market price ratio of exchange} \\
MP_{\text{acquiring}} &= \text{market price per share of the acquiring firm} \\
MP_{\text{target}} &= \text{market price per share of the target firm} \\
RE &= \text{ratio of exchange}
\end{aligned}
$$

E x a m p l e ▼ The market price of Grand Company's stock was $80, and that of Small Company's was $75. The ratio of exchange was 1.375. Substituting these values into Equation 19.1 yields a ratio of exchange in market price of 1.47 [($80 × 1.375) ÷ $75]. This means that $1.47 of the market price of Grand Company is ▲ given in exchange for every $1.00 of the market price of Small Company.

The ratio of exchange in market price is normally greater than 1, which indicates that to acquire a firm, the acquirer must pay a premium above its market price. Even so, the original owners of the acquiring firm may still gain because the merged firm's stock may sell at a price/earnings ratio above the individual premerger ratios. This results from the improved risk and return relationship perceived by shareholders and other investors.

E x a m p l e ▼ The financial data developed earlier for the Grand–Small merger can be used to explain the market price effects of a merger. If the earnings of the merged com-

---

8. To discover properly whether the merger is beneficial, the earnings estimates under each alternative would have to be made over a long period of time, say, 50 years, and then converted to cash flows and discounted at the appropriate rate. The alternative with the higher present value would be preferred. For simplicity, only the basic intuitive view of the long-run effect is presented here.

TABLE 19.7	Postmerger Market Price of Grand Company Using a P/E Ratio of 21

Item	Merged company
(1) Earnings available for common stock	$600,000
(2) Number of shares of common stock outstanding	152,500
(3) Earnings per share [(1) ÷ (2)]	$3.93
(4) Price/earnings (P/E) ratio	21
(5) Expected market price per share [(3) × (4)]	$82.53

pany remain at the premerger levels, and if the stock of the merged company sells at an assumed multiple of 21 times earnings, the values in Table 19.7 can be expected. Although Grand Company's earnings per share decline from $4.00 to $3.93 (see Table 19.5), the market price of its shares will increase from $80.00 to ▲ $82.53 as a result of the merger.

Although the behavior exhibited in this example is not unusual, the financial manager must recognize that only with proper management of the merged enterprise can its market value be improved. If the merged firm cannot achieve sufficiently high earnings in view of its risk, there is no guarantee that its market price will reach the forecast value. Nevertheless, a policy of acquiring firms with low P/Es can produce favorable results for the owners of the acquiring firm. Acquisitions are especially attractive when the acquiring firm's stock price is high, because fewer shares must be exchanged to acquire a given firm.

The Merger Negotiation Process

investment bankers
Financial intermediaries hired by acquirers in mergers to find suitable target companies and assist in negotiations.

Mergers are often handled by **investment bankers**—financial intermediaries hired by acquirers to find suitable target companies and assist in negotiations. Once a target company is selected, the investment banker negotiates with its management or investment banker. Likewise, when management wishes to sell the firm or an operating unit of the firm, it will hire an investment banker to seek out potential buyers.

If attempts to negotiate with the management of the target company break down, the acquiring firm, often with the aid of its investment banker, can make a direct appeal to shareholders by using *tender offers* (as explained below). The investment banker is typically compensated with a fixed fee, a commission tied to the transaction price, or a combination of fees and commissions.

Management Negotiations

To initiate negotiations, the acquiring firm must make an offer either in cash or based on a stock swap with a specified ratio of exchange. The target company then reviews the offer and, in light of alternative offers, accepts or rejects the

Career Key
Accounting personnel will assist in the financial evaluation of potential mergers, acquisitions, and divestitures. They will be a major source of information about the tax effects of the proposed action.

terms presented. A desirable merger candidate usually receives more than a single offer. Normally, certain nonfinancial issues must be resolved relating to the existing management, product-line policies, financing policies, and the independence of the target firm. The key factor, of course, is the per-share price offered in cash or reflected in the ratio of exchange. Sometimes negotiations will break down.

Tender Offers

When negotiations for an acquisition break down, tender offers may then be used to negotiate a "hostile merger" directly with the firm's stockholders. As noted in Chapter 13, a *tender offer* is a formal offer to purchase a given number of shares of a firm's stock at a specified price. The offer is made to all the stockholders at a premium above the market price. Occasionally, the acquirer will make a **two-tier offer** in which the terms offered are more attractive to those who tender shares early. For example, the acquirer offers to pay $25 per share for the first 60 percent of the outstanding shares tendered and only $23 per share for the remaining shares. The stockholders are advised of a tender offer through announcements in financial newspapers or through direct communications from the offering firm. Sometimes a tender offer is made to add pressure to existing merger negotiations. In other cases, the tender offer may be made without warning as an attempt at an abrupt corporate takeover.

two-tier offer
A *tender offer* in which the terms offered are more attractive to those who tender shares early.

Fighting Hostile Takeovers

If the management of a target firm does not favor a merger or considers the price offered in a proposed merger too low, it is likely to take defensive actions to ward off the *hostile takeover*. Such actions are generally developed with the assistance of investment bankers and lawyers who help the firm develop and employ effective **takeover defenses.** There are obvious strategies such as informing stockholders of the alleged damaging effects of a takeover, acquiring another company (discussed earlier in the chapter), or attempting to sue the acquiring firm on antitrust or other grounds. In addition, many other defenses exist (some with colorful names)—white knight, poison pills, greenmail, leveraged recapitalization, golden parachutes, and shark repellents.

The **white knight** strategy involves the target firm finding a more suitable acquirer (the "white knight") and prompting it to compete with the initial hostile acquirer to take over the firm. The basic premise of this strategy is that if being taken over is nearly certain, the target firm ought to attempt to be taken over by the firm that is deemed most acceptable to its management. **Poison pills** typically involve the creation of securities that give their holders certain rights that become effective when a takeover is attempted. The "pill" allows the shareholders to receive special voting rights or securities that make the firm less desirable to the hostile acquirer. **Greenmail** is a strategy by which the firm repurchases through private negotiation a large block of stock at a premium from one or more shareholders to end a hostile takeover attempt by those shareholders. Clearly, greenmail is a form of corporate blackmail by the holders of a large block of shares.

Another hostile takeover defense involves the use of a **leveraged recapitalization,** which is a strategy involving the payment of a large debt-financed cash div-

takeover defenses
Strategies for fighting hostile takeovers.

white knight
A takeover defense in which the target firm finds an acquirer more to its liking than the initial hostile acquirer and prompts the two to compete to take over the firm.

poison pill
A takeover defense in which a firm issues securities that give their holders certain rights that become effective when a takeover is attempted; these rights make the target firm less desirable to a hostile acquirer.

greenmail
A takeover defense under which a target firm repurchases through private negotiation a large block of stock at a premium from one or more shareholders to end a hostile takeover attempt by those shareholders.

leveraged recapitalization
A takeover defense in which the target firm pays a large debt-financed cash dividend, increasing the firm's financial leverage and deterring the takeover attempt.

idend. This strategy significantly increases the firm's financial leverage, thereby deterring the takeover attempt. In addition, as a further deterrent the recapitalization is often structured to increase the equity and control of the existing management. **Golden parachutes** are provisions in the employment contracts of key executives that provide them with sizable compensation if the firm is taken over. Golden parachutes deter hostile takeovers to the extent that the cash outflows required by these contracts are large enough to make the takeover unattractive to the acquirer. Another defense is use of **shark repellents,** which are antitakeover amendments to the corporate charter that constrain the firm's ability to transfer managerial control of the firm as a result of a merger. Although this defense could entrench existing management, many firms have had these amendments ratified by shareholders.

Because takeover defenses tend to insulate management from shareholders, the potential for litigation is great when these strategies are employed. Lawsuits are sometimes filed against management by dissident shareholders. In addition, federal and state governments frequently intervene when a proposed takeover is deemed to be in violation of federal or state law. A number of states have legislation on their books limiting or restricting hostile takeovers of companies domiciled within their boundaries.

golden parachutes
Provisions in the employment contracts of key executives that provide them with sizable compensation if the firm is taken over; deters hostile takeovers to the extent that the cash outflows required are large enough to make the takeover unattractive.

shark repellents
Antitakeover amendments to a corporate charter that constrain the firm's ability to transfer managerial control of the firm as a result of a merger.

Holding Companies

As defined earlier, a *holding company* is a corporation that has voting control of one or more other corporations. The holding company may need to own only a small percentage of the outstanding shares to have this voting control. In the case of companies with a relatively small number of shareholders, as much as 30 to 40 percent of the stock may be required. In the case of firms with a widely dispersed ownership, 10 to 20 percent of the shares may be sufficient to gain voting control. A holding company that wants to obtain voting control of a firm may use direct market purchases or tender offers to acquire needed shares. Although there are relatively few holding companies and they are far less important than mergers, it is helpful to understand their key advantages and disadvantages.

Advantages of Holding Companies

The primary advantage of holding companies is the *leverage effect* that permits the firm to control a large amount of assets with a relatively small dollar investment. In other words, the owners of a holding company can *control* significantly larger amounts of assets than they could *acquire* through mergers.

Example ▼ Carr Company, a holding company, currently holds voting control of two subsidiaries—company X and company Y. The balance sheets for Carr and its two subsidiaries are presented in Table 19.8. It owns approximately 17% ($10 ÷ $60) of company X and 20% ($14 ÷ $70) of company Y. These holdings are sufficient for voting control.

The owners of Carr Company's $12 worth of equity have control over $260 worth of assets (company X's $100 worth and company Y's $160 worth). Thus,

TABLE 19.8	Balance Sheets for Carr Company and Its Subsidiaries		
Assets		Liabilities and stockholders' equity	
Carr Company			
Common stock holdings		Long-term debt	$ 6
Company X	$10	Preferred stock	6
Company Y	14	Common stock equity	12
Total	$24	Total	$24
Company X			
Current assets	$ 30	Current liabilities	$ 15
Fixed assets	70	Long-term debt	25
Total	$100	Common stock equity	60
		Total	$100
Company Y			
Current assets	$ 20	Current liabilities	$ 10
Fixed assets	140	Long-term debt	60
Total	$160	Preferred stock	20
		Common stock equity	70
		Total	$160

the owners' equity represents only about 4.6% ($12 ÷ $260) of the total assets controlled. From the discussions of ratio analysis, leverage, and capital structure in Chapters 4 and 12, you should recognize that this is quite a high degree of leverage. If an individual stockholder or even another holding company owns $3 of Carr Company's stock, which is assumed to be sufficient for its control, it will in actuality control the whole $260 of assets. The investment itself in this case ▲ would represent only 1.15% ($3 ÷ $260) of the assets controlled.

The high leverage obtained through a holding company arrangement greatly magnifies earnings and losses for the holding company. Quite often, a **pyramiding** of holding companies occurs when one holding company controls other holding companies, thereby causing an even greater magnification of earnings and losses. The greater the leverage, the greater the risk involved. The risk-return trade-off is a key consideration in the holding company decision.

pyramiding
An arrangement among holding companies wherein one holding company controls other holding companies, thereby causing an even greater magnification of earnings and losses.

Another commonly cited advantage of holding companies is the *risk protection* resulting from the fact that the failure of one of the companies (such as Y in the preceding example) does not result in the failure of the entire holding company. Because each subsidiary is a separate corporation, the failure of one company should cost the holding company, at maximum, no more than its investment in that subsidiary. Other advantages include the following: (1) certain state *tax benefits* may be realized by each subsidiary in its state of incorporation; (2) *lawsuits or legal actions* against a subsidiary will not threaten the remaining companies;

and (3) it is *generally easy to gain control* of a firm, because stockholder or management approval is not generally necessary.

Disadvantages of Holding Companies

A major disadvantage of holding companies is the *increased risk* resulting from the leverage effect. When general economic conditions are unfavorable, a loss by one subsidiary may be magnified. For example, if subsidiary company X in Table 19.8 experiences a loss, its inability to pay dividends to Carr Company could result in Carr Company's inability to meet its scheduled payments.

Another disadvantage is *double taxation*. Before paying dividends, a subsidiary must pay federal and state taxes on its earnings. Although a 70 percent tax exclusion is allowed on dividends received by one corporation from another, the remaining 30 percent received is taxable. (In the event that the holding company owns between 20 and 80 percent of the stock in a subsidiary, the exclusion is 80 percent; if it owns more than 80 percent of the stock in the subsidiary, 100 percent of the dividends are excluded.) If a subsidiary were part of a merged company, double taxation would *not* exist.

The fact that holding companies are *difficult to analyze* is another disadvantage. Security analysts and investors typically have difficulty understanding holding companies because of their complexity. As a result, these firms tend to sell at low multiples of earnings (P/Es), and the shareholder value of holding companies may suffer.

A final disadvantage of holding companies is the generally *high cost of administration* resulting from maintaining each subsidiary company as a separate entity. A merger, on the other hand, would likely result in certain administrative economies of scale. The need for coordination and communication between the holding company and its subsidiaries may further elevate these costs.

International Mergers

Perhaps in no other area does U.S. financial practice differ more fundamentally from practices in other countries than in the field of mergers. Outside of the United States (and, to a lesser degree, Great Britain), hostile takeovers are virtually nonexistent, and in some countries (such as Japan), takeovers of any kind are uncommon. The emphasis in the United States and Great Britain on shareholder value and reliance on public capital markets for financing is generally inapplicable in continental Europe. This occurs because companies there are generally smaller and other stakeholders, such as employees, bankers, and governments, are accorded greater consideration. The U.S. approach is also a poor fit for Japan and other Asian nations.

Changes in Western Europe

Today, there are signs that Western Europe is moving toward a U.S.-style approach to shareholder value and public capital market financing. Since the final plan for European economic integration was unveiled in 1988, the number, size, and importance of cross-border European mergers have exploded.

Nationally focused companies want to achieve economies of scale in manufacturing, encourage international product development strategies, and develop distribution networks across the continent. They are also driven by the need to compete with U.S. companies, which have been operating on a continentwide basis in Europe for decades.

These larger European-based companies will probably prove to be even more formidable competitors once national barriers are fully removed. Although the vast majority of these cross-border mergers are friendly in nature, a few have been actively resisted by target firm managements. It seems clear that as European companies come to rely more on public capital markets for financing, and as the market for common stock becomes more truly European in character, rather than French or British or German, active markets for European corporate equity will inevitably evolve.

Foreign Takeovers of U.S. Companies

Both European and Japanese companies have been active as acquirers of U.S. companies in recent years. Foreign companies purchased U.S. firms for two major reasons: to gain access to the world's single largest, richest, and least regulated market and to acquire world-class technology at a bargain price. British companies have been historically the most active acquirers of U.S. firms. For example, Britain's Pearson PLC acquired Simon and Schuster for $4.6 billion in 1998. In the late 1980s, Japanese corporations surged to prominence with a series of very large acquisitions, including two in the entertainment industry: Sony's purchase of Columbia Pictures and Matsushita's acquisition of MCA. More recently, German firms have become especially active acquirers of U.S. companies as the cost of producing export goods in Germany has become prohibitively expensive. (German workers now have the world's highest wages and shortest workweek.) For example, Germany's Deutsche Bank AG purchased the U.S. bank Bankers Trust Corp. for $10.1 billion in 1998. It seems inevitable that in the years ahead, foreign companies will continue to acquire U.S. firms even as U.S. companies continue to seek attractive acquisitions abroad.

? Review Questions

19–6   Describe the procedures that are typically used by an acquirer to value a target company, whether it is being acquired for its assets or as a going concern.

19–7   What is the *ratio of exchange?* Is it based on the current market prices of the shares of the acquiring and target firms? Why may a long-run view of the merged firm's earnings per share change a merger decision?

19–8   What role do *investment bankers* often play in the merger negotiation process? What is a *tender offer?* When and how is it used?

19–9   Briefly describe each of the following *takeover defenses* against a hostile merger: (a) white knight, (b) poison pill, (c) greenmail, (d) leveraged recapitalization, (e) golden parachutes, and (f) shark repellents.

19-10 What are the key advantages and disadvantages cited for holding companies? What is *pyramiding* and what are its consequences?

19-11 Discuss the differences in merger practices between U.S. companies and companies in other countries. What changes are occurring in international merger activity, particularly in Western Europe and Japan?

19.4 Business Failure Fundamentals

A business failure is an unfortunate circumstance. Although the majority of firms that fail do so within the first year or two of life, other firms grow, mature, and fail much later. The failure of a business can be viewed in a number of ways and can result from one or more causes.

Types of Business Failure

A firm may fail because its *returns are negative or low.* A firm that consistently reports operating losses will probably experience a decline in market value. If the firm fails to earn a return that is greater than its cost of capital, it can be viewed as having failed. Negative or low returns, unless remedied, are likely to result eventually in one of the following more serious types of failure.

A second type of failure, **technical insolvency,** occurs when a firm is unable to pay its liabilities as they come due. When a firm is technically insolvent, its assets are still greater than its liabilities, but it is confronted with a *liquidity crisis.* If some of its assets can be converted into cash within a reasonable period, the company may be able to escape complete failure. If not, the result is the third and most serious type of failure, **bankruptcy.** Bankruptcy occurs when a firm's liabilities exceed the fair market value of its assets. A bankrupt firm has a *negative* stockholders' equity.[9] This means that the claims of creditors cannot be satisfied unless the firm's assets can be liquidated for more than their book value. Although bankruptcy is an obvious form of failure, *the courts treat technical insolvency and bankruptcy in the same way.* They are both considered to indicate the financial failure of the firm.

Major Causes of Business Failure

The primary cause of business failure is *mismanagement,* which accounts for more than 50 percent of all cases. Numerous specific managerial faults can cause the firm to fail. Overexpansion, poor financial actions, an ineffective sales force, and high production costs can all singly or in combination cause failure. For example, *poor financial actions* include bad capital budgeting decisions (based on unrealistic sales and cost forecasts, failure to identify all

technical insolvency
Business failure that occurs when a firm is unable to pay its liabilities as they come due.

bankruptcy
Business failure that occurs when a firm's liabilities exceed the fair market value of its assets.

---

9. Because on a balance sheet the firm's assets equal the sum of its liabilities and stockholders' equity, the only way a firm that has more liabilities than assets can balance its balance sheet is to have a *negative* stockholders' equity.

relevant cash flows, or failure to assess risk properly), poor financial evaluation of the firm's strategic plans prior to making financial commitments, inadequate or nonexistent cash flow planning, and failure to control receivables and inventories. Because all major corporate decisions are eventually measured in terms of dollars, the financial manager may play a key role in avoiding or causing a business failure. It is his or her duty to monitor the firm's financial pulse.

Economic activity—especially economic downturns—can contribute to the failure of a firm.[10] If the economy goes into a recession, sales may decrease abruptly, leaving the firm with high fixed costs and insufficient revenues to cover them. In addition, rapid rises in interest rates just prior to a recession can further contribute to cash flow problems and make it more difficult for the firm to obtain and maintain needed financing. During the early 1990s, a number of major business failures such as those of Olympia and York (real estate), America West Airlines, and Southmark Corporation (convenience stores) resulted from overexpansion and the recessionary economy.

A final cause of business failure is *corporate maturity*. Firms, like individuals, do not have infinite lives. Like a product, a firm goes through the stages of birth, growth, maturity, and eventual decline. The firm's management should attempt to prolong the growth stage through research, new products, and mergers. Once the firm has matured and has begun to decline, it should seek to be acquired by another firm or liquidate before it fails. Effective management planning should help the firm to postpone decline and ultimate failure.

Voluntary Settlements

voluntary settlement
An arrangement between a technically insolvent or bankrupt firm and its creditors enabling it to bypass many of the costs involved in legal bankruptcy proceedings.

When a firm becomes technically insolvent or bankrupt, it may arrange with its creditors a **voluntary settlement,** which enables it to bypass many of the costs involved in legal bankruptcy proceedings. The settlement is normally initiated by the debtor firm, because such an arrangement may enable it to continue to exist or to be liquidated in a manner that gives the owners the greatest chance of recovering part of their investment. The debtor arranges a meeting between itself and all its creditors. At the meeting, a committee of creditors is selected to analyze the debtor's situation and recommend a plan of action. The recommendations of the committee are discussed with both the debtor and the creditors, and a plan for sustaining or liquidating the firm is drawn up.

Voluntary Settlement to Sustain the Firm

extension
An arrangement whereby the firm's creditors receive payment in full, although not immediately.

Normally, the rationale for sustaining a firm is that it is reasonable to believe that the firm's recovery is feasible. By sustaining the firm, the creditor can continue to receive business from it. A number of strategies are commonly used. An **extension**

---

10. The success of some firms runs countercyclical to economic activity, and other firms are unaffected by economic activity. For example, the auto repair business is likely to grow during a recession, because people are less likely to buy new cars and therefore need more repairs on their unwarranted older cars. The sale of boats and other luxury items may decline during a recession, whereas sales of staple items such as electricity are likely to be unaffected. In terms of beta—the measure of nondiversifiable risk developed in Chapter 6—a negative-beta stock would be associated with a firm whose behavior is generally countercyclical to economic activity.

is an arrangement whereby the firm's creditors receive payment in full, although not immediately. Normally, when creditors grant an extension, they require the firm to make cash payments for purchases until all past debts have been paid. A second arrangement, called **composition**, is a pro rata cash settlement of creditor claims. Instead of receiving full payment of their claims, creditors receive only a partial payment. A uniform percentage of each dollar owed is paid in satisfaction of each creditor's claim. A third arrangement is **creditor control.** In this case, the creditor committee may decide that the only circumstance in which maintaining the firm is feasible is if the operating management is replaced. The committee may then take control of the firm and operate it until all claims have been settled. Sometimes, a plan involving some combination of extension, composition, and creditor control will result. An example of this would be a settlement whereby the debtor agrees to pay a total of 75 cents on the dollar in three annual installments of 25 cents on the dollar, and the creditors agree to sell additional merchandise to the firm on 30-day terms if the existing management is replaced by new management that is acceptable to them.

composition
A pro rata cash settlement of creditor claims by the debtor firm; a uniform percentage of each dollar owed is paid.

creditor control
An arrangement in which the creditor committee replaces the firm's operating management and operates the firm until all claims have been settled.

Voluntary Settlement Resulting in Liquidation

After the situation of the firm has been investigated by the creditor committee, the only acceptable course of action may be liquidation of the firm. Liquidation can be carried out in two ways—privately or through the legal procedures provided by bankruptcy law. If the debtor firm is willing to accept liquidation, legal procedures may not be required. Generally, the avoidance of litigation enables the creditors to obtain *quicker* and *higher* settlements. However, all the creditors must agree to a private liquidation for it to be feasible.

The objective of the voluntary liquidation process is to recover as much per dollar owed as possible. Under voluntary liquidation, common stockholders (the firm's true owners) cannot receive any funds until the claims of all other parties have been satisfied. A common procedure is to have a meeting of the creditors at which they make an **assignment** by passing the power to liquidate the firm's assets to an adjustment bureau, a trade association, or a third party, which is designated the *assignee*. The assignee's job is to liquidate the assets, obtaining the best price possible. The assignee is sometimes referred to as the *trustee*, because it is entrusted with the title to the company's assets and the responsibility to liquidate them efficiently. Once the trustee has liquidated the assets, it distributes the recovered funds to the creditors and owners (if any funds remain for the owners). The final action in a private liquidation is for the creditors to sign a release attesting to the satisfactory settlement of their claims.

assignment
A voluntary liquidation procedure by which a firm's creditors pass the power to liquidate the firm's assets to an adjustment bureau, a trade association, or a third party, which is designated the *assignee*.

❓ Review Questions

19–12 What are the three types of business failure? What is the difference between *technical insolvency* and *bankruptcy?* What are the major causes of business failure?

19–13 Define an *extension* and a *composition,* and explain how they might be combined to form a voluntary settlement plan to sustain the firm. How is a voluntary settlement resulting in liquidation handled?

19.5 Reorganization and Liquidation in Bankruptcy

If a voluntary settlement for a failed firm cannot be agreed upon, the firm can be forced into bankruptcy by its creditors. As a result of bankruptcy proceedings, the firm may be either reorganized or liquidated.

Bankruptcy Legislation

Bankruptcy in the legal sense occurs when the firm cannot pay its bills or when its liabilities exceed the fair market value of its assets. In either case, a firm may be declared legally bankrupt. However, creditors generally attempt to avoid forcing a firm into bankruptcy if it appears to have opportunities for future success.

The governing bankruptcy legislation in the United States today is the **Bankruptcy Reform Act of 1978,** which significantly modified earlier bankruptcy legislation. This law contains eight odd-numbered (1 through 15) and one even-numbered (12) chapters. A number of these chapters would apply in the instance of failure; the two key ones are Chapters 7 and 11. **Chapter 7** of the Bankruptcy Reform Act of 1978 details the procedures to be followed when liquidating a failed firm. This chapter typically comes into play once it has been determined that a fair, equitable, and feasible basis for the reorganization of a failed firm does not exist (although a firm may of its own accord choose not to reorganize and may instead go directly into liquidation). **Chapter 11** outlines the procedures for reorganizing a failed (or failing) firm, whether its petition is filed voluntarily or involuntarily. If a workable plan for reorganization cannot be developed, the firm will be liquidated under Chapter 7.

Reorganization in Bankruptcy (Chapter 11)

There are two basic types of reorganization petitions—voluntary and involuntary. Any firm that is not a municipal or financial institution can file a petition for **voluntary reorganization** on its own behalf.[11] **Involuntary reorganization** is initiated by an outside party, usually a creditor. An involuntary petition against a firm can be filed if one of three conditions is met:

1. The firm has past-due debts of $5,000 or more.
2. Three or more creditors can prove that they have aggregate unpaid claims of $5,000 against the firm. If the firm has fewer than 12 creditors, any creditor that is owed more than $5,000 can file the petition.
3. The firm is *insolvent,* which means that (a) it is not paying its debts as they come due, (b) within the preceding 120 days a custodian (a third party) was

Bankruptcy Reform Act of 1978
The current governing bankruptcy legislation in the United States.

Chapter 7
The portion of the *Bankruptcy Reform Act of 1978* that details the procedures to be followed when liquidating a failed firm.

Chapter 11
The portion of the *Bankruptcy Reform Act of 1978* that outlines the procedures for reorganizing a failed (or failing) firm, whether its petition is filed voluntarily or involuntarily.

voluntary reorganization
A petition filed by a failed firm on its own behalf for reorganizing its structure and paying its creditors.

involuntary reorganization
A petition initiated by an outside party, usually a creditor, for the reorganization and payment of creditors of a failed firm.

---

11. Firms sometimes file a voluntary petition to obtain temporary legal protection from creditors or from prolonged litigation. Once they have straightened out their financial or legal affairs—prior to further reorganization or liquidation actions—they will have the petition dismissed. Although such actions are not the intent of the bankruptcy law, difficulty in enforcing the law has allowed this abuse to occur.

Hint   Some firms, particularly those in the airline industry, have used the bankruptcy laws to prevent technical insolvency. The courts have allowed them to nullify labor contracts on the basis that to force the firm to continue to conform to the contract would cause the firm to eventually become insolvent.

debtor in possession (DIP)
The term for a firm that files a reorganization petition under Chapter 11 and then develops, if feasible, a reorganization plan.

appointed or took possession of the debtor's property, or (c) the fair market value of the firm's assets is less than the stated value of its liabilities.

Procedures

A reorganization petition under Chapter 11 must be filed in a federal bankruptcy court. Upon the filing of this petition, the filing firm becomes the **debtor in possession (DIP)** of the assets. If creditors object to the filing firm being the debtor in possession, they can ask the judge to appoint a trustee. After reviewing the firm's situation, the debtor in possession submits a plan of reorganization and a disclosure statement summarizing the plan to the court. A hearing is held to determine whether the plan is *fair, equitable,* and *feasible* and whether the disclosure statement contains adequate information. The court's approval or disapproval is based on its evaluation of the plan in light of these standards. A plan is considered *fair and equitable* if it *maintains the priorities* of the contractual claims of the creditors, preferred stockholders, and common stockholders. The court must also find the reorganization plan *feasible,* meaning that it must be *workable.* The reorganized corporation must have sufficient working capital, sufficient funds to cover fixed charges, sufficient credit prospects, and sufficient ability to retire or refund debts as proposed by the plan.

Once approved, the plan and the disclosure statement are given to the firm's creditors and shareholders for their acceptance. Under the Bankruptcy Reform Act, creditors and owners are separated into groups with similar types of claims. In the case of creditor groups, approval of the plan is required by holders of at least two-thirds of the dollar amount of claims as well as a numerical majority of creditors. In the case of ownership groups (preferred and common stockholders), two-thirds of the shares in each group must approve the reorganization plan for it to be accepted. Once accepted and confirmed by the court, the plan is put into effect as soon as possible.

Role of the Debtor in Possession (DIP)

Because reorganization activities are largely in the hands of the debtor in possession (DIP), it is useful to understand the DIP's responsibilities. The DIP's first responsibility is the valuation of the firm to determine whether reorganization is appropriate. To do this, the DIP must estimate both the *liquidation value* of the business and its value as a *going concern.* If the firm's value as a going concern is less than its liquidation value, the DIP will recommend liquidation. If the opposite is found to be true, the DIP will recommend reorganization and a plan of reorganization must be drawn up.

recapitalization
The reorganization procedure under which a failed firm's debts are generally exchanged for equity, or the maturities of existing debts are extended.

The key portion of the reorganization plan generally concerns the firm's capital structure. Because most firms' financial difficulties result from high fixed charges, the company's capital structure is generally *recapitalized* to reduce these charges. Under **recapitalization,** debts are generally exchanged for equity, or the maturities of existing debts are extended. When recapitalizing the firm, the DIP seeks to build a mix of debt and equity that will allow the firm to meet its debts and provide a reasonable level of earnings for its owners.

Once the revised capital structure has been determined, the DIP must establish a plan for exchanging outstanding obligations for new securities. The guiding principle is to *observe priorities*. Senior claims (those with higher legal priority) must be satisfied before junior claims (those with lower legal priority). To comply with this principle, senior suppliers of capital must receive a claim on new capital equal to their previous claim. The common stockholders are the last to receive any new securities. (It is not unusual for them to receive nothing.) Security holders do not necessarily have to receive the same type of security they held before; often they receive a combination of securities. Once the debtor in possession has determined the new capital structure and distribution of capital, it will submit the reorganization plan and disclosure statement to the court as described.

In Practice

J. Peterman Dusts Itself Off

It started out as a quirky company selling long cowboy-style dusters and other pricey, retro-style clothing and accessories through a catalog featuring unique and exotic item descriptions. J. Peterman Co. developed a loyal following and eventually even found itself satirized on Seinfeld.

But the company, founded in 1987 by John Henry Peterman, petered out in January 1999 when it filed bankruptcy under Chapter 11. At the time of the filing, which gave the retail mail order company time to reorganize its finances, J. Peterman had $40 million in liabilities and $35 million in assets. "J. Peterman will not be closing," said founder Peterman, who promised that the company's retail stores, which were posting solid sales, would remain open. The bankruptcy court allowed Peterman to continue operating through February 12 after it obtained a loan from a major lender, Heller Financial of Chicago, to pay its employees and shipping expenses.

Peterman attributed his firm's failure to several factors, "any one of which, though not desirable, would not have put the company out of business," he said. Catalog sales slowed despite expanded mailings, and a new home-furnishings catalog flopped. Peterman blamed the Asian financial upheaval and subsequent fall 1998 stock market plunge. In addition, a slowdown in plans to open retail stores and catalog outlets left the company with excess inventory in 1998. Heller turned down requests for more credit, and Peterman's efforts to interest other investors in providing capital to save the firm also failed. Although some analysts criticized Peterman for adding retail operations, he countered, "Yes, the catalog business would have gone on. But we had reached a plateau and took a chance on growing."

Peterman's vision was right, however. In the March 1999 liquidation auction, Paul Harris Stores Inc. of Indianapolis bought J. Peterman for $10 million, rescuing the catalog operation and most of its stores.

Liquidation in Bankruptcy (Chapter 7)

The liquidation of a bankrupt firm usually occurs once the bankruptcy court has determined that reorganization is not feasible. A petition for reorganization must normally be filed by the managers or creditors of the bankrupt firm. If no petition is filed, if a petition is filed and denied, or if the reorganization plan is denied, the firm must be liquidated.

Procedures

When a firm is adjudged bankrupt, the judge may appoint a *trustee* to perform the many routine duties required in administering the bankruptcy. The trustee takes charge of the property of the bankrupt firm and protects the interest of its creditors. A meeting of creditors must be held between 20 and 40 days after the bankruptcy judgment. At this meeting, the creditors are made aware of the prospects for the liquidation. The trustee is given the responsibility to liquidate the firm, keep records, examine creditors' claims, disburse money, furnish information as required, and make final reports on the liquidation. In essence, the trustee is responsible for the liquidation of the firm. Occasionally, the court will call subsequent creditor meetings, but only a final meeting for closing the bankruptcy is required.

Priority of Claims

secured creditors
Creditors who have specific assets pledged as collateral and in liquidation of the failed firm receive proceeds from the sale of those assets.

unsecured, or general, creditors
Creditors who have a general claim against all the firm's assets other than those specifically pledged as collateral.

It is the trustee's responsibility to liquidate all the firm's assets and to distribute the proceeds to the holders of *provable claims*. The courts have established certain procedures for determining the provability of claims. The priority of claims, which is specified in Chapter 7 of the Bankruptcy Reform Act, must be maintained by the trustee when distributing the funds from liquidation. Any **secured creditors** have specific assets pledged as collateral and, in liquidation, receive proceeds from the sale of those assets. If these proceeds are inadequate to meet their claim, the secured creditors become **unsecured, or general, creditors** for the unrecovered amount, because specific collateral no longer exists. These and all other unsecured creditors will divide up, on a pro rata basis, any funds remaining after all prior claims have been satisfied. If the proceeds from the sale of secured assets are in excess of the claims against them, the excess funds become available to meet claims of unsecured creditors. The complete order of priority of claims is listed in Table 19.9. In spite of the priorities listed in items 1 through 7, secured creditors have first claim on proceeds from the sale of their collateral. The claims of unsecured creditors, including the unpaid claims of secured creditors, are satisfied next, and, finally, the claims of preferred and common stockholders. An example of the application of these priorities is included on the text's web site at **www.awlonline.com/gitman.**

Final Accounting

After the trustee has liquidated all the bankrupt firm's assets and distributed the proceeds to satisfy all provable claims in the appropriate order of priority, he or she makes a final accounting to the bankruptcy court and creditors. Once the court approves the final accounting, the liquidation is complete.

TABLE 19.9	Order of Priority of Claims in Liquidation of a Failed Firm

1. The expenses of administering the bankruptcy proceedings.

2. Any unpaid interim expenses incurred in the ordinary course of business between filing the bankruptcy petition and the entry of an Order for Relief in an involuntary proceeding. (This step is *not* applicable in a voluntary bankruptcy.)

3. Wages of not more than $2,000 per worker that have been earned by workers in the 90-day period immediately preceding the commencement of bankruptcy proceedings.

4. Unpaid employee benefit plan contributions that were to be paid in the 180-day period preceding the filing of bankruptcy or the termination of business, whichever occurred first. For any employee, the sum of this claim plus eligible unpaid wages (item 3) cannot exceed $2,000.

5. Claims of farmers or fishermen in a grain-storage or fish-storage facility, not to exceed $2,000 for each producer.

6. Unsecured customer deposits, not to exceed $900 each, resulting from purchasing or leasing a good or service from the failed firm.

7. Taxes legally due and owed by the bankrupt firm to the federal government, state government, or any other governmental subdivision.

8. Claims of secured creditors, who receive the proceeds from the sale of collateral held, regardless of the preceding priorities. If the proceeds from the liquidation of the collateral are insufficient to satisfy the secured creditors' claims, the secured creditors become unsecured creditors for the unpaid amount.

9. Claims of unsecured creditors. The claims of unsecured, or general, creditors and unsatisfied portions of secured creditors' claims (item 8) are all treated equally.

10. Preferred stockholders, who receive an amount up to the par, or stated, value of their preferred stock.

11. Common stockholders, who receive any remaining funds, which are distributed on an equal per-share basis. If different classes of common stock are outstanding, priorities may exist.

? Review Questions

19–14 What is the concern of Chapter 11 of the Bankruptcy Reform Act of 1978? How is the *debtor in possession (DIP)* involved in (1) the valuation of the firm, (2) the recapitalization of the firm, and (3) the exchange of obligations using the priority rule?

19–15 What is the concern of Chapter 7 of the Bankruptcy Reform Act of 1978? Under which conditions is a firm liquidated in bankruptcy? Describe the procedures (including the role of the *trustee*) involved in liquidating the bankrupt firm.

19–16 In which order would the following claims be settled when distributing the proceeds from liquidating a bankrupt firm: (a) claims of preferred stockholders; (b) claims of secured creditors; (c) expenses of administering the bankruptcy; (d) claims of common stockholders; (e) claims of unsecured, or general, creditors; (f) taxes legally due; (g) unsecured deposits of customers; (h) certain eligible wages; (i) unpaid employee benefit plan contributions; (j) unpaid interim expenses incurred between the time of filing and the entry of an Order for Relief; and (**k**) claims of farmers or fishermen in a grain-storage or fish-storage facility?

SUMMARY

LG1 **Understand merger fundamentals, including basic terminology, motives for merging, and types of mergers.** Mergers result from the combining of firms. Typically, the acquiring company pursues and attempts to merge with the target company, on either a friendly or a hostile basis. Mergers are undertaken either for strategic reasons to achieve economies of scale or for financial reasons to restructure the firm to improve its cash flow. The overriding goal of merging is maximization of owners' wealth (share price). Other specific merger motives include growth or diversification, synergy, fund raising, increased managerial skill or technology, tax considerations, increased ownership liquidity, and defense against takeover. The four basic types of mergers are horizontal (the merger of two firms in the same line of business); vertical (acquisition of a supplier or customer); congeneric (acquisition of a firm in the same general industry but neither in the same business nor a supplier or customer); and conglomerate (merger between unrelated businesses).

LG2 **Describe the objectives and procedures used in leveraged buyouts (LBOs) and divestitures.** Leveraged buyouts (LBOs) involve use of a large amount of debt to purchase a firm. LBOs are generally used to finance management buyouts. Divestiture involves the sale of a firm's assets, typically an operating unit, to another firm or existing management; the spin-off of assets into an independent company; or the liquidation of assets. Motives for divestiture include cash generation and corporate restructuring.

LG3 **Demonstrate the procedures used to value the target company and discuss the effect of stock swap transactions on earnings per share.** The value of a target company can be estimated by applying capital budgeting techniques to the relevant cash flows. All proposed mergers with positive net present values are considered acceptable. In a stock swap transaction in which an acquisition is paid for by an exchange of common stock, a ratio of exchange must be established to measure the amount paid per share of the target company relative to the per-share market price of the acquiring firm. The resulting relationship between the price/earnings (P/E) ratio paid by the acquiring firm and its initial P/E affects the merged firm's earnings per share (EPS) and market price. If the P/E paid is greater than the P/E of the acquiring company, the EPS of the acquiring company decreases and the EPS of the target company increases.

LG4 **Discuss the merger negotiation process, the role of holding companies, and international mergers.** Investment bankers are commonly hired by the acquirer to find a suitable target company and assist in negotiations. A merger can be negotiated with the target firm's management or, in the case of a hostile merger, directly with the firm's shareholders by using tender offers. When the management of the target firm does not favor the merger, it can employ various takeover defenses—a white knight, poison pills, greenmail, leveraged recapitalization, golden parachutes, and shark repellents. A holding company can be created by one firm gaining control of other companies, often by owning as little as 10 to 20 percent of their stock. The chief advantages of holding companies are the leverage effect, risk protection, tax benefits, protection against lawsuits, and the ease of gaining control of a subsidiary. Disadvantages include increased risk due to the magnification of losses, double taxation, difficulty of ⬛⬛⬛⬛⬛⬛⬛⬛ cost of administration. In rec⬛⬛⬛⬛ companies in Western Europ⬛⬛⬛⬛ the U.S.-style approach to sh⬛⬛⬛ public capital market financi⬛⬛⬛ Japanese companies have be⬛⬛⬛ of U.S. companies.

Understand the types and major causes of business failure and the use of voluntary settlements to sustain or liquidate the failed firm. A firm may fail because it has negative or low returns, because it is technically insolvent, or because it is bankrupt. The major causes of business failure are mismanagement, downturns in economic activity, and corporate maturity. Voluntary settlements are initiated by the debtor and can result in sustaining the firm through an extension, a composition, creditor control of the firm, or a combination of these strategies. If creditors do not agree to a plan to sustain a firm, they may recommend voluntary liquidation, which bypasses many of the legal requirements and costs of bankruptcy proceedings.

 Explain bankruptcy legislation and the procedures involved in reorganizing or liquidating

a bankrupt firm. A failed firm that cannot or does not want to arrange a voluntary settlement can voluntarily or involuntarily file in federal bankruptcy court for reorganization under Chapter 11 or for liquidation under Chapter 7 of the Bankruptcy Reform Act of 1978. Under Chapter 11, the judge will appoint the debtor in possession, who with court supervision develops, if feasible, a reorganization plan. A firm that cannot be reorganized under Chapter 11 of the bankruptcy law or does not petition for reorganization is liquidated under Chapter 7. The responsibility for liquidation is placed in the hands of a court-appointed trustee, whose duties include the liquidation of assets, the distribution of the proceeds, and making a final accounting. Liquidation procedures follow a priority of claims for distribution of the proceeds from the sale of assets.

SELF-TEST PROBLEMS   (Solutions in Appendix B)

 ST 19–1 Cash acquisition decision Luxe Foods is contemplating acquisition of Valley Canning Company for a cash price of $180,000. Luxe currently has high financial leverage and therefore has a cost of capital of 14%. As a result of acquiring Valley Canning, which is financed entirely with equity, the firm expects its financial leverage to be reduced and its cost of capital therefore to drop to 11%. The acquisition of Valley Canning is expected to increase Luxe's cash inflows by $20,000 per year for the first 3 years and by $30,000 per year for the following 12 years.

a. Determine whether the proposed cash acquisition is desirable. Explain your answer.

b. If the firm's financial leverage would actually remain unchanged as a result of the proposed acquisition, would this alter your recommendation in **a**? Support your answer with numerical data.

ST 19–2 Expected EPS—Merger decision At the end of 2000, Lake Industries had 80,000 shares of common stock outstanding and had earnings available for common of $160,000. Butler Company, at the end of 2000, had 10,000 shares of common stock outstanding and had earned $20,000 for common shareholders. Lake's earnings are expected to grow at an annual rate of 5%, and Butler's growth rate in earnings should be 10% per year.

a. Calculate earnings per share (EPS) for Lake Industries for each of the next 5 years, assuming that there is no merger.

b. Calculate the next 5 years' earnings per share (EPS) for Lake if it acquires Butler at a *ratio of exchange* of 1.1.

c. Compare your findings in **a** and **b**, and explain why the merger looks attractive when viewed over the long run.

INTERMEDIATE

19–1   Tax effects of acquisition   Connors Shoe Company is contemplating the acquisition of Salinas Boots, a firm that has shown large operating tax losses over the past few years. As a result of the acquisition, Connors believes that the total pretax profits of the merger will not change from their present level for 15 years. The tax loss carryforward of Salinas is $800,000, and Connors projects annual earnings before taxes to be $280,000 per year for each of the next 15 years. These earnings are assumed to fall within the annual limit legally allowed for application of the tax loss carryforward resulting from the proposed merger (see footnote 4 on page 783). The firm is in the 40% tax bracket.

  a. If Connors does not make the acquisition, what are the company's tax liability and earnings after taxes each year over the next 15 years?

  b. If the acquisition is made, what are the company's tax liability and earnings after taxes each year over the next 15 years?

  c. If Salinas can be acquired for $350,000 in cash, should Connors make the acquisition, based on tax considerations? (Ignore present value.)

INTERMEDIATE

19–2   Tax effects of acquisition   Trapani Tool Company is evaluating the acquisition of Sussman Casting. Sussman has a tax loss carryforward of $1.8 million. Trapani can purchase Sussman for $2.1 million. It can sell the assets for $1.6 million—their book value. Trapani expects earnings before taxes in the 5 years after the merger to be as shown in the following table.

Year	Earnings before taxes
1	$150,000
2	400,000
3	450,000
4	600,000
5	600,000

The expected earnings given are assumed to fall within the annual limit that is legally allowed for application of the tax loss carryforward resulting from the proposed merger (see footnote 4 on page 783). Trapani is in the 40% tax bracket.

  a. Calculate the firm's tax payments and earnings after taxes for each of the next 5 years *without* the merger.

b. Calculate the firm's tax payments and earnings after taxes for each of the next 5 years *with* the merger.

c. What are the total benefits associated with the tax losses from the merger? (Ignore present value.)

d. Discuss whether you would recommend the proposed merger. Support your decision with figures.

CHALLENGE

19–3 **Tax benefits and price** Hahn Textiles has a tax loss carryforward of $800,000. Two firms are interested in acquiring Hahn for the tax loss advantage. Reilly Investment Group has expected earnings before taxes of $200,000 per year for each of the next 7 years and a cost of capital of 15%. Webster Industries has expected earnings before taxes for the next 7 years as shown in the following table.

Webster Industries	
Year	Earnings before taxes
1	$ 80,000
2	120,000
3	200,000
4	300,000
5	400,000
6	400,000
7	500,000

Both Reilly's and Webster's expected earnings are assumed to fall within the annual limit legally allowed for application of the tax loss carryforward resulting from the proposed merger (see footnote 4 on page 783). Webster has a cost of capital of 15%. Both firms are subject to 40% tax rates on ordinary income.

a. What is the tax advantage of the merger each year for Reilly?

b. What is the tax advantage of the merger each year for Webster?

c. What is the maximum cash price each interested firm would be willing to pay for Hahn Textiles? (*Hint:* Calculate the present value of the tax advantages.)

d. Use your answers in **a** through **c** to explain why a target company can have different values to different potential acquiring firms.

CHALLENGE

19–4 **Asset acquisition decision** Zarin Printing Company is considering the acquisition of Freiman Press at a cash price of $60,000. Freiman Press has liabilities of $90,000. Freiman has a large press that Zarin needs; the remaining assets would be sold to net $65,000. As a result of acquiring the press, Zarin would experience an increase in cash inflow of $20,000 per year over the next 10 years. The firm has a 14% cost of capital.

a. What is the effective or net cost of the large press?
b. If this is the only way Zarin can obtain the large press, should the firm go ahead with the merger? Explain your answer.
c. If the firm could purchase a press that would provide slightly better quality and $26,000 annual cash inflow for 10 years for a price of $120,000, which alternative would you recommend? Explain your answer.

  19–5 Cash acquisition decision   Benson Oil is being considered for acquisition by Dodd Oil. The combination, Dodd believes, would increase its cash inflows by $25,000 for each of the next 5 years and $50,000 for each of the following 5 years. Benson has high financial leverage, and Dodd can expect its cost of capital to increase from 12% to 15% if the merger is undertaken. The cash price of Benson is $125,000.
a. Would you recommend the merger?
b. Would you recommend the merger if Dodd could use the $125,000 to purchase equipment returning cash inflows of $40,000 per year for each of the next 10 years?
c. If the cost of capital does not change with the merger, would your decision in **b** be different? Explain.

 19–6 Ratio of exchange and EPS   Marla's Cafe is attempting to acquire the Victory Club. Certain financial data on these corporations are summarized in the following table.

Item	Marla's Cafe	Victory Club
Earnings available for common stock	$20,000	$8,000
Number of shares of common stock outstanding	20,000	4,000
Market price per share	$12	$24

Marla's Cafe has sufficient authorized but unissued shares to carry out the proposed merger.
a. If the *ratio of exchange* is 1.8, what will be the earnings per share (EPS) based on the original shares of each firm?
b. Repeat **a** if the *ratio of exchange* is 2.0.
c. Repeat **a** if the *ratio of exchange* is 2.2.
d. Discuss the principle illustrated by your answers to **a** through **c**.

 19–7 EPS and merger terms   Cleveland Corporation is interested in acquiring Lewis Tool Company by swapping 0.4 share of its stock for each share of Lewis stock. Certain financial data on these companies are given in the following table.

Item	Cleveland Corporation	Lewis Tool
Earnings available for common stock	$200,000	$50,000
Number of shares of common stock outstanding	50,000	20,000
Earnings per share (EPS)	$4.00	$2.50
Market price per share	$50.00	$15.00
Price/earnings (P/E) ratio	12.5	6

Cleveland has sufficient authorized but unissued shares to carry out the proposed merger.

a. How many new shares of stock will Cleveland have to issue to make the proposed merger?

b. If the earnings for each firm remain unchanged, what will the postmerger earnings per share be?

c. How much, effectively, has been earned on behalf of each of the original shares of Lewis stock?

d. How much, effectively, has been earned on behalf of each of the original shares of Cleveland Corporation's stock?

INTERMEDIATE **19–8 Ratio of exchange**   Calculate the *ratio of exchange* (1) of shares and (2) in market price for each of the cases shown in the following table. What does each ratio signify? Explain.

	Current market price per share		
Case	Acquiring company	Target company	Price per share offered
A	$50	$25	$ 30.00
B	80	80	100.00
C	40	60	70.00
D	50	10	12.50
E	25	20	25.00

CHALLENGE **19–9 Expected EPS—Merger decision**   Graham & Sons wishes to evaluate a proposed merger into the RCN Group. Graham had 2000 earnings of $200,000, has 100,000 shares of common stock outstanding, and expects earnings to grow at an annual rate of 7%. RCN had 2000 earnings of $800,000, has 200,000 shares of common stock outstanding, and expects its earnings to grow at 3% per year.

a. Calculate the expected earnings per share (EPS) for Graham & Sons for each of the next 5 years *without* the merger.

d. Use your finding in **c** to determine how much, if any, the *total market value* of Rome Industries will change as a result of acquiring Procras Corporation.

e. Determine how much each claimant will receive if Procras Corporation is liquidated under the terms given.

f. How much, if any, will Rome Industries recover of its $1.9 million balance due from Procras Corporation as a result of liquidation of Procras?

g. Compare your findings in **d** and **f**, and make a recommendation for Rome Industries with regard to its best action—acquisition of Procras or its liquidation.

h. Which alternative would the shareholders of Procras Corporation prefer? Why?

WEB EXERCISE

GOTO web site www.dnbeconomics.com. Click on BUSINESS FAILURE RECORD.

1. How many businesses have failed in the most recent year reported?
2. Is that more or less than the previous year?
3. What is the failure rate per 10,000 listed concerns?

GOTO web site www.moeb.uscourts.gov. Click TABLE OF CONTENTS. Click STATISTICS.

4. Which year had the greatest number of bankruptcy filings?
5. Is the trend increasing or decreasing?

Keep clicking the MORE STATISTICS button at the bottom of the screen until you come to a chart that is titled "Comparison of Chapter 13 and Chapter 7."

6. Under which Chapter is there a greater number of filings?

GOTO web site www.abiworld.org. Click on STATISTICS.

7. Which state has the most bankruptcies per household? (*Hint:* Find the state that has the rank of 1.)

Click ANNUAL FILINGS US, 1980–xxxx. (It's the first on the list of Annual Filings.)

8. Which year had the most businesses filing bankruptcy? How many?
9. Which year had the fewest businesses filing bankruptcy? How many?

International Managerial Finance

LEARNING GOALS

LG1 Understand the major factors influencing the financial operations of multinational companies (MNCs).

LG2 Describe the key differences between purely domestic and international financial statements—particularly consolidation, translation of individual accounts, and international profits.

LG3 Discuss exchange rate risk and political risk, and explain how MNCs manage them.

LG4 Describe foreign direct investment, investment cash flows and decisions, the factors that influence MNCs' capital structure, and the international debt and equity instruments that are available to MNCs.

LG5 Demonstrate use of the Eurocurrency market in short-term borrowing and investing (lending) and the basics of cash, credit, and inventory management in international operations.

LG6 Discuss the growth of and special factors relating to international mergers and joint ventures.

20.1 The Multinational Company and Its Environment

multinational companies (MNCs)
Firms that have international assets and operations in foreign markets and draw part of their total revenue and profits from such markets.

In recent years, as world markets have become significantly more interdependent, international finance has become an increasingly important element in the management of **multinational companies (MNCs).** These firms, based anywhere in the world, have international assets and operations in foreign markets and draw part of their total revenue and profits from such markets. The principles of managerial finance presented in this text are applicable to the management of MNCs. However, certain factors unique to the international setting tend to com-

"Goodbye—Let Us Know When You Get There"

In the year 1271, at the age of 17, Marco Polo left Venice, Italy. Traveling by ship across the Mediterranean and then by camel across Asia, he reached Cathay—China— more than three years later. (The first junior year abroad?) Able to speak four languages and having much knowledge of the world from his travels, Polo was warmly received. By the time he returned home 24 years later, Polo had logged about 15,000 miles. Today, it is not uncommon for businessmen and businesswomen to travel that distance in a little over a day. Modern transportation and communication systems have been like steroids (without the risks) in promoting the growth of global business opportunities. This chapter will demonstrate how the principles of managerial finance presented in this book can be applied in the international setting.

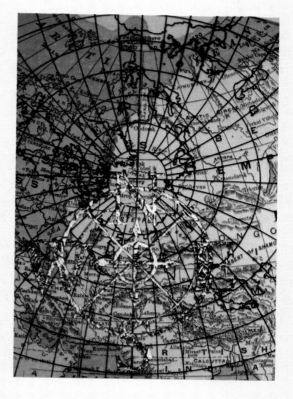

Hint One of the reasons that firms have operations in foreign markets is the portfolio concept that was discussed in Chapter 6. Just as it is not wise for the individual investor to put all of his or her investment into the stock of one firm, it is not wise for a firm to invest in only one market. By having operations in many markets, firms can smooth out some of the cyclical changes that occur in each market.

plicate the financial management of multinational companies. A simple comparison between a domestic U.S. firm (firm A) and a U.S.-based MNC (firm B), as illustrated in Table 20.1, indicates the influence of some of the international factors on MNCs' operations.

In the present international environment, multinationals face a variety of laws and restrictions when operating in different nation-states. The legal and economic complexities existing in this environment are significantly different from those a domestic firm would face. Here we take a brief look at the newly emerging trading blocs in North America and Western Europe, legal forms of business organization, taxation of MNCs, and financial markets.

TABLE 20.1   International Factors and Their Influence on MNCs' Operations

Factor	Firm A (Domestic)	Firm B (MNC)
Foreign ownership	All assets owned by domestic entities	Portions of equity of foreign investments owned by foreign partners, thus affecting foreign decision making and profits
Multinational capital markets	All debt and equity structures based on the domestic capital market	Opportunities and challenges arise from the existence of different capital markets where debt and equity can be issued
Multinational accounting	All consolidation of financial statements based on one currency	The existence of different currencies and of specific translation rules influences the consolidation of financial statements into one currency
Foreign exchange risks	All operations in one currency	Fluctuations in foreign exchange markets can affect foreign revenues and profits as well as the overall value of the firm

Emerging Trading Blocs: NAFTA, the European Union, and Mercosur

During the early 1990s, three important trading blocs emerged, centered in the Americas and Western Europe. Chile, Mexico, and several other Latin American countries began to adopt market-oriented economic policies in the late 1980s, forging very close financial and economic ties with the United States and with each other. In 1988, Canada and the United States negotiated essentially unrestricted trade between their countries, and this free trade zone was extended to include Mexico in late 1992 when the **North American Free Trade Agreement** (**NAFTA**) was signed by the presidents of the United States and Mexico and the prime minister of Canada. Eventually, the agreement will probably include Chile and other countries. NAFTA was, after much debate, ratified by the U.S. Congress in November 1993. This trade pact simply mirrors underlying economic reality—Canada is already the United States' largest trading partner, and Mexico is the third largest (after Japan) U.S. export market.

The **European Union**, or **EU**, has been in existence since 1956. It has a current membership of 15 nations. With a total population estimated at more than 350 million (compared to the U.S. population of about 270.5 million) and an overall gross national income paralleling that of the United States, the EU is a significant global economic force. Due to a series of major economic, monetary, financial, and legal provisions set forth by the member countries during the 1980s, the countries of Western Europe opened a new era of free trade within the union when intraregional tariff barriers fell at the end of 1992. This transformation is commonly called the **European Open Market.** Although the EU has managed to reach agreement on most of these provisions, debates continue on certain

North American Free Trade Agreement (NAFTA)
The treaty establishing free trade and open markets between Canada, Mexico, and the United States.

European Union (EU)
A significant economic force currently made up of 15 nations that permit free trade within the union.

European Open Market
The transformation of the European Union into a *single* market at year-end 1992.

other aspects (some key), including those related to automobile production and imports, monetary union, taxes, and workers' rights. As a result of the Maastricht Treaty of 1991, 11 of the 15 EU nations adopted a single currency, the **Euro,** as a continentwide medium of exchange beginning January 2, 1999. Currently, the Euro is being used for large financial transactions, but not yet as a currency among consumers. By the year 2002, the national currencies of all 11 countries participating in **monetary union** will disappear, to be completely replaced by the Euro.

At the same time that the European Union is struggling to implement monetary union (which also involved creating a new European Central Bank), the EU must also deal with a wave of new applicants from eastern Europe and the Mediterranean region. Whatever its final shape, the new community of Europe will offer both challenges and opportunities to a variety of players, including multinational firms. MNCs, especially those based in the United States, will face heightened levels of competition when operating inside the EU. As more of the existing restrictions and regulations are eliminated, for instance, U.S. multinationals will have to face other MNCs, some from within the EU itself.

The third major trading bloc that arose during the 1990s is the Mercosur Group of countries in South America. Beginning in 1991, the nations of Brazil, Argentina, Paraguay, and Uruguay began removing tariffs and other barriers to intraregional trade. The second stage of Mercosur's development began at the end of 1994, and involved the development of a customs union to impose a common tariff on external trade while enforcing uniform and lower tariffs on intragroup trade. To date, Mercosur has been even more successful than its founders had imagined. Its long-term importance will likely depend on whether the U.S. Congress overcomes its reluctance to extend NAFTA throughout Latin America. In any case, the Mercosur countries represent well over half of total Latin American GDP, and thus will loom large in the plans of any MNC wishing to access the growth markets of this region.

U.S. companies can benefit from the formation of Mercosur and the single European market, but only if they are prepared. They must offer a desirable mix of products to a collection of varied consumers and be ready to take advantage of a variety of currencies as well as financial markets and instruments (such as the Euro-equities discussed later in this chapter). They must staff their operations with the appropriate combination of local and foreign personnel and, when necessary, enter into joint ventures and strategic alliances.

General Agreement on Tariffs and Trade (GATT)

Although it may seem that the world is splitting into a handful of trading blocs, this is less of a danger than it may appear to be, because many international treaties are in force that guarantee relatively open access to at least the largest economies. The most important such treaty is the **General Agreement on Tariffs and Trade (GATT)**. In 1994, Congress ratified the most recent version of this treaty, which has governed world trade throughout most of the post-war era. The current agreement extends free trading rules to broad areas of economic activity—such as agriculture, financial services, and intellectual property rights—that had not previously been covered by international treaty, and which were

Euro
A single currency used by 11 of the 15 EU nations, as of 1/2/99.

monetary union
The eventual melding of the national currencies of the EU nations into one currency, the Euro, by the year 2002.

General Agreement on Tariffs and Trade (GATT)
A treaty that has governed world trade throughout most of the post-war era; it extends free trading rules to broad areas of economic activity and is policed by the *World Trade Organization (WTO)*.

thus effectively off-limits to foreign competition. The 1994 GATT treaty also established a new international body, the *World Trade Organization (WTO),* to police world trading practices and to mediate disputes between member countries. The WTO began operating in January 1995, and seems to be functioning effectively, but as of May 1999 one important nation—the People's Republic of China—remained a nonmember. Until China's status is resolved, there is unlikely to be true stability in world trading patterns, especially because of the stunning collapse of several East Asian economies that began in July 1997. To date, China has escaped the worst aspects of this regional crisis and has resisted the temptation to devalue its currency to maintain its price-competitiveness in Western markets. However, the long-term economic prognosis for China and for this formerly dynamic region of the world is unclear.

Legal Forms of Business

In many countries outside the United States, operating a foreign business as a subsidiary or affiliate can take two forms, both similar to the U.S. corporation. In German-speaking nations the two forms are the *Aktiengesellschaft* (A.G.) or the *Gesellschaft mit beschrankter Haftung* (GmbH). In many other countries the similar forms are a *Société Anonyme* (S.A.) or a *Société à Responsibilité Limitée* (S.A.R.L.). The A.G. and the S.A. are the most common forms, but the GmbH and the S.A.R.L. require fewer formalities for formation and operation.

Although establishing a business in a form such as the S.A. can involve most of the provisions that govern a U.S.-based corporation, to operate in many foreign countries, it is often essential to enter into joint-venture business agreements with private investors or with government-based agencies of the host country. A **joint venture** is a partnership under which the participants have contractually agreed to contribute specified amounts of money and expertise in exchange for stated proportions of ownership and profit. Joint ventures are common in most of the less-developed nations.

The governments of numerous countries, such as Brazil, Colombia, Mexico, and Venezuela in Latin America as well as Indonesia, Malaysia, the Philippines, and Thailand in East Asia, have in recent years instituted new laws and regulations governing MNCs. The basic rule introduced by most of these nations requires that the majority ownership of MNCs' joint-venture projects be held by domestically based investors. In other regions of the world, MNCs, especially those based in the United States and Japan, will face new challenges and opportunities, particularly in terms of ownership requirements and mergers.

The existence of joint-venture laws and restrictions has implications for the operation of foreign-based subsidiaries. First, majority foreign ownership may result in a substantial degree of management and control by host-country participants; this in turn can influence day-to-day operations to the detriment of the managerial policies and procedures that are normally pursued by MNCs. Next, foreign ownership may result in disagreements among the partners as to the exact distribution of profits and the portion to be allocated for reinvestment. Moreover, operating in foreign countries, especially on a joint-venture basis, can involve problems regarding the remittance of profits. In the past, the governments of Argentina, Brazil, Nigeria, and Thailand, among

joint venture
A partnership under which the participants have contractually agreed to contribute specified amounts of money and expertise in exchange for stated proportions of ownership and profit.

Career Key

The *marketing* department might decide that the best way to enter a new international market is to enter into a joint venture with a firm that understands and has access to this new market. Cultural nuances and distribution systems would probably be better understood by a firm already operating in that international market.

others, have imposed ceilings not only on the repatriation (return) of capital by MNCs, but also on profit remittances by these firms back to the parent companies. These governments usually cite the shortage of foreign exchange as the motivating factor. Finally, from a "positive" point of view, it can be argued that to operate in many of the less-developed countries, MNCs would benefit from joint-venture agreements, given the potential risks stemming from political instability in the host countries. This issue will be addressed in detail in subsequent discussions.

Taxes

Multinational companies, unlike domestic firms, have financial obligations in foreign countries. One of their basic responsibilities is international taxation—a complex issue because national governments follow a variety of tax policies. In general, from the point of view of a U.S.-based MNC, several factors must be taken into account.

Tax Rates and Taxable Income

First, the *level* of foreign taxes needs to be examined. Among the major industrial countries, corporate tax rates do not vary too widely. Many less industrialized nations maintain relatively moderate rates, partly as an incentive for attracting foreign capital. Certain countries—in particular, the Bahamas, Switzerland, Liechtenstein, the Cayman Islands, and Bermuda—are known for their "low" tax levels. These nations typically have no withholding taxes on *intra-MNC dividends*.

Next, there is a question as to the definition of *taxable income*. Some countries tax profits as received on a cash basis, whereas others tax profits earned on an accrual basis. Differences can also exist in treatments of noncash charges, such as depreciation, amortization, and depletion. Finally, the existence of tax agreements between the United States and other governments can influence not only the total tax bill of the parent MNC, but also its international operations and financial activities.

Tax Rules

Different home countries apply varying tax rates and rules to the global earnings of their own multinationals. Moreover, tax rules are subject to frequent modifications. In the United States, for instance, the Tax Reform Act of 1986 resulted in certain changes affecting the taxation of U.S.-based MNCs. Special provisions apply to tax deferrals by MNCs on foreign income; operations set up in U.S. possessions, such as the U.S. Virgin Islands, Guam, and American Samoa; capital gains from the sale of stock in a foreign corporation; and withholding taxes. Furthermore, MNCs (both U.S. and foreign) can be subject to national as well as local taxes. As an example, a number of individual state governments in the United States have in recent years introduced new measures—in the form of special **unitary tax laws**—that tax the multinationals on a percentage of their *total* worldwide income rather than on their earnings arising within the jurisdiction of each respective government. Obviously, these laws can make a big difference in a multinational's tax bill. (In response to unitary tax laws, MNCs have already

unitary tax laws
Laws in some U.S. states that tax multinationals (both U.S. and foreign) on a percentage of their *total* worldwide income rather than the usual taxation of the MNCs' earnings arising within their jurisdiction.

pressured a number of state governments into abolishing the laws. In addition, some MNCs have relocated their investments away from those states that continue to apply such laws.)[1]

As a general practice, the U.S. government claims jurisdiction over *all* the income of an MNC, wherever earned. (Special rules apply to foreign corporations conducting business in the United States.) However, it may be possible for a multinational company to take foreign income taxes as a direct credit against its U.S. tax liabilities. The following example illustrates one way of accomplishing this objective.

Example ▼ American Enterprises, a U.S.-based MNC that manufactures heavy machinery, has a foreign subsidiary that earns $100,000 before local taxes. All of the after-tax funds are available to the parent in the form of dividends. The applicable taxes consist of a 35% foreign income tax rate, a foreign dividend withholding tax rate of 10%, and a U.S. tax rate of 34%.

Subsidiary income before local taxes	$100,000
Foreign income tax at 35%	− 35,000
Dividend available to be declared	$ 65,000
Foreign dividend withholding tax at 10%	− 6,500
MNC's receipt of dividends	$ 58,500

Using the so-called *grossing up procedure,* the MNC will add the full before-tax subsidiary income to its total taxable income. Next, the U.S. tax liability on the grossed-up income is calculated. Finally, the related taxes paid in the foreign country are applied as a credit against the additional U.S. tax liability:

Additional MNC income		$100,000
U.S. tax liability at 34%	$34,000	
Total foreign taxes paid to be used as a credit ($35,000 + $6,500)	−41,500	−41,500
U.S. taxes due		0
Net funds available to the parent MNC		$ 58,500

Because the U.S. tax liability is less than the total taxes paid to the foreign government, *no additional U.S. taxes are due* on the income from the foreign subsidiary. In our example, if tax credits had not been allowed, then "double taxation" by the two authorities, as shown in what follows, would have resulted in a substantial drop in the overall net funds available to the parent MNC:

Subsidiary income before local taxes	$ 100,000
Foreign income tax at 35%	−35,000
Dividend available to be declared	$ 65,000
Foreign dividend withholding tax at 10%	−6,500
MNC's receipt of dividends	$ 58,500
U.S. tax liability at 34%	−19,890
Net funds available to the parent MNC	$ 38,610

---

1. For updated details on various countries' tax laws, consult relevant publications of international accounting firms.

The preceding example clearly demonstrates that the existence of bilateral tax treaties and the subsequent application of tax credits can significantly enhance the overall net funds available to MNCs from their worldwide earnings. Consequently, in an increasingly complex and competitive international financial environment, international taxation is one of the variables that multinational corporations should fully utilize to their advantage.

Financial Markets

Euromarket
The international financial market that provides for borrowing and lending currencies outside their country of origin.

During the last two decades the **Euromarket**—which provides for borrowing and lending currencies outside their country of origin—has grown rapidly. The Euromarket provides multinational companies with an "external" opportunity to borrow or lend funds with the additional feature of less government regulation.

Growth of the Euromarket

The Euromarket has grown so large for several reasons. First, beginning in the early 1960s, the Russians wanted to maintain their dollar earnings outside the legal jurisdiction of the United States, mainly because of the Cold War. Second, the consistently large U.S. balance of payments deficits helped to "scatter" dollars around the world. Third, the existence of specific regulations and controls on dollar deposits in the United States, including interest rate ceilings imposed by the government, helped to send such deposits to places outside the United States.

These and other factors have combined and contributed to the creation of an "external" capital market. Its size cannot be accurately determined, mainly because of its lack of regulation and control. Several sources that periodically estimate its size are the Bank for International Settlements (BIS), Morgan Guaranty Trust, the World Bank, and the Organization for Economic Cooperation and Development (OECD). The latest available estimates put the overall size of the Euromarket at over $4.0 trillion *net* international lending.

offshore centers
Certain cities or states (including London, Singapore, Bahrain, Nassau, Hong Kong, and Luxembourg) that have achieved prominence as major centers for Euromarket business.

One aspect of the Euromarket is the so-called **offshore centers.** Certain cities or states around the world—including London, Singapore, Bahrain, Nassau, Hong Kong, and Luxembourg—are considered major offshore centers for Euromarket business. The availability of communication and transportation facilities, along with the importance of language, costs, time zones, taxes, and local banking regulations, are among the main reasons for the prominence of these centers.

In recent years, a variety of new financial instruments have appeared in the international financial markets. One is interest rate and currency swaps. Another is various combinations of forward and options contracts on different currencies. A third is new types of bonds and notes—along with an international version of U.S. commercial paper—with flexible characteristics in terms of currency, maturity, and interest rate. More details will be provided in subsequent discussions.

Major Participants

The Euromarket is still dominated by the U.S. dollar. However, activities in other major currencies, including the Deutsche mark, Swiss franc, Japanese yen, British pound sterling, French franc, and, increasingly, the Euro, have in recent years grown much faster than those denominated in the U.S. currency. Similarly, although U.S. banks and other financial institutions continue to play a significant role in the global markets, financial giants from Japan and Europe have become major participants in Euromarkets. At the end of 1997, for example, six of the top ten largest banks in the world as measured in terms of total assets were based in Japan—though several huge mergers between U.S. banks in 1998 helped reestablish U.S. prominence in world banking.

Following the oil price increases by the Organization of Petroleum Exporting Countries (OPEC) in 1973–1974 and 1979–1980, massive amounts of dollars were placed in various Euromarket financial centers. International banks, in turn, began lending to different groups of borrowers. At the end of 1994, for example, a group of Latin American countries had total borrowings outstanding of about $437 billion. Also, many of the top corporations in the "Tiger economies" of East Asia had huge amounts of foreign-currency–denominated bank debt outstanding when these countries slid into financial crisis in the summer of 1997. Although developing countries have become a major borrowing group in recent years, the industrialized nations also continue to borrow actively in international markets. Included in the latter group's borrowings are the funds obtained by multinational companies. The multinationals use the Euromarket to raise additional funds as well as to invest excess cash. Both Eurocurrency and Eurobond markets are extensively used by MNCs.

? Review Questions

20–1 What are the three important international trading blocs? What is the *European Union* and what is its single new unit of currency? What is *GATT?*

20–2 What is a *joint venture?* Why is it often essential to use this arrangement? What effect do joint-venture laws and restrictions have on the operation of foreign-based subsidiaries?

20–3 From the point of view of a U.S.-based MNC, what key tax factors need to be considered? What are *unitary tax laws?*

20–4 Discuss the major reasons for the growth of the Euromarket. What is an *offshore center?* Name the major participants in the Euromarket.

20.2 Financial Statements

Career Key

Accounting personnel will have to be familiar with how to treat the foreign operations within their U.S. accounting system. They will also have to understand the difference between domestic and international financial statements.

Several features differentiate domestically oriented financial statements and internationally based reports. Among these are the issues of consolidation, translation of individual accounts, and overall reporting of international profits.

Consolidation

At the present time, U.S. tax rules require the consolidation of financial statements of subsidiaries according to the percentage of ownership by the parent company. Table 20.2 illustrates this point. As indicated, the regulations range

TABLE 20.2	U.S. Rules for Consolidation of Financial Statements

Beneficial ownership by parent in subsidiary	Consolidation for financial reporting purposes
0–19%	Dividends as received
20–49%	Pro rata inclusions of profits and losses
50–100%	Full consolidation[a]

[a]Consolidation may be avoided in the case of some majority-owned foreign operations if the parent can convince its auditors that it does not have control of the subsidiaries or if there are substantial restrictions on the repatriation of cash.

Source: Rita M. Rodriguez and E. Eugene Carter, *International Financial Management,* 3rd ed. (Englewood Cliffs, NJ: Prentice Hall, 1984), p. 492.

from a one-line income-item reporting of dividends to a pro rata inclusion of profits and losses to a full disclosure in the balance sheet and income statement.

Translation of Individual Accounts

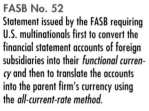

FASB No. 52
Statement issued by the FASB requiring U.S. multinationals first to convert the financial statement accounts of foreign subsidiaries into their *functional currency* and then to translate the accounts into the parent firm's currency using the *all-current-rate method.*

functional currency
The currency of the host country in which a subsidiary primarily generates and expends cash and in which its accounts are maintained.

Unlike domestic items in financial statements, international items require translation back into U.S. dollars. Since December 1982, all financial statements of U.S. multinationals have had to conform to Statement No. 52 issued by the Financial Accounting Standards Board (FASB). The basic rules of FASB No. 52 are given in Figure 20.1.

Under **FASB No. 52,** the *current rate method* is implemented in a two-step process. First, each subsidiary's balance sheet and income statement are *measured* in terms of their functional currency by using generally accepted accounting principles (GAAP). That is, foreign currency elements are translated by each subsidiary into the **functional currency**—the currency of the host country in which a subsidiary primarily generates and expends cash and in which its

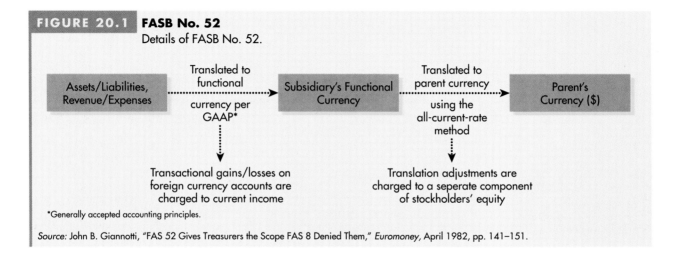

FIGURE 20.1 **FASB No. 52**
Details of FASB No. 52.

Assets/Liabilities, Revenue/Expenses → Translated to functional currency per GAAP* → Subsidiary's Functional Currency → Translated to parent currency using the all-current-rate method → Parent's Currency ($)

Transactional gains/losses on foreign currency accounts are charged to current income

Translation adjustments are charged to a seperate component of stockholders' equity

*Generally accepted accounting principles.

Source: John B. Giannotti, "FAS 52 Gives Treasurers the Scope FAS 8 Denied Them," *Euromoney,* April 1982, pp. 141–151.

accounts are maintained before financial statements are submitted to the parent for consolidation.

In the second step, the functional currency–denominated financial statements of the foreign subsidiary are translated into the parent's currency. This is done using the **all-current-rate method,** which requires the translation of all balance sheet items at the closing rate and all income statement items at average rates.

Each of these steps can result in certain gains or losses. The first step can lead to transaction (cash) gains or losses. Whether realized or not, these gains or losses are charged directly to current income. The completion of the second step can result in translation (accounting) adjustments, which are excluded from current income. Instead, they are disclosed and charged to a separate component of stockholders' equity.

all-current-rate method
The method by which the *functional currency–denominated* financial statements of an MNC's subsidiary are translated into the parent company's currency.

International Profits

Before January 1976, the practice for most U.S. multinationals was to utilize a special account called the *reserve account* to show "smooth" international profits. Excess international profits due to favorable exchange fluctuations were deposited in this account. Withdrawals were made during periods of high losses stemming from unfavorable exchange movements. The overall result was to display a smooth pattern in an MNC's international profits.

Between 1976 and 1982, however, FASB No. 8 required that both transaction gains or losses and translation adjustments be included in net income, with separate disclosure of only the aggregate foreign exchange gain or loss. This requirement caused highly visible swings in the reported net earnings of U.S. multinationals. Since the issuance of FASB No. 52, only certain transactional gains or losses are reflected in the income statement.

? Review Question

20–5 State the rules for consolidation of foreign subsidiaries. Under *FASB No. 52,* what are the translation rules for financial statement accounts?

20.3 Risk

The concept of risk clearly applies to international investments as well as purely domestic ones. However, MNCs must take into account additional factors including both exchange rate and political risks.

Exchange Rate Risks

exchange rate risk
The risk caused by varying exchange rates between two currencies.

Because multinational companies operate in many different foreign markets, portions of these firms' revenues and costs are based on foreign currencies. To understand the **exchange rate risk** caused by varying exchange rates between two currencies, we examine the relationships that exist among various currencies, the causes of exchange rate changes, and the impact of currency fluctuations.

Relationships Among Currencies

Since the mid-1970s, the major currencies of the world have had a *floating*—as opposed to *fixed*—relationship with respect to the U.S. dollar and to one another. Among the currencies regarded as being major (or "hard") currencies are the British pound sterling (£), the Swiss franc (Sf), the Deutsche mark (DM), the French franc (Ff), the Japanese yen (¥), the Canadian dollar (C$), and, of course, the U.S. dollar (US$). The new Euro does not yet circulate as a currency among consumers in European countries, but it is increasingly being used for financial transactions—particularly debt security issues.

> **foreign exchange rate**
> The value of two currencies with respect to each other.

The value of two currencies with respect to each other, or their **foreign exchange rate**, is expressed as follows:

$$US\$1.00 = Sf\ 1.4175$$
$$Sf\ 1.00 = US\$0.7055$$

Since the U.S. dollar has served as the principal currency of international finance for over 50 years, the usual exchange rate quotation in international markets is given as Sf 1.4175/US$, where the unit of account is the Swiss franc and the unit of currency being priced is one U.S. dollar. In this case, the dollar is the currency that is actually being priced. Expressing the exchange rate as US$0.7055/Sf would indicate a dollar price for the Swiss franc.

> **floating relationship**
> The fluctuating relationship of the values of two currencies with respect to each other.

> **fixed (or semifixed) relationship**
> The constant (or relatively constant) relationship of a currency to one of the major currencies, a combination (basket) of major currencies, or some type of international foreign exchange standard.

For the major currencies, the existence of a **floating relationship** means that the value of any two currencies with respect to each other is allowed to fluctuate on a daily basis. On the other hand, many of the nonmajor currencies of the world try to maintain a **fixed (or semifixed) relationship** with respect to one of the major currencies, a combination of major currencies, or some type of international foreign exchange standard.

On any given day, the relationship between any two of the major currencies will contain two sets of figures. One reflects the **spot exchange rate**—the rate on that day. The other indicates the **forward exchange rate**—the rate at some specified future date. The foreign exchange rates given in Figure 20.2 illustrate these concepts. For instance, the figure shows that on Wednesday, February 3, 1999, the spot rate for the Swiss franc was US$0.7055/Sf (or Sf 1.4175/US$, as usually stated), and the forward (future) rate was US$0.7075/Sf (Sf 1.4135/US$) for 30-day delivery. In other words, on February 3, 1999, one could execute a contract to take delivery of Swiss francs in 30 days at a dollar price of US$0.7075/Sf. Forward rates are also available for 90-day and 180-day contracts. For all such contracts, the agreements and signatures are completed on, say, February 3, 1999, but the actual exchange of dollars and Swiss francs between buyers and sellers will take place on the future date (say, 30 days later).

> **spot exchange rate**
> The rate of exchange between two currencies on any given day.

> **forward exchange rate**
> The rate of exchange between two currencies at some specified future date.

Figure 20.2 also illustrates the differences between floating and fixed currencies. All the major currencies previously mentioned have spot and forward rates with respect to the U.S. dollar. Moreover, a comparison of the exchange rates prevailing on Wednesday, February 3, 1999, versus those on Tuesday, February 2, 1999, indicates that the floating major currencies (currencies such as the

FIGURE 20.2

Currency Trading
Spot and forward exchange rate quotations.

CURRENCY TRADING

EXCHANGE RATES
Wednesday, February 3, 1999

The New York foreign exchange mid-range rates below apply to trading among banks in amounts of $1 million and more, as quoted at 4 p.m. Eastern time by Telerate Inc. and other sources. Retail transactions provide fewer units of foreign currency per dollar. Rates for the 11 Euro currency countries are derived from the latest dollar-euro rate using the exchange ratios set 1/1/99.

Country	U.S. $ equiv. Wed	U.S. $ equiv. Tue	Currency per U.S. $ Wed	Currency per U.S. $ Tue
Argentina (Peso)	**1.0005**	**1.0002**	**.9995**	**.9998**
Australia (Dollar)	.6412	.6376	1.5596	1.5684
Austria (Schilling)	**.08215**	**.08241**	**12.173**	**12.134**
Bahrain (Dinar)	2.6525	2.6525	.3770	.3770
Belgium (Franc)	**.02802**	**.02811**	**35.686**	**35.573**
Brazil (Real)	.5587	.5747	1.7900	1.7400
Britain (Pound)	1.6353	1.6389	.6115	.6102
1-month forward	1.6342	1.6377	.6119	.6106
3-months forward	1.6325	1.6361	.6126	.6112
6-months forward	1.6311	1.6348	.6131	.6117
Canada (Dollar)	.6616	.6602	1.5115	1.5148
1-month forward	.6615	.6581	1.5117	1.5195
3-months forward	.6615	.6581	1.5117	1.5195
6-months forward	.6617	.6603	1.5113	1.5145
Chile (Peso)	.002038	.002030	490.75	492.55
China (Renminbi)	.1208	.1208	8.2777	8.2779
Colombia (Peso)	.0006344	.0006324	1576.22	1581.27
Czech. Rep. (Koruna)				
Commercial rate	.03040	.03021	32.892	33.099
Denmark (Krone)	.1521	.1522	6.5725	6.5720
Ecuador (Sucre)				
Floating rate	.0001385	.0001379	7220.00	7250.00
Finland (Markka)	.1901	.1907	5.2598	5.2431
France (Franc)	**.1723**	**.1729**	**5.8029**	**5.7845**
1-month forward	.1726	.1730	5.7951	5.7797
3-months forward	.1731	.1737	5.7766	5.7584
6-months forward	.1740	.1745	5.7473	5.7295
Germany (Mark)	.5780	.5798	1.7302	1.7247
1-month forward	.5787	.5806	1.7279	1.7224
3-months forward	.5806	.5824	1.7224	1.7169
6-months forward	.5836	.5854	1.7136	1.7082
Greece (Drachma)	.003527	.003544	283.52	282.17
Hong Kong (Dollar)	.1291	.1290	7.7488	7.7495
Hungary (Forint)	.004555	.004547	219.55	219.92
India (Rupee)	.02355	.02353	42.462	42.496
Indonesia (Rupiah)	.0001183	.0001133	8450.00	8825.00
Ireland (Punt)	1.4353	1.4399	.6967	.6945
Israel (Shekel)	.2447	.2453	4.0869	4.0773
Italy (Lira)	.0005838	.0005857	1712.91	1707.47

Country	U.S. $ equiv. Wed	U.S. $ equiv. Tue	Currency per U.S. $ Wed	Currency per U.S. $ Tue
Japan (Yen)	.008862	.008917	112.84	112.14
1-month forward	.008862	.008918	112.84	112.14
3-months forward	.008863	.008918	112.83	112.13
6-months forward	.008864	.008919	112.81	112.11
Jordan (Dinar)	1.4104	1.4144	.7090	.7070
Kuwait (Dinar)	3.3135	3.3212	.3018	.3011
Lebanon (Pound)	.0006631	.0006638	1508.00	1506.50
Malaysia (Ringgit-b)	.2632	.2632	3.8000	3.8000
Malta (Lira)	2.6247	2.6076	.3810	.3835
Mexico (Peso)				
Floating rate	.09899	.09932	10.102	10.068
Netherland (Guilder)	.5130	.5146	1.9495	1.9433
New Zealand (Dollar)	.5496	.5449	1.8195	1.8352
Norway (Krone)	.1308	.1319	7.6458	7.5828
Pakistan (Rupee)	.01949	.01951	51.300	51.250
Peru (new Sol)	.2942	.2956	3.3985	3.3835
Philippines (Peso)	.02601	.02597	38.450	38.500
Poland (Zloty)	.2705	.2685	3.6975	3.7250
Portugal (Escudo)	.005638	.005656	177.35	176.79
Russia (Ruble) (a)	.04325	.04363	23.120	22.920
Saudi Arabia (Riyal)	.2666	.2666	3.7508	3.7506
Singapore (Dollar)	.5923	.5935	1.6882	1.6850
Slovak Rep. (Koruna)	.02665	.02641	37.530	37.860
South Africa (Rand)	.1663	.1662	6.0150	6.0180
South Korea (Won)	.0008545	.0008545	1170.30	1170.30
Spain (Peseta)	.006794	.006815	147.19	146.72
Sweden (Krona)	.1267	.1274	7.8903	7.8508
Switzerland (Franc)	**.7055**	**.7076**	**1.4175**	**1.4133**
1-month forward	.7075	.7096	1.4135	1.4092
3-months forward	.7119	.7141	1.4047	1.4004
6-months forward	.7183	.7205	1.3921	1.3879
Taiwan (Dollar)	.03101	.03099	32.251	32.271
Thailand (Baht)	.02717	.02729	36.800	36.650
Turkey (Lira)	.00000299	.00000299	334643.00	334314.50
United Arab (Dirham)	**.2723**	**.2723**	**3.6725**	**3.6725**
Uruguay (New Peso)				
Financial	.09149	.09141	10.930	10.940
Venezuela (Bolivar)	.001734	.001736	576.57	576.12
	- - -			
SDR	1.3950	1.3930	.7169	.7179
Euro	1.1304	1.1340	.8846	.8818

Special Drawing Rights (SDR) are based on exchange rates for the U.S., German, British, French, and Japanese currencies. Source: International Monetary Fund.
a-Russian Central Bank rate. Trading band lowered on 8/17/98.
b-Government rate.
The Wall Street Journal daily foreign exchange data from 1996 forward may be purchased through the Readers' Reference Service (413) 592-3600.

Source: The Wall Street Journal, February 4, 1999, p. C16.

Austrian schilling and the Belgian franc that float in relation to the U.S. dollar) experienced changes in rates. Other currencies, however, such as the Argentine peso or the United Arab Emirate's dirham, do not exhibit relatively large fluctuations on a daily basis with respect to either the U.S. dollar or the currency to which they are pegged. That is, those currencies have very limited movements with respect to either the U.S. dollar or other currencies.

A final point to note is the concept of changes in the value of a currency with respect to the U.S. dollar or another currency. For the floating currencies, changes in the value of foreign exchange rates are called *appreciation* or *depreciation*. For example, Figure 20.2 shows that the value of the French franc depreciated from US$0.1729/Ff on Tuesday to US$0.1723/Ff on Wednesday. In other words, it took fewer dollars (cents) to buy 1 franc on Wednesday than it did on Tuesday. It is equally correct to say that the dollar appreciated from Ff 5.7845/US$ on Tuesday to Ff 5.8029/US$ on Wednesday.

TABLE 20.4	Approaches for Coping with Political Risks	
Positive approaches		**Negative approaches**
Prior negotiation of controls and operating contracts		License or patent restrictions under international agreements
Prior agreement for sale	Direct	
Joint venture with government or local private sector		Control of external raw materials
Use of locals in management		Control of transportation to (external) markets
Joint venture with local banks		
Equity participation by middle class	Indirect	Control of downstream processing
Local sourcing		
Local retail outlets		Control of external markets
External approaches to minimize loss		
International insurance or investment guarantees		
Thinly capitalized firms:		
Local financing		
External financing secured only by the local operation		

Source: Rita M. Rodriguez and E. Eugene Carter, *International Financial Management,* 3rd ed. (Englewood Cliffs, NJ: Prentice Hall, 1984), p. 512.

expect that as MNCs comply with these regulations, the potential for acts of political risk will decline, thus benefiting MNCs as well.

? Review Questions

20–6   Define *spot* and *forward exchange rates.* Define and compare *accounting exposures* and *economic exposures* to exchange rate fluctuations.

20–7   Explain how differing inflation rates between two countries affect their exchange rate over the long term.

20–8   Discuss *macro* and *micro political risk.* Describe some techniques for dealing with political risk.

20.4 Long-Term Investment and Financing Decisions

Important long-term aspects of international managerial finance include foreign direct investment, investment cash flows and decisions, capital structure, long-term debt, and equity capital. Here we consider the international dimensions of these topics.

Foreign Direct Investment

foreign direct investment (FDI)
The transfer by a multinational firm of capital, managerial, and technical assets from its home country to a host country.

Foreign direct investment (FDI) is the transfer by a multinational firm of capital, managerial, and technical assets from its home country to a host country. The equity participation on the part of an MNC can be 100 percent (resulting in a wholly owned foreign subsidiary) or less (leading to a joint-venture project with foreign participants). In contrast to short-term, foreign portfolio investments undertaken by individuals and companies (e.g., internationally diversified mutual funds), FDI involves equity participation, managerial control, and day-to-day operational activities on the part of MNCs. Therefore, FDI projects will be subjected not only to business, financial, inflation, and exchange rate risks (as would foreign portfolio investments), but also to the additional element of political risk.

Career Key

The personnel in *operations* will prepare the additional documents and cope with extensive regulations involved in foreign operations. If the firm decides to locate production facilities outside the domestic market, the operations personnel will be major players in designing and starting up the facility.

For several decades, U.S.-based MNCs dominated the international scene in terms of both the *flow* and *stock* of FDI. The total FDI stock of U.S.-based MNCs, for instance, increased from $7.7 billion in 1929 to over $970.8 billion at the end of 1996. Since the 1970s, though, their global presence is being challenged by MNCs based in Western Europe, Japan, and other developed and developing nations. In fact, even the "home" market of U.S. multinationals is being challenged by foreign firms. For instance, in 1960, FDI into the United States amounted to only 11.5 percent of U.S. investment overseas. By the end of 1996, the *book value* of FDI into the United States, at US$729.1 billion, was comparable to the figure of US$970.8 billion for U.S. FDI abroad. The *market value* of U.S. FDI at year-end 1996—US$1,534 billion—is also comparable to (though larger than) the US$1,254 billion market value of FDI into the United States.

In Practice

The World's Largest Wireless Phone Company

For people accustomed to thinking of American firms as being unchallenged technology leaders, the January 1999 contest to buy San Francisco's Air Touch Communications ended shockingly. The giant Bell Atlantic Corp. was set to complete its acquisition of Air Touch when Britain's Vodafone Group plc swooped in with a counteroffer totaling $62 billion—topping Bell Atlantic's bid by a cool $17 billion. Not only did Vodafone, which is less than 20 years old, succeed in acquiring Air Touch, but this purchase enthroned the British firm as the world's largest cellular-phone operator. This amazing deal came sharply on the heels of a record year for takeovers (over $2.5 trillion worldwide) that saw British firms become the most active international acquirers of other businesses (with total purchases of $128 billion). The year 1998 also witnessed several other immense international corporate combinations involving European and U.S. companies, such as the merger between Daimler-Benz and Chrysler and between British Petroleum and Amoco.

Fueled by a decade of gradual deregulation and privatization, and given confidence by the successful launch of the Euro, European companies are now emerging as among the most efficient, innovative, and productive companies in the world. Although this development may worry U.S. commentators and politicians, the competition is good news for consumers everywhere.

Investment Cash Flows and Decisions

Measuring the amount invested in a foreign project, its resulting cash flows, and the associated risk is difficult. The returns and NPVs of such investments can significantly vary from the subsidiary's and parent's points of view. Therefore, several factors that are unique to the international setting need to be examined when making long-term investment decisions.

First, elements relating to a parent company's *investment* in a subsidiary and the concept of taxes must be considered. For example, in the case of manufacturing investments, questions may arise as to the value of the equipment a parent may contribute to the subsidiary. Is the value based on the market conditions in the parent country or the local host economy? In general, the market value in the host country is the relevant "price."

The existence of different taxes—as pointed out earlier—can complicate measurement of the *cash flows* to be received by the parent because different definitions of taxable income can arise. There are still other complications when it comes to measuring the actual cash flows. From a parent firm's viewpoint, the cash flows are those that are repatriated from the subsidiary. In some countries, however, such cash flows may be totally or partially blocked. Obviously, depending on the life of the project in the host country, the returns and NPVs associated with such projects can vary significantly from the subsidiary's and the parent's point of view. For instance, for a project of only 5 years' duration, if all yearly cash flows are blocked by the host government, the subsidiary may show a "normal" or even superior return and NPV, although the parent may show no return at all. On the other hand, for a project of longer life, even if cash flows are blocked for the first few years, the remaining years' cash flows can contribute toward the parent's returns and NPV.

Finally, there is the issue of *risk* attached to international cash flows. The three basic types of risk categories are (1) business and financial risks, (2) inflation and exchange rate risks, and (3) political risks. The first category relates to the type of industry the subsidiary is in as well as its financial structure. More details on financial risks are presented later. As for the other two categories, we have already discussed the risks of having investments, profits, and assets/liabilities in different currencies and the potential impacts of political risks.

The presence of the three types of risks will influence the discount rate to be used when evaluating international cash flows. The basic rule is this: The *local cost of equity capital* (applicable to the local business and financial environments within which a subsidiary operates) is the starting discount rate. To this rate, the risks stemming from exchange rate and political factors would be added and the benefits reflecting the parent's lower capital costs would be subtracted.

Hint The discount rates used by the parent and subsidiary to calculate the NPV will also be different. The parent company has to add in a risk factor based on the possibility of exchange rates changing and the risk of not being able to get the cash out of the foreign country.

Capital Structure

Both theory and empirical evidence indicate that the capital structures of multinational companies differ from those of purely domestic firms. Furthermore, differences are also observed among the capital structures of MNCs domiciled in various countries. Several factors tend to influence the capital structures of MNCs.

International Capital Markets

MNCs, unlike smaller-size domestic firms, have access to the Euromarket (discussed earlier) and the variety of financial instruments available there. Because of their access to the international bond and equity markets, MNCs may have lower long-term financing costs, thus resulting in differences between the capital structures of MNCs and those of purely domestic companies. Similarly, MNCs based in different countries and regions may have access to different currencies and markets, resulting in variances in capital structures for these multinationals.

International Diversification

It is well established that MNCs, in contrast to domestic firms, can achieve further risk reduction in their cash flows by diversifying internationally. International diversification may lead to varying degrees of debt versus equity. Empirically, mixed evidence exists on debt ratios. Some studies have found MNCs' debt proportions to be higher than those of domestic firms. Other studies have concluded the opposite, citing imperfections in certain foreign markets, political risk factors, and complexities in the international financial environment that cause higher agency costs of debt for MNCs.

Country Factors

A number of studies have concluded that certain factors unique to each host country can cause differences in capital structures. These factors include legal, tax, political, social, and financial aspects, as well as the overall relationship between the public and private sectors. Owing to these factors, differences have been found not only among MNCs based in various countries, but among the foreign subsidiaries of an MNC as well. However, because no one capital structure is ideal for all MNCs, each multinational has to consider a set of global and domestic factors when deciding on the appropriate capital structure for both the overall corporation and its subsidiaries.

Long-Term Debt

As noted earlier, multinational companies have access to a variety of international financial instruments. International bonds are among the most widely used, so we will begin by focusing on them. Next, we discuss the role of international financial institutions in underwriting such instruments. Finally, we consider the use of various techniques by MNCs to change the structure of their long-term debt.

international bond
A bond that is initially sold outside the country of the borrower and often distributed in several countries.

foreign bond
An *international bond* that is sold primarily in the country of the currency of the issue.

International Bonds

In general, an **international bond** is one that is initially sold outside the country of the borrower and often distributed in several countries. When a bond is sold primarily in the country of the currency of the issue, it is called a **foreign bond**. For example, an MNC based in West Germany might float a foreign bond issue in the French capital market underwritten by a French syndicate and denominat-

Eurobond
An *international bond* that is sold primarily in countries other than the country of the currency in which the issue is denominated.

ed in French francs. When an international bond is sold primarily in countries other than the country of the currency in which the issue is denominated, it is called a **Eurobond.** Thus, an MNC based in the United States might float a Eurobond in several European capital markets, underwritten by an international syndicate and denominated in U.S. dollars.

The U.S. dollar continues to be the most frequently used currency for Eurobond issues (accounting for 18 percent of 1998 issue volume), with the German mark and, especially, the Euro gaining popularity. (In fact, the total volume of newly issued Euro-dominated bonds exceeded that of dollar-denominated debt during January 1999, with the Euro accounting for one-half of the $120 billion total issued that very busy month.) In the foreign bond category, the U.S. dollar and the Swiss franc continue to be the major choices. Low interest rates, the general stability of the currency, and the overall efficiency of the Swiss capital markets are among the primary reasons for the ongoing popularity of the Swiss franc.

Eurobonds are much more widely used than foreign bonds. These instruments are heavily used, especially in relation to Eurocurrency loans in recent years, by major market participants, including U.S. corporations. The so-called *equity-linked Eurobonds* (i.e., convertible to equity), especially those offered by a number of U.S. firms, have found strong demand among Euromarket participants. It is expected that more of these innovative types of instruments will emerge on the international scene in the coming years.

A final point concerns the levels of interest rates in international markets. In the case of foreign bonds, interest rates are usually directly correlated with the domestic rates prevailing in the respective countries. For Eurobonds, several interest rates may be influential. For instance, for a Eurodollar bond, the interest rate will reflect several different rates, most notably the U.S. long-term rate, the Eurodollar rate, and long-term rates in other countries.

The Role of International Financial Institutions

For *foreign bonds,* the underwriting institutions are those that handle bond issues in the respective countries in which such bonds are issued. For *Eurobonds,* a number of financial institutions in the United States, Western Europe, and Japan form international underwriting syndicates. The underwriting costs for Eurobonds are comparable to those for bond flotation in the U.S. domestic market. Although U.S. institutions used to dominate the Eurobond scene, recent economic and financial strengths exhibited by some Western European (especially German) financial firms have led to an erosion in that dominance. Since 1986, a number of European firms have shared with U.S. firms the top positions in terms of acting as lead underwriters of Eurobond issues. However, U.S. investment banks continue to dominate most other international security issuance markets—such as international equity, medium-term note, syndicated loan, and commercial paper markets. U.S. corporations accounted for almost three-quarters of the $2.51 trillion in worldwide securities issues in 1998.

To raise funds through international bond issues, many MNCs establish their own financial subsidiaries. Many U.S.-based MNCs, for example, have created subsidiaries in the United States and Western Europe, especially in

Luxembourg. Such subsidiaries can be used to raise large amounts of funds in "one move," the funds being redistributed wherever MNCs need them. (Special tax rules applicable to such subsidiaries also make them desirable to MNCs.)

Changing the Structure of Debt

As will be more fully explained later, MNCs can use *hedging strategies* to change the structure/characteristics of their long-term assets and liabilities. For instance, multinationals can utilize *interest rate swaps* to obtain a desired stream of interest payments (e.g., fixed rate) in exchange for another (e.g., floating rate). With *currency swaps,* they can exchange an asset/liability denominated in one currency (e.g., U.S. dollar) for another (e.g., Swiss franc). The use of these tools allows MNCs to gain access to a broader set of markets, currencies, and maturities, thus leading to both cost savings and a means of restructuring the existing assets/liabilities. Such use has experienced significant growth during the last few years, and this trend is expected to continue.

Equity Capital

Here we look at how multinational companies can raise equity capital abroad. First, they can sell their shares in international capital markets. Second, they can use joint ventures, which are sometimes required by the host country.

Equity Issues and Markets

One means of raising equity funds for MNCs is to have the parent's stock distributed internationally and owned by stockholders of different nationalities. In the 1980s, the world's equity markets became more "internationalized." In other words, although distinct *national* stock markets (such as New York, London, and Tokyo) continue to exist and grow, an *international* stock market has also emerged on the global financial scene.

Euroequity market
The capital market around the world that deals in international equity issues; London has become *the* center of Euroequity activity.

In recent years, the terms **Euroequity market** and "Euroequities" have become widely known. Although a number of capital markets—including New York, Tokyo, Frankfurt, Zurich, and Paris—play major roles as hosts to international equity issues, London has become *the* center of Euroequity activity. For the year 1998, for instance, the *new issue* volume was close to $74 billion and included 575 offerings. As in most recent years, government sales of state-owned firms to private investors, referred to as *share-issue privatizations,* accounted for over half of the total volume of equity issues (over $50 billion in 1998 alone).

As the full financial integration of the EU approaches, some European stock exchanges continue to compete with each other. Others have called for more cooperation in forming a single market capable of competing with the New York and Tokyo exchanges. From the multinationals' perspective, the most desirable outcome would be to have uniform international rules and regulations with respect to all the major national stock exchanges. Such uniformity would allow MNCs to have unrestricted access to an international equity market paralleling that of the international currency and bond markets.

Joint Ventures

The basic aspects of foreign ownership of international operations were discussed earlier. Worth emphasizing here is that certain laws and regulations enacted by a number of host countries require MNCs to maintain less than 50 percent ownership in their subsidiaries in those countries. For a U.S.-based MNC, for example, establishing foreign subsidiaries in the form of joint ventures means that a certain portion of the firm's total international equity stock is (indirectly) held by foreign owners.

In establishing a foreign subsidiary, an MNC may wish to use as little equity and as much debt as possible, with the debt coming from local sources in the host country or the MNC itself. Each of these actions can be supported: The use of *local debt* can be a good protective measure to lessen the potential impacts of political risk. Because local sources are involved in the capital structure of a subsidiary, there may be fewer threats from local authorities in the event of changes in government or the enactment of new regulations on foreign business.

In support of the other action—having *more MNC-based debt* in a subsidiary's capital structure—many host governments are less restrictive toward intra-MNC interest payments than toward intra-MNC dividend remittances. The parent firm therefore may be in a better position if it has more MNC-based debt than equity in the capital structure of its subsidiaries.

? Review Questions

20–9   Indicate how NPV can differ if measured from the parent MNC's point of view or from that of the foreign subsidiary when cash flows may be blocked by local authorities.

20–10 Briefly discuss some of the international factors that cause the capital structures of MNCs to differ from those of purely domestic firms.

20–11 Describe the difference between *foreign bonds* and *Eurobonds*. Explain how each is sold, and discuss the determinant(s) of their interest rates.

20–12 What are the long-run advantages of having more *local* debt and less MNC-based equity in the capital structure of a foreign subsidiary?

20.5 Short-Term Financial Decisions

In international operations, the usual domestic sources of short-term financing, along with other sources, are available to MNCs. Included are accounts payable, accruals, bank and nonbank sources in each subsidiary's local environment, and the Euromarket. Our emphasis here is on the "foreign" sources.

The local economic market is a basic source of both short- and long-term financing for a subsidiary of a multinational company. Moreover, the subsidiary's borrowing and lending status, relative to a local firm in the same economy, can be superior, because the subsidiary can rely on the potential backing and guarantee of its parent MNC. One drawback, however, is that most local markets and local currencies are regulated by local authorities. A subsidiary may ultimately choose to turn to the Euromarket and take advantage of borrowing and investing in an unregulated financial forum.

The Euromarket offers nondomestic long-term financing opportunities through Eurobonds, which were discussed in Chapter 2. Short-term financing opportunities are available in **Eurocurrency markets.** The forces of supply and demand are among the main factors determining exchange rates in Eurocurrency markets. Each currency's normal interest rate is influenced by economic policies pursued by the respective "home" government. For example, the interest rates offered in the Euromarket on the U.S. dollar are greatly affected by the prime rate inside the United States, and the dollar's exchange rates with other major currencies are influenced by the supply and demand forces in such markets (and in response to interest rates).

Unlike borrowing in the domestic markets, where only one currency and a **nominal interest rate** is involved, financing activities in the Euromarket can involve several currencies and both nominal and effective interest rates. **Effective interest rates** are equal to nominal rates plus (or minus) any forecast appreciation (or depreciation) of a foreign currency relative to the currency of the MNC parent. An example will illustrate the issues involved.

Eurocurrency markets
The portion of the Euromarket that provides short-term, foreign-currency financing to subsidiaries of MNCs.

nominal interest rate
In the international context, the stated interest rate charged on financing when only the MNC parent's currency is involved.

effective interest rate
In the international context, the rate equal to the nominal rate plus (or minus) any forecast appreciation (or depreciation) of a foreign currency relative to the currency of the MNC parent.

Example ▼ A multinational plastics company, International Molding, has subsidiaries in Switzerland (local currency, Swiss franc, Sf) and Belgium (local currency, Belgian franc, Bf). Based on each subsidiary's forecast operations, the short-term financial needs (in equivalent U.S. dollars) are as follows:

Switzerland: $80 million excess cash to be invested (lent)
Belgium: $60 million funds to be raised (borrowed)

On the basis of all the available information, the parent firm has provided each subsidiary with the figures, given in the table below, regarding exchange rates and interest rates. (The figures for the effective rates shown are derived by adding the forecast percentage changes to the nominal rates.)

| | Currency | | |
Item	US$	Sf	Bf
Spot exchange rates		Sf 1.21/US$	Bf 30.44/US$
Forecast % change		+1.0%	−2.5%
Interest rates			
Nominal			
Euromarket	4.6%	6.2%	8.5%
Domestic	4.0	5.5	9.0
Effective			
Euromarket	4.6%	7.2%	6.0%
Domestic	4.0	6.5	6.5

From the MNC's point of view, the effective rates of interest, which take into account each currency's forecast percentage change (appreciation or depreciation) relative to the U.S. dollar, are the main considerations in investment and borrowing decisions. (It is assumed here that because of local regulations, a subsidiary is *not* permitted to use the domestic market of *any other* subsidiary.) The relevant question is, where should funds be invested and borrowed?

For investment purposes, the highest available rate of interest is the effective rate for the Swiss franc in the Euromarket. Therefore, the Swiss subsidiary should invest the $80 million in Swiss francs in the Euromarket. To raise funds, the cheapest source *open* to the Belgian subsidiary is the 4.6% in the US$ Euromarket. The subsidiary should therefore raise the $60 million in U.S. dollars. These two transactions will result in the most revenues and least costs, ▲ respectively.

Several points should be made with respect to the preceding example. First of all, this is a simplified case of the actual workings of the Eurocurrency markets. The example ignores taxes, intersubsidiary investing and borrowing, and periods longer or shorter than a year. Nevertheless, it shows how the existence of many currencies can provide both challenges and opportunities for MNCs. Next, the focus has been solely on accounting values; of greater importance would be the impact of these actions on market value. Finally, it is important to note the following details about the figures presented. The forecast percentage change data are those normally supplied by the MNC's international financial managers. Management may, instead, want a *range of forecasts,* from the most likely to the least likely. In addition, the company's management is likely to take a specific position in terms of its response to any remaining exchange rate exposures. If any action is to be taken, certain amounts of one or more currencies will be borrowed and then invested in other currencies in the hope of realizing potential gains to offset potential losses associated with the exposures.

Cash Management

In its international cash management, a multinational firm can respond to exchange rate risks by protecting (hedging) its undesirable cash and marketable securities exposures or by certain adjustments in its operations. The former approach is more applicable in responding to *accounting exposures,* the latter is better suited against *economic exposures.* Each of these two approaches is examined here.

Hedging Strategies

hedging strategies
Techniques used to offset or protect against risk; in the international context, these include borrowing or lending in different currencies, undertaking contracts in the forward, futures, and/or options markets, and also swapping assets/liabilities with other parties.

Hedging strategies are techniques used to offset or protect against risk. In international cash management, these strategies include actions such as borrowing or lending in different currencies; undertaking contracts in the forward, futures, and/or options markets; and swapping assets/liabilities with other parties. Table 20.5 briefly summarizes some of the major hedging tools available to MNCs. By far the most commonly used technique is to hedge with a forward contract.

TABLE 20.5	Exchange Rate Risk Hedging Tools	
Tool	Description	Impact on risk
Borrowing or lending	Borrowing or lending in different currencies to take advantage of interest rate differentials and foreign exchange appreciation/depreciation; can be either on a certainty basis with "up-front" costs or speculative.	Can be used to offset exposures in existing assets/liabilities and in expected revenues/expenses.
Forward contract	"Tailor-made" contracts representing an *obligation* to buy/sell, with the amount, rate, and maturity agreed upon between the two parties; has little up-front cost.	Can eliminate downside risk but locks out any upside potential.
Futures contract	Standardized contracts offered on organized exchanges; same basic tool as a forward contract, but less flexible because of standardization; more flexibility because of secondary market access; has some up-front cost/fee.	Can also eliminate downside risk, plus position can be nullified, creating possible upside potential.
Options	Tailor-made or standardized contracts providing the *right* to buy or to sell an amount of the currency, at a particular price, during a specified time period; has up-front cost (premium).	Can eliminate downside risk and retain unlimited upside potential.
Interest rate swap	Allows the trading of one interest rate stream (e.g., on a fixed-rate U.S. dollar instrument) for another (e.g., on a floating-rate U.S. dollar instrument); fee to be paid to the intermediary.	Permits firms to change the interest rate structure of their assets/liabilities and achieves cost savings due to broader market access.
Currency swap	Two parties exchange principal amounts of two different currencies initially; they pay each other's interest payments, then reverse principal amounts at a preagreed exchange rate at maturity; more complex than interest rate swaps.	All the features of interest rate swaps, plus it allows firms to change the currency structure of their assets/liabilities.
Hybrids	A variety of combinations of some of the preceding tools; may be quite costly and/or speculative.	Can create, with the right combination, a perfect hedge against certain exchange rate exposures.

Note: The participants in these activities include MNCs, financial institutions, and brokers. The organized exchanges include Amsterdam, Chicago, London, New York, Philadelphia, and Zurich, among others. Although most of these tools can be utilized for short-term exposure management, some, such as swaps, are more appropriate for long-term hedging strategies.

To demonstrate how you can use a forward contract to hedge exchange rate risk, assume you are a financial manager for Boeing Company, which has just booked a sale of three airplanes worth $100,000,000 to the Swiss national airline, Swissair. The sale is denominated in Swiss francs (international sales are generally denominated in the customer's currency), and the current spot exchange rate is Sf 1.4175/$ (or, equivalently, $0.7055/Sf). Therefore, you have priced this airplane sale at Sf 141,750,000. If delivery were to occur today, there would be no foreign exchange risk. However, delivery and payment will not occur for 90 days. If this transaction is not hedged, Boeing will be exposed to significant risk of loss if the Swiss franc depreciates over the next 3 months.

Let us say that between now and the delivery date, the dollar value of the Swiss franc changes from $0.7055/Sf to $0.6061/Sf. Upon delivery of the airplanes, the agreed-upon Sf 141,750,000 will then be worth only $85,914,675 (Sf 141,750,000 × $0.6061/Sf), rather than the $100,000,000 you originally planned for—a foreign exchange loss of over $14 million. If instead of remaining unhedged, you had sold the Sf 141,750,000 forward 3 months earlier at the 90-day forward rate of $0.7119/Sf offered to you by your bank, you could have locked in a net dollar sale price of $100,911,825 (Sf 141,750,000 × $0.7119/Sf). Of course, if you remained unhedged, and the Swiss franc appreciated, you would have experienced a foreign exchange profit for the firm—but most MNCs prefer to make profits through sales of goods and services rather than by speculating on the direction of exchange rates.

Adjustments in Operations

In responding to exchange rate fluctuations, MNCs can give some protection to international cash flows through appropriate adjustments in assets and liabilities. Two routes are available to a multinational company. The first centers on the operating relationships that a subsidiary of an MNC maintains with *other* firms—*third parties.* Depending on management's expectation of a local currency's position, adjustments in operations would involve the reduction of liabilities if the currency is appreciating or the reduction of financial assets if it is depreciating. For example, if a U.S.-based MNC with a subsidiary in Mexico expects the Mexican currency to *appreciate* in value relative to the U.S. dollar, local customers' accounts receivable would be *increased* and accounts payable would be reduced if at all possible. Because the dollar is the currency in which the MNC parent will have to prepare consolidated financial statements, the net result in this case would be to favorably increase the Mexican subsidiary's resources in local currency. If the Mexican currency were, instead, expected to *depreciate,* the local customers' accounts receivable would be *reduced* and accounts payable would be increased, thereby reducing the Mexican subsidiary's resources in local currency.

The second route focuses on the operating relationship a subsidiary has with its parent or with other subsidiaries within the same MNC. In dealing with exchange rate risks, a subsidiary can rely on *intra-MNC accounts.* Specifically, undesirable exchange rate exposures can be corrected to the extent that the subsidiary can take the following steps:

1. In appreciation-prone countries, intra-MNC accounts receivable are collected as soon as possible, and payment of intra-MNC accounts payable is delayed as long as possible.
2. In depreciation-prone countries, intra-MNC accounts receivable are collected as late as possible, and intra-MNC accounts payable are paid as soon as possible.

This technique is known as "leading and lagging," or simply as "leads and lags."

Example ▼ Assume that a U.S.-based parent company, American Computer Corporation (ACC), both buys parts from and sells parts to its wholly owned Mexican subsidiary, Tijuana Computer Company (TCC). Assume further that ACC has accounts payable of $10,000,000 that it is scheduled to pay TCC in 30 days, and in turn has accounts receivable of (Mexican peso) MP 75,900,000 due from TCC within 30 days. Because today's exchange rate is MP 7.59/US$, the accounts receivable are also worth $10,000,000. Therefore, parent and subsidiary owe each other equal amounts (though in different currencies), and both are payable in 30 days, but because TCC is a wholly owned subsidiary of ACC, the parent has complete discretion over the timing of these payments.

If ACC believes that the Mexican peso will depreciate from MP 7.59/US$ to, say, MP 9.00/US$ during the next 30 days, the combined companies can profit by collecting the weak currency (MP) debt immediately, but delaying payment of the strong currency (US$) debt for the full 30 days allowed. If parent and subsidiary do this, and the peso depreciates as predicted, the net result is that the MP 75,900,000 payment from TCC to ACC is made immediately and is safely converted into $10,000,000 at today's exchange rate, while the delayed $10,000,000 payment from ACC to TCC will be worth MP 90,000,000 (MP 9.00/US$ × $10,000,000). Thus, the Mexican subsidiary will experience a foreign exchange trading profit of MP 14,100,000 (MP 90,000,000 − MP 75,900,000), whereas the U.S. parent receives the full amount ($10 million) due from TCC and therefore is unharmed.

The example demonstrated that the manipulation of an MNC's consolidated intracompany accounts by one subsidiary generally benefits one subsidiary (or the parent) while leaving the other subsidiary (or the parent) unharmed. The exact degree and direction of the actual manipulations, however, may depend on the tax status of each country. The MNC obviously would want to have the exchange rate losses in the country with the higher tax rate. Finally, changes in intra-MNC accounts can also be subject to restrictions and regulations put forward by the respective host countries of various subsidiaries.

Credit and Inventory Management

Multinational firms based in different countries compete for the same global export markets. Therefore, it is essential that they offer attractive credit terms to potential customers. Increasingly, however, the maturity and saturation of developed markets is forcing MNCs to maintain and increase revenues by exporting and selling a higher percentage of their output to developing countries. Given the risks associated with the latter group of buyers, as partly evidenced by their lack of a major (hard) currency, the MNC must use a variety of tools to protect such revenues. In addition to the use of hedging and various asset and liability adjustments (described earlier), MNCs should seek the backing of their respective governments in both identifying target markets and extending credit. Multinationals based in a number of Western European nations and those based in Japan currently benefit from extensive involvement of government agencies that provide them with the needed service and financial support. For U.S.-based MNCs, government agencies such as the Export-Import Bank currently do not provide a comparable level of support.

In terms of inventory management, MNCs must consider a number of factors related to both economics and politics. In addition to maintaining the appropriate level of inventory in various locations around the world, a multinational

Preparing invoices in 6 foreign languages and 13 currencies was no easy task for Connecticut bicycle maker Cannondale, which derives 37% of its sales from European customers. To simplify the task, the company modified an available translation software package to create invoices in the correct currency and language for each of its customers. At first, Cannondale organized the system by country, but after discovering that a Swiss customer might speak German, French, or Italian, the company now groups customer files by language. The program also adjusts for currency fluctuations. When staff members enter rate changes once a month, the system automatically recalculates receivables balances. Cannondale's ability to translate invoices has won favor from its distributors and retailers, who appreciate not having to deal with currency and language translations. It has also helped this U.S. firm blend into the local business environment and compete more effectively.

firm is compelled to deal with exchange rate fluctuations, tariffs, nontariff barriers, integration schemes such as the EU, and other rules and regulations. Politically, inventories could be subjected to wars, expropriations, blockages, and other forms of government intervention.

? Review Questions

20–13 What is the *Eurocurrency market?* What are the main factors determining foreign exchange rates in that market? Differentiate between the *nominal interest rate* and *effective interest rate* in this market.

20–14 Discuss the steps to be followed in adjusting a subsidiary's accounts relative to *third parties* when that subsidiary's local currency is expected to *appreciate* in value in relation to the currency of the parent MNC.

20–15 Outline the changes to be undertaken in *intra-MNC accounts* if a subsidiary's currency is expected to *depreciate* in value relative to the currency of the parent MNC.

20.6 Mergers and Joint Ventures

The motives for domestic mergers—growth or diversification, synergy, fund raising, increased managerial skill or technology, tax considerations, increased ownership liquidity, and defense against takeover—are all applicable to MNCs' international mergers and joint ventures. Several additional points should also be made.

First, international mergers and joint ventures, especially those involving European firms acquiring assets in the United States, increased significantly beginning in the 1980s. MNCs based in Western Europe, Japan, and North America are numerous. Moreover, a fast-growing group of MNCs has emerged in the past two decades, based in the so-called newly industrializing countries (which include, among others, Brazil, Argentina, Mexico, Hong Kong, Singapore, South Korea, Taiwan, India, and Pakistan). Even though many of these companies were hit very hard by the economic problems arising in Asia after July 1997 and following the collapse of the Russian economy in August 1998, top firms from the region have been able to survive and even prosper. Additionally, many Western companies have taken advantage of these economies' weakness to buy into companies that were previously off-limits to foreign investors. This has added further to the number and value of international mergers.

Foreign direct investments in the United States have also gained popularity recently. Most of the foreign direct investors in the United States come from seven countries: Britain, Canada, France, the Netherlands, Japan, Switzerland, and Germany. The heaviest investments are concentrated in manufacturing, followed by the petroleum and trade/service sectors. Another trend is the current increase in the number of joint ventures between companies based in Japan and firms domiciled elsewhere in the industrialized world, especially U.S.-based MNCs. Although Japanese authorities continue their discussions and debates with other governments regarding Japan's international trade surpluses as well as perceived trade barriers, mergers and joint ventures continue to take place. In the eyes of some U.S. corporate executives, such business ventures are viewed as a "ticket into the Japanese market" as well as a way to curb a potentially tough competitor.

Developing countries, too, have been attracting foreign direct investments in many industries. Meanwhile, during the last two decades a number of these nations have adopted specific policies and regulations aimed at controlling the inflows of foreign investments, a major provision being the 49 percent ownership limitation applied to MNCs. Of course, international competition among MNCs has benefited some developing countries in their attempts to extract concessions from the multinationals. However, an increasing number of such nations have shown greater flexibility in their recent dealings with MNCs, as MNCs have become more reluctant to form joint ventures under the stated conditions. Furthermore, it is likely that as more developing countries recognize the need for foreign capital and technology, they will show even greater flexibility in their agreements with MNCs.

A final point relates to the existence of international *holding companies*. Places such as Liechtenstein and Panama have long been considered favorable spots for forming holding companies because of their conducive legal, corporate, and tax environments. International holding companies control many business entities in the form of subsidiaries, branches, joint ventures, and other agreements. For international legal (especially tax-related) reasons, as well as anonymity, such holding companies have become increasingly popular in recent years.

? Review Question

20–16   What are some of the major reasons for the rapid expansion in international mergers and joint ventures of firms?

SUMMARY

LG1 **Understand the major factors influencing the financial operations of multinational companies (MNCs).** Three important trading blocs have emerged in the 1990s: one in the Americas (primarily the United States, Mexico, and Canada) as a result of NAFTA; the European Union (EU); and the Mercosur Group in South America. The EU will become even more competitive when it achieves monetary union and all its members use the Euro as a single currency. Free trade among the largest economic powers is governed by the General Agreement on Tariffs and Trade (GATT) and is policed by the World Trade Organization (WTO).

Setting up operations in foreign countries can entail special problems due to the legal form of business organization chosen, the degree of ownership allowed by the host country, and possible restrictions and regulations on the return of capital and profits. Taxation of multinational companies is a complex issue because of the existence of varying tax rates, differing definitions of taxable income, measurement differences, and tax treaties.

The existence and expansion of dollars held outside the United States have contributed to the development of a major international financial market, the Euromarket. The large international banks, developing and industrialized nations, and multinational companies participate as borrowers and lenders in this market.

LG2 **Describe the key differences between purely domestic and international financial statements—particularly consolidation, translation of individual accounts, and international profits.** Regulations that apply to international operations complicate the preparation of foreign-based financial statements. Rulings in the United States require the consolidation of financial statements of subsidiaries according to the percentage of ownership by the parent in the subsidiary. Individual accounts of subsidiaries must be translated back into U.S. dollars using the procedures outlined in FASB No. 52. This standard also requires that only certain transactional gains or losses from international operations be included in the U.S. parent's income statement.

LG3 **Discuss exchange rate risk and political risk, and explain how MNCs manage them.** Economic exposure from exchange rate risk results from the existence of different currencies and the potential impact they can have on the value of foreign operations. Long-term changes in foreign exchange rates result primarily from differing inflation rates in the two countries. The money markets, the forward (futures) markets, and the foreign currency options markets can be used to hedge foreign exchange exposure. Political risks stem mainly from political instability and from the associated implications for the assets and operations of MNCs. MNCs can employ negative, external, and positive approaches to cope with political risk.

LG4 **Describe foreign direct investment, investment cash flows and decisions, the factors that influence MNCs' capital structure, and the international debt and equity instruments that are available to MNCs.** Foreign direct investment (FDI) involves an MNC's transfer of capital, managerial, and technical assets from its home country to the host country. The investment cash flows of FDIs are subject to a variety of factors, including taxes in host countries, regulations that may block the return (repatriation) of MNCs' cash flow, the usual business and financial risks, risks stemming from inflation and from currency and political actions by host governments, and the application of a local cost of capital.

The capital structures of MNCs differ from those of purely domestic firms because of the MNCs' access to the Euromarket and the financial instruments it offers; the ability to reduce risk in their cash flows through international diversification; and the impact of legal, tax, political, social, and financial factors unique to each host country. MNCs can raise long-term debt through the issuance of international bonds in various currencies. Foreign bonds are sold primarily in the country of the currency of issue; Eurobonds are sold primarily in countries other than the country of the currency in which the issue is denominated. MNCs can raise equity through the sale of their shares in the international capital markets or through joint ventures. In establishing foreign subsidiaries, it may be more advantageous to issue debt than MNC-owned equity.

 Demonstrate use of the Eurocurrency market in short-term borrowing and investing (lending) and the basics of cash, credit, and inventory management in international operations. Eurocurrency markets allow multinationals to invest (lend) and raise (borrow) short-term funds in a variety of currencies and to protect themselves against exchange rate risk exposures. Effective interest rates, which take into account each currency's forecast percentage change relative to the MNC parent's currency, are the main items considered by an MNC in making investment and borrowing deci-

sions. The MNC invests in the currency with the highest effective rate and borrows in the currency with the lowest effective rate. MNCs must offer competitive credit terms and maintain adequate inventories to provide timely delivery to foreign buyers. Obtaining the backing of foreign governments is helpful to the MNC in effectively managing credit and inventory.

 Discuss the growth of and special factors relating to international mergers and joint ventures. International mergers and joint ventures, including international holding companies, increased significantly in the last decade. Special factors affecting these mergers relate to various regulations imposed on MNCs by host countries and economic and trade conditions.

SELF-TEST PROBLEM (Solution in Appendix B)

 ST 20–1 Tax credits   A U.S.-based MNC has a foreign subsidiary that earns $150,000 before local taxes, with all the after-tax funds to be available to the parent in the form of dividends. The applicable taxes consist of a 32% foreign income tax rate, a foreign dividend withholding tax rate of 8%, and a U.S. tax rate of 34%. Calculate the net funds available to the parent MNC if:
a. Foreign taxes can be applied as a credit against the MNC's U.S. tax liability.
b. No tax credits are allowed.

PROBLEMS

  20–1 Tax credits   A U.S.-based MNC has a foreign subsidiary that earns $250,000 before local taxes, with all the after-tax funds to be available to the parent in the form of dividends. The applicable taxes consist of a 33% foreign income tax rate, a foreign dividend withholding tax rate of 9%, and a U.S. tax rate of 34%. Calculate the net funds available to the parent MNC if:

INTERMEDIATE

a. Foreign taxes can be applied as a credit against the MNC's U.S. tax liability.
b. No tax credits are allowed.

INTERMEDIATE   20–2 Translation of financial statements   A U.S.-based MNC has a subsidiary in France. The balance sheet and income statement of the subsidiary follow. On 12/31/00, the exchange rate is Ff 5.50/US$. Assume that the local (French franc,

Ff) figures for the statements remain the same on 12/31/01. Calculate the U.S. dollar-translated figures for the two ending time periods, assuming that between 12/31/00 and 12/31/01 the French currency has appreciated against the U.S. dollar by 6%.

Translation of Balance Sheet

	12/31/00		12/31/01
Assets	Ff	US$	US$
Cash	40.00		
Inventory	300.00		
Plant and equipment (net)	160.00		
Total	500.00		
Liabilities and stockholders' equity			
Debt	240.00		
Paid-in capital	200.00		
Retained earnings	60.00		
Total	500.00		

Translation of Income Statement

Sales	30,000.00		
Cost of goods sold	2,750.00		
Operating profits	250.00		

CHALLENGE 20–3 **Euromarket investment and fund raising**   A U.S.-based multinational company has two subsidiaries, one in Germany (local currency, Deutsche mark, DM) and one in Switzerland (local currency, Swiss franc, Sf). Forecasts of business operations indicate the following short-term financing position for each subsidiary (in equivalent U.S. dollars):

> Germany: $80 million excess cash to be invested (lent)
> Switzerland: $60 million funds to be raised (borrowed)

The management gathered the following data:

Item	US$	DM	Sf
		Currency	
Spot exchange rates		DM 1.48/US$	Sf 1.21/US$
Forecast % change		+1.5%	+1.0%
Interest rates			
Nominal			
Euromarket	5.0%	6.5%	6.2%
Domestic	4.5	6.1	5.7
Effective			
Euromarket			
Domestic			

Determine the *effective* interest rates for all three currencies in both the Euromarket and the domestic market; then indicate where the funds should be invested and raised. (*Note:* Assume that because of local regulations, a subsidiary is *not* permitted to use the domestic market of *any other* subsidiary.)

CASE   CHAPTER 20

Assessing a Direct Investment in Chile by U.S. Computer Corporation

David Smith is Chief Financial Officer for U.S. Computer Corporation (USCC), a successful and rapidly growing manufacturer of personal computers. He has been asked to evaluate an investment project calling for USCC to build a factory in Chile to assemble the company's most popular computer for sale in the Chilean market. David knows that Chile has been a real business success story in recent years—having achieved economic growth rates of over 7% per year from 1990 through 1998, even as it made the transition from military dictatorship to democracy—and USCC is eager to invest in this developing economy if an attractive opportunity arises. David's job is to use the information below to see whether this particular proposal meets the company's investment standards.

On the basis of the current Chilean peso (Ps)-to-dollar exchange rate of Ps 500/US$ (actually Ps 489.70/$ on February 8, 1999), David calculates that the factory would cost Ps 5,000,000,000 ($10,000,000) to build (including working capital) and would generate sales of Ps 10,000,000,000 ($20,000,000) per year for the first several years. Initially, the factory would import key components from the United States and assemble the computers in Chile using local labor. Smith estimates that half the company's costs will be dollar-denominated components, and half will be local currency (peso) costs, but all USCC's revenues will be in pesos. As long as the peso/dollar exchange rate is stable, the company's operating cash flow is expected to equal 20% of sales. If, however, the peso were to depreciate relative to the dollar, the company's peso cost of acquiring dollar-denominated components would increase, and its profit margin would shrink because the peso sale prices of its computers would not change.

If USCC made this investment, they would set up a subsidiary in Chile and structure the factory investment so that the subsidiary's capital structure was 60% debt and 40% equity. Therefore, to finance the Ps 5,000,000,000 factory cost, USCC must obtain Ps 3,000,000,000 ($6,000,000) in debt and Ps 2,000,000,000 ($4,000,000) in equity. The debt can be obtained either by issuing $6,000,000 of dollar-denominated bonds in the Eurobond market at a 6% annual rate and then converting the proceeds into pesos or by borrowing the Ps 3,000,000,000 in the Chilean market at a 14% annual interest rate. If borrowing is done in dollars, however, the parent company must also service and repay the debt in dollars, even though all project revenues will be in pesos.

For simplicity, assume the parent company decides to contribute the equity capital for the project itself. USCC would do this by contributing $4,000,000 to the subsidiary from either retained earnings or newly issued stock. This equity financing would then be converted to pesos. (Alternatively, the subsidiary could sell Ps 2,000,000,000 of stock to Chilean investors by listing shares on the Santiago Stock Exchange.) USCC has a 12% required return on equity on its dollar-denominated investments.

Required

a. Compute the weighted average cost of capital for this project, assuming that the long-term debt financing is in dollars.

b. Assuming that the peso/dollar exchange rate remains unchanged, compute the present value of the first 5 years of the project's cash flows, using the weighted average cost of capital computed in **a**. (*Note:* Round off your answer in **a** to the nearest 1% prior to making this calculation.) What happens to the present value if the dollar appreciates against the peso?

c. Identify the exchange rate risks involved in this project. Given that no forward, futures, or options markets exist for the Chilean peso, how might USCC minimize the exchange rate risk of this project by changes in production, sourcing, and sales? (*Hint:* Exchange rate risk can be minimized either by decreasing dollar-denominated costs or by increasing dollar-denominated revenue or both.)

d. What are the risks involved in financing this project as much as possible with local funds (pesos)? Which financing strategy—dollar versus peso—would minimize the project's exchange rate risk? Would your answer change if Chile began to experience political instability? What would happen to the attractiveness of the project if Chile joined NAFTA?

WEB EXERCISE

GOTO web site www.federalreserve.gov. Under DOMESTIC INTERNATIONAL RESEARCH, click STATISTICS: RELEASES AND HISTORICAL DATA. Under FOREIGN EXCHANGE RATES, click RELEASES. Click the date to the left of CURRENT RELEASE.

1. Using the data in the third column from the left, complete the following table:

Country and Currency		Number of U.S. Dollars
Canada	Dollar	$_____
EMU	Euro	_____
Japan	Yen	_____
South Africa	Rand	_____
South Korea	Won	_____
Thailand	Baht	_____

2. How many nations in this list denominate their currency in dollars?

GOTO web site www.pacific.commerce.ubc.ca. Under REFERENCE, click EXCHANGE RATE SERVICE.

3. Using the data from the table at the bottom of the page, how many CAD/USD?
4. Using the data from the table at the bottom of the page, how many GBP/USD?
5. Using the data from the table at the bottom of the page, how many USD/EUR?
6. Using the data from the table at the bottom of the page, how many EUR/CAD?

Click on SUPPLEMENTARY ISSUE.

7. How many countries are included in this list?
8. Which country's currency requires the greatest number of units/USD? (Look under the units/USD column.)

ORGANIC SOLUTIONS

Organic Solutions (OS), one of the nation's largest plant wholesalers in the Southeastern United States, was poised for expansion. Through strong profitability, a conservative dividend policy, and some recent realized gains in real estate, OS had a strong cash position and was searching for a target company to acquire. The executive members on the acquisition search committee had agreed that they preferred to find a firm in a similar line of business rather than one that would provide broad diversification. This would be their first acquisition, and they preferred to stay in a familiar line of business. Jennifer Morgan, director of marketing, had identified through exhaustive market research the targeted lines of business.

Ms. Morgan had determined that the servicing of plants in large commercial offices, hotels, zoos, and theme parks would complement the existing wholesale distribution business. Frequently, OS was requested by its large clients to bid on a service contract. However, Organic Solutions was neither staffed nor equipped to enter this market. Ms. Morgan was familiar with the major plant service companies in the Southeast and had suggested Green Thumbs, Inc. (GTI), as an acquisition target because of its significant market share and excellent reputation.

GTI had successfully commercialized a market that had been dominated by small local contractors and in-house landscaping departments. By first winning a contract from one of the largest theme parks in the United States, GTI's growth in sales had compounded remarkably over its 8-year history.

GTI had also been selected because of its large portfolio of long-term service contracts with several major Fortune 500 companies. These contracted clients would provide a captive customer base for the wholesale distribution of OS's plant products.

At the National Horticultural meeting in Los Angeles this past March, Ms. Morgan and OS's chief financial officer, Jack Levine, had approached the owner of GTI (a closely held corporation) to determine whether a merger offer would be welcomed. GTI's majority owner and president, Herb Merrell, had reacted favorably and subsequently provided financial data including GTI's earnings record and current balance sheet. These figures are presented in Tables 1 and 2 at the top of page 860.

Jack Levine had estimated that the incremental cash flow after taxes from the acquisition would be $18,750,000 for years 1 and 2; $20,500,000 for year 3; $21,750,000 for year 4; $24,000,000 for year 5; and $25,000,000 for years 6 through 30. He also estimated that the company should earn a rate of return of at least 16% on an investment of this type. Additional financial data for 2000 are available in Table 3 (on page 860) to analyze the acquisition potential of GTI.

REQUIRED

a. What is the maximum price Organic Solutions should offer GTI for a cash acquisition? (*Note:* Assume the relevant time horizon for analysis is 30 years.)

b. If OS planned to sell bonds to finance 80% of the cash acquisition price found in **a,** how might issuance of each of the following bonds impact the firm? Describe the characteristics and pros and cons of each bond.
   (1) Straight bonds.
   (2) Convertible bonds.
   (3) Bonds with stock purchase warrants attached.

c. (1) What is the *ratio of exchange* in a stock swap acquisition if OS pays $30 per share for GTI? Explain why.

TABLE 1   Green Thumbs, Inc., Earning Record

Year	EPS	Year	EPS
1993	$2.20	1997	$2.85
1994	2.35	1998	3.00
1995	2.45	1999	3.10
1996	2.60	2000	3.30

TABLE 2   Green Thumbs, Inc., Balance Sheet (December 31, 2000)

Assets		Liabilities and equity	
Cash	$ 2,500,000	Current liabilities	$ 5,250,000
Accounts receivable	1,500,000	Mortgage payable	3,125,000
Inventories	7,625,000	Common stock	15,625,000
Land	7,475,000	Retained earnings	9,000,000
Fixed assets (net)	13,900,000	Total liabilities and	
Total assets	$33,000,000	equity	$33,000,000

TABLE 3   OS and GTI Financial Data (December 31, 2000)

Item	OS	GTI
Earnings available for common stock	$35,000,000	$15,246,000
Number of shares of common stock outstanding	10,000,000	4,620,000
Market price per share	$50	$30[a]

[a]Estimated by Organic Solutions.

(2) What effect will this swap of stock have on the EPS of the original share-holders of (a) Organic Solutions and (b) Green Thumbs, Inc.? Explain why.

(3) If the earnings attributed to GTI's assets grow at a much slower rate than those attributed to OS's premerger assets, what effect might this have on the EPS of the merged firm over the long run?

d. What other merger proposals could OS make to GTI's owners?

e. What impact would the fact that GTI is actually a foreign-based company have on the foregoing analysis? Describe the added regulations, costs, bene-fits, and risks that are likely to be associated with such an international merger.

Appendix A

Financial Tables

TABLE A-1   Future Value Interest Factors for One Dollar Compounded at k Percent for n Periods:

$$FVIF_{k,n} = (1 + k)^n$$

TABLE A-2   Future Value Interest Factors for a One-Dollar Annuity Compounded at k Percent for n Periods:

$$FVIFA_{k,n} = \sum_{t=1}^{n} (1 + k)^{t-1}$$

TABLE A-3   Present Value Interest Factors for One Dollar Discounted at k Percent for n Periods:

$$PVIF_{k,n} = \frac{1}{(1 + k)^n}$$

TABLE A-4   Present Value Interest Factors for a One-Dollar Annuity Discounted at k Percent for n Periods:

$$PVIFA_{k,n} = \sum_{t=1}^{n} \frac{1}{(1 + k)^t}$$

TABLE A-1 Future Value Interest Factors for One Dollar Compounded at k Percent for n Periods: $FVIF_{k,n} = (1 + k)^n$

Period	1%	2%	3%	4%	5%	6%	7%	8%	9%	10%	11%	12%	13%	14%	15%	16%	17%	18%	19%	20%
1	1.010	1.020	1.030	1.040	1.050	1.060	1.070	1.080	1.090	1.100	1.110	1.120	1.130	1.140	1.150	1.160	1.170	1.180	1.190	1.200
2	1.020	1.040	1.061	1.082	1.102	1.124	1.145	1.166	1.188	1.210	1.232	1.254	1.277	1.300	1.322	1.346	1.369	1.392	1.416	1.440
3	1.030	1.061	1.093	1.125	1.158	1.191	1.225	1.260	1.295	1.331	1.368	1.405	1.443	1.482	1.521	1.561	1.602	1.643	1.685	1.728
4	1.041	1.082	1.126	1.170	1.216	1.262	1.311	1.360	1.412	1.464	1.518	1.574	1.630	1.689	1.749	1.811	1.874	1.939	2.005	2.074
5	1.051	1.104	1.159	1.217	1.276	1.338	1.403	1.469	1.539	1.611	1.685	1.762	1.842	1.925	2.011	2.100	2.192	2.288	2.386	2.488
6	1.062	1.126	1.194	1.265	1.340	1.419	1.501	1.587	1.677	1.772	1.870	1.974	2.082	2.195	2.313	2.436	2.565	2.700	2.840	2.986
7	1.072	1.149	1.230	1.316	1.407	1.504	1.606	1.714	1.828	1.949	2.076	2.211	2.353	2.502	2.660	2.826	3.001	3.185	3.379	3.583
8	1.083	1.172	1.267	1.369	1.477	1.594	1.718	1.851	1.993	2.144	2.305	2.476	2.658	2.853	3.059	3.278	3.511	3.759	4.021	4.300
9	1.094	1.195	1.305	1.423	1.551	1.689	1.838	1.999	2.172	2.358	2.558	2.773	3.004	3.252	3.518	3.803	4.108	4.435	4.785	5.160
10	1.105	1.219	1.344	1.480	1.629	1.791	1.967	2.159	2.367	2.594	2.839	3.106	3.395	3.707	4.046	4.411	4.807	5.234	5.695	6.192
11	1.116	1.243	1.384	1.539	1.710	1.898	2.105	2.332	2.580	2.853	3.152	3.479	3.836	4.226	4.652	5.117	5.624	6.176	6.777	7.430
12	1.127	1.268	1.426	1.601	1.796	2.012	2.252	2.518	2.813	3.138	3.498	3.896	4.334	4.818	5.350	5.936	6.580	7.288	8.064	8.916
13	1.138	1.294	1.469	1.665	1.886	2.133	2.410	2.720	3.066	3.452	3.883	4.363	4.898	5.492	6.153	6.886	7.699	8.599	9.596	10.699
14	1.149	1.319	1.513	1.732	1.980	2.261	2.579	2.937	3.342	3.797	4.310	4.887	5.535	6.261	7.076	7.987	9.007	10.147	11.420	12.839
15	1.161	1.346	1.558	1.801	2.079	2.397	2.759	3.172	3.642	4.177	4.785	5.474	6.254	7.138	8.137	9.265	10.539	11.974	13.589	15.407
16	1.173	1.373	1.605	1.873	2.183	2.540	2.952	3.426	3.970	4.595	5.311	6.130	7.067	8.137	9.358	10.748	12.330	14.129	16.171	18.488
17	1.184	1.400	1.653	1.948	2.292	2.693	3.159	3.700	4.328	5.054	5.895	6.866	7.986	9.276	10.761	12.468	14.426	16.672	19.244	22.186
18	1.196	1.428	1.702	2.026	2.407	2.854	3.380	3.996	4.717	5.560	6.543	7.690	9.024	10.575	12.375	14.462	16.879	19.673	22.900	26.623
19	1.208	1.457	1.753	2.107	2.527	3.026	3.616	4.316	5.142	6.116	7.263	8.613	10.197	12.055	14.232	16.776	19.748	23.214	27.251	31.948
20	1.220	1.486	1.806	2.191	2.653	3.207	3.870	4.661	5.604	6.727	8.062	9.646	11.523	13.743	16.366	19.461	23.105	27.393	32.429	38.337
21	1.232	1.516	1.860	2.279	2.786	3.399	4.140	5.034	6.109	7.400	8.949	10.804	13.021	15.667	18.821	22.574	27.033	32.323	38.591	46.005
22	1.245	1.546	1.916	2.370	2.925	3.603	4.430	5.436	6.658	8.140	9.933	12.100	14.713	17.861	21.644	26.186	31.629	38.141	45.923	55.205
23	1.257	1.577	1.974	2.465	3.071	3.820	4.740	5.871	7.258	8.954	11.026	13.552	16.626	20.361	24.891	30.376	37.005	45.007	54.648	66.247
24	1.270	1.608	2.033	2.563	3.225	4.049	5.072	6.341	7.911	9.850	12.239	15.178	18.788	23.212	28.625	35.236	43.296	53.108	65.031	79.496
25	1.282	1.641	2.094	2.666	3.386	4.292	5.427	6.848	8.623	10.834	13.585	17.000	21.230	26.461	32.918	40.874	50.656	62.667	77.387	95.395
30	1.348	1.811	2.427	3.243	4.322	5.743	7.612	10.062	13.267	17.449	22.892	29.960	39.115	50.949	66.210	85.849	111.061	143.367	184.672	237.373
35	1.417	2.000	2.814	3.946	5.516	7.686	10.676	14.785	20.413	28.102	38.574	52.799	72.066	98.097	133.172	180.311	243.495	327.988	440.691	590.657
40	1.489	2.208	3.262	4.801	7.040	10.285	14.974	21.724	31.408	45.258	64.999	93.049	132.776	188.876	267.856	378.715	533.846	750.353	1051.642	1469.740
45	1.565	2.438	3.781	5.841	8.985	13.764	21.002	31.920	48.325	72.888	109.527	163.985	244.629	363.662	538.752	795.429	1170.425	1716.619	2509.583	3657.176
50	1.645	2.691	4.384	7.106	11.467	18.419	29.456	46.900	74.354	117.386	184.559	288.996	450.711	700.197	1083.619	1670.669	2566.080	3927.189	5988.730	9100.191

USING THE CALCULATOR TO COMPUTE THE FUTURE VALUE OF A SINGLE AMOUNT

Before you begin, make sure to clear the memory, ensure that you are in the *end mode* and your calculator is set for *one payment per year,* and set the number of decimal places that you want (usually two for dollar-related accuracy).

SAMPLE PROBLEM

You place $800 in a savings account at 6 percent compounded annually. What is your account balance at the end of 5 years?

Hewlett-Packard HP 12C, 17 BII, and 19 BII[a]

Inputs:	800	5	6	
Functions:	PV	N	I%YR	FV
Outputs:				1070.58[b]

---

[a]For the 12C, you would use the n key instead of the N key, and the i key instead of the I%YR key.
[b]The minus sign that precedes the output should be ignored.

TABLE A-1 (Continued)

Period	21%	22%	23%	24%	25%	26%	27%	28%	29%	30%	31%	32%	33%	34%	35%	40%	45%	50%
1	1.210	1.220	1.230	1.240	1.250	1.260	1.270	1.280	1.290	1.300	1.310	1.320	1.330	1.340	1.350	1.400	1.450	1.500
2	1.464	1.488	1.513	1.538	1.562	1.588	1.613	1.638	1.664	1.690	1.716	1.742	1.769	1.796	1.822	1.960	2.102	2.250
3	1.772	1.816	1.861	1.907	1.953	2.000	2.048	2.097	2.147	2.197	2.248	2.300	2.353	2.406	2.460	2.744	3.049	3.375
4	2.144	2.215	2.289	2.364	2.441	2.520	2.601	2.684	2.769	2.856	2.945	3.036	3.129	3.224	3.321	3.842	4.421	5.063
5	2.594	2.703	2.815	2.932	3.052	3.176	3.304	3.436	3.572	3.713	3.858	4.007	4.162	4.320	4.484	5.378	6.410	7.594
6	3.138	3.297	3.463	3.635	3.815	4.001	4.196	4.398	4.608	4.827	5.054	5.290	5.535	5.789	6.053	7.530	9.294	11.391
7	3.797	4.023	4.259	4.508	4.768	5.042	5.329	5.629	5.945	6.275	6.621	6.983	7.361	7.758	8.172	10.541	13.476	17.086
8	4.595	4.908	5.239	5.589	5.960	6.353	6.767	7.206	7.669	8.157	8.673	9.217	9.791	10.395	11.032	14.758	19.541	25.629
9	5.560	5.987	6.444	6.931	7.451	8.004	8.595	9.223	9.893	10.604	11.362	12.166	13.022	13.930	14.894	20.661	28.334	38.443
10	6.727	7.305	7.926	8.594	9.313	10.086	10.915	11.806	12.761	13.786	14.884	16.060	17.319	18.666	20.106	28.925	41.085	57.665
11	8.140	8.912	9.749	10.657	11.642	12.708	13.862	15.112	16.462	17.921	19.498	21.199	23.034	25.012	27.144	40.495	59.573	86.498
12	9.850	10.872	11.991	13.215	14.552	16.012	17.605	19.343	21.236	23.298	25.542	27.982	30.635	33.516	36.644	56.694	86.380	129.746
13	11.918	13.264	14.749	16.386	18.190	20.175	22.359	24.759	27.395	30.287	33.460	36.937	40.745	44.912	49.469	79.371	125.251	194.620
14	14.421	16.182	18.141	20.319	22.737	25.420	28.395	31.691	35.339	39.373	43.832	48.756	54.190	60.181	66.784	111.119	181.614	291.929
15	17.449	19.742	22.314	25.195	28.422	32.030	36.062	40.565	45.587	51.185	57.420	64.358	72.073	80.643	90.158	155.567	263.341	437.894
16	21.113	24.085	27.446	31.242	35.527	40.357	45.799	51.923	58.808	66.541	75.220	84.953	95.857	108.061	121.713	217.793	381.844	656.841
17	25.547	29.384	33.758	38.740	44.409	50.850	58.165	66.461	75.862	86.503	98.539	112.138	127.490	144.802	164.312	304.911	553.674	985.261
18	30.912	35.848	41.523	48.038	55.511	64.071	73.869	85.070	97.862	112.454	129.086	148.022	169.561	194.035	221.822	426.875	802.826	1477.892
19	37.404	43.735	51.073	59.567	69.389	80.730	93.813	108.890	126.242	146.190	169.102	195.389	225.517	260.006	299.459	597.625	1164.098	2216.838
20	45.258	53.357	62.820	73.863	86.736	101.720	119.143	139.379	162.852	190.047	221.523	257.913	299.937	348.408	404.270	836.674	1687.942	3325.257
21	54.762	65.095	77.268	91.591	108.420	128.167	151.312	178.405	210.079	247.061	290.196	340.446	398.916	466.867	545.764	1171.343	2447.515	4987.883
22	66.262	79.416	95.040	113.572	135.525	161.490	192.165	228.358	271.002	321.178	380.156	449.388	530.558	625.601	736.781	1639.878	3548.896	7481.824
23	80.178	96.887	116.899	140.829	169.407	203.477	244.050	292.298	349.592	417.531	498.004	593.192	705.642	838.305	994.653	2295.829	5145.898	11222.738
24	97.015	118.203	143.786	174.628	211.758	256.381	309.943	374.141	450.974	542.791	652.385	783.013	938.504	1123.328	1342.781	3214.158	7461.547	16834.109
25	117.388	144.207	176.857	216.539	264.698	323.040	393.628	478.901	581.756	705.627	854.623	1033.577	1248.210	1505.258	1812.754	4499.816	10819.242	25251.164
30	304.471	389.748	497.904	634.810	807.793	1025.904	1300.477	1645.488	2078.208	2619.936	3297.081	4142.008	5194.516	6503.285	8128.426	24201.043	69348.375	191751.000
35	789.716	1053.370	1401.749	1861.020	2465.189	3258.053	4296.547	5653.840	7423.988	9727.598	12719.918	16598.906	21617.363	28096.695	36448.051	130158.687	*	*
40	2048.309	2846.941	3946.340	5455.797	7523.156	10346.879	14195.051	19426.418	26520.723	36117.754	49072.621	66519.313	89962.188	121388.437	163433.875	700022.688	*	*
45	5312.758	7694.418	11110.121	15994.316	22958.844	32859.457	46897.973	66748.500	94739.937	134102.187	*	*	*	*	*	*	*	*
50	13779.844	20795.680	31278.301	46889.207	70064.812	104354.562	154942.687	229345.875	338440.000	497910.125	*	*	*	*	*	*	*	*

*Not shown due to space limitations.

Texas Instruments BA-35, BAII, BAII Plus[c]

Inputs:	800	5	6

Functions:	PV	N	%i	CPT	FV

Outputs:					1070.58 [d]

[c]For the Texas Instruments BAII, you would use the 2nd key instead of the CPT key; for the Texas Instruments BAII Plus, you would use the I/Y key instead of the %i key.

[d]If a minus sign precedes the output, it should be ignored.

TABLE A-2   Future Value Interest Factors for a One-Dollar Annuity Compounded at k Percent for n Periods: $FVIFA_{k,n} = \sum_{t=1}^{n} (1 + k)^{t-1}$

Period	1%	2%	3%	4%	5%	6%	7%	8%	9%	10%	11%	12%	13%	14%	15%	16%	17%	18%	19%	20%
1	1.000	1.000	1.000	1.000	1.000	1.000	1.000	1.000	1.000	1.000	1.000	1.000	1.000	1.000	1.000	1.000	1.000	1.000	1.000	1.000
2	2.010	2.020	2.030	2.040	2.050	2.060	2.070	2.080	2.090	2.100	2.110	2.120	2.130	2.140	2.150	2.160	2.170	2.180	2.190	2.200
3	3.030	3.060	3.091	3.122	3.152	3.184	3.215	3.246	3.278	3.310	3.342	3.374	3.407	3.440	3.472	3.506	3.539	3.572	3.606	3.640
4	4.060	4.122	4.184	4.246	4.310	4.375	4.440	4.506	4.573	4.641	4.710	4.779	4.850	4.921	4.993	5.066	5.141	5.215	5.291	5.368
5	5.101	5.204	5.309	5.416	5.526	5.637	5.751	5.867	5.985	6.105	6.228	6.353	6.480	6.610	6.742	6.877	7.014	7.154	7.297	7.442
6	6.152	6.308	6.468	6.633	6.802	6.975	7.153	7.336	7.523	7.716	7.913	8.115	8.323	8.535	8.754	8.977	9.207	9.442	9.683	9.930
7	7.214	7.434	7.662	7.898	8.142	8.394	8.654	8.923	9.200	9.487	9.783	10.089	10.405	10.730	11.067	11.414	11.772	12.141	12.523	12.916
8	8.286	8.583	8.892	9.214	9.549	9.897	10.260	10.637	11.028	11.436	11.859	12.300	12.757	13.233	13.727	14.240	14.773	15.327	15.902	16.499
9	9.368	9.755	10.159	10.583	11.027	11.491	11.978	12.488	13.021	13.579	14.164	14.776	15.416	16.085	16.786	17.518	18.285	19.086	19.923	20.799
10	10.462	10.950	11.464	12.006	12.578	13.181	13.816	14.487	15.193	15.937	16.722	17.549	18.420	19.337	20.304	21.321	22.393	23.521	24.709	25.959
11	11.567	12.169	12.808	13.486	14.207	14.972	15.784	16.645	17.560	18.531	19.561	20.655	21.814	23.044	24.349	25.733	27.200	28.755	30.403	32.150
12	12.682	13.412	14.192	15.026	15.917	16.870	17.888	18.977	20.141	21.384	22.713	24.133	25.650	27.271	29.001	30.850	32.824	34.931	37.180	39.580
13	13.809	14.680	15.618	16.627	17.713	18.882	20.141	21.495	22.953	24.523	26.211	28.029	29.984	32.088	34.352	36.786	39.404	42.218	45.244	48.496
14	14.947	15.974	17.086	18.292	19.598	21.015	22.550	24.215	26.019	27.975	30.095	32.392	34.882	37.581	40.504	43.672	47.102	50.818	54.841	59.196
15	16.097	17.293	18.599	20.023	21.578	23.276	25.129	27.152	29.361	31.772	34.405	37.280	40.417	43.842	47.580	51.659	56.109	60.965	66.260	72.035
16	17.258	18.639	20.157	21.824	23.657	25.672	27.888	30.324	33.003	35.949	39.190	42.753	46.671	50.980	55.717	60.925	66.648	72.938	79.850	87.442
17	18.430	20.012	21.761	23.697	25.840	28.213	30.840	33.750	36.973	40.544	44.500	48.883	53.738	59.117	65.075	71.673	78.978	87.067	96.021	105.930
18	19.614	21.412	23.414	25.645	28.132	30.905	33.999	37.450	41.301	45.599	50.396	55.749	61.724	68.393	75.836	84.140	93.404	103.739	115.265	128.116
19	20.811	22.840	25.117	27.671	30.539	33.760	37.379	41.446	46.018	51.158	56.939	63.439	70.748	78.968	88.211	98.603	110.283	123.412	138.165	154.739
20	22.019	24.297	26.870	29.778	33.066	36.785	40.995	45.762	51.159	57.274	64.202	72.052	80.946	91.024	102.443	115.379	130.031	146.626	165.417	186.687
21	23.239	25.783	28.676	31.969	35.719	39.992	44.865	50.422	56.764	64.002	72.264	81.698	92.468	104.767	118.809	134.840	153.136	174.019	197.846	225.024
22	24.471	27.299	30.536	34.248	38.505	43.392	49.005	55.456	62.872	71.402	81.213	92.502	105.489	120.434	137.630	157.414	180.169	206.342	236.436	271.028
23	25.716	28.845	32.452	36.618	41.430	46.995	53.435	60.893	69.531	79.542	91.147	104.602	120.203	138.295	159.274	183.600	211.798	244.483	282.359	326.234
24	26.973	30.421	34.426	39.082	44.501	50.815	58.176	66.764	76.789	88.496	102.173	118.154	136.829	158.656	184.166	213.976	248.803	289.490	337.007	392.480
25	28.243	32.030	36.459	41.645	47.726	54.864	63.248	73.105	84.699	98.346	114.412	133.333	155.616	181.867	212.790	249.212	292.099	342.598	402.038	471.976
30	34.784	40.567	47.575	56.084	66.438	79.057	94.459	113.282	136.305	164.491	199.018	241.330	293.192	356.778	434.738	530.306	647.423	790.932	966.698	1181.865
35	41.659	49.994	60.461	73.651	90.318	111.432	138.234	172.314	215.705	271.018	341.583	431.658	546.663	693.552	881.152	1120.699	1426.448	1816.607	2314.173	2948.294
40	48.885	60.401	75.400	95.024	120.797	154.758	199.630	259.052	337.872	442.580	581.812	767.080	1013.667	1341.979	1779.048	2360.724	3134.412	4163.094	5529.711	7343.715
45	56.479	71.891	92.718	121.027	159.695	212.737	285.741	386.497	525.840	718.881	986.613	1358.208	1874.086	2590.464	3585.031	4965.191	6879.008	9531.258	13203.105	18280.914
50	64.461	84.577	112.794	152.664	209.341	290.325	406.516	573.756	815.051	1163.865	1668.723	2399.975	3459.344	4994.301	7217.488	10435.449	15088.805	21812.273	31514.492	45496.094

USING THE CALCULATOR TO COMPUTE THE FUTURE VALUE OF AN ANNUITY

Before you begin, make sure to clear the memory, ensure that you are in the *end mode* and your calculator is set for *one payment per year,* and set the number of decimal places that you want (usually two for dollar-related accuracy).

SAMPLE PROBLEM

You want to know what the future value will be at the end of 5 years if you place five end-of-year deposits of $1,000 in an account paying 7 percent annually. What is your account balance at the end of 5 years?

Hewlett-Packard HP 12C, 17 BII, and 19 BII[a]

Inputs:	1000	5	7
Functions:	PMT	N	I%YR	FV
Outputs:			5750.74 [b]

---

[a]For the 12C, you would use the n key instead of the N key, and the i key instead of the I%YR key.
[b]The minus sign that precedes the output should be ignored.

TABLE A-2 (Continued)

Period	21%	22%	23%	24%	25%	26%	27%	28%	29%	30%	31%	32%	33%	34%	35%	40%	45%	50%
1	1.000	1.000	1.000	1.000	1.000	1.000	1.000	1.000	1.000	1.000	1.000	1.000	1.000	1.000	1.000	1.000	1.000	1.000
2	2.210	2.220	2.230	2.240	2.250	2.260	2.270	2.280	2.290	2.300	2.310	2.320	2.330	2.340	2.350	2.400	2.450	2.500
3	3.674	3.708	3.743	3.778	3.813	3.848	3.883	3.918	3.954	3.990	4.026	4.062	4.099	4.136	4.172	4.360	4.552	4.750
4	5.446	5.524	5.604	5.684	5.766	5.848	5.931	6.016	6.101	6.187	6.274	6.362	6.452	6.542	6.633	7.104	7.601	8.125
5	7.589	7.740	7.893	8.048	8.207	8.368	8.533	8.700	8.870	9.043	9.219	9.398	9.581	9.766	9.954	10.946	12.022	13.188
6	10.183	10.442	10.708	10.980	11.259	11.544	11.837	12.136	12.442	12.756	13.077	13.406	13.742	14.086	14.438	16.324	18.431	20.781
7	13.321	13.740	14.171	14.615	15.073	15.546	16.032	16.534	17.051	17.583	18.131	18.696	19.277	19.876	20.492	23.853	27.725	32.172
8	17.119	17.762	18.430	19.123	19.842	20.588	21.361	22.163	22.995	23.858	24.752	25.678	26.638	27.633	28.664	34.395	41.202	49.258
9	21.714	22.670	23.669	24.712	25.802	26.940	28.129	29.369	30.664	32.015	33.425	34.895	36.429	38.028	39.696	49.152	60.743	74.887
10	27.274	28.657	30.113	31.643	33.253	34.945	36.723	38.592	40.556	42.619	44.786	47.062	49.451	51.958	54.590	69.813	89.077	113.330
11	34.001	35.962	38.039	40.238	42.566	45.030	47.639	50.398	53.318	56.405	59.670	63.121	66.769	70.624	74.696	98.739	130.161	170.995
12	42.141	44.873	47.787	50.895	54.208	57.738	61.501	65.510	69.780	74.326	79.167	84.320	89.803	95.636	101.840	139.234	189.734	257.493
13	51.991	55.745	59.778	64.109	68.760	73.750	79.106	84.853	91.016	97.624	104.709	112.302	120.438	129.152	138.484	195.928	276.114	387.239
14	63.909	69.009	74.528	80.496	86.949	93.925	101.465	109.611	118.411	127.912	138.169	149.239	161.183	174.063	187.953	275.299	401.365	581.858
15	78.330	85.191	92.669	100.815	109.687	119.346	129.860	141.302	153.750	167.285	182.001	197.996	215.373	234.245	254.737	386.418	582.980	873.788
16	95.779	104.933	114.983	126.010	138.109	151.375	165.922	181.867	199.337	218.470	239.421	262.354	287.446	314.888	344.895	541.985	846.321	1311.681
17	116.892	129.019	142.428	157.252	173.636	191.733	211.721	233.790	258.145	285.011	314.642	347.307	383.303	422.949	466.608	759.778	1228.165	1968.522
18	142.439	158.403	176.187	195.993	218.045	242.583	269.885	300.250	334.006	371.514	413.180	459.445	510.792	567.751	630.920	1064.689	1781.838	2953.783
19	173.351	194.251	217.710	244.031	273.556	306.654	343.754	385.321	431.868	483.968	542.266	607.467	680.354	761.786	852.741	1491.563	2584.665	4431.672
20	210.755	237.986	268.783	303.598	342.945	387.384	437.568	494.210	558.110	630.157	711.368	802.856	905.870	1021.792	1152.200	2089.188	3748.763	6648.508
21	256.013	291.343	331.603	377.461	429.681	489.104	556.710	633.589	720.962	820.204	932.891	1060.769	1205.807	1370.201	1556.470	2925.862	5436.703	9973.762
22	310.775	356.438	408.871	469.052	538.101	617.270	708.022	811.993	931.040	1067.265	1223.087	1401.215	1604.724	1837.068	2102.234	4097.203	7884.215	14961.645
23	377.038	435.854	503.911	582.624	673.626	778.760	900.187	1040.351	1202.042	1388.443	1603.243	1850.603	2135.282	2462.669	2839.014	5737.078	11433.109	22443.469
24	457.215	532.741	620.810	723.453	843.032	982.237	1144.237	1332.649	1551.634	1805.975	2101.247	2443.795	2840.924	3300.974	3833.667	8032.906	16579.008	33666.207
25	554.230	650.944	764.596	898.082	1054.791	1238.617	1454.180	1706.790	2002.608	2348.765	2753.631	3226.808	3779.428	4424.301	5176.445	11247.062	24040.555	50500.316
30	1445.111	1767.044	2160.459	2640.881	3227.172	3941.953	4812.891	5873.172	7162.785	8729.805	10632.543	12940.672	15737.945	19124.434	23221.258	60500.207	154105.313	383500.000
35	3755.814	4783.520	6090.227	7750.094	9856.746	12527.160	15909.480	20188.742	25596.512	32422.090	41028.887	51868.563	65504.199	82634.625	104134.500	325394.688	*	*
40	9749.141	12936.141	17153.691	22728.367	30088.621	39791.957	52570.707	69376.562	91447.375	120389.375	*	*	*	*	*	*	*	*
45	25294.223	34970.230	48300.660	66638.937	91831.312	126378.937	173692.875	238384.312	326686.375	447005.062	*	*	*	*	*	*	*	*

*Not shown due to space limitations.

Texas Instruments BA-35, BAII, BAII Plus[c]

Inputs:	1000	5	7		
Functions:	PMT	N	%i	CPT	FV
Outputs:					5750.74 [d]

[c]For the Texas Instruments BAII, you would use the 2nd key instead of the CPT key; for the Texas Instruments BAII Plus, you would use the I/Y key instead of the %i key.
[d]If a minus sign precedes the output, it should be ignored.

TABLE A-3 **Present Value Interest Factors for One Dollar Discounted at *k* Percent for *n* Periods:**

$$PVIF_{k,n} = \frac{1}{(1+k)^n}$$

Period	1%	2%	3%	4%	5%	6%	7%	8%	9%	10%	11%	12%	13%	14%	15%	16%	17%	18%	19%	20%
1	.990	.980	.971	.962	.952	.943	.935	.926	.917	.909	.901	.893	.885	.877	.870	.862	.855	.847	.840	.833
2	.980	.961	.943	.925	.907	.890	.873	.857	.842	.826	.812	.797	.783	.769	.756	.743	.731	.718	.706	.694
3	.971	.942	.915	.889	.864	.840	.816	.794	.772	.751	.731	.712	.693	.675	.658	.641	.624	.609	.593	.579
4	.961	.924	.888	.855	.823	.792	.763	.735	.708	.683	.659	.636	.613	.592	.572	.552	.534	.516	.499	.482
5	.951	.906	.863	.822	.784	.747	.713	.681	.650	.621	.593	.567	.543	.519	.497	.476	.456	.437	.419	.402
6	.942	.888	.837	.790	.746	.705	.666	.630	.596	.564	.535	.507	.480	.456	.432	.410	.390	.370	.352	.335
7	.933	.871	.813	.760	.711	.665	.623	.583	.547	.513	.482	.452	.425	.400	.376	.354	.333	.314	.296	.279
8	.923	.853	.789	.731	.677	.627	.582	.540	.502	.467	.434	.404	.376	.351	.327	.305	.285	.266	.249	.233
9	.914	.837	.766	.703	.645	.592	.544	.500	.460	.424	.391	.361	.333	.308	.284	.263	.243	.225	.209	.194
10	.905	.820	.744	.676	.614	.558	.508	.463	.422	.386	.352	.322	.295	.270	.247	.227	.208	.191	.176	.162
11	.896	.804	.722	.650	.585	.527	.475	.429	.388	.350	.317	.287	.261	.237	.215	.195	.178	.162	.148	.135
12	.887	.789	.701	.625	.557	.497	.444	.397	.356	.319	.286	.257	.231	.208	.187	.168	.152	.137	.124	.112
13	.879	.773	.681	.601	.530	.469	.415	.368	.326	.290	.258	.229	.204	.182	.163	.145	.130	.116	.104	.093
14	.870	.758	.661	.577	.505	.442	.388	.340	.299	.263	.232	.205	.181	.160	.141	.125	.111	.099	.088	.078
15	.861	.743	.642	.555	.481	.417	.362	.315	.275	.239	.209	.183	.160	.140	.123	.108	.095	.084	.074	.065
16	.853	.728	.623	.534	.458	.394	.339	.292	.252	.218	.188	.163	.141	.123	.107	.093	.081	.071	.062	.054
17	.844	.714	.605	.513	.436	.371	.317	.270	.231	.198	.170	.146	.125	.108	.093	.080	.069	.060	.052	.045
18	.836	.700	.587	.494	.416	.350	.296	.250	.212	.180	.153	.130	.111	.095	.081	.069	.059	.051	.044	.038
19	.828	.686	.570	.475	.396	.331	.277	.232	.194	.164	.138	.116	.098	.083	.070	.060	.051	.043	.037	.031
20	.820	.673	.554	.456	.377	.312	.258	.215	.178	.149	.124	.104	.087	.073	.061	.051	.043	.037	.031	.026
21	.811	.660	.538	.439	.359	.294	.242	.199	.164	.135	.112	.093	.077	.064	.053	.044	.037	.031	.026	.022
22	.803	.647	.522	.422	.342	.278	.226	.184	.150	.123	.101	.083	.068	.056	.046	.038	.032	.026	.022	.018
23	.795	.634	.507	.406	.326	.262	.211	.170	.138	.112	.091	.074	.060	.049	.040	.033	.027	.022	.018	.015
24	.788	.622	.492	.390	.310	.247	.197	.158	.126	.102	.082	.066	.053	.043	.035	.028	.023	.019	.015	.013
25	.780	.610	.478	.375	.295	.233	.184	.146	.116	.092	.074	.059	.047	.038	.030	.024	.020	.016	.013	.010
30	.742	.552	.412	.308	.231	.174	.131	.099	.075	.057	.044	.033	.026	.020	.015	.012	.009	.007	.005	.004
35	.706	.500	.355	.253	.181	.130	.094	.068	.049	.036	.026	.019	.014	.010	.008	.006	.004	.003	.002	.002
40	.672	.453	.307	.208	.142	.097	.067	.046	.032	.022	.015	.011	.008	.005	.004	.003	.002	.001	.001	.001
45	.639	.410	.264	.171	.111	.073	.048	.031	.021	.014	.009	.006	.004	.003	.002	.001	.001	.001	*	*
50	.608	.372	.228	.141	.087	.054	.034	.021	.013	.009	.005	.003	.002	.001	.001	.001	*	*	*	*

*PVIF is zero to three decimal places.

USING THE CALCULATOR TO COMPUTE THE PRESENT VALUE OF A SINGLE AMOUNT

Before you begin, make sure to clear the memory, ensure that you are in the *end mode* and your calculator is set for *one payment per year,* and set the number of decimal places that you want (usually two for dollar-related accuracy).

SAMPLE PROBLEM

You want to know the present value of $1,700 to be received at the end of 8 years, assuming an 8 percent discount rate.

Hewlett-Packard HP 12C, 17 BII, and 19 BII[a]

Inputs:	1700	8	8	
Functions:	FV	N	I%YR	PV
Outputs:				918.46 [b]

[a]For the 12C, you would use the **n** key instead of the **N** key, and the **i** key instead of the **I%YR** key.

[b]The minus sign that precedes the output should be ignored.

TABLE A-3   (Continued)

Period	21%	22%	23%	24%	25%	26%	27%	28%	29%	30%	31%	32%	33%	34%	35%	40%	45%	50%
1	.826	.820	.813	.806	.800	.794	.787	.781	.775	.769	.763	.758	.752	.746	.741	.714	.690	.667
2	.683	.672	.661	.650	.640	.630	.620	.610	.601	.592	.583	.574	.565	.557	.549	.510	.476	.444
3	.564	.551	.537	.524	.512	.500	.488	.477	.466	.455	.445	.435	.425	.416	.406	.364	.328	.296
4	.467	.451	.437	.423	.410	.397	.384	.373	.361	.350	.340	.329	.320	.310	.301	.260	.226	.198
5	.386	.370	.355	.341	.328	.315	.303	.291	.280	.269	.259	.250	.240	.231	.223	.186	.156	.132
6	.319	.303	.289	.275	.262	.250	.238	.227	.217	.207	.198	.189	.181	.173	.165	.133	.108	.088
7	.263	.249	.235	.222	.210	.198	.188	.178	.168	.159	.151	.143	.136	.129	.122	.095	.074	.059
8	.218	.204	.191	.179	.168	.157	.148	.139	.130	.123	.115	.108	.102	.096	.091	.068	.051	.039
9	.180	.167	.155	.144	.134	.125	.116	.108	.101	.094	.088	.082	.077	.072	.067	.048	.035	.026
10	.149	.137	.126	.116	.107	.099	.092	.085	.078	.073	.067	.062	.058	.054	.050	.035	.024	.017
11	.123	.112	.103	.094	.086	.079	.072	.066	.061	.056	.051	.047	.043	.040	.037	.025	.017	.012
12	.102	.092	.083	.076	.069	.062	.057	.052	.047	.043	.039	.036	.033	.030	.027	.018	.012	.008
13	.084	.075	.068	.061	.055	.050	.045	.040	.037	.033	.030	.027	.025	.022	.020	.013	.008	.005
14	.069	.062	.055	.049	.044	.039	.035	.032	.028	.025	.023	.021	.018	.017	.015	.009	.006	.003
15	.057	.051	.045	.040	.035	.031	.028	.025	.022	.020	.017	.016	.014	.012	.011	.006	.004	.002
16	.047	.042	.036	.032	.028	.025	.022	.019	.017	.015	.013	.012	.010	.009	.008	.005	.003	.002
17	.039	.034	.030	.026	.023	.020	.017	.015	.013	.012	.010	.009	.008	.007	.006	.003	.002	.001
18	.032	.028	.024	.021	.018	.016	.014	.012	.010	.009	.008	.007	.006	.005	.005	.002	.001	.001
19	.027	.023	.020	.017	.014	.012	.011	.009	.008	.007	.006	.005	.004	.004	.003	.002	.001	*
20	.022	.019	.016	.014	.012	.010	.008	.007	.006	.005	.005	.004	.003	.003	.002	.001	.001	*
21	.018	.015	.013	.011	.009	.008	.007	.006	.005	.004	.003	.003	.003	.002	.002	.001	*	*
22	.015	.013	.011	.009	.007	.006	.005	.004	.004	.003	.003	.002	.002	.002	.001	.001	*	*
23	.012	.010	.009	.007	.006	.005	.004	.003	.003	.002	.002	.002	.001	.001	.001	*	*	*
24	.010	.008	.007	.006	.005	.004	.003	.003	.002	.002	.002	.001	.001	.001	.001	*	*	*
25	.009	.007	.006	.005	.004	.003	.003	.002	.002	.001	.001	.001	.001	.001	.001	*	*	*
30	.003	.003	.002	.002	.001	.001	.001	.001	*	*	*	*	*	*	*	*	*	*
35	.001	.001	.001	.001	*	*	*	*	*	*	*	*	*	*	*	*	*	*
40	*	*	*	*	*	*	*	*	*	*	*	*	*	*	*	*	*	*
45	*	*	*	*	*	*	*	*	*	*	*	*	*	*	*	*	*	*
50	*	*	*	*	*	*	*	*	*	*	*	*	*	*	*	*	*	*

*$PVIF$ is zero to three decimal places.

Texas Instruments BA-35, BAII, BAII Plus[c]

Inputs:	1700	8	8	
Functions:	FV	N	%i	CPT PV
Outputs:				918.46 [d]

[c]For the Texas Instruments BAII, you would use the 2nd key instead of the CPT key; for the Texas Instruments BAII Plus, you would use the I/Y key instead of the %i key.
[d]If a minus sign precedes the output, it should be ignored.

TABLE A-4   Present Value Interest Factors for a One-Dollar Annuity Discounted at *k* Percent for *n*

$$\text{Periods: } PVIFA_{k,n} = \sum_{t=1}^{n} \frac{1}{(1+k)^t}$$

Period	1%	2%	3%	4%	5%	6%	7%	8%	9%	10%	11%	12%	13%	14%	15%	16%	17%	18%	19%	20%
1	.990	.980	.971	.962	.952	.943	.935	.926	.917	.909	.901	.893	.885	.877	.870	.862	.855	.847	.840	.833
2	1.970	1.942	1.913	1.886	1.859	1.833	1.808	1.783	1.759	1.736	1.713	1.690	1.668	1.647	1.626	1.605	1.585	1.566	1.547	1.528
3	2.941	2.884	2.829	2.775	2.723	2.673	2.624	2.577	2.531	2.487	2.444	2.402	2.361	2.322	2.283	2.246	2.210	2.174	2.140	2.106
4	3.902	3.808	3.717	3.630	3.546	3.465	3.387	3.312	3.240	3.170	3.102	3.037	2.974	2.914	2.855	2.798	2.743	2.690	2.639	2.589
5	4.853	4.713	4.580	4.452	4.329	4.212	4.100	3.993	3.890	3.791	3.696	3.605	3.517	3.433	3.352	3.274	3.199	3.127	3.058	2.991
6	5.795	5.601	5.417	5.242	5.076	4.917	4.767	4.623	4.486	4.355	4.231	4.111	3.998	3.889	3.784	3.685	3.589	3.498	3.410	3.326
7	6.728	6.472	6.230	6.002	5.786	5.582	5.389	5.206	5.033	4.868	4.712	4.564	4.423	4.288	4.160	4.039	3.922	3.812	3.706	3.605
8	7.652	7.326	7.020	6.733	6.463	6.210	5.971	5.747	5.535	5.335	5.146	4.968	4.799	4.639	4.487	4.344	4.207	4.078	3.954	3.837
9	8.566	8.162	7.786	7.435	7.108	6.802	6.515	6.247	5.995	5.759	5.537	5.328	5.132	4.946	4.772	4.607	4.451	4.303	4.163	4.031
10	9.471	8.983	8.530	8.111	7.722	7.360	7.024	6.710	6.418	6.145	5.889	5.650	5.426	5.216	5.019	4.833	4.659	4.494	4.339	4.192
11	10.368	9.787	9.253	8.760	8.306	7.887	7.499	7.139	6.805	6.495	6.207	5.938	5.687	5.453	5.234	5.029	4.836	4.656	4.486	4.327
12	11.255	10.575	9.954	9.385	8.863	8.384	7.943	7.536	7.161	6.814	6.492	6.194	5.918	5.660	5.421	5.197	4.988	4.793	4.611	4.439
13	12.134	11.348	10.635	9.986	9.394	8.853	8.358	7.904	7.487	7.013	6.750	6.424	6.122	5.842	5.583	5.342	5.118	4.910	4.715	4.533
14	13.004	12.106	11.296	10.563	9.899	9.295	8.745	8.244	7.786	7.367	6.982	6.628	6.302	6.002	5.724	5.468	5.229	5.008	4.802	4.611
15	13.865	12.849	11.938	11.118	10.380	9.712	9.108	8.560	8.061	7.606	7.191	6.811	6.462	6.142	5.847	5.575	5.324	5.092	4.876	4.675
16	14.718	13.578	12.561	11.652	10.838	10.106	9.447	8.851	8.313	7.824	7.379	6.974	6.604	6.265	5.954	5.668	5.405	5.162	4.938	4.730
17	15.562	14.292	13.166	12.166	11.274	10.477	9.763	9.122	8.544	8.022	7.549	7.120	6.729	6.373	6.047	5.749	5.475	5.222	4.990	4.775
18	16.398	14.992	13.754	12.659	11.690	10.828	10.059	9.372	8.756	8.201	7.702	7.250	6.840	6.467	6.128	5.818	5.534	5.273	5.033	4.812
19	17.226	15.679	14.324	13.134	12.085	11.158	10.336	9.604	8.950	8.365	7.839	7.366	6.938	6.550	6.198	5.877	5.584	5.316	5.070	4.843
20	18.046	16.352	14.878	13.590	12.462	11.470	10.594	9.818	9.129	8.514	7.963	7.469	7.025	6.623	6.259	5.929	5.628	5.353	5.101	4.870
21	18.857	17.011	15.415	14.029	12.821	11.764	10.836	10.017	9.292	8.649	8.075	7.562	7.102	6.687	6.312	5.973	5.665	5.384	5.127	4.891
22	19.661	17.658	15.937	14.451	13.163	12.042	11.061	10.201	9.442	8.772	8.176	7.645	7.170	6.743	6.359	6.011	5.696	5.410	5.149	4.909
23	20.456	18.292	16.444	14.857	13.489	12.303	11.272	10.371	9.580	8.883	8.266	7.718	7.230	6.792	6.399	6.044	5.723	5.432	5.167	4.925
24	21.244	18.914	16.936	15.247	13.799	12.550	11.469	10.529	9.707	8.985	8.348	7.784	7.283	6.835	6.434	6.073	5.746	5.451	5.182	4.937
25	22.023	19.524	17.413	15.622	14.094	12.783	11.654	10.675	9.823	9.077	8.422	7.843	7.330	6.873	6.464	6.097	5.766	5.467	5.195	4.948
30	25.808	22.396	19.601	17.292	15.373	13.765	12.409	11.258	10.274	9.427	8.694	8.055	7.496	7.003	6.566	6.177	5.829	5.517	5.235	4.979
35	29.409	24.999	21.487	18.665	16.374	14.498	12.948	11.655	10.567	9.644	8.855	8.176	7.586	7.070	6.617	6.215	5.858	5.539	5.251	4.992
40	32.835	27.356	23.115	19.793	17.159	15.046	13.332	11.925	10.757	9.779	8.951	8.244	7.634	7.105	6.642	6.233	5.871	5.548	5.258	4.997
45	36.095	29.490	24.519	20.720	17.774	15.456	13.606	12.108	10.881	9.863	9.008	8.283	7.661	7.123	6.654	6.242	5.877	5.552	5.261	4.999
50	39.196	31.424	25.730	21.482	18.256	15.762	13.801	12.233	10.962	9.915	9.042	8.304	7.675	7.133	6.661	6.246	5.880	5.554	5.262	4.999

USING THE CALCULATOR TO COMPUTE THE PRESENT VALUE OF AN ANNUITY

Before you begin, make sure to clear the memory, ensure that you are in the *end mode* and your calculator is set for *one payment per year,* and set the number of decimal places that you want (usually two for dollar-related accuracy).

SAMPLE PROBLEM

You want to know what the present value will be of an annuity of $700 per year at the end of each year for 5 years, given a discount rate of 8 percent.

Hewlett-Packard HP 12C, 17 BII, and 19 BII[a]

Inputs:	700	5	8	
Functions:	PMT	N	I%YR	PV
Outputs:				2794.90[b]

---

[a]For the 12C, you would use the n key instead of the N key, and the i key instead of the I%YR key.

[b]The minus sign that precedes the output should be ignored.

TABLE A-4 (Continued)

Period	21%	22%	23%	24%	25%	26%	27%	28%	29%	30%	31%	32%	33%	34%	35%	40%	45%	50%
1	.826	.820	.813	.806	.800	.794	.787	.781	.775	.769	.763	.758	.752	.746	.741	.714	.690	.667
2	1.509	1.492	1.474	1.457	1.440	1.424	1.407	1.392	1.376	1.361	1.346	1.331	1.317	1.303	1.289	1.224	1.165	1.111
3	2.074	2.042	2.011	1.981	1.952	1.923	1.896	1.868	1.842	1.816	1.791	1.766	1.742	1.719	1.696	1.589	1.493	1.407
4	2.540	2.494	2.448	2.404	2.362	2.320	2.280	2.241	2.203	2.166	2.130	2.096	2.062	2.029	1.997	1.849	1.720	1.605
5	2.926	2.864	2.803	2.745	2.689	2.635	2.583	2.532	2.483	2.436	2.390	2.345	2.302	2.260	2.220	2.035	1.876	1.737
6	3.245	3.167	3.092	3.020	2.951	2.885	2.821	2.759	2.700	2.643	2.588	2.534	2.483	2.433	2.385	2.168	1.983	1.824
7	3.508	3.416	3.327	3.242	3.161	3.083	3.009	2.937	2.868	2.802	2.739	2.677	2.619	2.562	2.508	2.263	2.057	1.883
8	3.726	3.619	3.518	3.421	3.329	3.241	3.156	3.076	2.999	2.925	2.854	2.786	2.721	2.658	2.598	2.331	2.109	1.922
9	3.905	3.786	3.673	3.566	3.463	3.366	3.273	3.184	3.100	3.019	2.942	2.868	2.798	2.730	2.665	2.379	2.144	1.948
10	4.054	3.923	3.799	3.682	3.570	3.465	3.364	3.269	3.178	3.092	3.009	2.930	2.855	2.784	2.715	2.414	2.168	1.965
11	4.177	4.035	3.902	3.776	3.656	3.544	3.437	3.335	3.239	3.147	3.060	2.978	2.899	2.824	2.752	2.438	2.185	1.977
12	4.278	4.127	3.985	3.851	3.725	3.606	3.493	3.387	3.286	3.190	3.100	3.013	2.931	2.853	2.779	2.456	2.196	1.985
13	4.362	4.203	4.053	3.912	3.780	3.656	3.538	3.427	3.322	3.223	3.129	3.040	2.956	2.876	2.799	2.469	2.204	1.990
14	4.432	4.265	4.108	3.962	3.824	3.695	3.573	3.459	3.351	3.249	3.152	3.061	2.974	2.892	2.814	2.478	2.210	1.993
15	4.489	4.315	4.153	4.001	3.859	3.726	3.601	3.483	3.373	3.268	3.170	3.076	2.988	2.905	2.825	2.484	2.214	1.995
16	4.536	4.357	4.189	4.033	3.887	3.751	3.623	3.503	3.390	3.283	3.183	3.088	2.999	2.914	2.834	2.489	2.216	1.997
17	4.576	4.391	4.219	4.059	3.910	3.771	3.640	3.518	3.403	3.295	3.193	3.097	3.007	2.921	2.840	2.492	2.218	1.998
18	4.608	4.419	4.243	4.080	3.928	3.786	3.654	3.529	3.413	3.304	3.201	3.104	3.012	2.926	2.844	2.494	2.219	1.999
19	4.635	4.442	4.263	4.097	3.942	3.799	3.664	3.539	3.421	3.311	3.207	3.109	3.017	2.930	2.848	2.496	2.220	1.999
20	4.657	4.460	4.279	4.110	3.954	3.808	3.673	3.546	3.427	3.316	3.211	3.113	3.020	2.933	2.850	2.497	2.221	1.999
21	4.675	4.476	4.292	4.121	3.963	3.816	3.679	3.551	3.432	3.320	3.215	3.116	3.023	2.935	2.852	2.498	2.221	2.000
22	4.690	4.488	4.302	4.130	3.970	3.822	3.684	3.556	3.436	3.323	3.217	3.118	3.025	2.936	2.853	2.498	2.222	2.000
23	4.703	4.499	4.311	4.137	3.976	3.827	3.689	3.559	3.438	3.325	3.219	3.120	3.026	2.938	2.854	2.499	2.222	2.000
24	4.713	4.507	4.318	4.143	3.981	3.831	3.692	3.562	3.441	3.327	3.221	3.121	3.027	2.939	2.855	2.499	2.222	2.000
25	4.721	4.514	4.323	4.147	3.985	3.834	3.694	3.564	3.442	3.329	3.222	3.122	3.028	2.939	2.856	2.499	2.222	2.000
30	4.746	4.534	4.339	4.160	3.995	3.842	3.701	3.569	3.447	3.332	3.225	3.124	3.030	2.941	2.857	2.500	2.222	2.000
35	4.756	4.541	4.345	4.164	3.998	3.845	3.703	3.571	3.448	3.333	3.226	3.125	3.030	2.941	2.857	2.500	2.222	2.000
40	4.760	4.544	4.347	4.166	3.999	3.846	3.703	3.571	3.448	3.333	3.226	3.125	3.030	2.941	2.857	2.500	2.222	2.000
45	4.761	4.545	4.347	4.166	4.000	3.846	3.704	3.571	3.448	3.333	3.226	3.125	3.030	2.941	2.857	2.500	2.222	2.000
50	4.762	4.545	4.348	4.167	4.000	3.846	3.704	3.571	3.448	3.333	3.226	3.125	3.030	2.941	2.857	2.500	2.222	2.000

Texas Instruments BA-35, BAII, BAII Plus[c]

Inputs:	700	5	8		
Functions:	PMT	N	%i	CPT	FV
Outputs:				2794.90 [d]	

---

[c]For the Texas Instruments BAII, you would use the 2nd key instead of the CPT key; for the Texas Instruments BAII Plus, you would use the I/Y key instead of the %i key.

[d]If a minus sign precedes the output, it should be ignored.

Appendix B

Solutions to Self-Test Problems

CHAPTER 3

ST 3-1   **a.** Capital gains = $180,000 sale price − $150,000 original purchase price = <u>$30,000</u>

   b. Total taxable income = $280,000 operating earnings + $30,000 capital gain = <u>$310,000</u>

   c. Firm's tax liability:

   Using Table 3.4:
   Total taxes due = $22,250 + [.39 × ($310,000 − $100,000)]
   = $22,250 + (.39 × $210,000) = $22,250 + $81,900
   = <u>$104,150</u>

   d. Average tax rate = $\dfrac{\$104{,}150}{\$310{,}000}$ = <u>33.6%</u>

   Marginal tax rate = <u>39%</u>

ST 3-2   **a.** Depreciation Schedule

Year	Cost^a (1)	Percentages (from Table 3.8) (2)	Depreciation [(1) × (2)] (3)
1	$150,000	20%	$ 30,000
2	150,000	32	48,000
3	150,000	19	28,500
4	150,000	12	18,000
5	150,000	12	18,000
6	150,000	5	7,500
	Totals	100%	$150,000

^{a}$140,000 asset cost + $10,000 installation cost.

870

b. Cash flow schedule

Year	EBDT (1)	Deprec. (2)	Net profits before taxes [(1) − (2)] (3)	Taxes [.4 × (3)] (4)	Net profits after taxes [(3) − (4)] (5)	Operating cash flows [(2) + (5)] (6)
1	$160,000	$30,000	$130,000	$52,000	$78,000	$108,000
2	160,000	48,000	112,000	44,800	67,200	115,200
3	160,000	28,500	131,500	52,600	78,900	107,400
4	160,000	18,000	142,000	56,800	85,200	103,200
5	160,000	18,000	142,000	56,800	85,200	103,200
6	160,000	7,500	152,500	61,000	91,500	99,000

c. The purchase of the asset allows the firm to deduct depreciation—a noncash charge—for tax purposes. This results in lower taxable income and therefore lower tax payments. As a result, the firm's operating cash flows (in column 6 of the preceding table) exceed its net profits after taxes (in column 5 of the table).

CHAPTER 4

ST 4-1

Ratio	Too high	Too low
Current ratio = current assets/current liabilities	May indicate that the firm is holding excessive cash, accounts receivable, or inventory.	May indicate poor ability to satisfy short-term obligations.
Inventory turnover = CGS/inventory	May indicate lower level of inventory, which may cause stockouts and lost sales.	May indicate poor inventory management, excessive inventory, or obsolete inventory.
Times interest earned = earnings before interest and taxes/interest		May indicate poor ability to pay contractual interest payments.
Gross profit margin = gross profits/sales	Indicates the low cost of merchandise sold relative to the sales price; may indicate noncompetitive pricing and potential lost sales.	Indicates the high cost of the merchandise sold relative to the sales price; may indicate either a low sales price or a high cost of goods sold.
Return on total assets = net profits after taxes/total assets		Indicates ineffective management in generating profits with the available assets.

ST 4-2

Balance Sheet
O'Keefe Industries
December 31, 2000

Cash	$ 30,000	Accounts payable	$ 120,000
Marketable securities	25,000	Notes payable	160,000^e
Accounts receivable	200,000^a	Accruals	20,000
Inventories	225,000^b	Total current	
Total current assets	$ 480,000	liabilities	$ 300,000^d
Net fixed assets	$1,020,000^c	Long-term debt	$ 600,000^f
Total assets	$1,500,000	Stockholders' equity	$ 600,000
		Total liabilities and	
		stockholders' equity	$1,500,000

^{a}Average collection period (ACP) = 40 days
ACP = accounts receivable/average sales per day
40 = accounts receivable/($1,800,000/360)
40 = accounts receivable/$5,000
$200,000 = accounts receivable

^{b}Inventory turnover = 6.0
Inventory turnover = cost of goods sold/inventory
6.0 = [sales × (1 − gross profit margin)]/inventory
6.0 = [$1,800,000 × (1 − .25)]/inventory
$225,000 = inventory

^{c}Total asset turnover = 1.20
Total asset turnover = sales/total assets
1.20 = $1,800,000/total assets
$1,500,000 = total assets
Total assets = current assets + net fixed assets
$1,500,000 = $480,000 + net fixed assets
$1,020,000 = net fixed assets

^{d}Current ratio = 1.60
Current ratio = current assets/current liabilities
1.60 = $480,000/current liabilities
$300,000 = current liabilities

^{e}Notes payable = total current liabilities −
accounts payable − accruals
= $300,000 − $120,000 − $20,000
= $160,000

^{f}Debt ratio = .60
Debt ratio = total liabilities/total assets
.60 = total liabilities/$1,500,000
$900,000 = total liabilities
Total liabilities = current liabilities + long-term debt
$900,000 = $300,000 + long-term debt
$600,000 = long-term debt

CHAPTER 5

ST 5-1   **a.** *Bank A:*

$$FV_3 = \$10,000 \times FVIF_{4\%/3yrs} = \$10,000 \times 1.125 = \underline{\$11,250}$$
$$\text{(Calculator solution} = \$11,248.64)$$

Bank B:

$$FV_3 = \$10,000 \times FVIF_{4\%/2,2 \times 3yrs} = \$10,000 \times FVIF_{2\%,6yrs}$$
$$= \$10,000 \times 1.126 = \underline{\$11,260}$$
$$\text{(Calculator solution} = \$11,261.62)$$

Bank C:

$$FV_3 = \$10,000 \times FVIF_{4\%/4,4 \times 3yrs} = \$10,000 \times FVIF_{1\%,12yrs}$$
$$= \$10,000 \times 1.127 = \underline{\$11,270}$$
$$\text{(Calculator solution} = \$11,268.25)$$

b. Bank A: $k_{EAR} = (1 + 4\%/1)^1 − 1 = (1 + .04)^1 − 1 = 1.04 − 1 = .04 = \underline{4\%}$
Bank B: $k_{EAR} = (1 + 4\%/2)^2 − 1 = (1 + .02)^2 − 1 = 1.0404 − 1 = .0404 = \underline{4.04\%}$
Bank C: $k_{EAR} = (1 + 4\%/4)^4 − 1 = (1 + .01)^4 − 1 = 1.0406 − 1 = .0406 = \underline{4.06\%}$

c. Ms. Martin should deal with Bank C: The quarterly compounding of interest at the given 4% rate results in the highest future value as a result of the corresponding highest effective annual rate.

d. *Bank D:*

$$FV_3 = \$10,000 \times FVIF_{4\%,3yrs} \text{ (continuous compounding)}$$
$$= \$10,000 \times e^{.04 \times 3} = \$10,000 \times e^{.12}$$
$$= \$10,000 \times 1.127497$$
$$= \underline{\$11,274.97}$$

This alternative is better than Bank C, because it results in a higher future value because of the use of continuous compounding, which with otherwise identical cash flows always results in the highest future value of any compounding period.

ST 5-2   **a.** On a purely subjective basis, annuity X looks more attractive than annuity Y. The fact that annuity Y's cash flows occur at the end of the year (an *ordinary annuity*) while annuity X's cash flows occur at the beginning of the year (an *annuity due*) favors annuity X, because its beginning-of-year cash flows will have more time to compound than the end-of-year cash flows of annuity Y. On the other hand, it would seem that the extra $1,000 per year in cash flow from annuity Y ($10,000 for annuity Y and $9,000 for annuity X) would outweigh the benefit of annuity X's longer compounding period. As noted in what follows, only after making necessary computations can the more attractive annuity be determined.

b. *Annuity X (annuity due):*

$$FVA_6 = \$9,000 \times FVIFA_{15\%,6yrs} \times (1 + .15)$$
$$= \$9,000 \times 8.754 \times 1.15 = \underline{\$90,603.90}$$

(Calculator solution = $90,601.19)

Annuity Y (ordinary annuity):

$$FVA_6 = \$10,000 \times FVIFA_{15\%,6yrs}$$
$$= \$10,000 \times 8.754 = \underline{\$87,540.00}$$

(Calculator solution = $87,537.38)

c. Annuity X is more attractive, because its future value at the end of year 6, FVA_6, of $90,603.90 is greater than annuity Y's end-of-year-6 future value, FVA_6, of $87,540.00. Clearly, the subjective assessment in **a** was incorrect. The benefit of receiving annuity X's cash flows at the beginning of the year more than offset the fact that its cash flows are $1,000 less than those of annuity Y, which has end-of-year cash flows. The high interest rate of 15% added to the attractiveness of annuity X (the annuity due), because each of its cash flows earns at this rate for an extra year, thereby enhancing its future value.

ST 5-3   *Alternative A:*

Cash flow stream:

$$PVA_5 = \$700 \times PVIFA_{9\%,5yrs}$$
$$= \$700 \times 3.890 = \underline{\$2,723}$$
(Calculator solution = $2,722.76)

Lump sum: $\underline{\$2,825}$

Alternative B:
Cash flow stream:

Year (n)	Cash flow (1)	$FVIF_{9\%,n}$ (2)	Present value [(1) × (2)] (3)
1	$1,100	.917	$1,088.70
2	900	.842	757.80
3	700	.772	540.40
4	500	.708	354.00
5	300	.650	195.00
		Present value	$2,855.90

(Calculator solution = $2,856.41)

Lump-sum: <u>$2,800</u>

Conclusion: Alternative B in the form of a cash flow stream is preferred because its present value of $2,855,90 is greater than the other three values.

ST 5-4 $FVA_5 = \$8,000$; $FVIFA_{7\%,5yrs} = 5.751$; $PMT = ?$
$FVA_n = PMT \times (FVIFA_{k,n})$ [Equation 5.15 or 5.29]
$\$8,000 = PMT \times 5.751$
$PMT = \$8,000/5.751 = \underline{\$1,391.06}$
(Calculator solution = $1,391.13)

Judi should deposit $1,391.06 at the end of each of the 5 years to meet her goal of accumulating $8,000 at the end of the fifth year.

CHAPTER 6

ST 6-1   **a.** Expected return, $\bar{k} = \dfrac{\Sigma \text{Returns}}{3}$ (*Equation 6.2a in footnote 9*)

$$\bar{k}_A = \frac{12\% + 14\% + 16\%}{3} = \frac{42\%}{3} = \underline{14\%}$$

$$\bar{k}_B = \frac{16\% + 14\% + 12\%}{3} = \frac{42\%}{3} = \underline{14\%}$$

$$\bar{k}_C = \frac{12\% + 14\% + 16\%}{3} = \frac{42\%}{3} = \underline{14\%}$$

b. Standard deviation, $\sigma_k = \sqrt{\dfrac{\sum\limits_{i=1}^{n}(k_i - \bar{k})^2}{n-1}}$ (*Equation 6.3a in footnote 10*)

$$\sigma_{k_A} = \sqrt{\frac{(12\% - 14\%)^2 + (14\% - 14\%)^2 + (16\% - 14\%)^2}{3-1}}$$

$$= \sqrt{\frac{4\% + 0\% + 4\%}{2}} = \sqrt{\frac{8\%}{2}} = \underline{2\%}$$

$$\sigma_{k_B} = \sqrt{\frac{(16\% - 14\%)^2 + (14\% - 14\%)^2 + (12\% - 14\%)^2}{3 - 1}}$$

$$= \sqrt{\frac{4\% + 0\% + 4\%}{2}} = \sqrt{\frac{8\%}{2}} = \underline{2\%}$$

$$\sigma_{k_C} = \sqrt{\frac{(12\% - 14\%)^2 + (14\% - 14\%)^2 + (16\% - 14\%)^2}{3 - 1}}$$

$$= \sqrt{\frac{4\% + 0\% + 4\%}{2}} = \sqrt{\frac{8\%}{2}} = \underline{2\%}$$

c.

Year	Annual expected returns	
	Portfolio AB	Portfolio AC
2001	$(.50 \times 12\%) + (.50 \times 16\%) = 14\%$	$(.50 \times 12\%) + (.50 \times 12\%) = 12\%$
2002	$(.50 \times 14\%) + (.50 \times 14\%) = 14\%$	$(.50 \times 14\%) + (.50 \times 14\%) = 14\%$
2003	$(.50 \times 16\%) + (.50 \times 12\%) = 14\%$	$(.50 \times 16\%) + (.50 \times 16\%) = 16\%$

Over the 3-year period:

$$\overline{k}_{AB} = \frac{14\% + 14\% + 14\%}{3} = \frac{42\%}{3} = \underline{14\%}$$

$$\overline{k}_{AC} = \frac{12\% + 14\% + 16\%}{3} = \frac{42\%}{3} = \underline{14\%}$$

d. AB is perfectly negatively correlated.

AC is perfectly positively correlated.

e. Standard deviation of the portfolios

$$\sigma_{k_{AB}} = \sqrt{\frac{(14\% - 14\%)^2 + (14\% - 14\%)^2 + (14\% - 14\%)^2}{3 - 1}}$$

$$= \sqrt{\frac{0\% + 0\% + 0\%}{2}} = \sqrt{\frac{0\%}{2}} = \underline{0\%}$$

$$\sigma_{k_{AC}} = \sqrt{\frac{(12\% - 14\%)^2 + (14\% - 14\%)^2 + (16\% - 14\%)^2}{3 - 1}}$$

$$= \sqrt{\frac{4\% + 0\% + 4\%}{2}} = \sqrt{\frac{8\%}{2}} = \underline{2\%}$$

f. Portfolio AB is preferred, because it provides the same return (14%) as AC but with less risk [$(\sigma_{k_{AB}} = 0\%) < (\sigma_{k_{AC}} = 2\%)$].

ST 6-2   a. When the market return increases by 10%, the project's required return would be expected to increase by 15% ($1.50 \times 10\%$). When the market return decreases by 10%, the project's required return would be expected to decrease by 15% [$1.50 \times (-10\%)$].

b. $k_j = R_F + [b_j \times (k_m - R_F)]$
$\quad = 7\% + [1.50 \times (10\% - 7\%)]$
$\quad = 7\% + 4.5\% = \underline{11.5\%}$

c. No, the project should be rejected, because its *expected* return of 11% is less than the 11.5% return *required* from the project.

d. $k_j = 7\% + [1.50 \times (9\% - 7\%)]$
$\quad = 7\% + 3\% = \underline{10\%}$

The project would now be acceptable, because its *expected* return of 11% is now in excess of the *required* return, which has declined to 10% as a result of investors in the marketplace becoming less risk-averse.

CHAPTER 7

ST 7-1   a. $B_0 = I \times (PVIFA_{k_d,n}) + M \times (PVIF_{k_d,n})$
$I = .08 \times \$1,000 = \$80$
$M = \$1,000$
$n = 12$ yrs

(1) $k_d = 7\%$
$B_0 = \$80 \times (PVIFA_{7\%,12\text{yrs}}) + \$1,000 \times (PVIF_{7\%,12\text{yrs}})$
$\quad = (\$80 \times 7.943) + (\$1,000 \times .444)$
$\quad = \$635.44 + \$444.00 = \underline{\$1,079.44}$
(Calculator solution = $\$1,079.43$)

(2) $k_d = 8\%$
$B_0 = \$80 \times (PVIFA_{8\%,12\text{yrs}}) + \$1,000 \times (PVIF_{8\%,12\text{yrs}})$
$\quad = (\$80 \times 7.536) + (\$1,000 \times .397)$
$\quad = \$602.88 + \$397.00 = \underline{\$999.88}$
(Calculator solution = $\$1,000$)

(3) $k_d = 10\%$
$B_0 = \$80 \times (PVIFA_{10\%,12\text{yrs}}) + \$1,000 \times (PVIF_{10\%,12\text{yrs}})$
$\quad = (\$80 \times 6.814) + (\$1,000 \times .319)$
$\quad = \$545.12 + \$319.00 = \underline{\$864.12}$
(Calculator solution = $\$863.73$)

b. (1) $k_d = 7\%$, $B_0 = \$1,079.44$; sells at a *premium*
(2) $k_d = 8\%$, $B_0 = \$999.88 \approx \$1,000.00$; sells at its *par value*
(3) $k_d = 10\%$, $B_0 = \$864.12$; sells at a *discount*

c. $B_0 = \dfrac{I}{2} \times (PVIFA_{k_d/2,2n}) + M \times (PVIF_{k_d/2,2n})$

$\quad = \dfrac{\$80}{2} \times (PVIFA_{10\%/2,2\times12\text{periods}}) + \$1,000 \times (PVIF_{10\%/2,2\times12\text{periods}})$

$\quad = \$40 \times (PVIFA_{5\%,24\text{periods}}) + \$1,000 \times (PVIF_{5\%,24\text{periods}})$

$\quad = (\$40 \times 13.799) + (\$1,000 \times .310)$

$\quad = \$551.96 + \$310.00 = \underline{\$861.96}$
(Calculator solution = $\$862.01$)

ST 7-2 **a.** $B_0 = \$1,150$

$\quad I = .11 \times \$1,000 = \$110$

$\quad M = \$1,000$

$\quad n = 18$ yrs

$\quad \$1,150 = \$110 \times (PVIFA_{k_d,18yrs}) + \$1,000 \times (PVIF_{k_d,18yrs})$

Because if $k_d = 11\%$, $B_0 = \$1,000 = M$, try $k_d = 10\%$.

$\quad B_0 = \$110 \times (PVIFA_{10\%,18yrs}) + \$1,000 \times (PVIF_{10\%,18yrs})$

$\quad\quad = (\$110 \times 8.201) + (\$1,000 \times .180)$

$\quad\quad = \$902.11 + \$180.00 = \$1,082.11$

Because $\$1,082.11 < \$1,150$, try $k_d = 9\%$.

$\quad B_0 = \$110 \times (PVIFA_{9\%,18yrs}) + \$1,000 \times (PVIF_{9\%,18yrs})$

$\quad\quad = (\$110 \times 8.756) + (\$1,000 \times .212)$

$\quad\quad = \$963.16 + \$212.00 = \$1,175.16$

Because the $\$1,175.16$ value at 9% is higher than $\$1,150$, and the $\$1,082.11$ value at 10% rate is lower than $\$1,150$, the bond's yield to maturity must be between 9 and 10%. Because the $\$1,175.16$ value is closer to $\$1,150$, rounding to the nearest whole percent, the YTM is 9%. (By using interpolation, the more precise YTM value is 9.27%.)

(Calculator solution = 9.26%)

b. The calculated YTM of 9+% is below the bond's 11% coupon interest rate, because the bond's market value of $\$1,150$ is above its $\$1,000$ par value. Whenever a bond's market value is above its par value (it sells at a *premium*), its YTM will be below its coupon interest rate; when a bond sells at *par,* the YTM will equal its coupon interest rate; and when the bond sells for less than par (at a *discount*), its YTM will be greater than its coupon interest rate.

ST 7-3 $D_0 = \$1.80$/share

$k_s = 12\%$

a. *Zero growth:*

$$P_0 = \frac{D_1}{k_s} = \frac{D_1 = D_0 = \$1.80}{.12} = \underline{\$15\text{/share}}$$

b. *Constant growth, g = 5%:*

$D_1 = D_0 \times (1 + g) = \$1.80 \times (1 + .05) = \$1.89$/share

$$P_0 = \frac{D_1}{k_s - g} = \frac{\$1.89}{.12 - .05} = \frac{\$1.89}{.07} = \underline{\$27\text{/share}}$$

c. *Variable growth, N = 3, $g_1 = 5\%$ for years 1 to 3 and $g_2 = 4\%$ for years 4 to ∞:*

$D_1 = D_0 \times (1 + g_1)^1 = \$1.80 \times (1 + .05)^1 = \$1.89$/share

$D_2 = D_0 \times (1 + g_1)^2 = \$1.80 \times (1 + .05)^2 = \$1.98$/share

$D_3 = D_0 \times (1 + g_1)^3 = \$1.80 \times (1 + .05)^3 = \$2.08$/share

$D_4 = D_3 \times (1 + g_2) = \$2.08 \times (1 + .04) = \$2.16$/share

$$P_0 = \sum_{t=1}^{N} \frac{D_0 \times (1+g_1)^t}{(1+k_s)^t} + \left(\frac{1}{(1+k_s)^N} \times \frac{D_{N+1}}{k_s - g_2} \right)$$

$$\sum_{t=1}^{N} \frac{D_0 \times (1+g_1)^t}{(1+k_s)^t} = \frac{\$1.89}{(1+.12)^1} + \frac{\$1.98}{(1+.12)^2} + \frac{\$2.08}{(1+.12)^3}$$

$$= [\$1.89 \times (PVIF_{12\%,1yr})] + [\$1.98 \times (PVIF_{12\%,2yrs})] + [\$2.08 \times (PVIF_{12\%,3yrs})]$$
$$= (\$1.89 \times .893) + (\$1.98 \times .797) + (\$2.08 \times .712)$$
$$= \$1.69 + \$1.58 + \$1.48 = \$4.75$$

$$\left[\frac{1}{(1+k_s)^N} \times \frac{D_{N+1}}{(k_s-g_2)} \right] = \frac{1}{(1+.12)^3} \times \frac{D_4 = \$2.16}{.12-.04}$$

$$= (PVIF_{12\%,3yrs}) \times \frac{\$2.16}{.08}$$

$$= .712 \times \$27.00 = \$19.22$$

$$P_0 = \sum_{t=1}^{N} \frac{D_0 \times (1+g_1)^t}{(1+k_s)^t} + \left[\frac{1}{(1+k_s)^N} \times \frac{D_{N+1}}{k_s-g_2} \right] = \$4.75 + \$19.22$$
$$= \underline{\$23.97/share}$$

CHAPTER 8

ST 8-1 **a.** Book value = installed cost − accumulated depreciation

Installed cost = $50,000

Accumulated depreciation = $50,000 × (.20 + .32 + .19 + .12)
$$= \$50,000 \times .83 = \$41,500$$

Book value = $50,000 − $41,500 = $\underline{\$8,500}$

b. Taxes on sale of old equipment:

Capital gain = sale price − initial purchase price
$$= \$55,000 - \$50,000 = \$5,000$$

Recaptured depreciation = initial purchase price − book value
$$= \$50,000 - \$8,500 = \$41,500$$

Taxes = (.40 × $5,000) + (.40 × $41,500)
$$= \$2,000 + \$16,600 = \underline{\$18,600}$$

c. Initial investment:

Installed cost of new equipment		
Cost of new equipment	$75,000	
+ Installation costs	5,000	
Total installed cost—new		$80,000
− After-tax proceeds from sale of old equipment		
Proceeds from sale of old equipment	$55,000	
− Taxes on sale of old equipment	18,600	
Total after-tax proceeds—old		36,400
+ Change in net working capital		15,000
Initial investment		$58,600

ST 8-2   **a.** Initial investment:

Installed cost of new machine

Cost of new machine	$140,000	
+ Installation costs	10,000	
Total installed cost—new (depreciable value)		$150,000
− After-tax proceeds from sale of old machine		
Proceeds from sale of old machine	$ 42,000	
− Taxes on sale of old machine[1]	9,120	
Total after-tax proceeds—old		32,880
+ Change in net working capital[2]		20,000
Initial investment		$137,120

---

[1]Book value of old machine = $40,000 − [(.20 + .32) × $40,000]
= $40,000 − (.52 × $40,000)
= $40,000 − $20,800 = $19,200

Capital gain = $42,000 − $40,000 = $2,000

Recaptured depreciation = $40,000 − $19,200 = $20,800

Taxes = (.40 × $2,000) + (.40 × $20,800) = $800 + $8,320 = $9,120

[2]Change in net working capital = +$10,000 + $25,000 − $15,000
= $35,000 − $15,000 = $20,000

b. Incremental operating cash inflows:

Calculation of Depreciation Expense for New Machine

Year	Cost (1)	Applicable MACRS depreciation percentages (from Table 3.8) (2)	Depreciation [(1) × (2)] (3)
With new machine			
1	$150,000	33%	$ 49,500
2	150,000	45	67,500
3	150,000	15	22,500
4	150,000	7	10,500
Totals		100%	$150,000

Calculation of Depreciation Expense for Old Machine

Year	Cost (1)	Applicable MACRS depreciation percentages (from Table 3.8) (2)	Depreciation [(1) × (2)] (3)
With old machine			
1	$40,000	19% (year-3 depreciation)	$ 7,600
2	40,000	12 (year-4 depreciation)	4,800
3	40,000	12 (year-5 depreciation)	4,800
4	40,000	5 (year-6 depreciation)	2,000
		Total	$19,200[a]

[a]The total of $19,200 represents the book value of the old machine at the end of the second year, which was calculated in part **a.**

Calculation of Operating Cash Inflows

		Year		
	1	2	3	4
With new machine				
Profits before depr. and taxes[a]	$120,000	$130,000	$130,000	$ 0
− Depreciation[b]	49,500	67,500	22,500	10,500
Net profits before taxes	$ 70,500	$ 62,500	$107,500	−$10,500
− Taxes (rate = 40%)	28,200	25,000	43,000	− 4,200
Net profits after taxes	$ 42,300	$ 37,500	$ 64,500	−6,300
+ Depreciation[b]	49,500	67,500	22,500	10,500
Operating cash inflows	$ 91,800	$105,000	$ 87,000	$ 4,200
With old machine				
Profits before depr. and taxes[a]	$ 70,000	$ 70,000	$ 70,000	$ 0
− Depreciation[c]	7,600	4,800	4,800	2,000
Net profits before taxes	$ 62,400	$ 65,200	$ 65,200	−$ 2,000
− Taxes (rate = 40%)	24,960	26,080	26,080	− 800
Net profits after taxes	$ 37,440	$ 39,120	$ 39,120	−$ 1,200
+ Depreciation	7,600	4,800	4,800	2,000
Operating cash inflows	$ 45,040	$ 43,920	$ 43,920	$ 800

[a]Given in the problem.
[b]From column 3 of the first table.
[c]From column 3 of the preceding table.

Calculation of Incremental Operating Cash Inflows

	Operating cash inflows		
Year	New machine[a] (1)	Old machine[a] (2)	Incremental (relevant) [(1) − (2)] (3)
1	$ 91,800	$45,040	$46,760
2	105,000	43,920	61,080
3	87,000	43,920	43,080
4	4,200	800	3,400

[a]From final row for respective machine in the preceding table.

c. Terminal cash flow (end of year 3):

After-tax proceeds from sale of new machine		
Proceeds from sale of new machine	$35,000	
− Tax on sale of new machine[1]	9,800	
Total after-tax proceeds—new		$25,200
− After-tax proceeds from sale of old machine		
Proceeds from sale of old machine	$ 0	
− Tax on sale of old machine[2]	− 800	
Total after-tax proceeds—old		800
+ Change in net working capital		20,000
Terminal cash flow		$44,400

---

[1]Book value of new machine at end of year 3
= $150,000 − [(.33 + .45 + .15) × $150,000] = $150,000 − (.93 × $150,000)
= $150,000 − $139,500 = $10,500
Tax on sale = .40 × ($35,000 sale price − $10,500 book value)
    = .40 × $24,500 = $9,800
[2]Book value of old machine at end of year 3
= $40,000 − [(.20 + .32 + .19 + .12 + .12) × $40,000] = $40,000 − (.95 × $40,000)
= $40,000 − $38,000 = $2,000
Tax on sale = .40 × ($0 sale price − $2,000 book value)
    = .40 × (− $2,000) = −$800 (i.e., $800 tax saving)

d.

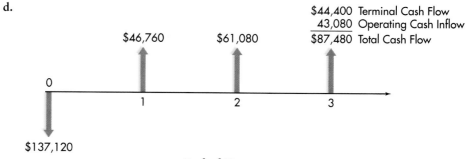

$44,400 Terminal Cash Flow
43,080 Operating Cash Inflow
$87,480 Total Cash Flow

$46,760

$61,080

0

1

2

3

$137,120

End of Year

Note: The year-4 incremental operating cash inflow of $3,400 is not directly included; it is instead reflected in the book values used to calculate the taxes on sale of the machines at the end of year 3 and is therefore part of the terminal cash flow.

CHAPTER 9

ST 9-1   a. Payback period:

Project M: $\dfrac{\$28,500}{\$10,000} = \underline{2.85 \text{ years}}$

Project N:

Year (t)	Cash inflows (CF_t)	Cumulative cash inflows
1	$11,000	$11,000
2	10,000	21,000 ←
3	9,000	30,000
4	8,000	38,000

$$2 + \frac{\$27,000 - \$21,000}{\$9,000} \text{ years}$$

$$2 + \frac{\$6,000}{\$9,000} \text{ years} = \underline{2.67 \text{ years}}$$

b. Net present value (NPV):

Project M: NPV $= (\$10,000 \times PVIFA_{14\%,4\text{yrs}}) - \$28,500$

$= (\$10,000 \times 2.914) - \$28,500$

$= \$29,140 - \$28,500 = \underline{\$640}$

(Calculator solution $= \$637.12$)

Project N:

Year (t)	Cash inflows (CF_t) (1)	$PVIF_{14\%,t}$ (2)	Present value at 14% [(1) × (2)] (3)
1	$11,000	.877	$ 9,647
2	10,000	.769	7,690
3	9,000	.675	6,075
4	8,000	.592	4,736
	Present value of cash inflows		$28,148
	− Initial investment		27,000
	Net present value (NPV)		$ 1,148

(Calculator solution $= \$1,155.18$)

c. Internal rate of return (IRR):

Project M: $\dfrac{\$28,500}{\$10,000} = 2.850$

$PVIFA_{\text{IRR},4\text{yrs}} = 2.850$

From Table A-4:

$PVIFA_{15\%,4\text{yrs}} = 2.855$

$PVIFA_{16\%,4\text{yrs}} = 2.798$

IRR $= \underline{15\%}$ (2.850 is closest to 2.855)

(Calculator solution $= 15.09\%$)

$$\text{Project N: Average annual cash inflow} = \frac{\$11,000 + \$10,000 + \$9,000 + \$8,000}{4}$$

$$= \frac{\$38,000}{4} = \$9,500$$

$$PVIFA_{k,4yrs} = \frac{\$27,000}{\$9,500} = 2.842$$

$$k \approx 15\%$$

Try 16%, because there are more cash inflows in early years.

Year (t)	CF_t (1)	$PVIF_{16\%,t}$ (2)	Present value at 16% $[(1) \times (2)]$ (3)	$PVIF_{17\%,t}$ (4)	Present value at 17% $[(1) \times (4)]$ (5)
1	$11,000	.862	$ 9,482	.855	$ 9,405
2	10,000	.743	7,430	.731	7,310
3	9,000	.641	5,769	.624	5,616
4	8,000	.552	4,416	.534	4,272
	Present value of cash inflows		$27,097		$26,603
−	Initial investment		27,000		27,000
	NPV		$ 97		−$ 397

IRR = <u>16%</u> (rounding to nearest whole percent)
(Calculator solution = 16.19%)

d.

	Project	
	M	**N**
Payback period	2.85 years	2.67 years[a]
NPV	$640	$1,148[a]
IRR	15%	16%[a]

[a]Preferred project.

Project N is recommended, because it has the shorter payback period and the higher NPV, which is greater than zero, and the larger IRR, which is greater than the 14% cost of capital.

e. Net present value profiles:

	Data	
	NPV	
Discount rate	**Project M**	**Project N**
0%	$11,500[a]	$11,000[b]
14	640	1,148
15	0	—
16	—	0

[a]($10,000 + $10,000 + $10,000 + $10,000)
− $28,500 = $40,000 − $28,500 = $11,500

[b]($11,000 + $10,000 + $9,000 + $8,000)
− $27,000 = $38,000 − $27,000 = $11,000

From the NPV profile that follows, it can be seen that if the firm has a cost of capital below approximately 6% (exact value is 5.75%), conflicting rankings of the projects would exist using the NPV and IRR decision techniques. Because the firm's cost of capital is 14%, it can be seen in part **d** that no conflict exists.

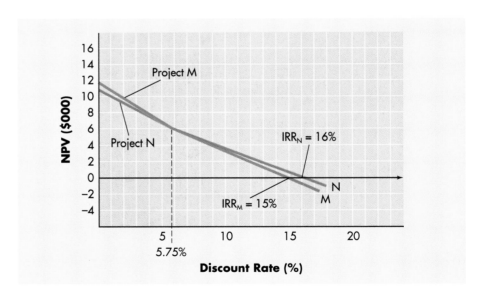

CHAPTER 10

ST 10-1   **a.** $NPV_A = (\$7,000 \times PVIFA_{10\%,3yrs}) - \$15,000$
$= (\$7,000 \times 2.487) - \$15,000$
$= \$17,409 - \$15,000 = \underline{\$2,409}$
(Calculator solution = $2,407.96)

$$NPV_B = (\$10,000 \times PVIFA_{10\%,3yrs}) - \$20,000$$
$$= (\$10,000 - 2.487) - \$20,000$$
$$= \$24,870 - \$20,000 = \underline{\$4,870}*$$
$$(\text{Calculator solution} = \$4,868.52)$$

*Preferred project, because higher NPV.

b. Project A:

Year (t)	Cash inflows (CF_t) (1)	Certainty equivalent factors (α_t) (2)	Certain CF_t [(1) × (2)] (3)	$PVIF_{7\%,t}$ (4)	Present value at 7% [(3) × (4)] (5)
1	$7,000	.95	$6,650	.935	$ 6,218
2	7,000	.90	6,300	.873	5,500
3	7,000	.90	6,300	.816	5,141
			Present value of cash inflows		$16,859
	−		Initial investment		15,000
			NPV		$ 1,859*

$$(\text{Calculator solution} = \$1,860.29)$$

Project B:

Year (t)	Cash inflows (CF_t) (1)	Certainty equivalent factors (α_t) (2)	Certain CF_t [(1) × (2)] (3)	$PVIF_{7\%,t}$ (4)	Present value at 7% [(3) × (4)] (5)
1	$10,000	.90	$9,000	.935	$ 8,415
2	10,000	.85	8,500	.873	7,421
3	10,000	.70	7,000	.816	5,712
			Present value of cash inflows		$21,548
	−		Initial investment		20,000
			NPV		$ 1,548

$$(\text{Calculator solution} = \$1,549.53)$$

*Preferred project, because higher NPV.

c. From the CAPM-type relationship, the risk-adjusted discount rate for project A, which has a risk index of 0.4, is 9%; for project B, with a risk index of 1.8, the risk-adjusted discount rate is 16%.

$$NPV_A = (\$7,000 \times PVIFA_{9\%,3yrs}) - \$15,000$$
$$= (\$7,000 \times 2.531) - \$15,000$$
$$= \$17,717 - \$15,000 = \underline{\$2,717}*$$
$$(\text{Calculator solution} = \$2,719.06)$$

$$NPV_B = (\$10,000 \times PVIFA_{16\%,3yrs}) - \$20,000$$
$$= (\$10,000 \times 2.246) - \$20,000$$
$$= \$22,460 - \$20,000 = \underline{\$2,460}$$
$$(\text{Calculator solution} = \$2,458.90)$$

*Preferred project, because higher NPV.

d. When the differences in risk were ignored in **a,** project B is preferred over project A; but when the higher risk of project B is incorporated in the analysis using either certainty equivalents (**b**) or risk-adjusted discount rates (**c**), *project A is preferred over project B.* Clearly, project A should be implemented.

CHAPTER 11

ST 11-1   **a.** Cost of debt, k_i (using approximation formula)

$$k_d = \frac{I + \dfrac{\$1,000 - N_d}{n}}{\dfrac{N_d + \$1,000}{2}}$$

$$I = .10 \times \$1,000 = \$100$$
$$N_d = \$1,000 - \$30 \text{ discount} - \$20 \text{ flotation cost} = \$950$$
$$n = 10 \text{ years}$$

$$k_d = \frac{\$100 + \dfrac{\$1,000 - \$950}{10}}{\dfrac{\$950 + \$1,000}{2}} = \frac{\$100 + \$5}{\$975} = 10.8\%$$

(Calculator solution = 10.8%)

$$k_i = k_d \times (1 - T)$$
$$T = .40$$
$$k_i = 10.8\% \times (1 - .40) = \underline{6.5\%}$$

Cost of preferred stock, k_p

$$k_p = \frac{D_p}{N_p}$$
$$D_p = .11 \times \$100 = \$11$$
$$N_p = \$100 - \$4 \text{ flotation cost} = \$96$$
$$k_p = \frac{\$11}{\$96} = \underline{11.5\%}$$

Cost of retained earnings, k_r

$$k_r = k_s = \frac{D_1}{P_0} + g$$

$$= \frac{\$6}{\$80} + 6.0\% = 7.5\% + 6.0\% = \underline{13.5\%}$$

Cost of new common stock, k_n

$$k_n = \frac{D_1}{N_n} + g$$
$$D_1 = \$6$$
$$N_n = \$80 - \$4 \text{ underpricing} - \$4 \text{ flotation cost} = \$72$$
$$g = 6.0\%$$
$$k_n = \frac{\$6}{\$72} + 6.0\% = 8.3\% + 6.0\% = \underline{14.3\%}$$

b. (1) Breaking point, BP

$$BP_{common\ equity} = \frac{AF_{common\ equity}}{w_{common\ equity}}$$

$$AF_{common\ equity} = \$225,000$$
$$w_{common\ equity} = 45\%$$

$$BP_{common\ equity} = \frac{\$225,000}{.45} = \$500,000$$

(2) WACC for total new financing < $500,000

Source of capital	Weight (1)	Cost (2)	Weighted cost [(1) × (2)] (3)
Long-term debt	.40	6.5%	2.6%
Preferred stock	.15	11.5	1.7
Common stock equity	.45	13.5	6.1
Totals	1.00		10.4%

Weighted average cost of capital = 10.4%

(3) WACC for total new financing > $500,000

Source of capital	Weight (1)	Cost (2)	Weighted cost [(1) × (2)] (3)
Long-term debt	.40	6.5%	2.6%
Preferred stock	.15	11.5	1.7
Common stock equity	.45	14.3	6.4
Totals	1.00		10.7%

Weighted average cost of capital = 10.7%

c. IOS data for graph

Investment opportunity	Internal rate of return (IRR)	Initial investment	Cumulative investment
D	16.5%	$200,000	$ 200,000
C	12.9	150,000	350,000
E	11.8	450,000	800,000
A	11.2	100,000	900,000
G	10.5	300,000	1,200,000
F	10.1	600,000	1,800,000
B	9.7	500,000	2,300,000

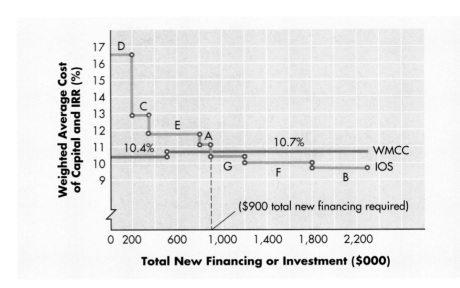

d. Projects D, C, E, and A should be accepted because their respective IRRs exceed the WMCC. They will require $900,000 of total new financing.

CHAPTER 12

ST 12-1   a. $Q = \dfrac{FC}{P - VC}$

$$= \frac{\$250,000}{\$7.50 - \$3.00} = \frac{\$250,000}{\$4.50} = \underline{\underline{55,556 \text{ units}}}$$

	+20%	
b. Sales (in units)	100,000	120,000
Sales revenue (units × $7.50/unit)	$750,000	$900,000
Less: Variable operating costs (units × $3.00/unit)	300,000	360,000
Less: Fixed operating costs	250,000	250,000
Earnings before interest and taxes (EBIT)	$200,000	$290,000

+45%

Less: Interest	80,000	80,000
Net profits before taxes	$120,000	$210,000
Less: Taxes ($T = .40$)	48,000	84,000
Net profits after taxes	$ 72,000	$126,000
Less: Preferred dividends (8,000 shares × $5.00/share)	40,000	40,000
Earnings available for common	$ 32,000	$ 86,000
Earnings per share (EPS)	$32,000/20,000 = $1.60/share	$86,000/20,000 = $4.30/share

+169%

c. $DOL = \dfrac{\% \text{ change in EBIT}}{\% \text{ change in sales}} = \dfrac{+45\%}{+20\%} = \underline{2.25}$

d. $DFL = \dfrac{\% \text{ change in EPS}}{\% \text{ change in EBIT}} = \dfrac{+169\%}{+45\%} = \underline{3.76}$

e. $DTL = DOL \times DFL$

$= 2.25 \times 3.76 = \underline{8.46}$

Using the other DTL formula:

$DTL = \dfrac{\% \text{ change in EPS}}{\% \text{ change in sales}}$

$8.46 = \dfrac{\% \text{ change in EPS}}{+50\%}$

$\% \text{ change in EPS} = 8.46 \times .50 = 4.23 = \underline{+423\%}$

ST 12-2

Data summary for alternative plans		
Source of capital	**Plan A (bond)**	**Plan B (stock)**
Long-term debt	$60,000 at 12% annual interest	$50,000 at 12% annual interest
Annual interest =	.12 × $60,000 = $7,200	.12 × $50,000 = $6,000
Common stock	10,000 shares	11,000 shares

a.

	Plan A (bond)		Plan B (stock)	
EBIT[a]	$30,000	$40,000	$30,000	$40,000
Less: Interest	7,200	7,200	6,000	6,000
Net profits before taxes	$22,800	$32,800	$24,000	$34,000
Less: Taxes ($T = .40$)	9,120	13,120	9,600	13,600
Net profits after taxes	$13,680	$19,680	$14,400	$20,400
EPS (10,000 shares)	$1.37	$1.97		
(11,000 shares)			$1.31	$1.85

[a]Values were arbitrarily selected; other values could have been utilized.

Coordinates		
	EBIT	
	$30,000	**$40,000**
Financing plan	**Earnings per share (EPS)**	
A (Bond)	$1.37	$1.97
B (Stock)	1.31	1.85

b.

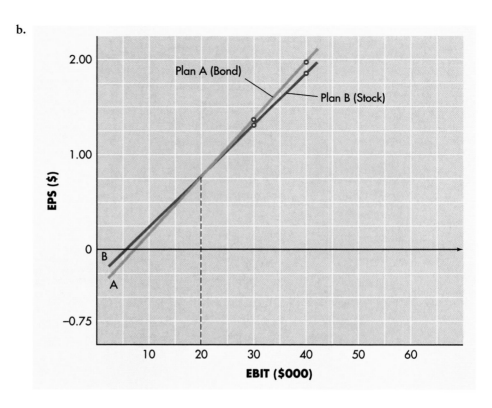

c. The bond plan (Plan A) becomes superior to the stock plan (Plan B) at *around $20,000* of EBIT, as represented by the dashed vertical line in the figure in **b.** (*Note:* The actual point is $19,200, which was determined algebraically by using the technique described in footnote 22.)

ST 12-3 **a.**

Capital structure debt ratio	Expected EPS (1)	Required return, k_s (2)	Estimated share value [(1) ÷ (2)] (3)
0%	$3.12	.13	$24.00
10	3.90	.15	26.00
20	4.80	.16	30.00
30	5.44	.17	32.00
40	5.51	.19	29.00
50	5.00	.20	25.00
60	4.40	.22	20.00

b. Using the table in **a**:
  (1) Maximization of EPS: *40% debt ratio,* EPS = $5.51/share (see column 1).
  (2) Maximization of share value: *30% debt ratio,* share value = $32.00 (see column 3).
c. Recommend *30% debt ratio,* because it results in the maximum share value and is therefore consistent with the firm's goal of owner wealth maximization.

CHAPTER 13

ST 13-1   **a.** Earnings per share (EPS) = $\dfrac{\$2{,}000{,}000 \text{ earnings available}}{500{,}000 \text{ shares of common outstanding}}$

$= \underline{\$4.00/\text{share}}$

Price/earnings (P/E) ratio = $\dfrac{\$60 \text{ market price}}{\$4.00 \text{ EPS}} = \underline{\underline{15}}$

b. Proposed dividends = 500,000 shares $\times$ $2 per share = $1,000,000

Shares that can be repurchased = $\dfrac{\$1{,}000{,}000}{\$62} = \underline{16{,}129 \text{ shares}}$

c. *After proposed repurchase:*

Shares outstanding = 500,000 − 16,129 = 483,871

EPS = $\dfrac{\$2{,}000{,}000}{483{,}871} = \underline{\$4.13/\text{share}}$

d. Market price = $4.13/share $\times$ 15 = $\underline{\$61.95/\text{share}}$

e. The earnings per share (EPS) are higher after the repurchase, because there are fewer shares of stock outstanding (483,871 shares versus 500,000 shares) to divide up the firm's $2,000,000 of available earnings.

f. In both cases, the stockholders would receive $2 per share—a $2 cash dividend in the dividend case or an approximately $2 increase in share price ($60.00 per share to $61.95 per share) in the repurchase case. (*Note:* The $.05 per share ($2.00 − $1.95) difference is due to rounding.)

CHAPTER 14

ST 14-1   **a.**

	Cash Budget Carroll Company April–June					Accounts receivable at end of June	
	February	**March**	**April**	**May**	**June**	**July**	**August**
Forecast sales	$500	$600	$400	$ 200	$200		
Cash sales (.30)	$150	$180	$120	$ 60	$ 60		
Collections of A/R							
Lagged 1 month [(.7 × .7) = .49]		245	294	196	98	$ 98	
Lagged 2 months [(.3 × .7) = .21]			105	126	84	42	$42
						$140 +	$42 = $182
Total cash receipts			$519	$ 382	$242		
Less: Total cash disbursements			600	500	200		
Net cash flow			$ (81)	$(118)	$ 42		
Add: Beginning cash			115	34	(84)		
Ending cash			$ 34	$ (84)	$(42)		
Less: Minimum cash balance			25	25	25		
Required total financing (notes payable)			—	$109	$ 67		
Excess cash balance (marketable securities)			$ 9	—	—		

b. Carroll Company would need a maximum of $109 in financing over the 3-month period.

c.

Account	Amount	Source of amount
Cash	$ 25	Minimum cash balance—June
Notes payable	67	Required total financing—June
Marketable securities	0	Excess cash balance—June
Accounts receivable	182	Calculation at right of cash budget statement

ST 14-2   **a.**

**Pro forma Income Statement
Euro Designs, Inc.,
for the year ended December 31, 2001**

Sales revenue (given)	$3,900,000
Less: Cost of goods sold (.55)[a]	2,145,000
Gross profits	$1,755,000
Less: Operating expenses (.12)[b]	468,000
Operating profits	$1,287,000
Less: Interest expense (given)	325,000
Net profits before taxes	$ 962,000
Less: Taxes (.40 × $962,000)	384,800
Net profits after taxes	$ 577,200
Less: Cash dividends (given)	320,000
To retained earnings	$ 257,200

[a]From 2000: CGS/Sales = $1,925,000/$3,500,000 = .55.
[b]From 2000: Oper. Exp./Sales = $420,000/$3,500,000 = .12.

b. The percent-of-sales method may underestimate actual 2001 pro forma income by assuming that all costs are variable. If the firm has fixed costs, which by definition would not increase with increasing sales, the 2001 pro forma income would likely be underestimated.

CHAPTER 15

ST 15-1   **a.**

Month	Total funds requirement (1)	Permanent funds requirement[a] (2)	Seasonal funds requirement [(1) − (2)] (3)
January	$7,400,000	$5,000,000	$2,400,000
February	5,500,000	5,000,000	500,000
March	5,000,000	5,000,000	0
April	5,300,000	5,000,000	300,000
May	6,200,000	5,000,000	1,200,000
June	6,000,000	5,000,000	1,000,000
July	5,800,000	5,000,000	800,000
August	5,400,000	5,000,000	400,000
September	5,000,000	5,000,000	0
October	5,300,000	5,000,000	300,000
November	6,000,000	5,000,000	1,000,000
December	6,800,000	5,000,000	1,800,000
Monthly average[b]		$5,000,000	$ 808,333

[a]Represents the lowest level of total funds required over the 12-month period.

[b]Found by summing the monthly amounts for 12 months and dividing the resulting totals by 12. For the permanent funds requirement, $60,000,000/12 = $5,000,000, and for the seasonal funds requirement, $9,700,000/12 = $808,333.

b. (1) *Aggressive strategy*—Applying this strategy would result in a perfect matching of long-term financing with the permanent funds requirement and short-term financing with the seasonal funds requirement. Therefore $5,000,000 of long-term financing and average monthly short-term financing of $808,333 would be used.

(2) *Conservative strategy*—Applying this strategy would result in enough long-term financing to meet all projected funds requirements; short-term financing would be used only to meet emergency or unexpected financial needs. In this case, $7,400,000 of long-term financing would be used to meet the peak funds requirement (during January), and no short-term financing would be used.

c. (1) *Aggressive strategy:*

$$\text{Total cost} = (\$5,000,000 \times .16) + (\$808,333 \times .10)$$
$$= \$800,000 + \$80,833 = \underline{\$880,833}$$

(2) *Conservative strategy:*

$$\text{Total cost} = (\$7,400,000 \times .16) + (\$0 \times .10)$$
$$= \$1,184,000 + \$0 = \underline{\$1,184,000}$$

d. The *aggressive strategy is more profitable,* because, as noted in **c**, its total cost is $880,833 compared to the total cost of $1,184,000 under the conservative strategy. This difference results because the aggressive strategy uses as much of the less expensive short-term (current liability) financing as possible, whereas the conservative strategy finances all needs with the more expensive long-term financing. Also, under the aggressive strategy, interest is paid only on necessary financing; under the conservative strategy, interest is paid on unneeded funds. (For example, under the conservative strategy, interest is paid on $7,400,000 in July when only $5,800,000 of financing is needed.)

The *aggressive strategy, on the other hand, is more risky,* because it relies heavily on the *limited* short-term financing, whereas the conservative strategy reserves short-term borrowing for emergency or unexpected financial needs. In addition, the aggressive strategy results in lower net working capital than the conservative strategy, thereby resulting in lower liquidity and a higher risk of technical insolvency.

ST 15-2 a.

Supplier	Approximate cost of giving up cash discount
X	$1\% \times [360/(55 - 10)] = 1\% \times 360/45 = 1\% \times 8\ = \underline{\ 8\%}$
Y	$2\% \times [360/(30 - 10)] = 2\% \times 360/20 = 2\% \times 18 = \underline{36\%}$
Z	$2\% \times [360/(60 - 20)] = 2\% \times 360/40 = 2\% \times 9\ = \underline{18\%}$

b.

Supplier	Recommendation
X	8% cost of giving up discount < 15% interest cost from bank; therefore, *give up discount.*
Y	36% cost of giving up discount > 15% interest cost from bank; therefore, *take discount and borrow from bank.*
Z	18% cost of giving up discount > 15% interest cost from bank; therefore, *take discount and borrow from bank.*

c. Stretching accounts payable for supplier Z would change the cost of giving up the cash discount to

$$2\% \times \{360/[(60 + 20) - 20]\} = 2\% \times 360/60 = 2\% \times 6 = \underline{12\%}$$

In this case, in light of the 15% interest cost from the bank, the recommended strategy in **b** would be to *give up the discount,* because the 12% cost of giving up the discount would be less than the 15% bank interest cost.

CHAPTER 16

ST 16-1

Basic data		
Time component	**Current**	**Proposed**
Average payment period (APP)	10 days	30 days
Average collection period (ACP)	30 days	30 days
Average age of inventory (AAI)	40 days	40 days

Cash conversion cycle (CCC) = AAI + ACP − APP

$$CCC_{current} = 40\ days + 30\ days - 10\ days = 60\ days$$
$$CCC_{proposed} = 40\ days + 30\ days - 30\ days = \underline{40\ days}$$
$$Reduction\ in\ CCC\quad \underline{20\ days}$$

Annual operating cycle investment = $18,000,000

Daily expenditure = $18,000,000 ÷ 360 = $50,000
Reduction in financing = $50,000 × 20 days = $1,000,000
Annual profit increase = .12 × $1,000,000 = $\underline{\$120,000}$

ST 16-2   Time reduction:

Mailing time	$1\frac{1}{2}$ days
Processing time	$1\frac{1}{2}$ days
Clearing time	1 day
Total time reduction	4 days

Float reduction:

$$4 \text{ days} \times \$300,000/\text{day} = \underline{\$1,200,000}$$

Gross annual benefit of float reduction:

$$.09 \times \$1,200,000 = \underline{\$108,000}$$

Because the annual earnings from the float reduction of $108,000 exceed the annual cost of $90,000, *the proposed lockbox should be implemented.* It will result in a net annual savings of $18,000 ($108,000 earnings − $90,000 cost).

CHAPTER 17

ST 17-1   **Tabular Calculation of the Effects of Easing Collection Efforts on Regency Rug Repair Company**

Additional profit contribution from sales			
[1,000 rugs × ($32 avg. sale price − $28 var. cost)]			$ 4,000
Cost of marginal investment in accounts receivable			
Average investment under proposed plan:			
$\dfrac{(\$28 \times 73,000 \text{ rugs})}{360/58} = \dfrac{\$2,044,000}{6.21}$		$329,147	
Average investment under present plan:			
$\dfrac{(\$28 \times 72,000 \text{ rugs})}{360/40} = \dfrac{\$2,016,000}{9}$		224,000	
Marginal investment in A/R		$105,147	
Cost of marginal investment in			
A/R (.24 × $105,147)			($25,235)
Cost of marginal bad debts			
Bad debts under proposed plan			
(.02 × $32 × 73,000 rugs)		$ 46,720	
Bad debts under present plan			
(.01 × $32 × 72,000 rugs)		23,040	
Cost of marginal bad debts			($23,680)
Annual savings in collection expense			$40,000
Net loss from implementation of proposed plan			($ 4,915)

Recommendation: Because a net loss of $4,915 is expected to result from easing collection efforts, *the proposed plan should not be implemented.*

ST 17-2   **a.** *Data:*

S = 60,000 gallons

O = \$200 per order

C = \$1 per gallon per year

Calculation:

$$EOQ = \sqrt{\frac{2 \times S \times O}{C}} = \sqrt{\frac{2 \times 60,000 \times \$200}{\$1}} = \sqrt{24,000,000} = \underline{4,899 \text{ gallons}}$$

b. Total cost = $(O \times S/Q) + (C \times Q/2)$

Q = EOQ = 4,899 gallons

Total cost = $[\$200 \times (60,000/4,899)] + [\$1 \times (4,899/2)]$

$= (\$200 \times 12.25) + (\$1 \times 2,449.5)$

$= \$2,450 + \$2,449.5 = \underline{\$4,899.50}$

c. Number of orders = S/Q

$= 60,000/4,899 = \underline{12.25 \text{ orders}}$

d. *Data:*

Lead time = 20 days

Daily usage = 60,000 gallons/360 days

$= 166.67$ gallons/day

Calculation:

Reorder point = lead time in days × daily usage

$= 20$ days × 166.67 gallons/day

$= \underline{3,333.4 \text{ gallons}}$

CHAPTER 18

ST 18-1   **a.** (1) and (2). In tabular form—after-tax cash outflows in column 3 and present value of the cash outflows in column 5.

End of year	Lease payment (1)	Tax adjustment [(1 − .40) = .60] (2)	After-tax cash outflows [(1) × (2)] (3)	Present value factors[a] (4)	Present value of outflows [(3) × (4)] (5)
1	\$5,000	.60	\$3,000	.917	\$ 2,751
2	5,000	.60	3,000	.842	2,526
3	5,000	.60	3,000	.772	2,316
4	5,000	.60	3,000	.708	2,124
5	5,000	.60	7,000[b]	.650	4,550
			Present value of cash outflows		\$14,267

[a]From Table A-3, *PVIF*, for 9% and the corresponding year.

[b]After-tax lease payment outflow of \$3,000 plus the \$4,000 cost of exercising the purchase option.

(Calculator solution = \$14,269)

b. (1) In tabular form—annual interest expense in column 3.

End of year	Loan payments (1)	Beginning of-year principal (2)	Payments Interest [.15 × (2)] (3)	Payments Principal [(1) − (3)] (4)	End-of-year principal [(2) − (4)] (5)
1	$5,967	$20,000	$3,000	$2,967	$17,033
2	5,967	17,033	2,555	3,412	13,621
3	5,967	13,621	2,043	3,924	9,697
4	5,967	9,697	1,455	4,512	5,185
5	5,967	5,185	778	5,189	—[a]

[a]The values in this table have been rounded to the nearest dollar, which results in a slight difference ($4) between the beginning-of-year-5 principal (in column 2) and the year-5 principal payment (in column 4).

(2) In tabular form—after-tax cash outflows in column 9.

End of year	Loan payments (1)	Maintenance costs (2)	Cost of oven (3)	Depreciation percentages[a] (4)	Depreciation [(3) × (4)] (5)	Interest[b] (6)	Total deductions [(2) + (5) + (6)] (7)	Tax shields [.40 × (7)] (8)	After-tax cash outflows [(1) + (2) − (8)] (9)
1	$5,967	$1,000	$20,000	.20	$4,000	$3,000	$8,000	$3,200	$3,767
2	5,967	1,000	20,000	.32	6,400	2,555	9,955	3,982	2,985
3	5,967	1,000	20,000	.19	3,800	2,043	6,843	2,737	4,230
4	5,967	1,000	20,000	.12	2,400	1,455	4,855	1,942	5,025
5	5,967	1,000	20,000	.12	2,400	778	4,178	1,671	5,296

[a]From Table 3.8 on page 96.
[b]From column 3 of table in **b**(1).

(3) In tabular form—present value of the cash outflows in column 3.

End of year	After-tax cash outflows[a] (1)	Present value factors[b] (2)	Present value of outflows [(1) × (2)] (3)
1	$3,767	.917	$ 3,454
2	2,985	.842	2,513
3	4,230	.772	3,266
4	5,025	.708	3,558
5	5,296	.650	3,442
		Present value of cash outflows	$16,233

[a]From column 9 of table in **b**(2).
[b]From Table A-3, *PVIF*, for 9% and the corresponding year.

(Calculator solution = $16,237)

c. Because the present value of the lease outflows of $14,267 is well below the present value of the purchase outflows of $16,233, *the lease is preferred.* Leasing rather than purchasing the oven should result in an incremental savings of $1,966 ($16,233 purchase cost − $14,267 lease cost).

ST 18-2   **a.** In tabular form:

Year(s)	Payments (1)	Present value interest factor at 13 percent (2)	Present value [(1) × (2)] (3)
1–25	$ 110ᵃ	7.330ᵇ	$806.30
25	1,000	.047ᶜ	47.00
		Straight bond value	$853.30

ᵃ$1,000 at 11% = $110 interest per year.
ᵇPresent value interest factor for an annuity, *PVIFA*, discounted at 13% for 25 years, from Table A-4.
ᶜPresent value interest factor for $1, *PVIF*, discounted at 13% for year 25, from Table A-3.

(Calculator solution = $853.40)

b. In tabular form:

Market price of stock (1)	Conversion ratio (2)	Conversion value [(1) × (2)] (3)
$20	40	$ 800
25 (conversion price)	40	1,000 (par value)
28	40	1,120
35	40	1,400
50	40	2,000

c. The bond would be expected to sell at the higher of the conversion value or straight value. In no case would it be expected to sell for less than the straight value of $853.30. Therefore, at a price of $20, the bond would sell for its straight value of $853.30, and at prices of $25, $28, $35, and $50 the bond would be expected to sell at the associated conversion values (calculated in **b**) of $1,000, $1,120, $1,400, and $2,000, respectively.

d. The straight bond value of $853.30.

CHAPTER 19

ST 19-1   **a.** Net present value at 11%:

Year(s)	Cash inflow (1)	Present value factor at 11%[a] (2)	Present value [(1) × (2)] (3)
1–3	$20,000	2.444	$ 48,880
4–15	30,000	(7.191 − 2.444)	142,410
		Present value of inflows	$191,290
		Less: Cash purchase price	180,000
		Net present value (NPV)	$ 11,290

[a]Present value interest factors for annuities, *PVIFA,* from Table A-4.

(Calculator solution = $11,289)

Because the NPV of $11,290 is greater than zero, *Luxe Foods should acquire Valley Canning.*

b. In this case, the 14% cost of capital must be used. Net present value at 14%:

Year(s)	Cash inflow (1)	Present value factor at 14%[a] (2)	Present value [(1) × (2)] (3)
1–3	$20,000	2.322	$ 46,440
4–15	30,000	(6.142 − 2.322)	114,600
		Present value of inflows	$161,040
		Less: Cash purchase price	180,000
		Net present value (NPV)	($ 18,960)

[a]Present value interest factors for annuities, *PVIFA,* from Table A-4.

[Calculator solution = ($18,951)]

At the higher cost of capital, the *acquisition of Valley by Luxe cannot be justified.*

ST 19-2   **a.** Lake Industries' EPS without merger:

		Earnings available for common			
Year	Initial value (1)	Future value factor at 5%[a] (2)	End-of-year value [(1) × (2)] (3)	Number of shares outstanding (4)	EPS [(3) ÷ (4)] (5)
2000	$160,000	1.000	$160,000	80,000	$2.00
2001	160,000	1.050	168,000	80,000	2.10
2002	160,000	1.102	176,320	80,000	2.20
2003	160,000	1.158	185,280	80,000	2.32
2004	160,000	1.216	194,560	80,000	2.43
2005	160,000	1.276	204,160	80,000	2.55

[a]Future value interest factors, FVIF, from Table A-1.

b. Number of postmerger shares outstanding for Lake Industries:

$$\frac{\text{Number of new}}{\text{shares issued}} = \frac{\text{Initial number of}}{\text{Butler Company shares}} \times \frac{\text{Ratio of}}{\text{exchange}}$$

= 10,000 × 1.1 = 11,000 shares

Plus: Lake's premerger shares   80,000

Lake's postmerger shares   91,000 shares

		Earnings available for common					
		Butler Company			Lake Industries		
					Without merger	With merger		
Year	Initial value (1)	Future value factor at 10%[a] (2)	End-of-year value [(1) × (2)] (3)	End-of-year value[b] (4)	End-of-year value [(3) + (4)] (5)	Number of shares outstanding[c] (6)	EPS [(5) ÷ (6)] (7)
2000	$20,000	1.000	$20,000	$160,000	$180,000	91,000	$1.98
2001	20,000	1.100	22,000	168,000	190,000	91,000	2.09
2002	20,000	1.210	24,200	176,320	200,520	91,000	2.20
2003	20,000	1.331	26,620	185,280	211,900	91,000	2.33
2004	20,000	1.464	29,280	194,560	223,840	91,000	2.46
2005	20,000	1.611	32,220	204,160	236,380	91,000	2.60

[a]Future value interest factors, FVIF, from Table A-1.
[b]From column 3 of table in part **a**.
[c]Calculated at beginning of this part.

c. Comparing the EPS without the proposed merger calculated in **a** (see column 5 of table in **a**) with the EPS with the proposed merger calculated in **b** (see column 7 of table in **b**), we can see that after 2002, the EPS *with* the merger rises above the EPS *without* the merger. Clearly, over the long run, the EPS with the merger will exceed those without the merger. This outcome is attributed to the higher rate of growth associated with Butler's earnings (10% versus 5% for Lake).

CHAPTER 20

ST 20-1   MNC's receipt of dividends can be calculated as follows:

Subsidiary income before local taxes	$150,000
Foreign income tax at 32%	−48,000
Dividend available to be declared	$102,000
Foreign dividend withholding tax at 8%	−8,160
MNC's receipt of dividends	$ 93,840

a. If tax credits are allowed, then the so-called grossing up procedure will be applicable:

Additional MNC income		$150,000
U.S. tax liability at 34%	$51,000	
Total foreign taxes paid to be used as a credit ($48,000 + $8,160)	−56,160	−56,160
U.S. taxes due		0
Net funds available to the MNC		$ 93,840

b. If no tax credits are permitted, then:

MNC's receipt of dividends	$93,840
U.S. tax liability at 34%	−31,906
Net funds available to the parent MNC	$61,934

Appendix C

Answers to Selected End-of-Chapter Problems

The following list of answers to selected problems and portions of problems is included to provide "check figures" for use in preparing detailed solutions to end-of-chapter problems requiring calculations. For problems that are relatively straightforward, the key answer is given; for more complex problems, answers to a number of parts of the problem are included. Detailed calculations are not shown—only the final and, in some cases, intermediate answers, which should help to confirm whether the correct solution is being developed. Answers to problems involving present and future value were solved by using the appropriate tables; calculator solutions are not given. For problems containing a variety of cases for which similar calculations are required, the answers for only one or two cases have been included. The only verbal answers included are simple yes-or-no or "choice of best alternative" responses; answers to problems requiring detailed explanations or discussions are not given.

The problems and portions of problems for which answers have been included were selected randomly; therefore, there is no discernible pattern to the choice of problem answers given. The answers given are based on what are believed to be the most obvious and reasonable assumptions related to the given problem; in some cases, other reasonable assumptions could result in equally correct answers.

1-1	a.	Ms. Harper has unlimited liability: $60,000
	c.	Ms. Harper has limited liability
1-2	b.	$150,000
1-3	a.	$460,000
2-1	b.	$175,000
2-3	a.	$100
2-4	c.	100,000 shares
2-5	b.	$1,002.50
	g.	($6.25)
		$1,008.75
2-6	b.	$81.75
	f.	$1.32
	h.	1,243,200
2-8	b.	4%
2-12	a.	B: 3%
		E: 3.1%
2-14	a.	C: 11%
		E: 14%
	c.	C: 13%
		E: 15%
3-4	b.	$27,050
3-5	a.	$1.16
3-9	a.	EPS = $1.9375
	b.	Total assets: $926,000
3-12	b.	Changes to cumulative translation adjustment account = +$1,300,000
	c.	US$9,860,000
3-13		1,000,000 shares
3-14	a.	$19,700
3-16	a.	15%; 25%; 34%; 39%; 34%
3-19	a.	X: $250
		Y: $5,000
3-22		$80,000
3-25	a.	$70,680
3-28	a.	Total sources: $2,900
3-29	a.	Total sources: $70,800
4-3	a.	Average age of inventory: 97.6 days
4-8	a.	(2) Pelican Paper, times interest earned = 62.5
	b.	(2) Timberland Forest, net profit margin = 13.8%
4-10	a.	1999 Johnson ROE = 22.13%
		Industry ROE = 16.92%

4-12	a.		*Actual 2000*
		Current ratio:	1.04
		Average collection period:	56 days
		Net profit margin:	4.1%
		Return on equity:	11.3%

4-14	a.	Net working capital = +5.45%
		Average collection period = −26.19%
		Return on assets = +39.66%
5-3	C:	3 years $< n <$ 4 years
5-4	A:	$530.60
	D:	$78.450
5-6	a.	(1) $15,456
5-10	a.	(1) Annual: $8,810
		Semiannual: $8,955
		Quarterly: $9,030
5-11	b.	B: 12.62%
		D: 16.99%
5-12	A:	$1,197.22

5-15	a.	B: (1) $4,057.50
		(2) $4,544.40
5-19	A:	$3,862.50
	B:	$138,450.00
	C:	$6,956.80
5-22	A:	$4,452.00
	D:	$80,250
5-25		$63
5-27	a.	A: $20,833.50
	c.	B
5-32	a.	PV of stream C = $52,410
5-33	a.	PV of stream A = $109,890
5-36	E:	$85,297.50
5-40	a.	$43,691.48
5-45		Future value of retirement home in 20 years = $272,595
		Annual deposit = $4,759.49
5-46	b.	Deposit = $3,764.82

5-49	*Year*	*Interest*	*Principal*
	2	$1,489.61	$4,970.34

5-54		$PVIFA_{k,10}$ = 5.303
		13% $< k <$ 14%
6-1	a.	X: 12.5%
		Y: 12.36%
6-2	A:	25%
6-4	a.	A: 8%
		B: 20%
6-5	a.	R: 10%
		S: 20%
	b.	R: 25%
		S: 25.5%
6-9	a.	(4) Project 257 CV: .368
		Project 432 CV: .354
6-10	a.	F: 4%
	b.	F: 13.38%
	c.	F: 3.345
6-12	b.	Portfolio return: 15.5%
	c.	Standard deviation: 1.638%
6-15	b.	Purchase price = US$2,225.84
6-18	a.	18% increase
	b.	9.6% decrease
	c.	No change
6-22	A:	8.9%
	D:	15%
6-23	c.	b = 1.18
6-24	b.	10%
6-25	d.	k_A = .088
7-2	C:	$16,660
	E:	$14,112
7-4	a.	$1,156.88
7-5	A:	$1,149.66
	D:	$450.80
7-10	a.	12.69%
7-12	a.	For Bond A, B_0 = $753.30
	d.	For Bond B, B_5 = $35,610.24
7-13		$841.15
7-18	a.	$68.82
	b.	$7.87
7-21	a.	$37.75
	b.	$60.40
7-22		$81.18

7-24	a.	$34.12
	b.	$20.21
	c.	$187.87
7-29		2.67
7-30	a.	14.8%
	b.	$29.55
8-1	a.	Current expenditure
	d.	Current expenditure
	f.	Capital expenditure
8-6	A:	$275,500
	B:	$26,800
8-9	a.	Total tax: $49,600
	d.	Total tax: ($6,400)
8-11	a.	$156,000
8-12		Initial investment: $22,680
8-13	a.	Initial investment: $18,240
	c.	Initial investment: $23,100
8-16	c.	Cash inflow, Year 3: $584,000
8-18	b.	Incremental cash flow, Year 3: $1,960
8-21		Terminal cash flow: $76,640
8-25	a.	Initial investment, Asset B: $51,488
	b.	Incremental cash flow, Year 2, Hoist A: $8,808
	c.	Terminal cash flow, Hoist B: $18,600
9-2	a.	Machine 1: 4 years, 8 months
		Machine 2: 5 years, 3 months
9-5	a.	(1) $2,675
		(2) Accept
9-8	a.	NPV = ($320); reject
9-10	a.	Project A: 3.08 years; Project C: 2.38 years
	b.	Project C: NPV = $5,451
9-11		Project A: 17%
		Project D: 21%
9-14	a.	NPV = $1,222
	b.	IRR = 12%
	c.	Accept
9-16	b.	A: $120,000; B: $105,000
9-18	a.	Project A
		NPV = $15,245
	b.	Project B
		IRR = 18%
9-21	a.	Initial Investment: $1,480,000

9-21 b.

Year	Cash Flow
1	$656,000
2	761,600
3	647,200
4	585,600
5	585,600
6	44,000

	c.	2.1 years
	d.	NPV = $959,289
		IRR = 35%
10-4	a.	Range A: $1,600
		Range B: $200
10-7	a.	NPV = $22,320
	b.	NPV = ($5,596)
10-9	a.	Project E: NPV = $2,130
		Project F: NPV = $1,678
		Project G: NPV = $1,144
	c.	Project E: NPV = $834
		Project F: NPV = $1,678
		Project G: NPV = $2,138

10-14	b.	X: $920.04
		Y: $1,079.54
		Z: $772.80
10-15	a.	Sell: $177,850
	b.	License: $61,234.40
10-17	b.	Projects C, F, and G
11-2	b.	12.4%
11-3	a.	$980
	c.	12.31%
	d.	Before-tax: 12.26%; after-tax: 7.36%
11-4	A:	5.66%
	E:	7.10%
11-9	c.	15.91%
	d.	16.54%
11-11	a.	11.3%
11-13	a.	Weighted cost: 8.344%
	b.	Weighted cost: 10.854%
11-15	c.	9.1%
11-17	a.	$k_i = 5.2\%; k_p = 8.4\%; k_n = 15.0\%; k_r = 13.8\%$
	b.	(1) $200,000
		(2) 10.1%
		(3) 10.7%
11-18	b.	$500,000 and $800,000
	c.	WACC over $800,000: 16.2%
11-19	c.	WACC, 0–$600,000 = 10.6%
12-4	a.	21,000 CDs
	d.	$10,500
12-8	a.	Q = 8,000 units
	e.	DOL = 5.00
12-10	a.	EPS = $0.375
12-12	a.	DFL = 1.5
12-13	a.	175,000 units
	d.	DTL = 2.40
12-15	b.	EBIT = $25,000

12-16

Debt ratio	Debt	Equity
40%	$400,000	$600,000

12-21	a.	At 30%, EPS = $5.99
	b.	At 15%, P_0 = $42.00
12-23	a.	EBIT: $60,000; $240,000; $420,000
	d.	At 15% debt ratio, EPS = $0.85, $4.02, $7.20
	e.	(1) At 15% debt ratio, expected EPS = $4.03
	g.	$0 < EBIT < $100,000; choose 0%
		$100,000 < EBIT < $198,000; choose 30%
		$198,000 < EBIT < ∞; choose 60%
	h.	At 15% debt ratio, share price = $38.38
	i.	Maximum EPS at 60% debt ratio
		Maximize share value at 30% debt ratio
12-24	c.	At 10%, EPS = $3.21; at 40%, EPS = $3.90
13-1	b.	Monday, July 3 (due to July 4 holiday)
	c.	Cash $170,000 Dividends payable $ 0
		Retained earnings $2,170,000
13-4	a.	$4.75 per share
	b.	$50.40 per share
	d.	A decrease in retained earnings and hence stockholder's equity by $80,000
13-6	a.	Pay-out ratio in 1998 = 22.73%
13-8	a.	1997 = $0.60
	b.	1997 = $0.50
	c.	1997 = $0.62
	d.	1997 = $0.62
13-9	a.	Retained earnings = $85,000
	b.	(1) Retained earnings = $70,000
		(2) Retained earnings = $40,000

13-11 a.   EPS = $2.00
     b.   1%
     c.   1%; stock dividends do not have a real value
13-13 b.   Common stock (400,000 shares @ $4.50 par) =
        $1,800,000
14-2   Accounts payable, 1-month lag, April = $168,000
     Wages and salaries, May = $48,700
     Accounts payable, 2-month lag, June = $146,400

14-4

		Feb.	Mar.	Apr.
			(in $000)	
a.	Ending cash	$37	$67	($22)
b.	Required total financing			$37
	Excess cash balance	$22	$52	

     c.   Line of credit should be at least $37,000 to
        cover borrowing needs for the month of April
14-8   a.   Net profit after taxes: $216,600
     b.   Net profit after taxes: $227,400
14-11 a.   Accounts receivable: $1,440,000
        Net fixed assets: $4,820,000
        Total current liabilities: $2,260,000
        External funds required: $775,000
        Total assets: $9,100,000
14-12 a.   Net profit after taxes: $67,500
     b.

	Judgmental
Total assets	$697,500
External funds required	11,250

15-1   b.   (1) $36,000
        (2) $10,333
15-2   Annual loan cost: $1,200
15-3   a. $908,333
15-6   c.   January 9
15-8   c.   For 1/15 net 45, the cost of giving up the cash
        discount = 12.12%
15-9   Effective annual rate = 31.81%
15-11 $1,300,000
15-18 a.   9.0%
     b.   13.06%
15-21 b.   Effective annual rate for 12 months = 13.5%
15-22 Total: $886,900
16-1   a.   OC = 150 days
     b.   CCC = 120 days
     c. $10,000,000
16-2   b.   CCC = 35 days
     c. $97,222
16-4   Plan E
16-8   a.   7 days
     b.   Opportunity cost = $21,450
16-11 a.   Maximum savings = $3,850
        Minimum savings = $1,100
16-16 $22,500 annual savings
17-1   a.   Credit score, applicant B: 81.5
17-2   b. $75,000
     c. $9,000
17-4   a.   Present plan: $20,000
        Proposed plan: $48,000
17-6   The credit standards should not be relaxed, because
     the proposed plan results in a loss of $4,721
17-7   Net profit on the proposal: $20,040
17-9   a. $14,000 additional profit contribution

     b. $36,432 marginal investment in accounts
        receivable
17-11 b. $52,000 net savings
17-14 c.   4,000 units
17-17 a.   200 units
     b.   123 units
     c.   33 units
18-4   b.   Lease: PV = $42,934
        Purchase: PV = $43,733
18-6   *Lease   Capitalized value*

A	$272,560
B	596,160
E	374,261

18-9   a. $1,250
     b. $525
     c. $1,050
18-13 a. $832.75
     b.   At $9: $720
     c.   At $9: $832.75
18-14 Bond A: $6.46 per warrant
18-17 a.   160 shares, 400 warrants
     b.   20%
     c.   125%
18-20 a. $800 profit
     b. $400 profit
     c. $6/share
19-1   a.   Total tax liability = $1,680,000
     b.   Tax liability: Year 1 = $0
                        Year 2 = $0
                        Year 3 = $16,000
                        Years 4–15 = $112,000/year
19-3   a.   Total tax advantage = $320,000;
        Years 1–4 = $80,000/year
     b.   Total tax advantage = $320,000
     c.   Reilly Investment Group: $228,400
        Webster Industries: $205,288
19-5   a.   Yes, the NPV is $42,150
     b.   No, the NPV for the equipment = $101,000
19-6   a.   EPS merged firm = $1.029
     b.   EPS Maria's = $1.00
     b.   EPS Victory = $2.139
19-8   Ratio of exchange of: (1) shares; (2) market price
     A: 0.60; 1.20
     D: 0.25; 1.25
     E: 1.00; 1.25
19-10 a.   1.125
     b.   Henry Co.: EPS = $2.50; P/E = 18
     c.   16.89
20-1   a.   Net funds available: $152,425
20-3   Effective rate, Euromarket
     US$ 5.0%
     DM   8.0%
     Sf   7.2%

Appendix **D**

Instructions for Using the *PMF* CD-ROM Software

The *PMF* CD-ROM contains three applications: the *PMF Tutor, PMF Problem-Solver,* and the *PMF Excel Spreadsheet Templates.* These solutions are designed to run on any computer running Windows 3.1, 95 or 98 and Microsoft Excel version 5.0 or higher.

The *PMF Tutor, PMF Problem-Solver,* and *PMF Excel Spreadsheet Templates* are arranged in the same order as the text discussions. For your convenience, text page references are shown on the screen for each associated computation in the *Problem-Solver* and the *Tutor.* As noted in the text preface as well as in Chapter 1, applicability of the software throughout the text and the study guide is keyed to related text discussions, end-of-chapter problems, and end-of-chapter and end-of-part cases by icons for all of the computational routines. Thus, you can integrate the procedures on the disk with the corresponding text discussions.

WHAT IS THE *PMF* TUTOR?

The *PMF Tutor* is an Excel workbook containing a collection of managerial finance problem types with the problem varied by random number generation. Its purpose is to give you an essentially unlimited number of problems to work through so that you can practice until you are satisfied that you understand a concept. In using the *Tutor,* the following sequence should produce the best results:

1. **Work the problem first yourself.** It is tempting to save time by letting the computer solve the problem for you and then studying the computer's answer. You won't learn much that way. Even if you make mistakes when you try the problem on your own, you will learn from those mistakes.
2. **Enter your answer.** The computer will check your answer against the correct answer.
3. **Check the solution.** If you do not get the same answer as the computer, check your work step by step against the correct solution displayed on the computer screen. Doing so will help you to pinpoint your mistakes. Practice each type of problem until you have genuinely mastered it. Don't have false pride about your mastery. When you take the course exams, you won't be able to fake your knowledge level. So don't stop until you're sure that you have mastered the concepts.

The *Tutor* uses random number generation to choose the specific numbers, so it is unlikely that you will ever see a combination of numbers twice. This gives you an effectively unlimited number of practice problems. The only limit is your willingness to practice.

WHAT IS THE *PMF* PROBLEM-SOLVER?

The *PMF Problem-Solver* is an Excel workbook containing a collection of financial computation worksheets. The purpose of the *PMF Problem-Solver* is to aid the student's learning and understanding of managerial finance by providing a fast and easy method for performing the often time-consuming mathematical computations required. It is not the intent of the *PMF Problem-Solver* to eliminate the need for learning the various concepts, but to assist in solving the problems once the appropriate formulas have been studied. The *PMF Problem-Solver* differs from the *Tutor* in that it solves for the answer, given the input data supplied by the user, whereas the *Tutor* supplies the input data and looks to the student to perform the calculations. The *Tutor* should be used to practice application of basic concepts; the *PMF Problem-Solver* should be used to save computational time once the concepts are understood.

WHAT ARE THE *PMF* EXCEL SPREADSHEET TEMPLATES?

The *PMF Excel Spreadsheet Templates* are preprogrammed Excel worksheets, with one file for each problem. The worksheets enable students to enter data and solve problems using Microsoft Excel—the most commonly used spreadsheet software. The worksheet files correspond to selected end-of-chapter problems, and the worksheet file names are based on the chapter number and the problem number. For selected problems, there are additional worksheets that are not tied to problems in the text. These worksheets can be used to provide additional opportunities for solving financial problems on their own.

HARDWARE AND SOFTWARE REQUIREMENTS

To use the *PMF CD-ROM,* you must have the following:

- an IBM compatible PC
- Microsoft Windows 3.1, Windows 95, or Windows 98
- Microsoft Excel Version 5.0, 7.0, 97 or 2000

INSTALLING THE SOFTWARE

If you are using Windows 95 or 98, do the following:

1. Insert the *PMF* CD-ROM into your CD-ROM drive.
2. An autorun will automatically lead you through the installation process. If your CD is configured to bypass this autorun, select Start | Run | X:setup.exe where X:\ is the drive letter of your CD-ROM.
3. Follow the instructions on the screen to install the files to your hard drive.

You can also access the spreadsheets directly on the CD-ROM. All of the individual files are available in folders for your respective version of Excel. The folder names are XL5, XL95, XL97, and XL2000.

If you are using Windows 3.1, there is no install— the files are available on the PMF CD-ROM in a folder called XL5.

Be sure to store the CD-ROM in a safe place in the event that you need to install the software again at a later time.

THE *PMF* TUTOR

RUNNING THE *PMF* TUTOR

To run the *PMF Tutor,* follow these steps:

1. Start Excel.
2. Select File / Open.
3. Select the *PMF* directory in which the *Tutor* is stored and then select the file Tutorial.xls.
4. Click the OK button and the *Tutor* will open, displaying its main menu.

When the *PMF Tutor* is loaded, you will see the following introductory screen:

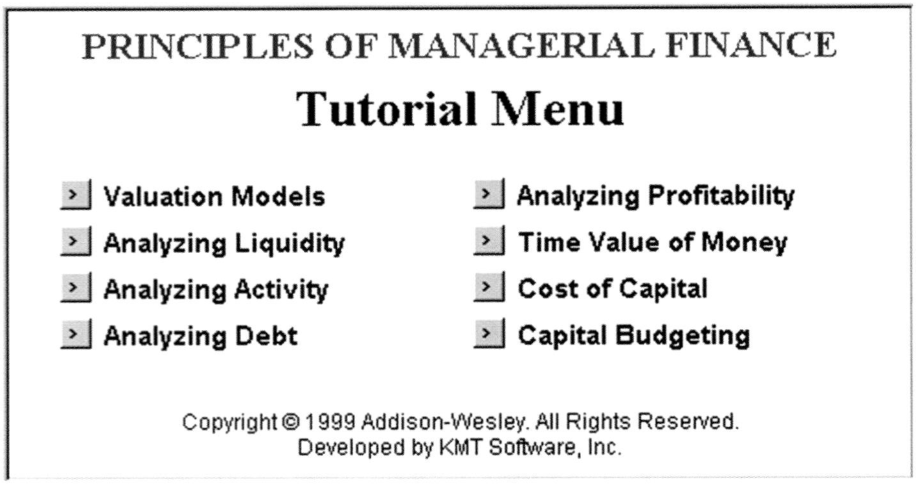

PRINCIPLES OF MANAGERIAL FINANCE
Tutorial Menu

> Valuation Models   > Analyzing Profitability
> Analyzing Liquidity   > Time Value of Money
> Analyzing Activity   > Cost of Capital
> Analyzing Debt   > Capital Budgeting

Copyright © 1999 Addison-Wesley. All Rights Reserved.
Developed by KMT Software, Inc.

FIGURE D-1

Excel *PMF Tutor* start-up screen showing the main menu

USING THE *PMF* TUTOR

From the *PMF Tutor* main menu, click the button of the problem category that you want to work with. When the category menu is displayed, select a specific problem type. Each tutorial will open with a new problem ready for you to solve. The following is an example *Tutor* problem:

Current Ratio

Cash	$11,100
Accounts Receivable	18,870
Inventory	22,200
Net Fixed Assets	58,830
Total Assets	111,000
Accounts Payable	12,210
Notes Payable (due in three months)	9,990
Long-term Liabilities	28,000
Retained Earnings	10,850

Enter the Current Ratio here -->

The correct answer is:

LEARNING OBJECTIVE

This problem tests you on the current ratio. Selected Balance Sheet data are given and you are asked to calculate this commonly used liquidity ratio.

See related text material on page 133.

FIGURE D–2

Excel *PMF Tutor* sample problem

There are five buttons at the top of the window for each tutorial:

- Solution—Click this to see the problem solution.
- New Problem—Click this to see new problem data.
- Prev—Click this to move to the previous tutorial problem.
- Main—Click this to return to the *PMF Tutor* main menu.
- Next—Click this to move to the next tutorial problem.

USING THE *PMF* TUTOR TOOLBAR

The *PMF Tutor* has a toolbar that also facilitates navigation and tasks. The twelve buttons of the toolbar are explained on the next page.

◻ Click this button to go to the main menu

◀ Click this button to go to the previous tutorial

▶ Click this button to go to the next tutorial

◻ Click this button to go to the summary sheet

⊕ Click this button to set the zoom factor for the tutorial

? Click this button to make a new problem in the current tutorial

✓ Click this button to check the solution to the current problem

▦ Click this button to open the Windows calculator to facilitate your solution

🖨 Click this button to print the current tutorial sheets

📄 Click this button to preview the printing of the current tutorial sheets

? Click this button to view Help for *PMF Tutor*

ⓘ Click this button to learn more about KMT Software, the developer of this application

When you are ready to solve a particular tutorial problem, you may want to follow these steps:

1. Review the learning objective. Each tutorial has a learning objective situated just below the problem. Learning objectives provide a brief description of what each problem is testing you on and note the associated pages in the textbook where the material is covered.
2. Review the problem data and calculate your answer.
3. Enter your answer in the yellow cell. Note: If the problem calls for a percentage, be sure to enter the percentage in decimal form (i.e., 20% as .2) or enter the number followed by the percent sign (i.e., type 20% and then press Enter).
4. Check your solution.
5. If you need more practice, click the New Problem button and begin with step 1.

THE *PMF* PROBLEM-SOLVER

RUNNING THE *PMF* PROBLEM-SOLVER

To run the *PMF Problem-Solver*, follow these steps:

1. Start Excel.
2. Select File / Open.
3. Select the *PMF* directory in which the *Problem-Solver* is stored and then select the file Solver.xls.
4. Click the OK button and the *Problem-Solver* will open, displaying its main menu.

USING THE *PMF* PROBLEM-SOLVER

From the *PMF Problem-Solver* main menu, click the button of the calculation category that you want to work with. When the category menu is displayed, select a specific calculation. Here is the *PMF Problem-Solver* main menu:

PRINCIPLES OF MANAGERIAL FINANCE
Solver Menu

> **Bond and Stock Valuation**   > **Cost of Capital**

> **Financial Statements**   > **Capital Budgeting**

> **Time Value of Money**   > **General Budgeting**

Copyright © 1999 Addison-Wesley. All Rights Reserved.
Developed by KMT Software, Inc.

FIGURE D–3

Excel *PMF Problem-Solver* start-up screen showing the main menu

Using a *PMF Problem-Solver* worksheet is simple. You enter your inputs in the yellow cells. You can move between these cells using your mouse or by pressing the Tab on your keyboard. If any of your inputs involve percentages (e.g., an interest rate of 10.5%), enter the percentage either in decimal form (i.e., enter .105 for 10.5%) or enter the percentage following the format number followed by the percent sign (i.e., type 10.5% and then press Enter).

The following is an example *Problem-Solver* problem:

Basic Bond Valuation

Par Value of the Bond	$1,000
Years to Maturity	10
Required Rate of Return	12.000%
Coupon Rate of Bond	10.000%
Payment of interest:	
Annual ◉ Semi-annual ○	

Value of the bond is:	$887.00

DESCRIPTION

Use this worksheet to determine the value of a bond. If the bond pays interest on an semi-annual basis (twice per year), be sure to selection the semi-annual option button.

This material is covered in chapter 7, pages 290 – 293.

FIGURE D–4

Excel *PMF Problem-Solver* sample problem

The *PMF Problem-Solver* has a toolbar that also facilitates navigation and tasks. The 10 buttons of the toolbar are explained below.

USING THE PROBLEM-SOLVER TOOLBAR

The *Problem-Solver* has a toolbar that performs a variety of functions depending on which button you select. The toolbar includes the following buttons and functions:

Click this button to go to the main menu

Click this button to go to the previous sheet

Click this button to go to the next sheet

Click this button to go to the summary sheet

Click this button to set the zoom factor for the solver

Click this button to open the Windows calculator to facilitate your solution

Click this button to print the solver sheets

Click this button to preview the printing of the current solver sheets

Click this button to view Help for *PMF Problem-Solver*

Click this button to learn more about KMT Software, the developer of this application

THE *PMF* EXCEL SPREADSHEET TEMPLATES

RUNNING THE *PMF* EXCEL SPREADSHEET TEMPLATES

To run one of the *PMF Excel Spreadsheet Templates*, follow these steps:

1. Start Excel.
2. Select File / Open.
3. Select the *PMF* directory in which the problems are stored and then select the appropriate file as described in the textbook (e.g. Ch02–15.xls).
4. Click the OK button and the problem will open.

USING THE PMF EXCEL SPREADSHEET TEMPLATES

The *PMF Excel Spreadsheet Templates* describe the problem from the chapter material. You then enter the inputs in the yellow highlighted cells. If any of your inputs involve percentages (e.g., an interest rate of 10.5%), enter the percentage either in decimal form (i.e., enter .105 for 10.5%) or enter the percentage following the format number followed by the percent sign (i.e., type 10.5% and then press Enter).

Each of the *PMF Excel Spreadsheet Templates* has a description of the problem at the top of the worksheet and the answer is listed below. The screen shot in Figure D-5 shows a typical problem description. The answer is made available as shown in Figure D-6 below the problem description.

PRINCIPLES OF MANAGERIAL FINANCE

Problem 3-18 Interest versus Dividend Expense

The Michaels Corporation expects earnings before interest and taxes to be $40,000 for this period, assuming an ordinary tax rate of 40%, compute the firm's earnings after taxes and earnings available for common stockholders (earnings after taxes and preferred stock dividends, if any) under the following conditions:

a.   The firm pays $10,000 in interest.

b.   The firm pays $10,000 in preferred stock dividends

FIGURE D-5

Example *PMF Excel Spreadsheet Templates* sample problem description

Answer:

a. EBIT $40,000
    Less: Interest expense   10,000
    Earnings before taxes $30,000
    Less: Taxes (40%)   12,000
    Earnings after taxes $18,000 *

    * This is also earnings available to common stockholders

b. EBIT $40,000
    Less: Taxes (40%)   16,000
    Earnings after taxes $24,000
    Less: Preferred Dividends   10,000
    Earnings available for common stockholders $14,000

FIGURE D-6

Example *PMF Excel Spreadsheet Templates* sample answer

The data entry cells are clearly highlighted in yellow. When you enter your data, the worksheet automatically calculates the new answer.

USING THE *PMF* SPREADSHEET TOOLBAR

Each *PMF Spreadsheet* has a toolbar that performs a variety of functions depending on which button you select. The toolbar includes the following buttons and functions:

 Click this button to set the zoom factor for the solver

 Click this button to open the Windows calculator to facilitate your solution

 Click this button to print the solver sheets

 Click this button to preview the printing of the current tutorial sheets

 Click this button to view Help for *PMF Spreadsheet*

 Click this button to learn more about KMT Sofware, the developer of this application

IN PRACTICE SOURCES

Bold page numbers indicate location of feature.

Chapter 1

14 "The Best of 1998," *CFO*, September 1998, downloaded from **www.cfonet.com**; "Bulletin Board: CFOs Should Lead, Not Push," *San Diego Union-Tribune*, August 18, 1998, p. C–1; "Measuring Up," *Financial Executive*, November/December 1998, pp. 33–36; and "Thomas J. Wilson—Allstate Insurance: Developing an Efficient Finance Function," *CFO*, September 1998, downloaded from **www.cfonet.com**.

20 John Elkington, "Healthy societies are good markets," *The Guardian*, June 13, 1998, downloaded from Electric Library Business Edition, **http://business.elibrary.com**; Leslie Kaufman, "Levi Strauss Pays Price for Allowing Jeans to Lose Cool," *The Patriot Ledger* (Quincy, MA), February 23, 1999, downloaded from Electric Library Business Edition, **http://business.elibrary.com**; Betsy Reed, "The Business of Social Responsibility," *Dollars & Sense*, May 15, 1998, downloaded from Electric Library Business Edition, **http://business.elibrary.com**; and Stratford Sherman, "Levi's: As Ye Sew, So Shall Ye Reap," *Fortune*, May 12, 1997, downloaded from Electric Library Business Edition, **http://business.elibrary.com**.

Chapter 2

49 Gaston F. Ceron, "IPO Pipeline Offers Firms No Guarantees," *The Wall Street Journal*, September 14, 1998, p. B11A; Inmoo Lee, Scott Lockhead, and Jay Ritter, "The Costs of Raising Capital," *The Journal of Financial Research* (Spring 1996), pp. 59–73; "Multicom Announces Fiscal 1997 Results," *Business Wire*, October 22, 1997, downloaded from **www.elibrary.com/s/elbec_/**; and Stephen D. Solomon, "Follow the Money," *Inc.*, June 1997, pp. 80–81.

61 "Confusing Curves," *The Economist*, September 5, 1998, downloaded from **www.elibrary.com/s/elbec_/**; Jonathan Lanser, "It's a Strange New World on the Yield Front," *The Orange County Register*, September 6, 1998, downloaded from **www.elibrary.com/s/elbec_/**; Jacob M. Schlesinger and David Wessel, "Fed Cuts Short-Term Rates by 0.25 Point," *The Wall Street Journal*, September 30, 1998, p. A3; "What Do the Market Drops Tell Us?" *Investor's Business Daily*, September 2, 1998, downloaded from **www.elibrary.com/s/elbec_/**.

Chapter 3

82 "Digits," *The Wall Street Journal*, October 29, 1998, p. B6; Earnings Roundup/Strong Gains for Microsoft, *Newsday*, October 21, 1998, downloaded from Electric Library, **http://business.elibrary.com**; "Microsoft Announces First Quarter Revenue and Income," Press Release, Microsoft Corp., Redmond, Washington, October 20, 1998.

91 Karen Hube, "Autumn Steps Can Cut Taxes in Spring," *The Wall Street Journal*, October 27, 1998, pp. C1, C17; Selena Maranjian and Roy Lewis, *The Motley Fool Investment Tax Guide*, 1998.

Chapter 4

146 John Barrickman, "Four Steps to Better Loan Structure," *Commercial Lending Review*, July 1, 1997, downloaded from **http://business.elibrary.com**; Kent Eastman, "EBITDA: An Overrated Tool for Cash Flow Analysis," *Commercial Lending Review*, April 1, 1997, downloaded from **http://business.elibrary.com**; and John Green, "Borrowers under the Microscope," *Treasury and Risk Management*, March 1998, downloaded from **http://www.cfonet.com**.

149 Robin Goldwyn Blumenthal, " 'Tis the Gift to Be Simple," *CFO*, January 1998, downloaded from **http://www.cfonet.com**; Peter C. Eisemann, "Return on Equity and Systematic Ratio Analysis," *Commercial Lending Review*, July 1, 1997.

Chapter 5

201 Russ Banham, "Making Your Mark," *CFO*, March 1998, downloaded from **http://www.cfonet.com**; and Thomas A. Stewart, "What's a Loyal Customer Worth?" *Fortune*, December 11, 1995, p. 182.

212 Carlos Tejada, "Sweet Fifteen: Shorter Mortgages Are Gaining Support," *The Wall Street Journal*, September 17, 1998, p. C1; Ann Tergesen, "It's Time to Refinance ... Again," *Business Week*, November 2, 1998, pp. 134–135.

Chapter 6

253 Christopher Rhoads, "Low Key GE Capital Expands in Europe," *The Wall Street Journal*, September 17, 1998, p. A18; Bill Shepherd, "GE Capital's M&A Strategy," *Global Finance*, November 1, 1998, downloaded from **www.business.elibrary.com**.

266 Peter Coy, "Taking the Angst out of Taking a Gamble," *Business Week*, July 14, 1997, pp. 52–53; and Paul Hom and Ron Tonuzi, "Value-at-risk: Safety Net or Abyss?" *Treasury & Risk Management*, November/December 1998, downloaded from **http://www.cfonet.com**; Bluford Putnam, "Lessons in Quantitative Risk Management," *Global Investor*, February 1, 1997, downloaded from **www.business.elibrary.com**.

Chapter 7

287 Jill Andresky Fraser, "Business for Sale: Western Credit Reporting Agency," *Inc.*, October 1998, p. 132.

296 Hope Hamashige, "More than Zero," *Los Angeles Times*, September 16, 1997, p. D–6; "Putting Compound Interest to Work Through Zero Coupon Bonds," The Bond Market Association, PR Newswire, June 24, 1998, downloaded from **www.business.elibrary.com**.

Chapter 8

331 "America's Best Technology Users," *Forbes ASAP* (August 24, 1998), p. 86; Heather Page, "Wired for Success," *Entrepreneur* (May 1997), pp. 132–140; and Edward Teach, "How to Succeed in IT," *CFO* (July 1997), downloaded from **http://www.cfonet.com**.

342 Stephen Barr, "Coors's New Brew," *CFO* (March 1998), downloaded from **http://www.cfonet.com**; and "Marking 125th Year, Coors Looks to Future," *Minneapolis Star Tribune* (April 1, 1998), p. 1D.

Chapter 9

377 Neil Cahill, "Automation: U.S. Textiles Close In," *Textile World* (May 1995), pp. 39–45.

386 Justin Martin, "Eli Lilly Is Making Shareholders Rich. How? By Linking Pay to EVA," *Fortune* (September 9, 1996), downloaded from **www.pathfinder.com/fortune/magazine/1996**; Randy Myers, "Measure for Measure," *CFO* (November 1997), downloaded from **http://www.cfonet.com**; Stern Stewart Web site, **www.sternstewart.com**; and Shawn Tully, "America's Greatest Wealth Creators," *Fortune* (November 9, 1998), pp. 193–204.

Chapter 10

410 Mary Addonizio, "Loanshop.com Measures Productivity in Terms of Leads and Sales," Mainspring ProofPoint (November 1998), downloaded from **http://www.mainspring.com/BaseAll/**; and Beth Lipton, "Net Investment Still Exceeds Return," *CNET News.com* (August 31, 1998), downloaded from **http://www.news.com**.

427 Edward Teach, "Opportunity Calling: U S West Communications," *CFO* (July 1997), downloaded from **http://www.cfonet.com**; and "U S West, Inc.," *Hoover's Company Profiles* (January 1, 1999), Electric Library Business edition, downloaded from **http://business.elibrary.com**.

Chapter 11

457 Russ Banham, "Larry Kellner—Continental Airlines: Managing External Stakeholders," *CFO* (September 1998), downloaded from **www.cfonet.com**; and "Continental Airlines Reports 15th Consecutive Profitable Quarter, Ends Year on High Note," *PR Newswire* (January 21, 1999), downloaded from Electric Library Business Edition, **http://business.elibrary.com**.

471 Randy Meyers, "GM Remeasures the Bar in Latin America," *CFO* (May 1998), downloaded from **http://cfonet.com**; and Dave Phillips, "Automakers Build, but Brazil Busts: Investments Continue Despite Economic Woes," *The Detroit News* (July 19, 1998), downloaded from Electric Library Business Edition, **http://business.elibrary.com**.

Chapter 12

503 Barnes & Noble, Inc. Briefing Book, *The Wall Street Journal Interactive Edition,* downloaded from **http://interactive.wsj.com**; Barnes & Noble, Inc. 1998 10-K, downloaded from **http://www.sec.gov/Archives/edgar**; "Barnes & Noble, Inc., Reports 1998 Record Retail Sales of $3.0 Billion," *Business Wire,* February 22, 1999, downloaded from Electric Library Business Edition, **http://business.elibrary.com**; Borders Group Briefing Book, *The Wall Street Journal Interactive Edition,* **http://interactive.wsj.com**; Patrick M. Reilly, "In the Age of the Web, a Book Chain Flounders," *The Wall Street Journal,* February 22, 1999, pp. B1, B4.

518 Stephen Barr, "USG Remodels Its Balance Sheet," *CFO,* November 1998, downloaded from **http://www.cfonet.com**; Carl Quintanilla, "USG Shows Signs of Shedding a Past Marked by Volatility," *The Wall Street Journal* (February 25, 1999); "USG Initiates Cash Dividend and Announces Share Repurchase Program," company press release, September 18, 1998, downloaded from USG Web site, **http://www.usg.com**; and *USG Corp. Annual Report 1997,* downloaded from USG Web site, **http://www.usg.com**.

Chapter 13

548 Don Bauder, "Dividends Keep Managers Honest," *The San Diego Union Tribune,* November 13, 1998, p. C–3; and Patricia Horn, "Philadelphia-Based Cable Company Cuts Out Cash Dividend," *The Philadelphia Inquirer,* March 4, 1999, downloaded from **http://www.phillynews.com**.

559 Daniel Kadlec, "The Dumb Money," *Time,* February 22, 1999, downloaded from Electric Library Business Edition, **http:// business.elibrary.com**; and Jim Rasmussen, "Investor-Pleasing Stock Splits Mostly an Exercise in Math," *Omaha World-Herald,* February 22, 1999, downloaded from **http://www.omaha.com**.

Chapter 14

582 Susan Arterian, "Sprint Retools the Budget Process," *CFO,* September 1997, downloaded from **http://cfonet.com**; and Cathy Lazere, "All Together Now," *CFO,* February 1998, downloaded from **http://cfonet.com**.

599 "Hands On: CEO's Notebook," *Inc.,* July 1997, p. 104; and "Just-in-Time Financials," *301 Great Ideas for Using Technology,* April 15, 1998, downloaded from **http://www.inc.com/301/ideas**.

Chapter 15

629 Linda Corman, "Cash Masters," *CFO,* July 1998, downloaded from **http://www.cfonet.com**; S. L. Mintz and Cathy Lazere, "The 1997 Working Capital Survey: Inside the Corporate Cash Machine," *CFO,* June 1997, downloaded from **http://www.cfonet.com**.

636 Timothy Middleton, "Lending by the Numbers," *Business Week Enterprise,* October 12, 1998, p. ENT 16–18; and Hal Plotkin, "The Few, the Proud, the Bankable," *Inc. 500,* October 20, 1998, p. 173.

Chapter 16

668 Russ Banham, "Upgrading Cash Flow at Dell," *CFO,* December 1997, downloaded from **http://www.cfonet.com**; Richard Gamble, "No More Dunning Days," *Treasury & Risk Management,* September 1998, downloaded from **http://www.cfonet.com**; and Ellen Leander, "The Honor Roll," *Treasury & Risk Management,* December 1997, downloaded from **http://www.cfonet.com**.

675 Gina Fann, "Banking in Your Bathrobe," *The Tennessean,* October 5, 1998, downloaded from Electric Library Business Edition, **http://business.elibrary.com;** Bill Wolf, "Online Banking: It's Convenient for User, But Banks Enjoy Biggest Savings," *The Courier-Journal* (Louisville, KY), January 5, 1998, downloaded from Electric Library Business Edition, **http://business.elibrary.com.**

Chapter 17

704 Lorrie Cohen, "Credit Card Lesson Can Carry High Price," *The Tucson Citizen,* February 2, 1998, downloaded from Electric Library Business Edition, **http://business.elibrary.com;** Jane Bryant Quinn, "Debt Counseling Can Be a Bulwark Against Bankruptcy," *Seattle Post-Intelligencer,* January 26, 1999, downloaded from Electric Library Business Edition, **http://business.elibrary.com;** and George Rodrigue, "FTC Targets 'Bogus' Credit Repair Firms," *The Dallas Morning News,* March 22, 1998, downloaded from Electric Library Business Edition, **http://business.elibrary.com.**
717 Jill Andresky Fraser, "The Recession Is Coming! The Recession Is Coming!" *Inc.,* September 1997, pp. 119–120.

Chapter 18

749 "Common Queries in Automobile Leasing," *The Arizona Republic,* September 3, 1998, downloaded from Electric Library Business Edition, **http://business.elibrary.com;** Tom Incantalupo, "Lease or Buy? A Checklist," *Newsday,* July 19, 1998, p. H05, downloaded from Electric Library Business Edition, **http://business.elibrary.com;** and Kathleen C. Thomas, "Leasing a Vehicle Can Be a Complicated Transaction," *Richmond Times-Dispatch,* February 28, 1999, downloaded from Electric Library Business Edition, **http://business.elibrary.com.**
759 Stephanie Gates, "Amazon's Junk Is in Demand," *Red Herring Online,* February 3, 1999, downloaded from **http://www.redherring.com/insider;** and Gregory Zukerman and George Anders, "Amazon.com Launches Convertible Bond Issue, as Internet Craze Enters New Financial Arenas," *The Wall Street Journal,* January 29, 1999, p. C17.

Chapter 19

783 Mike Hofman, "The Year of Dealing Dangerously," *Inc. 500 1998,* October 20, 1998, pp. 69–71; "PhotoDisc Leads the Stock Photo Industry," *Business Wire,* August 31, 1998, downloaded from Electric Library Business Edition, **http://business.elibrary.com;** and Paul Shukovsky, "Getty Images Pictures Seattle as HQ," *Seattle Post-Intelligencer,* March 16, 1999, downloaded from Electric Library Business Edition, **http://business.elibrary.com.**
808 Victoria Colliver, "J. Peterman Seeks a Suitor," *San Francisco Examiner,* February 2, 1999, Electric Library Business edition, downloaded from **http://business.elibrary.com;** David Goetz, "Judge OKs J. Peterman Disposal Plan," *The Courier-Journal* (Louisville, Kentucky), February 24, 1999, downloaded from Electric Library Business Edition, **http://business.elibrary.com;** "J. Peterman Co. Files Chapter 11," *Inc. Online,* January 28, 1999, **http://www.inc.com/news/newyork;** "J. Peterman Might Need 'Seinfeld' to Return," *CNNShowBuzz,* January 26, 1999, downloaded from **http://cnn.com/SHOWBIZ/News;** and Tim Whitmire, "J. Peterman Reflects on Catalog's Rise, Fall," *Tulsa World,* March 8, 1999, Electric Library Business edition, downloaded from **http://business.elibrary.com.**

INDEX

Page numbers in *italics* indicate figures; page numbers followed by *n* indicate footnotes; page numbers followed by *t* indicate tables. Marginal terms are bold.